Eleventh Edition

UNDERSTANDING ABNORMAL BEHAVIOR

DAVID SUE
Department of Psychology
Western Washington University

DERALD WING SUE
Department of Counseling and Clinical Psychology
Teachers College, Columbia University

DIANE SUE
Private Practice

STANLEY SUE
Professor of Psychology
Palo Alto University

CENGAGE

Australia • Brazil • Mexico • Singapore • United Kingdom • United States

Understanding Abnormal Behavior,
Eleventh Edition
**David Sue, Derald Wing Sue, Diane Sue,
and Stanley Sue**

Product Director: Jon-David Hague

Product Manager: Timothy Matray

Content Developer: Tangelique Williams-Grayer

Product Assistant: Nicole Richards

Media Developer: Jasmin Tokatlian

Marketing Manager: Jennifer Levanduski

Content Project Manager: Michelle Clark

Art Director: Vernon Boes

Manufacturing Planner: Karen Hunt

Production Service: Graphic World Inc

Photo and Text Researcher: Lumina Datamatics

Text and Cover Designer: Lisa Henry

Cover Image: Diana Ong / Superstock

Compositor: Graphic World Inc

For product information and technology assistance, contact us at
**Cengage Customer & Sales Support, 1-800-354-9706
or support.cengage.com.**

For permission to use material from this text or product, submit all requests online at **www.cengage.com/permissions.**

Library of Congress Control Number: 2014947907

ISBN: 978-0-357-67094-1

Cengage
200 Pier 4 Boulevard
Boston, MA 02210
USA

Cengage is a leading provider of customized learning solutions with employees residing in nearly 40 different countries and sales in more than 125 countries around the world. Find your local representative at: **www.cengage.com.**

To learn more about Cengage platforms and services, register or access your online learning solution, or purchase materials for your course, visit **www.cengage.com.**

Printed in Mexico
Print Number: 01   Print Year: 2020

BRIEF CONTENTS

CONTENTS

Chapter **14**
SEXUAL DYSFUNCTIONS, GENDER DYSPHORIA, AND PARAPHILIC DISORDERS
433

Chapter 17 LAW AND ETHICS IN ABNORMAL PSYCHOLOGY 541

FEATURES

DISORDERS CHARTS

PREFACE

We are all touched in one way or another by mental health issues, either directly through our own struggles with mental disorders or indirectly through friends or family. Thus, knowledge about the symptoms of, causes of, and treatments for mental disorders and about methods for maintaining optimal mental health is a highly relevant topic for all students. It is a privilege to write a textbook that summarizes information and research that is so meaningful to the lives of those who read the book.

The 11th edition of *Understanding Abnormal Behavior* has been extensively revised to accommodate the newest scientific, psychological, multicultural, and psychiatric research and is completely up-to-date with respect to the many changes and controversies surrounding the classification and diagnosis of mental disorders included in the American Psychiatric Association's *Diagnostic and Statistical Manual of Mental Disorders, Fifth Edition* (DSM-5). Because the 10th edition of *Understanding Abnormal Behavior* covered anticipated DSM-5 changes, you will find that most chapters in the 11th edition did not require extensive reorganization. However, we have included additional discussion of DSM-5 changes, as well as other key topics in the field of abnormal psychology. Although we have relied on the DSM-5 for much of our organizational framework and for the specific diagnostic characteristics of mental disorders, you will find that we do not follow the DSM in a mechanistic fashion. Instead, we remain committed to providing our readers with information from a variety of key organizations and from the multitude of medical and psychological publications that address mental health issues. Thus, you will find that our discussions of disorders, contemporary issues, controversies, and trends in the field rely on multiple sources of information from a variety of disciplines.

As authors of an abnormal psychology textbook, we feel a keen responsibility to keep our book fresh and to incorporate the burgeoning and immensely important research from the fields of neuroscience, psychology, and psychiatry that pertains to the study of abnormal psychology. In recent years, researchers from a variety of disciplines have made unprecedented contributions to our understanding of the causes of and most effective treatments for mental disorders. In addition to biological breakthroughs in treatment, there is excitement regarding how psychological forms of intervention can create lasting changes in brain functioning and improve the distressing emotional and behavioral symptoms associated with mental disorders. In keeping with our commitment to currency of information presented, you will find that we have included hundreds of new references in this edition of the text. Most important, consistent with our goal of a balanced presentation, the references come from a wide variety of journals and other resources. Further, we have made every attempt to determine which research is most critical to a comprehensive understanding of each mental disorder and to present that information in an understandable, nontechnical manner. Although we strive to avoid overwhelming students with extensive data or too much theory, we are strong believers in sharing research-based information and evidence-based mental health practices. As with previous editions of *Understanding Abnormal Behavior*, our goal has been to include recent and cutting-edge research from a variety of resources, but in a manner that engages the reader.

We continue to receive very positive feedback about our use of the Multipath Model of Mental Disorders; the model is considered a highly effective visual and conceptual framework that helps students understand the multitude of factors that influence the development of various mental health conditions. In keeping with this model, we once again emphasize the importance of considering biological, psychological, social, and sociocultural factors and their interactions in the etiology of mental disorders. Our four-dimensional model ensures that instructors consistently consider sociocultural influences that are associated with specific disorders—a dimension often neglected by contemporary models of psychopathology. Although we continue to emphasize the importance of multicultural issues in abnormal psychology, a topic that is increasingly salient given the growing diversity of the population, readers will find that we take a very balanced approach when discussing the etiology of mental disorders—emphasizing multicultural issues within the context of interactions between these cultural factors and biological, psychological, and social factors. In other words, we strive to provide an evenhanded, balanced approach to the topics we address throughout the text.

Readers will find that another signature feature of our text, Mental Disorders Charts, concisely describe symptoms and diagnostic criteria, prevalence, and gender data, as well as data on course and outcome for many of the disorders covered in the text. Students can easily compare and contrast the various disorders presented throughout the text by referring to these charts and the Multipath Model figures.

We are excited about the fresh focus and some of the innovative changes you will find in this newest edition of *Understanding Abnormal Behavior,* including our new Focus on Resilience feature that encompasses contributions from the field of positive psychology and highlights key information relevant to both prevention and recovery from the symptoms associated with various disorders. This emphasis is particularly important given all of the recent data on neuroplasticity and the changes that are possible with prevention efforts or with evidence-based therapy targeted toward ameliorating the distressing symptoms of many disorders.

Overall, we believe readers will find the text more engaging and captivating than ever before. We have made a consistent effort to align the information presented from chapter to chapter in order to enhance students' understanding of more complex topics. We also connect our discussions with current events whenever possible and with issues of particular importance to college-age populations. We have concentrated on providing students with information that is related not only to the field of abnormal psychology but also to their day-to-day lives—material students will find valuable both now and in the future. In fact, we view this text as a meaningful tool that students can refer to when they encounter questions regarding mental health issues in their personal lives or with co-workers or clientele within the workforce.

We have also prioritized putting a human face on the various disorders and issues we discuss thought the text. When writing, we have considered the fact that many students have direct experience with mental disorders, either because they are personally affected or because their friends or family members are experiencing or have experienced the distressing symptoms of a mental disorder. Many of the case studies are presented from the perspective of individuals coping with various disorders to allow readers to better comprehend the struggles involved.

As illustrated by the new information added to each chapter, this edition of our book provides current and relevant information on a wide variety of topics in the field of abnormal psychology.

New and Updated Coverage of the Eleventh Edition

Our foremost objective in preparing this edition was to thoroughly update the contents of the text and present the latest trends in research and clinical thinking, with a particular emphasis on the new DSM-5. This has led to updated coverage of many topics throughout the text, including the following:

Chapter 1—Abnormal Behavior

- Updated discussion of the DSM-5 definition of mental disorders.
- New statistics on the prevalence of mental disorders.
- Discussion of new topics, including the recovery movement; overcoming stigma and stereotypes (including the difference between public stigma and self-stigma); the importance of considering each person's strengths and assets; and technological advances that affect mental health research and treatment.

Chapter 2—Understanding and Treating Mental Disorders

- Expanded multipath model coverage, including a significantly expanded discussion of biological factors with a focus on key concepts that underlie later biological discussions throughout the text.
- New discussion of genetics and epigenetics, the enteric nervous system, neurohormones, neuroplasticity, and sex differences in brain development.
- Updated discussion of the social and sociocultural etiological dimensions, including a focus on stress associated with immigration (acculturative stress).
- Updated discussion of treatment techniques associated with the various theoretical models.

Chapter 3—Assessment and Classification of Mental Disorders

- Updated material on assessment, differential diagnosis, and classification of mental disorders.
- Expanded discussion of neuropsychological assessment, including new tables comparing structural and functional imaging techniques.
- Expanded discussion of the DSM-5 and controversies regarding the new classification system.
- Expanded coverage on cultural considerations in assessment and diagnosis.

Chapter 4—Research Methods for Studying Mental Disorders

- Updated sections on scientific evidence, the scientific method, and research design.
- New discussions about trends in research, including evidence-based practice and reducing research bias.

Chapter 5—Anxiety and Obsessive-Compulsive and Related Disorders

- New case studies.
- Expanded discussion of hoarding disorder.
- Expanded discussion of treatment for anxiety and obsessive-compulsive disorders, including research trends involving cognitive-behavioral therapies.

Chapter 6—Trauma- and Stressor-Related Disorders

- New case studies.
- Expanded discussion about the physiological and psychological effects of trauma.
- New discussion of adjustment disorders.
- Expanded discussion of biological factors contributing to stress disorders.
- Expanded discussion regarding treatment for trauma disorders.

Chapter 7—Somatic and Dissociative Disorders

- New disorders chart reflecting reorganization of somatic disorders in DSM-5.
- New discussion of self-reported medically self-sabotaging behaviors.
- New discussion regarding possible ramifications of the changes in the DSM-5 diagnostic criteria involving somatic symptoms.

Chapter 8—Depressive and Bipolar Disorders

- New tables outlining symptoms of depressive, hypomanic, or manic episodes and new figure regarding range of mood symptoms.
- New discussion of depressive reactions to grief and persistent complex bereavement disorder.
- New case studies and expanded discussion of depressive and hypomanic/manic symptoms.
- New discussion of seasonal patterns, maladaptive thinking patterns, and memory bias in depression.
- Reorganized and updated discussion of biological factors influencing depression.

Chapter 9—Suicide

- New figures with data on the frequency of suicidal thoughts and suicide attempts and ethnic and gender differences in completed suicide.
- New discussions regarding preventing suicide, coping with a suicidal crisis, suicide in the military, suicide among baby boomers, suicide in men, psychotherapy for clients with suicidal ideation, and the effects of suicide on friends and family.

Chapter 10—Eating Disorders

- Updated research on the etiology and treatment of eating disorders and obesity, including a discussion of the influence of hormones and intestinal bacteria.
- New discussions on prevention of eating disorders and online resources to counteract Web sites that encourage disordered eating.

Chapter 11—Substance-Related and Other Addictive Disorders

- Updated statistics and figures illustrating the prevalence of substance use and abuse, with a particular focus on alcohol.
- Expanded discussion regarding the abuse of illicit and prescription drugs.
- New topics, including the marijuana debate, e-cigarettes, and designer drugs.
- New discussion of other addictions, including gambling and Internet gaming disorders.

Chapter 12—Schizophrenia Spectrum Disorders

- Updated research on schizophrenia and explanations of the DSM-5 diagnostic categories.

- Expanded discussion of symptoms associated with schizophrenia spectrum disorders and cultural issues associated with schizophrenia.
- Updated discussion on attenuated psychosis syndrome.
- New discussion about the recovery model and early intervention for individuals at risk for psychotic disorders.

Chapter 13—Neurocognitive and Sleep–Wake Disorders

- Presentation of new research on various neurocognitive disorders, particularly Alzheimer's disease.
- Continued focus on neurocognitive disorders across the life span, with a strong emphasis on lifestyle changes that can help prevent the development of degenerative disorders such as dementia.
- Expanded discussion of traumatic brain injury and chronic traumatic encephalopathy.
- New discussion of normal sleep patterns and sleep–wake disorders, including the two major categories of sleep disorders included in DSM-5: dyssomnias and parasomnias.

Chapter 14—Sexual Dysfunctions, Gender Dysphoria, and Paraphilic Disorders

- Updated DSM-5 terminology related to sexual dysfunctions and paraphilic disorders.
- Updated application of the multipath model to sexual disorders.
- Discussion of new research on treatment for sexual dysfunctions and paraphilic disorders.

Chapter 15—Personality Psychopathology

- Chapter substantially reorganized to incorporate the 10 traditional personality disorders, as well as the DSM-5 alternative model for diagnosing personality psychopathology, including a new discussion of the dimensional and categorical assessment associated with the new alternative model.
- Expanded discussion of the 10 traditional personality categories, including updated research on etiology and treatment.
- Expanded discussion of the six personality types and five personality trait domains included in the DSM-5 alternative model for diagnosing a personality disorder.
- Critical discussion of the DSM-5 inclusion of two methods for diagnosing personality disorders and dimensional methods of personality assessment.
- Discussion of Dr. Marsha Linehan and her contributions to our understanding and treatment of borderline personality disorder.

Chapter 16—Disorders of Childhood and Adolescence

- Updated and expanded discussion of neurodevelopmental disorders, childhood anxiety, childhood post-traumatic stress disorder, reactive attachment disorder, tics and Tourette's syndrome.
- Updated discussion of new diagnostic categories, including nonsuicidal self-injury (a category undergoing further study), disruptive mood dysregulation disorder, and disinhibited social engagement disorder.
- New discussion regarding early prevention of lifelong mental illness and methods for enhancing resilience.

Chapter 17—Law and Ethics in Abnormal Psychology

- New cases illustrating dilemmas posed by the interaction of psychology and the law.

- Expanded discussion of the therapeutic and legal implications of disclosure by clients in regard to violent behaviors.

- New discussion of individual rights and the legal implications of suicide and assisted suicide.

In writing and revising this book, we have sought to engage students in the exciting process of understanding abnormal behavior and the ways that mental health professionals study and attempt to treat various disorders. In pursuing this goal, we have been guided by three major objectives:

- to provide students with scholarship of the highest quality;

- to offer an evenhanded treatment of abnormal psychology as both a scientific and a clinical endeavor, giving students the opportunity to explore topics thoroughly and responsibly; and

- to make our book inviting and stimulating to a wide range of students by focusing on meaningful topics such as eating disorders, traumatic head injury in sports, and the abuse of alcohol and other substances frequently encountered by college populations.

Our Approach

We take an eclectic, evidence- and research-based, multicultural approach to understanding abnormal behavior, drawing on important contributions from various disciplines and theoretical perspectives. The text covers the major categories of disorders in the updated *Diagnostic and Statistical Manual of Mental Disorders* (DSM-5), but it is not a mechanistic reiteration of the DSM. We believe that different combinations of life experiences and constitutional factors influence mental disorders, and we project this view throughout the text. This combination of factors is demonstrated in our multipath model, which was introduced in our 9th edition. There are several elements to our multipath model. First, possible contributors to mental disorders are divided into four dimensions: biological, psychological, social, and sociocultural. Second, factors in the four dimensions can interact and influence each other in any direction. Third, different combinations and interactions within the four dimensions can cause abnormal behaviors. Fourth, many disorders appear to be heterogeneous in nature; therefore, there may be different versions of a disorder or a spectrum of the disorder. Finally, distinctly different disorders (such as anxiety and depression) can be caused by similar factors.

Sociocultural factors, including cultural norms, values, and expectations, are given special attention in our multipath model. We are convinced that cross-cultural comparisons of abnormal behavior and treatment methods can greatly enhance our understanding of disorders; cultural and gender influences are emphasized throughout the text. *Understanding Abnormal Behavior* was the first textbook on abnormal psychology to integrate and emphasize the role of multicultural factors. Although many texts have since followed our lead, the 11th edition continues to provide the most extensive coverage and integration of multicultural models, explanations, and concepts available. Not only do we discuss how changing demographics increase the importance of multicultural psychology, we also introduce multicultural models of psychopathology in the opening chapters and address multicultural issues throughout the text whenever research findings and theoretical formulations allow. Such an approach adds richness to students' understanding of mental disorders. As psychologists (and professors), we know that learning is enhanced whenever material is presented in a lively and engaging manner. We therefore provide case vignettes and clients' descriptions of their experiences to complement and illustrate symptoms of various disorders and research-based explanations. Our goal is to encourage students to think critically rather than to merely assimilate a collection of facts and theories. As a result, we hope that students will develop an appreciation of the study of abnormal behavior.

Special Features

The 11th edition includes a number of new features, as well as features that were popularized in earlier editions and that, in some cases, have been revised and enhanced. These features are aimed at helping students to organize and integrate the material in each chapter.

As previously noted, our *Multipath Model of Mental Disorders* provides a framework through which students can understand the origins of mental disorders. The model is introduced in Chapter 2 and applied throughout the book, with multiple figures highlighting how biological, psychological, social, and sociocultural factors contribute to the development of various disorders.

Critical Thinking boxes provide factual evidence and thought-provoking questions that raise key issues in research, examine widely held assumptions about abnormal behavior, or challenge the student's own understanding of the text material.

Controversy boxes deal with controversial issues, particularly those with wide implications for our society. These boxes stimulate critical thinking, evoke alternative views, provoke discussion, and allow students to better explore the wider meaning of abnormal behavior in our society.

Contemporary Trends and Future Directions is a new feature with which we conclude most of the chapters, providing a final look at current trends in the field that are relevant to topics covered in each chapter.

Myth versus Reality discussions challenge the many myths and false beliefs that have surrounded the field of abnormal behavior and help students realize that beliefs, some of which may appear to be "common sense," must be checked against scientific facts and knowledge.

Did You Know? boxes found throughout the book provide fascinating, at-a-glance research-based tidbits for students.

Chapter Outlines and **Focus Questions**, appearing in the first pages of every chapter, provide a framework and stimulate active learning.

Chapter Summaries provide students with a concise recap of the chapter's most important concepts via brief answers to the chapter's opening Focus Questions.

A wide variety of **Case Studies** allow issues of mental health and mental disorders to "come to life" for students and instructors. Many cases are taken from journal articles and actual clinical files.

Streamlined **Disorder Charts** provide snapshots of disorders in an easy-to-read format.

Key Terms are highlighted in the text and appear in the margins.

MindTap for Sue's Understanding Abnormal Behavior

MindTap for Sue's *Understanding Abnormal Behavior* engages and empowers students to produce their best work—consistently. By seamlessly integrating course material with videos, activities, apps, and much more, MindTap creates a unique learning path that fosters increased comprehension and efficiency.

For students:

- MindTap delivers real-world relevance with activities and assignments that help students build critical thinking and analytical skills that will transfer to other courses and their professional lives.

- MindTap helps students stay organized and efficient with a single destination that reflects what's important to the instructor, along with the tools students need to master the content.
- MindTap empowers and motivates students with information that shows where they stand at all times—both individually and compared to the highest performers in their class.

Additionally, for instructors, MindTap allows you to:

- Control what content students see and when they see it with a learning path that can be used as is or aligned with your syllabus.
- Create a unique learning path of relevant readings and multimedia activities that move students up the learning taxonomy from basic knowledge and comprehension to analysis, application, and critical thinking.
- Integrate your own content into the MindTap Reader using your documents or pulling from sources such as RSS feeds, YouTube videos, Web sites, Googledocs, and more.
- Use powerful analytics and reports that provide a snapshot of class progress, time in course, engagement, and completion.

In addition to the benefits of the platform, MindTap for Sue's *Understanding Abnormal Behavior* features:

- Videos from the Continuum Video Project.
- Case studies to help students humanize psychological disorders and connect content to the real world.

Supplements

Continuum Video Project

The Continuum Video Project provides holistic, three-dimensional portraits of individuals dealing with psychopathologies. Videos show clients living their daily lives, interacting with family and friends, and displaying—rather than just describing—their symptoms. Before each video segment, students are asked to make observations about the individual's symptoms, emotions, and behaviors, and then rate them on the spectrum from normal to severe. The Continuum Video Project allows students to "see" the disorder and the person, humanly; the videos also illuminate student understanding that abnormal behavior can be viewed along a continuum.

Instructor's Manual

The *Online Instructor's Manual* contains chapter overviews, learning objectives, lecture outlines with discussion points, key terms, classroom activities, demonstrations, lecture topics, suggested supplemental reading material, handouts, video resources, and Internet resources. ISBN: 978-1-305-50449-3

Cognero

Cengage Learning Testing Powered by Cognero is a flexible, online system that allows you to author, edit, and manage test bank content from multiple Cengage Learning solutions, create multiple test versions in an instant, and deliver tests from your Learning Management System (LMS), your classroom, or wherever you want. ISBN: 978-1-305-50488-2

PowerPoint

The Online PowerPoint features lecture outlines, key images from the text, and relevant video clips. ISBN: 978-1-305-49302-5

Acknowledgments

We continue to appreciate the critical feedback received from reviewers and colleagues. The following individuals helped us prepare the 10th edition by sharing valuable insights, opinions, and recommendations:

Katheryn Lovell,
Thomas Nelson Community College

Joseph Falco,
Rockland Community College

Tiffany Rich,
East Los Angeles College

Sandra Terneus,
Tennessee Technological University

Dawn Lin,
Jackson State University

We also thank the reviewers of the previous editions of *Understanding Abnormal Behavior.*

Sandra K. Arntz,
Northern Illinois University

Julia C. Babcock,
University of Houston

Jay Brown,
Texas Wesleyan University

Jeffrey D. Burke,
University of Pittsburgh

Catherine Chambliss,
Ursinus College

Betty Clark,
University of Mary-Hardin

Irvin Cohen,
Hawaii Pacific University and Kapiolani Community College

Lorry Cology,
Owens Community College

Bonnie J. Ekstrom,
Bemidji State University

Greg A. R. Febbraro,
Drake University

Kate Flory,
University of South Carolina

David M. Fresco,
Kent State University

Jerry L. Fryrear,
University of Houston, Clear Lake

Michele Galietta,
John Jay College of Criminal Justice

Alice L. Godbey,
Daytona State College

Christina Gordon,
Fox Valley Technical College

Robert Hoff,
Mercyhurst College

Deborah Huerta,
The University of Texas at Brownsville

George-Harold Jennings,
Drew University

Kim L. Krinsky,
Georgia Perimeter College

Arlene Lacombe,
St. Joseph's University

Brian E. Lozano,
Virginia Polytechnic Institute and State University

Vicki Lucey,
Las Positas College

Polly McMahon,
Spokane Falls Community College

Jan Mohlman,
Rutgers University

Sherry Davis Molock,
George Washington University

Rebecca L. Motley,
University of Toledo

Gilbert R. Parra,
University of Memphis

Jeffrey J. Pedroza,
Santa Ana College

Kimberly Renk,
University of Central Florida

Mark Richardson,
Boston University

Alan Roberts,
Indiana University

Tom Schoeneman,
Lewis and Clark College

Daniel L. Segal,
University of Colorado at Colorado Springs

Michael D. Spiegler,
Providence College

Ma. Teresa G. Tuason,
University of North Florida

Theresa A. Wadkins,
University of Nebraska, Kearney

Susan Brooks Watson,
Hawaii Pacific University

Fred Whitford,
Montana State University

Jessica L. Yokley,
University of Pittsburgh

We also wish to acknowledge the support, and high quality of work, done by Tim Matray, Product Manager; Michelle Clark, Content Project Manager; Nicole Richards, Product Assistant; and Vernon Boes, Art Director. We also thank the text designer and the text and photo researchers. We are particularly grateful for the patience, efficiency, and creativity shown by content developer Tangelique Williams-Grayer and production editor Cassie Carey. Their positive contributions and flexibility were invaluable to the successful completion of this edition of the text.

D. S.
D. W. S.
D. M. S.
S. S.

ABOUT THE AUTHORS

 **DAVID SUE** is Professor Emeritus of Psychology at Western Washington University, where he is an associate of the Center for Cross-Cultural Research. He has served as the director of both the Psychology Counseling Clinic and the Mental Health Counseling Program. He co-authored the books *Counseling and Psychotherapy in a Diverse Society* and *Counseling the Culturally Diverse: Theory and Practice*. He received his Ph.D. in Clinical Psychology from Washington State University. His research interests revolve around multicultural issues in individual and group counseling. He enjoys hiking, snowshoeing, traveling, and spending time with his family.

 **DERALD WING SUE** is Professor of Psychology and Education in the Department of Counseling and Clinical Psychology at Teachers College, Columbia University. He has written extensively in the field of counseling psychology and multicultural counseling/therapy and is author of the best-selling book *Counseling the Culturally Diverse: Theory and Practice*. Dr. Sue has served as president of the Society of Counseling Psychology and the Society for the Psychological Study of Ethnic Minority Issues and has received numerous awards for teaching and service. He received his doctorate from the University of Oregon and is married and the father of two children. Friends describe him as addicted to exercise and the Internet.

 **DIANE M. SUE** received her Ph.D. from the University of Michigan, Ann Arbor. She has worked as a school psychologist and counselor, and with adults needing specialized care for mental illness and neurocognitive disorders. She has also served as an adjunct faculty member at Western Washington University. She received the Washington State School Psychologist of the Year Award and the Western Washington University College of Education Professional Excellence Award, and has co-authored the book *Counseling and Psychotherapy in a Diverse Society*. Her areas of expertise include child and adolescent psychology, neuropsychology, and interventions with ethnic minority children and adolescents. She enjoys travel and spending time with friends and family.

 **STANLEY SUE** is Distinguished Professor of Psychology and Co-Director of the Center for Excellence in Diversity at Palo Alto University. He was Assistant and Associate Professor of Psychology at the University of Washington (1971–1981); Professor of Psychology at University of California, Los Angeles (1981–1996); and Distinguished Professor of Psychology at University of California–Davis (1996–2010). He served as President of the Western Psychological Association in 2010 and as President of APA Division 45 (Society for the Psychological Study of Culture, Ethnicity, and Race) in 2015. His hobbies include working on computers and swimming.

1

ABNORMAL BEHAVIOR

IN THE EARLY MORNING HOURS of January 8, 2011, 23-year-old Jared Lee Loughner posted a message on social media, prefaced with the words "Goodbye." The post continued: "Dear friends... Please don't be mad at me. The literacy rate is below 5%. I haven't talked to one person who is literate. I want to make it out alive. The longest war in the history of the United States. Goodbye. I'm saddened with the current currency and job employment. I had a bully at school. Thank you."

Hours later, Loughner took a taxi to a supermarket in Tucson, Arizona, where Democratic Representative Gabrielle Giffords was meeting with her constituents. Loughner approached the gathering and opened fire on Giffords and numerous bystanders using a semi-automatic handgun, killing six people and injuring thirteen others. Giffords, believed to have been Loughner's target, was shot in the head and left in critical condition (Cloud, 2011). After his arrest, Loughner was declared incompetent to stand trial due to his extensive mental confusion. However, 19 months after the shooting, his mental condition improved enough for him to participate in court proceedings. He pleaded guilty to all charges related to the shooting and received a life sentence without the possibility of parole. Fortunately, Giffords has demonstrated remarkable resilience and recovery from her brain injury. Although she resigned her congressional seat in 2012 to continue her rehabilitation, she is determined to return to public service.

As with other mass shootings, many of us attempted to make sense out of this apparently senseless act, asking questions such as: What could have motivated Loughner to take so many innocent lives? Did he have a **mental disorder**? Was he a political extremist? Was he a callous, psychopathic killer? Was he suicidal? Was he high on drugs? What was Loughner like before the shooting? Were there warning signs that he was so dangerous? Could therapy or medication have helped Loughner? Could *anything* have prevented this tragedy?

These questions are extremely difficult to answer for a number of reasons. First, understanding what might cause behavior and mental disturbance like

focus
QUESTIONS

1. What is abnormal psychology?
2. How do we differentiate between normal and abnormal behaviors?
3. What societal factors affect definitions of abnormality?
4. How common are mental disorders?
5. Why is it important to confront the stigma and stereotyping associated with mental illness?
6. How have explanations of abnormal behavior changed over time?
7. What were early explanations regarding the causes of mental disorders?
8. What are some contemporary trends in abnormal psychology?

mental disorder psychological symptoms or behavioral patterns that reflect an underlying psychobiological dysfunction, are associated with distress or disability, and are not merely an expectable response to common stressors or losses

mental illness a mental health condition that negatively affects a person's emotions, thinking, behavior, relationships with others, or overall functioning

abnormal psychology the scientific study whose objectives are to describe, explain, predict, and modify behaviors associated with mental disorders

psychopathology the study of the symptoms, causes, and treatments of mental disorders

Loughner's is not an easy task. We still do not know enough about the specific causes of abnormal behavior and mental disorders to arrive at a definitive answer. We do know, however, that **mental illness** does not generally result from a single cause but instead arises from an interaction of many factors, a fact that we discuss in the next chapter.

Second, trying to assess someone's state of mind can be extremely difficult. In the case of Loughner, his thinking and reasoning were so confused that he was unable to assist in his own defense for over 18 months. Given such mental confusion, any attempt to construct a portrait of Loughner's state of mind around the time of the shooting requires the use of secondary sources such as observations by family and acquaintances, school records, and other data (Internet postings and media communications). Fortunately, unlike Loughner, many people recognize the need to seek help when they experience emotional distress or the behavioral, emotional, or physical symptoms of a mental disorder. It is very important to note that the vast majority of those affected by mental illness display neither the violence nor the extreme mental confusion shown by Loughner (Grann & Langstrom, 2007).

As you can see, understanding mental disorders is a complex topic. The purpose of this book is to help you understand the signs, symptoms, and causes of mental illness and to begin to answer questions such as those posed above. We also focus on research related to preventing mental disorders and successfully coping with and overcoming mental illness. Before we begin our exploration of mental health and mental illness, however, it helps to learn more about the study of abnormal behavior, including some of its history and emerging changes in the field. During our discussion, we will periodically refer to the Loughner case to illustrate issues in the mental health field.

AP Images/Pima County Sheriff's Dept. via *The Arizona Republic*, File/Anonymous

Untreated Mental Illness

This picture of Jared Lee Loughner was taken after his arrest for shooting Representative Gabrielle Giffords and killing numerous bystanders. It was not until after his arrest that he received a mental health evaluation and was diagnosed with paranoid schizophrenia.

The Field of Abnormal Psychology

Abnormal psychology focuses on **psychopathology**, the study of the symptoms and causes of mental distress and the various treatments for behavioral and mental disorders. Those who study psychopathology attempt to describe, explain, predict, and modify the behaviors, emotions or thoughts associated with various mental conditions. This includes behavior that ranges from highly unusual to fairly common—from the violent homicides, suicides, and mental breakdowns that are widely reported by the news media to unsensational (but more prevalent) concerns such as depression, anxiety, eating disturbances, and substance abuse. People who work in the field of psychopathology strive to alleviate the distress and life disruption experienced by those with mental disorders and the concerns of their friends and family members.

Describing Behavior

If you were experiencing emotional distress, you might decide to seek help from a **mental health professional**. If so, the therapist might begin by asking you some questions and observing your behavior and reactions. The therapist would then use these observations, paired with information you share about your background and symptoms, to formulate a **psychodiagnosis**, an attempt to describe, assess, and understand your particular situation and the possibility that you might be experiencing a mental disorder. After gaining a better understanding of your situation, you and the professional would work together to develop a **treatment plan**, beginning with a focus on your most distressing symptoms.

Loughner never worked with a mental health professional before the shooting, but received several psychiatric evaluations while imprisoned. In addition to receiving a psychiatric diagnosis, Loughner was evaluated to assess potential dangerousness, the degree to which he was in contact with reality, and whether he was mentally competent to assist in his own defense. Based on observations of Loughner and a review of available information, the examiners determined that Loughner had symptoms consistent with a diagnosis of schizophrenia (a serious mental disorder we discuss in Chapter 12).

Explaining Behavior

Identifying the **etiology**, or possible causes, for abnormal behavior is a high priority for mental health professionals. In the case of Loughner's actions, one popular explanation was that he was a right-wing political extremist who held positions diametrically opposed to those of Representative Giffords. However, Loughner's issues were much more complex. His Internet postings and YouTube videos suggested that he was convinced that the U.S. government was brainwashing people. Additionally, when he attended one of Giffords' political events in 2007, he asked the question "What is government if words have no meaning?" Giffords declined to comment (probably because the question made no sense to her). Loughner apparently felt slighted and angered by her lack of response. This interaction reportedly fueled his rage and obsession with Giffords.

A closer look at Loughner's background reveals many other possible causes for his rampage:

- Friends noted that he seemed to undergo a personality transformation around the time he dropped out of high school. He again experienced academic difficulties when attending community college; he was suspended because of poor academic performance, disruptive behavior, and a YouTube posting in which he described the school as "one of the biggest scams in America." Could this pattern of academic failure have contributed to his downward spiral and resultant anger?

- Others noted that Loughner was devastated following a breakup with a high school girlfriend. The failed relationship seemed to trigger increasing drug and alcohol abuse. He reportedly used marijuana, LSD, and other hallucinogens. When he tried to enlist in the U.S. Army, he was deemed unqualified because of his drug use. Did the breakup, his drug use, or being rejected from military service play a role in his actions?

- By all accounts, Loughner was fascinated with lucid dreaming, a state of consciousness where the dreamer is half awake but aware he or she is dreaming.

mental health professional health care practitioners (such as psychologists, psychiatrists, psychiatric nurses, social workers, or mental health counselors) whose services focus on improving mental health or treating mental illness

psychodiagnosis assessment and description of an individual's psychological symptoms, including inferences about what might be causing the psychological distress

treatment plan a proposed course of therapy, developed collaboratively by a therapist and client, that addresses the client's most distressing mental health symptoms

etiology the cause or causes for a condition

DID YOU KNOW?

It is very difficult to predict if someone will behave violently. However, risk factors such as youth, male gender, access to weapons, and a history of fire-setting, violence, substance abuse, impulsivity, cruelty to animals, or lack of compassion are all associated with increased potential for violence.

SOURCE: Buchanan, Binder, Norko, & Scwartz, 2012

The practice of lucid dreaming has a long history among some Eastern cultures that believe in altered states of consciousness. The ability to control dreams and to discern meaning is among the goals of those who engage in lucid dreaming. Loughner apparently became obsessed with lucid dreaming and kept a dream journal. Could lucid dreaming have caused his break with reality and his paranoid beliefs?

- Others have noted that biological factors may account for Loughner's mental breakdown. While incarcerated, he was diagnosed with schizophrenia. Research points to a biological basis for this disorder, particularly among those who use marijuana at an early age. Interestingly, the downward spiral of Loughner in his early twenties is very consistent with the onset of schizophrenia, as are his paranoid beliefs and nonsensical speech. What role did biological factors play in his deteriorating mental condition?

These snippets from Loughner's life suggest many possible explanations for his actions, including the following: a biological problem, perhaps made worse by his use of marijuana; his belief in extremist political rhetoric; his academic and military failures; his anger about the breakup with his girlfriend; his obsession with lucid dreaming; and his substance abuse. Some explanations may appear more valid than others. As you will see in the next chapter, no single explanation adequately accounts for complex human behavior. Normal and abnormal behaviors result from interactions among various biological, psychological, social, and sociocultural factors.

Predicting Behavior

Many believe that there was sufficient evidence to predict that Loughner was a seriously disturbed and potentially dangerous young man. At Pima Community College, concerned staff and students contacted campus police regarding Loughner's disruptive conduct on at least five occasions. He posted hate-filled rants about the college on YouTube, and at least one teacher and one classmate expressed concern that he was capable of a school shooting. To protect the campus, college administrators suspended Loughner, stipulating that he could return if (a) his behavior conformed to the codes of the college, and (b) he received a mental health clearance confirming that his presence on campus would not constitute a danger to himself or others. In light of these reports, why was it that Loughner never received any type of psychological help or treatment? How could he purchase firearms during a period of obvious mental deterioration? If college officials were concerned that he was dangerous, why did mental health professionals or police officials not intervene?

There appear to be several reasons. First, *civil commitment*, or involuntary confinement, represents an extreme decision that has major implications for an individual's civil liberties. Our legal system operates under the assumption that people are innocent until proven guilty. Locking someone up before he or she commits a dangerous act potentially violates that person's civil rights. In Loughner's case, there were concerns but no evidence that he presented an imminent threat. Second, because Loughner apparently never sought mental health treatment, he was not in contact with a mental health professional who would have recognized the potential danger from his deteriorating mental condition. However, even if Loughner had sought treatment, his therapy would have been confidential unless the therapist

Intervening Through Therapy

Group therapy is a widely used form of treatment for many problems, especially those involving interpersonal relationships. In this group session, participants are learning to develop adaptive skills for coping with social problems rather than relying on alcohol or drugs to escape the stresses of life.

©Monkey Business Images/Shutterstock.com

became aware of a clear and present danger to others. Regarding the purchase of firearms, Loughner met no criteria in Arizona that prevented him from purchasing weapons. Additionally, it is possible for someone with a deteriorating mental condition to appear relatively normal.

Modifying Behavior

Distressing symptoms can often be modified through **psychotherapy**, which is a program of systematic intervention designed to improve a person's behavioral, emotional, or cognitive state. Mental health professionals focus first on understanding the cause of a client's mental distress and then work with the client to plan treatment. Just as there are many ways to explain mental disorders, there are many therapies and many professional helpers offering their services. (Table 1.1 lists the qualifications and training of various mental health professionals.) Many believe that Loughner's violent rampage could have been prevented if he had received psychotherapy; his intense anger, disturbed thinking, and deteriorating mental condition would have been recognized as a serious concern. Treatment might have included appropriate medications, anger management and social skills training, educating Loughner and his family about schizophrenia, and perhaps even temporary hospitalization to stabilize his mental condition.

psychotherapy a program of systematic intervention with the purpose of improving a client's behavioral, emotional, or cognitive symptoms

Table 1.1 The Mental Health Professions

Clinical psychologist	• Must hold a Ph.D. or a Psy.D. • Training includes course work in psychopathology, personality, diagnosis, psychological testing, psychotherapy, and human physiology.
Counseling psychologist	• Academic and internship requirements are similar to those for a clinical psychologist, but with a focus on life adjustment problems rather than mental illness.
Mental health counselor; marriage/family therapist	• Training usually includes a master's degree in counseling or psychology and many hours of supervised clinical experience.
Neuropsychologist	• Ph.D.-level specialization focusing on brain-behavior relationships. • Conducts assessment, diagnosis, treatment planning, and research related to neurological, medical, developmental, or psychiatric conditions.
Psychiatrist	• Holds an M.D. degree; can prescribe medication. • Completes the 4 years of medical school required for an M.D., and an additional 3 or 4 years of training in psychiatry.
Psychiatric nurse	• Holds an R.N. degree from a nursing program, plus specialized psychiatric training. • Some are advanced practice registered nurses (APRNs) who have completed master's or doctoral degrees and are allowed to prescribe medication. • Specializes in the assessment, diagnosis, treatment, and evaluation of mental illness.
Psychiatric social worker	• Holds a master's degree from a social work graduate program. • Specializes in assessment, screening, and therapy with high-need clients and outreach to other agencies.
School psychologist	• Completes a master's or a doctoral degree in school psychology. • Specializes in assessing and intervening with the emotional and learning difficulties of students in educational settings.
Substance abuse counselor	• Professional training requirements vary; many practitioners have personal experience with addiction. • Works in agencies that specialize in the evaluation and treatment of drug and alcohol addiction.

© Cengage Learning®

Views of Abnormality

Understanding and treating the distressing behavior caused by mental illness is the main objective of abnormal psychology. But how do mental health professionals decide if a client is experiencing a mental disorder? How do professionals define a mental disorder? The *Diagnostic and Statistical Manual of Mental Disorders* (5th ed.; DSM-5; American Psychiatric Association [APA], 2013), the most widely used classification system of mental disorders, indicates that a mental disorder has the following components:

(a) involves a significant disturbance in thinking, emotional regulation, or behavior caused by a dysfunction in the basic psychological, biological, or developmental processes involved in normal development;

(b) causes significant distress or difficulty with day-to-day functioning; and

(c) is not merely a culturally expected response to common stressors or losses or a reflection of political or religious beliefs that conflict with societal norms.

This definition is quite broad and raises many questions. First, when are symptoms or patterns of behavior significant enough to have meaning? Second, is it possible to have a mental disorder without any signs of distress or discomfort? Third, what criteria do we use to decide if a behavior pattern is a reflection of an underlying psychological or biological dysfunction and not merely a normal variation or an expectable response to common stressors?

Complex definitions aside, most practitioners agree that mental disorders involve behavior or other distressing symptoms that depart from the norm and that harm affected individuals or others. Nearly all definitions of abnormal behavior use some form of statistical average to gauge deviations from normative standards. The four major factors involved in judging psychopathology are

- distress,
- deviance,
- dysfunction, and
- dangerousness.

Distress

Most people who seek the help of therapists are experiencing psychological distress that affects social, emotional, or physical functioning. In the social sphere, an individual may become withdrawn and avoid interactions with others or, at the other extreme, may engage in inappropriate or dangerous social interactions. In the emotional realm, distress might involve extreme or prolonged reactions such as anxiety and depression. Distress also surfaces physically in conditions such as asthma or hypertension or with symptoms of fatigue, pain, or heart palpitations. Of course, we all have social, emotional, and physical ups and downs. For example, you have probably felt temporarily depressed after experiencing a loss or a disappointment or anxious about situations involving friendships or school. However,

Societal Norms and Deviance

Societal norms often affect our definitions of normality and abnormality. When social norms begin to change, standards used to judge behaviors or roles also shift. Here we see a stay-at-home father cooking with his son. In the past, staying home to care for children was a role reserved for women. Role reversals in employment, hobbies, sports, and other activities are becoming more acceptable over time.

MGP/Digital Vision/Getty Images

if your reaction is so intense, exaggerated, or prolonged that it interferes with your ability to function adequately, the symptoms may reflect a mental disorder.

Deviance

Normal behavior is behavior that occurs frequently. Abnormal behaviors are those that occur least frequently. Thus, abnormal behaviors deviate—or represent a significant deviation from—social norms. Some examples of unusual behavior include false perceptions of reality (such as **hallucinations**), an intense preoccupation with repetitively washing one's hands, or demonstrating extreme panic in a social setting. Defining symptoms of mental illness can be extremely subjective; decisions about what is normal or abnormal are influenced by the background of the mental health professional evaluating the symptoms and the cultural context in which the behavior or symptoms occurs.

Certain sexual acts, criminal activities, and homicide are also behaviors that our society considers deviant. However, such activities do not necessarily involve the psychological or biological dysfunction associated with mental disorders. Additionally, social norms are far from static, and behavioral standards are not always absolute. Changes in societal attitudes toward human sexuality are a prime example. Many films and magazines now openly exhibit the naked human body and explicit sex acts, and topless and bottomless nightclub entertainment is hardly newsworthy. Additionally, compared to earlier generations, women are freer to question traditional gender roles and to act more assertively in initiating sex. Such changes in attitudes make it difficult to subscribe to absolute standards of normality.

However, certain behaviors are considered abnormal in most situations. These behaviors include refusal to leave your house; depression so severe that you sleep most of the day; starving yourself because you are so fearful of gaining weight; experiencing frequent nightmares involving a trauma you experienced; forgetting your own identity; feeling overwhelmed with fear at the sight of a spider; avoiding contact with objects such as doorknobs because of the fear of germs; believing that others can "hear" your thoughts; seeing aliens inside your home; collecting so many items that your health and safety are jeopardized; or intentionally making your own child sick with the purpose of receiving attention. Even taking varying cultural norms into account, these situations (which will be discussed throughout the book) would be seen as abnormal.

Personal Dysfunction

In everyday life, we all fulfill a variety of social and occupational roles, such as friend, family member, student, or employee. Emotional problems sometimes interfere with the performance of these roles. Therefore, role dysfunction is often considered when determining if someone has a mental disorder. One way to assess dysfunction is to compare someone's performance with the requirements of a role. An employee who suddenly cannot fulfill job demands may be experiencing emotional difficulties. Dysfunction can also be assessed by comparing an individual's performance with his or her potential. For example, a sudden drop in academic performance may signal that a college student is experiencing effects from substance abuse or from anxiety, depression, or other common mental disorders.

Dangerousness

Even though it is a statistical rarity for individuals who are mentally ill to commit violent crimes, media coverage of national tragedies has led the public to associate mental illness with violence. In reality, only a small minority of acts of

hallucination   a sensory experience (such as an image, sound, smell, or taste) that seems real but that does not exist outside of the mind

Determining What Is Abnormal

By most people's standards, the full-body tattoos of these three men would be considered unusual. Yet these three men openly and proudly display their body art at the National Tattoo Association Convention. Such individuals may be very "normal" and functional in their work and personal lives. This leads to an important question: What constitutes abnormal behavior, and how do we recognize it?

DID YOU KNOW?

It was not until 1986 that homosexuality was completely removed as a disorder from the DSM. The decision was based on the many studies that demonstrate that individuals with a homosexual orientation are as well-adjusted as the heterosexual population.

violence involve someone with a severe mental illness (Frazel & Grann, 2006). Drug and alcohol abuse is much more likely to result in violent behavior than are other kinds of mental illness (Friedman & Michels, 2013). Even though violence is rare, predicting the possibility that clients might be dangerous to themselves or to others has become an inescapable part of the role of mental health professionals (Scott & Resnick, 2009). Therapists are required by law to take appropriate action when a client is potentially homicidal or suicidal. In the case of potential harm to others, they have a duty to warn the intended victim or to contact officials who can provide protection, a topic we cover in Chapter 17. In the case of Loughner, some believed he was dangerous, but the circumstances were such that neither law enforcement nor mental health professionals were directly involved prior to the shooting.

Cultural Considerations in Abnormal Behavior

culture   the configuration of shared values, beliefs, attitudes, and behaviors that is transmitted from one generation to another by members of a particular group and symbolized by artifacts, roles, expectations, and institutions

cultural relativism   the belief that lifestyles, cultural values, and worldviews affect the expression and definition of mental disorders

Psychologists now recognize that all behaviors, whether normal or abnormal, originate from a cultural context. **Culture** is the learned behavior that members of a group transmit to the next generation. Culture includes shared values, beliefs, attitudes, and the group's views about the world (D. W. Sue & Sue, 2013). Our cultural background can significantly influence not only our behavior, but also our definition or view of mental illness. This is **cultural relativism**—the belief that lifestyles, cultural values, and worldviews affect the expression and determination of abnormal behavior (Becker & Kleiman, 2013). For example, a body of research supports the conclusion that acting-out behaviors associated with mental disorders are much higher in the United States than in Asia; even Asian Americans in the United States are less likely to express symptoms via acting out (D. W. Sue & Sue, 2013; Yang & WonPat-Borja, 2007). Researchers have proposed that Asian cultural values (restraint of feelings, emphasis on self-control, and use of subtlety in approaching problems) all contribute to this difference. According to cultural relativism, cultures vary in what they define as normal or abnormal behavior. In some cultural groups, hallucinating (having false sensory impressions) is considered normal in some situations, particularly religious ceremonies. Yet in the United States, hallucinating is typically viewed as a symptom of a psychological disorder.

Cultural universality, on the other hand, refers to the perspective that symptoms of mental disorders are the same in all cultures and societies (Eshun & Gurung, 2009). According to those who see mental illness as a universal phenomenon, specific mental disorders would have the same causes and symptoms throughout the world. Which point of view is correct? Should the criteria used to determine normality and abnormality be based on cultural universality or cultural relativism? Few mental health professionals today embrace the extreme of either position, although most gravitate toward one or the other. Proponents of cultural universality focus on specific disorders and minimize cultural factors, while proponents of cultural relativism focus on the cultural context within which symptoms are manifested. Both views are valid. Many disorders have symptoms that are very similar across cultures. In some cases, however, there are cultural differences in the definitions, descriptions, and understandings of mental illness.

Cultural Relativism

Cultural differences often lead to misunderstandings and misinterpretations. In a society that values technological conveniences and modern fashion, the lifestyles and cultural values of some groups may be perceived as strange. The Amish, for example, continue to rely on the horse and buggy for transportation. Women in both Amish and Islamic cultures wear simple, concealing clothing; according to the cultural norms of these communities, dressing in any other way would be considered deviant.

Sociopolitical Considerations in Abnormality

The criteria for defining abnormal behavior discussed so far are not without fault. Some scholars believe that we also need to consider behavior from a sociopolitical perspective—the social and political context within which a behavior occurs. The importance of considering the sociopolitical implications of defining mental illness was well-articulated by Thomas Szasz (1987). In a radical departure from conventional beliefs, he asserted that mental illness is a myth, a fictional creation that society uses to control and change people. According to Szasz, people may have "problems in living," but not "mental illness." His argument stems from three beliefs: (a) that abnormal behavior is so labeled by society because it is different, not necessarily because it reflects illness; (b) that unusual belief systems are not necessarily wrong; and (c) that abnormal behavior is frequently a reflection of something wrong with society rather than with the individual. Few mental health professionals would take the extreme position advocated by Szasz, but his arguments highlight an important

cultural universality the assumption that a fixed set of mental disorders exists whose manifestations and symptoms are similar across cultures

area of concern. Therapists and other practitioners must be sensitive to the fact that personal bias, sociopolitical factors, or societal norms and values may influence decisions about diagnosis and treatment.

How Common Are Mental Disorders?

Many of us have direct experiences with mental disorders, either personally or through our involvement with family and friends. You may have wondered, "Just how many people are affected by a mental disorder?" To answer this question and to understand societal trends and factors that contribute to the occurrence of specific mental disorders, we turn to data from **psychiatric epidemiology**, the study of the prevalence of mental illness in a society. The **prevalence** of a disorder is the percentage of people in a population who have the disorder during a given interval of time. For example, the results from three large studies from the Department of Health and Human Services revealed that 24.8 percent of adults have experienced a mental disorder (not including a drug or alcohol use disorder) during the last 12 months, with 5.8 percent facing a serious mental disorder such as schizophrenia (Bagalman & Napili, 2013). When looking at prevalence rates, it is important to consider the time interval involved. A **lifetime prevalence** rate refers to existence of the disorder during any part of a person's life, whereas the study just discussed involved a 12-month prevalence rate.

In a comprehensive study investigating the lifetime prevalence of mental disorders in U.S. youths (Merikangas et al., 2010), data from a face-to-face survey involving more than 10,000 teenagers (between the ages of 13 and 18) revealed that nearly half of those interviewed met the criteria for at least one psychological disorder (see Figure 1.1). Additionally, 40 percent of those with a disorder also met the criteria for at least one additional disorder. Anxiety disorder was the most common (31.9 percent), followed by behavior disorders (19.1 percent), mood disorders such as depression and bipolar disorder (14.3 percent), and substance-use disorders (11.4 percent). Among the adolescents surveyed who had a mental disorder, 22.2 percent reported that their symptoms caused severe impairment or distress. As you can see, mental disorders are very common, even among the young.

This kind of statistical information allows us to determine how frequently or infrequently various conditions occur in the population. We can also use prevalence data to compare how disorders vary by ethnicity, gender, and age. And by monitoring changes in rates we can tell whether current mental health practices are effective in preventing or treating various disorders.

The cost and distress associated with mental disorders is a major societal concern. The U.S. spends over $135 billion a year on mental health and substance abuse services (Mark, Levit, Vandivort-Warren, Buck, & Coffey, 2011). In addition, 25 percent of adults have a diagnosable mental health condition in a given year and many more people experience "mental health problems" that do not meet the exact criteria for a mental disorder. These problems may be equally distressing and debilitating unless adequately treated. These epidemiological findings are troubling, to say the least. Clearly, mental disturbances are widespread, and many people currently are coping with symptoms of mental distress. What is even more troubling is that up to 57 percent of adults with severe mental disorders are not receiving or seeking treatment (Substance Abuse and Mental Health Services Administration, 2012).

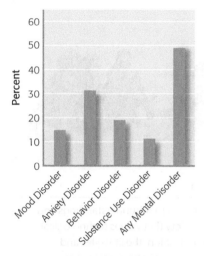

Figure 1.1

Lifetime Prevalence of Mental Disorders in a Sample of 10,000 U.S. Adolescents

SOURCE: Merikangas et al., 2010
© Cengage Learning®

psychiatric epidemiology the study of the prevalence of mental illness in a society

prevalence the percentage of individuals in a targeted population who have a particular disorder during a specific period of time

lifetime prevalence the percentage of people in the population who have had a disorder at some point in their lives

Overcoming Social Stigma and Stereotypes

> It frustrates me more than anything else to hear other people show their absolute ignorance about mental illness. They turn it into a joke or a prejudice remark. Such as, "the weather has been very bipolar lately!" or, "we should lock up all these crazy people before they shoot up another restaurant."... When you stop to think about it, many people in today's society hold a stigma over mental illness. It is as if society has put a sign on our foreheads saying, "I am a crazy person, also I am very dangerous. Please belittle me and make fun of me" (Schwerdtfeger, 2011).

DID YOU KNOW?

About 15 percent of Canadians and 20 percent of U.S. Americans stated they would probably not seek care for mental health problems even if they had a severe disorder. Negative attitudes toward help-seeking behavior are most common among less-educated and socioeconomically challenged young, single men and among those who abuse drugs. Aversion to seeking therapy may be associated with the social stigma surrounding mental illness.

SOURCE: Jagdeo, Cox, Stein, & Sareen, 2009

Amy Schwerdtfeger, who has been diagnosed with bipolar disorder, has personally experienced the distressing **stereotypes** and **social stigma** associated with mental illness. As Ms. Schwerdtfeger points out, despite the prevalence of mental disorders in families and communities across the country, many U.S. Americans hold negative stereotypes such as beliefs that people with mental disorders are dangerous, unpredictable, incompetent, or responsible for their condition. Research findings support her perceptions—that those with mental illness are often strongly disapproved of, devalued, and set apart from others (Kvaale, Haslam, & Gottdiener, 2013).

Individuals with mental illness often need to contend with two forms of stigma. First, they often must cope with public stigma that is expressed through **prejudice** (belief in negative stereotypes) and **discrimination** (actions based on this prejudice). Prejudice and discrimination are sometimes more devastating than the illness itself (Stuart, 2012). Second, **self-stigma** can also be very destructive to those coping with mental illness. Self-stigma occurs when individuals internalize negative beliefs or stereotypes regarding their group and accept the prejudice and discrimination directed against them. In doing so, they come to accept negative societal stereotypes of being different, dangerous, unpredictable, or incompetent and then incorporate these negative beliefs into their self-image (Rusch, Corrigan, Todd, & Bodenhausen, 2013). As you might imagine, this negative self-image can lead to further distress, and maladaptive reactions such as not socializing or not seeking work because of feelings of uselessness or incompetence (Corrigan & Rao, 2012). Unfortunately, self-stigma based on societal prejudices not only undermines feelings of self-worth and **self-efficacy** (belief in one's ability to succeed), but can also hinder recovery.

The belief that those who are mentally ill are somehow responsible for their condition also results in social stigma. Would stigma be reduced if the public better understood that mental illness is similar to medical conditions, such as cancer, that result from a variety of factors, including **biological vulnerability**, rather than voluntary actions by the individual? Beliefs about the causes of severe mental disorders and prejudice and discrimination toward the mentally ill were studied in 1996 and again in 2006 (Pescosolido et al., 2010). There has indeed been a shift toward increased public understanding about biological causes for mental illness rather than blaming families or personal characteristics. For example, more people cited biological reasons as the cause of major depression (80 percent in 2006 compared to 67 percent in 1996) and for schizophrenia (87 percent in 2006 compared to 78 percent in 1996). Has this increased understanding about the biological basis for these disorders resulted in a decrease in prejudice and discrimination? Surprisingly, the researchers found that increased focus on biological causes did not lessen social distance toward or perceived danger from individuals with schizophrenia or major depression. Of the respondents,

stereotype an oversimplified, often inaccurate, image or idea about a group of people

social stigma negative societal beliefs about a group, including the view that the group is somehow different from other members of society

prejudice an unfair, preconceived judgment about a person or group based on their supposed characteristics

discrimination unjust or prejudicial treatment toward a person based on the person's actual or perceived membership in a certain group

self-stigma acceptance of prejudice and discrimination based on internalized negative societal beliefs or stereotypes

self-efficacy belief in one's ability to succeed in a specific situation

biological vulnerability genetic or physiological susceptibility

62 percent reported they would not want to "work closely with" individuals with schizophrenia and 60 percent believed individuals with schizophrenia are "violent to others." Similarly, 47 percent of respondents would be unwilling "to work closely with" those with major depression and 32 percent expressed concern that people coping with major depression would be "violent to others." Although biological explanations reduced the tendency to blame those with mental illness for their situation, it may have had the "unintended side effect" of increasing the perception of dangerousness and creating a desire for greater social distance (Kvaale, Gottdiener, & Haslam, 2013). Mental health advocates continue to work to counter inaccurate perceptions about those with mental illness. Overcoming the stigma of mental illness can be particularly challenging for those who contend with "dual stigma" such as lesbian, gay, transgendered, and bisexual individuals or those subjected to societal stigma based on their religion, race, or ethnicity.

Because stigma continues to exist, there have been concerted efforts to increase public awareness and provide accurate information about mental illness via media messages such as those seen in the "You Are Not Alone" campaign launched by the National Alliance on Mental Illness (NAMI). NAMI and other organizations such as Mental Health America are strongly committed to the goal of educating the public about mental health issues and reducing the unfair stigma associated with mental illness (Corrigan, Sokol, & Rusch, 2013). Additionally, organizations are recognizing and commending those in the entertainment industry who are producing movies and television shows that humanize and present a more accurate portrayal of mental disorders. Many hope that public educational efforts will reduce both public stigma and self-stigma and improve the recovery chances for those coping with mental illness. Higher rates of help-seeking, feelings of empowerment, positive quality of life, and lower self-stigma are reported among those with mental disorders who reside in countries where there is less discrimination and prejudice (Evans-Lacko, Brohan, Mojtabai, & Thornicroft, 2012).

Media Portrayals of Mental Illness

Many people learn about mental disorders from watching movies and television. This scene, from the film Silver Linings Playbook, shows the main character who struggles with bipolar disorder interacting with his parents. Do media portrayals of mental illness add to our understanding of mental illness or simply perpetuate stereotypes?

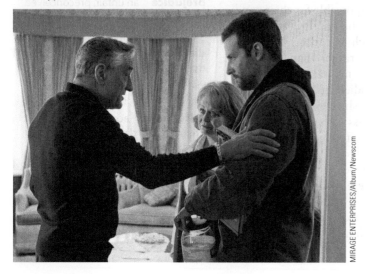

MIRAGE ENTERPRISES/Album/Newscom

Well-known public personalities who come forward to acknowledge and even openly discuss their own personal struggles with stress and various mental health symptoms also reduce stigma. Such public disclosure and openness has come from well-known people, including Oprah; performers Catherine Zeta-Jones, Brooke Shields, Vinny Guadagnino, Emma Stone, Janet Jackson, Richard Dreyfus, Heather Locklear, and Demi Lavoto; authors Patricia Cornwell, Terrie Williams, and Sherman Alexie; and sports figures, including NFL wide receiver Brandon Marshall and professional basketball player Royce White. Such public disclosure can also help open the topic for discussion among family and friends. There is no doubt that the social stigma surrounding mental illness is reduced when the public is able to see how talented people cope with and recover from distressing mental symptoms, rather than just hearing stories of untreated mental disturbance that ends in violence or tragedy.

Professionals in the mental health field are encouraged by attempts such as these to reduce stigma, stereotyping, and popular misconceptions about mental illness. Such efforts are important because social stigma can cause individuals and families to avoid seeking treatment or develop a "code of silence" regarding mental illness, especially when a family member has not "come out" regarding their situation.

Famous people with mental disorders who have made important contributions to the world include J. K. Rowling, Winston Churchill, and Virginia Woolf, pictured here, as well as Michelangelo, Abraham Lincoln, Isaac Newton, Ludwig van Beethoven, Patrick Kennedy, and Buzz Aldrin, among many others.

Personal **empowerment** through open discussion of mental illness is a first step in overcoming societal prejudice and discrimination (Corrigan & Rao, 2012).

A question we have asked ourselves as we write this book is: If so many individuals are affected by mental illness in today's society, is it really "abnormal" to have mental health challenges? When we look at the pervasiveness of anxiety, depression, eating disorders, and substance-use disorders, for example, it appears that dealing with stress and mental health concerns has become the new norm. The question then becomes: What can we do as a society to allow people to be open and honest about their mental health problems and to seek treatment without fear of being stigmatized? It is our hope that someday soon, the course you are now taking will no longer be called "abnormal psychology" but will instead have a more progressive title such as "Promoting Mental Health and Treating Mental Illness."

What can you do to help reduce stigma and stereotyping and assist those working to move mental illness out of the shadows? You can take care to be respectful when discussing someone who is experiencing mental distress, and encourage friends or family who are experiencing emotional symptoms to seek help, perhaps letting them know that the sooner they receive treatment the greater the likelihood of a full recovery. You can carefully consider your choice of words and avoid casual use of the many commonly used terms that perpetuate negative stereotypes about mental illness.

Historical Perspectives on Abnormal Behavior

Definitions of abnormal behavior are firmly rooted in the system of beliefs that operate in a given society at a given time. This next section covering historical details is based on writings by Alexander and Selesnick (1966), Neugebauer (1979), Plante (2013), Spanos (1978), and Wallace and Gach (2008). We must be aware, however, that our discussion is strongly influenced by Western understandings of mental health and mental disorders. Other, non-Western societies have historical journeys and beliefs about abnormal behavior that differ from those presented here.

empowerment increasing one's sense of personal strength and self-worth

Paul Bevitt/Alamy

Trephining: Evidence of Therapy?

Anthropologists speculate that this human skull is evidence of trephining, the centuries-old practice of chipping a hole in the skull to release the evil spirits causing symptoms of mental disturbance.

trephining   a surgical method from the Stone Age in which part of the skull was chipped away to provide an opening through which an evil spirit could escape

exorcism   treatment method used by the early Greeks, Chinese, Hebrews, and Egyptians in which prayers, noises, emetics, flogging, and starvation were used to cast evil spirits out of an afflicted person's body

brain pathology   a dysfunction or disease of the brain

Prehistoric and Ancient Beliefs

Prehistoric societies some half a million years ago did not distinguish between mental and physical disorders. According to historians, these ancient peoples attributed many forms of illness to demonic possession, sorcery, or retribution from an offended ancestral spirit. Certain symptoms and behaviors, from simple headaches to convulsions, were ascribed to evil spirits residing within a person's body. Within this system of belief, called *demonology*, the person displaying symptoms was often held at least partly responsible for the misfortune.

It has been suggested that Stone Age cave dwellers may have treated behavior and mental disorders with a surgical method called **trephining**, in which part of the skull was chipped away to provide an opening through which the evil spirits could escape, in hopes that the person would return to his or her normal state. Surprisingly, anthropologists have discovered some trephined skulls with evidence of healing, indicating that some individuals survived this extremely crude operation. Another treatment method used by the early Greeks, Chinese, Hebrews, and Egyptians was exorcism. In an **exorcism**, elaborate prayers, noises, emetics (drugs that induce vomiting), and extreme measures such as flogging and starvation were used to cast evil spirits out of an afflicted person's body.

Naturalistic Explanations: Greco-Roman Thought

With the flowering of Greek civilization and its continuation into the era of Roman rule (500 B.C.–500 A.D.), naturalistic explanations gradually became distinct from supernatural ones. Early thinkers, such as Hippocrates (460–370 B.C.), a physician sometimes referred to as the father of Western medicine, actively questioned prevailing superstitious beliefs and proposed much more rational and scientific explanations for mental disorders. He believed that, because the brain was the central organ of intellectual activity, deviant behavior was caused by **brain pathology**, that is, a dysfunction or disease of the brain. He also considered heredity and the environment important factors in psychopathology. He classified mental illnesses into three categories— mania, melancholia (sadness or depression), and phrenitis (brain fever)—and provided detailed clinical descriptions of symptoms such as paranoia, alcoholic delirium, and epilepsy. Many of his descriptions of disorders are still used today, eloquent testimony to his keen powers of observation. To treat melancholia, Hippocrates recommended tranquility, moderate exercise, a careful diet, abstinence from sexual activity, and bloodletting when necessary. His belief in environmental influences on behavior sometimes led him to separate disturbed individuals from their families.

Other thinkers who contributed to the organic explanation of behavior were the philosopher Plato and the Greek physician Galen, who practiced in Rome. Plato (429–347 B.C.) carried on the thinking of Hippocrates; he insisted that people who were mentally disturbed were the responsibility of their families and that they should not be punished for their behavior. Galen (A.D. 129–199) made major contributions through his scientific examination of the nervous system and his explanation of the role of the brain and central nervous system in mental functioning. His greatest contribution may have been the coding and classification of all European medical knowledge from Hippocrates's time to his own.

Reversion to Supernatural Explanations: The Middle Ages

With the upheavals in society associated with the collapse of the Roman Empire, the rise of Christianity, and the devastating plagues sweeping through Europe, rational and scientific thought gave way to a renewed emphasis on the supernatural. Religious dogma reinforced the idea that nature is a reflection of divine will and beyond human reason and that earthly life is a prelude to the "true" life experienced after death. Scientific inquiry—attempts to understand, classify, explain, and control nature—became less important than accepting nature as a manifestation of God's will. In fact, religious truths were viewed as sacred and those who challenged these ideas were denounced as heretics. Natural and supernatural explanations of illness were once again fused. Because of this atmosphere, rationalism and scholarly scientific works went underground for many years, preserved mainly by Arab scholars and European monks.

People once again believed that many illnesses were the result of supernatural forces. In some cases, religious monks treated the mentally ill with compassion, allowing them to rest and receive prayer in monasteries and at shrines. In other cases, treatment was quite brutal, particularly when the illness was seen as resulting from God's wrath or possession by the devil. When the illness was perceived to be punishment for sin, the sick person was assumed to be guilty of wrongdoing; relief could only come through atonement or repentance.

The humane treatment that Hippocrates had advocated centuries earlier was replaced by torturous exorcism procedures designed to combat Satan and eject him from the possessed person's body. Prayers, curses, obscene epithets, and the sprinkling of holy water—as well as such drastic and painful "therapies" as flogging, starving, and immersion in cold water—were used to drive out the devil. A time of trouble for everyone, the Middle Ages were especially bleak for the mentally ill.

Belief in the power of the supernatural became so prevalent and intense that it frequently affected whole populations. Beginning in Italy early in the 13th century, large numbers of people were affected by various forms of mass madness, or group **hysteria**, involving the sudden appearance of unusual symptoms that had no apparent physical cause. One of the better-known manifestations of this condition was **tarantism**, characterized by agitation and frenzied dancing. People would leap up, believing they were bitten by a spider. They would then run out into the street or marketplace, jumping and dancing about, joined by others who also believed that they had been bitten. The mania soon spread throughout the rest of Europe, where it became known as *Saint Vitus's dance*.

How can these phenomena be explained? Outbreaks of mass hysteria are often associated with stress and fear. During the 13th century, for example, there was enormous social unrest. The bubonic plague had decimated one third of the population of Europe. War, famine, and pestilence were rampant, and the social order of the times was crumbling.

DID YOU KNOW?

The belief in tarantism persisted into the mid-20th century in some regions of Italy. Peasants believed that engaging in a frenzied dance, called the tarantella, would remove the venom and cure them of aggressive, depressive, or lethargic symptoms.

SOURCE: De Martino, 2005

hysteria   an outdated term referring to excessive or uncontrollable emotion, sometimes resulting in somatic symptoms (such as blindness or paralysis) that have no apparent physical cause

tarantism   a form of mass hysteria prevalent during the Middle Ages, characterized by wild raving, jumping, dancing, and convulsing

Witchcraft: 15th Through 17th Centuries

During the 15th and 16th centuries, social and religious reformers increasingly challenged the authority of the Catholic Church. Martin Luther attacked the corruption and the abuses of the clergy, precipitating the Protestant Reformation of the 16th century. Church officials viewed such protests as insurrections that threatened their power. According to the church, Satan himself fostered the attacks on church practices. In effect, the church actively endorsed an already popular belief in demonic possession and witches.

To counter the satanic threat, Pope Innocent VIII issued a decree in 1484 calling on the clergy to identify and exterminate witches. This resulted in the 1486 publication of the Malleus Maleficarum, which officially confirmed the existence of witches, suggested means to detect them (such as red spots on the skin and areas of anesthesia on the body), and methods to force a confession. Confession could be designated as "with" or "without" torture. The latter allowed "mild" bone crushing. The church initially recognized two forms of demonic possession: willing and unwilling. The willing person made a blood pact with the devil and had the power to create floods,

Casting Out the Cause of Abnormality

During the Middle Ages, people with mental disorders were thought to be victims of a demonic possession. The most prevalent form of treatment was exorcism, usually conducted by religious leaders. Here a televangelist and his daughters are participating in a modern day exorcism.

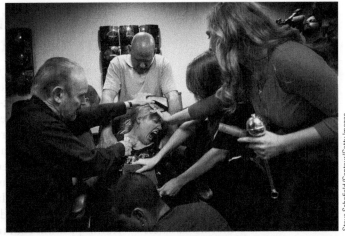

Steve Schofield/Contour/Getty Images

The practice of casting out evil spirits still occurs among some Pentecostals and other Christian groups who believe that physical or psychological illnesses result from possession by demons. Many believe that such illnesses are due to sins committed by the individual or the person's ancestors.

SOURCE: Mercer, 2013

MYTH A person who has a mental illness can never contribute anything of worth to the world.

REALITY Many people with mental illness were never "cured," but they nevertheless made great contributions to humanity. Abraham Lincoln and Winston Churchill, both world leaders, battled recurrent episodes of depression. Ernest Hemingway, one of the great writers of the 20th century and winner of a Nobel Prize for Literature, experienced lifelong depression, alcoholism, and frequent hospitalizations. The famous Dutch painter Vincent van Gogh produced great works of art even when hospitalized for severe mental illness. Others, such as Pablo Picasso and Edgar Allan Poe, contributed major artistic and literary works while seriously disturbed.

pestilence, storms, crop failures, and impotence. Although those deemed unwilling victims of possession initially received more sympathetic treatment than those believed to have willingly conspired with the devil, this distinction soon evaporated.

Thousands of innocent men, women, and even children were beheaded, burned alive, or mutilated during the period of the witch hunts. It has been estimated that over 100,000 people (mainly women) were executed as witches from the middle of the 15th century to the end of the 17th century. Witch hunts also occurred in colonial America. The witchcraft trials of 1692 in Salem, Massachusetts, were infamous. Several hundred people were accused, many were imprisoned and tortured, and 20 were killed. Most psychiatric historians believe that individuals who were mentally ill were those initially suspected of witchcraft. Additionally, the astonishingly high number of women who were accused and persecuted suggests that other sociological factors were involved, such as patriarchal (male-dominated) societal conditions (Reed, 2007). Although these events took place centuries ago, belief in witchcraft or supernatural causes for mental and physical disorders still exists today in the United States and other countries (Fottrell, Tollman, Byass, Golooba-Mutebi, & Kahn, 2012).

The Rise of Humanism

A resurgence of rational and scientific inquiry during the 14th through 16th centuries led to great advances in science and **humanism**, a philosophical movement emphasizing human welfare and the worth and uniqueness of the individual. Prior to this time, most asylums were at best custodial centers in which people who were mentally disturbed were chained, caged, starved, whipped, and even exhibited to the public for a small fee, much like animals in a zoo (Dreher, 2013). For example, the term *bedlam*, which has become synonymous with chaos and disorder, was the shortened name of Bethlehem Hospital, an asylum in London that has come to symbolize the cruel treatment of people experiencing severe mental illness. Patients were bound by chains, left untreated, and exhibited to the public in the courtyard.

Johann Weyer (1515–1588), a German physician, published a revolutionary book that challenged the prevailing beliefs about witchcraft. He personally investigated many cases of possession and asserted that many people who were tortured, imprisoned, and burned as witches were mentally disturbed, not possessed by demons (Metzger, 2013). Although both the church and state severely criticized and banned his book, it helped pave the way for the humanistic perspective on mental illness. With the rise of humanism, a new way of thinking developed—if people were "mentally ill" and not possessed, they should be treated as though they were sick. A number of new treatment methods reflected this humanistic spirit.

The Moral Treatment Movement: 18th and 19th Centuries

In France, Philippe Pinel (1745–1826), a physician, took charge of la Bicêtre, a hospital for mentally ill men in Paris. Pinel instituted what came to be known as the **moral treatment movement**—a shift to more humane treatment of people who were mentally disturbed. He removed patients' chains, replaced dungeons with sunny rooms, encouraged exercise outdoors on the hospital grounds, and treated patients with kindness and reason. Surprising many disbelievers, the freed patients did not become violent; instead, this humane treatment seemed to foster recovery and improve behavior. Pinel later instituted similar, equally successful, reforms at la Salpêtrière, a large mental hospital for women in Paris. In England, William Tuke (1732–1822), a prominent Quaker tea merchant, established a retreat at York for the "moral treatment" of mental patients. At this pleasant country estate, the patients worked, prayed, rested, and talked out their

humanism a philosophical movement that emphasizes human welfare and the worth and uniqueness of the individual

moral treatment movement crusade to institute more humane treatment of people with mental illness

problems—all in an atmosphere of kindness. This emphasis on moral treatment laid the groundwork for using psychological means to treat mental illness. Indeed, it resulted in much higher rates of "cure" than other treatments of that time (Charland, 2007).

In the United States, three individuals—Benjamin Rush, Dorothea Dix, and Clifford Beers—made important contributions to the moral treatment movement. Rush (1745–1813), widely acclaimed as the father of U.S. psychiatry, encouraged humane treatment of those residing in mental hospitals. He insisted that patients be treated with respect and dignity and that they be gainfully employed while hospitalized, an idea still evident in the modern concept of work therapy. Dorothea Dix (1802–1887), a New England schoolteacher, was a leader in 19th century social reform in the United States. At the time, people who were mentally ill were often incarcerated in prisons and poorhouses. While teaching Sunday school to female prisoners, she was appalled to find jailed mental patients living under deplorable conditions. For the next 40 years, Dix worked tirelessly on behalf of those experiencing mental disorders. She campaigned for reform legislation and funds to establish suitable mental hospitals. She raised millions of dollars, established more than 30 mental hospitals, and greatly improved conditions in countless others. But the struggle for reform was far from over. Although the large hospitals that replaced jails and poorhouses had better physical facilities, the humanistic focus of the moral treatment movement was lacking.

CONTROVERSY

What Role Should Spirituality and Religion Play in Mental Health Care?

The role of demons, witches, and possession in explaining abnormal behavior has been part and parcel of past religious teachings. Psychology's reluctance to incorporate religion into the profession may be understandable in light of the historical role played by the church in the oppression of people who are mentally ill. Furthermore, psychology as a science stresses objectivity and naturalistic explanations of human behavior; this approach is often at odds with religion as a belief system (D. W. Sue & Sue, 2013).

Until recently, the mental health profession was largely silent about the influence or importance of spirituality and religion in mental health. Therapists have generally avoided discussing such topics with clients (Saunders, Miller, & Bright, 2010). For example, many therapists (a) do not feel comfortable discussing spiritual or religious issues with their clients, (b) are concerned they will appear to be proselytizing or judgmental if they touch on such topics, (c) believe they may usurp the role of the clergy, or (d) feel inauthentic addressing client concerns, especially if the therapist is atheist or agnostic (Gonsiorek, Richards, Pargament, & McMinn, 2009; Saunders et al., 2010).

Because more than 82 percent of U.S. adults identify with a specific religion, many people are open to medical and mental health care providers discussing spiritual and faith issues with them. Additionally, many racial and ethnic minority group members believe that spiritual issues are intimately linked to their cultural identities (Gallup, 2013;

D. W. Sue & Sue, 2013). More compelling are findings that reveal a positive association between spirituality or religion and optimal health outcomes, longevity, and lower levels of anxiety, depression, suicide, and substance abuse (Kasen, Wickramaratne, & Gameroff, 2013). Many mental health professionals are becoming increasingly open to the potential benefits of incorporating spirituality into treatment. As part of that process, psychologists are making distinctions between spirituality and religion. Spirituality is a broad term that refers to the process of finding meaning, purpose, and connection to a higher power or something larger within the universe, whereas religion involves a specific doctrine and particular system of beliefs. Spirituality can be pursued outside of a specific religion because it involves spiritual growth associated with self-discovery and finding meaning in connections to others (Cornish & Wade, 2010). Mental health professionals are increasingly recognizing that people are thinking, feeling, behaving, social, cultural, and spiritual beings.

For Further Consideration

1. What thoughts do you have about the role of spirituality and religion in mental health and psychotherapy?

2. Should therapists avoid discussing religious or spiritual matters with clients?

3. If you were in therapy, how important would it be to discuss your religious or spiritual beliefs?

Dorothea Dix (1802–1887)

During a time when women were discouraged from political participation, Dorothea Dix, a New England schoolteacher, worked tirelessly as a social reformer to improve the deplorable conditions in which people who were mentally ill were forced to live.

The moral treatment movement was energized in 1908 with the publication of *A Mind That Found Itself,* a book by Clifford Beers (1876–1943) about his own mental collapse. His book describes the terrible treatment he and other patients experienced in three mental institutions, where they were beaten, choked, spat on, and restrained with straitjackets. His vivid account aroused public sympathy and attracted the interest and support of the psychiatric establishment, including such eminent figures as psychologist-philosopher William James. Beers founded the National Committee for Mental Hygiene (forerunner of the National Mental Health Association, now known as Mental Health America), an organization dedicated to educating the public about mental illness and advocating for effective treatment for people who are mentally ill. This organization continues to advocate against ineffective or inappropriate treatment of people with mental disorders. Even the severest critics of today's mental health system, however, would have to admit that conditions and treatment for people who are mentally ill have improved over the years.

Causes of Mental Illness: Early Viewpoints

Paralleling the rise of humanistic treatment of mental illness was an inquiry into its causes. Two schools of thought emerged. The biological viewpoint holds that mental disorders are the result of physiological damage or disease. The psychological viewpoint stresses an emotional basis for mental illness. It is important to note that most people tended to combine elements of both positions rather than adhering only to one view.

The Biological Viewpoint

Hippocrates's suggestion of a biological explanation for abnormal behavior was ignored during the Middle Ages but revived after the Renaissance. Not until the 19th century, however, did the **biological viewpoint**—the belief that mental disorders have a physical or physiological basis—flourish. The ideas of Wilhelm Griesinger (1817–1868), a German psychiatrist who believed that all mental disorders had physiological causes, received considerable attention. Emil Kraepelin (1856–1926), a follower of Griesinger, observed that certain symptoms tend to occur regularly in clusters, called **syndromes**. Kraepelin believed that each cluster of symptoms represented a mental disorder with its own unique—and clearly specifiable—cause, course, and outcome. In his *Textbook of Psychiatry* (1883/1923), Kraepelin outlined a system for classifying mental illnesses based on their physiological causes. That system was the foundation for the diagnostic categories in the *Diagnostic and Statistical Manual of Mental Disorders* (DSM), the classification system of the American Psychiatric Association that is still in use today.

Emil Kraepelin (1856–1926)

In an 1883 publication, psychiatrist Emil Kraepelin proposed that mental disorders could be directly linked to biologically based brain disorders and further proposed a diagnostic classification system for all disorders.

biological viewpoint the belief that mental disorders have a physical or physiological basis

syndrome certain symptoms that tend to occur regularly in clusters

The acceptance of an organic or biological cause for mental disorders was enhanced by medical breakthroughs such as Louis Pasteur's (1822–1895) germ theory of disease. The biological viewpoint gained even greater strength with the discovery of the biological basis of *general paresis*, a degenerative physical and mental disorder associated with late-stage syphilis (a sexually transmitted infection). In 1897, Richard von Krafft-Ebing, a German neurologist, proved conclusively that the serious mental symptoms associated with general paresis resulted from syphilis bacteria invading the brain. Finally, in 1905, a German zoologist, Fritz Schaudinn, isolated the microorganism that causes syphilis and develops into general paresis. These events strengthened the search for biological explanations for mental disorders. As medical breakthroughs in the study of the nervous system occurred, many scientists became hopeful that they would discover a biological basis for all mental disorders. As we discuss in the next chapter, the biological model, including the focus on genetic factors, brain structure, and biochemical processes within the body, continues to generate considerable interest (Deacon, 2013).

The Psychological Viewpoint

Some scientists noted, however, that certain types of emotional disorders do not appear to be associated with any obvious biological cause. Such observations led to the **psychological viewpoint**—the belief that mental disorders are caused by psychological and emotional factors. For example, personal challenges or interpersonal conflicts can lead to intense feelings of frustration, depression, and anger, which may consequently lead to deteriorating mental health. This perspective received support with the discovery that psychological interventions could both produce and treat hysteria, a condition involving physical symptoms that have a psychological rather than a physical cause.

Mesmerism and Hypnotism

The unique and exotic techniques to treat hysteria used by Friedrich Anton Mesmer (1734–1815), an Austrian physician who practiced in Paris, presented an early challenge to the biological viewpoint. Mesmer developed a theory of "animal magnetism" contending that disruptions in the flow of magnetic forces in the body could produce physical problems and that the use of magnetism could restore the flow to normal. Based on this theory, Mesmer developed a highly controversial treatment referred to as *mesmerism,* a technique that evolved into the modern practice of hypnotism. Mesmer performed his most miraculous cures by treating hysteria, successfully curing symptoms of blindness, deafness, loss of bodily feeling, and paralysis that seemed to have no biological basis. His system for curing hysteria involved inducing a sleeplike state, during which his patients became highly susceptible to suggestion. During this state, symptoms often disappeared. Mesmer's dramatic and theatrical techniques earned him censure, as well as fame. A committee of prominent thinkers, including U.S. ambassador to France, Benjamin Franklin, investigated Mesmer and declared him a fraud. The theory of animal magnetism also became popular in some circles in the United States, despite claims that practitioners were using deliberate deception (Quinn, 2012).

Although Mesmer's theatrics and basic assumptions were discredited, he succeeded in demonstrating that the power of suggestion could treat hysteria. Following Mesmer, two physicians, Ambroise-Auguste Liébeault (1823–1904) and Hippolyte-Marie Bernheim (1840–1919), hypothesized that hysteria was a form of self-hypnosis. In treating hysterical patients using hypnosis, they were often able to cure symptoms of paralysis, deafness, and blindness. They were also able to produce these symptoms in healthy persons through hypnosis. Their work demonstrated that suggestion could cause certain symptoms of mental illness and that mental and physical disorders could have a psychological rather than a biological explanation. This conclusion represented a major breakthrough in the understanding of mental disorders.

Science Photo Library/Science Source

Friedrich Anton Mesmer (1734–1815)

Mesmer's techniques were a forerunner of modern hypnotism. Although highly controversial and ultimately discredited, Mesmer's efforts stimulated inquiry into the possibility that psychological and emotional factors could cause mental disorders.

psychological viewpoint the belief that mental disorders are caused by psychological and emotional factors rather than biological influences

Breuer and Freud

The idea that psychological processes could produce mental and physical dysfunction soon gained credence among physicians who were using hypnosis. Among them was the Viennese doctor Josef Breuer (1842–1925). He discovered that after one of his female patients spoke quite freely about her past traumatic experiences while in a trance, many of her physical symptoms disappeared. There was even greater improvement when the patient recalled and talked about previously forgotten memories of emotionally distressing events. This technique became known as the **cathartic method**, the therapeutic use of verbal expression to release pent-up emotional conflicts. It foreshadowed the practice of psycho-analysis initiated by Sigmund Freud (1856–1939)—techniques that have had a lasting influence in the field of abnormal psychology, contributions we discuss in Chapter 2.

Behaviorism

Whereas psychoanalysis explained abnormal behavior as an **intrapsychic** phenomenon involving psychological processes occurring within the mind, another viewpoint that emerged, behaviorism, was firmly rooted in laboratory science. The behavioristic perspective stressed the importance of directly observable behaviors and the conditions that evoked, reinforced, and extinguished them. As we will see in Chapter 2, behaviorism not only provided an alternative explanation regarding the development of both normal and abnormal behaviors but also offered successful procedures for treating some psychological conditions.

Contemporary Trends in Abnormal Psychology

Our understanding and treatment of psychopathological disorders has changed significantly over the past 30 years. Views of abnormality continue to evolve as they incorporate the effects of several major events and trends in the field: (a) the influence of multicultural psychology, (b) the focus on resilience and positive psychology, (c) the recovery movement, and (d) changes in the therapeutic landscape such as psychiatric medications, managed health care and health care reform, evidence-based treatments, and the increased use of technology in treatment.

The Influence of Multicultural Psychology

We are fast becoming a multicultural, multiracial, and multilingual society (Figure 1.2). The U.S. Census Bureau reveals that within several decades, members of racial and ethnic minorities will become a numerical majority (D. W. Sue & Sue, 2013). Additionally, the number of individuals identifying as having a biracial or multiracial background is steadily increasing. These changes are sometimes referred to as the diversification of the United States or, literally, the changing complexion of society.

Diversity has had a major impact on the mental health profession, creating a field of study called **multicultural psychology**. Mental health professionals now recognize the need to (a) increase their cultural sensitivity; (b) acquire knowledge of the worldviews and lifestyles of a culturally diverse population, including those with a multiracial or multicultural background; and (c) develop culturally relevant therapy approaches in working with different groups (Morales & Norcross, 2010;

cathartic method a therapeutic use of verbal expression to release pent-up emotional conflicts

intrapsychic psychological processes occurring within the mind

multicultural psychology a branch of psychology that focuses on culture, race, ethnicity, gender, age, socioeconomic class, and other similar factors in its effort to understand behavior

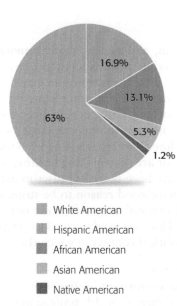

White American
Hispanic American
African American
Asian American
Native American

Figure 1.2

2012 Census Projections: Racial and Ethnic Composition of the United States

The rapid demographic transformation of the United States is illustrated by the fact that minorities now constitute an increasing proportion of the population. Several trends are evident. First, within several decades, people of color will constitute a numerical majority. Second, the number of Latino/ Hispanic Americans has surpassed the number of African Americans. Third, mental health providers will increasingly come into contact with clients who differ from them in race, ethnicity, and culture.

SOURCE: http://quickfacts.census.gov/qfd/states/00000.html

D. W. Sue & Sue, 2013). Culture, ethnicity, and gender are recognized as powerful influences on many aspects of normal and abnormal human development. Four primary dimensions related to cultural diversity—social conditioning, cultural values and influences, sociopolitical influences, and bias in diagnosis—help explain how cultural forces exert their influence.

Social Conditioning

How we are raised, the values we develop, and cultural expectations regarding our behavior can have a major effect on the types of symptoms we are most likely to experience. In U.S. culture, men are exposed to expectations regarding how to fulfill the masculine role—to be independent, assertive, courageous, active, unsentimental, and objective. Women, in contrast, are often raised to be dependent, helpful, self-deprecating, conforming, empathetic, and emotional. Some mental health professionals believe that, as a result, women are more likely to internalize their conflicts (resulting in anxiety and depression), whereas men are more likely to externalize and act out (resulting in drug or alcohol abuse). Although gender roles have begun to change, their effects continue to be widely felt.

Cultural Values and Influences

Mental health professionals now recognize that types of mental disorders differ from country to country. Additionally, differences in cultural traditions among various racial and ethnic minority groups in the United States may influence susceptibility to certain emotional disorders. Among Latino/ Hispanic Americans and Asian Americans, experiencing physical complaints is a common and culturally accepted means of expressing psychological and emotional stress (Yang & WonPat-Borja, 2007; Zaroff, Davis, Chio, & Madhavan, 2012). Within these cultural groups, many believe that physical problems cause emotional distress and that symptoms will disappear as soon as the physical illness is treated. In addition, Asian groups view physical illness as acceptable, whereas mental illness may be a source of shame and disgrace (D. W. Sue & Sue, 2013). Thus, mental health professionals might hear complaints involving headaches, fatigue, restlessness, and disturbances of sleep and appetite rather than discussion of stress or emotional distress.

Diversity Is a Fact of Life

This group of students represents the increasing diversity of the United States.

Anderson Ross/Blend Images/Corbis

Sociopolitical Influences

In response to a history of prejudice, discrimination, and racism, many minorities have adopted various behaviors (in particular, behaviors toward white people) that have proved important for their survival (D. W. Sue, 2010). Some people may define these actions as abnormal and deviant, yet from the minority group's perspective, the behaviors function as healthy survival mechanisms. Early personality studies of African Americans concluded that, as a group, they tend to appear more "suspicious," "mistrustful," and "paranoid" than their white counterparts. But are African Americans inherently suspicious, as studies suggest, or are they making healthy, adaptive responses? Members of minority groups who have been targets of discrimination and oppression in a society not yet free of racism have good reason to be suspicious and distrustful of white society. The "paranoid orientation" may reflect not only survival skills but also an accurate reflection of reality. Thus, we need to consider people's behaviors based on an understanding of the sociopolitical context in which they arise.

Cultural and Ethnic Bias in Diagnosis

It is important to be aware of potential cultural biases inherent in diagnosis and the diagnostic system. For example, bias on the part of mental health professionals can affect their view of symptoms and subsequent diagnosis. Mental health practitioners are not immune from inheriting the prejudicial attitudes and stereotypes of the larger society. It is possible for even the most enlightened and well-intentioned mental health professionals to be influenced by race, gender, and social class bias. One source of bias is the tendency to *overpathologize*—to exaggerate the severity of disorders—among clients from particular socioeconomic, racial, or ethnic groups whose cultural values or lifestyles differ markedly from the clinician's own. The overpathologizing of disorders has been found to occur in psychological evaluations of African Americans, Latino/Hispanic Americans, women, and lesbian/gay/bisexual/ transsexual populations (Singh, Hays, & Watson, 2011; D. W. Sue & Sue, 2013).

Multicultural psychology is now incorporating studies of brain functioning. In the growing field of cultural neuroscience, researchers are discovering that cultural diversity can influence the development of the brain (Chiao, Cheon, Pornpattananangkul, Mrazek, & Blizinsky, 2013). It appears that certain patterns of neural activity are associated with specific cultural practices. For example, individuals who meditate regularly show patterns of neural activity that are distinctly different from those who do not practice meditation (Craigmyle, 2013).

Positive Psychology

Positive psychology is a branch of the profession that seeks to add balance to our view of human functioning; its purpose is to study, develop, and achieve scientific understanding of the positive human qualities that build thriving individuals, families, and communities (Seligman & Csikszentmihalyi, 2000). Positive psychology and optimal human functioning focus on three domains (Seligman, 2007; Seligman & Csikszentmihalyi, 2000). First, there is interest in feelings of well-being, contentment, and satisfaction in the past; hope and optimism for the future; and flow and happiness in the present. Second, at the individual level, research concentrates on positive traits such as resilience, capacity for love, courage, interpersonal skills, **spirituality**, and wisdom. Third, at the group level, positive psychology addresses civic virtues and the institutions that move us toward better citizenship and responsibility.

What contributions does the field of positive psychology make to our understanding of mental health?

positive psychology the philosophical and scientific study of positive human functioning and the strengths and assets of individuals, families, and communities

spirituality belief in an animating life force or energy beyond what we can perceive with our senses

1. Considering clients' strengths and their capacity for resilience has become increasingly important in therapeutic assessment and treatment. Therapists realize that clients are not just passive beings, helpless to deal with life problems. Identifying strengths is a positive experience for clients and can assist with treatment and recovery. When therapists incorporate the positive qualities of

Psychology Is Also the Study of Strengths and Assets

Randy and Billy grew up in the same neighborhood, went to the same high school, joined the army together, and served two tours of duty in Iraq before leaving the service. In Iraq, they encountered threats of death, saw their buddies killed or wounded, and endured many hardships. While in the army, Billy frequently used drugs and alcohol, especially after witnessing traumatic events. Although Randy went drinking with his friends, he never drank excessively.

Upon their return home, Randy and Billy both enrolled in a community college with the hopes of opening a car repair business. However, Billy's mental health deteriorated quickly. He was very anxious and had flashbacks about the war. Before long, he was heavily involved in drugs, and dropped out of college. Randy finished his college program and opened a small, successful automobile repair shop with three employees. He has since married, and he and his wife are expecting their first child. In addition, he has become actively involved in helping other veterans at the local VA hospital.

After years of not seeing his friend Billy, Randy accidentally ran into him late one afternoon. Billy sat on a box on a street corner, talking to himself, and occasionally swearing at people who walked by. He had an unkempt appearance and wore dirty clothes. It was obvious he had not bathed for some time. He was begging for handouts and became verbally abusive to those who did not drop money into his hat. Billy did not seem to recognize Randy, even when addressed by name. He avoided eye contact, refused to speak, and simply pointed to his hat. Feeling sorry for his friend, Randy gave him all the cash he had.

Billy's mental state is understandable in light of his war trauma. Many soldiers returning from Iraq have experienced post-traumatic stress disorder, anxiety attacks, drug or alcohol abuse, and depression. The constant threat of death or bodily harm is a reality for soldiers serving in war zones, and the trauma they experience is often beyond human endurance. We know much about war trauma, post-traumatic stress disorders, and the psychological

©Straight 8 Photography/Shutterstock.com

harm that combat can produce. In many ways, we know more about pathology than about resilience and strength; we know more about mental illness than mental health, and thus we know more about Billy than we do about Randy.

It may sound strange to ask this question, but what *do* we know about Randy? He seems to have returned from Iraq unscathed, completed his college education, started a successful business, married, and become an active member of the community. Didn't he go through the same war traumas as his friend Billy? Why didn't he show psychological symptoms? What helped him remain mentally healthy? How did he cope with and overcome the hardships of war?

There are benefits to addressing these questions and realizing that psychology is not just the study of pathology and damage but also the study of strength, character, and virtue. For example, even after experiencing significant combat trauma, Randy exhibits many positive traits—grit, perseverance, integrity, social responsibility, kindness, and compassion. This may be due to Randy's personal characteristics and coping skills, but also may reflect other factors such his exposure to supportive social relationships before, during, and after his military service.

It is important for psychologists to study mental health as well as mental illness and to consider resilience, assets, strengths, and **optimal human functioning** (Seligman, 2007). Unfortunately, we often ignore these positive aspects of the human condition. For example, we know more about inadequacies than strengths, anxiety and fear than courage, depression than happiness, selfishness than altruism, stagnation than creativity, and ignorance than wisdom. By focusing on problems and symptoms, we inadvertently see a very narrow picture of the human functioning. Thus, as we learn about psychopathology, it is important to focus on factors that can help people remain resilient, bounce back from adversity, and facilitate recovery from mental disorders (Seery, 2011).

human functioning and adaptive coping into treatment, clients increase their confidence in coping with distressing emotional symptoms and in managing day-to-day challenges.

2. Positive psychology also focuses on prevention. Positive psychology addresses adaptive, healthy coping and the potential for positive emotions to influence

optimal human functioning
qualities such as subjective well-being, optimism, resilience, hope, courage, ability to cope with stress, self-actualization, and self-determinism

negative moods and build **psychological resilience** (Schutz et al., 2013). The goal is to identify the strengths and assets of people, to arm them with adaptive coping skills, and to promote mental health.

What distinguishes those who handle adversity well from those who do not? It is likely that you, and those around you, encounter stressful situations on a regular basis. Additionally, you may have also experienced a traumatic event or been subjected to violence, abuse, bullying, racism, or discrimination. What characteristics have helped you effectively cope with these kinds of stressors? Positive psychologists believe that if we identify qualities associated with effective coping and resilience, we can teach people—even children—strategies that allow them to effectively regulate emotions, cope with the demanding challenges of life, and avoid developing depression, anxiety, or other mental health conditions.

Positive psychology has reawakened an interest in optimizing human functioning and presenting a more balanced picture of the human condition. In chapters throughout this text, you will find a section called **Focus on Resilience** that covers the positive aspects of resilience, strengths, and psychological assets—information that relates to the prevention of or recovery from the various mental health conditions we discuss.

Recovery Movement

CASE STUDY Peter Ashenden was determined not to let his severe depression keep him from finishing his college degree and getting a job. The clinical staff at the day facility . . . had a different idea: a sheltered workshop for people with disabilities. "The workshop was putting caps on lipstick tubes for six hours a day," remembers Ashenden, who now directs consumer and family affairs at the insurance company OptumHealth (Clay, 2012, p. 53).

The recovery movement arose in response to the pessimistic views held by the public and mental health professionals regarding the life prospects of those coping with mental illness. Individuals with mental illness often received the devastating message that they would never recover, work on a job, complete school, or have a fulfilling future (Arboleda-Fiorex & Stuart, 2012). In contrast to this pessimistic message, a reconceptualization of the possible outcomes for those with severe mental illness resulted in the **recovery movement**—the perspective that those with mental illness can recover and live satisfying, hopeful, and contributing lives even with limitations caused by illness. Recovery involves the "development of new meaning and purpose in one's life as one grows beyond the catastrophic effects of mental illness" (Anthony, 1993, p. 16).

Indeed, there is a move away from the view that severe mental disorders have an inevitably poor prognosis. Instead, with appropriate support and treatment, those with mental illness can look forward to a meaningful future. The recovery model, emphasizing optimism and collaborative support targeting each individual's potential for recovery, views severe mental disorders as chronic medical conditions, such as diabetes or heart disease—illnesses that may interfere with optimal functioning but that do not define the individual (Warner, 2009). The recovery model is based on the following assumptions (Dilks, Tasker, & Wren, 2010):

1. Recovery or improvement in functioning is possible and begins when a person realizes that positive change is possible.
2. Recovery is not a continual movement forward; occasional setbacks can be viewed as opportunities for new learning.
3. Healing involves separating one's identity from the illness and developing the ability to cope with psychiatric symptoms.

psychological resilience the capacity to effectively adapt to and bounce back from stress, trauma, and other adversity

recovery movement philosophy that with appropriate treatment and support those with mental illness can improve and live satisfying lives even with any limitations caused by their illness

4. Self-acceptance and regaining belief in one's self is vital. Community and societal resources can help protect the rights of those with mental illness and eliminate discrimination and stigma.

5. Recovery involves learning about one's capabilities, talents, and coping skills and using these strengths to engage in new life roles.

6. Self-direction allows one to learn to control and exercise choice on the journey to recovery and to participate in all decisions that can affect one's life and well-being.

7. Empowerment of the individual helps correct the sense of powerlessness and dependence that results from traditional mental health care.

8. Establishing or strengthening social connections can facilitate healing. This can include sharing one's knowledge, skills, and encouragement to others in recovery; helping others can provide a sense of belonging and community.

9. Taking personal responsibility for one's self-care and the journey toward recovery begins with understanding one's experiences and identifying the most effective coping strategies and healing processes.

10. Understanding that barriers can be overcome allows one to confidently live, work, and participate in society.

There are more and more community and peer support resources available to assist with recovery. For example, NAMI sponsors NAMI on Campus, a student-led group that not only supports students coping with mental illness but also strives to educate campus communities regarding mental health thereby increasing the chances that students will have a positive college experience. The recovery model has also resulted in social justice actions such as identifying the impact of stigma and discrimination on mental health; fighting policies that neglect the rights of individuals with mental illness; and promoting healing, growth, and respect for those affected by severe mental disorders (Glynn, Cohen, Dixon, & Niv, 2006).

A focus on recovery assists those coping with mental illness to achieve their potential and live more meaningful and positive lives. Recognizing that many in the mental health field are still unfamiliar with or mistaken about what recovery encompasses, the Substance Abuse and Mental Health Services Administration (SAMHSA) has funded a 5-year initiative to develop recovery-focused training for mental health professionals so that they can provide recovery-oriented services (Keita, 2012).

Changes in the Therapeutic Landscape

The use of psychiatric medications combined with a focus on reducing health care costs, researching treatment effectiveness, and using technology in the treatment process have literally changed the therapeutic landscape of the mental health profession.

The Drug Revolution in Psychiatry

Many mental health professionals consider the introduction of **psychotropic medications** (psychiatric drugs) in the 1950s as one of the great medical advances of the 20th century (Norfleet, 2002). First, lithium, a naturally occurring chemical substance, was discovered to radically calm some mental patients who had been hospitalized for years. Several years later, the drug chlorpromazine (brand name Thorazine) was found to be extremely effective in treating agitation in patients with schizophrenia. Before long, drugs were available to treat disorders such as depression, phobias, and anxiety. These drugs were revolutionary because they could rapidly and dramatically decrease or eliminate troublesome symptoms. As a result, those with serious mental illness were able to focus their attention on their therapy. In many cases, confinement in mental hospitals was no longer necessary and treatment became

psychotropic medications drugs used to treat or manage psychiatric symptoms by influencing brain activity associated with emotions and behavior

CRITICAL THINKING

I Have It, Too: The Medical Student Syndrome

To be human is to encounter difficulties and problems in life. A course in abnormal psychology dwells on human problems—many of them familiar. As a result, as you read this text, you may be prone to the medical student syndrome: reading about a disorder may lead you to suspect that you have the disorder or that a friend or relative has the disorder. This reaction to the study of abnormal behavior is common and important for you to recognize. Similarly, medical students reading about physical disorders sometimes begin to imagine that they have the illnesses they are studying. "Diarrhea? Fatigue? Trouble sleeping? That's me!" In this way, a cluster of symptoms—no matter how mild or how briefly experienced—can lead some people to suspect that they are ill.

Students who take a course that examines psychopathology are equally prone to believing that they have one or more of the mental disorders described in their text. The problem is compounded by easy access to the Internet where brief research on mental disorders such as schizophrenia, depression, or anxiety can produce a multitude of descriptors that seem to fit them. It is possible, of course, that some students *do* have an undiagnosed psychological disorder and would benefit from counseling or therapy. Most, however, are merely experiencing an exaggerated sense of their vulnerability to disorders. Two influences in particular may make us susceptible to imagining that we have a disorder. One is the universality of the human experience. All of us have experienced misfortunes in life. Depressed mood following the loss of a loved one or anxiety before giving a speech to a large audience are perfectly normal reactions. We can all remember and relate to feelings of fear, apprehension, unhappiness, or euphoria. In most cases, however, these feelings are normal reactions to life situations, not symptoms of illness. Another influence is our tendency to compare our own functioning with our perceptions of how other people are functioning. The outward behaviors you observe your fellow students displaying may lead you to conclude that they experience few difficulties in life, are self-assured and confident, and are invulnerable to mental disturbance. If you were privy to their inner thoughts and feelings, however, you might be surprised to find that they share the same apprehensions and insecurities that you sometimes experience.

If you see yourself anywhere in the pages of this book, we hope you will take the time to discuss your feelings with a friend, a family member, one of your professors, or someone at the counseling center at your school. You may be responding to pressures that you have not encountered before—worries about friendships, your grades, or a heavy course load, for example—or may be experiencing other common difficulties associated with adjustment to college life. Other people can help point out these pressures to you. If you continue to suspect that you have a problem, we hope you will consider getting help from your campus counseling center or a mental health professional in your community. As you will read many times throughout this text, people who seek and receive treatment for mental health issues often find that their condition improves; by seeking help, they are able to prevent a downward spiral of increasing emotional distress.

more cost-effective. The new drug therapies were credited with the depopulation of mental hospitals, a movement we discuss in Chapter 17. To handle the large number of patients returning to the community, outpatient treatment became the primary mode of service for those with severe symptoms. In addition to changing treatment, the introduction of psychiatric drugs revived strong belief in the biological basis of mental disorders.

The Development of Managed Health Care

managed health care   the industrialization of health care, whereby large organizations in the private sector control the delivery of services

Managed health care refers to the industrialization of health care, whereby insurance organizations in the private sector monitor and control the delivery of services. Traditionally, psychotherapy has been provided by individuals working independently or in small group practices. Some clients paid for services out of their own pockets. Others had health plans that allowed their therapists to determine fees and the methods and duration of treatment. However, a rapid escalation of health expenditures and a need to control costs resulted in the implementation of managed health care

(Cantor & Fuentes, 2008). This industrialization of health care has brought about major changes in the mental health professions:

- The business interests of health insurers exert increasing control over psychotherapy by determining what mental conditions are eligible for treatment and the number of treatment sessions allowed.

- Some organizations, in an effort to reduce costs, prefer hiring therapists with master's degrees rather than those with doctoral degrees.

- Therapists are increasingly required to use therapies that have strong research support. If research reveals that certain forms of treatment are successful for a particular disorder, the insurance carrier may deny coverage for unproven treatments.

Many mental health professionals are alarmed by these trends, fearing that decisions are made for business reasons rather than in the best interests of clients. On a positive note, in 2010, mental health advocates celebrated the enactment of groundbreaking mental health and substance-abuse parity legislation—insurance companies are no longer allowed to deny or offer less coverage to subscribers with addictions or mental illness. Additionally, provisions of the recently implemented Affordable Health Care Act have allowed many people previously unable to purchase health insurance (due to high costs or pre-existing conditions such as mental illness) to access mental health services.

An Increased Appreciation for Research

Breakthroughs in neuroscience and increasing interest in exploring evidence-based forms of psychotherapy have produced another contemporary trend: a heightened appreciation for the role of research in evaluating the effectiveness of treatments for mental disorders. The success of psychopharmacology spawned renewed interest and research into brain-behavior relationships. Indeed, as we discuss in Chapter 2, more and more researchers are exploring the physiological basis of mental disorders and biologically based treatments. Additionally, researchers are comparing the effectiveness of biological treatment with that of psychological treatment, with the goal of highlighting or even combining effective treatments for each mental disorder (Castelnuovo, 2010).

Although the move toward evidence-based practice is important, it is not without controversy. Some claim that the call for empirically based treatments is biased against treatment connected with certain theoretical orientations. For example, studies reveal that 60 to 80 percent of those treatments identified as most effective are those based on cognitive-behavioral principles (Norcross, 2004). Others assert that evidence-based practice is too restrictive and does not recognize clinical intuition and the dynamic basis of therapy. In addition, some question whether treatment research is applicable to ethnic minorities without adaptations that take into account an individual's cultural background (Hall & Yee, 2014). Last, as noted earlier, some fear that managed care companies will use research information to place more restrictions on the types of treatments they are willing to reimburse.

Technology-Assisted Therapy

Researchers and practitioners committed to treating mental disorders are making increasing use of technology to supplement traditional therapies or as a stand-alone intervention. Many people seem open to these forms of treatment. For example, computer-assisted and online programs to treat psychological problems such as depression and anxiety are rapidly increasing. In general, computer-based programs that employ techniques used in traditional therapy have shown success in reducing troublesome symptoms involving stress, anxiety, and depression (Cavanagh et al., 2013). For example, as we discuss in Chapter 8, adolescents with depression reported improvement after participating in an interactive computer program in which they navigated through a fantasy world using skills that are effective in combatting depression (Merry et al., 2012). If you were depressed, would you prefer using a computer program for treatment or meeting with a counselor? Many hope that having a variety of treatment options available will increase interest in and access to therapy.

Therapists are also using technological devices in their work with clients. For example, virtual reality therapy, using helmets with computer screens that immerse the wearer into a realistic virtual world, has successfully treated phobias, stress disorders, and other problems. We will go into more detail about this technology as we discuss treatments for anxiety in Chapter 5. Another example involves the use of smart phones with a downloaded application that allows individuals with schizophrenia to monitor their symptoms, receive reminders to take medications, obtain information on medication side effects, receive suggestions on how to identify and avoid stressors, and, if their symptoms are intensifying, to access ideas for coping (Ben-Zeev et al., 2013). Many participants like using this technology, especially because support is readily available when needed. As applications such as this become more sophisticated, it is likely that the use of mobile devices for providing assistance to those in therapy will increase.

Social robots are another example of how technology is changing treatment options. In one example, researchers interested in treating depression in older adults developed Paro, a seal-like robot that reacts to sounds and voices by turning his head. Participants who interacted with Paro reported feeling less lonely, coped better when encountering stress, and increased their willingness to participate in group activities; they showed positive psychological and emotional changes similar to those obtained with animal-assisted therapies (Misselhorn, Pompe, & Stapleton, 2013). In Japan, scientists are developing robots that are more and more human-like—robots that are improving the health of hospitalized patients (Akinaga, 2013). These amazing robots can mimic facial expressions and communicate with people, including answering questions in complete sentences. Do you think that robots have a future in assisting with therapy or reducing loneliness and depression in our aging population or in other socially isolated groups? Are there disadvantages to the idea of using social robots? What ethical issues may be involved?

It is an exciting time in the field of abnormal psychology. Many advances have been made over the years regarding the understanding and treatment of mental illness, and technological advances are producing a surge of research into causes of and treatment for mental disorders, topics we cover extensively in Chapter 2.

Chapter SUMMARY

1 What is abnormal psychology?
- Abnormal psychology is the study of the symptoms and causes of behavioral and mental disorders; the objectives are to describe, explain, predict, and modify distressing emotions and behaviors.

2 How do we differentiate between normal and abnormal behaviors?
- Four criteria are used to determine and define abnormality: distress, deviance, dysfunction, and dangerousness.

3 What societal factors affect definitions of abnormality?
- Cultural context and sociopolitical factors can influence definitions of abnormality. Criteria used to define normality or abnormality must be considered in light of community standards, changes over time, cultural values, and sociopolitical experiences.

4 How common are mental disorders?
- Over the course of a year, approximately 25 percent of adults in the United States experience a mental disorder.

- Among U.S. youth between the ages of 13 and 18, almost half of those surveyed met the criteria for a mental health disorder at some point in their lives.

5 Why is it important to confront the stigma and stereotyping associated with mental illness?

- Much of the stigma and stereotyping surrounding mental illness is based on inaccurate information, such as beliefs that those with mental illness are prone to violence or cannot make important social, artistic, or career-related contributions; those coping with mental illness may internalize and come to believe this inaccurate information.
- Negative societal attitudes about mental illness and related discrimination produce additional barriers to recovery.
- A code of silence about mental illness allows inaccurate stereotypes to continue and may prevent people from seeking treatment.

6 How have explanations of abnormal behavior changed over time?

- Ancient peoples believed in demonology and attributed abnormal behaviors to evil spirits that inhabited the victim's body. Treatments consisted of trephining, exorcism, and bodily assaults.
- Rational and scientific explanations of abnormality emerged during the Greco-Roman era. Hippocrates believed that abnormal behavior was due to biological causes, such as a dysfunction or disease of the brain. Treatment became more humane.
- With the collapse of the Roman Empire and the increased influence of the church, belief in the supernatural again flourished. During the Middle Ages, some of those killed in church-endorsed witch hunts were people with mental illness.
- The 14th through 16th centuries brought a return to rational and scientific inquiry, along with a heightened interest in humanistic methods of treating the mentally ill.

7 What were early explanations regarding the causes of mental disorders?

- In the 19th and 20th centuries, major medical breakthroughs reignited a belief in the biological roots of mental illness. An especially important discovery of this period was the microorganism that causes the symptoms of general paresis.
- The uncovering of a relationship between hypnosis and hysteria corroborated the belief that psychological processes could produce emotional difficulties.

8 What are some contemporary trends in abnormal psychology?

- Multicultural psychology, positive psychology, the recovery movement, the drug revolution, managed care, evidence-based practice, and the use of technology have all influenced the field of abnormal psychology.

2

UNDERSTANDING AND TREATING MENTAL DISORDERS

STEVE V., A 21-YEAR-OLD COLLEGE STUDENT, is suffering from a crippling bout of depression. He has a long psychiatric history, including two hospitalizations for severe depression and confused thinking. Steve was born in a suburb of San Francisco, California, the only child of an extremely wealthy couple.

His father is a prominent businessman who works long hours and travels frequently. On those rare occasions when he is home, Mr. V. is frequently preoccupied with business and aloof toward his son. When they do interact, Mr. V. often criticizes and ridicules Steve. Mr. V. expresses disappointment that his son seems so timid, weak, and withdrawn. Mr. V. often comments that Steve inherited "bad genes" from his wife's side of the family. Although Steve is extremely bright and earns good grades, Mr. V. feels that he lacks the "toughness" needed to survive and prosper in today's competitive world. Once, when 10-year-old Steve was bullied and beaten up by classmates, his father berated Steve for losing the fight.

Although Mrs. V. experiences episodes of severe depression several times each year, she tries to remain active in civic and social affairs. She sometimes treats Steve lovingly, but spent little time with him as he was growing up and seldom defends Steve during Mr. V.'s insulting tirades. In reality, Mrs. V. is quite lonely. She feels abandoned by Mr. V. and harbors a deep resentment toward him, which she is frightened to express. When Steve was younger, Mrs. V. often allowed Steve to sleep with her when her husband was away on business trips. She usually dressed minimally on these occasions and was very demonstrative—holding, stroking, and kissing Steve. This behavior continued until Steve was 12, and Mrs. V. caught Steve masturbating under her sheets one morning; she then abruptly refused to allow Steve into her bed.

Steve was raised by a series of full-time nannies. He had few playmates. His birthdays were celebrated with a cake and candles, but the only celebrants were Steve and his mother. By age 10, Steve occupied himself with "mind games," letting his imagination carry him off on flights of fancy. He frequently imagined himself as a powerful figure—Spiderman or Batman. His fantasies were often extremely violent, involving bloody battles with his enemies.

During high school, Steve became convinced that external forces were controlling his mind and behavior. After seeing a horror movie about exorcism, he was convinced that he was possessed by the devil. He also began to experience episodes of severe depression. On two occasions, suicide attempts led to his hospitalization. He initially did well in college. Recently, however, he has little interest in attending classes or studying for exams.

focus
QUESTIONS

1 What models of psychopathology have been used to explain abnormal behavior?

2 What is the multipath model of mental disorders?

3 How is biology involved in mental disorders?

4 How do psychological models explain mental disorders?

5 What role do social factors play in psychopathology?

6 What sociocultural factors influence mental health?

7 Why is it important to consider mental disorders from a multipath perspective?

What do you make of Steve? He certainly fulfills our criteria of someone experiencing symptoms of a mental disorder. How do we explain his unusual thoughts and his deep depression? Is Steve correct in his belief that he is possessed by evil spirits? Is his father correct in suggesting that "bad genes" caused his disorder? What role did social isolation, constant criticism from his father, and confusing interactions with his mother play in the development of his problems? These complex questions lead us to a very important aspect of abnormal psychology: the **etiology**, or causes, of disorders. In this chapter, we propose an integrative *multipath model* for explaining abnormal behavior—a model that highlights how biological, psychological, social, and sociocultural factors influence the development of specific mental disorders. Before we begin, however, let's look at how traditional one-dimensional models might explain Steve's psychopathology.

One-Dimensional Models of Mental Disorders

Humanism helped change society's attitude toward mental disorders, as described in Chapter 1. The humanistic view led to modern perspectives regarding the causes of mental illness. Most contemporary explanations fall into four distinct camps: (a) biological views (including genetics and other physiological explanations); (b) psychological issues, rooted in the invisible complexities of the human mind; (c) dysfunctional social relationships, including stressful interactions with family members and peers; and (d) sociocultural influences, including the effects of discrimination and stressors related to race, gender, and socioeconomic status. Let's look at how each model might explain Steve's psychopathology.

- *Biological explanations:* Some form of biological dysfunction is causing Steve's difficulties. His problems are possibly due to a genetic predisposition to depression or perhaps abnormalities in his neurological makeup.

- *Psychological explanations:* Psychological explanations for Steve's behavior might focus on (a) early childhood experiences that created resentment and loneliness, (b) Steve's inability to confront his intense feelings of hostility toward his father and unresolved sexual longing toward his mother, or (c) irrational beliefs and distorted thinking processes that made him lose touch with objective reality.

- *Social explanations:* From a social-relational perspective, a dysfunctional family system and pathological upbringing contributed to Steve's issues. Parental neglect, rejection, and psychological abuse may explain many of his symptoms. The constant bullying of Steve by his father and the confusing messages and lack of support from his mother are the primary culprits. Steve also led a very isolated life, with few opportunities to develop appropriate social skills and behaviors. Additionally, Steve lacks a network of supportive relationships.

- *Sociocultural explanations:* Societal and cultural context are important considerations in understanding Steve's difficulties. He is a white European American, born to a wealthy family in the upper socioeconomic class. He is a male, raised in a cultural context that values individual achievement, assertiveness, and competitiveness. Because Steve does not live up to his father's standards of masculinity, he is considered a failure not only by his father, but by himself.

These four explanations, perspectives, or viewpoints of abnormal behavior are referred to as *models* by psychologists. A **model** describes a phenomenon or process that we cannot directly observe. Researchers studying psychopathology use a variety of models, each embodying a particular theoretical approach. Such models help researchers determine relevant information, ask probing questions, make educated

etiology   cause or origin of a disorder

model   an analogy used by scientists, usually to describe or explain a phenomenon or process they cannot directly observe

guesses about the causes of mental disorders, and organize information in a meaningful way. Theorists do not expect to develop one definitive model of human behavior because they recognize the complexities involved in being human. They realize that the models they construct are limited and cannot explain every aspect of the phenomena they are studying (Brooks-Harris, 2008). Rather, they use the models to visualize psychopathology as if it truly worked in the manner described.

Models of psychopathology, whether biological, psychological, social, or sociocultural, help us to organize and make sense of what we know about mental illness. These models, however, can foster a one-dimensional and linear explanation of mental disorders, thus limiting our ability to consider other perspectives. If, for example, we use a psychological explanation of Steve's behavior and consider his problems to be rooted in unconscious incestuous desires for his mother and competitiveness toward his father, we may unintentionally ignore research findings pointing to powerful biological, social, or sociocultural influences on his symptoms.

As you reviewed the one-dimensional explanations for Steve V.'s difficulties, it is likely that you concluded that each explanation contains kernels of truth, but that none of the explanations comprehensively addresses Steve's mental distress, including his unique physiology, experiences, and family background. You may have also concluded that it is more likely that a combination of biological, psychological, social, and sociocultural factors interacted and contributed to Steve's difficulties. If so, you are beginning to appreciate the complexities involved in understanding the causes of mental disorders.

Scientists now recognize that one-dimensional perspectives are overly simplistic because they (a) set up a false "either/or" dichotomy between accepting one explanation or another (e.g., nature vs. nurture), (b) neglect the possibility that a variety of factors contribute to the development of mental disorders, and (c) fail to recognize the reciprocal influences of the various contributing factors (T.-Y. Zhang & Meaney, 2010).

We will use our *multipath model*—an integration of biological, psychological, social, and sociocultural influences—to explain the mental disorders discussed throughout the text. The multipath model addresses the limitations associated with one-dimensional models and will help you conceptualize how various interacting factors can contribute to mental illness.

A Multipath Model of Mental Disorders

Nearly all abnormal psychology texts present a variety of theories to explain mental disorders. Research shows, however, that a variety of factors influence the development of a psychological disorder—influences that incorporate the perspectives of multiple theories. Some models do, in fact, consider multiple viewpoints. The **biopsychosocial model**, for example, suggests that interactions between biological, psychological, and social factors cause mental disorders. In Steve V.'s case, genetics and brain functioning (a biological perspective) may interact with ways of thinking (a psychological perspective) in a given family environment (a social perspective) to produce his distressing symptoms (J. J. Mann & Haghighi, 2010). Although the biopsychosocial model highlights the fact that multiple factors can influence the development of mental disorders, concerns remain: (a) there is limited focus on how factors interact to produce illness; (b) the model provides little guidance regarding how to treat the disorder; and (c) the model neglects the powerful influences of culture (Ghaemi, 2010b; Sue & Sue, 2013). Of particular concern is the relative neglect of **sociocultural influences** such as the effects of poverty or discrimination in explaining mental disorders.

What, then, is the "best" way to conceptualize the causes of mental disorders? The integrative and interacting **multipath model** we use throughout this text will prompt you

biopsychosocial model perspective suggesting that interactions between biological, psychological, and social factors cause mental disorders

sociocultural influences factors such as gender, sexual orientation, spirituality, religion, socioeconomic status, race/ethnicity or culture that can exert an effect on mental health

multipath model a model that provides an organizational framework for understanding the numerous influences on the development of mental disorders, the complexity of their interacting components, and the need to view disorders from a holistic framework to consider the multitude of factors that researchers have confirmed are associated with each disorder we discuss. The multipath model is not a theory but a way of looking at the variety and complexity of contributors to mental disorders. In some respects it is a *metamodel*, a model of models that provides an organizational framework for understanding the numerous factors that increase risk for the development of mental disorders, the complexity of potential interactions among factors, and the need to view disorders from a holistic framework. The multipath model operates under several assumptions:

- No one theoretical perspective is adequate to explain the complexity of the human condition and the development of mental disorders.

- There are multiple pathways to and influences on the development of any single disorder. Explanations of abnormal behavior must consider biological, psychological, social, and sociocultural elements.

- Not all dimensions contribute equally to a disorder. In the case of some disorders, current research suggests that certain etiological forces have the strongest influence on the development of the specific disorder. Additionally, our understanding of mental disorders often evolves as further investigation provides new insights into contributing factors.

- The multipath model is integrative and interactive. It acknowledges that factors may combine in complex and reciprocal ways so that people exposed to the same influences may not develop the same disorder and that different individuals exposed to different factors may develop similar mental disorders.

- The biological and psychological strengths and assets of a person and positive aspects of the person's social and sociocultural environment can help protect against psychopathology, minimize symptoms, or facilitate recovery from mental illness.

As you can see, understanding the causes of various disorders is a complex process. Let's look at the details of how our multipath model conceptualizes the development of mental disorders. As we explain various disorders throughout the book, we will focus on these four dimensions (see Figure 2.1).

- *Dimension One: Biological Factors*—Genetics, brain anatomy and physiology, central nervous system functioning, autonomic nervous system reactivity, and so forth.

Figure 2.1

The Multipath Model

Each dimension of the multipath model contains factors found to be important in explaining mental disorders. Reciprocal interactions involving factors within and between any of these dimensions can also influence the development of mental disorders.

© Cengage Learning®

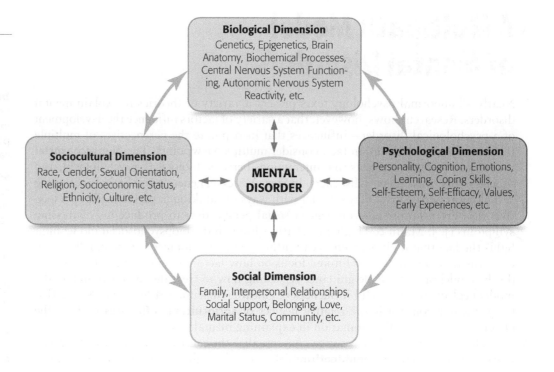

Biological Dimension
Genetics, Epigenetics, Brain Anatomy, Biochemical Processes, Central Nervous System Functioning, Autonomic Nervous System Reactivity, etc.

Sociocultural Dimension
Race, Gender, Sexual Orientation, Religion, Socioeconomic Status, Ethnicity, Culture, etc.

MENTAL DISORDER

Psychological Dimension
Personality, Cognition, Emotions, Learning, Coping Skills, Self-Esteem, Self-Efficacy, Values, Early Experiences, etc.

Social Dimension
Family, Interpersonal Relationships, Social Support, Belonging, Love, Marital Status, Community, etc.

- *Dimension Two: Psychological Factors*—Personality, cognition, emotions, learning, coping skills, self-efficacy, values, and so forth.
- *Dimension Three: Social Factors*—Family and other interpersonal relationships, social support, belonging, love, marital status, community connections, and so forth.
- *Dimension Four: Sociocultural Factors*—Race, gender, sexual orientation, spirituality or religion, socioeconomic status, ethnicity, culture, and so forth.

Let's consider some of the aspects of the multipath model. First, within each dimension, there may be distinct theories and, thus, multiple proposed explanations for a disorder; the theoretical perspective affects the explanations proposed and the research conducted. Let's take the psychological dimension as an example. Some theories highlight the importance of unconscious impulses in the development of psychopathology whereas others emphasize learned patterns of thinking and behaving. Thus, there are considerable differences of opinion regarding the purported causes of a disorder even within a particular dimension. Because some explanations, such as the effects of a stressful environment, can exert influence in more than one area—stressful experiences can have influence in all four dimensions—it is best to view the four dimensions as having permeable boundaries with considerable overlap.

Second, factors within each of the four dimensions can interact and influence each other in any direction. For example, let's talk about the association between **impulsivity** and addiction. Research shows that certain patterns of brain functioning (a biological characteristic) are associated with impulsivity (a psychological characteristic). Additionally, if you are impulsive, it is quite possible that you have a parent or sibling who behaves impulsively; this might have affected your family relationships or your experiences growing up (a social factor). Also, if you have a tendency to make decisions without carefully considering the consequences, you might be more likely to hang around with friends who also engage in higher-risk behaviors such as underage drinking or experimenting with drugs (a social factor that results in additional biological influences—substance use affects brain regions that guide decision making).

Your impulsive behavior may also affect your ability to complete your education or keep a job. This makes you vulnerable to the influences of poverty or discrimination because of your inconsistent employment history (a sociocultural factor). This may increase your tendency to turn to drugs, alcohol, or gambling and lead to a cycle of addictive behavior, a factor that may further affect your brain functioning, strain your relationships with family and friends, decrease your chances of stable employment, and so on.

impulsivity tendency to act quickly without careful thought

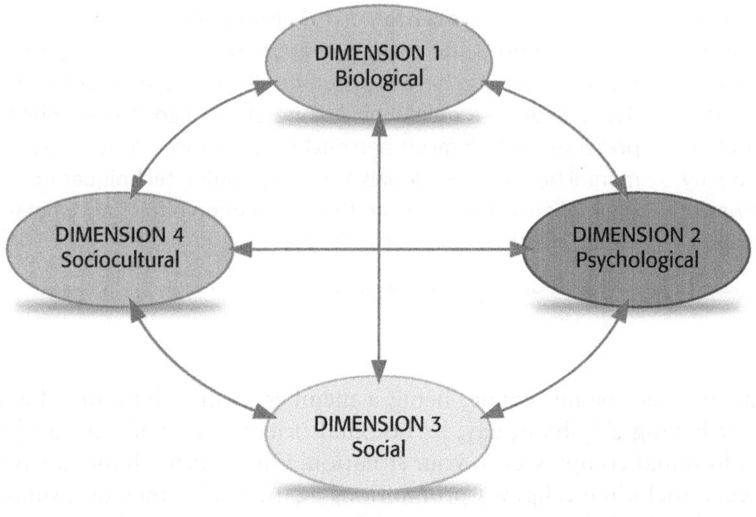

Figure 2.2

The Four Dimensions and Possible Pathways of Influence
Conceptually, mental disorders arise from four possible dimensions (biological, psychological, social, and sociocultural) and from reciprocal interactions between factors within a dimension or among factors in multiple dimensions.
© Cengage Learning®

A Multipath Model of Resilience

Most of us face various adversities during our lifetimes. How is it that some people bounce back quickly when affected by stressful circumstances? Just as biological, psychological, social, and sociocultural vulnerabilities contribute to mental disorders, these same factors influence our **resilience**—our ability to recover from stressful or challenging circumstances (see Figure 2.3). In other words, enhancing and using our strengths and relying on positive supports within our environment may decrease the likelihood that we develop a mental disorder. Similarly, if circumstances are such that we are coping with a mental health condition, these protective factors may decrease the duration or severity of our symptoms. Here are some examples of factors influencing resilience from a multipath perspective:

Biological Influences

Because adaptation is the key to our survival, our brains and bodies are primed for resilience. This biological ability to adapt and bounce back increases our chances of thriving even after we have faced challenging circumstances (Karatsoreos & McEwen, 2013). Because some people appear to have high internal resilience, researchers are attempting to identify genes associated with this characteristic. Additionally, researchers have found that lifestyle factors such as healthy dietary, exercise, and sleep patterns can exert positive effects on our mental health (Chatburn, Coussens, & Kohler, 2013; Minich & Bland, 2013). Biological researchers interested in increasing resilience are also using neuroimaging procedures to investigate methods for improving emotional regulation (van der Werff, van den Berg, Pannekoek, Elzinga, & van der Wee, 2013).

Psychological Influences

Psychological qualities such as mental flexibility, active coping, optimism, self-efficacy, and adaptability allow people to tackle life challenges and increase resilience (Baratta, Rozeske, & Maier, 2013; Schaefer et al., 2013). In one study involving nurses working in a high-stress intensive care unit, characteristics such as these were associated with less burnout and fewer symptoms of anxiety or depression (Mealer et al., 2013). Additionally, our mindset—our views about our ability to make positive changes in our lives—can exert a powerful influence on our well-being; if we have positive expectations that sustained effort will influence outcome, we are less likely to succumb to distressing life circumstances (Yeager, Walton, & Cohen, 2013).

Social Influences

Social support can play an important role in increasing our resilience. For example, adolescents who reported high levels of peer support were less reactive to stress compared to teens who reported average or low levels of support (Doane & Zeiders, 2013). Additionally, supportive family characteristics can help us cope with adversity (Bradley, Davis, Wingo, Mercer, & Ressler, 2013). Combining both psychological and social factors, the broaden-and-build theory of positive emotions posits that positive emotions increase our engagement in the world and thus enhance our resilience by building our coping skills and interpersonal resources (Fredrickson, 2013).

Sociocultural Influences

Cultural and community support can also increase our ability to deal with life's challenges. For example, Canadian minority youth who remained involved in the culture and customs of their ethnic community showed good resilience (Ungar & Liebenberg, 2013). Presumably, cultural connections serve as a buffer to adverse situations. Similarly, adherence to traditional cultural values such as *familismo* (importance of family), respect, and ethnic identity were associated with strength in overcoming adversity among Mexican American college students (Morgan Consoli & Llamas, 2013).

These are just a few of many possible examples illustrating how biological, psychological, social, and sociocultural factors play a role in resilience. As you read about the risk factors associated with mental disorders, we hope you will remember that we all have personal and social strengths—positive life outlook, social support, coping skills, and social group identities—that we can rely on to help us bounce back when life is challenging. Additionally, just as we can improve our physical health, we also have the opportunity to engage in activities that improve our mental health and our resilience, even when presented with difficult personal circumstances. In fact, many mental health professionals are incorporating techniques from the resilience literature into their prevention efforts and therapeutic practices (Bolier et al., 2013).

---

resilience   the ability to recover quickly from stress or adversity

protective factors   conditions or attributes that lessen or eliminate the risk of a negative psychological or social outcome

As you might imagine, being female, being a member of an ethnic or religious minority group, or having a lesbian, gay, or bisexual orientation (sociocultural factors) would add additional complexity to your situation. On the other hand, a variety of **protective factors**, including religious prohibitions against substance use, supportive family and friends who help you avoid impulsive actions, or engaging in certain

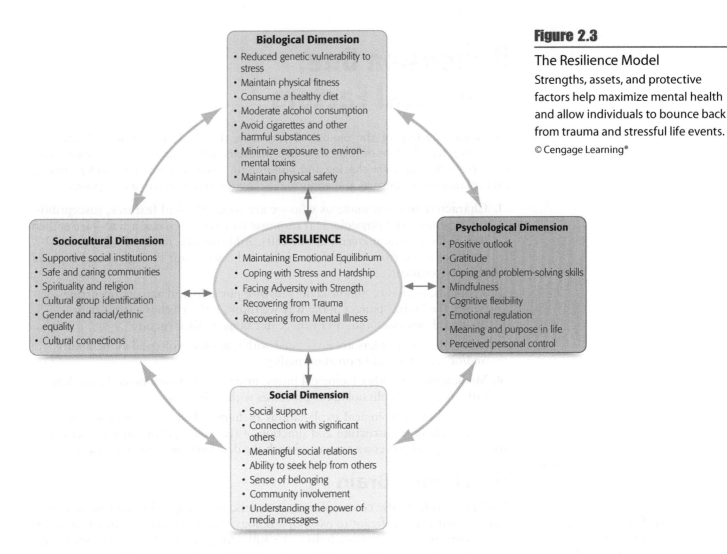

Figure 2.3

The Resilience Model
Strengths, assets, and protective factors help maximize mental health and allow individuals to bounce back from trauma and stressful life events.
© Cengage Learning®

Biological Dimension
- Reduced genetic vulnerability to stress
- Maintain physical fitness
- Consume a healthy diet
- Moderate alcohol consumption
- Avoid cigarettes and other harmful substances
- Minimize exposure to environmental toxins
- Maintain physical safety

Sociocultural Dimension
- Supportive social institutions
- Safe and caring communities
- Spirituality and religion
- Cultural group identification
- Gender and racial/ethnic equality
- Cultural connections

RESILIENCE
- Maintaining Emotional Equilibrium
- Coping with Stress and Hardship
- Facing Adversity with Strength
- Recovering from Trauma
- Recovering from Mental Illness

Psychological Dimension
- Positive outlook
- Gratitude
- Coping and problem-solving skills
- Mindfulness
- Cognitive flexibility
- Emotional regulation
- Meaning and purpose in life
- Perceived personal control

Social Dimension
- Social support
- Connection with significant others
- Meaningful social relations
- Ability to seek help from others
- Sense of belonging
- Community involvement
- Understanding the power of media messages

behaviors (exercise or meditating, for example), can reduce impulsivity and the likelihood of problematic behaviors. We will discuss factors associated with resilience throughout the text. As you can see, the etiology of mental disorders is complex and often involves the interaction of factors occurring within and between all four dimensions, as noted in Figure 2.2.

Third, different combinations within the four dimensions may influence the development of a particular condition. For instance, let's look at the severe depression experienced by Steve V.'s mother. Her depression may be related to a single factor (e.g., an unhappy marriage) or may involve an interaction of factors in different dimensions (e.g., biological vulnerability to depression, child abuse occurring in early life, and stressors in adulthood). Although a single factor may trigger a disorder such as depression, it is more likely the result of a combination of factors.

Fourth, many disorders appear to be **heterogeneous** in nature. That is, there may be different types or versions of a disorder. Different types of depression, for example, may be influenced by different factors; severe depression appears to have a stronger biological basis than mild depression.

Fifth, the same triggers or underlying vulnerabilities may cause different disorders. For example, child abuse appears to trigger or increase the risk of a number of disorders.

We discuss each of the four dimensions in more detail in the following sections, including the theories and data underlying each dimension.

heterogeneous   different or diverse

Dimension One: Biological Factors

Our understanding of the biological processes that influence mental disorders is expanding rapidly. Not only are research methods increasing in sophistication, scientists across the globe are sharing and building on available research. Modern biological explanations of normal and abnormal behaviors share certain assumptions:

1. Characteristics that make us who we are—our physical features, susceptibility to illness, and physiological response to stress, to name a few—are embedded in the genetic material of our cells. Additionally, many of our personal qualities result from complex interactions between our biological makeup and the environment.

2. Thoughts, emotions, and behaviors involve physiological activity occurring within the brain; changes in the way we think, feel, or behave affect these biological processes and, over time, can change brain structure.

3. Many mental disorders are associated with inherited biological vulnerability and/or some form of brain abnormality.

4. Medications and other biological interventions used to treat mental disorders influence various physiological processes within the brain.

Understanding biological explanations of human behavior requires some basic knowledge about the structure and function of the brain, particularly the structures and physiological processes associated with the development of mental disorders.

The Human Brain

The brain's role as the center of consciousness, including all thoughts, memories, and emotions, is significant to psychopathology. The brain coordinates a variety of highly complex functions, including the following: (a) regulating activities necessary for our survival (such as breathing and heartbeat); (b) receiving and interpreting sensory information (from both inside and outside our bodies); (c) transmitting information to our muscles and other organs; and (d) coordinating our responses to incoming stimuli.

Viewed in cross section, the brain has three parts (see Figure 2.4):

- *the forebrain*—responsible for higher-level mental processes;
- *the midbrain*—involved with basic functions such as hearing and vision, motor movement, alertness and sleep/wake cycles, and temperature regulation; and
- *the hindbrain*—the most primitive brain region; designed for self-preservation and survival; responsible for instinctive behavior, balance and equilibrium, and basic bodily functions such as heartbeat, respiration, and digestion.

Cerebrospinal fluid surrounds the entire brain; this fluid not only cushions and protects the delicate regions of the brain, but also fills the cerebral ventricles—the linked system of open spaces found within the brain. A deep groove divides the outer layers of the brain and the deeper brain structures into virtually identical halves—the left and right hemispheres. Each hemisphere's matching brain structures receive sensory input from and control muscle movement on the opposite side of the body. Each hemisphere has some specialized functions; the left hemisphere is associated with many language functions, whereas the right hemisphere is associated with visual-spatial abilities and has stronger connections to structures associated with emotion. Newer research suggests that although some brain activities occur primarily in one

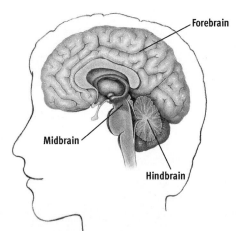

Figure 2.4

Three Major Divisions of the Brain

A cross-sectional view of the brain reveals the forebrain, midbrain, and hindbrain. Although the large size of the forebrain makes the other two divisions look trivial, the midbrain and hindbrain also play a key role in controlling vital functions such as vision, hearing, breathing, movement, and maintaining balance.

© 2016 Cengage Learning®

hemisphere, most mental performance involves complex communication between brain regions. Although all brain regions are critical for optimal functioning, some brain structures play a greater role in the development of mental disorders. Many of the structures relevant to psychopathology are in the forebrain.

The Forebrain

The forebrain contains brain structures associated with characteristics that make us human—thoughts, perceptions, intelligence, language, personality, imagination, planning, organization, and decision making. The forebrain holds the largest and most advanced part of the brain, the **cerebrum**. Another significant part of the forebrain is the **cerebral cortex**, which consists of layers of specialized nerve cells, called neurons, that transmit information to other nerve cells, muscles, and gland cells throughout the body.

The **prefrontal cortex**, the region of the cerebral cortex responsible for **executive functioning**, helps us manage our attention, behavior, and emotions so that we reach short-term and long-term goals. Executive functioning involves a combination of emotional, social, and intellectual capacities. The ability to foresee consequences of our actions, guided by memories from the past in combination with assessment of present circumstances, is an important aspect of executive functioning. When operating optimally, the prefrontal cortex helps inhibit many of the instinctual responses and reflexive actions that arise from the more primitive areas of the brain. In other words, the prefrontal cortex helps us exercise good judgment and keep our feelings and impulses in check. Unfortunately, many mental disorders involve dysfunction in the prefrontal cortex; when this occurs, a person may experience difficulty organizing and evaluating incoming stimuli and planning appropriate responses.

The **limbic system** is a group of deep brain structures associated with emotions, decision making, and the formation of memories (Figure 2.5). The intricate connections in this system link our emotions and our memories. One role that the **amygdala** plays in the limbic system is to facilitate recall of our emotional memories and our response to potential threat. It is sometimes referred to as a barometer of our emotions—the stronger the emotion, the greater the arousal in the amygdala. The amygdala activates in response to our thoughts or imagination, as well as real-world stimuli; this reactivity in response to our thoughts is a key factor in various mental disorders. Another structure in the limbic system is the **hippocampus**, which helps us form, organize, and store memory; this includes evaluating short-term memories and sending emotionally relevant memories to the cerebral cortex for long-term storage, as well as assisting with the recall of emotions associated with specific memories.

Emotional responses originating in the limbic system directly affect the **autonomic nervous system (ANS)**. The ANS coordinates basic functions such as digestion and respiration when we are at rest. It also regulates automatic physical responses associated with emotional reactions, most notably the "fight or flight" response (e.g., increased blood flow and heart rate that prepare us to respond to threat) that occurs when we perceive a situation as threatening. The **hypothalamus**, a structure that regulates bodily drives, such as hunger, thirst, and sexual response, and body conditions, such as body temperature and circadian rhythms, plays a key role in our reactions via the

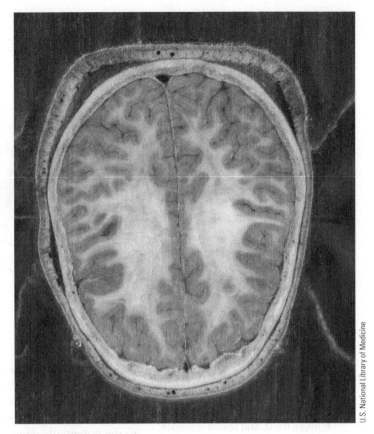

The Cerebral Cortex

This section of the brain of an adult female shows the cerebral cortex, with its extensive folding, and the underlying white matter—the connective networks of the brain.

cerebrum the largest part of the brain, consisting of the right and left hemisphere

cerebral cortex the outermost layers of brain tissue; covers the cerebrum

prefrontal cortex the outer layer of the prefrontal lobe responsible for inhibiting instinctive responses and performing complex cognitive behavior such as decision making

executive functioning mental processes that involve the planning, organizing, and attention required to meet short-term and long-term goals

limbic system group of deep brain structures associated with emotions, decision making, and memory formation

amygdala structure involved with physiological reactivity and emotional memories

Figure 2.5

Structures in the Limbic System

The limbic system, comprised of an interconnected group of brain structures, controls emotional reactions and basic human drives. It is also involved in motivation, decision making, and the formation of memories.

© 2016 Cengage Learning®

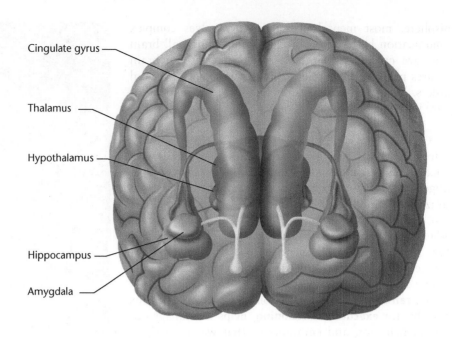

Cingulate gyrus
Thalamus
Hypothalamus
Hippocampus
Amygdala

hippocampus   structure involved with the formation, organization, and storing of emotionally relevant memories

autonomic nervous system (ANS)   coordinates basic physiological functions and regulates physical responses associated with emotional reactions

hypothalamus   brain structure that regulates bodily drives, such as hunger, thirst, and sexual response, and body conditions, such as body temperature and circadian rhythms

hypothalamic-pituitary-adrenal (HPA) axis   a system activated under conditions of stress or emotional arousal

pituitary gland   stimulates hormones associated with growth, sexual and reproductive development, metabolism, and stress responses

hormones   regulatory chemicals that influence various physiological activities, such as metabolism, digestion, growth, and mood

adrenal gland   releases sex hormones; releases other hormones, such as cortisol, in response to stress

neuron   nerve cell that transmits messages throughout the body

glia   cells that support and protect neurons

neural circuits   signal-relaying network of interconnected neurons

dendrite   short, rootlike structure on the neuron cell body that receives signals from other neurons

axon   extension on the neuron cell body that sends signals to other neurons, muscles, and glands

hypothalamic-pituitary-adrenal (HPA) axis, a system activated under conditions of stress or emotional arousal. When stress or perceived threat triggers the HPA axis, the hypothalamus stimulates the **pituitary gland** to release **hormones** that produce a sequence of events (including stimulation of the **adrenal gland**) that prepare the body to respond to the potentially dangerous situations. Biochemical processes associated with the HPA axis can have a cascading effect throughout the brain and produce symptoms associated with various mental disorders.

Biochemical Processes within the Brain and Body

Biochemical theories attempt to explain how irregularities in biochemical functioning trigger mental disorders. These theories are based on the involvement of the brain's biochemical actions in most physiological and mental processes, from sleeping and digestion to thinking and feeling. Research confirms the connection between biochemical processes within the brain and the etiology of specific mental disorders. To see how biochemical dysfunction is associated with psychopathology, it is important to understand the physiological processes underlying mental and emotional functioning.

The functioning of the brain involves a variety of interconnected activities. Our brains are composed of billions of **neurons** (nerve cells) and trillions of **glia**, cells that perform a variety of supportive roles, including shaping the brain's **neural circuits** or signal-relaying systems (Chung et al., 2013). Although neurons vary in the specific functions they perform, they all share certain characteristics. Each neuron has a cell body with the capacity to regulate the growth, metabolism, and repair of the neuron. On one end of the cell body are numerous **dendrites**, short, rootlike structures that receive chemical and electrical signals from other neurons (Figure 2.6). At the other end is an **axon**, a much longer extension that sends signals not only to other neurons but also to muscles and glands, often a considerable distance away. Incoming messages are received and transmitted to the cell body by a neuron's dendrites; the signal then is sent down the axon to bulblike swellings called axon terminals, usually located near dendrites of another neuron.

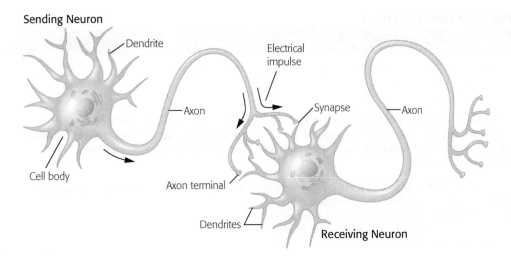

Sending Neuron

Dendrite

Electrical impulse

Axon

Synapse

Axon

Cell body

Axon terminal

Dendrites

Receiving Neuron

Figure 2.6

Synaptic Transmission
Electrical impulses travel along the axon, through the synapse, and to the dendrites of the next neuron. Neurotransmitters facilitate the transmission of the impulse across the synapse.

© Cengage Learning®

Thus, dendrites bring information *to* the body of the cell and axons carry information *away* from the cell. Many axons are covered with **myelin**, a fatty, insulating substance that forms a myelin sheath; **myelination** increases the efficiency of signal transmission and allows damaged nerve pathways to regenerate by providing tracks along which regrowth can occur. Some brain tissue (**white matter**) primarily consists of nerve pathways, myelinated axons, and the supportive glia cells that surround them, whereas other tissue (**gray matter**) consists of the cell bodies of neurons and glia (and the capillaries supplying them nutrients).

The functioning of the brain involves many continuous activities—neurons working in synchronization with processes occurring throughout the body. Effective communication between neurons relies on both electrical impulses and chemical signals. A variety of chemicals, called **neurotransmitters**, help relay messages by transmitting nerve impulses across the **synapse**, a tiny gap that exists between nerve cells (Figure 2.6). After crossing the synapse, the neurotransmitter binds to the correct receptor neuron on the other side, like a key fitting into a lock. Once neurotransmitters have performed their function, they are often reabsorbed by the axon that released them, a process called **reuptake**. If not reabsorbed, neurotransmitters are sometimes deactivated (neutralized) by enzymes in the synapse or removed by glial cells. (See Table 2.1 for some of the neurotransmitters and hormones most frequently involved in mental disorders.)

Depending on the specific neurotransmitter and other factors, the binding that occurs at the synapse (Figure 2.7) either excites the cell (stimulating continued transmission of the signal) or inhibits further signaling. Excitation causes electrical impulses to travel to other neurons, to muscles, or to gland cells that stimulate the release of hormones. Some neurotransmitters (such as gamma-aminobutyric acid [GABA] and serotonin) have inhibitory effects that decrease neural signaling whereas others (such as epinephrine and norepinephrine) have excitatory effects that promote signal transmission. Other neurotransmitters, such as acetylcholine and dopamine, can either increase or decrease the likelihood that neurons will fire depending on the type of receptors available. Additionally, some chemicals, such as epinephrine (also called adrenaline), can function both as a neurotransmitter and as a hormone.

The **enteric nervous system (ENS)**, embedded in the lining of the gastrointestinal system, is sometimes described as our "second brain" because it uses and manufactures many of the same neurotransmitters and hormones found in the brain. The ENS is an independent neural system involved in maintaining **homeostasis** in gastrointestinal processes such as digestion. Hormones and neurotransmitters in the ENS are capable of signaling the brain regarding stress and other emotions and can even influence higher-level thinking. In other words, bodily signals that originate within the ENS,

myelin white, fatty material that surrounds and insulates axons

myelination myelin sheaths increase the efficiency of signal transmission between nerve cells

white matter brain tissue comprised of myelinated nerve pathways

gray matter brain tissue comprised of the cell bodies of neurons and glia

neurotransmitter any of a group of chemicals that help transmit messages between neurons

synapse tiny gap that exists between the axon of the sending neuron and the dendrites of the receiving neuron

reuptake the reabsorption of a neurotransmitter after an impulse has been transmitted across the synapse

enteric nervous system (ENS) an independent neural system involved with digestion; capable of signaling the brain regarding stress and other emotions

homeostasis ability to maintain internal equilibrium by adjusting physiological processes

Table 2.1 Major Neurotransmitters and Their Functions

Neurotransmitter	Function	Associated Disorders
Acetylcholine (ACH)	Influences attention and memory, dream and sleep states, and muscle activation; has excitatory and inhibitory effects	Alzheimer's disease
Dopamine*	Influences motivation and reward-seeking behaviors; regulates movement, emotional responses, attention, and planning; has excitatory and inhibitory effects	Attention-deficit/hyperactivity disorder; autism; depression; schizophrenia; substance use disorders; Parkinson's disease
Epinephrine (adrenaline)* and norepinephrine (noradrenaline)*	Excitatory functions including regulating attention, arousal and concentration, dreaming, and moods; as a hormone, influences physiological reactions related to stress response (constricted attention, blood flow, heart rate, etc.)	Anxiety and stress disorders; sleep disorders
Glutamate	Major excitatory neurotransmitter involved in cognition, memory, and learning	Alzheimer's disease: autism; depression; obsessive-compulsive disorder; schizophrenia
Gamma-aminobutyric acid (GABA)	Major inhibitory neurotransmitter; calms the nerves; regulates mood and muscle tone	Anxiety disorders; attention-deficit/hyperactivity disorder; bipolar disorder; depression; schizophrenia
Serotonin	Inhibitory effects regulate temperature, mood, appetite, and sleep; reduced serotonin can increase impulsive behavior and aggression	Depression, suicide, obsessive-compulsive and anxiety disorders, post-traumatic stress disorder, eating disorders

Hormone	Function	Associated Disorders
Cortisol	Steroid hormone released in response to stress	Anorexia nervosa: depression; stress-related disorders
Ghrelin	Stimulates hunger and boosts the appeal of food	Eating disorders; obesity
Leptin	Suppresses appetite	Anorexia nervosa: schizophrenia
Melatonin	Regulates circadian sleep and wake cycles	Bipolar disorder; depression, particularly seasonal depression; schizophrenia; obsessive-compulsive disorder
Oxytocin	Neuropeptide hormone influencing lactation and complex social behavior (including nurturing and bonding)	Autism; anxiety; schizophrenia

*These neurotransmitters also function as a hormone.
© Cengage Learning®

and subsequent brain processing of these signals, are involved in emotional regulation. Additionally, small molecules called **neuropeptides** function as neurotransmitters and moderate biological processes within the ENS and the central nervous system; neuropeptides have the ability to both directly and indirectly influence a variety of hormones and neurotransmitters (Burbach, 2011).

Neurotransmitters, hormones, neuropeptides, and related biochemical processes play an important role in our overall functioning, affecting our mood, behavior, coordination, communication, and higher-level thinking, as well as basic physiological activities occurring throughout our brains and bodies. When hormonal and neurotransmission processes do not function appropriately, the result can be the symptoms seen in some mental disorders. Biochemical processes also play an important role in adaptive structural changes that occur in the brain and central nervous system.

neuropeptides small molecules that can directly and indirectly influence a variety of hormones and neurotransmitters

Neuroplasticity

The human brain evolves and adapts to ensure our survival. This process of frequent change, **neuroplasticity**, enables the brain to adjust to environmental circumstances or to compensate for injury. Many factors influence changes in our brains, including the following: our interactions with people, places, and events; our thoughts and emotional reactions; and biological factors such as health, nutritional intake, and exercise patterns. Throughout your lifetime, physical, sensory, and emotional stimulation have produced electrical and chemical changes within your central nervous system, as well as changes in the structures within your brain. Your brain responds to environmental circumstances by creating neural circuits as needed (for example, to facilitate new learning or to cope with environmental stressors) and by pruning the neural pathways that are no longer used. Although many of the neurons in our brain remain healthy over much of our lifetime, the synapses that connect neurons are constantly changing.

You may have heard the saying "neurons that fire together, wire together." This refers to another important concept related to neuroplasticity—nerve pathways that we use frequently become myelinated and thus become stronger and more efficient. Neural circuits are bolstered when you practice a new skill or new way of reacting to a situation—the neural circuits become "hardwired" into the brain. This is true for healthy, productive thoughts and behaviors, as well as for the distressing or dysfunctional thoughts and behaviors associated with mental disorders.

Neuroplasticity also involves brain changes associated with the birth of new neurons (**neurogenesis**). We all have **neural stem cells** (uncommitted cells) in certain regions of our brain, cells that can be stimulated to form new neurons and glia. This means we can alter brain functioning at any point in life by engaging in experiences that stimulate neurogenesis. Neural stem cells have the ongoing potential to generate neurons needed for new skills or experiences, as well as to compensate for brain damage or changes in the brain associated with illness or aging (Gage & Temple, 2013). Just as we know that conditions such as chronic stress can have negative effects on brain functioning, we also know that exercise, challenging mental activities, some forms of psychotherapy, and some medications can produce positive changes in brain activity and brain structure via neurogenesis, particularly in the hippocampus (Thakker-Varia & Alder, 2009).

Many mental disorders are associated with brain dysfunction. However, to fully understand the biological bases of psychopathology we need to move beyond brain processes alone. Researchers across the globe are finding hundreds—perhaps even thousands—of pieces to add to the biological puzzle through the study of genetics and epigenetics.

Genetics and Heredity

Research strongly indicates that **heredity**—the genetic transmission of **traits**—plays an important role in the development of mental disorders. Genetics is a fascinating but incredibly complex field of study. Let's review some basic information associated with genetics and how traits are inherited. Contained in the nucleus of each cell in the human body are the 23 pairs of chromosomes we inherit from our parents. Within each chromosome are **genes**; each gene contains specific information pertaining to the development of our cells, tissues, organs, and body systems, all coded as a DNA

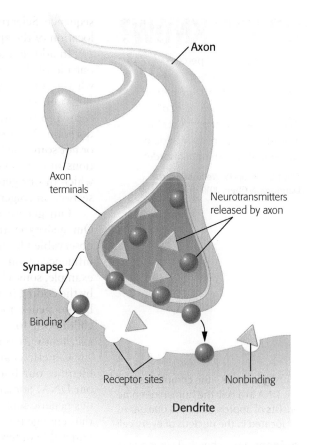

Figure 2.7

Neurotransmitter Binding

Neurotransmitters are released into the synapse and bind with receptor cells on the dendrites of the receiving neuron. Each neurotransmitter has a specific "shape" that corresponds to a receptor site. Like a jigsaw puzzle, binding occurs if the neurotransmitter fits into the receptor site.

© Cengage Learning®

neuroplasticity the process by which the brain changes to adapt to environmental changes or compensate for injury

neurogenesis birth and growth of new neurons

neural stem cells uncommitted cells that can be stimulated to form new neurons and glia

heredity the genetic transmission of personal characteristics

trait a distinguishing quality or characteristic

genes segments of DNA coded with information needed for the biological inheritance of various traits

genome the complete set of DNA in a cell; the human genome consists of approximately 21,000 genes located in the nucleus of every cell

epigenome chemical compounds found outside of the genome that modify gene expression; although the epigenome does not change DNA within the genome, epigenetic changes can be passed on to new cells during cell division and can be inherited

gene expression the process by which information encoded in a gene is translated into a specialized function or phenotype

genotype a person's genetic makeup

phenotype observable physical and behavioral characteristics resulting from the interaction between the genotype and the environment

genetic mutations an alteration in a gene that changes the instructions within the gene; some mutations result in biological dysfunction

polymorphisms a common DNA mutation or variation of a gene

alleles the gene pair responsible for a specific trait

critical periods a specific time in early development during which there is heightened sensitivity to environmental influences or experiences

sequence. Scientists have been able to map the entire human **genome** and determine the location of the approximately 21,000 genes located in the nucleus of every human cell.

In addition to the genetic information carried in our genes, chemical compounds outside of the genome (the **epigenome**) control **gene expression** and thus determine whether or not specific genes are "turned on" or "turned off." Each cell has a special function, so only a small number of genes within a cell are expressed—the genes related to the function of that cell. The remaining genes in the cell remain inactive or dormant. Most genetically determined differences between people, including whether or not someone has an increased risk of developing a mental disorder, are due to variations in our genes combined with variations in the epigenetic processes controlling which of our genes are expressed. (We will further discuss the epigenome in the next section on epigenetics.)

Our genetic makeup (the specific genes each of us inherit) is called our **genotype**. Our genotype and environmental factors interact and produce our **phenotype**, our observable physical and behavioral characteristics. Determining what exerts the most influence on our traits—our genotype or the environment—is sometimes difficult. For example, some characteristics, such as eye color, are determined solely by our genotype— by the coding in our genes. Other characteristics, such as height, are determined partly by our genes and partly by environmental factors. People who are malnourished in childhood, for instance, may not reach their genetically programmed height. Yet, excellent nutrition does not produce growth beyond what our genes dictate.

Genetic characteristics can also result from **genetic mutations**. Throughout our lifetime, our bodies create new cells; each cell has a copy of our chromosomes and our DNA. Sometimes, errors occur in the cell duplication process, causing a spontaneous genetic mutation. Genetic mutations change the instructions within the gene and thus change the outcome of the genetic coding. Some mutations are helpful or have no noticeable outcome whereas others result in biological dysfunction, including difficulties associated with mental illness. Toxins, viruses, or other environmental factors can produce genetic mutations. We can also inherit a genetic mutation. Additionally, some mental disorders are influenced by common genetic variations called **polymorphisms**; with polymorphic genes, people inherit various forms (**alleles**) of a particular gene. Any genetic variation—whether inherited or produced by cell division or environmental influences—can interact with environmental factors to produce varying phenotypes, including symptoms associated with mental disorders.

Certain triggers—environmental influences—can stimulate or inhibit gene expression. Triggers sometimes affect gene expression only during certain critical developmental periods. For example, in one classic longitudinal study of children from age 5 through their mid-20s, researchers assessed multiple variables such as early abuse, stressful life events, and depression (Caspi et al., 2003). They divided the participants into three groups based on variations in a particular polymorphic gene, the *serotonin transporter gene* (5-HTTLPR): (1) those with two short alleles (SS), (2) those with two long alleles (LL), and (3) those with one short and one long allele (SL). Those with the SS and the SL alleles who were abused as children were most likely to experience depression, as well as suicidal thoughts and behavior. Surprisingly, even when abused, those with the LL allele were unlikely to develop these symptoms.

In some cases, our genes appear to program our biological processes or our behavior in ways that help protect us against difficult environment circumstances. This may be the case with the LL variation of the 5-HTTLPR gene. Subsequent studies have similarly concluded that gene-environment interactions that occur during critical periods, such as early childhood, can set the stage for behavioral or physiological phenotypes that increase the likelihood of experiencing mental illness (Leonardo & Hen, 2006). It is clear that simply having a specific gene and encountering environmental stressors is not enough to increase the risk of developing a mental disorder. Rather, the configuration of the gene, the specific stressors, and the times at which stressors occur (**critical periods**) can all affect gene expression (Bale et al., 2010). This gene × environment interaction can affect cellular functioning in complex ways.

Epigenetics

Although genes program the sequence of human development, the environment shapes the path the development takes. **Epigenetics** refers to biochemical activities occurring outside of our genes. Epigenetic changes occur when environmental factors trigger processes that affect gene expression. When epigenetic processes leave biological markers on the DNA responsible for regulating gene expression, these markers can produce traits different from those coded in our DNA. We are learning more about how environmental influences can change our epigenome and alter development. To date, documented epigenetic alterations appear to result from four primary environmental influences: nutrition, behavior, exposure to stress, and contact with toxins (Faulk & Dolinoy, 2011). Even minor events that occur during certain critical periods of development can have significant epigenetic consequences (Relton & Davey-Smith, 2012).

There is mounting evidence that epigenetic changes that occur early in life may result in lifelong alterations in gene expression; in many cases, they serve an adaptive function by helping us respond to environmental circumstances and adversities (Szyf & Bick, 2013). Additionally, researchers are finding that some epigenetic alternations in gene expression can be passed down from parent to child (via epigenetic markers in the egg or sperm), perhaps as a means of assisting our offspring to adapt to the same environmental variables that triggered the changes in gene expression (Sasaki, de Vega, & McGowan, 2013). As with genetic mutations, not all epigenetic changes are positive. However, unlike genetic mutations, future changes in environmental influences (such as improved nutrition) can eliminate epigenetic markers and thus reverse the epigenetic processes that originally altered gene expression (Supic, Jagodic, & Magic, 2013).

Sex Differences in Brain Development

Brain differences between men and women are well documented (Zaidi, 2012). First, there are differences in the size of some brain structures. For example, men have more volume in the hypothalamus and amygdala (which regulates sexual behavior) whereas women have a larger hippocampus (associated with recall of emotional memories) and more volume in regions of the cortex associated with decision making and emotional regulation. The female brain has a thicker left hemisphere (associated with communication), whereas the male brain has a thicker right hemisphere (associated with spatial skills). Second, men and women tend to use different brain regions when recognizing and processing emotions, storing and retrieving memories, and making decisions. In general, the female brain is more integrated; women tend to use both hemispheres and display greater neural efficiency. Additionally, male and female brains have differences in key neurotransmitter systems, including those involving serotonin, dopamine, and GABA. Overall, the differences are extensive enough to suggest that nature has separate blueprints for the brain development in females as compared to males (Hines, 2011).

Some sex differences in brain development are probably evolutionary based: brain regions associated with spatial and navigational skills are larger in men and regions associated with fine motor and communication skills are larger in women. What causes these differences? Sex-linked genes and testosterone are believed to influence prenatal gender differences in brain development, as well as brain changes during critical periods such as puberty. Of course, it is likely that socialization and other environmental experiences strengthen the neural circuitry arising from genetic and hormonal influences (Hines, 2011).

Gender differences in brain functioning can help explain, to some degree, why the frequency and progression of mental disorders differs in men and women. For instance, the prevalence of disorders involving reactivity to stress (such as depression, anxiety, and eating disorders) is higher among women and girls whereas disorders involving impulsivity and risk-taking (such as substance abuse and attention-deficit

epigenetics field of biological research focused on understanding how environmental factors influence gene expression

disorder) are more prevalent among men and boys. This information may eventually assist in constructing gender-specific treatments or prevention efforts.

Biology-Based Treatment Techniques

Treatments based on biological principles aim to improve an individual's social and emotional functioning by producing changes in physiological functioning. Our increasing knowledge of human physiology and brain functioning has led to the development of more effective biologically based therapies for a variety of mental health conditions.

Psychopharmacology

Psychopharmacology is the study of how **psychotropic medications** affect psychiatric symptoms, including thoughts, emotions, and behavior. Psychotropic medications, prescribed after careful diagnosis and analysis of symptoms, are widely used to treat a variety of mental health conditions. Many psychiatric medications correct biochemical imbalances by normalizing biochemical processes (e.g., binding, reabsorption, or breakdown by enzymes) involving certain neurotransmitters, thereby increasing or decreasing the availability of the neurotransmitter. Some medications work by enhancing message transmission, while others block communication between neurons.

Classes of medication used to treat mental disorders include (a) antianxiety drugs (or minor tranquilizers), (b) antipsychotics (or major tranquilizers), (c) antidepressants (used for both depression and anxiety), and (d) mood stabilizers (sometimes called antimanic drugs). Antianxiety medications (minor tranquilizers) such as *benzodiazepines* (including Valium and Xanax) are used to calm people and to help them sleep. Benzodiazepines increase the activity of GABA, an inhibitory neurotransmitter, thereby reducing the transmission of nerve impulses, with a resultant reduction in symptoms of anxiety. Benzodiazepines are usually prescribed in low doses and on a short-term basis due to their addictive potential.

Antipsychotic medications (also referred to as *neuroleptics* or major tranquilizers) play a major role in treating the agitation, mental confusion, and loss of contact with reality associated with **psychotic symptoms**. In 1951, the first drug with antipsychotic properties (*chlorpromazine*; generic name Thorazine) was synthesized in France. Thorazine had the unexpected effect of significantly reducing agitation and mental confusion in severely ill psychiatric patients. Physicians around the world were soon prescribing Thorazine to treat psychotic symptoms, allowing many individuals to live and function outside of hospital settings (Ban, 2007). Thorazine and the many other antipsychotic medications developed using Thorazine as a prototype (a group referred to as *typical antipsychotics*) exert their effect by binding tightly to and blocking dopamine receptors, thereby stopping nerve activity that relies on dopamine.

Unfortunately, the sizeable reduction in dopamine associated with these first-generation antipsychotics also produces a constellation of side effects, referred to as **extrapyramidal symptoms**—these side effects include involuntary muscle contractions that affect gait, movement, and posture. A newer generation of antipsychotics, referred to as *atypical antipsychotics*, has emerged; these medications produce a variety of biochemical changes with fewer extrapyramidal symptoms. Some atypical antipsychotics reduce dopamine transmission by loosely binding to dopamine receptors (creating a less drastic reduction in dopamine), whereas others influence other neurotransmitters. Medical professionals prescribe atypical antipsychotics not only to control psychotic symptoms, but also to stabilize mood fluctuations in conditions such as bipolar disorder. These powerful medications require careful monitoring because they may produce a variety of possible side effects.

Antidepressant medications are prescribed to help relieve symptoms of depression and anxiety. Many of these medications increase the availability of neurotransmitters by blocking their reabsorption, allowing them to remain in the synapse and produce neural-communication effects for a longer period. There are several well-known classes of antidepressants. Among the most popular medications for both depression

psychopharmacology study of the effects of medications on thoughts, emotions, and behaviors

psychotropic medications drugs that treat or manage psychiatric symptoms by influencing brain activity associated with emotions and behavior

psychotic symptoms loss of contact with reality that may involve disorganized thinking, false beliefs, or seeing or hearing things that are not there

extrapyramidal symptoms side effects of antipsychotic medications that affect a person's gait, movement, or posture

and anxiety are the *selective serotonin reuptake inhibitors (SSRIs),* which increase the availability of serotonin. The drugs Prozac (fluoxetine hydrochloride), Paxil (paroxetine), and Zoloft (sertraline) are SSRIs. Another class of antidepressants, the *tricyclic antidepressants,* increase the availability of both serotonin and norepinephrine. *Monoamine oxidase inhibitors (MAOIs)* are antidepressants that inhibit the action of monoamine oxidase, an enzyme that deactivates neurotransmitters after they are released into the synapse. There are other antidepressant medications with distinct biochemical properties such as Wellbutrin (bupropion). The primary difference between the SSRIs and other antidepressants is that SSRIs specifically target the neurotransmitter serotonin whereas others target multiple neurotransmitters.

Mood-stabilizing medications are prescribed to treat the excitement associated with episodes of mania, as well as to help prevent future mood swings. Lithium, a naturally occurring chemical compound, is a well-known and frequently prescribed mood stabilizer. A variety of anticonvulsant (used to treat seizure disorders) and antipsychotic medications are also used for mood stabilization. The exact means by which these medications work to calm brain activity remain unclear.

The use of psychotropic medication has improved the lives of many people with mental illness, especially those with severe symptoms. Many individuals using these medications report symptom improvement and are better able to participate in other forms of treatment, such as psychotherapy. In most cases, severe mental illness no longer requires long periods of hospitalization. Remember, however, that although symptoms improve, medications do not cure mental disorders; they just help. Additionally, some people need to try many different medications before finding one that helps their symptoms. Further, some individuals are not helped by medication or are not able to tolerate the medication side effects.

Researchers hope to develop simple blood tests that will identify which medications work best for each person. A new field, *pharmacogenomics,* focuses on understanding the relationship between a person's genetic makeup and both positive and aversive responses to drug treatment. Also, given the communication occurring between the ENS and the brain, interventions aimed at modifying bacteria in the digestive tract, including beneficial bacteria (probiotics), have been proposed as a potential treatment for some psychological disorders (Cryan & Dinan, 2012). Many hope that such individualized treatment will be available in the near future.

Electroconvulsive Therapy

Electroconvulsive therapy (ECT) is a procedure that can change brain chemistry and reverse symptoms associated with some mental disorders. ECT, usually reserved for those who have not responded to other treatments, applies moderate electric voltage to the brain to induce a short convulsion (seizure). The person undergoing treatment receives a general anesthetic and muscle relaxant before the procedure. A related treatment currently being researched is magnetic seizure therapy, which involves the induction of seizures using magnetic stimulation instead of a direct electrical current (Soehle, Kayser, Ellerkmann, & Schlaepfer, 2014).

Neurosurgical and Brain Stimulation Treatments

During the 1940s and 1950s, *psychosurgery*—performing brain surgery in an attempt to correct a severe mental disorder—became increasingly popular. The treatment, which involves destruction or removal of a small area of the brain, raised many scientific and ethical objections. As a result, psychosurgery is now very uncommon and has been replaced by neurosurgical techniques that focus on stimulation rather than destruction of brain tissue.

A contemporary neurosurgical treatment, *deep brain stimulation (DBS),* involves implanting electrodes that produce ongoing stimulation of specific regions of the brain. Another approach, *vagus nerve stimulation,* involves surgically implanting a pacemaker-like device under the skin on the chest; when activated, the device sends signals along a wire connected to the vagus nerve (the longest cranial nerve), which then sends signals to various regions of the brain.

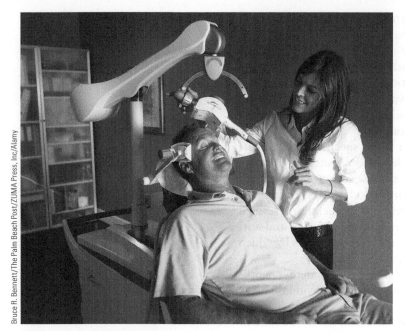

A noninvasive brain stimulation procedure, *repetitive transcranial magnetic stimulation (rTMS)*, involves weeks of daily stimulation of the prefrontal cortex and regions of the brain involved with mood regulation; this is done by means of magnetic pulses emitted from an electromagnetic coil held against the forehead (George, Taylor, & Short, 2013). Each rTMS treatment takes less than an hour and requires no sedation or anesthesia. All of these procedures aim to reduce symptoms by changing physiological processes within the brain; however, they are used only with certain conditions, such as severe depression, and when other treatments have not been effective.

Criticisms of Biological Models and Therapies

Most biological models of mental illness only minimally acknowledge psychological, social, or cultural influences. Biological models are criticized for their failure to consider the unique circumstances of the individual and environmental influences on the etiology of symptoms. Although biological models have traditionally focused only on biological explanations, this has changed in recent years. For example, most researchers now reject the simple linear explanation of genetic determinism; they no longer claim that mental disorders result primarily from "bad genes" or that there is "one gene for one disease" (Rucker & McGuffin, 2010).

The majority of biological research comes from physicians and researchers whose worldview strongly supports the medical model and the use of medication to treat mental disorders. This is a particular concern given the rapid growth in the sale and marketing of psychotropic medications and the frequent use of these medications without first conducting a careful mental health evaluation (Smith, 2012). There is also little discussion of where psychotherapy fits into treatment planning and when to consider medication in the course of comprehensive treatment. Prescribing multiple medications has also become common, increasing the importance of watching for side effects and possible **drug-drug interactions**. Another concern is the limited focus on ethnic or gender group differences in physiological response to medication. There is clearly a need for more discussion about how mental health professionals, health care providers, and clients can effectively collaborate in monitoring the effectiveness of medications and other biological interventions; however, it is equally important that all involved consider psychological factors that may be influencing symptoms and treatment outcome.

Repetitive Transcranial Magnetic Stimulation

Repetitive transcranial magnetic stimulation is used to treat a variety of disorders including depression. This man has been undergoing the treatment for almost two years. He describes his response as "instant" saying he "walks in feeling one way and walks out feeling another".

Dimension Two: Psychological Factors

A number of psychological factors contribute to the etiology of mental disorders. The psychological dimension focuses on emotions, conflicts in the mind, learned behavior, and cognitions. Interestingly, psychological explanations of abnormal behavior vary considerably depending on the underlying theory. In this section, we describe four major psychological perspectives that explain abnormal behavior: psychodynamic, behavioral, cognitive, and humanistic-existential.

drug-drug interactions when the effect of a medication is changed, enhanced, or diminished when taken with another drug, including herbal substances

Psychodynamic Models

Psychodynamic models view mental disorders as the result of childhood trauma, anxieties, and unconscious conflicts. The early development of psychodynamic theory is credited to Sigmund Freud (1938, 1949). Freud originally characterized much of human behavior as attempts to express, gratify, or defend against sexual or aggressive impulses—instinctual drives that operate at an unconscious level, continually seeking expression. Psychological symptoms are associated with these sexual or aggressive impulses. Further, certain experiences or mental conflicts are too threatening to face, so we block them from consciousness. As a result, we sometimes experience emotional symptoms, but do not understand their meaning. Freud believed that the therapist's role was to help individuals experiencing mental distress achieve insight into these unconscious processes.

Personality Components

Freud developed a model suggesting that all behavior is a product of interactions between three personality components: the id, the ego, and the superego. The *id*, a key part of our unconscious psyche, is present at birth. The id operates from the **pleasure principle**—the impulsive, pleasure-seeking aspect of our being—and seeks immediate gratification of instinctual needs, regardless of moral or realistic concerns. In contrast, the *ego* represents the realistic and rational part of the mind. It is influenced by the **reality principle**—an awareness of the demands of the environment and of the need to adjust behavior to meet these demands. The ego's decisions are dictated by realistic considerations rather than by moral judgments. Moralistic considerations are the domain of the *superego*. The *conscience* is the part of the superego that instills guilt in us and helps prevent us from engaging in immoral or unethical behavior.

Psychosexual Stages

Human personality develops through a sequence of five **psychosexual stages**, each of which brings a unique challenge. If unfavorable circumstances prevail, the personality may be drastically affected. Because Freud stressed the importance of early childhood experiences, he saw the human personality as largely determined in the first 5 years of life—during the *oral* (first year of life), *anal* (around the second year of life), and *phallic* (beginning around the third or fourth years of life) stages. The last two psychosexual stages are the *latency* (approximately 6 to 12 years of age) and *genital* (beginning in puberty) periods. The importance of each psychosexual phase for later development lies in whether fixation occurs during that phase. *Fixation* halts emotional development at a particular psychosexual stage. Someone who is fixated at a particular stage may experience emotional disturbance resulting from the distinct conflicts associated with that period of development.

Defense Mechanisms

According to psychodynamic theory, we often use **defense mechanisms** to distance ourselves from feelings of anxiety associated with unpleasant thoughts or other internal conflicts. Defense mechanisms are ways of thinking or behaving that share three characteristics: they protect us from anxiety, they operate unconsciously, and they distort reality. We all experience the self-deception associated with defense mechanisms from time to time. Defense mechanisms are considered maladaptive, however, when they are overused—that is, if they become our predominant means of coping with stress and interfere with our ability to handle life's demands. Table 2.2 lists some common defense mechanisms.

Library of Congress, Prints & Photographs Division, Washington

Sigmund Freud (1856–1939)

Freud began his career as a neurologist. He became increasingly intrigued with the relationship between illness and mental processes and ultimately developed psychoanalysis, a therapy in which unconscious conflicts are brought to the surface so they can be resolved.

psychodynamic model model that views disorders as the result of childhood trauma or anxieties and that holds that many of these childhood-based anxieties operate unconsciously

pleasure principle the impulsive, pleasure-seeking aspect of our being, from which the id operates

reality principle an awareness of the demands of the environment and of the need to adjust behavior to meet these demands, from which the ego operates

psychosexual stages in psychodynamic theory, the sequence of stages—oral, anal, phallic, latency, and genital—through which human personality develops

Table 2.2 Examples of Defense Mechanisms

Mechanism	Definition	Example
Repression	Preventing forbidden or dangerous thoughts or desires from entering one's consciousness.	A soldier who witnesses the death of a friend in combat blocks the event from conscious thought.
Reaction formation	Acting in a manner opposite to one's unconscious wishes or feelings.	A woman who gives birth to an unwanted child showers the child with superficial attention.
Projection	Distancing oneself from unwanted desires or thoughts by attributing them to others.	A worker masks feelings of inadequacy by claiming fellow workers are incompetent.
Rationalization	Explaining one's behavior by giving socially acceptable reasons unrelated to one's true motives.	A student explains his failing grade by complaining that the class is boring.
Displacement	Directing an emotion, such as hostility or anxiety, toward a substitute target.	A clerk who is belittled by her boss yells at her husband.
Undoing	Attempting to right a wrong or negate an unconscious thought, impulse, or act.	After making an insensitive comment to his daughter, a father makes amends by buying her a gift.
Regression	Retreating to an earlier developmental level that demands less mature responses and aspirations.	A dignified college president drinks too much and sings old school songs at a college reunion.

© Cengage Learning®

Contemporary Psychodynamic Theories

As psychodynamic theory continued to evolve, theorists such as Adler (1929/1964) and Erickson (1968), unhappy with the prominence given to instinctual drives, suggested that the ego had adaptive abilities, including the capacity to function independently from the id. Other psychoanalytic theorists (Bowlby, 1969; Mahler, 1968) proposed that having our social needs met—the need to be loved, accepted, and emotionally supported—are of primary importance in early development and identity formation. Thus, children who do not receive empathy or emotional support from caregivers may experience difficulty achieving a healthy self-identity. Mental distress and problem behaviors occur when people seek interpersonal experiences lacking in childhood. These views led to a variety of new therapeutic approaches.

Therapies Based on the Psychodynamic Model

We begin with a brief overview of some of the techniques used by Freud and his approach to therapy. However, very few psychodynamic therapists rely only on these traditional methods. Instead, they emphasize interpersonal relationships and the ego's ability to cope with life challenges.

Traditional Psychodynamic Therapy Many of you have probably heard of psychoanalysis, but what is it? Psychoanalytic therapy, or **psychoanalysis**, aims to overcome a client's defenses so that material blocked from consciousness can be uncovered, allowing clients to gain insight into inner thoughts and unresolved childhood conflicts. If you were to undergo psychoanalysis, your therapist might use some of these methods:

- In **free association**, you say whatever comes to your mind, regardless of how illogical or embarrassing it may seem. The idea is that if you spontaneously express your thoughts, you will reveal the contents of your unconscious, including unrecognized worries and conflicts.

- **Dream analysis** is a technique focused on interpreting the hidden meanings in dreams. Psychoanalysts believe that when people sleep, ego defenses and inhibitions weaken so that unacceptable impulses or repressed anxieties are more likely to surface. Your therapist would help you understand the underlying meaning of your dreams.

defense mechanism in psychoanalytic theory, an ego-protection strategy that shelters the individual from anxiety, operates unconsciously, and distorts reality

psychoanalysis therapy whose goals are to uncover repressed material, to help clients achieve insight into inner motivations and desires, and to resolve childhood conflicts that affect current relationships

free association psychoanalytic therapeutic technique in which clients are asked to say whatever comes to mind for the purpose of revealing their unconscious thoughts

dream analysis psychoanalytic technique focused on interpreting the hidden meanings of dreams

- Your therapist would look for and attempt to analyze evidence of **resistance**—your unconscious attempts to impede therapy and prevent exposure of conflicts you are repressing. Your therapist would remain alert to see if you missed appointments, or suddenly changed the subject, lost your train of thought, or became silent during therapy. If you appear to be demonstrating resistance, the next step would be to uncover and analyze any unconscious conflicts your resistance might be trying to conceal.

- Psychoanalysts believe that client reactions such as anger, love, or disappointment directed toward the therapist are signs of other relationship issues; they refer to this process as **transference**. If your therapist noticed you displaying frustration or anger during therapy, you would be encouraged to work through the true meanings of your reactions.

Because psychoanalysts believe that unconscious impulses and instinctual drives cause psychological symptoms, they focus almost exclusively on the internal world of clients and work to allow unconscious conflicts to surface. Psychoanalysts assume that healthy behavior patterns will develop once clients understand and resolve their unconscious issues. Traditional psychoanalysis is a slow process, sometimes involving up to five hourly sessions per week for a period of years.

Therapy Based on Later Psychodynamic Theories   Contemporary psychodynamic therapists view experiences with early attachment figures as having powerful effects on current interpersonal difficulties. Therefore, therapy focuses on existing social and interpersonal relationships rather than on unconscious conflicts. Some psychodynamic therapists attempt to change adult personality patterns by analyzing recurring themes in problematic relationships. One contemporary therapy, short-term psychodynamic psychotherapy, focuses on past relationship issues and how they affect current emotional and relationship experiences (Lindfors, Knekt, Virtala, & Laaksonen, 2012). Another approach, interpersonal psychotherapy, focuses on the link between childhood experiences and current relational patterns. Therapists using interpersonal psychotherapy focus on improving interpersonal relationships, decreasing social distress, and helping clients learn ways of interacting that are more effective than the maladaptive patterns acquired during childhood (Lipsitz & Markowitz, 2013).

Criticisms of Psychodynamic Models and Therapies

Psychodynamic theory has strongly influenced the field of psychology. Nonetheless, three major criticisms are leveled against psychodynamic theory and treatment. First, Freud relied heavily on case studies and on his own self-analysis as a basis for his theory. Second, his patients represented a very narrow spectrum of society—relatively affluent Victorian-era Austrian women. Thus, traditional psychoanalysis fails to address external issues such as social inequality, race, class, gender, and culture. A third criticism is that traditional psychoanalysis has a limited range of usefulness. It has limited therapeutic value with people who are less talkative, less psychologically minded, or more severely disturbed.

There are far fewer outcome studies evaluating psychodynamic therapies compared to the large number of studies conducted on other contemporary treatment techniques. This is, in part, because psychodynamic theories are difficult to investigate in a scientific manner; the processes and outcomes are dynamic rather than specific. Compounding this problem are the many different approaches to psychodynamic therapy.

Behavioral Models

The **behavioral models** of psychopathology are concerned with the role of learning in the development of mental disorders and are based on experimental research. The differences among the models lie in their explanations of how learning occurs. The

resistance   during psychoanalysis, a process in which the client unconsciously attempts to impede the analysis by preventing the exposure of repressed material

transference   process by which a client undergoing psychoanalysis reenacts early conflicts by applying to the analyst feelings and attitudes that the person has toward significant others

behavioral models   models of psychopathology concerned with the role of learning in abnormal behavior

three learning paradigms are *classical conditioning*, *operant conditioning*, and *observational learning*.

The Classical Conditioning Paradigm

Early in the 20th century, Ivan Pavlov (1849–1936), a Russian physiologist, discovered that automatic responses (such as salivation) can be learned through association. Pavlov was measuring dogs' salivation as part of a study of their digestive processes when he noticed that the dogs began to salivate at the sight of an assistant carrying their food. This response led to his formulation of the theory of **classical conditioning**, sometimes referred to as respondent conditioning. Pavlov reasoned that food is an **unconditioned stimulus (UCS)**, which automatically elicits salivation; this salivation is an unlearned or **unconditioned response (UCR)** to the food.

Pavlov then presented a previously *neutral* stimulus (the sound of a bell) to the dogs just before feeding them. Initially, no salivation occurred with just the bell alone. However, after several repetitions of the bell combined with food powder in the mouth, the dogs began to salivate when hearing the bell. The bell had become a **conditioned stimulus (CS)**; that is, the sound induced salivation due to its previous pairings with the food (UCS). The salivation elicited by the bell is a **conditioned response (CR)**—a learned response to a previously neutral stimulus. Each time a conditioned stimulus (CS) is paired with an unconditioned stimulus (UCS), the conditioned response is reinforced, or strengthened. Pavlov also discovered that if he kept presenting the bell (CS) without following it with the food powder (UCS), **extinction** would occur; eventually, the bell no longer produced salivation. Figure 2.8 illustrates Pavlov's conditioning process.

John B. Watson (1878–1958) is credited with recognizing how classical conditioning can help explain abnormal behavior. In a classic experiment, Watson and Rosalie Rayner (1920) demonstrated how classical conditioning experiences can create *phobias* (an extreme fear of particular objects or situations). They performed experiments with an 8-month-old infant, Albert, in an attempt to determine if there might be "simple methods" by which emotional responses develop. Could little Albert learn to fear objects through classical conditioning? They presented Albert with a number of objects, including a white rat. None of the items produced a

classical conditioning a process in which responses to new stimuli are learned through association

unconditioned stimulus (UCS) in classical conditioning, the stimulus that elicits an unconditioned response

unconditioned response (UCR) in classical conditioning, the unlearned response made to an unconditioned stimulus

conditioned stimulus (CS) in classical conditioning, a previously neutral stimulus that has acquired some of the properties of another stimulus with which it has been paired

conditioned response (CR) in classical conditioning, a learned response to a previously neutral stimulus that has acquired some of the properties of another stimulus with which it has been paired

extinction decrease or cessation of a behavior due to the gradual weakening of a classically or operantly conditioned response

| Stimulus: | UCS (food) | UCS & CS (food & bell) | CS (bell alone) |
| Response: | UCR (salivation) | UCR (salivation) | CR (conditioned salivation) |

Figure 2.8

A Basic Classical Conditioning Process

Dogs normally salivate when food is provided (left). With his laboratory dogs, Ivan Pavlov paired the ringing of a bell with the presentation of food (middle). Eventually, the dogs would salivate to the ringing of the bell alone, when no food was near (right).

© Cengage Learning®

fear response. They then again showed Albert the white rat, immediately followed by a loud bang from a hammer striking a steel bar. Albert was startled and began crying. After several pairings of the rat and the loud sound, Albert showed a fear response when presented with the rat alone. This finding has helped us understand the etiology of anxiety and fear responses. The passive nature of classical conditioning limits its usefulness, however, as an explanatory and treatment tool. Most human behavior, both normal and abnormal, tends to be much more active and voluntary.

The Operant Conditioning Paradigm

Operant conditioning was first formulated by Edward Thorndike (1874–1949) and further elaborated by B. F. Skinner (1904–1990). Their operant models are based on observations that behaviors are sometimes influenced by events that follow them. Rather than the involuntary reactions (e.g., sweating, salivating, and fear responses) involved in classical conditioning, **operant conditioning** involves voluntary behaviors. An **operant behavior** is a controllable behavior, such as walking or talking, that "operates" on an individual's environment. In an extremely warm room, for example, you would have difficulty consciously controlling your sweating (an involuntary response) because perspiring is controlled by the autonomic nervous system. You could, however, simply walk out of the uncomfortably warm room—an operant behavior.

Behaviors based on *classical* conditioning are controlled by events *preceding* the response: Salivation occurs only when it is preceded by a UCS (food) or a CS (the thought of a sizzling steak covered with mushrooms, for example). In *operant* conditioning, however, behaviors are controlled by **reinforcers**—anything that influences the frequency or magnitude of a behavior. **Positive reinforcement** involves actions that increase the likelihood and frequency of a behavior. For example, receiving good grades (a positive reinforcer) might increase the chances that you study and attend class regularly. As with classical conditioning, extinction occurs if reinforcement does not follow a behavior: if the reinforcer is no longer present the behavior will eventually diminish. For example, you might have noticed that class attendance decreases if an instructor does not consider class participation when assigning grades.

Studies have demonstrated a relationship between environmental reinforcers and certain abnormal behaviors. Self-injurious behavior, such as head banging, is a dramatic form of psychopathology that occurs in some individuals with autism or low intellectual functioning. If caregivers give attention and show concern whenever self-injurious behavior occurs, they may unwittingly be providing positive reinforcement for these behaviors. Can self-injurious behavior be learned and extinguished through operant conditioning?

Researchers trained two rhesus monkeys to demonstrate self-injurious behavior—to strike their heads with their paws until lacerations occurred. This behavior was shaped by giving food when the monkeys lifted a paw, moved the paw closer to the head, touched the head, and, finally, only when they hit their head. This process only took 12 minutes for one monkey and 20 minutes for the other. After this behavior was shaped, food reinforcement was only given when the experimenter said, "Poor boy. Don't do that. You'll hurt yourself." The monkeys soon only hit themselves when they heard these words. When the food rewards were halted, extinction occurred and the self-injurious behavior stopped (Schaefer, 1970).

Although positive reinforcement can account for some undesirable behaviors, other variables also influence behavior. For example, **negative reinforcement**—when behavior is reinforced because something aversive has been removed—can increase the likelihood of a behavior. For example, you may spend time reviewing your class notes because studying removes the anxiety associated with upcoming exams. Notice that

operant conditioning theory of learning that holds that behaviors are controlled by the consequences that follow them

operant behavior voluntary and controllable behavior, such as walking or thinking, that "operates" on an individual's environment

reinforcer anything that influences the frequency or magnitude of a behavior

positive reinforcement desirable actions or rewards that increase the likelihood that a particular behavior will occur

negative reinforcement increasing the frequency or magnitude of a behavior by removing something aversive

Christina Kennedy/PhotoEdit

Operant Conditioning in the Classroom

In operant conditioning, positive consequences increase the likelihood and frequency of a desired response. This is particularly important in teaching young children that appropriate behavior will be rewarded and inappropriate behavior will be punished. Here a pre-Kindergarten student receives a smiley face token as a reward for attention and reading efforts.

the focus is on the *effect* of the reinforcer. Negative reinforcement can also strengthen and maintain maladaptive behaviors. Imagine you are in a class in which the instructor requires oral reports. The thought of doing an oral presentation in front of the class terrifies you. If you decide to transfer to another class where the instructor does not require oral presentations, you will escape the aversive feelings. Thus, you would negatively reinforce your avoidance behavior; you might also be tempted to use similar escape tactics when confronted by other anxiety-provoking situations.

The Observational Learning Paradigm

The traditional behavioral theories of learning—classical conditioning and operant conditioning—require that the individual be directly involved in the learning process. In contrast, **observational learning theory** suggests that we can acquire new behaviors and emotional reactions simply by watching other people perform them (Bandura, 1997). The process of learning by observing models (and later imitating them) is called *vicarious conditioning* or **modeling**. Reinforcement for imitation of the model is not necessary for learning to occur. Watching someone respond fearfully to a stimulus can cause a fear reaction to develop. For example, Bandura and Rosenthal (1966) found that individuals who watched someone receive a shock when a buzzer sounded also began to react to the buzzer.

Voluntary behaviors are also learned through observation (Bandura, 1997). In a series of experiments, children exposed to models displaying "unique" behaviors later demonstrated the very same behavior themselves. Thus, observation of another individual can result in new behavior, including socially undesirable behaviors. Similarly, we sometimes inhibit a behavior if we see others punished for the behavior; for example, you may have reduced your driving speed after seeing someone receive a traffic ticket.

Social learning theory greatly expanded our understanding of the ways in which voluntary and involuntary behaviors are learned. Bandura (1982) further developed his social learning theory to encompass *self-efficacy*, individuals' belief in their ability to make changes in their environment. His work introduced the idea that humans are not merely the "subjects" of conditioning—we are quite capable of mastering situations and producing positive outcomes. Bandura's research also reinforced the idea that we learn to persevere when we observe others succeeding through sustained effort.

In explaining psychopathology, social learning theory posits that exposure to disturbed models is likely to produce disturbed behaviors. For example, when children watch their parents respond with fear, they learn to respond in a similar manner. Similarly, if we are exposed to models who display impulsivity, helplessness, or aggression, we are more likely to acquire these characteristics.

Behavioral Therapies

Classical conditioning and the concept of extinction are the basis for different therapies that involve having clients directly face their fears. **Exposure therapy**, also known as *extinction therapy*, can involve *graduated exposure*, gradually introducing a person to feared objects or situations, or *flooding*, which involves rapid exposure to produce high levels of anxiety. For example, if you had a spider phobia the therapist might ask you to imagine seeing a spider (graduated exposure) or may hand you a jar containing a live spider (flooding). Therapists often prefer to use the graduated approach because

observational learning theory
theory that suggests that an individual can acquire new behaviors by watching other people perform them

modeling   process of learning by observing models (and later imitating them)

exposure therapy   a treatment approach based on extinction principles that involves gradual or rapid exposure to feared objects or situations

of the amount of discomfort that can occur with flooding. Similarly, extinction therapy can also involve virtual reality procedures such as the use of computer-generated images that immerse clients in a realistic setting. For example, a therapist might treat your spider phobia by having you view spider images on a computer screen or through a helmet with video monitors.

In a related approach, therapists sometimes combine exposure with response prevention, exposing clients to feared objects or situations and "preventing" them from escaping the situation. Another effective behavioral technique, **systematic desensitization**, developed by Joseph Wolpe (1958), involves having the extinction process occur while the client is in a competing emotional state such as relaxation. If you were undergoing systematic desensitization to decrease your fear of public speaking, you would first learn to relax, and then imagine yourself engaged in a hierarchy of behaviors related to giving a speech (perhaps beginning with imagining yourself practicing the talk at home and ending with giving the speech to a large audience).

Social skills training, which involves the teaching of specific skills needed for appropriate social interactions, is an effective behavioral intervention for individuals who experience social difficulties. Social skills training includes modeling and the use of role-play activities to develop positive behaviors associated with appropriate social interactions. *Assertiveness training* is a form of social skills training that teaches individuals (especially those who tend to be overly timid or overly aggressive) the difference between nonassertive, aggressive, and assertive responses (Jakubowski & Lange, 1978). Clients describe difficult, real-life situations and then practice appropriate responses with a focus on clear verbal communication and nonverbal skills such as body posture, voice intonation, eye contact, and facial expression.

Learning by Observing

Observational learning is based on the theory that behavior can be learned through observation. Observational learning can have positive benefits, as you can see in this photo. However, children and adults also develop maladaptive behaviors by observing others demonstrate dysfunctional behavior.

Criticisms of the Behavioral Models and Therapies

Behavioral approaches to psychopathology have provided considerable insight into the etiology and treatment of mental disorders, and remain a strong force in psychology today. Opponents of the behavioral orientation, however, point out that they often neglect—or place minimal emphasis on—inner determinants of behavior. They also criticize behaviorists' use of results obtained from animal studies to solve human problems. Some also charge that the behaviorist perspective is mechanistic, viewing people as "empty organisms." These theories, like many others, also tend to view normal and abnormal human development in a linear and one-dimensional fashion.

Cognitive-Behavioral Models

Cognitive-behavioral theories focus not only on our observable behaviors but also on how our thoughts influence our emotions and behaviors. According to cognitive-behavioral models, we create our own problems (and symptoms) based on how we interpret events and situations. For example, you might believe that it is important to be loved and accepted by everyone. Is this a realistic belief? Is it logical to expect everyone we know to like us? If we harbor irrational beliefs such as this, we become susceptible to develop distressing emotions and maladaptive behaviors. Consider a friend who becomes depressed after an unsuccessful date. An appropriate emotional response might be frustration and temporary disappointment. However, if your friend

systematic desensitization
treatment technique involving repeated exposure to a feared stimulus while a client is in a competing emotional or physiological state such as relaxation

adds irrational thoughts, such as "I'm not surprised my date didn't like me. Why would they?" the friend might become discouraged and depressed, and avoid social activities. We often develop these patterns of irrational thinking in childhood, and then continue to respond as though these inaccurate assumptions are correct.

Cognitive Dynamics in Psychopathology

Cognitive theorists, such as Aaron Beck (1921–) and Albert Ellis (1913–2007), were among the first to break away from traditional behavioral approaches. They both theorized that the manner in which we interpret situations can profoundly affect our emotional reactions and behaviors (Rosner, 2012). Further, their theories link psychopathology with irrational and maladaptive assumptions and thoughts (A. T. Beck & Weishaar, 2010; A. Ellis, 2008). In other words, distressing emotional responses such as anger, depression, fear, and anxiety result from our *thoughts* about events rather than from the events themselves. For example, some students who fail a test might show only mild irritation and resolve to study harder next time, whereas others become discouraged and depressed. Why does the same event (failing a test) result in such different emotional responses? How do irrational thoughts develop in the first place?

The *A-B-C theory of emotional disturbance*, developed by Albert Ellis (1997, 2008), aims to describe how people develop irrational thoughts. *A* is an event, a fact, or someone's behavior or attitude. *C* is the person's emotional or behavioral reaction. The activating event *A* never causes the emotional or behavioral consequence *C*. Instead, *B*, the person's beliefs about *A,* causes *C*. Let's imagine you were interviewed for a job you really wanted, and then you learned someone else was hired for the job (activating event *A*). If your reaction was: "How awful to be rejected! I'll never get a good job." (irrational belief *B*), and you continued thinking this way, you might become depressed and withdrawn (emotional and behavioral consequence *C*). Imagine that instead when you learned you didn't get the job (activating event *A*) you responded by thinking, "I really wanted that job so it's hard being rejected. Everyone says it's frustrating looking for jobs. Maybe next time I'll be the best match for the job." (rational belief *B*), and you continued looking for another job (healthy consequence *C*).

The two sets of assumptions and expectations are very different. If you blame yourself for not getting a job and view your situation as hopeless, you are likely to feel discouraged and lose motivation. Thus, if you interpret the rejection as "awful and catastrophic" you are more likely to become distressed and postpone your job search efforts. If, on the other hand, you don't take the rejection personally and recognize that many people experience rejection during a job search, your motivation and self-esteem will remain intact and you will continue seeking employment, thereby increasing your chances of finding a job. Figure 2.9 illustrates the A-B-C relationship and shows how a cognitive therapist might work with a client who is depressed over the loss of a job.

A common type of irrational thinking involves *catastrophizing*, or envisioning the worst possible outcome for situations; for example, you would be catastrophizing if you concluded that you should drop out of school because you failed a class. Exaggerated or inaccurate thoughts such as this distort objective reality and may result in anxiety, depression, or other psychological symptoms of mental distress.

Cognitive-Behavioral Approaches to Therapy

Cognitive-behavioral therapy (CBT) is rapidly becoming the treatment of choice for many disorders. Cognitive approaches to psychotherapy help clients recognize patterns of illogical thinking and replace them with more realistic and helpful thoughts (A. T. Beck & Weishaar, 2010). Although these therapies emphasize cognitions (patterns of thinking), they are called cognitive-behavioral therapies because they also incorporate changes in social skills and other behaviors. Cognitive-behavioral therapists encourage clients to become actively involved in their treatment outside of therapy sessions by assigning homework that includes skills learned during therapy.

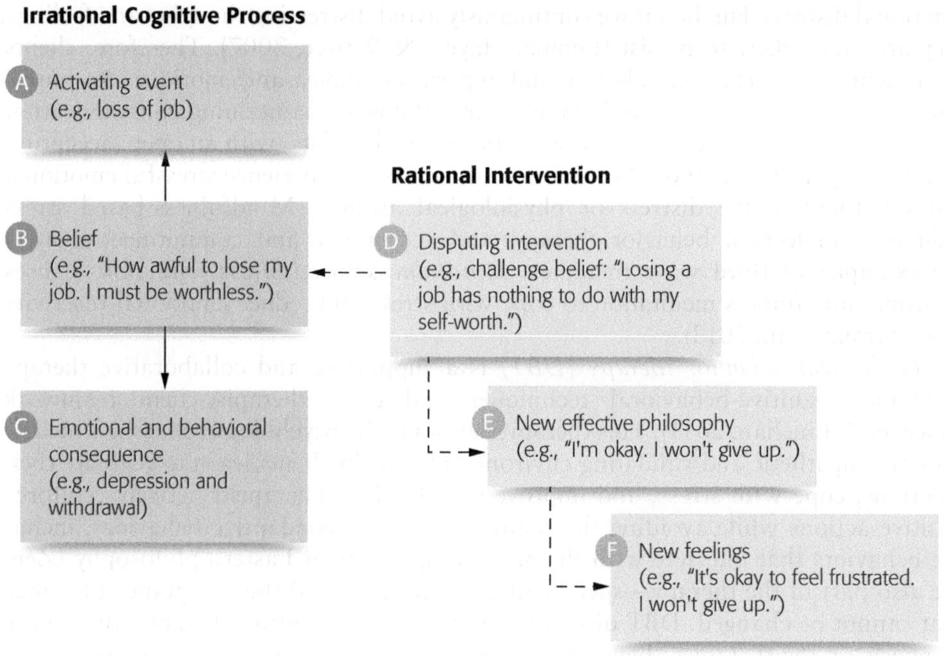

Irrational Cognitive Process

A — Activating event
(e.g., loss of job)

B — Belief
(e.g., "How awful to lose my job. I must be worthless.")

C — Emotional and behavioral consequence
(e.g., depression and withdrawal)

Rational Intervention

D — Disputing intervention
(e.g., challenge belief: "Losing a job has nothing to do with my self-worth.")

E — New effective philosophy
(e.g., "I'm okay. I won't give up.")

F — New feelings
(e.g., "It's okay to feel frustrated. I won't give up.")

Figure 2.9

Ellis's A-B-C Theory of Personality

The development of emotional and behavioral problems is often linked to dysfunctional thinking. Cognitive psychologists assist their clients to identify and modify irrational thoughts and beliefs.

© Cengage Learning®

Albert Ellis and Aaron Beck developed distinct varieties of therapy based on their views regarding the connection between thought processes and emotional reactions and behaviors. Rational Emotive Behavior Therapy (REBT) has a strong focus on challenging illogical thinking (Ellis, 1997). Ellis believed that mental distress occurs when someone takes a reasonable desire such as "I'd like to perform well and be approved by others" and changes it into an illogical expectation such as "I *must* perform well and be approved" (Ellis referred to this pattern of thinking as "musturbation"). Ellis often confronted clients about their irrational thinking patterns and encouraged them to change "*musts,*" or irrational demands, into more rational "preferences."

Beck's approach to cognitive therapy, which has strong research support for treating depression and other conditions, involves making clients aware of cognitive distortions and negative schemas and then learning how to change them. A **schema** is the framework from which we automatically organize and give meaning to information. We develop cognitive schemas so we can process information more efficiently. In effect, a schema is the lens through which we view the world and ourselves. Because dysfunctional schemas such as "I'm stupid," "I'm helpless," or "People are dangerous" result in emotional distress, Beck's therapy helps clients recognize dysfunctional attitudes and beliefs systems. Clients eventually learn to replace automatic negative thinking with more adaptive thoughts.

If you worked with a cognitive therapist, you would go through a very systematic process. First, you would first learn to identify your automatic, negative thoughts. The therapist would then help you recognize how your thoughts, feelings, and behaviors are all connected. Once you identified your negative thought patterns, the therapist would ask you to gather and examine evidence for and against your negative views. For example, if you noticed that you often find yourself thinking "Everyone seems to have more fun than I do" or "I never look good in anything I wear," your therapist would ask you to "prove" your statements. In all likelihood, you would discover that there is minimal evidence for your negative thinking. You would also learn to identify dysfunctional beliefs such as "I should be having fun most of the time" or "I won't look good unless I'm really thin" and substitute more realistic thoughts.

The newest cognitive-behavioral therapies, sometime referred to as the *third wave therapies*, also focus on cognitions and behaviors. However, instead of identifying irrational or negative thoughts and refuting them, the newer therapies are based on the premise that nonreactive attention to emotions can reduce their power to create

schema a preconceived world view based on certain underlying assumptions; the framework from which we automatically organize and give meaning to information

emotional distress. Further, if we continuously avoid distressing thoughts and feelings, they are more likely to persist (Luoma, Hayes, & Walser, 2007). Therefore, clients are taught to nonreactively observe and experience unpleasant emotions. An important component of third wave therapies is **mindfulness**, maintaining conscious attention to the present, including negative emotions or thoughts, with an open, accepting, and nonjudgmental attitude. Mindfulness allows us to experience stressful emotional states without undue distress or physiological arousal. Mindfulness-based stress reduction, dialectical behavior therapy, and acceptance and commitment therapy are examples of third wave therapies. *Mindfulness-based stress reduction* focuses on using mindfulness meditation to cope with stress and reduce emotional reactivity (Rosenkranz et al., 2013).

Dialectical behavior therapy (DBT) is a supportive and collaborative therapy involving cognitive-behavioral techniques and close therapist-client teamwork (Koerner & Linehan, 2011). This therapy, developed by psychologist Marsha Linehan, uses an empathetic and validating environment to help clients learn to regulate their emotions, cope with stress, and improve social skills. Therapists actively reinforce positive actions while avoiding the reinforcement of maladaptive behaviors, including behaviors that interfere with therapy. Components of Eastern philosophy (Zen) are also part of the therapy—specifically, mindfulness and the acceptance of things that cannot be changed. DBT differs from traditional cognitive therapies due to the emphasis on the therapist-client relationship and the priority given to accepting and validating the client.

DBT is very structured and relies on four interrelated modules:

- *Mindfulness*—Learning to tolerate and accept your emotions by observing them objectively and nonjudgmentally.

- *Distress Tolerance*—Viewing yourself and your circumstances in an objective and dispassionate manner so that you can take productive actions rather than being pulled into an emotional reaction.

- *Emotional Regulation*—Identifying and labeling your emotions rather than being emotionally reactive; learning to change your negative thoughts and increase your positive emotions.

- *Interpersonal Effectiveness*—Improving your skills in dealing with difficult interpersonal situations such as learning to make requests assertively and to say "no" when appropriate.

Using a similar approach, *acceptance and commitment therapy (ACT)* focuses on learning to notice, accept, and even embrace the uncomfortable thoughts and emotions that are associated with mental distress. Therapists who use ACT also help their clients develop **psychological flexibility**, the ability to adapt to situational demands, including decisions to change or persist with current behaviors based on the client's core values. ACT and the other third wave therapies have growing research support (Churchill et al., 2013).

Criticisms of the Cognitive-Behavioral Models and Therapies

Some behaviorists remain quite skeptical of the **cognitive models** and therapies. Just before his death, B. F. Skinner (1990) warned that cognitions are not observable phenomena and cannot form the foundations of empiricism. In this context, he echoed the beliefs of John B. Watson, who stated that the science of psychology was about observable behaviors, not "mentalistic concepts." Cognitive-behavioral theories are also criticized for failing to acknowledge that human behavior involves more than thoughts and beliefs (Corey, 2013). Others question the role of the therapist as teacher, expert, and authority figure, especially because some therapists are quite direct when identifying and attacking irrational beliefs. In such interactions, clients might be intimidated into acquiescing to the therapist's power and authority.

mindfulness nonjudgmental awareness of thoughts, feelings, physical sensations, and the environment

psychological flexibility the ability to mentally and emotionally adapt to situational demands

cognitive models explanations based on the assumption that conscious thought mediates an individual's emotional state or behavior in response to a stimulus

Humanistic-Existential Models

The humanistic-existential models include a group of theories that emphasize the whole person rather than looking at parts of the personality such as the id, ego, and superego (psychoanalysis) or specific behavior patterns (behavioral theories). In fact, the humanistic-existential approaches evolved in reaction to the failure of these early models of psychopathology to acknowledge the role of free will. Although each of the humanistic theories has a different emphasis, there is a common belief in the innate goodness of humanity, in our uniqueness and individuality, and in our capacity to choose our life direction. Humanistic approaches are philosophical in nature. They deal with values, decry the use of diagnostic labels, and prefer a holistic view of the person.

The humanistic-existential perspectives represent many schools of thought, but they share a set of assumptions that distinguishes them from other approaches. The first is that what we see as "reality" is a product of our unique experiences and perceptions of the world. Our subjective universe—how we construe events—is more important than the events themselves. Therefore, to understand a person's behavior, it is important to understand the person's perspective on the world. Second, humanistic theorists assume that we have the ability to make free choices and are responsible for our own decisions. Third, they believe in the wholeness or integrity of the person and assume that we will lead lives that are best suited to who we are.

The Humanistic Perspective

The best known of the humanistic psychologists is Carl Rogers (1902–1987). His theory of personality (C. R. Rogers, 1959, 1961) and **humanistic perspective** reflect his concern with human welfare and his deep conviction that humans are basically good, forward moving, and trustworthy. Humanistic theory is based on the idea that people are motivated not only to satisfy their biological needs (e.g., for food, warmth, and sex) but also to cultivate, maintain, and enhance the self. Related to this view is Abraham Maslow's concept of **self-actualization**—our inherent tendency to strive toward the realization of our full potential.

Humanistic Views on the Development of Psychopathology Applying humanistic approaches to the development of mental disorders is a major challenge. Instead of concentrating exclusively on problems, the humanistic approach focuses on bettering the state of humanity and helping people *actualize* their potential. Rogers believed that when allowed to grow and develop freely, unencumbered by societal restrictions, people will thrive. Anxiety, depression, and other problems occur when society blocks this innate tendency for growth by imposing conditions on whether we have personal value. These standards are transmitted via *conditional positive regard*—when significant others in our lives, such as parents, friends, or partners, value us only when our actions, feelings, and attitudes meet their expectations. Thus, we begin to believe we have worth only when we have the approval of others. This belief can prevent us from developing optimally and can result in mental distress. Rogers believed that when circumstances allow us to reach our full potential we avoid mental illness. The environmental condition most suitable for this growth is *unconditional positive regard*—feeling loved, valued, and respected for who we are, regardless of our behavior.

The Existential Perspective

The **existential approach** is not a systematized school of thought but a set of attitudes. It shares with humanistic psychology an emphasis on our individual uniqueness, our quest for freedom and for meaning in life, and a belief that we all have positive attributes that we express unless environmental factors interfere. However, existentialism differs from humanism in several ways: (a) existentialists focus on the

humanistic perspective   the optimistic viewpoint that people are born with the ability to fulfill their potential and that abnormal behavior results from disharmony between a person's potential and self-concept

self-actualization   an inherent tendency to strive toward the realization of one's full potential

existential approach   a set of philosophical attitudes that focus on human alienation, the individual in the context of the human condition, and personal responsibility to others as well as to oneself

irrationality, difficulties, and suffering all humans encounter in life; (b) humanists attempt to understand the subjective world of their clients through empathy, while existentialists believe we must be viewed within the context of the human condition; and (c) humanists emphasize that we have the responsibility to determine our life path, while existentialists stress that we have responsibility not only to ourselves, but also to others. Human unhappiness and psychopathology stem from these issues and our avoidance of important life challenges. Thus, for many of us, life is directionless and without meaning. Paradoxically, many of us are responsible for our own unhappiness because we have ignored choices available to us or "unconsciously" chosen an unfulfilling path.

Humanistic and Existential Therapies

The assumption that humans need unconditional positive regard has many implications for psychotherapy. For therapists, it means fostering conditions that allow clients to grow and fulfill their potential, an approach known as *person-centered therapy*. Rogers emphasized that therapists' attitudes and ability to communicate respect, understanding, and acceptance are more important than specific counseling techniques. Rogers believed that therapists help clients reactivate the tendency for self-actualization by providing an accepting therapeutic environment. With unconditional positive regard, clients can make constructive changes and learn to accept themselves, including any imperfections. This self-growth allows clients to cope with present and future problems. The relationship between the client and therapist (the therapeutic alliance) is, in fact, an important contributor to the outcome of psychotherapy (Del Re, Flückiger, Horvath, Symonds, & Wampold, 2012).

Existential therapy is rooted in philosophy and the universal challenges of existence faced by all humans. As with other humanistic therapies, the therapeutic-client relationship is important. It is through this relationship that a client can acknowledge or deal with universal challenges. Existential therapists work to have their clients consider ways in which their freedom is impaired so they can remove obstacles to autonomy and increase their opportunities for choice. They also look for underlying meaning in what clients say and challenge clients to examine their lives. When clients become aware of choices they have made, they are more able to choose a new direction rather than continue to react to external forces. The goal is to help people become intentional in directing their lives.

Criticisms of the Humanistic and Existential Models and Therapies

Critics of the humanistic-existential approaches point to their "fuzzy," ambiguous, and nebulous nature; lack of scientific grounding; and reliance on people's unique, subjective experiences. Others question the power of the self-actualizing tendency and whether the therapist-client relationship in and of itself is sufficient to promote change. Although these approaches have been extremely creative in describing the human condition, they have been less successful in constructing theory and treatment strategies. Moreover, they are not suited to scientific or experimental investigation. It is difficult, for example, to verify the humanistic concept of people as rational, inherently good, and moving toward self-fulfillment.

Although Carl Rogers studied the processes involved in his client-centered approach to therapy, such research has decreased since the 1960s and the existential therapies have never been subject to much research (Elliott, 2002). Nevertheless, the existential concepts of freedom, choice, and responsibility have had a profound influence on contemporary thought beyond the field of psychology. Another major criticism leveled at the humanistic-existential approaches is that they do not explain many mental disorders, nor do they address cultural diversity or acknowledge social factors such as poverty, discrimination, and prejudice. They seem to be most effective with well-educated individuals experiencing mild distress or adjustment difficulties. These limitations have hindered the application of these perspectives to the treatment of mental illness.

Dimension Three: Social Factors

The theories of psychopathology discussed so far focus primarily on the individual rather than on the social environment. They are relatively silent when it comes to addressing important aspects of our lives such as how current relationships, family, social support, community, and belonging affect the expression of mental distress. It is clear that we are social beings and that our relationships can influence the development, manifestation, and amelioration of mental disorders.

Social-Relational Models

Social-relational models consider a variety of interpersonal relationships, including those involving intimate partners, nuclear or extended family, or connections within the community. Social-relational explanations of mental distress make several important assumptions (D. W. Johnson & Johnson, 2003):

1. Healthy relationships are important for optimal human development and functioning.

2. Social relationships provide many intangible health benefits (social support, love, compassion, trust, sense of belonging, etc.).

3. When relationships prove dysfunctional or are absent, the individual may be vulnerable to mental distress.

Studies show that social isolation and lack of emotional support and intimacy are associated with a variety of symptoms of mental illness and difficulty coping with stress (Nagano et al., 2010).

Family, Couples, and Group Perspectives

In contrast to traditional psychological models, social-relational models emphasize how other people, especially significant others, influence our behavior. For example, the **family systems model** assumes that the behavior of one family member directly affects the entire family system. According to this model, we behave in ways that reflect both healthy and unhealthy family influences. There are three distinct beliefs underlying the family systems approach (Corey, 2013). First, our personality development is strongly influenced by our family's characteristics, especially the way our parents interacted with us and other family members. Second, mental illness in an individual often reflects unhealthy family dynamics, especially poor communication among family members. Thus, the cause of mental disorders resides within the family system, not within the individual. Third, therapy must focus on the family system, rather than the individual; treatment may be ineffective unless the entire family is involved.

Social-Relational Treatment Approaches

The family systems model has spawned a number of treatment approaches. One method, the *conjoint family therapeutic approach*, developed by Virginia Satir (1967), stresses the importance of clear and direct communication and teaches message-sending and message-receiving skills to family members. Like other family therapists, Satir believed that a family member experiencing mental distress or behavioral difficulties (referred to as the "identified patient") is a reflection of dysfunction in the family system. *Strategic family approaches* (Haley, 1963, 1987) consider

family systems model explanation that assumes that the behavior of one family member directly affects the entire family system

couples therapy a treatment aimed at helping couples understand and clarify their communications, role relationships, unfulfilled needs, and unrealistic or unmet expectations

group therapy a form of therapy that involves the simultaneous treatment of two or more clients and may involve more than one therapist

power struggles within the family and focus on developing a more healthy power distribution. *Structural family approaches* (Minuchin, 1974) attempt to reorganize family relationships based on the assumption that family dysfunction occurs when family members have too much or too little involvement with one another. All of these approaches focus on communication, equalizing power within the family, and restructuring the troubled family system.

Another social-relational approach, **couples therapy**, targets marital relationships and intimate relationships between unmarried partners. Treatment helps couples to understand and clarify their communications, role relationships, unfulfilled needs, and unrealistic or unmet expectations. Couples therapy has become an increasingly popular treatment for those who find that the quality of their relationship needs improvement (Nichols & Schwartz, 2005).

Another form of social-relational treatment is **group therapy**. Unlike couples and family therapy, members of the therapy group are often initially strangers. However, group members may share certain characteristics such as experiencing a similar life stressor (e.g., chronic illness, divorce, or death of a family member) or having similar mental disorders or similar therapeutic goals. Most group therapies focus on a specific topic or interactions among members. Despite their wide diversity, successful group therapies share several features that promote change in clients (Corey, 2013; Yalom, 2005). For example, the group experience:

- allows participants to become involved in a social situation and to see how their behavior affects others;
- permits the therapist to see how clients actually respond in a real-life social and interpersonal context;
- provides group members an opportunity to develop new communication skills, social skills, and insights;
- allows group members to feel less isolated and less fearful about their problems; and
- provides participants with strong social and emotional support.

Family Dynamics and Positive Self-Image

Family interaction patterns can exert tremendous influence on a child's personality development, determining the child's sense of self-worth and the acquisition of appropriate social skills. This picture shows a Hispanic/Latino family preparing dinner together. Notice how the family members are actively involved in working together, and how the children are experiencing family cohesion and belonging.

Hill Street Studios/ Blend Images/Getty Images

The feelings of intimacy, belonging, protection, and trust (which participants may not be able to experience outside the group) can provide powerful motivation for group members to confront and to overcome personal difficulties.

Criticisms of Social-Relational Models

There is no denying that we are social beings, and that the social-relational models provide important insight into our understandings of abnormal behavior. However, social-relational research studies are generally not rigorous in design; they have often lacked appropriate control groups or solid outcome measures (Cottrell & Boston, 2002). Further, considerable evidence exists that couples, marital, and family therapies do not adequately address cultural diversity (Sue & Sue, 2013). Other critics have voiced concern that family systems models may have unpleasant consequences. Too often, family therapists have pointed an accusing finger at the parents of children with certain disorders, despite an abundance of evidence that factors other than parental behaviors are likely involved. This burdens parents with unnecessary guilt over a situation that resulted from factors beyond their control.

Dimension Four: Sociocultural Factors

Sociocultural perspectives emphasize the importance of considering race, ethnicity, gender, sexual orientation, religious preference, socioeconomic status, and other such factors in explaining mental disorders. The importance of the sociocultural dimension is evident in the *Diagnostic and Statistical Manual of Mental Disorders* (DSM), which lists disorders that are limited to a specific society or cultural group. For example, *taijin kyofusho* is a culture-specific disorder (seen in Japan) in which individuals fear that their body parts or normal bodily functions are offensive to other people. Similarly, *ataque de nervios* is common in Puerto Rico and includes symptoms of uncontrollable shouting, seizure-like episodes, trembling, and crying.

It is clear that people's cultural experiences play an important role in their mental health (Sue & Sue, 2013). The cultural groups to which we belong may expose us to unique stressors or may influence how we express mental distress (Keller & Calgay, 2010). We briefly discuss four major sociocultural influences to illustrate their importance in understanding psychopathology: gender, socioeconomic class, acculturative stress, and race and ethnicity.

Gender Factors

There is little doubt that sociocultural factors related to gender influence mental health. The importance of gender in understanding psychopathology is evident when examining the much higher prevalence of depression, anxiety, eating disorders, and other mental health conditions among women (Ferrari et al., 2013). In Chapter 10 (on eating disorders), we discuss how stereotyped standards of beauty in advertisements and the mass media can affect the mental health of girls and women. Body dissatisfaction, eating disorders, and depression are all influenced by these sociocultural standards.

Women are also subjected to more stress than their male counterparts (L. Smith, 2010). For example, they are often placed in the unenviable position of fulfilling a variety of feminine social roles defined by society. Even when employed full-time outside of the home, women have more responsibility for domestic chores and childcare (Bureau of Labor Statistics, 2013). Additionally, significant wage disparities exist between men and women working in full-time jobs, with women earning only 77 percent of the wages earned by men (American Association of University Women, 2013). Women with limited income have an increased risk of depression, domestic violence, or having the extra responsibility of being the primary caregiver for children or older family members (Levy & O'Hara, 2010). Women are also more likely to experience the stress that comes from working in jobs that provide few decision-making opportunities (Verboom et al., 2011).

Exposure to sexual harassment often begins during the middle school years, with effects on both psychological well-being and learning (American Association of University Women, 2011). Further, women are much more likely to experience trauma related to sexual assault or intimate partner violence (U.S. Department of Commerce, 2011). For example, many college women report experiencing some form of sexual aggression (Yeater, Treat, Viken, & McFall, 2010). These are just a few of the many findings documenting stressors that have a major effect on the mental health of girls and women.

Socioeconomic Class

Social class and classism are two frequently overlooked sociocultural factors that influence mental health (L. Smith, 2010). Lower socioeconomic class is associated with a limited sense of personal control, poorer physical health, and higher incidence of depression (Sue, 2010). Increasingly, psychologists are recognizing the degree to which poverty subjects people to multiple stressors (L. Smith & Reddington, 2010). Life in poverty is associated with low wages, unemployment or underemployment, lack of savings, and lack of food reserves. Meeting even the most basic needs of food and shelter becomes a major challenge. In such circumstances, people are likely to experience feelings of hopelessness, helplessness, dependence, and inferiority.

Immigration and Acculturative Stress

Many immigrants face **acculturative stress**, the psychological, physical, and social pressures associated with a move to a new country. Not only do immigrants face the challenge of adjusting and adapting to new cultural customs, they sometimes receive a hostile reception from both the government and the public. Placed in unfamiliar settings and missing their accustomed social support from the communities they left behind, many experience severe culture shock (Breslau et al., 2011). Feelings of isolation, loneliness, helplessness, anxiety, and depression are common. Many immigrants face additional challenges as they negotiate the educational system, learn a new language, and seek employment. Male immigrants often experience a loss of status and develop a sense of powerlessness. Problems of gender inequities and spousal abuse can increase under these conditions (Ting & Panchanadeswaran, 2009). Acculturation conflicts are common, especially among first-generation immigrants and their children. The children may experience difficulty fitting in with their peers, yet may be considered "too Americanized" by their parents. Racism and discrimination can compound these already stressful circumstances (Sue & Sue, 2013).

Race and Ethnicity

Early attempts to explain differences between various minority groups and their counterparts in the majority culture tended to adopt one of two models. The first, the **inferiority model**, contended that racial and ethnic minorities are inferior in some respect to the majority population. For example, this model suggests that low academic achievement and higher unemployment rates among African Americans and Hispanics/Latinos are due to biological differences such as low intelligence. The second model—the deprivation or **deficit model**—explained differences as the result of "cultural deprivation." It implied that minority groups lacked the "right" culture. Both models are criticized as being inaccurate, biased, and unsupported by scientific research (Ridley, 2005; Sue & Sue, 2013).

During the late 1980s and early 1990s, a new and conceptually different perspective, the **multicultural model** (or the *culturally diverse model*; Sue & Sue, 2013), emerged in the literature. This approach emphasizes that being culturally different does not mean that someone is deviant, pathological, or inferior; instead, it is important to recognize that each culture has strengths and limitations. The multicultural model also points out that all theories of human development and psychopathology arise from a particular cultural context (Ivey, D'Andrea, Ivey, & Simek-Morgan, 2007). Thus, many traditional models of psychopathology operate from a European

Multicultural Perspectives

Multicultural models of human behavior regard race, culture, and ethnicity as central to the understanding of normality and abnormality. In China, children are taught to value group harmony over individual competitiveness. In contrast, in the United States, individual efforts and privacy are valued. These values are evident in the common use of cubicles in work settings to separate people from one another.

acculturative stress the psychological, physical, and social pressures experienced by individuals who are adapting to a new culture

inferiority model early attempt to explain differences in minority groups that contended that racial and ethnic minorities are somehow inferior to the majority population

deficit model early attempt to explain differences in minority groups that contended that differences are the result of "cultural deprivation"

multicultural model contemporary view that emphasizes the importance of considering a person's cultural background and related experiences when determining normality and abnormality

American worldview not experienced or shared by other cultural groups. For example, individualism and autonomy are valued in the United States; we raise children to become increasingly independent, to make their own decisions, and to "stand on their own two feet." In contrast, many traditional Asian Americans value collectivity; thus, the psychosocial unit of importance is the family rather than the individual. Whereas European Americans fear the loss of individuality, members of traditional Asian groups fear the loss of belonging and group membership.

Given these variations in experiences and values, unenlightened mental health professionals may make biased assumptions about human behavior—assumptions that influence their judgments of normality and abnormality among clients who differ from them in terms of race or ethnicity. For example, a mental health professional who does not understand that Asian Americans typically value a collectivistic identity might see clients with close family connections as overly dependent, immature, or unable to make decisions on their own. The same professional might perceive restraint of strong feelings—a valued characteristic among some Asian groups—as evidence of an inability to express emotions.

The Universal Shamanic Tradition: Wizards, Sorcerers, and Witch Doctors

Since the beginning of human existence, all societies and cultural groups have developed their own explanations of abnormal behavior and their own culture-specific ways of dealing with human suffering and distress (Moodley, 2005). A surprising consequence of the multicultural psychology movement has been a revival of interest in non-Western indigenous explanations of human disorders and their treatments. Much of this is due to our changing demographics, including an influx of immigrants who hold non-Western beliefs regarding illness, mental disorder, and treatment.

Western science focuses on what we can observe and measure through the five senses. However, many indigenous people believe that the nature of reality transcends the senses (R. Walsh & Shapiro, 2006). The **universal shamanic tradition** incorporates a belief in special healers who are blessed with powers to cure the sick (Moodley, 2005). Shamans treat mental and physical disorders using rituals, prayers, and sacred symbols that summon spiritual forces. They are admired for their ability to enter altered states of consciousness, journey to an existence beyond the physical world, and contact and communicate with spirits.

The *universal shamanic tradition* views illness, distress, and problematic behaviors as the result of an imbalance in human relationships, a disharmony between the person and the group, or a lack of synchrony among mind, body, spirit, and nature. Many cultures believe that accessing higher states of consciousness can enhance perceptual sensitivity, clarity, concentration, and emotional well-being. Interestingly, meditation and yoga are the most widely practiced forms of therapy in the world today. These ancient practices can help with anxiety, phobias, substance abuse, chronic pain, and high blood pressure, as well as enhance self-confidence, marital satisfaction, and sense of control (Sue & Sue, 2013).

For Further Consideration

1. How valid are shamanic explanations of illness? Can you identify commonalities between what therapists and shamans do?

2. What can we learn from indigenous forms of healing?

3. Are there dangers or downsides to shamanism as a belief system or form of treatment?

© Roger Bamber/Alamy

Social psychological studies on implicit bias reveal that we all learn societal stereotypes, biases, and prejudices. On a conscious level, most of us believe we would never deliberately or intentionally discriminate against others. Yet many of our stereotypes operate outside the level of conscious awareness, so we may unconsciously behave in a discriminatory fashion.

SOURCE: Dovidio, Kawakami, Smoak, & Gaertner, 2009

The multicultural model emphasizes that mental health difficulties are sometimes due to sociocultural stressors residing in the social system rather than conflicts within the person. Racism, bias, discrimination, economic hardships, and cultural conflicts are just a few of the realities faced by members of racial and ethnic minorities and other marginalized groups. As a result, it may be more productive for therapists to focus on ameliorating oppressive or detrimental social conditions rather than attempting therapy aimed at changing the individual. Individual therapy may be effective, however, for clients who could benefit from learning strategies for coping with environmental stressors.

Sociocultural Considerations in Treatment

Multicultural counseling has been called the "fourth force" in the field of psychotherapy following the other major schools of psychoanalytic, cognitive-behavioral, and humanistic-existential therapies. Therapists who use a multicultural approach take care to show respect for clients' ethnicity and cultural background and to incorporate cultural themes into traditional psychotherapeutic techniques. Multicultural counseling has assumed greater importance as our population has become more diverse. Cultural differences, such as family experiences and degree of assimilation, are essential to consider in assessment and treatment. At the same time, therapists need to be careful not to assume that just because their clients are part of a particular group, they strongly identify with or share the values of that group.

Criticisms of the Multicultural Model and Related Therapeutic Techniques

According to the multicultural model, normal and abnormal behavior should be evaluated from a cultural perspective. The reasoning is that behavior considered disordered in one context—seeing a vision of a dead relative, for example—might be considered acceptable within another cultural context. As indicated in the DSM, some cultural groups consider it normal to hear or see a deceased relative during bereavement or during religious ceremonies. For example, certain groups, including some American Indian and Hispanic/Latino groups, look upon hallucinations as a positive spiritual event.

Critics of the multicultural model argue that a disorder is a disorder, regardless of the cultural context in which it occurs. For example, they would contend that someone who is actively hallucinating (seeing, hearing, or feeling things that are not there) lacks contact with reality. This behavior would represent a dysfunction, according to this viewpoint, even if the person considers the hallucination desirable. Another criticism leveled at the multicultural model is that it relies heavily on case studies and ethnographic analyses and that formal research has not yet validated many of the concepts associated with the model. Multicultural psychologists note that criticisms such as these are based on a Western worldview that emphasizes precision and empirical definitions. They point out that there is more than one way to ask and answer questions about the human condition.

Contemporary Trends and Future Directions

universal shamanic tradition set of beliefs and practices from non-Western indigenous traditions that assume that special healers are blessed with powers to act as intermediaries or messengers between the human and spirit worlds

Unfortunately, we are seeing a steady increase in mental disorders, among children, adolescents, and adults. Thus, it is a high priority to learn as much as possible about the biological, psychological, social, and sociocultural influences associated with

Applying the Models of Psychopathology

A useful learning exercise to evaluate your mastery of the various models is to apply them to a case study. We invite you to try your hand at explaining the behavior of Bill, a hypothetical client, from the perspective of the various models we have discussed. Afterward, we invite you to attempt a more integrated multipath approach to explaining Bill's difficulties.

Bill was born in Indiana to extremely religious parents who raised him in a strict moralistic manner. His father, a Baptist minister, often told Bill and his two sisters to "keep your mind clean, heart pure, and body in control." He forbade Bill's sisters to date while they lived at home. Bill's own social life and contacts were extremely limited, and he recalls feeling very anxious around girls. Bill also remembers feeling very intimidated by his father throughout his childhood. No one in the family dared disagree with the father openly, lest they be punished. The father appeared to be hardest on Bill's two sisters, especially when they expressed any interest in boys. The arguments and conflicts between father and daughters were often loud and intense, disrupting the typical quietness of the home.

Bill recalls that his mother was often sick with what his father referred to as "the dark cloud," which seemed to visit her periodically; during these episodes, she withdrew from the family and spent her days in bed. Bill's relationships with his sisters, who were several years older, were uncomfortable. When Bill was young, they teased him mercilessly, and when he reached adolescence, they seemed to take sadistic delight in arousing him by flaunting their partially exposed bodies. The result was that Bill became obsessed with having sex with one of his sisters. Throughout his adolescence, he was tortured by feelings of guilt; he began to believe that he was, as his father put it, "an unclean and damned sinner."

By all external standards, Bill was a quiet and well-behaved child and adolescent. He did well in school, attended Sunday school without fail, never argued or spoke against his parents, and seldom ventured outside of the home. Although Bill did exceptionally well in high school, some of his teachers were concerned about his introverted and increasingly withdrawn behavior. When teachers brought Bill's depression to the attention of his father, however, Mr. M. assured them

there was no reason to worry. Mr. M. often complimented Bill on his good grades and unobtrusive behavior, rewarding him occasionally with small privileges for being "so good." In many ways, Bill felt that his worth as a person was dependent on "getting good grades" and "staying out of trouble."

As a young child, Bill had exhibited excellent artistic potential. His artistic interests continued into high school, where his art instructor entered one of Bill's drawings in a state contest. His entry won first prize. Unfortunately, Mr. M. discouraged Bill's artistic interest and told him "God calls you in another direction." Attempting to please his father, Bill became less involved in art and concentrated more on math and science. He did very well in these subjects, obtaining nearly straight A's in high school.

When Bill entered college, his prime objective was to remain a straight-A student. Although he had originally loved the excitement of learning and mastering new knowledge, he became cautious and obsessed with "safety"; he was fearful of upsetting his father by risking a B grade. He began to choose safe and easy topics for essays, to enroll in easy courses, and to take incompletes or withdrawals when courses appeared tough. Toward the end of his sophomore year, Bill became severely depressed, feeling overwhelming pessimism and hopelessness. He was hospitalized after he tried to take his own life.

Table 2.3 summarizes the various models to review as you begin this exercise:

- Consider what each theory would propose as the basis of Bill's severe depression. Consider the type of information that each perspective would consider most important.

- Compare and contrast the views of several of the models.

- As you attempt to explain Bill's mental distress, notice how your adoption of a particular framework influences the type of data you consider important. Is it possible that all the models hold some semblance of truth? Are their positions necessarily contradictory? How would you explain Bill's difficulties if you integrated all of the background information into a unified explanation using the multipath model?

this disturbing trend. All of the perspectives we have discussed have both strengths and weaknesses; no one approach can claim to tell "the whole truth." Each model represents different views of pathology. Each details a different perspective from which to interpret symptoms, the origin of disorders, and a therapeutic cure. As you have seen, many models of psychopathology focus on one aspect of the human

Table 2.3 Comparison of the Most Influential Models of Psychopathology

Model	Motivation for Behavior	Theoretical Foundation	Source of Abnormal Behavior	Treatment
Biological	State of biological integrity and health	Animal and human research, case studies, neuroimaging	Genetics, epigenetics, brain anatomy, and physiology; autonomic overreactivity	Medications, ECT, rTMS, DBS, vagus nerve stimulation
Psychodynamic	Unconscious influences	Case studies, correlational methods	Early childhood experiences	Psychoanalysis, uncovering unconscious conflict, dream analysis, free association, transference
Behavioral	External influences	Animal research, case studies, experimental methods	Learning maladaptive responses, not acquiring appropriate responses	Directly modifying behavior; analyzing and changing the environmental factors controlling behavior
Cognitive	External and cognitive influences	Human research, case studies, experimental methods	Learned patterns of irrational or negative thoughts or self-statements	Understanding relationship between thoughts and problem behavior, modifying internal dialogue
Humanistic	Self-actualization	Case studies, correlational methods	Incongruence between self and experiences	Nondirective reflection, unconditional positive regard
Existential	Capacity for self-awareness; freedom to decide one's fate	A philosophical approach to understanding the human condition	Failure to actualize human potential, avoidance of choice and responsibility	Providing conditions for maximizing self-awareness and growth and concern for others
Family Systems	Interaction with significant others	Case studies, social psychological studies, experimental methods	Faulty family interactions and inconsistent communication patterns	Treating the entire family, not just the identified patient
Multicultural	Cultural values and norms	Data about cultural groups from various disciplines	Culture conflicts, discrimination, and oppression	Adapting therapy to consider both individual and cultural factors

© Cengage Learning®

condition to the exclusion of others; many overlook important aspects of the individual or the social environment.

A truly comprehensive model of human behavior must address the likelihood that biological, psychological, social, and sociocultural factors are all involved. We hope it is now clear why it is important to consider mental disorders from a multipath perspective, and to embrace an integration of the various theories and treatment approaches. Fortunately, our evidence-based understanding of mental disorders has evolved in the past decades, guided by new theories as well as research and scientific findings regarding the relative merits of factors that purportedly influence the development of disorders. Let's take biological explanations as an example. Because the brain controls all aspects of human functioning, it is easy to conclude that mental disorders result from an interruption in normal brain function. However, researchers have increasingly come to reject a simple linear explanation of biological effects on mental disorders (Rucker & McGuffin, 2010). Rather, we now view mental disorders as resulting from complex interactive and oftentimes reciprocal processes (J. J. Mann & Haghighi, 2010). Further, epigenetic research is revealing how reciprocal gene × environment interactions modify gene expression. Additionally, we are learning how behavioral traits associated with certain genes or gene combinations can lead to stressful personal or environmental circumstances

(Diamond, 2009). For example, genetic factors may predispose a person to seek out situations (such as using drugs or alcohol or selecting unstable friends or romantic partners) that increase the risk of experiencing stressors that trigger depression. Accumulating evidence demonstrates that biochemistry, brain activity, and even brain structures and neural circuitry can change in response to a variety of psychological, social, cultural, and other environmental influences (J. A. Foster & MacQueen, 2008).

Researchers analyzing mental disorders from various perspectives are recognizing that the majority of mental disorders are indeed multifactorial, and that, in many cases, single factors have relatively small effects with respect to etiology. An early formulation of this perspective was the **diathesis-stress theory** originally proposed by Meehl (1962) and developed further by Rosenthal (1970). This theory suggests that it is not a particular abnormality that is inherited but rather a *predisposition to develop illness* (the diathesis). Certain environmental forces, called *stressors*, may activate the predisposition, resulting in a disorder. Alternatively, in a benign and supportive environment, the abnormality may never materialize. The diathesis-stress model is consistent with other theories that point to an interaction between biological vulnerabilities and environmental influences as a key factor in the development of mental disorders. However, epigenetic research has shown that the diathesis-stress theoretical focus on having a "predisposition" to develop a disorder is an oversimplification; we now know that brain functioning is best understood as a constant and reciprocal conversation between the genome and the environment (Zhang & Meaney, 2010).

Whether mental disorders result from biological, psychological, social, or sociocultural factors, we know that biological and other therapeutic strategies can change physiological processes occurring within the brain and body. We know, for example, that fear can cause the secretion of adrenaline and noradrenalin. Through brain imaging studies, we also know that psychotherapeutic interventions can "normalize" brain circuitry in people experiencing symptoms of various mental disorders. Thus, although biology influences the development of mental disorders, the environment can exert an equally powerful reciprocal influence on brain activity, brain circuitry, and biochemical processes.

Sociocultural factors are increasingly recognized as playing an important role in the etiology of psychological distress, particularly among diverse populations. Over the past few years, major research universities are focusing on *cultural neuroscience*—the study of how biology shapes culture and culture shapes biology. Fortunately, mental health professionals are learning more about the importance of using therapeutic practices that consider clients' diverse cultural backgrounds, their culturally based experiences, and their views regarding the causes of their difficulties and their opinions regarding treatment goals. In fact, we are seeing much more individualization of both psychologically and biologically based treatment approaches. As our understandings of the complex causes of mental disorders increase, it is likely that we will see earlier diagnosis, preventive interventions, and evidence-based treatments that are guided by a comprehensive understanding of a client's biological, psychological, social, and sociocultural characteristics.

MYTH If one member of a family has a mental health condition, other members will probably develop the same disorder.

REALITY The fact that mental health conditions run in certain families has caused undue anxiety for many people. Heredity does play a role in many mental disorders. However, even though genetics may predispose an individual to certain disorders, there is no certainty that a disorder will develop. Mental disorders result from interactions among biological, psychological, social, and cultural influences. Similarly, a variety of psychological, social, and cultural factors can help protect people from developing a disorder to which they are biologically predisposed.

diathesis-stress theory view that people inherit a predisposition to develop illness (diathesis) and that certain environmental forces (stressors) may activate the predisposition, resulting in a disorder

chapter SUMMARY

1 What models of psychopathology have been used to explain abnormal behavior?

- A variety of one-dimensional models have been traditionally used to explain disorders. They are inadequate because mental disorders are multidimensional.

2 What is the multipath model of mental disorders?

- The multipath model provides a framework for understanding biological, psychological, social, and sociocultural influences on mental disorders; the complexity of their interacting components; and the need to view disorders from a holistic framework.

3 How is biology involved in mental disorders?

- Genetics, brain anatomy, biochemical imbalances, central nervous system functioning, and autonomic nervous system reactivity are often involved. Neurotransmitters seem to play a significant role in abnormal behavior, and genetic inheritance and epigenetic factors are associated with many psychopathologies.

4 How do psychological models explain mental disorders?

- Psychodynamic models emphasize childhood experiences and the role of the unconscious in determining adult behavior.
- Behavioral models focus on the role of learning in symptoms of mental disorders. Abnormal behaviors are acquired through association (classical conditioning), reinforcement (operant conditioning), or modeling (observational learning).

- Cognitive models are based on the assumption that mental disorders are due to irrational beliefs or distorted cognitive processes.
- The humanistic-existential models view an individual's reality as a product of personal perception and experience, see people as capable of making free choices and fulfilling their potential, and emphasize the whole person.

5 What role do social factors play in psychopathology?

- Poor-quality or absent social relationships are associated with increased susceptibility to mental disorders.
- Family systems approaches view abnormal behavior as the result of distorted or faulty communication or unbalanced relationships within the family.

6 What sociocultural factors influence mental health?

- Proponents of the sociocultural approach believe that race, culture, ethnicity, gender, sexual orientation, religious preference, socioeconomic status, and other societal variables are powerful influences on the development and manifestation of mental disorders.

7 Why is it important to consider mental disorders from a multipath perspective?

- Focusing on only one theoretical perspective can overlook important aspects of the individual.
- The majority of mental disorders result from complex and reciprocal interactions among biological, psychological, social, and sociocultural factors.

3

ASSESSMENT AND CLASSIFICATION OF MENTAL DISORDERS

POLICE WERE CALLED When Ms. Y. Became Physically Aggressive, breaking several windows and leaving her home in disarray. Police officers described Ms. Y.'s behavior as threatening and violent. Because Ms. Y. was too confused to be interviewed, her boyfriend provided background information. He reported that Ms. Y. was hospitalized earlier in the year because she was hearing voices and claiming she was God, and on one previous occasion when she displayed similar symptoms after experimenting with drugs. Ms. Y.'s family history includes an aunt diagnosed with schizophrenia (Lavakumar, Garlow, & Schwartz, 2011).

Different conditions can cause the symptoms Ms. Y. exhibited. To determine the exact cause, a thorough assessment must be performed. In the case of Ms. Y., a drug screen ruled out alcohol and illicit drugs as causal factors. There was also no evidence of infections or other medical conditions that might produce her symptoms. However, when asked about the use of medications, Ms. Y. volunteered that she had been taking carnitine, an over-the-counter weight-loss supplement. In fact, Ms. Y. had been taking twice the recommended levels of carnitine. In addition, she had been drinking energy drinks containing carnitine as one of the main ingredients. The mental health team concluded that her mental confusion was due to carnitine intoxication.

In the mental health field, assessment is critical. Mental health professionals collect and organize information about a person's current condition and past history using observations, interviews, psychological tests, and neurological tests, as well as input from relatives and friends. Of course, it is always important to rule out physical causes for psychological symptoms (e.g., anemia, medication reactions, thyroid or cardiac irregularities), particularly when there is a sudden onset of symptoms without a precipitating event or precipitating environmental factors. Data gathered from a variety of sources allow a more thorough understanding of a client's symptoms and mental state. In the case of Ms. Y., the therapists relied on observations, laboratory tests, and interviews to arrive at their diagnosis. One of the first steps in assessment is to consider possible physical or biological causes for the symptoms. In the case of Ms. Y., knowledge about her excessive use of carnitine was an important piece of the puzzle regarding what might be

focus
QUESTIONS

1 How do we know if psychological tests and evaluation procedures are accurate?

2 How do mental health professionals evaluate a client's mental health?

3 How do professionals make a psychiatric diagnosis?

4 What changes are occurring that will affect assessment?

causing the sudden changes in her behavior. As we noted in Chapter 1, evaluation of all available information leads to a **psychodiagnosis**—a description of the individual's psychological state and judgments about possible causes of the psychological distress. The therapist comes up with a tentative diagnosis after considering the client's concerns, pattern of symptoms, and background information. Psychodiagnosis is usually the first step in the treatment process.

In this section, we examine assessment methods and tools used to make a psychodiagnosis. We also discuss the most widely used diagnostic classification system, as well as criticisms regarding labeling and classification. We begin with a discussion of the accuracy of assessment tools and diagnostic systems.

Reliability and Validity

There are many tests and procedures that professionals can use to assess clients who are seeking help for distressing social or emotional symptoms. The best assessment tools for accurately diagnosing psychological disorders are both reliable and valid.

Reliability is the degree to which a procedure, test, or classification system yields the same results repeatedly under the same circumstances. There are many types of reliability, including the following:

- *Test-retest reliability* determines whether a measure yields the same results when given at two different points in time. For example, if you take a personality test in the morning and then retake the test later in the day, the test is reliable if the results show stability (i.e., are consistent) from one point in time to another. If the test results vary, we would say the test has poor reliability.

- *Internal consistency reliability* requires that various parts of a test yield similar or consistent results. For example, on a test assessing anxiety, each test item should reliably measure characteristics related to anxiety.

- *Interrater reliability* refers to how consistent (or inconsistent) test results are when scored by different test administrators. For instance, imagine that two clinicians trained to diagnose individuals according to a certain classification system are given the same list of symptoms to review and are asked to formulate a psychodiagnosis. If one clinician diagnoses an anxiety disorder and one diagnoses depression, there would be poor interrater reliability.

It is also important to consider **validity**, the extent to which a test or procedure actually performs the function it was designed to perform. If a measure intended to assess depression actually measures motivation, the measure is an invalid measure of depression. The most common forms of validity considered in assessment are predictive, construct, and content validity (Weiner & Greene, 2008).

- *Predictive validity* is how well a test or measure predicts or forecasts a person's behavior, response, or performance. Colleges and universities often use applicants' SAT or ACT scores to predict future college grades. If the tests have good predictive validity, they should be able to differentiate students who will perform well in college from those who will perform poorly.

- *Construct validity* is how well a test or measure relates to the characteristics or disorder in question. For example, a test to measure social anxiety should be constructed to match other measures of social anxiety, including questions about physical symptoms seen in people who are socially anxious—muscle tension, sweating, or startle responses.

- *Content validity* is how well a test measures what it is intended to measure. For example, we know that depression involves cognitive, emotional, behavioral, and physiological symptoms. If a self-report measure of depression contains

psychodiagnosis assessment and description of an individual's psychological symptoms, including inferences about what might be causing the psychological distress

reliability the degree to which a procedure or test yields consistent results

validity the extent to which a test or procedure actually measures what it was designed to measure

Should Strengths Be Assessed?

A woman received a diagnosis of major depressive disorder. When talking about her symptoms with her therapist, she expressed feelings of hopelessness and despair. The clinician then conducted a strength assessment by asking her to describe a life story that would show her at her best. She relayed a story about defending a boy in school who was being laughed at by other students. As she discussed this story, her face lit up, and she described her strengths as courage and fairness. The therapist helped her to identify other strengths and apply them to the problems she was facing. After 20 sessions, the woman no longer met the criteria for major depressive disorder (Rashid & Ostermann, 2009).

Deficits, symptoms, problem behaviors, and emotional difficulties are emphasized in assessments and classification

Kevin Peterson/Photodisc/Getty Images

systems such as the DSM-5. The negative picture this emphasis creates can affect the client and the therapist's view of the client. Fortunately, therapists are beginning to recognize the importance of focusing not only on clients' problems but also on their strengths—their positive personal characteristics, accomplishments, and prior successes in dealing with adversities and stress (Corcoran & Walsh, 2010). Identifying and fostering strengths can increase resilience, improve quality of life, and reduce symptoms (Harbin, Gelso, & Rojas, 2013). Strength assessment can provide a more balanced picture for both the mental health professional and the client. Peterson and Seligman (2005) developed a classification system involving character strengths and virtues to complement the DSM; their system focuses on six overarching virtues (wisdom, courage, humanity, justice, temperance, and transcendence), characteristics that are important to assess and consider when working with mental disorders. What do you see as the advantages of assessing client strengths?

items that assess only cognitive features, such as items indicating pessimism, the measure has poor content validity because it fails to assess the other areas we know are associated with depression.

Let's look at the reliability and validity of a measure developed to assess the unusual thinking patterns and impaired sense of reality seen in **psychosis**. The test creators (Cicero, Kerns, & McCarthy, 2010) wanted to determine if the instrument they developed was a valid and reliable measure of individuals' likelihood of developing psychosis. The items for the test were based on descriptions of psychosis, including characteristics observed during the early stages of schizophrenia (a disorder involving symptoms of psychosis), and interviews with people diagnosed with schizophrenia. The test's internal consistency reliability—the consistency among the items—was high (0.89).

To determine the construct validity—how well the measure actually assesses the likelihood of developing psychosis—the inventory was compared to other scales that measure psychosis. It was highly correlated to other measures of psychosis, thus demonstrating good construct validity and increasing confidence in the measure. Because the inventory assesses the likelihood of developing psychosis, you would also expect that individuals with a history of psychosis would score higher on this test than individuals with other mental disorders. This was also found. Thus, the researchers concluded that their inventory is a useful measure of susceptibility to psychosis.

psychosis loss of contact with reality, including disorganized thinking, false beliefs, or seeing or hearing things that are not there

Test accuracy is also influenced by the conditions under which tests are administered. **Standardization**, or standard administration, requires professionals administering a test to follow common rules or procedures. If an examiner creates a tense or hostile environment for some individuals who are taking a test, for example, the test scores may vary simply due to differences in the testing situation. An additional concern is the **standardization sample**—the group of people who originally took the measure and whose performance is used as the standard or norm. Clinicians use the standardization sample to compare and interpret test results. For test scores to be valid, test-takers should be similar to the original group or sample. For example, would comparing the test score of a 20-year-old African American woman with a standardization sample consisting of middle-aged white men provide accurate information? Most would agree that the standardization group is too different to allow for valid interpretation of the results.

Assessment and Classification of Mental Disorders

Psychological assessment involves gathering information and drawing conclusions about the traits, skills, abilities, emotional functioning, and psychological problems of an individual; information from assessment is used to make a psychodiagnosis. Clinicians use four main methods of assessment: observations, interviews, psychological tests and inventories, and neurological tests. Using several different assessment methods can provide a more accurate view of the client and increase diagnostic accuracy (Godoy & Haynes, 2011).

Observations

CASE STUDY [A] 9-year-old boy … was referred to a neurologist for treatment of "hysterical paralysis." … Medical tests indicated no apparent neurological damage. … He reported that his legs simply did not work no matter how he tried. As the child was describing his difficulties, we noted that he would shift his feet and legs in his wheelchair so his legs could swing freely. … When we asked him to describe his paralysis, he would look at his feet and … his leg movements would diminish. However, when we asked him to discuss other topics (e.g., school, friends), he would look up, become engaged in the interview, and his feet would swing. (O'Brien & Carhart, 2011, p. 14)

standardization the use of identical procedures in the administration of tests

standardization sample the comparison group on which test norms are based

psychological assessment the process of gathering information and drawing conclusions about the traits, skills, abilities, emotional functioning, and psychological problems of an individual

In the case of this 9-year-old boy, observations provided critically important information—he seemed to be able to move his legs under some circumstances. Both formal and informal behavioral observation can provide key information. Sometimes observations are highly structured and specific. For example, a school psychologist observing a child in a classroom may count episodes of off-task behavior and the circumstances under which off-task behaviors occur. On other occasions, observations may be less formal and exact, as when the school psychologist observes the child interacting with peers on the playground. Informal observations such as this tend to be more subjective (Szymkowicz, Finnegan, & Dale, 2013).

Mental health professionals informally observe behavior when they interview or work with clients. Often, behavioral clues have diagnostic significance. A client's mode of dress, scars or tattoos, and even choice of jewelry provide information about the client. Similarly, behavioral characteristics, such as posture, facial expression, and speech patterns, can provide important clues, as seen in the following case.

> **CASE STUDY**   Margaret was a 37-year-old woman seen by one of the authors for treatment of severe depression. It was obvious from a casual glance that Margaret had not taken care of herself for weeks. Her face, hands, and hair were dirty. Her beat-up tennis shoes were only halfway on her sockless feet. Her disheveled appearance and stooped body posture made her appear much older than she was.
>
> When first interviewed, Margaret sat as though she did not have the strength to straighten her body. She avoided eye contact and stared at the floor. When asked questions, she responded in short phrases: "Yes," "No," "I don't know," "I don't care." There were long pauses between the questions and her answers.

Although Margaret did not have the energy for much conversation, her lack of grooming and low energy levels helped confirm that she was in the midst of a deep depression.

Interviews

The clinical interview is a time-honored means of psychological assessment. During interviews, the mental health professional gets to know a client and learn his or her life history, current situation, and personality. Verbal and nonverbal behaviors, as well as the specific information shared, provide important clues to analyze. Therapists listen carefully to what clients are saying and look for evidence of emotions such as anxiety, hopelessness, frustration, or anger. Client interviews can also explore social and sociocultural factors that may affect mental health. For example, do issues such as religion, sexual orientation, age, gender, social class, or disability play a role in the difficulties a client is experiencing? The identification of client strengths is also important as it helps clients to understand that they have positive qualities and supportive relationships, thus creating hope and motivation (Scheel, Davis, & Henderson, 2013).

Interviews can vary in their degree of structure and formality. The most structured interview is the formal standardized interview, which often includes a standard series of questions or the use of standardized rating scales. Although structured interviews limit conversation and in-depth probing of responses, they have the advantage of collecting consistent and comprehensive information and are less subject to interviewers' biases (Kotwicki & Harvey, 2013).

Mental Status Examination

A widely used clinical procedure is the mental status examination. This examination uses questions, observations, and tasks to briefly evaluate a client's cognitive, psychological, and behavioral functioning (Goldberg, 2009). As the exam is administered, the clinician considers the appropriateness and quality of the client's responses (behaviors, speech, emotions, and intellectual functioning) and then attempts to render an initial, tentative opinion regarding diagnosis and treatment needs (Brannon & Bienenfeld, 2013). A mental status report on Margaret (described in the previous case study) might indicate the following:

* Appearance—Poor self-care in grooming; disheveled appearance; shoes halfway off her feet; stooped body posture; avoidance of eye contact.

Naturalistic versus Controlled Observations

Naturalistic observations are made in natural environments. Here, in the top photo, a researcher is taking notes while observing children at a playground—a natural setting for the children. In the photo on the bottom, another researcher is rating the behaviors observed as a mother and child interact in a clinic laboratory. What are the advantages and disadvantages of naturalistic versus controlled observations?

Bill Aron/Photo Edit

Spencer Grant/Photo Edit

- Mood—Appears severely depressed. Margaret verified that she has felt "depressed," "exhausted," "hopeless," and "worthless" for months.
- Affect—Margaret shows minimal emotional responsiveness. Her overall demeanor is suggestive of depression.
- Speech—Margaret speaks and responds slowly, with short replies. She frequently stated "I don't know" and "I don't care."
- Thought Process—Margaret's lack of responsiveness made it difficult to assess her thought processes. There was no evidence of racing or tangential thinking.
- Thought Content—Margaret denies experiencing hallucinations or delusions (false beliefs). She reports thinking about suicide almost daily but denies having a suicide plan or thoughts of hurting someone else. She reports constantly worrying about what others think of her, especially her coworkers.
- Memory—Margaret seems to have good recall of family background, past events, jobs, and educational background. However, she had difficulty with short-term memory—she was able to recall only one out of three words after a 5-minute delay.
- Abstract Thought—Margaret was slow to respond but was able to explain the proverbs "a rolling stone gathers no moss" and "people in glass houses should not throw stones."
- General Knowledge—Margaret was able to name the last four presidents but gave up before determining the number of nickels in $135, explaining that she "just can't concentrate."

The mental status examination is a useful diagnostic tool that helps clinicians assess areas that are not included in most clinical interviews. However, many aspects of the exam are subjective and one's cultural background can influence the assessment. As Goldberg (2009) points out, "there is a major distinction between 'different' and 'abnormal.' A 'failure' to provide a correct interpretation of a proverb, for example, may have nothing to do with an individual's intellectual function but rather may simply reflect a different upbringing or background. Similarly, tests of memory which require the subject to recite past presidents may not be an appropriate measuring tool depending on a person's country of origin, language skills, educational level, etc." (p. 3). A client's eye contact and body posture may also reflect cultural factors. Individuals from diverse cultural backgrounds may show patterns of eye contact, dress, and body postures that appear atypical, but are consistent with the client's culture and upbringing (Sue & Sue, 2008a).

Psychological Tests and Inventories

Psychological tests and inventories are standardized tools that measure characteristics such as personality, social skills, intellectual abilities, or vocational interests. Tests differ in structure, degree of objectivity, content, and method of delivery (for example, some tests are administered individually and others in groups). To illustrate some of the differences, we examine several types of personality measures (projective and self-report inventories), tests of intelligence and cognitive impairment, and neuropsychological and neurological assessment procedures.

Projective Personality Tests

projective personality test
testing involving responses to ambiguous stimuli, such as inkblots, pictures, or incomplete sentences

If you were to take a **projective personality test**, the examiner would present you with ambiguous stimuli, such as inkblots, pictures, or incomplete sentences, and ask you to respond to them in some way. The stimuli would be unfamiliar and you would be unaware of the true purpose of the test: to reveal attitudes, unconscious conflicts, and personality characteristics. Projective tests presumably tap into a person's unconscious needs and motivations (Meyer et al., 2003).

The Rorschach test, created by Swiss psychiatrist Hermann Rorschach, consists of 10 cards that display symmetrical inkblot designs. Inkblots are considered appropriate stimuli because they are ambiguous, nonthreatening, and unfamiliar so learned responses are unlikely. If you were taking the Rorschach test, the examiner would show you the cards one at a time and ask you to describe what you see in the blots. The examiner would then analyze your personality based on your responses, paying close attention to what you see in the blots, whether you attend to large areas or to details, whether you respond to color, and whether your perceptions suggest movement—all of these factors are assumed to be symbolic of inner promptings, motivations, and conflicts (Woods & Nashat, 2012).

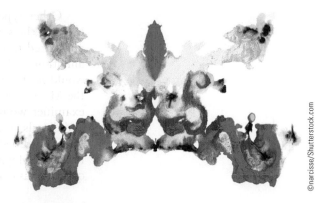
©narcisse/Shutterstock.com

The Rorschach Technique

Devised by Swiss psychiatrist Hermann Rorschach in 1921, the Rorschach technique uses a number of cards, each showing a symmetrical inkblot design similar to the one shown here. The earlier cards in the set are in black and white; the later cards are more colorful. A client's responses to the inkblots are interpreted according to assessment guidelines and can be compared with responses of individuals diagnosed with various disorders.

You may have correctly guessed that the Rorschach test and the interpretation of responses rely on psychoanalytic theory and an assumption that certain responses are associated with particular unconscious conflicts. For example, seeing eyes or buttocks may imply paranoid tendencies; seeing fierce animals may imply aggressive tendencies; seeing blood may imply strong uncontrolled emotions; and seeing food may imply dependency needs (Klopfer & Davidson, 1962). Although intriguing, research has found that interpretation of these "signs" is unreliable and highly subject to clinician bias. There are many questions about the validity and reliability of the Rorschach test and its utility in the assessment of mental disorders (Wood et al., 2010).

The Thematic Apperception Test (TAT), another projective personality test, was developed in 1935 (Murray & Morgan, 1938). It consists of 30 picture cards, most depicting two human figures. Their poses and actions are vague and ambiguous enough to be open to different interpretations. If you were to take the TAT, you would be shown 20 cards, one at a time, and the examiner would ask you to tell a story about what is going on in each picture, what led up to it, and what the outcome will be. As with the Rorschach technique, your responses to the TAT items would be analyzed to provide information about your personality and your unconscious conflicts, worries, or motives (Verdon, 2011).

Wikipedia and the Rorschach Test

In 2009, editors of the online encyclopedia Wikipedia decided to publish the entire set of Rorschach inkblot plates, the most common responses for each inkblot, and the characteristics each inkblot are purported to measure. One of the inkblots, for example, represents a "father figure"; responses to this card are supposed to reveal one's attitude toward males and authority figures.

Although the reliability and validity of the inkblot test is questionable, many clinicians still use this assessment tool. As Bruce Smith, president of the International Society of Rorschach and Projective Methods, states,

"The more test materials are promulgated widely, the more possibility there is to game the test" (Cohen, 2009, p. 1). In other words, knowing the typical answers may change the responses of individuals taking the test and invalidate the results.

In defense of their decision to publish the inkblot information, editors at Wikipedia argue that the Rorschach test is in the public domain because intellectual property rights have expired, and it does not have copyright protection. Did Wikipedia go too far in publishing the entire Rorschach inkblot test?

Other types of projective tests include sentence-completion and draw-a-person tests. In the *sentence-completion test*, you would be given a list of partial sentences and asked to complete each of them. You might see partial sentences such as "My ambition …," "My mother was always …," and "I can remember …" The examiner would try to interpret the meaning of your responses. In *draw-a-person tests*, such as the Machover D-A-P (Machover, 1949), you would be asked to draw a person. The examiner would analyze characteristics of your drawing, such as the size, position, and details you included, assuming that the drawings would provide clues about you. Well-controlled studies cast doubt on such diagnostic interpretations (Imuta, Scarf, Pharo, & Hayne, 2013). The validity of conclusions drawn from these tests is open to question, as can be seen in the following case.

CASE STUDY A 7-year-old girl was asked to draw a picture of her family doing something. She drew a picture of herself and her sister with their hands up in the air with the father standing next to them and smiling. The child told the psychologist that she and her sister were "cheering at a show" (Wakefield & Underwager, 1993, p. 55).

Instead of relying on the child's explanation of the picture, the psychologist focused on the "symbolism" inherent in the picture and her belief that the girls raising their hands in the air represented a sense of helplessness. Noting that the father's hands were large and asserting that sexually abused children often draw large hands on their perpetrators (this interpretation is not supported by research), she accused the father of sexually abusing the girl who had drawn the family picture. Even though the girl insisted no such acts had taken place, the psychologist argued that the girl needed protection to prevent further abuse.

As this case demonstrates, projective tests results do not meet reliability and validity standards, and therefore are subject to error and wide variation in interpretation. The low reliability, low validity, and limited cultural relevance of these instruments suggest that they should be used with caution and only in conjunction with other assessment measures (Butcher, 2010).

Self-Report Inventories

Self-report inventories are used to assess personality or other symptoms such as depression, anxiety, or emotional reactivity. Self-report inventories may involve the completion of open-ended questions or responding to a list of self-descriptive statements. For example, you might be asked to agree or disagree with a list of statements or to indicate the extent of your agreement with each statement. The inventory would be scored by comparing your responses to a standardization sample or to responses from individuals with specific mental disorders.

The *Minnesota Multiphasic Personality Inventory*, or *MMPI*, is the most widely used self-report personality inventory (Hathaway & McKinley, 1943). The updated version, the MMPI-2 (Butcher, 1990), consists of 567 statements; participants are asked to indicate whether each statement is true or false as it applies to them. The MMPI-2 scoring system rates the test-taker on 10 clinical scales, each measuring a specific psychological characteristic. The 10 scales were constructed by comparing the responses of diagnosed psychiatric patients with responses from participants not diagnosed with a mental condition; this allowed test developers to analyze response patterns associated with different psychiatric diagnoses. Interpreting the MMPI-2 scales is complicated and requires special training. Thus, it is a self-report inventory that should be used only by clinicians

The Thematic Apperception Test

In the Thematic Apperception Test, the person being assessed is asked to tell a story about each of a series of pictures. These pictures—often depicting one, two, or three people doing something—are less ambiguous than Rorschach inkblots.

Lewis J. Merrim / Science Source

who have mastered its intricacies, who understand relevant statistical concepts, and who can accurately interpret the client's responses (Graham, 2005).

Scales on the MMPI-2 can also measure factors that affect test score validity, including the person's degree of candor, confusion, or falsification; these validity scales help clinicians detect potential faking or symptom exaggeration (Groth-Marnat, 2009; Tolin, Steenkamp, Marx, & Litz, 2010). Although individuals can lower their psychopathology scores by trying to hide their symptoms on the MMPI (i.e., trying to fake being healthy when they are not), the MMPI scales alert clinicians to possible faking (Groth-Marnat, 2009). Interestingly, when researchers evaluated the validity scales by asking mental health professionals to complete the MMPI-2 and feign post-traumatic stress disorder (PTSD) symptoms, the validity scale accurately identified the overreporting of symptoms by the therapists (Goodwin, Sellbom, & Arbisi, 2013). Figure 3.1 shows the relationship between responses on 10 MMPI-2 items and its 10 clinical scales.

Unlike the MMPI-2, which assesses different personality characteristics, some self-report inventories or questionnaires focus only on certain personality traits or emotional problems, such as impulsivity, depression, or anxiety. For example, the *Beck Depression Inventory (BDI)* is composed of 21 items that measure various aspects of depression, such as mood, appetite, functioning at work, suicidal thinking, and sleeping patterns (Beck, Ward, Mendelson, Mock, & Erbaugh, 1961).

Though widely used, self-report inventories have limitations (Sollman, Ranseen, & Berry, 2010). First, the fixed number of answer choices can make it difficult for individuals to answer in a manner that clearly describes them. For example, if asked to answer "true" or "false" to the statement "I am suspicious of people," you would not have an opportunity to explain your answer. You might mark "yes" because you have had personal experiences to which suspiciousness is a logical reaction. Second, a person may have a unique response style or response set (i.e., a tendency to respond to test items in a certain way regardless of content) that may affect the test results. For example, if you have a tendency to present yourself in a favorable light (which many people do), your

CRITICAL THINKING

Should We Assess the Assessor?

A treatment team observing a clinical interview erupted in laughter when the foreign-born psychiatric resident attempted to find out what precipitated the client's problem. In poor and halting English, the resident asked, "How brought you to the hospital?" The patient responded, "I came by car" (Chambliss, 2000, p. 186). Later, during the case conference, the resident argued that the patient's response was a symptom of mental illness (concrete thinking), a quality that is sometimes displayed by people with schizophrenia. The rest of the treatment team, however, believed the response was due to a poorly worded question. Why was the resident unable to see that his questioning might have influenced the client's responses?

Researchers have found that errors in assessment due to attributes, beliefs, or personal values of the assessor can occur. For example, the biases or personal perspectives of mental health professionals have been found to influence IQ scores (McDermott, Watkins, & Rhoad, 2013), cross-cultural assessment results (Alcantara & Gone, 2014), and the diagnosis of attention-deficit/hyperactivity disorder (Bruchmüller, Margraf, & Schneider, 2012). In one study, 108 psychotherapists read an intake report regarding a male client whose sexual orientation (either heterosexual, gay, or bisexual) was revealed through a reference to his previous and present partners. While heterosexuality and gay sexual orientation had little impact on clinical ratings, the bisexual male was rated as more pathological even though all the information other than sexual orientation was the same. The researchers concluded that the difference was due to the stereotype of bisexual men being "confused and conflicted" (Mohr, Weiner, Chopp, & Wong, 2009). It is clear that the characteristics, attitudes, and beliefs of mental health professionals can influence the assessment process. Given this reality, should the assessor also be evaluated? And if so, how can this information result in more accurate assessments?

SAMPLE ITEMS

TEN MMPI CLINICAL SCALES WITH SIMPLIFIED DESCRIPTIONS	I like mechanics magazines.	I have a good appetite.	I wake up fresh and rested most mornings.	I think I would like the work of a librarian.	I am easily awakened by noise.	I like to read newspaper articles on crime.	My hands and feet are usually warm enough.	My daily life is full of things that keep me interested.	I am about as able to work as I ever was.	There seems to be a lump in my throat much of the time.
1. **Hypochondriasis (Hs)**—Individuals showing excessive worry about health with reports of obscure pains.		NO	NO				NO		NO	
2. **Depression (D)**—People suffering from chronic depression, feelings of uselessness, and inability to face the future.		NO		YES				NO	NO	
3. **Hysteria (Hy)**—Individuals who react to stress by developing physical symptoms (paralysis, cramps, headaches, etc.).		NO	NO			NO	NO	NO	NO	YES
4. **Psychopathic Deviate (Pd)**—People who show irresponsibility, disregard social conventions, and lack deep emotional responses.								NO		
5. **Masculinity-Femininity (Mf)**—People tending to identify with the opposite sex rather than their own.	NO			YES						
6. **Paranoia (Pa)**—People who are suspicious, sensitive, and feel persecuted.										
7. **Psychasthenia (Pt)**—People troubled with fears (phobias) and compulsive tendencies.			NO					NO		YES
8. **Schizophrenia (Sc)**—People with bizarre and unusual thoughts or behavior.								NO		
9. **Hypomania (Ma)**—People who are physically and mentally overactive and who shift rapidly in ideas and actions.										
10. **Social Introversion (Si)**—People who tend to withdraw from social contacts and responsibilities.										

Figure 3.1

The 10 MMPI-2 Clinical Scales and Sample MMPI-2 Tests

Shown here are the MMPI-2 clinical scales and a few of the items that appear on them. As an example, answering "no" or "false" (rather than "yes" or "true") to the item "I have a good appetite" would result in a higher scale score for hypochondriasis, depression, and hysteria. These sample questions do not pertain to some of the MMPI categories such as paranoia, hypomania, and social introversion.

SOURCE: Adapted from Dahlstrom & Welsh (1965). These items from the original MMPI remain unchanged in the MMPI-2.

answers might be socially acceptable but may not accurately reflect your mental state. Third, interpretations of responses of people from different cultural groups may be inaccurate if test norms for these groups are lacking (Knabb, Vogt, & Newgren, 2011). Fourth, cultural factors may shape the way a trait or characteristic is viewed. For example, although Asian Americans tend to score higher on measures of social anxiety, their scores may reflect cultural values of modesty and self-restraint rather than a sign of psychopathology; similarly, African Americans show a unique pattern of responding to measures of social anxiety (Melka, Lancaster, Adams, Howarth, & Rodriguez, 2010). Fifth, scores on inventories may not accurately reflect the client's perspective. For example, approximately half of a sample of 274 outpatients with major depressive disorder who showed "good" improvement according to the Hamilton Rating Scale for Depression (a questionnaire that measures the severity of depression) did not consider their symptoms to have lessened or resolved. As the researchers noted, the findings call into question the clinical usefulness of the scale, as well as the validity of studies that rely exclusively on questionnaire scores to document symptom improvement (Zimmerman et al., 2012). Despite these potential problems, self-report inventories are widely used. Many have been extensively researched and have excellent validity.

Intelligence Tests

Intelligence testing, intended to obtain an estimate of a person's current level of cognitive functioning, results in a score called the *intelligence quotient (IQ)*. An IQ score indicates an individual's level of performance relative to that of other people of the same age (see Figure 3.2). Through statistical procedures, IQ test results are converted into numbers, with 100 representing the mean, or average, score. An IQ score is an important aid in predicting school performance or detecting intellectual disability, a topic we discuss in Chapter 16.

The two most widely used intelligence tests are the Wechsler scales (Wechsler, 1981) and the Stanford-Binet scales (Terman & Merrill, 1960; Thorndike, Hagen, & Sattler, 1986). The *Wechsler Adult Intelligence Scale* (the *WAIS* and most recent version, *WAIS-IV*) is administered to persons age 16 and older. The WAIS-IV assesses four areas: Verbal Comprehension, Perceptual Organization, Working Memory, and Processing Speed (Saklofske, Hildebrand, & Gorsuch, 2000). The *Stanford-Binet Intelligence Scale*, now in its fifth edition, assesses intelligence in individuals ages 2 to 85. The Stanford-Binet is somewhat complicated to administer and score. If you were to take the Stanford-Binet, the examiner would first establish a basal age (the level where you pass all subtests) and a ceiling age (the level where you fail all subtests) as part of the process of calculating your IQ score. The Stanford-Binet is the standard to which other tests are compared because of its long history, careful revision, and periodic updating (Kline, 2005).

There are various critiques regarding the use of IQ tests. First, some psychologists believe that IQ tests largely reflect cultural and social factors rather than innate intelligence (Sternberg, 2005). The issue of racial differences in innate intelligence has a long history of debate. Publication of the controversial book *The Bell Curve* (Herrnstein & Murray, 1994) refocused attention on this issue when the book's authors proposed that racial differences in IQ scores are genetically determined; they further argued that there is little that can be done to overcome the social and status differences between racial groups because of these inherent IQ differences. More recently, Richwine (2009) made a similar claim about Hispanic immigrants, arguing that their IQ is "substantially lower than that of the white native populations" and that their children and grandchildren will continue to have low IQs. Assertions such as this fail to consider other important influences such as culture, poverty, discrimination, and oppression.

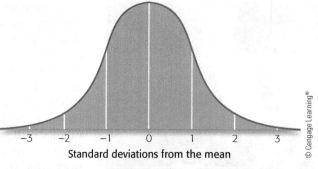

Standard deviations from the mean

© Cengage Learning®

Figure 3.2

A Bell Curve Showing Standard Deviations

The bell curve refers to the bell-shaped distribution of IQ scores in a population, with most scores hovering over the mean and fewer scores falling in the outlying areas of the distribution. IQ scores are transformed so that the mean equals 100, and deviations from the mean are expressed in terms of standard deviations. One standard deviation from the mean (about 15 IQ points above or below the mean, or IQ scores between 85 and 115) represents about 68 percent of the scores. Two standard deviations (about 30 IQ points above or below the mean, or IQs between 70 and 130) account for more than 95 percent of the scores.

A number of researchers have proposed that intelligence is a multidimensional attribute not adequately assessed by most IQ tests. For example, Sternberg (2004) describes intelligence as involving analytical proficiency (capacity to analyze and evaluate ideas, solve problems, and make decisions), creativity (ability to generate novel and interesting ideas), and practical skills (ability to meet the demands of the environment), characteristics not assessed by the most commonly used tests of intelligence. Others also argue that the assumption that IQ tests measure innate intelligence is false (e.g., Nisbett, 2005; Suzuki & Aronson, 2005). They also question the predictive validity of IQ tests, pointing out that IQ test scores do not accurately predict future behaviors or achievement. Many believe that characteristics such as motivation and work ethic are much better predictors of future success.

Tests for Cognitive Impairment

Clinical psychologists, especially those working in hospital settings, are concerned with detecting and assessing cognitive impairment resulting from brain damage, a topic we address in our discussion of neurocognitive disorders in Chapter 13. Brain dysfunction can have profound effects on both physical skills, such as motor coordination, and cognitive skills, such as memory, attention, and learning (Grant & Adams, 2009). A common method of screening for cognitive impairment is the *Bender-Gestalt Visual-Motor Test* (Bender, 1938; Brannigan, Decker, & Madsen, 2004), shown in Figure 3.3. Nine geometric designs, each drawn in black on a piece of white cardboard, are presented one at a time to the test taker, who is asked to copy them on a piece of paper. Certain drawing errors are characteristic of neurological impairment. Among these are rotation of figures, perseveration (unusual continuation of a pattern), and inability to copy angles.

Comprehensive neuropsychological tests are also used to assess cognitive impairment. In fact, they are far more accurate in documenting cognitive deficits than are interviews or informal observations (Malik, 2013). For example, the *Halstead-Reitan Neuropsychological Test Battery* successfully differentiates patients with brain damage from those without brain damage and can provide valuable information about the type and location of the damage (Goldstein & Beers, 2004). The full battery consists of 11 tests, which feature a series of tasks that assess sensorimotor, cognitive, and perceptual functioning, including abstract concept formation, memory and attention,

Testing for Intellectual Functioning

Intelligence tests can provide valuable information about intellectual functioning and can help psychologists assess intellectual disability and intellectual deterioration. Although these tests have been criticized for being culturally biased, if used with care, they can be beneficial tools. Here, a 3-year-old child is shown taking the Stanford-Binet test. The Stanford-Binet Intelligence Scale is a standardized test that assesses cognitive abilities in children and adults ages 2 to 85.

Figure 3.3

The Nine Bender Designs

The figures presented to participants are shown on the left. The distorted figures drawn by an individual with suspected brain damage are shown on the right.

SOURCE: Bender (1938).

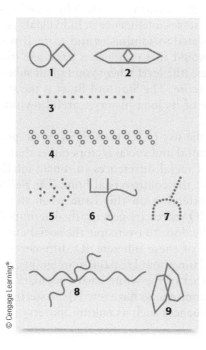
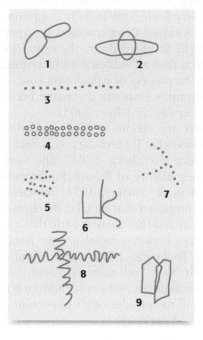

and auditory perception. The full battery takes more than 6 hours to administer, so it is an expensive and time-consuming assessment tool.

Neurological Tests

Various neurological tests are used to research and diagnose impairment associated with psychiatric and neurocognitive disorders. Neuroimaging techniques allow medical professionals and researchers to noninvasively visualize brain structures (**structural imaging**), as well as monitor the physiological processes occurring within the brain (**functional imaging**). We begin by discussing structural imaging procedures (see Table 3.1); the anatomical views of the brain obtained through these procedures can help detect skull fractures, brain tumors, bleeding within the brain, or significant changes in brain tissue associated with substance abuse and disorders such as schizophrenia, depression, and Alzheimer's disease.

A well-known and widely available structural imaging procedure is the computerized axial tomography (CT) scan. CT scans are three-dimensional, cross-sectional brain structure images generated by combining multiple X-rays. Although CT scans are useful for diagnosis, the radiation exposure may increase cancer risk, especially in children; children exposed to multiple CT scans have triple the risk of developing leukemia or brain cancer, so efforts are made to keep radiation doses as low as possible (Pearce et al., 2012).

Magnetic resonance imaging (MRI) is another structural imaging procedure. Radio waves within a magnetic field create images by scanning one layer at a time to produce an amazingly clear cross-sectional "picture" of the brain and its tissues; these images look remarkably similar to postmortem brain slices. Unlike CT scans, MRIs do not involve radiation exposure and cancer risk (Zondervan, Hahn, Sadow, Liu, & Lee, 2013). MRIs provide highly detailed pictures, but are more expensive and less widely available than CT scans.

Functional imaging methods (see Table 3.2) allow doctors and researchers to study physiological and biochemical processes in the brain. One of the most basic functional techniques is the *electroencephalograph (EEG)*. During an EEG, electrodes attached to the scalp record electrical activity (brain wave patterns); an EEG can detect even brief episodes of irregular electrical activity associated with seizures or other brain conditions. A newer procedure, *magnetoencephalography (MEG)*, uses electrodes within a helmet to measure electrical activity in the magnetic field close to the surface of the brain; the MEG process is even more precise in localizing brain dysfunction. Unfortunately, these techniques do not measure electrical activity occurring deep within the brain.

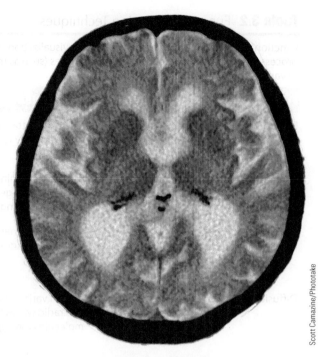

Scott Camazine/Phototake

CT Scan Showing Brain Atrophy

Cerebral CT scans, which involve multiple, cross-sectional X-rays of the brain, are able to document changes in brain tissue and brain structures. This CT scan of the brain of a 94-year-old woman shows enlarged ventricles and atrophy indicative of a loss of neurons in some brain regions.

structural imaging procedures that allow for visualization of brain anatomy

functional imaging procedures that provide data regarding physiological and biochemical processes occurring within the brain

Table 3.1 Structural Imaging Techniques

Structural imaging techniques allow noninvasive study of major brain structures and the detection of injury or disease, including skull fractures, brain tumors, bleeding within the brain, and changes in brain tissue associated with substance abuse and many mental disorders.

Structural Imaging Technique	Description	What Is Detected?
Computerized axial tomography (CT)	Uses multiple cross-sectional X-rays to rapidly produce brain images	Brain deterioration or major abnormality, including swelling, bleeding, skull fractures, or tumors
Magnetic resonance imaging (MRI)	Uses a constant magnetic field and radio waves to produce detailed images of the brain and its tissues	White matter and gray matter abnormalities seen in many psychiatric disorders

Table 3.2 Functional Imaging Techniques

Functional imaging techniques allow for direct visualization of brain activation patterns, including the physiological and biochemical processes associated with specific mental activities (such as thinking, feeling, or reacting to visual, auditory, or tactile stimuli) and symptoms of various mental disorders.

Functional Imaging Techniques	Description	What Is Detected?
Electroencephalograph (EEG)	Electrodes attached to the scalp detect electrical activity from neurons firing in the cortex	Confirms coma or brain death; detects seizures
Magnetoencephalography (MEG)	Electrodes within a helmet measure the magnetic field generated from electrical activity occurring close to the brain's surface	Provides even more precise localization and measurement of surface electrical activity than the EEG
Functional magnetic resonance imaging (fMRI)	Constant magnetic field and radio waves measure changes in blood flow and oxygenation	Can detect location and patterns of brain activation associated with different mental processes and reduced blood flow associated with clots
Diffusion tensor imaging (DTI)	An MRI variation that uses a magnetic field and radio waves to track diffusion of water molecules throughout the brain	Provides data regarding axons, nerve fibers, and connections, including how white matter injury relates to cognitive or motor symptoms
Positron emission tomography (PET)	Nuclear imaging technique using computer monitoring of a radioactive tracer injected into the bloodstream	Can detect neuronal damage and neurochemical changes, including gene expression and activity of some neurotransmitters, as well as other brain activity
Single photon emission computed tomography (SPECT)	Less expensive and less detailed nuclear imaging technique	Provides basic information about metabolism and blood flow for a longer time period than a PET scan

© Cengage Learning®

Other forms of functional imaging can measure metabolic processes on the brain's surface and much deeper. Rather than a static image of the brain's anatomy, it is possible to see the brain in action. In fact, functional imaging shows which brain regions are active during the resting state and the changes that occur during various mental activities or emotional states. For example, nuclear imaging procedures such as *positron emission tomography (PET)* reveal brain processes using small quantities of radioactive substances and special cameras that detect radioactivity. If you were to have a PET scan, you would be given an intravenous injection of glucose (sugar) combined with a radioactive (positron-emitting) tracer; the scanner then follows the tracer to see how your brain is metabolizing the glucose. Brain activity and subtle metabolic changes measured during PET imaging can indicate active disease or malignant tumors. Researchers also use PET scans to compare the outcomes of psychotherapy and medications by observing brain activity changes in regions of the brain associated with the disorder being treated (McGrath et al., 2013).

Although most neuroimaging techniques cannot show biochemical changes occurring within the brain, the radioactive tracers used in PET provide unique information regarding the release, uptake, and transport of neurotransmitters (Badgaiyan, 2011) and gene expression (Potter et al., 2013). Unfortunately, the tracers used in PET technology are short-lived, requiring close proximity to expensive generators (cyclotrons) equipped to produce radioactive substances. *Single photon emission computed tomography (SPECT)* imaging is a less expensive nuclear imaging technique that uses a longer-lived radioactive substance to produce images of metabolic activity and blood flow similar to those obtained through PET scans, but with less detail.

PET Scan

As can be seen in these PET scans comparing brain activity between someone with normal brain functioning (left) and someone with neurological dysfunction in which brain activity is significantly reduced (right).

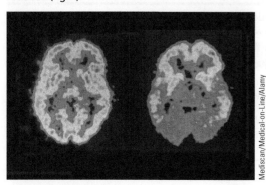

Mediscan/Medical-on-Line/Alamy

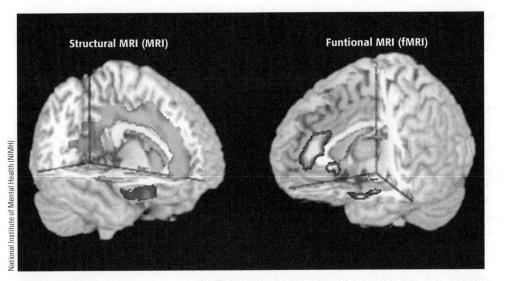

Structural MRI (MRI)   Funtional MRI (fMRI)

National Institute of Mental Health (NIMH)

AP Images/picture-alliance/dpa/Klaus Rose

MRI and EEG

These structural MRI (left) and functional MRI (right) scans reveal abnormalities in the brain regions associated with regulating impulses (blue area in the front part of the brain at the left and corresponding yellow area in brain at the right). The woman to the right is undergoing an electroencephalograph (EEG). Electrodes placed on her skull are measuring and recording her brainwaves.

Functional magnetic resonance imaging (fMRI) provides images of brain structures combined with physiological activity in different brain regions. It is a newer, noninvasive procedure that does not involve radioactivity. fMRI reveals brain activity, such as where blood is flowing and which nerve cells are actively using oxygen. Another variation of MRI technology is *diffusion tensor imaging (DTI)*, which tracks the diffusion (movement) of water molecules throughout the brain; this imaging provides pictures of axons and the networks of nerve fibers that connect different brain areas (white matter).

These techniques, either individually or in combination, allow the study of brain abnormalities and distinct metabolic patterns of people diagnosed with a mental disorder. Each of the neuroimaging techniques has strengths and weaknesses in terms of costs, benefits, and possible side effects. Evaluating the risks and benefits helps determine which tools to use for research, diagnosis, treatment, and monitoring of disease progression. Because of these techniques, our knowledge of brain structure and function associated with schizophrenia, depression, bipolar disorder, Alzheimer's disease, and substance abuse has increased significantly. Combining these procedures with other assessments helps us learn even more about how physiological processes relate to psychological processes. Some researchers predict that these techniques will eventually allow clinicians to make more rapid and more specific diagnoses, and provide information that helps guide treatment.

Diagnosing Mental Disorders

After gathering assessment data, clinicians formulate diagnoses using a psychiatric classification system. A classification system for abnormal behaviors aims to provide distinct categories and indicators for atypical behaviors, thought processes, and emotional disturbances. Psychiatric classification systems are like a catalog: a detailed description accompanies each mental disorder. Thus, the pattern of behavior associated with each diagnosis is distinctly different. For example, the symptoms associated with social phobia are different from the symptoms that define obsessive-compulsive disorder (APA, 2013). At the same time, each category also accommodates symptom variations. For example, the exact symptoms, symptom severity, and length of depressive episodes vary among people diagnosed with major depressive disorder.

The Diagnostic and Statistical Manual of Mental Disorders

The *Diagnostic and Statistical Manual of Mental Disorders* (DSM) is a widely used classification system for psychiatric disorders. The DSM lists all officially designated mental disorders and the characteristics or symptoms needed to confirm a diagnosis. Diagnostic criteria include physical, behavioral, and emotional characteristics associated with a disorder. For all disorders, the symptoms must cause significant distress or impairment in social, occupational, or other important areas of functioning (APA, 2013). The DSM affects consumers, health care providers, insurance companies, and the pharmaceutical industry. The most recent revision of the diagnostic manual, DSM-5 (APA, 2013), is touted as an improvement over previous editions of the manual. However, it is not without its own set of controversies.

Although the DSM is widely used in the United States, another important classification system is the International Classification of Disease (ICD). This system covers all health conditions, including mental disorders. The World Health Organization oversees the system. In recent years, the DSM diagnostic definitions have more closely resembled the ICD classification of mental disorders; however, there are significant differences between the two diagnostic systems.

All of the DSMs are based on the classification system Emil Kraepelin developed around 1850. Kraepelin believed that mental disorders were like physical disorders, each with a specific set of symptoms. Thus, the DSM has traditionally been a categorical system, listing disorders and the various characteristics, course, and outcome associated with each. Like physical disorders, the diagnostic process involves deciding whether a person has a particular disorder (Shorter, 2010). The process of diagnosing mental disorders, however, is complex because disorders often have overlapping symptoms, making it difficult to distinguish one from another. For example, depressive and anxiety disorders share some of the same symptoms and have common neurobiological underpinnings and responsiveness to antidepressant medications (Nasrallah, 2009).

To add to the complexity, the number of identified psychological disorders has increased dramatically over time. In 1840, the U.S. census had only two categories of mental disorders—idiocy or insanity (Cloud, 2010). Since then, the number of disorders acknowledged by the American Psychiatric Association, the organization that publishes the DSM, has increased:

- DSM, 1952: 106 mental disorders
- DSM-II, 1968: 182 mental disorders
- DSM-III, 1980: 265 mental disorders
- DSM-III-R: 292 mental disorders
- DSM-IV, 1994: 297 mental disorders

DSM-5, published in May 2013, did not significantly increase the number of diagnostic categories, although some new disorders were added and there were changes in some diagnostic criteria. Table 3.3 lists the DSM-5 categories of mental disorders, most of which are discussed in this book. Each new edition of the DSM has attempted to correct or refine problems in previous editions and improve reliability and validity.

The process involved in testing the reliability and validity of recent editions of the DSM has involved having two clinicians independently interview and formulate diagnoses for the same client, based on DSM criteria. Agreement between the clinicians

Table 3.3 DSM-5 Disorders

Categories of Disorders	Features
Neurodevelopmental Disorders	Cognitive, learning, and language disabilities evident early in life
Neurocognitive Disorders	Psychological or behavioral abnormalities associated with dysfunction of the brain
Substance-Related and Addictive Disorders	Excessive use of alcohol, illicit drugs, or prescription medications that results in impaired functioning; behavioral addictions such as gambling
Schizophrenia Spectrum and Other Psychotic Disorders	Disorders marked by severe impairment in thinking and perception; often involving delusions, hallucinations, and inappropriate affect
Bipolar and Related Disorders	Disorders characterized by episodes of mania or hypomania, alternating with periods of normal and/or depressed mood
Depressive Disorders	Disorders involve feelings of sadness, emptiness, and social withdrawal
Anxiety Disorders	Disorders characterized by excessive or irrational anxiety or fear, often accompanied by avoidance behaviors and fearful cognitions or worry
Obsessive-Compulsive and Related Disorders	Disorders characterized by obsessions (recurrent thoughts) and/or compulsions (repetitive behaviors) and other compulsive behavior such as hoarding
Trauma and Stressor-Related Disorders	Disorders associated with chronic or acute reactions to trauma and stress
Somatic Symptom and Related Disorders	Disorders involving physical symptoms that cause distress and disability, including high levels of health anxiety and disproportionate concern over bodily dysfunctions
Dissociative Disorders	Disturbance or alteration in memory, identity, or consciousness, including amnesia, having two or more distinct personalities, or experiencing feelings of depersonalization
Sexual Dysfunctions	Disorders involving the disruption of any stage of a normal sexual response cycle, including desire, arousal, or orgasm
Gender Dysphoria	Significant distress associated with conflict between biological sex and gender assigned at birth
Paraphilic Disorders	Recurrent, intense sexual fantasies or urges involving nonhuman objects, pain, humiliation, or children
Eating Disorders	Disturbed eating patterns and body dissatisfaction, involving bingeing, purging, and excessive dieting
Sleep-Wake Disorders	Problems in initiating/maintaining sleep, excessive sleepiness, sleep disruptions, sleepwalking, or repeated awakening associated with nightmares
Personality Disorders	Disorders involving stable personality traits that are inflexible and maladaptive and notably impair functioning or cause subjective distress

© Cengage Learning®

(interrater reliability) and data regarding the frequency of a diagnosis is then measured. Early studies of the DSM found poor agreement (poor interrater reliability) between clinicians making diagnoses based on the same information; one clinician reviewing case information on an individual might diagnose an anxiety disorder, whereas another clinician reviewing the same information might diagnose depression. Although the reliability and validity of many of the DSM diagnoses have been problematic over the years, they improved with each successive edition, with the exception of the newest DSM. With the DSM-5, some, but not all, diagnostic categories have good validity and reliability (see Figure 3.4). What is especially problematic is the "questionable" reliability of some of the most common diagnoses—major depressive disorder and generalized anxiety disorder, both of which rated lower than the reliability of these categories in the two previous DSM editions (Stetka, Christoph, & Correll, 2013).

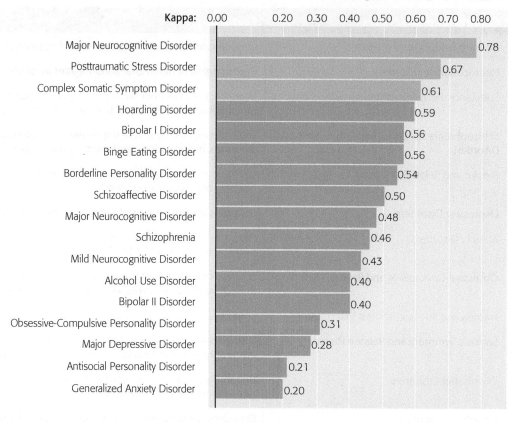

Adult Diagnoses

Kappa: 0.00   0.20   0.30   0.40   0.50   0.60   0.70   0.80

Disorder	Kappa
Major Neurocognitive Disorder	0.78
Posttraumatic Stress Disorder	0.67
Complex Somatic Symptom Disorder	0.61
Hoarding Disorder	0.59
Bipolar I Disorder	0.56
Binge Eating Disorder	0.56
Borderline Personality Disorder	0.54
Schizoaffective Disorder	0.50
Major Neurocognitive Disorder	0.48
Schizophrenia	0.46
Mild Neurocognitive Disorder	0.43
Alcohol Use Disorder	0.40
Bipolar II Disorder	0.40
Obsessive-Compulsive Personality Disorder	0.31
Major Depressive Disorder	0.28
Antisocial Personality Disorder	0.21
Generalized Anxiety Disorder	0.20

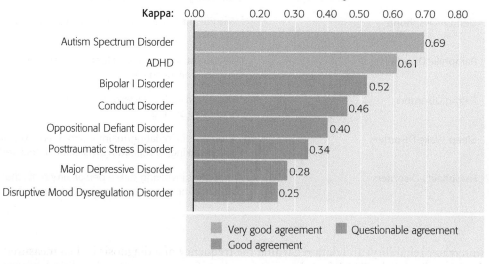

Child Diagnoses

Kappa: 0.00   0.20   0.30   0.40   0.50   0.60   0.70   0.80

Disorder	Kappa
Autism Spectrum Disorder	0.69
ADHD	0.61
Bipolar I Disorder	0.52
Conduct Disorder	0.46
Oppositional Defiant Disorder	0.40
Posttraumatic Stress Disorder	0.34
Major Depressive Disorder	0.28
Disruptive Mood Dysregulation Disorder	0.25

Very good agreement ■ Questionable agreement
■ Good agreement

Figure 3.4

Interrater Reliability of DSM-5 Diagnostic Categories
During the DSM-5 field trials, individuals undergoing diagnostic evaluation were assessed by two clinicians; each clinician interviewed the person and made a diagnosis. Kappa scores from the field trials (which take into account diagnostic agreement between clinicians and data regarding the frequency of a diagnosis) varied significantly for both adult and child/adolescent diagnostic categories.
Modified from Freedman et al. (2013).

Dimensional Perspective

The DSM-5 is a categorical model—it provides a category or label for each disorder. Some mental health professionals believe that a categorical model is ineffective for diagnosis. This opinion prompted much discussion among the work group members involved in revising the DSM; the discussion centered on the possibility of changing the DSM to a dimensional classification system. In a dimensional model of mental disorders, disorders reside on a continuum with "normality" appearing at one end of the continuum and severe forms of a disorder at the opposite end. From a dimensional perspective, anxiety, depression, and even psychotic-like experiences would not constitute an "either/or" phenomenon; instead, clinicians would rate the degree to which a person demonstrates characteristics of a particular condition (Pincus, 2011). The final decision of the work groups, however, was for DSM-5 to remain a categorical system with only a few exceptions. These exceptions included the following:

1. Replacing the different autism categories (each with distinct diagnostic characteristics) with one disorder called "autism spectrum disorder," and adding an alternative dimensional model for the diagnosis of personality disorders.

2. Adding "risk syndromes," which includes a few disorders (such as mild neurocognitive disorder) that represent milder forms of well-established disorders.

3. Enhancing assessment procedures to permit more than a simple "yes-or-no" option. For example, the DSM-5 uses subtypes, specifiers, disorder-specific severity measures, and cross-cutting assessments that allow mental health professionals to make finer distinctions within a diagnosis.

Subtypes are distinctly different subgroups within a diagnostic category. Only one subtype can apply to each diagnostic category. Therefore, the clinician making the diagnosis decides which subtype most closely fits the person's symptoms. Anorexia nervosa, for instance, includes two subtypes: a restricting type and a binge-eating/purging type.

Specifiers allow clinicians to indicate whether a person has certain characteristics associated with a diagnostic category. Specifiers are not mutually exclusive, so people can have multiple specifiers associated with a diagnosis. With major depressive disorder, for example, there are 12 possible specifiers, including "anxious distress," "melancholic features," and "seasonal pattern of depression." The DSM-5 also includes a dimensional rating scale with criteria to help clinicians specify the severity of symptoms associated with the diagnosis as mild, moderate, or severe. Specifiers also allow clinicians to indicate if a disorder is in full or partial **remission** or if someone had early or late onset of a disorder, a factor that affects **prognosis** (likely outcome) with some disorders.

The DSM-5 also includes client-rated and clinician-rated symptom measures called **cross-cutting measures** that "cut across" diagnostic boundaries. These measures highlight symptoms beyond those associated with a diagnosed disorder. There is a brief screening questionnaire involving various symptoms that are frequently seen in individuals coping with a mental disorder and a follow-up questionnaire that can be used to further assess areas that emerge as a possible concern. These questionnaires identify and address key symptoms that may affect prognosis and treatment. Additionally, they help clinicians track the severity of symptoms and monitor changes throughout treatment. They also help clinicians determine if a person has a **comorbid** disorder. **Comorbidity** refers to the presence of two or more disorders in the same person.

Clinicians assess and diagnose. They also identify other factors that may affect the **course**, prognosis, or treatment for the disorder. For example, therapists consider the causes of diagnosed disorders to help plan treatment. The DSM-5, therefore, includes a focus on "other conditions that may be a focus of clinical attention." Let's look at an example of a comprehensive diagnostic evaluation based on the DSM-5.

subtype mutually exclusive subgrouping within a diagnosis

specifier specific features associated with a diagnostic category

remission a diminution in the seriousness of an illness

prognosis prediction of the probable outcome of a disorder, including the chances of full recovery

cross-cutting measure assesses common symptoms that are not specific to one disorder

comorbid the presence of two or more disorders in the same person

comorbidity co-occurrence of different disorders

course usual pattern that a disorder follows

CASE STUDY   Mark is a 50-year-old machine operator referred for treatment by his work supervisor due to concerns about his frequent absenteeism and difficulty getting along with others. Coworkers complain that Mark distrusts others and overreacts with anger to any perceived criticism. The supervisor suspects that Mark drinks alcohol during work hours. The supervisor is unaware that Mark recently received a diagnosis of cirrhosis of the liver due to his heavy drinking. In his assessment interview, Mark acknowledged that he consumes a large quantity of alcohol daily. He also shared that his wife recently left him, claiming she could no longer tolerate his drinking, his withdrawal, his extreme jealousy, and his accusations of infidelity. Mark indicated he has no close friends although he does hang out with "regulars" at a local bar.

During interviews with the therapist, Mark revealed that he began drinking in his early teens to help him "get through the day." He admitted drinking on the job, but claimed it was "no big deal." He blames others for his drinking problems. He eventually shared that his father is an alcoholic who physically and verbally abused Mark and his siblings. Mark believes that his mother has stayed with his father only because of the family's Catholic religion.

Mark's pattern of heavy alcohol use is clearly interfering with his social and occupational functioning, and he continues drinking despite the loss of his marriage and risk of losing his job. This pattern is consistent with a diagnosis of alcohol use disorder with severe symptoms. Mark's distrust, suspiciousness, and hostility toward others has interfered with relationships since childhood and suggests a comorbid paranoid personality disorder.

Upon completing the DSM-5 cross-cutting screening measure, Mark's therapist noted problems with depression, sleep, memory, and excessive use of prescription medications as additional concerns. Further assessment revealed that Mark met the diagnostic criteria for a major depressive disorder with mild severity. His depressive symptoms have been evident since childhood and preceded his alcohol use. Assessments conducted by the therapist also revealed that Mark has some mild cognitive deficits, presumably resulting from his heavy alcohol consumption. Cirrhosis of the liver is a significant medical condition. The clinician noted Mark's pending divorce, work difficulties, and poor relationships with coworkers when assessing psychosocial functioning. Mark's treatment plan focused on specific needs noted during the assessment.

Mark's diagnosis:

- Alcohol use disorder; with a specifier of "severe"
- Paranoid personality disorder
- Major depressive disorder; with a specifier of "mild"
- Physical disorder: cirrhosis of the liver
- Causal or other factors

    1. *Biological/genetic*—There is a family history of alcohol abuse. The early onset of Mark's heavy drinking may be related to genetic vulnerability to alcohol abuse or depression.

    2. *Environmental*—Mark is in jeopardy of losing his job and is facing financial stress due to his upcoming divorce.

    3. *Developmental*—Mark's father exhibited paranoia and drank heavily. Mark endured physical and psychological abuse throughout childhood. Mark began drinking in early adolescence to cope with feelings of worthlessness; early substance use appears to have affected emotional maturation and social development.

4. *Social*—There is limited family support. Mark's wife is seeking a divorce. Mark has very few friends other than a few "drinking buddies."

5. *Cultural*—Mark is very concerned about family reactions to his upcoming divorce due to his Catholic upbringing.

6. *Behavioral*—Mark tends to blame others and reacts with anger to perceived criticism. Mark has a strong tendency to be suspicious of others, a characteristic that has consistently interfered with social relationships. Mark has a long history of withdrawing and using alcohol to cope at home and at work.

Mark also completed the *World Health Organization Disability Schedule*—an instrument used to assess overall level of impairment and disability. His total score of 72 suggests moderately severe impairment; he has severe problems getting along with other people, understanding and communicating and participating in society, and mild to moderate disability in getting around, self-care, and life activities. The therapist will use all of the information obtained from Mark's diagnostic assessment to develop a plan of treatment.

Cultural Factors in Assessment

CASE STUDY   David Henderson, an associate professor of psychiatry at Harvard Medical School, worked as a psychiatrist in Cambodia. While working in Cambodia, he found that every patient he interviewed reported hearing voices. He wondered why so many Cambodians had this symptom. When he later asked his Cambodian colleagues whether they had ever heard voices, they all answered affirmatively and observed, "it looks as if Dr. Henderson is the only one among us who has not been in touch with his ancestors" (Treichel, 2011).

Dr. Henderson's story is an excellent example of how our culture affects our worldview, including our view of psychological "symptoms." Determining whether or not a behavior is consistent with cultural norms or evidence of mental illness requires the clinician to understand a client's cultural background. Culture not only affects diagnosis, but also influences a person's willingness to seek help; it can also affect treatment variables such as how medication is metabolized (Bender, 2013). Unfortunately, mental health assessment, diagnosis, and treatment often fail to adequately consider racial or cultural factors (Carter et al., 2013). This is a serious problem since ethnic minorities constitute 37 percent of the U.S. population (U.S. Census Bureau, 2012). Advocates for cultural competence say that both clinicians and clients are unwilling to acknowledge that race might matter. Francis Lu, a psychiatrist at the University of California at San Francisco, summarizes the concern: "Bias is a very real issue, but we don't talk about it … We see ourselves as unbiased and rational and scientific" (Vedantam, 2005, p. 1).

The DSM-5 affirms that cultural factors can influence a person's symptoms and thus encourages consideration of cultural influences when making a diagnosis. To support increased consideration of culture, the DSM-5 includes culture-related and gender-related diagnostic issues along with the diagnostic characteristics for each disorder. Additionally, to improve the assessment and diagnosis of mental disorders among ethnic and cultural minorities, DSM-5 includes a list of topics to explore with culturally diverse clients. This list includes factors such as the degree to which they identify with their racial or ethnic background, the presence of acculturation conflicts or stressors within their social network, and whether factors such as race, ethnicity, or experiences of racism or discrimination might hamper the therapeutic relationship or influence interactions during assessment and treatment.

DID YOU KNOW?

Ethnic minorities are now the majority in four states and in the District of Columbia.

Hawaii	77.1 percent
DC	64.7 percent
California	60.3 percent
New Mexico	59.8 percent
Texas	55.2 percent

It is not surprising that the DSM-5 has devoted more attention to racial and ethnic diversity.

SOURCE: U.S. Census Bureau, 2012

DSM-5 also includes an in-depth guide for conducting a cultural assessment interview that includes 16 questions to help determine the possible impact of culture on a client's symptoms. Here are some sample questions:

- "What do you think is causing your problem?" This helps the therapist to understand the client's perception of the factors involved, including interpersonal, social, and cultural influences.

- "Why is this happening to you?" This question taps into the issue of causality and possible spiritual or cultural explanations for the problem.

- "What have you done to cope with or treat this condition?" This can lead to a discussion of previous interventions, the possible use of home remedies, and the client's evaluation of the usefulness of these treatments.

- "Your cultural identity or background can be a source of strength or can contribute to problems. How is it affecting your problem?" The client can discuss the positive aspects of cultural identity and the effects of factors such as discrimination and acculturation conflicts.

- "How has this condition affected your life?" This question helps identify individual, interpersonal, health, and social issues related to the concern.

In addition, there are questions regarding current stressors and supports, the role of cultural identity, and perceived barriers to seeking help. This new focus on cultural assessment in the DSM-5 has met with approval from many scholars and therapists involved with ethnic minorities and cultural groups (Bender, 2013).

Evaluation of the DSM-5 Classification System

The DSM-5 has received criticism regarding its construction, dimensional focus, changes in diagnostic criteria for disorders, and the addition of new disorders. Although the total number of disorders is similar to those in the previous edition of the DSM, some believe that the changes in the criteria for some disorders will allow a greater number of individuals to receive diagnoses. Along with the lower reliability for many diagnostic categories compared to previous DSM editions, other concerns include the following:

1. Viewing mental disorders more broadly or on a continuum may have the unexpected consequence of pushing diagnostic boundaries to encompass people with less severe symptoms (Frances, 2013).

2. Criteria for certain disorders, such as alcohol use disorder, have changed and may increase the number of individuals receiving a diagnosis. In one study assessing regular drinkers, the use of the DSM-5 criteria for alcohol use disorder resulted in a 61.7 percent increase in prevalence when compared to use of the DSM-IV criteria (Mewton, Slade, McBride, Grove, & Teesson, 2011).

3. Concern that decisions regarding the DSM-5 diagnostic categories were unduly influenced by outside pressure. For example, 70 percent of the professionals who developed the DSM-5 had direct ties to pharmaceutical companies. This raises the concern that there may have been subtle pressure to broaden diagnostic categories thereby increasing access to medication as a form of treatment (Cosgrove & Krimsky, 2012; Miller & Prosek, 2012).

4. Addictive disorders now include gambling disorder, which opens the possibility that other "behavioral addictions" (Internet, video games, shopping, or eating) may eventually be included in this category. Some believe such diagnostic expansion amounts to medicalizing behavioral problems (Frances, 2009).

5. Bereavement was removed as an exclusionary criteria when diagnosing depression; individuals who have severe depressive symptoms after the death of a loved one can now receive a diagnosis of major depressive disorder. This revision has been criticized as pathologizing the normal human process of grieving (Stetka et al., 2013; Wakefield, 2013).

Differential Diagnosis: The Case of Charlie Sheen

During the first week of March 2011, actor Charlie Sheen appeared on numerous television and radio shows. He appeared energized and made exaggerated gestures while claiming that he had "tiger blood" with "Adonis DNA." He referred to people that he disagreed with as "trolls," among other terms (Gardner, 2011). Some of the statements he made in the media included the following (Boudreault, 2011):

- "I am on a drug, it's called Charlie Sheen. It's not available, 'cause if you try it once, you will die. Your face will melt off and your children will weep over your exploded body."

- "I'm tired of pretending like I'm not special. I'm tired of pretending like I'm not bitchin', a total frickin' star from Mars."

- "I have cleansed myself. I closed my eyes and in a nanosecond, I cured myself. . . . The only thing I'm addicted to is winning."

- "[Regular guys] lay down with their ugly wives in front of their ugly children and just look at their loser lives and then they look at me and they say, 'I can't process it!' Well, no, and you never will . . ."

What additional information would a therapist need to determine if Sheen has a mental disorder or is simply an angry celebrity spouting off? A mental health professional conducting an assessment might hypothesize that Sheen was showing symptoms of:

- A manic episode, a condition characterized by rapid speech and pressure to keep talking; restlessness; irritability; decreased need to sleep; distractibility; poor judgment; grandiosity and inflated self-esteem; reckless behavior.

- A narcissistic personality, with characteristics such as reacting to criticism with rage; exaggerated sense of self-importance, achievement, and talent; preoccupation with fantasies of success, power, and ideal love; unreasonable expectations of favorable treatment; need for constant attention and admiration; pursuit of selfish goals; limited empathy; and disregard for the feelings of others (APA, 2013).

- A delusional disorder with grandiose features that includes an inflated sense of self, power, and knowledge.

- A psychotic reaction with grandiose features produced by substance use or substance withdrawal.

Of course, a clinician conducting an assessment would evaluate background information; self-reports of symptom onset, as well as reports from friends and family members; and medical tests (including drug screening), and would conduct observations and interviews and consider psychological and/or neurological assessment that could shed light on the nature of the difficulties. Important considerations would include information regarding the onset of symptoms, previous experiences with similar symptoms, and patterns of previous behaviors.

Charlie Sheen on Tour

Charlie Sheen speaks at Radio City Music Hall on April 10, 2011 during his "Violent Torpedo of Truth/Defeat Is Not An Option" tour.

Kevin Mazur/WireImage/Getty Images

Lavakumar, Garlow, & Schwartz, 2011.

6. Premenstrual Dysphoric Disorder has been the subject of heated discussion. Critics of this category contend that symptoms associated with hormonal changes during menses should be treated as a physiological or gynecological disorder and that it is stigmatizing to women to label severe premenstrual moods swings as a psychiatric disorder.

Eight "normal" researchers (pseudopatients) were sent to different psychiatric hospitals as part of a research study (Rosenhan, 1973). Their assignment was first to fake psychiatric symptoms to gain admission into psychiatric wards (i.e., they all reported hearing the words "empty," "hollow," and "thud"); once admitted, they behaved in a normal manner. Interestingly, no hospital staff detected that the pseudopatients were normal. However, other patients did. What might account for this difference?

7. Although DSM-5 strengthened cultural considerations in diagnosis, the cross-cultural applicability of the system is still questioned. The prevalence of some disorders differs across the globe. What accounts for this variability? It may be that some descriptions of disorders developed in Western countries do not fit other cultures.

Although there are many valid criticisms of the DSM, it is the most frequently used diagnostic and classification system in the United States and some other countries. Classification systems, like the DSM, not only facilitate diagnosing disorders, they also help diagnosticians differentiate one disorder from another. Classification systems also facilitate communication between mental health professionals and provide diagnostic consistency for researchers who study the etiology and treatment of mental disorders. Without a classification system to identify, differentiate, and group disorders, it would be difficult to accomplish the above goals. Debating the usefulness of the DSM system has generated new research, increased the role of research in developing the system, and stimulated the examination of conceptual, methodological, philosophical, and clinical assumptions in the classification of mental disorders.

Objections to Classification and Labeling

Although classification systems such as the DSM are essential for diagnosing disorders, communicating information about disorders, and conducting research, they are also subject to criticism because of the negative consequences that sometimes result from classification and labeling.

1. *Labeling a person as having a mental disorder can result in overgeneralization, stigma, and stereotypes.* Stereotypes about certain mental disorders can lead to inaccurate generalizations about individuals and assumptions that may result in discriminatory behavior. When we respond to someone according to stereotypes, we are less likely to see the person's strengths and unique qualities (Corrigan & Rao, 2012).

2. *A label may lead those who are labeled to believe that they do indeed possess characteristics associated with the label or may cause them to behave in accordance with the label.* When people are told that they have particular characteristics, they may come to believe what they are told; this may lead to cognitive and behavioral changes (Vogel, Bitman, Hammer, & Wade, 2013). Davies and his colleagues have shown that labels and stereotypes can influence individuals not only to act out the stereotypes but also to devalue their personal status (Davies, Spencer, & Steele, 2005). Internalized self-stigma can have a profound effect on a person's self-image.

3. *Although social systems often require labels, mental health labels do not provide the precise, functional information required by health care organizations.* Today, many organizations are responsible for efficiently providing mental health care. Although many of these systems rely on diagnoses for making decisions about treatment and health care reimbursement, a diagnosis itself does not provide information about treatment needs. The assessment of an individual's functioning at work, home, school, and elsewhere is often of much greater utility in treatment planning than a particular clinical diagnosis.

Contemporary Trends and Future Directions

Two current trends in assessment and classification, with somewhat opposing perspectives, have emerged in recent years: (1) increased reliance on the biological model to provide guidance in assessing and diagnosing mental disorders; and (2) increased and more careful consideration of psychological, social, and sociocultural factors, along with biological influences. Advocates for this second view believe that all clients should receive a comprehensive, multifaceted assessment, but let us first consider the biological perspective.

The DSM-5 is an inadequate diagnostic system based only on clusters of symptoms, according to Dr. Thomas Insel, director of the prestigious National Institute of Mental Health (NIMH). He strongly advocates for a "precision medicine" approach that identifies, classifies, and groups disorders based on biological markers such as genes, brain structure, and patterns of brain functioning. Consistent with this neuroscientific view of psychological disorders, the NIMH launched the Research Domain Criteria (RDoC) in 2010 in an effort to identify the specific biomarkers associated with many of the DSM disorders and biological similarities between disorders.

Other researchers believe that viewing mental disorders as biomedical illnesses similar to cancer or diabetes is a mistake, in spite of breakthroughs in neuroscience. They contend that it is impossible to learn all that we need to know about a client by studying genetics, brain structure, and brain circuits and that we cannot afford to ignore the influence of factors such as loss, discrimination, abuse, trauma, and poverty on the development and course of mental illness (Doward, 2013). Additionally, psychological processes, such as negative thinking patterns, play a role in the development of some mental disorders. It is also significant that certain psychotherapies, such as cognitive-behavioral therapy, have proven to be more effective than medication for many mental illnesses (Berenbaum, 2013).

Many researchers agree that we have not yet identified reliable biomarkers for the vast majority of mental disorders (Anderson, Mizgalewicz, & Illes, 2013). An extensive review of research on neuroimaging concluded that we have yet to locate biomarkers that reliably assist with the identification of causes, outcome, or treatment of mental illnesses. Despite this reality, some biological researchers characterize mental disorders as disorders of brain circuits (Stetka & Correll, 2013; Insel et al., 2010). Kupfer (2013), a leader in the development of the DSM-5, calls the search for biological and genetic markers a welcome effort, but believes success in our quest to locate such biomarkers remains "disappointingly distant."

Although biological research and neuroscience will continue to provide new discoveries in the study of mental disorders, many hope that we do not abandon research into the many psychological, social, and sociocultural influences associated with mental illness. Interestingly, although the DSM emerged from a medical or biological model, the recent focus on appropriate assessment practices for those from diverse backgrounds has highlighted the importance of ensuring that all clinicians understand how social and cultural factors can influence the assessment process and development of mental disorders.

Within the mental health field, there is a growing consensus that mental health professionals are not merely objective observers of illnesses. Instead, there is increasing acknowledgment that accurate diagnosis and treatment are dependent upon the characteristics, values, and worldview of both the clinician and client (APA Presidential Task Force on Evidence-Based Practice, 2006; Pumariega et al., 2013). Thus, it is increasingly recognized that self-assessment is a necessary step when clinicians work with clients whose backgrounds differ from their own; such self-assessment can help clinicians identify and counteract biases, errors in thinking, and stereotypes (Ridley, Mollen, & Kelly, 2011). For example, it is important for mental health professionals to consider assumptions they may hold about topics such as gender roles, sexual orientation, older individuals, social class, or political philosophy and other issues that may influence the diagnostic process (Ashley, 2014; Sue & Sue, 2013).

In the areas of diagnosis and assessment, we will continue to see advances based on biological research as proposed by NIMH, as well as from other professional organizations that focus on the importance of psychological, social, and sociocultural factors in the development of psychopathology. We believe that an integrative assessment model, considering the multitude of factors that can affect both mental health and mental illness, is essential if we want to effectively assess, diagnose, and treat mental disorders.

chapter SUMMARY

1 How do we know if psychological tests and evaluation procedures are accurate?

- In developing assessment tools and classification systems, it is important to consider reliability (the degree to which a procedure or test yields consistent results) and validity (the extent to which a test or procedure actually performs the function it was designed to perform).

2 How do mental health professionals evaluate a client's mental health?

- Clinicians primarily use four methods of assessment: observations, interviews, psychological tests and inventories, and neurological tests.
- Observations of behaviors and personal characteristics can have diagnostic significance.
- Interviews involve a face-to-face conversation, after which the interviewer reviews and interprets information obtained from the interviewee. The mental status examination is frequently used as an interview tool during assessment.
- Psychological tests and inventories provide a more formalized means of obtaining information.
- Neurological assessment can detect important information about abnormalities in brain structure or biochemical processes occurring within the brain.

3 How do professionals make a psychiatric diagnosis?

- Professionals consider all available information and evaluate the pattern of symptoms to determine if there is a mental disorder. The DSM, used by the majority of mental health professionals, contains detailed diagnostic criteria.
- DSM-5 primarily uses categorical assessment but includes some dimensional measures, symptom rating systems and culturally relevant interviews that enhance assessment.

4 What changes are occurring that will affect assessment?

- Agencies such as the National Institute of Health advocate for assessment systems that rely on biologically based data.
- Other groups advocate for the use of comprehensive assessment models that include psychological, social, and sociocultural as well as biological factors; the importance of considering the worldview and potential biases of those conducting assessment is also emphasized.

4

RESEARCH METHODS FOR STUDYING MENTAL DISORDERS

A 24-YEAR-OLD MARRIED WOMAN from Puerto Rico, Nayda, reported that she was in "utter anguish" and incapacitated by "epileptic fits." A strong headache usually preceded her seizures, which involved convulsions and a loss of consciousness. A neurologist diagnosed her condition as intractable (difficult-to-treat) epilepsy. The psychotherapist, however, believed that some of Nayda's symptoms were inconsistent with those seen in epilepsy. First, when regaining consciousness, Nayda sometimes did not recognize her husband or children. Second, during her seizures, she appeared fearful and would beg an invisible presence to have mercy and not to kill her. Third, during these episodes, Nayda often hit herself and burned items in the house. Her most recent seizures included hallucinations involving blood and an attempt to strangle herself with a rope.

Because Nayda's symptoms were not consistent with those commonly seen in seizures, the therapist wanted to determine if the seizures were psychogenic (generated from psychological causes). He asked if Nayda had suffered any significant trauma in her life. Nayda told of an event that had occurred when she was 17 years old—2 years before the seizures began. She tearfully related that one night at about 2 a.m., she was awakened by the smell of something burning. She was shocked to find her grandmother's house in flames (her grandmother lived in a small house in the backyard). Strangely, she decided to go back to sleep and repeatedly told herself, "Tomorrow I will tell my parents of the fire" (Martinez-Taboas, 2005, p. 8). A few minutes later, the smoke awakened the rest of the family. Their attempts to rescue the grandmother failed. It was later determined that the grandmother had set the fire to take her own life. When asked about her feelings regarding the incident, Nayda cried profusely, saying she was responsible for her grandmother's death.

The therapist concluded that it was highly probable that this traumatic event was causing the seizure episodes. She also wanted to investigate the possibility that cultural influences were contributing to Nayda's symptoms. In many Latin American countries, there is a belief in *espiritismo*—that the soul is immortal and, under certain circumstances, able to inhabit or possess a living person. Auditory or visual hallucinations are common among those experiencing *espiritismo*. When asked what she believed was causing the seizures, Nayda explained that the spirit of her grandmother was not at peace and was causing her seizures and other problems. She believed that her failure to help her grandmother resulted in a disturbed and revenge-seeking spirit. Using the case study method to understand Nayda's psychological distress and a therapeutic approach that combined cognitive therapy with Nayda's cultural beliefs, the therapist succeeded in eliminating Nayda's distressing seizure episodes.

1 What methods do researchers use to study the causes of and treatments for psychopathology?

2 How does biological research help us understand the causes of abnormal behavior?

3 Why is epidemiological research important in understanding mental illness?

4 What are current trends in research into psychopathology?

Science and research inform the study of abnormal behavior. Nayda's story illustrates several important points regarding clinical research. First, professionals tend to interpret events from a perspective that is consistent with their own background and field of study. For example, proponents of the biological model may focus on physical causes for symptoms, with little attention to psychological or environmental factors. In the case of Nayda, the neurologist believed that the seizures were due to epilepsy and prescribed an antiseizure medication to treat her condition. Conversely, psychological theorists tend to view disorders primarily from a psychological framework, placing less emphasis on biological, social, or sociocultural explanations. For example, a psychologist with a cognitive-behavioral perspective might focus on Nayda's irrational thoughts and intervene by challenging her illogical beliefs. Fortunately, in Nayda's case, the therapist viewed the symptoms from both a psychological and a sociocultural perspective; this broader perspective acknowledged both the distress associated with Nayda's intense self-blame and important aspects of Nayda's cultural belief system.

Similarly, researchers frequently design studies based on their personal perspectives about possible causes of psychopathology. When you review research, remembering this fact will help you keep an open mind and avoid inaccurate assumptions. Instead of concluding that a single factor is responsible for a condition, you can consider how a particular study intersects with other research and how various contributing factors may interact. For example, shortly after the discovery of a gene associated with obesity made headlines, media attention focused on the increased likelihood of obesity among those who socialize with people who are overweight. After reading such divergent explanations you might wonder: Is obesity due to genetic influences or is it related to our social relationships? To answer questions such as this it is important to evaluate the perspectives of the researchers and the quality of the research and to consider whether other researchers are coming to similar conclusions. We now know that the majority of mental health disorders are the result of a convergence of biological, psychological, social, and sociocultural risk factors. Thus, when you come across mental health research, it is essential to remember that mental disorders are complex and, therefore, best understood from an integrative perspective. Researchers and mental health practitioners must open-mindedly investigate all possible causes and consider alternative explanations for behavior, the approach taken by Nayda's therapist. Additionally, as you will discover in this chapter, understanding different research designs and their shortcomings will help you evaluate reported findings about psychopathology.

Research Methods Used to Study Mental Disorders

Mental health practitioners rely on scientifically verified information to guide both diagnosis and treatment. Thus, they rely on data generated using the **scientific method**—a process of inquiry that incorporates systematic collection of data, controlled observation, and the testing of hypotheses. A **hypothesis** is a tentative explanation for certain facts or observations—an idea that can be tested by further investigation. Examples of hypotheses investigated by researchers include: "Seasonal forms of depression are due to decreases in light," "Exposure to certain food dyes causes hyperactivity," or "Eating disorders develop due to exposure to extremely thin models and celebrities." A **theory**—a group of principles and hypotheses that together explain some aspect of a particular area of inquiry—is much broader than a hypothesis. Recalling the large number of theories developed to explain psychopathology that we covered in Chapter 2, you probably would not be surprised to learn that researchers generate

scientific method a method of inquiry that provides for the systematic collection of data, controlled observation, and the testing of hypotheses

hypothesis a tentative explanation for certain facts or observations

theory a group of principles and hypotheses that together explain some aspect of a particular area of inquiry

many different hypotheses when studying mental disorders. For example, hypothesized explanations for eating disorders include genetic vulnerability, fear of sexual maturity, societal demands for thinness in women, and unhealthy family relationships. Each of these hypotheses comes from a different theoretical perspective. Researchers in the field of psychopathology design studies to test hypotheses about the causes of and treatments for mental disorders.

Scientists are often described as skeptics. Rather than accept the conclusions from a single study, scientists demand that other researchers replicate (repeat) the results. As Nosek observed, "Learning new things is hard, and a single study is not enough to establish new knowledge" (Samarrai, 2013). Replicating research reduces the chance that findings are due to experimenter bias, methodological flaws, or unusual characteristics of the group studied (LeBel & Peters, 2011). Let's consider research findings that were initially reported as "conclusive" in the mass media. As you can see, the status of some changed after further investigation:

- *Childhood vaccines may cause autism.* Due to media reports suggesting that childhood vaccines cause autism, half of all parents report concerns about vaccine safety and side effects, and 11 percent of parents have refused at least one recommended vaccine (Freed, Clark, Butchart, Singer, & Davis, 2010).

  Status: Research does not support a link between vaccines and autism (DeStefano, Price, & Weintrau, 2013; Price et al., 2010). The single study that supported the link between the MMR (mumps, measles, and rubella) vaccine and autism was eventually deemed an "elaborate fraud" by the *British Medical Journal* after it was discovered that Dr. Wakefield, the researcher involved, falsified his data (Godlee, Smith, & Marcovitch, 2011).

- *Antidepressants raise suicide risk in children and adolescents.* In 2004, the Food and Drug Administration (FDA) required manufacturers of certain antidepressants to include a warning about increased risk of suicidal symptoms in children and adolescents.

  Status: Needs further research. Although some studies concluded that use of antidepressants is associated with a twofold increase in suicide attempts in youths taking these antidepressants (Olfson & Marcus, 2008; Spielmans, Jureidini, Healy, & Purssey, 2013), others have found no such relationship (Gibbons, Brown, Hur, Davis, & Mann, 2012).

- *Cannabis use leads to the development of psychosis.* Drug prevention efforts nationwide cite this concern regarding marijuana use.

  Status: A number of well-designed studies support an association between marijuana use during adolescence and an increased risk of psychosis, particularly among those with a preexisting genetic vulnerability (Davis, Compton, Wang, Levin, & Blanco, 2013; McGrath et al., 2010).

- *The majority of sexually abused children exhibit signs of trauma that can be reliably detected by experts in the field of child sexual abuse.* Many believe certain behaviors in children, including masturbating or mimicking movements of sexual activity, are signs of sexual abuse.

  Status: There are no signs or symptoms that characterize the majority of sexually abused children. In fact, a significant number of abused children have no apparent symptoms (Kellogg, 2009; Kuehnle & Connell, 2009).

As you can see, the search for "truth" is often a long journey. Reports regarding the causes of psychopathology come and go, and questions sometimes remain unanswered, as the following example illustrates.

New Research Methods

Researchers are investigating the use of new technologies to understand and treat mental disorders. Pictured here, a technique called cortical magnetic stimulation is being researched as a possible treatment for depression. Participants in this study received magnetic stimulation of the cortex 30 minutes per day for two weeks.

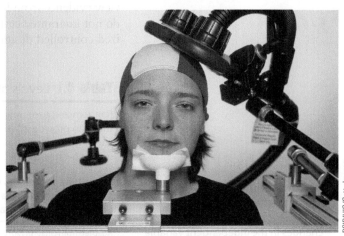

BSIP/UIG/Getty Images

A mysterious illness involving uncontrolled bodily tics and verbal outbursts was reported in 15 teenagers (14 girls and 1 boy) in upstate New York. One girl spent most of her time in a wheelchair due to the severity of her symptoms. All of the afflicted attended Le Roy High School when these behavioral changes began (Graham, 2012). The New York Department of Health and local physicians have found no medical or environmental explanations for the symptoms (Moisse & Davis, 2012).

Clinical phenomena such as the behaviors displayed by these teenagers need to be assessed and evaluated. Quality clinical research requires the development of specific hypotheses and decisions about which variables to investigate. Examples of hypotheses regarding the cause of the mysterious illness in New York have included suggestions that the symptoms may have resulted from (1) an environmental toxin, (2) an infection or other medical condition, or (3) psychological stressors. Researchers used the scientific method to evaluate these hypotheses and other possible causes of the behaviors displayed by the teens. Specialists assessed the background and personal characteristics of each teen. Many of the girls had family issues that could cause psychological symptoms; for example, one was assaulted by her father and one witnessed her father's suicide (Porter, 2012). Doctors also looked for common medical conditions or environmental exposures that might explain the symptoms, but found nothing. Unfortunately, this situation remains unsolved. Some professionals are convinced that the symptoms are due to psychological factors, whereas others remain adamant that the teen's distressing symptoms resulted from unidentified environmental influences, such as toxins, and that more inquiry is needed.

In evaluating research, we must consider the adequacy of the design used. Case studies (used with Nayda and the teens in New York), correlational approaches, and experimental designs are tools used in the field of abnormal psychology to study the characteristics, causes, and appropriate treatment for mental disorders. As Hunsley (2007) observed, "not all evidence is created equal" (p. 114). Some types of studies provide stronger evidence (more accuracy, reliability, and generalizability) because of their methodological or conceptual soundness (see Table 4.1).

If we were to construct an evidence hierarchy based on **internal validity** considerations (i.e., confidence that one thing causes another), expert opinion and case studies would be placed on the lowest level of the hierarchy. Group research designs (such as correlational studies) and single-participant experimental designs generally provide stronger evidence, and thus appear in the middle. Randomized controlled designs that involve random assignment of participants to experimental and control conditions provide the most reliable evidence and are thus the "gold standard" in research (Maughan, 2013).

Each kind of study has its own strengths and weaknesses. In general, scientists view evidence from higher levels of the hierarchy as most valid, although higher levels do not guarantee certainty without replication (Ghaemi, 2010a). Even when randomized controlled designs are used to compare different forms of therapy, for example,

Table 4.1 Levels of Evidence

Randomized experimental designs are considered the gold standard in research because they can provide information regarding cause and effect relationships. Correlational and case studies furnish other important information, including ideas for hypotheses that can be tested using an experimental design.

Level 1: Randomized, controlled studies
Level 2: Observational studies and single-subject research design
Level 3: Case studies and clinical judgment or opinions

Adapted from Ghaemi (2010a).

internal validity the degree to which changes in the dependent variable are due solely to the effect of changes in the independent variable

researcher bias (such as the belief that a certain therapy is superior) can influence the outcome of studies (Munder, Brütsch, Leonhart, Gerger, & Barth, 2013). It is particularly important for practitioners to choose treatment methods based on solid scientific evidence, as you will see in the following case:

> **CASE STUDY**   A 10-year-old girl named Candace was diagnosed with a reactive attachment disorder, a condition that interferes with the formation of trusting relationships. In an attempt to help Candace bond with her adoptive mother, her therapist decided to use "rebirthing therapy." Candace was wrapped in a blanket, surrounded by four adults pressing pillows against her, in a process intended to simulate birth. During the 70-minute session, Candace complained that she was unable to breathe. After being unwrapped, Candace had no pulse—the "treatment" caused her to die from suffocation (Kohler, 2001). Because of this case, Colorado now has a law prohibiting rebirthing therapy (Associated Press, 2001).

This heartbreaking story is an example of the importance of using scientifically verified approaches to treating mental illness. The research literature is replete with studies designed to evaluate the effectiveness of various treatment methods in alleviating symptoms of mental disorders. Some treatment outcome studies, designed to investigate conditions associated with treatment effectiveness, analyze the therapy process itself—how therapists, clients, or situational factors influence one another during the course of treatment. You are probably wondering if therapists actually use the scientific method to determine the effectiveness of approaches they choose when treating mental disorders. Fortunately, many practitioners choose therapies based on data from rigorous experimental studies that have proven that the treatments are effective for specific disorders (Hagermoser Sanetti & Kratochwill, 2014). However, some proponents of **evidence-based therapies**—those that have the highest level of research support—are concerned that many psychotherapists value their own experience and judgment over that of research (Baker, McFall, & Shoham, 2008).

Characteristics of Clinical Research

Clinical research relies on various characteristics of the scientific method, including the potential for self-correction, the development of hypotheses about relationships, the use of operational definitions, consideration of reliability and validity, the acknowledgment of base rates, and the evaluation of research findings based on their statistical significance. These characteristics allow us to understand exactly what researchers are studying and how much confidence we can place in research findings.

Potential for Self-Correction

One of the unique characteristics of the scientific method is the potential for self-correction. Under ideal conditions, research data and conclusions are freely exchanged and experiments are replicable (reproducible). Clinical research is most easily replicated when hypotheses are explicitly stated and when the variables of concern are clearly defined and easily measurable. Open discussion, testing, and verification of research minimize influence from scientists' personal beliefs, perceptions, biases, values, attitudes, and emotions.

Operational Definitions

Operational definitions are concrete definitions of the variables researchers are studying. Operational definitions are important because they encourage researchers to be very explicit about what they are measuring. Additionally, researchers choose participants or assessment measures based on the operational definitions they use. For example, researchers studying treatments for depression have the option of defining depression in a variety of ways, including (1) a specific pattern of responses to a self-report depression inventory,

evidence-based therapies treatment techniques that have strong research support

operational definition concrete description of the variables that are being studied

Attacks on Scientific Integrity

- *Studies that are financed by pharmaceutical companies report more favorable efficacy results and fewer side effects than research from studies with other sources of sponsorship (Lundh, Sismondo, Lexchin, Busuioc, & Bero, 2012).*

- *Eighty-seven percent of researchers who expressed "favorable views" of GlaxoSmithKline's diabetes drug Avandia, despite indications that it might increase the risk of heart attacks, had some financial involvement with the drug's manufacturer (Seife, 2012, p. 58).*

- *The manufacturers of popular antidepressant medications did not publish nearly one-third of the studies evaluating their effectiveness, particularly results not favoring the medication. In addition, some studies with negative or questionable results were written as if the drugs were effective (Turner, Matthews, Linardatos, Tell, & Rosenthal, 2008).*

There is suspicion that many findings unfavorable to "interested parties" (drug developers or manufacturers) are not published. In some cases, the publication of any data resulting from a company-sponsored study is subject to the approval of the company. The scientific method requires a commitment from researchers to search for the truth and to remain objective. When personal beliefs, values, political position, or conflicts of interest are allowed to influence the interpretation or dissemination of data, scientific integrity is threatened. We rely on scientists to maintain high ethical standards so we can make informed decisions based on valid research. Unfortunately, when financial considerations intersect with science, research can become a tool of interested parties rather than a mechanism to promote the welfare of society.

Should individuals be excluded from research or other activities in which they have a financial conflict of interest? Are clinical researchers or practitioners with financial ties to drug companies able to provide objective feedback regarding the effectiveness of the medications their clients are taking? These are important questions. Additionally, some have expressed concern because over two-thirds of the mental health professionals who assisted in developing the DSM-5 worked for pharmaceutical companies as consultants, researchers, or promoters of certain medications (Cosgrove & Krimsky, 2012). With researchers and key decision makers receiving funding from pharmaceutical companies, how can the interests of consumers be promoted and scientific integrity be maintained?

Animal Research

Research on animals can provide clues to the development of emotions in humans. For example, rats appear to show "regret" when making a food choice that does not produce a desired outcome (Steiner & Redish, 2014).

AP Images/dpa/picture-alliance/Waltraud Grubitzsch

(2) a rating assigned by an observer using a depression checklist, or (3) a specific pattern of neuroimaging results associated with depression. This specificity allows others to agree or disagree with the definition used.

When operational definitions of a phenomenon differ, comparing research is problematic, and conclusions can be faulty. Let's consider the definition of child sexual abuse, a stressor associated with a number of negative effects such as anxiety, eating disorders, depression, and substance abuse (Knapik, Martsolf, Draucker, & Strickland, 2010). Unfortunately, studies exploring this important topic define it differently (Haugaard, 2000). Consider the following operational definitions of *child sexual abuse* used in the research literature:

- A child or adolescent under the age of 16 being involved in sexual activities she does not and cannot fully comprehend and to which she does not fully consent (Williamson, 2009, p. 3).

- Any sexual contact between a child of 13 years or younger with another person who was at least 5 years older or a family member who was at least 2 years older (Lab & Moore, 2005, p. 325).

Other definitions of child sexual abuse used in research include "unwanted sexual experiences ranging from overt verbal advances, exposure to sexual media, unwanted touching or penetration" (Noll, Shenk, & Putnam, 2009) and "being made to look at private parts using force or surprise" (Finkelhor, Ormrod, Turner, & Hamby, 2005). The use of so many different definitions of child sexual abuse makes conclusions difficult when evaluating the research. Operational definitions need to be clear, precise, and consistent.

Reliability and Validity of Measures and Observations

The scientific method requires that measures provide accurate results. **Reliability** refers to the degree to which a measure or procedure yields the same results repeatedly. Consider, for example, an individual who has been diagnosed, by means of a questionnaire, as having a personality disorder. If the questionnaire is reliable, the individual should receive the same diagnosis after filling out the questionnaire on another occasion. Results must be consistent if we are to have any faith in them. Even if consistent results are obtained, questions can arise over the **validity** of a measure. Does the testing instrument really measure what it was developed to measure? For example, if our research uses a test to determine the severity of anxiety, we must demonstrate that the test can accomplish this task.

Base Rates

A **base rate** is the rate of natural occurrence of a phenomenon in the population studied. Research findings can be misinterpreted if we fail to consider the base rate of the variables we are studying. For example, both unwanted sexual events and eating problems are reported by a high percentage of females (Fischer, Stojek, & Hartzell, 2010). As a result, clinicians may find that many of their clients with eating problems report a history of sexual abuse. A researcher, not recognizing that both of these conditions occur with high frequency (have high base rates), may mistakenly conclude that one causes the other.

Base rate data is helpful in interpreting phenomena such as sexual behaviors in children. Is the presence of "sexualized" behaviors in children a sign of sexual abuse or a normative type of behavior? Primary caregivers reported a wide range of sexual behaviors in 1,114 children who were not sexually abused. Knowledge of the base rate of specific behaviors can help us avoid jumping to inaccurate conclusions. Regarding sexual touching, researchers stated: "Simply because a five-year-old boy touches his genitals occasionally, even after a weekend visit with his noncustodial parent, it does not mean he has been sexually abused. Rather, it is a behavior that is seen in nearly two-thirds of boys at that age" (Friedrich, Fisher, Broughton, Houston, & Shafran, 1998, p. 8). Although base rate data provide us with basic information about the frequency of some behaviors, decisions about something as significant as sexual abuse must be determined on an individual basis.

The importance of base rates in clinical research is evident from the responses of individuals in the general population to questionnaires designed to measure psychotic traits, the unusual thoughts or reactions seen in individuals with schizophrenia. When adolescents completed one such questionnaire, 30.2 percent reported having psychotic-like symptoms, including unusual thoughts or reactions. The researchers therefore cautioned others against using a single symptom when screening for risk of developing a psychotic disorder among adolescents (Menge et al., 2009). Similarly, using another questionnaire, Johns and colleagues (2004) found that 66 percent of a control group of adults endorsed having one or more psychotic symptoms (Figure 4.1).

Knowing these base rates is important—reports of having odd or bizarre thoughts or being watched by others may not always reflect psychosis. Similarly, a cross-cultural study found significant differences in reports of psychotic symptoms between countries. For example, the prevalence of hallucinations ranged from

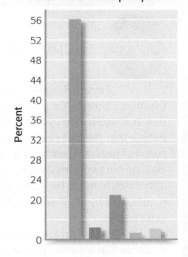

Percent regarding thoughts and behaviors over the past year.

- Feeling very happy without a break for days on end
- Thoughts being interfered with or controlled by some outside force or person
- Felt that people were against you
- Heard voices or saw things that other people could not
- Felt like something strange was going on

Figure 4.1

Base Rate Responses to Psychosis Screening Questionnaire

It is important to know the base rate of responses when interpreting questionnaire data. This figure shows the percentage of "normal" individuals endorsing items on a questionnaire used to identify psychotic thinking and beliefs. Based on these data, do you think this questionnaire is a valid measure of psychotic thinking?

SOURCE: Data from Johns et al. (2004).

reliability degree to which a measure or procedure yields the same results repeatedly

validity degree to which an instrument measures what it was developed to measure

base rate the rate of natural occurrence of a phenomenon in the population studied

Repressed Memories: Issues and Questions

Patricia Burgus claimed that when undergoing psychiatric therapy for postpartum depression, treatment that included hypnosis and hypnotic drugs, she came to believe that she had eaten human flesh, was part of a satanic cult, had been abused by numerous men, and was sexually abusing her two sons (Ewing, 1998). Burgus's memories were later determined to be the result of suggestions and techniques used by her therapists. She was awarded $10.6 million in damages.

Elizabeth Loftus argues that there is little scientific evidence that a memory, however painful, can be banned from consciousness and return years later (Loftus, Garry, & Hayne, 2008). Similarly, Pope and Hudson (2007) believe that repressed memory is not a scientifically valid phenomenon but rather a condition "manufactured" after the 1800s. In fact, they offered a $1,000 reward to anyone who could produce a published case of the phenomenon in fiction or nonfiction before 1800. They argue that if "repressed memory" were genuine, it would have been the subject of writings in the past. After reviewing over 100 submissions, they did find that one character (Nina, from a 1786 opera) met their criteria and they awarded the money. However, they still maintain that genuine psychological phenomena such as depression,

anxiety, and hallucinations are abundantly represented in historical works, unlike repressed memories (Pope, Poliakoff, Parker, Boynes, & Hudson, 2009).

Differences in opinion regarding the existence of "repressed memory" is especially pronounced between experimental psychologists and therapists. In one study, only 34 percent of the research psychologists reported that they believed in the validity of the phenomenon, compared with over 60 percent of clinicians (Dammeyer, Nightingale, & McCoy, 1997). The study also revealed some differences among the clinicians themselves. Those with psychodynamic orientations believed more strongly in repressed memories than did those with cognitive or behavioral orientations. Many clinicians also believe that some therapeutic techniques can lead to false memories.

For Further Consideration

1. Do you believe repressed memories are real? How would you decide whether to maintain or abandon repressed memory as a genuine phenomenon? What would be the implications of your decision?

2. Why are research psychologists more likely than clinicians to have doubts regarding the existence of repressed memories?

0.1 percent in Vietnam to 31.0 percent in Nepal; these data suggest that clinicians and researchers should take into account base rates from a client's country of origin when interpreting psychotic symptoms. The researchers did find, however, that the more symptoms reported, the greater the likelihood the individual had a mental illness (Nuevo et al., 2012).

Statistical versus Clinical Significance

The scientific method also requires that research findings be evaluated in terms of their **statistical significance**—the statistical probability that the findings are not due to chance alone. Even a statistically significant finding may have little practical significance in a clinical setting, as demonstrated in the following studies: Wearing compression stocking significantly reduced the number of episodes of sleep apnea (cessation of breathing) from 48 to 31 episodes per hour, a highly significant finding from a statistical perspective. However, the results were not clinically significant since the number of apnea episodes remained in the severe range (Redolfi et al., 2011). Similarly, in depression studies with large sample sizes, a change of two points on the Hampton Depression Rating Scale (HDRS) may be statistically significant to a researcher but not of clinical significance to depressed clients (Pies, 2012). When evaluating research, you must determine whether the statistical significance reported is truly "clinically" significant. This problem—a finding being statistically significant but not necessarily meaningful—is most likely to occur in studies with large sample sizes.

statistical significance the likelihood that a research finding is not due to chance alone

Experiments

The **experiment** is perhaps the best tool for testing cause and effect relationships. In contrast to case study and correlational methods, experiments allow researchers to investigate causal relationships. When researchers manipulate (change) experimental variables, they can draw conclusions about the effects of the manipulated variables on other variables. In its simplest form, an experiment involves the following:

1. An **experimental hypothesis**, which is a prediction concerning how an independent variable will affect a dependent variable

2. An **independent variable** (the possible cause), which the experimenter manipulates to determine its effect on a dependent variable

3. A **dependent variable**, which is expected to change as a result of changes in the independent variable

Let's clarify these concepts by examining an actual research study.

> **CASE STUDY**   Melinda N., a 19-year-old sophomore who needed dental treatment for several painful cavities, went to a university psychology clinic looking for help for her dental phobia. Melinda's therapist had heard that antianxiety medication and psychological methods (relaxation training and changing fearful thoughts about the procedure) were both successful in treating dental phobia. Before deciding which treatment to recommend, she reviewed research studies that compared the effectiveness of these approaches.
>
>   Research conducted by Thom, Sartory, and Johren (2000) seemed to provide some direction. In their study of individuals with dental phobia, 50 patients who needed dental surgery were assigned to one of three groups: psychological treatment, medication, or no treatment. The psychological treatment consisted of one stress management training session (relaxation exercises, visualization of dental work, use of coping thoughts) followed by 1 week of practicing these techniques at home. Those in the medication group took an antianxiety pill 30 minutes before the dental procedure. All participants (including those in the no-treatment control group) were told that their surgeon specialized in patients with dental anxiety and would treat them carefully.

The Experimental Group

An experimental group is a group exposed to an independent variable. In their study, Thom and her colleagues created two experimental groups: One group received a single-session of stress management training plus 1 week of daily home-based stress reduction activities. The other experimental group received antianxiety medication. Because the investigators were interested in how treatment affects levels of anxiety and reports of panic, their dependent variables included pretreatment and post-treatment self-reports of dental fear and ratings of pain during the procedure. The investigators also tabulated how many of the patients completed dental treatment with further appointments. Thus, the dependent variables were self-reports of fear, ratings of pain when undergoing dental surgery, and participation in further dental care.

The Control Group

If the participants in the two experimental groups in the study by Thom and her colleagues showed a reduction in dental fear

experiment   a technique of scientific inquiry in which a prediction is made about two variables; the independent variable is then manipulated in a controlled situation, and changes in the dependent variable are measured

experimental hypothesis   a prediction concerning how an independent variable will affect a dependent variable in an experiment

independent variable   a variable or condition that an experimenter manipulates to determine its effect on a dependent variable

dependent variable   a variable that is expected to change when an independent variable is manipulated in a psychological experiment

MYTH Building more controls into an experiment always results in greater generalizability of the findings.

REALITY Although a tightly controlled study increases internal validity, problems can occur with external validity— that is, the findings may not be generalizable to other populations because the conditions existing in an experimental setting may not resemble those found in real-life situations. Both internal and external validity have to be considered when designing a study.

between pretesting and post-testing measures, could the researchers conclude that the treatments were effective forms of therapy? The answer would be no, because participants may have shown less anxiety about dental procedures merely due to the passage of time or as a function of completing the assessment measures. The use of a control group enables researchers to eliminate such possibilities. A control group is a group that is similar in every way to the experimental group except they are not exposed to the independent variable. In the study by Thom and her colleagues, the control group also took the pretest measures, received reassurance about their surgeon, underwent dental surgery, and took the post-test measures. However, those in the control group did not receive medication or stress management training, the treatments being investigated. Because of this, we can be more certain that any differences found between the control and experimental groups were due to the independent variable (i.e., the treatment received).

The findings revealed that the groups who received stress management training or antianxiety medication reported significantly less fear and pain when undergoing surgery than the control group. However, those treated with medication continued to display dental phobia following their surgery, whereas those who received stress management training showed sustained improvement and continued their dental treatment. Of those who completed additional dental procedures, 70 percent had been in the psychological intervention group, 20 percent in the medication group, and 10 percent in the control group. Given these findings, the therapist told Melinda that both treatments could help during her dental appointment but that psychological intervention is more likely to produce long-term effects.

The Placebo Group

Some researchers have found that if participants have an expectation that they will improve from treatment, it may be this expectancy—referred to as the **placebo effect**—rather than specific treatment that accounts for improvement. To control for placebo effects, researchers often design their experiment to include a placebo control group. In fact, studies developed to test the effectiveness of medication often use a **placebo**—an inactive substance—for the purpose of making a comparison. Interestingly, placebos can actually produce biological changes in the brain such as triggering dopamine release or increasing endorphins that result in symptom improvement (Brown, 2012).

Researchers sometimes build a placebo control group into their research design. For example, Thom and her colleagues could have given another group a medication capsule containing a placebo or designed a presumably ineffective single-session intervention such as a therapist reading an informational pamphlet and asking the client to review the pamphlet daily for 1 week. If the experimental (i.e., medication or psychological treatment) groups improved more than the placebo control groups, the researchers could be even more confident that the treatment, rather than expectancy, was responsible for the results.

Additional Controls in Experimental Research

Because experimenter and participant expectations can also influence the outcome of a study, researchers sometimes use either a **single-blind design**, in which experiment participants are unaware of the purpose of the research, or a **double-blind design**, in which the impact of both experimenter and participant expectations is reduced. In the latter procedure, neither the individual working directly with the participant (such as a therapist or physician) nor the participant is aware of the experimental conditions. The effectiveness of this design is dependent on whether participants are truly "blind" to the intervention, which may not always be the case. For example, in medication studies, over 75 percent of subjects may correctly guess their treatment assignment due to either the presence or absence of physical symptoms or other side effects (Perlis et al., 2010). Physicians are also able to distinguish between placebos and actual medications based on

placebo effect improvement produced by expectations of a positive treatment outcome

placebo an ineffectual or sham treatment, such as an inactive substance, used as a control in an experimental study

single-blind design experimental design in which only the participants are unaware of the purpose of the research

double-blind design experimental design in which neither those helping with the experiment nor the participants are aware of experimental conditions

Double-Blind Design

When researching the effects of a drug, researchers often use a double-blind design to ensure that neither participants nor experimenters are aware of the experimental conditions. Here a physician is holding a bottle containing either medication or placebo pills. Neither she nor the participants in the study will know the type of pill received. This design is used to control for expectancy effects.

patient reactions. Many researchers attempt to design experiments that increase the degree of "blindness" while simultaneously decreasing expectancy effects.

Although experimental studies have the greatest credibility with respect to cause and effect relationships, shortcomings also exist. Questions are sometimes raised about the generalizability of the results of experimental studies. For example, some wonder if findings generated in clinics or research settings are generalizable to other environments. The tight control of variables that might possibly influence the outcome of a study may not resemble problems faced in the real world where this kind of control does not exist.

Additionally, some variables cannot be manipulated. For example, for ethical reasons, we cannot conduct an experiment to investigate if child abuse increases risk of depression. Investigating this hypothesis using an experimental design would require randomly assigning children to conditions of child abuse or no child abuse to determine if those in the abuse condition were more likely to develop depression. In this case, a correlational study analyzing the association between child abuse and depression would be the most appropriate research approach.

Correlational Studies

Correlational studies allow researchers to look at data from a large group to determine if variations in one variable are accompanied by increases or decreases in a second variable. If we wanted to investigate a possible link between child abuse and depression, we would operationally define both variables (child abuse and depression), find a large sample where we had access to data on these variables, and then perform a statistical analysis to see if degree of exposure to child abuse was associated with increases in symptoms of depression. The statistical analysis would tell us if there was a **correlation**—a relationship between the variables.

For example, in a correlational study involving 3,000 5-year-olds, greater consumption of soft drinks was associated with increased frequency of aggressive behavior (Suglia, Solnick, & Hemenway, 2013). This study demonstrates a *positive correlation* in which an increase in one variable (soft drink consumption) was accompanied by an increase in the other (aggressive behavior). When an increase in one variable is accompanied by a decrease in the other variable, there is a *negative correlation*. The greater the value of correlation, positive or negative, the stronger the relationship between the variables. See Figure 4.2 for examples of correlations. Correlational studies are very important to scientific inquiry because they allow analysis of variables that cannot be controlled—variables such as age, annual income, or frequency of exposure to traumatic experiences.

Although correlational studies provide data regarding the degree to which two variables are related, they do not explain the reason for the relationship. For example, eating certain processed foods (e.g., sweets, fried food, refined grains, high-fat dairy) is correlated with increased likelihood of depression (Sánchez-Villegas &

correlation the extent to which variations in one variable are accompanied by increases or decreases in a second variable

Ethical Considerations—Risk/Benefit versus Social Value

Randomized controlled experiments that include components such as placebo trials and random assignment represent the "gold standard" of research designs. However, all experiments must consider the risk/benefit ratio to the participants and the social value of the data obtained. Consider the following experiment and decide if you have concerns with the study.

Romanian officials asked researchers to conduct a study regarding the effects of institutional care. One hundred thirty-six young children living in a Romanian orphanage were randomly assigned to either continued institutional care or to placement in foster care (Zeanah et al., 2009). These Romanian orphans received mental health assessments (1) before the random assignment and (2) after the children were 54 months of age. Noninstitutionalized Romanian children served as a comparison group. The findings revealed that children assigned to foster care had fewer psychiatric problems than those who remained in the orphanage. It was concluded that placement in foster care can ameliorate some of the effects of early institutionalization.

For Further Consideration:
1. What is your reaction to this study?
2. What are the potential risks or benefits of this study?
3. Are there other research designs that might furnish the same information?

An Ethical Study?

Romanian children living in an orphanage.

Martínez-González, 2013). However, because these data come from correlational studies, it is possible that the relationship between dietary patterns and depression is due to variables other than those studied. In other words, we cannot conclude that consuming processed foods causes depression; it is possible that depressed individuals are more prone to eating unhealthy foods or that a third variable affects both dietary habits and depression.

Let's consider another study assessing the relationship between hours of television viewing and the number of aggressive behaviors exhibited by viewers over a 17-year period (Johnson, Cohen, Smailes, Kasen & Brook, 2002). A significant correlation was found. The greater the number of hours spent watching television per day, the greater the number of aggressive acts (assaults, robbery, threats to injure someone, or using a weapon to commit a crime). The study took into consideration possible confounding variables such as childhood neglect, low family income, unsafe neighborhoods, and psychiatric disorders.

Because this was a correlational study, the authors cautioned, "It should be noted that a strong inference of causality cannot be made without conducting a controlled experiment, and we cannot rule out the possibility that some other covariates that were not controlled in the present study may have been responsible for these associations" (Johnson et al., 2002, p. 2,470). Such cautions are common with respect to interpreting correlational studies—correlations do not demonstrate cause and effect.

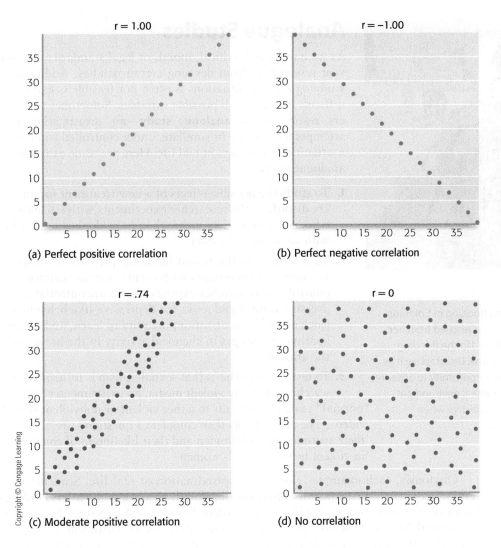

Figure 4.2

Possible Correlation between Two Variables

The more closely the data points approximate a straight line, the greater the magnitude of the correlation. The slope of the regression line rising from left to right in example (a) indicates a perfect positive correlation between two variables, whereas example (b) reveals a perfect negative correlation. Example (c) shows a lower positive correlation. Example (d) shows no correlation whatsoever.

(a) Perfect positive correlation

(b) Perfect negative correlation

(c) Moderate positive correlation

(d) No correlation

Copyright © Cengage Learning

There are numerous ways that a third variable might affect a correlation. Consider the following observations. What third-variable explanations can you suggest?

- There is a positive correlation between the number of churches in a city and the number of individuals living in the city who have been diagnosed with depression.
- There is a positive correlation between the number of mental health professionals working in a community and the number of violent crimes committed in the region.

When interpreting correlational data it is always important to remember that "correlation does not mean causation" and to consider alternative possibilities. Some of the misinformation regarding immunizations causing autism mentioned earlier in the chapter resulted, in part, because the age of onset of autism is correlated with the timing of childhood vaccines; this association resulted in the widespread but inaccurate assumption that childhood vaccines cause autism—a conclusion that has since been dispelled by many studies.

In summary, correlational studies are a very important method of scientific inquiry. Because sample sizes are large and the research can be replicated, this method of investigation has a broader scientific foundation than case studies. However, interpreting the outcome of correlational studies can be problematic. Even when variables are causally related, the direction of causality may be unclear. It is also possible that variables that are highly correlated are, in fact, causally unrelated or influenced by an additional, not-yet-identified variable.

Analogue Studies

As we have noted, ethical, moral, or legal standards may prevent researchers from devising certain studies. Additionally, studying real-life situations is often not feasible because it is difficult to control all possible variables. Sometimes researchers resort to an **analogue study**—an investigation that attempts to replicate or simulate, under controlled conditions, a situation that occurs in real life. Here are some examples of analogue studies:

1. To study the possible effects of a new treatment for anxiety disorders, the researcher experiments with students who have test anxiety rather than individuals diagnosed with an anxiety disorder.

2. To test the hypothesis that human depression is caused by continual encounters with events that one cannot control, the researcher exposes rats to uncontrollable aversive stimuli and looks for depressive-like behaviors (such as lack of motivation, inability to learn, and general apathy) or changes in chemical activity in the brains of the animals.

3. To test the hypothesis that sexual sadism is influenced by watching sexually violent media, an experimenter exposes "normal" male participants to either violent or nonviolent sexual videos. The participants then complete a questionnaire assessing their attitudes toward women and their likelihood of engaging in violent behaviors with women.

Obviously, each example is only an approximation of real life. Students with test anxiety may not be equivalent to individuals with an anxiety disorder. Findings based on rats may not be applicable to human beings. And exposure to one violent sexual film and the use of a questionnaire may not be sufficient to allow a researcher to draw the conclusion that sexual sadism is caused by long-term exposure to such films. However, analogue studies can give researchers insight into the processes that might be involved in abnormal behavior and facilitate the search for effective treatment.

Field Studies

In some cases, it may be too difficult to develop an analogue study that accurately reflects a real-life situation. Investigators may then resort to a **field study**, in which they observe and record behaviors and events in their natural environment. Field studies sometimes examine behavior after events of major consequence, such as wars, floods, and earthquakes or explore personal crises, as in military combat, major surgery, or terminal disease. Field studies sometimes employ data collection techniques, such as questionnaires, interviews, and analysis of existing records, but the primary technique is observation. Observers must be highly trained and have enough self-discipline to avoid disrupting or modifying the behavioral processes they are observing and recording.

Although field studies offer a more realistic investigative environment than other types of research, they suffer from certain limitations. First, as with other nonexperimental research, field work does not provide information about causality. Second, so many factors affect real-life situations that it is impossible to control—and sometimes even distinguish—all possible variables. As a result, the findings may be difficult to

AP Images/The Daily Camera, Mark Leffingwell, Pool

Field Studies

Many people were affected by devastating flooding in Colorado. Here a rescue worker helps a woman who was rescued from her home by helicopter. Many individuals involved in the flooding suffered severe emotional and physical trauma. Disasters such as this provide a unique, though unwelcome, opportunity to observe events and reactions of individuals in the natural environment. Can social scientists remain detached and objective when recording a tragedy of such magnitude?

analogue study an investigation that attempts to replicate or simulate, under controlled conditions, a situation that occurs in real life

field study an investigative technique in which behaviors and events are observed and recorded in their natural environment

interpret. Third, observers can never be absolutely sure that their presence did not influence the interactions they observed.

Single-Participant Studies

Most researchers believe we learn the most when a study includes large numbers—the more people studied, the easier it is to uncover the basic principles governing behavior. This approach, called the *nomothetic orientation*, is concerned with formulating general laws or principles while deemphasizing individual variations or differences. Experiments and correlational studies are nomothetic. Other scientists advocate the in-depth study of one person, exemplified by the single-participant study. This approach is called the *idiographic orientation*. There is much debate regarding which method is more fruitful in studying psychopathology.

Although the idiographic method of studying a single participant has many limitations, especially lack of generalizability, it has proven very valuable in applied clinical work. Furthermore, is not productive to argue about which method is more helpful because both approaches provide important insight into abnormal behavior. The nomothetic approach seems appropriate for researchers, whereas the idiographic approach seems appropriate for psychotherapists, who regularly face the challenge of providing effective treatment.

There are two types of single-participant studies: the **case study** and the **single-participant experiment**. Both techniques may be used to examine a rare or an unusual phenomenon, demonstrate a novel diagnostic or treatment procedure, test an assumption, generate future hypotheses on which to base controlled research, or collect comprehensive information to better understand an individual. Only the single-participant experiment, however, can determine cause and effect relationships. Nevertheless, case studies often provide crucial information.

The Case Study

In psychology, a case study is an in-depth look at data about an individual, including observations, medical and psychological tests, and historical and biographical information. Clinicians using the case study method, such as the therapist working with Nayda, develop a strong therapeutic relationship with the client and make every effort to understand the client's background, symptoms, and distress (Josselson & Matilla, 2012). The therapist can then formulate hypotheses regarding possible causes of the client's behavior or distress and test out different therapeutic strategies. Innovative methods of assessment or treatment often arise from case studies—strategies that can be evaluated with further research. In Nayda's case, the therapist adapted a therapeutic approach to incorporate Nayda's cultural beliefs. In addition to facilitating new therapeutic or diagnostic techniques, case studies are also used to study rare psychological phenomena such as the symptoms experienced by the teenagers in New York. A case study is illustrated in the following example.

CASE STUDY Around 18 months of age, Craig's behavior around others changed. He started to communicate in a very unusual manner (echoing what was said to him) and no longer seemed interested in his parents or other children. He began to line up his toys rather than play with them and became highly distressed with even minor changes in his environment. By age 3 he was given a provisional diagnosis of autism.

At 12 years of age, Craig expressed serious concerns about his identity. He complained that he did not want to be autistic, saying he would rather have something like Down syndrome so he could look like and fit in with other children in his special education classes. He became preoccupied with his appearance, complaining that he was too

case study an intensive study of one individual that relies on clinical data, such as observations, psychological tests, and historical and biographical information

single-participant experiment an experiment performed on a single individual in which some aspect of the person's behavior is used as a control or baseline for comparison with future behaviors

tall, too heavy, and too "old looking." His obsession with his appearance continued during his teen years despite psychotherapy and pharmacological interventions. He complained of boredom, anxiety, and suicidal thoughts. His deepening feelings of unhappiness resulted in an additional diagnosis of major depressive disorder. He started taking an antidepressant medication and his mood gradually improved. Although he continued to have some concern about his appearance and weight, his anxiety and distress decreased significantly (Warren, Sanders, & Veenstra-VanderWeele, 2010).

This case study provides information regarding the early development of an autism spectrum disorder (which involves impaired socialization and communication skills, and repetitive and restrictive behaviors). Of interest is Craig's development of additional mental disorders—body dysmorphic disorder (intense anxiety and distress over one's physical appearance) and major depressive disorder (severe, disabling depression). Initial therapies were ineffective until a medication prescribed to treat his depression also helped diminish the other concerns. A case study such as this provides in-depth information about the development and experience of a disorder, as well as insight into possible treatments.

However, case studies have limitations. First, because the study involves a single individual or specific situation, questions arise about whether the findings are applicable to other individuals with similar problems. For example, would the technique devised by Nayda's therapist also work with other clients with psychogenic seizures—even those with the same cultural background? Second, the data gathered in case studies often reflect the theoretical perspective or bias of the investigator. The clinician may operate from a biological, psychological, sociocultural, or other perspective and ignore other viewpoints. Third, case studies do not generally provide scientifically reliable information about causes. Because of these problems, group designs such as correlational and experimental studies that allow for replication and larger sample sizes provide a more solid research foundation for investigating mental disorders. In summary, case studies provide detailed information regarding the development and features of psychopathology in a specific individual but lack the control and objectivity of many other methods.

The Single-Participant Experiment

The single-participant experiment involves research on one person; the person's current behavior is used as a control or baseline for comparison with future behaviors. To determine the effectiveness of a treatment, for example, the experimenter first determines the frequency of a behavior before intervention. The treatment occurs, and the person's behavior is again observed. Once behavior change occurs, the treatment is withdrawn. If, after the withdrawal of treatment, the person's behavior again resembles that observed during the baseline condition, we can be fairly certain that the treatment was responsible for the behavior changes observed earlier. In the final step, the treatment is reinstated.

A **multiple-baseline study** is a single-participant experimental design in which baselines on two or more behaviors or the same behavior in two or more settings are obtained prior to intervention. An intervention is first introduced for one behavior or setting, its effects are observed, and then the intervention is applied to the next behavior or setting. If the behaviors change only with the intervention, confidence is increased that the intervention caused the behavior change.

Bock (2007) used a multiple-baseline approach to determine the effectiveness of a training program for four children with Asperger's syndrome, an autism spectrum disorder characterized by difficulty developing peer relationships and understanding social customs. Baseline information for each child's behaviors was obtained during (1) cooperative learning activities, (2) recess, and (3) lunch with peers. Prior to

multiple-baseline study a single-participant experimental design in which baselines on two or more behaviors or the same behavior in two or more settings are obtained prior to intervention

the intervention, the four children used very few appropriate social behaviors in any of these settings. The intervention program, called "SODA," taught each child how to attend to social cues and to respond appropriately. The children were prompted to use the SODA strategies in different settings—first in the cooperative learning situation, then during recess, and finally when eating lunch in the school cafeteria. Figure 4.3 demonstrates how one of the students, Bob, increased appropriate behaviors in each of the three conditions after the intervention. (The other three students showed similar improvement.)

Single-participant designs can provide valuable information, but are seldom used because researchers often rely on research designs that involve group comparisons. Because only one participant is observed at a time in a single-participant design, questions are raised about **external validity**, or the generalizability of the findings, even when the approach is applied to several children as in the evaluation of the SODA intervention.

Biological Research Strategies

Researchers in the field of psychopathology often rely on biological research to enhance their understanding of factors influencing the development of mental disorders, as well to guide research on effective treatment. Researchers study biological processes involved in mental illness from many directions, including endophenotypes, twin comparisons, genetic studies, and, more recently, study of the epigenetic processes.

The Endophenotype Concept

Endophenotypes are measurable characteristics, such as atypical cognitive functioning or anatomical or chemical differences in the brain—traits that indicate the genetic pathways involved in a disorder. To be considered an endophenotype, the characteristic must be heritable (can be inherited), seen in family members who do not have the disorder, and occur more frequently in affected families than in the general population. For example, as many as 80 percent of individuals diagnosed with schizophrenia (a severe mental illness we will discuss in Chapter 12) and 45 percent of their close relatives show irregularities in the way they track objects with their eyes. In families without schizophrenia, only 10 percent have this trait.

This irregularity thus qualifies as an endophenotype: It is inherited, is seen in families with a particular disorder (schizophrenia), and occurs more often in those families than in the general population. Although the majority of **asymptomatic** relatives never develop the disorder, identifying endophenotypes associated with a disorder can guide prevention and early treatment efforts (Gottesman & Gould, 2003). Despite strong interest in the use of endophenotypes, progress has been slow. As we learned in Chapter 2, there are many possible pathways leading to the development of a disorder, not just those involving genetics. Additionally, the search for clear-cut indicators of risk for specific disorders is complicated because the symptoms and severity of symptoms can vary significantly even for those given the same diagnosis (Viding & Blakemore, 2007).

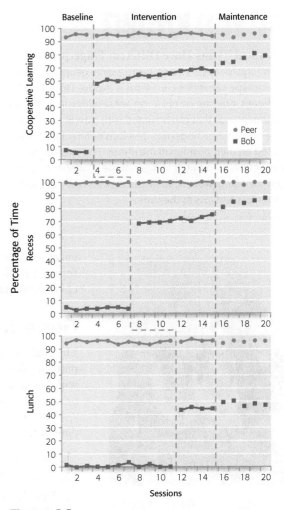

Figure 4.3

A Multiple-Baseline Study

The figures show the percentage of time Bob and a classmate spent behaving appropriately during cooperative learning, recess, and lunch. During baseline, Bob displayed appropriate behaviors less than 10 percent of the time. With the SODA intervention, the percentage increased to about 70 percent during cooperative learning and recess and to more than 40 percent during lunch. At a 5-month follow-up, Bob maintained his gains in appropriate behaviors.
SOURCE: From Bock (2007, p. 92).

external validity the degree to which findings of a particular study can be generalized to other groups or conditions

endophenotypes measurable characteristics (neurochemical, endocrinological, neuroanatomical, cognitive, or neuropsychological) that can give clues regarding the specific genes involved in disorders

asymptomatic without symptoms

Carlos Osorio/Toronto Star/Getty Images

Identical Twins Reared Apart

Researchers learn about environmental and genetic influences on mental health by comparing similarities and differences between identical and fraternal twins. Rare cases of identical twins reared apart provide a unique opportunity to closely investigate the effects of nature vs. nurture. Here you see identical twin girls who were separated as babies in China and adopted by two different Canadian families. Since the girls were reunited, the adoptive parents have ensured that the sisters have regular contact with one another.

genetic linkage studies studies that attempt to determine whether a disorder follows a genetic pattern

penetrance the proportion of individuals carrying a specific variant of a gene (allele or genotype) who also express the associated trait (phenotype)

Twin Studies

Ongoing developments in the field of genetic research are contributing to our understanding of psychopathology. Researchers often study monozygotic (MZ) twins, commonly called identical twins, because they originate from the same egg; MZ twins not only share the same DNA, but they also experience similar environmental influences prenatally and during childhood. Fraternal or dizygotic (DZ) twins also provide important information; although they originate from two eggs and thus have no more genetic similarity than non-twin siblings (sharing approximately half of inherited traits), fraternal twins do share the same prenatal and childhood environments. Researchers often make comparisons between identical and fraternal twins to evaluate hereditary and environmental influences on development. In rare cases, twins are raised apart; when this occurs researchers have even more opportunity to investigate the influence of genetic and environmental factors.

Genetic Linkage Studies

The goal of a **genetic linkage study** is to determine whether a disorder follows a genetic pattern. With genetically linked disorders, individuals closely related to the person with the disorder (who is called the *proband*) are more likely to display that disorder or a related disorder.

Genetic studies of psychiatric disorders often employ the following procedure (Smoller, Shiedly, & Tsuang, 2008):

1. The proband and his or her family members are identified.
2. The proband is asked about the psychiatric history of family members.
3. Family members are contacted and given some type of assessment such as psychological tests, brain scans, or neuropsychological examinations to determine whether they have the same or a related disorder.

This research strategy depends on the accurate diagnosis of both the proband and the relatives. Caution must be used in employing the family history method in genetic linkage studies. Variables such as psychiatric status ("ill" or "well") may influence the accuracy of a person's assessment of the mental health of relatives. Researchers often reduce this bias by using multiple informants or assessing family members directly. In one comprehensive study looking at psychological disorders in more than 11,000 twins, researchers increased the reliability of their findings by interviewing each twin and co-twin at least twice and at different points of time; they also relied on independent assessments of the psychiatric status of family members to increase the accuracy of their research (Kendler & Prescot, 2006).

Genetic research is also complicated by the fact that genes vary in their penetrance. **Penetrance** refers to the proportion of individuals with a particular genotype (carrying a specific gene) who manifest the phenotype (observable characteristics) associated with the gene. Complete penetrance occurs when a carrier *always* manifests the characteristic associated with the gene. In mental disorders, incomplete penetrance is the rule—many people carry the genotype but do not display the trait. Even in cases of schizophrenia (a disorder with high heritability), only about half of the identical twins of a proband develop the disorder. When genes have lower penetrance, it is particularly difficult to differentiate between genetic and environmental influences. Additionally, epigenetic effects can influence whether or not a gene is expressed and thus affect gene penetrance; not surprisingly, epigenetics has become a major focus of research.

Epigenetic Research

Epigenetic researchers are looking closely at the role of epigenetic influences on gene expression. In particular, they focus on environmental factors that influence whether or not a gene is expressed; the manner in which epigenetic changes regulate how and when genes are turned on or turned off; and how epigenetic modifications influence an individual's risk of developing a mental disorder. Researchers are also attempting to build on research that suggests that certain environmental stressors have the greatest impact during certain sensitive periods in early development (Mann & Haghighi, 2010).

Not only do children's experiences early in life affect their own development, researchers have found that certain experiences in childhood can change traits inherited by their descendants. This occurs when epigenetic changes leave an *imprint*, a genetic marker, on eggs or sperm, a marker that turns off or turns on specific genetic characteristics in future generations (Weinhold, 2006). Epigenetic researchers conduct laboratory studies to learn more about the molecular and chemical processes involved with epigenetic regulation of genes. They also research genomewide distribution of epigenetic changes, sometimes using human epidemiological studies to look for changes that may have affected large numbers of people in a population.

Using Animals in Biological Research

The use of *animal models*, relying on animals as surrogates for humans in research, is a frequent practice in biological research, particularly in genetic and epigenetic studies. Such experiments allow for considerable control over the variables studied and analysis across multiple generations. Animal studies also permit experimental

Biological challenge tests are used to determine the effect of a substance on behavior. For example, to determine if a specific additive is responsible for hyperactivity in a child, behavior after eating food with the additive (the "challenge" phase) is compared with behavior after eating the same food without the additive. If the behavior is present during the challenge phase and absent during the other phase, the additive will most likely be removed from the child's diet.

Researching Human Genetics

The Human Genome Project, an international effort to sequence and map all human genes—the human genome—was completed in April 2003. The data gathered resulted in a comprehensive genetic blueprint for understanding the approximately 20,000 genes found in all humans. The technology for sequencing DNA has rapidly progressed and scientists continue to use this data to research genetic patterns that may contribute to disease and mental disorders. Here you see a computer rendering of a fragment of the human genome.

procedures that would not be practical to use with humans. In one such study, newborn mice were exposed to frequent, unpredictable separation from their mothers; follow-up with the mice and their offspring yielded the highly important findings that separation not only affected the behavior, emotional development, and expression of genes in the original mice but also exerted similar effects among their offspring, particularly male offspring (Franklin et al., 2010). The researchers were also able to pinpoint the exact biological processes that occurred in the mice and their offspring. Advocates of animal research point to the critical information gleaned from such studies, particularly with respect to understanding causality and possible treatment strategies. We now examine other major techniques used in clinical research, techniques that vary in their adherence to the scientific method.

Epidemiological Research

Epidemiological research examines the frequency and distribution of mental disorders in a population. This important type of research is used to determine both the extent of mental disturbance found in a targeted population and the factors that influence the rate of mental disturbance. Two terms, *prevalence* and *incidence,* are used to describe the frequency with which mental disorders occur. As noted in Chapter 1, **prevalence** tells us the percentage of individuals in a targeted population who have a particular disorder during a specific period of time. For example, we might be interested in how many school-age children had a spider phobia during the previous 6 months (6-month prevalence), during the previous year (1-year prevalence), or at any time during their lives (**lifetime prevalence**). In general, shorter time periods have lower prevalence rates. Determining the prevalence rate is vital for planning treatment services because mental health workers need to know the base rates and the percentage of people who are affected by particular disorders.

Epidemiological studies also provide information regarding **incidence**—the number of new cases of a disorder that appear in an identified population within a specified time period. The incidence rate is lower than the prevalence rate because incidence involves only new cases, whereas prevalence includes both new and existing cases. Incidence rates are important for examining hypotheses about the causes or origins of a disorder. For example, if we find an increased incidence of a disorder (i.e., more new cases) in a population exposed to a particular stressor compared with another population not exposed to the stressor, we can hypothesize that the stressor caused the disorder. Epidemiological research, then, is important not only in describing the frequency and distribution of disorders but also in determining possible causal factors.

Surveys, which involve collecting data from all or part of a population to assess the relative prevalence, distribution, and interrelationships of different phenomena, are frequently used in epidemiological research. For instance, survey researchers often collect data and then correlate certain variables, such as family income and frequency of psychiatric hospitalization, to discover whether they are related. Surveys are also used in **longitudinal research**, a methodology that involves observing, assessing, and evaluating people's behaviors over a long period. In fact, researchers often combine elements of different methods in their research. For example, an investigator conducting treatment outcome studies may use both surveys and longitudinal studies.

iatrogenic effects unintended effects of an intervention—such as an unintended change in behavior resulting from a medication or a psychological technique used in treatment

epidemiological research the study of the prevalence and distribution of mental disorders in a population

prevalence the percentage of individuals in a targeted population who have a particular disorder during a specific period of time

lifetime prevalence the percentage of people in the population who have had a disorder at some point in their lives

incidence number of new cases of a disorder that appear in an identified population within a specified time period

longitudinal research method that involves observing, assessing, or evaluating a group of people over a long period of time

Contemporary Trends and Future Directions

Clinical practice continues to be defined by research. Therefore, mental health professionals must be able to easily sort though and evaluate research data. Several contemporary trends are facilitating this effort. For example, meta-analysis has simplified the process of comparing research results from the many studies published each year. **Meta-analysis** is a statistical method in which researchers combine and analyze the results from numerous studies focused on the same or similar phenomena. In general, the studies included in a meta-analysis meet particular criteria, such as having a certain sample size or research design. However, unless studies chosen for inclusion are well designed and use meaningful operational definitions, the outcome may be suspect. Additionally, a meta-analysis is only as good as the information going into it—or, as some say, "garbage in, garbage out."

In the field of psychology and psychiatry, there is also increasing emphasis on **evidence-based practice**. Evidence-based practice is based on the principle that treatment decisions must incorporate three components: (1) high-quality research such as randomized controlled studies; (2) clinician judgment and experience; and (3) client culture, values, needs, and perspectives (Morales & Norcross, 2010). Following this trend, the American Psychological Association and other organizations maintain a list of evidence-based therapies that are effective for specific mental disorders. Although some clinicians believe that psychotherapy is a personal process that cannot be evaluated using randomized controlled studies, therapies receiving the designation of empirically supported are becoming the treatment of choice for many disorders. The validity of evidence-based therapies for minority group members is questionable, however, because many studies do not include diverse populations (Bernal & Sáez-Santiago, 2006).

Another contemporary trend is the concerted effort to reduce bias and misconduct in research. Retractions of articles due to fraud, plagiarism, and duplication of previously published data have been increasing, especially in the last few decades (Fang, Steen, & Casadevall, 2012). Publication bias, such as only publishing studies that demonstrate that a treatment is effective, is also getting increasing attention. For example, Carrasco, Volkmar, and Bloch (2012) conducted a meta-analysis of published studies related to the effectiveness of an antidepressant medication in reducing repetitive behaviors in autistic children. Although the original meta-analysis concluded that the medication was somewhat effective, the authors later discovered five unpublished studies on the same topic. When the data were reanalyzed including the unpublished studies, the results changed: There was insufficient evidence to conclude that the medication had an effect on repetitive behavior. Publication bias in research can be reduced by:

- facilitating access to both published and unpublished studies (Turner, Knoepflmacher, & Shapley, 2012);
- reducing conflicts of interest by identifying pharmaceutical or other financial ties for all researchers;
- congressional action such as the Physician Payments Sunshine Act, passed in 2013, which compels pharmaceutical companies to publicly report any payments they make to medical researchers or mental health professionals;
- increasing the transparency of research by having researchers register their studies, including their hypotheses and statistical methods; and
- encouraging all researchers to demand openness in research.

Finally, biological researchers are continuing to focus on locating biomarkers and endophenotypes for particular disorders. Locating specific neurochemical,

meta-analysis   statistical method in which researchers combine and analyze the results from numerous studies focused on the same or similar phenomena

evidence-based practice treatment decisions based on best current research combined with clinician judgment and client needs

neuroanatomical, cognitive, or neuropsychological traits associated with specific disorders will provide important information regarding possible genetic pathways and physiological processes involved in their etiology. If we know who is at greatest risk to develop a particular disorder, it is then possible to focus efforts on prevention or on rapid diagnosis and treatment if symptoms develop.

Chapter SUMMARY

1 What methods do researchers use to study the causes of and treatments for psychopathology?

- The scientific method is a method of inquiry involving the systematic collection of data, controlled observation, and the testing of hypotheses.

- Characteristics such as the potential for self-correction, the development of hypotheses, the use of operational definitions, the consideration of reliability and validity, an acknowledgment of base rates, and the evaluation of the statistical significance of the results enable us to have greater faith in research findings.

- The experiment is the most powerful research tool we have for determining and testing cause and effect relationships. In its simplest form, an experiment involves an experimental hypothesis, an independent variable, and a dependent variable.

- Correlational studies measure the degree to which two variables are related to each other. Correlational techniques provide less precision, control, and generality than experiments, and they cannot be taken to prove cause and effect relationships.

- Analogue studies are used to create a situation as close to real life as possible. They permit the study of phenomena under controlled conditions when such study might otherwise be ethically, morally, legally, or practically impossible.

- Field studies rely on naturalistic observations in real-life situations; events are observed as they naturally occur. However, a field study cannot determine causality, and it may be difficult to sort out all the variables involved.

- A case study is an intensive study of one individual that relies on clinical data, such as observations, psychological tests, and historical and biographical information.

- Single-participant experiments differ from case studies in that cause and effect relationships can be determined. A multiple-baseline study is a type of single-participant experimental design in which baselines on two or more behaviors or the same behavior in two or more settings are obtained prior to intervention.

2 How does biological research help us better understand the causes of abnormal behavior?

- Biological research strategies allow us to search for genetic and epigenetic factors involved in psychological disorders and to identify biological indicators of a disorder.

- Biological researchers study biological processes involved in mental illness from many directions, including endophenotypes, the measurable and heritable traits that give clues regarding the genetic pathways involved in a disorder.

- Researchers often make comparisons between monozygotic (MZ) or identical twins and fraternal twins or dizygotic (DZ) twins to evaluate hereditary and environmental influences on development.

- Genetic linkage studies allow researchers to determine whether a disorder follows a genetic pattern by assessing individuals with a mental disorder and their close relatives.

- Epigenetic researchers seek to determine which environmental factors influence whether or not a gene is expressed and how gene expression is associated with the development of mental disorders.

- Researchers frequently use animals as surrogates for humans, particularly in genetic and epigenetic studies.

3 What is epidemiological research and what does it tell us about mental illness?

- Epidemiological research examines the rate and distribution of mental disorders in a population. It can also provide insight into what groups are at risk for mental disturbance and what factors may influence the development of mental disorders.

- There is often confusion between prevalence and incidence rates. Prevalence rates include both new and existing cases during a specified time period. Incidence rates involve only new cases.

4 What are current trends in research into psychopathology?

- Meta-analytic research combines and analyzes the results from numerous studies focused on the same or similar phenomena.

- The recent focus on evidence-based practice helps ensure that therapies for mental disorders are based on solid research.
- Professionals are concerned about reducing bias and misconduct in research.
- Biological researchers continue to focus on locating biomarkers for particular disorders with the goal of preventing or intervening early to treat mental disorders.

5 ANXIETY AND OBSESSIVE-COMPULSIVE AND RELATED DISORDERS

"I'VE FROZEN, MORTIFYINGLY, ONSTAGE at public lectures and presentations, and on several occasions I have been compelled to bolt from the stage . . . I've abandoned dates: walked out of exams; and had breakdowns during job interviews, plane flights, train trips, and car rides, and simply walking down the street. My anxiety can be intolerable" (Stossel, 2014).

Scott Stossel, a Harvard graduate, is the editor of *Atlantic* magazine and author of several best-selling books. He has suffered from anxiety his entire life beginning in childhood, when he was often terrified by worries that his parents might die. Anxiety has also been an ongoing issue throughout his adult years. While making his wedding vows he leaned on his bride so that he would not collapse from anxiety; during the birth of his child, the nurses had to stop attending to his wife so they could help him as he turned pale and keeled over. Even today, Stossel drinks a small quantity of alcohol and takes several antianxiety medications to cope with the strong physiological reactions he experiences before making a public presentation.

Anxiety takes many forms. People vary in how they express anxiety and what triggers their anxiety. People also differ in the severity of their anxiety reactions. Why do so many of us, like Scott Stossel, feel our hearts race, our muscles tense, and our bodies tremble during public speaking or other social situations when no actual danger exists? Why do some people have extreme fears of clowns, spiders, flying, or enclosed places; experience constant worry; or feel compelled to perform rituals?

In this chapter, we answer these questions and discuss three major conditions involving extreme anxiety—*phobias, panic disorder,* and *generalized anxiety disorder*. We also cover obsessive-compulsive and related disorders (*obsessive-compulsive disorder, body dysmorphic disorder, hair-pulling disorder, and skin-picking disorder*) in this chapter because of their strong association with anxiety. We begin our discussion with the multipath model outlined in Chapter 2 to illustrate some of the etiological factors associated with anxiety disorders.

1 According to the multipath model, how are biological, psychological, social, and sociocultural factors involved in the development of anxiety disorders?

2 What are phobias, what contributes to their development, and how are they treated?

3 What is panic disorder, what produces it, and how is it treated?

4 What is generalized anxiety disorder, what are its causes, and how is it treated?

5 What are characteristics of obsessive-compulsive and related disorders, what causes these disorders, and how are they treated?

Understanding Anxiety Disorders from a Multipath Perspective

We have all experienced the uneasiness or apprehension associated with anxiety. **Anxiety** often produces tension, worry, and physiological reactivity. Anxiety is frequently an anticipatory emotion—a sense of unease about a dreaded event or situation that has not yet occurred. What causes so many of us to experience anxiety? From an evolutionary perspective, anxiety may be adaptive, producing bodily reactions that prepare us for "fight or flight." Thus, mild or moderate anxiety prevents us from ignoring danger and allows us to cope with potentially hazardous circumstances. **Fear** is a more intense emotion experienced in response to a threatening situation. In some cases, as we saw with Scott Stossel's reactions to various events in the opening vignette, fear and anxiety occur even when no danger is present. Unfounded fear or anxiety that interferes with day-to-day functioning and produces clinically significant distress or life impairment is a sign of an **anxiety disorder**.

Those who are affected by anxiety have plenty of company. Anxiety disorders are the most common mental health condition in the United States and affect about 18 percent of adults—40 million people—in a given year (R. C. Kessler, Chiu, Demler, & Walters, 2005). In a large survey of adolescents, 31.9 percent had experienced an anxiety disorder (lifetime prevalence), with 8.3 percent experiencing severe impairment (Merikangas, He, Burstein, Swanson, et al., 2011). The prevalence of anxiety disorders is quite high when adolescents and adults are both considered (see Figure 5.1). Anxiety disorders are responsible for a great deal of distress and dysfunction, especially because they are often accompanied by depression or substance abuse (Barrera &

anxiety a fundamental human emotion that produces bodily reactions that prepare us for "fight or flight"; anxiety is anticipatory—the dreaded event or situation has not yet occurred

fear an intense emotion experienced in response to a threatening situation

anxiety disorder fear or anxiety symptoms that interfere with an individual's day-to-day functioning

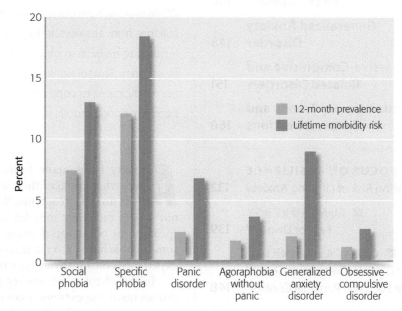

Figure 5.1

12-month Prevalence and Lifetime Morbidity Risk of Anxiety Disorders in Individuals 13 and Older in the United States

*Lifetime morbidity risk is the estimate of the likelihood of developing an anxiety disorder based on the age of the individual during the survey and the risk period for the specific disorder.

SOURCE: Kessler, Petukhova, Sampson, Zaslavsky, & Wittchen (2012).

Norton, 2010). Anxiety reactions, such as a *phobia,* can significantly interfere with a person's quality of life, as you can see from the following case of a young woman who developed a fear of dogs.

CASE STUDY Emily was hiking with her dog when another dog attacked her and bit her wrist. She was terrified. The wound became badly infected and very painful, requiring medical treatment. On another occasion, her sister, Marian, was walking in the fields when three large, growling dogs chased her. The owner heard the commotion and intervened before she was physically injured. Marian developed a fear of dogs—she became fearful of visiting friends who have dogs or participating in leisure activities where dogs might be present. In contrast, Emily, who suffered painful injuries, did not develop a fear of dogs. What could account for these differences in reactions between the sisters? (Mineka & Zinbarg, 2006)

Emily experienced a traumatic dog attack, but it was her sister, Marian, who developed a phobia. What might be some factors that increased Marian's vulnerability to experiencing anxiety and fear around dogs and what might have protected Emily from developing a phobia? In general, single **etiological models**, whether biological, psychological, social, or sociocultural, do not adequately explain why people vary in their responses to fearful situations. A number of factors play a role in the acquisition of disorders involving anxiety and fear, including biological factors such as genetically based vulnerabilities and psychological factors such as personality variables, an individual's sense of mastery or control, attention to body sensations, and learning experiences (van Almen & van Gerwen, 2013). In addition, social stressors and cultural rules or norms can influence the development and expression of anxiety. You can see the variety of factors that can potentially influence the development of an anxiety disorder in the multipath model shown in Figure 5.2. We begin our etiological discussion with a focus on the biological underpinnings of anxiety.

etiological model model developed to explain the cause of a disorder

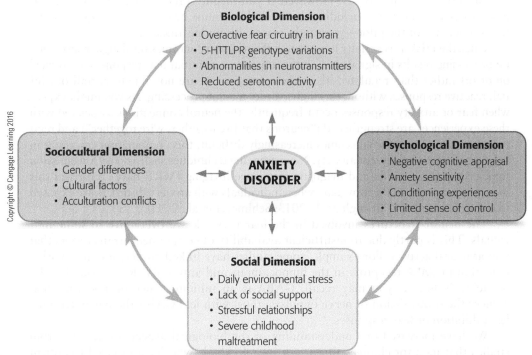

Figure 5.2

Multipath Model of Anxiety Disorders

The dimensions interact with one another and combine in different ways to result in a specific anxiety disorder. The importance and influence of each dimension vary from individual to individual.

Copyright © Cengage Learning 2016

Biological Dimension

For phobias and all anxiety disorders, it is important to rule out possible medical or physical causes of anxiety symptoms, such as hyperthyroidism (overactive thyroid), cardiac arrhythmias, asthma medications, stimulants (e.g., excessive caffeine intake), or withdrawal from alcohol (Yates, 2014). Beyond these physiological causes of anxiety symptoms, two main biological factors influence the development of anxiety disorders: fear circuitry in the brain and genetics.

Fear Circuitry in the Brain

A variety of brain structures and processes are involved in fear and anxiety responses. The **amygdala** (the part of the brain that helps us form and store memories associated with emotional events) plays a central role in triggering a state of fear or anxiety. As you may recall, the amygdala is involved in our recollection of intense emotions, particularly memories associated with danger. But how is the amygdala involved in fear reactions? When we react to a fearful situation, two separate neural circuits (neural pathways) are activated (B. J. Casey et al., 2011). In the first, when we encounter a possible threat, the potentially dangerous stimulus rapidly activates the amygdala, triggering the hypothalamic-pituitary-adrenal (HPA) axis to prepare for immediate action—the "fight or flight" response. The ensuing chemical cascade prepares us to defend ourselves or to flee. Our emotional reaction may be so strong that our perceptions are narrowed and primitive survival responses take over, interfering with rational thinking.

Fortunately, the stimulus simultaneously activates the second and slower pathway in which sensory signals travel to the **hippocampus** and **prefrontal cortex**. These structures process the sensory input and evaluate any potential danger associated with the situation. Once this secondary fear circuit determines that no threat exists, signals are sent to the amygdala to curtail the HPA axis activity, thus overriding the initial fear response. For example, if you were on an airplane, sudden turbulence might activate your amygdala and produce an immediate fear response. However, more precise mental processing of the event involving your hippocampus and prefrontal cortex—putting the turbulence in context perhaps by activating memories of prior air travel where you remained safe despite turbulence—would provide reassurance, inhibit your fear, and reduce your anxiety. However, if you misinterpret or magnify the environmental signals—such as concluding that turbulence must be dangerous or questioning the competence of the pilot—you might react with undue anxiety.

Once the HPA axis activity is activated, the reaction continues until higher-level mental processing results in signals to halt the response; our initial fear responses are turned on or off rather than regulated like a thermostat so we are not able to curtail our initial, reactive responses without this higher-order mental processing. As you might expect, when fear or anxiety responses occur frequently, the neural connections associated with these experiences are strengthened ("neurons that fire together, wire together") and regulating emotional reactivity becomes increasingly difficult; this combination can result in heightened or more frequent anxiety. Neuroimaging techniques such as positron emission tomography (PET) scans and magnetic resonance imaging (MRI) have confirmed this increased reactivity in the amygdala when individuals with anxiety disorders are exposed to emotional stimuli (Hattingh et al., 2013; Sehlmeyer et al., 2011).

The neural structures involved in the fear network are overactive in some individuals. This is partly due to insufficient availability of certain neurotransmitters that inhibit neural activity. For example, some studies have linked anxiety and fear with a reduction in **GABA** receptors in the hippocampus and amygdala (Roy-Byrne, Craske, & Stein, 2006). As you may recall, GABA is an inhibitory neurotransmitter that reduces the transmission of nerve impulses; thus, with less GABA there is potentially less inhibition of fear responses.

We have increased our understanding of the biological aspects of anxiety from studies that monitor changes that occur in individuals who have received treatment

amygdala brain structure associated with the processing, expression, and memory of emotions, especially anger and fear

hippocampus the part of the brain involved in forming, organizing, and storing memories

prefrontal cortex the region of the cortex responsible for executive functioning; allows us to manage our attention, behavior, and emotions

GABA gamma-aminobutyric acid, an inhibitory neurotransmitter involved in inducing sleep and relaxation

for an anxiety disorder. For example, neuroimaging techniques allow us to observe the effects of both medication and psychotherapy on anxiety symptoms. Medication appears to directly decrease activity in the amygdala and thus "normalize" anxiety reactions, whereas therapy appears to reduce physiological arousal by strengthening distress tolerance and the ability of the prefrontal cortex to inhibit fear responses (Britton, Lissek, Grillon, Norcross, & Pine, 2011) (see Figure 5.3). Interestingly, some psychotherapies appear to enhance amygdala–prefrontal cortex connectivity, which suggests that the neurological mechanisms that inhibit fear responses have been strengthened (Hölzel et al., 2013).

Genetic Influences

Genes modestly contribute to anxiety disorders, particularly when genetic factors interact with other important environmental influences (Bienvenu, Davydow, & Kendler, 2011). Researchers are now trying to identify how genes influence the development of anxiety symptoms. As you learned in Chapter 2, **neurotransmitters** are chemicals that help transmit messages in the brain. One specific neurotransmitter, **serotonin**, is implicated in both depressive and anxiety disorders. Consequently, a variation in the serotonin transporter gene (5-HTTLPR) has been the focus of research.

In the case of the 5-HTTLPR genotype, a **polymorphic variation** (a common DNA mutation) affects the length of one region of the associated **alleles** (the gene pair responsible for each trait); it is possible to inherit two short alleles, two long alleles, or one short and one long allele. Researchers have found that short alleles of the 5-HTTLPR gene are associated with (a) a reduction in serotonin activity and (b) increased fear- and anxiety-related behaviors. This means that carriers of the short allele are more likely to show reactivity of the amygdala when exposed to threatening stimuli (Pezawas et al., 2005). For example, individuals with this genotype demonstrate heightened neural activity in response to film clips with scenes depicting injury and death (Papousek et al., 2013). Having two short alleles appears to exert greater influence on the amygdala reactivity of females compared to males (Cerasa et al., 2013).

It is likely that numerous genes affect vulnerability to anxiety disorders. Additionally, identified genes only influence an individual's **predisposition** to develop an anxiety disorder. The presence of certain alleles increases the chances that a characteristic such as anxiety is expressed. Actual expression of the gene, however, depends on interactions between the genotype and the environment (Klauke, Deckert, Reif, Pauli, & Domschke, 2010).

Interactions between Biological and Environmental Influences

How do environmental variables influence the expression of genes related to anxiety? Researchers were initially puzzled by conflicting findings regarding carriers of the short allele of the 5-HTTLPR gene and **behavioral inhibition** (Leonardo & Hen, 2006). If the short allele of the 5-HTTLPR genotype is associated with anxiety, why are only some children who are carriers of this allele shy or behaviorally inhibited?

N. A. Fox and colleagues (Nichols & Schwartz, 2005) hypothesized that behavioral inhibition occurs when certain environmental factors such as parental behaviors interact with a child's genetic predisposition. Using a longitudinal design, researchers observed and rated characteristics of behavioral inhibition in 153 children at age 14 months and again at 7 years. They also rated the mothers' nurturing behaviors and tendency to provide social support to their children. Based on DNA genotyping, they divided the children into two groups: those with and those without a short 5-HTTLPR allele. The researchers found that children with the short allele showed behavioral inhibition only when they were raised in a stressful environment with low levels of maternal social support.

As Fox observed:

"If you have two short alleles of this serotonin gene, but your mom is not stressed, you will be no more shy than your peers as a school age child. . . . But . . . if you are raised in a stressful environment, and you inherit the short

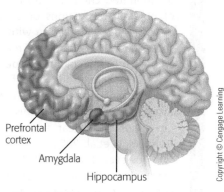

Prefrontal cortex

Amygdala

Hippocampus

Copyright © Cengage Learning

Figure 5.3

Neuroanatomical Basis for Panic and Other Anxiety Disorders
The fear network in the brain is centered in the amygdala, which interacts with the hippocampus and areas of the prefrontal cortex. Antianxiety medications appear to desensitize the fear network. Some psychotherapies also affect brain processes associated with anxiety.

neurotransmitter any of a group of chemicals that help transmit messages between neurons

serotonin a neurotransmitter associated with mood, sleep, appetite, and impulsive behavior

polymorphic variation a common mutation of a gene

alleles the gene pair responsible for a specific trait

predisposition a susceptibility to certain symptoms or disorders

behavioral inhibition shyness

Reducing Risk of Lifelong Anxiety

When young children have a biological predisposition to shyness and anxiety, environmental factors can either contribute to or protect against anxiety symptoms. For example, some infants and toddlers show high levels of behavioral inhibition characterized by distress and emotional overreactivity to environmental stimuli. Inhibited children tend to be cautious, shy, and wary of unfamiliar situations or people. New experiences are difficult because children with these characteristics show negative emotional reactions to novelty and attempt to avoid or escape from uncomfortable social situations (Hirshfeld-Becker et al., 2007). Such behavioral inhibition is thought to result from biological predispositions involving heightened fear responses (N. A. Fox, Henderson, et al., 2005).

However, less than half of children who are biologically predisposed to anxiety continue to be inhibited in middle childhood (Degnan & Fox, 2007). What protective factors enhance the resilience of these children? Nurturing behaviors on the part of parents and other caretakers play a key role in reducing symptoms of inhibition. A warm, sensitive parenting style can help reduce anxiety by building a child's self-confidence and feelings of

Kevin Peterson/Photodisc/Getty Images

mastery, including the belief that it is possible to control anxiety (Ursache, Blair, Stifter, & Voegtline, 2013).

Other helpful parental behaviors include encouraging the child to explore new situations by reinforcing independent behaviors, supporting the child's attempts to approach situations that evoke anxiety, and giving comfort when needed (Degnan & Fox, 2007). Such exposure allows children to develop the skills needed to regulate their emotional reactivity. As children with anxiety increasingly engage with anxiety-evoking situations, they begin to focus on positive aspects of the situation rather than solely on their anxiety and vigilance to threats (G. E. Miller, Lachman, et al., 2011). As they increase their sense of mastery and learn to regulate their emotions, they decrease their risk of developing an anxiety disorder (L. White, McDermott, Degnan, Henderson, & Fox, 2011).

Thus, the behaviors of parents or other caretakers can produce adaptive emotional regulation skills in young children and help them overcome their biological predisposition toward behavioral inhibition; in fact, such support can reduce the innate physiological reactivity and emotional overarousal associated with anxiety disorders (Maier & Watkins, 2010).

---

form of the gene, there is a higher likelihood that you will be fearful, anxious or depressed." (Association for Psychological Science, 2007)

Similarly, severe childhood abuse is associated with epigenetic alterations affecting the expression of genes linked to the hippocampus and the amygdala—areas associated with emotional expressiveness and anxiety responses (Labonté et al., 2012). Thus, understanding interactions between genetic and environmental factors yields insight into the causes of anxiety-related behaviors.

Psychological Dimension

An individual's psychological characteristics can also interact with his or her biological predispositions to produce anxiety symptoms. Those of us who engage in **negative appraisal**—interpreting events, even ambiguous ones, as threatening—have an increased likelihood of developing an anxiety disorder. Similarly, if you have **anxiety sensitivity**—a tendency to interpret physiological changes in your body as signs of danger—you might be particularly vulnerable to developing anxiety symptoms

negative appraisal interpreting events as threatening

anxiety sensitivity trait involving fear of physiological changes within the body

(M. W. Gallagher et al., 2013). In contrast, individuals who practice adaptive forms of emotional regulation such as using the skill of **reappraisal**—minimizing negative responses by looking at a situation from various perspectives—demonstrate fewer anxiety symptoms (Miu, Vulturar, Chiş, Ungureanu, & Gross, 2013).

One's sense of control may also be a factor in the development of an anxiety disorder. Young monkeys reared in environments in which they could control access to water and food showed less fear when exposed to anxiety-provoking situations compared to monkeys without this control. Having a sense of self-control and mastery also appears to reduce susceptibility to anxiety in humans (M. G. Gallagher, Naragon-Gainey, & Brown, 2014). Thus a number of psychological characteristics can affect individual vulnerability to anxiety disorders.

Social and Sociocultural Dimensions

Any etiological theory of anxiety disorders should consider the influence of social and sociocultural factors and stressors. Daily environmental stress can produce anxiety, especially in individuals who have biological or psychological vulnerabilities. For example, experiencing financial stress due to a low income is associated with higher rates of anxiety disorders (R. C. Kessler, Berglund, Demler, Jin, Merikangas, et al., 2005). Living in poverty or in an unsafe environment can exacerbate both stress and anxiety. Traumatic events such as terrorist attacks, school shootings, and natural disasters are also associated with increased rates of anxiety disorders (Weems et al., 2007). Similarly, adverse working conditions can increase anxiety (Liu et al., 2013). Perceptions of having limited social support from family, friends, and peers can exacerbate anxiety reactions, especially among those genetically predisposed to anxiety sensitivity (Reinelt et al., 2014).

Gender plays a role in the development of anxiety disorders. Females are more likely to experience anxiety disorders than males. Is the reason biological, social, or a combination of the two? Women are more likely to be diagnosed with emotional disorders due to their lack of power, status, and stressors associated with poverty, lack of respect, and limited choices, according to Nolen-Hoeksema (2004). These social factors produce stress hormones that may make women more vulnerable to both depression and anxiety. Thus interactions between psychological, social, and biological factors may help explain why women are more likely to develop anxiety disorders.

Cultural factors such as acculturation conflicts also contribute to anxiety disorders among ethnic minorities. Among Native Americans and Asian American undergraduate students, there is evidence of high levels of self-reported anxiety (De Coteau, Anderson, & Hope, 2006; Okazaki, Liu, Longworth, & Minn, 2002). Exposure to discrimination and prejudice can increase the anxiety of people who are members of ethnic minorities or other marginalized groups, such as individuals with disabilities or sexual minorities. Culture can also influence how anxiety is expressed. For example, in the United States and other Western countries social anxiety involves fear of embarrassing oneself, whereas in some Asian countries social anxiety concerns involve worries about being offensive to others (e.g., having a foul odor, staring inappropriately, displaying unusual facial expressions) (S. F. Hofmann, Asnaani, & Hinton, 2010). Awareness of cultural

reappraisal minimizing negative responses by looking at a situation from various perspectives

Self-Control and Mastery Decrease Anxiety

Children who develop a sense of control and mastery are less susceptible to anxiety disorders. In this case, the child is mastering the skill of using utensils independently.

©iStock.com/Fertnig

Table 5.1 Anxiety Disorders

DISORDERS CHART			
Disorder	**DSM-5 Criteria**	**Prevalence**	**Age of Onset**
Social Anxiety Disorder	• Excessive fear of being watched or judged by others • Extreme self-consciousness in social situations • Fear that anxiety symptoms will be humiliating or offend others • Social situations are avoided or endured with intense fear and anxiety	12-month prevalence of 7% to 8.7% 2 times more common in females; in Asian cultures, may involve fear of offending others	Mid-teens
Specific Phobia	• Excessive fear of specific objects or situations • Intense fear or panic attacks produced by exposure to objects or situations • Object or situation avoided or endured with great anxiety	12-month prevalence from 7% to 9% Approximately twice as common in females, although it depends on type of phobia	Childhood or early adolescence (depends on type of phobia)
Agoraphobia	• Anxiety or panic in situations where escape is difficult or embarrassing • Situations nearly always produce panic and are avoided	12-month prevalence rate of up to 1.7% More prevalent in females	Usually late adolescence, with two thirds before age 35
Panic Disorder	• Recurrent and unexpected intense attacks of fear or terror • Worry about future panic attacks • Can occur with or without agoraphobia	12-month prevalence 2.7% 2 times more common in females; may involve intense fear of the supernatural in some cultures	Late adolescence and early adulthood
Generalized Anxiety Disorder	• Excessive anxiety and worry over life circumstances (e.g., money, family, or school) • Difficulty controlling worry • Vigilance, muscle tension, restlessness, edginess, and difficulty concentrating	12-month prevalence ranges from 1.2% to 2.9% Up to 2 times more prevalent in females	Median age of about 30 but wide range of age of onset

SOURCE: American Psychiatric Association, 2013; Lewis-Fernández et al. (2010); National Institute of Mental Health (2009a); Wittchen, Gloster, Beesdo-Baum, Fava, & Craske (2010).

manifestations of anxiety in different groups is essential for clinicians working with clients from diverse backgrounds.

You now have some ideas about some of the factors associated with anxiety—the emotion underlying the disorders we discuss in this chapter. Keep these influences in mind as we turn our attention to the specific anxiety disorders, beginning with phobias (see Table 5.1.).

Phobias

phobia   a strong, persistent, and unwarranted fear of a specific object or situation

The word *phobia* comes from the Greek word for "fear." A **phobia** is a strong, persistent, and unwarranted fear of some specific object or situation. Phobias are the most common mental disorder in the United States (see Table 5.2). Individuals with a phobia often experience extreme anxiety or panic when encountering the phobic stimulus. Adults with phobias usually realize that their fear is excessive, although children may not. There are three categories of phobias: *social anxiety disorder*, *specific phobias*, and *agoraphobia*. These disorders require that symptoms are present for at least 6 months.

Social Anxiety Disorder

CASE STUDY   In any social situation, I felt fear. I would be anxious before I even left the house, and it would escalate as I got closer to a college class, a party, or whatever. When I would walk into a room full of people, I'd turn red, and it would feel like everybody's eyes were on me. I was embarrassed to stand off in a corner by myself, but I couldn't think of anything to say.... It was humiliating.... I couldn't wait to get out. (National Institute of Mental Health , 2009a, p. 9)

A **social anxiety disorder (SAD)**, sometimes referred to as a *social phobia,* involves an intense fear of being scrutinized or of doing something embarrassing or humiliating in the presence of others. According to DSM-5, the fear is out of proportion to the circumstances and results in avoidance of the situation or experiencing intense fear or anxiety when enduring the situation. Individuals with SAD are so self-conscious that they literally feel sick with fear at the prospect of public activities. SAD often involves high levels of anxiety in most social situations, although some people experience anxiety only in situations in which they must speak or perform in public *(performance only type).* The most common forms of SAD involve public speaking and meeting new people (APA, 2013).

SAD affects 8.7 percent of adults in a given year; women are twice as likely as men to have this disorder. More than 48 percent of those with SAD rate the severity of their symptoms as "mild" (R. C. Kessler, Berglund, et al., 2005). However, SAD can be chronic and disabling, especially for those who develop the disorder early in life (Dalrymple & Zimmerman, 2011). In a 5-year naturalistic follow-up study, only 40 percent of those with SAD recovered (Beard, Moitra, Weisberg, & Keller, 2010). The 2-year recovery rate is much lower for African Americans and Hispanic Americans, with less than 1 percent reporting a significant reduction in symptoms according to one study (Sibrava et al., 2013; Bjornsson et al., 2014). SAD is often **comorbid** with (i.e., often occurs with) major depressive disorders, substance-use disorders, and suicidal thoughts or attempts (El-Gabalawy, Cox, Clara, & Mackenzie, 2010).

Individuals with high social anxiety tend to believe that others are evaluating them or viewing them negatively (Cody & Teachman, 2011). Thus, they remain alert for "threat" cues such as signs of disapproval or criticism (Shorey & Stuart, 2012). They avoid drawing attention to themselves by engaging in "safety behaviors" such as avoiding eye contact, talking less, sitting alone, holding a glass tightly to prevent tremors, or wearing makeup to hide blushing (Moukheiber et al., 2010). Those with SAD also tend to be socially submissive in an effort to avoid conflicts with others (Russell, Moskowitz, Zuroff, Bleau, & Young, 2010).

Not surprisingly, individuals with SAD often report stressful interpersonal relationships (Rodebaugh, 2009). Among romantic couples, partners with high levels of social anxiety attended more to negative information, showed less interest in and support for their partners when communicating, and made fewer supportive comments in response to shared positive events; not surprisingly, these couples were more likely to have ended their relationship 6 months later (Kashdan, Ferssizidis, Farmer, Adams, & McKnight, 2013).

Specific Phobias

A **specific phobia** is an extreme fear of a specific object (such as snakes) or situation (such as being in an enclosed place). Exposure to the stimulus nearly always produces intense panic or anxiety that is out of proportion to the actual danger

Table 5.2 Examples of Phobias

Phobia	Object of Phobia
Acrophobia	Heights
Ailurophobia	Cats
Algophobia	Pain
Astrapophobia	Storms, thunder, lightning
Dementophobia	Insanity
Genophobia	Fear of sexual relations
Hematophobia	Blood
Microphobia	Germs
Monophobia	Being alone
Mysophobia	Contamination/germs
Nyctophobia	Dark
Pathophobia	Disease
Phobophobia	Phobias
Pyrophobia	Fire
Xenophobia	Strangers

DID YOU KNOW?

Men with social anxiety disorder are most likely to report fear regarding dating situations and to use alcohol and illicit drugs to cope with their anxiety. Women have a wider variety of social fears and are more likely to be treated with medications.

SOURCE: Xu et al., 2012

social anxiety disorder (SAD)   an intense fear of being scrutinized in social or performance situations

comorbid   existing simultaneously with another condition

specific phobia   an extreme fear of a specific object (such as snakes) or situation (such as being in an enclosed place)

National News/Topham/The Image Works

ALBERTO PIZZOLI/AFP/Getty Images

Phobias

Coulrophobia, a fear of clowns, may result from their painted eyes and smiles and never-changing expressions. Celebrities reported to have a fear of clowns include Johnny Depp, Daniel Radcliffe, Billy Bob Thornton, and Sean "P. Diddy" Combs. Uma Thurman is reported to have claustrophobia (fear of enclosed places).

remit diminish or disappear

represented by the object or situation (APA, 2013). The primary types of specific phobias involve:

- living creatures (e.g., spiders, insects, dogs, snakes),
- environmental conditions (e.g., heights, earthquakes, thunder, water),
- blood/injections or injury (e.g., needles, dental treatment, invasive medical procedures), or
- situational factors (e.g., enclosed places, flying, driving, being alone, the dark, or traveling in tunnels or over bridges).

The following case study illustrates a common specific phobia exhibited by a 26-year-old public relations executive.

CASE STUDY If I see a spider in my house, I get out! I start shaking, and I feel like I'm going to throw up. I get so scared, I have to bolt across the street to drag my neighbor over to get rid of the spider. Even after I know it's gone, I obsess for hours. I check between my sheets 10 times before getting in bed, and I'm so creeped out that I won't get up and go to the bathroom at night, even if my bladder feels like it's about to burst. (Kusek, 2001, p. 183)

This case illustrates how phobias can be extremely distressing and how they can interfere with daily life, especially if it is difficult to avoid the feared object or situation. It is not unusual for an individual to have more than one phobia. Scott Stossel, introduced at the beginning of the chapter, not only had social anxiety disorder but also had phobias involving germs, vomiting, enclosed spaces, heights, flying, and cheese.

Specific phobias affect approximately 19 million adults in a given year in the United States (approximately 8.7 percent of the population) and are twice as common in women as in men (R. C. Kessler, Berglund, et al., 2005; NIMH, 2009). Specific phobias often begin during childhood. Animal phobias tend to have the earliest onset (age 7), followed by blood phobia (age 9), dental phobia (age 12), and claustrophobia (age 20) (APA, 2013; Öst, 1992). Figure 5.4 illustrates ages at which different phobias typically begin. Early fears are common and most **remit**, or disappear, without treatment (Broeren, Lester, Muris, & Field, 2011).

The most common childhood fears used to include spiders, the dark, frightening movies, and being teased, while adolescents most frequently feared heights, animals, and speaking in class or speaking to strangers (Muris, Merckelbach, & Collaris, 1997). Contemporary fears of adolescents now include "being raped," "terrorist attacks," "having to fight in a war," "drive-by shootings," and "snipers at school" (Burnham, 2009).

Blood phobias differ from other phobias because they are associated with a unique physiological response: fainting in the phobic situation. Fainting appears to result from an initial increase in physiological arousal followed by a sudden drop in blood pressure and heart rate (Ritz, Meuret, & Simon, 2013). Nearly 70 percent of those with blood phobias report a history of fainting in medical situations; many avoid medical examinations or are unable to care for injured family members (Hellstrom, Fellenius, & Öst, 1996).

Agoraphobia

Agoraphobia is an intense fear of at least two of the following situations: (a) being outside of the home alone; (b) traveling via public transportation; (c) being in open spaces (e.g., parking lot or playground); (d) being in stores or theaters; or (e) standing in line or being in a crowd. These situations are feared because escape or help may not be readily available. The fears are out of proportion to actual dangers and result in avoidance of the situation or intense fear or anxiety when enduring the situation (APA, 2013).

People coping with agoraphobia have a fear that they might become incapacitated or severely embarrassed by fainting, losing control over bodily functions, or displaying

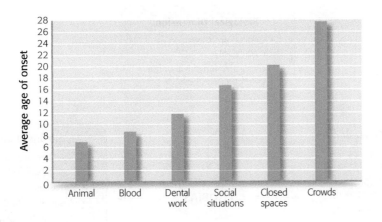

Figure 5.4

Phobia Onset

This graph illustrates the average ages at which 370 people said their phobias began. Animal phobias began during childhood, whereas the onset of agoraphobia did not occur until the individuals were in their late twenties. What accounts for the differences reported in the age of onset for the types of phobias?

SOURCE: Based on Öst (1987, 1992)

excessive fear in public. In some cases, anxiety about the possibility of a **panic attack**, which is an episode of intense fear accompanied by various physiological symptoms, can prevent people from leaving their homes. Individuals who have agoraphobia often have *anxiety sensitivity,* the tendency to misinterpret and overreact to normal physiological changes. This precipitates anxiety, which further increases bodily sensations (e.g., sweating or heart palpitations), resulting in a vicious cycle that can culminate in a panic attack (Rudaz, Craske, Becker, Ledermann, & Margraf, 2010).

Agoraphobia occurs much more frequently in females compared to males. Although this phobia is relatively uncommon (affecting less than 1 percent of U.S. adults in a given year), 41 percent of those affected rate their symptoms as serious (R. C. Kessler, Chiu, et al., 2005). The prevalence of agoraphobia among older adults is relatively high with about 11 percent experiencing their first episode at age 65 or older. Risk factors for late-onset agoraphobia include severe depression or a tendency to be anxious (Ritchie, Norton, Mann, Carrière, & Ancelin, 2013).

Etiology of Phobias

How do such strong and "irrational" fears develop? In most cases, predisposing genetic factors interact with psychological, social, and sociocultural influences, as discussed earlier. Scott Stossel, for example, has a family history of anxiety that traces back to his great grandfather. His mother, an attorney, has panic attacks and many of the same phobias that Scott experiences. In addition to these biological factors, Scott also mentions that the unhappy relationship between his mother and father and their divorce may have played a role in his phobias. Although his parents' child-rearing practices were well intentioned and loving, Scott believes that he had few opportunities to develop "autonomy and a sense of self-efficacy." So, were Scott's phobias a result of genetics, psychological influences, social pressures, or their combination? In this section, we examine the factors related to the etiology of phobias, as shown in Figure 5.5.

Biological Dimension

All phobia subtypes involve a moderate genetic contribution (heritability of 31 percent), according to studies of twin pairs (Kendler & Prescott, 2006). Individuals with phobias may have an innate tendency to be anxious and have strong emotional responses; thus their chances of developing an irrational fear response are increased. Exaggerated

agoraphobia an intense fear of being in public places where escape or help may not be readily available

panic attack episode of intense fear accompanied by symptoms such as a pounding heart, trembling, shortness of breath, and fear of losing control or dying

Figure 5.5

Multipath Model of Phobias
The dimensions interact with one
another and combine in different
ways to result in a phobia.

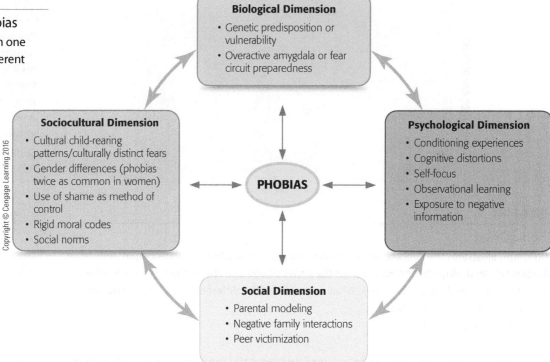

Biological Dimension
• Genetic predisposition or vulnerability
• Overactive amygdala or fear circuit preparedness

Sociocultural Dimension
• Cultural child-rearing patterns/culturally distinct fears
• Gender differences (phobias twice as common in women)
• Use of shame as method of control
• Rigid moral codes
• Social norms

PHOBIAS

Psychological Dimension
• Conditioning experiences
• Cognitive distortions
• Self-focus
• Observational learning
• Exposure to negative information

Social Dimension
• Parental modeling
• Negative family interactions
• Peer victimization

Copyright © Cengage Learning 2016

DID YOU KNOW?

- 3.5 percent of Americans have a severe injection phobia.

- 50 percent of individuals who use medications that require self-injections are unable to perform the injections.

- Those with an injection phobia fear pain or have unrealistic thoughts such as "the needle might break off."

SOURCE: Mohr, Cox, & Merluzzi, 2005

responsiveness of the amygdala and other areas of the brain associated with fear may make an individual more susceptible to developing a phobia. Neuroimaging studies have confirmed that individuals with phobias show increased physiological fear responses in reaction to phobic-related stimuli (Schweckendiek et al., 2011).

A different biological view of the development of fear reactions is that of *preparedness*. Proponents of this position argue that fears do not develop randomly. They believe that it is easier for humans to develop fears to which we are physiologically predisposed, such as a fear of heights or snakes. Such quickly aroused (or "prepared") fears may have been necessary to human survival. In fact, evolutionarily prepared fears (e.g., fear of fire or deep water) occur even without exposure to traumatic conditioning experiences (Muhlberger, Wiedemann, Herrmann, & Pauli, 2006). Although preparedness is an interesting theory, it is hard to believe that most phobias stem from prepared fears. Many simply do not fit into the prepared-fear model. It would be difficult, for example, to explain the survival value of social phobias, as well as many of the other specific phobias. In addition, phobias involving snakes and spiders (prepared fears) are usually not difficult to eliminate.

Psychological Dimension

There are multiple psychological pathways that can lead to the development of phobias: (a) fear conditioning, (b) observational learning or modeling, (c) negative informational effects, and (d) cognitive processes. The factors involved often depend on the specific type of phobia. For example, modeling—watching someone else display the fear—seems to be more important in spider phobia, whereas direct conditioning plays a major role in blood or injection phobia (Coelho & Purkis, 2009).

Classical Conditioning Perspective   The view that phobias are conditioned fear responses evolved from psychologist John B. Watson's classic conditioning experiment with an infant, Little Albert. Watson caused Little Albert to develop a fear of white rats by pairing a white rat with a loud sound (Watson & Rayner, 1920), demonstrating that fears can result through an association process. Similarly, conditioning occurred when women undergoing chemotherapy for breast cancer were given lemon-lime Kool-Aid in a container with a bright orange lid. After repeated pairings of the drink and the chemotherapy, the women reported emotional distress and nausea when presented with the container (Jacobsen et al., 1995). Many children with severe phobias report that conditioning experiences caused their fear (N. J. King, Eleonora, & Ollendick, 1998). Many of us find that our childhood fears can be retriggered in adulthood if we are faced with sounds, smells, or events that bring up memories of those fears and how we responded to them. However, many people with phobias report something other than a direct conditioning experience as the "key" to their phobia.

Observational Learning Perspective   Fears can develop through observational learning. For example, after being told that they would participate in a similar experiment, participants in a study watched a video in which a man received an uncomfortable shock in response to a stimulus. After viewing the video, they were shown the stimulus that was associated with the shock. Not surprisingly, the participants responded with fear. Their fear response was documented by neuroimaging scans that showed activation of the amygdala (Olsson, Nearing, & Phelps, 2007).

Children can develop fear responses by observing others displaying fear in real life or in the media. In one study, parents of children ages 8 to 12 were trained to act anxiously or in a relaxed manner before their child took a spelling test (Burstein & Ginsburg, 2010). Children exposed to an anxious-acting parent reported higher anxiety levels, more anxious thoughts, and a greater avoidance of the spelling test than did those in the relaxed parent condition. In another study, watching peers who showed either calm or anxious behaviors when interacting with a novel animal influenced how much fear children displayed when asked to interact with the animal (Broeren et al., 2011). Thus, it appears that observational learning can play a role in the development of fear.

Negative Information Perspective   Can information cause someone to fear an object or situation? To determine this, parents were given descriptions regarding an unfamiliar animal (a cuscus) and were asked to use the information to tell their children how the cuscus might behave in certain situations. Parents received one of three descriptions: (a) negative (has sharp claws and long teeth, can jump at your throat); (b) ambiguous (has white teeth, can jump, likes to drink all sorts of things); or (c) positive (has nice tiny teeth, eats tasty strawberries, likes to play with other animals). Children whose parents received the negative description reacted with more fear

Fear or Disgust?

Do phobias such as fears of spiders and rats result from feelings of disgust rather than from a threat of physical danger? Some researchers have pointed out that spiders and rats are, in general, harmless. These researchers believe that phobias result from an inborn or "prepared" fear of disease or contamination, rather than a threat of physical danger (Bianchi & Carter, 2012). In an experiment to determine whether disgust is involved in spider phobia, Mulkens, de Jong, and Merckelbach (1996) asked women with and without spider phobias to indicate their willingness to eat a cookie that a "medium sized" spider had walked across. The researchers reasoned that if disgust was a factor, those with a spider phobia should be more reluctant to eat the "contaminated" cookie. Results supported this idea: Only 25 percent of women with spider phobia eventually ate some of the cookie, compared with 70 percent of the control group participants. Does the avoidance of spiders and snakes stem from fear, disgust, or both? Since insects such as cockroaches, maggots, and slugs also elicit disgust, why do they not result in phobias?

Scary or Cute?

Fears can be induced through negative information. Children's reactions to the cuscus depended on the descriptions furnished to their parents about the unfamiliar animal.

to the cuscus than those whose parents received positive or ambiguous information (Muris, van Zwol, Huijding, & Mayer, 2010). Thus, fears can be induced through negative or threatening information.

Cognitive-Behavioral Perspective Why do individuals with a spider phobia react with such terror at the sight of a spider? Some researchers believe that catastrophic thoughts and cognitive distortions (including overestimating threat) may cause strong fears to develop (Rinck & Becker, 2006). For example, people with spider phobia overestimate the size of spiders they encounter (Vasey et al., 2012). Others report thinking that the spider "will attack" or "will take revenge" (Mulkens, de Jong, & Merckelbach, 1996). Individuals with SAD believe they are being scrutinized by others and think, "Everyone in the room is watching me. I know I am going to do something stupid!" (Vassilopoulos, Banerjee, & Prantzalou, 2009).

Social Dimension

Parental behaviors can influence the course of behavioral inhibition and the development of social anxiety in children. Overprotection of socially withdrawn children and lack of support for their independence can increase their sense of insecurity and decrease opportunities for them to practice approaching novel situations (K. Burgess, Rubin, Cheah, & Nelson, 2001). The children are thus prevented from developing emotional regulation and coping skills—and social anxiety is more likely to continue (Muris & Dietvorst, 2006).

Family interaction patterns can also influence the development of phobias and social anxiety. Behavioral inhibition (shyness) and family interactions were measured in a sample of 242 boys and girls at age 3 and again 4 years later. Negative family interactions at age 3 and family stress in middle childhood were both associated with social anxiety symptoms (Schmidt, Richey, Buckner, & Timpano, 2009). A punitive maternal parenting style (based on child report) has been linked with an increased tendency to have fearful beliefs (Field, Ball, Kawycz, & Moore, 2007). Victimization by peers during childhood can also increase social anxiety (R. E. McCabe, Miller, Laugesen, Antony, & Young, 2010).

Sociocultural Dimension

Females are more likely to have phobias, with the gender difference showing up as early as 9 years of age. However, this difference is found mainly for repulsive animals, such as snakes, rather than harmless animals such as dogs. Some of the gender differences in phobias may occur because women show a stronger disgust response than men and because some phobic objects produce both fear and disgust responses (Rohrmann, Hopp, & Quirin, 2008). Fewer gender differences exist for social fears, fears of bodily injury, and fears of enclosed spaces. Gender differences may be due to a combination of biological and temperamental factors, as well as social norms and values (C. P. McLean & Anderson, 2009).

Social anxiety appears to be more common in collectivistic cultures in which individual behaviors are seen to reflect on the entire family or group (Sue & Sue, 2013). It also occurs more frequently when parents are highly concerned about the opinions of others and use shame as a method of control (M. A. Bruch & Heimberg, 1994). These are common child-rearing practices among some cultural groups, including Asians; not surprisingly, fear of being evaluated by others is more common in Chinese children and adolescents than in Western comparison groups (Dong, Yang, & Ollendick, 1994). In one study, higher levels of social anxiety found in people of Asian heritage appeared to be due, in part, to discrepancies between traditional cultural behavioral norms and social expectations of the mainstream culture (Hsu et al., 2012).

SAD is common among Arab college students, with a prevalence rate between 12 percent and 13 percent. These high rates of SAD may be due to cultural factors such as a strong sense of personal responsibility for social behaviors, a perceived need to follow a set of rigid moral codes and rituals, and the threat of being ostracized for deviations from social norms (Iancu et al., 2011).

It is important to note that social fears may be expressed differently in different cultures. *Taijin kyofusho*, for instance, is a culturally distinctive phobia found in Japan that is similar to a social anxiety disorder. However, instead of a fear involving social or performance situations, *taijin kyofusho* is a fear of offending or embarrassing others, a concept consistent with the Japanese cultural emphasis on maintaining interpersonal harmony (K. Suzuki, Takei, Kawai, Minabe, & Mori, 2003). Individuals with this disorder are fearful that their appearance, facial expression, eye contact, body parts, or body odor are offensive to others.

Treatment of Phobias

Phobias are successfully treated by both pharmacological and cognitive-behavioral methods (Koszycki, Taljaard, Segal, & Bradwejn, 2011).

Biological Treatments

In treating phobias, a number of medications demonstrate some effectiveness, although symptoms often recur when the medication is discontinued (Sundel & Sundel, 1998). Both benzodiazepines (a class of antianxiety medication) and the antidepressant selective serotonin reuptake inhibitors (SSRIs) have shown evidence of efficacy for SAD; benzodiazepines are also used for treating specific phobias (Otto et al., 2010). You may recall that benzodiazepines reduce symptoms of anxiety by increasing the activity of the inhibitory neurotransmitter GABA. Short-acting benzodiazepines, such as lorazapam (Ativan) and alprazolam (Xanax), are used for acute panic attacks or in short-term situations such as a traveler with a fear of flying.

Long-acting benzodiazepines, such as diazepam (Valium), are used for more generalized anxiety and for longer-term treatment needs. As with most medications, side effects can occur. Benzodiazepines can produce dependence, withdrawal symptoms, and paradoxical reactions such as increased talkativeness, excessive movement, and even hostility and rage (Mancuso, Tanzi, & Gabay, 2004). Among older adults, those who use benzodiazepines have an increased risk of developing dementia or experiencing falls and fractures (Billioti de Gage et al., 2012).

Because of these problems, other medications, such as SSRI antidepressants, are often prescribed to treat chronic forms of anxiety. Although SSRIs begin to alter brain chemistry after the very first dose, they require about 4 to 6 weeks before they begin to reduce symptoms. Beta-blockers, such as propranolol (Inderal), which is used to treat high blood pressure and heart conditions, can also reduce the physical symptoms that accompany certain anxiety disorders, particularly social phobia. When a feared situation is anticipated (such as giving a speech), physicians sometimes prescribe a beta-blocker to keep physical symptoms of anxiety under control (NIMH, 2010).

D-cycloserine, a drug used to treat tuberculosis, is sometimes used in combination with psychotherapy in the treatment of phobias. This medication appears to affect brain regions associated with the unlearning of fear. One study found that adding D-cycloserine to cognitive-behavioral therapy (CBT) for SAD resulted in more rapid symptom improvement compared to placebo plus CBT (S. G. Hofmann et al., 2013). However, not everyone appears to respond to D-cycloserine. Individuals with high contentiousness or low extroversion had the best outcome when combining the drug with behavioral fear extinction treatment (de Kleine, Hendriks, Smits, Broekman, & van Minnen, 2014). There is some concern that if D-cycloserine is not effective during an extinction trial, fear memory reconsolidation may occur and be strengthened by the drug, thus increasing the person's fear and anxiety symptoms (Hofman, 2014).

Cognitive-Behavioral Treatments

Phobias are also successfully treated with a variety of cognitive-behavioral approaches. These approaches include:

- *Exposure therapy*: gradually introducing the individual to the feared situation or object until the fear dissipates.
- *Systematic desensitization*: exposure techniques combined with an additional response, such as relaxation.
- *Cognitive restructuring*: identifying and changing irrational or anxiety-arousing thoughts associated with the phobia.
- *Modeling therapy*: viewing another person's successful interactions with the feared object or situation.

Exposure Therapy   Exposure therapy is frequently used to treat phobias. In **exposure therapy**, treatment involves gradual and increasingly difficult encounters with a feared situation. For example, when treating a client with a fear of leaving the house, a therapist may first ask the client to visualize or imagine the anxiety-evoking situation. Eventually, the client might walk outside the home together with the therapist and then independently.

A variant of exposure therapy has been successful for the treatment of blood and injection phobia, at least for individuals who show the physiological pattern of a sudden drop in blood pressure (Ritz et al., 2013). A procedure known as *applied tension* (described in the following case study) is combined with exposure techniques (Mednick & Claar, 2012).

CASE STUDY   Mr. A. reported feeling faint when exposed to any stimuli involving blood, injections, injury, or surgery. Even hearing an instructor discuss the physiology of the heart caused Mr. A. to feel sweaty and faint. Mr. A. was taught to recognize the first signs of a drop in blood pressure and then to combat this autonomic response by tightening (tensing) the muscles of his arms, chest, and legs until his face felt warm. He was then taught to stop the tension for about 15 to 20 seconds and then to reapply the tension, repeating the procedure about five times. (The rise in blood pressure that follows this process prevents fainting, and the fear becomes extinguished.) After going through this process, Mr. A. was able to watch a video of thoracic surgery, watch blood being drawn, listen to a talk about cardiovascular disease, and read an anatomy book—stimuli that in the past would have produced fainting (K. W. Anderson, Taylor, & McLean, 1996).

Devices such as virtual reality screens can enhance the effects of exposure-based psychotherapy. For example, after successful behavioral treatment, phobias sometimes recur if the person encounters the feared object in a context that is different from the one used in treatment. Can the use of virtual reality exposure to multiple contexts reduce the likelihood of symptom renewal? Thirty individuals with spider phobias were exposed four times to a virtual spider either in a single context (e.g., the spider was pictured on a chair) or in multiple contexts. Each successive exposure produced a reduction in skin conductance and behavioral measures of fear. However, those exposed to the spider in a single context showed a renewal of fear when the spider was shown in a novel context whereas those who had been exposed to multiple contexts did not. Thus, virtual reality techniques improve treatment outcome for phobias by reducing the chances that phobic responses will reappear (Shiban, Pauli, & Mühlberger, 2013).

Systematic Desensitization   **Systematic desensitization** uses muscle relaxation to reduce the anxiety associated with phobias. Wolpe (1958, 1973), who developed the

exposure therapy treatment that involves introducing the client to increasingly difficult encounters with a feared situation

systematic desensitization exposure strategy that uses muscle relaxation to reduce the anxiety associated with specific and social phobias

Online Program for Social Anxiety

Pictured are sample items from a computerized treatment program dealing with social phobia in children and adolescents.

SOURCE: Reprinted with permission of the authors from Spence, S.H.; Donovan, C. L.; March, S.; Gamble, A.; Anderson, R.; Prosser, S.; Kercher, A.; & Kenardy, J. (2008). Online CBT in the treatment of child and adolescent anxiety disorders: Issues in the development of BRAVE-ONLINE and two case illustrations. Behavioural and Cognitive Psychotherapy, 36, 411–430.

treatment, first taught clients to relax their muscles. Second, he had them visualize feared stimuli (arranged from least to most anxiety provoking) while in the relaxed state. This continued until clients reported little or no anxiety with the stimuli. This procedure was adapted for a man who had a fear of urinating in restrooms when others were present. He was trained in muscle relaxation and, while relaxed, learned to urinate under the following conditions: no one in the bathroom, therapist in the stall, therapist washing hands, therapist at adjacent urinal, therapist waiting behind client. The easier items were practiced first until anxiety was sufficiently reduced (McCracken & Larkin, 1991).

Cognitive Restructuring   In **cognitive restructuring**, unrealistic thoughts believed to be responsible for phobias are altered (Kendall, Khanna, Edson, Cummings, & Harris, 2011). Individuals with social phobias, for example, tend to be intensely self-focused and fearful that others will see them as anxious, incompetent, or weak. Their own self-criticism is the basis for their phobia (Britton et al., 2011). Therapists use cognitive strategies to help clients "normalize" social anxiety by encouraging them to interpret emotional and physical tension as "normal anxiety" and redirect their attention away from themselves in social situations (Goldin et al., 2012).

cognitive restructuring   cognitive strategy that attempts to alter unrealistic thoughts that are believed to be responsible for phobias

Modeling Therapy In **modeling therapy**, the individual with the phobia observes a model (either on screen or in person) coping with or responding appropriately to the fear-producing situation. The individual with the phobia may be asked to repeat the model's interactions with the phobic object (V. L. Kelly, Barker, Field, Wilson, & Reynolds, 2010). In one study testing this process, 99 children saw a film in which a peer interacted positively with an unfamiliar animal. After watching positive peer modeling, the children's fear toward the animal decreased significantly (Broeren et al., 2011).

Panic Disorder

modeling therapy procedure involving observation of a nonphobic individual successfully coping with the phobic object or situation

panic disorder condition involving recurrent, unexpected panic attacks with apprehension over future attacks or behavioral changes to avoid attacks

CASE STUDY Rachel had her first panic attack at work during a period in which she was experiencing high stress, including problems with her partner, financial difficulties, and job pressures. The second attack followed 3 days later. She now experiences panic attacks on a daily basis. To try to minimize the risk of a panic attack, Rachel avoids anything that might result in physiological arousal (Lindner, Lacefield, Dunn, & Dunn, 2014).

According to DSM-5, a diagnosis of **panic disorder** involves recurrent unexpected panic attacks in combination with (a) apprehension over having another attack or worry about the consequences of an attack (e.g., feeling a loss of control or inability to breathe) or (b) changes in behavior or activities designed to avoid another panic attack. These reactions must be present for a period of 1 month or more. As you could see in the case of Rachel, the attacks are extremely distressing because they often occur unpredictably and without warning. The following description of a panic attack by someone with a panic disorder highlights the strong physiological reactions that occur.

Modeling

Watching a fear-producing act being performed successfully can help people overcome their fear. In this photo, the girl on the left is confidently touching the snake. Why do you think modeling works?

Paul Wood/Alamy

CASE STUDY For me, a panic attack is almost a violent experience.... My heart pounds really hard, I feel like I can't get my breath and there's an overwhelming feeling that things are crashing in on me.... In between attacks, there is this dread and anxiety that it's going to happen again. I'm afraid to go back to places where I've had an attack. Unless I get help, there soon won't be any place where I can go and feel safe from panic. (NIMH, 2009, p. 3)

Panic disorder is diagnosed in only a small percentage of individuals, but panic attacks are fairly common. The 12-month prevalence for panic attacks is about 11.2% among U.S. adults. Panic attacks often begin in late adolescence or early adulthood (APA, 2013). Approximately 40 percent of the general population experience panic attack symptoms at some point in their lifetime.

The 12-month prevalence rate for panic disorder is 2.7 percent (R. C. Kessler, Chiu, et al., 2005); it is twice as common in women as in men (NIMH, 2009a). Those who have more recurrent panic symptoms tend to have comorbid depression, generalized anxiety, or substance abuse (Bystritsky et al., 2010). Many individuals diagnosed with a panic disorder also develop agoraphobia associated with their fear of having a panic episode in a public place (Cosci, 2012).

Etiology of Panic Disorder

As with the other disorders we have discussed so far, biological, psychological, social, and sociocultural factors and their interactions play a role in the etiology of panic disorder, as shown in Figure 5.6.

Biological Dimension

Higher **concordance rates** (i.e., percentages of relatives sharing the same disorder) for panic disorder have been found in monozygotic (identical) twins compared to dizygotic (fraternal) twins. Heritability is estimated to be about 32 percent, which is considered a modest contribution (Kendler & Prescott, 2006). Research has focused on identifying specific gene × environment interactions, neural structures, and a neurochemical basis for panic disorder (Klauke et al., 2010).

As we mentioned earlier, brain structures (such as the amygdala) are involved in anxiety disorders (including panic disorder), and neurotransmitters (such as serotonin and GABA) play an important role in emotions such as fear. Neuroimaging has revealed that individuals with panic disorder have fewer serotonin receptors, which results in decreased availability of serotonin (Klauke et al., 2010). It is interesting to note that SSRIs, antidepressant medications designed to increase levels of serotonin, are effective in treating panic disorders, as well as other anxiety disorders.

Psychological Dimension

Certain psychological characteristics have been associated with panic disorder. Individuals with this disorder score high on anxiety sensitivity measures and show heightened fear responses to bodily sensations (Schmidt, Keough, et al., 2010); they display hypervigilance over changes such as heart rate, blood pressure, and respiration

DID YOU KNOW?

The following questions are used to screen for panic disorder:

- Do you sometimes have sudden attacks of fear that last for several minutes?
- Do you feel like you are having a heart attack or cannot breathe?
- Do these attacks occur at unpredictable times, causing you to worry about the possibility of having another attack?

SOURCE: NIMH, 2013c

concordance rate degree of similarity between twins or family members with respect to a trait or disorder

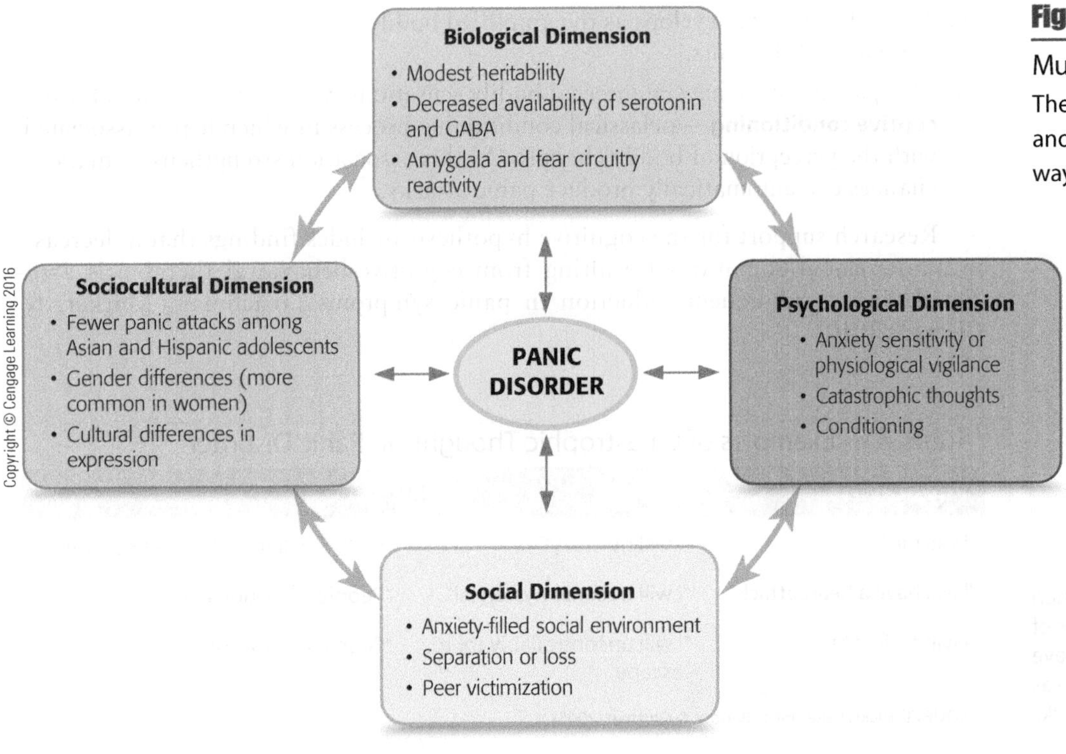

Figure 5.6

Multipath Model of Panic Disorder

The dimensions interact with one another and combine in different ways to result in panic disorder.

Figure 5.7

Role of Cognitions in Panic Attacks

A positive feedback loop between cognitions and somatic symptoms leads to panic attacks.

SOURCE: Roy-Byrne, Craske, & Stein (2006), p. 1,027.

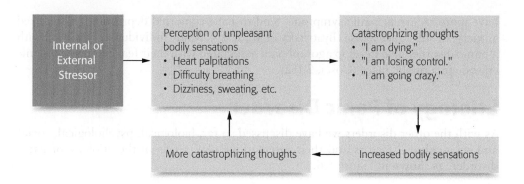

(see Figure 5.7). When these physiological changes are detected, anxiety increases, resulting in even more physical symptoms and more anxiety; this cycle often culminates in a panic attack (Domschke, Stevens, Pfleiderer, & Gerlach, 2010). It is possible that physiological sensitivity is learned via modeling—by watching parents or friends express fears about physical sensations or by using avoidance to cope with fear-producing situations (Lindner et al., 2014).

Cognitive-Behavioral Perspective   The cognitive-behavioral model proposes that panic attacks occur when unpleasant bodily sensations are misinterpreted as indicators of an impending disaster. These inaccurate cognitions (see Table 5.3) and somatic symptoms create a feedback loop that results in increasing anxiety. Thus, the following pattern is associated with the development of a panic disorder (Rudaz et al., 2010):

1. A physiological change occurs (e.g., faster breathing or increased heart rate) due to factors such as exercise, excitement, or stress.

2. Catastrophic thoughts develop, such as "Something is wrong," "I'm having a heart attack," or "I'm going to die."

3. These thoughts result in increased apprehension and fear, resulting in even more physiological changes.

4. A circular pattern develops as the amplified bodily changes now result in even more fearful thoughts.

5. This pairing of changes in internal bodily sensations with fear results in **interoceptive conditioning**—a classical conditioning process in which fear is associated with the perception of bodily changes. As this association strengthens, somatic changes can automatically produce panic attacks.

Research support for the cognitive hypothesis includes findings that a decrease in panic-related cognitions (resulting from cognitive-behavioral therapy) is associated with a subsequent reduction in panic symptoms (Teachman, Marker, & Clerkin, 2010).

Table 5.3 Examples of Catastrophic Thoughts in Panic Disorder

Physical	Mental	Social
"I will die"	"I will go crazy"	"People will think I'm crazy or weird"
"I will have a heart attack"	"I will become hysterical"	"People will laugh at me"
"I will suffocate"	"I will uncontrollably try to escape"	"People will stare at me"

SOURCE: Hicks, Leitenberg, Barlow, & Gorman (2005).

interoceptive conditioning   when internal bodily sensations of fear and anxiety that have preceded panic attacks serve as signals for new panic attacks

Social and Sociocultural Dimensions

Many individuals with panic disorder report a stressful childhood involving separation anxiety, family conflicts, school problems, or loss of a loved one (Klauke et al., 2010). Being a victim of bullying increases the likelihood of developing panic disorder (Copeland, Wolke, Angold, & Costello, 2013). Such environmental stressors may interact with a biological predisposition toward anxiety and result in panic symptoms.

Culture can also play a role in panic disorder. Asian American and Latino/Hispanic adolescents report higher anxiety sensitivity compared to European American adolescents but are less likely to have panic attacks. This may be due to cultural differences in the way Asian American and Latino/Hispanic adolescents interpret anxiety or bodily symptoms (Weems, Hayward, Killen, & Taylor, 2002). Symptom differences are also found in people from India, where panic attacks are associated with physiological symptoms (e.g., increased heart rate, shortness of breath) rather than with catastrophic thoughts (Neerakal & Srinivasan, 2003).

Treatment of Panic Disorder

Both medication and cognitive-behavioral therapies have been effective in treating panic disorder (Hicks, Leitenberg, Barlow, & Gorman, 2005). With either therapy, an important step involves teaching clients about panic disorders and providing reassurance about normal physiological changes.

Biological Treatment

Different classes of medications have been used successfully to treat panic disorder. Benzodiazepines (antianxiety medications) can help reduce the frequency of panic attacks (Nardi et al., 2012). Panic disorder is also treated with antidepressants, although they usually take 4 to 6 weeks to become fully effective. Beta-blockers are sometimes used to reduce panic symptoms such as excessive sweating, heart palpitations, and dizziness (NIMH, 2013a). Unfortunately, relapse rates after cessation of drug therapy are quite high (Biondi & Picardi, 2003).

MYTH Because brain activity associated with anxiety disorders can be "normalized" with medication, biological therapies provide the best alternatives for treatment.

REALITY Psychotherapy is highly effective with anxiety disorders and can also normalize brain functioning. Medications appear to influence the fear network at the level of the amygdala, whereas cognitive-behavioral therapy leads to fear inhibition mediated by the prefrontal cortex and hippocampus.

Cognitive-Behavioral Treatment

Cognitive-behavioral treatment is successful in treating panic disorder and promotes self-efficacy by helping clients develop the sense that they can effectively deal with panic symptoms (M. W. Gallagher et al., 2013). Cognitive-behavioral intervention involves extinction of the fear associated with both internal bodily sensations (e.g., heart rate, sweating, dizziness, breathlessness) and fear-producing environmental situations, such as being in crowds or in unfamiliar areas (S. G. Hofmann et al., 2007). In general, cognitive-behavioral treatment for panic disorder involves the following steps (D. B. Pincus, May, Whitton, Mattis, & Barlow, 2010):

1. educating the client about panic disorder and correcting misconceptions regarding the symptoms;

2. identifying and correcting catastrophic thinking—for example, the therapist might comment, "Maybe you are overreacting to what is going on in your body" or "A panic attack will not stop your breathing";

3. teaching the client to self-induce physiological symptoms associated with panic (such as hyperventilating or breathing through a straw) in order to extinguish the interoceptive conditioning that has occurred in response to bodily cues or sensations;

4. encouraging the client to face the symptoms, both within the session and in the outside world, using statements such as "Allow your body to have its reactions and let the reactions pass";

Panic Disorder Treatment: Should We Focus on Personal Control?

Imagine standing in the middle of a busy mall when suddenly your heart starts to pound and you begin to sweat. You may not realize it but you are experiencing a panic attack. Soon you feel nauseated and disoriented, and can barely breathe. You fear you are going to either pass out or die. What is happening to you? What brought on this terrifying experience? Will it happen again? When you regain your composure, you think about what has just happened. You decide to explore treatment options. What treatment techniques will you choose? Consider the following studies.

Abraham Bakker and his colleagues (Bakker, Spinhoven, Van Balkom, & Van Dyck, 2002) compared two groups of individuals with panic disorder. One group was treated with cognitive-behavioral therapy (CBT)—a therapy that encouraged clients to accept personal control over their panic reactions. The other group was treated with antidepressant medications without psychotherapy. Clients in the CBT group had lower relapse rates than those treated pharmacologically, perhaps because those in the CBT group learned to view their gains as the result of their own efforts rather than due to medication.

Biondi & Picardi (2003) compared medication alone with a combination of medication and CBT. The CBT strategies included sharing information about panic disorders, challenging catastrophic misinterpretations, considering alternative explanations for bodily sensations, practicing relaxation strategies, facing feared situations, and understanding the implications of having a panic disorder. Before, during, and at the end of treatment, the researchers assessed participants' beliefs concerning what accounted for their recovery. After the treatment, relapse rate was 78.1 percent for those in the medication group, compared with 14.3 percent for the CBT group.

A common factor in the cognitive-behavioral approaches used in both studies was the enhancement of self-efficacy—a belief that recovery and the ability to manage anxiety are under personal control. Individuals who believe (or come to believe) that success is up to them are significantly more likely to reduce anxiety symptoms than those who attribute their improvement to external factors, such as medication (Golding et al., 2012). How might therapists help their clients increase self-efficacy?

5. teaching coping statements such as "This feeling is not pleasant, but I can handle it"; and

6. helping the client to identify the antecedents of the panic: "What stress am I facing?"

Generalized Anxiety Disorder

CASE STUDY Lana, age 12, has worried about many things over the past year, including what will happen if her mother gets sick, if her parents cannot afford their house, or if she fails a math test. She has trouble concentrating and becomes easily fatigued. Usually, if she starts worrying about one issue, she starts thinking about others, and often seeks reassurance from her mother. (Rynn et al., 2011, p. 77)

Many of us have had specific concerns and worries, but how do these differ from what Lana is experiencing? **Generalized anxiety disorder (GAD)** is characterized by persistent, high levels of anxiety and excessive and difficult-to-control worry over life circumstances; these feelings are accompanied by physical symptoms such as feeling restless or tense. For a DSM-5 diagnosis of GAD, the symptoms must be present on the majority of days for at least 6 months and cause significant distress or impairment in life activities. As we saw with Lana, the worry and anxiety associated with GAD can significantly interfere with optimal functioning. Worry appears to be the

generalized anxiety disorder (GAD) condition characterized by persistent, high levels of anxiety and excessive worry over many life circumstances

defining characteristic of GAD, and some believe a better term for this disorder would be "pathological worry behavior" (Andrews, Hobbs, et al., 2010). Most people with GAD spend up to 6 hours a day worrying and feeling anxious versus an average of about 1 hour a day for nonclinical samples (Donegan & Dugas, 2012).

GAD develops gradually, often beginning in childhood or adolescence (Rynn et al., 2011). In any given year, about 1.2 percent to 2.9 percent of the U.S. population is affected by GAD (Cuijpers et al., 2014); women are twice as likely to receive this diagnosis compared to men (R. C. Kessler, Berglund, et al., 2005).

Etiology of Generalized Anxiety Disorder

GAD is the result of biological factors combined with psychosocial stressors, as shown in Figure 5.8. Let's take a look at each of the factors that may contribute to the etiology of GAD.

Biological Dimension

Heritability appears to play a small but significant role in the development of GAD (Kendler & Prescott, 2006). As discussed earlier, genes may be expressed in terms of serotonin or GABA abnormalities or overactivity of brain regions associated with anxiety.

As mentioned earlier, our prefrontal cortex modulates our responses to threatening situations. GAD may involve a disruption in this system. In an MRI investigation, 18 adolescents with GAD and 15 without GAD were exposed to angry faces (Monk et al., 2006). Those with GAD showed greater activation of the prefrontal cortex in response to the faces, suggesting that the prefrontal cortex was attempting to regulate the anxiety aroused by the faces. Individuals with GAD not only report higher anxiety levels, but also show greater sensitivity to bodily changes than individuals without this disorder (Hoehn-Saric, McLeod, Funderburk, & Kowalski, 2004).

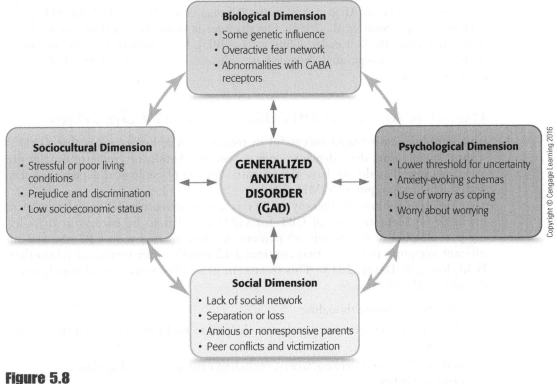

Figure 5.8

Multipath Model of Generalized Anxiety Disorder (GAD)

The dimensions interact with one another and combine in different ways to result in generalized anxiety disorder (GAD).

Intrusive thoughts are common among college students.

- 50 percent of men and 42 percent of women have thoughts of hurting a family member.

- 24 percent of men and 14 percent of women have thoughts of indecently exposing themselves.

- 19 percent of men and 7 percent of women have thoughts of sex with a child or minor.

SOURCE: Purdon & Clark, 2005

Psychological Dimension

Cognitive theories emphasize the role of dysfunctional thinking and beliefs in the development of GAD. Individuals with this disorder have a lower threshold for uncertainty, which leads to worrying. They also have erroneous beliefs regarding worry and assume that worry is an effective way to deal with problems or that it prevents negative outcomes from occurring (Ladouceur et al., 2000). A. T. Beck (1985) believes that negative **schemas** (mental frameworks for organizing and interpreting information) play a key role in anxiety disorders. Schemas may involve beliefs such as "I am incompetent" or "The world is dangerous." When someone interprets everyday occurrences through the filter of a negative schema, ambiguous or even positive situations may be viewed with concern and apprehension.

Some researchers believe that the roots of GAD lie in beliefs regarding the function of worrying (A. Wells, 2005, 2009). In this model, there are two types of worry. The first involves the frequent use of worry to cope with stressful events or situations that might occur. However, the stress of constantly generating solutions to "what if" scenarios eventually results in a belief that worry is uncontrollable, harmful, and dangerous. GAD develops when the second type of worry ("worrying about worry") occurs. This dynamic (worrying about worry) leads to increased anxiety and thus reinforces the view that worry has negative effects (D. M. Ellis & Hudson, 2010).

Social and Sociocultural Dimensions

A variety of social factors may influence the development of GAD. Mothers who themselves have anxiety symptoms may be less responsive and engaged with their infants than mothers who are not anxious. These behaviors appear to increase the likelihood that the child will develop GAD (A. Stein et al., 2012). Conflict in peer relationships, including being a victim of bullying, can increase the chances of developing GAD (Copeland et al., 2013). Stressful conditions such as poverty, poor housing, prejudice, and discrimination also contribute to GAD and may be responsible for the high prevalence of GAD in African Americans (Sibrava et al., 2013) and Latino/Hispanic Americans (Bjornsson et al., 2014). The disorder is twice as prevalent among those with low income (R. C. Kessler, Chiu, et al., 2005). It is also seen more frequently in individuals who are separated, divorced, or widowed and in the unemployed (Wittchen & Hoyer, 2001).

Treatment of Generalized Anxiety Disorder

Benzodiazepines have been successful in treating GAD; however, because GAD is a chronic condition, drug dependence is a concern. Antidepressants are usually preferred because they do not have the potential for the physiological dependence seen with the benzodiazepines (NIMH, 2013a).

Cognitive-behavioral therapy (CBT) is an effective psychological treatment for GAD. A meta-analysis of CBT for GAD found it to be successful in reducing pathological worry; nearly 60 percent of those treated with CBT showed significant symptom reduction that continued 12 months after treatment (Hanrahan, Field, Jones, & Davey, 2013). This treatment generally involves teaching clients to (Stanley et al., 2003):

- identify worrisome thoughts;
- discriminate between worries that are helpful to problem solving and those that are not;
- evaluate beliefs concerning worry, including evidence for and against any distorted beliefs;
- develop self-control skills to monitor and challenge irrational thoughts and substitute more positive, coping thoughts; and
- use muscle relaxation to deal with somatic symptoms.

schema   mental framework for organizing and interpreting information

We now discuss another set of disorders characterized by persistent troublesome thoughts and underlying anxiety: obsessive-compulsive and related disorders.

Obsessive-Compulsive and Related Disorders

CASE STUDY Mrs. A. is a 32-year-old married mother of two who spends at least 4 hours each day cleaning and making sure everything in her house is in its perfect place. If Mrs. A. sees or hears words pertaining to death she immediately begins to repeat the Lord's Prayer in her mind 100 times. She believes that failure to perform this ritual will lead to the untimely death of her children (W. M. Greenberg, 2010).

Obsessive and compulsive symptoms such as those experienced by Mrs. A. can be extremely distressing and debilitating. In this section we will learn more about obsessive-compulsive and related disorders, including *obsessive-compulsive disorder, hoarding disorder, body dysmorphic disorder, hair-pulling disorder (trichotillomania)*, and *excoriation (skin-picking) disorder* (Table 5.4). These disorders are grouped together because they have similar symptoms, such as repetitive disturbing thoughts

Table 5.4 Obsessive-Compulsive Spectrum Disorders

DISORDERS CHART			
Disorder	**DSM-5 Criteria**	**Gender and Cultural Factors**	**Age of Onset**
Obsessive-Compulsive Disorder	• Repeated disturbing and intrusive thoughts or impulses • Inability to control or suppress the thoughts or behaviors • Brief relief after performing the behaviors	12-month prevalence rate about 1.2% About equally common in males and females; less prevalent among African Americans, Asian Americans, and Latino/Hispanic Americans	Usually adolescence or early adulthood; 25% of cases begin by age 14
Body Dysmorphic Disorder	• Distressing and impairing preoccupation with imagined or slight defects in appearance	Prevalence rate of 2.4%; up to 15% in those seeing dermatologists Equally common in males and females	Early adolescence to twenties; may be sudden or gradual
Hair-Pulling Disorder (Trichotillomania)	• Repeated pulling out of hair, resulting in hair loss	12-month prevalence rate of 1%–2%; lifetime prevalence up to 4 percent; up to 10 times more common in females	Usually before age 17; may periodically recur
Excoriation (Skin-Picking) Disorder	• Repeated picking at the skin, resulting in lesions	Lifetime prevalence rate of 1.4%; 75% of those affected are female	Usually begins in adolescence, although can occur at any age
Hoarding Disorder	• Difficulty discarding items because of perceived need, resulting in cluttered and unsafe living areas	From 2% to 6% at any given time; females more prevalent in clinical samples; 3 times more prevalent in older adults	Usually begins by age 15 and produces clinically significant impairment by the thirties

SOURCE: Based on American Psychiatric Association, 2013; Leckman et al. (2010); K. A. Phillips, Stein, et al. (2010); K. A. Phillips, Wilhelm, et al. (2010); Tucker, Woods, Flessner, Franklin, & Franklin (2011).

OCD may be underdiagnosed. If it is suspected, screening questions such as these are asked:

■ Do you feel the need to check and recheck things over and over?

■ Do you constantly have the same thoughts?

■ Do you feel a very strong need to perform certain rituals repeatedly and feel like you have no control over what you are doing?

SOURCE: NIMH, 2013b

and irresistible urges, and are believed to have similar neurobiological causes. They also have much in common with anxiety disorders (Mathews & Grados, 2011).

Obsessive-Compulsive Disorder

The primary symptoms in **obsessive-compulsive disorder (OCD)** are **obsessions**, which are persistent, anxiety-producing thoughts or images (e.g., Mrs. A.'s concern that her children might die), and **compulsions**, which involve an overwhelming need to engage in activities or mental acts to counteract anxiety or prevent the occurrence of a dreaded event (e.g., Mrs. A.'s mental repeating of the Lord's Prayer 100 times). The obsessions and compulsions consume at least 1 hour of time per day and cause significant distress or impairment in life activities. You can probably imagine how upsetting it must feel to be unable to control disturbing thoughts or refrain from performing ritualistic acts.

People who experience the intrusive and often irrational thoughts or images associated with obsessions find it difficult to control their thinking. Although they may try to ignore the obsession or push it from their minds, the thoughts persist (Leisure, 2013). Common themes associated with obsessions include:

- contamination, including concern about dirt, germs, body wastes, or secretions and fear of being polluted by contact with items, places, or people considered to be unclean or harmful (Cisler, Adams, et al., 2011);
- errors or uncertainty, including obsessing over decisions or anxiety regarding daily behaviors such as locking the door or turning off appliances;
- unwanted impulses, such as thoughts of sexual acts or harming oneself or others; and
- orderliness, including striving for perfect order or symmetry (Yadin & Foa, 2009).

Compulsions involve repetitive actions, in contrast to the recurring thoughts or distressing images associated with obsessions. Compulsions often entail observable behaviors such as hand washing, checking, or ordering objects. They can also involve mental acts such as praying, counting, or repeating words silently. Distress or anxiety occurs if the behavior is not performed or if it is not done "correctly."

Table 5.5 Clinical Examples of Obsessions and Compulsions

Client Age	Gender	Duration of Obsession in Years	Content of Obsession or Compulsion
21	M	6	Teeth are decaying, particles between teeth
55	F	35	Fetuses lying in the street, people buried alive
29	M	14	Shoes dirtied by dog excrement
32	F	7	Contracting AIDS
42	F	17	Hand washing triggered by touching surfaces touched by other people
21	M	2	Intense fear of contamination after touching money
9	M	4	Going back and forth through doorways 500 times

SOURCE: Based on W. M. Greenberg (2010); Jenike (2001); Kraus & Nicholson (1996); Rachman, Marks, & Hodgson (1973); Zerdzinski (2008).

obsessive-compulsive disorder (OCD) condition characterized by intrusive, repetitive anxiety-producing thoughts or a strong need to perform acts or dwell on thoughts to reduce anxiety

obsession intrusive, repetitive thought or image that produces anxiety

compulsion the need to perform acts or mental tasks to reduce anxiety

Although obsessions and compulsions sometimes occur separately, they frequently occur together; in fact, only 25 percent of those with OCD report distressing obsessions without compulsive behaviors (Markarian et al., 2010). Compulsions are frequently performed to neutralize or counteract a specific obsession. For example, individuals with an obsession about contamination may compulsively wash their hands. Table 5.5 contains additional examples of obsessions and compulsions.

Individuals with OCD often describe their obsessive or compulsive thoughts and actions as being out of character for them and not under their voluntary control. Most recognize that their thoughts and impulses are senseless, yet they feel unable to control them. If they try to avoid engaging in their rituals, they feel more and more anxious. As one individual noted, "The reason I do these kinds of rituals and obsessing is that I have a fear that someone is going to die. This is not rational thinking to me. I know I can't prevent somebody from dying by putting 5 ice cubes in a glass instead of 4" (Jenike, 2001, p. 2,122). See Figure 5.9 for some clinical examples of disabling obsessions and compulsions.

In a given year, about 1 percent of the U.S. adult population experience OCD symptoms significant enough to constitute a disorder. Over half of those affected report the severity of the disorder as "serious" (R. C. Kessler, Chiu, et al., 2005). OCD usually begins in childhood or adolescence (Yadin & Foa, 2009). The disorder is about equally common in males and females but is less common in African Americans and Latino/Hispanic Americans (A. Y. Zhang & Snowden, 1999). Many people with this disorder are depressed and may abuse substances, possibly because of the emotional distress associated with the OCD symptoms (Canavera, Ollendick, May, & Pincus, 2010).

How common are intrusive, unacceptable thoughts and impulses? Many people report experiencing occasional intrusive ideas or impulses to behave in an uncharacteristic manner. In fact, about one fourth of the general population report having obsessive-compulsive symptoms, but without the severity required to meet the diagnostic criteria for OCD (Fullana et al., 2009). Additionally, the content of obsessions reported by individuals with OCD overlaps considerably with intrusive thoughts reported by the general population. However, with OCD, the obsessions last longer, are more intense, produce more discomfort, and are more difficult to dismiss (Morillo, Belloch, & Garcia-Soriano, 2007). For all of us, intrusive thoughts are more likely to occur during times of stress. For example, some new mothers report intrusive thoughts such as worries that the baby might stop breathing or that they might scream at, slap, or drop the baby (Abramowitz, Metzer-Brody, et al., 2010).

Compulsions are also common in the general population (Muris, Merckelbach, & Clavan, 1997). A continuum appears to exist between "normal" rituals and "pathological" compulsions. Mild compulsions include superstitions such as refusing to walk under a ladder, throwing salt over one's shoulder, or knocking on wood. In individuals with OCD, the compulsions are much more frequent and intense, and they produce more discomfort. Additionally, the behaviors are repetitive and are often performed in a mechanical fashion; if compulsive acts are not performed in a certain manner or a specific number of times, the individual is flooded with anxiety.

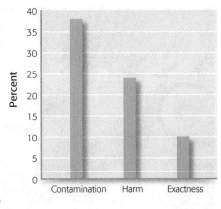

Obsessions

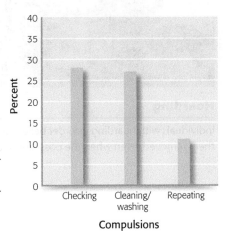

Compulsions

Figure 5.9

Common Obsessions and Compulsions

About half of the clients reported both obsessions and compulsions. Twenty-five percent believed that their symptoms were reasonable.

SOURCE: Based on Foa & Kozak (1995)

Hoarding Disorder

CASE STUDY Rose, a 39-year-old woman with two children, came into treatment for compulsive hoarding. Over 75 percent of her house was inaccessible because of piles of boxes, small appliances, food items, cans, and clothes. The dining room was unusable because the chairs, tables, and floor were covered with objects and boxes. She could not use her stove because of all of the items piled on top of it. Even a portion of her bed was covered with clothes and boxes. She was unable to discard items because she thought, "Maybe I will need this item in the future" and "If I throw it away, I will regret it" (St-Pierre-Delorme, Lalonde, Perreault, Koszegi, & O'Connor, 2011).

Hoarding

Individuals with hoarding disorder believe that the items collected are valuable and resist having them removed, even when the possessions are worthless or unsanitary or create a fire danger.

According to DSM-5, **hoarding disorder** is diagnosed when there is (a) an inability to discard items regardless of their value, (b) a perceived need for items and distress over the thought of giving or throwing them away, and (c) an accumulation of items that produces congestion and clutter in the living area. The hoarding results in distress or impairment in life activities or interferes with safety within the home. For example, Rose was unable to perform daily activities because about 75 percent of her house was inaccessible, and the accumulated objects posed a fire hazard. She also avoided inviting friends and family to her house because of the clutter and because she believed that they might try to convince her to give away, sell, or junk the excess items. Social pressure to discard possessions or cease hoarding is distressing for individuals with hoarding disorder because of their irrational emotional attachment to the items (Rachman, Elliott, Shafran, & Radomsky, 2009).

The prevalence of hoarding disorder ranges from 2 percent to 5 percent of adults (Iervolino et al., 2009; Mueller, Mitchell, Crosby, Glaesmer, & de Zwaan, 2009); up to 25 percent of individuals with anxiety disorders report significant hoarding symptoms (Tolin, Meunier, Frost, & Steketee, 2011).

Body Dysmorphic Disorder

CASE STUDY   A 14-year-old girl complained of dark under-eye circles and too-large eyebrows, which, she said, made her "look dead" or "punched in both eyes." She was also concerned about her uneven skin tone and blemishes. She spent between 5 and 9 hours a day tweezing her eyebrows and applying makeup to cover her perceived defects. To be able to get to school on time, she had to get up at 1 a.m. to begin this routine and refused to leave her home unless she felt that her "defects" were adequately covered (Burrows, Slavec, Nangle, & O'Grady, 2013).

The DSM-5 criteria for **body dysmorphic disorder (BDD)** include (a) preoccupation with a perceived physical defect in a normal-appearing person or excessive concern over a slight physical defect; (b) repetitive behaviors such as checking one's appearance in mirrors, applying makeup to mask "flaws," and comparing one's appearance to those of others; and (c) significant distress or impairment in life activities due to these symptoms. The preoccupation may be underdiagnosed because individuals are unwilling to bring attention to their "problem" (Bjornsson, Didie, & Phillips, 2010).

Although some individuals with BDD recognize that their beliefs are untrue, most maintain strong **delusions** (false beliefs) about their bodies (H. E. Reese, McNally, & Wilhelm, 2011). Individuals with BDD regard their "defect" with embarrassment and loathing and are concerned that others may be looking at or thinking about the defect. Some make frequent requests for cosmetic surgery.

hoarding disorder   condition involving congested living conditions due to accumulation of items and distress over the thought of discarding them

body dysmorphic disorder (BDD)   condition involving a preoccupation with a perceived physical defect or excessive concern over a slight physical defect

delusion   a firmly held false belief

Concern commonly focuses on bodily features such as excessive hair, lack of hair, or the size or shape of the nose, face, or eyes (see Figure 5.10).

The prevalence of BDD ranges from 0.7 percent to 2.4 percent of community samples, but has been found to be as high as 13 percent among individuals undergoing psychiatric hospitalization. Sixty percent of individuals with BDD have experienced an anxiety disorder, including 38 percent who have social anxiety (Mufaddel, Osman, Almugaddam, & Jafferany, 2013). BDD tends to be chronic and difficult to treat. In a 1-year follow-up of 183 individuals with BDD (84 percent had received mental health treatment), only 9 percent had full remission and 21 percent had partial remission of symptoms (K. A. Phillips, Pagano, Menard, & Stout, 2006). However, another study showed a more favorable outcome, with 76 percent recovering over an 8-year period (Bjornsson, Dyck, et al., 2011).

Muscle dysphoria, the belief that one's body is too small or insufficiently muscular, is a type of BDD (Ahmed, Cook, Genen, & Schwartz, 2014). Some bodybuilders who show a pathological preoccupation with their muscularity also suffer from BDD; these individuals have high body dissatisfaction and mistakenly believe they are "small" even though they are large and very muscular (Babusa & Túry, 2011).

Hair-Pulling Disorder (Trichotillomania)

Trichotillomania involves recurrent and compulsive hair pulling despite repeated attempts to stop the behavior. Trichotillomania results in hair loss and significant distress. The hair pulling may occur sporadically during the day or continue for hours

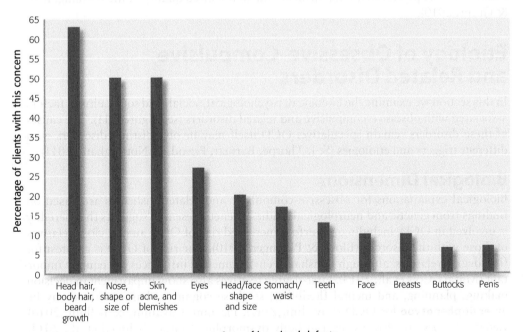

Figure 5.10

Imagined Defects in Patients with Body Dysmorphic Disorder

This graph illustrates the percentage of 30 patients who targeted different areas of their body as having "defects." Many of the patients selected more than one body region.

SOURCE: K. A. Phillips (2005)

muscle dysphoria belief that one's body is too small or insufficiently muscular

trichotillomania recurrent and compulsive hair pulling that results in hair loss and causes significant distress

at a time (Neal-Barnett et al., 2010). There is a lifetime prevalence of 4 percent, with woman having a 10 times greater likelihood of developing the disorder. Symptoms usually begin before age 17; however, many younger children outgrow the behavior (D. J. Stein et al., 2010; Trichotillomania, 2010).

Excoriation (Skin-Picking) Disorder

CASE STUDY A woman initiated therapy due to her 3-year history of skin picking resulting in lesions around her lips, cheeks, chin, and nose. The urge to pick occurred many times during the day and was followed by feelings of relief as soon as she engaged in the behavior. This activity was frequent, lasting for hours and preceded by emotional stress. Attempts to resist the urge were highly distressing (Luca, Vecchio, Luca, & Calandra, 2012).

Excoriation (skin-picking) disorder involves repetitive and recurrent picking of the skin that results in skin lesions (Snorrason, Smari, & Olafsson, 2011). Individuals with excoriation disorder spend 1 hour or more per day thinking about, resisting, or actually picking the skin. Episodes are preceded by rising tension; picking results in feelings of relief or pleasure (Tucker, Woods, Flessner, Franklin, & Franklin, 2011). According to DSM-5, a diagnosis of excoriation disorder occurs only when the behavior causes clinically significant distress or impairment and when there are repeated unsuccessful attempts to decrease or stop the behavior.

The lifetime prevalence of skin picking disorder is approximately 1.5 percent in adults and is most prevalent during adolescence. About three quarters of individuals with this disorder are females (APA, 2013). It is often comorbid with body dysmorphic disorder or trichotillomania. As with trichotillomania, individuals with excoriation disorder report psychosocial impairment and an impaired quality of life (Odlaug, Kim, & Grant, 2010).

Etiology of Obsessive-Compulsive and Related Disorders

In this section we examine the biological, psychological, social, and sociocultural factors associated with obsessive-compulsive and related disorders (see Figure 5.11). The causes of these disorders remain speculative. OCD itself may involve distinct disorders with different triggers and etiologies (S. J. Thorpe, Barnett, Friend, & Nottingham, 2011).

Biological Dimensions

Biological explanations for obsessive-compulsive and related disorders are based on findings from genetic and neurological studies. Genetic research suggests that heredity is involved in OCD, including a fourfold increased risk of OCD among close relatives of those with the disorder (Bloch & Pittenger, 2010). The risk of OCD is greatest for first-degree relatives, although nonshared environmental influences are equally important (Mataix-Cols et al., 2013). First-degree relatives also show impairment in decision making, planning, and mental flexibility, so these cognitive characteristics may be an **endophenotype** for OCD (Cavedini, Zorzi, Piccinni, Cavallini, & Bellodi, 2010). Genetic factors are also involved in body dysmorphic disorder (Ahmed et al., 2014), compulsive hoarding (Lervolino et al., 2009), and skin picking disorder (Monzani et al., 2012b), although environmental factors play a greater role in their etiology compared with OCD.

OCD may result from impairment in the functioning of brain circuits and structures that help mediate strong emotions and behavioral reactions to these emotions. Neuroimaging has revealed that some people with OCD show increased metabolic activity in the frontal lobe of the left hemisphere of the brain, suggesting that this

excoriation (skin-picking) disorder distressing and recurrent compulsive picking of the skin resulting in skin lesions

endophenotype measurable characteristics that can give clues regarding the specific genetic pathways involved in a disorder

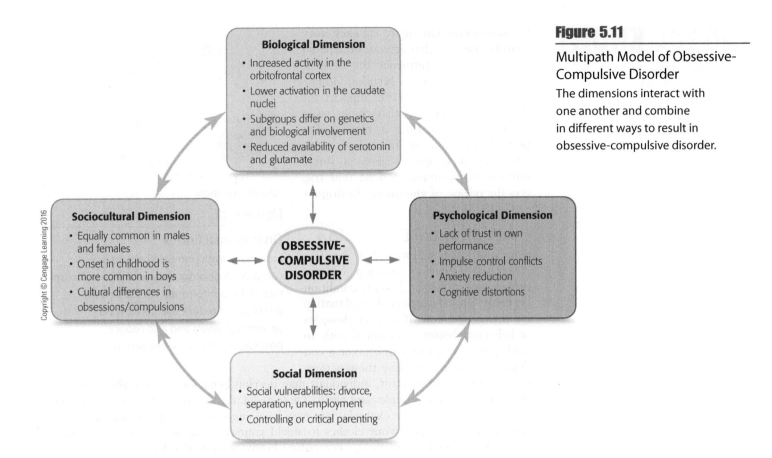

Figure 5.11

Multipath Model of Obsessive-Compulsive Disorder

The dimensions interact with one another and combine in different ways to result in obsessive-compulsive disorder.

Biological Dimension
- Increased activity in the orbitofrontal cortex
- Lower activation in the caudate nuclei
- Subgroups differ on genetics and biological involvement
- Reduced availability of serotonin and glutamate

Sociocultural Dimension
- Equally common in males and females
- Onset in childhood is more common in boys
- Cultural differences in obsessions/compulsions

OBSESSIVE-COMPULSIVE DISORDER

Psychological Dimension
- Lack of trust in own performance
- Impulse control conflicts
- Anxiety reduction
- Cognitive distortions

Social Dimension
- Social vulnerabilities: divorce, separation, unemployment
- Controlling or critical parenting

Copyright © Cengage Learning 2016

area—the **orbitofrontal cortex**—and related neural networks are associated with obsessive-compulsive behaviors (Beucke et al., 2013; Freyer et al., 2011) (see Figure 5.12). Symptoms of obsessive-compulsive disorder similarly suggest dysregulation involving the orbitofrontal-caudate circuit. The orbitofrontal cortex alerts the rest of the brain when something is wrong. When it is hyperactive, it may not only trigger the feeling that something is not right but also produce the feeling that something is "deadly wrong." Further, individuals with OCD show decreased activity in the brain region that regulates transmission of impulses (the **caudate nuclei**); this may allow disturbing thoughts to continue unchecked (Markarian et al., 2010). Interestingly, MRI scans have documented increased activity in the caudate nuclei of individuals with OCD who were successfully treated with cognitive-behavioral therapy (Freyer et al., 2011).

Excessive neural connectivity between the orbitofrontal cortex and the prefrontal cortex, a region associated with executive functions such as impulse control, has been documented using neuroimaging techniques. Interestingly, SSRI medications reduce OCD symptoms by targeting overactive neural connections (Cheng et al., 2013) while behavioral treatments appears to induce neuroplasticity that results in more functional connectivity. The latter treatment retrains the brain so that the fear circuitry no longer activates when a cue for obsessions or compulsions is present (Ressler & Rothbaum, 2012). Not surprisingly, hyperconnectivity between the visual processing areas of the brain and the prefrontal cortex and amygdala has been found in BDD (Ahmed et al., 2014; Buchanan et al., 2013).

Abnormalities in serotonin availability are presumed to be associated with OCD based on findings that SSRIs, medications that increase the availability of serotonin in the brain, are effective in treating many individuals with OCD. Additionally, drugs that are effective with other anxiety disorders but that do not increase serotonin availability are not effective with OCD symptoms (Zohar, Hollander, Stein, Westenberg, & Cape Town Consensus Group, 2007). Recent research also suggests that disrupted

orbitofrontal cortex brain region associated with planning and decision making

caudate nuclei brain region that regulates transmission of impulses warning that something is amiss

transmission of glutamate (an excitatory neurotransmitter that activates the firing of neurons) may influence the development of OCD (Kariuki-Nyuthe, Gomez-Mancilla, & Stein, 2014). Support for the role of glutamate also comes from research demonstrating a rapid reduction of symptoms in individuals with severe OCD symptoms given a single infusion of ketamine, a drug that triggers the release of glutamate (Rodriguez et al., 2013).

Psychological Dimension

Some researchers maintain that obsessive-compulsive behaviors develop because they reduce anxiety. Classical conditioning theory provides a possible explanation for this connection. If certain thoughts or behaviors become associated with an unpleasant event, they can become a conditioned stimulus. Because these actions or thoughts are unpleasant, individuals may develop behaviors or thoughts that help them avoid the initial unpleasant event. These avoidance behaviors reduce anxiety and are thus reinforcing. For example, you may have engaged in escape activities such as repeatedly reorganizing your clothes to shield yourself from anxiety over upcoming exams. If this occurs frequently, a compulsive behavior could develop.

Psychologists have also studied cognitive factors that lead to the severe doubts associated with obsessive-compulsive behavior. As we have discussed, individuals with OCD believe that if they do not act in a certain way, negative consequences will occur (Ghisi, Chiri, Marchetti, Sanavio, & Sica, 2010). Individuals with OCD show certain cognitive characteristics, including distorted thinking in the following areas:

* *Exaggerated estimates regarding the probability of harm*—"If the door isn't locked, I'll be killed by an intruder."
* *Control*—"If I am not able to control my thoughts, I will be overwhelmed with anxiety."
* *Intolerance of uncertainty*—"I have to be absolutely certain that I turned off the computer."

Similarly, individuals with OCD display *thought-fusion,* in which distressing thoughts regarding (a) an action (e.g., shouting obscenities during church services), (b) an event (e.g., thoughts of an injury to a loved one), or (c) an object (e.g., seeing a black cat means misfortune) become "fused" with the action, event, or object. In other words, having these thoughts produces the same emotions as if the event occurred or the actions were carried out (Myers & Wells, 2013). Because of this, individuals with OCD attempt to prevent these occurrences by suppressing the distressing thoughts (which paradoxically make them more likely to occur) or performing some type of ritual to negate the thought.

Individuals with OCD often have a *disconfirmatory bias*—that is, they search for evidence that might show that they failed to perform the ritual correctly. Compulsions occur because they are unable to trust their own memories or judgment and feel a need to determine whether they actually performed the behavior or performed it "correctly." Further, there may be a need to repeat the ritual multiple times until it is "just right" Thus, individuals with a compulsive need to check things may repeatedly lock their doors (even though they have seen and heard the lock engage) because they are unable to convince themselves that the door is indeed locked.

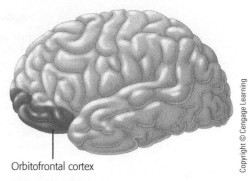

Orbitofrontal cortex

Copyright © Cengage Learning

Figure 5.12

Orbitofrontal Cortex

Individuals with untreated obsessive-compulsive disorder show a high metabolism rate in the orbitofrontal cortex. Certain medications reduce metabolic rates to "normal" levels and also reduce obsessive-compulsive symptoms.

Cognitive influences or beliefs also play an important role in hoarding disorder. Individuals with this disorder appear to have the conviction that objects that they have collected are extensions of themselves. They feel a sense of responsibility toward the items and have guilty feelings at the thought of discarding them. Individuals who hoard believe "I might need this someday," or "If I give it away, and need it in the future, I might ruin myself financially" (St-Pierre-Delorme et al., 2011). Such cognitive biases maintain the hoarding behavior.

Social and Sociocultural Dimensions

Family variables such as a controlling, overly critical style of parenting, minimal parental warmth, and discouragement of autonomy are associated with the development of OCD symptoms (Challacombe & Salkovskis, 2009). Individuals raised in adverse environments may develop maladaptive beliefs relating to personal responsibility; they may believe it is up to them to prevent harm to themselves or others and overestimate threats and feeling of responsibility (Briggs & Price, 2009). Individuals with OCD who perceive their relatives to be critical or hostile tend to have more severe symptoms (Van Noppen & Steketee, 2009).

Although we tend to think about OCD as an individual problem, it often develops within an interpersonal context. Friends, roommates, and family members also have to deal with OCD symptoms, as seen in the following case.

CASE STUDY   "... as soon as I'd go into the bathroom, they'd be banging on the door. 'How long are you going to be in there?'... I'd have to lock myself in the bathroom ... and I'd shake a third of this thing of Ajax in the toilet, a third in the sink and a third in the bath and I'd be there about an hour scrubbing everything up until it was pristine ..." (Murphy & Perera-Delcourt, 2014, p. 118)

Understandably, the long wait to use the bathroom was frustrating for family members; however, such negative reactions to OCD symptoms can increase symptom severity. Interestingly, symptoms also increase when loved ones provide assistance (e.g., helping someone clean or check doors and locks) or reassurance regarding the rituals. Although this might temporarily reduce distress, such assistance may actually reinforce or prolong the symptoms and contribute to poorer treatment outcome (Boeding et al., 2013).

OCD is more common among young people and among individuals who are divorced, separated, or unemployed (Karno & Golding, 1991). African Americans and Latino/Hispanic Americans are less likely to receive a diagnosis of OCD than are European Americans (A. Y. Zhang & Snowden, 1999). Culture may affect how the symptoms of OCD are expressed. For example, African Americans show greater concern about animals and about contamination than do European Americans (M. T. Williams, Abramowitz, & Olatunji, 2012).

Treatment of Obsessive-Compulsive and Related Disorders

The primary methods of treatment for obsessive-compulsive and related disorders are either biological or cognitive-behavioral in nature. Behavioral therapies have been used successfully for many years, but treatment with medication is becoming more common.

Biological Treatments

Antidepressant medications that increase serotonin availability (SSRIs) are often used to treat OCD and related disorders. Unfortunately, only about 60 percent of people with OCD respond to SSRIs, and often the relief is only partial (Brandl, Muller, & Richter, 2012). In one group of individuals with moderate OCD symptoms treated with SSRIs, many had significantly reduced symptoms after 2 years, although about

DID YOU KNOW?

The postpartum period is associated with obsessive and compulsive symptoms in women. Up to 11 percent of new mothers have persistent symptoms such as thoughts about injuring the baby, checking to see if the baby is breathing, or worrying about germs. These symptoms are usually temporary and may result from hormonal changes or adaptations to motherhood.

SOURCE: E. S. Miller, Chu, Gollan, & Gossett, 2013

one third experienced a recurrence of symptoms during a 5-year follow-up period; the likelihood of relapse was lowest for those who had a full remission of symptoms (Cherian, Math, Kandavel, & Reddy, 2014). Greater improvement is achieved in treating OCD when behavioral interventions are combined with SSRIs (Simpson et al., 2013). Additional medications such as antipsychotics are sometimes prescribed for individuals with OCD who do not improve with SSRIs; however, caution is advised because adverse reactions can occur (Andrade, 2013). Additionally, adding antipsychotic or antianxiety medications to cognitive-behavioral therapy does not significantly reduce symptom severity for those with OCD (Van Ameringen et al., 2014). There has, however, been increasing interest in the use of medications that modulate glutamate in the treatment of OCD (Grados, Specht, Sung, & Fortune, 2013).

Behavioral Treatments

The treatment of choice for OCD is a combination of exposure and response prevention (McKay & Storch, 2014; Olatunji et al., 2013). In treating OCD, exposure therapy involves continued actual or imagined exposure to a fear-arousing situation; it can involve gradual exposure to a distressing stimulus or **flooding**, which is the immediate presentation of the most frightening stimuli. **Response prevention** involves not allowing the individual with OCD to perform the compulsive behavior. The steps in exposure therapy with response prevention generally include (Simpson et al., 2013):

1. education about OCD and the rationale for exposure and response prevention;
2. development of an exposure hierarchy (from somewhat fearful to most-feared situations);
3. exposure to feared situations until anxiety has diminished; and
4. prevention of the performance of compulsive rituals such as hand washing.

Cognitive-behavioral therapy that focuses on correcting dysfunctional beliefs can also assist with OCD symptoms; unfortunately, up to 30 percent of those treated with CBT for OCD do not achieve symptom relief (Murphy & Perera-Delcourt, 2014). Cognitive-behavioral therapy has also produced promising results in the treatment of body dysmorphic disorder (Wilhelm, Phillips, Fama, Greenberg, & Steketee, 2011) and compulsive hoarding (St-Pierre-Delorme et al., 2011), although attrition rates are high (Mancebo, Eisen, Sibrava, Dyck, & Rasmussen, 2011). In fact, about half of the individuals treated for hoarding disorder do not complete treatment due to their extreme distress at the idea of parting with their possessions (Steketee, Frost, Tolin, Rasmussen, & Brown, 2010). Combining CBT with SSRIs may be a more effective means of treating hoarding disorder (Saxena, 2011).

Contemporary Trends and Future Directions

CASE STUDY   . . . I have, since the age of 10 . . . tried in various ways to overcome my anxiety . . . individual psychotherapy (three decades of it), family therapy, group therapy, cognitive-behavioral therapy, rational emotive behavior therapy, acceptance and commitment therapy, hypnosis, meditation, role-playing, interoceptive exposure therapy, in vivo exposure therapy, self-help workbooks, massage therapy, prayer, acupuncture, yoga, Stoic philosophy, and audiotapes. . . . Lots of medication. (Stossel, 2014)

flooding   a technique that involves inducing a high anxiety level through continued actual or imagined exposure to a fear-arousing situation

response prevention   treatment in which an individual with OCD is prevented from performing a compulsive behavior

Although there have been many advancements in treating the disorders covered in this chapter, many of those affected continue to experience distressing symptoms even after receiving treatment, as is the case for Scott Stossel. Cognitive-behavioral therapies are considered to be the most effective treatments for anxiety and obsessive-compulsive and related disorders. Yet, even among those who show improvement, many later relapse. As Schmidt (2012) observed, "we appear to have reached somewhat of a plateau with regard to treatment response, which would suggest a need to consider novel methods and approaches" (p. 465). Three areas that are receiving attention in the field of cognitive behavioral therapies are (a) specialized therapy programs that target specific disorders, (b) treatment protocols that can be used across different anxiety disorders, and (c) technology to improve CBT outcome and outreach (Schmidt, 2012). We will consider examples of research in these areas.

Therapy Modifications to Target Specific Disorders

Can CBT programs that are targeted to specific characteristics of a disorder improve treatment outcome? Consider BDD, which is very difficult to treat with traditional CBT approaches. Wilhelm and his colleagues (2014) developed a modified CBT-BDD program that focused on the "core" components of the disorder. Along with psycho-education regarding BDD, the approach involves:

- motivational enhancement to address ambivalence about complying with treatment;
- cognitive restructuring focused specifically on negative thoughts about personal appearance;
- exposure and response prevention focused on eliminating mirror checking, seeking reassurance, and the camouflaging of imagined defects; and
- mindfulness training focused on learning to observe and describe one's body without judgment.

Participants also learn to move away from self-focus, to pay attention to others and to their environment, and to base their self-esteem on qualities such as being a good friend rather than attractiveness. The participants also choose one of four treatment modules on topics such as mood management or concerns with shape/weight/muscularity.

How successful was this modified treatment? Of the participants, 83 percent responded favorably to the treatment, an outcome that is very promising because the participants were severely ill. Follow-up assessment at 3 and 6 months showed that participants maintained their treatment gains. The success of this program has prompted the development of modified CBT treatments for other difficult-to-treat disorders.

Treatment Protocols for Multiple Disorders

Paradoxically, not only is there interest in improving treatment outcome by modifying CBT for specific anxiety disorders, there is interest in developing CBT interventions that can be used with most anxiety disorders. Why is this necessary? Farchione and his colleagues (2012) believe that current treatments have resulted in a "proliferation of diagnosis-specific treatment manuals, many of which have only minor and somewhat trivial variations in treatment procedures" (p. 519). They wondered: Is there a unifying factor that is common across different anxiety disorders and, if so, can we develop a treatment package that adheres to a "single set of therapeutic principles"? Thus, they developed the Unified Protocol for Transdiagnostic Treatment of Emotional Disorders, which is a CBT program that is applicable to all anxiety and depressive disorders. It targets aspects of emotional processing and regulation that are assumed to underlie these disorders and consists of five modules: (a) increasing present emotional awareness, (b) increasing cognitive flexibility, (c) identifying and preventing patterns of emotion avoidance, (d) increasing awareness and tolerance of emotion-related physical sensations, and (e) exposure to physiological and emotional triggers.

Of the individuals with GAD, SAD, panic disorder, and OCD who were treated with this approach, more than half no longer met the criteria for the diagnosis at follow-up. Similarly, positive results were obtained using a modified "transdiagnostic" application of CBT in treating GAD, SAD, and panic disorder (Schmidt et al., 2012). Further, a study that directly compared the results of "transdiagnostic" CBT with group-specific treatments for GAD, SAD, and panic disorder found that both treatments produced similar improvements (Norton & Barrera, 2012). Greater attention and research pertaining to "universal" CBT treatments for anxiety disorders will continue, although it remains to be seen if this approach can also be successful with difficult to treat disorders such as BDD and hoarding disorder.

Technology to Improve CBT Outcome and Outreach

Use of computerized programs to treat anxiety disorders is increasing. This approach is reaching many individuals who do not have easy access to traditional treatment. A 6-week, self-administered CBT program for GAD based on computer-delivered cognitive and behavioral treatment modules was developed by Amir and Taylor (2012). Of the individuals who completed the program, 79 percent no longer met the criteria for a GAD diagnosis. While this program was based on treatment for a single diagnosis, an Internet-based program using mindfulness principles was found to be effective for individuals with GAD, SAD, and panic disorder (Boettcher et al., 2014). These findings again support the view that certain treatments may be effective across different diagnostic categories. Given the pervasiveness of disorders associated with anxiety and the number of people who do not respond to or cannot access traditional therapy, novel approaches to treatment are certainly warranted.

chapter SUMMARY

1 According to the multipath model, how are biological, psychological, social, and sociocultural factors involved in the development of anxiety disorders?

- The multipath model stresses the importance of considering the contribution of and *interaction* between biological, psychological, social, and sociocultural factors in the etiology of anxiety disorders.

- For example, genetically predisposed individuals (e.g., those with inherited overactivity of the fear circuitry in the brain) who grow up in a supportive family or social environment may not develop an anxiety disorder. Similarly, although sociocultural factors (e.g., discrimination, poverty) can increase the risk of anxiety disorders, personality variables, such as a sense of control and mastery, can help mitigate the impact of stressors.

2 What are phobias, what are their causes, and how are they treated?

- Phobias are strong, irrational fears. Social anxiety disorder involves anxiety over situations in which others can observe the person. Agoraphobia is an intense fear of being in public places where escape or help may not be possible. Specific phobias include a variety of irrational fears involving objects and situations.

- Biological explanations are based on studies of the influence of genetic, biochemical, and neurological factors and on the idea that humans are predisposed to develop certain fears. Psychological explanations include classical conditioning, observational learning, and distorted cognitions.

- The most effective treatments for phobias seem to be biochemical (antidepressants) and cognitive-behavioral (exposure, systematic desensitization, modeling, and graduated exposure).

3 What is panic disorder, what causes it, and how is it treated?

- Panic disorder is marked by unexpected episodes of extreme anxiety and feelings of impending doom.

- The causes of panic disorder include biological factors (genetics, neural structures, and neurotransmitters), psychological factors (catastrophic thoughts regarding bodily sensations), and social and sociocultural factors (a disturbed childhood environment and gender-related issues).

- Treatments for panic disorder include biochemical treatments (benzodiazepines and antidepressants) and behavioral treatments (identifying catastrophic thoughts, correcting them, and substituting more realistic ones).

4 What is generalized anxiety disorder, what are its causes, and how is it treated?

- Generalized anxiety disorder (GAD) involves chronically high levels of anxiety and excessive worry.

- There appears to be less support for the role of genetics in GAD than in other anxiety disorders, although overactivity of the anxiety circuitry in the brain is implicated. Cognitive-behavioral theorists emphasize erroneous beliefs regarding the purpose of worry or the existence of dysfunctional schemas. Social and sociocultural factors such as poverty and discrimination can also contribute to GAD.

- Antidepressant medications and cognitive-behavioral therapies are used for treatment.

5 What are obsessive-compulsive and related disorders, what causes these disorders, and how are they treated?

- Obsessive-compulsive disorder (OCD) and related disorders involve thoughts or actions that are involuntary, intrusive, repetitive, and uncontrollable.

- OCD is associated with increased metabolic activity in the orbitofrontal cortex and excessive neural connectivity involving the prefrontal cortex. According to the anxiety-reduction hypothesis, obsessions and compulsions develop because they reduce anxiety. Cognitive-behavioral therapists have focused on cognitive factors such as an intolerance of uncertainty or overestimating the probability of harm.

- Body dysmorphic disorder involves excessive concern or preoccupation with a perceived body defect.

- Hair-pulling disorder (trichotillomania) involves the compulsive pulling out of one's hair, resulting in noticeable hair loss.

- Excoriation (skin-picking) disorder involves the repetitive picking of one's skin, resulting in the development of lesions.

- Hoarding disorder involves accumulating possessions and difficulty discarding items, including items that appear to have little or no value.

- Antidepressant medications and cognitive-behavioral therapies are used to treat these disorders.

6

TRAUMA- AND STRESSOR-RELATED DISORDERS

GRISHAM, AN ARMY VETERAN, experienced a number of traumatic events when serving in Iraq, including shooting a person being used as a human shield and helping a distressed Iraqi family recover a dead loved one from a burned-out car. He had flashbacks and nightmares of these events. Even after returning to the United States, he remained extremely vigilant and fearful of crowded situations; he searched for exits before entering any building and always sat with his back against the wall so he could observe people approaching him (Tucker, 2012).

How does stress affect our mental and physical health? The answer is that stress can affect us in a variety of ways and that we all differ in our vulnerability to the effects of stressors. **Stressors** are external events or situations that place physical or psychological demands on us. We all encounter numerous stressors throughout our life—ranging from daily situations that may result in irritation or frustration to life-changing, traumatic events such as those experienced by Grisham, the army veteran in the introductory vignette.

Stress is the internal psychological or physiological response to a stressor. Most of us understand that traumatic events can affect us physically and psychologically. However, exposure to worrisome but less traumatic events can also significantly influence our health and well-being. Unfortunately, most of us experience stress on a regular basis. According to the Stress in America Survey, 44 percent of the adults responding indicated that their stress levels had increased over the past 5 years. Symptoms of stress reported by respondents included irritability or anger (45 percent), fatigue (41 percent), feeling nervous or anxious (36 percent), headache (36 percent), feeling depressed (34 percent), and muscle tension (23 percent) (American Psychological Association, 2010b).

Everyday stress can negatively influence our health and lead to the development of both psychological and physical conditions. Additionally, exposure to traumatic stressors can result in the distressing symptoms associated with trauma-related disorders. But how does this occur? And why are some people who are exposed to stressors, even traumatic ones, able to adjust without too much difficulty, whereas others develop intense, long-lasting

1 What do we know about disorders caused by exposure to specific stressors or traumatic events?

2 In what ways can stress affect our physical health?

psychological or physical symptoms? As you will see, the answers are complex, involving interactions among a variety of biological, psychological, social, sociocultural, and resiliency factors. In this chapter, we focus on disorders in which stress plays a major role—trauma- and stressor-related disorders and stress-related physical conditions.

Trauma- and Stressor-Related Disorders

The DSM-5 trauma and stressor-related disorder category includes disorders involving intense reactions to traumatic or stressful events. We will discuss three of these disorders: adjustment, acute stress, and post-traumatic stress disorders. The remaining trauma- and stressor-related disorders, reactive attachment disorder and disinhibited social engagement disorder, result from childhood trauma and are covered in our discussion of childhood disorders in Chapter 16.

Adjustment Disorders

An **adjustment disorder (AD)** occurs when someone has difficulty coping with or adjusting to a specific life stressor—the reactions to the stressor are disproportionate to the severity or intensity of the event or situation. Common stressors such as interpersonal or family problems, divorce, academic failure, harassment or bullying, loss of a job, or financial problems may lead to an AD. When do these common stressors cause diagnosable AD? According to DSM-5, the following is necessary for diagnosis of AD (American Psychiatric Association, 2013):

1. Exposure to an identifiable stressor that results in the onset of significant emotional or behavioral symptoms that occur within 3 months of the event.

2. Emotional distress and behavioral symptoms that are out of proportion to the severity of the stressor (normal bereavement is excluded from the AD diagnosis) and result in significant impairment in social, academic, or work-related functioning, or other life activities.

3. These symptoms last no longer than 6 months after the stressor or consequences of the stressor have ended.

AD can be acute, occurring after a specific one-time stressor, or chronic, involving multiple or repeated stressors. For example, individuals who experience repeated distressing stressors (e.g., employment problems or relationship conflicts) may qualify for a diagnosis of AD for up to 6 months after each stressor (APA, 2013).

Adjustment disorders often involve mood or behavioral changes, including symptoms of anxiety or depression. It is not always easy to distinguish between normal adaptive stress, adjustment disorders, and depressive and anxiety disorders (Fernández et al., 2012). The main differentiating factor is that a specific stressor precedes the symptoms seen in AD and that the person experiences an unusually intense reaction to the stressor. To increase diagnostic accuracy and to rule our preexisting mental health conditions, clinicians also consider a person's emotional functioning prior to the stressor (Kangas, 2013).

Some are concerned that an AD diagnosis may result in labeling and medicating individuals who are experiencing normative reactions to stressors (Doka, 2013). Determining whether someone's reaction to a stressful situation is "out of proportion" can be difficult. Is a young woman with children who received a diagnosis of cancer 3 weeks earlier and who is overwhelmed with feelings of depression demonstrating an AD, a normal adaptive emotional reaction, or a depressive disorder? Examples

stressor an external event or situation that places a physical or psychological demand on a person

stress the internal psychological or physiological response to a stressor

adjustment disorder (AD) condition involving reactions to life stressors that are disproportionate to the severity or intensity of the event or situation

such as this highlight the difficulty of differentiating between these three conditions (Casey & Doherty, 2013).

We have limited data on the prevalence of AD in the general population. However, it is a common diagnosis among people seeking help from medical or mental health professionals. The prevalence in that population ranges from 7 to 28 percent (Casey, 2009; Mitchell et al., 2011; Pelkonen, Marttunen, Henriksson, & Lönnqvist, 2007). AD is particularly common among those who have received a worrisome medical diagnosis; for example, up to one third of those diagnosed with cancer have symptoms qualifying for an AD diagnosis.

As you will see in the next section, in contrast to an AD diagnosis that involves exposure to stressors that range in their level of severity, other trauma-related disorders (acute and post-traumatic stress disorders) require the presence of certain traumatic stressors (see Table 6.1).

Table 6.1 Trauma- and Stressor-Related Disorders

DISORDERS CHART				
Disorder	**DSM-5 Criteria**[a]	**Prevalence (%)**	**Gender and Cultural Factors**	**Course**
Adjustment Disorder	• Exposure to stressor of any type or severity • Begins within 3 months of exposure to stressor • Lasts no longer than 6 months after termination of stressor or consequences from the stressor	Prevalence unknown in general population From 7–28% in medical and psychiatric samples	More common in women and higher-income groups	Most adults recover Adolescents may be at risk for other disorders

Acute Stress Disorder	• Direct or indirect exposure to traumatic stressor involving actual or threatened death, serious injury, or sexual violence
	• Nine or more symptoms involving
	  • intrusive memories
	  • avoidance of reminders of event
	  • negative thoughts or emotions
	  • heightened arousal
	  • dissociation or inability to remember details
	• Disturbance persists from 3 days to 1 month after exposure to trauma
		Up to 20% for most traumatic events; higher rates for those involving interpersonal situations
		Varies according to the type, intensity, and personal meaning of the traumatic stressor
			More prevalent in women, possibly due to more interpersonal trauma
			Symptoms may vary cross-culturally
				Over half will later receive a PTSD diagnosis; the remainder will remit within 30 days

Post-traumatic Stress Disorder	• Direct or indirect exposure to traumatic stressor involving actual or threatened death, serious injury, or sexual violence
	• One or two symptoms involving each of the following:
	  • intrusive memories
	  • avoidance of reminders of the event
	  • negative thoughts or emotions
	  • heightened arousal and hypervigilance
	• symptoms are present for at least 1 month
		Lifetime for U.S. adults is about 8.7%; 12- month prevalence is 3.5%
		Varies according to the traumatic stressor and population involved; higher rates for rape, military combat, and emergency responders
			Twice as prevalent in women
			Female adolescents have higher prevalence (6.6%) compared to males (1.6%)
			Low prevalence in Asian Americans
			Higher prevalence in Latinos and African Americans
			Symptoms may vary cross-culturally
				Symptoms fluctuate
				Over 50% recover within the first 3 months; for a minority, PTSD is a chronic condition

[a]Symptoms produce significant distress or impairment in social interactions, ability to work, or other areas of functioning.
SOURCE: Data from Alcantara et al., 2013; APA, 2013; Benton et al., 2012; Kobayashi et al., 2012; Merikangas et al., 2010.

Trauma-Related Disorders

> **CASE STUDY** I was raped when I was 25 years old. For a long time, I spoke about the rape as though it was something that happened to someone else. I was very aware that it had happened to me, but there was just no feeling. Then I started having flashbacks. They kind of came over me like a splash of water. I would be terrified. Suddenly I was reliving the rape. Every instant was startling. I wasn't aware of anything around me. I was in a bubble, just kind of floating. And it was scary. (National Institute of Mental Health, 2009, p. 7)

Unfortunately, exposure to trauma, such as the terrifying sexual assault described in this case, is not uncommon. In fact, as many as 85 percent of undergraduate students have experienced a traumatic event sometime in their lives (Table 6.2), with family violence and unwanted sexual attention or assault producing the highest levels of distress. People who face severe psychological or physical trauma such as military combat, sexual assault, or other life-threatening situations often display short-term psychological or physical reactions. However, some people who undergo these traumatic events experience few trauma-related symptoms.

After exposure to traumatic incidents, there are four common outcomes or trajectories (Bryant, 2013):

1. *Resilience*—relatively stable functioning and few symptoms resulting from the trauma
2. *Recovery*—initial distress with reduction in symptoms over time
3. *Delayed symptoms*—few initial symptoms followed by increasing symptoms over time
4. *Chronic symptoms*—consistently high trauma-related symptoms that begin soon after the event

Most individuals who experience trauma recover; they show a marked decrease or remission in symptoms with time (Santiago et al., 2013). For example, among people

Table 6.2 Undergraduates' Lifetime Exposure to Traumatic Events

	Women	Men
Unexpected death of close friend or loved one	49%	41%
Another's life-threatening event	31%	25%
Witnessing of family violence	25%	20%
Unwanted sexual attention	27%	5%
Severe injury (self or someone else)	18%	22%
Motor vehicle accident	17%	15%
Threat to one's life	11%	19%
Stalking	15%	4%
Childhood physical abuse	7%	7%
Partner violence	7%	3%
Unwanted sexual contact	8%	3%

SOURCE: Frazier et al., 2009.

directly affected by the September 11, 2001, attacks (i.e., people who were injured or who were in the attacked buildings), only about 15 percent developed a trauma-related disorder (DiGrande, Neria, Brackbill, Pulliam, & Galea, 2011).

The trauma-related disorders we will discuss—**acute stress disorder (ASD)** and **post-traumatic stress disorder (PTSD)**—both begin with normal adaptive responses to extremely upsetting circumstances. However, individuals who develop these disorders find that their anxiety and reactivity to cues associated with the traumatic circumstances do not fade away soon after the event. As you will see from our discussion, the risk of developing either ASD or PTSD depends on a number of variables, including the type of trauma and degree of perceived threat, the magnitude of the event, the extent of exposure to the stressor, and risk and protective factors specific to the individual.

Diagnosis of Acute and Post-Traumatic Stress Disorders

Trauma-related disorders begin with direct or indirect exposure to specific traumatizing stressors, including actual or threatened death, serious injury, or sexual violence. Initial stress reactions that occur shortly after a traumatic event are normative responses to an overwhelming and threatening stimulus. For some people, however, the response to a traumatic experience lasts for more than several days and results in the heightened reactivity and ongoing fear, alarm, and distress characteristic of ASD or PTSD. The trauma may be so overwhelming that the person finds it difficult to process or make sense of the event. Indirect exposure to trauma such as witnessing a traumatic event involving others, learning of a traumatic event involving loved ones, or repeated contact with aversive details of a traumatic event (such as professionals frequently exposed to details of violence or abuse) can also result in ASD or PTSD.

A diagnosis of ASD or PTSD requires direct or indirect exposure to the traumatic event, as well as symptoms from these major symptom clusters (APA, 2013):

- **Intrusion symptoms**—*intrusive thoughts, including distressing recollections, nightmares, or flashbacks of the trauma; psychological distress triggered by external or internal reminders of the trauma; physical symptoms such as increased heart rate or sweating.* Carmen, a 19-year-old college student, was raped by her best friend's father when she was 13 years old. The release of the perpetrator when she was in college increased her PTSD symptoms. Flashbacks of the assault began to occur, sometimes triggered by her boyfriend touching her or older men looking at her (Frye & Spates, 2012).

- **Avoidance**—*avoidance of thoughts, feelings, or physical reminders associated with the trauma, as well as places, events, or objects that trigger distressing memories of the experience.* One Iraq War veteran avoided social events and cookouts: Even grilling hamburgers reminded him of the burning flesh he encountered during combat in Iraq (Keltner & Dowben, 2007).

- **Negative alterations in mood or cognition**—*difficulty remembering details of the event; persistent negative views about oneself or the world; distorted cognitions leading to self-blame or blaming others; frequent negative emotions; limited interest in important activities; feeling emotionally numb, detached, or estranged from others; persistent inability to experience positive emotions.* The woman in the vignette presented earlier poignantly described her experience of numbness and detachment resulting from her rape. "I spoke about the rape as though it was something that happened to someone else. I was very aware that it had happened to me, but there was just no feeling. . . . I was in a bubble, just kind of floating."

- **Arousal and changes in reactivity**—*feelings of irritability that may result in verbal or physical aggression; engaging in reckless or self-destructive behaviors;* **hypervigilance** *involving constantly remaining alert for danger; heightened physiological reactivity such as exaggerated startle response; difficulty concentrating; sleep*

acute stress disorder (ASD) disorder characterized by flashbacks, hypervigilance, and avoidance symptoms that last up to 1 month after exposure to a traumatic stressor

post-traumatic stress disorder (PTSD) disorder characterized by flashbacks, hypervigilance, avoidance, and other symptoms that last for more than 1 month and that occur as a result of exposure to extreme trauma

hypervigilance state of ongoing anxiety in which the person is constantly tense and alert for threats

DID YOU KNOW?

Although PTSD was not officially recognized as a diagnosis until 1980, its symptoms have been recorded throughout history and known by different names:

- Soldier's heart during the Civil War (most prevalent among soldiers ages 9–17)
- Shell shock during World War I
- Battle fatigue during World War II
- Post-Vietnam syndrome after the Vietnam War

SOURCE: Pizarro, Silver, & Prause, 2006

disturbance. War veterans can become "unglued" at the sound of a door slamming, a nail gun being used, or a camera clicking. An Iraq War veteran who almost attacked some strangers at a sports event remarked, "When friends say 'I know where you're coming from,' . . . how could they? They didn't have to deal with insects, the heat, not knowing who the enemy is, not knowing where the bullet is coming from" (Lyke, 2004, p. A8).

In addition to the symptoms already described, clinicians also specify if there are recurrent symptoms of *depersonalization* (feeling detached from one's body or thoughts) or *derealization* (a persistent sense of unreality).

The diagnostic criteria for ASD and PTSD are very similar. A diagnosis of ASD requires the presence of at least nine symptoms from any of the symptom clusters, whereas a PTSD diagnosis requires that the individual exhibit one or two symptoms from each of the symptom clusters. Additionally, ASD involves symptoms that persist for at least 3 days but no longer than 1 month after the traumatic event; for a PTSD diagnosis the symptoms must be present for at least 1 month (APA, 2013). If someone with ASD experiences distressing symptoms for more than 30 days, the diagnosis may be changed to PTSD (Bryant, 2013). PTSD has a variable course; it may remit after several months or last for years (Santiago et al., 2013). In some cases, expression of PTSD is delayed—symptoms are not evident or sufficiently distressing to warrant a diagnosis until 6 months or more after the trauma.

Having the symptoms of PTSD can be quite distressing. Intrusive memories of the traumatic event via nightmares or flashbacks often occur unexpectedly and can be very upsetting both physically and psychologically. Trauma can shatter our sense of safety and security, and lead to feelings of disillusionment or helplessness. Irritability and verbal or physical reactivity or feelings of numbness and disconnection from others can strain friendships and other close relationships. Avoiding cues associated with the trauma can become a priority and further interfere with normal functioning. It is not surprising that up to half of individuals with PTSD develop depression (Rytwinski, Scur, Feeny, & Youngstrom, 2013).

What traumatic situations can cause a trauma-related disorder? Events associated with ASD and PTSD include the following:

- Combat (Peterson, Luethcke, Borah, Borah, & Young-McCaughan, 2011)
- Sexual assaults (Walsh et al., 2012)
- Violent crime or domestic violence (Hornor, 2013)
- Sexual harassment (Larsen & Fitzgerald, 2011)
- Natural disasters, such as hurricanes and earthquakes (Arnsberg, Johannesson, & Michel, 2013)
- Car accidents, work-related accidents, or other situations that produce a fear of severe injury or death (Buodo et al., 2011)

Current diagnostic guidelines for ASD and PTSD require direct or indirect exposure to a "traumatic" stressor—according to DSM-5, the person must be exposed to "death, threatened death, actual or threatened serious injury, or actual or threatened sexual violence" (APA, 2013). What happens when an individual develops ASD or PTSD symptoms after exposure to a traumatic stressor other than those defined in DSM-5? For example, a man developed trauma symptoms after eating part of a candy bar and discovering the candy was infested with maggots. He developed flashbacks to the event, imagined maggots in his food, and had nightmares of the incident (Christensen, 2012). Eating maggots may be horrifying but it does not meet the DSM-5 definition of a traumatic stressor. (His severe reactions would meet the criteria for an adjustment disorder diagnosis.) Some mental health professionals

CONTINUUM Video Project

Darwin: **PTSD**

© Cengage Learning®

"I led men into combat. And sometimes when I made decisions, people died."

Access the Continuum Video Project in MindTap at
www.cengage.com

believe that individuals with ASD or PTSD symptoms should receive a trauma-related diagnosis even in the absence of a traumatic stressor as described in DSM-5 (Cameron, Palm, & Follette, 2010; Christensen, 2012).

The lifetime prevalence of PTSD for adults in the United States is about 8.7 percent while the 12-month prevalence is about 3.5 percent (APA, 2013). Among U.S. adolescents 13 to 18 years of age, the lifetime prevalence rate is 4 percent, with females having a much higher rate of PTSD (6.6 percent) compared to males (1.6 percent) (Merikangas et al., 2010). The prevalence of PTSD varies across cultural groups and may reflect differential exposure to traumatic stressors, cultural differences in response to trauma, or differences in symptom expression (Hinton & Lewis-Fernández, 2011). For example, panic-like *khyâl attacks* induced by environmental triggers associated with trauma are a key feature of PTSD among Cambodian refugees (Hinton, Nickerson, & Bryant, 2011).

The lifetime prevalence of PTSD is highest among African Americans (9 percent), intermediate among Latino/Hispanic Americans (7 percent) and European Americans (7 percent), and lowest among Asian Americans (4 percent). Asian Americans have lower exposure to trauma and are less likely to develop PTSD after exposure (Roberts, Gilman, Breslau, Breslau, & Koenen, 2010). Women are twice as likely as men to be diagnosed with PTSD (Kobayashi, Cowdin, & Mellman, 2012).

Of the few studies available on ASD, it is estimated that up to 20 percent of those who experience a traumatic event develop ASD (Benton, Ifeagwu, Aronson, & Talavera, 2012). Rates of ASD of up to 50 percent are reported in cases involving interpersonal trauma such as rape or sexual assault (Elklit & Christiansen, 2010). However, the prevalence of ASD may be underestimated, as many of those with the symptoms may not seek treatment within the 30-day period that defines the disorder.

Impact of Natural Catastrophes

Acute stress disorder is often observed among people who experience natural disasters. Here Leona Watts sits in a chair in the wreckage of her home of 61 years. She had returned to look for some of her belongings.

Etiology of Trauma- and Stressor-Related Disorders

Only a minority of those exposed to trauma develop a disorder. What factors increase risk? Certain stressors such as severe physical injuries or more personalized trauma are more likely to result in PTSD (see Table 6.3). For example:

- Individuals who experience a stroke (Edmondson et al., 2013) or serious injuries to the head or extremities have increased risk of developing PTSD (Haagsma et al., 2012). Approximately one third of individuals hospitalized with major burn injuries demonstrated PTSD symptoms either initially or in the year after their trauma (McKibben, Bresnick, Wiechman Askay, & Fauerbach, 2008).

- Approximately one third of those who are raped or sexually assaulted develop PTSD (Kilpatrick, Amstadter, Resnick, & Ruggiero, 2007).

- PTSD rates are higher among those exposed to intentional trauma (e.g., assaults, war) than nonintentional trauma (e.g., car accidents, earthquakes) (Santiago et al., 2013).

PTSD symptoms are more likely when the perpetrator of an interpersonal trauma such as sexual assault is someone with whom the person has a close relationship (Martin, Cromer, Deprince, & Freyd, 2013). Factors such as a person's cognitive style, childhood history, genetic vulnerability, and availability of social support also moderate the impact of a traumatic event (Lindstrom, Cann, Calhoun, & Tedeschi, 2013; Schmidt, Kaltwasser, & Wotjak, 2013). In this section we use the multipath model to consider biological,

Table 6.3 Lifetime Prevalence of Exposure to Stressors by Gender and PTSD Risk

Trauma	Lifetime Prevalence (%)		PTSD Risk (%)	
	Male	Female	Male	Female
Life-threatening accident	25.0	13.8	6.3	8.8
Natural disaster	18.9	15.2	3.7	5.4
Threat with weapon	19.0	6.8	1.9	32.6
Physical attack	11.1	6.9	1.8	21.3
Rape	0.7	9.2	65.0	45.9

Some traumas are more likely to result in PTSD than others. Significant gender differences were found in reactions to "being threatened with a weapon" and "physical attack." What accounts for the differences in risk for developing PTSD among the specific traumas and for the two genders?

SOURCE: Ballenger et al., 2000.

psychological, social, and sociocultural factors associated with the development of trauma-related disorders (see Figure 6.1). Although we refer to PTSD throughout the discussion, the information also pertains to the acute reactions to trauma seen in ASD.

Biological Dimension

Many individuals who develop trauma-related disorders have a nervous system that is more reactive to fear and stress when compared to people who are exposed to trauma but do not develop a disorder (Medina, 2008). Although our biological systems are designed for rapid recovery from traumatic events and for **homeostasis** (physiological balance), some people are more prone to the physiological reactivity associated with chronic stress reactions.

homeostasis   state of metabolic equilibrium

Figure 6.1

Multipath Model for Post-Traumatic Stress Disorder
The dimensions interact with one another and combine in different ways to result in post-traumatic stress disorder (PTSD).

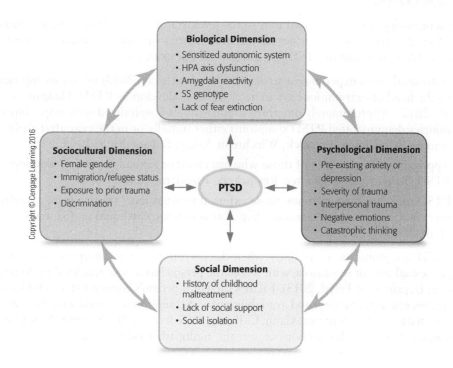

Copyright © Cengage Learning 2016

Biological Dimension
- Sensitized autonomic system
- HPA axis dysfunction
- Amygdala reactivity
- SS genotype
- Lack of fear extinction

Sociocultural Dimension
- Female gender
- Immigration/refugee status
- Exposure to prior trauma
- Discrimination

Psychological Dimension
- Pre-existing anxiety or depression
- Severity of trauma
- Interpersonal trauma
- Negative emotions
- Catastrophic thinking

Social Dimension
- History of childhood maltreatment
- Lack of social support
- Social isolation

PTSD

The normal response to a fear-producing stimulus is quite rapid, occurring in milliseconds, and involves the **amygdala**, the part of the brain that is the major interface between events occurring in the environment and physiological fear responses. In response to a potentially dangerous situation, the amygdala sends out a signal to the sympathetic nervous system, preparing the body for action (i.e., to fight or to flee). The **hypothalamic-pituitary-adrenal (HPA) axis** (the system involved in stress and trauma reactions) then releases hormones, including **epinephrine** and **cortisol**. These hormones prepare the body for "fight or flight" by raising blood pressure, blood sugar levels, and heart rate; the body is thus prepared to react to the potentially dangerous situation (Stahl & Wise, 2008). Cortisol also helps the body return to normal (i.e., restore homeostasis) after the stressor is removed.

Individuals with PTSD, however, continue to demonstrate these physiological stress reactions even when the stressor is no longer present. For example, neuroimaging studies of individuals with PTSD have shown heightened amygdala reactivity in response to stimuli associated with their trauma (Sherin & Nemeroff, 2011). Individuals with trauma-related disorders also show minimal **fear extinction**, or decline in fear responses associated with the trauma. In a study involving testing of soldiers before they were deployed, participants who showed less fear extinction (more prolonged reactivity to a fearful stimulus) were the most likely to exhibit PTSD after returning home. The researchers believe that deficiencies in fear extinction occur when the medial prefrontal cortex is unable to adequately inhibit fear responses; when fear extinction does not occur, various trauma-related cues continue to trigger fear reactions (Lommen, Engelhard, Sijbrandij, van den Hout, & Hermans, 2013). Impaired fear inhibition and difficulty discriminating safe situations is a hallmark of PTSD (Jovanovic et al., 2013). Thus, those with PTSD demonstrate an enhanced startle response, exaggerated physiological sensitivity to stimuli associated with the traumatic event, and diminished ability to inhibit fear responses (Schmidt et al., 2013). This reactivity may not be permanent, however, as over half of those with PTSD eventually recover (Santiago et al., 2013).

Why this reactivity occurs in the first place (i.e., why homeostasis is not restored soon after the trauma) is unclear. It is possible that the chronic release of stress hormones such as cortisol alters brain structures associated with stress regulation. The brain is particularly vulnerable to the effects of cortisol during childhood, a time when the brain is still developing. Disruptions caused by excess cortisol can lead to neuronal loss and affect brain areas such as the hippocampus, amygdala, and cerebral cortex (Gerson & Rappaport, 2013).

Genetic differences are also implicated in vulnerability to trauma-related disorders. Genetic research involving PTSD focuses on individuals with two short alleles (SS genotype) of the serotonin transporter gene (5-HTTLPR). Those with this genotype appear to have increased stress sensitivity and are more prone to the heightened anxiety reactions associated with PTSD. Recent research indicates that this increased risk among those with the SS genotype occurs only under conditions of severe trauma (Gressier et al., 2013). Other research suggests that this genetic variation increases risk of developing PTSD primarily when individuals exposed to a severe trauma have limited social support (Kilpatrick et al., 2008).

Psychological Dimension

What psychological factors contribute to the development of a trauma-related disorder? Preexisting conditions such as anxiety and depression (Weems et al., 2007) and negative emotions such as hostility and anger (DiGangi et al., 2013) are risk factors for the development of PTSD. Individuals with higher anxiety or negative emotions may react more intensely to a traumatic event because they ruminate about the event (DiGangi et al., 2013) or overestimate the probability that aversive events will follow (Engelhard, de Jong, van den Hout, & van Overveld, 2009).

amygdala   brain structure associated with the processing, expression, and memory of emotions, especially anger and fear

hypothalamic-pituitary-adrenal (HPA) axis   the system involved in stress and trauma reactions and regulation of body processes such as "fight or flight" responses

epinephrine   hormone released by the adrenal gland in response to physical or mental stress; also known as *adrenaline*

cortisol   hormone released by the adrenal gland in response to stress

fear extinction   elimination of conditioned fear responses associated with a trauma

A tendency to generalize trauma-related stimuli to other situations (e.g., a rape survivor avoiding contact with men) and to avoid situations associated with the trauma can maintain the fear response because the person is not able to learn that such situations are not dangerous; in other words, there is less opportunity for fear extinction (Frye & Spates, 2012).

As with anxiety disorders, individuals with specific cognitive styles or dysfunctional thoughts about themselves (e.g., "I feel so helpless") or the environment (e.g., "The world is a dangerous place") are more likely to develop PTSD (S. A. Bennett, Beck, & Clapp, 2009). They may interpret stressors in a catastrophic manner and thereby increase the psychological impact of trauma. For example, among child and adolescent survivors of assault and motor vehicle accidents, those with thoughts such as "I will never be the same" were more likely to develop PTSD symptoms (Meiser-Stedman, Dalgleish, Gluckman, Yule, & Smith, 2009). Negative thoughts such as these may produce sustained and heightened physiological reactivity, making the development of PTSD more likely. On the other hand, a positive cognitive style that results in active problem-solving, reframing traumatic events in a more positive light, and optimistic thinking can increase resilience and reduce risk of PTSD (Gupta & Bonanno, 2010; Prati & Pietrantoni, 2009). Not surprisingly, helping trauma survivors decrease dysfunctional trauma-related appraisals is effective in reducing PTSD symptoms (Kleim et al., 2013).

Social Dimension

CASE STUDY Ebaugh was traumatized when she was abducted and raped by a man with a knife. She begged him to release her but instead he handcuffed her and threw her from a bridge four stories above the water. She was able to swim on her back to shore. This terrifying ordeal resulted in PTSD (Hughes, 2012).

Ebaugh recovered from this trauma and was eventually free of PTSD symptoms. She attributes her resilience to the support from caring people. The truck driver who found her took her to a nearby store and gave her a cup of tea, the police were very sympathetic when questioning her, the physician at the hospital treated her like a daughter, and a close friend took her in. In addition, her family was supportive. Social support can prevent or diminish PTSD symptoms by affecting brain processes (such as the release of endorphins) that reduce stress and anxiety (Hughes, 2012).

In contrast, individuals who are socially isolated and lacking in support systems appear to be more vulnerable to PTSD when encountering traumatic events. Social support may dampen the anxiety associated with a trauma or prevent negative cognitions from occurring. In one study, those who reported low social support in the 6 months prior to exposure to the September 11, 2001 attacks were more than twice as likely to report symptoms of PTSD (Galea et al., 2002).

Additionally, less than optimal social support during childhood or exposure to childhood traumas such as physical or sexual abuse or severe bullying can contribute to the development of trauma-related disorders. Preexisting family conflict or overprotectiveness may also increase the impact of stress following exposure to a traumatic event (Bokszczanin, 2008). Conflicts or maltreatment in an individual's family of origin may increase anxiety, lead to negative cognitive styles, alter stress-related physiological activity and HPA axis dysfunction, or "trigger" a genetic predisposition toward greater physiological reactivity and thus increase the risk of developing PTSD (Kidd, Hamer, & Steptoe, 2011; McGowan, 2013).

Sociocultural Dimension

Ethnic differences have been found in the prevalence of PTSD, as mentioned earlier. In a survey of 1,008 adult New York residents following the terrorist attacks

Stress Following a Disaster

Many survivors of the Boston Marathon bombings recounted the terror they felt after two explosions went off near the finish line of the marathon on April 15, 2013.

Nicolas Czarnecki/METRO US/ZUMA Press, Inc. / Alamy

Post-Traumatic Stress Disorder and Abuse

In this photo, Cheryl, center, consoles Catherine, 24, during group therapy. Catherine is recalling the physical and emotional abuse she received during her childhood. Post-traumatic stress disorder is not isolated to combat situations. Women who have been battered or have suffered sexual assaults often report high rates of acute stress or post-traumatic stress disorder.

BananaStock/Jupiter Images/Getty Images

of September 11, 2001: 3.2 percent of Asian Americans, 6.5 percent of European Americans, 9.3 percent of African Americans, and 13.4 percent of Latino/Hispanic Americans reported symptoms consistent with PTSD (Galea et al., 2002). Among a sample of Hawaiian veterans of the wars in Iraq and Afghanistan, Asian Americans had lower rates of PTSD than Native Hawaiian/Pacific Islanders and European Americans (Wheatlin et al., 2013). Another survey found that Latino Americans have elevated rates of PTSD relative to non-Latino whites (Alcantara, Casement, & Lewis-Fernandez, 2013).

Ethnic group differences may be due to preexisting variables such as differential exposure to previous trauma or cultural differences in responding to stress (Triffleman & Pole, 2010). For example, African Americans and Latino/Hispanic Americans report higher levels of childhood trauma and interpersonal violence, experiences that can increase risk for PTSD (A. L. Roberts, Gilman, et al., 2010). Perceived discrimination based on race or sexual orientation is also associated with increased risk for PTSD (Flores, Tschann, Dimas, Pasch, & de Groat, 2010). Experiences or perceptions of discrimination can increase anxiety and lead to the development of negative thoughts about oneself and the world.

Women are twice as likely as men to suffer from a trauma-related disorder (Kobayashi et al., 2012). This may result from physiological differences or because women have greater risk of exposure to stressors that are likely to result in PTSD. In analyzing the data from the National Violence Against Women Survey, Cortina and Kubiak (2006) concluded that the greater prevalence of trauma-related disorders in women was due, in part, to more frequent exposure to violent interpersonal situations.

Female police officers face greater assaultive violence than civilian women, yet they are less likely to have symptoms of PTSD (Lilly, Pole, Best, Metzler, & Marmar, 2009). Similarly, female veterans deployed to Iraq and Afghanistan appear to be as resilient as men to combat-related stress (Maguen, Luxton, Skopp, & Madden, 2012; Vogt et al., 2011). What accounts for the difference in PTSD prevalence among civilian women and women who join the police force or the military? Women who choose these career paths may differ biologically from civilian women, may engage in emotional suppression to cope with the challenges of their work, or may conform to male

DID YOU KNOW?

About 5 percent of the 650 military dogs exposed to explosions, gunfire, and other combat violence in Afghanistan develop PTSD and display symptoms of hypervigilance, fear, and avoidance.

SOURCE: Dao, 2011

norms (Lilly et al., 2009). It is also possible that training for combat or police duties increases resilience.

Treatment of Trauma- and Stressor- Related Disorders

Studies on treatments for adjustment disorders are rare. Most researchers suggest using brief forms of therapy that focus on developing more adaptive responses to the immediate stressor or removing or modifying the stressor (Carta, Balestrieri, Murru, & Hardoy, 2009; Casey & Doherty, 2013). Fortunately, there is more research on treatment for the distressing trauma-related symptoms seen in those with ASD and PTSD.

Is There a Silver Lining to Adverse Life Events?

Stressful and traumatic life events are common. Although some people develop trauma or stressor-related disorders, many individuals appear to be resilient to stressors—that is, they are able to rebound after exposure to adversity. In fact, many who encounter significant stressors not only recover but also show "post-traumatic growth" and a greater capacity for future resilience (Seery, 2011). Adversity can produce mental and physiological "toughness" by decreasing physiological reactivity to stressors and increasing a sense of control and skill in dealing with difficult situations. Similarly, the concepts of stress inoculation (Meichenbaum, 2007) and "steeling" (Rutter, 2006) involve the assumption that some exposure to stress can actually strengthen an individual's resilience when encountering future stressors.

In a study to determine the accuracy of these perspectives, Seery, Holman, and Silver (2010) assessed the cumulative lifetime exposure to 37 negative events (e.g., death of family members, serious illness or injury, divorce, physical or sexual assaults, and exposure to natural disasters) experienced by several thousand respondents. Participants completed measures of mental health and well-being, involving life satisfaction, overall psychological distress, distress during the previous week, and post-traumatic stress (PTSD) symptoms, including impairment in day-to-day functioning. For the next 2 years, respondents completed periodic questionnaires regarding stressors encountered and current mental health. The researchers found an interesting relationship between adversity and mental health: Those who reported experiencing moderate amounts of prior adverse events showed better mental health (higher life satisfaction, lower global distress, fewer PTSD symptoms) than those who had either minimal or high levels of prior adversity. In addition, those with moderate exposure to adversity appeared to be more resilient to the adversities encountered within the 2-year follow-up period.

Thus, it does appear that moderate amounts of adversity can generate resiliency to future stressors. This may be because individuals who encounter adversities learn that challenges can be overcome, thereby increasing a sense of mastery and control. These qualities may buffer the impact of future stressors and reduce physiological stress reactions. Individuals with very limited exposure to adversity may not have had the opportunity to develop the skills necessary for overcoming challenges. Conversely, individuals confronted by multiple adverse events may feel overwhelmed and develop feelings of hopelessness and helplessness. Neither of these situations maximizes resilience or allows "toughness" to develop. Although more research is needed to determine if certain stressors or traumas are more toxic than others, it appears that "in moderation, whatever does not kill us may indeed make us stronger" (Seery et al., 2010, p. 1,038).

Photodisc/Getty Images

Medication Treatment for Trauma-Related Disorders

Certain antidepressant medications show moderate effects in some individuals with ASD and PTSD (Jonas et al., 2013). These medications appear to help by altering serotonin levels, decreasing reactivity of the amygdala and desensitizing the fear network. However, they are effective in less than 60 percent of people with PTSD; additionally, only about 20–30 percent of those who respond to antidepressants show full recovery (Berger et al., 2009). Friedman (2013) expresses concern about pharmaceutical companies' policies of marketing already-developed medications used with other disorders rather than searching for new medications that specifically target PTSD symptoms.

Several other medications treat PTSD symptoms with variable success. In clinical trials, D-cycloserine, a medication that appears to act on the brain to boost fear extinction processes, initially had promising results. However, further studies produced mixed results—although some individuals with PTSD improved, others reported increases in symptom severity (Hofmann, Wu, & Boettcher, 2013). Prazosin, a hypertension medication prescribed to reduce nightmares associated with PTSD, has shown some promising results (Kung, Espinel, & Lapid, 2012). Propranolol, a beta-blocker believed to reduce memory consolidation of a recent trauma (if given within 6 hours of the event), has been investigated as a treatment for the intrusive memories associated with PTSD. Although some studies showed support for propranolol (Klemm, 2010), a recent randomized, placebo-controlled study found little benefit and concluded that "the clinical results from this study do not support the preventive use of propranolol in the acute aftermath of a traumatic event" (Hoge et al., 2012). All three drugs are undergoing additional clinical trials.

GARVEY SCOTT/MCT/Landov

Psychiatric Service Dogs

Trained service dogs can mitigate PTSD symptoms in veterans by entering and checking out anxiety-evoking environments before the veteran enters and by reducing panic symptoms by giving the veteran a friendly nudge. Service dogs are also trained to place themselves as a barrier to reduce the chance of the veteran being startled by people unexpectedly approaching.

Psychotherapy for Trauma-Related Disorders

Prolonged exposure therapy (PE), cognitive-behavioral therapy (CBT), trauma-focused cognitive-behavioral therapy (TF-CBT), and eye movement desensitization and reprocessing (EMDR) are more effective in treating PTSD than other psychotherapies (Bisson, Roberts, Andrew, Cooper, & Lewis, 2013; Foa, Gillihan, & Bryant, 2013; Kleim et al., 2013). These therapies have generally focused on extinguishing the fear of trauma-related stimuli and correcting dysfunctional cognitions that perpetuate PTSD symptoms.

Prolonged exposure therapy involves imaginary and real-life exposure to trauma-related cues. Prolonged exposure to avoided thoughts, places, or people can help individuals with PTSD realize that these situations do not present a danger and thus extinguish associated fear reactions. The process of exposure sometimes involves asking participants to re-create the traumatic event in their imagination. For example, trauma survivors may be asked to repeatedly imagine and describe the event "as if it were happening now," verbalizing not only details, but also their thoughts and emotions regarding the incident. This exposure process allows extinction of the fear to occur (Foa et al., 2013).

In a meta-analytic review of PE, individuals treated using prolonged exposure fared better than 86 percent of individuals in control conditions (Powers, Halpern, Ferenschak, Gillihan, & Foa, 2010). PE is a preferred treatment modality among military personnel (Reger et al., 2013). Traumatized combat veterans have also benefited from PE techniques presented in a group format (Mott et al., 2012) and using visual immersion

> **MYTH** When individuals exposed to a traumatic event engage in psychological debriefing and emotional reprocessing of the event in a *critical incident stress debriefing* session, they are less likely to develop PTSD.
>
> **REALITY** There is no evidence that providing single-session psychological debriefing to trauma victims or rescue workers reduces psychological distress or prevents the development of PTSD. In fact, psychological debriefing may actually increase the risk of PTSD and depressive symptoms in some individuals (Rose, Bisson, Churchill, & Wessely, 2009; Wei, Szumilas, & Kutcher, 2010).

helmets that simulate combat scenes (McLay et al., 2012). Although reduced depression is not a direct treatment goal, PE has reduced depressive symptoms among veterans (Eftekhari et al., 2013). For PTSD resulting from child abuse, a therapeutic focus on helping individuals regulate their emotions appears to augment the effects of PE (Cloitre et al., 2010). Further, antidepressant medication may be more effective when combined with exposure therapy (Schneier et al., 2012).

Cognitive-behavioral therapy (CBT) and **trauma-focused cognitive-behavioral therapy (TF-CBT)**, which uses a combination of CBT techniques and trauma-sensitive principles, focus on helping clients identify and challenge dysfunctional cognitions about the traumatic event and current beliefs about themselves and others. These therapies address underlying dysfunctional thinking or pervasive concerns about safety. For example, battered women with PTSD often have thoughts associated with guilt or self-blame. Cognitions such as "I could have prevented it," "I never should have . . . ," or "I'm so stupid" can maintain PTSD symptoms. Therapy involving education about PTSD, developing a solution-oriented focus, reducing negative self-talk, and receiving therapeutic exposure to fear triggers (such as photos of their abusive partner or movies involving domestic violence) reduced PTSD symptoms in 87 percent of battered women receiving this treatment (Kubany et al., 2004). Mindfulness training, which involves paying attention to emotions and thoughts on a nonjudgmental basis without reacting to symptoms, also shows promise as an intervention for PTSD (Kearney, McDermott, Malte, Martinez, & Simpson, 2012; Kim et al., 2013).

Eye movement desensitization and reprocessing (EMDR) is a nontraditional and somewhat controversial therapy used to treat PTSD. In this unique approach, clients undergoing EMDR visualize their traumatic experience while following a therapist's fingers moving from side to side. The therapist prompts the client to substitute positive cognitions (e.g., "I am in control") for negative cognitions associated with the experience (e.g., "I am helpless"). Processing the trauma in a more relaxed state allows the client to detach from negative emotions and replace them with more adaptive appraisals of the trauma. After a series of EMDR sessions, many individuals with PTSD find significant reductions in hyperarousal and other symptoms associated with PTSD.

The exact mechanisms responsible for the success of EMDR are a subject of controversy. EMDR practitioners contend that the technique increases access to traumatic memories and allows the brain to reprocess emotional experiences with less distress (Jeffries & Davis, 2013). EMDR also includes aspects of prolonged exposure since visualization of the trauma allows desensitization and fear extinction to occur; EMDR also employs cognitive reappraisal strategies used in CBT. Researchers who have compared EMDR with and without the eye movement component, to see if the treatment effects are due to the eye movements or more traditional aspects of the therapy, have concluded that eye movements appear to play a role in enhancing treatment effects (Lee & Cuijpers, 2013). However, positive results have also occurred when other dual tasks replace eye movements during visualization of the trauma; thus, the emotional vividness of the traumatic memory may diminish due to other factors, including the taxing of working memory that occurs with dual tasks (van den Hout & Engelhard, 2012). Research into the mechanisms underlying EMDR therapy will no doubt continue.

Psychological Factors Affecting Medical Conditions

CASE STUDY Data from 200 patients who happened to have cardiac defibrillators implanted prior to the World Trade Center attack on September 11, 2001, provided interesting information regarding the physiological impact of the stressful event. The defibrillators, which record and respond to serious heart arrhythmias, showed a doubling of life-threatening arrhythmias during the month following the terrorist attacks (Steinberg et al., 2004).

Stress causes a multitude of physiological, psychological, and social changes that influence health conditions. Unfortunately, stress is pervasive. Among a national sample of college students, nearly 43 percent felt "more than average stress" and over 10 percent had "tremendous stress" during the last 12 months (American College Health Association, 2012). As we mentioned earlier, U.S. adults are also quite stressed. (See Figure 6.2 for the major causes of stress.) Further, stress experienced by parents is often apparent to their children; more than 90 percent of children report that their parents are more likely to argue, yell, or complain when stressed (American Psychological Association, 2010b). In this part of the chapter, we consider the ways in which stress and other psychological factors affect physical illness.

Although stress can have beneficial functions such as alerting us to the need to deal with a challenging situation or energizing us to accomplish important goals, most researchers acknowledge that excessive stress can negatively affect our physical well-being. In the past, *psychosomatic* was the term applied to physical disorders—such as asthma, hypertension, and headaches—made worse by psychological factors or behaviors. This term attempted to distinguish physical disorders affected by psychological factors from conditions considered strictly physical in nature. Now, however, medical and mental health professionals recognize that psychological factors influence many medical conditions.

In DSM-5, the diagnostic category "Psychological Factors Affecting Other Medical Condition" applies to situations where psychological or behavioral factors adversely influence the course or treatment of a medical disorder, constitute an additional risk factor for the medical condition, or make the illness worse (APA, 2013). For the sake of brevity, we sometimes substitute the term **psychophysiological disorder**—which references any physical disorder that has a strong psychological basis or component—instead of "psychological factors affecting other medical conditions." Emotional states, patterns of interpersonal interaction, and coping styles are just a few examples of how psychological factors can affect physical illness. We begin by discussing how stress and other psychological factors or behaviors influence the development of and exacerbate symptoms of a variety of medical conditions.

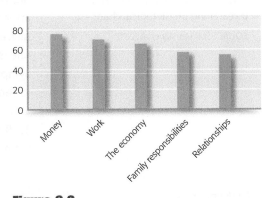

Figure 6.2

Five Leading Causes of Stress in America

The Stress in America survey, documenting high levels of stress among U.S. adults, suggests that the economic recession has taken a toll on the well-being of adults in the U.S.

SOURCE: American Psychological Association (2010b)

MYTH Psychophysiological disorders are merely psychological in nature. Real physical problems are not present. Therefore, the only recommended treatment is psychotherapy.

REALITY Although psychophysiological disorders do have a psychological component, actual physical processes or conditions are involved. Any physical condition can be considered a psychophysiological disorder if psychological factors contribute to the development of the disorder, make the condition worse, or delay improvement. In most cases, both medical and psychological treatments are needed.

Medical Conditions Influenced by Psychological Factors

CASE STUDY Cyndy Bizon was under a great deal of stress. Her husband, Joe, suffered a heart attack while in recovery from routine surgery. Cyndy became increasingly stressed over her husband's condition and camped out in the hospital. Two days after his heart attack, she walked up to the nurses' station, felt faint, and dropped to the floor. A rush of stress hormones (e.g., adrenalin) had stunned her heart muscle. The hospital staffers were able to revive her and get her heart back to its normal rhythm. She had suffered from "broken heart" syndrome (Naggiar, 2012).

psychophysiological disorder
any physical disorder that has a strong psychological basis or component

Broken heart syndrome, a reversible cardiac condition, results from toxic levels of epinephrine (i.e., adrenaline) associated with sudden stress. Any strong emotional reaction can produce this physiological response. In one study, researchers described 19 adults who developed severe cardiac symptoms after exposure to a highly emotional event (e.g., car accident, news of a death, surprise birthday party, armed robbery, court appearance). The emotional stress resulted in the cardiac distress associated with broken heart syndrome (Wittstein et al., 2005). A massive release of stress hormones paralyzes the heart muscle, causing it to shut down. Symptoms and test results associated with broken heart syndrome are very similar to those of a heart attack. However, there is no evidence of blocked heart arteries and most people make a full recovery within weeks (American Heart Association, 2013). For some unknown reason, this condition is 7.5 times more likely to occur in women. Fortunately, only about 1 percent of cases are fatal (Deshmukh, 2012).

Medical conditions influenced by psychological factors can involve actual tissue damage (e.g., coronary heart disease), a disease process (e.g., impairment of the immune system), or physiological dysfunction (e.g., asthma, migraine headaches). Both medical treatment and psychotherapy may be required. The relative contributions of physical and psychological factors to a physical disorder can vary greatly. Although it is sometimes difficult to determine the exact psychological factors that are contributing to a medical condition, repeated association between a stressor and symptoms of the disorder provides important information regarding psychological influences that may be involved. The case of broken heart syndrome is more clear-cut than many psychophysiological conditions; it is evident that a psychological stressor set off a cascade of physiological events that affected the heart.

In this section we discuss several of the more prevalent psychophysiological disorders—coronary heart disease, hypertension (high blood pressure), headaches, and asthma—and then consider the topic of how stress influences the immune system. We also review research identifying biological, psychological, social, and sociocultural influences on specific psychophysiological disorders.

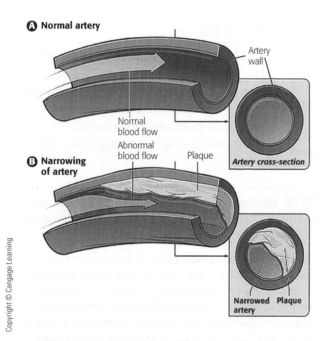

A Normal artery

Artery wall

Normal blood flow

Abnormal blood flow

B Narrowing of artery

Plaque

Artery cross-section

Narrowed artery

Plaque

Copyright © Cengage Learning

Figure 6.3

Atherosclerosis

Atherosclerosis occurs when fat, cholesterol, and other substances build up in arteries and form a hard structure called *plaque*. The buildup of plaque and resultant narrowing of the arteries can result in arteriosclerosis, or hardening of the arteries, a condition that can reduce or even stop blood flow to tissues and major organs.

Coronary Heart Disease

Coronary heart disease (CHD) involves the narrowing of cardiac arteries due to **atherosclerosis** (plaque buildup within the arterial walls), resulting in complete or partial blockage of the flow of blood and oxygen to the heart, as seen in Figure 6.3. When coronary arteries are narrowed or blocked, less oxygen-rich blood reaches the heart muscle. This can result in angina (chest pain) or, if blood flow to the heart is significantly blocked, a heart attack.

One out of every six deaths in the United States is due to CHD. Each year, about 600,000 people have an initial heart attack and almost 300,000 have a recurrent attack (Go et al., 2014). A variety of psychological and behavioral factors increase risk and affect prognosis with CHD, including poor eating habits (resulting in high cholesterol levels), hypertension, cigarette smoking, obesity, lack of physical activity, and psychosocial factors such as depression, perceived stress, and difficult life events (American Heart Association, 2010).

Stress plays both a biological and psychological role in CHD. Biologically, stress causes the release of hormones that activate the sympathetic nervous system, which can lead to changes in heart rhythm such as *ventricular fibrillation* (rapid, ineffective contractions of the heart), *bradycardia* (slowing of the heartbeat), *tachycardia* (speeding

coronary heart disease (CHD) disease process involving the narrowing of cardiac arteries, resulting in the restriction or partial blockage of the flow of blood and oxygen to the heart

up of the heartbeat), or *arrhythmia* (irregular heartbeat). Figure 6.4 shows an example of ventricular fibrillation.

Hypertension

CASE STUDY On October 19, 1987, the stock market drastically dropped 508 points. By chance, a 48-year-old stockbroker was wearing a device measuring stress in the work environment on that day. The instrument measured his pulse every 15 minutes. At the beginning of the day, his pulse was 64 beats per minute and his blood pressure was 132 over 87. As stock prices fell dramatically, the man's physiological system surged in the other direction. His heart rate increased to 84 beats per minute and his blood pressure hit a dangerous 181 over 105. His pulse was "pumping adrenaline, flooding his arteries, and maybe slowly killing him in the process" (Tierney, 1988).

The stockbroker's reaction in the case study illustrates the impact of a stressor on **blood pressure,** the measurement of the force of blood against the walls of the arteries and veins. **Normal blood pressure** is considered a **systolic pressure** (force when the heart contracts) lower than 120 and a **diastolic pressure** (the arterial pressure that occurs when the heart is relaxed after a contraction) lower than 80. We all experience transient physiological responses to stressors, but some people develop a chronic condition called **hypertension,** in which the systolic blood pressure equals or exceeds 140 and the diastolic pressure is 90 or higher. **Prehypertension** involves increases in blood pressure (systolic pressure between 120 and 139 and diastolic pressure between 80 to 89) and is believed to be a precursor to hypertension, stroke, and heart disease (Zhang & Li, 2011); prehypertension is found in 34 percent of men and 22 percent of women in the United States (Ostchega, Yoon, Hughes, & Louis, 2008).

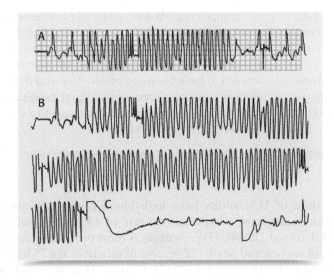

atherosclerosis condition involving the progressive thickening and hardening of the walls of arteries due to an accumulation of fats and cholesterol along their inner linings

blood pressure the measurement of the force of blood against the walls of the arteries and veins

normal blood pressure the normal amount of force exerted by blood against the artery walls; systolic pressure is less than 120 and diastolic pressure is less than 80

systolic pressure force on blood vessels when the heart contracts

diastolic pressure arterial force exerted when the heart is relaxed and the ventricles of the heart are filling with blood

hypertension a chronic condition, which increases risk of stroke and heart disease, characterized by a systolic blood pressure of 140 or higher or a diastolic pressure of 90 or higher

prehypertension a condition believed to be a precursor to hypertension, stroke, and heart disease, characterized by systolic blood pressure of 120 to 139 and diastolic pressure from 80 to 89

Figure 6.4

Ventricular Fibrillation in Sudden Unexplained Death
A Thai man fitted with a defibrillator showed ventricular episodes (rapid spikes on the graph) when asleep. Part A represents a transient episode that resolved itself. Part B depicts a sustained ventricular episode accompanied by labored breathing. Part C shows that his defibrillator was set off, which normalized the heart rate. Is this the explanation for sudden unexplained death syndrome?
SOURCE: Nademanee et al. (1997)

The Hmong Sudden Death Syndrome

CASE STUDY Vang Xiong is a Hmong (Laotian) former soldier who, with his wife and child, resettled in Chicago in 1980. City life in a new country was a significant change from the familiar farm life and rural surroundings of his native village. Vang had experienced the trauma of seeing people killed prior to his escape from Laos, and expressed feelings of guilt about leaving his brothers and sisters behind. His physical difficulties began soon after his move to Chicago:

[He] could not sleep the first night in the apartment, nor the second, nor the third. After three nights of sleeping very little, Vang went to see his resettlement worker, a bilingual Hmong man named Moua Lee. Vang told Moua that the first night he woke suddenly, short of breath, from a dream in which a cat was sitting on his chest. The second night, the room suddenly grew darker, and a figure, like a large black dog, came to his bed and sat on his chest. He could not push the dog off, and he grew quickly and dangerously short of breath. The third night, a tall, white-skinned female spirit came into his bedroom from the kitchen and lay on top of him. Her weight made it increasingly difficult for him to breathe, and as he grew frantic and tried to call out he could manage but a whisper. He attempted to turn onto his side, but found he was pinned down. After fifteen minutes, the spirit left him, and he awoke, screaming. (Tobin & Friedman, 1983, p. 440)

The terrifying dream-state symptoms experienced by Vang are connected to *Hmong sudden death syndrome*—the term used to describe hundreds of cases of sudden death involving Southeast Asian refugees. Almost all cases involved men and most occurred within the first 2 years of residence in the United States. Autopsies produced no identifiable cause for the deaths. All of the reports were the same: People in apparently good health went to sleep and died in their sleep. Often, victims displayed labored breathing, screams, and frantic movements just before death. Some consider the deaths to represent an extreme and very specific example of the impact of psychological stress on physical health (see Figure 6.4). Similar cases of sudden unexplained death have been reported in Asian countries (Aoki et al., 2003).

Vang was one of the lucky people with the syndrome—he survived. He went for treatment to a Hmong woman, a highly respected shaman in Chicago's Hmong community. She believed unhappy spirits were causing his problem and performed ceremonies to release them. After that, Vang reported no more physical problems or nightmares during sleep.

In many non-Western cultures, physical or mental problems are attributed to supernatural forces such as witchcraft or evil spirits (Sue & Sue, 2013). The spiritual treatment Vang received using non-Western methods seemed to have been successful. How would a doctor practicing Western medicine interpret Vang's symptoms? Would you have recommended consulting a shaman in this case? Why or why not?

DID YOU KNOW?

During the recent recession, there was a 26 percent increase in Google searches for stress-related conditions such as headaches and chest and stomach pain.

SOURCE: Althouse, Allem, Childers, Dredze, & Ayers, 2014

About one third of U.S. adults have high blood pressure requiring treatment. African American adults have a hypertension rate of 44 percent, which is the highest in the world (Go et al., 2014). Hypertension is most prevalent among older adults. Over 81 percent of women and nearly 72 percent of men over age 75 have hypertension (National Center for Health Statistics, 2012). Chronic hypertension leads to *arteriosclerosis* (hardening of the arteries) and to increased risk of stroke and heart attack. In 90–95 percent of the cases, the exact cause of the hypertension is not known, but psychological and behavioral factors can play a role (American Heart Association, 2010). Figure 6.5 shows age, gender, and ethnic comparisons of hypertension among adults.

Migraine, Tension, and Cluster Headaches

Headaches are among the most common stress-related psychophysiological complaints. About 90 percent of males and 95 percent of females have at least one headache during a given year. Among adolescents, headaches are common and more prevalent and

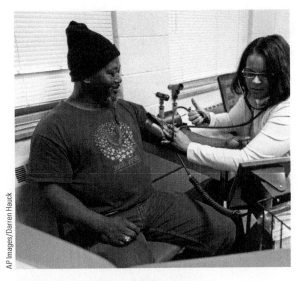

Undiagnosed Hypertension

David Thomas was buying groceries and decided to get a blood pressure check at a clinic located in the store. He found that he had high blood pressure and was a prime candidate for a stroke.

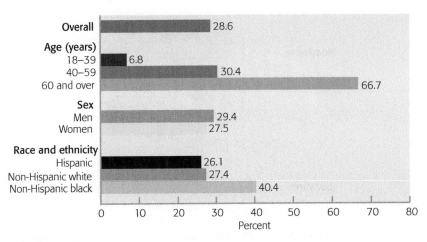

Figure 6.5

Gender and Ethnic Differences in Hypertension among Adults in the United States, 2009–2010 Data

SOURCE: Yoon, Burt, Louis & Carroll (2012) and CDC/NCHS, National Health and Nutrition Examination Survey

severe in girls (Larsson & Fischtel, 2012). More than 45 million U.S. Americans suffer from chronic, recurring headaches (Meeks, 2004). The pain of a headache can vary in intensity from dull and annoying to excruciating. A number of biological, psychological, social, and sociocultural factors have been associated with the onset of headaches.

In addition to stress, headaches can be precipitated by negative emotions, noise, too much or too little sleep, exposure to smoke or strong odors, hormonal factors in women, and certain foods (Martin & MacLeod, 2009; National Institute of Neurological Disorders and Stroke, 2012). Although we discuss migraine, tension, and cluster headaches separately, the same person can be susceptible to more than one type of headache. (Figure 6.6 illustrates some differences among the three types.)

Migraine Headaches

CASE STUDY   A 42-year-old woman described her headaches as a throbbing that pulsed with every heartbeat. Visual effects, such as sparklers flashing across her visual field, accompanied the pain. The symptoms would last for up to 3 days (Adler & Rogers, 1999).

Migraine headaches are associated with inflammation and dilation of cranial arteries; the pressure on nearby nerves and chemical changes within the brain produce pain (NINDS, 2012). Pain from a migraine headache may be mild, moderate, or severe. Most people with migraines report having them once or twice a month; 10 percent have them weekly, 20 percent have them every 2 or 3 days, and 15 percent have them more than 15 days a month (Dodick & Gargus, 2008).

Migraines may last from a few hours to several days and are often accompanied by nausea and vomiting. Up to one third of individuals with migraines experience an **aura**—involving unusual physical sensations or visual symptoms such as flashes of light, unusual visual patterns, or blind spots—prior to the headache (Steiner, MacGregor, & Davies, 2007). Individuals with severe migraine headaches accompanied by symptoms such as flashes of light, tingling, or blind spots show anomalies in

migraine headache   moderate to severe head pain resulting from abnormal brain activity affecting the cranial blood vessels and nerves

aura   a visual or physical sensation (e.g., tingling of an extremity or flashes of light) that precedes a headache

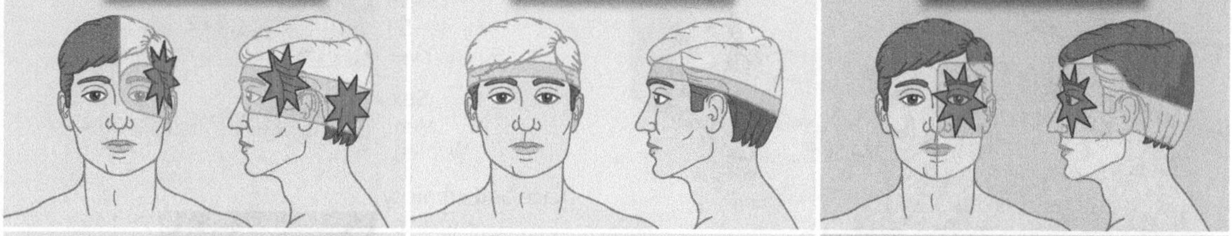

Headache	Migraine	Tension	Cluster
Location	Often one side of head but location varies	Both sides of head, often concentrated	Centered on one eye on same side of head
Duration	Hours to 4 days	Hours to days	Usually less than an hour
Severity of Pain	Mild to severe	Mild to moderate	Excruciating
Symptoms	Nausea, sensitivity to light, sound, odors, and movement	Tightness or pressure around neck, head, or shoulders	Eye often teary, nose clogged on side of head with pain; pacing and rubbing head
Sex Ratio	More common in young adult women	More common in women	More common in men
Heredity	Often hereditary	Probably not hereditary	Sometimes hereditary

Figure 6.6

Three Types of Headaches

Some differences in the characteristics of migraine, tension, and cluster headaches have been reported, although similarities between them also exist.

SOURCE: Data adapted from "Headaches" (2006); Silberstein (1998)

the white matter of the brain. This suggests that severe migraines may be associated with structural changes in the brain (Bashir, Lipton, Ashina, & Ashina, 2013).

Based on 19 studies of adults, the 1-year prevalence of definite migraine headaches is 11.5 percent (17.1 percent in women and 5.6 percent in men) while an additional 7 percent have probable migraine headaches (Merikangas, 2013). Over 8 percent of college students report being treated for migraine headaches in a 12-month period (American College Health Association, 2012). Prevalence peaks in midlife and is lower in adolescents and those over age 60. Migraine headaches are common not only among women but also among people with lower incomes. They are more common among European Americans than African Americans (Lipton et al., 2007).

Tension Headaches **Tension headaches** are produced when stress creates prolonged contraction of the scalp and neck muscles, resulting in vascular constriction and steady pain. They are the most common form of headache and tend to disappear once the stress producing the muscle tension is over (Singh & Crystal, 2013). The vast majority of adults experience tension headaches; additionally, about one third of children report having tension headaches (Monteith & Sprenger, 2010). Tension headaches are generally not as severe as migraine headaches, and can usually be relieved with aspirin or other analgesics.

tension headache head pain produced by prolonged contraction of the scalp and neck muscles, resulting in constriction of the blood vessels and steady pain

Cluster Headaches

CASE STUDY A patient seeking help for excruciating headaches described the pain in the following manner: "It feels like someone walked up to me, took a screwdriver and jammed it up in my right eye and kept digging it around for 20 minutes" (Linn, 2004, p. A1).

Cluster headaches involve an excruciating stabbing or burning sensation located in the eye or cheek. The attacks are extremely painful and have a very rapid onset (Bakbak, Gedik, Koktekir, & Okka, 2012). The symptoms are so severe that 55 percent of individuals experiencing a cluster headache report suicidal thoughts (Rozen & Fishman, 2012). Cluster headaches occur in cycles, and incapacitating attacks can arise several times a day (Meeks, 2004). In about 20 percent of cases, the headaches are preceded by an aura (Rozen, 2010). Each attack may last from 15 minutes to 3 hours before ending abruptly.

Along with the headache, the individual may experience tears or a stuffy nose on one side of the head. Headache cycles may last from several days to months, followed by pain-free periods. Only about 10 to 20 percent of cluster headaches are chronic. Cluster headaches sometimes run in families and, in contrast to other headaches, are more common in men (Rozen & Fishman, 2012).

Asthma

Asthma, a chronic inflammatory disease of the lungs, can be aggravated by stress or anxiety. During asthma episodes, stress or other triggers cause excessive mucus secretion combined with spasms and swelling of the airways, which reduces the amount of air that can be inhaled (Figure 6.7). Symptoms range from mild and infrequent wheezing or coughing to severe respiratory distress requiring emergency care. In severe asthma attacks, respiratory failure can occur.

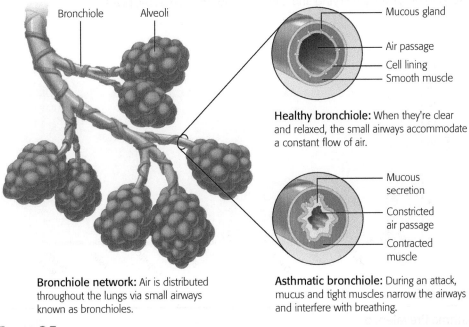

Bronchiole network: Air is distributed throughout the lungs via small airways known as bronchioles.

Healthy bronchiole: When they're clear and relaxed, the small airways accommodate a constant flow of air.

Asthmatic bronchiole: During an attack, mucus and tight muscles narrow the airways and interfere with breathing.

Figure 6.7

An Asthma Attack

Asthma attacks and deaths have increased dramatically since the 1980s.

SOURCE: Cowley & Underwood (1997, p. 61)

cluster headache excruciating stabbing or burning sensations located in the eye or cheek

asthma a chronic inflammatory disease of the airways in the lungs

In the United States, prevalence of asthma has increased dramatically since the 1980s. It affects up to 8.2 percent of the population, or about 24.6 million individuals, with a disproportionate recent increase among women (Akinbami, Moorman, & Liu, 2011; Centers for Disease Control and Prevention, 2013). The increase in the number of asthma cases in the United States is puzzling. Suspicion grows that, in addition to increasingly stressful life circumstances, a number of different pollutants (cigarette smoke, industrial toxins, pollution, pet hair and dander, indoor molds, and cockroaches) may be responsible (Global Initiative for Asthma, 2010; Schultz et al., 2012).

Exposure to pollutants and other environmental stressors may be responsible for the finding that ethnic minority children living in inner cities and African American, American Indian, and Filipino children are more vulnerable to asthma (Brim, Rudd, Funk, & Callahan, 2008; Forno & Celedón, 2009). Figure 6.8 shows asthma prevalence among different groups.

People with asthma often underestimate the magnitude of airflow obstruction during an asthma attack (Ritz, Meuret, Trueba, Fritzsche, & von Leupoldt, 2013). Unfortunately, when there is a delay in seeking emergency assistance, death can result. In fact, asthma is the sixth leading cause of death in children 5–14 years of age (Katon, 2010). Additionally, for reasons that are not clearly understood, adolescents with asthma are twice as likely to die from suicide compared to their peers without asthma (Kuo et al., 2010).

Stress and the Immune System

CASE STUDY Florida was hit by four hurricanes within a 6-week period. One woman was able to deal with the first, even though it smashed her windows, flooded her carpets, and caused her to throw food away. Then a second hurricane struck, causing similar damage. She had to wait in the hot sun to get ice and was without food or water for her children. As she related, "The first one, I stayed strong. But this second one, I started crying and couldn't stop" (Barton, 2004, p. A3).

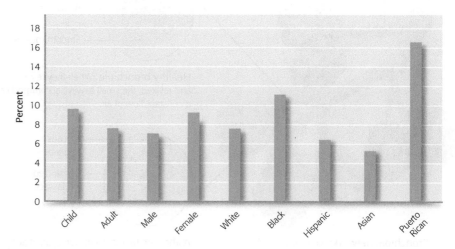

Figure 6.8

Asthma Prevalence

This figure shows the prevalence of asthma among adults and children, men and women, and members of different ethnic groups. Of these groups, Puerto Ricans, African Americans, females, and children appear to be especially vulnerable.

SOURCE: Akinbami et al. (2011)

We know that stress is associated with illness, but what is the precise relationship between the two? How does stress affect health? Although stress itself does not cause infections, it does appear to decrease the immune system's efficiency, thereby increasing a person's susceptibility to disease. Part of our physiological stress response involves the release of hormones such as cortisol that suppress immune functioning. When stress results in excessive production of cortisol, the suppressed immune system may fail to combat infection; additionally, white blood cells, responsible for destroying pathogens such as bacteria, viruses, fungi, and tumors, may be unable to multiply (Powell, Tarr, & Sheridan, 2013). If natural defenses are weakened, infections and diseases are more likely to develop or become more serious.

Researchers are attempting to demonstrate how exposure to chronic stress increases vulnerability to infection and accelerates the progression of disease (Dhabhar, 2013). Cohen and colleagues (1998) asked 276 volunteers to complete a life stressor interview and a physical evaluation. They then quarantined those who were healthy, after giving them nasal drops containing a cold virus. Of this group, 84 percent became infected with the virus, but only 40 percent developed cold symptoms. Participants who reported undergoing severe stress (e.g., conflicts with family or friends or unemployment) for 1 or more months were much more likely to develop colds.

Similarly, researchers queried law students about their optimism regarding their law school experience multiple times over a period of 6 months. On each occasion they were also injected with an antigen designed to generate an immune response. A stronger immune response was noted when students were feeling optimistic. Thus, perceptions about their performance in school influenced their immunity (Segerstrom & Sephton, 2010).

Deterioration in immune system functioning can increase vulnerability to certain illnesses, but can it also lead to the development of diseases such as cancer? Consider the following case study.

CASE STUDY Anne is an unhappy, passive individual who always accedes to the wishes and demands of her husband. She has difficulty expressing strong emotions, especially anger, and represses her feelings. She has few friends and no one to confide in. She often feels a pervasive sense of hopelessness and depression. During a routine physical exam, Anne's doctor discovers a lump in her breast. A biopsy reveals that the tumor is malignant.

Did Anne's personality or emotional state contribute to the formation or growth of the malignant tumor? Can she now alter the course of her disease by changing her emotional state, thereby improving her immune functioning? Several problems exist in research investigating the effects of mood and personality on the development of cancer (Honda & Goodwin, 2004). First, *cancer* is a general name for a variety of disease processes, each of which may have a varying susceptibility to psychological influences. Second, cancer develops over a relatively long period of time. Determining a relationship between its occurrence and a specific mood or personality is not possible. Third, most studies examining the relationship between psychological variables and cancer are retrospective—that is, personality or mood states are usually assessed after the cancer is diagnosed. People who receive the life-threatening diagnosis of cancer may respond with depression, anxiety, and confusion. Thus, instead of being a cause, negative emotions may be an emotional response to having a serious disease.

Does stress or certain personality characteristics increase susceptibility to cancer or increase the severity of the disease? Stressors and negative emotions have been associated with decreases in immune system functioning; when the immune system is compromised, it is possible that cancer can gain a foothold (Kiecolt-Glaser, 2009). Nevertheless, the connection between stress and cancer has yet to be demonstrated.

At this time, negative emotions and stressors have not been found to cause cancer. Additionally, reducing the stress of cancer victims does not appear to increase longevity, although quality of life is improved (National Cancer Institute, 2012).

Etiological Influences on Physical Disorders

As we have seen, not everyone who faces stressful events develops a psychophysiological disorder or shows reduced immune functioning. Daily living involves constant exposure to stressors, including work expectations at school or on the job, relationship problems, and illness, to name a few. Why do only some individuals develop a physical disorder when engaging in unhealthy behaviors or when exposed to stressors? In this section, we use the multipath model to explore some of the biological, psychological, social, and sociocultural dimensions of the disease process, as shown in Figure 6.9. Although we are discussing these dimensions separately, many interactions can occur among factors within and between dimensions.

Biological Dimension

Stressors, especially chronic ones, can dysregulate physiological processes occurring throughout the brain and body. When a stressor activates the HPA axis and the **sympathetic nervous system**, a cascade of hormones is released, including epinephrine, norepinephrine, and cortisol. These hormones, along with the activation of the sympathetic nervous system, prepare the body for emergency action by increasing heart rate, respiration, and alertness while simultaneously decreasing vulnerability to inflammation. This preparation helps us respond quickly to a crisis situation. However, when such activation occurs over an extended period of time (i.e., there are chronic stressors), a psychophysiological disorder can develop (Kendall-Tackett, 2009).

sympathetic nervous system part of the nervous system that automatically performs functions such as increasing heart rate, constricting blood vessels, and raising blood pressure

Figure 6.9

Multipath Model of Psychophysiological Disorders

The dimensions interact with one another and combine in different ways to result in a specific psychophysiological disorder.

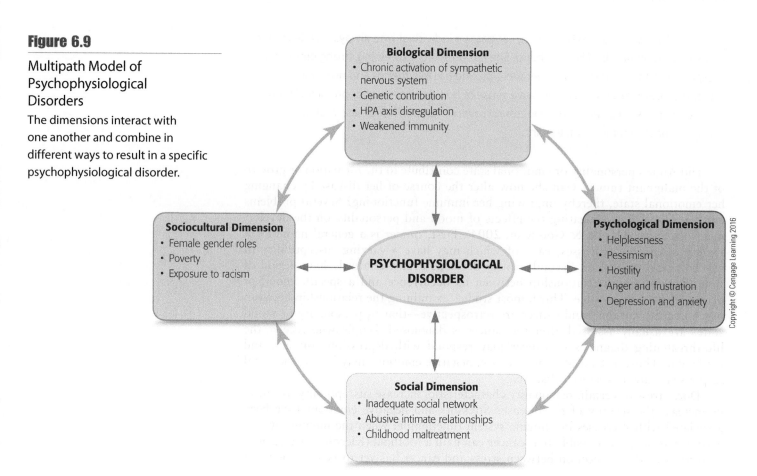

Biological Dimension
- Chronic activation of sympathetic nervous system
- Genetic contribution
- HPA axis disregulation
- Weakened immunity

Psychological Dimension
- Helplessness
- Pessimism
- Hostility
- Anger and frustration
- Depression and anxiety

PSYCHOPHYSIOLOGICAL DISORDER

Sociocultural Dimension
- Female gender roles
- Poverty
- Exposure to racism

Social Dimension
- Inadequate social network
- Abusive intimate relationships
- Childhood maltreatment

Copyright © Cengage Learning 2016

Research supports the view that while brief exposure to stressors enhances immune functioning, long-lasting stress can impair immune response (Schuster, Bornovalova, & Hunt, 2012). Heightened or ongoing preparedness to face stress results in increased cortisol production: Excess cortisol has been linked with coronary artery calcification, a contributor to coronary heart disease (Hamer, O'Donnell, Lahiri, & Steptoe, 2010). Table 6.4 compares short-term adaptive responses to stress with symptoms that can result from chronic stress.

Early environmental influences such as traumatic childhood experiences may produce changes in stress-responsive neurobiological systems, resulting in increased vulnerability to the development of a psychophysiological disorder (Midei, Matthews, Chang, & Bromberger, 2013). Additionally, genetic influences contribute to psychophysiological disorders. For example, cardiovascular stress reactivity as measured by blood pressure is more similar among identical twins than among fraternal twins (De Geus, Kupper, Boomsma, & Snieder, 2007). Genetic factors also appear to play a role in asthma: If one parent has asthma, a child has a 1 in 3 chance of developing asthma; if both parents have asthma, the chances increase to 7 in 10 (Asthma and Allergy Foundation of America, 2007). Among African American men, having purer African ancestry increases risk of developing severe asthma (Rumpel et al., 2012). Migraine headaches may involve a biological predisposition that affects the reactivity of brain cells and pain receptors (Dodick & Gargus, 2008). Although genetics and physiological response to chronic stress play a role in physical illness, so do psychological, social, and sociocultural factors.

Psychological Dimension

Psychological and personality characteristics can influence health status. Positive affect, such as optimism, happiness, joy, and contentment, can help regulate heart rate, blood pressure, and other physiological stress reactions, whereas negative emotions accentuate the stress response (Trudel-Fitzgerald, Boehm, Kivimaki, & Kubzansky, 2014). For example, a longitudinal study of individuals who remained employed in a down-sized company where nearly half of the workforce was laid off demonstrate how people respond differently to stress; although two thirds of the retained employees developed health problems, the remaining third appeared to thrive. The individuals who did well had three characteristics: (1) commitment—rather than allowing themselves to feel isolated and helpless, they became involved in the change process; (2) control—they refused to feel powerless and attempted to influence decisions; and (3) openness to challenge—they viewed changes within the company as opportunities

Table 6.4 Adaptive and Maladaptive Responses to Stress

Adaptive Responses (Short-term Stress)	Maladaptive Responses (Chronic Stress)
Increased glucose	Hyperglycemia (diabetes)
Increased blood pressure	Hypertension, breakage of plaque in arteries
Increased immunity	Impaired immune response to illnesses
Increased vigilance	Hypervigilance
Diminished interest in sex	Global loss of interest in sex
Improved cognition and memory	Increased focus on traumatic events, lack of attention to current environment
Faster blood clotting	Increased thickness of coronary artery walls (coronary vascular disease, strokes)

SOURCE: Data from Carels et al., 2003; Keltner & Dowben, 2007.

(Maddi, 2002). These characteristics are sometimes together described as "hardiness," a trait that appears to protect people from the harmful effect of stressors (Hamer et al., 2010).

Control and the perception of control over the environment and its stressors can influence the effects of stress (Christie & Barling, 2009). People who believe they have limited influence over life circumstances ("I have little control over things that happen to me") have an increased risk of mortality from CHD (Surtees et al., 2010). A group of older adults agreed to keep a daily journal describing stressful situations and their perceptions of perceived control over life events. Individuals who reported greater daily stress and lower control were more likely to have thickening of the lining of the carotid artery, a marker of atherosclerosis (Kamarck, Muldoon, Shiffman, & Sutton-Tyrrell, 2007). Similarly, women with demanding jobs involving little personal control had nearly double the chance of having a heart attack compared to women with more personal control over stressful jobs (Albert, Glynn, & Buring, 2010). In contrast, among older adults with physical health problems, those who vowed to take charge of their health by engaging in health-improving strategies and seeking help to address their physical problems were less likely to show the pattern of biological decline typical of those with health issues (Wrosch, Schulz, Miller, Lupien, & Dunne, 2007).

Positive emotions may increase heart health. High levels of well-being (feeling energetic, cheerful and happy with life) are associated with reduction in cardiovascular disease even in those with many risk factors for heart disease (Yanek et al., 2013). In a comprehensive study involving nearly 10,000 women studied for 8 years, those who scored high on optimism ("In unclear times, I usually expect the best") had a 9 percent lower risk of developing heart disease and a 14 percent lower risk of dying. In contrast, women who had hostile thoughts about others were 16 percent more likely to die during the same time period (Tindle et al., 2009). People who were satisfied with their lives had less CHD risk than their dissatisfied counterparts (Boehm, Peterson, Kivimaki, & Kubzansky, 2011).

Negative emotional states such as depression, hostility, anxiety, and cynicism are related to airway constriction in individuals with asthma (Goodwin, Bandiera, Steinberg, Ortega, & Feldman, 2012; Ritz et al., 2013), symptoms of CHD (Hamer, Kivimaki, Stamatakis, & Batty, 2012), and stroke risk (Pendlebury, 2012). Depression and anxiety can influence both physiological functioning and behaviors that affect health. Individuals with high levels of these emotions exhibit irregularities in the autonomic nervous system (e.g., elevated levels of the adrenal hormones epinephrine and norepinephrine) that suggest exaggerated cardiovascular responses to stressors (Lambiase, Kubzansky, & Thurston, 2014). In addition, depression may result in behaviors—such as excessive sleep, reduced exercise, consumption of unhealthy food, or increased use of caffeine, alcohol, or cigarettes—that increase susceptibility to illness.

Hostility is associated with several psychophysiological disorders, particularly CHD (Wong, Na, Regan, & Whooley, 2013). The association between hostility and CHD may exist because negative emotions such as hostility can increase cardiovascular reactivity, subsequently increasing the risk of developing CHD. Additionally, young healthy males who responded to unfair treatment with anger or frustration showed elevated cholesterol levels, a factor associated with increased risk of developing CHD (Richards, Alvarenga, & Hof, 2000). Among African American and European American adolescents, those who scored low on social skills and high on anger or hostility measures had increased abdominal fat and greater arterial stiffness (hardening of the arteries); these associations were particularly strong for the African American participants (Midei & Matthews, 2009).

Social Dimension

Social stressors have been associated with impaired immunological functioning and other adverse health outcomes (Dickerson & Kemeny, 2004). A lack of social support can lead to immune system dysregulation with less natural killer cell activity and elevated inflammation (Jaremka et al., 2013).

Maltreatment in social relationships can have significant health consequences. Childhood adversities such as physical, emotional, or sexual abuse are associated with headaches (Tietjen, Khubchandani, Herial, & Shah, 2012) and hypertension (Kidd et al., 2011). Those who reported a greater number of childhood adversities had a greater likelihood of developing hypertension in adulthood (S. E. Taylor, 2010). Early childhood or chronic adversities can affect physiological stress reactions and result in the suppression of immune functioning. Similarly, an "astonishing number" of health consequences occur when there is physical or emotional abuse in intimate partner relationships; the acute and chronic stress caused by relationship violence can influence a wide range of health conditions (Black, 2011).

However, having social support (i.e., feelings of being loved, valued, and cared for) is associated with positive health (S. E. Taylor, 2010). In fact, good relationships may moderate the link between hostility and poor health. In one study, hostile individuals in high-quality relationships showed reduced physiological reactivity to stress (Guyll, Cutrona, Burzette, & Russell, 2010). Social support may exert an indirect influence on health. For example, individuals with supportive family relationships or with a large social network may receive encouragement for healthy eating habits, exercise, and other health-promoting activities, thus increasing resistance to disease.

Sociocultural Dimension

Sociocultural factors such as gender roles can have a major impact on health. For example, women have an increased likelihood of exposure to stressors associated with their role as caregivers for children, partners, and parents (Stambor, 2006). Additionally, woman

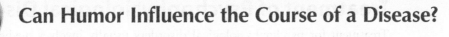

CONTROVERSY

Can Humor Influence the Course of a Disease?

Can humor reduce the severity of or even cure a physical illness? Author Norman Cousins, who suffered from rheumatoid disease, described how he recovered his health through laughter. He claimed that 10 minutes of laughter would provide 2 hours of pain relief (Cousins, 1979). In 1999, Patch Adams, a physician known for using humor with his patients, received an award for "excellence in the field of therapeutic humor." Some research has shown that exposing participants to humorous videos reduces stress and improves immune system functioning (Bennett, Zeller, Rosenberg, & McCann, 2003). Watching funny videos is associated with improved blood flow (Sugawara, Tarumi, & Tanaka, 2010), and laughter is associated with improved heart functioning (Sakuragi, Sugiyama, & Takeuchi, 2002).

How might humor influence the disease process? Several routes are possible:

- Humor may directly affect immune functioning.
- Humor may serve as a psychological buffer to stress, thus reducing the impact of stressors on physical health.

- Humor may increase social connections and enhance social support from friends and family, thus exerting an indirect positive influence on health.

Although laughter can produce positive physiological benefits, it may exacerbate certain conditions such as asthma and headaches (Ferner & Aronson, 2013). Overall, the evidence regarding positive health benefits of humor is mixed and relatively weak (Bennett & Lengacher, 2006). Even if humor does not directly benefit health outcomes, are there circumstance where humor might improve psychological well-being and reduce a person's stress levels?

David Sacks/Stone/Getty Images

Maintaining Tradition and Reducing Risk

Japanese Americans who maintain traditional lifestyles have a lower rate of coronary heart disease than those who have acculturated to mainstream U.S. culture. The difference does not appear to be due to diet or other investigated risk factors.

are more likely to live in poverty and experience the sociocultural stressors and chronic disparities associated with having limited economic resources (L. Smith, 2010). Given the importance of social relationships for most women, social isolation is more likely to negatively affect the health of women. In a longitudinal study of men and women, high loneliness in women (discrepancy between actual and desired social relationships) was associated with a nearly 80 percent increase in CHD; this association was not found in men (Thurston & Kubzansky, 2009).

Although genetic and other biological factors may perhaps partially explain the high rate of hypertension in African Americans, another line of research supports a sociocultural explanation. Exposure to racism and perceived discrimination can heighten stress responses and elevate blood pressure and heart rate (Pascoe & Richman, 2009). Even exposure to subtle racism can cause cardiovascular reactivity (Merritt, Bennett, Williams, Edwards, & Sollers, 2006). Experiencing discrimination may function as a chronic stressor and thus explain the increased rates of hypertension (Dolezsar, McGrath, Herzig, & Miller, 2014). This relationship may be complex, however, at least among African American women. When exposed to racism, those who are least likely to seek social support experienced the greatest increases in blood pressure; those who frequently reach out for social support did not show this tendency (R. Clark, 2006). Thus, coping skills, resources, and social support may mitigate vascular reactivity in response to racism. This clearly warrants further research.

Treatment of Psychophysiological Disorders

Treatment for psychophysiological disorders usually involves medical treatment for the physical symptoms and psychotherapy to eliminate stress and anxiety. For example, individuals who learn specific techniques to help manage stress show reductions in stress hormones and autonomic reactivity, and report less pain, less anxiety, improved sleep, and a higher quality of life (Blume, Brockman, & Breuner, 2012). Similarly, therapeutic interventions such as relaxation training, cognitive therapy, and biofeedback can reduce headaches (Ezra, Gotkine, Goldman, Adahan, & Ben-Hur, 2012). Newer cognitive-behavioral therapies such as acceptance and commitment therapy (which focuses on accepting the difficulties that come with life and committing to behaviors that are consistent with one's values) appear to improve the well-being of individuals with serious health conditions (Masters & Hooker, 2013). Other psychological approaches for stress management include relaxation training, biofeedback, or cognitive-behavioral therapy.

Relaxation Training

relaxation training a therapeutic technique in which a person acquires the ability to relax the muscles of the body in almost any circumstance

Relaxation training is a therapeutic technique in which a person acquires the ability to relax the muscles of the body under almost any circumstances. Imagine that you are a client who is beginning relaxation training. You are instructed to concentrate on one set of muscles at a time—first tensing and then relaxing them. You might tightly clench your fists for approximately 10 seconds, then release the tension. As your tightened muscles relax, you are asked to focus on the sensation of warmth and looseness in your hands. You practice this tightening and relaxing cycle several times before proceeding to the next muscle group, perhaps in your lower arms. After you have practiced tensing and relaxing various muscle groups, you might be asked to tighten and then relax your entire body.

The emphasis throughout the procedure is on the contrast between the feelings produced during tensing and those produced during relaxing. For a novice, the entire exercise lasts about 30 minutes. Progressive muscle relaxation has been effective in reducing physiological arousal and mitigating the physiological impact of stressors (Trautmann & Kroner-Herwig, 2010).

Biofeedback Training

Biofeedback is a self-regulation technique that allows people to alter physiological processes in order to improve physical or mental health (Frank, Khorshid, Kiffer, Moravec, & McKee, 2010). In **biofeedback training**, a therapist teaches you to *voluntarily* control a physiological function, such as heart rate or blood pressure. During training, you would receive second-by-second information (feedback) regarding a specific physiological activity. If you were trying to lower blood pressure, for example, you would receive feedback on your blood pressure, presented visually on a screen or via auditory signals. After repeated training sessions, you would be able to maintain your blood pressure in the desired range. The goal of biofeedback training is to continue improved physiological responses outside of the training setting, similar to the results seen in this case study:

Controlling Physiological Responses

Meditation is associated with a deeply relaxed bodily state produced by minimizing distractions and focusing internally or on a positive image, mantra, or word. Meditation can help regulate emotions and decrease stress hormones.

CASE STUDY A 23-year-old man reported that when he was nervous about exams his resting heart rate increased to 95–120 beats per minute. He sought treatment, concerned that this anxiety might lead to a serious cardiac condition. He received eight sessions of biofeedback training, involving both visual and auditory feedback regarding his heart rate. After the treatment, his heart rate stabilized and was within normal limits (73 beats per minute). Even a year later, he was able to control his heart rate during stressful situations by both relaxing and concentrating on reducing the heart rate (Janssen, 1983).

Biofeedback works because the visual and auditory feedback reinforces relaxation responses. It has been used to help people lower their heart rates and decrease their blood pressure during stressful situations (Peira, Fredrikson, & Pourtois, 2013), treat migraine and tension headaches (Blume et al., 2012), and decrease the need for asthma medication (Lehrer et al., 2004).

Cognitive-Behavioral Therapy

Cognitive strategies designed to enhance coping skills and stress management can improve both physiological functioning and psychological distress in individuals with chronic illness (Sung, Woo, Kim, Lim, & Chung, 2012). For example, improved immune functioning and reduced cortisol levels (associated with a reduction in stress) were found among breast cancer patients who participated in cognitive-behavioral treatment, whereas patients in a control group continued to show deterioration in their immune response (Witek-Janusek et al., 2008). Similarly, in a 1-year follow-up study, prostate and breast cancer patients who learned techniques to cope with stress showed improved quality of life and lower cortisol levels (Carlson, Speca, Faris, & Patel, 2007).

With many diseases, having the opportunity to express emotions, to process beliefs about illness, and to develop adaptive strategies can improve feelings of well-being and physical health. For example, cognitive reappraisal can help individuals facing a life-threatening disease adjust and find validation and meaning in the experience. In a study of 70 female cancer patients, opportunities to talk about their health

biofeedback training a physiological and behavioral approach in which an individual receives information regarding particular autonomic functions and is rewarded for influencing those functions in a desired direction

situation helped predict adjustment to cancer (Cordova, Cunningham, Carlson, & Andrykowski, 2001). Those who were did not talk about (i.e., cognitively process) their disease because of invalidation ("When I talk about cancer, my husband tells me I'm living in the past") or discomfort ("It's difficult to share with those you love, as they are scared, too") reported more depressive symptoms. In contrast, women who had opportunities to openly discuss their cancer were less depressed and better adjusted. Emotional regulation strategies such as acceptance and positive reappraisal are also beneficial for individuals with cancer (Y. Wang et al., 2013).

Because negative emotions are associated with psychophysiological disorders, cognitive-behavioral programs sometimes focus on emotional regulation strategies for managing strong emotions such as anger. In one study, individuals with hypertension significantly reduced their blood pressure after participating in a 6-week anger management program (Larkin & Zayfert, 1996). When initially exposed to confrontational role-playing activities, the participants experienced sharp increases in blood pressure. The participants learned muscle relaxation techniques and strategies for changing their thoughts about confrontational situations. They also learned how to express their views calmly and assertively. The combination of techniques resulted in significant reductions in blood pressure.

Contemporary Trends and Future Directions

Many questions remain about the biological underpinnings of trauma-related disorders and psychophysiological illness. For example, can psychotherapy or preventive interventions alter the biological predisposition to fear reactivity associated with trauma and stressor-related disorders? Is it possible to reverse the changes in brain functioning and other physiological processes that result from trauma or stress? Neuroimaging and psychological studies are currently underway to provide answers to these questions.

There are also continuing questions regarding the influence of psychological factors on individual responses to stress or trauma. As we have discussed, negative emotions amplify the consequences of trauma or stressful events, whereas cognitive characteristics such as perceived control, optimism, and self-efficacy appear to moderate the impact of stressors. Research continues to focus on how positive emotions such as optimism affect stress responses and influence risk of infection or disease. Do positive psychological states directly influence brain structure and biochemical processes occurring in the brain, or do positive emotions primarily promote resilience more indirectly? Future research will likely provide more clarification about the role that psychological factors play in the etiology of cancer and other serious diseases, as well as the prevention of certain medical conditions.

Social influences and sociocultural factors also affect our health and reactions to stress. Research will continue to examine why there are gender and racial/ethnic differences in trauma- and stress-related disorders. For example, why are women and Latinos so much more likely to develop PTSD following severe trauma and why do Asian Americans have such a low incidence of trauma-related disorders? Are these findings a result of biological, socialization, or culture-related factors? As you can see, many questions remain that can be answered only by continuing to examine the multitude of possible contributors to the trauma- and stress-related disorders.

chapter SUMMARY

1 What do we know about disorders caused by exposure to specific stressors or traumatic experiences?

- Adjustment disorder involves clinically significant emotional distress and significant impairment in life's activities within 3 months after exposure to a stressor. It persists no longer than 6 months after the end of the stressor or consequences from the stressor.

- Acute and post-traumatic stress disorders involve direct or indirect exposure to a life-threatening or violent event, resulting in intrusive memories of the occurrence, attempts to forget or repress the memories, emotional withdrawal, and increased arousal.

- In acute stress disorder (ASD) symptoms last up to 1 month; post-traumatic stress disorder (PTSD) is diagnosed when symptoms continue for more than 1 month after the traumatic event.

- Many factors contribute to vulnerability to trauma-related disorders. Possible biological factors involve stress hormones and a sensitized autonomic nervous system. Psychological factors include anxiety, depression, and maladaptive cognitions. Maltreatment or inadequate social support during childhood is a risk factor, as are various sociocultural factors, such as experiences with discrimination or racism.

- Certain medications are somewhat effective in treating AD, ASD, and PTSD. Prolonged exposure therapy, cognitive-behavioral therapies, and eye movement desensitization and reprocessing (EMDR) are often effective with ASD and PTSD.

2 What role does stress play in our physical health?

- External events that place a physical or psychological demand on a person can serve as stressors and can affect physical health.

- A psychophysiological disorder is any physical disorder that has a strong psychological component. Psychophysiological disorders can involve actual tissue damage, a disease process, or physiological dysfunction.

- Not everyone develops an illness when exposed to the same stressor or traumatic event. Individuals may react to the same stressor in very different ways.

- Biological explanations for stress-related physical conditions include chronic activation of the sympathetic nervous system and continual release of stress hormones, as well as genetic influences.

- Psychological contributors include characteristics such as helplessness, isolation, cynicism, pessimism, and hostility, as well as feelings of depression or anxiety.

- Social contributors include having an inadequate social network; abusive intimate partner interactions; or childhood maltreatment.

- Sociocultural factors such as gender, racial, and ethnic background increase risk of some psychophysiological disorders. Stressful environments associated with poverty, prejudice, and racism are associated with increased risk of illness.

- Psychophysiological disorders are treated with interventions aimed at reducing stress and physiological reactivity combined with medical treatment for associated physical symptoms.

7

SOMATIC AND DISSOCIATIVE DISORDERS

A BOY OF 12 was referred for evaluation because he suddenly began to walk in an unusual staggering manner, which on close inspection appeared to be voluntary and deliberate. A comprehensive clinical examination showed no neurological abnormality. Shortly before his symptoms developed, he had been promoted to an academically rigorous secondary school. He was unable to meet the high academic expectations, and the teacher who taught his favorite subject humiliated him by rejecting classwork he had done and throwing his workbook on the floor (P. M. Leary, 2003, p. 436).

JOE BIEGER, A BELOVED HUSBAND, FATHER, GRANDFATHER, AND HIGH SCHOOL ASSISTANT ATHLETIC DIRECTOR, walked out of his front door one morning with his two dogs. Minutes later, his identity was seemingly wiped from his brain's hard drive. For the next 25 days he wandered the streets of Dallas, unable to remember what his name was, what he did for a living, or where he lived. Finally, a contractor he worked with happened to recognize him and notified his family (Associated Press, 2007a).

I n this chapter, we discuss (a) somatic symptom disorder and related disorders, including conditions that involve highly distressing thoughts related to bodily symptoms; and (b) dissociative disorders, which involve alterations in memory, consciousness, or identity. These disorders, and the distress they cause, often occur because of underlying biological, psychological, cognitive, or social factors. We discuss somatic symptom and dissociative disorders together because research shows they have common etiological roots (Baslet & Hill, 2011). Those with somatic symptom disorders often express stress through physical symptoms, while dissociative disorders involve psychological mechanisms for coping with overwhelming stress (Cloninger & Dokucu, 2008). We begin with a discussion of the somatic symptom disorders.

1 What are the somatic symptom and related disorders and what do they have in common? What are the causes and treatments of these conditions?

2 What are dissociations? Why do they occur, and how are they treated?

Somatic Symptom and Related Disorders

The **somatic symptom and related disorders** are a disparate group of disorders that include somatic symptom disorder; illness anxiety disorder; conversion disorder (functional neurological symptom disorder); and factitious disorder (see Table 7.1). DSM-5 groups these disorders together because they all have prominent **somatic symptoms** (physical or bodily symptoms) that are associated with significant impairment or distress. According to the DSM-5, actual physical illnesses may or may not be present. However, these diagnoses emphasize the presence of "distressing somatic symptoms plus abnormal thoughts, feelings and behaviors in response to these symptoms" (APA, 2013, p. 309). In one study, over 30 percent of individuals with illnesses such as heart disease or arthritis met the criteria for somatic symptom disorder because of "persistently high levels of anxiety" or "excessive time and energy devoted to" their disorder (Häuser & Wolfe, 2013). Psychophysiological disorders, discussed in Chapter 6, are also considered part of the somatic symptom disorder category. (Differences between the somatic symptom disorders are shown in Table 7.2.) We begin with a discussion of somatic symptom disorder.

Table 7.1 Somatic Symptom and Related Disorders

DISORDERS CHART			
Disorder	**DSM-5 Criteria**	**Prevalence**	**Course**
Somatic symptom disorder	At least one distressing somatic symptom and one of the following: a. Persistent thoughts b. High anxiety c. Excessive time devoted to symptoms	• Symptoms in up to 7% of general population	• Tends to be chronic and comorbid with depression
Illness anxiety disorder	• Preoccupation with health and excessive worry about serious illness • No somatic symptoms or very mild symptoms • Excessive health anxiety • Repeatedly checks for signs of illness or avoids medical contact for fear that illness will be confirmed	• Up to 6% • Similar prevalence in men and women	• Begins in adulthood • Considered chronic
Conversion disorder	• Motor or sensory disturbances • Symptoms incompatible with medical findings	• 2–3% of new referrals to neurologists	• Substantial minority stay the same or get worse • Prognosis better for children
Factitious disorder, imposed on self or others	• Physical or mental symptoms fabricated or induced in oneself or others • Presents self or other as ill or injured • Absence of external rewards for illness	• About 1% in hospital settings • Diagnosed more often in women	• Varies from single episode to persistent or chronic

SOURCE: American Psychiatric Association (2013); Ani, Reading, Lynn, Forlee, & Garralda (2013); Yates (2013).

Table 7.2 Comparison of DSM-5 Somatic Symptom and Related Disorders

Disorder	Identifiable Medical Condition?	Voluntarily Produced?	Cognitive Distortions Regarding Illness?
Psychophysiological disorders*	Yes	No	No
Somatic symptom disorder	Sometimes	No	Yes
Illness anxiety disorder	Sometimes	No	Yes
Conversion disorder	No, but involves physical symptoms	No	No
Factitious disorder	Possibly, but self-induced	Yes	No

© Cengage Learning®

*Covered in Chapter 6.

Somatic Symptom Disorder

CASE STUDY Cheryl, a 38-year-old, separated Italian American woman, is raising her 10-year-old daughter, Melanie, without much support. Cheryl has been involved in several abusive relationships and has struggled with unresolved grief about the loss of her mother. Cheryl is extremely distressed by episodes of vertigo and a variety of vague somatic complaints, including neck pain. When Cheryl becomes incapacitated, Melanie helps comfort her, providing remedies such as back rubs and hot compresses or taking over activities such as grocery shopping if Cheryl feels dizzy in the store. Cheryl and Melanie both describe the efficiency with which Melanie provides comfort and assistance (McDaniel & Speice, 2001).

Individuals diagnosed with **somatic symptom disorder (SSD)** have a pattern of reporting and reacting to pain or other distressing physical or bodily symptoms. This pattern occurs for at least 6 months and also involves persistent thoughts or high anxiety regarding the symptoms and associated health concerns (APA, 2013). Thus, SSD involves not only excessive focus on somatic symptoms, but also catastrophic thoughts related to these symptoms (Dimsdale & Levenson, 2013). See Table 7.3 for examples of somatic complaints reported by individuals with SSD.

Individuals with SSD (previously known as *somatization disorder*) report a variety of physical complaints that can involve discomfort in different parts of the body; gastrointestinal symptoms such as nausea, diarrhea, and bloating; sexual symptoms such as sexual indifference, irregular menses, or erectile dysfunction; and pseudoneurological symptoms such as breathing difficulties (Yates, 2013). Diagnostic tests that rule out disease or other physical conditions do little to reassure individuals with SSD or reduce their anxiety. They remain convinced they have a serious disease (Rolfe & Burton, 2013). In some cases, it may be true. It is estimated that up to 10 percent of symptoms that are initially considered to be psychologically based are later discovered to be the first signs of a disease or medical condition (Morriss, 2012).

Approximately 2 percent of women and less than 0.2 percent of men have been diagnosed with SSD (Yates, 2013). The diagnosis is more prevalent in African Americans. It is also prevalent among those with less than a high school education

somatic symptom and related disorders broad grouping of psychological disorders that involve physical symptoms or anxiety over illness, including somatic symptom disorder, illness anxiety disorder, conversion disorder (functional neurological symptom disorder), and factitious disorder

somatic symptoms physical or bodily symptoms

somatic symptom disorder (SSD) condition involving a pattern of reporting distressing physical symptoms combined with extreme concern about health or fears of having an undiagnosed medical condition

Table 7.3 Symptoms Reported by Patients with Somatic Symptom Disorder (SSD)

Gastrointestinal Symptoms	Pseudoneurological Symptoms
Vomiting	Amnesia
Abdominal pain	Difficulty swallowing
Nausea	Loss of voice
Bloating and excessive gas	Difficulty walking Seizures

Pain Symptoms	Reproductive Organ Symptoms
Diffuse pain	Burning sensation in sex organs
Pain in extremities	Pain during intercourse
Joint pain	Irregular menstrual cycles
Headaches	Excessive menstrual bleeding

Cardiopulmonary Symptoms	Other Symptoms
Shortness of breath at rest	Vague food allergies
Palpitations	Hypoglycemia
Chest pain	Chronic fatigue
Dizziness	Chemical sensitivity

SOURCE: So (2008).

or lower socioeconomic status (Noyes, Stuart, Watson, & Langbehn, 2006). The presence is much higher in hospital settings, involving as many as 50 percent of the cases in which psychiatric consultations were requested (Yates, 2013). Because the criteria for SSD are less restrictive in DSM-5, the prevalence rate may increase and include up to 7 percent of the general adult population (APA, 2013).

When SSD is diagnosed in adolescents, there is an increased likelihood that the adolescent will experience a serious mental illness later in life. In a 15-year longitudinal study, adolescents with somatic symptoms were likely to develop depression and other mental disorders during adulthood. Those with the most severe somatic symptoms during adolescence were also most likely to have suicide attempts later in life (Bohman et al., 2012); these findings reinforce the importance of early identification and intensive treatment for adolescents with SSD. Remission of symptoms can also occur. Although SSD is considered a chronic condition, in one large study only about half of those diagnosed with SSD with predominantly somatic complaints met the criteria 12 months later (Steinbrecher & Hiller, 2011).

Sometimes pain is the primary complaint expressed by someone with an SSD, as seen in the following case.

> **CASE STUDY** Ms. J is a 37-year-old woman who presents to the emergency department with abdominal pain. She reports that she has suffered from chronic pain since her adolescence. She has a history of multiple abdominal surgeries; the most recent was for pain due to scar tissue from her previous surgeries. These operations have failed to reduce her complaints of pain.... The treatment plan includes regular appointments to monitor her chronic pain complaints.... Outpatient visits focus on identifying sources of stress and encouraging healthy coping mechanisms (Yates, 2013).

Ms. J has been diagnosed with **somatic symptom disorder (SSD) with predominant pain**, previously known as *pain disorder*. According to the DSM-5, those with this pattern experience persistently high levels of distress over pain along with an excessive amount of time and energy devoted to the pain symptoms. In one study (J. R. Walker & Furer, 2008), pain complaints associated with SSD included back pain (30 percent), joint pain (25 percent), pain in the extremities (20 percent), headache (19 percent), abdominal pain (11 percent), and chest pain (5 percent). These pain complaints result in frequent medical appointments. However, diagnostic tests cannot identify specific causes for the chronic pain. As you can imagine, those with SSD who are experiencing pain may feel angry and frustrated if they believe that medical staff are questioning their reports of pain (Furness, Glazebrook, Tay, Abbas, & Slaveska-Hollis, 2009).

Deciding if someone meets the diagnostic criteria for SSD can be problematic. Chronic pain is relatively common and affects 30 percent of the U.S. population (Turk, Swanson, & Tunks, 2008). However, a diagnosis of SSD occurs only when there is excessive distress associated with the pain symptoms. From 10 to 50 percent of all patients are described as expressing excessive concerns over physical symptoms,

somatic symptom disorder (SSD) with predominant pain SSD involving severe or lingering pain that appears to have no physical basis

depending on the primary care setting (McCarron, 2006; McGorm, Burton, Weller, Murray, & Sharpe, 2010). Many undergo unnecessary surgical or assessment procedures. Although medical professionals sometimes believe that those with SSD are faking their symptoms (So, 2008), mental health professionals do not agree. They do not believe that SSD involves feigning (faking) or exaggerating symptoms. Rather, they understand that for those with SSD the symptoms are very real and extremely distressing (Parish & Yutzy, 2011). However, researchers and clinicians are moving away from the view that SSD is *only* "psychological" in nature and now acknowledge that many people with SSD have accompanying medical conditions (Dimsdale, 2011).

Illness Anxiety Disorder

CASE STUDY   A 41-year-old woman, Linda, reported having a history of concerns about cancer, especially stomach or bowel cancer. Her grandmother had bowel cancer when Linda was 22. Media stories of illness, medical documentaries, or reading about people who are ill all trigger her worries: "I notice a feeling of discomfort and bloating in my abdomen. I wonder if this could be an early sign of cancer. Cancer is something that can happen at my age. People can have very few symptoms and then suddenly it is there and a few months later they are gone." (Furer & Walker, 2005, p. 261)

©Paul Hakimata Photography/Shutterstock.com

Linda's distress is associated with an **illness anxiety disorder**. According to the DSM-5, the primary characteristic of this disorder is a chronic pattern (at least 6 months) of preoccupation with having or contracting a serious illness or illnesses. In contrast with SSD, illness anxiety disorder involves minimal or no somatic symptoms. However, those with illness anxiety disorder are very anxious and easily alarmed about their health. This anxiety may result in excessive health-related behaviors such as continual checking of one's body for signs of illness, or avoidance behaviors (e.g., refusing to go to the doctor) due to extreme fear of possible illness. Some people with illness anxiety disorder have an actual medical condition or a high risk of developing a medical condition (perhaps due to a strong family history of a disease); in these cases, illness anxiety disorder is diagnosed when there is impairment due to excessive or disproportionate worry about this situation (APA, 2013). See Table 7.4 for examples of the fears related to health seen in individuals with illness anxiety disorder.

Illness anxiety disorder is strongly associated with a person's cognitions; that is, the individual misinterprets bodily variations or sensations as indications of a serious illness or undetected disease and becomes distressed (K. S. White, Craft, & Gervino, 2010). When unpleasant or "unusual" symptoms are identified, this bodily focus produces feelings of extreme distress and alarm (Sorensen, Birket-Smith, Wattar, Buemann, & Salkovskis, 2011). Those with illness anxiety disorder have a strong tendency to:

- *catastrophize* and view ambiguous or mild somatic symptoms as indications of a severe or catastrophic illness;
- *overgeneralize* by believing that serious illness and fatal conditions are prevalent;
- *display all-or-none thinking,* such as believing they must be symptom free to be healthy; and
- *show selective attention* to medical information and focus primarily on threatening information (Fulton, Marcus, & Merkey, 2011).

A Physical or Psychological Disorder?

Somatic symptom disorder with pain is most frequently diagnosed in women, in members of minority groups, and in people living in poverty. How can we determine if the cause of the pain is psychological, physical, or both?

illness anxiety disorder
persistent health anxiety and/or concern that one has an undetected physical illness; the person has few or no somatic complaints

Table 7.4 Percentage of Adults with Illness Anxiety Disorder Who Endorse Selected Fears Related to Health

Item	Much Agree or Very Much Agree (%)
When I notice my heart beating rapidly, I worry I might have a heart attack.	51
When I get aches or pains, I worry that there is something wrong with my health.	75
It scares me when I feel "shaky" (trembling).	47
It scares me when I feel tingling or prickling sensations in my hands.	50
When I feel a strong pain in my stomach, I worry it might be cancer.	62

SOURCE: J. R. Walker & Furer (2008).

- Worldwide, the most common somatic symptoms are gastro-intestinal complaints or abnormal skin sensations, whereas in the United States menstrual pain, abdominal pain, and chest pain are the most common somatic symptoms.

- Distinctive cultural somatic symptoms include concerns about body odor (Japan), body heat and coldness (Nigeria), loss of semen while urinating (India), and kidney weakness (China).

SOURCE: B. S. Singh, 2007

Those with illness anxiety disorder frequently check for signs of illness or disease, seek reassurance from others, continuously research and gather information on diseases, and avoid activities or circumstances they believe might result in an illness. Paradoxically, these behaviors only serve to increase anxiety (Olatunji, Etzel, Tomarken, Ciesielski, & Deacon, 2011). It is estimated that approximately 4 to 6 percent of those who visit doctors have illness anxiety disorder (Yates, 2013). This condition is found equally in men and women (APA, 2013).

Conversion Disorder (Functional Neurological Symptom Disorder)

CASE STUDY   A., a 34-year-old woman, described frequent attacks of sudden onset, often resembling sleep but sometimes involving violent jerking of her arms and legs and arching of her back. She experienced violent outbursts. She viewed herself as disabled and needing constant care and was extremely dependent on her partner and teenage stepsons (Howlett & Reuber, 2009, p. 129). Interviews revealed that she was raped at age 13 by her biological father and was very traumatized by the death of her grandparents.

CASE STUDY   A boy, age 10, was first believed to have a case of juvenile myasthenia gravis (weakening of the voluntary muscles). For 5 weeks he had been unable to open his eyes, and the consequent "blindness" had stopped him from attending school. On detailed physical examination, no other abnormalities were found. In the hospital ward it was noted that he did not walk into furniture. He was the village football star and had been blamed for his team's defeat, and from that day he had been unable to open his eyes (P. M. Leary, 2003, p. 436).

Conversion disorder (functional neurological symptom disorder) involves motor, sensory, or seizure-like symptoms that are inconsistent with any recognized neurological or medical disorder and result in significant distress or impairment in life activities. Symptoms such as muscle weakness or paralysis, unusual movements, swallowing difficulties, problems with speech, seizures, or loss of sensation may be involved (APA, 2013). The most common conversion symptoms seen in neurological clinics involve **psychogenic** movement disorders, such as disturbances of stance and walking; sensory symptoms, such as blindness, loss of voice, or dizziness; and psychogenic seizures (Marshall et al., 2013). Among children and adolescents, the most common symptoms are motor weakness and abnormal movements (Ani, Reading, Lynn, Forlee, & Garralda, 2013).

Diagnosis is confirmed when the symptoms are incompatible with neurological findings. For example, one woman had seizure-like attacks that were preceded by seeing white spots, followed by twitching of her upper and lower extremities involving one or sometimes both sides of her body and lasting for about 20 minutes. Electroencephalograph (EEG) monitoring during the episodes revealed no abnormalities that would suggest any form of epilepsy (Baslet & Hill, 2011). In some cases, the presenting symptoms—such as glove anesthesia (Figure 7.1), which involves a loss of feeling in the hand ending in a straight line at the wrist, or an inability to talk or whisper combined with the ability to cough—are easily diagnosed as symptoms of conversion disorder. The diagnosis is not complicated because coughing indicates intact vocal cord function and in glove anesthesia, the area of sensory loss does not correspond to the distribution of nerves in the body (R. J. Brown, 2004). Other symptoms may require extensive neurological and physical examinations to rule out a true medical disorder before professionals are able to make a diagnosis of conversion disorder.

conversion disorder (functional neurological symptom disorder)   a condition involving sensory or motor impairment suggestive of a neurological disorder but with no underlying medical cause

psychogenic   originating from psychological causes

Discriminating between conversion disorder and actual medical conditions can be difficult, because there are no specific tests to confirm the diagnosis (J. H. Friedman & LaFrance, 2010). For this reason, neurologists and other physicians are reluctant to make a diagnosis of conversion disorder unless they are absolutely certain that the condition is psychologically based (Kanaan, Armstrong, & Wessely, 2009). Neurologists report that about 2 to 3 percent of new referrals involve cases of conversion disorder (J. H. Friedman & LaFrance, 2010). This disorder occurs more frequently in women (Powsner, 2013).

In general, individuals with conversion disorder are not physically damaged by the symptoms. For example, a person with psychogenic paralysis of the legs rarely shows the atrophy of the lower limbs that occurs when there is paralysis due to an underlying biological cause. In some persistent cases, however, long-term disuse of muscles can result in atrophy (Schonfeldt-Lecuona, Connemann, Spitzer, & Herwig, 2003).

Individuals with conversion disorder are not consciously faking symptoms. In other words, they are not **malingering** (feigning illness for an external purpose such as getting out of work duties). People with conversion disorder believe that the problem is genuine and not under their control, and they are stressed by their symptoms (Voon et al., 2010). Most individuals with the disorder report that their conversion symptoms developed soon after experiencing a stressor (Ani, Reading, Lynn, Forlee, & Garralda, 2013). These cases of conversion disorder illustrate how conversion symptoms are related to trauma or stressors (Becker, Scheele, Moessner, Maier, & Hurlemann, 2013; Gillig, 2013):

- Development of seizures by a college honors student after he failed an introductory biology exam
- Falling and motor weakness in a man after his wife abruptly left him for someone else
- Bilateral vision loss after a 25-year-old man discovered that his close boyhood friend had accidentally died due to autoerotic asphyxiation

What is the prognosis for individuals with conversion disorder? The long-term outcome is variable among adults with conversion symptoms. In a review of 25 long-term outcomes studies, about 39 percent of individuals with this disorder reported that their symptoms remained the same or became worse. A sudden onset of symptoms, early diagnosis, shorter duration of symptoms, and a good premorbid (before the illness) personality increase the likelihood of a positive outcome (Gelauff, Stone, Edwards, & Carson, 2014). The prognosis may be better for children and adolescents. In a sample of 204 children and adolescents between the ages of 7 and 15 with conversion disorder, a 12-month follow-up showed that all had symptomatic improvement (Ani, Reading, Lynn, Forlee, & Garralda, 2013).

Factitious Disorder and Factitious Disorder Imposed on Another

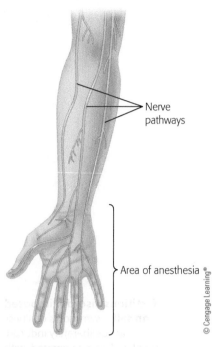

Figure 7.1

Glove Anesthesia
In glove anesthesia, the lack of feeling covers the hand in a glovelike shape. It does not correspond to the distribution of nerve pathways. This discrepancy leads to a diagnosis of conversion disorder (functional neurological symptom disorder).

CASE STUDY   Mandy was not hesitant to discuss how she was diagnosed with leukemia at age 37, right after her husband left her. She shared how chemotherapy damaged her immune system, liver, and heart, resulting in a stroke and weeks in a coma. She posted her story and updates on a Web site and the virtual community rallied to support her as she shared details of additional surgeries and bouts of life-threatening infections. It was later discovered that Mandy was not sick and had made up the entire story (Kleeman, 2011).

Factitious disorders are mental disorders in which a person deliberately induces or simulates symptoms of physical or mental illnesses with no apparent incentive other than attention from medical personnel or others (Catalina, Gomez, & de Cos, 2008).

malingering   feigning illness for an external purpose

factitious disorder   condition in which a person deliberately induces or simulates symptoms of physical or mental illness with no apparent incentive other than attention from medical personnel or others

DSM-5 includes **factitious disorder imposed on self**, which involves inducing or simulating illness in oneself, and **factitious disorder imposed on another**, which involves inducing or falsifying illness in someone else.

Before we discuss the factitious disorders, we should note that these disorders are completely different from malingering—faking a disorder to achieve some goal, such as an insurance settlement. With malingering, the specific goal is usually evident, and the individual can "turn off" the symptoms whenever they are no longer useful. In factitious disorders, the purpose of the simulated or induced illness is much less apparent. Complex psychological variables are involved, and those with a factitious disorder are usually unaware of the motivation for their behavior. Simulation of illness is often done almost compulsively.

Factitious Disorder Imposed on Self

Factitious disorder imposed on self is characterized by the presentation of oneself to others as ill or impaired through the recurrent falsification or induction of physical or psychological symptoms. This is done without any obvious external rewards (APA, 2013). However, the symptoms do provide attention, support, and social relationships that the individual may not have otherwise obtained (IsHak et al., 2010). Sabotaging or intentionally interfering with medical care is surprisingly common, particularly among individuals with other mental health conditions (Sansone & Sansone, 2012b); in some cases, such behaviors meet the criteria for a factitious disorder (see Table 7.5). In the past, this condition was referred to as *hospital addiction* or *professional patient syndrome*. In 1951, it was given the name Munchausen syndrome after an 18th-century German nobleman who was noted for making up fanciful stories (Bande & Garcia-Alba, 2008).

In the case of Mandy, she obtained online attention and social support due to completely fabricated stories of "illness." In other situations, people engage in behaviors that produce actual physical problems. One young woman, for example, requested

factitious disorder imposed on self symptoms of illness are deliberately induced, simulated, or exaggerated, with no apparent external incentive

factitious disorder imposed on another a pattern of falsification or production of physical or psychological symptoms in another individual

Table 7.5 Prevalence of Self-Reported Medically Self-Sabotaging Behaviors in Samples of Family Medicine Outpatient (n = 411) and Psychiatric Inpatients (n = 120).

Item	Family Medicine (%)	Psychiatry (%)
Have you ever, intentionally or on purpose		
• Not taken a prescribed medicine to hurt yourself	25.1	24.2
• Damaged self on purpose, and sought medical treatment	2.4	28.3
• Not gone for medical treatment, despite needing it, to purposefully hurt self	37.2	27.5
• Created additional symptoms to attract the attention of a health care provider	0.7	10.8
• Exaggerated physical symptoms to attract the attention of a health care provider	1.2	15.8
• Not followed directions of a health care provider to intentionally prolong physical illness	1.2	12.5
• Purposefully misused medications to worsen a physical illness	.5	12.5
• Lied about symptoms to purposefully confuse a health care provider	1.0	12.5
• Lied about the cause of physical symptoms to hide self-injury	1.2	18.3
• Tampered with medical equipment to cause false readings	0.5	5.0
• Mixed prescription drugs with intent to harm self	0.2	16.7
• Prevented wounds from healing	0.5	13.3

SOURCE: Adapted from Sansone & Sansone (2012b, p. 40).

medical attention for pain and infection in her limbs. It was discovered that she was inserting thin wires into different parts of her body to produce injury and infection (Sinha-Deb, Sarkar, Sood, & Khandelwall, 2013). In another case, a 27-year-old woman went to the emergency room complaining of abdominal pain and bleeding from her rectum. Comprehensive tests, including computed tomography (CT) scans, upper gastrointestinal endoscopy, colonoscopy, and biopsies, came out negative. Later, a nurse found the patient in a bathroom inserting a toothbrush in her rectum, producing the blood she had been complaining of (IsHak et al., 2010).

Signs of factitious disorder may include lingering, unexplained illnesses with multiple surgical or complex treatments; "remarkable willingness" to undergo painful or dangerous treatments; a tendency to become angry if the illness is questioned; and the involvement of multiple doctors (Worley, Feldman, & Hamilton, 2009). Depending on the study, factitious disorder imposed on self has a prevalence rate of 1.3 percent for adults and 0.7 percent for adolescents (Ehrlich, Pfeiffer, Salbach, Lenz, & Lehmkuhl, 2008). Factitious disorder is most often diagnosed in women, but the more chronic forms of the disorder are found in middle-aged men (Elwyn, Ahmed, & Dunayevich, 2014).

Factitious Disorder Imposed on Another

> **CASE STUDY**   A hidden camera at a children's hospital captured the image of a mother suffocating the baby she had brought in for treatment of breathing problems. In another case, a child was admitted for treatment of ulcerations on his back; hospital staff discovered the mother had been rubbing oven cleaner on his skin. Another "sick" infant had been fed laxatives for nearly 4 months (Wartik, 1994). In each of these cases, there was no apparent motive other than the attention the parent received from the hospital staff caring for the child's "illness."

If an individual deliberately feigns or induces physical or psychological symptoms in another person (or even a pet) in the absence of any obvious external rewards, the DSM-5 diagnosis is **factitious disorder imposed on another**; this condition is sometimes referred to as *Munchausen syndrome by proxy* (Brannon & Dunayevich, 2011). In the case examples, the mothers produced symptoms in their children. Little information is available on prevalence, age of onset, or familial patterns with this diagnostic category. In the vast majority of cases, the individual is a mother who appears to be loving and attentive toward her infant or young child while simultaneously sabotaging the child's health, sometimes by poisoning or suffocation (Kannai, 2009). Warning signs involve physical symptoms that occur only when the mother or caretaker is around and insistence on medical tests that are unnecessary or invasive. A mortality rate of up to 9 percent of those targeted has been reported, either from the abuse itself or from unnecessary, invasive medical procedures (Abdulhamid & Pataki, 2011).

Diagnosis of this condition is difficult, and some believe that the diagnosis is so unclear, unreliable, and subject to misdiagnosis that it should be eliminated as a psychiatric diagnosis (Butz, Evans, & Webber-Dereszynski, 2009). Cases of false accusations against parents have been reported (C. Smith, 2002). What safeguards should be put in place to balance protection of a child with the possibility of a false accusation against a parent?

Etiology of Somatic Symptom and Related Disorders

In the majority of cases, multiple factors contribute to the development of somatic symptom, illness anxiety, conversion, and factitious disorders, as evidenced by the multipath model, which includes biological, psychological, social, and sociocultural dimensions (Figure 7.2).

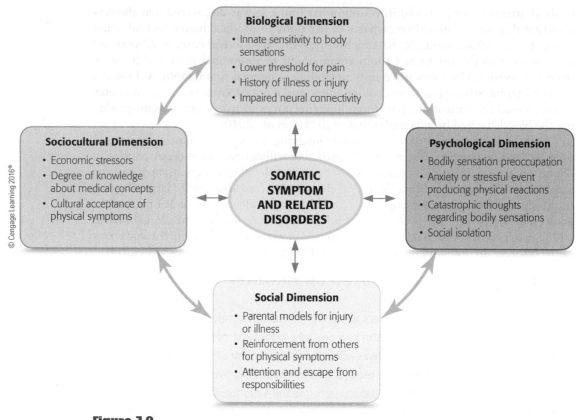

Biological Dimension
- Innate sensitivity to body sensations
- Lower threshold for pain
- History of illness or injury
- Impaired neural connectivity

Sociocultural Dimension
- Economic stressors
- Degree of knowledge about medical concepts
- Cultural acceptance of physical symptoms

SOMATIC SYMPTOM AND RELATED DISORDERS

Psychological Dimension
- Bodily sensation preoccupation
- Anxiety or stressful event producing physical reactions
- Catastrophic thoughts regarding bodily sensations
- Social isolation

Social Dimension
- Parental models for injury or illness
- Reinforcement from others for physical symptoms
- Attention and escape from responsibilities

© Cengage Learning 2016®

Figure 7.2

Multipath Model of Somatic Symptom and Related Disorders
The dimensions interact with one another and combine in different ways to result in a somatic symptom or related disorder.

Biological Dimension

What causes the development of SSD and related disorders? Genetic factors only modestly contribute to these disorders, according to twin and family studies (K. Kato, Sullivan, Evengard, & Pedersen, 2009). Environment plays a much greater role. However, biological vulnerabilities, such as lower pain thresholds, heightened sensitivity to pain, and greater sensitivity to somatic cues, are suspected of playing a key role in the development of somatic symptoms and health anxiety (Katzer, Oberfeld, Hiller, Gerlach, & Witthoft, 2012). A biological predisposition, hardwired into the central nervous system, can result in (a) hypervigilance or exaggerated focus on bodily sensation, (b) increased sensitivity to even mild bodily changes, and (c) a tendency to react to somatic sensations with alarm (S. Taylor, Jang, Stein, & Asmundson, 2008).

It is also possible that repetitive activation of the sympathetic nervous system due to chronic exposure to stressors can lead to increased sensitivity of the nerves associated with pain and subsequent increases in pain sensation (Baliki et al., 2012). The finding that war veterans with combat exposure are more likely to report high levels of somatic symptoms than are veterans without exposure to trauma supports this hypothesis (Ginzburg & Solomon, 2010).

Dysregulated connectivity in brain regions associated with symptoms have been found for conversion disorder; interestingly, neural connections normalize after successful psychological treatment. In one case of functional visual blindness in a 25-year-old man, magnetic resonance imaging (MRI) showed overreactivity in the frontoparietal regions of the brain along with suppressed responses in interconnected visual areas, indicating that visual cues were being suppressed (Becker, Scheele, Moessner, Maier, &

Hurleman, 2013). Other researchers suggest that conversion disorder may result from abnormal actions of inhibitory neural systems. For example, they compared MRI scans of a patient with conversion disorder (involving an inability to speak) before and after successful psychotherapy. Before treatment, there was evidence of impaired connectivity in the speech network; this abnormality was no longer evident after treatment (R. A. Bryant & Das, 2012).

In contrast, individuals with SSD with predominant pain show increased excitability between areas of the brain related to emotional behaviors (Baliki et al., 2012). Can brain reactivity involving brain regions associated with pain be reduced or inhibited? Some studies have found that those with chronic pain conditions had reduced cerebral gray matter in the prefrontal areas of the brain. Following cognitive-behavioral therapy, gray matter increased in these areas. The researchers hypothesized that increases in gray matter increased cognitive control over pain, reducing the perception of pain (Seminowicz et al., 2013).

Psychological Dimension

Psychological theoretical explanations for somatic symptom and related disorders have focused on psychodynamic and cognitive-behavioral perspectives. Certain psychological characteristics have also been associated with these disorders.

Psychodynamic Perspective   In psychodynamic theory, somatic symptoms defend against the awareness of unconscious emotional issues (Marshall et al., 2013). Freud believed that hysterical reactions (biological complaints of pain, illness, or loss of physical function) were caused by the repression of some type of conflict, usually sexual in nature. To protect the individual from intense anxiety, this conflict is converted into a physical symptom (Breuer & Freud, 1895/1957). The psychodynamic view suggests that two mechanisms produce and then sustain somatic symptoms. The first provides a *primary gain* for the person by protecting him or her from the anxiety associated with the unacceptable desire or conflict; the need for protection gives rise to the physical symptoms. This focus on the body keeps the person from becoming aware of the underlying conflict (Simon & VonKorff, 1991). Then a *secondary gain* accrues when the person's dependency needs are fulfilled through attention and sympathy. In one study of 25 patients with conversion symptoms, all relied on family members and friends to complete domestic tasks and were receiving disability allowances (Allanson, Bass, & Wade, 2002).

Cognitive-Behavioral Perspective   Reinforcement, modeling, cognitions, or a combination of these factors are important in the development of SSD, according to cognitive-behavioral researchers. Some contend that people with SSD, conversion disorder, and factitious disorders assume the "sick role" because it is reinforcing and because it allows them to escape unpleasant circumstances or to avoid responsibilities (Turk, Swanson, & Tunks, 2008). A study of men experiencing pain associated with SSD revealed the importance of reinforcement. Men with supportive wives (attentive to pain cues) reported significantly greater pain when their wives were present than when their wives were absent. The reverse was true of patients whose wives were nonsupportive: Reports of pain were greater when their wives were absent (Williamson, Robinson, & Melamed, 1997). Not surprisingly, many individuals with SSD and related disorders have experiences associated with convalescence, including serious illness, physical injury, and depression (Burton et al., 2010); in fact, these situations are all associated with an increased risk of developing SSD (Leiknes, Finset, Moum, & Sandanger, 2008).

Catastrophic misinterpretations of bodily sensations or changes in bodily functions might be important in the etiology of SSD and illness anxiety disorder. Health anxiety arises because symptoms are interpreted as being very serious or due to catastrophic conditions that could result in disability or death (Rachman, 2012). Individuals' preoccupation with disease and inordinately high anxiety levels are fueled by intrusive imagery such as "visualizing that the doctor tells me that I have cancer" or "I'm lying on my death bed with my children and partner crying" (Muse, McManus, Hackmann, Williams, & Williams, 2010).

According to this perspective, catastrophic cognitions related to somatic symptoms are more likely to develop in individuals who are biologically or psychologically predisposed to having these thoughts—people who have somatic sensitivity, a low pain threshold, a history of illness, or who or have received parental attention for somatic symptoms. It is hypothesized that distressing cognitions develop in the following manner (Abramowitz, Taylor, & McKay, 2010; J. R. Walker & Furer, 2008):

1. External triggers (traumatic or anxiety-evoking stressors) or internal triggers (anxiety-producing thoughts such as "My father died of cancer at age 47") result in physiological arousal.

2. The individual perceives bodily changes associated with these triggers such as increased heart rate or respiration.

3. Thoughts and worries about possible disease begin in response to these physical sensations.

4. These thoughts amplify bodily sensations, causing further physical reactions and concern.

5. Catastrophic thoughts increase in response to the magnified bodily sensations, creating a circular feedback pattern.

Consistent with this perspective, individuals with SSD tend to misinterpret and overestimate the dangerousness of bodily symptoms (P. G. Williams, Smith, & Jordan, 2010). One group of individuals with SSD involving chest pain in the absence of cardiac pathology were highly attuned to cardiac-related symptoms and exhibited anxiety reactions in response to heart palpitations and chest discomfort (K. S. White et al., 2010). Similarly, individuals with health anxiety interpreted nine common bodily sensations as indications of disease, whereas healthy controls were more likely to use normalizing explanations and view the symptoms as insignificant (Neng & Weck, 2014).

Social Dimension

A variety of social factors appear to influence somatic symptom and related disorders. Some individuals with SSD report being rejected or abused by family members and feeling unloved (Tunks, Weir, & Crook, 2008). A history of sexual abuse or rape has been associated with chronic pelvic pain and gastrointestinal disorders in women (Paras et al., 2009). More than 50 percent of a sample of individuals with somatic symptom, illness anxiety, or conversion disorder had experienced a serious physical illness in the preceding 12 months (G. C. Smith, Clarke, Handrinos, Dunsis, & McKenzie, 2000). Some individuals may seek out contact with medical staff as a source of attention or comfort because of social isolation or an inability to connect with family or friends (S. Stuart & Noyes, 2005).

The development of illness or injury sensitivity appears to be closely linked with parental characteristics such as being preoccupied with or overly attentive to somatic complaints expressed by their children (Watt, O'Connor, Stewart, Moon, & Terry, 2008). Additionally, individuals with SSD frequently have parents or family members with chronic physical illnesses (Schulte & Petermann, 2011) or high health anxiety (Schulte, Petermann, & Noeker, 2010).

Sociocultural Dimension

There is a long history of sociocultural explanations for some somatic disorders. Conversion disorder, initially called *hysteria*, was originally viewed as a problem that afflicted only women; in fact, it derived its name from *hystera*, the ancient Greek word for uterus. Hippocrates believed that a shift or movement of the uterus resulted in complaints of breathing difficulties, paralysis, and seizures. He presumed that the movement was due to the uterus "wanting a child." However, others argued that hysteria was more prevalent in women because restrictive social mores did not provide them with appropriate channels for the expression of aggression or sexuality (Satow, 1979).

Anna O., a patient of physician Josef Breuer, was a 21-year-old woman who developed a variety of symptoms, including muscle rigidity and insensitivity to feeling. Breuer later coauthored a book with Sigmund Freud, in which they proposed that hysterical symptoms such as those experienced by Anna O. result from intrapsychic conflicts. However, they did not consider the impact of social role restrictions on psychogenic symptoms. According to Hollender (1980), Anna O. was highly intelligent, but her educational and intellectual opportunities were severely restricted because she was a woman. Breuer described her as "bubbling over with intellectual vitality."

As Hollender pointed out, "Not only was Anna O., as a female, relegated to an inferior position in her family with future prospects limited to that of becoming a wife and mother, but at the age of twenty-one she was suddenly called on to assume the onerous chore of nursing her father" (Hollender, 1980, p. 798). It is possible that many of her physical symptoms resulted from her resentment of this duty—the symptoms also allowed her to maintain the intellectually stimulating contact with Breuer. Anna O. was supposedly cured after her "talk therapy" with Breuer but eventually required additional treatment in an institution. Later in her life, Anna O. made significant contributions to the field of social work, and became recognized as a feminist leader.

Cultural factors can influence the frequency, expression, and interpretation of somatic complaints. Risk factors associated with SSD and related disorders include lower educational levels, ethnicity, and immigrant status (Noyes, Stuart, et al., 2006). Among Asian populations, physical complaints often occur in reaction to stress (Sue & Sue, 2013). Some African groups express somatic complaints, such as feelings of heat, crawling sensations, and numbness, that differ from those expressed in Western cultures (R. J. Brown & Lewis-Fernández, 2011). Reports of pain also differ between white and Latino patients with Latinos reporting more pain, perhaps due to the cultural acceptance of physical problems as an expression of distress (Hernandez & Sachs-Ericsson, 2006).

Differences such as those just described may reflect different cultural views of the relationship between mind and body. The dominant view in Western culture is the *psychosomatic* perspective—that psychological conflicts are sometimes expressed via physical symptoms. But many other cultures have a *somatopsychic* perspective—that physical problems produce psychological and emotional symptoms. Although many of us believe that our psychosomatic view is the correct one, the somatopsychic view is the dominant perspective in most cultures.

Functional Neurological Symptom Disorder or Society's Victim?

Anna O., whose real name was Bertha Pappenheim, was diagnosed as being severely disturbed, even though her later years were extremely productive. Were the paralysis and other physical disturbances she experienced products of societal restrictions on the role of women in the late 1800s or her inability to conform to that role? Or was it something totally different?

Treatment of Somatic Symptom and Related Disorders

Although somatic symptom and related disorders are considered difficult to treat, newer biological and psychological treatments are showing some success. Therapists now realize that it is necessary to focus on mind-body connections, understand clients' perspectives regarding their somatic symptoms, and acknowledge the role of stressors in the development of physical complaints, as seen in the following case study.

CASE STUDY   Mr. X, a 68-year-old Chinese man, reported sleep disturbance, loss of appetite, dizziness, and a sensation of tightness around his chest. Several episodes of chest pain led to admission and medical evaluation at the local hospital. All results, including tests for heart disease, were normal. He was referred for psychiatric consultation. Because traditional Chinese views of medicine recognize an interconnection between mind and body, the psychiatrist accepted and

Culture and Somatic Symptom and Dissociative Disorders

- A 56-year-old Brazilian man requested an evaluation and treatment due to an ongoing somatic complaint. He had the firm belief that his penis was retracting and entering his abdomen, and he was reacting with a great deal of anxiety. He attempted to pull on his penis to prevent the retraction, a strategy he felt had been effective with a previous episode that occurred when he was 19 (Hallak, Crippa, & Zuardi, 2000).

- Dibuk ak Suut, a Malaysian woman, goes into a trancelike state in which she follows commands, blurts out offensive phrases, and mimics the actions of people around her. This happens when she has been suddenly frightened. She displays profuse sweating and increased heart rate, but claims to have no memory of what she says or does (Osbourne, 2001).

The symptoms of the first case study fit the description of *koro*, a culture-bound syndrome that is seen primarily in Southeast Asia, although cases have also been reported in West Africa (Dzokoto & Adams, 2005) and South America. Symptoms of koro involve an intense fear that the penis—or, in a woman, the labia, nipples, or breasts—is receding into the body. Episodes of koro are usually brief and responsive to positive reassurances. In the second case study, Dibuk is displaying symptoms related to *latah*, a condition found in Malaysia and many other parts of the world that consists of dissociation or a trancelike state associated with mimicking or following the instructions or behaviors of others. Other culture-bound disorders related to either somatic symptom or dissociative disorders include the following:

- *Brain fag.* Found primarily in West Africa, this condition affects high school and college students who report somatic symptoms involving a fatigued brain, neck or head pain, or blurring of vision due to difficult course work or classes.

- *Dhat syndrome.* This is a term used in India to describe illness anxiety concerns and severe anxiety over the discharge of semen. The condition produces feelings of weakness or exhaustion.

- *Ataque de nervios.* Commonly found in Latino/Hispanic people residing in the United States and Latin America, the somatic and dissociative symptoms of this condition can include brain aches, stomach disturbances, anxiety symptoms, and trancelike states.

- *Piblokto.* Generally found in Inuit communities, this condition involves dissociative-type episodes accompanied by extreme excitement that are sometimes followed by convulsions and coma. The individual may perform aggressive and dangerous acts and report amnesia after the episode.

- *Zar.* This condition, found in Middle Eastern or North African societies, involves the experience of being possessed by a spirit. Individuals in a dissociative state may engage in bizarre behaviors, including shouting or hitting their head against a wall.

Culture-bound syndromes are interesting because they point to the existence of a pattern of symptoms that are associated primarily with specific societies or groups. These "disorders" do not fit easily into the DSM-5 classification or into many of the biological and psychological models used to explain dissociative and somatic symptom disorders. What does it mean when unusual behavioral patterns are discovered that do not fit into Western-developed classification systems?

showed interest in the somatic concerns, such as their onset, duration, and factors that relieved or increased the symptoms. Arguments between Mr. X and his wife appeared to be a significant stressor. The psychiatrist prescribed medication as a supportive treatment. He also shared strategies for improving communication with Mrs. X, which led to a decrease in physical complaints (Yeung & Deguang, 2002).

Biological Treatment

Antidepressant medications such as selective serotonin reuptake inhibitors are sometimes used to treat SSD (S. Taylor, Asmundson, & Coons, 2005) and illness anxiety disorder (Schweitzer, Zafar, Pavlicova, & Fallon, 2011). Although medication treatment for somatic and related disorders is rarely successful in isolation, medication sometimes helps reduce anxiety and depression (Yates, 2013).

Psychological Treatments

Treatment for SSD and related disorders focuses primarily on understanding the client's view of his or her problem. Individuals with somatic symptom, illness anxiety, and conversion disorders are often frustrated, disappointed, and angry following years of encounters with the medical profession. They believe that treatment strategies have been ineffective and resent the implication that they are "fakers" or "problem patients" (Frohm & Beehler, 2010). Medical personnel often do, in fact, show negative reactions when interacting with individuals with these disorders (P. G. Williams et al., 2010). Because of these reactions, it may be difficult for patients to establish a positive therapeutic relationship with medical personnel.

A newer approach to treating SSD and illness anxiety disorder involves demonstrating empathy regarding the physical complaints, accepting them as genuine, and providing information about symptoms that are often stress-related such as hypertension and headaches. Medical professionals can also describe how emotions such as anxiety can produce symptoms such as queasiness before making a public speech or increased heart rate when asking someone out for a date. They further explain how various physiological symptoms are quite common and emphasize that, due to the absence of medical findings, the chances for a positive outcome are very good. Similarly, eliciting the patient's views and providing psychoeducation regarding the relationship between stress, somatic symptoms, and emotional states can enhance working relationships between therapists and clients and help reduce anxiety (Marshall et al., 2013).

In another approach, SSD is viewed within a social context—somatic complaints are seen as reflecting unsatisfying or inadequate social relationships. Individuals who assume a "sick role" often control others through bodily complaints or receive some reinforcement, such as escape from responsibility. Therapy is directed toward developing and improving the individual's social network and adaptive coping skills. A therapist may say something such as: "There is treatment available that may be helpful to you, if you would like to participate. This involves learning new ways of understanding and coping with stresses, other than going to the nearest emergency room. Treatment will also involve learning more about yourself and finding out what gets in the way of developing more fulfilling relationships" (Gregory & Jindal, 2006, p. 34).

Because many patients with somatic symptom and health anxiety disorders appear to have cognitive distortions, such as a conviction that they are especially vulnerable to disease, cognitive-behavioral approaches focused on correcting these misinterpretations are successful (Schroder et al., 2012). In one program, individuals with illness anxiety disorder who feared having cancer, heart disease, or other fatal diseases were educated about the relationship between misinterpretations of bodily sensations and selective attention to illness themes. Six 2-hour group sessions covered topics such as "What Is Illness Anxiety?" "The Role of Your Thoughts," "Bodily Attention and Illness Anxiety," "Stress and Bodily Symptoms," and "Your Own Vicious Cycle." As homework, participants monitored and challenged illness-related anxiety thoughts. After completing these sessions, most participants showed considerable improvement or no longer met the criteria for the disorder; the gains were maintained at a 6-month follow-up (Hiller, Leibbrand, Rief, & Fichter, 2002). A similar cognitive-behavioral program also led to marked reductions in somatic symptoms and illness concerns in individuals with SSD (Schroder et al., 2012).

Because individuals with SSD often show a fear of internal bodily sensations, cognitive-behavioral therapists include *interoceptive* exposure (exposure to bodily sensations) during treatment. Therapists ask clients to perform activities that typically trigger anxiety symptoms, such as breathing through a straw, hyperventilating, spinning, or climbing stairs, until feared reactions such as light-headedness, chest discomfort, or increased heart rate occur. The activities are repeated until the bodily sensations no longer elicit anxiety or fear (Flink, Nicholas, Boersma, & Linton, 2009).

DID YOU KNOW?

A physician was called in to assist a woman in labor. She had a melon-sized abdomen and was writhing and groaning with pain. The physician later found that the woman was not pregnant but instead had pseudocyesis, a rare somatic symptom disorder involving numerous signs of pregnancy, including abdominal and breast enlargement and cessation of menses. With pseudocyesis, psychological factors appear to trick the body into secreting hormones that result in outward symptoms of pregnancy.

SOURCE: Svoboda, 2006

Relaxation training can also effectively reduce the sympathetic nervous system activity found in individuals with somatic symptoms (Sauer et al., 2010). Mindfulness-based cognitive therapy is another approach that can lower anxiety. Clients learn to experience and observe their problematic thoughts and symptoms without judgment or emotion, and without reacting to them. Instead of responding with fear and anxiety, the individual merely observes and reflects on thoughts and physical reactions. This process weakens the connection between emotional arousal and the symptoms and thoughts. Mindfulness cognitive therapy has been effective in treating somatic symptom and illness anxiety disorders (Blacker, Herbert, Forman, & Kounios, 2012; McManus, Surawy, Muse, Vazquez-Montes, & Williams, 2012).

Dissociative Disorders

CASE STUDY   A 29-year-old woman who was in China for an academic trip was found unconscious in the hotel bathroom. The woman was unable to remember her identity or any information about her life. Examinations showed no neurological abnormalities or evidence of substance use. She remained in an amnesiac state for 10 months, until blood on her fingers triggered memories of witnessing a murder in China and being unable to help the victim because of her fear. Once this memory surfaced, she began to remember other aspects of her life (Reinhold & Markowitsch, 2009).

The **dissociative disorders**—dissociative amnesia (localized, generalized, and fugue), depersonalization/derealization disorder, and dissociative identity disorder (multiple-personality disorder)—are shown in Table 7.6. Each of these DSM-5 disorders involves some sort of dissociation, or separation, of a part of the person's consciousness, memory, or identity. Although dissociative disorders are highly publicized and sensationalized, they are considered rare.

Dissociative Amnesia

According to DSM-5, **dissociative amnesia** occurs when a traumatic event or stressful circumstances result in a sudden partial or total loss of important personal information or memory of a specific event (APA, 2013). An affected individual may be unable to recall information such as his or her name, address, or names of relatives, yet remember the necessities of daily life—how to read, write, and drive (Spiegel et al., 2011). As you can imagine, it is highly distressing to discover that there are lapses in your memory, that you have done things you are not aware of, or you are unable to do something you ordinarily could do (Dell, 2013). Fortunately, unlike amnesia associated with strokes, substance abuse, or other medical conditions, dissociative amnesia results from psychological factors or stressors so the memory is potentially retrievable (Schauer & Elbert, 2010). In a community sample in New York, a 12-month prevalence of 1.8 percent was reported for dissociative amnesia, with over twice as many women experiencing symptoms of the disorder (Johnson, Cohen, Kasen, & Brook, 2006).

Localized Amnesia

The most common form of dissociative amnesia, **localized amnesia**, involves an inability to recall events that happened in a specific period, often centered on some highly painful or disturbing event. The following case study is typical of localized amnesia.

dissociative disorders   a group of disorders, including dissociative amnesia, dissociative identity disorder, and depersonalization/derealization disorder, all of which involve some sort of dissociation, or separation, of a part of the person's consciousness, memory, or identity

dissociative amnesia   sudden partial or total loss of important personal information or recall of events due to psychological factors

localized amnesia   lack of memory for a specific event or events

Table 7.6 Dissociative Disorders

DISORDERS CHART				
Disorder	**DSM-5 Criteria**	**Prevalence**	**Age of Onset**	**Course**
Dissociative amnesia	• Sudden inability to recall information of specific events or of one's identity or life history—results from stress or a traumatic event	1.8% in a community sample with 1% for males and 2.6% for females	Any age group	Acute forms may remit spontaneously, although may become chronic
Dissociative amnesia, with dissociative fugue	• Sudden confusion, e.g., wandering to a new area with inability to recall one's past and confusion about personal identity	0.2%; may increase during natural disasters or wartime	Usually adulthood	Related to stress or trauma; recovery is generally rapid
Depersonalization/ derealization disorder	• Persistent changes in perception and detachment from one's own thoughts and body • May feel things are unreal or a sense of being in a dreamlike state • Intact reality testing	About 2%; although 50–75% of adults may experience brief episodes of stress-related depersonalization	Adolescence or adulthood	May be short-term or chronic
Dissociative identity disorder (multiple-personality disorder)	• Identity disrupted by two or more distinct personality states or by the experience of possession (self-reported or observed) • Altered behavior, mood, sense of self, memories, emotions, cognitions, and perceptions • Frequent gaps in memory of everyday events or inability to recall important personal information	Sharp rise in reported cases since the 1980s; up to 9 times more frequent in women in clinic settings; 1.5% in a community sample	Childhood to adolescence, but misdiagnosis may result in late reporting	Fluctuating; tends to be chronic and recurrent

SOURCE: Data from APA (2013); Johnson, Cohen, Kasen, & Brook (2006); Spiegel et al. (2011).

CASE STUDY   An 18-year-old woman who survived a dramatic fire claimed not to remember it or the death of her child and husband in the fire. She claimed her relatives were lying about the fire. She became extremely agitated and emotional several hours later, when her memory abruptly returned.

As this case demonstrates, localized amnesia often begins and ends very abruptly, particularly when it is in response to an overwhelming traumatic event. People vary in the degree and type of memory that is lost in localized amnesia. Some individuals display **systematized amnesia**, which involves the loss of memory for certain categories of information. Individuals may be unable to recall memories of their families or of a particular person. In one case, shortly after the sudden death of her only daughter, an elderly woman appeared to have no recall of having had a daughter, but other memories were unaffected.

Some people display **selective amnesia**, an inability to remember certain details of an incident. For example, a man remembered having an automobile accident but could not recall that his child had died in the crash. Selective amnesia is often claimed by people accused of violent criminal offenses; many murderers report that they remember arguments but do not remember killing anyone. In some cases, this may be

systematized amnesia   loss of memory for certain categories of information

selective amnesia   an inability to remember certain details of an event

Hypnosis as Therapy

Some practitioners continue to use hypnosis to assess and treat dissociative disorders, based on the belief that these disorders may be inadvertently induced by self-hypnosis.

DID YOU KNOW?

Some individuals experience a rare form of amnesia called *continuous amnesia*, which involves an inability to recall any events that occur between a specific time in the past and the present time. The individual remains alert and attentive but forgets each successive event after it occurs.

SOURCE: Spiegel et al., 2011

true since extreme emotions may have prevented the encoding of a traumatic memory. Because the diagnosis of dissociative amnesia depends primarily on self-report, the possibility of feigning must be considered. According to one estimate, about 70 percent of criminals who say they have amnesia regarding their crime are feigning (Merryman, 1997).

In some cases of localized amnesia, the amnesia comes to light only after the individual begins to recall details of a traumatic event—a **repressed memory**. Cases of repressed memory are believed to result from exposure to trauma that is so overwhelming or threatening that the individual represses the event, often for a sustained period of time (McNally, 2007). For example, it was 20 years after the event that one woman recovered memories of a teacher molesting her when she was in the sixth grade. These memories were uncovered after years of psychiatric treatment. The teacher was convicted, but the case was later overturned because of the weakness of the evidence (Loftus, 2003).

Not all researchers believe in the validity of repressed memory and the hypothesis that certain threatening memories can be pushed out of consciousness. Laney and Loftus (2005) point out the complexities involved in interpreting reports of repressed memories:

- Many abuse survivors with recovered memories claim that they had forgotten their abuse, but this does not necessarily mean that they repressed their memories.

- Many abuse survivors do not mention abuse when initially asked, but this is not proof of repression.

- Memory is malleable. Details can be distorted, and wholly false memories can be planted, intentionally or unintentionally.

- Just because a memory report is detailed, confidently expressed, and emotional does not mean that it reflects a true experience. False memories can have these same features (p. 823).

repressed memory memory of a traumatic event has been repressed and is, therefore, unavailable for recall

Some further argue that parents or therapists can unintentionally plant or strengthen implausible memories (Pezdek, Blandon-Gitlin, & Gabbay, 2006). At this point, it is not clear how many cases of genuine repressed memory actually exist, or whether the phenomenon exists at all. Belief in repressed memory is still high among undergraduates and many clinicians. Those least likely to believe the phenomenon is real are research-oriented psychologists and memory experts (Patihis, Ho, Tingen, Lilienfeld, & Loftus, 2014).

Dissociative Fugue

Another form of dissociative amnesia is **dissociative fugue**, which involves bewildered wandering or purposeless travel accompanied by amnesia for one's identity and life history. The following case study illustrates the extensive loss of personal identity that occurs during a dissociative fugue state.

Dissociative Fugue

Jeff Ingram was on his way to visit a terminally ill friend in Alberta and woke up 4 days later in Denver without any memory of his life. He was without his car or any personal identification. Ingram now wears a necklace flash drive and a bracelet that contains his personal information.

> **CASE STUDY**   When she awoke, Joan looked around and realized that she did not know her own name, where she was, or how she got there. She did not recognize herself in the mirror. She figured out that she was in a motel room in Albuquerque, New Mexico . . . She then took a bus downtown in hopes of finding something familiar. She felt disoriented, and became anxious, afraid and paranoid. . . . For Joan, her life began when she awoke in the motel room (Howley & Ross, 2003, pp. 110–111).

Similar to others who experience a fugue state, Joan awoke in a new location, with no recall of her identity. As with localized amnesia, recovery from a fugue state is often abrupt and complete, although the gradual return of bits of information may also occur. Kopelman (2002) believes that genuine cases are short lived: "Fugue states usually last only a few hours or days, if prolonged, suspicion of simulation must always arise" (p. 2,171). However, it appears that some fugue states may last for an extended period and may recur, as seen in the following case study.

> **CASE STUDY**   Mr. A, a 74-year-old man, was brought to the hospital emergency room after awakening on a park bench not knowing who or where he was. He reported having no memory of how he got to the park, nor did he know his name or where he was from (Ballew, Morgan, & Lippmann, 2003, p. 347). Mr. A was treated with an antianxiety medication and recovered his memory. His family was contacted, and his sister reported that Mr. A had disappeared on two other occasions when under stress.

Some individuals who, like Mr. A, have experienced several fugue episodes decide to wear personal identification in the event of a future occurrence. Because of the complete loss of memory, law enforcement agencies or hospitals often become involved. However, some individuals act completely normal during a fugue episode and slowly begin to take on a new identity, until someone recognizes them or bits of information about the past begin to return.

Depersonalization/Derealization Disorder

Depersonalization/derealization disorder is the most common dissociative disorder. According to the DSM-5, it is characterized by recurrent or persistent symptoms of *depersonalization* (feelings of unreality, detachment, being an outside observer of

dissociative fugue   episode involving complete loss of memory of one's life and identity, unexpected travel to a new location, or assumption of a new identity

depersonalization/derealization disorder   dissociative condition characterized by feelings of unreality concerning the self and the environment

DID YOU KNOW?

Compared to those who attended a lecture on internal medicine, general medical practitioners who attended a lecture on dissociation reported significantly more dissociative experiences and symptoms, more suicidal ideas, and more abuse of alcohol. Why might the two groups of physicians differ in their views of dissociative disorders?

SOURCE: Damsa et al., 2009

one's own thoughts, feelings, or behaviors) and/or *derealization* (sense of unreality or dreamlike detachment from one's environment) that cause significant impairment or distress. During depersonalization/derealization episodes, the person remains in contact with reality (APA, 2013).

Questions used to screen for this disorder may include "Have you had the feeling that things around you are unreal?" "Have you ever felt completely detached from your feelings?" "Have you ever felt like your thoughts are not your own?" or "Have you found yourself somewhere and not known how you got there?" One woman described her depersonalization symptoms this way: "It is as if the real me is taken out and put on a shelf and stored somewhere inside of me. Whatever makes me me is not there" (Simeon, Gross, et al., 1997, p. 1,110). Episodes of depersonalization can be chronic, and can produce great anxiety, as the following case study illustrates.

> **CASE STUDY** Ms. A., age 23, sought counseling because she had been feeling "detached" for the past 4 years, and was feeling increasingly worried about her symptoms. She explained to the therapist that she feels "fuzzy all the time, like I lost touch of reality." She also complained of confused thinking: "It feels like I'm watching my life on television; I don't feel any emotions." Her symptoms began immediately after a college party, which the police stopped because of underage drinking (Janjua, Rapport, & Ferrara, 2010, p. 62).

A DSM-5 diagnosis of depersonalization/derealization disorder occurs only when the feelings of unreality and detachment, disembodiment, and emotional numbing cause major impairment in social or occupational functioning. Depersonalization/derealization disorder is often accompanied by mood and anxiety disorders (Janjua et al., 2010).

Depersonalization episodes are sometimes brief or they may last for decades, depending on individual circumstances. In a community sample in New York, a 12-month prevalence of 0.8 percent was reported for depersonalization/derealization disorder (Johnson et al., 2006). The lifetime prevalence of the disorder, which typically begins in the teenage years, is about 2 percent; it is equally common in men and women (APA, 2013). Transient depersonalization/derealization symptoms are much more common. For example, fleeting experiences of depersonalization are reported in up to 70 percent of college students and 23 percent of the general population (Sierra, 2012).

Dissociative Identity Disorder

> **CASE STUDY** "Little Judy" is a young child who laughs and giggles. "Gravelly Voice" is a man who speaks with a raspy voice. "The one who walks in darkness" is blind and trips over furniture. "Big Judy" is articulate, competent, and funny. These are 4 of the 44 personalities that existed within Judy Castelli. She was initially diagnosed with schizophrenia, but was later told that dissociative identity disorder was the appropriate diagnosis. She is a singer, a musician, an inventor, and an artist who has also become a lay expert on mental health issues (Woliver, 2000).

dissociative identity disorder (DID) a condition in which two or more relatively independent personality states appear to exist in one person, including experiences of possession; also known as *multiple-personality disorder*

possession the replacement of a person's sense of personal identity with a supernatural spirit or power

Dissociative identity disorder (DID), formerly known as *multiple-personality disorder*, is a disruption of identity as evidenced by two or more distinct personality states. According to DSM-5, those with DID have a disrupted sense of self and show alterations in behaviors, attitudes, and emotions when these alternate personality states occur. Recurrent gaps in memory for personal information or for everyday or traumatic events are also evident. These symptoms (which may be self-reported or observed by others) cause significant distress and impairment in functioning (APA, 2013). DID can also involve an experience of **possession**, in which the person's sense of personal identity is replaced by a supernatural presence. Possession was added to the DID definition in DSM-5 to encompass cultural symptoms of dissociation involving alternate personality states (Spiegel et al., 2011). Many individuals with DID report experiencing trance states, sleepwalking, paranormal and possession episodes (C. A. Ross, 2011), symptoms of conversion disorder (APA, 2013), and high rates of post-traumatic stress disorder (PTSD) (Rodewald, Wilhelm-Gobling, Emrich, Reddemann, & Gast, 2011). The estimated 12-month prevalence of dissociative identity disorder in a community sample was about 1.5 percent with the rate being slightly higher in males than females (Johnson et al., 2006). In inpatient and outpatient settings, the lifetime prevalence of DID is estimated to be around 5 percent (Sar, 2011).

In situations in which two or more personality states are observed, only one personality is evident at any moment. However, one or more personalities may be aware of the existence of the others. The personality states usually differ from one another and sometimes are direct opposites, as we saw in the case of Judy Castelli. In many cases, the role of the alternate personality (alter) is to protect the emotional well-being of the main personality from stress or trauma. The process of dissociation and switching to an alternate personality state usually occurs during highly stressful situations and may be preceded by trance-like behavior, blinking, rolling of the eyes, or changes in posture (Gentile, Dillon, & Gillig, 2013).

The alters often make their appearance to help deal with difficult situations faced by the primary personality. For example, Kristen, a 19-year-old, reported being overwhelmed with stress during interactions or confrontations with her peers or parents. Her primary personality was compliant, depressed, and helpless—even to the point of depending on her mother's advice as to what to wear. Zac was the alter who displayed anger and aggression. She spoke with a clear, forceful voice, defined herself as a lesbian, and served as Kristen's protector. During childhood, when Kristen was bullied by other children, Zac would appear to make them stop. Zac was initially concerned about therapy, worried that she would be "killed off" once Kristen no longer needed her, but later became a willing part of Kristen's fully integrated personality (Humphreys, Rubin, Knudson, & Stiles, 2005).

Gaps in memories similar to symptoms of dissociative amnesia and fugue are present in individuals with DID. For example, one 28-year-old woman mentioned receiving messages from people she did not know saying that they had a "great time" with her. Her phone contained phone numbers that she did not recognize and she had a feeling she might have been sexually involved with a man but had no memory of it (Gentile et al., 2013). Many individuals with DID also report finding themselves at a different location without knowing how they got there (APA, 2013).

Complex legal debate arises regarding acts performed when an individual with dissociative identity disorder is purportedly in a dissociated state. The following examples offer an additional glimpse into this controversy:

- A therapist claimed that it was one of her client's 24 personalities who kidnapped and sexually assaulted her and that the main personality was not responsible (Haley, 2003).
- A man was charged with the rape of a woman with multiple personalities because one of the personalities said she did not consent to sexual activity with the man.

Former NFL Star and Heisman Trophy Winner Herschel Walker

Herschel Walker wrote about his ongoing struggle with dissociative identity disorder and his efforts to integrate his 12 alters in his recent book, "Breaking Free: My Struggle With Dissociative identity Disorder." He describes his alters as including "The Warrior" who appeared as he played football and "The Hero" who had the role of making public appearances.

DID YOU KNOW?

Individuals with DID often report that information about events happening to one personality is unavailable to other personalities. Research, however, has found that learning does in fact transfer between the different personalities.

SOURCE: Huntjens, Verschuere, & McNally, 2012

Dissociative Identity Disorder

Judy Castelli, reported to have 44 personalities, stands beside her stained-glass artwork. The people in her art have no faces but are connected and touching each other. Castelli considers her artistic endeavors a creative outlet for her continuing struggle with dissociative identity disorder.

- A South Carolina woman going through a divorce had 21 personalities. She claimed that she had not committed adultery and that she had tried to stop the responsible personality, "Rosie," from becoming involved in an extramarital affair.

- A woman with multiple personality claimed it was one of her alternate personalities who did not know right from wrong who killed four of her relatives (Collins, 2013).

Cases such as these raise questions regarding dissociative disorders and responsibility. Does a diagnosis of dissociative identity disorder constitute mitigating circumstances and "diminished capacity"? Are people with DID responsible for the behaviors and actions of their alternate personalities?

Diagnostic Controversy

DID is both complex and intriguing, especially because the characteristics associated with DID have changed over time. Goff and Simms (1993) compared professional and historical case reports from the years 1800 to 1965 with those from the 1980s. The earlier cases involved an average of three personality states (versus 12 in the more recent cases), a later age of onset of first dissociation (age 20, as opposed to age 11 in the 1980s), a greater proportion of males, and a much lower prevalence of child abuse (Figure 7.3).

Similarly, H. G. Pope, Jr., Barry, Bodkin, and Hudson (2006) tracked publications related to DID and dissociative amnesia over a 20-year period. The number of articles related to these disorders was low in the 1980s, rose to a sharp peak in the mid-1990s, and then declined sharply by 2003. No other disorder showed a similar phenomenon. The researchers concluded that both DID and dissociative amnesia "enjoyed a brief period of fashion that has now waned. . . . These diagnostic entities presently do not command widespread scientific acceptance" (p. 19).

Before the case of Sybil—a woman who appeared to have 16 different personalities—became popularized in a movie and book in the 1970s, there had been fewer than 200 reported cases of DID worldwide. Now, each year thousands of new cases are reported. However, DID is still a rare diagnosis. The disorder has become a source of controversy between clinicians and researchers in the field (Gentile et al., 2013). Some clinicians contend that DID is relatively common but that it is often not recognized and diagnosed (Foote, Smolin, Kaplan, Legatt, & Lipschitz, 2006). Other practitioners, however, believe that DID is rare and that the increase in numbers may be due to clinician bias, the use of faulty assessment, or the use of therapeutic techniques that increase the likelihood of a DID diagnosis (Gharaibeh, 2009). Temporary dissociation symptoms such as alterations in memory, thoughts, and perceptions or a sense of depersonalization (feeling detached or numb) are fairly common symptoms during periods of stress (Carlson, Dalenberg, & McDade-Montez, 2012). Some clinicians may mistakenly interpret these symptoms as evidence of DID. Additionally, the use of hypnosis or suggestion appears to increase the likelihood that a client is viewed as having a dissociative disorder involving multiple personality states (P. R. McHugh, 2009).

Questions have also been raised regarding reports of memories retrieved from very early ages. Clients with DID have reported the emergence of alternate personalities at age 2 or earlier (Dell & Eisenhower, 1990), and in one study, 11 percent reported being abused before age 1 (C. A. Ross et al., 1991). Reports regarding memories of events at these ages would be highly suspect. Whether the increase in diagnosis of DID is the result of more accurate diagnosis, false positives, hypnosis, or an actual increase in the incidence of the disorder is still being debated.

MYTH Dissociative identity disorder is relatively easy to diagnose, and most mental health professionals accept the category.

REALITY There are no objective measures from which a diagnosis can be made, and cases involving feigning the disorder have been reported. Those who question the category suggest that symptoms of the disorder are inadvertently produced through suggestion or hypnosis.

Etiology of Dissociative Disorders

The possible causes of dissociative disorders are subject to much conjecture. Because diagnosis depends heavily on self-report, feigning or faking is always a possibility. Fabricated amnesia, dissociative fugue, or DID can be produced by individuals who are attempting to avoid social, legal, or financial consequences of their behaviors. However, true cases of these disorders may also result from these types of stressors. Differentiating between genuine cases of dissociative disorders and faked ones is difficult.

In this section, we consider the multipath dimensions that contribute to the dissociative disorders (Figure 7.4). Although two models—the psychologically based *posttraumatic model* and the *sociocognitive model*—are currently the most influential etiological perspectives, neither is sufficient to explain why only some individuals develop these disorders. It is likely that biological, psychological, social, and sociocultural vulnerabilities all play a role (Dalenberg et al., 2012).

Biological Dimension

Biological explanations for dissociative disorders have focused on disruptions in encoding of memories due to acute stress and the inability to retrieve autobiographical material because of the release of hormones such as glucocorticoid, which may impede the recall of traumatic events (Bourget & Whitehurst, 2007). Atypical brain functioning in the structures associated with memory encoding and retrieval has been documented in various dissociative disorders (Arzy et al., 2011). In dissociative amnesia, MRI scans show inhibited neural activity in the hippocampus apparently associated with memory repression (Kikuchi et al., 2010), and positron emission tomography (PET) scans show reduced metabolism in an area of the prefrontal cortex that is involved in the retrieval of autobiographical memories (M. Brand et al., 2009).

A number of studies using PET and MRI scans with individuals diagnosed with DID have found variations in brain activity when comparing different personality states (Sheehan, Sewall, & Thurber, 2005). Switching between personalities is associated with activation or inhibition of certain brain regions, particularly the hippocampus (G. E. Tsai et al., 1999), an area involved in memories and hypothesized to be involved in the generation of dissociative states and amnesia (Staniloiu & Markowitsch, 2010). However, these patterns of brain activity are difficult to interpret because it is unclear what causes them and what specific role they play, if any, in dissociative disorders.

M. H. Teicher and colleagues (2002) believe that chronic activation of stress responses due to childhood trauma can result in permanent structural changes in the brain. Similarly, Spiegel (2006) has suggested that reduced volume in the hippocampus and amygdala may hamper the ability of the brain to encode, store, and retrieve memory; comprehend contradictory information; and integrate emotional memories. Such alterations may play an etiological role in dissociative amnesia, DID, and depersonalization (Janjua et al., 2010).

Psychological Dimension

The primary psychological explanations for the dissociative disorders come from psychodynamic theory, although individual vulnerabilities such as hypnotizability or suggestibility are also thought to play an important role. According to psychodynamic theory, dissociative disorders are caused by an individual's use of repression to block unpleasant or traumatic events from consciousness (L. F. Richardson, 1998). This process protects the individual from painful memories or conflicts. In dissociative amnesia and fugue, for example, memories of specific events or large parts of the individual's personal identity are no longer available to conscious awareness. Dissociation is carried to an extreme in DID. Here, the splits in mental processes become so persistent that independent identities are formed, each with a unique set of memories (K. Baker, 2010).

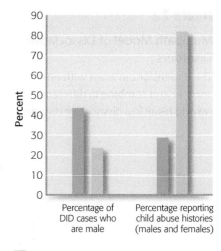

■ Between 1800 and 1965

■ 1980s

Figure 7.3

Comparison of Characteristics of Reported Cases of Dissociative Identity Disorder (Multiple-Personality Disorder)

This graph illustrates characteristics of dissociative identity disorder (DID) cases reported in the 1980s versus those reported between 1800 and 1965. What could account for these differences?

SOURCE: Based on Goff & Simms (1993).

Figure 7.4

Multipath Model of Dissociative Disorders

The dimensions interact with one another and combine in different ways to result in a dissociative disorder.

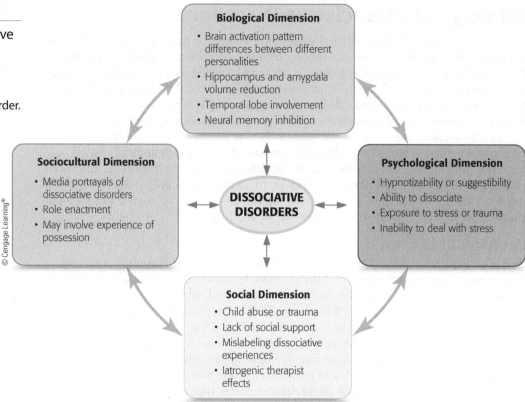

© Cengage Learning®

Biological Dimension
- Brain activation pattern differences between different personalities
- Hippocampus and amygdala volume reduction
- Temporal lobe involvement
- Neural memory inhibition

Sociocultural Dimension
- Media portrayals of dissociative disorders
- Role enactment
- May involve experience of possession

DISSOCIATIVE DISORDERS

Psychological Dimension
- Hypnotizability or suggestibility
- Ability to dissociate
- Exposure to stress or trauma
- Inability to deal with stress

Social Dimension
- Child abuse or trauma
- Lack of social support
- Mislabeling dissociative experiences
- Iatrogenic therapist effects

Contemporary psychodynamic theorists propose a post-traumatic model of DID that focuses on the role of severe childhood abuse, parental neglect or abandonment, or other early traumatic events (Dalenberg et al., 2012; Kluft, 1987). According to this model, the factors necessary for the development of DID include:

- being exposed to overwhelming childhood stress, such as traumatic physical or sexual abuse;
- genetic or biological predispositions, psychiatric vulnerabilities, life stressors, and having the capacity to dissociate;
- encapsulating or walling off the experience; and
- developing different memory systems.

Thus, according to the post-traumatic model, the split in personality develops because of traumatic early experiences combined with an inability to escape them. If a supportive environment is not available or if the personality is not resilient, these factors can result in DID (Irwin, 1998; see Figure 7.5). In the case of Sybil, who was severely abused by her mother, Dr. Wilbur—Sybil's psychiatrist—speculated that Sybil escaped "an intolerable and dangerous reality" by dividing into different personalities (F. R. Schreiber, 1973). Consistent with this perspective, most individuals diagnosed with DID do report a history of physical or sexual abuse during childhood (Barlow, 2011). In fact, individuals with DID have the highest rate of childhood psychological trauma compared to people with other psychiatric disorders (Sar, 2011).

To develop DID, the individual must have the capacity to dissociate—or separate—certain memories or mental processes in response to traumatic events. Some researchers believe that pathological dissociation represents an escape from unpleasant experiences through self-hypnosis (L. D. Butler, Duran, Jasiukaitis, Koopman, & Spiegel, 1996). In fact, people who have DID are very susceptible to hypnotic suggestion. Additionally, females with DID report various experiences involving alterations in consciousness, including trance states and sleepwalking (APA, 2013). As with most

DID YOU KNOW?

Many individuals with DID report hearing voices before the age of 18. They hear two or more voices (often child and adult) and also report tactile and visual hallucinations.

SOURCE: Dorahy et al., 2009

psychodynamic conceptualizations, it is difficult to formulate and test hypotheses. In addition, the post-traumatic model presupposes exposure to childhood trauma. In most studies, information on child abuse is based on self-reports, is not independently corroborated, and involves varying definitions and degrees of abuse (Gharaibeh, 2009).

Social and Sociocultural Dimension

The sociocognitive model of DID takes both social and sociocultural factors into consideration. It was developed by Spanos (1994) and further elaborated by Lilienfeld, Lynn, Kirsch, and colleagues (1999). In this perspective, DID is conceptualized as

> *displays of multiple role enactments that have been created, legitimized, and maintained by social reinforcement. Patients with DID synthesize these role enactments by drawing on a wide variety of sources of information, including the print and broadcast media, cues provided by therapists, personal experiences, and observations of individuals who have enacted multiple identities.* (Lilienfeld, Lynn, Kirsch, et al., 1999, p. 507)

According to this model, individuals with the disorder learn about DID and its characteristics through the mass media and, under certain circumstances, begin to act out these roles. Vulnerable individuals may demonstrate these behaviors when therapists inadvertently use questions or techniques that evoke dissociative types of problem descriptions by clients. Proponents of the sociocognitive model cite the large increase in DID cases after mass media portrayals of this disorder as support for their perspective. For example, after the 1973 publication of *Sybil*, which detailed her 16 personalities, the mean number of personalities for those diagnosed with DID rose from 3 to 12 (Goff & Simms, 1993).

Therapists are also exposed to mass media portrayals of DID and may unconsciously encourage reports of DID from clients. This would be referred to as an **iatrogenic disorder**—a condition unintentionally produced by a therapist through mechanisms such as selective attention, suggestion, reinforcement, and expectations that are placed on the client. Could some or even most cases of dissociative identity disorder be iatrogenic? A number of researchers and clinicians say yes. They believe that many of the cases of DID and dissociative amnesia have unwittingly been produced by therapists, self-help books, and the mass media (Lilienfeld, Lynn, & Lohr, 2004; Piper & Mersky, 2004). Clients most sensitive to these influences may have predisposing characteristics. Research findings indicate that individuals who report dissociations score high on fantasy proneness and fantasy susceptibility (Giesbrecht, Lynn, Lilienfeld, & Merckelbach, 2008).

The authenticity of one well-known case of DID—that of Sybil (mentioned earlier)—has also been questioned (Borch-Jacobsen, 1997). Herbert Spiegel, a hypnotist, worked with Sybil and used her to demonstrate hypnotic phenomena in his classes. He described her as extremely easy to hypnotize, calling her a "hypnotic virtuoso," something found in only 5 percent of the population. Sybil told Spiegel that her psychiatrist, Cornelia Wilbur, had wanted her to be "Helen," a name given to a feeling she expressed during therapy; this may have facilitated the conversion of different memories or emotions into "personalities." Tapes of sessions between Wilbur and Sybil suggest that Wilbur may have described various personalities for Sybil. Sybil eventually wrote a letter denying that she had multiple

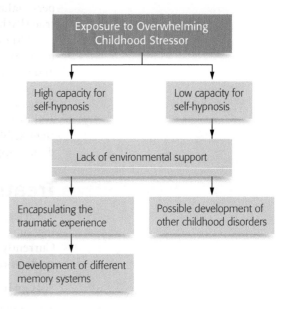

Figure 7.5

The Post-Traumatic Model of Dissociative Identity Disorder

Note the importance of each of the factors in the development of dissociative identity disorder.

SOURCE: Adapted from Kluft (1987); Loewenstein (1994).

iatrogenic disorder a condition unintentionally produced by a therapist's actions and treatment strategies

Cross-Cultural Factors and Dissociation

Dissociative trance states are part of certain cultural or religious practices, as demonstrated by this Haitian woman participating in a voodoo ceremony.

Thony Belizaire/AFP/Getty Images

personalities and stating that the "extreme things" she told about her mother were not true (Rieber, 2006).

Although iatrogenic influences can occur in any disorder, such effects may be more common with dissociative disorders, because of the high levels of hypnotizability and suggestibility found in individuals with these conditions. As Goff has stated, it is "no coincidence that the field of [multiple-personality disorder] studies in the United States largely originated among practitioners of hypnosis" (1993, p. 604). Hypnosis and other memory-retrieval methods may *create* rather than uncover personalities in suggestible clients. Although some cases of DID are probably therapist produced, most do not appear to be a result of this process.

Treatment of Dissociative Disorders

A variety of treatments for the dissociative disorders have been developed, including supportive counseling and the use of hypnosis and personality reconstruction. Currently, there are no specific medications for the dissociative disorders. However, medications are sometimes prescribed to treat concurrent anxiety or depression.

Treating Dissociative Amnesia and Dissociative Fugue

The symptoms of dissociative amnesia and fugue tend to end, or abate, spontaneously. It has been noted that depression is often associated with the fugue state and that severe stress is associated with both dissociative amnesia and fugue (Kopelman, 2002). A reasonable therapeutic approach is to treat these dissociative

"Suspect" Techniques Used to Treat Dissociative Identity Disorder

Bennett Braun, who founded the International Society for the Study of Multiple Personality and Dissociation and trained many therapists to work with clients with dissociative identity disorder, was brought up on charges by the Illinois Department of Financial and Professional Regulation. A former patient, Patricia Burgus, claimed that Braun inappropriately used hypnotic drugs, hypnosis, and leather strap restraints to stimulate abuse memories. Under this "repressed-memory therapy," Burgus became convinced that she possessed 300 personalities, was a high priestess in a satanic cult, ate meatloaf made of human flesh, and sexually abused her children. Burgus later began to question her "memories." In November 1997, she won a $10.6 million lawsuit, alleging inappropriate treatment and emotional harm (Associated Press, 1998). Braun lost his license to practice for 2 years and was placed on probation for an additional 5 years (Bloomberg, 2000). Another former patient, Elizabeth Gale, won a $7 million settlement against Braun and other staff at the hospital where he worked. She had been convinced she was raised as a "breeder" to produce babies who would be subjected to sexual abuse. She has since sought to reestablish relationships with family members whom she accused of being part of a cult (Dardick, 2004).

Such lawsuits create a quandary for mental health practitioners. Many feel intimidated by the threat of legal action if they attempt to treat adult survivors of childhood sexual abuse, especially cases involving recovered memories. However, discounting the memories of clients could result in further victimization. Especially worrisome is the use of techniques such as hypnosis, trance work, body memories, and age regression, because they may produce inaccurate "memories" (J. G. Benedict & Donaldson, 1996).

For Further Consideration

1. In the case of repressed memories, should clients be told that some techniques may produce inaccurate information?

2. Under what conditions, if any, should a therapist express doubt about information remembered by a client?

3. Given the high prevalence of child sexual abuse and the indefinite nature of repressed memories, how should clinicians proceed if a client discusses early memories of abuse?

disorders indirectly by alleviating the depression and the stress that may underlie dissociative symptoms with antidepressants, cognitive-behavioral therapy, and stress management techniques.

Treating Depersonalization/Derealization Disorder

Depersonalization/derealization disorder is also subject to spontaneous remission, but at a much slower rate than is seen with dissociative amnesia and fugue. Treatment generally concentrates on alleviating the feelings of anxiety or depression or the fear associated with the symptoms of detachment. Various antidepressants and antianxiety medications may be prescribed to treat these symptoms (Janjua et al., 2010). Because catastrophic attributions and appraisals sometimes play a role in the development of depersonalization/derealization symptoms, some therapists focus on "normalizing" minor dissociative reactions and thoughts in response to stressful situations (Hunter, Salkovskis, & David, 2014). Mindfulness techniques in which the individual focuses on the breathing process itself while nonjudgmentally observing dissociative sensations can help reduce the fear and anxiety associated with depersonalization/derealization symptoms (Michal et al., 2013).

Behavioral techniques are occasionally used to treat depersonalization/derealization disorder. For example, behavior therapy was successfully used to treat the disorder in a 15-year-old girl who had blackouts that she described as "floating in and out." These episodes were associated with headaches and feelings of detachment, but neurological and physical examinations revealed no biological cause. Treatment involved encouraging her family to provide attention and reinforcement when she decreased the frequency of blackouts; she was also taught strategies for coping with stressful situations (Dollinger, 1983).

Treating Dissociative Identity Disorder

The mental health literature contains more information on treating dissociative identity disorder than on all of the other dissociative disorders combined. For DID, trauma-focused therapy is used to help the individual develop healthier ways of dealing with stressors. Trauma-focused therapy for DID also helps the different identities or alters become aware of one another, consider each as legitimate parts of the individual, and resolve their differences. Each of the personalities is validated for helping the main personality cope with stressors and traumatic events. The desired outcome is an integration or harmony among the different alters and a final fusion of the personality states. In other words, the goal is for the alters to be completely integrated, merged, and assimilated into one personality (International Society for the Study of Trauma and Dissociation, 2011).

A hierarchical treatment approach for integrated functioning involves the following steps (Brand et al., 2012; Brand & Loewenstein, 2010; International Society for the Study of Trauma and Dissociation, 2011):

1. working on safety issues, emotional stabilization, and the reduction of symptoms;
2. reducing cognitive distortions;
3. identifying and working through the traumatic memories underlying the disorder;
4. stabilizing and learning to identify and deal with current stressors;
5. developing healthy relationships and practicing self-care;
6. assisting all identities to view themselves as a legitimate part of the self; and
7. integration and final fusion.

Treatment for this disorder is not always successful. Chris Sizemore (who was the inspiration for the book and movie *The Three Faces of Eve*) developed additional personalities after therapy but has now recovered. She is a writer, lecturer, and artist. Sybil also recovered (although questions remain regarding her diagnosis), and

A Famous Case of Dissociative Identity Disorder

Chris Sizemore, whose experiences with dissociative identity disorder inspired the book and movie *The Three Faces of Eve*, is seen in this 1993 photo with one of her paintings.

eventually became a college art professor (M. Miller & Kantrowitz, 1999). Successful treatment of DID, however, may be difficult to achieve. In a 30-month follow-up involving 119 individuals with DID who underwent comprehensive treatment, it was concluded that therapy resulted in fewer symptoms of dissociation and PTSD and increased adaptive behaviors such as socializing, attending school, or engaging in work or volunteer activities. However, these individuals were not "cured"; they still experienced some dissociative and other stress symptoms (Brand et al., 2013).

Other researchers reported that trauma-focused therapy addressing the child abuse experienced by a group of adults with DID reduced symptoms of dissociation by a moderate degree (Jepsen, Langeland, Sexton, & Heir, 2013). Similarly, a review of 16 treatment outcome studies found that individuals with DID tended to have lower rates of dissociation, suicidality, and depression following treatment (B. L. Brand, Classen, McNary, & Zaveri, 2009). Those who were able to integrate their personalities showed the greatest reduction in symptoms.

Contemporary Trends and Future Directions

With each edition of the DSM, some new disorders are added, some removed, and the criteria for others changed. Sometimes these changes are improvements, but some diagnostic changes create controversy. The criteria for somatic symptom disorder (formerly somatization disorder) have changed dramatically with the DSM-5; these changes will affect the prevalence of this disorder and individuals affected by this condition. Let's look at the different characteristics of these disorders.

Somatization Disorders (DSM-IV)

1. History of multiple distressing physical complaints and treatment-seeking before age 30.

2. At least eight symptoms involving pain, gastrointestinal symptoms, sexual symptoms, and pseudoneurological symptoms.

3. The symptoms or somatic complaints are "medically unexplained."

Somatic Symptom Disorder (DSM-5)

1. The existence of one or more somatic complaints.

2. This is accompanied by at least one of the following:

   • Persistent thoughts and concerns about the seriousness of the symptom(s)

   • Chronically high levels of anxiety over health

   • Spending excessive time or energy in regard to these symptoms

As you can see, the change from somatization disorder to somatic symptom disorder as described in DSM-5 is quite dramatic; the former required a more extensive history of physical complaints, many more somatic symptoms, and documentation that the symptoms were "medically unexplained." The DSM-5 Work Group believed the previous criteria were too restrictive and were especially concerned with the "medically unexplained" aspect of the criteria. It was difficult for physicians to verify that there was no physical basis for the somatic complaints. This situation sometimes resulted in an adversarial relationship between the health care professional and patient, particularly when patients believed their symptoms were considered "imaginary." Because of these concerns, the DSM-5 Work Group decided to eliminate the emphasis on the "medically unexplained" nature of the symptoms and focused instead on the degree of distress and impairment caused by somatic complaints and renamed the disorder *somatic symptom disorder*.

However, does the removal of "medically unexplained" and a focus on fewer symptoms produce its own set of problems? To receive the diagnosis of somatic symptom disorder only one problematic physical symptom is needed. A physician or clinician can decide if the individual has persistent, distressing thoughts about the symptom(s), has high levels of anxiety about the symptom(s), or devotes excessive time and energy to the symptom(s). Only one of these needs to be present for the diagnosis.

Because actual illnesses are not excluded, individuals with physical conditions may meet the criteria for somatic symptom disorder. For example, in one sample, 26 percent of the individuals with irritable bowel syndrome or fibromyalgia and 15 percent with cancer or heart disease would meet the new DSM-5 criteria for somatic symptom disorder (Frances, 2013). These statistics suggest that it will be difficult to decide if people with a chronic or potentially life-threatening illness have too much anxiety over their condition, spend an inordinate amount of time or energy on their symptoms, or have excessive thoughts regarding the seriousness of their illness.

In removing the "medically unexplained" aspect from somatic symptom disorder, are we now in danger of giving a psychiatric diagnosis to individuals with legitimate concerns about their diagnosed physical conditions? Who is to say whether a person with an illness such as HIV, heart disease, or cancer is devoting "excessive time or energy" or showing too much anxiety in response to their condition? The change in the criteria for this disorder is controversial. Time will tell if the changes are beneficial or have instead created a new set of concerns that will require further revisions in future editions of the DSM.

CONTINUUM Video Project

Lani and Jan: Dissociative Identity Disorder

"It's like living with 13 roommates . . . and your responsibility is to make sure everyone's needs get met."

Access the Continuum Video Project in MindTap at **www.cengage.com**

© Cengage Learning

chapter SUMMARY

1 What are the somatic symptom and related disorders and what do they have in common? What are the causes and treatments of these conditions?

- Somatic symptom and related disorders involve prominent somatic complaints that cause significant distress or impairment in the life of the individual and includes somatic symptom, illness anxiety, conversion, and factitious disorders.

- Somatic symptom disorder (SSD) is characterized by at least one physical complaint accompanied by excessive anxiety, thoughts, or behaviors associated with health concerns.

- Illness anxiety disorder is characterized by a belief that one has a serious and undetected illness or physical problem. In contrast to somatic symptom disorder, somatic symptoms are not a major feature of the disorder.

- Conversion disorder (functional neurological symptom disorder) involves neurological-like symptoms that are incompatible with a medical condition.

- Factitious disorders involve self-induced or feigned physical complaints, or symptoms induced in others.

- Biological explanations have suggested that there is increased vulnerability to somatic symptom disorders when individuals have high sensitivity to bodily sensations, a lower pain threshold, or a history of illness or injury.

- Psychological factors include high anxiety or stress, and catastrophic thoughts regarding bodily sensations.

- Social explanations suggest that the role of "being sick" is reinforcing. Parental models for injury or illness and social isolation can also be influential.

- From a sociocultural perspective, somatic symptom disorders result from societal restrictions placed on women, who are affected by these disorders to a much greater degree than are men. Additionally, social class, limited knowledge about medical concepts, and cultural acceptance of physical symptoms can play a role.

- Treatment includes the use of antidepressants to improve anxiety or depression and the use of cognitive-behavioral strategies. The process involves psychoeducation about physical complaints, the role of distorted cognitions, and strategies for tolerating changes in bodily sensations.

2 What are dissociations? Why do they occur, and how are they treated?

- Dissociation involves a disruption in consciousness, memory, identity, or perception, and may be transient or chronic.

- Dissociative amnesia, including localized amnesia and dissociative fugue, involves a selective form of forgetting in which the person cannot remember information that is of personal significance. Depersonalization/derealization disorder is characterized by feelings of unreality—distorted perceptions of oneself and one's environment. Dissociative identity disorder (DID) involves the presence of two or more personality states in one individual, or an experience of possession.

- Biological explanations for DID have focused on variations in brain activity during dissociative states that may demonstrate an inhibition of brain areas associated with memory. Some researchers believe that childhood trauma and chronic stress can result in permanent structural changes in the brain.

- Psychoanalytic perspectives attribute these disorders to the repression of impulses that are seeking expression and ways of coping with childhood abuse.

- Social explanations include childhood abuse, subtle reinforcement, mislabeling of dissociative experiences, and responding to the expectations of a therapist.

- Sociocultural explanations for dissociation include exposure to media portrayals of dissociation and role enactment.

- Dissociative amnesia and dissociative fugue tend to remit spontaneously; behavioral therapy has also been used successfully. Dissociative identity disorder is often treated with trauma-focused cognitive therapy that addresses integration of the personality states and learning strategies to reduce cognitive distortions and deal with current stressors.

8 DEPRESSIVE AND BIPOLAR DISORDERS

CHELSEA, RAISED IN A STABLE AND LOVING FAMILY, was an A student and star athlete throughout much of high school. However, in her senior year, she became uncharacteristically irritable, frequently snapping at her parents and sister without reason. She began to miss swimming practice and fell behind in her school assignments. She seemed uninterested when friends contacted her. When her parents tried to talk to her, she asked to be left alone and retreated to her bedroom. She spent most of her weekends sleeping. As graduation approached, Chelsea became increasingly withdrawn from family and friends. She felt guilty about how she was treating everyone and finally agreed to see a therapist. During her first visit she told the therapist, "I don't know what's wrong with me. Everything had seemed so right, and now everything seems so wrong."

Mood refers to our emotional state or our prevailing frame of mind. Our mood can significantly affect our perceptions of the world, sense of well-being, and interactions with others. Persistent changes in mood, such as the depressive symptoms demonstrated by Chelsea, are concerning, especially when they occur for no apparent reason. You can probably imagine how discouraging it is to want to return to a normal mood, but be unable to do so. As you will learn in this chapter, a variety of factors, including genetic predisposition, early life events, and current stressors, can interact to produce mood changes such as those experienced by Chelsea.

Two groups of mental disorders involve significant mood changes—depressive and bipolar disorders. We include depressive and bipolar disorders in the same chapter because they both entail pervasive, life-altering disturbances in mood. Both depressive and bipolar disorders are associated with an increased risk of suicide, a topic we discuss extensively in Chapter 9.

1 What are symptoms of depression and mania?

2 What are depressive disorders, what causes them, and how are they treated?

3 What are bipolar disorders, what causes them, and how are they treated?

Symptoms Associated with Depressive and Bipolar Disorders

Most of you experience minor mood changes throughout the day, but are able to stay emotionally balanced and on an even keel. You may also have times where you feel depressed or times when you experience an emotional high—normal reactions to the events going on around you. You may have occasional, brief episodes of more significant mood changes—experiencing overwhelming sadness over the loss of a friendship or feeling extremely energized or even ecstatic when you hear great news. Unlike these temporary, normal emotional reactions, the mood symptoms in depressive and bipolar disorders:

- affect the person's well-being and school, work, or social functioning;
- continue for days, weeks, or months;
- often occur for no apparent reason; and
- involve extreme reactions that cannot be easily explained by what is happening in the person's life.

Depression and mania, opposite ends of a continuum that extends from deep sadness to wild elation, represent the extremes of mood. Whereas depressive disorders involve only one troubling mood (depression), those with bipolar disorders (previously called manic-depression) often cope with two mood extremes—overwhelming depression and periods involving an elevated or abnormally energized mood. Bipolar refers to the fact that the condition involves mood extremes at both emotional "poles." Experiencing these mood extremes on a regular basis can be very distressing and disruptive to everyday life.

Let's begin by looking at the symptoms associated with a depressed or energized mood state (see Table 8.1), and how clinicians determine if a person has a depressive or bipolar disorder.

Symptoms of Depression

Depression involves intense sadness or loss of interest in normally enjoyed activities. Depression is the core feature of depressive disorders. We can usually tell if someone is depressed because we notice changes in their emotional reactions, thinking, behavior, or physical well-being.

mood emotional state or prevailing frame of mind

depression a mood state characterized by sadness or despair, feelings of worthlessness, and withdrawal from others

Emotional Changes in Bipolar Disorder

Individuals with bipolar disorder may talk excessively during hypomanic or manic episodes; in contrast, they may withdraw from social interactions when experiencing depression.

13/picturegarden/Ocean/Corbis

Table 8.1 Symptoms of Depression and Hypomania/Mania

Domain	Depression	Hypomania/Mania
Mood	Sadness, emptiness and worthlessness, apathy, hopelessness	Elevated mood, extreme confidence, grandiosity, irritability, hostility
Cognitive	Pessimism, guilt, difficulty concentrating, negative thinking, suicidal thoughts	Disorientation, racing thoughts, decreased focus and attention, creativity, poor judgment
Behavioral	Social withdrawal, crying, low energy, lowered productivity, agitation, poor hygiene	Overactivity, rapid or incoherent speech, impulsivity, risk-taking behaviors
Physiological	Appetite and weight changes, sleep disturbance, aches and pain, loss of sex drive	High levels of arousal, decreased sleep, increased sex drive

© Cengage Learning®

Emotional Symptoms in Depression

The most striking symptom of depression—depressed mood—involves feelings of sadness, emptiness, hopelessness, worthlessness, or low self-esteem. The following quote from a college student coming out of a deep depression illustrates the hopelessness and emotional numbness she was experiencing.

CASE STUDY   It's hard to describe the state I was in several months ago. The depression was total—it was as if everything that happened to me passed through this dark filter, and I kept seeing the world through this dark cloud. Nothing was exciting. I felt I was no good, completely worthless, and deserving of nothing. The people who tried to cheer me up just couldn't understand how down I felt. There were many days when I couldn't even make it to class.

As this young woman so clearly expresses, people experiencing depression have little enthusiasm for things they once enjoyed, including spending time with family and friends. Feeling irritable or anxious and worried is also common.

Cognitive Symptoms in Depression

Certain thoughts and ideas, including pessimistic, self-critical beliefs, are typical among people who are depressed. **Rumination**, continually thinking about certain topics or repeatedly reviewing distressing events, often occurs during a depressive episode. Ruminating can intensify feelings of depression, especially when it involves self-criticism, feelings of guilt, irrational beliefs, or other negative thoughts (Auerbach, Ho, & Kim, 2014). Depression can also cause distractibility and interfere with our ability to concentrate, remember things, or make decisions. We may then feel frustrated over our inability to handle tasks we normally manage without difficulty.

Thoughts of suicide are also common among those who are depressed. This may result from feelings of being a burden to friends and family or a belief that there is little hope for the future. People who are suicidal may feel that there is no end to the distressing emotional pain. As we discuss in Chapter 9, it is crucial to intervene if someone is feeling suicidal. By encouraging someone who has suicidal thoughts to seek professional assistance, you might help save a life.

Behavioral Symptoms in Depression

Behavioral symptoms such as fatigue, social withdrawal, and reduced motivation are common with depression. Some people who are depressed speak slowly or quietly; they

rumination repeatedly thinking about concerns or details of past events

may respond only in short phrases or not respond at all. Some appear agitated and restless, pacing and finding it difficult to sit still. They may cry for no particular reason or in reaction to sadness, frustration, or anger. It may appear that they no longer care about their grooming or personal cleanliness. This occurs because daily activities such as getting out of bed, bathing, dressing, or preparing for work or class take immense effort and feel overwhelming. Not surprisingly, a person's grades or job performance may slip during a depressive episode.

Physiological Symptoms in Depression

We often focus on the emotional and behavioral changes that occur with depression. However, there are also physiological symptoms associated with depressive episodes:

- *Appetite and weight changes.* Depression sometimes causes changes in weight due to either increased or decreased eating. While some people have almost no appetite and lose weight, others eat even if they are not hungry (especially sweets and carbohydrates) and find that they are gaining weight.

- *Sleep disturbance.* Many people with depression have difficulty falling asleep or staying asleep. Others sleep much more than usual, but wake up feeling tired and unrefreshed.

- *Unexplained aches and pain.* Headaches, stomachaches, or other body aches commonly occur during depression, especially among those with severe or chronic depression (Huijbregts et al., 2010). In some cultural groups, unexplained aches and pains are the main symptoms of depression (Kung & Lu, 2008).

- *Aversion to sexual activity.* Depression often produces dramatically reduced sexual interest and arousal.

Symptoms of Hypomania or Mania

Individuals with bipolar disorder experience mood states characterized by increased energy, emotional changes, and other significant transformations in behavior. This **elevated mood** includes two levels of intensity—hypomania and mania (APA, 2013). The milder form, **hypomania**, is characterized by increased levels of activity or energy combined with a self-important, **expansive mood** or an irritable, agitated mood. Someone with hypomania may appear quite distractible, change topics frequently, and have many ideas. The person may feel creative and start many projects, sometimes involving topics he or she knows nothing about. Impulsivity and risk taking may also appear during a hypomanic episode. The person may talk excessively or dominate conversations. All of these symptoms are uncharacteristic of how the person normally functions.

Mania is a state of even more pronounced mood change involving extremely exaggerated activity levels and emotionality that impair normal functioning. Behaviors demonstrated during mania can range from extreme giddiness, excitement, and **euphoria** (exceptionally elevated mood) to extreme irritability, hostility, or agitation. Aside from hypomania being a milder version of mania, another notable difference is that manic episodes cause marked impairment in social or occupational functioning and may involve **psychosis** (loss of contact with reality) and a need for psychiatric hospitalization. When someone is experiencing a manic episode it is obvious to others that something is amiss; in contrast, hypomania is often more subtle, does not impair normal functioning, and may be evident only to those who know the person well. As with depression, hypomania and mania involve emotional, cognitive, behavioral, and physiological symptoms.

Emotional Symptoms of Hypomania/Mania

People experiencing hypomania may appear to be in unusually high spirits and full of energy and enthusiasm. They also may be uncharacteristically irritable, have a low tolerance for frustration, and overreact with anger or hostility in response to environmental stimuli (e.g., noises, a child crying) or the people around them. People

elevated mood a mood state involving extreme confidence and exaggerated feelings of energy and well-being

hypomania a milder form of mania involving increased levels of activity and goal-directed behaviors combined with an elevated, expansive, or irritable mood

expansive mood person may feel extremely confident or self-important and behave impulsively

mania mental state characterized by very exaggerated activity and emotions including euphoria, excessive excitement, or irritability that result in impairment in social or occupational functioning

euphoria exceptionally elevated mood; exaggerated feeling of well-being

psychosis condition involving loss of contact with or distorted view of reality

with mania exhibit unstable and rapidly changing emotions and mood, or **emotional lability**. Inappropriate use of humor, poor judgment in expressing feelings or opinions, and **grandiosity** (inflated self-esteem and beliefs of being special, chosen, or superior to others) can result in interpersonal conflicts and aggressive interactions.

Cognitive Symptoms of Hypomania/Mania

Individuals experiencing hypomania often display energized, goal-oriented behavior at home, school, or work. They may seem excited and talk more than usual, engage in one-sided conversations, and demonstrate little concern about giving others an opportunity to speak. They may have difficulty focusing their attention, show poor judgment, and fail to recognize the inappropriateness of their behavior. Those experiencing mania are much more likely to appear disoriented and exhibit cognitive difficulties. Their impaired thinking may be apparent from their speech, sometimes referred to as **pressured speech**, which may be rapid, loud, and difficult to understand. Those experiencing mania frequently have extreme difficulty maintaining focus and display a **flight of ideas**; that is, they change topics, become distracted with new thoughts, or make irrelevant or illogical comments.

Behavioral Symptoms of Hypomania/Mania

Individuals experiencing hypomania or mania may seem uninhibited and act impulsively, engaging in uncharacteristic behaviors such as reckless driving, excessive drinking, illegal drug use, promiscuous behavior, uncontrolled spending, or making impulsive decisions such as changing jobs or developing plans to move to a new location. Similarly, they may have difficulty delaying gratification and insist on following through with their impulsive actions, becoming irritable if loved ones interfere with or encourage them to reconsider their plans (Strakowski et al., 2010). Failure to evaluate the consequences of decisions can lead to unsafe sexual practices or illegal activity, or other behaviors that are highly uncharacteristic for the individual. As you might imagine, the behaviors that occur during a hypomanic/manic episode can create significant tensions in family and other interpersonal relationships.

Other behavioral changes are also likely. The person might seem energetic and productive and display an expansive mood of extreme confidence and self-importance, taking on a variety of complex or creative tasks. The person also may seem agitated and react angrily with little provocation. During mania, motor movement is often rapid and speech may be incoherent. Wild excitement, ranting, raving (thus the stereotype of a raving "maniac"), constant movement, and agitation characterize severe mania. Psychotic symptoms including paranoia, hallucinations, and delusions (false beliefs) may also occur during a manic episode. Individuals experiencing extreme mania may require hospitalization if they become dangerous to themselves or to others.

Physiological Symptoms of Hypomania/Mania

Individuals experiencing hypomania or mania have high levels of physiological arousal that results in intense activity, extreme restlessness, or a need to be constantly "on the go." Increased libido (sex drive) often leads to reckless sexual activity or other impulsive behaviors. A decreased need for sleep is often the first sign of a hypomanic or manic episode; this sleep disturbance often escalates just before an episode and worsens during the episode (Gujar, Yoo, Hu, & Walker, 2011). This arousal results in less sleep, yet the person does not feel tired. During a manic episode, a person may go for days without sleep. The high expenditure of energy and limited sleep characteristic of elevated episodes often results in unplanned weight loss.

Evaluating Mood Symptoms

Careful assessment of mood symptoms is essential for diagnosing depressive and bipolar disorders, especially because brief depressive or hypomanic symptoms also occur in people who do not have a mood disorder. Diagnosis is even more complicated because depression occurs in both depressive and bipolar disorders and because the symptoms

emotional lability unstable and rapidly changing emotions and mood

grandiosity an overvaluation of one's significance or importance

pressured speech rapid, frenzied, or loud, disjointed communication

flight of ideas rapidly changing or disjointed thoughts

of these disorders may vary considerably from person to person. Also, you may have noticed that both depressive and hypomanic/manic symptoms include irritability; this further confounds diagnosis, especially when someone's symptoms during hypomania/mania are predominately irritable or agitated. Additionally, people often fail to report hypomanic symptoms because they do not cause significant problems or impair functioning. Therefore, when evaluating someone who is depressed, clinicians are careful to inquire if the individual has ever had any hypomanic or manic symptoms.

Diagnosis is further complicated because people experiencing a depressive or hypomanic/manic episode sometimes exhibit symptoms from the opposite pole. For example, someone who is experiencing hypomania/mania may cry excessively or talk of suicide; similarly, someone who is depressed may experience extreme restlessness and have racing thoughts. When this occurs, the clinician specifies that the mood episode has *mixed features*. Clinicians also ask about the frequency and duration of the mood episodes and about any seasonal changes in mood. They are also interested in whether the symptoms have been mild, moderate, or severe.

Of course, clinicians also consider other factors that can cause mood changes, such as medical conditions or the use or abuse of alcohol, illegal drugs, or prescription medications. Careful symptom evaluation prior to diagnosis is important because, as you will see, interventions for depressive and bipolar disorders are quite different. Therapists also monitor symptoms throughout treatment; a diagnosis may change from a depressive disorder to a bipolar disorder if hypomanic or manic symptoms develop. In the next section, we focus on depressive disorders and then conclude the chapter with a discussion of bipolar disorders.

Depressive Disorders

Depressive disorders, a group of related disorders characterized by depressive symptoms, include major depressive disorder, persistent depressive disorder (dysthymia), and premenstrual dysphoric disorder (Table 8.2).

Diagnosis and Classification of Depressive Disorders

An important aspect to diagnosing a depressive disorder is making sure the person has never experienced an episode of mania or hypomania (see Table 8.6 on page 255). Information about such episodes helps the clinician differentiate between a bipolar and a depressive disorder (Phillips & Kupfer, 2013). When diagnosing depressive disorders, clinicians also consider how severe and how chronic the depressive symptoms have been.

Major Depressive Disorder

CASE STUDY Antonio finally agreed to stop by the university counseling center. His parents were concerned about him, and now his roommate was suggesting he get some help. They all noticed that Antonio was losing weight and that he stayed in his room as much as possible, avoiding his friends and often sleeping for hours. Antonio has always been a good student, but now he is barely passing several of his classes because he is having such difficulty concentrating. Antonio has not told anyone, but he has been feeling sad almost constantly. He does not know why, but he has also been feeling incredibly hopeless about his future and worried that he will never find a good job. He had been excited about starting college, and now he can barely wait until summer break so he can sleep without worrying about missing class.

Table 8.2 Depressive Disorders

DISORDERS CHART				
Depressive Disorder	**DSM-5 Criteria**	**Lifetime Prevalence (%)**	**Gender Difference**	**Age of Onset**
Major depressive disorder	• Occurrence of at least one major depressive episode (2-week duration) • No history of mania or hypomania	14.0–16.0	Much higher in females	Any age; average onset in late 20s
Persistent depressive disorder (dysthymia)	• Depressed mood that has lasted for at least 2 years (with no more than 2 months symptom-free)[a]	4.0; including 3.1 for chronic MDD and 0.9 for pure dysthymic syndrome	Much higher in females	Often childhood or adolescence
Premenstrual dysphoric disorder	• Severe depression, mood swings, anxiety, or irritability occurring before the onset of menses • Improvement of symptoms within a few days of menstruation and minimal or no symptoms following menstruation	2.0–5.0 of women of reproductive age	Most common in women with personal or family history of depression	Late 20s, although earlier onset is possible

SOURCE: Data from APA (2013); Blanco et al. (2010); Epperson et al. (2012); Hasin, Goodwin, et al. (2005); Kessler, Chiu, Demler, & Walters (2005).

[a] In children and adolescents, mood can be irritable and diagnosis can occur if symptoms have been present for at least 1 year.

After the evaluation at the counseling center, Antonio was diagnosed as having a **major depressive disorder (MDD)**. This diagnosis occurs following impaired functioning due to a **major depressive episode**, which involves *severe* depressive symptoms that have negatively affected functioning most of the day, nearly every day, for at least 2 full weeks (see Table 8.3). According to DSM-5, a major depressive episode involves a consistent pattern of (a) depressed mood, feelings of sadness, or emptiness and/or (b) loss of interest or pleasure in previously enjoyed activities. The individual must *also* experience at least four additional changes in functioning involving: significant alteration in weight or appetite; atypical sleep patterns; restlessness or sluggishness; low energy; feelings of guilt or worthlessness; difficulty concentrating or making decisions; or preoccupation with death or suicide (APA, 2013).

Table 8.3 DSM-5 Criteria for a Major Depressive Episode

A major depressive episode involves *a change in functioning that includes at least one of these symptoms most of the day nearly every day over a period of 2 weeks (or longer)*:

(a) depressed mood, feelings of sadness, or emptiness and/or
(b) loss of interest or pleasure in previously enjoyed activities.

The person must *also* experience at least four of these symptoms during the same period:

(a) significant weight gain or weight loss (without dieting) or increases or decreases in appetite,
(b) persistent changes in sleep patterns, involving increased sleep or inability to sleep,
(c) observable restlessness or slowing of activity,
(d) persistent fatigue or loss of energy,
(e) excessive feelings of guilt or worthlessness,
(f) persistent difficulty with concentration or decision making, or
(g) suicidal behaviors or recurrent thoughts of death or suicide.

The symptoms cause significant impairment and are not due to the physiological effects of a medical condition, a prescribed medication, or drug or alcohol abuse.

SOURCE: APA (2013).

major depressive disorder (MDD) condition diagnosed if someone (without a history of hypomania/mania) experiences a depressive episode involving severe depressive symptoms that have negatively affected functioning most of the day, nearly every day, for at least 2 full weeks

major depressive episode a period involving severe depressive symptoms that have impaired functioning for at least 2 full weeks

Many people experience **anxious distress** during a depressive episode. For example, Antonio had difficulty functioning not only due to depressive symptoms, but also because of his persistent worry about his future. Individuals who experience anxious distress often feel unusually tense or restless or experience pervasive worries that make it difficult to concentrate. They may also worry that they will lose self-control or that something bad will happen. It is important for clinicians to inquire about anxious distress because it is associated with longer depressive episodes and a heightened risk of suicide (Coryell et al., 2012).

Suicide is a significant concern for anyone with MDD. People who feel hopeless or behave impulsively may act on suicidal thoughts, especially if they are under the influence of drugs or alcohol (Ali et al., 2013). Nearly one third of those with MDD also have a substance-use disorder; this combination further increases suicide risk (L. Davis, Uezato, Newell, & Frazier, 2008). Similarly, people who have chronic depressive symptoms or who developed depression in response to grief have increased risk of suicide (APA, 2013).

MDD with a Seasonal Pattern   Some people with MDD (and bipolar disorder) report a seasonal pattern to their depressive episodes—they begin to develop depression when daylight decreases as the seasons change. In individuals with this pattern, depressive symptoms typically begin in the fall or winter and remit during the spring or summer (a small number of those affected display the opposite pattern). Seasonal depression typically involves "vegetative depressive symptoms," including low energy, social withdrawal, increased need for sleep, and carbohydrate craving. Winter depressive episodes occur most frequently among younger individuals, in regions with less light in the winter months (northern latitudes), and among those who are sensitive to the influence of environmental light on their circadian rhythm (APA, 2013).

Many clinicians use the term *seasonal affective disorder (SAD)* to refer to this seasonal pattern. However, SAD is not an official DSM-5 diagnostic category; the manual instead describes **MDD with a seasonal pattern**, a condition involving at least two seasonal episodes of severe depression ending at a predictable time of year combined with a pattern of depressive episodes that occur seasonally more than nonseasonally (APA, 2013). Thus, the many people who experience milder seasonal depressive symptoms would not meet the DSM-5 criteria for MDD with a seasonal pattern.

Persistent Depressive Disorder (Dysthymia)

Persistent depressive disorder (dysthymia) involves chronic depressive symptoms that are present most of the day for more days than not during a 2-year period (with no more than 2 months symptom-free). According to the DSM-5, dysthymia involves the ongoing presence of at least two of the following symptoms: feelings of hopelessness, low self-esteem, poor appetite or overeating, low energy or fatigue, difficulty concentrating or making decisions, or sleeping too little or too much (APA, 2013). In addition to those who meet the above criteria for a **pure dysthymic syndrome**, this category also includes individuals who have chronic symptoms of MDD. For many, dysthymia is a lifelong, pervasive disorder with long periods of depression, few periods without symptoms, and poor response to treatment. Dysthymia is often associated with negative thinking patterns and a pessimistic outlook on the future (Torpey & Klein, 2008).

Premenstrual Dysphoric Disorder

Premenstrual dysphoric disorder (PMDD) is a controversial diagnostic category involving serious symptoms of depression, irritability, and tension that appear the week before menstruation and disappear soon after menstruation begins. A PMDD diagnosis requires the presence of five premenstrual symptoms; at least one of the symptoms must involve significantly depressed mood, mood swings, anger, anxiety, tension, irritability, or increased interpersonal conflict. Other symptoms considered in making a diagnosis include difficulty concentrating; social withdrawal; lack of energy; food cravings or overeating; insomnia or excessive sleepiness; feeling overwhelmed;

anxious distress   symptoms of motor tension, difficulty relaxing, pervasive worries, or feelings that something catastrophic will occur

MDD with a seasonal pattern   major depressive episodes occur seasonally more than nonseasonally; at least two seasonal episodes of severe depression have occurred ending at a predictable time of year

persistent depressive disorder (dysthymia)   condition involving chronic depressive symptoms that are present most of the day for more days than not during a 2-year period with no more than 2 months symptom-free

pure dysthymic syndrome   the individual meets the criteria for persistent depressive disorder (dysthymia) and has not had a major depressive episode in the previous 2 years

premenstrual dysphoric disorder   condition involving distressing and disruptive symptoms of depression, irritability, and tension that occur the week before menstruation or physical symptoms such as bloating, weight gain, or breast tenderness. These are similar to the physical and emotional symptoms of *premenstrual syndrome*; however, PMDD produces much greater distress and interferes with social, interpersonal, academic, or occupational functioning (APA, 2013). Some researchers have argued against designating symptoms of a normal biological function (menstruation) as a psychiatric disorder (Chekoudjian, 2009).

Depressive Reactions to Grief

CASE STUDY Mrs. Lee is a 48-year-old-married mother of two teenagers who works full-time as a store manager. Over the past 2 months, she has developed symptoms of fatigue, irritability, general aches and pains, loss of appetite, and reduced libido. Mrs. Lee had been her mother's primary caregiver until 4 months ago when her mother lost her battle with cancer. Her husband is supportive but feels overwhelmed by her depressive symptoms; her children avoid her because of her temper and frequent outbursts of anger. In recent months, Mrs. Lee no longer attends church or participates in social events. She finally agreed to see her doctor about her symptoms. Although her physical examination was normal, she burst into tears midway through the examination and admitted that she feels that life is hopeless (Lie, 2012).

Normal grief reactions occur in response to situations such as the death of a loved one or catastrophic events associated with loss such as a natural disaster or sudden serious illness or disability. The DSM-5 makes it clear that it is important to distinguish normal grief-related reactions from the severe depression and impaired functioning associated with MDD. Grief often involves feelings of emptiness associated with the loss rather than the more persistent depressed mood or inability to experience pleasure that occurs with MDD. Although normal grief reactions may last for several years, the frequency and intensity of these episodes decrease over time. Of course, bereavement can be a significant stressor and result in the development of MDD, as was the case with Mrs. Lee.

persistent complex bereavement disorder diagnostic category undergoing study; proposed disorder involves persistent sorrow or preoccupation continuing a year after the death of a loved one

Persistent complex bereavement disorder is a condition undergoing study as a diagnostic category in DSM-5. This diagnosis would apply to individuals who have intense and persistent preoccupation or debilitating sorrow that continues for over a year after the death of a loved one. Those with persistent complex bereavement may also experience continued longing for the deceased, preoccupation with the way the person died, distress or anger over the death, or difficulty accepting the death. A diagnosis would require that the death have a significant effect on the person's interpersonal relationships or sense of identity (APA, 2013). These symptoms may occur in up to 4.8 percent of the population (Kersting, Brähler, Glaesmer, & Wagner, 2011). Of course, clinicians would need to take cultural, religious, and age-appropriate norms associated with bereavement into account when considering this diagnosis.

Loss as a Source of Depression

Mourning the death of a loved one occurs in all cultures and societies, as illustrated by these women mourning an Iraqi tae kwon do team who were kidnapped and killed. What characteristics or symptoms help distinguish between "normal" grief, major depressive disorder, and persistent complex bereavement?

AP Images/Karim Kadim

Prevalence of Depressive Disorders

Depression is one of the most common psychiatric disorders and the second leading cause of

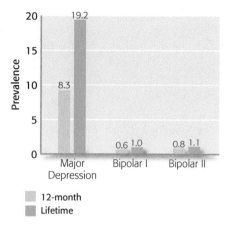

Figure 8.1

12-Month and Lifetime U.S. Prevalence of Major Depressive and Bipolar Disorders

SOURCE: Based on Merikangas, Jin, et al. (2011)

disability worldwide, affecting approximately 298 million people each year (Ferrari et al., 2013). Approximately 19 percent of the U.S. population will experience a major depressive episode at some point in their lives (see Figure 8.1). Women have a significantly greater risk of experiencing major depression compared to men (Merikangas, Jin, et al., 2011). Additionally, approximately 2–5 percent of women experience symptoms of PMDD during their reproductive years (Epperson et al., 2012).

For many people, depression is a chronic disorder. If depressive symptoms do not completely resolve with treatment, the chances of a relapse or chronic depression are greatly increased (Conradi, Ormel, & de Jonge, 2010). The most common lingering symptoms of depression include poor concentration, lack of decisiveness, low energy, and sleep difficulties (Conradi et al., 2010). Approximately 15 percent of those treated for depression fail to show any significant reduction in symptoms (Berlim & Turecki, 2007); some researchers believe that many of these cases represent undiagnosed bipolar disorder (Bowden, 2010a). In an 8-year follow-up of individuals diagnosed with MDD, approximately 10 percent eventually received a bipolar diagnosis, including 25 percent of those who did not improve after taking antidepressant medications (C. T. Li et al., 2012). People who are misdiagnosed often experience greater impairment, presumably because they initially received ineffective treatment due to the inaccurate diagnosis (Kamat et al., 2008).

Etiology of Depressive Disorders

Given the pervasiveness of depressive disorders, a great deal of research has been devoted to searching for answers as to why some people develop the distressing symptoms of depression. Consistent with our multipath approach, we will discuss how biological, psychological, social, and sociocultural factors interact in complex ways to cause depressive disorders (Figure 8.2). For example, you will see the complexity of interactions between genetic susceptibility, timing of stressful life events, and the type of stressors encountered (Pemberton et al., 2010). As you read, keep in mind that environmental factors have more influence on childhood depression, whereas hereditary factors have greater influence in adolescence and adulthood. The transition between

Figure 8.2

Multipath Model of Depression

The dimensions interact with one another and combine in different ways to result in depression.

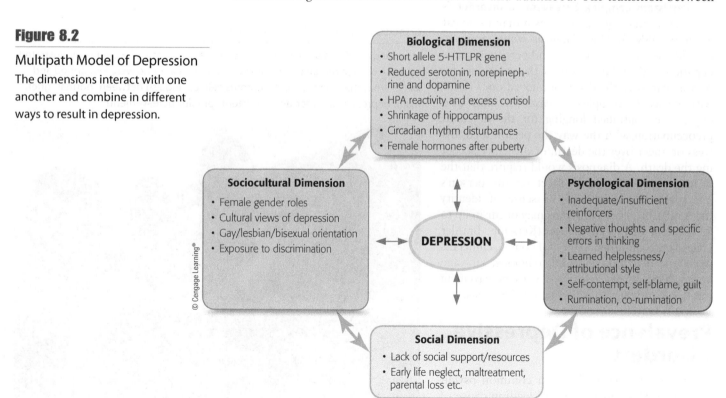

middle and late adolescence is considered a time when genetic influences begin to surpass environmental influences (Tully, Iacono, & McGue, 2010).

Biological Dimension

Biological explanations regarding depressive disorders generally focus on neurotransmitters and stress-related hormones, genetic influences, structural or functional brain irregularities, circadian rhythm disruption, or interactions among these factors.

Neurotransmitters and Depressive Disorders Low levels of certain neurotransmitters, including serotonin, norepinephrine, and dopamine, are associated with depression. When our biochemical systems are functioning normally, neurotransmitters regulate our emotions and basic physiological processes involving appetite, sleep, energy, and libido; however, biochemical irregularities can produce the physiological symptoms associated with depression. Evidence regarding the importance of neurotransmission in depression comes from a variety of sources. Years ago, it was accidentally discovered that when the drug reserpine was used to treat hypertension, many patients became depressed (reserpine depletes certain neurotransmitters). Similarly, the drug isoniazid, given to patients with tuberculosis, induced biochemical changes that resulted in mood elevation (Ramachandraih, Subramanyam, Bar, Baker, & Yeragani, 2011). Findings that antidepressant medications function by increasing the availability of the neurotransmitters norepinephrine and serotonin have also pointed to the role of neurotransmission (Stahl & Wise, 2008). More recently, therapies involving electrical stimulation of brain regions that have high concentrations of brain cells that release dopamine have implicated dopamine deficiencies in depression, particularly **treatment-resistant depression** that does not respond to antidepressant medications (Conway et al., 2013).

The Role of Heredity Depression tends to run in families, and the same types of depressive disorders are often found among members of the same family (Hettema, 2010). Studies comparing the prevalence of depressive disorders among the biological and adoptive families of individuals with depression indicate that the incidence is significantly higher among biological relatives compared to adoptive family members (Levinson, 2006). Interestingly, the chances of inheriting depression are greatest for female twins, suggesting gender differences in heritability (D. Goldberg, 2006). As mentioned previously, genetic influence on depression becomes most evident after puberty. As with many other mental disorders, it appears that many different genes, each with relatively small influence, interact with environmental factors to produce depression (Lohoff, 2010).

Because many antidepressants work on serotonin, genes that affect the serotonin system are of particular interest to researchers. As you may recall, the short allele of the serotonin transporter gene (5-HTTLPR) is associated with depression, particularly among those who experience childhood maltreatment (Caspi, Sugden, et al., 2003). A comprehensive meta-analysis affirmed that variations in this gene mediate the relationship between stress and depression, with the short allele increasing risk of depression in those exposed to stressors, particularly trauma in childhood (Karg, Burmeister, Shedden, & Sen, 2011). This gene × environment interaction is particularly evident in those with chronic depression (Brown et al., 2013). Chronic depression may occur because individuals with the risk allele of the 5-HTTLPR gene who are exposed to early childhood stress have more difficulty effectively using the neurotransmitter serotonin and because they also release more of the stress hormone cortisol. Interestingly, while the short 5-HTTLPR allele increases vulnerability to depression, the long allele of this gene appears to promote resilience to depression (Hornung & Heim, 2014).

Cortisol, Stress, and Depression Dysregulation and overactivity of the hypothalamic-pituitary-adrenal (HPA) axis and overproduction of stress-related hormones such as cortisol appear to play an important role in the development of depression in

treatment-resistant depression depressive episode that has not improved despite an adequate trial of antidepressant medication or other traditional forms of treatment

both youth and adults (Guerry & Hastings, 2011). In explaining stress disorders in Chapter 5, we focused on the stress circuitry of the brain and discussed how stressors can increase levels of *cortisol*. Interestingly, throughout the world, people with depression have higher blood levels of cortisol (Schnittker, 2010).

Exposure to stress during early development affects cortisol levels and can increase susceptibility to depression in later life, especially among those who have genetic vulnerability. Many individuals with depression have early life traumas or stressors such as child abuse, neglect, or loss of a parent. In fact, researchers have linked depression to an interaction between childhood adversities and certain genes that increase cortisol release; in other words, environmental stressors trigger these genes to release excess cortisol (H. J. Grabe et al., 2010). For example, people who have an increased genetic risk of depression (such as carriers of the short allele of the 5-HTTLPR) who experience maltreatment in childhood release more cortisol (Karg et al., 2011). Thus, genetic predisposition, stress, and the timing of stress can interact to increase cortisol production and produce depressive symptoms.

Research consistently points to the harmful effects of cortisol and other stress-related hormones on biochemical functioning and neuroplasticity in brain regions associated with depression (Detka et al., 2013). But how does cortisol influence depression? The answer is complicated. We know chronic stress and associated high levels of cortisol can damage the hippocampus (i.e., neurons die and fail to regenerate) and interfere with systems involved in our stress response. In fact, excess cortisol may explain why individuals with depression have inhibited neurogenesis (birth of neurons) in the hippocampus (Snyder, Soumier, Brewer, Pickel, & Cameron, 2011).

An overactive stress response system and excessive cortisol production may also cause depressive symptoms by depleting certain neurotransmitters, particularly serotonin (Leonard, 2010). Additionally, stress can affect the production of enzymes that are necessary for our brains to use serotonin effectively (J. M. Miller et al., 2009). Of course these reactions can be circular—depression can result in lifestyle changes (sleep disruption, lack of exercise, alcohol use) that heighten our stress reactivity and further interfere with optimal biochemical functioning.

Functional and Anatomical Brain Changes with Depression Neuroimaging studies document decreased brain activity and other brain changes in people with depression (Stahl & Wise, 2008). For example, researchers have found that individuals experiencing depression have increased connectivity in the brain regions referred to as the *default mode network*, regions that are associated with a wakeful resting state. Interestingly, antidepressant medications appear to normalize connectivity in this region (Posner et al., 2013). Variations in the 5-HTTLPR gene are also associated with the changes in brain anatomy seen in some people with depression; for example, individuals with the short 5-HTTLPR allele who experienced emotional neglect in childhood show stress-induced changes in the hippocampus, the brain structure involved in regulating stress and emotions (Frodl et al., 2010). In addition, depression is associated with reduced neuroplasticity, including reduced neurogenesis in the hippocampus and in synapses within the cortex (Hayley & Litteljohn, 2013).

"Faulty wiring" of emotional circuits may explain why some people experience persistent depression. A meta-analysis of neuroimaging findings concluded that individuals with depression show different patterns of neural reactivity compared to controls; interestingly, the pattern of neural activation depends on whether the emotional stimuli are positive or are negative. In some brain regions, for example, individuals with depression show heightened activity in response to negative stimuli but reduced activation with positive stimuli (Groenewold, Opmeer, de Jonge, Aleman, & Costafreda, 2013). Even those who have the milder depressive symptoms associated with pure dysthymic syndrome have abnormalities in neurological functioning, including reduced activation in the prefrontal cortex and increased activity in the amygdala (Ravindran et al., 2009).

Circadian Rhythm Disturbances in Depression   Our circadian rhythms appear to play a role in physiological disturbances associated with depression, particularly seasonal depression (De Berardis et al., 2013). **Circadian rhythms** are internal biological rhythms, maintained by the hormone melatonin, that influence a number of our bodily processes, including body temperature and sleeping patterns. Depression is associated with disruptions in this system, both among those with and without seasonal patterns of depression (Pail et al., 2011).

Circadian rhythm disturbances affecting sleep can increase risk of depression. For example, insomnia (difficulty falling or staying asleep) doubles the risk of developing depression and intensifies depressive symptoms (Baglioni et al., 2011). In a study involving twin pairs, excessively short or long sleep duration appeared to activate genes related to depression. Compared to a 27 percent genetic risk of depression for twins with normal sleep patterns, the risk of depressive symptoms increased to 53 percent for those who averaged less than 5 hours and to 49 percent for those who slept more than 10 hours per night (Watson et al., 2014). Disrupted sleep is also linked to the onset of postpartum depression (Goyal, Gay, & Lee, 2009). It has long been recognized that people with depression have irregularities in rapid eye movement sleep, the stage of sleep during which dreaming occurs (Ebdlahad et al., 2013). Interestingly, reducing the rapid eye movement sleep of people with depression can improve depressive symptoms (Howland, 2011).

Whether circadian system disturbances, hormonal or neurotransmitter abnormalities, or other brain irregularities exert the greatest influence on depressive disorders cannot be resolved at this time. It certainly appears that complex interactions between biological influences, stressful experiences, and psychological, social, and sociocultural factors influence the development of depression.

Psychological Dimension

A number of psychological theories address the etiology of depression. It is important to note that although these theories may help explain the development of depressive symptoms in some people, they are not necessarily associated with all cases of depression.

Behavioral Explanations   Behavioral explanations suggest that depression occurs when people receive insufficient social reinforcement (Lejuez, Hopko, Acierno, Daughters, & Pagoto, 2011). Losses such as unemployment, divorce, or the death of a friend or family member can reduce available reinforcement (e.g., love, affection, companionship) and produce depression. Consistent with this perspective, behaviorists believe that it is possible to reduce depressive symptoms by becoming more socially active, thereby increasing environmental reinforcement (Gawrysiak, Nicholas, & Hopko, 2009).

One of the most comprehensive behavioral explanations for depression identifies variables that can increase or decrease a person's chances of receiving positive reinforcement (Lewinsohn, Muñoz, Youngren, & Zeiss, 1994). For example, risk of depression is increased when:

- *A person participates in few events or activities that are potentially reinforcing.* Opportunities to participate in reinforcing activities may vary depending on the person's age, gender, or physical attributes.

- *There are few reinforcements available in the environment.* Harsh or isolating environments contain fewer possible reinforcers, whereas warm, nurturing environments increase the likelihood of social reinforcement.

- *A person's behavior and social skills* result in limited reinforcement. Individuals experiencing depression often display fewer behaviors associated with positive reinforcement, such as making eye contact or smiling. They interact with fewer people, respond less, and are less likely to initiate conversation. This behavior may result in subdued responses from others. Interestingly, people with negative personality traits or few positive interpersonal traits experience depression at an early age and are more likely to develop chronic depression (Robison, Shankman, & McFarland, 2009).

circadian rhythm   an internal clock or daily cycle of internal biological rhythms that influence various bodily processes such as body temperature and sleep–wake cycles

Magnification of Events

People become depressed because of the way they interpret situations, according to cognitive explanations for depression. They may overly magnify events that happen to them. In this photo, an adolescent football player sits alone in a locker room after losing a football game.

Stressful circumstances can also produce depression by disrupting predictable patterns of social reinforcement and initiating a cycle that further reduces social opportunities and increases vulnerability to depression (Lewinsohn, Hoberman, Teri, & Hautzinger, 1985). For example, when distressing events result in self-criticism, negative expectancies, and loss of self-confidence, a person may begin to withdraw from social interactions; this social withdrawal may further exacerbate depressive symptoms.

Cognitive Explanations Cognitive psychologists contend that depression is caused by the way people think and that negative thoughts and errors in thinking result in pessimism, damaging self-views, and feelings of helplessness. In other words, depression may result from our internal responses to what is happening around us.

Depression is a disturbance in thinking rather than a disturbance in mood, according to some theories (Beck, 1976). In other words, the way we interpret our experiences affects our emotions. According to Beck's theory, individuals experiencing depression tend to have a negative **self-schema** or way of looking at themselves; they have a pessimistic outlook regarding their present experiences and their expectations regarding the future (see Table 8.4). They may draw sweeping conclusions about their ability, performance, or worth from a single experience, or focus on trivial details taken out of context. For example, if no one initiates conversation at a party, someone with a negative self-schema may conclude, "People dislike me"; or if a supervisor makes a minor corrective comment, the person may focus on the possibility of losing the job, even when the supervisor's overall feedback is highly positive. Similarly, a job loss due to budgetary cuts may lead to self-perceptions of inadequacy or worthlessness. These negative thinking patterns may become so

Table 8.4 Beck's Six Types of Faulty Thinking

Arbitrary inference	Drawing conclusions about oneself or the world without sufficient and relevant information. *Example:* A man not hired by a potential employer concludes that he is "totally worthless" and that he will never find a job.
Personalization	Relating external events to one another when there is no objective basis for such a connection. *Example:* A man who does not receive a response to an e-mail he sent to his supervisor concludes that the supervisor must dislike him.
Overgeneralization	Holding extreme beliefs on the basis of a single incident and applying these inaccurate beliefs to other situations. *Example:* A woman who does not get along with her father believes she will fail in all relationships with men.
Magnification and exaggeration	Overestimating the significance of negative events. *Example:* A woman misses an important social event at work and concludes that all of her co-workers are criticizing her for not attending.
Polarized thinking	An "all-or-nothing," "good or bad," and "either/or" approach to viewing the world. *Example:* A woman feels that she needs to be perfect in all she does at work; if she makes a mistake, she considers herself totally incompetent.
Selective abstraction	Drawing conclusions from very isolated details and events without considering the larger context. *Example:* A student who receives a C on an exam stops attending classes and considers dropping out of school despite having A's and B's in all other courses.

SOURCE: Beck, 1976

self-schema   stable set of beliefs and assumptions about the self that are based on the person's experiences, values, and perceived capabilities

Dennis MacDonald/PhotoEdit

©wavebreakmedia ltd/Shutterstock.com

Talk it Over with a Friend?

People with depression often cope with negative events by ruminating or co-ruminating—constantly talking over their issues with friends. Unfortunately, both coping mechanisms increase the risk for developing depression.

ingrained that they consistently affect a person's emotional reactions. Once this pattern of pessimistic thinking develops, it is easy to succumb to hopelessness and pessimism; in other words, depression can become chronic. *Not surprisingly,* exaggeration of personal limitations and minimization of accomplishments, achievements, and capabilities is common among those experiencing depression.

These negative thinking patterns often lead to exaggerated, irrational, or catastrophic thinking involving self-blame and self-criticism (A. Ellis, 1989). Confirming this line of thought, a longitudinal study involving adolescents found that those with negative thinking patterns were much more likely to experience depression in response to high stress (J. S. Carter & Garber, 2011). Individuals with a negative outlook on life not only become stuck in dysfunctional thinking patterns, but also lack the psychological flexibility that would allow them to consider alternative explanations or disengage from negative thoughts (Kashdan & Rottenberg, 2010). They may also experience difficulty using positive events to regulate negative moods (Gotlib & Joormann, 2010). Evidence of a link between cognition and depression is strengthened by studies of memory bias. For example, researchers testing the theory of cognitive vulnerability to depression found that even when no longer depressed, individuals with a history of depression have more thoughts that are negative and have greater recall of negative information about themselves compared to individuals without a history of depression (Romero, Sanchez, & Vazquez, 2014).

Other cognitive processes can also influence depression. For example, individuals with depression often cope with stressful circumstances via rumination (repeatedly thinking about concerns or events) rather than active problem solving. Having a ruminative response style increases the likelihood of depressive symptoms among youth and adults, particularly females and people who tend to be anxious (Hankin, 2008). **Co-rumination**, the process of constantly talking over problems or negative events with others, also increases risk for depression, especially in girls (Stone, Hankin, Gibb, & Abela, 2011). Early negative temperament may influence the tendency to ruminate and thus increase risk of depression. In a group of youth followed from birth through adolescence, negative emotionality at age one was associated with self-reported rumination at age 13 and depressive symptoms at ages 13 and 26; the link between rumination and depressive symptoms in this group was particularly strong for girls (Mezulis, Priess, & Hyde, 2011). Not surprisingly, adolescents and adults who have experienced stressful life events are more likely to develop a pattern of rumination (Michl, McLaughlin, Shepherd, & Nolen-Hoeksema, 2013).

Learned Helplessness and Attributional Style Our **attributional style** (how we explain events that occur in our lives) can have powerful effects on our mood, according to Martin Seligman and his colleagues (Nolen-Hoeksema, Girgus, & Seligman, 1992; Seligman, 1975). Specifically, they suggest that depression is more likely to occur if we display thinking patterns associated with **learned helplessness**—a belief that we have little influence over what happens to us. People who have developed

co-rumination extensively discussing negative feelings or events with peers or others

attributional style characteristic way of explaining why a positive or negative event occurred

learned helplessness a learned belief that one is helpless and unable to affect outcomes

an attributional style of learned helplessness often make erroneous assumptions about their experiences. These beliefs can result in depressive symptoms.

Individuals with a negative attributional style focus on causes that are *internal,* *stable,* and *global,* according to research on learned helplessness. If something distressing occurs, they might conclude that it is *their* fault, that things will *always* turn out poorly, and that it will affect *all* aspects of their life. Not surprisingly, they are more likely to experience depression. In contrast, those with a positive attributional style focus on explanations that are *external, unstable,* and *specific.* If something bad occurs, they may see it as a one-time event resulting from circumstances beyond their control (M. C. Morris, Ciesla, & Garber, 2008). For instance, suppose that you received a low grade in a math class despite studying extensively. If you had a negative attributional style you might attribute the low grade to personal factors ("*I* don't do well in math") rather than external factors ("The *teacher* didn't teach very well"). You might also assume the low grade is due to unchangeable factors ("*I'm the type of person* who will never do well in math") rather than a temporary, changeable situation ("My low math grade was due to *my heavy workload this quarter*"). Additionally, you might tend to think globally ("I'm a *lousy student*") rather than specifically ("I'm *struggling with math but am good in other subjects*"). Unfortunately, when someone develops a pattern of making these kinds of negative attributions, they are much more vulnerable to the passive, apathetic, and hopeless reactions that lead to depression.

Factors Associated with Negative Thinking Patterns   Cognitive-behavioral theories make an important contribution to understanding how depression might develop. Moreover, patterns of pessimistic thinking often interact with biological and social factors. For example, carriers of two short 5-HTTLPR alleles (the serotonin transporter gene associated with increased risk of depression following stressful circumstances) show increased attention to negative information when undergoing acute stress (Markus & De Raedt, 2011). Further, if we develop a pattern of negative thinking or ruminating, it eventually becomes our normal way of looking at the world and interacting with others.

As we have mentioned, maltreatment occurring during childhood is associated with increased risk of depression. Early stressful interactions with parents or caregivers may lead to negative thinking patterns. For example, emotional abuse and neglect in childhood may set the stage for feelings of vulnerability, shame, or inadequacy; beliefs that our interpersonal needs will never be met; or expectations that loving someone will lead to rejection (Eberhart, 2011). These cognitive factors can further shape our expectations, perspectives, and interpretations of situations we encounter. Self-contempt, self-criticism, guilt, and shame may also increase vulnerability to depression because emotions such as these can interfere with the development of positive interpersonal relationships.

These maladaptive patterns of thinking are particularly destructive when they influence our self-concept. For example, self-criticism is strongly associated with depression (Auerbach, Ho, & Kim, 2014). Similarly, individuals who have experienced a major depressive episode are more likely to have a self-contempt bias in their thinking (a tendency to blame themselves rather than others) compared to individuals without a history of depression (Green, Moll, Deakin, Hulleman, & Zahn, 2013). Emotions such as shame and guilt are particularly prominent in individuals with depressive episodes; in one study, individuals with MDD continued to demonstrate

Learned Helplessness Leads to Depression

Born without a right hand, former Major League Baseball pitcher Jim Abbott fought feelings of helplessness and won multiple awards for overcoming obstacles and adversity through determination and courage. According to Martin Seligman, feelings of helplessness can lead to depression. Jim Abbott did not feel helpless.

JOHN ZICH/AFP/Getty Images

neural reactivity in response to thoughts of shame even after their symptoms subsided (Pulcu et al., 2014). Thus, negative thinking patterns can exert lifelong psychological, physiological, and social effects.

Social Dimension

Stressful interpersonal events can exert a powerful influence on our mood and increase the risk of depression. Severe acute stress (e.g., serious illness or death of a loved one) often precedes the onset of major depression (Stroud, Davila, Hammen, & Vrshek-Schallhorn, 2011) and is much more likely to cause a first depressive episode than is chronic stress (Muscatell, Slavich, Monroe, & Gotlib, 2009). However, after an initial episode of depression, less severe stressors can trigger further depression (Stroud et al., 2011). Chronic social stress often interacts with personal vulnerabilities to produce depression (M. C. Morris, Ciesla, & Garber, 2010). For example, individuals who are highly conscientious and who have chronically high levels of work stress coupled with few decision-making opportunities have increased risk of depression (Verboom et al., 2011).

Why do some people who encounter stressful life events develop depression, whereas others do not? The relationship between stress and depression is complex and interactive. Stress itself may activate a genetic predisposition for depression. As previously discussed, individuals who are predisposed to depression (carriers of the short allele of the 5-HTTLPR gene) develop depression when exposed to childhood maltreatment (Caspi, Sugden, et al., 2003). This may also explain why some people with genetic predispositions do not develop depression (i.e., significant stressors are absent) and why others who have encountered the same stressors as a person who is depressed do not experience depression (i.e., they do not have the genetic vulnerability).

Individuals who fail to develop secure attachments and trusting relationships with caregivers early in life have increased vulnerability to depression when confronted with stressful life events (T. E. Morley & Moran, 2011). For example, parental depression appears to have both a genetic and a social influence on intergenerational transmission of depression (Silberg, Maes, & Eaves, 2010). Among children born by assisted conception, depression in either parent (but especially the mother) increases the likelihood of childhood depression even when the children are not biologically related to the depressed parent (G. Lewis, Rice, Harold, Collishaw, & Thapar, 2011). Parental depression is associated with both fewer positive and more negative parent–child interactions; this pattern appears to initiate a cascade of social and psychological risk factors that culminate in depression (Garber & Cole, 2010).

Distressing social interactions are also linked with depression. For example, social rejection increases risk of depression, particularly among those who have genetic vulnerability, prior life stressors, or prior depressive episodes or who react with self-conscious emotions (such as shame or humiliation) or by internalizing negative beliefs about the self (Slavich, O'Donovan, Epel, & Kemeny, 2010). Additionally, *targeted rejection* (active, intentional social exclusion or rejection) has a particularly strong link with depressive symptoms (Slavich, Way, Eisenberger, & Taylor, 2010). Unfortunately, not only does stress increase risk of depression, but depression can also increase social stress. For example, individuals with depressive disorders are more likely to generate stressors that are within their control such as initiating arguments (Hammen, 2006). R. T. Liu and Alloy (2010) similarly concluded that *stress generation* (i.e., engaging in behaviors that lead to stressful events) plays an important role in depression.

Sociocultural Dimension

Sociocultural factors found to be associated with depression include culture, race and ethnicity, sexual orientation, and gender.

Cultural Influences on Depression A person's cultural background may influence descriptions of depressive symptoms, decisions about treatment, doctor–patient interactions, and the likelihood of outcomes such as suicide (Kleinman, 2004). In

Can We Immunize People against Depression?

Just as vaccines can protect people against the flu and other diseases, considerable research now suggests that various interventions can prevent or reduce depressive symptoms. For example, recognizing the strong connection between behaviors associated with depression (withdrawal, listlessness, agitation) and the learned helplessness that develops when aversive situations seem inescapable, positive psychologists have developed programs to "psychologically immunize" children against depression and to combat learned helplessness. Youth who learn to think optimistically (e.g., recognize how their efforts result in successful outcomes) and cope effectively with disappointments and challenges are much less likely to experience depression (Seligman, Ernst, Gillham, Reivich, & Linkins, 2009).

The Penn Resiliency Program has concentrated on classroom teaching of cognitive-behavioral and social problem-solving skills (Seligman, Ernst, et al., 2009). Premised on understandings that people's beliefs about events play a critical role in their emotional reactions and behaviors, students are taught to evaluate the accuracy of various thoughts, detect inaccurate thoughts (especially negative beliefs), and consider alternate interpretations of events. Youth also practice coping and problem-solving strategies that can be used in stressful situations (e.g., learning to relax, respond assertively, or negotiate resolutions to conflicts). Prevention program effects are particularly impressive for high-risk populations, including youth displaying high levels of depressive symptoms (Brière, Rohde, Shaw, & Stice, 2014). The outcome is further enhanced when parents are taught depression-prevention strategies (Stice, Shaw, Bohon, Marti, & Rohde, 2009).

Programs for adolescent girls target gender-related risk factors such as media messages, body image, and rumination, and teach emotion regulation and strategies for dealing with relational aggression and interpersonal conflicts (Gillham, Chaplin, Reivich, & Hamilton, 2008). In one study, adolescents who demonstrated the most optimism were half as likely as others to be depressed and were more able to cope effectively with life challenges (Patton et al., 2011).

Other interventions that can help protect against depression include:

- *Mobilizing social support.* Friendships and family support can help youth and adults cope with difficult life circumstances and decrease the incidence of depression (Kollannoor-Samuel et al., 2011). Religious participation is also associated with decreased risk of depression (Kasen, Wickramaratne, Gameroff, & Weissman, 2012), as is trust in neighbors and neighborhood cohesion (Bassett & Moore, 2013).

- *Increasing positive emotions.* Participating in enjoyable or meaningful activities, reflecting on personal strengths, positive reappraisal of challenging situations, focusing on gratitude, and performing acts of kindness can significantly increase positive emotions, particularly when multiple strategies are used on an ongoing basis (Sin & Lyubomirsky, 2009). The ability to boost one's mood by finding pleasure in daily activities ("in-the-moment" pleasure) is also protective against depression (Geschwind, Peeters, Van Os, Drukker, & Wichers, 2011).

- *Maintaining a healthy lifestyle.* Higher levels of physical activity are associated with lower depression risk (Lucas et al., 2011). Both aerobic and weight-training activities can boost mood (Greer & Trivedi, 2009). Eating a healthy diet is also linked with better mental health (Jacka, Kremer, et al., 2011), and eating vegetables, fruit, meat, fish, nuts, legumes, and whole grains is associated with a reduced risk of depression (Jacka, Pasco, et al., 2010). Sufficient sleep (7–9 hours) is also strongly associated with positive mood and psychological well-being (S. Brand & Kirov, 2011).

In summary, just as a variety of factors contribute to the development of depressive illness, a variety of protective factors can reduce the risk of depression.

Photodisc/Getty Images

some cultures, depression is expressed in the form of somatic or bodily complaints, rather than as sadness. For example, depression is often experienced as "nerves" and headaches in Latino and Mediterranean cultures; weakness, tiredness, or "imbalance" in Chinese and other Asian cultures; problems of the "heart" in Middle Eastern cultures; and being "heartbroken" among the Hopi (American Psychiatric Association, 2000).

Do triggers for depression differ among different cultural groups? Greenberger, Chen, Tally, and Dong (2000) gained some insight into this question by comparing factors associated with depressed mood among adolescents in China and the United States. In both cultures, certain "culture-general" stressors such as serious illness or family economic distress had similar effects on depressed mood. However, cultural differences emerged for other variables. For instance, depressed mood among Chinese adolescents was frequently associated with poor academic performance or conflicts with parents, perhaps reflecting the Chinese cultural emphasis on family and achievement. Similarly, family conflict and intergenerational stress is a risk factor for depression among adolescents with immigrant parents (S. Y. Kim, Chen, Li, Huang, & Moon, 2009).

Perceived discrimination based on gender, race or ethnicity, or sexual orientation, especially among those who do not talk to others about their experiences, is also associated with depression (Juang & Cookston, 2009; McLaughlin, Hatzenbuehler, & Keyes, 2010). Analysis of everyday encounters with discrimination among African American women revealed that those subjected to frequent discrimination were most likely to have depressive symptoms (Schulz et al., 2006). Another study involving African Americans found perceived discrimination to be related to severity of depressive symptoms; overall, discrimination was more stressful for the women compared to the men in the study (J. Wagner & Abbott, 2007). Perceived racial discrimination is also associated with lower self-esteem and depressive symptoms among Hispanic/Latino adolescents (Zeiders, Umaña-Taylor, & Derlan, 2013).

Societal stressors such as prejudice and discrimination related to having a gay, lesbian, or bisexual orientation can also result in depression, as can be seen in the following case.

CASE STUDY   Gabriel, a 24-year-old college upperclassman, began therapy complaining of depressed mood and high anxiety, as well as guilt and disappointment regarding his failure to complete his undergraduate degree on time while his parents continued to pay for his education. . . . Gabriel had experienced anxieties about school when he was an adolescent, in addition to a depressive episode that he attributed to anticipated difficulties in revealing his homosexuality to his family. Gabriel insisted that this latter problem had been resolved, in spite of the fact that he had never disclosed his sexual orientation to his father. (Newman, 2010, pp. 25–26)

Gabriel was encountering a common stressor among young adults who are lesbian, gay, or bisexual—how and when to disclose their sexual orientation to family and friends. The decision to *come out* is complex and can result in fear of rejection and feelings of social isolation. However, maintaining secrets about sexual orientation also creates distress and may affect relationships with friends and family. Negative reactions that sometimes occur during the disclosure process can further increase risk of depression (Chaney, Filmore, & Goodrich, 2011). Unfortunately, the prevalence of attempted suicide is much greater for gay, lesbian, or bisexual adolescents compared to their heterosexual peers (21.5 percent versus 4.2 percent); suicide attempts were 20 percent more likely among those who reported an unsupportive social environment with respect to sexual orientation (Hatzenbuehler, 2011).

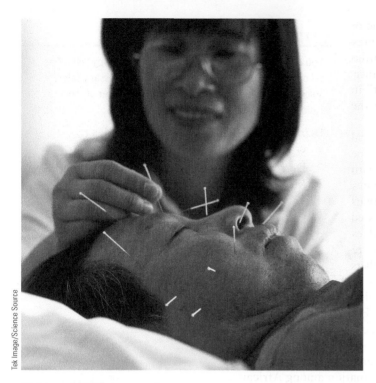

Cultural Differences in Symptoms and Treatment

People from different cultures vary in the way they express depression. Individuals of Chinese descent often report somatic or bodily complaints instead of psychological symptoms, such as sadness or loss of pleasure. They also are more likely to rely on Chinese medicine and acupuncture to treat their symptoms.

Gender and Depressive Disorders Depression is far more common among women than among men, regardless of region of the world, race and ethnicity, or social class (R. C. Kessler, 2003). Some suggest that clinicians or diagnostic systems may be biased toward finding depression in women (Caplan, 1995). Others wonder if women are simply more likely to seek treatment or to report their depression to physicians or those conducting surveys regarding emotional well-being. That is, do gender differences reflect differences in self-report of depressive symptoms or willingness to seek treatment rather than differences in actual depression rates? Evidence suggests that women do, in fact, have higher rates of depression compared to men and that the differences are real rather than an artifact of self-reports or biases (Rieker & Bird, 2005). Gender differences in depression begin appearing during adolescence and are greatest during the reproductive years. Attempts to explain these differences have focused on physiological and social or psychological factors (Table 8.5).

Variations in hormone levels that begin in puberty and continue until menopause appear to influence gender differences in depression (Graziottin & Serafini, 2009). The phase of the menstrual cycle appears to affect women's ability to integrate and process emotional information. For example, many women experience more physiological and subjective stress reactivity just prior to menstruation (Hoyer et al., 2013). Interestingly, girls who experience early physical maturity are at particular risk of depression (Joinson, Heron, Lewis, Croudace, & Araya, 2011). Additionally, up to 13 percent of women experience mood changes associated with pregnancy, including depression (Breese-McCoy, 2011). Menopause is another occasion when women are particularly vulnerable to severe depression (Graziottin & Serafini, 2009), especially when menopause is combined with poor health or negative views regarding aging (Woods, Mitchell, Percival, & Smith-DiJulio, 2009).

Life stressors may interact with physiological factors to influence gender differences in depression (Vigod & Stewart, 2009). For example, among children who have experienced early traumatic experiences (such as death, divorce, violence, sexual abuse, or illness), both boys and girls show alterations in connectivity in the fear circuitry of the brain (less connectivity between the hippocampus and prefrontal cortex). However, the girls showed additional irregularities—reduced connectivity between the amygdala and hippocampus, a factor that can cause less inhibition of fear responses and increased emotional reactivity (Herringa et al., 2013). Although these

Table 8.5 Possible Explanations for the Higher Frequency of Depression among Women

- Women may be more willing to acknowledge and seek help for depression.

- Genetic or hormonal differences may result in higher rates of depression among women.

- Women are subjected to societal factors such as unfulfilling gender roles or limited occupational opportunities that lead to feelings of helplessness and hopelessness.

- Cognitive styles (such as ruminating or co-ruminating) that increase depression are more common in women.

- Women are more likely to have experienced childhood trauma (sexual abuse, childhood maltreatment) and other stressors associated with depression.

© Cengage Learning®

brain differences most likely represent neuroplastic accommodations designed to allow individuals who experience early life stress to adapt to their environment, such biological changes are associated with increased risk for anxiety and depression. Additionally, girls and women have increased risk of encountering certain environmental stressors such as sexual abuse that produce ongoing changes in physiological reactivity; not surprisingly, sexual abuse has a strong association with lifetime risk of depression, particularly persistent depression (Garcia-Toro et al., 2013).

Social or psychological factors related to traditional gender roles can also influence the development of depressive disorders. Specifically, social modeling and socialization practices can influence feelings of self-worth. While males are socialized to value autonomy, self-interest, and achievement-oriented goals, females learn to value social goals and interdependent functioning (e.g., caring about others, not wanting to hurt others). Therefore, the opinions of others are more likely to influence the self-perceptions of women; this may increase vulnerability to interpersonal stress, particularly stressors involving close friends or family. Interestingly, some researchers suggest that gender socialization and early social learning contribute to gender differences in the regulation and metabolism of stress hormones (Dedovic, Wadiwalla, Engert, & Pruessner, 2009).

The way women respond to depressed moods also contributes to the severity, chronicity, and frequency of depressive episodes, suggests Nolen-Hoeksema (2012). In her view, women tend to ruminate and amplify their depressive moods, whereas men often find ways to minimize sad feelings through methods such as drinking alcohol. As we have mentioned, rumination is linked to increases in depressive symptoms (Hankin, 2009). Adolescent girls who are depressed are also more likely to generate interpersonal stress, which in turn can lead to chronic depression (Rudolph, Flynn, Abaied, Groot, & Thompson, 2009).

Some researchers contend that men are as likely as women to experience depression. They suggest that gender disparities in depression rates result from the fact that traditional symptoms of depression (such as sadness and hopelessness) are more likely to be displayed by women, whereas men who are depressed are more likely to display nontraditional symptoms such as anger, aggression, burying themselves in their work, or substance abuse (Martin, Neighbors, & Griffith, 2013).

Treatment for Depression

Finding the correct treatment or combination of treatments for depression is very important, because longer depressive episodes are associated with negative long-term outcomes, more frequent depressive episodes, and reduced likelihood of symptom improvement (Shelton, Osuntokun, Heinloth, & Corya, 2010). When someone is not responding to initial treatment for depression, adding on a therapy is generally preferred over switching from one therapy to another, particularly if the initial treatment had some effect (Shelton et al., 2010). If depression does not respond to treatment, it is important to inquire about hypomanic/manic symptoms to ensure that the person does not, in fact, have a bipolar disorder (Fornaro & Giosue, 2010). We now turn to various treatment strategies used with depressive disorders.

Biomedical Treatments for Depressive Disorders

Biomedical treatments include the use of medication and other interventions that affect various brain systems, such as circadian-related treatments (light therapy and sleep deprivation) and brain stimulation techniques.

Medication   Antidepressant medications increase the availability of certain neurotransmitters in the brain. Three classes of antidepressants—the *tricyclics, monoamine oxidase*

CRITICAL THINKING

Antidepressants and Suicidality: Risk versus Benefit

In 2004, the U.S. Food and Drug Administration (FDA) required manufacturers of SSRI antidepressants to provide warnings regarding the possibility of increased risk for suicidal thinking and behavior in children and adolescents taking these medications. In 2007, the FDA expanded the warning to include those ages 18–24. The FDA (2007) warned:

> Antidepressants increased the risk compared to placebo of suicidal thinking and behavior (suicidality) in children, adolescents, and young adults in short-term studies of major depressive disorder (MDD) and other psychiatric disorders. . . . All patients being treated with antidepressants for any indication should be monitored appropriately and observed closely for clinical worsening, suicidality, and unusual changes in behavior, especially during the initial few months of a course of drug therapy, or at times of dose changes, either increases or decreases.

Although the data cited by the FDA showed that suicidal thoughts and behaviors occurred among 4 percent of youth taking antidepressants compared to 2 percent of those taking placebo, some believe the FDA warning has resulted in more harm than good. There is concern that the warnings led to reductions in the diagnosis and treatment of depression in children, adolescents, and young adults (Brent, 2009b). In the year following the FDA warning, the suicide rate in children

and adolescents increased 18 percent, the first increase in 10 years (Hamilton et al., 2007). Considering the risk/benefit ratio based on available current research, some claim that the benefits of using FDA-approved SSRIs in children and adolescents with moderate to severe depression outweigh the risk of suicide (Soutullo & Figueroa-Quintana, 2013).

The debate regarding the effect of SSRIs on suicidal thoughts and behavior among those younger than age 25 continues (Spielmans, Jureidini, Healy, & Purssey, 2013). A comprehensive analysis of data on antidepressant use in children and young adults over a 12-year period revealed that heightened risk of deliberate self-harm occurred primarily among youth started on higher than average dosages of antidepressants. The authors cautioned clinicians to avoid excessive antidepressant doses and to monitor any young person taking antidepressants for signs of suicidality (Miller, Swanson, Azrael, Pate, & Stürmer, 2014). Most professionals agree that it is important for treatment providers to remain alert for suicidal ideation in anyone who is depressed, especially during the first months of antidepressant treatment.

For Further Consideration:

1. Should the FDA warnings regarding antidepressants be reviewed?

2. What factors should be considered when treating children, adolescents, and young adults experiencing depression?

inhibitors (MAOIs), and *serotonin-norepinephrine reuptake inhibitors* (SNRIs)—block the reabsorption of norepinephrine and serotonin, whereas the *selective serotonin reuptake inhibitors* (SSRIs) block the reuptake of serotonin. *Atypical antidepressants*, a group of unique antidepressant medications, affect other neurotransmitters, including dopamine. Medications within each class are similar in their chemical makeup, but they often differ in their side effects.

Antidepressants have a variety of potential side effects, including possible increased risk of suicidality in those younger than 25 (Miller, Swanson, Azrael, Pate, & Stürmer, 2014). Medical providers consider a variety of factors when deciding which antidepressant to prescribe for someone experiencing depression. For example, they take into account the presence of other symptoms (such as anxiety, overeating, or nicotine addiction) that might also be helped by certain antidepressants; the person's prior response to antidepressants (or family patterns of response); or the desire to avoid certain side effects such as weight gain, sexual side effects, or gastrointestinal problems (Brunoni, Fraguas, et al., 2009).

Despite the popularity of antidepressants, there are many questions about their effectiveness. First, publication bias in research involving antidepressant medication is a significant concern. One review of studies evaluating the effectiveness of antidepressants found that although 94 percent of the studies supportive of antidepressants

Computer-based Interventions for Depression

Computer-based therapies have proven successful in treating anxiety disorders. However, are these limited-contact interventions a safe alternative for treating depression, a disorder consistently associated with risk of suicidality? Is it possible to adequately monitor the severity of a person's depressive symptoms and associated suicide risk as they engage in computer-based treatment? Face-to-face contact is currently not a part of many computer-based interventions; thus, there is no clinician to identify signs of severe depression, hypomanic or manic symptoms, or suicidality.

Those who support use of computer-based interventions cite the large number of people with depression who receive no treatment (Williams et al., 2007), the accessibility of computer-based interventions, and the research supporting intervention effectiveness for those who participate. In a review of studies, Proudfoot (2004) found a high degree of satisfaction among users of computer therapy programs. Respondents reported greater comfort self-disclosing to a computer and indicated that they would be more likely to disclose suicidal plans online rather than to a human. A meta-analysis of various studies using computer-based CBT found therapy effects that were equal to face-to-face CBT and superior to attention-only control conditions; symptom improvement continued beyond the treatment period and satisfaction with treatment was good. Computer-assisted CBT modules have helped prevent depression relapse for up to 2 years after the intervention (Andrews, Cuijpers, Craske, McEvoy, & Titov, 2010).

Similar positive results occur for children and adolescents participating in computer-based CBT interventions designed to prevent and treat depression (Richardson, Stallard, & Velleman, 2010). A new interactive computer program designed for adolescents with depression involves participants choosing an avatar to represent themselves in a fantasy world. Participants undertake a series of challenges to restore balance in a world in which GNATs (Gloomy, Negative, Automatic Thoughts) rule. Modules in the program focus on finding hope; staying active; dealing with emotions; solving problems; and recognizing and challenging unhelpful thoughts. A "guide" in the fantasy provides information about the coping strategies needed to move to the next level. Participants who learned strategies to combat negative thoughts and cope with problems though this program made as much progress in reducing depressive symptoms as participants who received face-to-face counseling with a therapist (Merry et al., 2012).

More research is needed to determine the most appropriate role of computer-based interventions in treating depression. Unfortunately, high dropout rates and noncompletion of the full computer intervention are an ongoing concern (Kaltenthaler et al., 2008). Greater severity and chronicity of depressive symptoms are associated with higher dropout rates; adherence is particularly low with open-access treatment Web sites (Christensen, Griffiths, & Farrer, 2009). Data from behavior change research may help researchers develop techniques and modes of delivery that maximize adherence and long-term change (Webb, Joseph, Yardley, & Michie, 2010). For example, in studies focused on other health-related behaviors, computerized interventions are most effective when combined with some personal contact such as periodic text or e-mail messages prompting continued involvement (Fry & Neff, 2010). What do you see as advantages and disadvantages of computer-based treatment for depression?

were submitted for publication and were published, many studies that did not support the effectiveness of antidepressants were never published or were written to give the impression of a positive antidepressant outcome (E. H. Turner, Matthews, Linardatos, Tell, & Rosenthal, 2008). Even with this publication bias, the research evidence for antidepressant efficacy is rather weak.

In fact, many individuals affected by depression show no improvement with antidepressant medications (M. P. Ward & Irazoqui, 2010). Their effectiveness is particularly limited with mild depression; in fact, placebos are often as effective as antidepressants in treating mild depression (Barbui, Cipriani, Patel, Ayuso-Mateos, & van Ommeren, 2011). A comprehensive study evaluating the effectiveness of antidepressant medication concluded that the benefit of these medications over placebo for treating mild or moderate depression was "minimal or nonexistent." Antidepressants were somewhat more effective for those with severe depression, with about half showing some response to the first antidepressant prescribed (Fournier et al., 2010). A large meta-analysis provided support for the effectiveness of antidepressants with premenstrual syndrome and premenstrual dysphoric disorder, although side effects were commonly reported (Marjoribanks, Brown, O'Brien, & Wyatt, 2013). Even when antidepressants are effective, they do not cure depression; that is, once medication is stopped, symptoms often return.

A recent trend is to add other medications, particularly antipsychotics such as aripiprazole (Abilify) and quetiapine (Seroquel), to boost the effectiveness of antidepressants. Although this adjunctive therapy sometimes produces mild to moderate improvement, caution is urged due to potential side effects of these powerful medications and because the added medication often does not significantly improve a person's quality of life (Spielmans et al., 2013).

For many individuals who do not fully respond to antidepressant medication, participating in moderate to intense levels of daily exercise can significantly reduce residual symptoms of depression (Trivedi, Greer, et al., 2011). Omega-3 supplements can also reduce depressive symptoms, particularly for those without concurrent anxiety symptoms (Lespérance et al., 2011).

Circadian-Related Treatments   Some treatments for depression involve efforts to reset the circadian clock. For example, a night of total sleep deprivation followed by a night of sleep recovery can improve depressive symptoms (Howland, 2011). Additionally, use of specially designed lights is an effective and well-tolerated treatment for those with a seasonal pattern of depression (Roecklein, Schumacher, Miller, & Ernecoff, 2012). This therapy involves dawn-light simulation (timer-activated lights that gradually increase in brightness) or daily use of a box, visor, or lighting system that delivers light of a particular intensity for a designated period of time (Gooley et al., 2010). A well-designed study evaluating treatment for seasonal depression compared light therapy alone to light therapy combined with antidepressants; both groups made similar improvement (67 percent showed improvement and 50–54 percent showed remission of symptoms), but light therapy produced more rapid improvement and fewer side effects (R. W. Lam, Levitt, et al., 2006). An analysis of randomized controlled trials suggested that light therapy is as beneficial as antidepressant treatment not only for seasonal depression, but also for depression that occurs without a seasonal pattern (R. N. Golden et al., 2005).

Brain Stimulation Therapies   Electroconvulsive therapy, vagus nerve stimulation, and transcranial magnetic stimulation are sometimes used to treat severe or chronic treatment-resistant depression, especially when life-threatening symptoms such as refusal to eat or intense suicidal intent are present (Andrade et al., 2010). Electroconvulsive therapy (ECT) has U.S. Food and Drug Administration (FDA) approval for treating depression that does not respond to other treatments, and is a preferred treatment for profound depression (George, Taylor, & Short, 2013). ECT, which is typically conducted several times weekly, involves application of moderate electrical voltage to the brain in order to produce a convulsion (seizure) lasting at least 15 seconds; appropriate use of anesthetics during ECT minimizes side effects such as headaches, confusion, and memory loss (Mayo, Kaye, Conrad, Baluch, & Frost, 2010).

The FDA has also approved vagus nerve stimulation for people with chronic, recurrent depression that has not responded to at least four prior treatment attempts. This technique uses an implanted pacemaker-like device that delivers a frequent, 30-second electronic impulse that travels from the vagus nerve to the brain; this eventually produces changes in metabolic activity within the brain, including increased dopamine availability, and subsequent reduction in depressive symptoms. Regularly implemented vagus nerve

Seasonal Patterns of Depression

Some individuals with depressive and bipolar disorders find that their depressive symptoms occur or intensify during the winter. Many individuals who do not have a diagnosed mental disorder also report that they experience seasonal symptoms of depression. Here the store manager at the Indoor Sun Shoppe in Seattle, Washington displays one of many doctor-prescribed sunlamps available for purchase.

Kevin P. Casey/Bloomberg / Getty Images

stimulation has produced profound and sustained improvement in some individuals with treatment-resistant depression (Conway et al., 2013).

Another FDA-approved technique used with treatment-resistant depression is repetitive transcranial magnetic stimulation. This procedure, which uses an electromagnetic field to stimulate the brain, has proven effective for acute depressive episodes and for maintaining remission of depressive symptoms (Connolly, Helmer, Cristancho, Cristancho, & O'Reardon, 2012). Although a meta-analysis concluded that this technique has sufficient research for use with major depressive disorder (Slotema, Blom, Hoek, & Sommer, 2010), other literature reviews have expressed more skepticism, in part because of the weak design of many studies evaluating the procedure. A factor confounding the research may be intensity of stimulation; high-intensity stimulation appears to produce the most significant results (Levkovitz et al., 2009).

Psychological and Behavioral Treatments for Depressive Disorders

Three approaches (behavioral activation, interpersonal therapy, and cognitive-behavioral therapy) have received extensive research support for treating depression, and another technique (mindfulness-based cognitive therapy) has shown promise in treating depression. Although there is evidence that antidepressant medications can be beneficial in cases of severe depression (Fournier et al., 2010), psychotherapies appear to have longer-lasting effects. That is, effective psychological treatment appears to produce enduring results, whereas medication produces relief from depressive symptoms only during active treatment (Hollon, Stewart, & Strunk, 2006). Recently, researchers have been using PET scans to observe activity in different regions of the brain in an attempt to compare the effectiveness of psychotherapy and antidepressants in treating depression (McGrath et al., 2013).

Behavioral Activation Therapy   Behavioral activation therapy, based on principles of operant conditioning, focuses on helping those who are depressed to increase their participation in enjoyable activities and social interactions. The goal is to have clients improve their mood by actively engaging in life (Kanfer, Busch, & Rusch, 2009). This emphasis is very important because individuals with depression often lack the motivation to participate in social activities. Behavioral activation therapy is based on the idea that depression results from diminished reinforcement. Consistent with this perspective, treatment focuses on increasing exposure to pleasurable events and activities, improving social skills, and facilitating social interactions. The steps involved in treatment include:

1. identifying and rating different activities in terms of the pleasure or feelings of self-confidence they might produce;
2. performing some of the selected activities, thereby increasing feelings of pleasure or mastery;
3. identifying day-to-day problems and using behavior techniques to deal with them; and
4. improving social and assertiveness skills (Lejuez et al., 2011).

Because of the focus on actions that a depressed individual can take rather than talking about problems, this approach is also effective with people from other countries and ethnic backgrounds (Kanter, Puspitasari, & Nagy, 2012).

Interpersonal Psychotherapy   Interpersonal psychotherapy is an evidence-based treatment focused on current interpersonal problems. Because this approach presumes that depression occurs within an interpersonal context, therapy focuses on relationship issues. Clients learn to evaluate their role in interpersonal conflict

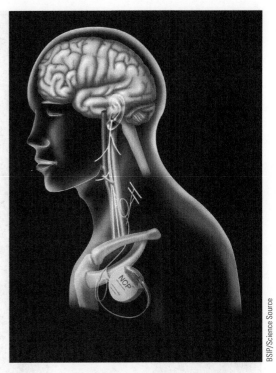

Treating Depression with Vagus Nerve Stimulation

Vagus nerve stimulation is a newer treatment for severe depression that does not respond to other treatment methods. A neurostimulator, surgically implanted under the skin on the chest, is connected to the left vagus nerve. When activated, the device sends electrical signals along the vagus nerve to the brainstem, which then sends signals to other areas of the brain.

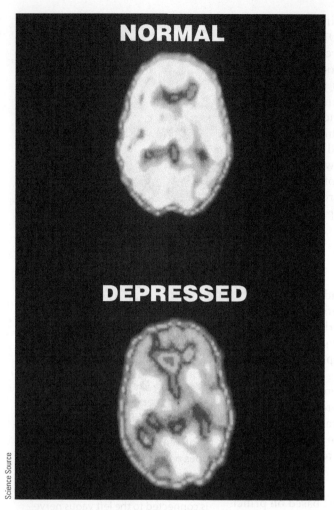

NORMAL

DEPRESSED

Reduced Brain Activity in Depression

These positron emission tomography scans comparing normal brain activity with the cerebral metabolism of a person with depression show the decreased brain activity seen in depressive disorders. Researchers hope that brain scans will soon guide treatment for depressive and bipolar disorders.

and make positive changes in their relationships. By improving communication, identifying role conflicts, and increasing social skills, clients develop more satisfying relationships. Although interpersonal psychotherapy acknowledges the role of early life experiences and trauma, it is oriented primarily toward present, not past, relationships. It has proven to be an efficacious treatment for acute depression (Levenson et al., 2010) and is as effective as continuing use of antidepressant medication in preventing recurrence of depressive symptoms (K. S. Dobson et al., 2008).

Cognitive-Behavioral Therapy Cognitive-behavioral therapy (CBT) focuses on altering the negative thought patterns and distorted thinking associated with depression. Cognitive therapists teach clients to identify thoughts that precede upsetting emotions, distance themselves from these thoughts, and examine the accuracy of their beliefs (DeRubeis et al., 2008). Clients learn to identify negative, self-critical thoughts and the connection between negative thoughts and negative feelings. They then learn to replace inaccurate thoughts with realistic interpretations.

Individuals treated with CBT are less likely to relapse after treatment has stopped compared to individuals taking antidepressants (K. S. Dobson et al., 2008). Changes in explanatory styles and alterations in negative self-biases may help prevent recurrence of depressive symptoms (DeRubeis et al., 2008). Interestingly, CBT produces changes in the same brain regions affected by the use of antidepressants (Goldapple et al., 2004). CBT has effectively helped adolescents from diverse backgrounds (E. Marchand, Ng, Rohde, & Stice, 2010), and adapted versions of the therapy are used in non-Western cultures (Naeem, Waheed, Gobbi, Ayub, & Kingdon, 2011). CBT has also reduced depression risk and symptoms among children whose parents have a history of depression (Compas et al., 2011).

Mindfulness-Based Cognitive Therapy Mindfulness-based cognitive therapy (MBCT) involves calm awareness of one's present experience, thoughts, and feelings, and promotes an attitude of acceptance rather than judgment, evaluation, or rumination. Mindfulness allows those affected by depression to disrupt the cycle of negative thinking by directing attention to the present (B. D. Gilbert & Christopher, 2010). Focusing on experiences with curiosity and without judgment prevents the development of maladaptive beliefs and thus reduces depressive thinking (Frewen, Evans, Maraj, Dozois, & Partridge, 2008). Clinical studies have found that MBCT reduces residual symptoms in chronic depression, is effective in treatment-resistant depression, and reduces the risk of recurrence of depressive symptoms (Godfrin & van Heeringen, 2010). The increases in positive emotions and appreciation of pleasant daily activities associated with MBCT appear to produce protective effects against depressive relapse (Geschwind, Peeters, Van Os, et al., 2011).

Other Psychological Interventions for Depression Less costly interventions for depression, including brief training to reduce negative attentional bias (T. T. Wells & Beevers, 2010), computerized skill-building sessions (Andrews, Cuijpers, Craske, McEvoy, & Titov, 2010), and cognitive-behavioral therapy delivered online (D. Kessler et al., 2009), have also shown promise in the treatment of depression. Similarly, participants in treatment focused on anticipation of a more positive future showed significant reductions in depressive symptoms (Vilhauer et al., 2011). Cognitive bias modification, a guided self-help intervention aimed at minimizing rumination and overgeneralization and enhancing specific problem-solving skills, is another low-cost, accessible treatment for depression (Watkins, Taylor, et al., 2012). However, individuals who tend to ruminate have shown an increase in depressive symptoms when using self-directed workbooks; those who ruminate may have difficulty identifying and disputing negative thoughts without the help of a trained professional (Haeffel, 2010).

Bipolar Disorders

Up to this point, we have discussed disorders that involve only depressive symptoms. In this section, we discuss bipolar disorders, a group of disorders that involve episodes of hypomania and mania (see Table 8.6) that may alternate with episodes of depression. Although depressive symptoms occur in bipolar disorders, depressive disorders and bipolar disorders are very different conditions. First, bipolar disorders have a very strong genetic component. In fact, there is strong evidence of physiological overlap (i.e., shared biological etiology) between bipolar disorders and schizophrenia, a severe mental health disorder involving loss of contact with reality, which we discuss extensively in Chapter 12. Second, people with bipolar disorders respond to medications that have little effect with depressive disorders. Third, the peak age of onset is somewhat earlier for bipolar disorders (teens and early twenties) than for depressive disorders (late twenties). And finally, bipolar disorders occur much less frequently than depressive disorders (see Figure 8.1) (Merikangas, Jin, et al., 2011).

Diagnosis and Classification of Bipolar Disorders

Bipolar disorders are diagnosed when careful assessment confirms the presence of hypomanic or manic symptoms. The clinician also inquires about the severity and pattern of any depressive symptoms. Understanding these symptoms is important because

Table 8.6 DSM-5 Criteria for a Hypomanic or Manic Episode

Hypomanic and manic episodes involve a specific period in which there is *a definite, observable change in behavior occurring most of the day, nearly every day during the episode.* The behavior change involves a *consistently elevated, expansive, or irritable mood* and *unusual increases in energy or goal-directed activity.*

In addition, the person exhibits at least three of the following symptoms (four are required if the mood is irritable rather than elevated or expansive):

1. Exaggerated self-esteem or feelings of grandiosity and extreme self-importance
2. Decreased need for sleep; feeling rested after minimal sleep
3. Usually talkative or seems pressured to keep talking
4. Racing thoughts or frequent change of topics or ideas
5. Distractibility that may involve attention to unimportant environmental stimuli
6. Increased social or work-related goal-directed activity, sexual activity, or physical restlessness
7. Impulsive involvement in activities that may have negative consequences (e.g., excessive spending, sexual promiscuity, gambling)

A hypomanic episode involves continuation of these symptoms for at least 4 days.

A manic episode involves continuation of these symptoms for at least 1 week (or less if psychiatric hospitalization occurs and shortens the duration of the episode). The symptoms are severe enough to require hospitalization or to result in impairment in social or work functioning. Psychotic symptoms may be present.

In both hypomanic and manic episodes, the symptoms are not due to the physiological effects of a medical condition, a prescribed medication, or drug or alcohol abuse.

SOURCE: APA (2013).

depression is often the most debilitating aspect of bipolar disorders (Michalak, Torres, Bond, Lam, & Yatham, 2013). Although clinicians are also interested in the frequency of normal mood states, they differentiate between the bipolar diagnostic categories by reviewing the severity of depressive and hypomanic/manic symptoms and the pattern of mood changes (see Figure 8.3). The three types of bipolar disorders are bipolar I, bipolar II, and cyclothymic disorder (see Table 8.7).

Figure 8.3

Mood States Experienced in Bipolar Disorders

Bipolar disorders differ in terms of the range of mood symptoms experienced. The widest range of symptoms occurs with bipolar I, although not everyone with bipolar I experiences depressive episodes.

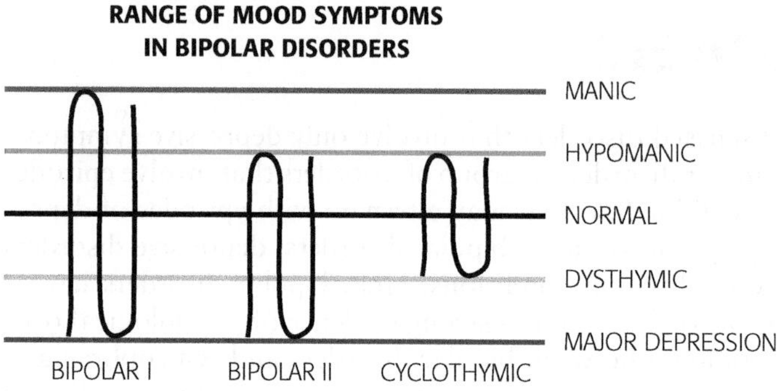

RANGE OF MOOD SYMPTOMS IN BIPOLAR DISORDERS

MANIC
HYPOMANIC
NORMAL
DYSTHYMIC
MAJOR DEPRESSION

BIPOLAR I   BIPOLAR II   CYCLOTHYMIC

© 2003 Julie Carboni, M.A.

Table 8.7 Bipolar Disorders

DSM-5 DISORDERS CHART				
Disorder	DSM-5 Criteria	Lifetime Prevalence (%)	Gender Difference	Age of Onset
Bipolar I disorder	• At least one weeklong manic episode • Mania impairs functioning • Mixed features or depressive episodes are common, but not required, for diagnosis • Possible psychotic features	0.4–1.0	No major difference, although depressive episodes, rapid cycling, and mixed features are more common in females	Any age; usually late adolescence or early adulthood, although later onset is possible
Bipolar II disorder	• At least one major depressive episode • At least one hypomanic episode • No history of mania	0.6–1.1	Mixed results, but appears to occur more frequently in females; rapid cycling and mixed features are more common in females	Any age; usually early adulthood, but diagnosis often occurs long after onset
Cyclothymic disorder	• Periods involving milder hypomanic symptoms alternating with milder depression for at least 2 years (with no more than 2 months symptom-free)[a] • Symptoms have never met the criteria for a hypomanic, manic, or major depressive episode	0.4–1.0	No difference	Often adolescence or early adulthood

SOURCE: Data from APA (2013); R. C. Kessler, Chiu, Demler, & Walters (2005); Merikangas, Akiskal, et al. (2007); Merikangas, Jin, et al. (2011).
[a]In children and adolescents, mood can be irritable and diagnosis can occur if symptoms have been present for at least 1 year.

Bipolar I Disorder

CASE STUDY   It took ten years, a suicide attempt, an acute manic episode and a psychotic break for me to finally get an accurate diagnosis of bipolar disorder. By that time, I was 29, and I had already graduated law school, passed the bar, earned a Master's in Public Health, published my first book and won an award for it. . . . It took roughly a month for me to believe and acknowledge my diagnosis. The antipsychotics worked remarkably fast, and soon, I was confronting the reality of my hallucinations, delusions, and erratic and irrational behavior from the perspective of someone who was neither acutely manic nor psychotic. I couldn't very well deny the diagnosis after looking back at the things I'd done while manic: disrobing in public, yelling obscenities at an infant, trying to give away all my money and belongings— and that's not even the half of it . . .

   I'm now able to make a living as a full-time writer. . . . I'm not cured by any stretch. I struggle with this illness every day. . . . Living with bipolar disorder, writing and speaking about it, and gaining strength from others who share in this fight, I've learned never to underestimate the power of compassion, perseverance, resilience and faith. (Moezzi, 2014)

Melody Moezzi is the author *Haldol and Hyacinths*, a memoir about her experiences living with bipolar I disorder. **Bipolar I disorder** is diagnosed when someone (with or without a history of severe depression) experiences at least one manic episode (see Table 8.6). For a diagnosis of bipolar I disorder, manic symptoms need to significantly affect normal functioning and be present most of the day, nearly every day, for at least 1 week. Manic episodes significantly interfere with common activities and interpersonal interactions. The uncharacteristic behaviors that occur during manic periods often produce feelings of guilt or worthlessness once the episode has ended. Although not everyone with bipolar I experiences depression, it is a common and disabling characteristic of this disorder. Both depressive and manic episodes may involve psychotic symptoms or end in hospitalization. As was the case with Ms. Moezzi, a diagnosis can be a turning point in a person's life—an opportunity to receive help and end the roller coaster of mood swings.

Bipolar II Disorder

CASE STUDY   For many years, Daniel had no idea what was wrong. His depression began in his midteens and sometimes lasted for months. In his twenties he began to have weeks when everything seemed great. He felt energetic, clever, productive, creative, and empowered. He saw himself as athletic, physically strong, and very sexy. He felt unusually social, frequently texting or messaging friends or posting on social media. He was not tired so he went out dancing and drinking, hooking up with women he met at the local clubs. At work, he had ideas he enthusiastically shared, but became irritable and impatient when co-workers asked questions or mentioned that his ideas seemed unrealistic. These energized times would sometimes last for weeks. He might then become "grouchy" and easily agitated, crashing into a dark world of depression. It seemed like the depressions were getting longer, and it was getting harder to undo the damage that occurred during his "good times." After years of telling his family to "lay off" and not to worry about him, he finally agreed that he needed to get some help.

bipolar I disorder diagnosis involves at least one manic episode that has impaired social or occupational functioning; the person may or may not experience depression or psychotic symptoms

Bipolar II disorder is diagnosed when there has been at least one major depressive episode (see Table 8.3) lasting at least 2 weeks and at least one hypomanic episode (see Table 8.6) lasting at least 4 consecutive days. The behavior associated with hypomania often surprises, annoys, or creates concern in friends and family. As was the case with Daniel, those with bipolar II often fail to seek treatment until their mood swings and periods of depression begin to feel overwhelming. Family members are often the first to express concern about the uncharacteristic behavior seen during energized episodes. Depression is the most pronounced feature of bipolar II, with almost three fourths of those with bipolar II reporting severe impairment while depressed (Merikangas, Jin, et al., 2011). Bipolar II is considered an underdiagnosed disorder, in part because many physicians prescribe antidepressants without adequately assessing for periods of highly energetic, goal-directed activity and other hypomanic symptoms (Benazzi, 2007).

The primary distinction between bipolar I and bipolar II is the severity of the symptoms during energized episodes. A bipolar I diagnosis requires at least one manic episode (including severe impairment that lasts at least 1 week); a bipolar II diagnosis requires at least one major depressive episode and one hypomanic episode, lasting at least 4 days (APA, 2013). Although you may have heard that bipolar II is a "milder" form of bipolar disorder, this is not accurate. The depressive symptoms associated with bipolar disorder can be as debilitating as the mood extremes see in bipolar I.

Cyclothymic Disorder

Cyclothymic disorder involves impairment in functioning resulting from milder hypomanic symptoms that are consistently interspersed with milder depressed moods for at least 2 years. For this diagnosis, the depressive moods must not reach the level of a major depressive episode and the energized symptoms must not meet the criteria for a hypomanic or manic episode. Additionally, the person must experience mood symptoms at least half of the time and never be symptom-free for more than 2 months. Cyclothymic disorder is similar to persistent depressive disorder (dysthymia) because the mood symptoms are chronic; however, with cyclothymic disorder there are also periods of hypomanic behavior. Some individuals diagnosed with cyclothymic disorder eventually meet the criteria for bipolar II if their mood symptoms become more severe (APA, 2013).

The DSM-5 includes a diagnostic category undergoing research, depressive episodes with short-duration hypomania, which includes individuals who have had a major depressive episode and at least two hypomanic periods that last at least 2–3 days (thus, not quite meeting the criteria for bipolar II).

Features and Conditions Associated with Bipolar Disorder

Bipolar disorder is associated with various features and comorbid conditions. For example, approximately one third of those with bipolar disorder exhibit both mixed features and rapid cycling (Koszewska & Rybakowski, 2009). **Mixed features** (i.e., three or more symptoms of hypomania/mania or depression occurring during an episode from the opposite pole) are common with both bipolar I and bipolar II (Judd et al., 2012). Mixed features is important to note because when hypomanic/manic symptoms occur with depressive symptoms, the risk of impulsive behaviors such as suicidal actions or substance abuse increases; those who have this pattern often require more intensive treatment (Valentí et al., 2011).

Rapid cycling, a pattern where there are four or more mood episodes per year, occurs in some individuals with bipolar disorder; this pattern is especially common among those who develop bipolar symptoms at an early age. Rapid cycling can be triggered by a variety of factors, including sleep deprivation and certain antidepressants (Fountoulakis, Kontis, Gonda, & Yatham, 2013). Rapid cycling increases the chance that the disorder will be chronic and that symptoms of mania, depression, and anxiety will be more severe (Nierenberg et al., 2010).

Those with bipolar disorder often have comorbid (concurrent) anxiety disorders (especially panic attacks), attention-deficit/hyperactivity disorder, and substance-use

bipolar II disorder diagnosis involves at least one major depressive episode and at least one hypomanic episode

cyclothymic disorder condition involving milder hypomanic symptoms that are consistently interspersed with milder depressed moods for at least 2 years

mixed features concurrent hypomanic/manic and depressive symptoms

rapid cycling the occurrence of four or more mood episodes per year

disorders. In fact, approximately three fourths of those with a bipolar disorder also have an anxiety disorder (APA, 2013). Unfortunately, both manic and depressive symptoms are more severe when accompanied by anxiety (Swann, Steinberg, et al., 2009). Surprisingly, many people with bipolar disorder meet the diagnostic criteria for three or more additional disorders (Merikangas, Jin, et al., 2011). Men with a bipolar disorder have an increased likelihood of having a coexisting substance-use disorder, whereas women with a bipolar diagnosis frequently have eating disorders, particularly binge-eating disorder and bulimia (McElroy et al., 2011; Suominen et al., 2009). Substance abuse is also common among those with bipolar disorder and can significantly increase the degree of impairment (Merikangas, Jin, et al., 2011). For example, more than half of one sample of individuals diagnosed with a bipolar disorder had a concurrent alcohol-use disorder and suicidal ideation (Oquendo et al., 2010). Those with coexisting conditions tend to develop bipolar disorder earlier and have longer episodes, as well as increased suicidal behavior (Baldassano, 2006).

Bipolar disorder is also associated with increased rates of physical illnesses such as hypertension, cardiovascular disease, and diabetes, as well as increased rates of death from suicide (Fagiolini, 2008; Ketter, 2010). In fact, individuals with bipolar disorder have a 20–30 times greater risk of completed suicide compared to the general population (Pompili et al., 2013). Antidepressant-induced suicidal behavior is a significant concern that affects some people with bipolar disorder; in fact, undiagnosed bipolar disorder may be responsible for some cases of suicidal ideation among adolescents and young adults taking antidepressants (Rihmer & Gonda, 2011).

Prevalence of Bipolar Disorders

The lifetime prevalence for bipolar I is 1.0 percent and 1.1 percent for bipolar II (see Figure 8.1), according to a large-scale national survey. Cyclothymic disorder has a lifetime prevalence rate between 0.4 and 1 percent (APA, 2013). Thus, bipolar disorders are far less prevalent than depressive disorders. It is important to recall, however, that bipolar disorder may be underdiagnosed. It is estimated that more than 10 percent of those diagnosed with a depressive disorder will eventually be diagnosed with a bipolar disorder (C. T. Li et al., 2012); in other words, a depressive disorder diagnosis can change to a bipolar diagnosis if hypomanic/manic symptoms become evident. Assessment instruments that contain self-ratings of hypomanic/manic symptoms and daily mood monitoring can help avoid misdiagnosis (Picardi, 2009). Although bipolar disorder can begin in childhood, onset more frequently occurs in late adolescence or early adulthood, suggesting that it is particularly important to monitor signs of depression and hypomania/mania among those in this age range.

Research on gender differences in bipolar disorder is mixed. Most researchers agree that there are no marked gender differences in the prevalence of bipolar I (Merikangas, Akiskal, et al., 2007), but that depressive and mixed features, bipolar II, and rapid cycling occur more frequently in women (Diflorio & Jones, 2010; Ketter, 2010). Women also have a higher risk that symptoms will recur (Suominen et al., 2009). As with depressive disorders, reproductive cycle changes, especially childbirth, can precipitate or worsen depressive bipolar episodes (Diflorio & Jones, 2010). The transition to menopause can also increase the frequency of depressive episodes (W. K. Marsh, Ketter, & Rasgon, 2009).

Although bipolar disorders are much less prevalent than depressive disorders, their costs are high. Bipolar disorder is associated with high unemployment and decreased work productivity (Ketter, 2010). In one study, bipolar disorder was associated with 65.5 annual lost workdays per ill worker, compared to 27.2 days for those with major depressive disorder; this is because those with bipolar disorder tend to have more severe and persistent depressive episodes (R. C. Kessler, Akiskal, et al., 2006). Furthermore, those with bipolar disorder often find that their symptoms recur; as the number of bipolar episodes increases, so does the likelihood of future episodes (Hollon, Stewart, et al., 2006).

Etiology of Bipolar Disorders

What explains the mood roller coaster experienced by those with bipolar disorders? Many of the psychological, social, and sociocultural factors that influence depressive disorders can also contribute to depressive episodes in bipolar disorder. In this section, we focus on factors that contribute to the hypomanic/manic episodes and mood switching seen in bipolar disorder. We conclude with a brief discussion of the overlap between bipolar disorder and another serious mental illness, schizophrenia.

Biological Dimension

Genetic factors contribute to bipolar disorder, a well-established finding from twin, adoption, and family studies. For example, the chance of developing bipolar I, bipolar II, or cyclothymic disorder when a twin is diagnosed with the condition is quite high—up to 72 percent for identical twins, compared to 14 percent for fraternal twins (Edvardsen et al., 2008). Bipolar disorders appear to have a complex genetic basis involving interactions among multiple genes, including several genes influenced by lithium, a chemical compound (Craddock & Sklar, 2013). Because individuals with bipolar disorders (like those with depressive disorders) have circadian rhythm abnormalities, it is not surprising that genes that influence our circadian cycle are also linked with vulnerability to bipolar disorder (Soria et al., 2010). Despite the high heritability of bipolar disorders, the exact biological mechanisms by which the various risk genes contribute to the development of these disorders remains unclear (Chuang, Kao, Shih, & Kuo, 2013). The variability of symptoms among those with bipolar disorders is likely due to varied combinations of risk genes combined with variations in the psychosocial stressors encountered by each individual.

Various neurological abnormalities are associated with bipolar symptoms. For example, irregularities in the way the brain processes and responds to stimuli associated with reward are associated with both manic and depressive symptoms. Consistent with this *dysregulation model of bipolar disorder*, individuals with bipolar disorders may show hypomanic/manic symptoms after reaching a goal; they also have a tendency to show anger and irritability in response to obstructed goals (Alloy & Abramson, 2010). Due to this high sensitivity to reward, mania can develop due to overly ambitious pursuit of goals and the brain dysregulation (i.e., excessive brain activation and increased energy output) that occurs when goals are attained (S. L. Johnson, Edge, Holmes, & Carver, 2012). This same hypersensitivity can cause a shutting down (i.e., deactivation) of motivational systems within the brain in response to perceived failures; this deactivation results in symptoms of depression, including decreased goal-directed activity, low energy, loss of interest, hopelessness, and sadness (Alloy & Abramson, 2010). Thus, individuals with hypersensitive neurological systems appear to have a vulnerability to bipolar disorder that is triggered by events that activate or deactivate brain systems involved in regulating energy and motivation.

It is likely that multiple biochemical pathways contribute to the symptoms associated with bipolar disorder. In a review of the literature, goal attainment, antidepressant medication use, disrupted circadian cycles, and seasonal increases in light triggered the onset of hypomanic/manic episodes in certain individuals (Proudfoot, Doran, Manicavasagar, & Parker, 2010). Some classes of drugs such as antidepressants (especially SSRIs) and stimulants such as cocaine and methamphetamine can trigger mania, thus implicating certain neurotransmitters (serotonin, norepinephrine, or dopamine) in the etiology of bipolar disorders (Soreff & McInnes, 2014). As with depressive disorder, hormonal influences and disruptions in the stress circuitry of the brain also contribute to bipolar symptoms. For example, multiple brain imaging studies have documented elevated glutamate neurotransmission (a neurotransmitter with stimulatory functions) in the brains of individuals with bipolar disorder (Gigante et al., 2012).

Evidence from neuroimaging studies suggests that individuals with bipolar disorders have functional and anatomical irregularities in brain networks, including reduced gray matter and decreased brain activation in regions associated with experiencing and regulating emotions and increased activation in regions associated with emotional responsiveness (Houenou et al., 2011). Bipolar I disorder, for example, is associated with irregularities in brain structure and function in regions of the brain involved with emotional regulation, particularly the limbic system and the amygdala; these abnormalities may explain the onset of mania and the chronic course of bipolar disorders (Strakowski et al., 2012). Brain injury has been found to precipitate manic episodes, especially in individuals with a family history of bipolar disorder (Mustafa, Evrim, & Sari, 2005); in fact, manic episodes are reported to affect up to 9 percent of those with traumatic brain injury (Oster, Anderson, Filley, Wortzel, & Arciniegas, 2007).

Other Etiological Factors Associated with Bipolar Disorders

Psychological and social factors may also influence the development and progression of bipolar disorders. For example, a major stressful event sometimes occurs just prior to the onset of bipolar symptoms (R. E. Bender & Alloy, 2011). Inadequate social support and strained social relationships are sometimes evident prior to the onset of both manic and depressive symptoms (Eidelman, Gershon, Kaplan, McGlinchey, & Harvey, 2012). Similar to patterns seen with depressive disorders, individuals with bipolar disorder tend to have selective attention for and recall of negative information about themselves (Molz-Adams, Shapero, Pendergast, Alloy, & Abramson, 2014). Rumination is common among individuals with bipolar disorder who experience depression; researchers theorize that rumination results from deficits in both executive functioning and emotional regulation (Ghaznavi & Deckersbach, 2012). While rumination is associated with depressive episodes, self-focused thinking patterns, perfectionism, and self-criticism are predictive of hypomanic/manic episodes (Alloy, Abramson, Walshaw, et al., 2009). Overall, however, biological factors appear to play a much more prominent role in the development of bipolar disorders compared to other factors. Additionally, evidence is mounting regarding common genetic vulnerabilities between bipolar disorders and schizophrenia.

Commonalities between Bipolar Disorders and Schizophrenia

It is now commonly accepted that bipolar disorder and schizophrenia, both chronic disorders with neurological irregularities and psychotic features, share genetic, neuroanatomical, and cognitive abnormalities. In fact, some contend that bipolar disorders (particularly bipolar I) are much more similar to schizophrenia than they are to depressive disorders (D. P. Goldberg, Krueger, Andrews, & Hobbs, 2009). Genome-wide studies have discovered risk alleles that contribute to both schizophrenia and bipolar disorder (Craddock & Sklar, 2013). Additionally, the increased prevalence of either bipolar disorder or schizophrenia among first-degree relatives of individuals with attention-deficit/hyperactivity disorder is attributed to shared genetic factors among the three disorders (Larsson et al., 2013).

Research comparing the neuroanatomy of schizophrenia and bipolar disorder reveals similar gray matter abnormalities in two brain regions; however, neuroimaging has also documented structural irregularities that are unique to each disorder. In the case of bipolar disorder, the brain regions affected tend to be less extensive and primarily involve areas related to emotional processing (Ellison-Wright & Bullmore, 2010). Additionally, there is substantial overlap in affected brain regions when comparing individuals with schizophrenia and people with bipolar disorder who experience psychosis during mood episodes (Khadka et al., 2013). Early environmental factors such as viral infections during pregnancy, birth complications, or other early stressors resulting in abnormal brain development early in life are implicated in both schizophrenia and bipolar disorder (Schmitt, Malchow, Hasan, & Falkai, 2014).

Bipolar disorder and schizophrenia also involve similar cognitive deficits, including confused thought processes and *poor insight* (failure to recognize symptoms of one's own mental illness). In schizophrenia, these difficulties are common throughout the course of the disorder. In bipolar disorder, this lack of insight and failure to recognize the inappropriateness of behavior occurs during hypomanic/manic episodes; insight is usually adequate during depressive episodes (F. Cassidy, 2010). Neurocognitive deficits that affect psychosocial competence and daily functioning are also present in both disorders, although the deficits are usually more severe and more pervasive in schizophrenia and in individuals with bipolar disorder who have experienced a psychotic episode (Hill et al., 2013; Vöhringer et al., 2013). Significant impairment in vocational functioning due to cognitive deficits involving attention, processing speed, and memory occur in both disorders (Bearden, Woogen, & Glahn, 2010).

Treatment for Bipolar Disorders

Therapy for bipolar disorders aims to eliminate symptoms to the greatest degree possible. As with depression, lingering or residual symptoms increase the likelihood of relapse and ongoing impairment (Marangell, Dennehy, et al., 2009). Intervention efforts, therefore, target current symptoms, as well as prevention of future hypomanic/manic and depressive episodes. Treatment focuses on the person's primary symptoms. For example, individuals with depressive episodes often benefit from the psychotherapies used to treat depressive disorders.

Effective treatment often involves a combination of psychotherapy, mood-stabilizing medications, and psychoeducation geared toward helping those with bipolar disorder (and their family members) understand the importance of regular use of prescribed medications and the mood regulation strategies learned in therapy. Additionally, clients benefit from learning how their sleep and circadian rhythm patterns influence mood fluctuations (Geddes & Miklowitz, 2013). It is important for those with bipolar disorder and their family members to remember that although bipolar disorder is a recurrent illness, each distressing mood episode is only temporary and that mood symptoms often become less severe with treatment.

Biomedical Treatments for Bipolar Disorders

Treatment for bipolar disorders can be complicated. It is not unusual for individuals with a bipolar disorder to take multiple medications, or to have multiple medication changes before discovering the correct combination of medications. Choices about medication vary depending on a person's present and past symptoms (e.g., severe mania; severe depression; rapid cycling; mixed or psychotic features). Most agree that medication is an essential component of treatment, not only in managing acute symptoms, but also in preventing relapse. Mood-stabilizing medications such as lithium are the foundation of treatment for bipolar disorder (J. O. Brooks et al., 2011). Although anticonvulsant and antipsychotic medications with mood-stabilizing properties are also used, lithium is considered the most effective mood-stabilizing medication for those who respond to its effects (Kessing, Hellmund, Geddes, Goodwin, & Andersen, 2011). Many studies have demonstrated that lithium decreases the risk of attempted and completed suicide (Cipriani, Hawton, Stockton, & Geddes, 2013). Lithium also appears to have neuroprotective effects, reducing the progressive shrinkage of the hippocampus associated with recurrent depressive episodes (Hajek, Kopecek, Höschl, & Alda, 2012). Lithium and other mood stabilizers are usually prescribed on an ongoing basis to prevent recurrence of depression or hypomania/mania. Antidepressants are sometimes added to deal with depressive symptoms. However, antidepressants are used cautiously with bipolar disorder—although they target depressive symptoms, there is a significant risk that they will produce or intensify hypomanic/manic symptoms (Geddes & Miklowitz, 2013).

Lisa O'Connor/Zuma/Corbis Wire/Corbis

Allstar Picture Library/Alamy

Overcoming Bipolar Disorder

Actor Ben Stiller has bipolar disorder, as do other members of his family. Following a stressful year and a brief hospital stay for treatment of bipolar II disorder, award-winning actress Catherine Zeta-Jones expressed hope that telling the public about her diagnosis would encourage others struggling with similar symptoms to seek help rather than suffer silently.

The generally positive results achieved with lithium and some other mood stabilizers may be overshadowed by serious side effects that can occur if blood levels of the medication and other physiological effects are not regularly monitored (McKnight et al., 2012). Fortunately, blood tests provide the information required to ensure safety and adjust medications or dosages, if necessary. If medications are taken regularly, symptoms of bipolar disorder can often be effectively controlled (Berk et al., 2010). When someone abruptly decreases or discontinues a medication, however, mood changes can occur rapidly.

Unfortunately, failure to take medication as prescribed is a major problem associated with lithium and other mood stabilizers. Individuals with bipolar disorder often report discontinuing or adjusting their own medication. This occurs for a variety of reasons, including weight gain; feelings of sedation; difficulty remembering to take medications; a desire to re-create the energetic or excited experience of hypomania; or a belief that the medication is no longer needed (Velligan et al., 2009). Making medication changes against medical advice is most likely to occur if judgment is impaired by hypomania/mania or by drug or alcohol abuse (Sajatovic et al., 2009). Psychoeducation that emphasizes the link between the regular use of medication and long-term improvement is an important aspect of treatment (Berk et al., 2010).

Various biomedical interventions are used with bipolar disorder. Many people with bipolar disorder benefit from social rhythm therapy, a treatment that teaches participants to avoid disruption of bodily rhythm patterns by developing regular eating, sleeping, and exercise routines (D. Lam, 2009). Light therapy is used cautiously, if at all, in individuals with bipolar disorder, due to concerns about light exposure precipitating hypomanic/manic episodes (McClung, 2007). ECT is sometimes successful in treating severe depression or acute mania (Loo, Katalinic, Mitchell, & Greenberg. 2011).

Psychosocial Treatments for Bipolar Disorders

CASE STUDY   Learning about bipolar disorder has helped Gabriela manage her symptoms. She takes her mood-stabilizing medications regularly, and has an antianxiety medication she uses when anxiety symptoms develop when she is depressed. She tries to go to bed and wake up around the same time each day, and has another medication she takes if she starts waking up alert after only a few hours of sleep, a sign that she might be moving into an energized episode. She has several friends who have learned about bipolar disorder and who let her know if it seems like her mood is changing. She has also stopped self-medicating with alcohol or marijuana. Instead, she tries to use the mindfulness meditation skills, relaxation, and problem-solving strategies she is learning in therapy. She realizes that managing her symptoms will be a lifelong challenge, but is confident that she is learning the strategies she needs to cope when symptoms develop.

Psychosocial therapies such as family-focused therapy, interpersonal therapy, and cognitive-behavioral therapy play a key role in helping those with bipolar disorder address the psychological and social factors that contribute to mood instability and thus help reduce symptom severity, prevent relapse, and enhance psychosocial functioning (Geddes & Miklowitz, 2013). Educating families about bipolar disorder and teaching communication and problem-solving skills to all family members is effective in reducing the risk of relapse and hospitalization (C. D. Morris, Miklowitz, & Waxmonsky, 2007). As we saw with Gabriela, individuals with bipolar disorder benefit from learning strategies to help manage their illness. Thus, therapists teach clients to avoid stress and overly ambitious goal setting, practice emotional regulation techniques, identify signs of an impending mood episode, and understand the dangers of substance abuse (Miklowitz et al., 2012). Additionally, because sleep deprivation is linked with poor emotional regulation and exaggerated brain reactivity to both negative and positive experiences (Gujar, Yoo, Hu, & Walker, 2011), interventions focused on regulating sleep patterns can help prevent the vicious cycle of disrupted sleep leading to increased emotional reactivity (Eidelman, Talbot, Gruber, & Harvey, 2010). Mindfulness interventions have proven successful in helping those with bipolar disorder regulate their moods, especially when mindfulness practices are used at the onset of a mood episode (Chadwick, Kaur, Swelam, Ross, & Ellett, 2011).

Contemporary Trends and Future Directions

Researchers and mental health professionals are directing considerable effort toward preventing depressive and bipolar disorders, taking into consideration the fact that child maltreatment and other early adverse experiences increase vulnerability to depressive symptoms. Our brains have high neuroplasticity early in life, recording memories of our interactions with the environment so we can effectively adapt to the circumstances we may need to confront. Unfortunately, stressors occurring in early childhood set the stage for brain changes that are associated with depression and mood dysregulation. Researchers are increasingly aware that epigenetic changes that occur during critical periods such as fetal development or early childhood can exert lifelong effects on our physiological reactivity in response to life stressors (Reynolds, 2013). Thus, efforts to prevent early childhood stress and trauma are essential if we hope to decrease the prevalence of depressive and bipolar disorders. Some researchers are even hoping to develop medications that increase the brain's neuroplasticity in adulthood, making it possible to undo some of the "faulty wiring" and maladaptive neurological patterns that develop based on damaging early life experiences (Hayley & Litteljohn, 2013).

Accurate diagnosis and effective treatment of depressive and bipolar disorders are also a high priority, especially because the symptoms of these disorders often strike in the prime of a person's life and frequently follow a chronic course. Thus, researchers are searching for the best psychological and medical treatments for those who develop early symptoms of these disorders. For example, some researchers are attempting to identify psychological factors that increase risk of depression, such as rumination, so that interventions can occur before these behaviors become habitual (Michl, McLaughlin, Shepherd, & Nolen-Hoeksema, 2013).

Researchers are also hoping to revolutionize the treatment for bipolar and depressive disorders though **personalized medicine**; once available, this approach would determine a person's vulnerability to developing certain illnesses and identify which therapies would be most effective based on the individual's unique genetic profile or physiological characteristics (Ozomaro, Wahlestedt, & Nemeroff, 2013). Thus, biologically based diagnostic tests rather than subjective symptoms would guide treatment. Personalized medicine will not only improve diagnosis, but will also determine the most efficient treatment with the least side effects. Clinicians will be able to choose the most optimal pharmacological and psychotherapeutic treatments at different stages of depressive or bipolar illnesses (Geddes & Miklowitz, 2013).

Fortunately, scientists are making some progress in using genetic testing to determine how an individual might respond to certain antidepressant medications; however, this work is still in its infancy (Miller & O'Callaghan, 2013). It is hoped that at some point in the near future brain imaging will be able to guide diagnosis and treatment decisions (Savitz, Rauch, & Drevets, 2013). The use of biological technologies will be particularly helpful in differentiating between recurring major depressive disorder and bipolar II disorder early in the course of the illness so that appropriate treatment can be initiated when symptoms first appear (Phillips & Kupfer, 2013).

personalized medicine use of a person's genetic profile to guide decisions about prevention and treatment of disease and mental disorders

chapter SUMMARY

1 What are the symptoms of depression and mania?

- Depression involves feelings of sadness or emptiness, social withdrawal, loss of interest in activities, pessimism, low energy, and sleep and appetite disturbances.

- Mania produces significant impairment and involves high levels of arousal, elevated or irritable mood, increased activity, poor judgment, grandiosity, and decreased need for sleep. Hypomania refers to milder manic symptoms, which may be accompanied by productive, goal-directed behaviors.

2 What are depressive disorders, what causes them, and how are they treated?

- Depressive disorders are diagnosed only when depressive symptoms occur without a history of hypomania/mania. Depressive disorders include major depressive disorder, persistent depressive disorder (dysthymia), and premenstrual dysphoric disorder.

- Biological factors, including heredity, increase vulnerability to depression. Biochemical irregularities involving neurotransmitters, stress reactivity, and cortisol levels are associated with depression.

- Behavioral explanations for depression focus on reduced reinforcement following losses. Cognitive explanations focus on negative attributions and thinking patterns, irrational beliefs, and rumination.

- Social explanations focus on relationships and interpersonal stressors that increase vulnerability to depression. Early childhood stressors are particularly important.

- Sociocultural explanations have focused on cultural factors, including gender, ethnicity, and sexual orientation.

- Behavioral activation therapy, cognitive-behavioral therapy, and interpersonal psychotherapy have received extensive research support as treatments for depression; mindfulness-based cognitive therapy has also shown promising results. Biomedical treatments include light therapy and electrical stimulation of the brain. Antidepressant medications are frequently used to treat depression; they are most effective with severe depression, but produce only temporary effects. Psychotherapy is more likely to prevent the return of depressive symptoms.

3 What are bipolar disorders, what causes them, and how are they treated?

- Bipolar disorders involve symptoms of mania or hypomania. Depressive episodes are also common in bipolar disorder.

- Bipolar I involves at least one weeklong manic episode and impaired functioning. Psychotic symptoms are sometimes present. Bipolar II is diagnosed only if there is a history of hypomania and at least one major depressive episode. Cyclothymic disorder is a chronic disorder involving milder hypomanic episodes that alternate with depressed mood for at least 2 years.

- Bipolar disorders have a strong genetic basis involving multiple, interacting genes. Biological factors, including neurochemical and neuroanatomical abnormalities and circadian rhythm disturbances, contribute to bipolar disorder. There are many overlaps between bipolar disorder and schizophrenia.

- The most effective treatment for bipolar disorders is ongoing use of mood-stabilizing medication combined with psychotherapy, psychoeducation, and psychosocial interventions.

9

SUICIDE

Chapter Outline

LATE ONE EVENING, CARL JOHNSON, MD, LEFT HIS DOWNTOWN OFFICE, got into his Mercedes-Benz S600, and drove toward his expensive suburban home. He was in no hurry, because the house would be empty anyway; his wife had divorced him and moved back east with their children. Although he had been drinking heavily for 2 years before his wife left him, he had always been able to function at work. Now he was unable to stop thinking about his failed marriage. For the past several months, his private practice had declined dramatically. He had once found his work meaningful, but now his patients bored and irritated him. Although he had suffered from depression in the past, this time it was different. The future had never looked so bleak and hopeless. Carl knew he was in serious trouble—he was, after all, a psychiatrist.

Carl parked carelessly, not bothering to press the switch that closed the garage door. Once in the house, he headed directly for his den. There he pulled out a bottle of bourbon and three glasses, filled each glass to the rim, and lined them up along the bar. He drank them down, one after the other, in rapid succession. For a good hour he stood at the window, staring out into the night. Then Carl sat down at his mahogany desk and unlocked one of the drawers. Taking a loaded .38-caliber revolver from the desk drawer, Carl held it to his temple and pulled the trigger. He died instantly.

Suicide—the intentional, direct, and conscious taking of one's own life—is as old as human history itself, so its occurrence is not rare. Suicide is not only a tragic act; it is also difficult to comprehend. Why would someone like Dr. Johnson choose to take his own life? Granted, he was depressed and obviously feeling the loss of his family, but most people under similar circumstances are able to cope and move forward. Why couldn't he see that he had other options? Unfortunately, we will never know the answer. Research on suicide, however, offers clues. First, he had a history of alcohol abuse, a biological factor implicated in suicide (Akbarian & Halene, 2013). Second, psychological factors such as hopelessness and depression are associated with suicide (Ali et al., 2013). Third, social factors clearly influenced Dr. Johnson's mental distress; perhaps the loss of his family made him believe life was no longer meaningful. People who lack or who

focus
QUESTIONS

1 What do we know about suicide?

2 How is suicide unique in different age groups?

3 How does suicide affect friends and family?

4 What might cause someone to commit suicide?

5 How can we prevent suicide?

6 What are future directions in the field of suicidology?

have ruptured social relationships are more likely to commit suicide (Rudd, Joiner, & Rajab, 2004). Finally, there are sociocultural aspects to Dr. Johnson's suicide. His gender and occupation are significant factors. Men are more likely to kill themselves compared to women. And occupationally, psychiatrists have one of the highest rates of suicide (Comtois & Linehan, 2006). Clearly, Dr. Johnson was at high risk for suicide on a number of risk dimensions.

Suicide has been extensively researched. We are able to identify suicide risk factors, delineate protective factors, and even develop strategies to successfully intervene with people contemplating suicide. But there is much we don't know. We still have no definitive answer to the question: "Why do people kill themselves?" Most of us believe that life is precious, and we operate under strong moral, religious, and cultural sanctions against taking our own lives. In fact, individuals who commit suicide are often described as weak, cowardly, selfish, or sinful (Sand, Gordon, & Bresin, 2013). Although explanations abound for suicide, we can never be entirely certain why people knowingly and deliberately end their own lives. Research suggests that people kill themselves for many different reasons (Granello, 2010).

A separate chapter on suicide is provided in this text for several reasons. First, although DSM-5 does not include suicide as a specific mental disorder, people who contemplate suicide usually have psychiatric symptoms. Up to 90 percent have a mental illness, often undiagnosed, such as depression, bipolar disorder, post-traumatic stress disorder (PTSD), substance-use disorder, anxiety disorders, personality disorders, or schizophrenia (APA, 2013; Soreff, 2013). In fact, it is common for people with these disorders to have suicidal thoughts and exhibit suicidal behavior (Nock et al., 2014). Although there is no current diagnostic category for those who contemplate or attempt suicide, some researchers and clinicians believe that suicide and **suicidal ideation**—thoughts about suicide—represent a distinct clinical condition warranting a unique diagnostic label; we will discuss this perspective later in the chapter.

Additionally, the fact that suicide is the tenth leading cause of death for all U.S. Americans reinforces the importance of this topic (Murphy, Xu, & Kochanek, 2013). Unfortunately, throughout history, people have avoided discussing suicide; the shame and stigma involved in taking one's life have produced a "conspiracy of silence." Even mental health professionals find the topic uncomfortable and deeply disturbing (R. A. Friedman, 2004). Discussing suicide is of critical importance, however, because it is an irreversible act. The decision to commit suicide is often an ambivalent one, clouded by many personal and social stressors. Unfortunately, once the action is taken, there is no going back. Many mental health professionals believe that when people who are feeling suicidal are given appropriate support in coping with personal and social crises, their pain lessens and they begin to see options beyond taking their own life. Most do not want to die; they simply want their pain to end and are unable to see other solutions (Granello & Granello, 2007). Thus, it is extremely important to understand factors associated with suicide; it is even more critical to understand and implement strategies for preventing suicide. Suicide prevention is also crucial because of the devastating psychological effects experienced by the friends and family of those who commit suicide.

suicide the intentional, direct, and conscious taking of one's own life

suicidal ideation thoughts about suicide

psychological autopsy the systematic examination of existing information after a person's death for the purpose of understanding and explaining the person's behavior before death

Facts about Suicide

People who commit suicide—who complete their suicide attempt—can no longer share their thoughts, motives, or emotional state. We have only indirect information, such as case records and reports by others, to help us understand what led to their heartbreaking act. Systematically examining information after a person's death in an effort to understand and explain a person's behavior before death is called a **psychological autopsy** (C. A. King & Merchant, 2008). Psychological autopsies are patterned on the *medical autopsy*, which involves the examination of a corpse to determine the cause of death. A psychological autopsy attempts to make psychological sense of a suicide by compiling and analyzing background information, including recollections of therapists, interviews with relatives and friends, information obtained from crisis phone calls, social media postings, and messages left in suicide notes.

Unfortunately, these sources are not always available or reliable. Often there is no suicide note and no previous contact with a therapist. Additionally, the judgment of friends and family may be clouded by their intense feelings of hurt and shock. Another strategy involves studying those who survive suicide attempts. This method, however, assumes that people who attempt suicide are no different from those who complete the act. Despite these limitations, researchers use all available data to better understand the personal characteristics and demographics associated with suicide, and to develop profiles for at-risk individuals (SAMHSA, 2012a). Table 9.1 summarizes some of the characteristics associated with suicide.

Table 9.1 Common Characteristics of Suicide

1. Belief that things will never change and that suicide is the only solution.

2. Desire to escape from psychological pain and distressing thoughts and feelings.

3. Triggering events including intense interpersonal conflicts and feelings of depression, hopelessness, guilt, anger, or shame.

4. Perceived inability to make progress toward goals or to solve problems; related feelings of failure, worthlessness, and hopelessness.

5. Ambivalence about suicide; there is a strong underlying desire to live.

6. Suicidal intent is communicated directly or indirectly through verbal or behavioral cues.

SOURCE: Shneidman (1998); Van Heeringen & Marusic (2003).

Prevalence of Suicidal Behavior

Suicidal behavior and ideation begin with an individual's initial suicidal thoughts. Some people then develop a plan and an even smaller number attempt suicide. Suicide without prior planning is rare (see Figure 9.1). Fleeting suicidal thoughts are not uncommon; even among those with more serious thoughts of suicide, most never attempt suicide. However, about 1 million U.S. adults make a suicide attempt each year. It is estimated that there is one completed suicide for every 25 suicide attempts; for the young (those 15 to 24 years of age), the ratio of attempts to completed suicides is much greater (CDC, 2012c).

Sadly, every 15 minutes or so, someone in the United States succeeds in taking his or her own life. Approximately 38,000 people kill themselves each year. Suicide is among the top 10 causes of death in industrialized parts of the world; it is the eighth leading cause of death among U.S. American males, the third leading cause of death among young people ages 15–24, and the second leading cause of death among college students (Drum, Brownson, Denmark, & Smith, 2009; SAMHSA, 2012a). Some evidence shows that the number of actual suicides is probably 25–30 percent higher than that recorded.

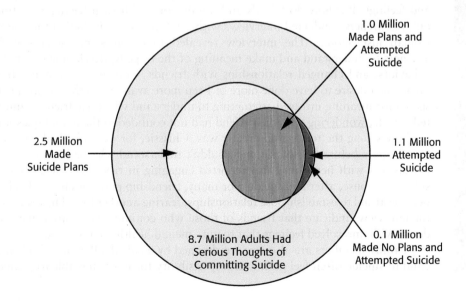

1.0 Million Made Plans and Attempted Suicide

2.5 Million Made Suicide Plans

1.1 Million Attempted Suicide

8.7 Million Adults Had Serious Thoughts of Committing Suicide

0.1 Million Made No Plans and Attempted Suicide

Figure 9.1

According to data from the 2010 National Survey on Drug Use and Health (NSDUH), an estimated 8.7 million adults (3.8 percent of those age 18 and over) had serious thoughts of suicide during the year. However, the vast majority (88 percent) of those with serious suicidal thoughts did not attempt suicide.
SOURCE: SAMHSA (2012b).

Suicide Methods

The most common methods of suicide in the United States in 2010 included:

Firearms: 50.5 percent

Suffocation/hanging: 24.7 percent

Poisoning/drug overdose: 17.2 percent

Cutting/piercing: 1.8 percent

Drowning: 1.1 percent

SOURCE: CDC WISQARS, 2013

Many deaths deemed accidental—such as single-auto crashes, drownings, and falls from great heights—are actually suicides (CDC, 2010d).

Choice of Method

More than 50 percent of completed suicides are committed with the use of firearms, and 70 percent of suicide attempts involve drug overdose (NIMH, 2011c). Hanging/suffocation, another common method, has increased in recent years for all age groups, especially among those ages 45–59 (Baker, Hu, Wilcox, & Baker, 2013). Older adolescents most frequently try hanging, jumping, and firearms; girls are more likely to use drug or alcohol intoxication (Hepp, Stulz, Unger-Köppel, & Ajdacic-Gross, 2012). Among children younger than 15, the most common suicide methods involve jumping from buildings or running into traffic. Younger children attempt suicide impulsively and thus use whatever means is most readily available.

Occupation

Physicians, lawyers, law enforcement personnel, and dentists have higher than average rates of suicide (Soreff, 2013). Among medical professionals, psychiatrists have the highest rate and pediatricians the lowest. It is unknown whether the specialty influences susceptibility or whether people who are prone to suicide are more likely to be attracted to certain specialties. The suicide rate for female physicians is 4 times higher than that of women of a similar age. Researchers speculate that burnout, stress, the availability of drugs, and guilt over medical errors increase the risk of suicide among physicians (Joelving, 2011).

Depression and Suicide

Paris Jackson, daughter of singer Michael Jackson, was hospitalized after a suicide attempt in January, 2014. Like many youth who attempt suicide, she was reportedly overwhelmed by stress and severe depression. Here she attends a party 15 months prior to her suicide attempt.

ZUMA Press, Inc./Alamy

Effects of Suicide on Friends and Family

> I probably should have helped a bit more. . . . I regret not having rung him up or checked up on him, I heard he was doing better, he was picking up again and then they found him hanging (Bartik, Maple, Edwards, & Kiernan, 2013, p. 214).

Friends of those who commit suicide often experience these kinds of thoughts and feelings. But how do friends and family cope with such feelings? To find out, researchers conducted interviews with 10 "survivors," including the young woman just quoted. The interview revealed four consistent themes—guilt, attempts to understand and make meaning of the tragedy, development of risky behaviors, and changed relationships with friends. Guilt was common, often involving a desire to have done more or been more available to the friend. Their search for meaning involved attempting to understand why their friend committed suicide, wondering why their friend had not confided in them, and questioning how strong the relationship really was. Chrissie, for example, had seen her friend hours before his suicide and couldn't understand why he hadn't shared his distress with her. Some also reported engaging in risky behavior, such as substance abuse, after the suicide. For many, friendship patterns changed. They became afraid to establish close relationships, fearing another loss. The results of the interviews indicate that friends of those who commit suicide are often burdened with unresolved feelings that require mental health intervention.

Family members are also forever changed by a suicide. Parents who lose a child to suicide often feel guilt and responsibility for not being able to protect

Bob Daemmrich/The Image Works

Shepard Sherbell/Corbis

Religion and Suicide

Many religions have strong taboos and sanctions against suicide. In countries in which Catholicism and Islam are strong, for example, the rates of suicide tend to be lower than in countries with fewer religious sanctions against suicide.

their child. Rates of depression, anxiety, alcohol abuse and marital difficulties increase, especially in the 2 years following a child's suicide (Bolton et al., 2013). In cases of the death of a child, recovery sometimes involves finding a new purpose to life (Rogers, Floyd, & Hong, 2008). Losing a parent to suicide is also incredibly painful.

CASE STUDY   I am 27 years old. . . . I lost my father . . . to suicide 26 years ago. He was 53 years old at the time and suffered from manic depression. I did not know him. I did not know his pain, but I have grown up wondering who he was, what his life was like? I have been haunted with so many questions over the years. Wondering why I wasn't enough for him to live. . . . As a teenager, this grief, mixed with my own personal struggles, accumulated into a huge messy, confusing ball of emotions. And in my own deepest times of sadness, I convinced myself that I no longer wanted to live. That the pain of life was too great. . . . I decided I wanted to die. I . . . started swallowing all of the pills. . . . I remember feeling content in dying. And then, what seems like hours later, but was only minutes later, I felt really, really scared. I started feeling the physical effects of the medication, and it shook me so hard that I went and woke up my mom in the next room and told her what I had done. That I needed her help. That I did not want to die anymore. . . . I am now a young adult who has known many great joys in life. I have travelled. I have loved. . . . If my story can help anyone in realizing how serious depression and mental illness is, and how necessary it is to seek help and look for signs, then I am happy to share it (Diles, 2013).

Suicide Prevention: Reinforcing Protective Factors

The majority of people who are suicidal do not truly wish to end their lives (Granello & Granello, 2007). When helped to understand the origins of their distress and the resources and options available to them, they inevitably choose life over death. This motivation to live is one of the primary protective mechanisms for individuals who are suicidal. One of the most effective ways to prevent someone from following through with a suicide plan is to use a strength-based approach, guided by questions such as: "What are the factors that protect against suicide? How can I use this information to help mobilize coping skills and social support?"

Four protective techniques are especially effective in preventing suicide: (1) reawakening and reinforcing the desire to live, (2) expanding perceptual outlook by reducing suicide myopia, (3) enhancing social connectedness, and (4) increasing the repertoire of coping skills.

1. *Reawakening and reinforcing the desire to live.* Most people possess a natural barrier against suicide. Once we cross that barrier, however, it becomes easier to act against our moral, ethical, or religious upbringing and to ignore the consequences of suicidal actions (P. N. Smith, Cukrowicz, Poindexter, Hobson, & Cohen, 2010). When speaking with someone who is suicidal, it helps to immediately and forcefully reinforce this barrier to prevent it from being crossed; it is especially helpful to focus on concrete actions aimed at connecting the person with friends and loved ones so that purpose and meaning in life can be revived or further developed (Joiner, 2005).

2. *Expanding perceptual outlook by reducing suicide myopia.* Most people contemplating suicide are overwhelmed by powerful emotions. This often results in confused thinking and a very constricted and narrow perception of problems and options. Conversation can help the person broaden his or her outlook and begin to consider solutions other than suicide. Additionally, our perspective often broadens when we engage in interesting or meaningful activities, including volunteer or leisure activities.

3. *Enhancing social connectedness.* Research increasingly reveals that social support, integration with family, and connectedness to schools, peers, and friends are powerful antidotes to suicide (Roy, Carli, & Sarchiapone, 2011). People who are suicidal often feel lonely, isolated, and disconnected from others, especially those who love them. Many people who consider suicide fail to recognize that friends and family care deeply about them and that there is a purpose to their lives. Therefore, effective interventions often involve reestablishing and strengthening relationships with friends and family. If a client has few social supports, involvement with clubs, support groups (such as NAMI on Campus), volunteer activities, or religious or spiritual pursuits can help fill this void.

4. *Increasing the repertoire of coping skills.* Contemplation of suicide is often associated with difficulty coping with a loss, relationship conflicts, or problematic life events. The more a person is able to regulate emotions and handle difficult situations, the less likely the person is to attempt suicide. Therefore, it helps to broaden the person's repertoire of coping strategies and possible steps to take when feeling overwhelmed—actions that can act as a buffer to suicide. Some possible actions might include:

   - Reaching out to supportive friends, family, or professionals.

   - Engaging in relaxing, enjoyable, or stress-reducing activities.

   - Practicing good self-care, including eating healthy foods, exercising, and getting sufficient sleep.

   - Contacting local crisis resources if there is a need for emergency support.

Therapists often help clients rehearse what specific actions to take if or when suicidal thoughts emerge. Another possible method of enhancing coping comes from a recent innovative study using positive psychology techniques: Individuals hospitalized for suicidal thoughts or behaviors who participated in exercises involving (1) gratitude (either recalling and writing about recent events for which they were grateful or writing a letter of gratitude to thank someone for a kind act) or (2) personal strengths (taking a survey to identify personal strengths, using one of the strengths for the next 24 hours, and then writing about the experience) exhibited increased optimism and decreased hopelessness, changes that would be predicted to decrease suicidality (Huffman et al., 2014). In summary, it is of critical importance for anyone who has been contemplating or who has attempted suicide to focus on activities that increase optimism and social connection and to realize that there is hope for a positive future once current, overwhelming concerns are resolved.

Photodisc/Getty Images

As you can see from this poignant story shared by Katrina Diles, suicide of a parent can have lifelong effects, even when a child is young at the time of the death. Children who have lost a parent to suicide not only have an increased risk for developing mental health problems, but, like Katrina, they have an increased risk of suicide attempts themselves; the risk is greatest if the deceased parent was the mother. Children whose fathers committed suicide have an increased likelihood of being hospitalized for depression or anxiety (Kuramoto et al., 2010). In a study of 26,096 offspring who experienced parental suicide, two different patterns of suicide attempts were found depending on the age of the child when the suicide occurred. For children who lost their parent to suicide during early childhood (up to 12 years of age) the rate of suicide attempts requiring hospitalization steadily increased over decades. In contrast, those who experienced parental suicide during adolescence or early adulthood (13 to 24 years of age) had the highest risk of hospitalization for suicide attempts during the first 2 years after the suicide—a risk that declined over time (Kuramoto, Runeson, Stuart, Lichtenste, & Wilcox, 2013).

CASE STUDY   My husband of only 8 months took his life in front of me all while I was pregnant with our daughter. Early in our marriage, I noticed he had changed. He had once attempted suicide with his gun in front of me. That time, I'm not exactly sure how I was able to diffuse the situation but we got through it. I didn't know how to take it because I was not educated on signs of suicide or depression. Each time my husband had been extremely intoxicated. I wish I would have known that he was suffering from some type of depression. My husband never asked for help. The day he committed suicide was the saddest day of my life. I keep asking myself why. I wonder why he made me a witness to his suicide. I wonder if he even loved me and the children. I will never know why. I now realize how important it is to get the ones we love the help they need when they show signs. I deeply regret not being aware . . . (Ester, 2013).

Her husband's decision to end his life has clearly had an everlasting change on Ester. We can only wonder what the effect has been for her children, including the child born after his death. As these stories demonstrate, those who are left behind after a suicide are forever touched by the traumatic loss of their loved one.

Suicide and Specific Populations

In this section, we discuss the occurrence of suicide in various groups: children and adolescents, college students, baby boomers, military personnel, and those who are elderly.

Suicide among Children and Adolescents

Suicide among young people is an unmentioned tragedy in our society. We find it difficult to acknowledge that children and teens find life so painful that they consciously and deliberately take their own lives. Suicide is now the third leading cause of death among persons 15 to 24 years old. According to an extensive national survey, 15.8 percent of high school students had seriously considered attempting suicide and another 7.8 percent had made an actual attempt in the previous 12 months. Overall, female students (19.3 percent) more frequently reported having seriously considered attempting suicide compared to male students (12.5 percent) (CDC, 2012c). Among students in grades 9 through 12, Hispanic/Latino and American Indian/Alaska Native females have the highest incidence of attempted suicide (13.5 percent and 19.9 percent, respectively), compared to 7.9 percent for European American, 8.8 percent for African American, and 15.0 percent for Asian American female students (CDC, 2012c).

Many reasons have been proposed for recent increases in suicide among young children and teenagers: attempts to regain control of their lives, retaliation or revenge against wrongs, reunion fantasies with a loved one, relief from unbearable pain, escape from being a family scapegoat, and acting out their parents' covert or overt desire to be rid of them. Drug use is also a factor associated with increased suicide risk among adolescents, particularly those using heroin, methamphetamine, and steroids (Wong, Zhou, Goebert, & Hishinuma, 2013). Adolescence and young adulthood are often periods of confusing emotions, identity formation, and questioning. It is a difficult and turbulent time for most teenagers, and suicide may seem to be a logical response to the pain and stress of growing up. Some point to three other possible reasons for the increase in suicide among children and adolescents—bullying, copycat suicides, and the decreased use of antidepressants with this age group (Bates & Bowles, 2012).

The Role of Bullying

CASE STUDY   Rebecca Ann Sedwich, a 12-year-old Florida girl, died after jumping from the roof of a concrete factory, allegedly after being bullied online by over a dozen girls. Some of the messages she received suggested she should kill herself. The situation was so distressing that Rebecca researched methods of suicide. Just before she jumped to her death, she changed her online name to "That Dead Girl" (AP, 2013).

The parents of the 15 girls who allegedly participated in the bullying were cooperative with the police and handed over cellphones and laptops to assist with the investigation. Two of the girls were charged with aggravated stalking, but the charges were eventually dropped.

It is evident from the tragic death of Rebecca Ann Sedwich that bullying can have serious consequences. Unfortunately, bullying is pervasive, especially during the teen years. Data from a 2009 survey revealed that one third of teens reported being bullied at school, including physical bullying, threats, and being the target of teasing, rumors, gossip, or coercion. This statistic is of particular concern because victims of bullying are 2 to 9 times more likely to consider suicide than those not subjected to bullying; nearly 50 percent of young people who commit suicide have experienced bullying (Bullying Statistics, 2009). Victims of bullying also have a high risk for developing an anxiety disorder, and those who are both bullies and victims are at risk for developing depression, panic disorder, and suicidality (Copeland, Wolke, Angold, & Costello, 2013).

If people observe bullying, do they intervene? As you might imagine, speaking up against a bully takes courage. Researchers recently set up an experiment in which two confederates participated in a Facebook discussion with 37 undergraduate females regarding the topic of same-sex marriage; one of the confederates began to bully the other confederate about her comments in the discussion. This resulted in 90.6 percent of the participants attempting to intervene in some way (attacking the bully, changing the subject, offering comfort to the victim, or directly asking that the bullying stop). It is a promising sign to see that most individuals realized that bullying was occurring and tried to intervene (Freis & Gurung, 2013). This supports the finding that the most effective way to curtail bullying is to unequivocally state that bullying is occurring and that it needs to stop (Aboud & Miller, 2007).

Copycat Suicides

Considerable attention has been directed to so-called copycat suicides (suicide contagion) in which youngsters in a particular school or community attempt suicide in response to the suicide of a peer (Alcantara & Gone, 2008). Among children and youth 12 to 17 years old, personally knowing someone who committed suicide is associated with an increase in suicidal thoughts and attempts (Swanson & Colman, 2013). Suggestion and imitation seem to play an especially powerful role in the increased risk of suicide among peers following a suicide. For this reason, schools implement suicide prevention and intervention programs so that students have an opportunity to receive support in an environment equipped to respond appropriately.

Media reports of suicides, especially by celebrities, also seem to spark an increase in suicide (Niederkrotenthaler et al., 2012). Research has indicated that publicizing a suicide may have the effect of glorifying and drawing attention to it. People who are depressed may identify with the pain of someone who has committed suicide, increasing their own suicide risk. This pattern appears to be especially true for youngsters who may already be thinking about killing themselves; stable, well-adjusted teenagers do not seem to be at risk in these situations. Although young people may be especially vulnerable to the phenomenon of suicide contagion, studies indicate that highly publicized suicides such as those of a celebrity or another well-known person, or the suicide of a close friend, relative, or co-worker, also increase suicide attempts in adults (Gould, 2007).

Tragic Consequences of Bullying

Rehtaeh Parsons, of Halifax, Nova Scotia, was taken off life support after attempting to commit suicide by hanging. Her family says she decided to end her own life following months of bullying, including online distribution of a digital photograph of her taken during an alleged gang rape. Here friends and family are holding pictures of Rehtaeh as they remember her during a community vigil.

Decrease in Antidepressant Medication

Another explanation for the increase in youth suicides relates to the 2004 U.S. Food and Drug Administration (FDA) warning of an increased suicide risk for children and adolescents taking selective serotonin reuptake inhibitor (SSRI) antidepressants. Although antidepressants can sometimes help youth experiencing depression, the FDA noted an increase in suicidal thoughts and actions among some youth taking SSRIs, and required that a warning to this effect be distributed with all such medication. There is considerable controversy over the actions of the FDA (Brent, 2009b; Ludwig, Marcotte, & Norberg, 2009). Although the effect of SSRIs on the suicide rates in young people is still unresolved (Gibbons, Brown, Hur, Davis, & Mann, 2012; Spielmans, Jureidini, Healy, & Purssey, 2013), it remains best practice for medical and mental health professionals to monitor suicidal ideation in anyone who is depressed, especially during the first 4 weeks of medication use (NIMH, 2013d). As we discussed in Chapter 8, researchers are continuing to search for biological indicators that will accurately predict who might experience suicidal ideation when taking antidepressants.

Suicide among Military Veterans

CASE STUDY   Leslie McCaddon listened with alarm when she overheard her husband, an Army physician, calling home during a break in his work at a local military hospital, tell their 9-year-old daughter, "Do me a favor . . . Give your mommy a hug and tell her that I love her." A few minutes later, he sent her an e-mail message stating, "This is the hardest e-mail I've ever written . . . Please always tell my children how much I love them, and most importantly, never, ever let them find out how I died . . . I love you. Mike." He was later found hanging in a room at the hospital where he worked (Thompson & Gibbs, 2012, p. 24).

There has been a surge in suicides in the military over the last few years with 349 deaths in 2012—more than the 295 combat-related deaths reported in Afghanistan during the same period (Chappel, 2013). What accounts for this increase in suicides among military members? Is it due to deployments in war zones, separation from families, or perhaps the military experience itself? There have been many reports suggesting that the military creates a culture that tends to dismiss and to stigmatize mental health issues; this culture may inhibit individuals from seeking help for mental stress.

Sadly, Leslie McCaddon's husband was battling depression and had reportedly tried to get help six times during the 3 days before his death. Additionally, Leslie met with her husband's commander to try to explain the anguish that her husband was feeling. Although barriers to seeking mental health care may contribute to the rates of suicide among the military, service members also face other significant stressors, including frequent separation from family, deployments, access to alcohol and drugs, loss of comrades, PTSD, and financial or personal problems associated with serving in the military. Additionally, traumatic brain injuries sustained in combat can lead to depression and suicidal thoughts. The greater the number of brain injuries sustained, the greater the suicide risk (Bryan & Clemans, 2013).

Among military service persons who committed suicide in recent years, only 45 percent had a mental health disorder, according to a Department of Defense report. This statistic is much lower than the 90 percent generally reported with civilian suicides. Strikingly, only 15 percent of those who committed suicide had direct combat experience. Similar to civilian suicides, interpersonal problems appear to play a significant role in military suicides—nearly half of those who killed themselves had experienced divorce or relationship conflicts before the suicide (Luxton et al., 2012). Suicide risk remains high even after individuals leave the service. In a study of 525 military veterans attending college, 46 percent reported having suicidal thoughts at some time during their life, 20 percent had made a suicide plan, 10 percent had frequent thoughts of suicide, 8 percent had made a suicide attempt, and 4 percent indicated that a suicide attempt was likely or very likely (Rudd, Goulding, & Bryan, 2011). These rates are much higher than those found in the general population (CDC, 2012c). The reasons for the high prevalence of suicidality among military personnel are still under investigation.

Suicide among College Students

Due to high-profile suicides on several college campuses, national interest in college-student suicides has increased (Drum et al., 2009). When you consider how fortunate most college students are—with youth, intelligence, and boundless opportunity—you might wonder why college suicides occur. Was the transition of leaving home, family, and friends too stressful? Did college work prove too challenging? Did they have problems with drugs and alcohol or a mental health condition? Or did loneliness, isolation, and alienation play a role in their deaths? As with all suicides, we can never be certain.

In one of the most comprehensive studies of college-student suicide risk, students at 70 participating colleges and universities were surveyed about suicidal ideation, attempts, preparation, and other demographic factors (Drum et al., 2009). The study revealed the following:

- More than 50 percent of undergraduate and graduate students reported suicidal thoughts.

- Eighteen percent of undergraduates and 15 percent of graduate students had *seriously considered* attempting suicide.

  Among those who had seriously contemplated suicide in the past 12 months:

- Ninety-two percent of undergraduates and 90 percent of graduate students had a specific plan for killing themselves.

- Fourteen percent of undergraduates and 8 percent of graduate students had made an attempt.
- Twenty-three percent of undergraduates and 27 percent of graduate students who had made a first attempt were considering a second try.

This study highlights the importance of addressing issues of suicide risk on college campuses. Unfortunately, approximately 80 percent of students who die by suicide do not seek professional help for their distress, despite the ease of access to services through college counseling centers (Kisch, Leino, & Silverman, 2005), and 45 percent never tell anyone about their serious intentions (Drum et al., 2009). Those who do share their anguish and thoughts of suicide with someone are most likely to do so with a fellow student. It is important to note that verbalizing thoughts of suicide is not the only sign of suicidal risk—other signs include withdrawal, depression, giving away prized possessions, and other risk factors discussed elsewhere in this chapter. Remember, many of those who commit suicide communicate their intent in one way or another. Campus prevention and intervention efforts are critically important in identifying students at risk for suicide. Many colleges and universities have developed programs and resources to (1) educate students and staff about warning signs related to suicide; (2) provide counselors, faculty, staff, and students with strategies for intervening if someone appears suicidal; and (3) publicize campus and community resources equipped to deal with a suicidal crisis.

DID YOU KNOW?

In order of frequency, the following were listed as contributing to suicidal thoughts and attempts for undergraduates:

- Emotional or physical pain
- Problems with romantic relations
- A desire to end one's life
- School problems
- Friend problems
- Family problems
- Financial problems

SOURCE: Drum et al., 2009

Suicide among Baby Boomers

CASE STUDY   Frank Turkaly took an overdose of tranquilizers. He was a retiree living on disability, had a large amount of debt, had little contact with friends or family, and was coping with depression, diabetes, and high blood pressure. He felt estranged from society—life was different than he had envisioned it in the 1960s and 1970s when the world seem to have endless possibilities (Bahrampour, 2013).

The baby boom generation includes individuals born between 1946 and 1964. This generation has consistently had higher suicide rates than earlier or subsequent generations. Characteristics of the baby boom generation that may increase suicide risk include their youth-oriented perspective and a belief in a limitless future (Bahrampour, 2013). The higher suicide rate among baby boomers may also be responsible for the substantially increased suicide rates among men and women ages 35–64 years that occurred between 1999 and 2010; the suicide rate among this age group increased 28.4 percent, with those in their fifties showing a 50 percent rate increase (MMWR, 2013). Because suicide rates tend to be highest in older adult populations, there are concerns that we may see additional suicides as the baby boomers age (Conwell, Van Orden, & Caine, 2011). Although suicide prevention efforts often focus on youths and older adults, many now advocate for prevention programs that address the stresses and challenges that middle-aged adults commonly face. Such stresses include economic pressure, dual-caregiver responsibilities (children and aging parents), and age-related changes in health.

Suicide among the Elderly

Suicide rates among older adults are high compared to the general population; indeed, suicide rates for elderly men are the highest for any age group (CDC, 2013). In one study comparing rates of suicide among different ethnic groups, it was found that elderly European Americans committed almost 18 percent of all suicides, although they

Coping with a Suicidal Crisis: A Top Priority

If you or someone you know is experiencing suicidal thoughts, the situation needs to become a top priority. So, what do you? First and foremost, remember that it is important to seek help from someone who has experience dealing with this kind of issue—there is help available day and night. In the United States, you can access free and confidential 24-hour services by calling the National Suicide Prevention Lifeline at 1-800-273-TALK. You can also contact a local crisis hotline or mental health resources that may be available on your campus. Of course, another option is to contact 911 or to go to the local emergency room for immediate assistance. Whether you are the one having the suicidal thoughts, or if you are aware that someone you know is possibly suicidal, seeking help can make the difference between life and death.

If You Are Having Suicidal Thoughts

What are some things that you can do if you are the one coping with suicidal thoughts? These five steps can help (Jaffe, Robinson, & Segal, 2013):

1. *Promise yourself not to do anything right now.* Even though you are in a lot of emotional pain, make a commitment to yourself that you will wait and put some distance between your suicidal thoughts and any suicidal action. Seeking support can help you keep this commitment. In most situations, suicidal thoughts are associated with mental health problems (such as depression, anxiety, mood swings, or the effects of drugs or alcohol) that can be successfully treated or with problems (such as breaking up, having conflicts with your friends or family, getting bad grades, worries about money) that have solutions. It is likely you will feel much better once these issues are addressed.

2. *Avoid using alcohol or drugs.* It is very important to avoid alcohol or recreational drugs if you are depressed or experiencing suicidal thoughts—they may impair your judgment or make you more likely to act impulsively. Also, they may cause your suicidal thoughts to become even stronger.

3. *Make your environment safe or go to a safe environment.* Try to avoid being alone, or thinking about things that make you feel worse. Remove anything you could use to hurt yourself or go somewhere where you know you will be safe.

4. *Remember there is always hope—people who go through hard times find that, with time, their situation improves.* Extreme emotional distress interferes with our ability to

see solutions to problems. No matter how painful your life is right now, if you give yourself time and find support, things will get better—usually *much* better. Reach out for help. Even if you have tried sharing your feelings with someone who didn't seem to understand, try again. There are people out there who will listen to your concerns with compassion and acceptance, including the people who staff suicide hotlines. They have helped many people like you—they understand.

5. *Don't keep your suicidal feelings to yourself.* Even though it's difficult to discuss your suicidal urges, it is important that you share your thoughts and feelings, including any suicide plans you have made. You can confide in someone you know and trust (a friend, family member, clergy, or therapist, for example). It also helps to talk with someone experienced in helping people who are having suicidal thoughts. Be honest about what you have been thinking and feeling. Talking can help you put things in perspective—it is very possible that you will discover ways to cope or solutions for some of your worries. Sharing your situation and your thoughts can help you see that your distress is temporary and that things will get better. You will find it is a big relief to seek help.

If Someone Else Is Emotionally Distressed or Expressing Suicidal Thoughts

What do you do if someone shares suicidal thoughts with you or if you are with someone who seems very emotionally distressed? By making the person a priority and taking the time to ask, to listen, and to seek help, you may save a life. These steps can help (National Institutes of Health, 2013):

1. *Ask—start a conversation so they can share their thoughts and feelings.* If you are concerned about someone, you can start a conversation, with openers such as "Are you doing okay? I've been concerned about you" or "You haven't seemed yourself lately. Can we talk about it?" Your goal is to make it clear that you care and want to help. If you are concerned that your friend might be considering suicide, it is important to bring up the topic. You may feel tempted to avoid directly discussing suicide due to fear that, if you bring up the subject, you will inadvertently encourage suicidal actions. Nothing could be further from the truth. Someone who is serious about suicide has entertained those thoughts for some time. Reluctance to discuss suicidal thoughts can have a devastating effect: It prevents a suicidal person from examining the situation

Coping with a Suicidal Crisis: A Top Priority—cont'd

more objectively and accessing life-saving help and support. Remember that even if your friend denies suicidal thoughts or plans, that does not necessarily mean there is limited risk; if you feel your friend needs mental health help, continue to encourage that help. If you are unsure what to do after having a conversation, you can contact a suicide hotline, share the specifics of the situation, and seek their advice.

2. *Listen—calmly, empathetically, and without judgment.* Your goal is to allow your friend to talk openly, without fear of being criticized or judged. It is important that you avoid minimizing or discounting what your friend it sharing; avoid arguing or making invalidating comments such as "That's not such a big deal" or "It's not worth killing yourself over that." If your friend is considering suicide, try not to seem frightened, shocked, or overwhelmed by the discussion. Even if the conversation is personally difficult for you, you have an opportunity to help by instilling hope—listening and validating powerful emotions can allow people to move beyond the feelings. You can also help your friend understand that, even though the emotional pain may seem unending, the strong feelings she or he is experiencing can and will get better. Most of the crises we experience in our lives are temporary—suicide is an irreversible solution to a temporary problem.

3. *Seek help.* If you become aware that someone is considering suicide, your goal will be to help connect the

person to professional support, as soon as possible. If a suicide attempt seems likely, you can immediately call a crisis hotline or 911. Meanwhile, you would stay with the person in a safe environment—somewhere where there is limited access to lethal objects. If your friend has shared any information related to a suicide plan, you would communicate that information to anyone involved in the crisis intervention. This is a situation where getting help is more important than confidentiality; even if you were sworn to secrecy, the main priority is helping your friend stay safe and access needed support. Helping out during a suicidal crisis can be very traumatic. If you are involved in a situation of this nature, consider seeking support from your school's counseling center or local crisis clinic.

For Further Consideration

1. If you were to feel distressed and overwhelmed, who are some people you could confide in? What crisis supports are available at your school or in your city?

2. Why is it so important to check in if you notice that a friend seems withdrawn or is expressing hopelessness? What would you do if you noticed that a classmate or other acquaintance seemed depressed or distressed?

3. For you, what might be the most difficult aspects of helping a friend who shares suicidal thoughts? Would you agree that this is a situation where safety is more important than confidentiality?

comprised only about 11 percent of the population (Leong & Leach, 2008). Another study found that suicide rates for elderly Chinese, Japanese, and Filipino Americans were even higher than the rate for elderly European Americans. Among females, Asian American women between the ages of 65 and 84 had the highest suicide rate of any other racial/ethnic group (AAPA, 2012).

Aging inevitably results in unwelcome physical changes, including illness and diminishing physical strength. In addition, older adults often encounter a succession of stressful life changes. Friends and relatives die, social isolation may increase, it may be difficult to live on a fixed income, and the prospect of death becomes more real. Such conditions make depression one of the most common psychiatric issues for aging adults—a depression associated more with "feeling old" than with their actual age or poor physical health (Rosenfeld, 2004).

For these reasons, suicide is more likely to accompany depression among the elderly. In particular, older adults who experience significant health issues and physical limitations, loss of independence, bereavement, and serious financial and relationship problems have an increased risk of suicide (Conwell, Van Orden, & Caine, 2011). Given the high rates of suicide among the elderly and other demographic groups, it is crucial to gain as much insight as possible into factors associated with suicide.

A Matter of Respect

Suicide is less likely to occur among the elderly in cultures that revere, respect, and esteem people of increasing age. In Asian and African countries, increasing age is equated with greater privilege and status. However, in the United States, growing old is often associated with declining worth and social isolation. What do you think accounts for the high rates of suicide among older adults in the United States?

DID YOU KNOW?

According to a Harvard research study that followed over 200,000 individuals for up to 16 years, those who drink two to four cups of coffee per day have a 50 percent lower rate of suicide compared to those who drink decaffeinated coffee or little or no coffee. Caffeine stimulates the central nervous system and boosts neurotransmitters such as dopamine and serotonin; the researchers speculate that this may produce a mild antidepressant effect and thus lower suicide rates.

SOURCE: Lucas et al., 2013

A Multipath Perspective of Suicide

A variety of biological, psychological, social, and sociocultural factors can influence a person's decision to commit suicide (see Figure 9.2). A single risk factor does not cause suicide. Instead, suicide often results from interactions among cumulative or collective influences. Especially when other risk factors are present, a situation, an event, or a series of events can become the final catalyst for suicide.

Biological Dimension

Suicide may have a biological component, according to biochemical and genetic studies, as well as other medical research. In the mid-1970s, scientists identified a chemical called *5-hydroxyindoleacetic acid* (5-HIAA). This chemical is produced when the body metabolizes serotonin. Low levels of 5-HIAA have been found in those who died from suicide and those who used more violent methods of suicide (Pandey, 2013). This research suggests that reduced availability of serotonin and low serotonin levels are associated with suicide; these abnormalities are also seen in depression. It is also significant that decreased serotonin is linked with increased aggression and impulsivity, characteristics that may increase suicidality (Ali et al., 2013).

Researchers believe that suicidal tendencies are not simply the result of depression. We already know that some individuals with depression also have low levels of 5-HIAA. What is startling is that low levels of 5-HIAA are found in some people who are suicidal but do not have a history of depression and in individuals who are suicidal and have mental disorders other than depression. Researchers believe that low 5-HIAA may indicate a vulnerability to environmental stressors that affect suicidality (J. J. Mann, Arango, et al., 2009). Additionally, researchers compared the levels of neuropeptides (a type of neurotransmitter involved in emotional regulation) in people who attempt or complete suicide with levels found in those without suicidal behaviors. Their findings revealed differences in neuropeptide levels between the two groups (Serafini, Pompili, Lindqvist, Dwivedi, & Girardi, 2013). All of this evidence, of course, is correlational in nature; it does not tell us whether low levels of 5-HIAA or neuropeptide differences cause suicidal behavior—or even whether the two are directly related.

Genetics are also implicated in suicidal behavior, but the relationship is far from clear. Research investigating possible genetic contributions to suicidal behavior suggests that multiple genes are involved, each contributing only small effects (Schosser et al., 2011) and that suicidal risk is increased when specific genes interact with stressful life events (Antypa, Serretti, & Rujescu, 2013). It is likely that these genetic contributions influence both biological processes and certain traits associated with suicide risk. For example, endophenotypes (heritable traits) that are associated with suicide include early-onset major depression, elevated cortisol reactivity, serotonin dysfunction, and traits such as aggressive/impulsive tendencies and impaired decision making (Courtet, Gottesman, Jollant, & Gould, 2011; Mann et al., 2009).

Some families have higher rates of suicide and suicide attempts (Brent & Melhem, 2008). As always, great care must be used in drawing conclusions—increased suicide in the family might be due to factors other than genetics. To separate genetic effects from environmental influences, one group of researchers decided to search for the biological siblings of adoptees who committed suicide (Petersen, Sørensen, Andersen, Mortensen, & Hawton, 2013). The prevalence of suicidal behaviors in

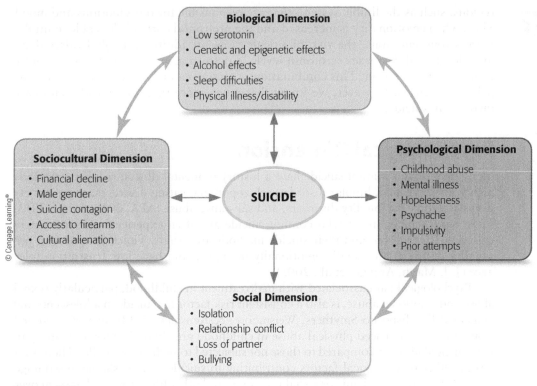

Figure 9.2

Multipath Model of Suicide

A variety of biological, psychological, social, and sociocultural factors may influence a person's decision to commit suicide. Cumulative risk factors interact with a situation, an event, or a series of events that become the final catalyst for suicide.

this sibling group was significantly higher than a comparison group comprised of siblings of adoptees who died from other causes. This result supports the presence of genetic risk factors in suicide. This genetic link to suicide may be expressed in many ways, including traits such as stress reactivity or impulsivity that increase the likelihood of suicidality.

Epigenetic research (the study of alterations in gene expression) is also shedding light on biological processes that may be associated with suicidality. Certain genes known to be influenced by epigenetic factors seem to be dysregulated in suicide (Labonté & Turecki, 2010). Similarly, analysis of postmortem tissue samples from individuals who committed suicide revealed epigenetic changes involving unique DNA alterations in the hippocampus (Labonté et al., 2013). These alterations, which represent a response to environmental influences, could affect gene expression involving characteristics associated with increased risk of suicide.

Other biological processes may also be involved in suicide. Among both adolescents and adults, sleep difficulties (including nightmares and trouble falling or staying asleep) are a strong predictor of both suicidal ideation and suicide attempts; this effect is present even in the absence of depression. Given the strength of these findings, some researchers propose that preventing or intervening with sleep difficulties may decrease the likelihood of suicide (Pigeon, Pinquart, & Conner, 2012; Wong & Brower, 2012).

Alcohol use is also implicated in suicides. Alcohol appears to act as a "lubricant," increasing suicidality in vulnerable individuals. Alcohol reduces the inhibitory control of our prefrontal cortex, raises our pain threshold, and affects brain

DID YOU KNOW?

In 2012, 150 workers in China threatened to commit mass suicide by leaping off the rooftop of the building where they worked; after 2 days of negotiations, they left without incident. Two years earlier, a cluster of 14 suicides had occurred at the same factory, apparently related to feelings of hopelessness over the work environment.

SOURCE: Goyette, 2012

regions, such as the limbic system, that are responsible for our emotions and mood. Thus, when emotionality is increased and the prefrontal cortex is less able to inhibit these strong emotions, the risk of suicide rises. In addition, alcohol raises dopamine levels and decreases serotonin levels, a pattern associated with poor impulse control and aggression. This combination of factors can increase the risk of suicide (Ali et al., 2013). However, we know that much more than biological factors are involved in suicide.

Psychological Dimension

Many people who commit suicide have a history of mental illness; risk is particularly high with depression, bipolar disorder, schizophrenia, eating disorders, some anxiety disorders, some personality disorders, and substance abuse (APA, 2013; Soreff, 2013). Those with schizophrenia who commit suicide are often experiencing a concurrent episode of depression, and their suicide methods are usually violent; those with personality disorders are usually emotionally immature and have low frustration tolerance (J. J. Mann, Arango, et al., 2009).

Psychological pain associated with maltreatment in childhood, particularly sexual abuse and emotional abuse, is also a consistent risk factor for suicide in adolescents and adults (Miller, Esposito-Smythers, Weismoore, & Renshaw, 2013). In fact, men and women who experienced physical abuse in childhood are about 5 times more likely to have suicidal ideation compared to those not subjected to such abuse (Fuller-Thompson, 2012). Other psychological factors contributing to suicide include shame, discouragement, distress over academic or social pressures, and other life stressors that seem overwhelming (SAMHSA, 2010b).

Depression and Hopelessness

The psychological states most strongly associated with suicide are depression and hopelessness (NIMH, 2011c). Suicidal thoughts sometimes develop when someone is experiencing the overwhelming hopelessness, fatigue, and loss of pleasure associated with depression. Shneidman (1998) has described the feeling as a "**psychache**," an intolerable pain created from an absence of joy. Psychache has, in fact, been strongly associated with suicidal ideation, even more so than depression or hopelessness (Troister & Holden, 2010). We know that having a depressive disorder is associated with suicidal thoughts and behaviors, but what about milder symptoms of depression? In a sample of 12,395 adolescents from 11 countries, 29 percent had symptoms of mild depression and another 10.5 percent had symptoms severe enough to meet the criteria for depressive disorder. Among this group, those with mild depression had 3 times more suicidal thoughts compared to adolescents without depressive symptoms; those who were clinically depressed had 9 times more suicidal thoughts (Balazs et al., 2013). Thus, even milder depression may increase suicide risk.

Although depression is associated with suicidal thoughts and behavior, the relationship is complex. For example, in some cases, the limited energy associated with severe depression makes suicide less likely. The danger period often comes when the depression begins to lift. Energy and motivation increase, enhancing the likelihood of follow-through with suicide plans. Why do some people with depression commit suicide, whereas most do not? Some people experiencing depression may experience emotions that increase the likelihood of suicide, such as heightened feelings of anxiety,

psychache a term created to describe the unbearable psychological hurt, pain, and anguish associated with suicide

Politically Motivated Suicide

In some cultures, self-immolation is conducted as a form of protest against the government. In this photo, a Tibetan man, living in exile in India, screams as he runs engulfed in flames after setting himself on fire to protest China's control over Tibet. He suffered burns over 98 percent of his body and died several days later.

Manish Swarup/AP Images

anger, or shame. For example, in a sample of individuals who were hospitalized for psychiatric issues, men with a disposition to anger, especially those with a background of childhood sexual abuse, and women with physiological arousal and a history of child sexual abuse were more likely to make a suicide attempt in the 1-year period after their release (Sadeh & McNiel, 2013). Some researchers believe that hopelessness, or negative expectations about the future, is the major catalyst in suicide, possibly an even more important factor than depression and other moods (D. Lester, 2008).

Alcohol Consumption

One of the most consistently reported correlates of suicidal behavior is alcohol consumption (Ali et al., 2013; Soreff, 2013). As many as 70 percent of people who attempt suicide drink alcohol before the act, and autopsies of suicide victims suggest that many are legally intoxicated (Jones, Holmgren, & Ahlner, 2013; Kaplan et al., 2012). Not only does alcohol have biological effects such as decreasing judgment, it also has psychological effects such as lowering inhibitions related to the fear of death, thus making it easier to carry out suicide plans. Heavy alcohol consumption, such as binge drinking, also seems to deepen feelings of remorse during dry periods, resulting in an increased risk even when the person is sober.

Several classic studies, however, suggest another explanation for the effects of alcohol: The strength of the relationship between alcohol and suicide may result from "alcohol-induced myopia," a constriction of cognitive and perceptual processes (J. R. Rogers, 1992). Alcohol use may increase personal distress by focusing people's thoughts on negative aspects of their personal situations. Alcohol does seem to constrict cognitive and perceptual processes. Although drinking may relieve depression and anxiety by distracting the person from the problem, it is equally likely to intensify distress by narrowing the person's focus and attention to problems (Cha, Najmi, Park, Finn, & Nock, 2010). Thus, a psychological link between alcohol and suicide may be due to the myopic qualities of alcohol exaggerating a previously existing depressed state.

Social Dimension

> **CASE STUDY**   Ten-year-old Tammy Jimenez was the youngest of three girls—a loner who had attempted suicide at least twice in the previous 2 years. Tammy's parents always seemed to be arguing and threatening divorce. Their father often lashed out at the children when he was intoxicated. One evening in late February, Tammy was struck and killed by a truck when she darted out into the highway that passed by her home. The incident was declared an accident. However, her older sister reported that Tammy had deliberately killed herself. On the evening of her death, an argument with her father had upset and angered her. Her sister said that seconds before Tammy ran out onto the highway, she cried out that no one wanted her around and that she wanted to die.

As in Tammy's tragic death, many suicides are interpersonal in nature and occur following relationship conflicts. Social factors that separate people or make them less connected to families, friends, religious institutions, or communities can also increase susceptibility to suicide (Alcantara & Gone, 2008). For example, unhappiness over a broken relationship, marital discord, disputes with parents, and recent bereavements all increase suicide risk (Rudd et al., 2004). Family instability, stress, and a chaotic family atmosphere are factors in suicide attempts by younger children, as we saw in the death of Tammy. Children who consider suicide are more likely to have experienced abuse, unpredictable traumatic events, and the loss of a significant parenting figure before age 12 (C. A. King & Merchant, 2008). It is not surprising that suicide prevention efforts often focus on increasing social support and connectedness and decreasing social isolation.

Thomas Joiner's interpersonal-psychological theory of suicide has received considerable attention (Joiner, 2005; Joiner, Van Orden, et al., 2009). In an attempt to integrate the many factors associated with suicide, he proposed that two social factors are strongly associated with suicide attempts: (a) perceived burdensomeness—feelings of being a burden to family, friends, or society; and (b) thwarted belongingness—feelings of alienation and a lack of meaningful connections to others. How important are interpersonal relationship issues in suicides? Investigators studied 100 suicide attempters to determine if some type of negative life event occurred within 48 hours of the attempt. As predicted by Joiner's theory, many reported recent interpersonal issues with a partner or other relationship conflicts (Bagge, Glenn, & Lee, 2013).

A unique third condition must exist before a suicide attempt occurs, according to Joiner's theory: the acquired capacity for suicide. People must experience a reduction in fear of taking their own life that is sufficient to overcome self-preservation reflexes. Unfortunately, repeated exposure to traumatic life events (physical or emotional abuse, rape, bullying, exposure to wartime atrocities, etc.) may result in habituation to painful life circumstances and may lower the fear of inflicting self-injury; this is the acquired capacity for suicide. Studies have found that people who attempt suicide do indeed report higher levels of fearlessness and pain insensitivity, as well as greater frequency of painful life events (P. N. Smith et al., 2010). Statistics indicating that suicide risk increases when a friend, family member, or acquaintance has committed suicide may also relate to the concept of acquired capacity (Crepeau-Hobson & Leech, 2013).

Marital Status

A stable marriage or relationship makes suicide less likely. Additionally, for women, having children decreases suicide risk (Denney, 2010). Not surprisingly, people who are divorced, separated, or widowed have higher suicide rates than those who are married (Navaneelan, 2013). In fact, the death of a spouse is associated with a 50 percent higher risk of suicide for men, and divorced men have a 39 percent higher risk of suicide compared to married men (Denney, Rogers, Krueger, & Wadsworth, 2009).

Sociocultural Dimension

French sociologist Émile Durkheim (Durkheim, 1897/1951) studied suicides in different countries, across different periods, and proposed one of the first sociocultural explanations of suicide. Suicide, as theorized by Durkheim, results from an inability to integrate oneself with society. In Durkheim's view, failing to maintain close ties with the community deprives a person of the support systems that are necessary for adaptive functioning. Without such support, the person becomes isolated and alienated from other people. Some **suicidologists** believe that our modern, mobile, and technological society, which deemphasizes the importance of extended families and a sense of community, is partially responsible for increased suicide rates. Similarly, the sense of alienation experienced by many lesbian, gay, bisexual, and transgender youth may explain their increased suicide risk; the risk is particularly high for those subjected to bullying due to cross-gender appearance or traits

suicidologist a professional who studies the manifestation, dynamics, and prevention of suicides

and those who experience strong feelings of isolation and low family support (Haas et al., 2011; Mustanski & Liu, 2013).

Ethnic and Cultural Variables

Suicidal ideation and rates of suicide vary among ethnic minority groups in the United States. American Indian/Alaska Native and European American males have the highest rates of completed suicides; rates are much lower among African American, Hispanic/Latino, and Asian American/Pacific Islander males (Murphy, Xu, & Kochanek, 2013). Although females in all groups have lower rates of suicide compared to men, the pattern of ethnic distribution among females is similar to that seen with men (see Figure 9.3). For American Indians, suicide is the second leading cause of death among youth ages 10–24 (Suicide Prevention Resource Center, 2013). In fact, the suicide rate of American Indian/Alaska Native adolescents and young adults is two and a half times higher than the national average for that age group (CDC, 2012c).

Social change and social disorganization, which reduces integration with one's community, may predispose members of a particular group to suicide. A regrettable example of this is the disorganization imposed on American Indians by U.S. society: Families were deprived of their lands, torn apart, and forced to live on reservations, while their children were sent to boarding schools only to become trapped on the margins of two different cultural traditions. Many American Indians became alienated and isolated from their communities and from larger society (Goldston et al., 2008). Similarly, perceived discrimination by Asian international students combined with a lack of feeling of belonging in a new cultural environment has been associated with an increase in suicidal ideation among this group (Wang, Wong, & Fu, 2013).

In contrast, aspects of the African American culture such as close family relationships, strong community connections, and religious and personal values that discourage suicide may decrease suicide risk. Similarly, the strong social connections and religiosity seen in Hispanic/Latino communities may account for the lower incidence of completed suicide. In contrast, the perception that suicide would bring shame to the family might account for the relatively low suicide rates among Asian Americans (Sue & Sue, 2013).

Gender

Females have higher rates of suicidal thoughts and suicide attempts, but death from suicide occurs much more frequently among males, representing 79 percent of all U.S. suicides. Although the rate of completed suicide is about 4 times higher for men compared to women, recent findings suggest that the gap is closing (CDC, 2012c). Males tend to choose more lethal methods of suicide, including firearms (males 56 percent, females 30 percent) and suffocation/hanging (males 24 percent, females 21 percent). Drug overdose/poisoning (males 13 percent, females 40 percent) is the most common means for women (NIMH, 2011c).

Although the use of lethal methods partially explains the high rate of suicide among males, the issue is more complex. Suicide among men is particularly perplexing because many men who commit suicide have no history of mental illness and

Iraq/Reuters/Corbis

Suicide Bombings

These events have become an all too common sight in Iraq. In the aftermath of a suicide bombing in Baghdad, two men try desperately to move a car away to clear the way for help. A suicide truck bomb was used in an attempt to destroy a satellite television station and take as many lives as possible.

American Indian and Proud of It

Suicide rates among American Indian youth are extremely high, due perhaps to a lack of validation of their cultural lifestyle. Here American Indian children perform a traditional dance. Many tribes are attempting to keep their children and adolescents connected with their cultural heritage.

Mark Ralston/AFP/Getty Images

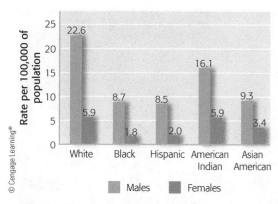

Figure 9.3

Suicide Rates by Race/Ethnicity and Gender, United States, 2010

During 2010, the annual suicide rate varied by race/ethnicity and gender, ranging from lows of 1.8 suicides per 100,000 for African American females to 22.6 suicides per 100,000 for European American males.

SOURCE: Murphy, S L., Xu, J. & Kochanek, K. D. (2013) Deaths: Final Data for 2010. National Vital Statistics Reports, 61, p. 63.

no previous suicide attempts (Kaplan et al., 2012). Cultural conditioning related to the male gender role combined with events that threaten a masculine ideal (such as job loss or broken relationships) may partially explain the high suicide rate for men. Most men are socialized to believe they must meet perceived social expectations (e.g., self-reliance, strength, financial success). Additionally, when under stress or experiencing loss, men may avoid seeking help or confiding in others about their problems and instead respond with anger, violence, or alcohol use. This pattern of behavior can lead to a narrowed view of possible solutions and impulsive actions. Men may also acquire a greater capacity for suicide due to work-related exposure to death (e.g., law enforcement and military careers) and access to lethal methods, such as firearms (Coleman, Kaplan, & Casey, 2011).

A group in Colorado recently launched a multimedia campaign (called Man Therapy) with the goal of encouraging men to seek help for mental health concerns, including suicidal ideation or intent. The project uses humor and traditional male values and language to confront serious issues; the Web site also provides information on community mental health resources (Spencer-Thomas, Hindman, & Conrad, 2012). In a similar attempt to engage masculine concepts, the U.S. Department of Veterans Affairs initiated a campaign with the slogan "It takes the strength and courage of a warrior to ask for help." Do you think these efforts will succeed in encouraging men to seek help when under stress?

Socioeconomic Stressors

Economic issues can have a significant impact on suicide rates. During the recession that began in 2008, the suicide rate in the United States increased by an additional 1,580 suicides per year from 2008–2010. European countries also experienced a recession during this time; in counties with the greatest economic challenges such as Greece, the suicide rated increased by more than 60 percent (Reeves et al., 2012). Suicide also increased among those who declared bankruptcy (Kidger, 2011). Consistent with these data, unemployed adults are over twice as likely to have serious thoughts of suicide, and over 4 times more likely to make suicide plans or attempt suicide compared to fully employed adults. Also, individuals who qualify for Medicaid (subsidized medical assistance for those with low income) have higher suicide rates compared to those who can afford health insurance (SAMHSA, 2012b).

Religious Affiliation

Religious affiliation is associated with suicide rates. The U.S. suicide rate is 11.4 per 100,000. However, the suicide rate is lower (less than 10 per 100,000) in countries, such as Brazil, Argentina, Ireland, Spain, and Italy, where the Catholic Church has a strong influence (CDC, 2010d). Islam, too, condemns suicide; low lifetime prevalence of suicidal thoughts (17.5 percent) and suicide attempts (1.8 percent) were reported by medical students in the United Arab Emirates, consistent with religious beliefs regarding the unacceptability of suicide and potential punishment after death (Amir et al., 2013). Where religious sanctions against suicide are absent or weaker, as they are in Scandinavian countries and Hungary, higher suicide rates are observed. In fact, rates in Hungary are quite high—40.7 per 100,000 (De Leo, 2009).

Preventing Suicide

Suicide is irreversible, of course, so prevention is critical. Early detection and successful intervention rely on understanding risk and protective factors associated with suicide (see Table 9.2). Suicide prevention can occur at several levels. Crisis intervention sometimes results from self-referrals or referrals from concerned family, friends,

Table 9.2 Risk and Protective Factors in Suicide Assessment and Intervention

Risk Factors	Protective Factors
• Previous suicide intent or attempt; self-injurious behavior or talk about suicide, dying, or self-harm	• Good emotional regulation, problem-solving, and conflict-resolution skills
• Substance abuse, chronic pain or physical illness, insomnia, and certain mental disorders	• Willingness to talk about problems
• Hopelessness, shame, humiliation, despair, anxiety/panic, self-loathing; impulsive or aggressive tendencies	• Cultural and religious beliefs that discourage suicide
• Recent loss or significant traumatic event including a failed relationship, bereavement, unemployment	• Open to seeking treatment for mental, physical, or substance-use disorders
• Relational conflicts, loneliness, and social isolation	• Family and community support
• Seeking out or easy access to lethal methods, especially guns	• Connection to or responsibility for children or beloved pets
• Family turmoil; history of physical or sexual abuse	• Restricted access to lethal means of suicide
• Family members, peers, or favored celebrities have died from suicide	

SOURCE: SAMHSA (2009); Smith, Segal, & Robinson (2013).

or co-workers. Another promising intervention is gatekeeper training; with this model, designated people within a system (such as schools or the military) learn about risk factors associated with suicide and methods for screening people at high risk (Klimes-Dougan, Klingbeil, & Meller, 2013, Robinson et al., 2013). If screening results are suggestive of suicide risk, comprehensive assessment and intervention occur.

Working with a potentially suicidal individual is a three-step process that involves (1) knowing which factors increase the likelihood of suicide; (2) determining whether there is high, moderate, or low probability that the person will act on the suicide wish; and (3) implementing appropriate actions (Isaac et al., 2009). Figure 9.4 summarizes the process of assessing risk and intervening based on different levels of risk. People trained in working with people who are suicidal often begin by looking for clues to suicidal intent.

Clues to Suicidal Intent

CASE STUDY   Marilyn Monroe had taken a large number of barbiturates, and then called people telling them she was in trouble. She had made similar suicide attempts in the past and had always been rescued. This time help came too late. Had she truly wanted to die? Could something have been done to prevent her death? (Fernández-Cabana, García-Caballero, Alves-Pérez, García-García, & Mateos, 2013.)

Preventing suicide depends on recognizing signs of potential suicide. Therapists, friends, family, or those trained in gatekeeper programs (such as the programs used on many college campuses) are the first line of defense against suicide—when they recognize warning signs of suicide, they can take actions to intervene. In almost every case of suicide, there are clues (some subtle and some not so subtle) that the act is about to occur. Clues to suicidal intent may be demographic or specific. We have already discussed a number of demographic factors, such as the fact that men are 4 times more likely to kill themselves than are women, and that older age is associated with an increased probability of suicide (CDC, 2012c).

Specific risk factors associated with suicide also provide important clues. In the case of Marilyn Monroe, a key indicator was her history of previous suicide

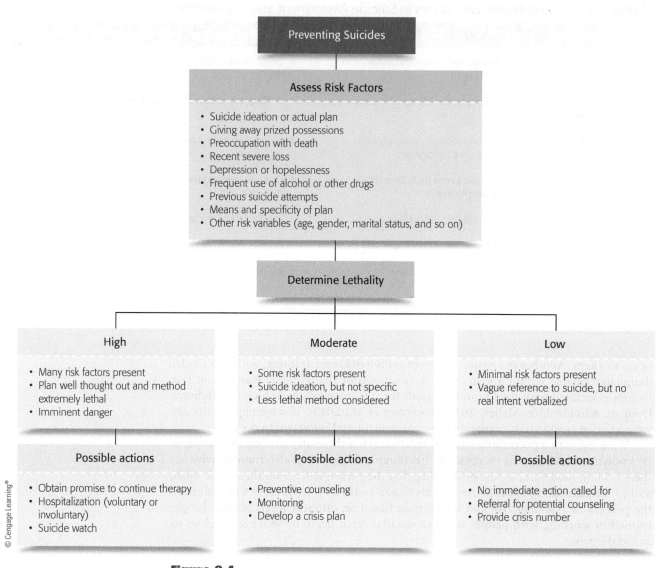

Figure 9.4

The Process of Preventing Suicide

Suicide prevention involves the careful assessment of risk factors to determine lethality—the probability that a person will choose to end his or her life. Working with an individual who is potentially suicidal is a three-step process that involves (1) knowing what risk factors are associated with suicide; (2) determining whether there is high, moderate, or low probability that the person will act on suicidal thoughts; and (3) implementing appropriate actions.

attempts. Even when suicide attempts are not lethal, they often reflect deep suicidal intent that will be carried out in the future. (Although suicide attempts are distinctly different from **nonsuicidal self-injury**, a topic we discuss in Chapter 16, both are reasons for concern.) Although some believe the myth that frequent suicide attempts are simply a cry for attention and shouldn't be taken too seriously, many people who commit suicide do, in fact, have a history of suicide attempts. So, ignoring a suicide attempt or suicide threat can have devastating consequences. All suicidal threats or attempts should be taken seriously. In fact, a previous suicide attempt is the most robust predictor of a future attempt (Beghi & Rosenbaum, 2010).

nonsuicidal self-injury
self-harm intended to provide relief from negative feelings or to induce a positive mood state

Another key piece of information to assist with prevention is knowing if a person is having suicidal ideation or has made a suicide plan. Therapists who are working with someone who might be at risk of suicide often ask very direct questions, such as:

"Are you feeling unhappy and down most of the time?" (If yes . . .)
"Do you feel so unhappy that you sometimes wish you were dead?" (If yes . . .)
"Have you ever thought about taking your own life?" (If yes . . .)
"What methods have you thought about using to kill yourself?" (If the client specifies a method . . .)
"When do you plan to do this?"

This openness will not adversely affect those who are suicidal. Instead, direct and straightforward discussion may help diminish distress and free a person to see problems and situations from a broader perspective. Many people considering suicide are relieved to be able to discuss a taboo topic openly and honestly, and to have someone help them look at their situation more objectively. Additionally, the amount of detail involved in a suicide plan is a clue to the potential seriousness of the situation. A person who provides specific details, such as method, time, and place, is much more at risk than one who has no detailed plan.

Suicide potential increases if the person has direct access to the means of suicide, such as a loaded pistol. Also, suicide is often preceded by a precipitating event. Triggers such as the breakup of an important relationship, perceiving oneself to be a burden, difficulties at school or at work, public humiliation, loss of a loved one, family discord, chronic pain, or terminal illness may contribute to a person's decision to end his or her life.

Many people contemplating suicide verbally communicate their intent. Some people make very direct statements: "I wish I were dead," or "If this happens again, I'll kill myself." Others make indirect statements: "Goodbye," "I've had it," "Everyone would be better off without me," "I'm so tired of feeling depressed," or "I've been thinking a lot about death lately." Sometimes these communications occur in person, but it is equally likely for messages to be sent via e-mail, text, or social media posts, sometimes shortly before the suicidal act.

Although some clues are very direct, many cues are much more subtle. Indirect behavioral clues include withdrawal, restlessness or changes in sleep patterns, reckless behavior, increased drinking or drug use, giving away possessions, or a prolonged or unexpected farewell. Concern is greatest when behavior deviates from what is normal for the person. Some clinicians divide warning signs into two categories: (a) early signs, such as depression, expressions of guilt or remorse, tension or anxiety, insomnia, or loss of appetite; and (b) critical signs, such as sudden changes in behavior (uncharacteristic risk-taking or calmness after a period of anxiety or depression), unusual or unexpected contact with family or friends, saying goodbye, giving away belongings, putting affairs in order, direct or indirect threats, and actual attempts (Smith, Segal, & Robinson, 2013). Recognizing clues to intent is a critical first step—the next step is seeking immediate help if you believe someone is suicidal.

Suicide Hotlines and Telephone Crisis Intervention

National agencies and local communities that sponsor suicide prevention centers and suicide hotlines recognize that a suicidal crisis requiring immediate preventive assistance can occur at any time, day or night. These resources are available to those considering suicide and to people concerned about a friend, family member, or co-worker. Suicide hotlines typically operate 24 hours a day, 7 days a week. Because most contacts are by phone, crisis lines publicize their numbers throughout the community. One well-known hotline in the United States is the National Suicide Prevention Lifeline (1-800-273-TALK). Volunteers, paraprofessionals, and mental

Intervening Before It Is Too Late

Suicide prevention centers operate 24 hours a day, 7 days a week, and have well-publicized telephone numbers because most contacts are made by phone.

health professionals who staff suicide prevention centers are trained in a variety of crisis intervention techniques, including:

1. *Maintaining contact and establishing a relationship.* Establishing a good relationship with a suicidal caller by demonstrating interest and concern and keeping the caller on the line increases the chances that the caller will realize that there are solutions other than suicide.

2. *Obtaining necessary information.* The worker elicits demographic data and the caller's name and address. This information is very valuable in case there is an urgent need to locate the caller.

3. *Evaluating suicidal potential.* The staff person taking the call must quickly determine the seriousness of the caller's self-destructive intent. Most centers use **lethality** rating scales to help workers determine suicide potential. These usually contain questions about age, gender, onset of symptoms, situational plight, prior suicidal behavior, and access to lethal methods.

4. *Clarifying the nature of the caller's distress.* Crisis workers help callers (1) clarify the exact nature of their concerns, (2) recognize that they may be under so much duress that they are not thinking clearly, and (3) realize that there are other solutions besides suicide. Because feelings of hopelessness often interfere with logical thinking, a key goal is to help callers recognize that there are options they might not have considered. When callers seem disoriented or confused, workers ask very specific questions to help bring them back to reality.

5. *Assessing strengths and resources.* In working out a crisis plan, workers often mobilize a caller's strengths or available resources. In their agitation and distress, callers may forget coping strategies that have helped them previously. The worker explores potential social resources, including family, friends, and co-workers, as well as professional resources such as doctors, clergy, or therapists.

6. *Recommending and initiating an action plan.* Besides being supportive, crisis workers are highly directive in developing a course of action. Whether the recommendation entails immediately seeing the person, calling the person's family, or referring the person for a crisis counseling appointment the next day, the worker presents a systematic plan of action.

Both the approach and the order of these steps will vary depending on the needs of the individual caller and the potential lethality of the situation. Today, hundreds of suicide hotlines function in the United States. There is evidence that suicide prevention efforts such as these can help meet the immediate needs of callers—to decrease psychological pain and feelings of hopelessness (Gould, Kalafat, Harrismunfakh, & Kleinman, 2007). However, the key to enhancing the success of suicide prevention efforts is the availability of mental health services during and immediately after a crisis. Many centers provide crisis treatment. Centers that lack such resources develop cooperative service arrangements with community mental health agencies equipped to provide crisis services.

Suicide Crisis Intervention

Suicide crisis intervention can be highly successful for (1) those who independently seek professional help for suicidal ideation, (2) clients who bring suicidal thoughts or intentions to the attention of their therapist, and (3) people encouraged to seek professional help by concerned family, friends, teachers, or co-workers. In addition to preventing suicide, the goal is to resolve feelings of hopelessness and concerns about immediate life crises. Crisis workers focus on the person's emotional pain and operate

lethality capability of causing death

under the assumption that anyone considering suicide is ambivalent about the act; they exert great effort to preserve the drive to live (Granello, 2010). They may point out that the person's willingness to share his or her despair and thoughts of suicide reflects a desire for help and a desire to live.

Similarly, the person intervening may explain that suicidal thoughts often represent the depth of a person's feelings rather than a true intent to take action, particularly considering the finality of death. They may also reassure the suicidal person that, although it may seem that the pain will go on forever, there are resources to help them cope and resolve whatever feels so overwhelming. Although discussions often begin by validating the person's emotional anguish, the conversation moves on to practical matters such as ideas for decreasing stress and managing immediate problems. Unlike traditional psychotherapy, in which sessions are spaced out and treatment is provided on a more leisurely long-term basis, crisis intervention recognizes the immediacy of the person's need for hope and support.

A common approach used in interventions with someone expressing suicidal intent is a "no-harm" agreement, sometimes referred to as a "no-suicide contract" or "suicide-prevention contract." Typically, this is a written agreement developed between the suicidal person and a therapist or the person involved in crisis intervention. Generally, the agreement involves a commitment that the suicidal person will not engage in self-harm for a designated period of time; a plan is also developed in the event that suicidal impulses continue. Although agreements such as these are frequently used, there is a lack of research supporting their effectiveness. In fact, suicide completers frequently have "no-harm" contracts in effect (Kroll, 2007). For this reason, therapists, friends, and family should not reduce their vigilance about suicide risk just because there is a no-harm agreement in place.

In some cases, the safest plan for those with strong suicidal urges is temporary hospitalization. In a hospital environment, there is close monitoring and the opportunity to receive assistance from a psychiatric team until the immediate crisis has passed. The hospital team helps determine what supports are needed once patients leave the hospital. After returning to a more stable emotional state and with the immediate risk of suicide behind them, patients can begin more traditional outpatient treatment. Relatives and friends are often enlisted to help monitor their loved one's safety and well-being following hospitalization and are given guidance on how to provide support between therapy sessions and whom to notify if problems arise outside of the hospital.

Psychotherapy for Suicidal Individuals

Treatment for those who have attempted suicide or who have suicidal ideation often involves both medication (which will vary depending on the underlying mental disorder) and psychotherapy. Psychotherapy techniques proven to reduce suicide risk include cognitive-behavioral therapy (CBT) and dialectical behavior therapy (DBT). Cognitive-behavioral therapy with individuals who have attempted suicide has been found to reduce repeat attempts by 50 percent compared to traditional follow-up treatment (Brown et al., 2005). The CBT program focuses on vulnerabilities associated with suicide such as feelings of hopelessness, social isolation, poor impulse control, poor problem solving, and difficulty refuting thoughts, images, and beliefs associated with suicide.

Dialectical behavior therapy (DBT) is also effective with severely suicidal individuals. DBT focuses on helping clients accept their current lives and the emotional anguish they feel. An important goal for suicidal clients is learning to regulate and tolerate their emotions rather than allowing emotions to overwhelm them and result in a suicidal act (DeAngelis, 2009). DBT with suicidal adolescents resulted in reductions in depression, self-injury, and suicidal feelings (Mujoomdar, Cimon, & Nkansah, 2010). DBT also reduced suicide attempts in adults by 50 percent when compared to other forms of therapy (Linehan et al., 2006).

Cognitive-behavioral therapy for suicide prevention, an innovative program for adolescents, combines features of both CBT and DBT (Stanley et al., 2009). Risk factors and stressors, including emotional, cognitive, behavioral, and interpersonal processes that occurred just before and after the suicide attempt or suicidal crisis, are discussed. Other difficulties such as an inability to regulate emotions, poor problem-solving skills, or negative thoughts and beliefs are also identified. The treatment program includes:

1. *Chain analysis*—During this phase, the teen describes all the events, stressors, thoughts, interpersonal conflicts, and other factors, such as drug use, that led to the suicide attempt. This information allows the mental health professional to devise a specific treatment plan based on the teen's unique circumstances.

2. *Safety planning*—Clients work with the therapist to develop a prioritized list of internal and external coping strategies and social supports that can be relied on during a suicidal crisis.

3. *Psychoeducation*—The client and family learn about suicide prevention, safety issues, and strategies for regulating emotions.

4. *Building hope and addressing reasons for living*—The therapist helps the client articulate reasons for hope and for staying alive; this might involve spending time with friends and family, plans for the future, or things the client would like to do or accomplish. Coping strategies make more sense if there is hope for the future.

5. *Learning and using adaptive strategies from CBT and DBT to deal with specific problems*—The client is given homework that involves making use of strategies learned in therapy.

Over half of the adolescents who completed the program felt positive about their progress and 86 percent indicated that they would recommend the therapy to a friend.

Contemporary Trends and Future Directions

Suicide is a global concern—over three quarters of a million people take their own life each year (Värnik, 2012). Each death brings incredible pain for the families and friends left behind. Given the tragic nature of suicide, researchers across the globe are devoting considerable energy to understanding this perplexing phenomenon. Many research endeavors focus on the many risk factors that underlie the propensity to consider and engage in suicidal behaviors. Other efforts involve searching for ways to most effectively detect and intervene with individuals contemplating suicide.

In the United States, there is debate about whether considering suicide a psychiatric disorder in its own right would improve the assessment, diagnosis, and treatment of this mental health issue. The DSM-5 includes "suicidal behavior disorder" as a condition for further study—a category being evaluated for possible inclusion as a disorder in future editions of the DSM (APA, 2013). The proposed criteria include: (a) a suicide attempt within the previous 24 months and (b) the individual must have had at least some intent to die. This definition excludes those who engage in nonsuicidal self-injury. It also excludes those whose suicidal behavior is the result of delirium, confusion, or political or religious goals. Additionally, suicidal thoughts, plans, or preparation are not sufficient for the diagnosis.

According to proponents of this diagnosis, having suicide as a distinct disorder will increase the likelihood that mental health professionals will recognize, assess, and identify both internal and external triggers associated with suicidal behavior (Kupfer, 2013). Using current standards, therapists often fail to address the possibility that a client is having suicidal thoughts and behaviors. Even when a client discloses suicidal ideation

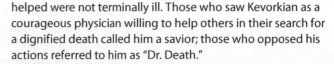

Do People Have a Right to Die?

Under what conditions, if any, should people have the right to take their own lives? Is suicide acceptable if someone has a terminal illness, degenerating physical condition, poor quality of life, or "unbearable psychological anguish"? We will present examples of each of these situations for you to consider.

Physician-Assisted Suicide

Physician-assisted suicide for terminal conditions is allowed in three states (Oregon, Washington, and Vermont) and is being considered in others. There are strict rules associated with these laws. For example, in Oregon and Washington, it is permitted only if:

- two physicians confirm that the person has a terminal condition and less than 6 months to live;

- two verbal requests and one written request are made in the presence of witnesses (the second verbal request must be made at least 15 days after the first); and

- the individual is of sound mind (a mental health evaluation may be required).

People in Oregon who requested physician-assisted suicide based their request on concerns about a deteriorating quality of life, loss of ability to engage in activities that make life enjoyable, loss of autonomy, and loss of dignity (Oregon Public Health Division, 2013).

Assisted Suicide for Other Than Terminal Conditions

On November 22, 1998, over 15 million viewers of *60 Minutes* watched in either horror or sadness as 52-year-old Thomas Youk died from a lethal injection. This was not, however, a death sentence carried out for a murder conviction, but rather the wishes of a man in the latter stages of Lou Gehrig's disease. Youk's wife stated, " so grateful to know that someone would relieve him of his suffering. . . . I consider it the way things should be done." The man who videotaped the event was Dr. Jack Kevorkian, a retired physician who helped nearly 130 people end their lives using a device he called a "suicide machine." His first client, Janet Adkins, had Alzheimer's disease. She did not want to put her family through the agony of the disease and believed that choosing death was a rational decision. Many others whom Kevorkian

helped were not terminally ill. Those who saw Kevorkian as a courageous physician willing to help others in their search for a dignified death called him a savior; those who opposed his actions referred to him as "Dr. Death."

Suicide Because of "Unbearable Psychological Anguish"

Nathan Verhelst, 44, who was born a female named Nancy, believed that he was male; in 2009 he began taking hormones to assist his transformation into a man. Along with this treatment, Nathan also had two surgeries—a mastectomy and the construction of a penis. Disappointed and disgusted with the results of the sex-change surgeries, he said he found living unbearable and elected to die from euthanasia. Two 45-year-old deaf twins also elected to undergo euthanasia after learning that they were going blind. The men had always lived together and communicated with one another through a special sign language only understood by them and close family members. They were terrified at the prospect of losing their independence and not being able to see each other. On the grounds of "unbearable psychological suffering," they both received a lethal injection (Gayle, 2013). Both of these cases involved euthanasia in Belgium, where there is also proposed legislation that would allow children under certain circumstances to have the right to request euthanasia (Cheng, 2013).

For Further Consideration

1. Under what conditions do individuals have the right to elect to die? Do you think the conditions for physician-assisted suicide are too strict or too lax?

2. Are physical or mental disabilities or declining physical conditions such as Alzheimer's disease sufficient reasons for suicide?

3. How would you define "unbearable psychological anguish"? Did Nathan Verhelst or the 45-year-old twins have a right to end their lives?

4. Does a doctor—or, for that matter, anyone—have a right to help others terminate their lives?

Transgender Nathan Verhelst (born Nancy Verhelst) one day before committing euthanasia.

or actions, suicide prevention may not be a primary target for therapeutic intervention. Having "suicide behavior disorder" as a diagnostic category would force clinicians to assess and treat this serious mental health condition (Oquendo, Baca-Garcia, Mann, & Giner, 2008).

Although including suicide as a diagnostic category would certainly draw more attention to this issue, questions remain about whether this change should occur. "Suicidal behavior disorder" would be a diagnosis associated with a single behavior—a suicide attempt. Is there sufficient rationale for creating a diagnostic category? Is it better to conceptualize suicide as a risk factor associated with other mental disorders, as we do currently? Would a "suicidal behavior disorder" diagnosis have a stigmatizing effect on clients and make them less willing to talk about suicide attempts since it would appear as a diagnosis on their records? Would this designation be permanent? Under the proposed criteria, an individual who made a suicide attempt 12 to 24 months previously without subsequent attempts would have a "suicidal behavior disorder in early remission."

As we discussed in Chapter 3, the DSM-5 now encourages therapists to ask about suicidal thoughts during initial assessment and to track changes in clients' mental health symptoms (including suicidal ideation) during treatment, especially for disorders associated with an increased suicide risk. DSM-5 currently mentions heightened risk of suicide as part of the diagnostic descriptions for approximately 20 disorders. For example, it is noted that individuals with specific phobias are "up to 60 percent more likely to make a suicide attempt" than people without this disorder (APA, 2013). This additional focus on suicide should result in better assessment and monitoring during treatment. This certainly is a step in the right direction—*if* practitioners use these methods consistently. Is this approach adequate, or do we need a "suicidal behavior disorder" diagnostic category to ensure adequate focus on suicidal behaviors? Research in the coming years should help answer this important question.

Researchers continue to search for the best methods for identifying and assisting individuals who are at risk for suicide. An innovative prevention program, the Durkheim Project, uses sophisticated linguistic-based prediction models to analyze postings on Facebook, Twitter, and LinkedIn to estimate an individual's suicide risk. High-tech computer programs work 24 hours a day to analyze social media data from the many veterans and active-duty military members who have chosen to participate in the program—the goal is to detect messages suggesting social isolation, interpersonal conflicts, or extreme emotional distress that might indicate a high risk for suicide or mental illness.

The hope is to detect suicide risk in real time and then alert pre-identified people who can provide support, such as a therapist, trusted family member, or designated buddy. The goal is to have at least 100,000 military personnel provide contact information and agree to have their social media messages monitored (Ramachandran, 2013). There is some optimism that the use of technology and innovative programs such as this will reduce suicide. Those working in the field are hopeful that "with improved diagnosis and care, the nation may finally be able to turn the tide on this loss and grief" (Kupfer, 2013).

chapter SUMMARY

1 What do we know about suicide?

- Suicide is the intentional, direct, and conscious taking of one's own life. The topic is often avoided, even among those directly affected by a suicide.

- A variety of demographic and specific risk factors are associated with suicide.

- Although women make more suicide attempts, men are more likely to kill themselves.

2 How is suicide unique in different age groups?

- In recent years, childhood and adolescent suicides have increased at an alarming rate.

- Suicide among college students is also a serious concern.

- Suicide rates are high among the baby boomer generation and among the elderly.

3 How does suicide affect friends and family?

- Suicide can affect surviving friends and family for years—feelings of guilt and responsibility are common.

4 What might cause someone to commit suicide?

- Genetic risk and biochemical abnormalities involving serotonin and neuropeptides are associated with suicide; alcohol use also exerts biological effects that increase suicide risk.

- Psychological factors include mental disturbance, depression, hopelessness, psychache, and suicide myopia resulting from excessive alcohol consumption.

- Lack of positive social relationships, feelings of loneliness and disconnection, interpersonal conflicts, and loss of a significant other can increase the chances of suicide.

- Race/ethnicity, economic downturns, male gender, and other demographic variables are all associated with increased risk of suicide.

5 How can we prevent suicide?

- The best way to prevent suicide is to recognize risk factors and intervene before it occurs.

- Crisis intervention strategies can help individuals who are contemplating suicide become more hopeful and consider other options. Intensive short-term therapy is used to stabilize the immediate crisis.

- Suicide prevention centers operate 24 hours a day to provide intervention services to people contemplating suicide.

- After a suicidal crisis has been resolved, ongoing therapy can help teach coping skills and treat underlying mental disorders. Cognitive-behavioral therapy (CBT) and dialectical behavior therapy (DBT) can help reduce suicidal ideation and suicide attempts.

6 What are future directions in the field of suicidology?

- Researchers worldwide are attempting to stem the tide of suicide by focusing on risk factors associated with suicide and effective methods of intervention.

- "Suicidal behavior disorder" is being considered for possible inclusion as a diagnostic category in future editions of the DSM.

- There is hope that the use of technology and innovative programs such as the Durkheim Project will reduce the number of suicides.

Hisayoshi Osawa/Getty Images

10

EATING DISORDERS

I LOOKED IN THE BATHROOM MIRROR AND A SKULL STARED BACK. A skull with a thin, very thin lining of pallid skin. Blanched lips, cheekbones so sharp they looked hurtful. Inanimate eyes. It seemed as if someone barely alive was looking through someone already dead. . . . I felt a shudder run through my bruised, emaciated body. . . Then a tingle of satisfaction. I was well on my way to succeeding! All I needed was to lose a few more pounds. . . . I stood 5'6" and weighed 79 pounds. . . . Two years later, I was dying. (Negreponti, 2012)

. . .

I purge about 4 times a day. . . . I have to be skinny, I want to be skinny. . . . I feel guilty and stupid if I don't purge everything out of my stomach. . . . I'm really scared. I don't want to die, but I don't know who to go to. (lcouvrely@yahoo.com, 2009)

. . .

My friends and I put on weight our first semester of college. . . . We ate dinner as a group, trying to stick to salad and grilled chicken, until one of us said "screw it," and we shared a heaping bowl of our favorite makeshift dessert: marshmallow fluff and butter melted in the dining hall microwave and mixed with sugary cereal and chocolate chips. (Kapalko, 2010)

In the United States, eating disorders and **disordered eating** patterns are becoming increasingly prevalent. Over 90 percent of college women have attempted to control their weight through dieting and 25 percent have used purging as a weight control method (Anorexia Nervosa and Associated Disorders, 2014). Adolescents also show concerns over weight or body size. Nearly 50 percent of adolescent girls and 20 percent of adolescent boys diet to control their weight. Weight concerns are so great that 13.4 percent of girls and 7.1 percent of boys have engaged in disordered eating patterns (Table 10.1). Unfortunately, disordered eating is often accompanied by depression, substance use, and suicidal ideation (Franco et al., 2013).

Despite frequent dieting and increasing societal emphasis on thinness—especially for women—people in the United States are getting heavier. As of 2012, 68 percent of adults were overweight; 35 percent of those were obese, as were 17 percent of children and adolescents (CDC, 2013; Flegal, Carroll, Kit, & Ogden, 2012). Weight and body shape concerns are now common

focus
QUESTIONS

1 What kinds of eating disorders exist?

2 What are some causes of eating disorders?

3 What are some treatment options for eating disorders?

4 What causes obesity and how is it treated?

Table 10.1 Prevalence of Weight Concerns of Youth in Grades 5–12

	Girls	Boys
Very important not to be overweight	68.5%	54.3%
Ever been on a diet	45.4%	20.2%
Diet recommended by parent	14.5%	13.6%
Diet to "look better"	88.5%	62.2%
Engage in binge/purge behaviors	13.4%	7.1%
Binge/purge at least once a day	8.9%	4.1%

SOURCE: Data from Neumark-Sztainer, Hannan, & Stat (2000).

not only among young white women and girls (the group most affected by eating disorders) but also among older women and members of ethnic minorities (Gagne et al., 2012).

Men and boys, especially those who compare themselves to others, are also demonstrating more behaviors associated with body dissatisfaction, such as exercising excessively and obsessively monitoring their weight (Bucchianeri, Serrano, Pastula, & Corning, 2014). Body dissatisfaction among men ranges from 9.0 percent to 28.4 percent according to various studies (Fallon, Harris, & Johnson, 2014). Weight dissatisfaction in men and boys most frequently involves a desire to be heavier and more muscular (Calzo, Corliss, Blood, Field, & Austin, 2013).

In a cross-cultural study in Germany, France, and the United States (H. G. Pope, Gruber, et al., 2000), pictures of men differing in size and muscularity were shown to male college students. The students were asked to choose images that represented their own bodies, the bodies they would like to have, and the male body they thought women preferred. In all three countries, the men picked an ideal body that was about 28 pounds heavier and more muscular than their own. Participants also believed that women preferred a very muscular male body. (Women actually preferred ordinary male bodies without added muscle.) An extreme dissatisfaction with one's muscularity is called **muscle dysmorphia** (S. B. Murray, Rieger, Touyz, & De la Garza Garcia, 2010).

Body dissatisfaction in men, as with women, may be due to social comparison processes involving media images portraying body types that few can achieve. A study of advertisements in *Sports Illustrated* magazine from 1975 to 2005 revealed an increase in muscular and lean male models. Male adolescents and college-age men exposed to these types of images are more likely to evaluate themselves negatively (Hobza & Rochlen, 2009). These unrealistic images may be responsible for the fact that over 4 percent of high school boys have taken steroids to gain more muscle mass; the prevalence of steroid use is even higher (21 percent) among male adolescents who self-identify as gay or bisexual (Blashill, & Safren, 2014).

In this chapter, you will learn why disordered eating patterns are increasing and about the characteristics, causes, and treatment of eating disorders. We also include a discussion of obesity, another condition with serious physical and psychological consequences.

disordered eating physically or psychologically unhealthy eating behavior such as chronic overeating or dieting with the goal of losing or controlling weight or managing emotions

muscle dysmorphia extreme dissatisfaction with one's muscularity

Eating Disorders

Preoccupation with weight and body dimensions can become extreme and lead to eating disorders such as anorexia nervosa, bulimia nervosa, or binge-eating disorder (Table 10.2). In a survey using DSM-5 criteria, the lifetime prevalence of anorexia

Table 10.2 Eating Disorders

DISORDERS CHART			
Disorder	**DSM-5 Criteria**	**Prevalence (%) and Gender Difference**	**Age of Onset**
Anorexia nervosa types: • Restricting • Binge-eating/purging	• Restricted caloric intake resulting in body weight significantly below the minimum normal weight for one's age and height • Intense fear of gaining weight or becoming fat, which does not diminish even with weight loss • Body image distortion (not recognizing one's thinness) or self-evaluation unduly influenced by weight	0.5–0.9; about 90% are female in clinical samples	Usually after puberty or in early adulthood
• Bulimia nervosa	• Recurrent episodes of binge eating and compensatory behaviors (one or more times per week for 3 or more months) • Loss of control over eating behavior when bingeing • Use of vomiting, exercise, laxatives, or fasting to control weight • Self-evaluation unduly influenced by weight or body shape	1–2.6%; about 90% are female	Late adolescence or early adulthood
• Binge-eating disorder (BED)	• Recurrent episodes of binge eating (one or more binges a week for 3 or more months) • Loss of control when bingeing • Eating until uncomfortably full or when not hungry • No regular use of inappropriate compensatory activities to control weight • Marked distress (guilt, embarrassment, depression) over bingeing	0.7–4%; 1.5 times more prevalent in females than in males; about 20–40% in weight-control clinics have this disorder	Late adolescence or early 20s

SOURCE: Data from APA (2013); Hudson, Hiripi, Pope, & Kessler (2007); Stice, Marti, & Rohde (2013).

nervosa, bulimia nervosa, and binge-eating disorder among 20-year-old females was 0.8 percent, 2.6 percent, and 3.0 percent, respectively (Stice, Marti, & Rohde, 2013). For men, using DSM-IV-TR criteria, the lifetime prevalence rate for anorexia nervosa, bulimia nervosa, and binge-eating disorder is 0.3 percent, 0.5 percent, and 2 percent (Hudson, Hiripi, Pope, & Kessler, 2007). In addition, many people exhibit disordered eating that does not quite meet the criteria for these eating disorders (Stice et al., 2013). We begin our discussion of eating disorders with a focus on a life-threatening condition: anorexia nervosa.

Anorexia Nervosa

CASE STUDY   Portia DeGeneres, known for her starring roles in the television shows *Ally McBeal*, *Arrested Development*, and *Better Off Ted*, weighed 82 pounds, at 5 ft. 7 in. tall, when coping with an eating disorder in her mid-20s. In her quest to become a model, she became consumed with bingeing, purging, exercising, dieting, and using laxatives. In her autobiography *Unbearable Lightness: A Story of Loss and Gain*, DeGeneres recounts eating only 300 calories per day, taking up to 20 laxatives a day, and exercising for hours. She received a "wakeup call" when her brother broke down and said he was afraid she was going to die. When she collapsed on a movie set, her

Portia DeGeneres

Portia DeGeneres' eating disorder had its roots in attempts to meet an idealized standard of beauty and turmoil over her sexual identity.

doctors said her organs were close to failing. These events helped her make changes in her life. With the development of self-confidence and self-acceptance, and coming out as a lesbian, DeGeneres now maintains a normal weight (de Rossi, 2010).

One of the most obvious symptoms of **anorexia nervosa** is extreme thinness. Individuals with this puzzling disorder starve themselves, relentlessly pursuing thinness, and detest weigh gain. Their body image is distorted (i.e., they see themselves as fat) and they deny the seriousness of the physical effects of their low body weight (National Institute of Mental Health, 2014).

Anorexia nervosa has been recognized for centuries. It occurs primarily in adolescent girls and young women, although 10 percent of those with this condition are male (APA, 2013). A very frightening characteristic of anorexia nervosa is that most people with the disorder, even when clearly emaciated, continue to insist they are overweight. Some may acknowledge that they are thin but maintain that some parts of their bodies are too fat. In most cases, the body image disturbance is profound. As one researcher noted more than 35 years ago, people with this disorder "vigorously defend their often gruesome emaciation as not being too thin. . . . They identify with the skeleton-like appearance, actively maintain it, and deny its abnormality" (H. Bruch, 1978, p. 209).

Subtypes of Anorexia Nervosa

Although the popular view of an individual with anorexia nervosa is a person who eats very little, there are actually two subtypes of the disorder: the restricting type and the binge-eating/purging type. The *restricting type* involves weight loss through severe dieting or exercising. The *binge-eating/purging type* involves self-induced vomiting or use of laxatives or diuretics to control weight, often after binge eating. Although both groups vigorously pursue thinness, they differ in some aspects. Those with the restricting type of anorexia nervosa are more introverted and tend to deny psychological distress or feelings of hunger. Those with the binge-eating/purging type are more extroverted and impulsive; report more anxiety, depression, and guilt; often have a strong appetite; and tend to be older (Sansone & Sansone, 2011).

Physical Complications

Anorexia nervosa is associated with serious medical complications. The mortality rate is up to 6 times higher than that of the general population due to suicide, substance abuse, and the physiological effects of starvation (Franko et al., 2013; Papadopoulous, Ekbom, Brandt, & Ekselius, 2009). Self-starvation produces a variety of physical problems such as irregular heart rate and low blood pressure. In addition, starvation causes the heart to become damaged when the body is forced to use muscles as a source of energy. Other physical changes include extreme fatigue, dry skin, brittle hair, low body temperature, and kidney disease (Bouquegneau, Dubois, Krzesinski, & Delanaye, 2012).

Those who **purge** often develop enlarged salivary glands, resulting in a "chipmunk look" to the face (NIMH, 2014). Bone loss is another common side effect of low caloric intake (Olmos et al., 2010). Portia DeGeneres experienced osteoporosis (weakening of the bones) and cirrhosis of the liver and was near death as a result of her self-starvation. Unfortunately, even with the severe health and emotional damage associated with the disorder, Web sites advocating anorexia as a lifestyle choice continue to appear on the Internet.

Course and Outcome

The course of anorexia nervosa is highly variable and can range from full recovery after one episode to a fluctuating pattern of weight gain and relapse to a chronic and deteriorating course ending in death (APA, 2013). In follow-up studies, about 20 percent of those with anorexia nervosa remained severely ill, with over 50 percent

anorexia nervosa an eating disorder characterized by low body weight, an intense fear of becoming obese, and body image distortion

purge to rid the body of unwanted calories by means such as self-induced vomiting or misuse of laxatives, diuretics, or other medications

Anorexia's Web

- Drink ice-cold water ("Your body has to burn calories to keep your temperature up") and hot water with bouillon cubes ("only 5 calories a cube, and they taste wonderful") (Springen, 2006).

- "Starvation is fulfilling.... The greatest enjoyment of food is actually found when never a morsel passes the lips" (Irizarry, 2004).

- "I will be thin, at all costs, it is the most important thing, nothing else matters" (Bardone-Cone & Cass, 2007).

Tips to reduce caloric intake, testimonials regarding the satisfaction of not eating, ways to conceal thinness from friends and family members, and rules to remain thin are part of pro-ana (anorexia) and pro-mia (bulimia) Web sites (Bond, 2012; Borzekowski et al., 2010). Some of the screen names used in online discussion groups include "thinspiration," "puking pals," "disappearing acts," "anorexiangel," and "chunkee monkeee." Participants on the Anorexic Nation Web site talk about how it is important to have friends who are like them, and argue that anorexia is a lifestyle choice and not an illness. In one study, 43 percent of those who visited the Web sites indicated that they received emotional support: "I kind of lost all of my friends at school and in my neighborhood but I still have my pro-ana and pro-mia friends" (Csipke & Horne, 2007, p. 202).

Such Web sites are visited by thousands of people each day, including many adolescents experimenting with disordered eating (Rouleau & von Ranson, 2011). Medical experts are deeply concerned that the sites are increasing the incidence of eating disorders, especially among susceptible individuals.

For Further Consideration

1. How much danger do you feel these Web sites pose to people with and without eating disorders?

2. What types of messages from these Web sites might resonate with young girls?

3. What kinds of restrictions, if any, should be placed on pro-ana and pro-mia Web sites?

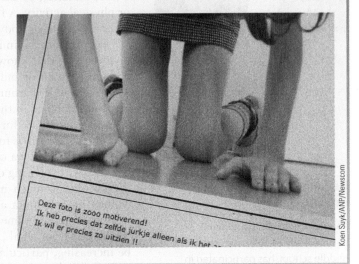

Deze foto is zooo motiverend! Ik heb precies dat zelfde jurkje alleen als ik het ... Ik wil er precies zo uitzien !!

Koen Suyk/ANP/Newscom

continuing to display disordered eating patterns. Purging, vomiting, and obsessive-compulsive eating behaviors are associated with an unfavorable outcome. There is a high mortality rate among those with anorexia nervosa, including those who commit suicide (Steinhausen, 2009).

Associated Characteristics

Depression, anxiety, impulse control problems, loss of sexual interest, and substance use often occur concurrently with anorexia nervosa (Pinheiro et al., 2010). Many individuals with anorexia nervosa have difficulty regulating their emotions, a factor that may maintain disordered eating patterns (Manuel & Wade, 2013; Naumann, Tuschen-Caffier, Voderholzer, & Svaldi, 2014). For some, the excessive control associated with restricted eating may occur to counteract feelings of powerlessness: "I feel so strong when I'm not eating and I feel success and such power and such control when I am not feeding my body" (Battiste & Effron, 2012). Additionally, weight loss is equated with success, temporarily boosting self-esteem (Draxler & Hiltunen, 2012).

Obsessive-compulsive behaviors and thoughts that may or may not involve food are common in those with anorexia nervosa (APA, 2013). For example, one woman worried that touching or even breathing around food would cause her to gain weight (Bulik & Kendler, 2000). The manner in which these symptoms are related to anorexia

Splash/Splash News/Corbis

Recovering from Societal Pressure to Be Thin

Popular singer, Ke$ha , who has battled body image issues since middle school, has participated in intensive inpatient treatment for an eating disorder. Her eating disorder reportedly developed in response to criticism about her weight from individuals managing her career.

bulimia nervosa an eating disorder in which episodes involving rapid consumption of large quantities of food and a loss of control over eating are followed by purging (vomiting, use of laxatives, diuretics, or enemas) or excessive exercise or fasting in an attempt to compensate for binges

binge eating rapid consumption of large quantities of food during a discrete period of time

nervosa is unclear because of the possibility that malnutrition or starvation may cause or exacerbate obsessive symptoms.

Bulimia Nervosa

CASE STUDY   "At first, after eating too much, I would just go to the toilet and make myself sick. I hadn't heard of bulimia. . . . I started eating based on how I was feeling about myself. If my hair looked bad, I'd stuff down loads of candy. After a while, I started exercising excessively because I felt so guilty about eating. I'd run for miles and miles and go to the gym for three hours." (Dirmann, 2003, p. 60)

Bulimia nervosa is an eating disorder characterized by (1) recurrent episodes of **binge eating** (rapid consumption of large quantities of food) that occur at least once a week for 3 months or more and (2) a loss of control over eating during the binge episode. Individuals with bulimia nervosa attempt to avoid weight gain by vomiting; using laxatives, diuretics, or enemas; restricting food intake; or engaging in excessive exercise or physical activity. A final characteristic is that self-evaluation is strongly influenced by one's weight or body shape (APA, 2013).

People with bulimia realize that their eating patterns are not normal, and are distressed by that knowledge. Eating episodes sometimes continue until they develop abdominal pain or induce vomiting. They often feel disgusted or ashamed of their eating and hide it from others. Some individuals eat nothing during the day but lose control and binge in the late afternoon or evening. For those who vomit or use laxatives to compensate for overeating, the temporary relief (from physical discomfort or fear of weight gain) is followed by feelings of shame and despair. Binge-eating episodes may be followed by a commitment to fasting, severely restricting eating, or engaging in excessive exercising or other physical activity (NIMH, 2014).

Bulimia is much more prevalent than anorexia nervosa. Up to 2.6 percent of women have bulimia at some point in their lifetime, and an additional 10 percent of women report some symptoms but do not meet all the criteria for the diagnosis (Hudson, Hiripi, et al., 2007; Stice et al., 2013). The incidence of bulimia appears to be increasing, particularly in urban areas. Fewer men and boys exhibit the disorder, presumably because there is less cultural pressure for them to remain thin; however, up to 10 percent of those affected by this disorder are males (APA, 2013).

Physical Complications

People with bulimia use a variety of measures—fasting, self-induced vomiting, diet pills, laxatives, and exercise—to control the weight gain that accompanies binge eating. Side effects from self-induced vomiting or from excessive use of laxatives include erosion of tooth enamel from vomited stomach acid; dehydration; swollen salivary glands; and lowered potassium, which can weaken the heart and cause heart irregularities and cardiac arrest (Nashoni, Yaroslavsky, Varticovschi, Weizman, & Stein, 2010). Other possible gastrointestinal disturbances include inflammation of the esophagus, stomach, and rectal area.

Associated Characteristics

Individuals with bulimia often use eating as a way of coping with distressing thoughts or external stressors (C. B. Peterson et al., 2010). As one woman stated, "Purging was the biggest part of my day. . . . It was my release from the stress and monotony of my life" (Erdely, 2004, p. 117). There is a close relationship between emotional states and disturbed eating. For example, among individuals with bulimia, the highest rates of binge eating occur during negative emotional states, including periods of anger or depression (Crosby et al., 2009). Negative moods such as sadness, hostility, and fear increase before bingeing and purging episodes, and decrease after these activities

(Berg et al., 2013). These studies seem to suggest that bulimic behaviors may represent maladaptive attempts at emotional regulation.

Course and Outcome

Bulimia nervosa has a somewhat later onset than anorexia nervosa, often beginning in late adolescence or early adult life. The mortality and suicide rates for this disorder are elevated, particularly among those who exercise excessively (Smith et al., 2012). Outcome studies have shown a mixed course, although the prognosis is more positive than for anorexia nervosa. In one follow-up study, about one third of individuals showed complete remission, one third showed partial remission, and the remaining one third continued to meet the criteria for bulimia nervosa (Zeeck, Weber, Sandholz, Joos, & Hartmann, 2011). Based on an analysis of the results of 27 studies involving 5,653 individuals with bulimia nervosa, approximately 45 percent made a full recovery, 27 percent demonstrated considerable improvement, and 23 percent showed little or no improvement. Those with better emotional functioning and positive social support had better outcomes, whereas psychosocial stress and low social status increased the likelihood of continued difficulties (Steinhausen & Weber, 2009). Because suicide risk is high for those with bulimia nervosa, some researchers recommend suicide risk assessments for individuals with bulimic symptoms (Bodell, Joiner, & Keel, 2013).

Binge-Eating Disorder

CASE STUDY   Ms. A, a 38-year-old African American woman, was single, lived alone, and was employed as a personnel manager. She weighed 292 pounds. Her chief reason for coming to the clinic was that she felt her eating was out of control, and as a result, she had gained approximately 80 pounds over the previous year. A typical binge episode consisted of the ingestion of two pieces of chicken, one small bowl of salad, two servings of mashed potatoes, one hamburger, one large serving of french fries, one large chocolate shake, one large bag of potato chips, and 15 to 20 small cookies—all within a 2-hour period. She was embarrassed by how much she was eating, and felt disgusted with herself and very guilty after eating. (Goldfein, Devlin, & Spitzer, 2000, p. 1,052)

Binge-eating disorder (BED) is similar to bulimia nervosa in that it involves bingeing, an accompanying feeling of loss of control, and marked distress over eating during the episodes. To be diagnosed with BED, an individual must have a history of binge-eating episodes at least once a week for a period of 3 months. Additionally, those with BED also exhibit at least three of the following with binge-eating episodes: eating more rapidly than normal; uncomfortable feeling of fullness; eating large amounts of food even when not hungry; eating alone due to embarrassment about the quantity eaten; or feeling depressed or guilty after bingeing. Unlike bulimia nervosa, those with BED do not use compensatory behaviors such as vomiting, excessive exercising, or fasting (APA, 2013).

Women and girls are 1.5 times more likely to have this disorder than are men and boys; the lifetime prevalence rate is 3.5 percent in women and 2 percent in men (Hudson, Hiripi, et al., 2007). White women make up the vast majority of those seeking treatment, whereas in community samples, the percentages of African American and white women with BED are roughly equal (Wilfley, Pike, Dohm, Striegel-Moore, & Fairburn, 2001).

Associated Characteristics

In contrast to those with bulimia nervosa, individuals with BED are often overweight (Bull, 2004). About 20–40 percent of individuals in weight control programs have

Body Revolution 2013

Aware of societal pressures on weight, Lady Gaga, who struggled with bulimia and anorexia in her teens, launched a project called Body Revolution 2013 to help her fans accept their bodies rather than focus on perceived shortcomings. Lady Gaga recently gained weight but reports feeling happier than ever with her body.

binge-eating disorder (BED)   an eating disorder that involves the consumption of large amounts of food over a short period of time with accompanying feelings of loss of control and distress over the excess eating; behaviors to compensate for overeating are not typically seen with this disorder

Table 10.3 Do You Have an Eating Disorder?

Questions for Possible Anorexia Nervosa
1. Are you considered to be underweight by others? (Screening question. If yes, continue to next questions.)
2. Are you intensely fearful of gaining weight or becoming fat even though you are underweight?
3. Do you feel that your body or a part of your body is too fat?
4. Do you diet, exercise, or make yourself vomit or take laxatives to lose weight even though you are underweight?

Questions for Possible Bulimia Nervosa
1. Do you have binges in which you eat a lot of food? (Screening question. If yes, continue to next questions.)
2. When you binge, do you feel a lack of control over eating?
3. Do you make yourself vomit, take laxatives, or exercise excessively because of overeating?
4. Are you very dissatisfied with your body shape or weight?

Questions for Possible Binge-Eating Disorder
1. Do you have binges in which you eat a lot of food?
2. When you binge, do you feel a lack of control over eating?

3. When you binge, do three or more of the following apply?
  a. You eat more rapidly than usual.
  b. You eat until uncomfortably full.
  c. You eat large amounts even when not hungry.
  d. You eat alone because of embarrassment from overeating.
  e. You feel disgusted, depressed, or guilty about binge eating.

4. Do you feel great distress regarding your binge eating?

Note: These questions are derived from the diagnostic criteria for eating disorders (APA, 2013).

BED. Binges are often preceded by poor mood, decreased alertness, feelings of poor eating control, and cravings for sweets (Hilbert & Tuschen-Caffier, 2007). Although overvaluation of weight and shape is not part of the diagnostic criteria for BED, many with this condition are unduly influenced by their weight or shape, a factor associated with feelings of depression, anxiety, and low self-esteem (Grilo, White, & Masheb, 2012). When experiencing weight or shape concerns, women with BED report that their negative emotions result in increased craving for food (Svaldi, Caffier, Blechert, & Tuschen-Caffier, 2009). Those who expect that eating will help relieve emotional distress are more likely to engage in binge eating (DeYoung, Zander, & Anderson, 2014). Complications from BED include medical conditions associated with obesity, such as type 2 diabetes, high blood pressure, and high cholesterol levels. (See Table 10.3 for questions used to assess for an eating disorder.)

Course and Outcome

The onset of BED is similar to that of bulimia nervosa in that it typically begins in late adolescence or early adulthood. There is limited information on the natural course of BED, although remission rates appear to be higher than anorexia nervosa or bulimia nervosa. In one study, most individuals with BED made a full recovery over a 5-year period, even without treatment, with only 18 percent continuing to demonstrate an eating disorder of clinical severity. However, their weight remained high, including 39 percent who were obese (Fairburn, Cooper, Doll, Norman, & O'Connor, 2000).

Other Specified Feeding or Eating Disorders

The category **other specified feeding or eating disorders** includes seriously disturbed eating patterns that do not fully meet the criteria for anorexia nervosa, bulimia nervosa, or binge-eating disorder. This is the most commonly diagnosed eating disorder and accounts for up to 30 percent of eating disorder diagnoses (Allen, Byrne, Oddy, & Crosby, 2013; Swanson, Crow, LeGrange, Swendsen, & Merikangas, 2011). Examples of people who fit in this category include the following:

- Individuals of normal weight who meet the other criteria for anorexia nervosa
- Individuals who meet the criteria for bulimia nervosa or binge-eating disorder except that binge eating occurs less than once a week or has been present for less than 3 months
- Individuals with *night-eating syndrome*, a distressing pattern of binge eating late at night or after awakening from sleep
- Individuals who do not binge but frequently purge (self-induced vomiting, misuse of laxatives, diuretics, or enemas) as a means to control weight (APA, 2013)

Other specified feeding or eating disorders is a problematic diagnostic category because it includes a variety of symptoms and nonspecific symptom severity. Although individuals with this diagnosis often feel that their condition is not as serious as the other eating disorders, they may be equally vulnerable to serious health complications (Battiste & Effron, 2012). Additionally, many individuals who receive this diagnosis have emotional problems (J. J. Thomas, Vartanian, & Brownell, 2009) and later develop bulimia nervosa or binge-eating disorder (Stice, Marti, Shaw, & Jaconis, 2009). As with other eating disorders, individuals in this category show increased risk of mortality and higher risk of suicide (Crow, Peterson, et al., 2009).

Etiology of Eating Disorders

The search for the causal factors associated with eating disorders is complicated because biological, psychological, social, and sociocultural factors interact to produce vulnerability to these disorders. We examine each of these influences to determine how they might explain the development of the severe dieting, bingeing, and purging behaviors found in eating disorders. Understanding etiology involves looking for conditions that both precede the development of disordered eating and maintain the disorder. Keeping this in mind, we use the multipath model (Figure 10.1) to consider the risk factors associated with eating disorders.

Psychological Dimension

Psychological risk factors increase an individual's chances of developing an eating disorder. These include body dissatisfaction, perfectionism, depression, low levels of interpersonal competence, and use of control over eating as a method of dealing with stress (T. A. Myers & Crowther, 2009).

Body dissatisfaction arises when someone's weight or body shape differs significantly from an imagined ideal. Up to one third of young people and a large percentage

other specified feeding or eating disorders a seriously disturbed eating pattern that does not fully meet criteria for another eating disorder diagnosis

Figure 10.1

Multipath Model of Eating Disorders

The dimensions interact with one another and combine in different ways to result in an eating disorder.

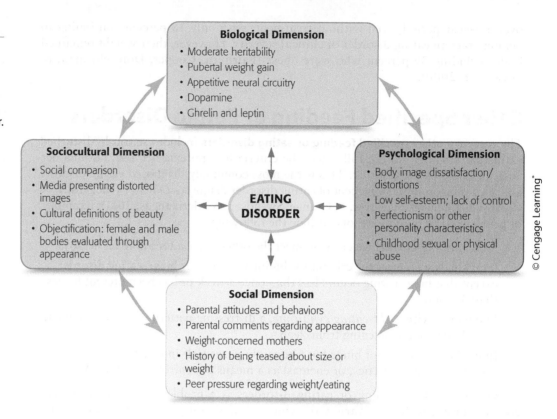

Biological Dimension
- Moderate heritability
- Pubertal weight gain
- Appetitive neural circuitry
- Dopamine
- Ghrelin and leptin

Sociocultural Dimension
- Social comparison
- Media presenting distorted images
- Cultural definitions of beauty
- Objectification: female and male bodies evaluated through appearance

EATING DISORDER

Psychological Dimension
- Body image dissatisfaction/ distortions
- Low self-esteem; lack of control
- Perfectionism or other personality characteristics
- Childhood sexual or physical abuse

Social Dimension
- Parental attitudes and behaviors
- Parental comments regarding appearance
- Weight-concerned mothers
- History of being teased about size or weight
- Peer pressure regarding weight/eating

© Cengage Learning

DID YOU KNOW?

Men who score high on measures of sexist attitudes and the objectification of women are also more focused on their own muscularity.

SOURCE: Swami & Voracek, 2013

of women between the ages of 35 and 65 have significant levels of body dissatisfaction (Gagne et al., 2012; McLean et al., 2010). There are significant ethnic differences in body dissatisfaction. For example, among female college students, European American and Asian American women reported greater frequency of body checking and thin-ideal internalization than African American and Latina women (White & Warren, 2013). Women highly dissatisfied with their bodies are more likely to compare their bodies to those of other women and report lower self-satisfaction after this process (Trampe, Stapel, & Siero, 2010). And men who highly value personal attractiveness and appearance report lower body satisfaction when exposed to TV commercials featuring muscular men (Hargreaves & Tiggemann, 2009). Body dissatisfaction is a robust risk factor in the development of eating disorders in longitudinal studies (Wade, George, & Atkinson, 2009). For example, many individuals with BED have internalized societal weight biases and stigma associated with weight—a factor that contributes to their emotional distress and binge eating (Durso et al., 2012).

Maladaptive perfectionism is also a risk factor; it may interact with body dissatisfaction to influence the development of anorexia nervosa and other eating disorders. Maladaptive perfectionism is composed of two dimensions: (a) inflexible high standards and (b) negative self-evaluations following mistakes. In fact, perfectionistic traits in early childhood are associated with the development of anorexia nervosa (Halmi et al., 2012). As you might imagine, imposing perfectionist standards on someone's weight, shape, or dieting may cause disordered eating (Boone, Soenens, Braet, & Goossens, 2010).

Individuals with eating disorders also appear to use food or weight regulation as a means of handling stress or anxiety (Battiste & Effron, 2012). Dieting may represent an effort to demonstrate self-control or to improve self-esteem and body image (C. Jones, Leung, & Harris, 2007). One

CONTINUUM Video Project

Sara: **Bulimia Nervosa**

"The refrigerator became my confidante."

Access the Continuum Video Project at
www.cengage.com

© Cengage Learning

woman stated, "We can be told what to do and what to think. We can be pressured in all sorts of ways. But we decide what, if anything, crosses our lips" (L. Carroll, 2011). In contrast, people who binge often view eating as a source of comfort and a way to counteract depression and other negative emotions (Bergstrom & Neighbors, 2006). Individuals who believe eating will relieve negative affect such as depression are more likely to binge (DeYoung et al., 2014).

Perceived or actual inadequacies in interpersonal skills are also associated with eating disorders, particularly when combined with maladaptive perfectionism (Ferrier-Auerbach & Martens, 2009). Individuals with eating disorders often perceive low levels of social support, which may be due to a passive interpersonal style (Bodell et al., 2011). For both men and women, characteristics such as passivity, low self-esteem, dependence, and nonassertiveness are associated with disordered eating (Arcelus, Haslam, Farrow, & Meyer, 2013; A. Hartmann, Zeeck, & Barrett, 2010). Not only do individuals with eating disorders appear to have interpersonal anxiety and perfectionistic tendencies, they also possess "self-uncertainty," which involves a low self-concept and limited sense of self (von Lojewski & Abraham, 2014).

Mood disorders such as depression often accompany eating disorders. Rates of depression are also higher in relatives of individuals with eating disorders than in control populations, suggesting that, in some cases, disordered eating may be a symptom of depression (Mischoulon et al., 2011). At this point, we still do not know the precise relationship between depression and eating disorders. Depression may be the result, not the cause, of having an eating disorder.

Social Dimension

Can certain relationship patterns increase the likelihood of developing an eating disorder? Some individuals coping with eating disorders report that their parents or family members frequently criticized them, had a negative reaction to their eating issues, or blamed them for their condition (Di Paola, Faravelli, & Ricca, 2010). Childhood maltreatment and negative family relationships possibly produce a self-critical style that causes depression and body dissatisfaction (Dunkley, Masheb, & Grilo, 2010).

Research findings to support this relationship are difficult to interpret. First, most research depends on the individual's perceptions regarding family relationships, and recollections that may or may not be accurate. Additionally, family interaction patterns may be a response to disordered eating rather than the cause of the disorder.

Myrleen Pearson/PhotoEdit

Body Consciousness

Women and girls are socialized to be conscious of their bodies. Although most of the attention has been directed to concerns over appearance among young white girls, rates of disordered eating and body dissatisfaction are also high among Latina/Hispanic American and American Indian girls.

Parents may become "controlling" because they are concerned about extreme weight loss or unhealthy eating patterns (Le Grange, Lock, Loeb, & Nicholls, 2010). At this point we do not know whether the described negative interaction patterns reported in the families of individuals with eating disorders are causal factors or reactions to disordered eating.

Peers or family members can inadvertently produce pressure to be thin through discussions of weight and encouragement to diet or exercise (T. Jackson & Chen, 2010). Among college-age women, "fat talk" is common. It involves the discussion of being overweight with friends who usually deny this observation. Although women who engage in fat talk believe it makes them feel better about their bodies, this pattern of conversation can increase body dissatisfaction and lower self-esteem (Rudigera & Winstead, 2013).

Certain social relationship patterns may increase the risk of developing an eating disorder. For example, mothers who diet are indirectly transmitting the message of the importance of slimness and a thin-ideal to their daughters (Keel, Forney, Brown, & Heatherton, 2013). Also, teasing and criticism about weight or body shape by family members is associated with body dissatisfaction, dieting, and eating problems (Vincent & McCabe, 2000). Peers can also produce pressure to lose weight, particularly when exposure to the ideal of thinness occurs during a critical period of development such as adolescence or early adulthood. In a longitudinal study, girls who reported that their friends were very focused on dieting at the beginning of the study were most likely to engage in extreme dieting and unhealthy weight control behaviors 5 years later (Eisenberg & Neumark-Sztainer, 2010). Similarly, women whose college friends and roommates focused on dieting were more likely to exhibit disordered eating during adulthood even though friendships, life roles, and the living environment had changed (Keel et al., 2013).

Sociocultural Dimension

A great deal of research has focused on the influence of sociocultural norms and values in the etiology of eating disorders. In the United States and most Western cultures, physical appearance is considered a very important attribute, especially for women and girls (Hausenblas et al., 2013). Teenage girls often strive to be very thin; although this body type is far from the norm, it is consistent with body images portrayed in the media. Table 10.4 provides data on the average weights of adults in the United States, data that differ significantly from this "thin-ideal."

Table 10.4 Average Weight for Women and Men 20–74 Years (in Pounds) for 1994–2010

	1994	2010
Women	153.0	166.2
Men	181.3	195.5
By ethnicity and gender		
White women	151.4	165.4
African American women	169.7	187.9
Mexican American women	152.6	161.5
White men	183.7	199.2
African American men	181.2	199.4
Mexican American men	172.3	185.4

SOURCE: Ogden, Fryar, Carroll, & Flegal (2004); Fryar, Gu, & Ogden (2012).

Women are socialized to be conscious of their body shape and weight. At an early age, girls are sexualized and objectified through television, music videos, song lyrics, magazines, and advertising (American Psychological Association, Task Force on the Sexualization of Girls, 2007) (see Figure 10.2). Following exposure to these messages, girls begin to (a) believe that their primary value comes from being attractive, (b) define themselves according to the body standards shown in media, and (c) see themselves as objects rather than as having the capacity for independent action and decision making. As girls and women adopt these unrealistic standards, many internalize a *thin-ideal* and begin to agree with statements such as "slender women are more attractive" or "I would like to look like the women that appear in TV shows and movies" (J. K. Thompson & Stice, 2004, p. 99). In a random sample of 100 teenage girls, more than 60 percent reported trying to change their appearance to resemble that of a celebrity (Seitz, 2007).

What kind of predisposition or characteristic leads some people to interpret images of thinness in the media as evidence of their own inadequacy? Are people who develop eating disorders chronically self-conscious to begin with, or do they develop eating disorders because their social environment makes them chronically self-conscious? How does exposure to portrayals of thinness in the mass media influence the values and norms of young people? The development of disordered eating and preoccupation with body image appears to involve multiple processes (T. A. Myers & Crowther, 2009).

A process of *social comparison* occurs in which women and girls begin to evaluate themselves according to external standards (see Figure 10.3). Because these standards are unattainable for most women, body dissatisfaction occurs. Studies on the topic suggest that one third of the women in the United States are dissatisfied with their body shape and weight (Fallon et al., 2014). Self-consciousness and frequent monitoring of one's external appearance can lead to anxiety or shame about the body. When women compare their body shape or weight with other women's, those with high body dissatisfaction report increased feelings of guilt and depression. Thoughts of "solutions" such as dieting, purging, and extreme exercise increase, especially among those with the greatest body dissatisfaction (Leahey, Crowther, & Ciesla, 2011). Thus, social comparison appears to be a strong risk factor for eating disorders, especially among women who are dissatisfied with their bodies. Although societal emphasis on thinness may increase disordered eating, it does not explain why only a small percentage of individuals in our media-conscious society develop eating disorders.

As noted in the beginning of the chapter, mass media portrayals of lean, muscular male bodies are increasing. There appears to be a gradual shift away from traditional measures of masculinity, such as wealth and power, to physical appearance. Given this trend, is body image dissatisfaction among men increasing? It appears so. More men

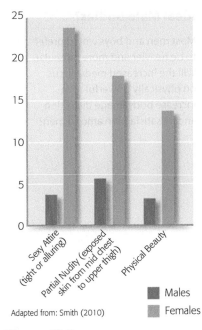

Adapted from: Smith (2010)

Males
Females

Figure 10.2

Objectification of Women and Girls

In family films (those with a G, PG, or PG-13 rating), women and girls often are "scantily clad" and very attractive, and have an unrealistic body shape. Does this contribute to the objectification of girls and women?

SOURCE: S. L. Smith & Choueiti (2010).

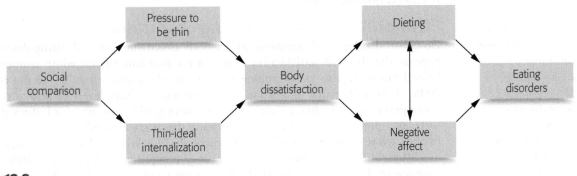

Figure 10.3

Route to Eating Disorders

Social comparison can lead to the development of eating disorders.

SOURCE: Adapted from Stice (2001).

Ideal Male Bodies?

Most men and boys would prefer to be heavier and more muscular. Will the increased media focus on physically powerful men increase body image distortion and dissatisfaction among men?

©Istvan Csak/Shutterstock.com

are reporting body fat dissatisfaction (A. R. Smith, Hawkeswood, Bodell, & Joiner, 2011) and displeasure with their musculature (Farquhar & Wasylkiw, 2007). Muscle enhancing behaviors such as the use of protein powders, steroids, and exercising are becoming common in male adolescents (Eisenberg & Neumark-Sztainer, 2010; Field et al., 2014).

Compared to heterosexual men, gay men tend to place greater emphasis on physical attractiveness. This focus on physical attributes often results in concern over body size and a greater prevalence of disturbed eating patterns (Blashill & Vander Wal, 2009). Similarly, body fat dissatisfaction and media images of attractive males are linked to appearance-related anxiety and disordered eating in gay men (Carper, Negy, & Tantleff-Dunn, 2010; A. R. Smith, Hawkeswood, Bodell, & Joiner, 2011). The fact that steroid use is prevalent among gay adolescents suggests that this socialization process begins early (Blashill & Safren, 2014). Subcultural influences on attractiveness are also apparent in the fact that lesbians appear to be less concerned about physical appearance, have lower levels of body dissatisfaction and a better body image, and express a larger ideal body size compared to heterosexual women (Alvy, 2013; Boehmer, Bowen, & Bauer, 2007).

Ethnic Minorities and Eating Disorders

Do cultural values and standards affect body dissatisfaction and eating disorders? It appears that body dissatisfaction is not just a problem among white women in the United States; it also exists among women in ethnic minorities (S. Grabe & Hyde, 2006). Latina/Hispanic and Asian American women have levels of body dissatisfaction equal to that of white women, although strong ethnic identity for Latina girls may serve as a protective factor in negating body dissatisfaction when exposed to images of thin white women (Schooler & Daniels, 2014). African American women show much less body dissatisfaction than all other comparison groups. Although African American girls and women tend to be heavier, on average, than their white counterparts, they tend to be more satisfied with their body size, weight, and appearance and less interested in being thin (Chandler-Laney et al., 2009). In a study evaluating the ethnic identity and self-esteem of African American, white, and Latina/Hispanic American adolescent girls, high ethnic identity and high self-esteem appeared to protect against

Table 10.5 Differences in Body Image and Weight Concerns among African American and White Women and Girls

	African American	White
Satisfied with current weight or body shape	70%	11%
Body image	Perceived selves to be thinner than they actually were	Perceived selves to be heavier than they actually were
Attitude toward dieting	Believed that it is better to be a little overweight than underweight	Believed in the importance of dieting to produce a slender body; feared being overweight
Definition of beauty	Good grooming, "style," and overall attractiveness; beauty is the right "attitude and personality"	Slim; 5 ft. 7 in.; 100–110 lb; a perfect body can lead to success and the good life
Being overweight	Of those who were overweight, 40% considered their figures attractive or very attractive	Those who believed they did not have a weight problem were 6–14 lb underweight
Age and beauty	Believed they would get more beautiful with age	Believed that beauty is fleeting and decreases with age

SOURCE: Boyington et al. (2008); Desmond, Price, Hallinan, & Smith (1989); Lovejoy (2001); Parker, Nichter, Vuckovic, Sims, & Ritenbaugh (1995).

disordered eating among the African American girls (Rhea & Thatcher, 2013). Nearly two thirds of overweight or obese African American women in a study reported high self-esteem compared to 41 percent of average sized or thin white women (*Washington Post*, 2012). Table 10.5 compares some differences in body image and weight concerns between African American and white women.

Why are African American women and girls somewhat insulated from unrealistic standards of thinness? It is possible that several cultural factors exert a protective influence. First, because many do not identify with white women and girls, media messages of thinness may have less influence. Second, the definition of attractiveness within the African American community encompasses dress, personality, and confidence, rather than focusing primarily on physical characteristics such as body shape and weight. Third, African American women are generally less influenced by gender-restrictive messages. For example, assertiveness and belief in egalitarian relationships may allow some African American women to have important roles in the home and community.

However, not all African American women and girls are immune to majority-culture messages (Rogers-Wood & Petrie, 2010). African American girls do, for example, diet, binge, and purge, but with less frequency than other groups (Story, Neumark-Sztainer, Sherwood, Stang, & Murray, 1998). And although fewer African American women appear to have either anorexia nervosa or bulimia nervosa, they are as likely as other groups of women to have binge-eating disorder (Franko et al., 2012).

In general, acculturation to mainstream U.S. values appears to be a risk factor for developing an eating disorder (Talleyrand, 2010). This relationship is greatest among those who have internalized societal values concerning attractiveness (S. Grabe & Hyde, 2006). Some studies have shown that American Indian, Asian American,

Mango Productions/Comet/Corbis

and Latina/Hispanic American girls show greater body image dissatisfaction than European American girls, possibly due to attempts to fit into societal definitions of beauty (S. C. Gilbert, 2003). Thus, it appears that ethnic minorities are becoming increasingly vulnerable to societal messages regarding attractiveness; the fact that an increasing number of children and adults from ethnic minorities, especially females, are overweight may further increase the risk of eating disorders (Madsen, Weedn, & Crawford, 2010).

Cross-Cultural Studies on Eating Disorders

Although far fewer reports of eating disorders are found in Latin American, South American, and Asian countries than in European countries, Israel, and Australia, the incidence is increasing (M. N. Miller & Pumariega, 2001; Palavras, Kaio, Mari, & Claudino, 2011). Of concern is the finding that exposure to Western values is associated with increased incidence of body dissatisfaction and disordered eating in women and girls in other countries (Steiger & Bruce, 2007). For example, although fuller figures have traditionally been equated with beauty in South Africa, when black teenage girls in this region were exposed to Western standards of thinness, there was a dramatic increase in eating disorders (Simmons, 2002). Asian countries have also reported increases in body shape concerns and distorted eating attitudes following exposure to Western media (Liao et al., 2010).

Cultural values and norms affect views on body shape and size. Our perspectives on what is considered a normal weight are influenced by our cultural beliefs and practices. For example, Micronesians view thinness as a sign of illness. As one parent responded, "The culture on Saipan, the fat one is the healthy one . . . but when they are skinny, 'Oh, my goodness, nobody is feeding that child'" (Bruss, Morris, & Dannison, 2003). Feeding signifies love and care from parents toward their children. Historically, eating disorders in Chinese populations have been rare because plumpness in women and girls has been considered desirable and attractive. However, S. Lee, Lam, Kwok, and Fung (2010) found that individuals with eating disorders in Hong Kong were increasingly demonstrating a fat-phobic pattern similar to that seen in Western countries.

What happens when other cultures are exposed to Western standards of beauty? Becker (2004) reported on the impact of television on adolescent girls living in a rural community in western Fiji. Traditional cultural norms support robust appetites and body sizes. Food and feasts are socially important, and plump bodies are considered aesthetically pleasing. After 3 years of exposure to Western television programs, girls revealed admiration for Western standards: "The actresses and all those girls, especially those European girls, I just like, I just admire them and want to be like them. I want their body, I want their size" (p. 546). The girls also paid attention to TV commercials advertising exercise equipment, which portrayed the ease with which weight could be lost. "When they show exercising on TV . . . I feel I should . . . lose my weight" (p. 542). This media exposure dramatically increased body dissatisfaction and purging among Fijian girls (Becker, Burwell, Herzog, Hamburg, & Gilman, 2002).

Biological Dimension

At this point, we have considered psychological, social, and sociocultural dimensions associated with eating disorders. However, an unanswered question remains: "If all young girls are exposed to these sociocultural pressures, why do only a small fraction go on to develop anorexia nervosa and bulimia nervosa?" (Striegel-Moore & Bulik, 2007, p. 188). Considering biological factors and possible gene χ environment interactions helps us answer this question. For example, if someone has a genetic predisposition toward severe dieting, exposure to certain environmental factors (e.g., family pressures or societal emphasis on being thin) may increase the risk of developing an eating disorder. Conversely, those without the predisposition might find severe dieting to be extremely aversive. In this section we consider possible genetic influences on eating disorders.

Disordered eating appears to run in families, especially among female relatives (Steiger & Bruce, 2007). Strober, Freeman, Diamond, and Kaye (2000) examined the lifetime rates of anorexia nervosa and bulimia nervosa among close relatives of individuals with and without eating disorders and found that anorexia nervosa and bulimia nervosa occurred with much greater frequency among close relatives of those with eating disorders. Heritability estimates from twin studies are 41 percent for binge-eating disorder, 46–76 percent for anorexia nervosa, and 50–83 percent for bulimia nervosa (Bulik, Thornton, et al., 2010; Striegel-Moore & Bulik, 2007).

Genetic influences may be triggered by physical changes such as puberty. In a sample of twins, heritability appeared to be low among preadolescent teens but was substantial after puberty. This suggests that either puberty itself or social processes associated with puberty (e.g., increasing awareness of sexuality and body shape) may influence the expression of genes for disordered eating through gene χ environment interactions. In other words, the eating disorder only shows up when certain environmental factors interact with the presence of genetic risk factors (Culbert, Burt, McGue, Iacono, & Klump, 2009).

Genetics may also influence the availability of neurotransmitters associated with eating behaviors. Research has focused on dopamine, which is considered the primary neurotransmitter involved in the reinforcing effects of food (Bello & Hajnal, 2010). Low levels of dopamine can increase hunger, whereas increased dopamine concentrations can decrease appetite (Y. Lee & Lin, 2010). Differences in dopamine levels may explain why those with bulimia nervosa are more attentive to food stimuli and why individuals with anorexia nervosa show less appetitive response to food images (S. Brooks, Prince, Stahl, Campbell, & Treasure, 2011). Additionally, having genes associated with lower dopamine availability may interact with adverse childhood rearing experiences to result in emotional eating patterns (van Strien, Snoek, van der Zwaluw, & Engels, 2010).

People with lower levels of dopamine may need greater quantities of food or other rewarding substances, such as drugs, to obtain pleasure. The possible influence of dopamine in eating disorders is supported by examining medications that affect dopamine levels. For example, some stimulant medications such as methylphenidate appear to decrease appetite by increasing dopamine availability (L. H. Epstein, Leddy,

DID YOU KNOW?

The addiction-like qualities of binge eating (desperation for food and loss of control over eating) have led some researchers to investigate neurobiological similarities between eating disorders and substance-use disorders.

SOURCE: Kaye et al., 2013

Should Underweight Models and Digitally "Enhanced" Photos Be Banned from Advertisements?

Former Ralph Lauren model Filippa Hamilton was fired for being too fat. She was 5 ft. 10 in. tall, weighed 120 pounds, and wore size 4 clothing. "They fired me because they said I was overweight and I couldn't fit in their clothes anymore," she said (Melago, 2009, p. 1). Later, Hamilton was shocked when she encountered a digitally retouched advertisement in which her hips appeared smaller than her head. (Ralph Lauren has since apologized for this action.) Similarly, singer Kelly Clarkson was digitally slimmed for the cover of *Self* magazine, as was country singer Faith Hill for *Redbook*. Altering photos to make women on magazine covers and in advertisements appear slimmer and "flawless" is a common practice (Carmichael, 2010).

By using models in a state of malnourishment or airbrushed photos, the fashion industry has created an unattainable image of the "ideal" woman (Lis, 2011). Young women exposed to these types of images show increases in depression and body dissatisfaction that can lead to eating disorders (S. Grabe, Ward, & Hyde, 2008). The American Medical Association (2011) and the Royal College of Psychiatrists in the United Kingdom (Berman, 2010) have called for the cessation of practices such as the use of underweight models and airbrushed photos because of their link with unhealthy body image and eating disorders (Berman, 2010). In 2013, Israel banned the use of "too skinny" models and now requires advertisers to make it clear when they have retouched a model's body (Greenfield, 2013).

Do you believe we should ban the use of ultrathin models and digitally manipulated images? Would this reduce the incidence of body dissatisfaction and eating disorders? How could the mass media help youth develop more realistic and healthy body images?

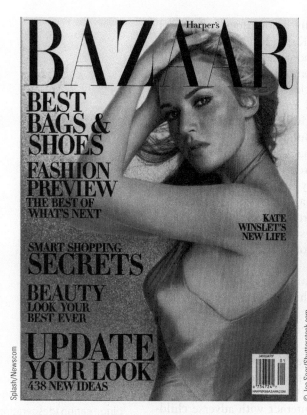

Kate Winslet Photoshopped?

Actress Kate Winslet, pictured on the right, has frequently been the target of image manipulation. *Harper's Bazaar* has been accused of grafting Winslet's head onto another woman's body for the cover shot on the left. Why do magazines go to such lengths in their portrayal of thinness?

Temple, & Faith, 2007). Although dopamine seems like a promising lead in explaining eating disorders, other neurotransmitters such as serotonin also appear to be involved. More research is needed to determine the precise relationship between genetic factors, neurotransmitters, and environmental influences.

Altered functioning of the appetitive neural circuitry (brain structures and processes that mediate appetite) also appears to influence disordered eating patterns. Magnetic resonance imaging (MRI) scans were used to study neural regions associated with response to pleasant-tasting foods. Individuals who had recovered from anorexia nervosa or bulimia nervosa were compared with women without these disorders in their response to the sweet taste of sucrose. As compared to the control group, the women recovered from anorexia nervosa showed a significantly diminished response to sucrose, whereas those recovered from bulimia nervosa showed a highly elevated response to the sweet flavor. Thus, the restricted eating in anorexia nervosa and overeating in bulimia nervosa may be due to alterations in appetitive neural circuitry that affect the reward aspects of taste (Oberndorfer, 2013).

Ghrelin, a gastrointestinal hormone capable of stimulating hunger, regulating taste sensation, and increasing interest in food, is also a focus of research. When the appetitive circuitry is operating normally, ghrelin levels rise before meals and decrease after eating. Ghrelin works in conjunction with leptin, a hormone that signals satiety and suppresses appetite. Abnormalities in these hormones have been found in those with eating disorders. Manipulating ghrelin levels as a method of promoting weight gain in those with anorexia nervosa or decreasing interest in food for those with who eat excessively is being explored as a mechanism for treating obesity and eating disorders (Müller & Tschöp, 2013).

Treatment of Eating Disorders

Although there are some similarities in treatment strategies used for anorexia nervosa, bulimia nervosa, and binge-eating disorder (Stice & Shaw, 2004), the approach, priorities, and physical effects addressed differ among the disorders.

Treatment of Anorexia Nervosa

> **CASE STUDY** A young woman who began treatment for anorexia nervosa weighing 81 lb reported:
>
> *I did gain 25 pounds, the target weight of my therapist and nutritionist. But every day was really difficult. I would go and cry. A big part of anorexia is fear. Fear of fat, fear of eating. But [my therapist] taught me about societal pressures to be ultra-thin that come from the media, TV, advertising. . . . She talked me through what I was thinking and how I had completely dissociated my mind from my body. . . . I'm slowly reintroducing foods one thing at a time. I'd like to think I am completely better, but I'm not. I'm still extremely self-conscious about my appearance. But I now know I have a problem and my family and I are finding ways to cope with it. (K. Bryant, 2001, p. B4))*

As you have seen, eating disorders, especially anorexia nervosa, can be life threatening. Weight gain is vital for a successful outcome (Brewerton & Costin, 2011). Unfortunately, as is evident from this case study, it can be extremely difficult to change eating patterns. Because anorexia nervosa is a complex disorder, there is a need for teamwork among physicians, psychiatrists, and therapists.

Treatment occurs in an outpatient therapy setting or in a hospital, depending on the weight and health of the individual. Regardless of the setting, developing a strong therapeutic relationship with treatment providers and enhancing readiness for change can help overcome denial of illness, ambivalence, and resistance to treatment and improve outcome (Abbate-Daga, Amianto, Delsedime, De-Bacco, & Fassino, 2013).

Because an individual being treated for anorexia nervosa is starving, the initial goal is to restore weight and address the physical complications associated with starvation. The physical condition of the person is carefully monitored, because sudden and severe physiological reactions can occur during re-feeding. During the weight restoration period, new foods are introduced to supplement food choices that are not sufficiently high in calories. Because these foods may be "forbidden," phobic-like reactions can occur. One woman described her response to spaghetti in the following manner. "My chest is tight, my stomach just feels very full . . . I feel like I want to cry. I'm trying to control my breathing or else I'll start hyperventilating . . ." (Battiste & Effron, 2012). As you can see, consuming higher-calorie food can be very distressing and require a great deal of psychological support. Those with anorexia nervosa are often terrified of gaining weight and need the opportunity to discuss these reactions in therapy.

Psychological interventions help the client (a) understand and cooperate with nutritional and physical rehabilitation, (b) identify and understand the dysfunctional attitudes related to the eating disorder, (c) improve interpersonal and social functioning, and (d) address other psychological disorders or conflicts that reinforce disordered eating behavior (American Psychiatric Association, 2006). Focusing on improving quality of life and mood disorder symptoms is particularly important in treating severe cases of anorexia nervosa (Touyz et al., 2013).

Family therapy is often an important component of the treatment plan, as seen in the case of one 18-year-old woman who remained emaciated despite inpatient treatment, dietary training, and cognitive-behavioral therapy (L. A. Sim, Sadowski, Whiteside, & Wells, 2004). Her family was enlisted to participate in family therapy. The therapy involved (a) having the parents assist in the re-feeding process by planning meals, (b) learning new family relationship patterns, (c) and reducing parental criticism by helping them understand that anorexia nervosa is a serious disease. The parents were encouraged to help their daughter develop skills, attitudes, and activities appropriate to her developmental stage. This form of family therapy resulted in the woman's gaining more than 22 pounds. Overall, family therapy is an important component in the treatment of adolescents with anorexia nervosa (Brown & Keel, 2012).

Treatment of Bulimia Nervosa

During the initial assessment of individuals with bulimia nervosa, conditions that result from purging are identified and treated; these may include dental erosion, muscle weakness, cardiac arrhythmias, dehydration, electrolyte imbalance, or gastrointestinal problems involving the stomach or esophagus. As with anorexia nervosa, treatment involves an interdisciplinary team that includes a physician and a psychotherapist. To normalize eating patterns and eliminate the binge/purge cycle is a primary goal of treatment.

Cognitive-behavioral approaches can help individuals with bulimia develop a sense of self-control (Poulsen et al., 2013). Common components of cognitive-behavioral treatment involve encouraging the consumption of three or more balanced meals a day, reducing rigid food rules and body image concerns, identifying triggers for bingeing, and developing strategies for coping with emotional distress. Even with these approaches, only about 50 percent of those with bulimia fully recover (Agras, Crow, et al., 2000). Adding exposure and response prevention procedures to therapy (i.e., exposure to cues associated with bingeing and prevention of purging following a binge) appears to improve long-term outcomes for individuals with bulimia nervosa (McIntosh, Carter, Bulik, Frampton, & Joyce, 2010). Antidepressant medications such as selective serotonin reuptake inhibitors are sometimes helpful in treating bulimia (NIMH, 2014).

Treatment of Binge-Eating Disorder

Treatments for binge-eating disorder are similar to those for bulimia nervosa, although binge-eating disorder presents fewer physical complications because of the lack of purging. Individuals with binge-eating disorder do differ in some ways from those with bulimia nervosa. Most are overweight and have to deal with societal prejudices regarding their weight. Due to the health consequences of excess weight, many therapy programs also focus on healthy approaches to weight loss.

In general, treatment follows two phases (Shelley-Ummenhofer & MacMillan, 2007). First, factors that trigger overeating are determined; then clients learn strategies to reduce eating binges, as seen in the following case study.

CASE STUDY Mrs. A. had very rigid rules concerning eating that, when violated, would result in her "going the whole nine yards." Two types of triggers were identified for her binges—emotional distress (anger, anxiety, sadness, or frustration) and work stress (long hours, deadlines). Interventions were applied to help her develop more flexible rules regarding eating and to deal with her stressors. She learned about obesity, proper nutrition, and physical exercise. Her body weight was recorded weekly, and a healthy pattern of three meals and two snacks a day was implemented. She used a food diary to record the type and amount of food consumed and her psychological state preceding eating. Second, the therapist used cognitive strategies to help change distorted beliefs about eating. Mrs. A. developed a list of "forbidden" foods and ranked them in order of "dangerousness." Gradually these foods were introduced into normal eating routines, beginning with those perceived as being least dangerous.

The prejudices of society about body size were discussed, and realistic expectations about change were addressed. Mrs. A. was asked to observe attractive individuals with a larger body size so that she could consider positive qualities rather than focusing solely on the body. After performing this "homework," she discovered that overweight women can look attractive, and began to buy more fashionable clothes for herself. She was astonished at the positive reactions and comments from friends and co-workers, and attributed the attention to her confidence and improved body image. (Goldfein et al., 2000)

Medications are sometimes effective in reducing or stopping binge eating; however, psychological interventions tend to produce the best long-term results. Unfortunately, combining medication and psychological treatments does not substantially enhance outcome (Reas & Grilo, 2014). Although cognitive-behavioral therapy (CBT) can produce significant reductions in binge eating, it has less effect on weight reduction (Hilbert et al., 2012). A newer form of CBT incorporates ways to address interpersonal difficulties and strategies for regulating negative emotions that can trigger bingeing and purging, a focus similar to the emotional regulation and distress tolerance skills taught in dialectical behavior therapy (Wilson, 2011). Further research is necessary to determine if the addition of these modules improves the efficacy of CBT for binge eating disorder.

Obesity

CASE STUDY   When I'm uptight, I often overeat. I know that I often use food to calm me when I'm upset and even find myself feeling that when things don't go my way, I'll just have my way by eating anything and all I want. Like an alcoholic who can't stop drinking once he or she starts, I don't seem to be able to stop myself from eating once I start. (LeCrone, 2007, p. 1)

obesity   a condition involving a body mass index (BMI) greater than 30

body mass index (BMI)   an estimate of body fat calculated on the basis of a person's height and weight

Obesity is a worldwide phenomenon that affects more than 500 million individuals (World Health Organization, 2013). **Obesity** is defined as having a **body mass index (BMI)** greater than 30. Our BMI, an estimate of our body fat, is calculated based on our height and weight. According to BMI standards, 68 percent of U.S. adults are overweight, which includes 35 percent who are obese. In the United States, the prevalence of overweight and obesity has doubled since the 1970s, and it is estimated that by 2015, 75 percent of adults and 24 percent of children and adolescents will fall into one of these categories. Figure 10.4 shows the projected adult obesity rate by states in 2030 if current trends continue. African Americans, Mexican Americans, American Indians, and women have the higher rates of obesity (CDC, 2013). A promising sign is that obesity and extreme obesity appear to have gone down in recent years among low-income, preschool-age children and among all racial and ethnic group children with the exception of American Indians/Alaska Natives (CDC, 2014).

Obesity is second only to tobacco use as a preventable cause of disease and death. Being overweight or obese increases the risk of high cholesterol and triglyceride levels, type 2 diabetes, cancer, coronary heart disease, stroke, gallbladder disease, arthritis, sleep apnea, and respiratory problems (CDC, 2013). Among adolescents, it is also associated with reduced cognitive performance and acceleration of changes in brain structure and function associated with aging (Chan, Yan, & Payne, 2013). In addition, children and adolescents who are overweight or obese have an increased risk of developing an eating disorder (Sim, Lebow, & Billings, 2013).

Childhood obesity also has a significant health impact, especially for girls. Girls who are obese are 9 times more likely to develop high blood pressure compared to their peers who are not obese, whereas boys have a threefold increase in risk (Ortiz, 2011). Being overweight or obese in childhood is associated with an increased risk of coronary heart disease in adulthood (J. L. Baker, Olsen, & Sorensen, 2007).

DID YOU KNOW?

Fitness may counter some of the health problems associated with obesity. In a 12-year study of American adults 60 years and older, those who were obese but fit had similar survival rates to individuals with normal weight.

SOURCE: Sui et al., 2007

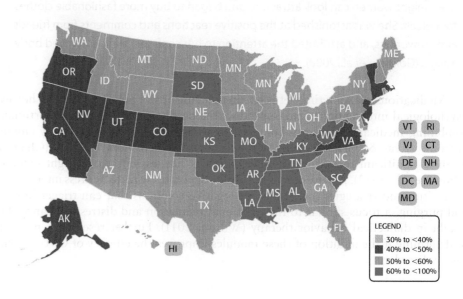

Figure 10.4

Projected State-Specific Obesity Prevalence among Adults, 2030

This map shows the state by state projected percentage of adults age 18 and older who will be considered obese in 2030 if current trends continue.

SOURCE: Trust for America's Health (2013).

Paradoxically, in a review of 97 studies involving nearly 3 million adults 65 and older, being overweight was not associated with an increase in mortality; in fact, overweight individuals died at a slightly lower rate than those of normal weight and older adults with mild obesity died no more frequently than their normal-weight peers (Flegal, Kit, Orpana, & Graubard, 2013).

DSM-5 does not yet recognize obesity as a specific disorder, despite its devastating medical and psychological consequences. Some researchers believe that forms of obesity that are characterized by an excessive drive for food should be recognized as a "food addiction" (Flint et al., 2014). We include obesity in this chapter because it is often accompanied by depression and anxiety, low self-esteem, poor body image, and unhealthy eating patterns; binge eating is also common among those who are obese (Peterson, Latendresse, Bartholome, Warren, & Raymond, 2012). Also, obese individuals are five times more likely to display behaviors characteristic of night-eating syndrome—consuming at least 25 percent of their food after their evening meal (Vander Wal, 2012).

MYTH Body mass index standards represent unvarying thresholds that remain constant from year to year.

REALITY In 1998, the BMI scores were lowered for all weight classes. This resulted in an increased prevalence of individuals considered overweight or obese. For example, the BMI cutoff score for the category of overweight was lowered from 27 to 25. This resulted in 29 million Americans being added to the overweight category—an overnight increase of 42 percent.

Etiology of Obesity

Obesity stems from many causes, including genetic and biological factors; our sedentary lifestyle combined with easy access to attractive, high-calorie foods; and some of the same disturbed eating patterns seen in eating disorders. Thus, obesity is a product of biological, psychological, social, and sociocultural influences, as shown in Figure 10.5. How these dimensions interact is still a matter of debate. For example, one theory, termed the "thrifty genotype" hypothesis, points to the role of both genetics and the environment in accounting for the rapid rise in obesity. According to this perspective, certain genes helped our ancestors survive famines by storing body fat. These same genes, however, may be dysfunctional in an environment in which high-fat foods are now plentiful (CDC, 2010c). Although "thrifty" genes and access to foods can account for some cases

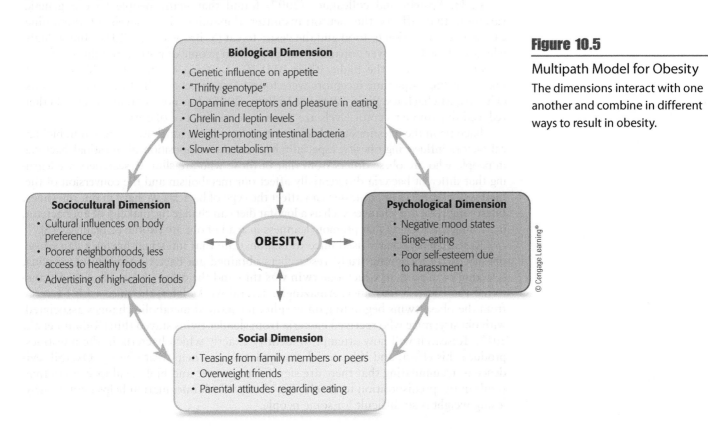

Figure 10.5

Multipath Model for Obesity
The dimensions interact with one another and combine in different ways to result in obesity.

of obesity, other factors must be involved, because rates of obesity also vary according to variables such as class, gender, and race or ethnicity.

Biological Dimension

Researchers focus on a variety of factors associated with obesity, including genetic influences and neurological and hormonal functioning. Although it is evident that the availability of high-calorie foods and a more sedentary lifestyle influence obesity, some individuals have particular difficulty maintaining a normal weight. For example, African American women appear to have more difficulty losing weight when participating in weight-loss programs, even when they follow prescribed calorie restrictions and physical activity recommendations. It is hypothesized that some people, including African American women, have a lower resting metabolism and thus expend less energy than other people attempting to lose weight (Delaney et al., 2013).

Obesity may involve more than just the excessive intake of food. In fact, researchers are increasingly implicating neurocircuitry associated with appetite regulation in the obesity epidemic. They consider obesity a "neurobiological disease" rather than merely a matter of faulty intake of food (Jauch-Chara & Oltmanns, 2014). In a study involving 2,100 severely obese children, genetic mutations involving the KSR2 gene were associated with an increased sense of hunger and a slower metabolism rate (Pearce et al., 2013). In another genetic study, individuals with a high-risk variant of the FTO gene—an allele associated with increased food intake—had a 70 percent greater chance of becoming obese compared to individuals with a low-risk version of the gene. Individuals with the high-risk allele found pictures of high-fat foods more appealing than those with the low-risk gene; additionally, the hormone ghrelin (responsible for stimulating hunger) was slow to decline after eating and then rose more rapidly in those with the high-risk variant (Karra et al., 2013). The appetite-regulating hormone, leptin, is also implicated in obesity. For example, a group of children who weighed more than 200 lb by age 10 were found to have a chromosomal abnormality that affected nine of the genes that influence leptin production (Bochukova et al., 2010).

L. H. Epstein and colleagues (2007) found that many people have a genetic variation that affects the neurotransmitter dopamine. Low levels of dopamine can increase attention to food and the desire to eat (S. Brooks et al., 2011). Individuals who are obese have fewer dopamine receptors than people of normal weight; the fewer receptors they have, the higher their BMI (G. J. Wang et al., 2001). Similar findings regarding dopamine receptors were found among genetically lean and obese rats (Thanos, Michaelides, Piyis, Wang, & Volkow, 2008). It is not clear, however, whether reduced dopamine receptor levels are a cause or an effect of obesity.

Bacteria in the intestines (gut bacteria) are also a focus for those interested in biological factors influencing obesity, especially because the composition of intestinal bacteria in people who are obese differs from that of those who are slim. Researchers are learning that different bacteria differentially affect our metabolism and the conversion of the food we consume to fat. Our diet can affect the type of bacteria we have in our intestines. Interestingly, dietary changes such as a low-fat diet can change the makeup of gut bacteria, increasing the bacteria that promote leanness instead of obesity (Rothe & Blaut, 2013).

Researchers recently used mice to demonstrate that intestinal bacteria can cause obesity. In an intriguing study, researchers obtained gut bacteria from human twins, selecting twin pairs in which one twin was thin and the other obese. They then transferred the bacteria into mice. Amazingly, several weeks later, the mice with bacteria from the obese twins began to gain weight and showed metabolic changes associated with obesity; mice who received bacteria from slender twins stayed thin (Ridaura et al., 2013). Research will now attempt to identify exactly which bacteria in the intestines produce this effect, and if bacterial manipulation can help treat obesity. Overall, evidence is accumulating that there are significant genetic and biological influences that result in the predisposition to developing obesity. Such information helps explain why losing weight is so difficult for some people.

Psychological Dimension

Adults who are obese often report feeling stressed, anxious, or depressed. African American women struggling to overcome obesity requested strategies to manage stress and increase self-esteem as a component of their weight-loss efforts (James, 2013). These responses are likely associated with the weight stigma that exists in society and the resultant harassment and discrimination in school, work, and hiring practices (Levi, Vinter, St. Laurent, & Segal, 2010). Mood and anxiety disorders were common among a sample of 122 overweight youth; more than one third of this group reported engaging in binge eating when upset (Eddy, Tanofsky-Kraff, et al., 2007). It is not clear whether negative mood states cause overeating, but it is easy to imagine how they can be a result of societal responses to excess weight.

Physical and sexual abuse during childhood also appears to be a risk factor for the development of obesity. In a study involving 57,321 nurses, over 8 percent reported severe physical abuse in childhood and 5.3 percent reported severe sexual abuse. Those who experienced childhood abuse had a greater risk of being overweight and engaging in out-of-control eating. It is possible that such a background increases the tendency to use eating as a means of coping with stressful emotions (Mason, Flint, Field, Austin, & Rich-Edwards, 2013).

Social Dimension

Negative social interactions are common among those struggling with weight issues and obesity. Classmates and acquaintances often ostracize children and adolescents who are overweight (Puhl & Heuer, 2009). Almost two thirds of adolescents attending a weight-loss camp reported weight-based victimization with the majority of perpetrators being friends and peers; physical education and other teachers, sport coaches, and family members also engaged in teasing and bullying regarding weight. More than half of the adolescents reported that bullying from peers involved social media or texting (Puhl, Peterson, & Luedicke, 2013). Far from helping weight reduction, those who face weight discrimination are more likely to become or remain obese than individuals who do not suffer from such discrimination (Sutin & Terracciano, 2013). Additionally, fear of victimization or bullying may lead individuals to avoid physical activities such as walking that can assist in weight reduction.

Stress within the family has been associated with excess weight during childhood, adolescence, and even adulthood. Longitudinal follow-up found that teens who had a "poor relationship" with their mothers between the ages of 1 and 3 were twice as likely to become obese during adolescence compared to those rated as having a good relationship with their mother (Anderson, Gooze, Lemeshow, & Whitaker, 2012). Teasing by family members about weight issues is also associated with obesity (Eddy, Tanofsky-Kraff, et al., 2007). Family eating patterns and attitudes may also influence food intake in children. For example, in families with a positive mealtime atmosphere, adolescents were less likely to engage in disordered eating (Neumark-Sztainer, Wall, Story, & Fulkerson, 2004).

In an interesting study, Christakis and Fowler (2007) followed the social networks of 12,067 adults over a period of 32 years to determine social factors associated with obesity. They wanted to see if a person's friends, siblings, partners, or neighbors had an impact on weight gain. Some of the findings were quite surprising. If someone a person considers a friend becomes obese, the person's chances of becoming obese increase by 57 percent. If both individuals consider each other friends, the chances increase by 171 percent. The chances for obesity in an individual also increased when an adult sibling (40 percent) or a spouse (37 percent) became obese. There was no increase if a neighbor became obese, unless the people were also friends. It is possible that people influence others in their social network regarding the acceptability of weight gain (Hill, Rand, Nowak, & Christakis, 2010).

Gregg DeGuire/FilmMagic/Getty Images

Plus Size Models—A Passing Fad?

Fashion model Whitney Thompson, an ambassador for the National Eating Disorders Association, is worried that the use of full-figured models is only a temporary phenomenon. Is she right?

Childhood Obesity

Overweight boys speed walk as part of a childhood obesity program called "Committed to Kids."

Mark Richards/Corbis

Sociocultural Dimension

Attitudes regarding food and acceptable weight are developed in the home and community. Rates of obesity tend to be highest among ethnic minorities (CDC, 2013). In some ethnic groups, there is less pressure to remain thin and being moderately overweight is not a big concern. As noted earlier, among African Americans there is greater acceptance of fuller figures; this may partially account for the fact that African American women have the highest rates of obesity of any group (James, 2013).

Rates of obesity also tend to be higher among individuals in lower social classes and may be a product of limited availability of fruits, vegetables, low-fat food, access to sports, and opportunities for exercise (playing outside or walking to school) in poorer neighborhoods (Frederick, Snellman, & Putnam, 2014). Similarly, advertising and availability of high-calorie, lower-cost foods may contribute to obesity in communities where there are fewer options to purchase healthy, fresh food.

Treatments for Obesity

Treatments for obesity have included dieting, lifestyle changes, medications, and surgery. In general, dieting alone may produce short-term weight loss but tends to be ineffective in the long term; some individuals gain back more weight than was lost. Dieting may be somewhat more successful for children (Moens, Braet, & Van Winckel, 2010). T. Mann and colleagues (2007) concluded that most adults would be better off not dieting, because weight fluctuations create considerable stress on the body. The "yo-yo" effect in dieting (cycles of weight gain and loss) is associated with increased risk of cardiovascular disease, stroke, and decreased immune functioning. Among those with a genetic predisposition to obesity, physical activity can reduce the risk of becoming overweight (Kilpeläinen et al., 2011). Comprehensive intervention programs appear to be the most promising. In a meta-analysis of studies incorporating "rigorous randomized trials" of obesity treatments that included a minimum of 2 years of follow-up, L. H. Powell, Calvin, and Calvin (2007) concluded that lifestyle interventions incorporating a healthy diet and regular exercise were successful in producing sustained reductions in weight. Lifestyle interventions are also moderately effective with overweight children (Ho et al., 2012).

Surgical methods such as gastric banding (placing an adjustable inflatable band around the upper stomach) or gastric bypass (creating a small pouch from the upper stomach and attaching it to the intestine) are used in the treatment of morbid obesity. Although these methods facilitate weight loss by severely limiting the amount of food that can be consumed, gastric surgery also appears to promote changes in intestinal bacteria that are conducive to weight loss (Kong et al., 2013). Gastric bypass seems to be more effective for weight loss but has higher complication rates (Angrisani, Cutolo, Formisano, Nosso, & Vitolo, 2013). Dietary counseling is recommended because follow-up studies report that many individuals have inadequate intake of essential nutrients after surgery (Shah et al., 2013).

Contemporary Trends and Future Directions

It is clear that media depictions of thin women have a negative impact on female body satisfaction and are a major contributor to eating disorders. Similarly, images of idealized masculine bodies are affecting the body image of males. To counter the impact of unrealistic images, physician and mental health groups in many countries are demanding

Preventing Eating Disorders

Prevention programs are attempting to reduce the incidence of eating disorders and disordered eating patterns. Programs geared toward women and girls target protective factors such as social support and strong social bonds and characteristics such as self-determination, autonomy, and social competence (Ferrier-Auerbach & Martens, 2009). Girls who have a sense of personal power and who recognize the positive attributes of their bodies are less likely to exhibit disordered eating or become obsessed with their weight or body shape (Steck, Abrams, & Phelps, 2004). Programs designed to reduce body dissatisfaction help women and girls to not only accept their weight and body shape, but also their overall appearance (T. Wade et al., 2009). Interventions to achieve this goal generally emphasize:

- increasing awareness of societal messages of what it means to be female and the role the media plays in creating unrealistic views of an ideal body,
- developing a more positive body image by eliminating "fat talk" and teasing about body size,
- incorporating moderate eating and exercising into a healthy lifestyle,
- increasing comfort in openly expressing feelings to peers and family members,

Kevin Peterson/Photodisc/Getty Images

- developing healthy ways of coping with stress and pressure, and
- increasing assertiveness skills.

These topics are addressed through group discussions and the use of videos, magazines, and examples from mass media (C. Chapman, Gilger, & Chestnutt, 2010; Richardson & Paxton, 2010).

There has been less focus on preventing eating disorders in men and boys. One program attempting to fill this gap (S. Friedman, 2007) focuses on:

- expanding the definition of masculinity to include prosocial characteristics such as caring, nurturance, and cooperation;
- examining beliefs regarding what it means to be male (e.g., needing to be brave and strong, not showing emotions, taking charge) and understanding how these beliefs affect men's feelings about their bodies;
- identifying and developing a positive sense of self that include qualities other than appearance;
- developing a broader range of emotions and feelings and learning to express them in a healthy manner; and
- developing skills to effectively deal with stressors.

It is hoped that bolstering protective factors such as social support, critical evaluation of unrealistic societal messages, and coping and communications skills will help stem the tide of eating disorders.

that advertisers include more images of women of varying sizes and weights. We know that women exposed to thin models increase their preference for thinness. Research is also finding that exposure to more normative body images can produced a shift toward more realistic body preference (Boothroyd, Tovée, & Pollet, 2012). Promoting a wider range of body types in mass media and advertising may promote healthier lifestyles and greatly reduce the body dissatisfaction that is so rampant in society today.

Researchers are also developing online resources to counteract the Web sites that encourage disordered eating. For example, Weigh2Rock.com offers an online support group for children, adolescents, and individuals up to age 25 who are struggling with eating and weight issues. This anonymous social networking is easily accessible and provides medical information and advice about nutrition, coping with weight issues, and healthy ways to manage eating. Members can share success stories, team up with a weight loss buddy, or post in chat rooms and on message boards. Dr. Robert Pretlow developed the Web site to help children, adolescents, and young adults receive positive social support in their attempts to lose weight and to combat the isolation and discrimination that overweight individuals face. Such supportive programs can help individuals struggling with weight or eating difficulties who may be too embarrassed to talk to health care providers or others about weight issues.

Additionally, research is delving into biological aspects of eating disorders, including similarities between compulsive starving, eating or exercising, and other addictive disorders (Jauch-Chara & Oltmanns, 2014). Ongoing research into effective prevention and treatment for these life-threatening disorders includes a focus on methods for achieving and maintaining a healthy weight and body image, including strategies that are effective for both men and women and for all cultural groups (Iacovino, Gredysa, Altman, & Wilfley, 2012).

Chapter SUMMARY

1 What kinds of eating disorders exist?

- Individuals with anorexia nervosa exhibit severe body image distortion. They are afraid of getting fat and engage in self-starvation. There are two subtypes of anorexia nervosa: the restricting type and the binge-eating/purging type.

- Individuals with bulimia nervosa engage in recurrent binge eating, feel a loss of control over eating, and use vomiting, exercise, or laxatives to attempt to control weight.

- Individuals with binge-eating disorder also engage in recurrent binge eating and feel a loss of control over eating; however, they do not regularly use purging or exercise to counteract the effects of overeating and are often overweight.

- Individuals who show atypical patterns of severely disordered eating that do not fully meet the criteria for anorexia nervosa, bulimia nervosa, or binge-eating disorder are given the diagnosis of other specified feeding or eating disorder.

2 What are some causes of eating disorders?

- Genetic abnormalities, neurotransmitters, appetitive neural circuitry, and intestinal bacteria are implicated in eating disorders.

- It is believed that societal emphasis on thinness plays a key role in the prevalence of eating disorders.

- Parental attitudes regarding the importance of thinness and peer attitudes about body size and weight can contribute to disordered eating.

- Countries that are influenced by Western standards have seen an increasing incidence of eating disorders.

3 What are some treatment options for eating disorders?

- Many of the therapies for eating disorders attempt to teach clients to identify the impact of societal messages regarding thinness and encourage them to develop healthier goals and values.

- For individuals with anorexia nervosa, medical as well as psychological treatment is necessary, because the body is in starvation mode. The goal is to help clients gain weight, normalize their eating patterns, understand and alter their thoughts related to body image, and develop healthier methods of dealing with stress.

- With both bulimia nervosa and binge-eating disorder, therapy involves normalizing eating patterns, developing a more positive body image, and dealing with stress in a healthier fashion.

- With bulimia nervosa, medical assistance may be required because of the physiological changes associated with purging.

- Because many people with binge-eating disorder are overweight or obese, weight reduction strategies are often included in treatment.

4 What causes obesity and how is it treated?

- The causes of obesity vary from individual to individual and involve combinations of biological predispositions and psychological, social, and sociocultural influences.

- In general, lifestyle changes that include reduced intake of high-calorie foods combined with exercise have proven to be the most effective treatment for obesity. Some individuals with extreme obesity have benefited from gastric surgery.

11 SUBSTANCE-RELATED AND OTHER ADDICTIVE DISORDERS

Chapter Outline

JAY, AGE 20, WAS ARRESTED FOR INITIATING A FIGHT and was brought to the emergency room due to his extreme agitation and violent behavior. In the emergency room, he yelled and made threats if anyone approached him. Periods of calm alternated with extreme emotionality and violent outbursts. At times, Jay sobbed uncontrollably and talked about suicide. When Jay eventually calmed down, he shared that he had smoked some "really great pot" earlier that day. He was eventually transferred to the inpatient psychiatric unit, where the staff was able to obtain a urine sample. Jay tested positive for both cannabis and PCP. Apparently, someone had laced the marijuana he had smoked with PCP (Schmetze & McGrath, 2014).

Throughout history, people have used a variety of chemical substances to alter their mood, level of consciousness, or behavior. These substances can lead to addiction or acute psychiatric symptoms such as those experienced by Jay. Our society consumes vast amounts of alcohol, tobacco, prescription medication, and illegal drugs. Each year, the Substance Abuse and Mental Health Services Administration (SAMHSA) obtains data regarding the use of alcohol, tobacco, and illicit substances based on interviews with approximately 67,500 adolescents and adults throughout the United States. Based on this data, researchers estimated that in 2012 there were 23.9 million adolescents and adults—9.2 percent of the population—who used illicit drugs such as cannabis, cocaine, or illegally obtained prescription medications. Illicit drug use occurs with greater frequency in some age groups and some ethnic groups (Figures 11.1 and 11.2). Addiction specialists are particularly concerned that young adults (ages 18–25) are reporting high rates of heavy and binge drinking and marijuana use, as well as nonmedical use of prescription drugs (SAMHSA, 2013a). Prescription drug misuse among older adults is also causing concern (Wang & Andrade, 2013).

As these statistics suggest, **substance abuse**, the excessive or harmful use of drugs or alcohol, is pervasive in our society. In 2012, an estimated 22.5 million adolescents and adults (8.5 percent of the population) met the criteria for a **substance-use disorder** at some time during the year; of this group, 2.8 million abused alcohol *and* illicit drugs, 4.5 million abused illicit drugs but not alcohol, and 14.9 million abused only alcohol. As you can see, alcohol is the most commonly abused substance. Marijuana is the most frequently abused illicit drug, followed by pain relievers and cocaine

focus
QUESTIONS

1 What are substance-use disorders?

2 What substances are associated with addiction?

3 Why do people develop substance-use disorders?

4 What kinds of interventions and treatments for substance-use disorders are most effective?

5 Can behaviors such as gambling be addictive?

(SAMHSA, 2013a). Substance abuse is twice as prevalent in men and boys, although abuse rates are almost equal for girls and boys ages 12–17 (Figure 11.3).

You may wonder which substances are considered the most dangerous. A comprehensive analysis concluded that heroin, crack cocaine, and methamphetamine present the greatest danger for the user, but that alcohol is the most dangerous drug when both personal and societal consequences are considered (Nutt, King, & Phillip, 2010). As you proceed through this chapter, consider the personal and societal effects of the substances discussed, as well as the vast number of people affected directly and indirectly by substance abuse.

We first examine the various substances involved in substance-use disorders. We next use the multipath perspective to understand possible causes of drug and alcohol addiction. We then review addiction treatment and conclude with a focus on other addictions, including gambling disorder.

Substance-Related Disorders

Substance-related disorders arise when **psychoactive substances**—substances that alter moods, thought processes, or other psychological states—are used excessively. Heavy substance use causes changes in the brain that result in the behaviors that characterize addiction (Wise & Koob, 2014). **Addiction** involves compulsive drug-seeking behavior and a loss of control over drug use. Once addiction develops, it is difficult to stop using the substance, not only because of the pleasurable feelings associated with use, but also because of the **withdrawal** symptoms—negative psychological and physiological effects such as shaking, irritability, or emotional distress—that occur when use is discontinued (Koob et al., 2014).

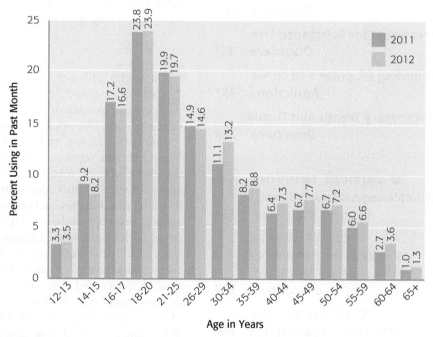

substance abuse pattern of excessive or harmful use of any substance for mood-altering purposes

substance-use disorder condition in which cognitive, behavioral, and physiological symptoms contribute to the continued use of alcohol or drugs despite significant substance-related problems

psychoactive substance a substance that alters mood, thought processes, or other psychological states

addiction compulsive drug-seeking behavior and a loss of control over drug use

withdrawal adverse physical and psychological symptoms that occur after reducing or ceasing intake of a substance

Figure 11.1

Two-Year Comparison of Past-Month Illicit Drug Use across Age Groups

In comparing 2011 and 2012, the rates of illicit drug use (cannabis, cocaine, heroin, hallucinogens, inhalants, and nonmedical use of prescription drugs) remained stable or decreased for those under age 30; however, rates of use increased slightly among older age groups, with the greatest increase occurring among 30- to 34-year-olds.

SOURCE: Substance Abuse and Mental Health Services Administration (2013).

What causes these withdrawal symptoms? Withdrawal occurs when chronic exposure to a substance results in **physiological dependence**—our bodies adapt and we need the substance to feel normal. In other words, withdrawal symptoms develop if we have become accustomed to regular use of a substance and then we suddenly stop. Different substances produce different withdrawal symptoms. Evidence of either withdrawal symptoms or **tolerance**, which involves progressive decreases in the effectiveness of the substance, indicates that physiological dependence has developed. The DSM-5 incorporates all of these concepts into the criteria for diagnosing a substance-use disorder (see Table 11.1).

DSM-5 differentiates substance-use disorders based on the substance used, such as alcohol-use disorder, cannabis-use disorder, or hallucinogen-use disorder. A substance-use disorder is considered mild when 2–3 of the designated symptoms are present and moderate if there are 4–5 symptoms. The presence of 6 or more symptoms indicates a severe substance-use disorder.

The DSM-5 also outlines the specific effects of intoxication and withdrawal associated with different substances. **Intoxication** refers to the distinct and recognizable pattern of problematic behavioral or psychological changes associated with use or abuse of a substance. For example, some of the DSM-5 criteria for alcohol intoxication (slurred speech, unsteady gait, inappropriate sexual or aggressive behavior, etc.) differ from

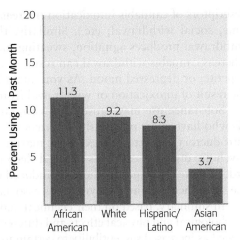

Figure 11.2

Comparison of Past-Month Illicit Drug Use across Ethnic Groups

In 2012, there were significant differences among ethnic groups in the use of illicit drugs.

SOURCE: Substance Abuse and Mental Health Services Administration (2013).

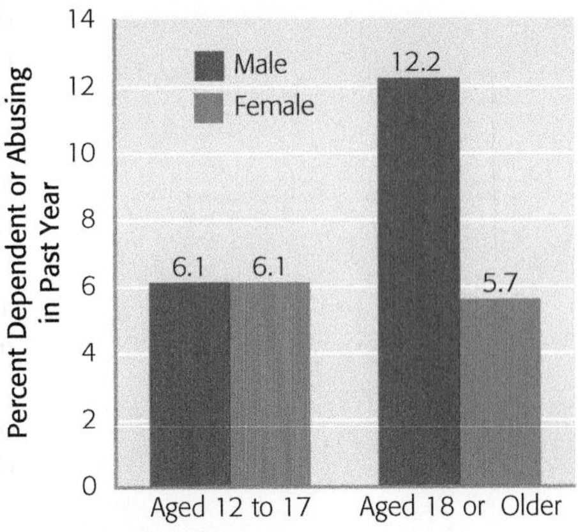

Figure 11.3

Age and Gender Differences in Substance-Use Disorder

In 2012, males and females ages 12–17 had similar frequency of past-year substance-use disorder diagnosis. However, among those age 18 years and older, males were twice as likely to receive a substance-use disorder diagnosis compared to females.

SOURCE: Substance Abuse and Mental Health Services Administration (2013a).

Table 11.1 DSM-5 Criteria for a Substance-Use Disorder

According to DSM-5, a substance-use disorder may be an appropriate diagnosis when *at least two* of the following characteristics occur within a 12-month period and cause significant impairment or distress:

- the quantity of the substance used or the amount of time spent using is often greater than intended;
- efforts to control use of the substance are unsuccessful due to a persistent desire for the substance;
- considerable time is spent using the substance, recovering from its effects, or attempting to obtain the substance;
- a strong desire, craving, or urge to use the substance is present;
- substance use interferes with major role obligations at work, school, or home;
- use of the substance continues despite harmful social or interpersonal effects caused or made worse by substance use;
- participation in social, work, or leisure activities is avoided or reduced due to substance use;
- substance use occurs in situations where substance use may be physically hazardous;
- continued substance use occurs even when the substance is causing physical or psychological problems or making these problems worse;
- tolerance for the substance develops, including a need for increasing quantities of the substance to achieve intoxication or desired effects or a noticeable decrease in effects when using the same amount of the substance;
- after heavy or sustained use of a substance, reduction in or abstinence from the substance results in withdrawal symptoms or precipitates resumption of use of the substance or similar substances to relieve or avoid withdrawal symptoms.

Adapted from APA (2013).

physiological dependence state of adaptation that occurs after chronic exposure to a substance; can result in craving and withdrawal symptoms

tolerance decreases in the effects of a substance that occur after chronic use

intoxication pattern of problem behaviors or psychological changes associated with use or abuse of a substance

descriptors of cannabis intoxication (increased appetite, euphoria, sensation of slowed time, social withdrawal, etc.). Similarly, the withdrawal symptoms differ: Alcohol withdrawal produces agitation, sweating, insomnia, hand tremor, and hallucinations, whereas cannabis withdrawal can result in irritability, anger, or aggression; decreased appetite; or depressed mood. As you might imagine, many emergency room visits are the result of intoxication or withdrawal from various substances.

Substance use may cause depressive, anxiety, or psychotic disorders in individuals who have never previously experienced such symptoms, as we saw with Jay in the introductory vignette. For example, marijuana users may develop a cannabis-induced psychotic disorder, cannabis-induced sleep disorder, or cannabis-induced anxiety disorder. These substance/medication-induced disorders develop within 1 month of using the substance and involve symptoms associated with the particular substance.

In summary, based on their chemical makeup, different substances produce different psychological and physical effects and different symptoms of intoxication and withdrawal, as well as increased susceptibility to certain mental disorders. We now move on to discuss the various substances that can lead to the development of a substance-use disorder.

Substances Associated with Abuse

Substances that are abused include prescription medications used to treat anxiety, insomnia, or pain; legal substances such as alcohol, caffeine, tobacco, and household chemicals; and illegal substances such as cocaine and heroin. Most of the substances discussed in this chapter can create significant physical, social, and psychological problems. Table 11.2 lists abused substances and their effects, as well as their addictive potential.

Table 11.2 Commonly Abused Substances

Substance	Short-Term Effects[a]	Addictive Potential
Central nervous system depressants		
Alcohol	Relaxation, impaired judgment	High
Opioids	Pain relief, sedation, drowsiness	High
Sedatives, hypnotics, anxiolytics	Sedation, drowsiness, reduced anxiety, impaired judgment	Moderate to high
Central nervous system stimulants		
Caffeine	Energy, enhanced attention	Moderate
Amphetamines	Energy, euphoria, enhanced attention	High
Cocaine	Energy, euphoria	High
Hallucinogen		
LSD, psilocybin, mescaline, salvia	Altered perceptions, sensory distortions	Low
Dissociative anesthetics		
Phencyclidine (PCP)	Confusion, sensory distortions, feelings of detachment	Moderate
Ketamine, methoxetamine (MXE)	Confusion, sensory distortions, feelings of detachment	Moderate
Dextromethorphan (DXM)	Confusion, sensory distortions, feelings of detachment	Moderate
Substances with multiple effects		
Nicotine	Energy, relaxation	High
Cannabis	Relaxation, euphoria	Moderate
Inhalants	Disorientation	Variable
Ecstasy (MDMA)	Energy, sensory distortions, feelings of connection	Moderate
Gamma hydroxybutyrate (GHB)	Relaxation, euphoria, enhanced strength	High

[a] Specific effects depend on the quantity used, the extent of previous use, and other substances concurrently ingested, as well as on the experiences, expectancies, and personality of the person using the substance.

Depressants

Depressants cause the central nervous system to slow down. Individuals taking depressants may feel relaxed and sociable due to lowered interpersonal inhibitions. Let's begin by examining the most widely used depressant—alcohol.

Alcohol

CASE STUDY   Jim, a married father of two teenage sons, recently lost his job, in large part due to his heavy drinking. Jim began drinking in high school, hoping it would help him feel less anxious; at first, he disliked the taste of alcohol, but forced himself to continue drinking. Over the next several years, Jim acquired the ability to consume large amounts of alcohol and was proud of his drinking capacity. He remained anxious about social gatherings, but after a few drinks he was the "life of the party." His heavy drinking continued throughout college.

Soon after Jim married and began his career, he began drinking throughout the week, claiming drinking was the only way he could relax. He attributed his increased drinking to pressures at work and a desire to feel comfortable in social situations. Despite frequent arguments with his wife regarding his alcohol use, loss of his job because he was drinking at work, and a physician's warning that alcohol was causing liver damage, Jim could not control his alcohol consumption.

Jim's problem drinking is typical of many people who develop an alcohol-use disorder. Although he initially found the taste of alcohol unpleasant, he continued drinking. Heavy drinking served a purpose: It helped him fit in socially and it reduced his anxiety in work and social situations. His preoccupation with alcohol and deterioration in social and occupational functioning are also characteristic of problem drinkers. His alcohol consumption continued despite obvious negative consequences, including arguments with family members, loss of his job, and health problems. Like many with an alcohol-use disorder, Jim claimed that he did not have a serious problem with drinking. Would things have turned out differently if Jim had sought professional help for his anxiety rather than trying to self-medicate with alcohol?

We begin our discussion of alcohol by clarifying terminology. One drink is defined as 12 oz. of beer, 5 oz. of wine, or 1.5 oz. of hard liquor. **Moderate drinking** refers to lower-risk patterns of drinking, generally no more than one drink for women or two drinks for men. **Heavy drinking** involves consumption of more than two drinks per day or 14 drinks per week for men and more than one drink per day or 7 drinks per week for women. **Binge drinking** is episodic drinking involving five or more drinks on a single occasion for men and four or more drinks for women.

Slightly more than half of U.S. adolescents and adults recently surveyed said they consumed at least one alcoholic drink in the previous month, but the vast majority (about 75 percent) do not drink excessively—they either abstain or drink in moderation. However, nearly one fourth of U.S. Americans age 12 or older binge drink, including 6.5 percent who engage in "heavy drinking" (defined by SAMHSA as binge drinking 5 or more days per month). Males in all age groups are more likely to consume alcohol and engage in binge and heavy drinking compared to females. Ethnic group data reveal that Asian Americans (followed by African Americans) have the lowest levels of excessive drinking (SAMHSA, 2013a). Native Americans of both genders begin drinking at the earliest age and have the highest weekly alcohol consumption, whereas Latino/Hispanic men have the highest rates of daily alcohol consumption (Chartier & Caetano, 2010).

Let's focus on statistics for the college-age population. As illustrated in Figure 11.4, binge drinking and heavy drinking are especially problematic among those ages 21–25, with 45.1 percent of those in this age group engaging in binge drinking, including 14.4 percent who binge drink at least 5 days per month (SAMHSA, 2013a). Binge drinking occurs more frequently in young adults (ages 18–22) who attend college full-time

depressant   a substance that causes a slowing of responses and generalized depression of the central nervous system

moderate drinking   a lower-risk pattern of alcohol intake (no more than one or two drinks per day)

heavy drinking   chronic alcohol intake of more than two drinks per day for men and more than one drink per day for women

binge drinking   episodic intake of five or more alcoholic beverages for men or four or more drinks for women

Figure 11.4

Comparisons of Alcohol Use across Age Groups

In 2012, almost half of those ages 18–20 reported underage alcohol use in the previous month, including 30.5 percent who reported binge drinking at least once and 10 percent who were heavy drinkers, binge drinking on at least five occasions. The highest level of binge drinking and heavy alcohol use is seen in the 21–25 age group.

SOURCE: Substance Abuse and Mental Health Services Administration (2013a).

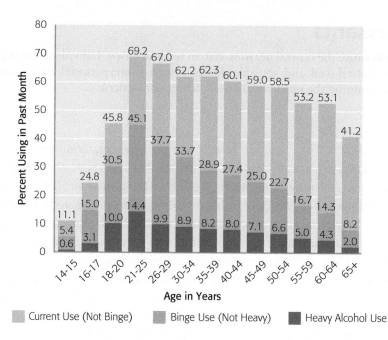

Figure 11.5

Trends in Binge Drinking among 18- to 22-Year-Olds

There are significant differences in binge drinking between 18- to 22-year-olds who attend college full-time and those who attend part-time or not at all, with college attendees consistently reporting higher rates of heavy drinking.

SOURCE: Substance Abuse and Mental Health Services Administration (2013a).

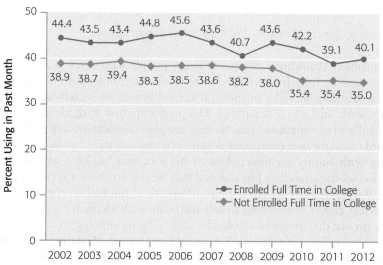

DID YOU KNOW?

College-age binge drinkers are much more likely to show deficits in information processing and working memory compared to alcohol drinkers who do not binge.

SOURCE: Courtney & Polich, 2009

compared to those who do not (Figure 11.5). College students also engage in other unsafe drinking practices such as skipping meals to compensate for high-caloric binge drinking or to get drunk faster, a practice that not only hastens intoxication but also increases risk of dehydration, blackouts, seizures, or cardiac arrest (Piazza-Gardner & Barry, 2013).

How does alcohol affect the body? Once swallowed, alcohol is quickly absorbed into the bloodstream and begins to depress central nervous system functioning. When the blood alcohol level, or alcohol content in the bloodstream, is about 0.1 percent—for many, the equivalent of drinking 3 oz. of whiskey or three glasses of beer—muscular coordination and judgment are impaired. Higher levels of blood alcohol, 0.3 percent in some individuals, can result in a loss of consciousness or even death. Alcohol lowers inhibitions, impairs judgment, and can increase aggression and impulsivity. This combination may partially explain why alcohol is frequently associated with suicidal behavior (Ali et al., 2013).

Our bodies produce "cleanup" enzymes, including aldehyde dehydrogenase (ALDH), to counteract toxins that build up as our bodies metabolize alcohol. Production of ALDH is affected by gender (males, especially younger males, produce more than females) and genetic makeup (some people, especially Asians, produce less ALDH). Recently ingested food, beverages, or medications also affect how we metabolize alcohol. For example, carbonated beverages and aspirin accelerate alcohol absorption and reduce the efficiency of the ALDH cleanup, whereas food slows absorption, giving the enzymes more time to work. Intoxication occurs more rapidly in those who have a low body weight or consume alcohol rapidly. Large amounts of alcohol consumed quickly can result in impaired breathing, coma, and death; this condition, known as **alcohol poisoning**, can be exacerbated by the vomiting and dehydration that occur as the body attempts to rid itself of excess alcohol.

Now, let's talk about people who have an alcohol-use disorder (refer to Table 11.1 and recall that impaired functioning and two of the symptoms may reflect an alcohol-use disorder). The lifetime prevalence of alcohol-use disorder in the U.S. adult population is 18 percent. European Americans, Native Americans, males, and those who are younger and unmarried with lower incomes are most likely to become **alcoholic** (Hasin, Stinson, et al., 2007). Although men are twice as likely to develop an alcohol-use disorder, **alcoholism** in women progresses more rapidly (Anthenelli, 2010). Some people become physiologically dependent on alcohol. That is, if they stop drinking, alcohol withdrawal symptoms (e.g., headache, fatigue, sweating, body tremors, and mood changes) develop. Severe withdrawal can produce a life-threatening condition called **delirium tremens**, which begins with profound anxiety, agitation, and confusion followed by seizures, disorientation, hallucinations, or extreme lethargy.

There are multiple physiological consequences associated with excessive alcohol use. Tolerance to alcohol develops rapidly, so drinkers wanting to feel the effects of alcohol often increase their intake. Unfortunately, tolerance does not decrease the toxicity of alcohol, so heavy drinkers progressively expose their brains and bodies to greater physiological risk. Neurological effects include impaired motor skills, reduced reasoning and judgment, memory deficits, distractibility, and reduced motivation (E. V. Sullivan, Harris, & Pfefferbaum, 2010). Additionally, alcohol affects the liver and the entire cardiovascular system. People with alcoholism who continue to drink demonstrate declines in neurological functioning. Although sustained **abstinence** can lead to cognitive improvement, those who were heavy drinkers often demonstrate ongoing impairment (Fortier et al., 2011).

In stark contrast to the stereotype of the skid row alcoholic, many people with an alcohol-use disorder are able to function without obvious disruption to their life—many of these so-called *high-functioning alcoholics* work, raise families, and maintain social relationships. Although aware of the negative physical and social consequences of their drinking, and distressed over their inability to control alcohol intake, they often deny they have a problem with alcohol or hide their drinking (Willenbring, 2010). It is common for individuals with alcohol-use disorder to alternate between periods of excessive drinking and sobriety, often in an attempt to prove they can abstain (E. V. Sullivan et al., 2010).

Opioids

CASE STUDY Throughout the evening of June 24, 2009, Michael Jackson energetically rehearsed for a concert series. The next morning he was found in his bedroom, not breathing. Paramedics could not revive him. His death appeared to be the result of a drug overdose. Battling pain, anxiety, and chronic insomnia, Jackson used a variety of prescription medications. His addiction reportedly began with pain medication prescribed after he was burned when filming a Pepsi commercial. The details of his later drug use are unclear, but prescription painkillers, stimulants, and antianxiety and sleeping medications are often mentioned. Lyrics written by Jackson—"Demerol, oh God he's taking Demerol"—from a song called "Morphine" added to speculation about continued drug use and opioid dependence.

Medications became less effective as Jackson developed tolerance to the drugs. Jackson continued to battle chronic insomnia and was desperate to rest, resorting to increasingly dangerous substances. On June 25, 2009, he suffered a cardiac arrest. The coroner found multiple medications in Jackson's system, including a powerful anesthetic, propofol; it was concluded that Jackson's death resulted from acute propofol intoxication.

alcohol poisoning toxic effects resulting from rapidly consuming alcohol or ingesting a large quantity of alcohol; can result in impaired breathing, coma, and death

alcoholic person who has become dependent on alcohol and who exhibits characteristics of an alcohol-use disorder

alcoholism broad term referring to a condition in which the individual is dependent on alcohol and has difficulty controlling drinking

delirium tremens life-threatening withdrawal symptoms that can result from chronic alcohol use

abstinence refraining from use of alcohol, drugs, or other addictive substances

What Messages Is Society Sending about Alcohol Use?

What messages are we sending regarding alcohol use in contemporary society? Alcohol advertising and media glamorization of alcohol is pervasive. The myth persists that "everyone drinks," despite the fact that the majority of American adults consume alcohol only occasionally or not at all. Although efforts to prevent alcohol abuse stress the personal and societal risk of excess alcohol consumption and the risk of underage drinking, these messages receive only minimal attention. Should we be making more effort to balance marketing and social media messages with information regarding the potential dangers of alcohol?

Professionals focused on addiction prevention assert that we need to find innovative ways to nullify societal messages that normalize and even glamorize alcohol use and to heighten awareness of risk factors, especially among those who are most vulnerable to addiction—adolescents and young adults. This is particularly important because we know that the effects of alcohol (along with other substances) on the developing brain are most profound through the mid-20s. The college years are a very high-risk period for beginning the addiction process

because students who participate in underage alcohol use often drink heavily (Beseler, Taylor, Kraemer, & Leeman, 2012). Although college-bound high school students are less likely to binge drink, this trend reverses after college entrance; additionally, students with the greatest genetic risk of developing alcoholism tend to drink the most (Timberlake et al., 2007). Given the data on heavy drinking among college students, there is a need for new strategies for educating students about alcohol and the addiction process. Although alcohol-abuse prevention campaigns are attempting to correct social misperceptions about the frequency of drinking (H. W. Perkins, Linkenbach, Lewis, & Neighbors, 2010), it will be difficult to reduce the prevalence of alcohol abuse as long as our society tolerates binge drinking and underage alcohol consumption.

Do you think the college environment plays a role in decisions to participate in heavy or underage drinking? What aspects of alcohol abuse do you think are most relevant to college students, and how can these be incorporated into prevention messages? What kinds of prevention efforts do you think would be the most effective on your college campus?

DID YOU KNOW?

The number of deaths due to prescription drug overdoses has tripled in the past decade. Almost two thirds of overdose deaths involve prescription opioids.

SOURCE: CDC, 2013

opioid a painkilling agent that depresses the central nervous system, such as heroin and prescription pain relievers

gateway drug a substance that leads to use of additional substances that are even more lethal

Opioids are painkilling agents that depress the central nervous system. Heroin and opium, both derived from the opium plant, are the best-known illicit opioids. All opioids (including the medications morphine, codeine, and oxycodone) are highly addictive and require careful medical management when prescribed for pain and anxiety. Misuse of illegally obtained prescription opioids is rising (Paulozzi et al., 2012). In fact, nonmedical use of pain relievers such as oxycodone is a leading form of drug abuse (SAMHSA, 2013a).

Prescription opioids are considered a **gateway drug**—a substance leading to the use of more dangerous drugs. This may have been what occurred with Michael Jackson following his burn injury. Many people who abuse opioids begin their habit with prescribed medication, eventually buying prescription drugs illegally or trying a less expensive and even more lethal opioid—heroin (Canfield et al., 2010). Those who misuse prescription opioids often rationalize their use because the substances are prescription medications (Daniulaityte, Falck, & Carlson, 2012). Given the increase in opioid-use disorders since physicians were first allowed to prescribe opioids for pain management in patients without cancer, some physicians question whether the benefits of prescribing opioids outweigh the addictive risks (Kissin, 2013).

Opioids produce both euphoria and drowsiness. Tolerance builds quickly, resulting in dependency and a need for increased doses to achieve desired effects. Opioid withdrawal symptoms (including restlessness, muscle pain, insomnia, and cold flashes) are often severe. Lethargy, fatigue, anxiety, and disturbed sleep may persist for months, and drug craving can persist for years. Unfortunately, deaths from accidental opioid overdose are common and often involve concurrent use of alcohol or other drugs (CDC, 2013).

Sedatives, Hypnotics, and Anxiolytics

Sedatives, including hypnotics (sleeping pills) and anxiolytics (antianxiety medications), have calming effects and are prescribed to reduce muscle tension, insomnia, agitation, and anxiety. **Hypnotics** induce sleep and combat insomnia. **Anxiolytics** are used to treat anxiety; they are sometimes referred to as minor tranquilizers, so named to distinguish them from the major tranquilizing medications used with psychotic disorders. The drug classes of *barbiturates*, such as Seconal and phenobarbital, and *benzodiazepines*, such as Valium, Ativan, and Xanax, provide rapid anxiety-reducing effects when used in moderate doses; higher doses are prescribed to produce hypnotic, or sleep-inducing, effects.

Sedative, hypnotic, or anxiolytic substance-use disorders can develop if someone takes high prescription doses, or deliberately misuses or illegally obtains these medications. Individuals who have difficulty dealing with stress or who experience anxiety or insomnia are particularly prone to overusing and becoming dependent on sedatives. Additionally, some use sedatives recreationally or to counteract cocaine withdrawal symptoms (Sola, Chopra, & Rastogi, 2010). Sedatives are quite dangerous when misused. Even in low doses, they cause drowsiness, impaired judgment, and diminished motor skills. As with opioids, systems are in place to monitor their legal use in an attempt to reduce risk of drug dependence; however, misuse is difficult to control due to their availability via illegal drug markets. Excessive use of sedatives can lead to accidental overdose and death. Combining alcohol with sedatives can be especially dangerous because alcohol compounds their depressant effects, slowing breathing and increasing risk of coma or lethal outcomes.

There is high potential for tolerance and physiological dependence with all sedatives; when they are discontinued, sedative withdrawal can produce insomnia, nervousness, headache, and drowsiness. Due to concerns regarding addictive potential and lethality with overdose, many medical practitioners avoid prescribing sedatives to treat anxiety, and instead prescribe antidepressants. This stance is supported by data from a 35,000-participant national survey revealing that individuals prescribed sedatives for anxiety are twice as likely to develop a sedative-use disorder (Fenton, Keyes, Martins, & Hasin, 2010). The risk of sedative dependence is greatest when doses are high, sedatives are used for more than 1 month, or there is a personal or family history of substance abuse (Sola et al., 2010).

Stimulants

Stimulants, substances that speed up central nervous system activity, are used for a variety of reasons: to produce feelings of euphoria and well-being, improve mental and physical performance, reduce appetite, and prevent sleep. Unwanted physiological effects include heart arrhythmias, dizziness, tremors, and sweating. Psychological side effects can include anxiety, restlessness, agitation, hostility, and paranoia. Binge use of illicit stimulants is common, with sequential high doses leading to exhaustion and acute psychotic symptoms. Tolerance to the stimulant effects develops rapidly, leading to increased drug use; stimulant withdrawal can produce depression, anxiety, and extreme fatigue. Our discussion begins with a commonly used mild stimulant, caffeine.

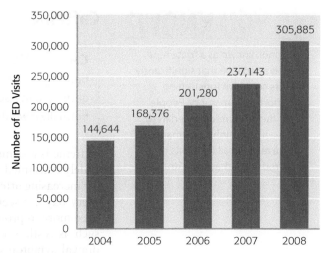

Figure 11.6

Emergency Department Visits Related to Illicit Use of Prescription Opioids

The number of emergency department visits due to illicit use of prescription pain medications increased 111 percent between 2004 and 2008, more than doubling in all age groups and for both males and females.

SOURCE: Substance Abuse and Mental Health Services Administration (2010a).

sedatives a class of drugs that have a calming or sedating effect

hypnotics a class of medications that induce sleep

anxiolytics a class of medications that reduce anxiety

stimulant a substance that energizes the central nervous system

DID YOU KNOW?

Rohypnol, known as a "date rape" drug, is a sedative that significantly impairs cognitive functioning and short-term memory. People given the drug may feel sedated, behave in an uninhibited manner, and have no recall of events that occurred while they were drugged.

Caffeine

> **CASE STUDY**   I use energy drinks to stay awake while I study at night. I am noticing that I need more and more energy drinks to stay awake and keep alert. It's getting to the point where I need over four or five cans to get through a night, when normally it would take me only one can.

Caffeine is a stimulant found in coffee, chocolate, tea, and soft drinks. It is the most widely consumed psychoactive substance in the world, prized by almost every culture for increasing attentiveness. About 90 percent of adults in North America use caffeine every day. As seen in the case example, we often develop tolerance to caffeine, and need more to produce the desired effect. Caffeine intoxication can produce symptoms such as restlessness, nervousness, insomnia, and cardiac arrhythmia. Caffeine withdrawal symptoms include headache, fatigue, irritability, and difficulty with concentration. DSM-5 contains a proposed diagnostic category of caffeine-use disorder for those who display impairment due to caffeine addiction (APA, 2013).

Caffeine is usually consumed in moderate doses (a cup of tea has 40–60 mg, coffee 70–175 mg, and cola 30–50 mg), but caffeine consumption has increased due to the widespread marketing and consumption of energy drinks. Energy drinks, now a multibillion-dollar industry, typically have 80–150 mg of caffeine in addition to sweeteners and energy-boosting additives (Bigard, 2010). Thirty percent of middle and high school students report regular use of energy drinks (Terry-McElrath, O'Malley, & Johnston, 2014). Frequent consumption of energy drinks can produce caffeine intoxication and caffeine withdrawal symptoms (Ishak, Ugochukwu, Bagot, Khalili, & Zaky, 2012). Emergency room and urgent care center visits associated with intoxication from energy drinks have dramatically increased, particularly when energy drinks are combined with alcohol or illicit drugs (SAMHSA, 2013b).

Amphetamines

Amphetamines, also known as "uppers," significantly speed up central nervous system activity. Amphetamines, such as Ritalin, Adderall, and Dexedrine, prescribed to treat attention and sleep disorders, are increasingly used illicitly, particularly among young adults (SAMHSA, 2013a). Of particular concern is the increase in nonmedical use of Adderall among high school students (Johnston et al., 2014), especially those who also use other illicit drugs (Sweeney, Sembower, Ertischek, Shiffman, & Schnoll, 2013).

Methamphetamine Effects

This pair of mug shots is part of the Faces of Meth project started when justice officials noticed the significant physical decline among methamphetamine users arrested more than once. As seen here, many of the second, later mug shots clearly demonstrate the gauntness and facial lesions associated with ongoing methamphetamine use.

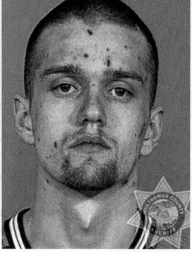

About 2 percent of U.S. adults have experienced an amphetamine-use disorder. Addiction is most common in those who take amphetamines intravenously or nasally ("snorting") and in high doses. Although amphetamines can induce feelings of euphoria and confidence, agitation, psychosis, and assaultive or suicidal behaviors also occur. Brain damage can result from chronic stimulant abuse (S. M. Berman, Kuczenski, McCracken, & London, 2009).

Methamphetamine ("meth"), a particularly dangerous amphetamine that is eaten, snorted, injected, or heated and smoked in rock "crystal" form, is used by 0.2 percent of the population (SAMHSA, 2013a). Popular due to its low cost and rapid euphoric effects, methamphetamine has serious health consequences, including permanent damage to the heart, lungs, and immune system (Hauer, 2010). Although many are aware of the profound dental and aging

Multnomah County Sheriff/Splash/Newscom

effects of methamphetamine (Rusyniak, 2011), significant psychological changes also occur, including psychosis, depression, suicide, and violent behavior (Lecomte et al., 2013). As with other stimulants, methamphetamine has high potential for abuse and addiction.

Cocaine

CASE STUDY A 49-year-old woman, previously diagnosed with congestive heart failure, was admitted to the hospital with a severe cough and labored breathing. She reported that she had never smoked cigarettes, consumed alcohol, or used drugs other than cocaine, which she had been smoking for 30 years. Due to her severe emphysema and continued cocaine use, she was not a candidate for heart transplantation. She died from respiratory failure and cardiac arrest (Vahid & Marik, 2007).

Cocaine, a stimulant extracted from the coca plant, induces feelings of energy and euphoria. Crack is a potent form of cocaine produced by heating cocaine with other substances ("freebasing"); it is sold in small, solid pieces ("rocks") and is typically smoked. Crack produces immediate but short-lived effects. Cocaine has a high potential for addiction, sometimes after only a short period of use. In 2012, there were an estimated 1.6 million cocaine users (0.6 percent of the population), with a large number of them (1.1 million) demonstrating a stimulant-use disorder (SAMHSA, 2013a).

Due to cocaine's intense effects, cocaine withdrawal causes lethargy and depression; users often take multiple doses in rapid succession trying to re-create the high. The constant desire for cocaine coupled with the high monetary cost and need for increased doses to achieve a high can cause users to resort to crime to feed their habit. Because cocaine stimulates the sympathetic nervous system, irregular heartbeat, stroke, and death may occur. Cocaine users sometimes experience acute psychiatric symptoms such as delusions, paranoia, and hallucinations; more chronic difficulties such as anxiety, depression, sexual dysfunction, and sleep difficulties also occur. Similar to the woman in the case example, regular cocaine users often have a shortened life span.

CONTROVERSY

Stimulants and Performance Enhancement: A New Source of Addiction?

The nonmedical use of prescription medications is on the rise, including illicit use of stimulant medications by high school and college students and young professionals who want to enhance their functioning and outperform the competition. Eighteen percent of one group of undergraduates reported such use, and another 26 percent of students with attention-deficit/hyperactivity disorder reported overuse of their own medication (Arria et al., 2008); many of these same students also reported extensive marijuana and alcohol use. Medical students, a group who should clearly understand the consequences of nonmedical use of prescription stimulants, are also a high-risk population for illicit stimulant use (Tuttle, Scheurich, & Ranseen, 2010). On the other hand, many university students indicate that they would not use stimulants to avoid sleep or enhance performance due to health risks, as well as ethical factors (Sattler, Sauer, Mehlkop, & Graeff, 2013). Some physicians are also speaking out against this practice, pointing out the addictive potential of stimulants and possible effects on the developing brain (Graf et al., 2013). What do you see as the biggest concerns arising from the illicit use of prescription medication to enhance performance?

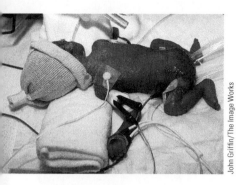

Cocaine Addiction from Mother to Child

Women who use drugs during pregnancy sometimes give birth to drug-addicted, underweight babies who are at risk for serious developmental problems. Pictured here is a newborn baby being monitored as it goes through cocaine withdrawal symptoms.

Hallucinogens

Hallucinogens are substances that can produce vivid sensory experiences, including hallucinations. Traditional hallucinogens are derived from natural sources: lysergic acid diethylamide (LSD) from a grain fungus, psilocybin from mushrooms, mescaline from the peyote cactus, and salvia from an herb in the mint family. Some synthetic drugs (such as PCP, ketamine, and Ecstasy) have hallucinogenic effects combined with other properties (e.g., stimulant or tranquilizing effects) and are discussed later in the chapter. Natural hallucinogens have been used in cultural ceremonies and religious rites for thousands of years. Approximately 1.1 million people, 0.4 percent of the U.S. adolescent and adult population, used hallucinogens in 2012 (SAMHSA, 2013a). Approximately 4.2 percent of hallucinogen users develop *hallucinogen persisting perception disorder* in which they experience distressing recurrence of hallucinations or other sensations weeks or even years after drug intake (APA, 2013).

The effects and emotional reactions from hallucinogen use can vary significantly, even for the same person. The altered state hallucinogens produce is sometimes pleasant, but can be an extremely traumatic experience. "Good trips" are associated with sharpened visual and auditory perception, heightened sensation, and perceptions of profound insight. "Bad trips" can produce severe depression, disorientation, delusions, and sensory distortions that result in fear and panic. Hallucinogens are not addictive and therefore do not cause compulsive drug-seeking behavior. However, tolerance does develop, so users frequently need larger quantities to re-create the initial effects of the drug (L. Wu, Ringwalt, Weiss, & Blazer, 2009). Large doses are not typically fatal, although there are reports of people who have unwittingly committed suicide while under the influence of hallucinogens.

Dissociative Anesthetics

Phencyclidine (known as PCP) and ketamine (sometimes referred to as Special K), both highly dangerous and potentially addictive substances, are classified as **dissociative anesthetics**; developed for use as anesthetics in veterinary medicine, they produce a dreamlike detachment in humans. PCP and ketamine are very similar chemically, and have the potential to produce a *phencyclidine-use disorder*. They have dissociative, stimulant, depressant, amnesic, and hallucinogenic properties. PCP and ketamine are among the most dangerous of the so-called club drugs, a term that comes from the popular use of certain drugs at dance clubs. These drugs cause disconnection, perceptual distortion, euphoria, and confusion, as well as delusions, hostility, and violent psychotic behavior, as seen in the case of Jay discussed at the beginning of the chapter. Additionally, frequent users demonstrate cognitive and memory deficits and depressive, dissociative, and delusional symptoms; delusions can persist even after cessation of use (C. J. Morgan, Muetzelfeldt, & Curran, 2010).

Dextromethorphan (DXM), an active ingredient in many over-the-counter cold medications and cough suppressants, is another frequently misused dissociative anesthetic. Despite industry efforts to control misuse of these products, approximately 5 percent of 12th graders report using cough and cold medicines to get high (Johnston et al., 2014). Effects of DXM abuse can include disorientation, confusion, and sensory distortion. The large quantities consumed by those who misuse DXM can result in **hyperthermia** (elevated body temperature), high blood pressure, and heart arrhythmia; as with PCP and ketamine, health consequences are intensified when DXM is combined with alcohol or other drugs. A recent trend of concern to medical personnel and drug enforcement officials is "sizzurp," which is a dangerous combination of cough syrup containing DXM, soda, and candy.

Substances with Mixed Chemical Properties

A number of abused substances have varied effects on the brain and central nervous system. We begin by briefly discussing nicotine, an addictive drug with both depressant and stimulant features. We then discuss cannabis, inhalants, and designer

hallucinogen a substance that induces perceptual distortions and heightens sensory awareness

dissociative anesthetic a substance that produces a dreamlike detachment

hyperthermia significantly elevated body temperature

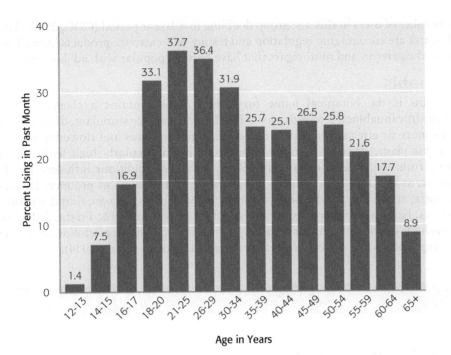

Figure 11.7

Past-Month Cigarette Use among Adolescents and Adults across Age Groups

Cigarette smoking increases significantly during late adolescence and peaks between ages 21 and 29.

SOURCE: Substance Abuse and Mental Health Services Administration (2013a).

drugs, including Ecstasy, as well as the unique dangers involved when substances are combined.

Nicotine

Nicotine, a drug most commonly associated with cigarette smoking, is highly addictive and can result in a tobacco-use disorder. Nicotine is a stimulant in low doses and a relaxant in higher doses. Almost 70 million adults and adolescents (26.7 percent of the population) use tobacco products, primarily cigarettes. Nicotine use increases significantly during late adolescence, peaking in the 20s, as shown in Figure 11.7. Tobacco use is more common among males (33 percent) than females (20.9 percent). Full-time college students (21.3 percent) are less likely to smoke than their age peers (37.2 percent; SAMHSA, 2013a). Many current tobacco users find it extremely difficult to quit due to the strength of their nicotine addiction (Boardman et al., 2011).

Nicotine releases both adrenaline and dopamine, which deliver a burst of energy and feelings of pleasure, respectively. A smoker's first cigarette of the day produces the greatest stimulant effect; as the day progresses, euphoric effects decrease (Benowitz, 2010). As tolerance develops, more nicotine is needed to experience energy, pleasure, and relaxation. Tobacco withdrawal symptoms include difficulty concentrating, restlessness, anxiety, depressed mood, and irritability. Five million people die each year throughout the world due to tobacco use. It is considered the single most preventable cause of premature death (World Health Organization, 2014).

Electronic cigarettes are gaining popularity among nonsmokers and those trying to quit smoking. These unregulated battery-powered devices allow users to simulate smoking by "vaping" a substance that combines both nicotine and flavorings. Proponents of e-cigarettes argue that they provide smokers with an alternative, less harmful source of nicotine (Polosa, Rodu, Caponnetto, Maglia, & Raciti, 2013). Other express concern about the limited research on the health effects of vaping and the fact that e-cigarettes are introducing nonsmokers to the addictive effects of nicotine (Palazzolo, 2013). It is particularly worrisome that the rate of experimentation and use of e-cigarettes among U.S. middle and high school students is increasing rapidly, with

DID YOU KNOW?

Feeling "relaxed" immediately after the first puff of a cigarette was the leading predictor of becoming dependent on cigarettes and being unable to quit. About 29 percent of adolescents interviewed said they had experienced such a feeling after their first cigarette.

SOURCE: DiFranza et al., 2007

Smoking's Effects on the Lungs

A New York City exhibit of real, whole human body specimens provides an actual view of the healthy lungs and heart of a nonsmoker versus the blackened lungs and heart of a smoker. The human body specimens are preserved through a revolutionary technique called polymer preservation. All bodies are from people who died of natural causes.

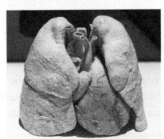

Nancy Kaszerman/ZUMA/Corbis Wire/Corbis

the number of users in this age group doubling in a 1-year period (CDC, 2013). Health advocates are encouraging regulation and testing of e-cigarette products, as well as the flavored cigarettes and mini-cigars that have become popular with adolescents.

Cannabis

Cannabis is the botanical name for a plant that contains a chemical (delta-9-tetrahydrocannabinol, referred to as THC) that can produce stimulant, depressant, and hallucinogenic effects. Marijuana is derived from the leaves and flowering top of the cannabis plant, whereas hashish, which contains particularly high levels of THC, comes from the pressed resin of the plant. Growing conditions influence the THC content, as well as other chemicals in cannabis plants. Cannabis produces feelings of euphoria, tranquility, and passivity combined with mild perceptual and sensory distortions, but can also increase anxiety and depression (Fattore & Fratta, 2010). Some individuals develop chronic psychotic symptoms or schizophrenia following cannabis use, especially when use occurs at a young age (Donoghue et al., 2014).

A Closer Look at Legalizing Pot

Although possession of cannabis is illegal under federal law, discussions about legalizing the recreational use of marijuana are occurring across the United States. Additionally, despite the fact that the Food and Drug Administration does not consider cannabis a safe or effective medical treatment, 20 states now allow the production and distribution of marijuana for certain medical conditions. Furthermore, many municipalities have decriminalized the possession of marijuana for personal use and voters in several states have gone farther—legalizing the commercialization, production, and sale of cannabis and allowing adults age 21 and older to possess small quantities of marijuana for personal use.

Proponents of legalization contend that marijuana is safe and poses fewer serious health consequences than legal substances such as alcohol or tobacco. Additionally, they point out the benefits associated with the taxation and regulation of marijuana sales. They also hope that legalization will reduce violence associated with the illegal drug trade and allow law enforcement officials to focus on other priorities. Professionals in the addiction field are attempting to counter the assertion that cannabis use poses limited physical or psychological risk. Instead, they emphasize that marijuana is a potent, addictive substance that can have long-term negative effects on brain functioning. They also express concern that increased availability of marijuana combined with the potency of today's cannabis will lead to a variety of health and personal problems, including addiction (American Society of Addiction Medicine, 2012).

Some researchers are concerned that cannabis use is increasing because legalization debates have normalized the use of marijuana and because there has been limited public education regarding the health consequences associated with cannabis. Increases in marijuana use, especially among adolescents and young adults, have paralleled increases in the legalization debate. For example, recent adolescent surveys reveal a decrease in the number of high school students who believe that marijuana poses health risks, with less than 40 percent believing that regular marijuana use is potentially harmful. Additionally, 34 percent of 12th graders who used marijuana in states allowing medical marijuana reported acquiring marijuana from someone who had a prescription (Johnston et al., 2014). Mental health professionals are concerned that these increases in cannabis use will result in increases in psychotic disorders, especially for those who initiate marijuana use during adolescence (Donoghue et al., 2014).

Research will be important as states implement laws legalizing the recreational or medical use of marijuana. There is no doubt that the debate will continue as marijuana becomes more available and states that have legalized marijuana contend with realities such as oversight of the marijuana industry and penalties for legal violations involving public or underage use, as well as traffic safety violations.

For Further Consideration

1. If chemicals in cannabis are found to be safe and effective for certain medical conditions, should they be distributed in herbal form by marijuana dispensaries or prepared in a standardized manner and dispensed in pill or liquid form by pharmacies?

2. What methods of research can we use to assess the effects of laws allowing the recreational or medical use of marijuana? What outcome variables should researchers monitor?

Marijuana is the most commonly used illicit drug worldwide (United Nations Office on Drugs and Crime, 2013). In the United States, almost 20 million adults and adolescents report current use, with males more likely than females to use marijuana (9.6 percent vs. 5 percent). As seen in Figure 11.8, of the 2.9 million adolescents and adults who first used illicit drugs in 2012, 65.6 percent reported the first drug they experimented with was marijuana. Marijuana use is particularly widespread among adolescents and young adults (SAMHSA, 2013a). An annual survey of high school students revealed that 29.8 percent of 10th graders and 36.4 percent of 12th graders used marijuana in the previous year; additionally, daily marijuana use among 8th, 10th, and 12th graders is increasing (Johnston et al., 2014).

These statistics are of particular concern because many addiction specialists view cannabis as a gateway drug associated with later use of other illicit substances; this is especially true for those who begin use during adolescence (Van Gundy, Cesar, & Rebellon, 2010). Additionally, marijuana has addictive potential and is the drug most frequently associated with a substance-use disorder diagnosis; more than 4 million adolescents and adults demonstrated a cannabis-use disorder in 2012 (SAMHSA, 2013a). Approximately 10 percent of those who use marijuana become dependent on the drug. A unique characteristic of marijuana dependence is a pervasive lack of concern regarding the consequences of drug use (Munsey, 2010). Cannabis withdrawal symptoms include irritability, anxiety, insomnia, restlessness, and depression, as well as distressing physical symptoms such as stomach pain, tremors, sweating, fever, and headache. Withdrawal symptoms cause many users to return to cannabis use or to resort to using other drugs (APA, 2013).

Long-term use of cannabis is associated with impaired judgment, memory, and concentration. Diminished cognitive functioning involving attention, memory, and learning can persist for years, especially for those who begin use during adolescence (Meier et al., 2012). Adolescents who engage in frequent marijuana use also have lower academic achievement (Martins & Alexandre, 2009), as well as subtle abnormalities in brain structure (Bava, Jacobus, Thayer, & Tapert, 2013). These cognitive effects may be more pronounced and persistent in adolescents because their brains are undergoing a critical period of development, thus increasing vulnerability to the effects of drug use (Gruber, Sagar, Dahlgren, Racine, & Lukas, 2012).

Inhalants

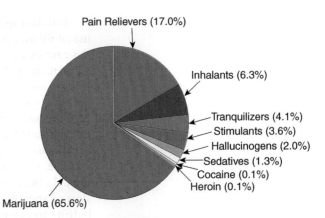

Figure 11.8

Drugs Involved in First-Time Illicit Drug Use in 2012

Among the 2.9 million adolescents and adults who first used an illicit drug during 2012, 65.6 percent reported that their first illicit drug was marijuana.

SOURCE: Substance Abuse and Mental Health Services Administration (2013a).

DID YOU KNOW?

The risk of having a car accident is doubled after marijuana use; this risk is further increased when the driver has also consumed alcohol.

SOURCE: M. Li et al., 2012

CASE STUDY   "The spray makes me talk slow. Besides the headache I get when I'm not doing it, it makes me slower. The high is good but it makes me slow. When it's wearing off, it makes me like I am stupid. I have to talk slow because the words don't come out." . . .

"Sometimes I get suicidal. I don't know why. I just do. I just don't give a damn. I just get out in the street in front of cars. Sometimes I remember that I'm doing it and sometimes I don't know it. When I do know it, I don't give a damn. I just want to stop my life because the headaches I get when I stop the spray paint just make me crazy." (Ramos, 1998, pp. 14, 24, 28)

Inhalant abusers become intoxicated from chemical vapors found in a variety of common household products, including solvents (paint removers, gasoline, lighter fluid), office supplies (marker pens, correction fluids), aerosol sprays (spray paints, hair spray), and compressed air products (computer and electronics duster sprays). Inhalation of these substances (known as "huffing") is accomplished through sniffing fumes from containers, bags, or balloons; directly inhaling aerosol sprays; or using inhalant-soaked rags.

Inhalant use is most common amongst those ages 12–17 (SAMHSA, 2013a). The use of inhalants by children and adolescents is considered a silent epidemic, although the rate of use is declining. In a recent school survey, 10.8 percent of 8th graders, 8.7 percent of 10th graders, and 6.9 percent of 12th graders reported using inhalants at least once (Johnston et al., 2014). Experimental use of inhalants in younger adolescents typically occurs before experimentation with tobacco or alcohol. Fortunately, experimentation with inhalants does not appear to be a gateway to more serious drug use, although those who chronically abuse inhalants often initiate marijuana and cocaine use (Ding, Chang, & Southerland, 2009).

The immediate effects of inhalants vary depending on the chemicals involved; typical effects include impaired coordination and judgment, euphoria, dizziness, and slurred speech. The intoxicating effects of inhalants are brief, resulting in repeated huffing to extend intoxication. Hypoxia (oxygen deprivation) results in the persistent cognitive deficits such as severe memory impairment and slow information processing seen in the case study. Any episode of inhalant use, even in first-time users, can result in stroke, acute respiratory distress, or sudden heart failure (referred to as "sudden sniffing death"). Fatal outcome is most common with compressed air products, aerosol sprays, air fresheners, butane, propane, and nitrous oxide (Marsolek, White, & Litovitz, 2010).

Inhalant use produces a number of emotional and interpersonal difficulties, including paranoid thinking and suicidal ideation. In one sample of inhalant abusers, 67 percent had contemplated suicide and 20 percent had attempted suicide (M. O. Howard, Perron, Sacco, et al., 2010). Additionally, chronic inhalant abuse is associated with high levels of anxiety and depression, as well as antisocial behavior and interpersonal violence (Howard, Perron, Vaughn, Bender, & Garland, 2010).

Designer Drugs

The term "designer drug" refers to substances manufactured as recreational drugs, using a variety of chemicals; these synthetic drugs are created to mimic the effects of hallucinogenic or stimulant drugs while evading legal restrictions. Many of these drugs are available in the form of pills, powders, or liquids and are sold over the Internet under a variety of product names.

Designer drugs include substances such as the following:

- Ecstasy (methylenedioxymethamphetamine, or MDMA)
- Synthetic marijuana, made from a combination of herbs and chemicals
- MDPV marketed as "bath salts" or "plant food"
- DOM, known as STP or Serenity, Tranquility, and Peace
- Bromo-Dragonfly or B-fly, with persistent hallucinogenic effects
- Methoxetamine or MXE, with effects similar to PCP and ketamine

Similarly, some natural drugs (such as the opiate-like plant, kratom) are labeled and sold as products such as incense, to avoid regulatory restrictions. One of the major concerns with these unregulated drugs is that they can affect multiple systems of the body. For example, authorities issued an international alert regarding MDPV (bath salts) due to the cardiac and neurological danger of the substance (Coppola & Mondola, 2012). Similarly, concern about the dangers of synthetic marijuana has resulted in federal efforts to ban chemicals used in its manufacture. A newer injectable opioid substance, Krokodil, has led unsuspecting users to have limbs amputated due to extensive ulceration of the skin (Grund, Latypov, & Harris, 2013). Unfortunately, efforts at regulation often result in the manufacture of new substances using alternate unregulated chemicals.

Ecstasy Ecstasy (methylenedioxymethamphetamine, or MDMA), which has both stimulant and hallucinogenic properties, is a designer drug that has gained popularity as a party drug. Short-term effects of Ecstasy, including euphoria, mild sensory and cognitive distortion, and feelings of intimacy and well-being, are often followed by intense depression. Users frequently experience hyperthermia or the need to suck on lollipops or pacifiers to counteract involuntary jaw spasms and teeth clenching. Following a period of increasing use, Ecstasy use among high school students is decreasing (Johnston et al., 2014).

Ecstasy appears to have unique chemical properties that accelerate the development of physiological dependence, even among those who do not use it regularly (Bruno et al., 2009). In one study, 59 percent of Ecstasy users met the criteria for dependence, with many reporting withdrawal symptoms including depression, irritability, and social withdrawal (Cottler, Leung, & Abdallah, 2009). Ecstasy is also linked to long-lasting damage in brain areas critical for thought and memory (J. Brown, McKone, & Ward, 2010).

A review of 82 cases in which Ecstasy was a cause of death revealed the following: Ecstasy was the sole cause of death in 23 percent of the cases; combined drug toxicity caused 59 percent of the deaths; and significant cardiovascular changes contributed to the remaining deaths. Surprisingly, despite the youth of the decedents, *atherosclerosis* (hardening of the arteries, a condition typically associated with aging) was found in 58 percent of decedents. This effect, typically seen in cocaine and methamphetamine users, may relate to the stimulant properties of Ecstasy (S. Kaye, Darke, & Duflou, 2009).

Club Drugs   Many of the designer drugs, including Ecstasy, and substances such as PCP, ketamine, and Rohypnol are considered "club drugs" because they are often used in a club or party context. Club drugs are used to induce energy and excitement, reduce inhibitions, and create feelings of well-being and connection with others. Although positive effects may last for hours, they are typically followed by a crash—lethargy, low motivation, and fatigue. Unfortunately, energy exertion in a warm environment intensifies harmful effects of drug use, particularly hyperthermia and dehydration. Extreme depression and anxiety (as well as acute physical symptoms due to dehydration or changes in blood pressure and heart rhythm) can occur, particularly when drugs are combined or taken with alcohol.

Cocaine is also used within the club drug culture. In one large sample of individuals using drugs in a club context, 90 percent reported cocaine use; in fact, 59 percent demonstrated cocaine dependence (Parsons, Grov, & Kelly, 2009). Another common club drug with high addictive potential is gamma hydroxybutyrate (GHB), a substance used primarily by males because of its purported strength-enhancing properties. Because GHB (sometimes referred to as liquid ecstasy) is a central nervous system depressant with strong sedative effects, it is particularly dangerous when combined with alcohol.

Stephen Lovekin/Getty Images

Relapse Leads to Overdose Death

Philip Seymour Hoffman, a renowned stage and screen actor, was found dead on the bathroom floor of his apartment with a syringe in his left arm. The medical examiner determined that he died from acute mixed drug intoxication. Prior to his death, Hoffman had maintained 23 years of sobriety. However, his addiction progressed rapidly after he resumed using drugs. Hoffman is pictured here at an event in New York City less than 3 months before his death.

Combining Multiple Substances

CASE STUDY   Kelly M., age 17, lived with her divorced mother. Kelly was hospitalized after her mother found her unconscious from an overdose of tranquilizers; her blood alcohol level was 0.15. The overdose was apparently accidental. Kelly was regularly using tranquilizers to help her relax and relieve her stress. Arguments with her mother would precipitate heavy use of the drugs. Eventually she found that she needed more of the pills to relax, occasionally stealing money to buy them from classmates. She sometimes used alcohol as a substitute for or in combination with the tranquilizers. Her mother reported that she had no knowledge of her daughter's drug or alcohol use, although she had noticed that Kelly was increasingly isolated and sleepy. Hospital personnel informed Kelly of the dangers of sedatives, especially when combined with alcohol, and recommended that she begin drug treatment.

The practice of combining substances can be extremely dangerous. Chemicals taken simultaneously may exhibit a **synergistic effect**; interactions between the substances intensify effects or create unique side effects. For example, when tranquilizers are combined with alcohol, both depress the central nervous system, and the synergistic effect can result in respiratory distress or even death. Furthermore, some substances (such as alcohol) may reduce judgment, resulting in excessive (or lethal) use of other substances. Equally dangerous is the use of one drug to counteract the effects of another substance, such as taking stimulants and later taking a sleeping pill to counteract insomnia from the stimulant.

Of particular concern is multiple drug use involving Ecstasy. One group of rave attendees taking Ecstasy tested positive for an average of four other drugs; those who illicitly manufacture drugs such as Ecstasy often adulterate them with other substances, a factor that may have affected the findings (D. L. Black et al., 2009).

There is also a concern about the increased intoxication that occurs from combining alcohol and energy drinks. Research suggests that students who combine alcohol and caffeine have more heavy-drinking episodes, drunkenness, and alcohol-related consequences such as sexual assault, physical injury, and driving while intoxicated (Kponee, Siegel, & Jernigan, 2014).

Etiology of Substance-Use Disorders

Why do people abuse substances, despite knowing that alcohol and drug abuse can have devastating consequences? What leads people down the path to drug or alcohol addiction? In general, the progression from initial substance use to substance abuse follows a typical sequence (H. J. Walter, 2001). First, an individual decides to experiment with alcohol or drugs—perhaps to satisfy curiosity, enhance self-confidence, rebel against authorities, imitate others, or conform to social pressure. Second, the substance begins to serve an important purpose (such as reduce anxiety, produce feelings of pleasure, or enhance social relationships) and so consumption continues. Third, brain chemistry becomes altered from substance use. In many cases, physiological dependency develops, resulting in craving for the substance and withdrawal symptoms if use is discontinued; it also becomes difficult to experience pleasure without the substance. Fourth, lifestyle changes occur due to chronic substance use. These changes may include loss of interest in previous activities and social relationships and preoccupation with opportunities to use the substance (Figure 11.9). Consistent with the multipath model, in all four phases, biological, psychological, social, and sociocultural influences are involved (Figure 11.10).

synergistic effect the result of chemicals (or substances) interacting to multiply one another's effects

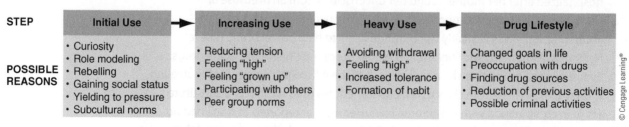

Figure 11.9

Typical Progression toward Drug Abuse or Dependence

The progression from initial substance use to substance abuse typically begins with curiosity about a drug's effects and casual experimentation.

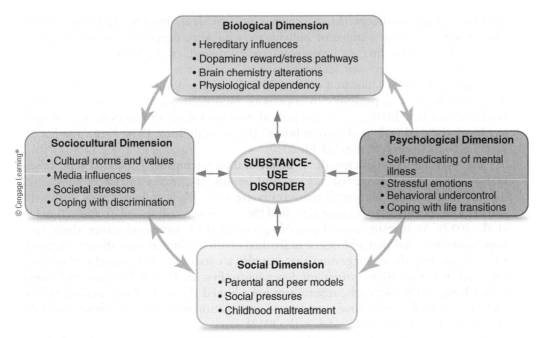

Figure 11.10

Multipath Model of Substance-Use Disorders

The dimensions interact with one another and combine in different ways to result in a substance-use disorder.

Psychological Dimension

Coping with psychological stress and emotional symptoms appears to be a major motive for substance use. Of the 20 million adults with a substance-use disorder in 2010, 45 percent had a concurrent psychiatric disorder. The use of illicit drugs is much higher among individuals with mental illness (26 percent) than among those without such difficulties (12 percent) (SAMHSA, 2012b). Individuals with psychiatric symptoms often use drugs and alcohol to self-medicate, an attempt to cope with emotions such as depression and anxiety.

Research suggests that four categories of life stressors influence substance use and the development of substance-use disorders: (a) general life stress (e.g., relationship or work difficulties), (b) stress resulting from trauma or catastrophic events, (c) childhood maltreatment, and (d) the stress of discrimination based on being a member of a sexual or racial/ethnic minority (Keyes, Hatzenbuehler, Grant, & Hasin, 2012). A desire to cope with stressors such as these is associated with marijuana use (C. L. Fox, Towe, Stephens, Walker, & Roffman, 2011) and the development of alcoholism (Anthenelli, 2010). Individuals with post-traumatic stress disorder also report using drugs and alcohol to cope with their distressing symptoms (Leeies, Pagura, Sareen, & Bolton, 2010). In one study of individuals participating in drug treatment, those with the most severe post-traumatic stress disorder symptoms—especially hyperarousal and reexperiencing the trauma—reported the greatest dependence on marijuana, supporting the self-medication hypothesis (Villagonzalo et al., 2011). Similarly, a large number of problem drinkers reported using alcohol to cope with mood symptoms; those with this pattern had an increased likelihood of developing an alcohol-use disorder (Crum et al., 2013).

Internalizing disorders such as depression and anxiety often precede substance use and abuse (O'Neil, Conner, & Kendall, 2011). For example, in a longitudinal study involving low-income adults seen at a public health clinic, symptoms of stress, depression, and anxiety preceded and predicted binge drinking, illegal drug use, and smoking (Walsh, Senn, & Carey, 2013). Anxiety and depressive symptoms that begin in early childhood and persist into adulthood appear to increase risk of alcohol abuse, particularly when accompanied by social withdrawal (Hussong, Jones, Stein, Baucom, & Boeding, 2011). Among individuals trying to quit smoking, 24 percent had major depression and 17 percent had symptoms of mild depression (Hebert, Cummins, Hernández, Tedeschi, & Zhu, 2011). Anxiety diagnoses are also common among smokers seeking treatment (M. E. Piper, Cook, Schlam, Jorenby, & Baker, 2010). Almost half of a large sample of individuals who were dependent on methamphetamine had a mood or anxiety disorder (Glasner-Edwards et al., 2010).

Adolescent girls have an increased risk of using pain medications to deal with stress and depression (Johnston et al., 2014). Similarly, adolescent girls with eating disorders often use depressants to cope with bulimic urges (J. H. Baker, Mitchell, Neale, & Kendler, 2010). Adolescent girls also report using substances to help "forget troubles" or "deal with problems at home" (Partnership for a Drug-Free America & MetLife Foundation [PFDFA/MET], 2010).

The personality characteristic of **behavioral undercontrol**, associated with rebelliousness, novelty seeking, risk taking, and impulsivity, increases risk of substance use and abuse. Individuals with these traits are more likely to experiment with substances and continue use because they find the effects rewarding and exciting (Beseler et al., 2012). An investigation of possible genetic links between substance abuse and impulsivity revealed that siblings of individuals with a stimulant-use disorder tended to be highly impulsive, suggesting that impulsivity may be a behavioral *endophenotype* that increases risk for stimulant dependence (Ersche, Turton, Pradhan, Bullmore, & Robbins, 2010). Similarly, researchers have linked the trait of risk taking with a pattern of neurological response to reward anticipation that occurs in those with substance-use disorders (S. Schneider et al., 2012).

What psychological factors might account for the increases in drug and alcohol use observed in college students? Undergraduates report using drugs and alcohol to cope with anxiety and depression (V. V. Grant, Stewart, O'Connor, Blackwell, & Conrod, 2007); academic, social, and financial pressures; and being away from home for the first time, living in a new environment, and having increased responsibility (C. Sloane et al, 2010). College students high in impulsivity and behavioral undercontrol, particularly those in fraternities or sororities, are most vulnerable to alcohol dependence (Grekin & Sher, 2006). Similarly, college students with high levels of sensation seeking are more likely to exhibit alcohol or cannabis dependence (Kaynak et al., 2013). Impulsivity has a particularly strong association with alcohol abuse among college students who are also risk takers and poor planners (Siebert & Wilke, 2007). Although some college students decrease their alcohol use when they experience negative consequences associated with drinking (Merrill, Read, & Barnett, 2013), negative events resulting from drinking—such as sexual assault, embarrassment over behavior while intoxicated, and poor academic performance—can also exacerbate the cycle of college drinking or drug use (Dams-O'Conner, Martens, & Anderson, 2006).

CONTINUUM Video Project

Mark: **Substance-Use Disorder**

©Cengage learning

"That's what drugs are, they are your savior but also they are also there to kill, maim, and destroy you. It's awesome, but true."

Access the Continuum Video Project in MindTap at
www.cengage.com

Social Dimension

The influence of social factors on substance abuse varies across the life span, exerting different effects at different ages (K. J. Sher, Dick, et al., 2010). Victimization and stressful events in childhood, including neglect and emotional, physical, and sexual abuse, are strongly associated with substance use later in life, especially for those with multiple victimization experiences (H. T. McCabe, Wilsnack, West, & Boyd, 2010). Many individuals receiving residential treatment for substance abuse report childhood trauma (Banducci, Hoffman, Lejuez, & Koenen, 2014). One variable linking child abuse with risk for substance-use disorders is the earlier onset of drinking or drug use among individuals exposed to childhood maltreatment (Keyes, Hatzenbuehler, Grant, & Hasin, 2012). Childhood trauma may increase the likelihood of impulsive behaviors in response to distress, such as turning to substance use as a means of coping (Weiss, Tull, Lavender, & Gratz, 2013). Not surprisingly, adolescents with parents with an alcohol-use disorder reported drinking heavily and drinking alone, with the goal of becoming intoxicated in order to forget their problems (Chalder, Elgar, & Bennett, 2006).

behavioral undercontrol
personality trait associated with rebelliousness, novelty seeking, risk taking, and impulsivity

As you might expect, adolescence and early adulthood are particularly vulnerable periods with respect to social influences on substance use, even for those without other life stressors. Patterns of alcohol or drug abuse often begin in early adolescence. In a recent survey, among the 15 percent of adolescents who had developed an alcohol-use disorder and the 16.4 percent who were dependent on other drugs by late adolescence, the mean age of onset of drinking or illicit drug use was 14 (Swendsen et al., 2012). Various social factors affect decisions to initiate drinking or drug use, including pressure from peers, a wish to fit in socially, attempts to rebel and challenge authority, a desire to assert independence or escape from societal or parental pressures for achievement, or interest in having fun or taking risks. Adolescent boys often report that drugs help them "relax socially" and "have more fun at parties" (PFDFA/MET, 2010). Association with friends who get drunk increases high-risk drinking (Siebert & Wilke, 2007). Friends with a high social status can exert a particularly strong influence with respect to substance use (J. P. Allen, Chango, Szwedo, Schad, & Marston, 2012).

Family attitudes and behaviors toward drinking and drugs (including the use of prescription medication) affect adolescents' likelihood of experimenting with substances. As you might imagine, when parents uses drugs or alcohol liberally, so do their children. Additionally, adolescents who receive less parental monitoring have increased substance use, as do those whose parents feel unable to enforce rules or influence decisions related to substance use and those whose parents believe cultural myths such as "all adolescents experiment" or "it's okay to have teens drink at home" (K. D. Wagner et al., 2010).

College presents its own unique set of sociocultural influences. The first year of college is a particularly vulnerable transitional period due to abrupt changes in levels of parental supervision, increased competition and pressure for academic achievement, easy access to alcohol, and exposure to peers engaged in heavy drinking. Unofficial social events that promote partying and peers who minimize the consequences of drinking also contribute to college drinking (C. M. Lee, Geisner, Patrick, & Neighbors, 2010). Social media also increases the acceptability and frequency of alcohol use in college: Recent research shows that problem drinking is associated with the frequency of online posting about alcohol use (Moreno, Christakis, Egan, Brockman, & Becker, 2012). Additionally, exposure to online postings about alcohol can lead students to overestimate the prevalence of college drinking (Fournier, Hall, Ricke, & Storey, 2013). In general, college students and other young adults significantly overestimate the extent of alcohol and marijuana use by their peers, thus inflating the social acceptability of substance use. Not surprisingly, those who overestimate peer use of alcohol and marijuana have an increased likelihood of using these substances (Bertholet, Faouzi, Studer, Daeppen, & Gmel, 2013).

Sociocultural Dimension

Although substance use varies according to sociocultural factors such as gender, age, socioeconomic status, ethnicity, religion, and nationality, the use and abuse of alcohol and other substances pervades all social classes. Certain substances—alcohol, nicotine, and, to some extent, marijuana and prescription drugs—are an accepted part of U.S. culture, as we have seen from prevalence data. Additionally, the data suggest that drug use and alcohol use are becoming a normative part of adolescent culture. Declines in the number of teens who view substance use as harmful and increases in peer approval for getting high are associated with increased use of substances in social situations and party environments (Johnston et al., 2014; PFDFA/MET, 2010). Adolescents whose peer group lacks school commitment and connectedness are particularly prone to engaging in substance use with their peers (Latimer & Zur, 2010).

It is common to see marketing messages regarding tobacco, alcohol, and prescription drugs, as well as depictions of these products in songs, movies, television, and social media. Exposure to positive drug and alcohol information on the Internet is increasing, whereas warnings from parents, schools, and antidrug advertising are decreasing (PFDFA/MET, 2010). The effects of exposure to media images and substance use can be

DID YOU KNOW?

People in the United States spent almost $326 billion on prescription medications in 2012.

SOURCE: Thomas, 2013

very powerful. For example, exposure to movies depicting alcohol use is associated with increased drinking (Stoolmiller, Wills, et al., 2012). Similarly, factors such as perceived prevalence of smoking, exposure to smokers, and exposure to tobacco advertising are all associated with smoking in young adults (Hanewinkel, Isensee, Sargent, & Morgenstern, 2011). Media messages promoting smoking appear to be most powerful when friends are present (Setodji, Martino, Scharf, & Shadel, 2013). Some researchers believe that the effect is strong enough to require showing anti-tobacco messages before any movie with tobacco imagery (Glantz, Iaccopucci, Titus, & Polansky, 2012). Similarly, there is concern that public debate regarding legalization of marijuana appears to be normalizing its social acceptability, with resultant increases in use (Johnston et al., 2014).

Use and abuse of alcohol and illicit drugs varies both within and between ethnic groups, as discussed earlier. Cultural values affect not only the substances used and amount consumed but also the cultural tolerance of substance abuse. Overall, African Americans adolescents show lower rates of using alcohol or illicit drugs than European Americans and Latino/Hispanic Americans at most age levels, although the gap is narrowing due to recent increases in marijuana use among younger African Americans. Latino/Hispanic Americans have the highest prevalence of illicit drug use, although European American adolescents have the highest rate of prescription drug misuse (Johnston et al., 2014). Another study evaluating racial differences in adolescent substance use concluded that among middle school students, Latino/Hispanic Americans are more likely to smoke cigarettes, consume alcohol, and use marijuana compared to other racial groups, whereas Asian American middle school students were least likely to engage in these activities. Latino/Hispanic American students reported less concern about potential negative consequences of substance use and less confidence using refusal skills. Asian American students reported that few of their friends and siblings used substances and that they wanted to respect parental expectations regarding substance use (Shih, Miles, Tucker, Zhou, & D'Amico, 2010).

Additional factors affecting variability among ethnic groups include racial discrimination; increased availability of alcohol in urban areas with high ethnic populations; decreased community safety; social and economic disadvantage, including limited job opportunities and inadequate health care; and stress related to acculturation, particularly for Latino/Hispanic Americans (Chartier & Caetano, 2010). The experience of unfair treatment and racial discrimination is associated with increased risk of substance-use disorders among Asian Americans, African Americans, and Latino/Hispanic Americans, especially among those who develop a pattern of using substances as a coping mechanism (Gerrard et al., 2012; Lo & Cheng, 2012). Among Hispanic/Latino adults, discrimination appears to increase risk of alcohol abuse for women and drug abuse for men (Otiniano-Verissimo, Gee, Ford, & Iguchi, 2014) and is also linked to heavier smoking and difficulty with smoking cessation (Kendzor et al., 2014). Discrimination encountered by gay, lesbian, and transgender youth and adults is also associated with risk for substance use and abuse, especially when there is a history of childhood abuse or victimization (H. T. McCabe et al., 2010).

Although psychological, social, and sociocultural influences have a pronounced effect on both the initiation and the continuation of substance use, the question remains: Why are some individuals able to use drugs or alcohol in moderation, whereas others succumb to heavy use and addiction? Biological explanations provide considerable insight into this issue, as we see in the following section.

Effects of Cocaine Use

These positron emission tomography scan images compare the cerebral metabolic activity of a control subject (top row) with those of a person who formerly abused cocaine at 10 days after discontinuing the substance (middle row) and after 100 days of abstinence (bottom row). Red and yellow areas reveal efficient brain activity, whereas blue regions indicate minimal brain activity. As you can see, after 100 days of abstinence, brain activity is improved but remains far from normal.

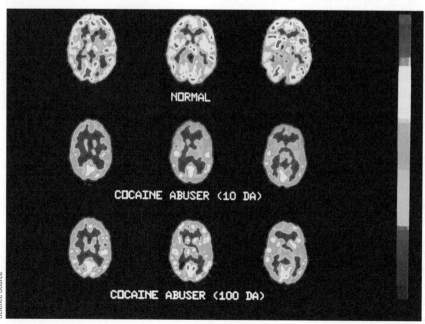

Science Source

NORMAL

COCAINE ABUSER (10 DA)

COCAINE ABUSER (100 DA)

Biological Dimension

Biological factors affect the development of substance-use disorders in various ways. First, substance use alters brain functioning. Some drugs (such as cannabis) produce changes by mimicking the actions of various neurotransmitters. Other drugs (such as stimulants) flood the brain with dopamine and alter the dopamine reward circuit, the neurological pathway associated with pleasure. Feelings of euphoria or pleasure ensue. The "high" resulting from excessive dopamine reinforces continued drug use. Eventually, substance use crowds out other pleasures and turns into an all-consuming, compulsive desire.

When exposed to excessive dopamine, brain cells adapt to the overstimulation by decreasing the number of dopamine receptors. The brain goes into this self-protective mode in order to maintain equilibrium. As the brain becomes less sensitive to the effects of dopamine and drug tolerance develops, the brain requires more of the substance to re-create the original "high" (Nestler & Malenka, 2004). This decreased sensitivity to dopamine means that drugs and alcohol (as well as other normally enjoyable activities) bring limited pleasure.

Furthermore, substance-induced changes in the prefrontal cortex result in impaired judgment and decision making. These changes also reduce self-control, making it difficult to resist the cravings associated with substance use. Thus, compulsive drug-seeking behavior ensues without consideration of negative consequences (Crews & Boettiger, 2009). Adolescence through early adulthood is a critical period for nuanced development of the prefrontal cortex; when drug or alcohol use affects this process, disruptions in reasoning, goal setting, and impulse control can lead to a lifelong pattern of neurological dysregulation and substance abuse (Silveri, 2012).

Genetic factors also play an important role in the development of substance abuse. There is strong evidence that substance abuse runs in families based on twin studies and analyses of family patterns of addiction (Edenberg, 2012). However, because family members usually share both genetic and environmental influences, researchers face the challenge of somehow separating the contributions of these two sets of factors. Kendler and Prescott (2006), using data from more than 4,500 pairs of identical and fraternal twins to isolate genetic and environmental factors involved in substance abuse, concluded the following:

- Genetic factors accounted for 56 percent of the risk of alcohol dependence and 55 percent of the risk of nicotine dependence.
- Genetic factors accounted for 75 percent of the risk of illicit drug abuse, with cannabis dependence having the strongest genetic risk.

Although collective findings support the importance of heredity in the etiology of substance use, the manner by which specific genes or gene combinations influence addiction is complex. For example, genetics influence personality traits such as impulsivity, risk taking, and novelty seeking that increase the likelihood that someone will experiment with drugs or alcohol, as well as protective characteristics such as self-control (Kendler & Prescott, 2006).

We also know that genes affect individual responses to specific drugs and risk of drug dependence. For example, one person may be susceptible to alcoholism, whereas another has genetic risk of marijuana dependence. And some gene combinations produce risk of addiction to multiple substances (Agrawal et al., 2012). Additionally, genetic variations can influence the degree of pleasure (or aversion) experienced during initial use of specific substances, as well as the negative and positive effects of ongoing use. For example, in a comprehensive longitudinal study, teens who experimented with smoking and who had high genetic risk for smoking were 43 percent more likely to enjoy smoking and to progress to heavy smoking compared to those without these high-risk genes (Belsky et al., 2013).

Genes can also decrease the risk of substance abuse. For example, some people have genetic variations associated with decreased production of the alcohol cleanup enzyme

Kurt Krieger/Corbis Entertainment/Corbis

Family Ties

Drew Barrymore entered a rehabilitation program at the age of 13 to deal with her addiction to drugs and alcohol. Although it is difficult to separate environmental and genetic influences in cases of alcohol abuse, both were likely operating in Barrymore's case. Not only did she experience the stress of young stardom, but she also had a family history of alcohol abuse—her grandfather drank himself to death and her father abused alcohol and drugs.

ALDH; when individuals with this variant consume alcohol, toxins from metabolized alcohol accumulate and cause unpleasant physical reactions. This naturally occurring effect makes alcohol consumption aversive and thus reduces risk of alcoholism. The protective effects of ALDH variations are quite strong—up to a sevenfold lowered risk in some Asian populations (Foroud et al., 2010). Similar protective genetic variations are common in certain regions of the Middle East and Africa.

Sex differences in the physiological effects of substances are also important in understanding addiction. Women who use drugs or alcohol show a more rapid progression to addiction compared to men, are more reactive to drug-related cues, and are more susceptible to relapse. Investigation into the neurobiological basis of these

---

Curbing the Tide of Substance Abuse

Substance-use disorders are unique among mental disorders because they are completely preventable—refraining from substance use *guarantees* that a substance-use disorder will not occur. In fact, some individuals with family members with substance-use disorders decide to never tempt fate—to never use substances—thus halting familial patterns of addiction (M. R. Pearson, D'Lima, & Kelley, 2011). Unfortunately, because substance abuse is a complex issue affected by a variety of processes operating over time, the solution is often not so simple (Masten, Faden, Zucker, & Spear, 2008).

We know that each day in the United States, approximately 7,900 adolescents or adults experiment with illicit drugs for the first time (SAMHSA, 2013a). Thus, a key to developing resilience is providing youth with the tools to refrain from such experimentation. Programs developed to prevent substance use and abuse often target critical periods of change—especially transitions during adolescence and early adulthood, when physiological addiction processes proceed most rapidly. Because youth develop within the broader context of family, school, community, and cultural groups, programs supporting healthy development typically aim at enhancing protective factors in a variety of areas (Hawkins et al., 2012; C. Jackson, Geddes, Haw, & Frank, 2012), including the following:

- Family—encouraging parents to build strong family relationships; articulate expected behavior (including abstinence from substance use); monitor activities and friendships; and interact with schools and other institutions

- Individual assets—helping youth develop a positive identity, understand the importance of education, acquire positive values, and build strong social competencies (especially self-control, self-efficacy, and assertiveness)

- Schools—providing students with effective learning opportunities; interactive prevention education regarding abused substances and how substance-use disorders develop (including peer and media influences); and skills for making positive decisions resisting peer pressure

- Community connections—developing community activities that build connection and assist youth to develop a sense of purpose and commitment beyond the self

Prevention and early intervention efforts are crucial if we hope to reduce the prevalence of substance abuse, especially among individuals with multiple risk factors. Interventions to prevent early experimentation with substances can have far-reaching consequences, not only in terms of decreasing the likelihood of substance abuse but also in terms of preventing detrimental effects on the academic and social competence of youth (Masten et al., 2008).

Photodisc/Getty Images

---

sex differences has implicated the effects of estrogen, which can influence dopamine levels and susceptibility to the reinforcing effects of addictive substances (Bobzean, Denobrega, & Perrotti, 2014). Other physiological differences may explain the more rapid development of alcoholism that occurs in women: Women tend to weigh less, produce fewer enzymes to metabolize alcohol, possess less total body fluid to dilute alcohol in the blood, and are more likely to limit food intake—factors that can increase toxicity and physiological changes associated with alcohol dependence (C. Sloane et al., 2010). Further, sex differences in physiological reactions to stress (combined with differential exposure to traumatic life events) may help explain the more severe course of alcoholism in women (Anthenelli, 2010).

In summary, gender and genetic predispositions, as well as physiological changes from heavy or chronic substance exposure, influence susceptibility to addiction. However, many factors beyond physiological effects contribute to the development and maintenance of substance abuse (Enoch, 2012). The psychological, social, and sociocultural explanations previously discussed provide substantial insight into forces involved in decisions to initiate substance use, factors that can also influence continued use and response to treatment.

Treatment for Substance-Use Disorders

Many of us have friends, family members, or acquaintances recovering from addiction to drugs or to alcohol. In fact, over 20 million adolescents and adults in the United States are now in recovery, living free from the addictive behaviors that previously controlled their lives (Faces and Voices of Recovery, 2014). There is a huge disparity, however, between the estimated 22.2 million who had a substance-use disorder in 2012 and the 4 million who received some form of intervention such as assistance from a physician, a self-help group, or inpatient or outpatient treatment. Unfortunately, many who recognize that they have a serious substance-abuse problem are unable to initiate treatment; cost is often a significant barrier. As seen in Figure 11.11, treatment most frequently involves alcohol-use disorders (2.4 million), followed by addiction to prescription pain relievers or cannabis (SAMHSA, 2013a).

Treatment and supportive intervention take place in a variety of settings, including self-help groups, mental health clinics, and inpatient or outpatient drug and alcohol treatment centers. Self-help group meetings are the most common means of substance-abuse intervention in the United States, with almost 2.2 million individuals participating in groups such as Alcoholics Anonymous (AA) and Narcotics Anonymous (SAMHSA, 2013a). Rather than specialized treatment, self-help groups provide a supportive approach to addiction, emphasizing fellowship and spiritual awareness to support abstinence. Self-help groups are often included as a component of ongoing treatment or as a mechanism to support sustained recovery once abstinence has been achieved.

Treatment is most effective when it incorporates best practices based on high-quality addiction research (Willenbring, 2010). Additionally, the inclusion of

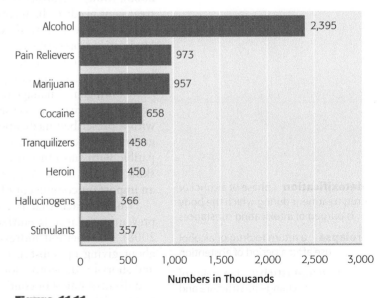

Figure 11.11

Substances for Which Treatment Was Received

In 2012, U.S. Americans sought treatment most frequently for alcohol abuse (2.4 million), with 973,000 receiving treatment for pain relievers and 957,000 for marijuana use.

SOURCE: SAMHSA (2013a).

integrated care that addresses underlying emotional difficulties enhances treatment outcome (Kuehn, 2010). Goals of treatment include achieving sustained abstinence, maintaining a drug-free lifestyle, and functioning productively in family, work, and other environments. This requires changing habits, minimizing thoughts of drugs or alcohol and substance-related social activities, and learning to cope with daily activities and stressors without substance use. Additionally, because drugs so often disrupt multiple aspects of an individual's life, there is a need to rebuild family, friend, and work relationships.

Most alcohol and drug treatment programs have two phases. In the first phase, called **detoxification**, the user ceases or reduces use of the substance. If the person is physiologically dependent on the substance, medical supervision may be necessary to help manage withdrawal symptoms. In the second phase, intervention focuses on preventing **relapse**, a return to use of the substance. Support is very important at this stage because relapse is common among those attempting to recover from alcohol or drug addiction.

Understanding and Preventing Relapse

Relapse prevention considers the physiological and psychological withdrawal symptoms a person might be experiencing, as well as neurological changes that occurred due to substance use; these physiological changes can influence motivation, impulsivity, learning, or memory. **Neuroplasticity**, the ability of the brain to change its structure and function in response to experience, is an important concept in addiction treatment. Just as an addict's brain became conditioned to needing a substance, treatment and abstinence can help recondition the brain, create new neural pathways, and undo changes caused by addiction. Sustained abstinence is necessary for permanent neurological changes to occur and is thus essential for maximizing treatment results.

Relapse prevention is a critical component of effective treatment because many individuals with substance-use disorders discontinue treatment when craving occurs. A single lapse in abstinence often leads to complete relapse (B. A. Moore & Budney, 2003). Many therapists view relapse not as a treatment failure but as an indicator that treatment needs to be intensified. People in treatment sometimes take medications to help prevent withdrawal symptoms, craving, and relapse (Jupp & Lawrence, 2010). Medications prescribed vary depending on the substance abused. It is important to remember that although medication can assist with cravings and withdrawal, medication alone—given the complexities of addiction—is not sufficient to prevent relapse.

Contingency management procedures in which participants receive either voucher or cash incentives for verified abstinence, adherence to treatment goals, or compliance with a prescribed medication plan can significantly reduce relapse. Contingency programs also increase treatment participation and maximize behaviors that are incompatible with substance use, such as exercising, attending school, or learning new job skills (Stitzer, Petry, & Peirce, 2010). Verifying abstinence via toxicology screening is an important component of these interventions (N. M. Petry, Alessi, et al., 2006).

An approach that is effective in setting the stage for successful treatment and preventing relapse is **motivational enhancement therapy** (Rollnick, Miller, & Butler, 2008). This method addresses a common barrier to effective treatment—ambivalence about giving up substance use. Unless this ambivalence is resolved, change is slow and short-lived. Motivational interviewing helps clients consider both the advantages and disadvantages of continued substance use; once there is a commitment to change, relapse risk is reduced and therapy moves forward with an emphasis on life modifications required for abstinence (Barnett et al., 2014).

As we have seen from our exploration of the etiology of substance abuse, the development of addiction is a complicated process made even more complex by the addictive characteristics of different substances. What all substances have in common are the long-lasting, difficult-to-reverse physiological and psychological changes that occur with chronic use. Some people are very susceptible to environmental triggers associated

detoxification phase of alcohol or drug treatment during which the body is purged of intoxicating substances

relapse a return to drug or alcohol use after a period of abstention

neuroplasticity the ability of the brain to change its structure and function in response to experience

motivational enhancement therapy a therapeutic approach that addresses ambivalence and helps clients consider the advantages and disadvantages of continuing substance use

with drugs or alcohol, so treatment strategies that help people avoid or cope with such triggers can reduce drug-seeking behavior and relapse (Robinson, Yager, Cogan, & Saunders, 2014). Thus, effective treatment targets the variety of psychological, social, and sociocultural factors associated with continued substance use. In the following sections we discuss research-validated treatment for the most commonly abused substances: alcohol, opioids, stimulants (including cocaine), cannabis, and nicotine.

Treatment for Alcohol-Use Disorder

Participation in AA is a common intervention for alcoholism. AA regards alcoholism as a disease and advocates total abstinence. Comparing the effects of AA with mental health treatment, Moos and Moos (2006) found that AA participation is more strongly associated with positive long-term outcomes than is professional treatment alone; however, the best outcome occurred for those who participated in both interventions. There is a strong association between regular attendance at AA meetings and decreased alcohol use. AA members also develop friendships and increase their coping skills and motivation for abstinence (J. F. Kelly et al., 2011).

Consistent with the position of AA, alcoholism specialists who believe alcoholism is a disease argue that chronic alcoholism changes cerebral functioning in fundamental and long-lasting ways (Nestler & Malenka, 2004) and that people who are recovering from alcoholism must completely abstain from drinking because any consumption will set off the disease process (Wollschlaeger, 2007). On the other hand, proponents of **controlled drinking** assume that, under the right conditions, people with alcoholism can learn to limit their drinking to appropriate levels. Although there is evidence that controlled drinking may work for some people with an alcohol-use disorder, abstinence increases the likelihood of continued recovery (D. A. Dawson, Goldstein, & Grant, 2007). A major task is to discover which individuals can handle controlled drinking without major relapse.

Medications are frequently used to treat alcohol abuse. Antabuse (disulfiram), a medication that produces an aversion to alcohol by creating highly unpleasant symptoms if alcohol is consumed, has been used for decades. Although it can be effective in those who take it as prescribed, many people avoid taking Antabuse once they have experienced the adverse effects caused by drinking (Skinner, Lahmek, Pham, & Aubin, 2014). The medication acamprosate can also help maintain abstinence and reduce relapse rates, especially among those who have undergone detoxification. Additionally, naltrexone, a medication used to reduce desire for and pleasure in using alcohol, is sometimes effective in reducing heavy drinking, especially for individuals who stopped drinking before starting the medication (Maisel, Blodgett, Wilbourne, Humphreys, & Finney, 2013). Nalmefene, recently approved for use with alcohol dependence, helps reduce the amount of alcohol consumed. It is most frequently prescribed as a harm-control measure, with the goal of reducing heavy drinking in individuals who have not achieved abstinence (Müller, Geisel, Banas, & Heinz, 2014).

Given the modest effects seen with pharmaceutical intervention, K. Mann and Hermann (2010) proposed an individualized approach to assessing the effectiveness of medications—assessing medication effects with subgroups of people with alcoholism based on biologically defined endophenotypes. They give the example of naltrexone being more effective with carriers of a specific gene variant and in those individuals with the strongest MRI evidence of brain reactivity in response to pictures of alcohol. Similarly, Ooteman and colleagues (2009) found that genetic characteristics of individuals undergoing alcohol treatment were associated with differential response to both acamprosate and naltrexone.

Overall, psychological and pharmacological approaches to alcohol treatment demonstrate only modest effects (K. Mann & Hermann, 2010). Interventions supported by research show the greatest promise. For example, a comprehensive analysis of interventions to decrease college drinking revealed that individual, face-to-face interventions using motivational interviewing and providing information correcting

DID YOU KNOW?

Life changes needed for long-term recovery include:

- eliminating cues associated with substance use;
- learning to manage drug craving;
- developing skills to cope with stress, depression, or anxiety;
- learning effective interpersonal skills;
- rebuilding family relationships;
- cultivating friendships with those who are not using substances;
- developing new hobbies and activities;
- addressing financial issues; and
- enhancing job skills.

controlled drinking   consuming no more than a predetermined amount of alcohol

Overcoming Addiction

Former Boston Celtic Chris Herren struggled with substance abuse for much of his basketball career. He has been drug-free and alcohol-free since August 1, 2008, attends daily meetings to support his sobriety and speaks to the public about the dangers of addiction. In this photo Herren pumps his fist in the air following a Celtics victory over the Atlanta Hawks.

misperceptions of social norms regarding drinking yielded the greatest reduction in alcohol-related problems (K. B. Carey, Scott-Sheldon, Carey, & DeMartini, 2007). These methods combined with challenging positive expectancies regarding alcohol use successfully reduced heavy drinking in another group of students (M. D. Wood, Capone, Laforge, Erickson, & Brand, 2007).

More research regarding treatments for alcoholism, as well as more access to alcohol treatment, is needed. This is particularly important because a decision to enter treatment appears to be a crucial change point for those with alcohol dependence (Willenbring, 2010). In 2012, almost 7 percent of adolescents and adults, more than 18.3 million individuals, needed treatment for an alcohol-use disorder; however, only about 4 million received treatment (SAMHSA, 2013a).

Treatment for Opioid-Use Disorder

Almost 3 million Americans received some form of treatment for opioid dependence in 2012, including 773,000 individuals addicted to prescription opioids and 450,000 with heroin addiction (SAMHSA, 2013a). Early detoxification and treatment are critical with opioid dependence, because treatment becomes more difficult for those who have used opioids longer (S. F. Butler et al., 2010). Due to the strong symptoms associated with opioid withdrawal, physicians often prescribe synthetic opioids such as methadone to reduce cravings without producing euphoria. Although methadone was initially considered a simple solution to the problem of prescription opioid abuse or heroin addiction, it has an important drawback—tolerance develops, resulting in an addictive need for methadone. The following case illustrates this problem, as well as other facets of treatment for opioid addiction.

CASE STUDY   After several months of denying the seriousness of his heroin habit, Gary B. finally enrolled in a residential treatment program that featured methadone maintenance, peer support, cognitive-behavioral therapy, and job retraining. Although Gary initially responded well to the program, he soon began to feel depressed. The staff reassured him that experiencing depression during opioid withdrawal is common. Gary began taking an antidepressant medication and started seeing a psychologist for individual therapy. Psychotherapy helped Gary identify unhealthy relationships in his life and examine the parallels between his dependence on these relationships and his dependence on drugs. He also began to understand how he often turned to drugs to escape his problems. The therapy then focused on practicing coping skills and exploring healthy alternatives to drug use. Gary worked hard during his therapy and made considerable progress.

Gary was satisfied with the changes he was making in his life until the day he realized that he was eagerly looking forward to his daily methadone dose. Although Gary had friends who became addicted to methadone, it was a shock when it happened to him. He decided almost immediately to terminate his methadone maintenance program. The withdrawal process was physically and mentally painful, and Gary often doubted his ability to function without methadone. However, by joining a support group composed of others who were discontinuing opioid use, he was eventually able to complete methadone withdrawal. Gary had never imagined that the most difficult part of his heroin treatment would be giving up methadone.

Although methadone is still used for treatment of opioid-use disorders, alternative medications are now available. For example, buprenorphine is a less addictive synthetic opioid that can ease opioid withdrawal and prevent cravings and relapse. Buprenorphine is most effective when the dose is reduced slowly and psychological treatment also occurs (Nielsen, Hillhouse, Thomas, Hasson, & Ling, 2013). Naltrexone (the medication designed to block pleasurable sensations in those who use alcohol) is sometimes used with opioid abuse, but appears to have limited effectiveness unless delivered in extended-release injections (Bart, 2012).

Opioid addiction is often associated with psychological drug dependence and feelings of being overwhelmed and unable to cope with daily activities. Thus, it is not surprising that being married and having a close relationship with one's spouse predicted better treatment outcome for heroin users (Heinz, Wu, Witkiewitz, Epstein, & Preston, 2009). Contingency management with incentives for abstinence (K. M. Carroll & Onken, 2005) and behaviorally oriented individual and family counseling (Fals-Stewart & O'Farrell, 2003) have improved treatment outcomes.

Treatment for Stimulant-Use Disorder

Over 1 million Americans received treatment for stimulant abuse in 2012, including almost 658,000 receiving treatment for cocaine dependence (SAMHSA, 2013a). There are currently no effective pharmacological interventions for stimulant abuse (Montoya & Vocci, 2008). Incentives for stimulant-free toxicology reports have increased rates of continuous abstinence in individuals receiving treatment for stimulant dependence (Stitzer, Petry, et al., 2010). One group of researchers found that teaching people who use cocaine to cope with temptations and high-risk situations was beneficial not only in lowering cocaine use but also in lowering the amount of cocaine used during a relapse (Rohsenow, Monti, Martin, Michalec, & Abrams, 2000). People who are married and who have a close spousal relationship have better treatment outcomes (Heinz et al., 2009).

Researchers are testing a vaccine (called TA-CD) to help individuals who are dependent on cocaine. Antibodies produced from the vaccine prevent cocaine from reaching the brain, thus eliminating any pleasurable effects. Clinical trials are underway to test this vaccine and a vaccine for individuals dependent on methamphetamine (Kosten, Domingo, Orson, & Kinsey, 2014).

Treatment for Cannabis-Use Disorder

In 2012, almost 1 million Americans received some form of treatment for cannabis abuse (SAMHSA, 2013a). Increases in treatment admissions and recent recognition of a cannabis withdrawal syndrome have led to a search for medications to assist in the withdrawal process and to help prevent relapse (Vandrey & Haney, 2009). Research efforts are focusing on the brain systems uniquely affected by THC, particularly the cannabinoid system (Elkashef et al., 2008).

Psychological approaches such as brief therapy, cognitive-behavioral therapy, and motivational enhancement have shown promise with cannabis-use disorder (Benyamina, Lecacheux, Blecha, Reynaud, & Lukasiewcz, 2008). However, individuals who are dependent on marijuana have trouble both initiating and maintaining abstinence (B. A. Moore & Budney, 2003). Because of the ongoing cognitive and motivational deficits associated with marijuana use, some researchers advocate using short, frequent therapy sessions and focusing on increased self-efficacy (Munsey, 2010).

The use of vouchers to reinforce negative urine toxicology has shown some promise (Nordstrom & Levin, 2007). In one study, rewards for verified abstinence from cannabis use initially produced the highest rates of abstinence; however, those who participated in contingency management combined with motivational enhancement and cognitive-behavioral therapy had higher abstinence in a later follow-up (Kaddena, Litt, Kabela-Cormiera, & Petrya, 2007). A review of outpatient therapies for cannabis dependence revealed low rates of abstinence even with cognitive and contingency management approaches; the researchers concluded that cannabis dependence may not be easily treated in outpatient settings (Denis, Lavie, Fatséas, & Auriacombe, 2006).

Treatment for Tobacco-Use Disorder

Among middle-aged and older adults, those who smoke are at least 3 times more likely to die compared to others their age who never smoked; however, smoking cessation at any age can decrease the likelihood of smoking-related death (Thun et al., 2013). Statistics such as these highlight the importance of smoking cessation programs. Unfortunately, even once cessation occurs, relapse to smoking remains high, emphasizing the highly addictive nature of nicotine and the need for long-term treatment strategies (Hatsukami, Stead, & Gupta, 2008). Relapse rates and withdrawal-related discomfort are higher in people who also have depression, anxiety, or other substance-use disorders; thus, it is important to address underlying emotional issues (K. K. Hebert et al., 2011). For example, those who have anxiety sensitivity (fear of aversive anxiety symptoms) have more difficulty coping with and tend to avoid the negative feelings associated with tobacco withdrawal, a factor that can interfere with smoking cessation (Johnson, Farris, Schmidt, Smits, & Zvolensky, 2013).

Three pharmaceutical products are used for smoking cessation—nicotine replacement, bupropion, and varenicline. Nicotine replacement therapy (NRT) involves delivering increasingly smaller doses of nicotine using a patch, inhaler, nasal spray, gum, or sublingual tablet. NRT helps reduce the urge to smoke by preventing withdrawal symptoms and also helps reduce relapse. Similarly, electronic cigarettes can help smokers ease tobacco withdrawal symptoms as they quit smoking, with rates of abstinence comparable to NRT; e-cigarettes also help prevent relapse in former smokers (Bullen et al., 2013). Additionally, some smokers are turning to e-cigarettes as an alternative method of obtaining nicotine and having a smoking experience (Etter & Bullen, 2014).

Bupropion (marketed under the name Zyban as an antismoking agent and Wellbutrin as an antidepressant) is frequently mentioned in the smoking cessation literature. Bupropion reduces activation of brain regions associated with craving, even in the presence of smoking-related cues (Culbertson et al., 2011). As with other antidepressant medications, caution is urged in the use of bupropion due to concerns about side effects, including agitation, depression, and suicidal ideation. Unfortunately, both NRT and bupropion have limited long-term effectiveness even when combined with psychological approaches (Mitrouska et al., 2007).

A newer medication, varenicline (marketed as Chantix), has shown success in reducing cue-activated cravings and withdrawal symptoms, as well as decreasing smoking satisfaction in healthy, adult smokers (T. Franklin et al., 2011). In one study, smokers taking varenicline had significantly higher continuous abstinence rates after 12–24 weeks of use compared to placebo, bupropion, or NRT; however, close monitoring for side effects involving agitation, depression, and suicidal thoughts is recommended for those taking varenicline, especially individuals with coexisting psychiatric disorders (Keating & Lyseng-Williamson, 2010).

Various psychological strategies have been helpful in reducing the urge to smoke, including learning to cope with negative emotions (K. A. O'Connell, Hosein, Schwartz, & Leibowitz, 2007). This is important because some smokers have difficulty tolerating negative moods and thus return to smoking when they feel depressed or anxious (Lerman & Audrain-McGovern, 2010). Intervention to address anxiety issues is particularly important in smokers with anxiety disorders; they tend to have greater nicotine dependence and are less responsive to standard pharmacological interventions (M. E. Piper et al., 2010). Smoking quitlines that include abstinence-related support and counseling have proven to be an effective intervention (Lichtenstein, Zhu, & Tedeschi, 2010).

Women have a more difficult time with smoking cessation compared to men; one variable that affects success is the phase of the menstrual cycle at the time of smoking cessation (S. S. Allen, Allen, & Pomerleau, 2009). Other factors that appear to make it more difficult for women to stop smoking include stress and negative mood, enjoyment of the routine of smoking, sensitivity to smoking cues, and fear of weight gain (K. A. Perkins, 2009). A study investigating methods to help women who were concerned about weight gain achieve cessation found success when bupropion was used in combination with cognitive-behavioral therapy focused on the issue of weight control (M. D. Levine et al., 2010).

Gambling Disorder and Other Addictions

Gambling disorder, involving a compulsive desire to engage in gambling activities despite negative consequences, is the first non–substance-related addiction added to the DSM. In contrast to people who occasionally gamble without negative consequences, people with a gambling disorder experience distress or impairment in social or professional functioning due to their gambling. A gambling disorder may be diagnosed when someone exhibits at least four of the following characteristics over a 12-month period:

- Needs to bet larger quantities of money to achieve the desired excitement
- Feels irritable or restless following attempts to reduce or stop gambling
- Is unsuccessful when attempting to control, reduce, or stop gambling
- Experiences frequent preoccupation with gambling, including previous or future gambling activities
- Turns to gambling when feeling upset or distressed
- Returns for more gambling after losing money, trying to break even
- Deceives others to conceal the extent of involvement with gambling
- Has risked or lost jobs, relationships, or important opportunities because of gambling
- Turns to others for money due to financial desperation resulting from gambling

Gambling disorder may be mild (4–5 of the symptoms), moderately severe (6–7 symptoms), or severe (8–9 symptoms). A person can have persistent or chronic symptoms or distinct episodes of pathological gambling. Some people with gambling disorder tend to be impulsive and overconfident, whereas others gamble when feeling depressed or lonely. Gambling disorder is relatively uncommon, with a lifetime prevalence of less than 1 percent (APA, 2013).

People often develop a gambling disorder gradually, although some rapidly progress to pathological gambling. Some individuals with gambling disorder prefer games of strategy (such as poker or sports betting) whereas others choose nonstrategic games (such as slot machines), with the latter group showing more aversion to loss and less effective decision making when gambling. Although gambling disorder has been associated with impulsivity, underlying emotional issues may be as important as poor impulse control in understanding problem gambling (Lorains, Stout, Bradshaw, Dowling, & Enticott, 2014).

Group approaches to therapy including facilitated 12-step groups and cognitive-behavioral therapy (focusing on changing dysfunctional cognitions and reactivity to triggers associated with gambling) have shown promise in decreasing gambling behavior (Marceaux & Melville, 2011). Improving financial management skills is also an important component of treatment. Similar to trends in treatment for substance-use disorders, researchers are attempting to use neuroimaging and monitoring of brain changes associated with addiction-related cues to determine which treatments are most effective for gambling addiction. For example, fMRI imaging is used to help determine which treatments increase impulse control and the ability to cope with distressing emotions, as well as decrease reactivity to cues associated with gambling (Potenza et al., 2013).

Internet Gaming Disorder

DSM-5 includes Internet gaming disorder—a condition involving excessive and prolonged engagement in computerized or Internet games either alone or with other players—as a proposed diagnostic category. Although gambling and associated financial difficulties are not involved, the criteria are very similar to those for gambling disorder, including the fact that gaming interferes with social relationships and day-to-day responsibilities (APA, 2013). Internet gaming disorder is a significant concern in Asian countries and is most common among adolescent males. Treatment approaches include both a focus on behavioral change and treating underlying emotions such as anxiety and depression (Winkler, Dörsing, Rief, Shen, & Glombiewski, 2013).

There is much debate about where Internet gaming and other excessive behaviors such as compulsive sex, eating, buying, or Internet use constitute an addiction. Because some compulsive behaviors share behavioral and neurological similarities with substance addiction (disrupting biological processes associated with sensitivity to reward and reducing impulse control), some researchers propose that they be considered addictions (Volkow, Wang, Tomasi, & Baler, 2013). It is argued that classification of these behaviors as addictions would provide reliable definitions for research, destigmatize people distressed by these behaviors, and facilitate the development of preventive and treatment strategies (Kuss, 2013). Time will tell if the mental health profession heads in the directions of broadening the definition of addiction. Certainly, inclusion of gambling disorder and a proposal for Internet gaming disorder in the DSM-5 are a step in that direction.

Contemporary Trends and Future Directions

Research into addiction remains a high priority given the significant personal and societal toll that results from substance-use and gambling disorders. Because so many people with substance-use disorders begin experimenting during early adolescence, professionals in the addiction field continue to focus on educating youth regarding the potential dangers of substance use, particularly the effects of substance abuse during adolescence or young adulthood when the brain is still developing. Fortunately, the data collected annually by the SAMHSA and the University of Michigan's Monitoring the Future surveys highlight trends in substance use and help guide prevention and intervention efforts. These comprehensive annual substance-use surveys also provide important information on which groups and substances to target for intervention; the data also help with the evaluation of significant policy changes such as the decriminalization and legalization of marijuana.

Researchers are focusing on the individual and environmental circumstances that increase risk for experimentation with alcohol and illegal substances. There is particular interest in helping youth understand the real-life consequences of current or escalating substance use (Mallett et al., 2013). Researchers are searching for ways to counteract media and social media messages that inflate perceptions about the acceptability of substance use, particularly alcohol. They also hope to find methods to help parents more accurately estimate their own children's use of alcohol or other substances and to enhance communication between parents and their children regarding the potential consequences of substance use (Labrie, Napper, & Hummer, 2014).

It is apparent that there is a considerable gap between those needing and those receiving treatment for substance use and gambling addictions. Developing affordable and accessible treatment opportunities is crucial if we hope to decrease the number of individuals and families affected by addiction. Additionally, researchers are continuing to use current technology such as neuroimaging techniques to help assess the effectiveness of addiction treatments (Potenza et al., 2013). A promising development is the National Drug Abuse Treatment Clinical Trials Network, which facilitates the sharing of research regarding psychological, pharmacological, and integrated treatments. Professionals and researchers in the field of addiction hope that easy access to research will enable practitioners to offer effective interventions in the community and to adapt the interventions to address the needs of diverse populations (Shmueli-Blumberg et al., 2013).

chapter SUMMARY

1 What are substance-use disorders?

- People often use chemical substances that alter their mood, level of consciousness, or behavior.
- The use of such substances is considered a disorder when there is a maladaptive pattern of recurrent use over a 12-month period and the person is unable to reduce or cease intake of the substance despite social, occupational, psychological, medical, or safety problems.

2 What substances are associated with addiction?

- Substances are classified on the basis of their effects. Substances that are abused include depressants, stimulants, hallucinogens, dissociative anesthetics, and substances with multiple properties.
- Widely used depressants include alcohol, opioids (such as heroin and prescription pain relievers), and prescription medications that produce sedation and relief from anxiety.
- Stimulants energize the central nervous system, often inducing elation, grandiosity, hyperactivity, agitation, and appetite suppression. Amphetamines, cocaine, and caffeine are all stimulants.
- Hallucinogens produce altered states of consciousness, perceptual distortions, and sometimes hallucinations. Included in this category are LSD, psilocybin, and mescaline.
- Dissociative anesthetics produce a dreamlike detachment. Phencyclidine (PCP), ketamine,

and dextromethorphan (DXM) are included in this category.
- Substances with multiple chemical properties include nicotine, cannabis, inhalants, and Ecstasy.

3 Why do people develop substance-use disorders?

- No single factor accounts for the development of a substance-use disorder. Biological, psychological, social, and sociocultural factors are all important.
- In terms of biological factors, heredity can significantly affect the risk of developing a substance-use disorder. Additionally, chronic drug or alcohol use alters brain chemistry, crowds out other pleasures, impairs decision making, and produces a compulsive desire for the substance.
- Psychological approaches to understanding substance-use disorders have emphasized personality characteristics such as behavioral undercontrol and self-medicating with substances to cope with stressful emotions and life transitions.
- Social factors are important in the initiation of substance use. Teenagers and adults use drugs because of parental models, social pressures from peers, and a desire for increased feelings of comfort and confidence in social relationships.
- Sociocultural factors affecting alcohol and drug use include media influences, cultural and subcultural norms, and societal stressors such as discrimination.

4 What kinds of interventions and treatments for substance-use disorders are most effective?

- The complex nature of addiction underscores the importance of a research-based, multifaceted treatment approach that is tailored to the individual's specific substance-use disorder and any concurrent social, emotional, or medical problems.

- Treatment for substance-use disorders has had mixed success. Intervening earlier in the addiction process increases success.

- Even after physiological withdrawal from a substance, individuals who abuse substances often relapse. Relapse prevention is enhanced through the use of motivational enhancement techniques to increase readiness for change, combined with pharmacological products to minimize withdrawal symptoms and with incentives for abstinence. Relapse indicates that longer-lasting or more intensive treatment is needed.

5 Can behaviors such as gambling be addictive?

- The definition of addiction has expanded to include behavioral addictions.

- The DSM-5 now includes gambling disorder, a compulsive desire to engage in gambling activities despite negative consequences, as a diagnostic category.

- Internet gaming disorder, which involves excessive engagement in computerized or Internet games, is a proposed diagnostic category.

12

SCHIZOPHRENIA SPECTRUM DISORDERS

AT THE AGE OF 8, Elyn Saks began to experience the hallucinations and fears of being attacked that have accompanied her throughout her life. She understood the importance of not talking openly about what ran through her mind. In fact, she was able to hide her delusional thoughts and hallucinations and maintain top grades throughout college. In graduate school, she experienced full-blown psychotic episodes (e.g., believing that someone had infiltrated her research and dancing on the roof of the law library) that resulted in her hospitalization and subsequent diagnosis of schizophrenia. Many of her symptoms persisted even after she began treatment. During one period, she believed her therapist had been replaced by an evil person with an identical appearance. In her book *The Center Cannot Hold: My Journey through Madness*, Saks (2007) recounts her lifelong struggle with mental illness, describing schizophrenia as a "slow fog" that becomes thicker over time.

Saks's struggle with schizophrenia, as well as her experience with forced treatment, resulted in an intense interest in mental health and the law. Her doctors had painted a bleak picture of her future. They believed that she would not complete her degree or be able to hold a job or get married. However, Saks did marry and complete graduate school. She is a professor of law, psychology, and psychiatry at the University of Southern California, where she also has served as an associate dean.

Like Elyn Saks, individuals with schizophrenia and some of the related disorders we discuss in this chapter lose contact with reality, see or hear things that are not actually present (hallucinations), or develop false beliefs about themselves or others (delusions). **Schizophrenia** is a serious chronic mental illness on the severe end of the **schizophrenia spectrum**. The disorders on the schizophrenia spectrum all involve specific symptoms: **psychosis** (an impaired sense of reality that frequently involves hallucinations and delusions); impaired cognitive processes (including disorganized speech); unusual or disorganized motor behavior; and a constellation of uncommon behaviors that affect social interactions. The

1 What are the symptoms of schizophrenia spectrum disorders?

2 Is there much chance of recovery from schizophrenia?

3 What causes schizophrenia?

4 What treatments are currently available for schizophrenia, and are they effective?

5 How do other psychotic disorders differ from schizophrenia?

schizophrenia spectrum disorders vary in severity, duration of symptoms, causes, and outcome. Schizophrenia is one of the most serious disorders on the spectrum (Frankenburg, 2010).

The schizophrenia spectrum disorders, particularly schizophrenia, receive a great deal of attention because they profoundly affect the individual, family members, and friends. People who have experienced a psychotic episode often mention that the experience is very confusing. A psychotic episode can significantly damage a person's sense of control and confidence. Initial psychotic episodes can be particularly scary because the person has no explanation for what is happening to him or her. To illustrate, let's consider the reactions of two individuals to their first episode of psychosis (Tan, Gould, Combes, & Lehmann, 2014, p. 87):

> *"I didn't understand what was happening to me, I didn't understand what I was seeing…. This isn't me, where's me gone?"*
> *"… Your thoughts are irrational but there's a strange logic to it."*

As you can see, psychosis is highly distressing because the hallucinations seem real and the delusions seem logical. The period after a psychotic breakdown is often full of chaos and confusion, especially if the individual is separated from family and friends due to hospitalization.

A diagnosis of schizophrenia in a member of the family affects all members of the unit. Common family reactions to a diagnosis include feelings of despair, worry that they might have somehow contributed to the illness, feelings of being unable to talk about their experiences with friends and family due to the stigma of mental illness, and economic strain. As one parent described the emotional and financial impact, "My son was off school for like, ten months and I was off work because he… couldn't be left on his own… and I just lost my confidence…" (Wainwright, Glentworth, Haddock, Bentley, & Lobban, 2014, p. 5). In the following first-person account, Eric Sundstrom presents a personal perspective on the changes he witnessed in his older sister after she developed schizophrenia.

CASE STUDY My family spent 3 years in Holland when my sister was in middle school. I think she was truly happy then, forming friendships and teaching me about the things she loved. It seems incredible she was once an ordinary girl, full of vibrant personality. I still remember how she taught me to read, using a now-ancient copy of *The Cat in the Hat*. When our family returned to America, all of her friends signed the clogs for her to remember them by. The clogs and a few memories are my only window into who she was then and who she should be now. (Sundstrom, 2004, p. 191)

Eric recalls how his sister developed delusions and violent behavior during her sophomore year in high school. Auditory hallucinations insulted her and commanded her to break things. One day, his sister's hallucinations intensified and, following the commands, she began to destroy items throughout the house. After Eric and his brother cleaned up the broken glass and silently began eating their dinner, they realized that their sister had thoughtfully baked quiche for them. Eric felt a profound sense of loss for the person that existed before the illness struck. As you can see, when psychotic symptoms develop, the experience can be confusing, frightening, and heart wrenching for everyone involved.

In this chapter, we begin with an in-depth discussion of symptoms associated with schizophrenia and other disorders on the schizophrenia spectrum. We then discuss the diagnosis, etiology, and treatment of schizophrenia and conclude with an overview of other disorders on the schizophrenia spectrum.

schizophrenia disorder characterized by severely impaired cognitive processes, personality disintegration, mood disturbance, and social withdrawal

schizophrenia spectrum group of disorders that range in severity and that have similar clinical features, including some degree of reality distortion

psychosis condition involving loss of contact with or distorted view of reality

Symptoms of Schizophrenia Spectrum Disorders

The symptoms associated with schizophrenia spectrum disorders fall into four categories: *positive symptoms, psychomotor abnormalities, cognitive symptoms, and negative symptoms.*

Positive Symptoms

> **CASE STUDY** Over a month before he committed the Navy yard shooting, Aaron Alexis called police to report that three people—two black males and a black female—were following him. He explained that he was unable to sleep because these people talked to him through the walls, ceiling, and floors of his hotel room. He also reported that they were using a microwave to send vibrations into his body (Winter, 2013).

Positive symptoms associated with schizophrenia spectrum disorders involve delusions, hallucinations, disordered thinking, incoherent communication, and bizarre behavior. These symptoms can range in severity, and persist or fluctuate. In the case above, Alexis experienced two positive symptoms: auditory hallucinations (hearing voices) and a delusion that three people were following him, keeping him awake and sending vibrations into his body. Many people with positive symptoms do not understand that their symptoms are the result of mental illness (Islam, Scarone, & Gambini, 2011). Failing to recognize symptoms of one's own mental illness, or having *poor insight*, is most common among those with severe symptoms and those who had difficulties functioning before the onset of their mental illness (Campos et al., 2011).

Delusions

Many individuals with psychotic disorders experience delusions. **Delusions** are false personal beliefs that are firmly and consistently held despite disconfirming evidence or logic. Individuals experiencing delusions are not able to distinguish between their private thoughts and external reality. Lack of insight is particularly common among individuals experiencing delusions; in other words, they do not recognize that their thoughts or beliefs are extremely illogical. In the following case study, therapists confront a graduate student's delusion that rats were inside his head, consuming a section of his brain.

> **CASE STUDY** Erin's therapists reminded him that he was a scientist and asked him to explain how it would be possible for rats to enter his brain. Erin had no explanation, but he was certain that he would soon lose functions controlled by the area of the brain that the rats were consuming. To prevent this from happening, he banged his head so that the "activated" neurons would "electrocute" the rats. Realizing he was not losing his sight even though the rats were eating his visual cortex, he entertained two possible explanations: Either his brain had a capacity for rapid regeneration or the remaining brain cells were compensating for the loss. Whenever information became too discrepant, Erin depended on his enhanced thought processes or "Deep Meaning," a system he believed transcended scientific logic (Stefanidis, 2006).

Image courtesy of Elyn Saks. Photo copyright Will Vinet.

Firsthand Experience

Elyn Saks teaches mental health law; has academic appointments at the University of Southern California (USC) and the University of California, San Diego; and has served as an associate dean at USC. Dr. Saks has accomplished many personal and professional goals despite her lifelong struggle with schizophrenia.

positive symptoms symptoms of schizophrenia that involve unusual thoughts or perceptions, such as delusions, hallucinations, disordered thinking, or bizarre behavior

delusion a false belief that is firmly and consistently held

Although some individuals with delusions, like Erin, attempt to maintain some sense of logic, most are either unaware or only moderately aware of the illogical nature of their delusional beliefs (Figure 12.1).

Individuals with schizophrenia spectrum disorders experience a variety of delusional themes:

- *Delusions of grandeur.* Individuals may believe they are someone famous or powerful (from the present or the past).

- *Delusions of control.* Individuals may believe that other people, animals, or objects are trying to influence or take control of them.

- *Delusions of thought broadcasting.* Individuals may believe that others can hear their thoughts.

Instilling Hope After a Schizophrenia Diagnosis

I am no longer defined by myself or by others as my mental illness or disability, nor am I limited in opportunity, responsibility or direction. It is not who I am—though it may be a small part of me at times (Andresen, Oades, & Caputi, 2003, p. 588).

There has been a move away from the view that schizophrenia is a chronic disorder with an inevitably poor prognosis. This newer perspective, referred to as the *recovery model*, mobilizes optimism and collaborative support for recovery. It also envisions substantial return of function for many individuals with schizophrenia. The model views schizophrenia as a chronic medical condition, such as diabetes or heart disease, which may interfere with optimal functioning but does not define the individual (R. Warner, 2009). The recovery model is based on the following assumptions (Bellack, 2006; Meyera, Johnson, Parks, Iwanskia, & Penn, 2012):

- Recovery or improvement in functioning is possible.

- Healing involves separating one's identity from the illness and developing the ability to cope with psychiatric symptoms.

- Empowerment of the individual helps correct the sense of powerlessness and dependence that results from traditional mental health care.

- Establishing or strengthening social connections can facilitate healing.

Kevin Peterson/Photodisc/Getty Images

- Recovery themes of hope, optimism, self-determination, self-respect, happiness, and engagement in life can change one's experiences and self-identity.

Recovery may include—but does not require—a complete remission of symptoms. Recovery is a process that involves overcoming the label of a "mental health patient" through personal growth, self-direction, identifying and building on strengths, assumption of responsibility for self-care, and establishment of a personally fulfilling and meaningful life. It is learning to engage in new roles, such as partner, friend, spouse, worker, and parent (Frese, Knight, & Saks, 2009).

The recovery model also supports social justice actions such as fighting policies that neglect the rights of individuals with schizophrenia, identifying the impact of stigma and discrimination on mental health, and promoting healing, growth, and respect for those affected by schizophrenia (Glynn, Cohen, Dixon, & Niv, 2006). Optimism about schizophrenia may be justified, as about 40 percent of people with the disorder show either complete recovery, defined as remission of symptoms and return to pre-illness function, or social recovery, which involves the return of independence and economic functioning (Warner, 2010).

- *Delusions of persecution.* Individuals may believe that others are plotting against, mistreating, or even trying to kill them.
- *Delusions of reference.* Individuals may believe they are the center of attention or that all happenings revolve around them.
- *Delusions of thought withdrawal.* Individuals may believe that someone or something is removing thoughts from their mind.

A common delusion involves **paranoid ideation**, or suspiciousness about the actions or motives of others as illustrated in the following case.

CASE STUDY I was convinced that a foreign agency was sending people out to get rid of me. I was so convinced because I kept receiving messages from them via a device planted inside my brain.... I decided to strike first: to kill myself so they wouldn't have a chance to carry out their plans and kill me. (Kean, 2011, p. 4)

Those with paranoid thinking often experience **persecutory delusions**, or beliefs that others are plotting against them, talking about them, or out to harm them in some way. The man in the case study was so concerned about the conspiracy against him that he decided to take his own life to prevent their plot from succeeding. Fortunately, he received help before his delusional thinking resulted in suicide. Those with paranoid ideation often have high levels of anxiety and worry, as well as angry reactions to perceived persecution (Startup, Freeman, & Garety, 2006). They are suspicious, and their delusional thinking causes them to misinterpret the behavior and motives of others. A busy clerk who fails to offer help is part of a plot to mistreat them. A telephone call that was a wrong number is an act of harassment or an attempt to monitor their comings and goings. As you can see, such interpretations can further reinforce paranoid thinking.

Delusions can produce strong emotional reactions such as fear, depression, or anger. Those with persecutory delusions may respond to perceived threats by leaving "dangerous" situations, avoiding areas where they might be attacked, or

MYTH Individuals experiencing delusions or hallucinations steadfastly accept them as reality.

REALITY The strength of hallucinations and delusions can vary significantly among individuals with schizophrenia spectrum disorders. Some believe in them 100 percent, whereas others are less certain. Even without treatment, many people cope by testing out the reality of their thinking. When faced with delusions or hallucinations, one person learned to ask himself, "What's the evidence for that?" Some individuals with schizophrenia are able to combat delusions and hallucinations through a combination of conscious effort, cognitive skills, and medication (Saks, 2013).

paranoid ideation suspiciousness about the actions or motives of others

persecutory delusions beliefs of being targeted by others

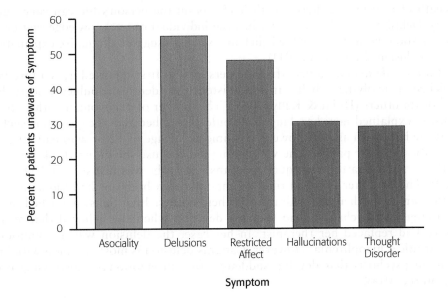

Figure 12.1

Lack of Awareness of Psychotic Symptoms in Individuals with Schizophrenia

Most individuals with schizophrenia are unaware or only somewhat aware that they have signs or symptoms of mental illness. The symptoms they are most unaware of include asociality, delusions and restricted affect.

SOURCE: Amador, X. (2006) Percentage of patients with schizophrenia who were unaware of these signs and symptoms of their illness. http://mentalillnesspolicy.org/medical/lack-of-insight-schizophrenia.pdf. Used by permission of Dr. Xavier Amador.

Paintings by People with Schizophrenia

The inner turmoil and private fantasies of people with schizophrenia are often revealed in their artwork. This painting was created by an individual with schizophrenia. What do you think the painting symbolizes?

becoming more vigilant. Paradoxically, these "safety" behaviors may prevent them from encountering **disconfirmatory evidence** (information that contradicts the delusional belief), thus reinforcing the idea that the lack of catastrophe was due to their cautionary behaviors. In one sample of individuals with delusions, between 80 percent and 90 percent had engaged in safety-seeking behavior in the previous month (Gaynor, Ward, Garety, & Peters, 2013).

Delusions may be unconnected or may involve a single theme. One woman had multiple delusions, including a belief that celebrities were talking to her through the television, that her deceased husband was still alive and cheating on her, and that her internal organs were getting infected (Mahgoub & Hossain, 2006). Delusions may include plausible themes, such as being followed or spied on, as well as bizarre beliefs, such as plots to remove internal organs or thoughts being placed in their minds. The strength of delusional beliefs and their effects on the person's life can vary significantly. Delusions have less impact when the individual can acknowledge that others may question the accuracy of the belief and is able to suggest alternative explanations for the delusion (Islam et al., 2011).

Capgras delusion, named after the person who first reported it, is a rare type of delusion involving a belief in the existence of identical doubles who replace significant others (Dulai & Kelly, 2009). The mother of one woman with Capgras delusion explained how her daughter would phone her and ask questions such as what she had worn as a Halloween costume at the age of 12 or who had attended a specific birthday party: "She was testing me because she didn't think I was her mother. . . . No matter what question I answered, she was just sobbing" (J. Stark, 2004). The daughter believed that an impostor in a bodysuit had kidnapped her mother and was then pretending to be her mother. Elyn Saks, described at the beginning of this chapter, had Capgras delusion when she believed that an evil double had replaced her therapist. In her case, the delusion was a symptom of her chronic schizophrenia. However, Capgras delusion is most common with brief forms of psychosis that develop suddenly after an emotionally distressing event (Salvatore, 2014).

disconfirmatory evidence information that contradicts a delusional belief

Hallucinations

CASE STUDY   An individual describes his experience with auditory hallucinations while hospitalized with schizophrenia:

"You're alone," an insidious voice told me. "You're going to get what's coming to you." . . . No one moved or looked startled. It was just me hearing the voice. . . . I had seen others screaming back at their voices. . . . I did not want to look mad, like them. . . . Never admit you hear voices. . . . Never question your diagnosis or disagree with your psychiatrist . . . or you will never be discharged. (Gray, 2008, p. 1006)

A **hallucination** is a perception of a nonexistent or absent stimuli; it may involve a single sensory modality or a combination of modalities, including hearing (*auditory hallucination*), seeing (*visual hallucination*), smelling (*olfactory hallucination*), touching (*tactile hallucination*), or tasting (*gustatory hallucination*). Auditory hallucinations are most common; the voices can be malicious or benevolent or involve both qualities (M. Hayward, Berry, & Ashton, 2011). As you can see from the case study, some individuals with hallucinations recognize that their perceptions are not real and try their best to "look normal" even when the hallucinations are occurring. Hallucinations are particularly distressing when they involve dominant, insulting voices. Negative hallucinations can be quite unsettling; those who hear negative voices often try to cope by ignoring them or by keeping busy with other activities (Jepson, 2013). Not all auditory hallucinations are negative, however. One individual reported hearing positive voices: "I thought I could hear the voice of God, and it was God who told me to refer myself for mental health help . . ." (Jepson, 2013, p.483).

Auditory hallucinations often seem very real to the individual experiencing them and sometimes involve relationship-like qualities (Chin, Hayward, &

hallucination   a sensory experience (such as an image, sound, smell, or taste) that seems real but that does not exist outside of the mind

---

CONTROVERSY

Should We Challenge Delusions and Hallucinations?

The doctor asked a patient who insisted that he was dead: "Look. Dead men don't bleed, right?" When the man agreed, the doctor pricked the man's finger, and showed him the blood. The patient said, "What do you know, dead men do bleed after all." (Walkup, 1995, p. 323)

Clinicians are often unsure about whether to challenge psychotic symptoms. Some contend that delusions and hallucinations serve an adaptive function and that any attempt to change them would be useless or even dangerous. The example of the man who believed he was dead illustrates the apparent futility of using logic with delusions. However, many clinicians have found that some clients respond well to challenges to their hallucinations and delusions (K. Ross, Freeman, Dunn, & Garety, 2011).

For example, Coltheart, Langdon, and McKay (2007) found that a "gentle and tactful offering of evidence" was successful in treating a man who believed his wife was not

his wife but was, instead, his business partner. The man was asked to entertain the possibility that the woman was actually his wife. The therapist pointed out that the woman was wearing a wedding ring identical to the one he had bought for his wife. The man said that the woman probably bought the ring from the same shop. He was then shown the initials engraved in the ring—those of his wife. Within 1 week, he accepted the fact that the woman was his wife. This approach of gently presenting contradictory information and having clients consider alternative explanations appears to be a successful approach to weakening delusions.

For Further Consideration

1. Should we challenge psychotic symptoms? If so, what is the best way of doing so?

2. In what ways might hallucinations or delusions serve an adaptive function?

In one study, individuals with schizophrenia and healthy controls wore a head-mounted virtual reality display that gave them the sense of going through a neighborhood, a shopping center, and a market. Fifty incoherencies such as a mooing dog, an upside-down house, and a red cloud were presented during the journey. Almost 90 percent of those with schizophrenia failed to detect these inconsistencies. Even when the inconsistencies were identified, about two thirds of the participants had difficulty explaining them.

SOURCE: Sorkin, Weinshall, & Peled, 2008

Drinnan, 2009). In one study involving individuals hospitalized with acute psychosis, 61 percent of respondents reported that the voice they heard had a distinct gender; 46 percent believed that the voice was that of a friend, family member, or acquaintance; and 80 percent reported having back-and-forth conversations with the voice. Most believed the voices were independent entities. Some even conducted "research" to test the reality of the voices. One woman said she initially thought that the voice might be her own but rejected it when the voice called her "Mommy," something she would not call herself. Another woman explained, "They are not imaginary. They see what I do. They tell me that I'm baking a cake. They must be there. How else would they know what I'm doing?" (Garrett & Silva, 2003, p. 447).

Cognitive Symptoms

Disordered thinking, communication, and speech are common characteristics of schizophrenia. Individuals experiencing these symptoms may have difficulty focusing on one topic, speak in an unintelligible manner, or reply tangentially to questions. **Loosening of associations**, also referred to as *cognitive slippage*, is another characteristic of disorganized thinking. This involves a continual shifting from topic to topic without any apparent logical or meaningful connection between thoughts. This may occur when cognitive confusion makes it difficult for the person to pay attention or respond to appropriate cues during conversation (Morris, Griffiths, LePelley, & Weickert, 2013). Disorganized communication often involves the kind of incoherent speech or bizarre, idiosyncratic responses seen in the following case study.

> **CASE STUDY** INTERVIEWER: "You just must be an emotional person, that's all."
> PATIENT: "Well, not very much I mean, what if I were dead? It's a funeral age. Well, I . . . um. Now I had my toenails operated on. They got infected and I wasn't able to do it. But they wouldn't let me at my tools." (P. Thomas, 1995, p. 289)

The beginning phrase in the person's first sentence appears appropriate to the interviewer's comment. However, the reference to death later in the sentence is not. Slippage appears in the comments referring to a funeral age, having toenails operated on, and getting tools. None of these thoughts are related to the interviewer's comment. They have no hierarchical structure or organization and thus represent disorganized thinking. People with schizophrenia may also demonstrate difficulty with abstractions and thus respond to words or phrases in a very concrete manner. For example, a saying such as "a rolling stone gathers no moss" might be interpreted as meaning no more than "moss cannot grow on a rock that is rolling."

Individuals with schizophrenia also show *overinclusiveness*, or abnormal categorization in their thinking. For example, when asked to sort cards with pictures of animals, fruit, clothing, and body parts into piles of things that go together, one man placed an ear, apple, pineapple, pear, strawberry, lips, orange, and banana together in a category he named "something to eat." When asked the reason for including the ear and lips in the "something to eat" category, he explained that an ear allows you to hear a person asking for fruit, and lips allow you to ask for and eat fruit (Doughty, Lawrence, Al-Mousawi, Ashaye, & Done, 2009).

Cognitive symptoms of schizophrenia also include problems with attention and memory and difficulty making decisions. As compared with healthy controls,

loosening of associations continual shifting from topic to topic without any apparent logical or meaningful connection between thoughts

individuals with schizophrenia have moderately severe to severe cognitive impairment, as evidenced by poor executive functioning—deficits in the ability to sustain attention, to absorb and interpret information and to make decisions based on recently learned information (Costafreda et al., 2011). Difficulties with social-cognitive skills, social perspective taking, and understanding one's own and other's thoughts, motivations, and emotions are also common. Cognitive symptoms are generally present even before the onset of the first psychotic episode (P. E. Bailey & Henry, 2010), tend to persist even with treatment, and are found (to a lesser degree) among nonpsychotic relatives of individuals with schizophrenia (Reichenberg & Harvey, 2007).

Grossly Disorganized or Abnormal Psychomotor Behavior

The symptoms of schizophrenia that involve motor functions can be quite bizarre and extremely distressing to family members, as is evident in the following case study.

CASE STUDY   At age 20, patient A . . . was found sitting at the edge of the bed for hours, displaying simple repetitive movements of the right hand while simultaneously holding his left hand in a bizarre posture and repeating "I do, I do, I do." (Stober, 2006, pp. 38–39)

This young man was experiencing an episode of **catatonia**, a condition involving extremes in activity level (either unusually high or unusually low), peculiar body movements or postures, strange gestures and grimaces, or a combination of these (see Figure 12.2 for symptoms associated with catatonia) (Enterman & van Dijk, 2011). People with *excited catatonia* have very disorganized behavior and may be very agitated, hyperactive, and lack inhibitions. They may talk and shout constantly, moving or running until they drop from exhaustion. They may appear to be acting "silly"

catatonia   a condition characterized by marked disturbance in motor activity—either extreme excitement or motoric immobility

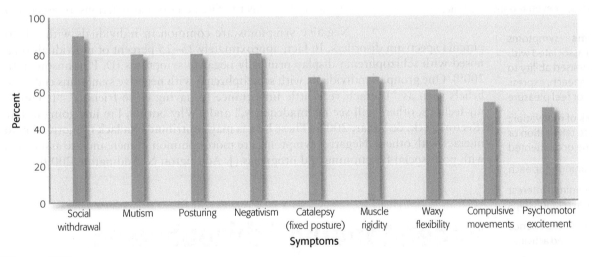

Figure 12.2

Prevalence of Symptoms in 30 Young Patients with Catatonia
Catatonic symptoms can vary significantly.
SOURCE: Cornic, Consoli, & Cohen (2007).

and display loud, inappropriate laughter. They sleep little and are continually on the go. Their behavior can become dangerous and involve violent acts. In one sample of 568 individuals with schizophrenia, 7.6 percent had experienced excited catatonia (Kleinhaus et al., 2012).

In sharp contrast, people experiencing *withdrawn catatonia* are extremely unresponsive, as was the young man in the case study. They show prolonged periods of stupor and mutism, despite an awareness of all that is going on around them. Some may adopt and maintain strange postures and refuse to move or change position. They may stand for hours at a time, perhaps with one arm stretched out to the side. They also may lie on the floor or sit awkwardly on a chair, staring, aware of what is occurring but not responding or moving. If someone attempts to change the person's position, they may persistently resist. Others exhibit a waxy flexibility, allowing their bodies to be arranged in almost any position and then remaining in that position for long periods. The extreme withdrawal associated with a catatonic episode can be life-threatening when it results in inadequate food intake (Aboraya, Chumber, & Altaha, 2009).

Negative Symptoms

Negative symptoms of schizophrenia are associated with an inability or decreased ability to initiate actions or speech, express emotions, or feel pleasure (Barch, 2013). Such symptoms include:

- **avolition**—an inability to initiate or persist in goal-directed behavior;
- **alogia**—a lack of meaningful speech;
- **asociality**—minimal interest in social relationships;
- **anhedonia**—reduced ability to experience pleasure from positive events; and
- **diminished emotional expression**—reduced display of emotion involving facial expressions, voice intonation, or gestures in situations in which emotional reactions are expected.

Negative symptoms are common in individuals with schizophrenia spectrum disorders. In fact, approximately 15–25 percent of individuals diagnosed with schizophrenia display primarily negative symptoms (D. P. Johnson et al., 2009). One group of individuals with schizophrenia with negative symptoms endorsed beliefs such as "I attach very little importance to having close friends," "If I show my feelings, others will see my inadequacy," and "Why bother, I'm just going to fail" (Rector, Beck, & Stolar, 2005). These beliefs may contribute to a lack of motivation to interact with others. Negative symptoms are more common in men and are associated with poor social functioning and prognosis (J. Addington & Addington, 2009).

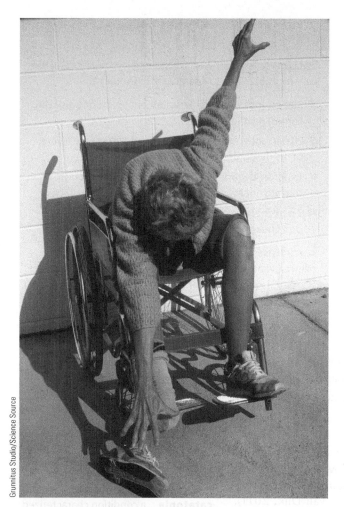

An Episode of Withdrawn Catatonia

The woman in the wheelchair is experiencing a form of catatonia that involves unresponsiveness and the adoption of a rigid body posture. Positions such as this are sometimes held for hours, days, weeks, or even months at a time.

negative symptoms symptoms of schizophrenia associated with an inability or decreased ability to initiate actions or speech, express emotions, or feel pleasure

avolition lack of motivation; an inability to take action or become goal oriented

alogia lack of meaningful speech

asociality minimal interest in social relationships

anhedonia inability to experience pleasure from previously enjoyed activities

diminished emotional expression reduced display of observable verbal and nonverbal behaviors that communicate internal emotions

Understanding Schizophrenia

According to DSM-5, a diagnosis of schizophrenia requires the presence of two of the following: delusions, hallucinations, disorganized speech, gross motor disturbances, or negative symptoms. At least one of the two indicators must be delusions, hallucinations, or disorganized speech (see Table 12.3). Additionally, there is deterioration from a previous level of functioning in areas such as work, interpersonal relationships, or self-care. The symptoms must be present most of the time for at least 1 month, and the disturbance must persist for at least 6 months, unless the symptoms subside due to successful treatment (APA, 2013).

Schizophrenia receives considerable attention because the financial costs of hospitalization, treatment, and loss of productivity that it causes are huge—an estimated $62.7 billion annually (E. Q. Wu et al., 2005). Because the lifetime prevalence rate of schizophrenia in the United States is about 1.1 percent, it affects millions of people (National Institute of Mental Health, 2014). In addition, because the causes of schizophrenia are not well understood, it has been difficult to find effective treatments for individuals diagnosed with the disorder.

It is popularly believed that overwhelming stress can cause a well-adjusted and relatively normal person to experience a psychotic breakdown and develop schizophrenia. Although sudden onset of psychotic behaviors can occur in previously well-functioning people (Kastelan et al., 2007), in most cases of schizophrenia, there is evidence of impairment in **premorbid** functioning; that is, individuals often show some abnormalities before the onset of major symptoms. Similarly, most people with schizophrenia recover from an illness episode gradually rather than suddenly. The typical course of schizophrenia consists of three phases: prodromal, active, and residual.

The *prodromal phase* includes the onset and buildup of schizophrenic symptoms. Social withdrawal and isolation, peculiar behaviors, inappropriate affect, poor communication patterns, and neglect of personal grooming may become evident during this phase. Friends and relatives often notice these differences and consider the changes in behavior as odd or peculiar. Often, excessive demands on the individual or other psychosocial stressors in the prodromal phase result in the onset of prominent psychotic symptoms, or the *active phase* of schizophrenia. In this phase, the person shows full-blown symptoms of schizophrenia, including severe disturbances in thinking, marked deterioration in social relationships, and restricted or markedly inappropriate affect.

Eventually, the person may enter the *residual phase*, in which the symptoms are no longer prominent. In the residual phase, the psychotic behavior and symptom severity decline. Frequently, the individual once again demonstrates the milder impairment seen in the prodromal phase. Although long-term studies have shown that many people with schizophrenia can lead productive lives, complete recovery is rare. (Figure 12.3 illustrates different courses schizophrenia may take.)

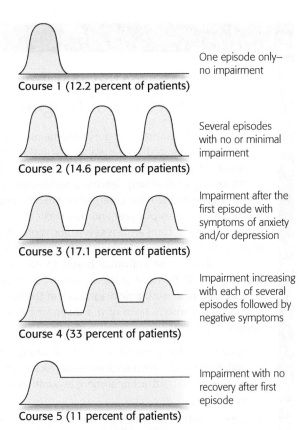

Course 1 (12.2 percent of patients) — One episode only—no impairment

Course 2 (14.6 percent of patients) — Several episodes with no or minimal impairment

Course 3 (17.1 percent of patients) — Impairment after the first episode with symptoms of anxiety and/or depression

Course 4 (33 percent of patients) — Impairment increasing with each of several episodes followed by negative symptoms

Course 5 (11 percent of patients) — Impairment with no recovery after first episode

Figure 12.3

Varying Outcomes with Schizophrenia

This figure shows five of the many outcomes possible with schizophrenia in individuals during a 15-year follow-up study.

SOURCE: Wiersma, Nienhuis, Sloof, & Giel (1998).

Long-Term Outcome Studies

What are the chances of recovering from or showing significant symptom improvement after an episode of schizophrenia? Recent developments in both psychotherapy and medication have led to increased optimism regarding the course of the disorder. In a 10-year follow-up study of individuals hospitalized for schizophrenia, the majority of participants improved over time, whereas only a minority appeared to deteriorate (Rabinowitz, Levine, Haim, & Hafner, 2007). Similarly, during a 15-year follow-up involving individuals with schizophrenia, a sizable minority were not on any medication and more than 40 percent showed one or more periods of substantial recovery (Harrow, Grossman, Jobe, & Herbener, 2005).

premorbid before the onset of major symptoms

Attenuated Psychosis Syndrome: A Beneficial or Harmful Diagnosis?

A proposed diagnostic category, *attenuated psychosis syndrome*, has generated considerable discussion and debate. **Attenuated psychosis syndrome** involves symptoms such as distressing or disabling delusions, hallucinations, or disorganized speech that have emerged or become progressively worse over the previous year and that occur at least once per week; these symptoms are less severe and more transient than those experienced by individuals with schizophrenia. Despite these symptoms, the individual is able to stay in touch with reality (APA, 2013). Whether these "milder" signs of psychosis should warrant a psychiatric diagnosis is at the heart of extensive debate. Those in favor of this diagnostic category make several arguments:

1. Symptoms of attenuated psychosis syndrome occurring in childhood and adolescence increase risk for schizophrenia and other psychiatric impairment in adulthood (Polanczyk et al., 2010).

2. Rapid deterioration often occurs during the early years of psychosis, so early intervention and treatment might diminish the effects of the illness in those who develop schizophrenia (Amminger et al., 2010; McGlashan & Woods, 2011).

3. This diagnosis allows treatment for people who are highly distressed by these milder psychotic symptoms.

Opponents of including the attenuated psychosis syndrome diagnosis in the DSM argue that many individuals with this diagnosis will not develop a psychotic disorder ("false positives") and that premature diagnosis could result in unnecessary stigma and unwarranted use of antipsychotic medications (Bola, Kao, & Soydan, 2012; Moncrieff, 2012). They also point out that psychotic-type experiences are present not only in those with schizophrenia spectrum disorders but also in the general population (Freeman, McManus, et al., 2010; Kelleher & Cannon, 2010). For example, reports of psychotic symptoms such as beliefs of persecution, thought interference, and auditory hallucinations are common among adolescents but, in most cases, are only transitory (Dominguez, Wichers, Lieb, Wittchen, & Van Os, 2011; B. Nelson & Yung, 2011). Because of the controversy, DSM-5 included attenuated psychosis syndrome as a "condition that requires further research" rather than a specific diagnostic category. Considering the arguments for and against having attenuated psychosis syndrome as a specific diagnosis, which position do you favor and why?

---

attenuated psychosis syndrome condition being researched that involves distressing or disabling early signs of delusions, hallucination, or disorganized speech that emerged or became progressively worse over the previous year; reality testing remains relatively intact

What factors appear to influence recovery from schizophrenia? Factors associated with a positive outcome include gender (women have a better outcome), higher levels of education, being married, and having a higher premorbid level of functioning (Irani & Siegel, 2006). In a 10-year follow-up study examining baseline predictors associated with recovery, researchers found that fewer negative symptoms, a prior history of good work performance and ability to live independently, and lower levels of depression and aggression were all associated with improved outcome (Shrivastava, Shah, Johnston, Stitt, & Thakar, 2010).

An 8-year follow-up of adults with first-episode psychosis documented the effectiveness of intervention early in the course of the illness. The comprehensive intervention increased chance of remission, reduced positive symptoms, and resulted in an overall more favorable course of the illness (Mihalopoulos, Harris, Henry, Harrigan, & McGorry, 2009). Intervention to decrease stress from issues such as self-stigmatization, negative beliefs, and social skills deficits can significantly enhance recovery (Tsang et al., 2010). Having a social network with friends and being single or married as opposed to separated or divorced are also associated with a more positive outcome (Sibitz, Unger, Woppmann, Zidek, & Amering, 2011). Peer support, work opportunities, and reducing the stigma of schizophrenia play an important role in the recovery process (Warner, 2009).

LHB Photo/Alamy

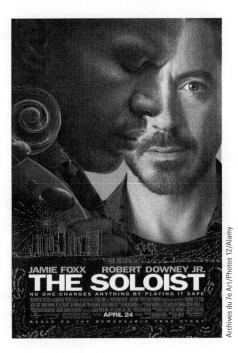

JAMIE FOXX   ROBERT DOWNEY JR.
THE SOLOIST
NO ONE CHANGES ANYTHING BY PLAYING IT SAFE

APRIL 24

BASED ON THE REMARKABLE TRUE STORY

Archives du 7e Art/Photos 12/Alamy

Obstacles to Recovery

The film, *The Soloist*, is based on the true story of Nathaniel Ayers (pictured on the left), a homeless musician coping with schizophrenia. When *Los Angeles Times* columnist Steve Lopez attempted to help Ayers after writing an acclaimed series of articles about the talented musician, he ran into many of the obstacles facing people who are homeless and mentally ill.

Etiology of Schizophrenia

CASE STUDY   A 13-year-old boy who was having behavioral and academic problems in school was taking part in a series of family therapy sessions. Family communication was negative in tone, with a great deal of blaming. Near the end of one session, the boy suddenly broke down and cried out, "I don't want to be like her." He was referring to his mother, who had been receiving treatment for schizophrenia. He had often been frightened by her bizarre behavior, and he was concerned that his friends would find out about her condition. But his greatest fear was that he would inherit the disorder. Sobbing, he turned to the therapist and asked, "Am I going to be crazy, too?"

If you were the therapist in the case study, how would you respond? At the end of this section on the etiology of schizophrenia, you should be able to reach your own conclusion about what to tell the boy.

Schizophrenia and other psychotic conditions are best understood using a multipath model that integrates heredity (genetic influences on brain structure and neurocognitive functioning), psychological characteristics, cognitive processes (e.g., faulty psychological processing of information), and social adversities such as low social or economic status. To develop an accurate etiological framework, all of these dimensions must be considered, as shown in Figure 12.4.

Although we discuss the biological, psychological, social, and sociocultural dimensions separately, keep in mind that each dimension interacts with the others. For example, emotional or sexual abuse, cannabis use, and trauma are all hypothesized to affect dopamine levels and neurocognitive functioning in those susceptible to schizophrenia. In one sample, each of these factors increased the risk of persistent psychotic symptoms, especially among individuals who were exposed to all three influences (Cougnard, Marcelis, et al., 2007).

Figure 12.4

Multipath Model of Schizophrenia
The dimensions interact with one another and combine in different ways to result in schizophrenia.

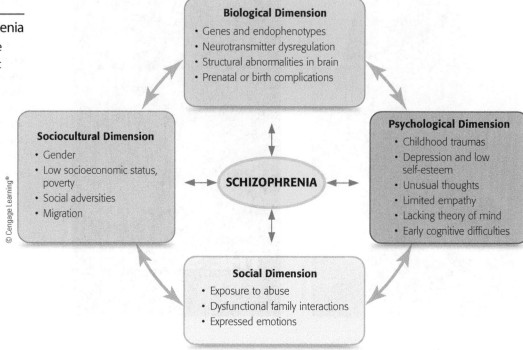

Biological Dimension
- Genes and endophenotypes
- Neurotransmitter dysregulation
- Structural abnormalities in brain
- Prenatal or birth complications

Sociocultural Dimension
- Gender
- Low socioeconomic status, poverty
- Social adversities
- Migration

SCHIZOPHRENIA

Psychological Dimension
- Childhood traumas
- Depression and low self-esteem
- Unusual thoughts
- Limited empathy
- Lacking theory of mind
- Early cognitive difficulties

Social Dimension
- Exposure to abuse
- Dysfunctional family interactions
- Expressed emotions

© Cengage Learning®

The interactive model of schizophrenia (see Figure 12.5) demonstrates how an underlying biological vulnerability combined with other risk characteristics (e.g., male sex, lower age) can result in the development of prodromal symptoms of schizophrenia. As time progresses, psychotic features may appear or intensify if additional environmental risk factors (e.g., cannabis use, trauma) occur. If the environmental exposures are chronic or severe, the risk of developing schizophrenia further increases. We now begin the discussion of specific risk factors associated with schizophrenia.

Biological Dimension

Genetics and heredity play an important role in the development of schizophrenia. Whereas past research focused on the attempt to identify the specific gene or genes that cause schizophrenia, the disorder is now understood to result from interactions among a large number of different genes; single genes appear to make only minor contributions toward the illness (Lyon et al., 2011). Researchers have found that closer blood relatives of individuals diagnosed with schizophrenia run a greater risk of developing the disorder (Figure 12.6). Thus, the boy described in the case study earlier who is

Figure 12.5

Interactive Variables and the Onset of Clinical Psychosis

This model shows how psychological and social factors may interact with genetic vulnerability to result in psychosis.

SOURCE: Dominguez, M. D. G., Saka, M. C., Lieb, R., Wittchan, H.-U., & Van Os, J. (2010). Early expression of negative/disorganized symptoms predicting psychotic experiences and subsequent clinical psychosis: A 10-year study. *American Journal of Psychiatry, 167*, 1075–1082.

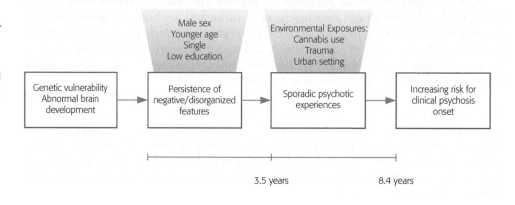

Male sex
Younger age
Single
Low education

Environmental Exposures:
Cannabis use
Trauma
Urban setting

Genetic vulnerability Abnormal brain development → Persistence of negative/disorganized features → Sporadic psychotic experiences → Increasing risk for clinical psychosis onset

3.5 years   8.4 years

concerned about developing schizophrenia like his mother has a 16 percent chance of being diagnosed with schizophrenia, whereas his mother's nieces or nephews have only a 4 percent chance. (It should be noted that the risk for the general population is 1.1 percent.)

However, even among monozygotic (identical) twins, if one twin receives the diagnosis of schizophrenia, the risk of the second twin developing the disorder is less than 50 percent. This is because environmental influences also play a significant role in genetic expression of the disorder. For example, low birth weight and other pregnancy and delivery complications are associated with an increased risk for schizophrenia. Yet most infants with these types of complications do not develop the disorder. Instead, it is primarily those with genetic susceptibility (such as having family members with schizophrenia) where the risk is the greatest (Forsyth et al., 2013).

Endophenotypes

The strategy in genetic research has moved from demonstrating that heredity is involved in schizophrenia to attempting to identify the genes that are responsible for the specific characteristics or traits that are evident in this disorder. This approach involves the identification and study of **endophenotypes**—measurable, heritable traits (Braff, Freedman, Schork, & Gottesman, 2007). Endophenotypes are hypothesized to underlie heritable illnesses (such as schizophrenia) and thus exist in the individual before the disorder, during it, and following remission. These characteristics are found with higher frequency, although in milder forms, among "non-ill" relatives of individuals with schizophrenia (Gur, Calkins, et al., 2007). Researchers have identified several possible endophenotypes that occur in those with schizophrenia and in their unaffected biological relatives. These traits include irregularities in working memory, executive function, sustained attention, and verbal memory (Chan, Di, McAlonan, & Gong, 2011; Reichenberg & Harvey, 2007; Turetsky et al., 2007).

Neurostructures

How do genes produce a vulnerability to schizophrenia? Clues to the ways that genes might increase susceptibility to developing schizophrenia have involved the identification of structural and neurochemical differences between individuals with and without schizophrenia. Individuals with schizophrenia have decreased volume in the cortex and other areas of the brain (Haijma et al., 2013), as well as ventricular enlargement (enlarged spaces in the brain; Ettinger et al., 2012). Ventricular enlargement may be an early indication of an increased susceptibility to schizophrenia, because it is sometimes present in healthy siblings of individuals with schizophrenia (Staal et al., 2001).

A striking loss of brain cells in the cortex over a period of 6 years among young people with schizophrenia was reported in a longitudinal study comparing brain changes in youth with and without schizophrenia. The loss was so rapid that it was likened to a "forest fire" (P. M. Thompson et al., 2001). Interestingly, healthy siblings of adolescents with child-onset schizophrenia also showed similar cortical loss (Gogtag, 2008).

How might decreased cortex volume and enlarged ventricles predispose someone to develop schizophrenia? These structural characteristics may result in atypical or weak connectivity between the various brain regions, leading to reductions in integrative functioning in the brain and impaired cognitive processing (Salgado-Pineda et al., 2007). Thus, ineffective communication between different brain regions may lead to the **cognitive symptoms** (e.g., disorganized speech and impairment in memory, decision making, and problem solving), negative symptoms (e.g., lack of drive or initiative), and positive symptoms (e.g., delusions and hallucinations) that are found in schizophrenia. However, the differences in brain structure between individuals with and without schizophrenia are relatively small. In addition, some of the abnormalities found in the brains of individuals with schizophrenia may result from the use of antipsychotic medication rather than the disorder itself (B.-C. Ho, Andreasen, Ziebell, Pierson, & Magnotta, 2011).

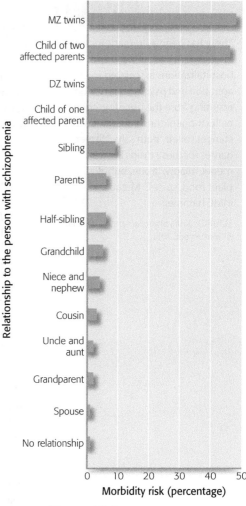

Figure 12.6

Risk of Schizophrenia among Blood Relatives of Individuals Diagnosed with Schizophrenia
This figure reflects the estimate of the lifetime risk of developing schizophrenia—a risk that is strongly correlated with the degree of genetic influence.
SOURCE: Data from Gottesman (1978, 1991).

endophenotype measurable characteristics (neurochemical, endocrinological, neuroanatomical, cognitive, or neuropsychological) that can give clues regarding the specific genes involved in a disorder

cognitive symptoms symptoms of schizophrenia associated with problems with attention and memory and with difficulty in developing a plan of action

There has been a dramatic increase in emergency room visits and hospitalizations associated with agitation and psychotic symptoms resulting from the use of synthetic hallucinogenic and stimulant substances called "bath salts." Street names for these drugs include meow, miaow, drone, bubbles, plant food, spice E, M-cat, and MMC hammer.

SOURCE: Kolli, Sharma, Amani, Bestha, & Chaturvedi, 2013

Biochemical Influences

Abnormalities in certain neurotransmitters (chemicals that allow brain cells to communicate with one another) including dopamine, serotonin, GABA, and glutamate have also been linked to schizophrenia (Benes, 2009; de la Fuente-Sandoval et al., 2013). Particular attention is given to the neurotransmitter dopamine (Howes, Kambeitz, et al., 2012). According to the **dopamine hypothesis**, schizophrenia may result from excess dopamine activity in certain areas of the brain. Support for the dopamine hypothesis has come from research with three types of drugs: phenothiazines, L-dopa, and amphetamines.

- *Phenothiazines* are conventional antipsychotic drugs that decrease the severity of disordered thinking, decrease social withdrawal, alleviate hallucinations, and improve the mood of individuals with schizophrenia. Phenothiazines reduce dopamine activity in the brain by blocking dopamine receptor sites.

- *L-dopa* is used to treat symptoms of Parkinson's disease, such as muscle and limb rigidity and tremors. L-dopa increases levels of dopamine; schizophrenic-like side effects often occur in individuals with Parkinson's disease who take this medication. (In contrast, the phenothiazines, which reduce dopamine activity, can produce side effects that resemble Parkinson's disease.)

- *Amphetamines* are stimulants that increase the availability of dopamine and norepinephrine (another neurotransmitter) in the brain. When individuals not diagnosed with schizophrenia use amphetamines, they sometimes show symptoms very much like those of acute paranoid schizophrenia. Also, even small doses of amphetamine can increase the severity of symptoms in individuals diagnosed with schizophrenia.

Thus, one group of drugs that blocks dopamine reception has the effect of reducing the severity of schizophrenic symptoms, whereas two drugs that increase dopamine availability either produce or worsen these symptoms. Such evidence suggests that excess dopamine may be responsible for schizophrenic symptoms.

The evidence is not clear-cut, however. Phenothiazines are not effective in treating many cases of schizophrenia, and newer antipsychotics work mainly by blocking serotonin receptors rather than dopamine receptors (Canas, 2005). This suggests that researchers may be looking for an oversimplified explanation by focusing on dopamine alone without considering the interactive biochemical functioning throughout the brain. Because schizophrenia involves multiple neurochemicals and brain regions, it is unlikely that one "magic bullet" medication will successfully treat all forms of schizophrenia (Desbonnet, O'Tuathaigh, & Waddington, 2012).

The use of cocaine, amphetamines, alcohol, and especially cannabis appears to increase the chances of developing a psychotic disorder (Callaghan et al., 2012; Zammit, Owen, Evans, Heron, & Lewis, 2012). Methamphetamine use may result in a fivefold increase in the likelihood of psychotic symptoms during intoxication (McKetin, Lubman, Baker, Dawe, & Ali, 2013). When distressing psychotic symptoms such as delusions or hallucinations develop during substance use or intoxication, a diagnosis of substance/medication-induced psychotic disorder may be appropriate (APA, 2013).

The effects of cannabis occurs in a dose-dependent manner—the higher the intake of cannabis, the greater the likelihood of psychotic symptoms (Davis, Compton, Wang, Levin, & Blanco, 2013). Adolescents who use cannabis are more likely to report prodromal symptoms (e.g., "Something strange is taking place in me," "I feel that I am being followed," or "I am being influenced in a special way"; Miettunen et al., 2008). Among cannabis users who develop schizophrenia, the onset of psychosis is nearly 3 years earlier in comparison to nonusers (Large, Sharma, Compton, Slade, & Nielssen, 2011).

Several possible interpretations may explain the relationship between cannabis use and psychosis (Foti, Kotov, Guey, & Bromet, 2010):

1. the increased risk of developing psychosis may be due to cannabis use itself;
2. individuals with a predisposition for psychosis may also be predisposed to use cannabis;

dopamine hypothesis the suggestion that schizophrenia may result from excess dopamine activity at certain synaptic sites

3. individuals with prodromal symptoms or psychotic-type experiences may use cannabis to self-medicate for these symptoms; or

4. cannabis may influence dopamine levels or increase vulnerability through interactions with environmental stressors associated with cannabis use (e.g., family conflict or poor school or work performance).

Although the prevalence of schizophrenia is roughly equal between men and women, the age of onset is earlier in males than in females (Segarra et al., 2012). The gender ratio shifts by the mid-40s and 50s, when the percentage of women receiving the diagnosis exceeds that of men. This trend is especially pronounced in the mid-60s and later (Thorup, Waltoft, Pedersen, Mortensen, & Nordentoft, 2007). Researchers have hypothesized that the later age of onset found in women is due to the protective effects of estrogen, which diminish after menopause (E. Hayes, Gavrilidis, & Kulkarni, 2012).

In a study of premenopausal women with schizophrenia, significant improvements in psychotic symptoms were observed during the luteal phase of their menstrual cycle (the period after ovulation), when estrogen levels are highest (Bergemann et al., 2008). Levels of estrogen also affect the availability of dopamine, which may influence cognitive functions such as working memory (Jacobs & D'Esposito, 2011). Interestingly, women with schizophrenia who have estrogen replacement therapy report improved cognitive functioning (Bergemann et al., 2008). These studies support the view that estrogen may protect against psychotic symptoms.

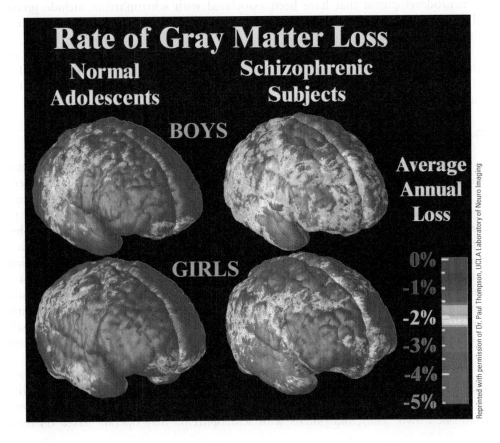

Reprinted with permission of Dr. Paul Thompson, UCLA Laboratory of Neuro Imaging

Rate of Gray Matter Loss in Teenagers with Schizophrenia

Male and female adolescents with schizophrenia show progressive loss of gray matter in the parietal, frontal, and temporal areas of the brain that is much greater than that found in adolescents without schizophrenia.

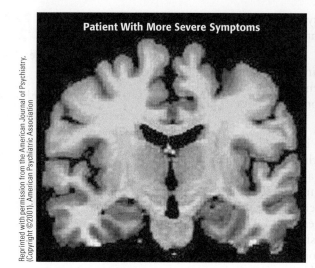

Patient With More Severe Symptoms

Reprinted with permission from the American Journal of Psychiatry, (Copyright ©2001). American Psychiatric Association

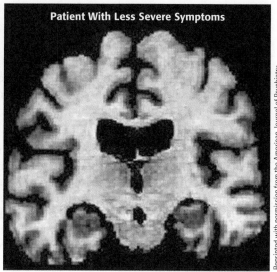

Patient With Less Severe Symptoms

Reprinted with permission from the American Journal of Psychiatry, (Copyright ©2001). American Psychiatric Association

Brain Changes Associated with Severe Schizophrenia

Structural brain abnormalities have been found in most individuals with schizophrenia. Patients with poor outcome (represented by the right photo) show significantly greater loss of cerebral gray matter and greater enlargement of the ventricles than those with less severe symptoms (represented by the photo on the left).

Because the **concordance rate**—the likelihood that both members of a twin pair show the same characteristic—is less than 50 percent when one identical twin has schizophrenia, physical, psychological, or social influences that are not shared between the twins must also play a role. Conditions influencing prenatal or postnatal neurodevelopment that have been associated with schizophrenia include prenatal infections, obstetric complications, and head trauma (Mittal, Ellman, & Cannon, 2008; Stahl, 2007).

Although a variety of biological influences appear to increase susceptibility to schizophrenia, specific psychological, social, and sociocultural variables can also influence development of schizophrenia. We now examine these influences as possible contributors to the disorder.

Psychological Dimension

Individuals who develop schizophrenia have certain cognitive attributes, dysfunctional beliefs, and interpersonal functioning that may predispose them to the development of psychotic symptoms. For example, deficits in empathy (understanding the feelings of others) and a tendency to focus only on one's own thoughts and feelings appear to compromise social interactions (Harvey, Zaki, Lee, Ochsner, & Green, 2013). This problem is also apparent during nonverbal communication; individuals with schizophrenia tend to gesture less when speaking and nod less frequently when listening compared to individuals without the disorder. Such a communication pattern may interfere with the development of interpersonal rapport and emotional connection (Lavelle, Healey, & McCabe, 2013). Among healthy adolescents, poorer interpersonal functioning during adolescence predicted bizarre experiences, perceptual abnormalities, and persecutory ideation (e.g., "Have you ever felt as if the thoughts in your head are being taken away from you?") later in life (Collip et al., 2013).

These communication problems and the lack of insight that frequently occurs with schizophrenia may result, in part, from deficits in the **theory of mind**—the ability to recognize that others have emotions, beliefs, and desires that may be different from one's own. Thus, individuals with schizophrenia may operate based on their

concordance rate the likelihood that both members of a twin pair show the same characteristic

theory of mind the ability to recognize that others have emotions, beliefs, and desires that may be different from one's own

own perspectives without understanding that others have their own viewpoint. As you might imagine, this could create major difficulties in communication and interpersonal interactions. In an interesting study, 79 individuals with psychotic symptoms described their delusions to an interviewer and were asked if the situation was believable for them and for the interviewer. The vast majority of participants indicated that they found the situation believable; 85 percent also thought the interviewer would find it believable. Two weeks later, all participants went through the same interview process. During this second interview session, a few more participants reported that the delusion was not believable, and 75 percent indicated that the interviewer might not find it believable. The researchers concluded that by considering a third-person perspective (e.g., the interviewer's perspective on the situation), some participants were able to increase their insight and understanding that their beliefs were not based on reality (Islam et al., 2011).

Early cognitive deficits are also associated with schizophrenia. Numerous studies have documented an association between early developmental delay and schizophrenia. One large prospective population study found that infants who later developed schizophrenia were slower to smile, lift their heads, sit, crawl, and walk compared to infants who did not develop schizophrenia (Sørensen et al., 2010). Similarly, early behavioral disturbances and cognitive and language deficits were evident in some individuals diagnosed with schizophrenia (Welham, Isohanni, Jones, & McGrath, 2009). Further, low cognitive ability test scores in childhood and adolescence predicted the presence of psychotic-like experiences and clinically significant psychotic symptoms in middle age; the low scores may represent early evidence of abnormalities in neural development (Barnett et al., 2012). Additionally, in a group of young men, a decline in verbal ability between ages 13 and 18 was associated with an increased risk of developing a psychotic disorder (MacCabe et al., 2013). These cognitive decrements may be an indication of brain abnormalities that result in less "cognitive reserve" and reduced opportunity for the brain to bounce back from neurological insult (Barnett et al., 2012).

Certain personal cognitive processes involving misattributions or negative attitudes can lead to or maintain psychotic symptoms such as delusions. For example, negative symptoms such as limited motivation and **restricted affect** may be due to individuals' beliefs that they are worthless and that their condition is hopeless (Beck, Grant, Huh, Perivoliotis, & Chang, 2013). The combination of low expectancy for pleasure and success combined with low motivation may maintain negative symptoms. In fact, some researchers believe that an individual's interpretation of events may be the primary cause of the distress and disability associated with schizophrenia (Garety, Bebbington, Fowler, Freeman, & Kuipers, 2007). In other words, pessimistic interpretations may produce and maintain negative symptoms. Table 12.1 presents patterns of thinking that may be associated with negative symptoms.

> **DID YOU KNOW?**
>
> Characteristics that sharply increase the likelihood of developing schizophrenia include:
>
> 1. genetic risk;
> 2. recent deterioration in functioning, especially social withdrawal;
> 3. increasing frequency of unusual thoughts;
> 4. high levels of suspiciousness and paranoia;
> 5. social impairment; and
> 6. substance abuse.
>
> SOURCE: Cannon et al., 2008

restricted affect severely diminished or limited emotional responsiveness

Table 12.1 Negative Expectancy Appraisals Associated with Negative Symptoms

Negative Symptom	Low Self-Efficacy (Success)	Low Satisfaction (Pleasure)	Low Acceptance	Low Available Resources
Restricted affect	If I show my feelings, others will see my inadequacy.	I don't feel the way I used to.	My face appears stiff and contorted to others.	I don't have the ability to express my feelings.
Alogia	I'm not going to find the right words to express myself.	I take so long to get my point across that it's boring.	I'm going to sound weird, stupid, or strange.	It takes too much effort to talk.
Avolition	Why bother, I'm just going to fail.	It's more trouble than it's worth.	It's best not to get involved.	It takes too much effort to try.

SOURCE: Rector, Beck, & Stolar (2005), p. 254.

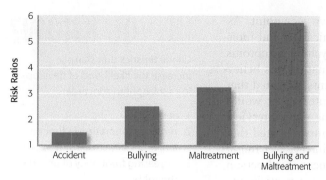

Figure 12.7

Risk of Psychotic Symptoms at Age 11 Associated with Cumulative Childhood Trauma

Youth exposed to both bullying and childhood maltreatment demonstrate a significantly increased risk of developing psychotic symptoms.

SOURCE: Based on Arseneault et al. (2011).

Social Dimension

The role of social relationships in the development of schizophrenia has been extensively studied. In fact, not long ago, dysfunctional family patterns, rather than biology, were considered the primary cause of schizophrenia (Walker & Tessner, 2008). However, as Lehman and Steinwachs (1998) note, "Research has failed to substantiate hypothesized causal links between family dysfunction and the etiology of schizophrenia" (p. 8). Unfortunately, blaming families for schizophrenia still occurs today. One parent whose son was hospitalized for psychosis heard a nurse say, "Well, no wonder he's ill—look at the state of his mother." The staff member apparently failed to understand that the mother's state of mind was the result of weeks of stress attempting to help her adult son cope with his psychotic symptoms prior to his hospitalization (Wainwright, Glentworth, Haddock, Bentley, & Lobban, 2014, p. 8). It is quite probable, however, that among individuals with a biological predisposition, the social environment does increase risk of schizophrenia. We will consider social factors that are associated with increased vulnerability to schizophrenia.

Maltreatment during childhood or other significant social stressors may alter neurodevelopment in a manner that increases susceptibility to schizophrenia. Certain social events appear to influence the appearance of psychotic symptoms. In a longitudinal study focused on 2,232 twins, those who experienced maltreatment by an adult or bullying by peers had a higher risk of psychotic symptoms at age 12 (see Figure 12.7); the risk was magnified among those exposed to both bullying and maltreatment. In contrast, being in a traumatic accident was associated with only a slightly increased risk of psychotic symptoms (Arseneault et al., 2011).

In one sample of 12-year-old children followed from age 7, the risk of psychotic symptoms doubled for those who were bullied between ages 8 and 10; the association was stronger with more severe or chronic forms of bullying (Schreier et al., 2009). Similarly, another study found a dose-dependent relationship between the severity of bullying and the risk for psychotic experiences in school-age adolescents—the more severe the bullying, the greater the risk of schizophrenia. The study reported another finding that has important implications for prevention programs—the psychotic symptoms in affected youth often decreased or subsided if the bullying stopped (Kelleher et al., 2013).

Relationships within the home can also influence the development of schizophrenia. Individuals with psychosis were 3 times more likely to report severe physical abuse from mothers before 12 years of age than were individuals without psychosis (H. L. Fisher et al., 2010). In contrast, among adolescents with symptoms that appeared to put them "at imminent risk" for the onset of psychosis, positive remarks and warmth expressed by caregivers were associated with decreases in negative and disorganized symptoms and improvement in social functioning (M. P. O'Brien et al., 2006). Children at higher biological risk for schizophrenia may be more sensitive to the effects of both adverse and healthy child-rearing patterns (Aas et al., 2012).

Expressed emotion (EE), a negative communication pattern found among some relatives of individuals with schizophrenia, has been associated with higher relapse rates in individuals diagnosed with schizophrenia (Breitborde, Lopez, & Nuechterlein, 2009). EE is determined by a variety of factors, including critical comments made by relatives; statements of dislike or resentment directed toward the individual with schizophrenia by family members; and statements reflecting emotional overinvolvement, overconcern, or overprotectiveness with respect to the

expressed emotion (EE) a negative communication pattern found among some relatives of individuals with schizophrenia

family member with schizophrenia. Although high EE has been associated with an increased risk of relapse, the studies are correlational in nature and are therefore subject to different interpretations. Figure 12.8 indicates three possible interpretations.

- A high EE environment is stressful and may lead directly to relapse in the family member who has schizophrenia (Cutting & Docherty, 2000).
- An individual who is more severely ill has a greater chance of relapse and may cause more negative or high EE communication patterns in relatives.
- The effects of EE and illness are bidirectional: Odd behaviors or symptoms of schizophrenia may increase the likelihood that family members criticize, overprotect, or react to the symptoms with frustration, which in turn produces increases in psychotic symptoms (Rosenfarb, Goldstein, et al., 1995).

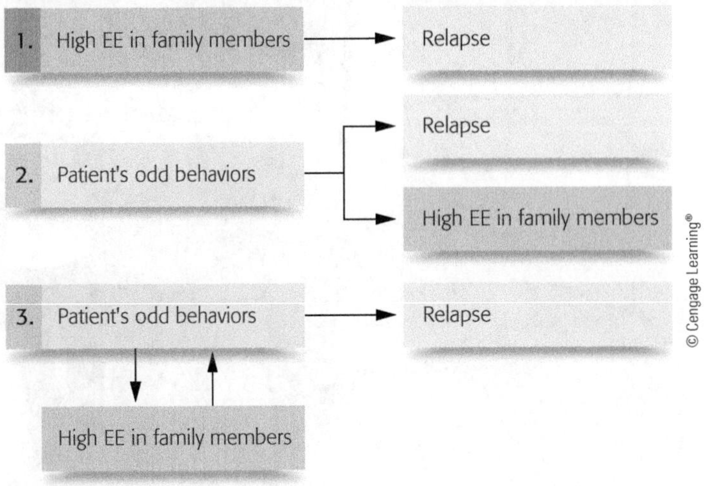

The EE construct appears to have less meaning for different cultural groups. It is possible that this occurs because cultural factors may influence whether family members view the symptoms as burdensome. For example, family criticism scores were not associated with relapse for Mexican Americans with schizophrenia (Rosenfarb, Bellack, & Aziz, 2006). Among a sample of African Americans and European Americans with schizophrenia, high levels of critical and intrusive behavior by family members (high EE) were associated with *better* outcomes for African American clients over a 2-year period, whereas European American clients had better outcomes with low levels of EE. Within some African American families, seemingly negative family communication may, in fact, reflect caring and concern (Rosenfarb, Bellack, et al., 2006). Lopez, Hipke, and associates (2004) concluded that different cultural groups interpret family communication processes such as emotional overprotection or overinvolvement differently. In fact, therapists who focus on reducing critical and intrusive communication patterns in culturally diverse families may inadvertently increase family stress.

Figure 12.8

Possible Relationships between High Rates of Expressed Emotion and Relapse Rates in Patients with Schizophrenia

This figure shows several ways in which expressed emotions and relapse rates can be related.

Sociocultural Dimension

There are ethnic differences in the rates of schizophrenia. Immigrant groups, particularly those of African descent, have the highest rates of schizophrenia in Western Europe. Similarly, follow-up of a large birth cohort in the United States revealed that African Americans were 2 to 3 times more likely to receive a diagnosis of schizophrenia compared to European Americans (Bresnahan et al., 2007). Why do clinical interviews result in higher rates of schizophrenia in African Americans? It is not clear whether these findings reflect clinician bias or actual differences in rates of the disorder. Elevated rates of schizophrenia among African Americans occur even when assessment data are reanalyzed by clinicians unaware of the ethnicity of clients. It is possible that previous discriminatory experiences lead to cultural mistrust and a "healthy paranoia" that is picked up during clinical assessments. In other words, discriminatory experiences may cause African Americans to respond in a manner that represents normative responses to ongoing discrimination; the responses may appear delusional to clinicians who do not understand these sociocultural realities (Gara et al., 2012).

It is also possible that there are cultural differences in how symptoms are expressed. In a study in which a structured assessment was used to interview 215 African Americans and 537 European Americans seeking mental health treatment,

DID YOU KNOW?

Individuals who recently experienced a psychotic breakdown attributed their emotional collapse to a variety of factors, including drug use (especially cannabis), adult trauma (e.g., sexual assault, violence, or abuse), personal sensitivity (e.g., not fitting in, bottling up feelings, discomfort around others), and developmental problems (e.g., being teased or bullied as a child, childhood abuse).

SOURCE: Dudley, Siitarinen, James, & Dodson, 2009

Visions of America/UIG/Getty Images

Socioeconomic Status and Schizophrenia

Schizophrenia is much more prevalent in poorer neighborhoods. Some believe that the increased stress from living in poverty may be the cause; others believe that individuals with schizophrenia move into poorer neighborhoods because of their decreased ability to function in society.

African Americans were over 3 times more likely to receive a diagnosis of schizophrenia. The researchers wanted to determine what accounted for this difference. Demographic and clinical characteristics contributed modestly to the disparity; however, the greatest contributor to the disparity in diagnosis was a simple question rated on a five-point scale regarding perceived honesty of the client ("Did the subject appear to be answering honestly?"). In general, clinicians believed that African American clients were less honest compared to European American clients. The researchers concluded that clinicians' personal perspectives or biases may affect the therapist-client relationship and the diagnostic process (Eack, Bahorik, Newhill, Neighbors, & Davis, 2012).

A number of other social factors have been identified as risk factors for schizophrenia, such as lower educational level of parents, lower occupational status of fathers, and residing in poorer areas at birth (Werner, Malaspina, & Rabinowitz, 2007; Wicks, Hjern, & Dalman, 2010). These forms of social adversity, especially when combined with other risk factors, appear to produce a threefold increase in the risk of developing schizophrenia compared to children not exposed to these adversities (Wicks, Hjern, Gunnell, Lewis, & Dalman, 2005). Interestingly, living among members of one's own ethnic group reduces the risk of experiencing psychotic symptoms. Residing in a neighborhood or community with others of the same ethnic background may serve as a buffer to social adversity and reduce risk of developing psychotic symptoms (Das-Munshi et al., 2012).

Stress associated with immigration experiences may increase risk of schizophrenia. Migration was identified as a risk factor for schizophrenia among first- and second-generation immigrants to the United Kingdom, especially for those with African ancestry (Schofield, Ashworth, & Jones, 2011). Similarly, the incidence of schizophrenia is very high among several ethnic groups in the Netherlands, particularly Moroccan immigrants (Veling, Selten, Mackenbach, & Hoek, 2007). The stress of migration and experiences of discrimination as a member of a visible minority may act as additional stressors in predisposed individuals. Although we do not know the exact relationship between social stress and increased risk of schizophrenia, one hypothesis points to the excess dopamine release that occurs in response to chronic stress (Mizrahi, 2010).

Cultural Issues with Schizophrenia

Culture may affect how people view or interpret symptoms of schizophrenia. In Japan, for example, schizophrenia is highly stigmatized. The condition was previously called *seishin-bunretsu-byou*, which roughly translates to "a split in mind or spirit," a term that implies it is an irreversible condition. Because of this connotation, only about 20 percent of those diagnosed with schizophrenia in Japan were told of their diagnosis in the years preceding 2000 (Y. Kim & Berrios, 2001). In 2002, the name was changed to *togo-shitcho-sho* (integration disorder), which is a less stigmatizing term. After this change, almost 70 percent of the psychiatrists surveyed said they would now inform a patient of the diagnosis (Takahashi, Tsunoda, et al., 2011). Similarly, a negative reaction to the term *schizophrenia* is part of the reason that many psychiatrists in Turkey will not mention the diagnosis to clients or family members (Ucok, 2007).

Culture also affects how a disorder is viewed, as evidenced by the case of a 13-year-old child of a Tongan mother and Caucasian father living in the United States.

CASE STUDY The parents were concerned because the girl began to isolate herself and appeared to have visual hallucinations, was observed talking to herself, and reported hearing voices of a woman who sounded like her mother and a man who sounded like her dead grandfather. Although she showed some improvement after taking antipsychotic medication, the girl still reported that people were talking about her and ghosts were disturbing her.

The mother decided that her daughter suffered from "fakama-haki," a culture-bound syndrome in which deceased relatives can inflict illness or possess the living when customs have been neglected. She took her daughter to Tonga to be treated. For 5 days, a traditional healer ("witch doctor") treated the girl with herbal potions that induced vomiting in order to remove toxins from the girl's body. She also visited her grandfather's gravesite to allow proper mourning. When the girl returned to the United States and was reevaluated, there were no symptoms of psychosis. Follow-up contact revealed that the girl was continuing to do well. (Takeuchi, 2000)

This case is interesting because medication was only minimally successful, whereas traditional healing seemed to be effective. Although it is also possible that the disorder was time-limited, it is important to consider how taking into account cultural beliefs might enhance treatment of severe mental disorders.

As noted throughout this book, the study of cross-cultural perspectives on psychopathology is important because indigenous belief systems influence views of etiology and treatment. In India, for example, the belief in supernatural causation of schizophrenia is widespread, leading families to consult with and rely on treatment from indigenous healers (G. Banerjee & Roy, 1998). In a study of individuals with schizophrenia from four ethnic groups (Anglos in the United Kingdom, African Caribbeans, Bangladeshi, and West Africans), distinct differences in explanatory models were found for the disorder (Table 12.2) (R. McCabe & Priebe, 2004). The different models included biological (e.g., physical illness or substance abuse), social (e.g., interpersonal problems, stress, negative childhood events, personality), supernatural (e.g., evil forces, evil magic), and various nonspecific explanations.

The United Kingdom group was the most likely to attribute the condition to biological causes and least likely to identify supernatural causes—the explanation selected by a substantial minority of individuals from the other ethnic groups—as a potential causal factor. Differing views on etiology also influenced response to taking medication for their symptoms. Those who cited biological causes believed they were receiving the correct treatment (medication), whereas those who supported a supernatural explanation wanted alternative forms of treatment, such as religious activities. Thus,

Table 12.2 Explanatory Models of Illness in Schizophrenia among Four Ethnic Groups

	Biological Explanation	Social Explanation	Supernatural Explanation	Nonspecific Explanation
African Caribbean	6.7%	60.0%	20.0%	23.3%
Bangladeshi	0.0%	42.3%	26.9%	30.8%
West African	10.7%	31.0%	28.6%	21.4%
Anglo (in the United Kingdom)	34.5%	31.0%	0.0%	34.5%

SOURCE: McCabe & Priebe (2004).

views of etiology can affect our understanding of schizophrenia, including its severity, prognosis, and appropriate treatment.

Treatment of Schizophrenia

Through the years, schizophrenia has been treated by a variety of means, including performing a **prefrontal lobotomy**—a surgical procedure in which the frontal lobes are disconnected from the remainder of the brain. Today schizophrenia is often treated with antipsychotic medication, along with some type of psychosocial therapy. In recent years, the research and clinical perspective on people with schizophrenia has shifted from a focus on illness and deficit to one of recovery and promotion of health, competencies, independence, and self-determination (Bellack, 2006; Lysaker & Roe, 2012). This change of focus is affecting therapists' views regarding clients and their families and their own role in the treatment process. We first discuss medication in the treatment of schizophrenia, and then the psychological and social therapies.

Antipsychotic Medications

CASE STUDY Peter, a 29-year-old man, was diagnosed with chronic paranoid schizophrenia.... When on medication, he heard voices talking about him and felt that his phone was bugged. When off medication, he had constant hallucinations and his behavior became unpredictable.... He was on 10 milligrams of haloperidol (Haldol) three times a day.... Peter complained that he had been quite restless, and did not want to take the medication. Over the next 6 months, Peter's psychiatrist gradually reduced Peter's medication to 4 milligrams per day.... At this dose, Peter continued to have bothersome symptoms, but they remained moderate.... He was no longer restless. (Liberman, Kopelowicz, & Young, 1994, p. 94)

The case study illustrates several points. First, **antipsychotic medication** can reduce intensity of symptoms; second, dosage levels should be carefully monitored; and third, side effects can occur as a result of medication and may affect a person's willingness to take prescribed medications.

Many consider the 1955 introduction of *Thorazine*, the first antipsychotic drug, to be the beginning of a new era in treating schizophrenia. For the first time, a medication was available that sufficiently relaxed even those most severely affected by schizophrenia and helped organize their thoughts to the point that straitjackets were no longer needed for physical restraint. Although medications have improved the lives of many with schizophrenia, they do not cure the disorder. Earlier antipsychotic drugs are known as *first-generation medications; atypical antipsychotic medications* are more recently developed and have somewhat different chemical properties than the earlier drugs.

First-generation antipsychotics (also called conventional or typical antipsychotics) are still viewed as effective treatments for schizophrenia, although their use has been largely supplanted by the newer **atypical antipsychotics**. Conventional antipsychotic medications (such as chlorpromazine/Thorazine or haloperidol/Haldol) have dopaminergic receptor–blocking capabilities (i.e., they reduce dopamine levels), a factor that led to the dopamine hypothesis of schizophrenia.

The newer atypical antipsychotics (such as risperidone/Risperdal, olanzapine/Zyprexa, quetiapine/Seroquel, aripiprazole/Abilify, and lurasidone/Latuda) act on both dopamine and serotonin receptors. These newer medications are purportedly less likely to produce side effects such as the rigidity, persistent muscle spasms, tremors, and

prefrontal lobotomy a surgical procedure in which the frontal lobes are disconnected from the remainder of the brain

antipsychotic medication medicine developed to counteract symptoms of psychosis

first-generation antipsychotics a group of medications originally developed to combat psychotic symptoms by reducing dopamine levels in the brain; also called *conventional* or *typical antipsychotics*

atypical antipsychotics newer antipsychotic medications that are chemically different and less likely to produce the side effects associated with first-generation antipsychotics

restlessness that occur with the older antipsychotics (Bobo, 2013). However, some researchers have raised questions about the side effects of these newer antipsychotic medications (Foley & Morley, 2011).

Conventional and atypical antipsychotics can effectively reduce the severity of the positive symptoms of schizophrenia, such as hallucinations, delusions, bizarre speech, and disordered thought. In one study, over 75 percent of those taking atypical antipsychotics felt that the medication helped them manage their symptoms and prevent hospitalization (Jenkins et al., 2005). Most of these medications, however, offer little relief from negative symptoms such as social withdrawal, apathy, and impaired personal hygiene (M. F. Green, 2007). Moreover, a "relatively large group" of people with schizophrenia do not benefit at all from antipsychotic medication. Additionally, from one half to three quarters of patients discontinue use of antipsychotics for the following reasons (Moritz et al., 2013):

- Too many side effects (80 percent)
- Did not need believe they needed antipsychotics (58 percent)
- Mistrust of the physician or therapist (31 percent)
- Rejection of medication in general (28 percent)
- Friends or relatives advised them not to take the medication (20 percent)

Many individuals treated with antipsychotic medications develop **extrapyramidal symptoms**, which include *parkinsonism* (muscle tremors, shakiness, and immobility), *dystonia* (involuntary muscle contractions involving the limbs and tongue), *akathisia* (motor restlessness), and *neuroleptic malignant syndrome* (muscle rigidity and autonomic instability, which can be fatal if untreated). Other symptoms may involve the loss of facial expression, shuffling gait, tremors of the hand, rigidity of the body, and poor balance. Although many symptoms are reversible once medication is stopped, some symptoms (e.g., involuntary movements) can be permanent (D. E. Casey, 2006).

In a study of 4621 patients, 12.6 percent had increased hospitalizations, emergency room visits, and health care costs resulting from extrapyramidal symptoms (Abouzaid et al., 2014). *Tardive dyskinesia*, a more chronic or permanent condition, is another side effect of antipsychotics. This condition involves involuntary and rhythmic movements of the tongue; chewing, lip smacking, and other facial movements; and jerking movements of the limbs. The risk of developing this disorder is greatest for those who take antipsychotic medications over an extended period. Antipsychotic medications are also associated with increased risk of **metabolic syndrome**, a condition associated with obesity, diabetes, high cholesterol, and hypertension (Bener, Al-Hamaq, & Dafeeah, 2014).

Newer antipsychotic medications cost 10 times more than older antipsychotics. But are these newer antipsychotic medications safer and more effective? The effectiveness of an older antipsychotic (perphenazine) was compared with that of several newer antipsychotic medications (olanzapine, quetiapine, risperidone, and ziprasidone) in the treatment of chronic schizophrenia (average length of illness in the participants was 14.4 years) as part of a comprehensive nationwide comparative drug study. Surprisingly, the older, less expensive medication (perphenazine) used in the study performed about as well as the four newer medications and did not produce significantly more extrapyramidal symptoms (Lieberman et al., 2005). In addition, a review of studies published between 1974 and 2012 comparing conventional and atypical antipsychotics found a lack of evidence that the latter offer an advantage in treating schizophrenia (Hartling et al., 2012).

The most beneficial treatment for schizophrenia is a combination of antipsychotic medication and psychotherapy, according to most clinicians today. Although medications can reduce many symptoms of schizophrenia, one fact is clear. Individuals with

CONTINUUM Video Project

Andre: Schizophrenia

"I believe that other people are pathological liars, and I'm not. So why should I even have to listen to them?"

Access the Continuum Video Project in MindTap at
www.cengage.com

extrapyramidal symptoms side effects such as restlessness, involuntary movements, and muscular tension produced by antipsychotic medications

metabolic syndrome a medical condition associated with obesity, diabetes, high cholesterol, and hypertension

schizophrenia discharged from protective hospital environments are often confronted with real-world stress once they return to the community. Dealing with chronic stress can result in the return of psychotic symptoms and rehospitalization; medication alone is often not enough to help those with schizophrenia function in their natural environments.

There is also concern that antipsychotic medications have a negative impact on brain anatomy and biochemical functioning and can also affect cognitive functioning (Sweeney, 2013). Because of these troubling findings, questions have arisen about whether it is possible for antipsychotic medications to be reduced or discontinued. Although there is a tendency for relapse in the first 6 to 10 months for individuals with schizophrenia who do not take or discontinue their medication, those who remain stable after this period have favorable outcomes (Harrow & Jobe, 2013). So it appears that continuous medication may not be needed for some individuals with schizophrenia. Additionally, dose reduction may be another option. Reducing the dosage of antipsychotic medication by half resulted in a significant improvement in cognitive functioning, including verbal memory and processing speed (Takeuchi et al., 2012). In a 7-year follow-up study, dose-reduction patients were twice as likely to recover compared to patients receiving ongoing maintenance medication (Wunderink, Nieboer, Wiersma, Systema, & Nienhuis, 2013).

The Marketing of Atypical Antipsychotic Medications

The woman in the Abilify ad says, "I'm taking an antidepressant but I think I need more help." According to the ad, two out of three individuals taking an antidepressant alone continue to experience symptoms of depression. The ad goes on to suggest that Abilify can be helpful when combined with current antidepressant medications. Abilify is an atypical antipsychotic medication, but that fact is not mentioned (Westberg, 2010).

Surprisingly, the top-selling class of medications in the United States is atypical antipsychotic medications, a drug class accounting for $18.2 billion of 3.1 million U.S. prescriptions in 2011 (Friedman, 2012), including more than $1 billion in annual sales for quetiapine (Seroquel), aripiprazole (Abilify), olanzapine (Zyprexa), and risperidone (Risperdal) (G. C. Alexander, Gallagher, Mascola, Moloney, & Stafford, 2011). These profitable drugs are heavily promoted by the pharmaceutical companies, with resultant increases in the number of people taking both antidepressants and antipsychotics. However, many of these combinations are of "unproven efficacy" (Mojtabai & Olfson, 2010).

Even more problematic is that off-label use (i.e., prescribing medication for unapproved indications, such as for treatment of a different disorder or age group) of atypical antipsychotics has increased dramatically. Antipsychotics are increasingly prescribed for a range of mental disorders, including attentional, conduct, and anxiety disorders,

although they have never been evaluated or approved for use with these conditions (Zito, Burcu, Ibe, Safer, & Magder, 2013). More than half of the prescriptions in 2008 for atypical antipsychotic medications were off-label and of "uncertain efficacy" (G. C. Alexander et al., 2011).

The increased use of atypical antipsychotic medications is of particular concern due to their association with troublesome side effects. After only 12 weeks on Abilify, Risperdal, Seroquel, or Zyprexa, children were found to gain up to 19 lb (Correll et al., 2010). In a 5-year study of atypical antipsychotics in middle-aged and older individuals with schizophrenia, 29.7 percent had serious adverse physical effects that were probably or possibly due to the medication. Increases in cholesterol levels and weight gain can occur in individuals taking atypical antipsychotic medications for as little as 3 months (Foley & Morley, 2011). The U.S. Food and Drug Administration (2011) has warned that infants born to mothers taking antipsychotic medications during the third trimester of pregnancy are at high risk of having abnormal muscle tone, tremors, sleepiness, severe difficulty breathing, and difficulty sucking.

Should regulations be in place to protect consumers from the increasing off-label use of antipsychotic medications? Should advertisements promoting atypical antipsychotic medications identify them as such? Should physicians and psychiatrists be required to inform patients about off-label prescriptions?

Psychosocial Therapy

CASE STUDY   Philip's psychotic symptoms were significantly reduced with medication. However, he was unable to obtain employment because of cognitive and behavioral peculiarities. Philip did not seem to understand social conventions such as appropriate conversational topics or attire. His therapist suggested that his clothing (sweatshirt, exercise pants, headband, and worn sneakers) might be inappropriate for job interviews. He coached Philip to observe attire worn by individuals in different businesses. He also gave Philip opportunities to practice engaging in informal conversation and answering job interview questions. When interviewing for a landscape job, Philip wore a work shirt, blue jeans, and construction boots and was hired by the landscaping contractor (Heinssen & Cuthbert, 2001).

Psychotherapeutic work with individuals with schizophrenia often focuses on the direct teaching of social skills, including conversational skills. Heinssen and Cuthbert (2001) found that eccentricities in the appearance, attire, and communication patterns of individuals with schizophrenia, as well as lack of discretion in discussing their illness, can impede employment or the establishment of social networks. Social communication may also be problematic because of difficulties with emotional perception and understanding the beliefs and attitudes of others (Combs et al., 2007). Thus, it is beneficial when communication skills are taught directly and practiced in role-play situations.

Inpatient Approaches

Both milieu therapy and behavioral therapy can be beneficial for individuals with schizophrenia receiving inpatient treatment. In milieu therapy, the hospital environment operates as a community within which those with schizophrenia exercise a wide range of responsibilities and help make decisions. Psychosocial skills training focuses on increasing appropriate self-care behaviors, conversational skills, and job skills. Undesirable behaviors such as "crazy talk" or social isolation are decreased through reinforcement and modeling techniques. These approaches have been effective in helping many people with schizophrenia achieve independent living. Living in community homes (halfway houses) can also assist with the transition from inpatient programs to community living. In a study of nearly 100 individuals with chronic schizophrenia placed in community facilities, almost all improved (Leff, 1994).

Cognitive-Behavioral Therapy

Major advances have been made in the use of cognitive and behavioral strategies in treating the symptoms of schizophrenia; this is particularly important for those who do not respond to medication. Therapists teach coping skills that allow clients to manage their positive and negative symptoms, as well as the cognitive challenges associated with schizophrenia (Hansen, Kingdon, & Turkington, 2006). An 18-month follow-up of 216 individuals with persisting psychotic symptoms found that those receiving cognitive-behavioral therapy demonstrated 183 days of normal functioning, compared to 106 days of normal functioning for those who received treatment as usual consisting of pharmacotherapy and contact with a psychiatric nurse (van der Gaag, Stant, Wolters, Burkens, & Wiersma, 2011).

The following case study provides an example of symptoms of schizophrenia that might be effectively addressed with cognitive-behavioral treatment strategies.

A young African American woman with auditory hallucinations, paranoid delusions, delusions of reference, a history of childhood verbal and physical abuse, and adult sexual assault felt extremely hopeless about her prospects for developing social ties. She believed that her "persecutors" had informed others of her socially undesirable activities. . . . She often loudly screamed at the voices she was hearing. . . . When she did leave her home, she often covered her head with a black kerchief and wore dark sunglasses, partly in an effort to disguise herself from her persecutors. (Cather, 2005, p. 260)

Cognitive-behavioral treatment to address concerns such as these often includes the following steps (Cather, 2005; Sivec & Montesano, 2013):

- *Engagement.* The therapist explains the therapy and works to foster a safe and collaborative method of looking at causes of distress, drawing out the client's understanding of stressors and ways of coping.

- *Assessment.* Clients are encouraged to discuss their fears and anxieties; the therapist shares information about how symptoms are formed and maintained. In the preceding case study, the therapist helped the woman make sense of her persecutory experiences. It was explained that victims of abuse often internalize beliefs that they are responsible for the abuse, and that her view that she was "bad" led to expectations of negative reactions from others and the need to disguise herself.

- *Identification of negative beliefs.* The therapist explains to the client the link between personal beliefs and emotional distress, and the ways that beliefs such as "Nobody will like me if I tell them about my voices" can be disputed and changed to "I can't demand that everyone like me. Some people will and some won't" (Hansen et al., 2006, p. 50). This reinterpretation often leads to less sadness and isolation.

- *Normalization.* The therapist works with the client to normalize and decatastrophize the psychotic experiences. Information that many people can have unusual experiences can reduce a client's sense of isolation.

- *Collaborative analysis of symptoms.* Once a strong therapeutic alliance has been established, the therapist begins critical discussions of the client's symptoms, such as "If voices come from your head, why can't others hear them?" Evidence for and against the maladaptive beliefs is discussed, combined with information about how beliefs are maintained through cognitive distortions or inferences.

- *Development of alternative explanations.* The therapist helps the client develop alternatives to previous maladaptive assumptions, using the client's ideas whenever possible.

Family Communication and Education

Therapy that includes the family members of individuals with schizophrenia reduces relapse rates and is more effective than drug treatment alone.

More recently, instead of trying to eliminate or combat hallucinations, therapists teach clients to accept them in a nonjudgmental manner. In mindfulness training, clients learn to let go of angry or fearful responses to psychotic symptoms; instead, they are taught to let the psychotic symptoms come into consciousness without reacting (e.g., just noticing the voices or thoughts rather than believing them or acting on them; accepting them even if one does not like them). This process enhances feelings of self-control and significantly reduces negative emotions (Dannahy et al., 2011; Shawyer et al., 2012). The approach was used with men who had heard malevolent and powerful voices for more than 30 years. Their attempts to stop the voices or to distract themselves were

©iStock.com/JodiJacobson

ineffective. After undergoing mindfulness training, the men were less distressed with the voices and more confident in their ability to live with them (K. N. Taylor, Harper, & Chadwick, 2009). Similarly, malevolent and persecuting voices became less disturbing when individuals with schizophrenia learned to access positive emotions such as warmth and contentment during psychotic episodes (Mayhew & Gilbert, 2008).

A form of cognitive therapy, *integrated psychological therapy (IPT)*, has also produced promising results. IPT specifically targets deficits found in individuals with schizophrenia, such as basic impairments in neurocognition (e.g., attention, verbal memory, cognitive flexibility, concept formation), deficits in social cognition (e.g., social-emotional perception, emotional expression), interpersonal communication (e.g., verbal fluency and executive functioning), and problem-solving skills. In a meta-analysis of treatment studies involving IPT, Roder and colleagues (2006) concluded: "IPT is an effective rehabilitation approach for schizophrenia that is robust across a wide range of patients and treatment conditions" (p. 81).

Interventions Focusing on Family Communication and Education

A serious mental illness such as schizophrenia can have a powerful effect on family members, who may feel stigmatized or responsible for the disorder. As one woman stated, "All family members are affected by a loved one's mental illness. The entire family system needs to be addressed" (Stalberg, Ekerwald, & Hultman, 2004).

Siblings without the disorder may display a variety of emotional reactions to the mental illness experienced by their sibling—love ("She's really kind and loves me so very much it's never been a problem."); loss ("Somehow I've lost my sister the way she was before and I think I won't get her back."); anger ("Yes, it's hell. . . . She's incredibly mean to our mother and she sure as hell doesn't deserve that."); guilt and shame ("Yes, you can think about how he got ill and I didn't."); and fear ("You worry a lot about getting it yourself.") (Stalberg, Ekerwald, & Hultman, 2004, p. 450).

More than half of those recovering from a psychotic episode return to live with their families, and new psychological interventions address this fact. Family intervention programs have not only reduced relapse rates but have also lowered the cost of care. They have been beneficial for families with and without negative communication patterns. Most programs include the following components (Glynn et al., 2006; Mueser et al., 2001):

- normalizing the family experience;
- demonstrating concern, empathy, and sympathy to all family members;
- educating family members about schizophrenia;
- avoiding blaming the family or pathologizing their coping efforts;
- identifying the strengths and competencies of the client and family members;
- developing skills in solving problems and managing stress;
- teaching family members to cope with the symptoms of mental illness and its repercussions on the family; and
- strengthening the communication skills of all family members.

Family approaches and social skills training are much more effective in preventing relapse than drug treatment alone (Xia, Merinder, & Belgamwar, 2011). Combining cognitive-behavioral strategies, family counseling, and social skills training seems to produce the most positive results (Penn et al., 2004). The use of medication combined with psychosocial interventions has provided hope for many individuals with schizophrenia. In fact, recent research suggests that "optimism about outcome from schizophrenia is justified" and that "a substantial proportion of people with the illness will recover completely and many more will regain good social functioning" (R. Warner, 2009, p. 374).

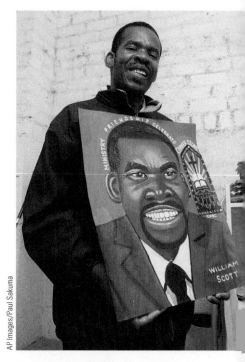

AP Images/Paul Sakuma

Artwork to Demonstrate Creative Talents

Diagnosed with schizophrenia and an autism spectrum disorder, paintings and sculptures by William Scott are sold around the world at cutting-edge art galleries. Scott is pictured here with a self-portrait.

Other Schizophrenia Spectrum Disorders

Disorders on the schizophrenia spectrum include some or all of the symptoms we discussed at the beginning of this chapter. The spectrum includes disorders that differ from schizophrenia in a variety of ways, including the specific symptoms involved, the duration of symptoms, or the presence of additional symptoms. With all of the schizophrenia spectrum disorders, clinicians must first determine that the symptoms do not result from medication side effects, medical conditions, substance use or abuse, or other mental disorders. Additional disorders on the schizophrenia spectrum include delusional disorder, brief psychotic disorder, schizophreniform disorder, and schizoaffective disorder (see Table 12.3).

Delusional Disorder

CASE STUDY A woman working as an intern in a firm and studying for a master's degree was convinced that the neighbors above her floor were making noises because they disapproved of her intense sexual desires. She reacted angrily, shouting at her neighbors and knocking on the ceiling. She believed that her Facebook friends and colleagues also disapproved of her for the same reasons (Salvatore, Russo, Russo, Popolo, & Dimaggio, 2012).

Table 12.3 Schizophrenia Spectrum and Other Psychotic Disorders

DISORDERS CHART				
Disorder	**Symptoms**	**Prevalence**	**Gender Differences**	**Age of Onset**
Schizophrenia	Two or more psychotic symptoms of which at least one must be delusions, hallucinations, or disorganized speech Impaired life functioning	• About 1% of the population	About equal	• 18–24 for men • 24–35 for women
Brief psychotic disorder	One or more psychotic symptoms, of which at least one must be delusions, hallucinations, or disorganized speech lasting at least 1 day but less than 1 month	• Up to 9% of new cases of psychosis • Much higher in developing countries	Twice as common in women	• Can occur at any age • Most common in 30s
Schizophreniform disorder	Two or more psychotic symptoms, of which at least one must be delusions, hallucinations, or disorganized speech lasting at least 1 month but less than 6 months	• Much lower rate than schizophrenia • Higher in developing countries	About equal	• 18–24 for men • 24–35 for women
Delusional disorder	One or more delusions continuing for at least 1 month	• About 0.03%–0.018%	About equal	• More prevalent in older adults
Schizoaffective disorder	Episode of mania or major depression concurrent with delusions, hallucinations, or disorganized speech; psychotic symptoms persist after the mood episode ends	• About 0.32%	More females	• Usually early adulthood

SOURCE: APA (2013); Bhalla (2013); Brannon & Bienenfeld (2012); Memon (2013).

Delusional disorder is characterized by persistent delusions that are not accompanied by other unusual or odd behaviors—other than those related to the delusional theme (Chopra & Bienenfeld, 2011). According to DSM-5, the delusions must persist for at least 1 month (APA, 2013). The individuals in both of these cases experienced persisting delusions, but had no other evidence of psychosis. Thus, they both received a diagnosis of delusional disorder. Delusional disorder is distinct from the other psychotic disorders due to the absence of additional disturbances in thoughts or perceptions, beyond occasional hallucinations that may be associated with the delusion (e.g., sensations of insects crawling on the skin within the context of a delusion that one's home is infested with insects). This disorder is rarely diagnosed (the prevalence is 0.03–0.18 percent); however, it is believed that many with the disorder do not perceive they have a problem and therefore do not seek assistance. People with delusional disorder generally behave normally when they are not discussing or reacting to their delusional ideas. Common themes involved in delusional disorders include the following (Chopra & Bienenfeld, 2011):

- *Erotomania*—the belief that someone is in love with the individual; this delusion typically has a romantic rather than sexual focus.
- *Grandiosity*—the conviction that one has great, unrecognized talent, special abilities, or a relationship with an important person or deity.
- *Jealousy*—the conviction that one's spouse or partner is being unfaithful.
- *Persecution*—the belief that one is being conspired or plotted against.
- *Somatic complaints*—convictions of having body odor, being malformed, or being infested by insects or parasites.

Women are more likely to develop erotomanic delusions, whereas men tend to have paranoid delusions involving persecution (Chopra & Khan, 2009). The following cases illustrate some features of delusional disorders:

- A woman was convinced that people were watching her and following her because she saw the same people day after day in her neighborhood and in the stores where she shopped (Muller, 2006).
- A 37-year-old man was arrested for stalking and harassing Tyra Banks, a model and television personality. He had followed her for 2 months, appeared at her TV studio, made repeated phone calls, and sent multiple letters and flowers, claiming that they had a "thing together" (Serpe, 2009).
- A woman complained of insects that wandered in her body; when she scratched her legs, she insisted she saw insects (Mercan et al., 2007).

In a rare form of delusional disorder (shared psychotic delusion), a person who has a close relationship with an individual with delusional or psychotic beliefs comes to accept those beliefs (Wehmeier, Barth, & Remschmidt, 2003), as seen in the following case.

delusional disorder persistent delusions without other unusual or odd behaviors; tactile and olfactory hallucinations related to the delusional theme may be present

Morgellons Disease: Delusional Parasitosis or Physical Disease?

More than 10 years ago, "Mary Leitao plucked a fiber that looked like a dandelion fluff from a sore under her two-year-old son's lips.... Sometimes the fibers were white, and sometimes they were black, red, or blue" (Devita-Raeburn, 2007). Leitao was frustrated by the inability of physicians to diagnose her son's skin condition. In fact, many of the professionals she consulted indicated that they could find no evidence of disease or infection. Frustrated by the medical establishment, Leitao put a description of the condition on a Web site in 2001, calling it Morgellons disease after a 17th-century French medical study involving children with similar symptoms (Mason, 2006).

The Web site has since compiled 11,000 worldwide reports of the condition among adults and children. Sufferers report granules and fiber-like threads emerging from the skin at the site of itching; sensations of crawling, stinging, or biting; and rashes and skin lesions that do not heal (M. Paquette, 2007). Some describe the fibers as "inorganic but alive" and report that the fibers pull back from a lit match (Browne, 2011). Symptoms of vision changes, joint pain, fatigue, mental confusion, and short-term memory difficulties have been reported in connection with Morgellons disease (Centers for Disease Control and Prevention, 2011).

What could cause this disorder? Many dermatologists, physicians, and psychiatrists believe that Morgellons disease results from self-inflicted injury or is a somatic type of delusional disorder such as *delusional parasitosis*, a condition in which individuals (often those with psychosis or a substance-use disorder) maintain a delusional belief that they are afflicted with living organisms or other pathogens (Freudenmann & Lepping, 2009). Stephen Stone, past president of the American Academy of Dermatology, does not believe Morgellons is a real disease. He argues that the Internet community is allowing individuals with somatic delusions to band together (Marris, 2006). Some physicians, however, believe there is an underlying physical disorder, citing those with Morgellons

symptoms who test positive for Lyme disease or whose symptoms are alleviated with antibacterial or antiparasitic medications (Savely, Leitao, & Stricker, 2006). Other medical professionals report that individuals with Morgellons symptoms show evidence of infectious disease such as immune system deficiency and markers of chronic inflammation (W. T. Harvey et al., 2009).

Because of the controversy and the increasing number of complaints, the Centers for Disease Control and Prevention (CDC) initiated an investigation into the characteristics and epidemiologic data related to Morgellons, including psychological testing, environmental analysis, examination of skin biopsies, and laboratory study of fibers or threads obtained from people with the condition (CDC, 2011). Researchers concluded that no medical condition or infection could explain the reported symptoms and that the skin lesions were probably produced by scratching. Fibers found at the site of skin inflammation were cotton or nylon, not organisms. Psychological tests revealed that individuals studied were more likely to be depressed and attentive to physical symptoms than the general population, but that they were not delusional (Pearson et al., 2012). Some researchers believe that "the rapid rise of Morgellons could not have occurred without the internet...which can spread information—without regard for accuracy or usefulness" (Freudenreich, Kontos, Tranulis, & Cather, 2010, p. 456).

For Further Consideration

1. Are Internet Web sites on diseases such as Morgellons creating disorders among vulnerable individuals, or do they provide comfort for those with an actual disease?

2. How might a psychologist or a physician determine if an individual reporting symptoms of Morgellons was suffering from a somatic delusion?

Shared delusions (sometimes referred to as *folie à deux*) are more prevalent among those who are socially isolated. In the preceding case, the daughter never married, lived with and was submissive to her mother, and had no close relationships with others. The pattern generally involves a family member or partner acquiring the delusional belief from the dominant individual. The other individual is often younger, highly suggestible, more passive, and has lower self-esteem (Lew-Starowicz, 2012). In many cases, an individual who shares another person's delusional beliefs loses faith in those beliefs when the two individuals are separated.

A decreased ability to obtain corrective feedback, combined with preexisting personality traits of suspiciousness, may increase a person's susceptibility to developing delusional beliefs. For example, hearing impairment in early adolescence is associated with an increased risk of developing delusions (van der Werf et al., 2011). There is a significant genetic relationship between delusional disorder and schizophrenia; a small proportion of those with the disorder eventually develop schizophrenia (APA, 2013). Delusional disorder can be treated with antipsychotic medications or cognitive-behavioral therapy (Chopra & Khan, 2009).

Brief Psychotic Disorder

CASE STUDY   Eve was a 20-year-old student studying forensic medicine when she first experienced a chaotic world of delusions. She believed that her body was decaying, deteriorating, and rotting away. She feared seeing her reflection in mirrors, worried that it would show that her skin was falling apart revealing a rotted monster. She pasted paper over windows and smashed the mirror in the bathroom. She splashed perfume over everything to hide the stench of her rotting body. She stayed in constant motion because she believed that remaining still would cause her body to deteriorate more quickly. At some point all she could do was scream.

During an interview after she was hospitalized, Eve was asked if she was aware that something was wrong. Eve replied that the disturbances produced by the delusions were so strong that she could not logically evaluate the experience. Eve received a diagnosis of brief psychotic disorder and the psychiatrist prescribed an antipsychotic medication, an antidepressant, and a sleeping aid. Within two and one-half weeks, her symptoms had subsided and she moved back in with her family (Purse, 2013).

A DSM-5 diagnosis of **brief psychotic disorder** requires the presence of one or more psychotic symptoms, including at least one symptom involving delusions, hallucinations, or disorganized speech, that continue for at least 1 day but last less than 1 month. The symptoms sometimes occur during pregnancy or within 4 weeks of childbirth (APA, 2013). Because of the abrupt and distressing nature of the disorder, prevention of self-harm through hospitalization and use of antipsychotic drugs is sometimes necessary (Memon, 2013). If there is rapid symptom remission after administration of antipsychotic medication, differential diagnosis becomes more difficult. A psychological trauma can also produce the short-term psychotic episodes seen in brief psychotic disorder. For example, among soldiers engaged in combat in Croatia, 20 percent reported hallucinations and delusions (Kastelan et al., 2007).

A significant stressor often precedes the onset of symptoms, although in some cases the precipitating event is not apparent. Eve experienced a number of stressors before her psychotic episode. She had just lost her best friend to an accident, was struggling with academic demands, had two jobs, had moved into a new apartment, was dealing with the divorce of her parents, and had just broken up with her boyfriend.

Brief psychotic disorder accounts for up to 9 percent of individuals who seek help for first-time psychotic symptoms and is twice as common in women (APA, 2013). In contrast to schizophrenia and other psychotic disorders, there is often a full return to normal functioning after the episode. When the psychotic symptoms persist, a different diagnosis from the schizophrenia spectrum may be appropriate.

Schizophreniform Disorder

According to the DSM-5, a diagnosis of **schizophreniform disorder** requires the presence of two or more of the following symptoms: delusions, hallucinations, disorganized speech, gross motor disturbances, or negative symptoms. At least one of the two symptoms must involve delusions, hallucinations, or disorganized speech. This condition lasts between 1 month and 6 months (APA, 2013).

DID YOU KNOW?

Individuals with severe mental disorders such as schizophrenia have higher rates of violence than healthy people—but *only* if they have risk factors for violent behavior, such as substance abuse or a history of violence or physical abuse. Severe mental illness alone does *not* predict violence. This is different from portrayals in 40 contemporary movies where 83 percent of individuals with schizophrenia were violent toward others.

SOURCE: Elbogen & Johnson, 2009; Owen, 2012

brief psychotic disorder   psychotic episodes with a duration of at least 1 day but less than 1 month

schizophreniform disorder psychotic episodes with a duration of at least 1 month but less than 6 months

Table 12.4 Comparison of Brief Psychotic Disorder, Schizophreniform Disorder, and Schizophrenia

	Brief Psychotic Disorder	Schizophreniform Disorder	Schizophrenia
Duration	Less than 1 month	Less than 6 months	6 months or more
Psychosocial stressor	Likely present	Usually present	May or may not be present
Onset of symptoms	Abrupt onset of psychotic symptoms	Often abrupt psychotic symptoms	Gradual onset of psychotic symptoms
Outcome	Return to premorbid functioning	Possible return to premorbid functioning	Occasional return to premorbid functioning
Risk factors	More common in females	Some increased risk of schizophrenia among family members	Higher prevalence of schizophrenia among family members

SOURCE: APA (2013); Bhalla & Ahmed (2011); Memon (2013).

Schizophreniform disorder occurs equally in men and women and shares some of the anatomical and neural deficits found in schizophrenia (Bhalla & Ahmed, 2011). Like schizophrenia, the onset peaks between the ages of 18–24 in men and 24–35 in women. Good prognostic signs for schizophreniform disorder include an abrupt onset of symptoms, good premorbid functioning, and the absence of negative symptoms. As with schizophrenia, there is a significant risk from suicide, especially when the disorder is accompanied by depression (Bhalla, 2013). One third of individuals with this diagnosis recover within the 6-month time frame, and the other two thirds eventually receive a diagnosis of schizophrenia or schizoaffective disorder (APA, 2013).

Brief psychotic disorder and schizophreniform disorder share many commonalities with schizophrenia (see Table 12.4) and are often considered **provisional diagnoses**. For example, an initial diagnosis of brief psychotic disorder may change to schizophreniform disorder if symptoms last longer than 1 month and to schizophrenia if they last longer than 6 months and impair social or occupational functioning.

Schizoaffective Disorder

CASE STUDY By her last year of college, Beth Baxter, MD, an honors student and class president, knew there was something wrong with her brain; during the previous 4 years, she had routinely slept only 4 hours a night. . . . She fought suicidal urges and had already made several half-hearted attempts. In her second year of medical school, she became convinced that the songs being played on the radio were carrying messages to her. Her grades began to slip for the first time, so she took a break and visited her grandparents' cattle ranch in Texas. While there, she went missing. She left on an imagined meeting with friends and followed some "messages" on the radio. Found wandering a day later, she was picked up by police on the side of a highway. So began Dr. Baxter's first hospitalization when she was diagnosed as having bipolar disorder. She managed to return and graduate from medical school, hiring a tutor to talk through all of her class notes.

After her residency, Dr. Baxter became increasingly depressed and suicidal; she tried to slash her neck and was hospitalized for a year. Due to the extent of her psychotic symptoms, her diagnosis was changed to schizoaffective disorder. She gradually began to recover, encouraged by a hospital psychiatrist who gave her hope for a full recovery. The psychiatrist was correct in her optimism. Dr. Baxter is now a psychiatrist herself, with a successful private practice. She understands the importance of taking her medications regularly to control her symptoms (Solovitch, 2014).

provisional diagnosis an initial diagnosis based on currently available information

Schizoaffective disorder is diagnosed when someone demonstrates psychotic symptoms that meet the diagnostic criteria for schizophrenia combined with symptoms of a major depressive or manic episode that continue for the majority of the time the schizophrenic symptoms are present. Additionally, according to DSM-5, the psychotic features must sometimes continue for at least 2 weeks after symptoms of the manic or depressed episode have subsided. Thus, schizoaffective disorder has features of both schizophrenia and a depressive or bipolar disorder (Brannon, 2013). If a person experiences manic episodes, the clinician specifies that he or she has the bipolar subtype of schizoaffective disorder rather than the depressive subtype. Diagnosis is difficult because many people with depressive or bipolar disorder experience hallucinations or delusions during a manic or depressive episode. However, individuals with mood disorders do not have psychotic symptoms in the absence of a major mood episode. DSM-5 recognizes the diagnostic difficulty and states: "There is growing evidence that schizoaffective disorder is not a distinct nosological category" (APA, 2013, p. 90). It will be interesting to see if this diagnosis continues to appear in future editions of the DSM.

Schizoaffective disorder is relatively rare, occurring in only 0.32 percent of the population, and is more prevalent in women (Brannon & Bienenfeld, 2012). Younger individuals with this disorder tend to have the bipolar subtype whereas older people are more likely to have the depressive subtype. As with schizophrenia, the age of onset is later for women than men. In a twin study, schizoaffective disorder and schizophrenia showed substantial familial overlap (Cardno & Owen, 2014). Similar biochemical and brain structure abnormalities have been found in individuals with schizoaffective disorder and schizophrenia (Radonic et al., 2011). Prognosis with schizoaffective disorder, including degree of social disability, is better than that seen with schizophrenia but somewhat worse than prognosis for bipolar or depressive disorders (Brannon, 2013). Treatment includes antipsychotic medication combined with mood stabilizers and individual and group psychotherapies.

Contemporary Trends and Future Directions

Two trends are gaining importance in the field of schizophrenia—the move from pessimistic views regarding outcome for the disorder to the recovery model and the early identification and treatment of individuals at high risk for developing schizophrenia. Dr. Elyn Saks, who has faced a lifelong struggle with schizophrenia, is part of the first trend. As she notes:

> Although I fought my diagnosis for years, I came to accept that I have schizophrenia and will be in treatment for the rest of my life. . . . What I refused to accept was my prognosis. . . . There are others with schizophrenia and active symptoms such as delusions and hallucinations who have significant academic and professional achievement (Saks, 2013).

Because of her success, Dr. Saks has had to contend with disbelief at her diagnosis and claims from others that she could not possibly have schizophrenia. In response, she asks doubters to "please tell that to the delusions crowding my mind." She and some of her colleagues are studying individuals with schizophrenia who are functioning well in spite of their schizophrenia diagnosis. This group includes graduate students, managers, technicians, and professionals. More than 75 percent of the group have been hospitalized from two to five times because of their illness. In spite of this, with medication and therapy, these individuals are examples of the principles of the recovery model—it is not necessary to be completely free of symptoms in order to move beyond the label of being mentally ill and work to one's potential (Bargenquast & Schweitzer, 2013; Saks, 2013).

schizoaffective disorder a condition involving the existence of both symptoms of schizophrenia and major depressive or manic symptoms

Researchers are also emphasizing the importance of early identification and treatment of individuals at risk for psychotic disorders. Although psychotic experiences are common in children and adolescents and the majority who experience these symptoms find that the symptoms disappear by age 18 (Zammit et al., 2013), there are solid reasons for pursuing early treatment. First, those with continuing psychotic symptoms have increased risk of developing psychosis or a chronic mental disorder such as depression. Additionally, many youth feel distressed by their psychotic symptoms (Kelleher et al., 2012). Interviews with at-risk young people show that they are very receptive to talking to clinicians about their symptoms, making comments such as, "You've helped. I feel I've finally gotten somewhere and I can get people to listen to me and I can talk to people whereas before I was sort of shut in. I was just sort of just sitting around with the voices pounding" (Shawyer et al., 2012, p. 120).

Many youth with these experiences are worried that they are "going crazy" and they find the opportunity to talk about their unusual experiences with a calm and receptive individual very comforting. In many cases, stressors such as bullying or isolation are identified as contributing to their symptoms and plans are made to modify these and other stressors. The teens reported that working with a therapist helped them normalize their experiences, learn to gather evidence to confront false perceptions, and look at possible explanations for their delusional or paranoid beliefs. As compared to treatment as usual, these cognitive-behavioral interventions have been successful in reducing the frequency and severity of psychotic symptoms (Byrne & Morrison, 2013; Morrison et al., 2012; van der Gaag et al. 2012). Successes such as these have encouraged researchers to focus on early identification and treatment of youth at high risk of psychosis.

chapter SUMMARY

1 What are the symptoms of schizophrenia spectrum disorers?

- Positive symptoms involve unusual thoughts or perceptions, such as delusions, hallucinations, disordered thinking, and bizarre behavior.

- Negative symptoms include an inability or decreased ability to initiate actions (avolition) or speech (alogia), express emotions, or feel pleasure.

- Cognitive symptoms include disorganized speech and problems with attention, memory, and developing plans of action.

- Grossly disorganized or abnormal psychomotor behaviors such as catatonia may occur in those with schizophrenia.

2 Is there much chance of recovery from schizophrenia?

- Prognosis for schizophrenia is variable and is associated with premorbid levels of functioning. Many individuals with schizophrenia experience minimal lasting impairment and recover enough to lead relatively productive lives.

3 What causes schizophrenia?

- The best conclusion is that genetics and environmental factors (physical, psychological, social and sociocultural) combine to cause the disorder. Biological risk factors include genetics and abnormalities in neurotransmitters or brain structures. Early negative childhood experiences, use of substances such as cannabis and amphetamines, and sociocultural stressors may interact with genetic predisposition to produce schizophrenia.

4 What treatments are currently available for schizophrenia, and are they effective?

- Schizophrenia involves both biological and psychological factors; treatment that combines medication with psychotherapy appears to hold the most promise.

- Drug therapy usually involves conventional antipsychotics or the newer atypical antipsychotics.

- The accompanying psychosocial therapy consists of either supportive counseling or behavior therapy, with an emphasis on cognitive and social skills training and facilitation of positive communication between those with schizophrenia and their family members.

5 How do other psychotic disorders differ from schizophrenia?

- Brief psychotic disorder is usually associated with a stressor and is characterized by psychotic symptoms that last less than 1 month.

- Schizophreniform disorder is characterized by psychotic symptoms that are usually associated with a stressor and that last from 1 to 6 months.

- Delusional disorder is characterized by persistent delusions and the absence of other unusual or odd behaviors.

- Schizoaffective disorder involves symptoms of schizophrenia combined with episodes of major depression or mania.

13

NEUROCOGNITIVE AND SLEEP–WAKE DISORDERS

MR. C., AGE 42, WAS IN A COMA FOR 2 WEEKS AFTER FALLING FROM A LADDER. Before his fall, he was respectful, reliable, and easygoing. After the fall, socially inappropriate and impulsive behaviors, such as getting into arguments and groping women, occurred frequently and interfered with all aspects of his life. Brain scans and neuropsychological testing documented residual brain injury, including damage to the frontal lobe of his brain, an area associated with decision making and impulse control. Although additional rehabilitation resulted in significant improvement in his cognitive skills, lasting effects from the injury prevented complete recovery (Rao et al., 2007).

Mr. C.'s life, and his family's, changed significantly due to the residual effects of his brain injury. Like many others who have experienced serious head trauma, Mr. C. qualifies for a diagnosis of **neurocognitive disorder** due to traumatic brain injury. Temporary (transient) or permanent brain malfunctions triggered by changes in brain structure or biochemical processes cause neurocognitive disorders. These structural and chemical changes result in impaired thinking, memory, or perception (the ability to recognize and interpret stimuli). Changes in behavior and emotional stability, as seen in the case of Mr. C., are also common among individuals diagnosed with a neurocognitive disorder. In fact, many individuals who sustain severe injury to the front regions of the brain display impulsive behavior, including saying or doing things without thinking. As you can imagine, these changes in functioning can be very frustrating for everyone involved.

In this chapter, we discuss the assessment of neurocognitive functioning, and then focus on how DSM-5 classifies neurocognitive disorders, as well as some of the causes for these disorders and methods of prevention, treatment, and rehabilitation. We also discuss sleep–wake disorders, many of which have a neurological basis.

1 How can we determine whether someone has a neurocognitive disorder?

2 What are the different types of neurocognitive disorders?

3 What are the causes of neurocognitive disorders?

4 What treatments are available for neurocognitive disorders?

5 What do we know about disorders that affect our sleep?

Types of Neurocognitive Disorders

Although DSM-5 defines only three major categories of neurocognitive disorders (major neurocognitive disorder, mild neurocognitive disorder, and delirium), the classification system recognizes that the symptoms of these disorders result from many disease processes or medical conditions. Therefore, medical assessment and determining specific etiology are important components of the diagnostic process. Thus, before we present the DSM-5 neurocognitive disorder categories, we discuss an important first step—assessing and documenting a person's brain function and adaptive, day-to-day mental functioning.

The Assessment of Brain Damage and Neurocognitive Functioning

Medical professionals and medical procedures play a key role in assessing and diagnosing neurocognitive disorders (Blaze, 2013). Physicians sometimes evaluate patients for brain damage during hospitalization following a traumatic event. Additionally, physicians often initiate assessment when an individual or family member is concerned about declining memory or other changes in day-to-day mental functioning.

Clinicians begin by gathering background information, paying particular attention to mental changes involving memory, thinking, or self-help skills. They carefully evaluate overall mental functioning, personality characteristics, and coping skills, as well as behaviors and emotional reactivity. They rule out sensory conditions (such as impaired hearing or vision) or emotional factors such as depression as the primary cause of the cognitive decline. Assessment may include screening of mental status, including memory and attentional skills and orientation to time and place. Additionally, psychologists may perform more extensive neuropsychological testing to pinpoint areas of cognitive difficulty or to evaluate emotional functioning. The goal is to see how a person's cognitive performance compares with others of the same gender, age range, and educational level.

Medical tests help medical professionals rule out easily treatable physical causes for the symptoms. In some cases, something as simple as a urinary tract infection can impair cognitive functioning. Similarly, blood tests can detect treatable medical conditions such as impaired thyroid or liver functioning or low levels of vitamin B_{12}. Structural and functional neurological testing procedures discussed in Chapter 3, such as an electroencephalograph (EEG), computed tomography (CT), magnetic resonance imaging (MRI), and positron emission tomography (PET), are sometimes used to assess current brain functioning, as well as to monitor progression of **brain pathology**. Physicians decide which tests to use based on the person's specific symptoms, as well as the risks and benefits of the procedures.

After reviewing all of the data from medical and psychological tests, the professionals involved have a much better understanding of probable causes of the impairment. Neuropsychological testing and standardized cognitive screening also provide objective information about the severity of cognitive difficulties. Comprehensive baseline assessments objectively monitor progress or decline in functioning. Although neuropsychological and neurological tests can assist with diagnosis, they provide limited information regarding prognosis or course of the disorder (Karceski, 2013). Even when there is no cure for a condition, early diagnosis may provide an opportunity for interventions that delay the progression of the disease or allow the individual to make decisions about future care needs before symptoms worsen.

CTE and Suicide

An autopsy of Junior Seau, a former NFL linebacker who committed suicide in 2012, revealed that he suffered from chronic traumatic encephalopathy, a condition resulting from recurrent head trauma that can lead to depression and cognitive difficulties. Autopsies on other NFL players who committed suicide have revealed similar brain pathology.

Margaret Bowles/SCG/ZUMAPRESS.com/Alamy

We will now review the three major categories of neurocognitive disorders described in DSM-5: (a) major neurocognitive disorder, (b) mild neurocognitive disorder, and (c) delirium (see Table 13.1).

Major Neurocognitive Disorder

CASE STUDY Ms. B., an 80-year-old woman, became increasingly agitated, screaming, spitting, striking staff. . . . Her speech was loud, disarticulate. . . . She repeatedly yelled "get out." Ms. B. had recently moved to an assisted-living facility due to her declining language, social, and self-care skills (Bang, Price, Prentice, & Campbell, 2009, p. 379).

Individuals diagnosed with **major neurocognitive disorder** show *significant* decline in both of the following:

- one or more areas of cognitive functioning, involving attention and focus, decision making and judgment, language, learning and memory, visual perception, or social understanding (Table 13.2); and
- the ability to independently meet the demands of daily living (this can involve more complex skills such as managing bills or medications).

The evidence from cognitive screening, neuropsychological testing, and interviews with the individual and others knowledgeable about the person's functioning must confirm that the person is demonstrating a significant skill deficit that represents a decline from prior levels of functioning. When known, clinicians specify the underlying medical circumstances causing the disorder. In the case of Ms. B., screening tests and input from her family members and caregivers revealed significant impairment involving declines in many areas of functioning. Although diagnosis of major neurocognitive disorder requires a significant deficit in only one cognitive area, deficits in multiple areas are common.

Dementia is the decline in mental functioning and self-help skills that result from a major neurocognitive disorder. People with dementia may forget the names of significant others or past events. They may also display difficulties with problem solving and impulse control. Agitation due to confusion or frustration is also common (Morris, 2012). Dementia typically has a gradual onset followed by continuing cognitive decline.

neurocognitive disorder a disorder that occurs when brain dysfunction affects thinking processes, memory, consciousness, or perception

brain pathology a dysfunction or disease of the brain

major neurocognitive disorder condition involving significant decline in independent living skills and one or more areas of cognitive functioning

dementia condition with symptoms involving deterioration in cognition and independent functioning

Table 13.1 Neurocognitive Disorders

Disorder	DSM-5 Criteria
Major neurocognitive disorder	Significant decline in one or more cognitive areas severe enough to interfere with independence
Mild neurocognitive disorder[a]	Moderate decline in performance in one or more cognitive areas; compensatory strategies may be required to maintain independence
Delirium[b]	Sudden changes in cognition, e.g., diminished awareness, impaired attention, and focus

[a]Mild and major neurocognitive disorder are sometimes earlier and later stages of the same disorder.
[b]Delirium can occur with major and mild neurocognitive disorder but can also occur independent of these conditions.
SOURCE: Based on information from APA (2013).

Table 13.2 Areas of Possible Neurocognitive Dysfunction

Cognitive Domain	Skills Affected
Complex attention	Focus, planning, working memory
Executive ability	Decision making, mental flexibility
Learning and memory	Long-term and recent memory; ability to learn new tasks
Language	Understanding and use of language
Visual-perceptual ability	Construction, visual perception
Social cognition	Recognition of emotions, understanding of social situations, behavioral self-control

SOURCE: APA (2013).

Age is the most studied and the strongest risk factor for dementia. The longer a person lives, the greater the chance of developing dementia. In the United States, approximately 15 percent of individuals over age 70 have dementia (Hurd, Martorell, Delavande, Mullen, & Langa, 2013). Because women have a longer life span than men, they are more likely to develop dementia.

Mild Neurocognitive Disorder

Individuals diagnosed with **mild neurocognitive disorder** demonstrate a *modest* decline in at least one major cognitive area (see Table 13.2). The degree of cognitive impairment is more subtle than that seen in major neurocognitive disorder. Individuals with a mild neurocognitive disorder are often able to participate in their normal activities, although they may require extra time or effort to complete complex tasks. Although accommodations to maintain independence may be required (e.g., hiring someone to manage finances), overall independent functioning is not compromised.

Mild neurocognitive disorder is often an intermediate stage between normal aging and major neurocognitive disorder or dementia. One of the major challenges in diagnosing mild neurocognitive disorder is ensuring that the symptoms are, in fact, a disorder and not the effects of physical or emotional difficulties associated with aging (Blaze, 2013). The cognitive slowing and occasional memory lapses associated with normal aging have less of an effect on daily functioning compared to the declines associated with mild or major neurocognitive disorder (see comparisons in Table 13.3).

The primary distinction between major and mild neurocognitive disorder is the severity of the decline in cognitive and independent functioning (Blaze, 2013). In fact, mild and major neurocognitive disorders are sometimes earlier and later stages of the same disease process. For example, someone in the early stages of a progressive disorder such as Alzheimer's disease may initially remain independent and display only moderate changes in cognitive functioning. As the disease progresses, however, the symptoms will increase in severity and begin to affect independent functioning. Unfortunately, the mild cognitive impairment associated with early dementia often

mild neurocognitive disorder condition involving a modest decline in at least one major cognitive area

Table 13.3 Normal Aging or Neurocognitive Disorder?

Normal Aging	Neurocognitive Disorder
Is independent in most activities, but may need occasional assistance with electronic devices, etc.	Has difficulty or requires assistance with normal, day-to-day activities
Occasionally misplaces things and locates them after searching	Places items in unusual locations; may not recall objects are missing or may accuse others of stealing
Occasionally forgets a name, word, or appointment	Frequently forgets words or recently learned information; uses incorrect words; repeats the same questions or comments
Is slower to complete mental or physical activities	Has difficulty performing familiar tasks
Shows concern about occasional forgetfulness	Is unaware or unconcerned about memory difficulties
Experiences occasional distractibility	Exercises poor judgment; fails to remember important dates or details
Continues interacting socially; occasionally feels tired	Exhibits decreasing social skills, declining social interest, and passivity; difficulty following or contributing to conversations
Occasionally gets lost	Experiences increasing disorientation and confusion; becomes lost or unaware of present location
Undergoes normal changes in mood	Has personality changes or drastic mood shifts; may seem apathetic, anxious, confused, or depressed

© Cengage Learning®

goes undiagnosed; when this occurs, those affected do not have the benefit of receiving practical information about the condition or the opportunity to plan for future care before experiencing more severe cognitive difficulties (Prince, Bryce, & Ferri, 2011).

In some situations, a diagnosis is upgraded from major to mild neurocognitive disorder; this might occur following partial recovery from a stroke or traumatic brain injury. In some cases, early diagnosis and treatment of nondegenerative conditions can result in a return to normal functioning (R. C. Petersen, 2011). Unfortunately, individuals with either major or mild neurocognitive disorder can show an abrupt decline in functioning if they experience an episode of delirium, the third type of neurocognitive disorder.

Delirium

> **CASE STUDY** Police brought an 18-year-old high school senior to the emergency department after he was picked up wandering in traffic. He was angry, agitated, and aggressive. In a rambling, disjointed manner he explained that he had been using "speed." In the emergency room he had difficulty focusing his attention, frequently needed questions repeated, and was disoriented as to time and place (Spitzer, Gibbon, Skodol, Williams, & First, 1994, p. 162).

Delirium is an acute state of confusion characterized by disorientation and impaired attentional skills. Delirium results from an underlying medical condition such as exposure to a toxin or medication or from alcohol or drug intoxication or withdrawal (APA, 2013). Although delirium can emerge in the context of a major or mild neurocognitive disorder, it often appears independently as seen in the case of the teenager using drugs. Delirium differs from mild and major neurocognitive disorder based on its core characteristics (disturbance in awareness and difficulty focusing, maintaining, or shifting attention), as well as its abrupt onset and fluctuating course. Delirium typically develops over a period of several hours or days. Symptoms can be mild or quite severe, and can be brief or last for several months. People experiencing delirium often have significant cognitive difficulties, including confusion regarding where they are or the time of day. Wandering attention, disorganized thinking, and rambling, irrelevant, or incoherent speech may be present. Psychotic symptoms such as delusions or hallucinations may also occur. Symptoms of delirium fluctuate and can range from agitation and combativeness to drowsy, unresponsive behavior.

Because delirium is caused by relatively sudden neurological dysfunction (Choi et al., 2012), treatment involves identifying the underlying cause. Possible causes include high fever; severe dehydration or malnutrition; acute infection; sensitivity to a medication or combination of medications; alcohol, drug, or inhalant intoxication; physiological withdrawal from alcohol, sedatives, or sleeping medications; or brain changes associated with a neurocognitive disorder. Delirium also develops in some sleep–wake disorders, a topic we discuss later in the chapter. Additionally, when people are ill or elderly, they are more likely to develop delirium with medical illness, severe stress, or surgical procedures. Given the multiple stressors experienced during hospitalization (illness, sleep deprivation, recovery from surgery and anesthetics), episodes of hospital-associated delirium are common, especially among older adults. Delirium associated with hospitalization is illustrated in the following case study.

delirium an acute state of confusion involving diminished awareness, disorientation, and impaired attentional skills

Hospital Delirium

Delirium is frequently experienced by individuals who are hospitalized, especially among those who are seriously ill and receiving intensive care. Here a daughter comforts her father in the critical care unit in Denver, Colorado.

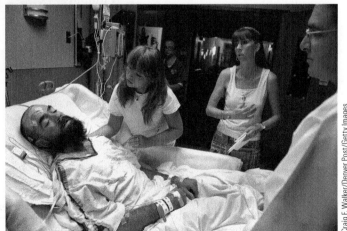

In a simulated driving experiment, individuals with dementia received more speeding tickets, ran more stop signs, and were involved in more accidents than individuals of a similar age and gender with no dementia.

SOURCE: de Simone, Kaplan, Patronas, Wassermann, & Grafman, 2006

DID YOU KNOW?

As you can see from the case of Mr. Kaplan, the severe symptoms of hospital delirium can distress loved ones, especially because there is usually no prior history of such behavior. Hospital delirium is more common in older individuals and can result in longer hospital stays, lower rates of survival, and persistent cognitive impairment (Patel, Poston, Pohlman, Hall, & Kress, 2014). Fortunately, many hospitals attempt to detect and intervene with delirium in its earliest stages to prevent these consequences.

Etiology of Neurocognitive Disorders

Neurocognitive disorders result from a variety of medical conditions. Therefore, rather than an etiological discussion using our multipath model, we focus on some of the *sources* of neurocognitive disorders. We do this because, in most cases, neurocognitive disorders involve an identified or suspected medical condition or disease process. As you will see, some neurocognitive disorders involve specific events such as stroke or head injury (Table 13.4) whereas others involve neurodegenerative conditions in which symptoms become worse over time (Table 13.5). **Neurodegeneration** refers to progressive brain damage due to neurochemical abnormalities and the death of brain cells. In contrast with the recovery that is possible in cases of stroke, traumatic brain injury, or substance abuse, individuals with neurodegenerative disorders such as Alzheimer's disease show decline in function rather than improvement. Neurodegenerative disorders vary greatly in terms of age of onset, skills affected, and course of the disorder.

As we discuss the various medical conditions associated with neurocognitive disorders, it is important to remember that even with the same underlying brain condition, a variety of factors can influence outcome. For example, people with similar brain trauma

Table 13.4 Neurodegenerative Disorders

Etiology	Characteristics
Alzheimer's disease	Declining cognitive functioning, including early, prominent memory impairment
Dementia with Lewy bodies	Visual hallucinations, fluctuating cognitive impairment, dysfunction in motor skills
Parkinson's disease	Tremor, muscle rigidity, slow movement, and possible cognitive decline
Huntington's disease	Involuntary movement, cognitive decline, and emotional instability
Frontotemporal lobar degeneration	Brain degeneration in frontal or temporal lobes that affects language and behavior
AIDS dementia complex	Cognitive decline due to HIV or AIDS

© Cengage Learning®

neurodegeneration declining brain functioning due to progressive loss of brain structure, neurochemical abnormalities, or the death of neurons may recover quite differently, depending on their personalities, their coping skills, and the availability of resources such as rehabilitation and family support systems. Additionally, the disruptions in brain function seen in neurocognitive disorders can lead to a variety of behavioral and emotional changes; factors such as apathy, depression, anxiety, or difficulty with impulse control can significantly affect recovery (H. J. Rosen & Levenson, 2009). Furthermore, insensitivity or impatience toward people with neurocognitive disorders can add to their stress and negatively affect their functioning. Indeed, stress can exacerbate symptoms that stem from the brain pathology itself. From the perspective of our multipath model, the specific brain pathology is the primary biological factor for each condition; however, psychological, social, and sociocultural factors can interact with the neurological condition to affect outcome, as shown in Figure 13.1. We now begin our discussion of medical conditions that can result in a neurocognitive disorder.

Table 13.5 Event Causes of Neurocognitive Disorders

Etiology	Characteristics
Ischemic stroke	Blockage of blood flow in the brain
Hemorrhagic stroke	Bleeding within the brain
Traumatic brain injury	Head wound or trauma
Substance abuse	Results from oxygen deprivation or other factors associated with intoxication, withdrawal, or chronic substance use

© Cengage Learning®

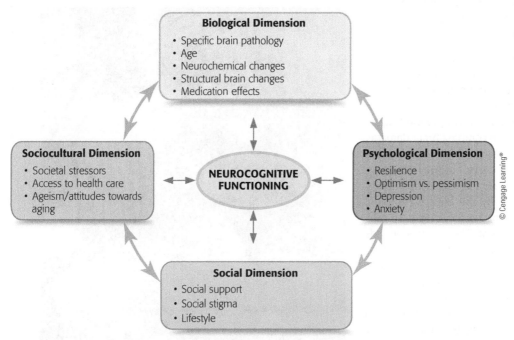

Figure 13.1

Multipath Model of Neurocognitive Disorders

The dimensions interact with specific brain pathology to produce the symptoms and pattern of recovery seen in various neurocognitive disorders.

Neurocognitive Disorder due to Traumatic Brain Injury

CASE STUDY   United States representative Gabrielle Giffords, age 40, was shot in the head at point-blank range on January 8, 2011. The bullet entered into and exited from the left side of her brain. Following surgery, Representative Giffords remained in a **medically induced coma**, a state of deep sedation that allows time for the brain to heal. Part of her skull was removed to accommodate the anticipated swelling of her brain and to prevent further damage. Giffords' purposeful movements and responsiveness to simple commands were early, encouraging signs. Although extensive therapy helped Giffords regain many language and motor skills, 1 year after the shooting she officially resigned her congressional seat, recognizing that she needed to continue to participate in specialized cognitive and physical rehabilitation in order to maximize her recovery.

medically induced coma   a deliberately induced state of deep sedation that allows the brain to rest and heal

Head Injury: What Do Soldiers Need to Know?

- A 28-year-old soldier with six separate blast-related concussions reports that he has daily headaches and difficulty performing simple mental tasks.

- After a bomb explosion hurled an Army enlistee against a wall, he continued working despite being dazed and suffering shrapnel wounds. Confusion, headaches, and problems with balance persisted for months; he later developed seizures.

- The driver of a vehicle hit by a roadside bomb did not appear to be seriously injured. However, in the months following the explosion, his speech was slurred and he had difficulty reading and completing simple tasks.
(T. C. Miller & Zwerdling, 2010)

A confidential survey conducted by the Rand Corporation (2010) revealed that almost 20 percent of veterans returning from Iraq and Afghanistan reported experiencing probable traumatic brain injury (TBI) during combat; injuries often involved blasts from hidden land mines and improvised explosive devices. These explosions cause complex brain damage, including (a) scattered brain injury resulting from shock waves that bruise the brain and damage nerve pathways, (b) penetrating injury from fragments of shrapnel or flying debris, and (c) injury from being thrown by the blast (Champion, Holcomb, & Young, 2009). Just what are the long-term risks from head injuries sustained in combat? The answer depends on many factors, including the source, location, and intensity of the injury, as well as interventions following the injury. Civilians treated for TBI are encouraged to allow the brain to rest to facilitate full recovery. However, in combat situations, mild head injuries are often not recognized, documented, and treated; soldiers often return immediately to combat (Murray et al., 2005).

Soldiers may not be receiving quality, evidence-based care for their brain injuries in a timely manner (T. C. Miller & Zwerdling, 2010). Additionally, because the long-term consequences of brain injury resulting from blast exposure are unknown, some researchers wonder if soldiers exposed to multiple blast injuries are at risk for degenerative neurocognitive conditions such as *chronic traumatic encephalopathy* (Rosenfeld et al., 2013). Researchers also stress the importance of intervening with the symptoms of depression and post-traumatic stress disorder that frequently occur in military personnel who have experienced a TBI (Vasterling et al., 2012).

Should standard recommendations for TBI for civilians also apply to soldiers? What protocols might be beneficial to ensure that soldiers in combat receive appropriate care for TBI sustained in battle?

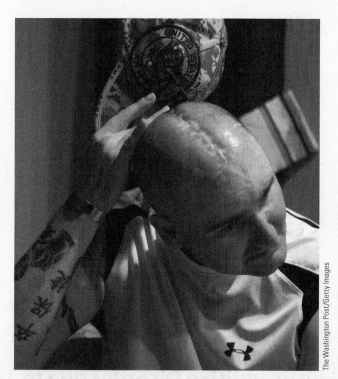

The Washington Post/Getty Images

John Barnes incurred a traumatic brain injury in Iraq when mortar shrapnel entered his brain. Due to extensive damage involving his frontal lobe, he continues to exhibit impulsive behavior and lack of inhibition.

CASE STUDY At age 53, H. N. sustained multiple injuries, including mild bleeding in the brain, when he was hit by a car. Although his initial delirium subsided, other behavioral changes, including pervasive apathy punctuated by angry outbursts, persisted for months. Subsequent MRI scans revealed damage in the orbitofrontal cortex, an area of the brain involved in emotion and decision making (adapted from Namiki et al., 2008, p. 475).

Recovery from Traumatic Brain Injury

Gabrielle Giffords waves to the delegates at the 2012 Democratic National Convention. Giffords captivated the audience by reciting the Pledge of Allegiance in a halting but strong voice while holding her right hand over her heart with the help of her stronger left hand.

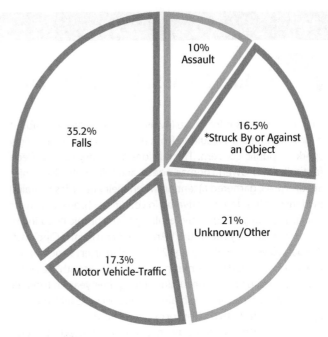

Figure 13.2

Leading Causes of Traumatic Brain Injury

*These data do not include injuries that occurred during military deployment.

SOURCE: Faul, Xu, Wald, & Coronado (2010).

CASE STUDY P. J. M., a 38-year-old woman, remained in a coma for several weeks after a bicycle accident. After regaining consciousness, she had severe short- and long-term memory deficits (including no recall of the year before her accident) and difficulty using the right side of her body. Despite some improvement, P. J. M. remains unable to drive or return to her work as a university professor (adapted from Rathbone, Moulin, & Conway, 2009, pp. 407–408).

Traumatic brain injury (TBI) can result from a bump, jolt, blow, or physical wound to the head. As you can see from the cases presented, the degree of impairment and course of recovery associated with a neurocognitive disorder due to TBI can vary significantly. Each year in the United States, approximately 1.7 million people receive emergency room care for head injury; TBI occurs most frequently in young children, older adolescents, and older adults. Approximately 2 percent of the population has a disability related to TBI (APA, 2013). Additionally, head injury contributes to almost one third of injury-related deaths (Faul, Xu, Wald, & Coronado, 2010). Falls, vehicle accidents, and striking or being struck by objects are the leading causes of TBI (Figure 13.2).

A neurocognitive disorder due to TBI is diagnosed when there is persisting cognitive impairment due to a brain injury; additionally, diagnosis requires that the person experienced loss of consciousness, amnesia, disorientation, or confusion following the event or received neurological testing that documented brain dysfunction (APA, 2013). The effects of TBI can be temporary or permanent and can result in mild to severe cognitive impairment. You have probably heard stories about people who have made a remarkable recovery following TBI. For example, the much-publicized progress of Gabrielle Giffords after her injury reinforces the capacity for brain recovery. In her

traumatic brain injury (TBI)
a physical wound or internal injury to the brain

Just How Safe Are Contact Sports?

How important is it for those involved in sports to know about concussion? Injuries resulting from team sports are increasingly sparking public concern. The suicides of Pennsylvania college football player Owen Thomas, age 21, and NFL linebacker Junior Seau, age 43, garnered attention when their autopsies revealed evidence of the degenerative brain condition chronic traumatic encephalopathy (CTE), likely resulting from chronic head injury incurred while playing football. An autopsy on former Cincinnati Bengals player Chris Henry, age 26, who died after falling out of a truck, also revealed CTE. Amazingly, none of these athletes were ever diagnosed with a concussion during their years in football. How could such significant brain damage occur at such a young age, particularly with no history of concussion?

A groundbreaking study involving a high school football team (Talavage et al., 2010) shed some light on the issue. Researchers compared cognitive testing and brain imaging of the players (obtained before, during, and after the football season) with data regarding the frequency and intensity of head impact during the football season (obtained by equipping the players' helmets with special impact-monitoring sensors). As expected, players who had experienced a concussion during the season showed MRI changes and related cognitive declines. However, so did half of the other players; data from the impact-monitoring sensors revealed that the players who experienced brain changes but no recorded concussions had sustained *multiple* impacts during the season. For example, one affected player had experienced 1,600 significant head

blows during the season. A similarly designed study involving college varsity football and ice hockey players wearing instrumented helmets revealed that those with more measured physical contact and head impact showed deterioration in performance on tests involving verbal learning and reaction time. The researchers concluded that repetitive head impact throughout a single sports season has the potential to impair learning in college athletes (McAllister et al., 2012).

Professional medical organizations have created guidelines for school-age athletes suspected of having a concussion. Recommendations include immediate removal from play and restriction of physical activity for at least 7–10 days. Return to play should occur only after all acute symptoms subside and a health professional knowledgeable about head injury agrees that it is safe to resume athletic activities (American Academy of Neurology, 2013). If followed, these guidelines could significantly increase safety for athletes. Careful monitoring of athletes with possible neurological damage (e.g., headache, confusion, poor balance, speech, vision, or hearing difficulties) is certainly a step in the right direction. Unfortunately, it is also recognized that some athletes deny concussion symptoms so they can continue playing even when they know the risks (Strand, 2013). Are there adequate protections in place for those who experience a blow to the head but show no symptoms of a concussion? Are the potential dangers of head injuries in sports such as basketball, soccer, baseball, hockey, or cycling receiving sufficient attention?

DID YOU KNOW?

Individuals given a simulated driving test after receiving emergency care for a mild TBI demonstrated significantly reduced response time and diminished hazard perception; this suggests that it may be hazardous to drive immediately after sustaining a TBI.

SOURCE: Preece, Horswill, & Geffen, 2010

case, immediate intervention, an excellent rehabilitation program, personal resilience, and social support all played a key role in her progress. Similar conditions facilitated the recovery of news anchor Bob Woodruff, who sustained a life-threatening brain injury resulting from a roadside bomb explosion while he was covering the war in Iraq. After surgery, he spent 36 days in a medically induced coma. He underwent extensive rehabilitation and has since returned to work. In both cases, prompt medical attention and surgery played an important role in survival and recovery.

A far different outcome resulted from what initially appeared to be a minor head injury sustained by actress Natasha Richardson. Her first symptom, a headache, did not appear until almost an hour after she hit the back of her head during a ski lesson; however, unrecognized neurological injury (i.e., bleeding between the skull and brain) resulted in her rapid and unexpected death. Sometimes referred to as the "talk and die" syndrome, such an injury can have severe, even fatal, consequences. All of these stories highlight the importance of immediate medical intervention when a head injury occurs.

As seen in the case studies, the severity, duration, and symptoms of TBI can vary significantly depending on the extent and location of the brain damage, as well as the person's age. Symptoms can include headaches, disorientation, confusion, memory loss, deficits in attention, poor concentration, fatigue, and irritability, as well as emotional and behavioral changes. Generally, the greater the damage to brain tissue or cells, the more impaired the functioning.

Acute head injuries include concussions, contusions, and cerebral lacerations. **Concussion**, the most common form of traumatic brain injury, refers to trauma-induced changes in brain functioning, typically caused by a blow to the head. The injury affects the functioning of neurons and causes disorientation or loss of consciousness. Symptoms of concussion can include headache, dizziness, nausea, impaired coordination, and sensitivity to light. Following a concussion, physicians recommend resting, minimizing stimulation or mental challenge, and refraining from any activity that can produce subsequent head injury (Harmon et al., 2013). Symptoms of a concussion are usually temporary, lasting no longer than a few weeks; however, in some cases they persist for much longer. Amnesia for events prior to a concussion appears to be a strong predictor of severity of impairment following a concussion (Dougan, Horswill, & Geffen, 2014). It is estimated that U.S. children and adults incur almost 4 million concussions per year while involved in competitive sports or recreational activities; however, approximately half of these concussions go unreported. Having one concussion increases the likelihood of sustaining another concussion and requiring a longer period of recovery (Eisenberg, Andrea, Meehan, & Mannix, 2013; Harmon et al., 2013).

A **cerebral contusion** (bruising of the brain) results when the brain strikes the skull with sufficient force to cause bruising. Unlike the disruption in cellular functioning seen in a concussion, contusions involve actual tissue damage in the areas bruised. Symptoms are similar to those seen with a concussion. Contusions and concussions commonly occur together. When someone receives a blow to the head, brain injury often occurs both at the site of impact and on the opposite side of the brain (i.e., the initial blow causes the brain to move and hit the other side of the skull). Neuroimaging can detect brain damage and monitor swelling. Unfortunately, brain imaging cannot always detect the more subtle changes caused by damage to neurons (a concussion), mild bruising of brain tissue (a contusion), or mild bleeding within the brain.

A **cerebral laceration** is an open head injury in which brain tissue is torn, pierced, or ruptured, usually from a skull fracture or an object that has penetrated the skull. As with a contusion, damage is localized and immediate medical care focuses on reducing bleeding and preventing swelling. As with other brain injuries, symptoms of cerebral lacerations can be quite serious, depending on the extent of damage to the brain tissue, the amount of hemorrhaging or swelling within the brain, and the medical care received. Severe brain trauma can have long-term effects, and, as you saw in the introductory case studies, recovery does not always ensure a return to prior levels of functioning. Along with the physical or cognitive difficulties produced by the injury, sleep difficulties and emotional symptoms commonly associated with TBI (e.g., depression, anxiety, irritability, or apathy) can also affect recovery (Bryan, 2013).

A type of brain injury receiving considerable media attention, **chronic traumatic encephalopathy (CTE)**, is a progressive, degenerative condition diagnosed when autopsy reveals diffuse brain damage resulting from ongoing head trauma. CTE occurs in individuals who have had multiple episodes of head injury, such as athletes or those who serve in the military (Baugh et al., 2012). CTE is associated with psychological symptoms such as depression and poor impulse control, as well as a significantly increased risk of dementia. Symptoms associated with different stages of CTE include the following (McKee et al., 2013):

Stage I—headache and loss of attention and concentration
Stage II—depression, explosive outbursts, and short-term memory loss
Stage III—cognitive impairment, including difficulties with planning and impulse control
Stage IV—dementia, word-finding difficulty, and aggression

concussion trauma-induced changes in brain functioning, typically caused by a blow to the head

cerebral contusion bruising of the brain, often resulting from a blow that causes the brain to forcefully strike the skull

cerebral laceration open head injury in which brain tissue is torn, pierced, or ruptured

chronic traumatic encephalopathy (CTE) a progressive, degenerative condition involving brain damage resulting from multiple episodes of head trauma

Similar to the neurodegenerative disorders we discuss later in the chapter, the neurological damage associated with CTE progresses slowly over decades, eventually resulting in dementia.

Vascular Neurocognitive Disorders

CASE STUDY Kate McCarron's stroke symptoms started on a Friday, with a little tingle in her leg. On Saturday, McCarron, age 46, felt uncharacteristically tired. Sunday she seemed a bit under the weather. Monday, her left side felt numb. Tuesday morning, she couldn't move her left side. She was rushed to the hospital. A small blood vessel leading to a deep part of her brain was closing, choking off a region of her brain that controlled motion (A. Dworkin, 2009).

Vascular neurocognitive disorders can result from a one-time **cardiovascular** event such as a stroke or from unnoticed, ongoing disruptions to blood flow within the brain. Predominant cognitive symptoms of vascular neurocognitive disorder involve complex attention, information processing, planning, and problem solving. Changes in motivation, personality, or mood are also common. Vascular neurocognitive disorders often begin with **atherosclerosis**, clogging of the arteries resulting from a buildup of plaque. This **plaque** (composed of fat, cholesterol, and other substances) accumulates over time, thickens, and narrows artery walls; the result is reduced blood flow to the brain and other organs.

A **stroke** occurs when there is an obstruction in blood flow to or within the brain; the sudden halt of blood flow results in death of neurons and loss of brain function. There are two major types of strokes: *hemorrhagic strokes* and *ischemic strokes*. A **hemorrhagic stroke**, unrelated to plaque buildup, occurs when a blood vessel bursts and bleeds into the brain. An **ischemic stroke** is caused by a clot or severe narrowing of the arteries; approximately 87 percent of strokes are ischemic (Go et al., 2013). A **transient ischemic attack (TIA)** is a "mini-stroke" or "warning stroke" resulting from temporary blockage of blood vessels in the brain; symptoms often last for only a few minutes. Seeking medical attention for transient stroke symptoms is important because these episodes often precede an ischemic stroke (Gupta, Farrell, & Mittal, 2014). When people seek emergency medical care for stroke symptoms, medications can dissolve the clot and prevent serious brain damage. In both ischemic and hemorrhagic strokes, brain damage occurs when brain cells die due to lack of blood, oxygen, and nutrients (Figure 13.3).

Strokes can occur at any age; in fact, approximately one third of those people who experience a stroke each year are under age 65 (Hall, Levant, & DeFrances, 2012). Immediate medical attention and careful management of neurological complications from stroke (e.g., bleeding or swelling within the brain) reduces mortality and improves prognosis (Balami, Chen, & Grunwald, 2011). However, stroke remains the fourth leading cause of death in the United States; stroke risk and mortality from stroke are particularly high for African Americans (Go et al., 2013).

Those younger than 50 years of age who experience a stroke often have risk factors such as hypertension, diabetes, high cholesterol, smoking, or exposure to secondhand smoke (Balci, Utku, Asil, & Celik, 2011). Cigarette smoking is a major contributor in about 1 in 4 strokes; however, when young adults experience a stroke, the contribution of smoking approaches 50 percent. An analysis of worldwide data revealed that men and women who smoke have a 60–80 percent increase in stroke risk; the risk of having a deadly hemorrhagic stroke is particularly high for women who smoke (Peters, Huxley, & Woodward, 2013). Use of oral contraceptives (i.e., "the pill") can increase stroke risk, particularly when combined with smoking (Raval, Borges-Garcia, Diaz, Sick, & Bramlett, 2013). Worldwide data regarding stroke risk point to stress, poor eating and sedentary lifestyles, and heavy or binge drinking as other major contributors to stroke (O'Donnell et al., 2010). Additionally, depression is associated with a 34 percent increase

vascular neurocognitive disorder condition involving decline in cognitive skills due to reduced blood flow to the brain

cardiovascular pertaining to the heart and blood vessels

atherosclerosis clogging of the arteries resulting from a buildup of plaque

plaque sticky material (composed of fat, cholesterol, and other substances) that builds up on the walls of veins or arteries

stroke a sudden halting of blood flow to a portion of the brain, leading to brain damage

hemorrhagic stroke a stroke involving leakage of blood into the brain

ischemic stroke a stroke due to reduced blood supply caused by a clot or severe narrowing of the arteries supplying blood to the brain

transient ischemic attack (TIA) a "mini-stroke" resulting from temporary blockage of arteries

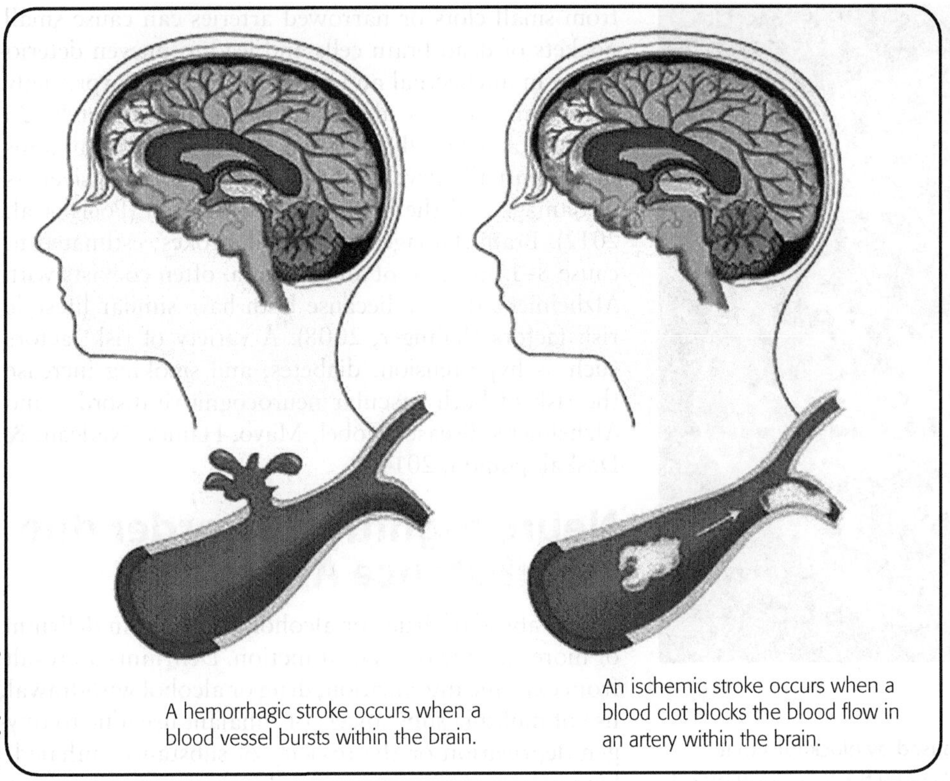

Figure 13.3

Types of Stroke
Ischemic strokes resulting from a blocked artery account for approximately 87 percent of all strokes.

A hemorrhagic stroke occurs when a blood vessel bursts within the brain.

An ischemic stroke occurs when a blood clot blocks the blood flow in an artery within the brain.

in risk for stroke; it is possible that unhealthy lifestyle factors associated with both disorders are the cause of this increased risk (Pan, Sun, Okereke, Rexrode, & Hu, 2011).

Stroke is not only a leading cause of death but also a significant cause of disability (J. A. Young & Tolentino, 2011). Prompt medical intervention decreases the chances of death and vastly improves prognosis (Saver et al., 2013); this underscores the importance of recognizing signs of a stroke (Table 13.6). Because many people do not recognize stroke symptoms (e.g., slurred speech, blurry vision, or numbness on one side of the body), or hesitate to treat these symptoms as an emergency, public health campaigns continue to stress the importance of immediate intervention. Additionally, many are unaware that women may display unique stroke symptoms, including sudden nausea, hiccups, facial pain, overall weakness, and shortness of breath (National Stroke Association, 2014).

Stroke survivors who do not receive immediate intervention often require long-term care because residual physical and psychological symptoms impair independent functioning. Strokes damaging the left side of the brain typically affect speech and language proficiency, as well as physical movement on the right half of the body. Strokes occurring within the right hemisphere can increase impulsivity and impair judgment, short-term memory, and motor movement on the left side of the body. Visual problems (blurry or double vision) may occur in those with a right-hemisphere stroke. Cognitive, behavioral, and emotional changes that occur following stroke depend not only on the extent of brain damage but also on the individual's personality, emotional resilience, and coping skills. Some stroke survivors experience frustration and depression, whereas others actively and optimistically participate in therapeutic rehabilitation activities.

A series of small asymptomatic (symptomless) strokes due to small bleeds in the brain (microbleeds) or a decrease in blood flow

DID YOU KNOW?

In a longitudinal study of over 10,000 middle-aged women, depressed women had a 2.4 times increased risk of stroke compared to those who were not depressed.

SOURCE: Jackson & Mishra, 2013

Table 13.6 Stroke Symptoms: Know When to Act

Emergency medical attention immediately following the onset of stroke symptoms can significantly improve outcomes for both ischemic and hemorrhagic strokes.

- Numbness or weakness, including drooping of facial features or weakness on one side of the body
- Confusion or difficulty understanding questions or conversation
- Slurred or incoherent speech
- Vision difficulty in one or both eyes
- Sudden dizziness, loss of balance, or difficulty with coordination
- Severe headache with no known cause

© Cengage Learning®

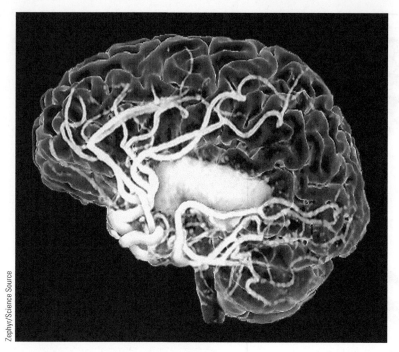

Results of a Stroke on the Brain

The brain damage associated with a stroke is caused by blockages that cause an interruption in the brain's blood supply or by the leakage of blood through blood vessel walls. Here, a three-dimensional magnetic resonance angiogram scan shows a human brain after a hemorrhagic stroke. Major arteries are shown in white. The central region in yellow is an area in which bleeding occurred.

from small clots or narrowed arteries can cause small pockets of dead brain cells and lead to uneven deterioration in intellectual and physical abilities. Surprisingly, these mini-strokes may occur in approximately 25 percent of older adults (Blum et al., 2012). Symptoms may eventually develop depending on the extensiveness of damage and the brain regions involved (Poels et al., 2012). Brain damage from small strokes, estimated to cause 8–15 percent of all dementia, often coexists with Alzheimer's disease because both have similar lifestyle risk factors (Jellinger, 2008). A variety of risk factors such as hypertension, diabetes, and smoking increase the risk of both vascular neurocognitive disorder and Alzheimer's disease (Nobel, Mayo, Hanley, Nadeau, & Daskalopoulou, 2014).

Neurocognitive Disorder due to Substance Abuse

Use or abuse of drugs or alcohol can result in delirium or more chronic brain dysfunction. Delirium can result from extreme intoxication, drug or alcohol withdrawal, use of multiple substances, or inhalant use (due to oxygen deprivation or the toxicity of substances inhaled). Symptoms consistent with mild neurocognitive disorder are common in individuals with a history of heavy substance use and those who continue using after age 50 (APA, 2013). The symptoms usually continue during initial abstinence, but may improve with time. For example, many of the deficits associated with alcohol-induced neurocognitive disorder require a full year of abstinence before they fully subside (Stavro, Pelletier, & Potvin, 2013). Older individuals and chronic substance users recover less brain function during abstinence (Yeh, Gazdzinski, Durazzo, Sjöstrand, & Meyerhoff, 2007).

Neurocognitive Disorder due to Alzheimer's Disease

CASE STUDY Elizabeth R., a 46-year-old woman diagnosed with Alzheimer's disease, is trying to cope with her increasing memory difficulties. She writes notes to herself and rehearses conversations, anticipating what might be said. After reading only a few sentences, she forgets what she has read. She sometimes forgets where the bathroom is located in her own house and is depressed by the realization that she is becoming a burden to her family (M. Clark et al., 1984, p. 60).

Alzheimer's disease (AD)
dementia involving memory loss and other declines in cognitive and adaptive functioning

Alzheimer's disease (AD), the most prevalent neurodegenerative disorder, affects more than 5 million Americans. It is estimated that by 2030 over 7 million adults in the United States will have AD, with the prevalence reaching 13.8 million by 2050 (Hebert, Weuve, Scherr, & Evans, 2013). Although AD can strike adults in midlife, risk of the disease significantly increases with age; those who are 65 have a 1 percent risk, whereas those who are 95 have a 40–50 percent risk (X. P. Wang & Ding, 2008). The prevalence and the severity of AD symptoms are greater among women than

Can We Prevent Brain Damage?

Given the serious consequences of neurocognitive disorders, you may wonder: "Is there anything that can be done to reduce the chances of experiencing a stroke, suffering a head injury, or developing a degenerative disorder?" The answer is yes, especially when prevention efforts begin at an early age. For example, the use of car seats and seat belts can help prevent head injury in children, as can the use of safe practices and properly fitting protective headgear during sports (Rivara et al., 2011). Similarly, allowing the brain to rest and recover after a blow to the head or a concussion can reduce the likelihood of long-term brain damage (American Academy of Neurology, 2013).

Lifestyle changes focused on maintaining a healthy cardiovascular system such as exercising regularly and eating a well-balanced diet also reduce the risk of both stroke and dementia (Lövdén, Xu, & Wangy, 2013). Varied exercise of higher intensity or longer duration enhances neuroprotective effects and helps prevent cognitive decline in older adults (Kirk-Sanchez & McGough, 2014). A healthy lifestyle protects against dementia not only by reducing risk factors but also by promoting neurogenesis, the formation of new brain cells (Lazarov, Mattson, Peterson, Pimplika, & van Praag, 2010). Prevention efforts focus on modifiable risk factors (e.g., avoiding smoking and excessive consumption of salt, sugar, saturated fats, and alcohol), because these unhealthy behaviors account for almost 90 percent of the risk of stroke (Hankey, 2011) and much of the risk of dementia (L. D. Baker et al., 2010). Preventing or treating hypertension is a key modifiable risk factor associated with cognitive decline and dementia (Gąsecki, Kwarciany, Nyka, & Narkiewicz, 2013). Regular participation in cognitively stimulating activities across the life span (especially during early and middle adulthood) is also associated with fewer pathological brain changes (less beta-amyloid) later in life (Landau et al., 2012). Prevention efforts really can make a difference in maintaining brain health.

Kevin Peterson/Photodisc/Getty Images

men, but the reasons for this difference are not fully understood (Mielke, Vemuri, & Rocca, 2014).

AD usually begins gradually and involves a pattern of progressive cognitive decline. Using the newest guidelines, a clinician can diagnose mild or major neurocognitive disorder due to AD by incorporating biological data such as genetic testing into the diagnostic process or by looking only at evidence of declines in cognitive and self-help skills (Howe, 2013). Although the main feature of AD is memory impairment, clinicians avoid diagnosing AD based solely on memory difficulties. Clear physiological indicators (e.g., evidence of genetic mutations or brain changes associated with AD) are required to predict which patients with mild memory impairment will likely develop AD (Ballard, Corbett, & Jones, 2011). Individuals seeking treatment for impaired memory develop AD at a rate of 12–15 percent per year; however, individuals with memory impairment in the general population (i.e., not just those who seek treatment) are less likely to develop AD, and in some cases show a reversal of symptoms (APA, 2013).

Characteristics of Alzheimer's Disease

Impaired memory and learning associated with AD develop quite gradually, followed by a progressive decline in cognitive and behavioral functioning. Unfortunately, the physiological processes that produce AD begin years before the onset of symptoms (Howe, 2013). As early symptoms—memory dysfunction, irritability, and cognitive impairment—gradually worsen, other symptoms such as social withdrawal, depression, apathy, delusions, impulsive behaviors, and neglect of personal hygiene often appear. Some individuals with AD become loving and childlike, whereas others become increasingly agitated and combative. At present, no curative or disease-reversing interventions exist for AD.

As we saw in the case of Elizabeth, deterioration of memory is one of the most disturbing symptoms for those who have AD and for their family members. Initially, they may forget appointments, phone numbers, and addresses, but as AD progresses, they lose track of the time of day, have trouble remembering recent and past events, and forget who they are. But even when memory is gone, emotions remain. In fact, researchers have found that although those with AD may forget details of an emotional event (such as the plot of a sad movie), the emotions of the experience continue (Feinstein, Duff, & Tranela, 2010).

Other Factors Affecting Memory Loss

A common concern of older adults is whether occasional memory lapses are signs of AD. Memory loss occurs for a variety of reasons. In some cases, it is an early symptom of AD. However, occasional lapses of memory are common in healthy adults. As we age, neurons are gradually lost, our brains become smaller, and we process information more slowly. Thus, occasional difficulty with memory or learning new material is normal. Many older adults experience only minimal decline in cognitive function; this is because, as we age, we continue to generate new brain cells and the brain reorganizes itself in a way that maximizes cognitive efficiency (Moran, Symmonds, Dolan, & Friston, 2014).

Memory loss and confusion can also result from temporary conditions such as infections or reactions to prescription drugs. Medications sometimes interact with one another or with certain foods to produce side effects, including memory impairment. In addition, various physical conditions and nutritional deficiencies can produce memory loss and symptoms resembling dementia. This type of memory loss usually disappears once the medical condition is diagnosed and treated.

Alzheimer's Disease and the Brain

Individuals with AD exhibit a variety of changes in the brain. First, those with end-stage AD have marked shrinkage of brain tissue due to the widespread death of neurons. Second, autopsies of people with AD reveal two abnormal structures—neurofibrillary tangles

Did Alzheimer's Disease Affect His Presidency?

Former president Ronald Reagan was diagnosed with Alzheimer's disease at age 83. Many believe he began to show symptoms of the disease, such as memory difficulties, while still in office. Five years prior to the diagnosis, Reagan was treated for a traumatic head injury that occurred when he was thrown from a horse. Some have speculated that this head injury accelerated the progression of his Alzheimer's disease.

AP Images/Ron Schumacher

and beta-amyloid plaque. Both affect metabolic processes and health of neurons in the hippocampus and in areas of the cortex associated with memory and cognition. **Neurofibrillary tangles**, found inside nerve cells, are comprised of twisted fibers of *tau*, a protein that helps transport nutrients in healthy cells; in those with AD, biochemical alterations in tau proteins result in cellular dysfunction. **Beta-amyloid plaques** develop when beta-amyloid proteins aggregate in the spaces between neurons (see Figure 13.4). Neurofibrillary tangles and beta-amyloid plaques are associated with decreased neurogenesis, as well as inflammation, loss of cellular connections, and other changes that eventually result in the death of neurons and shrinking of the brain (Lazarov, Mattson, Peterson, Pimplika, & van Praag, 2010).

Brain changes associated with AD appear years before dementia develops (Bernard et al., 2014). First, beta-amyloid deposits appear; as these structures multiply, neurodegeneration begins. Next, mild cognitive symptoms develop, usually followed by progressive cognitive decline and impairment in daily functioning (Blaze, 2013). We are learning more about this process due to recent advances in positron emission tomography (PET) imaging involving tracers that attach to beta-amyloid proteins, thus allowing the detection and monitoring of beta-amyloid plaques in the living brain (Johnson et al., 2013). Additionally, new fluorescent compounds are allowing PET imaging of tau protein clusters and neurofibrillary tangles in the brains of people with AD and other neurodegenerative disorders (Mathis & Klunk, 2013). It appears that tau creates brain changes more rapidly than beta-amyloid plaques and that beta-amyloid plaques somehow accelerate the spread of tau within the brain (Jack & Holtzman, 2013).

It is still not possible to definitively diagnose AD before autopsy, although a person may have multiple indicators suggestive of AD (e.g., memory loss, brain scans showing brain shrinkage). Although the monitoring of tau and beta-amyloid proteins in cerebrospinal fluid (CSF), the liquid that surrounds the brain and spinal cord, and the detection of beta-amyloid plaques via PET imaging are used for research, these biological markers are not sufficiently sensitive or accurate to make an AD diagnosis (Blaze, 2013).

Etiology of Alzheimer's Disease

A number of factors increase the risk of AD, including both hereditary and environmental influences. We are learning more about genetic influences on AD. Our bodies produce a chemical, apolipoprotein E (ApoE), that helps clear beta-amyloid by-products from the brain. The gene associated with this process (the APOE gene) has three variants (alleles). One of these variants, the e4 version of the APOE gene, appears to decrease production of ApoE thus increasing risk for AD. Although the APOE-e4 allele increases the likelihood of developing AD and contributes to approximately 25 percent of all AD, people with this genotype do not necessarily develop AD; however, risk is further increased when the APOE-e4 allele is inherited from both parents.

Researchers have also identified three rare genetic mutations (deterministic genes) that result in *autosomal-dominant Alzheimer's disease;* these genes are responsible for the multigenerational inheritance of early-onset AD in some families (Pilotto, Padovani, & Borroni, 2013). Those affected by these mutations usually develop AD in midlife, sometimes as early as the mid-30s. People who inherit these mutations appear to produce large quantities of a stickier version of the beta- amyloid protein that exits more slowly from the brain (Potter et al., 2013). One particular deterministic genetic variant, the TREM2 gene, appears to double the rate at which neurons are lost in AD (Guerreiro et al., 2013). Genetic association studies involving AD are shedding light on other genetic pathways and possible biological mechanisms underlying the

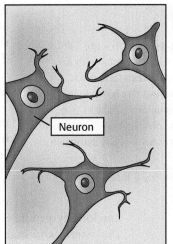

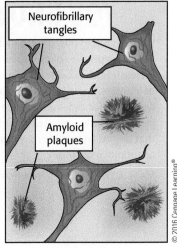

Normal brain   Alzheimer's brain

© 2016 Cengage Learning®

Figure 13.4

Brain Changes Associated with Alzheimer's Disease

Autopsies of the brains of individuals with Alzheimer's Disease reveal beta-amyloid plaques in the spaces between neurons and neurofibrillary tangles inside nerve cells. These brain changes begin years before symptoms of the disease appear.

DID YOU KNOW?

Among families with a genetic mutation responsible for early-onset Alzheimer's disease, changes in the brain and nervous system have been detected in individuals as young as 18 years of age.

SOURCE: Reiman et al., 2012

neurofibrillary tangles twisted fibers of tau protein found inside the nerve cells of individuals with Alzheimer's disease

beta-amyloid plaques clumps of beta-amyloid proteins found in the spaces between neurons in individuals with Alzheimer's disease

Various studies have found that depression (especially multiple episodes of depression) is associated with an increased risk of both Alzheimer's disease and other dementias. Some researchers believe this is because depression and dementia have similar risk factors (e.g., poor diet, little exercise); others contend that depression that begins later in life may represent an early symptom of cognitive decline.

SOURCE: G. Li et al., 2011; Spira, Rebok, Stone, Kramer, & Yaffe, 2012

Dementia with Lewy bodies (DLB) dementia involving visual hallucinations, cognitive fluctuations, and atypical movements

Alzheimer's Disease

As can be seen in these PET scans comparing brain activity between someone with Alzheimer's disease and a healthy control, Alzheimer's disease causes degeneration and death of nerve cells and significantly reduces metabolic activity in the brain. The associated brain dysfunction results in symptoms such as memory loss, disorientation, and personality change.

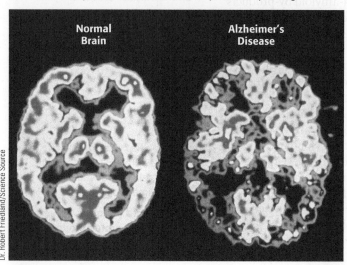

disorder (Medway & Morgan, 2014). Interestingly, some carriers of genes associated with AD have shown neurological abnormalities in brain pathways associated with AD but no overt symptoms (Lampert, Choudhury, Hostage, Petrella, & Doraiswamy, 2013). As you might imagine, following the progression of biomarkers in asymptomatic individuals is of great interest to researchers.

Lifestyle variables associated with stroke and cardiovascular disease also increase risk of AD. Researchers interested in determining how dietary intake affects beta-amyloid studied older adult volunteers who were randomly assigned to consume a diet either high or low in saturated fat; the high-fat diet resulted in increases in circulating beta-amyloid and reductions of ApoE, the chemical that helps clear the brain of beta-amyloid by-products (Hanson et al., 2013). Conversely, low levels of "bad" (LDL) cholesterol and high levels of "good" (HDL) cholesterol are associated with fewer beta-amyloid deposits in the brain (Reed et al., 2013). Another environmental factor we have already mentioned as associated with AD is traumatic brain injury (APA, 2013).

There is also a link between sleep and the amount of beta-amyloid in the brain. Older adult volunteers who report poor sleep quality or quantity had more beta-amyloid deposits in the brain compared to those reporting adequate sleep (Spira et al., 2013). Additionally, in a group of asymptomatic individuals involved in an ongoing study, those with evidence of beta-amyloid abnormalities had the poorest documented sleep quality (Ju et al., 2013). These findings are consistent with data suggesting that beta amyloid and other proteins are cleared from the brain during sleep. Researchers are attempting to determine if the buildup of beta-amyloid plaque disrupts sleep, or if loss of sleep contributes to the development of beta-amyloid plaque. Efforts to better understand the genes and biological processes associated with AD continue, with the hope that someday we will be able to prevent or treat this devastating disease (Bateman et al., 2011).

Neurocognitive Disorder due to Dementia with Lewy Bodies

Dementia with Lewy bodies (DLB), the second most common form of dementia, results in cognitive decline combined with the development of unusual movements similar to those seen in Parkinson's disease, a disorder we discuss later in the chapter. Characteristics of DLB include (a) significant fluctuations in attention and alertness (e.g., staring spells and periods of extreme drowsiness); (b) recurrent, detailed visual hallucinations; (c) impaired mobility (frequent falls, a shuffling gait, muscular rigidity, and slowed movement) that occurs after the onset of cognitive decline; and (d) sleep disturbance, including acting out dreams. Depression is common among those with DLB. Compared to the cognitive deficits associated with AD, memory and language skills are usually more intact in those with DLB, whereas visual-spatial tasks (such a reproducing a drawing) are more impaired. Although DLB tends to develop more rapidly than AD, the two diseases have a similar survival period of approximately 8 years after diagnosis (Lewy Body Dementia Association, 2014).

Individuals with DLB have brain cell irregularities, called Lewy bodies, which result from the buildup of abnormal proteins in the nuclei of neurons. These unique cell structures (named after Frederick Lewy, who first discovered them) are also present in Parkinson's disease. When Lewy bodies develop in the cortex, they deplete the neurotransmitter acetylcholine, resulting in the perceptual, cognitive, and behavioral symptoms seen in DLB and in later stages of Parkinson's disease. Lewy bodies in the brain stem cause the depletion of dopamine and the motor dysfunction seen in Parkinson's disease and later stages of DLB.

The incidence of DLB increases with age and occurs more frequently in men (Savica et al., 2013). DLB may account for up to 30 percent of all dementias; however, prevalence data may be inaccurate because of the overlap in symptoms with other neurodegenerative disorders and because DLB can only be confirmed by autopsy (National Institute of Neurological Disorders and Stroke, 2014). Additionally, professionals who are not dementia specialists are often less familiar with DLB. Although researchers have not yet identified any genes associated with DLB, the disorder occurs more frequently in some families (Nervi et al., 2011).

Neurocognitive Disorder due to Frontotemporal Lobar Degeneration

Frontotemporal lobar degeneration (FTLD), the fourth leading cause of dementia, is characterized by progressive declines in language or behavior; these deficits result from degeneration and atrophy in the frontal and temporal lobes of the brain (Galimberti & Scarpini, 2012). FTLD has several variants that involve either behavioral or language symptoms. Symptoms associated with these variants include (a) significant changes in behavior, personality, and social skills (e.g., impulsive or uninhibited actions, apathy, loss of empathy, stereotyped behavior patterns, or overeating); or (b) progressive difficulty with fluent speech or word meaning (e.g., understanding words or naming objects). Muscle weakness or other motoric abnormalities are sometimes present. There is usually minimal decline in learning, memory, or perceptual-motor skills. Behavioral symptoms are associated with atrophy in the frontal lobe whereas communication symptoms occur when temporal lobe damage is predominant (APA, 2013).

The average age of onset is between 45 and 64 years of age, making FTLD the second leading cause of early-onset dementia. Neuroimaging can assist with diagnosis by documenting the atrophy in the frontal or temporal lobes characteristic of FTLD (Association for Frontotemporal Degeneration, 2014). Genetic mutations appear to contribute to FTLD, with up to 40 percent of individuals with FTLD reporting a family history of neurodegenerative illness (Seltman & Matthews, 2012).

Neurocognitive Disorder due to Parkinson's Disease

Parkinson's disease (PD) involves four primary symptoms: (a) tremor of the hands, arms, legs, jaw, or face; (b) rigidity of the limbs and trunk; (c) slowness in initiating movement; and (d) drooping posture or impaired balance and coordination (National Institute of Neurological Disorders and Stroke, 2014). As the disease progresses, motor tremors and incoordination can interfere with daily activities. In neurocognitive disorder due to PD, motor symptoms are evident at least 1 year prior to notable cognitive decline. Mild cognitive impairment often develops early in the course of PD and affects about 27 percent of those with the disorder (Litvan et al., 2012); the dementia commonly seen in the later stages of PD results in cognitive and behavioral symptoms similar to those seen in

Parkinson's Disease

Actor Michael J. Fox, who has Parkinson's disease, performs at a benefit for the Michael J. Fox Foundation for Parkinson's Research in New York City.

frontotemporal lobar degeneration (FTLD)   dementia involving degeneration in the frontal and temporal lobes of the brain causing declines in language and behavior

Parkinson's disease (PD)   a progressive disorder characterized by poorly controlled motor movements sometimes followed by cognitive decline

DLB (Lewy Body Dementia Association, 2014). Personality and mood changes including apathy, depression, or anxiety, as well as hallucinations and delusions, occur with PD (APA, 2013). Individuals who have predominant damage in the right hemisphere may have difficulty visually recognizing emotional cues, especially faces conveying sadness, a characteristic that can strain interpersonal interactions (Ventura et al., 2012). The severity and progression of symptoms varies significantly from person to person.

PD is the second most common neurodegenerative disorder in the United States, affecting about 630,000 individuals with the prevalence expected to double by 2040 (Kowal, Dall, Chakrabarti, Storm, & Jain, 2013). The prevalence of PD increases with age and affects 3 percent of those older than 85. PD strikes more men than women, but the reasons for this discrepancy are unclear (APA, 2013). The neurotransmitter dopamine is essential for optimal and physical functioning. The symptoms of PD result from the accelerated aging of neurons and the death of dopamine-producing neurons in the midbrain, as well as Lewy body proteins in the motor area of the brain stem (Sharma et al., 2013).

Because genetic mutations account for only 5 percent of PD cases, researchers are trying to learn more about what causes the pattern of brain cell death seen in the disease (Trinh & Farrer, 2013). Twin studies have revealed that occupational exposure to certain toxins (contained in solvents and household cleaners) increases the risk of PD (Goldman et al., 2012). Exposure to herbicides and pesticides also appears to increase the likelihood of developing PD (APA, 2013). The disorder occurs more frequently in the northern Midwest and the Northeast and in urban settings; this geographic distribution has raised questions about whether environmental toxins common to these areas are associated with the development of PD (A. W. Willis, Bradley, et al., 2010).

Neurocognitive Disorder due to Huntington's Disease

Huntington's disease (HD) is a rare, genetically transmitted degenerative disorder characterized by involuntary movement, progressive dementia, and emotional instability. Age of onset is variable, ranging from childhood to late in life; onset most typically occurs during midlife (APA, 2013). Initial symptoms often involve neurocognitive decline and changes in personality and emotional stability. The progressive cognitive deficits associated with HD typically begin with difficulties in executive functioning involving complex attention, planning, and problem solving. Additionally, many individuals with HD become uncharacteristically apathetic, moody, and quarrelsome. As the disorder progresses, physical symptoms such as facial grimaces, difficulty speaking, and abrupt, repetitive movements often develop. Eventually, the severity of motor and cognitive impairment results in total dependency and the need for full-time care. There is no effective treatment for HD; death typically occurs 15–20 years after the onset of symptoms (Clabough, 2013).

Because HD is transmitted from parent to child through a dominant genetic mutation, offspring of someone with HD have about a 50/50 chance of developing the disorder. Predictive genetic testing is available for family members who want to know if they will develop HD. Additionally, neuroimaging to monitor glucose metabolism in the cortex can help predict rate of disease progression in those with HD (Shin et al., 2013). Genetic counseling is extremely important in preventing transmission of the disease.

Neurocognitive Disorder due to HIV Infection

Many people know about the serious complications associated with HIV infection and AIDS (acquired immune deficiency syndrome), including susceptibility to diseases, physical deterioration, and death. Relatively few people realize that cognitive impairment is sometimes the first sign of untreated HIV infection. Symptoms can vary significantly but often include slower mental processing, difficulty with complex mental tasks, and difficulty concentrating or learning new information (APA, 2013). In serious cases, a diagnosis of *AIDS dementia complex* (ADC) is made. ADC, a major neurocognitive disorder, develops when HIV becomes active within the brain resulting

Huntington's disease (HD) a genetic disease characterized by involuntary twitching movements and eventual dementia

Genetic Testing: Helpful or Harmful?

DNA testing is now available to provide information regarding risk for a variety of neurocognitive disorders. Genotyping (gathering information about specific genes by examining an individual's DNA) brings up a number of interconnected issues. When genotyping is performed on individuals who have a family member with a *genetically determined* condition such as Huntington's disease (HD) or early-onset Alzheimer's disease (AD), the outcome of the test reveals life-changing information—they know *with certainty* if they will develop the disorder afflicting their parent or other family members. In cases where genetic tests only indicate *possible* risk (e.g., the APOE-e4 genotype associated with later-onset AD), clinicians often discourage genetic testing due to concerns that knowledge of *possible risk* can be more harmful than helpful (Howe, 2010). For example, someone who learns that he or she has the APOE-e4 genotype knows there is approximately a 25 percent chance of developing AD—not the 100 percent risk revealed through genotype analysis involving HD or early-onset AD.

Those who encourage genetic testing for individuals who may carry *deterministic genes* (e.g., when family members have HD or early-onset AD) emphasize benefits such as being able to plan for the future, including decisions about whether or not to have children. However, others discourage such testing because of the social and economic stigma associated with these conditions and the lack of specific treatments or interventions if gene mutations are detected (*The Lancet Neurology*, 2010). Those who support genetic testing when there is *possible* risk of AD (e.g., families who have the APOE-e4 genotype) believe that learning about an increased risk of AD may motivate lifestyle changes that ultimately reduce the risk of developing the disease. Additionally, individuals with the APOE-e4 genotype may be able to participate in research studies aimed at preventing or slowing the progression of AD (Sleegers et al., 2010). Once such interventions exist, some of the debate may subside.

For Further Consideration

1. If your parent had Huntington's disease or early-onset Alzheimer's disease, would you want to know if you would eventually develop the disorder?

2. If your family members had later-onset Alzheimer's disease, would you want to know if you carried the APOE-e4 genotype and had a 25 percent risk of developing the disorder?

in significant alteration of mental processes. HIV-related infection can also produce inflammation throughout the brain and central nervous system.

Although the antiretroviral therapies used to treat HIV infection and AIDS can prevent or delay the onset of the severe cognitive dysfunction associated with ADC, HIV-related brain changes still occur in almost half of those taking antiretroviral medications. For example, neuroimaging studies revealed that 33 percent of one group receiving treatment had HIV-related neurological changes but without symptoms of cognitive decline; in addition, 12 percent of the group had mild neurocognitive impairment and 2 percent had ADC. The percentages of those affected were even higher when individuals with comorbid conditions were included (Heaton et al., 2010). Researchers hope that the prevalence of HIV-related neurocognitive disorder will decrease once antiretroviral medications are able to more efficiently penetrate the brain and central nervous system (Vassallo et al., 2014).

Treatment Considerations with Neurocognitive Disorders

Because neurocognitive disorders have many different causes and are associated with different symptoms and dysfunctions, treatment approaches vary widely. First, any underlying medical conditions are addressed. Beyond that, the major interventions for neurocognitive disorders include rehabilitation services, biological interventions, cognitive and behavioral treatment, lifestyle changes, and environmental support.

Rehabilitation Services

The key to recovery for those affected by stroke or traumatic brain injury is participation in comprehensive, sustained rehabilitation services. Physical, occupational, speech, and language therapy help individuals relearn skills or compensate for lost abilities. Rehabilitative interventions are often guided by the individual's physical and cognitive strengths, as well as deficits. A person's commitment to and participation in therapy plays an important role in recovery. Depression, pessimism, and anxiety can stall progress. Fortunately, those participating in rehabilitation become encouraged when the brain begins to reorganize and skills return. Neuroimaging techniques are increasingly used to document brain changes achieved through rehabilitation (J. A. Young & Tolentino, 2011); in fact, neuroimaging can help determine which physical and occupational therapies best enhance brain recovery (K. C. Lin et al., 2010). For example, very encouraging signs of brain reorganization and related recovery of motor function have been documented in individuals treated with *constraint-induced therapy*, a technique that encourages repeated and intensive use of the side of the body affected by brain damage by preventing the use of the unaffected side by means such as putting the individual's "good arm" in a sling (Stevenson, Thalman, Christie, & Poluha, 2012). This technique helps prevent the "learned nonuse" frequently seen in those with brain damage.

Biological Treatment

Medications can help prevent, control, or reduce the symptoms of some neurocognitive disorders. Treating vitamin deficiencies can also improve or reduce symptoms in some conditions. For example, the persistent memory and learning difficulties seen in Wernicke-Korsakoff's syndrome, a disorder caused by thiamine (vitamin B_1) deficiencies associated with chronic alcohol abuse, can improve when nutritional supplements are provided

Effective Rehabilitation

Sgt. Dan DaRosa plays a game to help with his memory at the traumatic brain injury clinic on Elmendorf Air Force base in Anchorage, Alaska. Structured activities such as this can play a key role in the recovery of cognitive skills.

AP Images

during alcohol treatment (Isenberg-Grzeda, Kutner, & Nicolson, 2012). Higher blood levels of an amino acid, homocysteine, are also associated with increased risk of AD. Fortunately, certain vitamins, such as vitamin B_6 or B_{12}, can decrease cognitive impairment in some individuals with high homocysteine levels. MRI scans of individuals with mild cognitive impairment taking high doses of B vitamins over a 2-year period revealed that brain atrophy was slowed by about 30 percent; not surprisingly, atrophy was reduced most (up to 53 percent) in those with the highest initial levels of homocysteine (Smith et al., 2010). High doses of vitamin E prescribed and monitored by a physician can also slow the progression of AD (Karceski, 2013).

Medications, including levodopa, a drug that increases dopamine availability, can provide relief from both cognitive and physical symptoms of PD; however, it can also produce problems with impulse control, hallucinations and other psychotic symptoms, and difficulty with voluntary motor movement (Poletti & Bonuccelli, 2013). Thus, physicians often delay pharmacological treatment for PD until it is certain that the benefits clearly outweigh the risks. For some patients, implanted electrodes and deep brain stimulation produced neurological changes and symptom improvement (van Hartevelt et al., 2014). Gene therapy (administering genes into the brains of PD patients) is also being tested with PD patients with the goal of sufficiently modifying brain cells so that they once again produce dopamine (Palfi et al., 2014).

The two classes of drugs (acetylcholinesterase inhibitors and memantine) approved to help slow the progression of AD have not shown robust effects (Howe, 2013). Efforts continue to focus on developing medications that might help prevent the development of beta-amyloid and tau protein irregularities in those at high risk for AD (Ghezzi, Scarpini, & Galimberti, 2013). Other proposed treatments for AD are still in the early stages, including deep brain stimulation to improve neural circuit function in those with AD (Lyketsos, Targum, Pendergrass, & Lozano, 2012).

Medication can help prevent recurrence of stroke by treating hypertension or diabetes. Antidepressants can also help alleviate the depression associated with stroke and other neurocognitive disorders. In one study, individuals with moderate to severe motor impairment resulting from an ischemic stroke took an antidepressant (fluoxetine) for 3 months. This group not only reported fewer depressive symptoms than did individuals in a placebo control group but also regained more muscle function; the antidepressant may have enhanced progress by reducing brain inflammation, improving neurotransmitter functioning, or enhancing participation in physical therapy due to improved mood (Chollet et al., 2011). Although low doses of antipsychotic medication sometimes reduce neurocognitive symptoms such as paranoia, hallucinations, and agitation, these medications are used cautiously, especially in older individuals (Declercq et al., 2013). As mentioned previously, it is often necessary to balance the positive effects and side effects of medications, taking particular care to monitor potential interactions of multiple medications.

Cognitive and Behavioral Treatment

Cognitive deficits and emotional changes caused by neurocognitive disorders (e.g., emotional reactivity and diminished ability to concentrate) can hinder recovery and interfere with well-being. For example, depression, common among those with vascular neurocognitive disorder, can decrease follow-through with treatment recommendations and increase risk of subsequent strokes (Sibolt et al., 2013).

Psychotherapy can enhance coping and participation in rehabilitation efforts. For example, a cognitive-behavioral treatment targeting depression in individuals with PD included identifying life stressors and teaching the participants self-care, stress management, and relaxation techniques. The treatment was found to be both feasible and effective (Dobkin et al., 2006). Cognitive and behavioral techniques can also reduce

Connecting with Positive Memories

Although dementia cannot be cured, individuals with the condition benefit from social contact and activities associated with positive memories. Here a volunteer reads poetry to a woman with dementia.

the frequency or severity of problem behaviors associated with neurocognitive disorders such as aggression or socially inappropriate conduct. Strategies may include teaching the individual social skills, reducing complex tasks (e.g., dressing or eating) into simpler steps, or simplifying the environment to avoid confusion and frustration. Additionally, preliminary research has demonstrated positive neurological changes including reduced brain atrophy in individuals with mild neurocognitive impairment who participated in meditation and mindfulness-based stress reduction (Wells et al., 2013).

Lifestyle Changes

Lifestyle changes can help prevent or reduce progression of some neurocognitive disorders. For example, changes in lifestyle may help slow the progression of AD (Rolland, van Kan, & Vellas, 2010). Among one group of adults with early-stage AD, those with good cardiovascular fitness had less brain atrophy than those who did not exercise regularly (Honea et al., 2009). Treatment for vascular neurocognitive disorders often targets smoking cessation, weight reduction, and blood sugar, cholesterol, or blood pressure control (Peters, Huxley, & Woodward, 2013).

Increased social interaction and mental stimulation involving enjoyable, social activities that provide an opportunity to concentrate and use memory skills can improve communication skills and reduce cognitive decline in individuals with dementia (Woods, Aguirre, Spector, & Orrell, 2012). However, the use of specific cognitive training programs does not have strong research support, nor do the results of the training appear to generalize to daily living activities among those exhibiting cognitive decline (Lövdén, Xu, & Wangy, 2013).

Environmental Support

Although rehabilitation can be very effective with acute conditions such as TBI or stroke, neurodegenerative disorders involving dementia are irreversible and best managed by providing a supportive environment. There are many ways to help those with declining abilities to feel happier and live comfortably and with dignity (Howe, 2011). For example, exposure to bright lighting throughout the day can improve sleep and decrease agitation and depression in individuals with dementia (Hanford & Figueiro, 2013). Techniques such as writing answers to repeatedly asked questions or labeling family photos can decrease frustration resulting from memory difficulties. Family visits enhance the lives of those with dementia because emotional memories (e.g., happiness at seeing a loved one) persist even when the visit itself is no longer recalled (Feinstein, Duff, et al., 2010). Modifying the environment can increase safety and comfort while decreasing confusion and agitation.

Family and friends who provide care may themselves need support. They may feel overwhelmed, helpless, frustrated, anxious, or even angry at having to take care of someone with neurocognitive impairment. Caring for someone with dementia or other degenerative conditions can be very stressful, especially because of the need for constant supervision and extensive assistance with personal care. Sometimes, agonizing decisions must be made about whether the affected individual can remain at home versus living in a skilled nursing or assisted-living facility.

Sleep–Wake Disorders

Sleep is an important topic because sleep difficulties increase the risk of stress and psychiatric disorders. In contrast, good-quality sleep is associated with mental and physical resilience. Most adults require 7 to 9 hours of sleep to function optimally (see Table 13.7). However, obtaining restful and adequate sleep is difficult for many adults, particularly those with mental disorders (Krystal, 2012). Inadequate sleep can also affect safety. Among individuals in one large study, those who reported occasions of excessive sleepiness were twice as likely to have had an accident while driving in the previous year (Ohayon, 2012).

What is a normal sleep pattern? Normal sleep has two phases: *Non–rapid eye movement (NREM) sleep* is a quiet sleep state in which the muscles are relaxed and loss of consciousness occurs; during this stage, our bodies perform important functions such as building bone and muscle, repairing tissues, and strengthening the immune system. The second phase is *rapid eye movement (REM) sleep*, in which breathing and heart rate are irregular and muscle tone is greatly reduced. REM sleep, which is associated with dreaming, occupies about 25 percent of sleep and usually alternates with NREM sleep every 90 minutes (National Sleep Foundation, 2014).

Many of us experience interruptions in normal sleep patterns, daytime sleepiness, or difficulty falling or staying asleep, perhaps after a traumatic experience or when dealing with stressful circumstances. Over 26 percent of college students indicate having troublesome sleep difficulties (American College Health Association, 2012b). However, in most cases, these difficulties are temporary and do not interfere with our daytime functioning.

When excessive sleepiness, ongoing problems initiating or maintaining sleep, or other sleep abnormalities result in daytime distress and impairment, the individual may meet the criteria for one of the sleep disorders. There are two major categories of sleep disorders: dyssomnias and parasomnias (APA, 2013). We will discuss several disorders from each of these categories.

Dyssomnias

Dyssomnias involve difficulties in falling asleep or maintaining sleep, as well as excessive sleepiness during the day. They include insomnia disorder, hypersomnolence disorder, narcolepsy, obstructive sleep apnea (a breathing-related sleep disorder), and circadian-rhythm sleep–wake disorder.

Insomnia Disorder

> It happens two or three times a week. I get in bed, turn off the light and wait to fall asleep ... and wait ... and wait. It might be two or three hours before I drop off. And even then, I might wake up a couple of hours later to go through the whole thing again. (Lemonick, 2004, p. 100)

Insomnia disorder, the most prevalent of all sleep disorders, involves a distressing and disruptive pattern of difficulty falling asleep or remaining asleep. Various factors cause insomnia, including stress, worry, or anxiety. Excessive daytime sleepiness is a common result of chronic insomnia and may impair cognitive functioning and alertness, performance at work, and enjoyment of family or recreational activities. Many individuals with insomnia have comorbid physical or mental health conditions. For example, up to 50 percent of those with cancer experience insomnia; this can affect recovery by suppressing the immune system or impeding the restorative processes that occur during sleep (Ishak et al., 2012). In a study of 700 children between the ages of 5 and 12, 19.3 percent had insomnia symptoms; the prevalence was highest (30.6 percent) in girls 11–12 years of age (Calhoun, Fernandez-Mendoza, Vgontzas, Liao, & Bixler, 2014). Older adults and women also show high rates of insomnia (APA, 2013).

Table 13.7 How Much Sleep Do You Really Need?

Age	Sleep Needs
Preschoolers (3–5 years)	11–13 hours
School-age children (5–10 years)	10–11 hours
Teens (10–17 years)	8.5–9.25 hours
Adults	7–9 hours

SOURCE: National Sleep Foundation (2014).

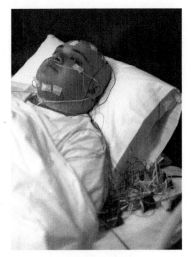

Studying Biological Functioning During Sleep

Emmanuel Michael, 29, prepares for a sleep disorder test at a University of Chicago clinic. Sleep evaluations usually involve an overnight stay at a sleep disorders clinic so that technicians can monitor biological changes that occur during sleep.

dyssomnias disorders involving abnormalities in the quality, amount, or timing of sleep

insomnia disorder chronic difficulty falling asleep or remaining asleep

Hypersomnolence Disorder

> **CASE STUDY**   A 27-year-old carpenter sought help because he always had difficulty waking up. His excessive daytime sleepiness began during adolescence, when he often slept for the rest of the day after returning from school. He was sometimes able to resist falling asleep in important situations but had several car accidents related to sleepiness. He sometimes fell asleep during the day (remaining asleep for up to 2 hours) but did not feel refreshed after sleeping (Bassetti & Aldrich, 1997)

Hypersomnolence (excessive sleepiness) disorder is characterized by a pattern of difficulty waking up after sleeping, excessive daytime sleepiness, or prolonged nighttime sleep with a tendency to wake up unrefreshed. Those with this disorder sleep at least 7 hours, but, as seen in the case vignette, may lapse into sleep or feel compelled to nap during the day; however, naps do not provide relief from sleepiness. Many individuals with hypersomnolence disorder experience **sleep inertia**, which involves significant grogginess and impaired alertness on awakening (Preda, 2012). How common is excessive sleepiness and hypersomnolence disorder? Among 16,000 U.S. adults interviewed about sleep symptoms, 27.8 percent reported experiencing periodic excessive sleepiness; 1.5 percent of the group reported symptoms consistent with hypersomnolence disorder (Ohayon, Dauvilliers, & Reynolds, 2012).

Narcolepsy

> **CASE STUDY**   A 14-year-old adolescent falls asleep 30 times or more per day, often in class, and has gone missing when operating on "dreamlike autopilot." She takes medication to reduce the excessive daytime sleepiness and the episodes of muscle weakness associated with her narcolepsy (Francis, 2014).

Narcolepsy, a very rare sleep disorder, results in an irresistible or overwhelming need for sleep in the daytime even when adequate sleep occurs during the night. Drowsiness or sudden sleep can occur without warning. Individuals with narcolepsy often go immediately into REM sleep, whereas a normal sleep cycle begins with 90 minutes of NREM sleep (NIH, 2014). Many individuals with narcolepsy experience *cataplexy*, a sudden loss of muscle function, varying from slight muscular weakness to complete physical collapse that can last for seconds or minutes; the person remains completely conscious during these episodes. Cataplexy is often triggered by laughter or by emotional states such as anger or fear. Surprisingly, in one sample, narcolepsy went undiagnosed for up to 16 years for men and 28 years for women (Won et al., 2014).

Obstructive Sleep Apnea

hypersomnolence (excessive sleepiness) disorder condition involving difficulty waking up after sleeping and excessive daytime sleepiness or prolonged unrefreshing sleep

sleep inertia significant grogginess and impaired alertness after sleeping or napping

obstructive sleep apnea (OSA) a breathing-related sleep disorder involving partial or complete upper-airway obstruction

> **CASE STUDY**   Forty-year-old Mike Palomar suffers from constant sleepiness and struggles to complete daily activities. He can fall asleep at any moment, is unable to control his weight, and feels sluggish. His wife complains of his loud snoring and is alarmed when he appears to stop breathing during sleep. During a sleep assessment it was found that he had 78 breathing pauses each hour (Simons, 2014).

Mike Palomar was surprised when he received the diagnosis of **obstructive sleep apnea (OSA)**, a common breathing-related sleep disorder. When asleep, those with this condition experience a collapse of the soft tissue in the rear of the throat resulting in partial or complete upper-airway obstruction. The frequent sleep disruption associated with OSA often results in significant daytime sleepiness. The obstruction repeatedly interferes with breathing during sleep. After detecting low levels of oxygen, the brain sends a signal to resume breathing, which results in snoring or gasping for breath. Having extra tissue around the airway due to excessive weight increases vulnerability to OSA (Lurie, 2011).

Symptoms of OSA include disruptive snoring, breathing pauses, snorting or gasping, and excessive daytime sleepiness (De Backer, 2013). OSA can cause high blood pressure, cardiovascular disease, and weight gain (Lee & Jeong, 2014) and is associated with increased risk of stroke (Wilson, Frontera, Thomas, & Duncan, 2014). Sleep apnea has been associated with shortened telomere length, suggesting that the condition may accelerate cellular aging (Savolainen, Eriksson, Kajantie, Lahti, & Räikkönen, 2014).

OSA is a relatively common disorder that remains undiagnosed in about 90 percent of women and 80 percent of men with the condition (Downey et al., 2013). In the general population the prevalence of OSA is estimated to range from 3 percent to 7 percent in men and 2 percent to 5 percent in women (Lurie, 2011) and is most prevalent among older adults (APA, 2013).

Circadian Rhythm Sleep Disorder

Circadian rhythm sleep disorder is a pattern of recurrent sleep disturbance caused by a disrupted biological sleep–wake cycle or a mismatch between environmental demands and a person's internal "clock." Circadian rhythm sleep disorder can result in insomnia or excessive sleepiness. **Circadian rhythms** are internal biological rhythms that influence a number of our bodily processes, including sleeping patterns. Our circadian rhythms are influenced by light, which also affects production of the sleep-inducing hormone, melatonin. Many of us have experienced jet lag, a temporary disruption in circadian rhythm that results from travel between time zones. Shift work can also produce problems with the circadian rhythm, because the schedule of work is in opposition to sleep-regulating cues associated with sunlight. Over 36 percent of night-shift workers and 26 percent of rotating workers show disruptions in the normal circadian rhythm pattern (Sack et al., 2007). There is little information on the prevalence of circadian rhythm sleep disorder.

Parasomnias

Parasomnias involve unusual behaviors or events occurring during sleep or the sleep–wake transition; in other words, the physiological systems associated with sleep do not function normally. The parasomnias include non–rapid eye movement (NREM) sleep arousal disorders, nightmare disorder, and rapid eye movement (REM) sleep behavior disorder (APA, 2013).

Non–Rapid Eye Movement (NREM) Sleep Arousal Disorders

Non–rapid eye movement (NREM) sleep arousal disorders involve simultaneous wakefulness and NREM sleep; these episodes of incomplete arousal, which involve talking or motor activity with eyes open but minimal conscious awareness, occur early in the night and usually last no more than 10 minutes. In general, there is little or no memory of the episode the next day. Many individuals exhibit both subtypes of this disorder: sleep terrors and sleepwalking. (Matwiyoff & Lee-Chiong, 2010).

Sleep Terrors **Sleep terrors** are abrupt episodes of intense fear (including sweating, rapid breathing, or increased heart rate) that occur during deep sleep. Those who experience sleep terrors often cry out in panic, but are not fully aroused. They are difficult to calm and may become more agitated if awakened (Haupt, Sheldon, & Loghmanee, 2013). The prevalence of sleep terror disorder is unknown, but about one third of young children experience sleep terror episodes (APA, 2013).

circadian rhythm sleep disorder sleep disturbance due to a disrupted sleep–wake cycle

circadian rhythm internal biological rhythms that influence bodily processes such as the sleep–wake cycle

parasomnias sleep abnormalities occurring during sleep or in the sleep–wake transition

sleep terrors episodes of intense fear that occur during deep sleep

Sleepwalking   Sleepwalking typically involves sitting up or walking during sleep; someone who is sleepwalking usually has a blank stare, does not respond if spoken to and is not easily awakened. Sleepwalking occurs in a state of reduced alertness and involves behaviors requiring little complexity. During sleepwalking episodes, some individuals eat or engage in sexual activity (without conscious awareness) or unusual behavior such as urinating in inappropriate places.

Experiencing an occasional sleepwalking episode is not uncommon; in fact, 29.2 percent of adults in one sample reported occasional sleepwalking (Ohayon, Mahowald, Dauvilliers, Krystal, & Léger, 2012). Repeated sleepwalking episodes causing distress and impairment affect up to 5 percent of the adult population. This disorder tends to disappear during early adolescence, but when it occurs in adults, it tends to follow a chronic waxing and waning course (APA, 2013).

Nightmare Disorder

Nightmare disorder involves dreams with themes of danger that are frightening enough to produce awakening. Nightmares often involve threats to our survival or sense of security. These story-like episodes occur almost exclusively during REM sleep. The associated fear and anxiety associated with the nightmare causes the person to become alert; distress from the dream often makes it difficult for the person to resume sleep.

Nightmares are most common during adolescence and young adulthood and more prevalent in females; approximately 1 to 2 percent of adults have frequent nightmares (APA, 2013). Individuals with psychiatric disorders have greater likelihood of experiencing nightmare disorder; prevalence rates range from about 18 percent in individuals with depression, schizophrenia, and insomnia to 50 percent or over in those with PTSD and borderline personality disorder (Swart, van Schagen, Lancee, & van den Bout, 2013).

REM Sleep Behavior Disorder

REM sleep behavior disorder involves vocalizations and motor behavior (often of a violent nature) during REM sleep. The movement or speaking is often associated with the content of a person's dreams. Sometimes, people with this disorder scream and hit or otherwise injure their sleeping partner. Once awakened, the person is alert and oriented (APA, 2013). This potentially dangerous disorder is more prevalent among middle-aged and older males (Sakuma-Sasai & Inoue, 2013).

Etiology of Sleep–Wake Disorders

Problems in sleep can result from neurological vulnerabilities; psychological factors such as stress, anxiety, and depression; environmental factors such as noise, light, or other stimuli; or from various health or behavioral habits, including substance use or abuse. Clinicians assessing someone for a sleep disorder inquire about the age of onset, predisposing characteristics (being a light sleeper, family history of sleep problems, current stressors, illnesses, or medications), lifestyle, and daily activity patterns. They also seek input from the bed partner about snoring, breathing pattern changes, or movement or verbalizations during sleep.

Dyssomnias tend to be associated with lifestyle and psychological factors, including the following:

- Intrusive, uncontrollable thoughts associated with stress, worry, anxiety, or depression and preoccupation with sleep and distress over sleep difficulties. For example, in one sample of sleep-disordered adolescents, catastrophizing thoughts regarding interpersonal relationships and school performance played a key role in delayed sleep onset (Hiller, Lovato, Gradisar, Oliver, & Slater, 2014).

- Lifestyle factors, such as irregular schedules resulting from shift work, retirement, napping, early bedtimes, or long periods spent in bed.

- Nocturnal activities that interfere with sleep, such as the consumption of heavy meals, caffeine, or alcohol or exercising in the evening.

nightmare disorder   condition involving frightening dreams that produce awakening

REM sleep behavior disorder   condition involving dream-related vocalizations and motor behavior that occur during REM sleep

- Medical conditions such as congestive heart failure or stroke.
- Drug or alcohol abuse and psychiatric conditions, particularly depression, PTSD, and anxiety disorders (Lubit, Bonds & Lucia, 2013).

Many people with sleep disorders, particularly parasomnias, have family members with sleep difficulties (APA, 2013). A genetic predisposition to physiological arousal, coupled with preoccupation with getting enough sleep and distress when unable to sleep, can create a vicious cycle that results in insomnia and the disruption of normal sleep patterns (Harvey, Gehrman, & Espie, 2014). Epigenetic processes affecting biological rhythms and physiological processes associated with sleep are also implicated in the etiology of sleep–wake disorders (Qureshi & Mehler, 2014). There is less known about etiology with the parasomnias; fortunately, parasomnias often remit spontaneously.

Treatment of Sleep-Wake Disorders

Treatment for insomnia involves techniques that help people psychologically and physically prepare for a good night's sleep (Holmqvist, Vincent & Walsh, 2014). Successful strategies include the following:

- Maintaining a regular sleep-and-wake schedule.
- Exercising regularly, but not too late in the day.
- Avoiding caffeine, long naps during the day, and heavy meals, alcohol, or nicotine within 2 hours of sleep.
- Creating a relaxed attitude or frame of mind when going to bed and practicing relaxation procedures and mindfulness techniques to calm the body and the mind.
- Minimizing worry about sleep and avoiding clock-watching if unable to sleep.
- Eliminating distractions and competing behaviors from the bedroom, thus creating a sleep-conducive environment and strengthening the association between the bedroom and sleep; going to sleep only when sleepy; avoiding use of the bed for anything except sleep (and sex); and leaving the bedroom if unable to sleep, returning only when sleepy.

Treatment for Obstructive Sleep Apnea.

Continuous positive airway pressure (CPAP) therapy is often used to treat obstructive sleep apnea. Here you see a man sleeping as the machine keeps his airways open by providing steady air pressure.

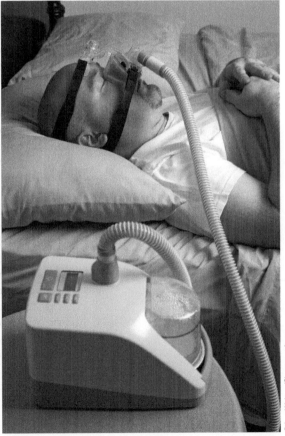

©Amy Walters/Shutterstock.com

Cognitive-behavioral therapy (CBT) is effective for the treatment of insomnia; additionally, CBT results in the decrease of symptoms associated with comorbid psychiatric disorders, especially anxiety, depression, and trauma-related disorders (Sánchez-Ortuño & Edinger, 2012). For mild sleep apnea, recommendations include avoiding alcohol or medications that make it harder for the throat to remain open during sleep; losing weight (if overweight); and sleeping on the side rather than the back, as this position is more likely to keep the throat open. People with moderate to severe sleep apnea often use a continuous positive airway pressure mask—a device that forces air through the nasal passages to prevent the throat from collapsing during sleep.

Medications are used to treat sleep disorders. Medications that maintain alertness treat the symptoms of excessive sleepiness seen in narcolepsy, sleep apnea, and sleepiness due to shift work (Darwish et al., 2010). Sodium oxybate can help control the cataplexy or sudden muscle weakness associated with narcolepsy, but is tightly controlled by the FDA because misuse can result in seizures, coma, and death (Simon & Zieve, 2012). The sedating properties of clonazepam, a benzodiazepine, and the sleep-inducing effects of the hormone melatonin are sometimes successful in reducing the aggressive movement that occurs in REM sleep behavior disorder, with melatonin producing fewer adverse effects compared to clonazepam (McCarter et al., 2013).

A variety of sleep-inducing medications such as zolpidem (Ambien), zaleplon (Sonata), and eszopiclone (Lunesta) are used to treat insomnia.

These medications can also reduce anxiety symptoms (Richey & Krystal, 2011). However, they may remain in effect after the person awakens and result in motor incoordination, cognitive confusion, and traffic accidents. Antidepressant medications are also used to treat underlying symptoms of anxiety or depression that interfere with sleep. Antianxiety medications (benzodiazepines) are prescribed with caution due to the increased likelihood of drug dependence.

Contemporary Trends and Future Directions

There is extensive research occurring related to neurocognitive and, to a lesser extent, sleep–wake disorders. The increasing economic and psychological burden associated with neurodegenerative diseases has invigorated the search for methods of prevention and treatment. Simultaneously, medical professionals continue to emphasize lifestyle changes we can make to reduce our vulnerability to neurocognitive or sleep–wake disorders. Of course, there is also hope we will learn more about how environmental factors, such as toxins or head injuries, trigger neurodegenerative disorders.

Researchers are addressing these disorders from a variety of perspectives, sharing and building on studies from across the globe. Because symptoms of the degenerative neurocognitive disorders do not appear until significant cell death and brain damage have already occurred, researchers continue to focus on identification of early biomarkers associated with each neurodegenerative disorder (Sharma et al., 2013). Some teams are contributing to the discussion by addressing the role of epigenetic dysregulation in neurodegenerative disorders, hoping that insight gained from research on one disorder will advance our understanding of related disorders (Valor & Guiretti, 2013). There is also a quest for biomarkers that can help individualize treatment.

Additionally, there is a continued shift from research focused on treatment to research addressing early identification and intervention with neurodegenerative disorders; this includes therapies to prevent the onset of biological processes associated with neurodegenerative conditions or to stop degenerative processes once they begin (Trinh & Farrer, 2013). For example, researchers have recently begun to use beta-amyloid protein tracers with positron emission tomography (PET) to detect and monitor the development of plaques in the living brain (Johnson et al., 2013). In fact, there are now five specific biomarkers validated for research with Alzheimer's disease. Advances such as these will allow clinicians to detect and monitor the progression of brain abnormalities in high-risk individuals even before symptoms develop (Jack & Holtzman, 2013). At some point in the future, those at risk for neurodegenerative diseases may be able to take medications or receive gene therapy to delay or prevent the development of a disorder. In addition to these biological advances, psychologists hope to develop more sensitive neuropsychological tests that can detect early declines in cognitive skills (Marras et al., 2013).

Additionally, research is beginning to emphasize the bidirectional relationship between sleep impairment and psychiatric disorders (Krystal, 2012) with the hope that treatment or prevention of sleep disorders can avert the development of psychiatric conditions (Spiegelhalder, Regen, Nanovska, Baglioni, & Riemann, 2013). This is particularly important given the mounting evidence that sleep disorders increase the risk of, or even directly contribute to, some psychiatric disorders, including anxiety, depressive, bipolar, and trauma-related disorders and conditions associated with aging such as Alzheimer's disease (Anderson & Bradley, 2013).

chapter SUMMARY

1 How can we determine whether someone has a neurocognitive disorder?

- The effects of brain damage vary greatly. The most common symptoms include confusion, attentional deficits, and impairments in consciousness, memory, and judgment.

- Brain damage is assessed using interviews, psychological tests, neurological tests, and other observational or biological measures.

2 What are the different types of neurocognitive disorders?

- There are three main types of neurocognitive disorders: major neurocognitive disorder, mild neurocognitive disorder, and delirium.

- Major neurocognitive disorder involves significant declines in independent-care skills and cognitive functioning.

- In mild neurocognitive disorder, cognitive declines are subtle and independent functioning is not compromised.

- Delirium is an acute condition characterized by diminished awareness (including disorientation) and impaired attentional skills.

3 What are the causes of neurocognitive disorders?

- Various events or conditions can cause neurocognitive disorders, including head injuries, substance abuse, and lack of blood flow to the brain.

- The incidence of memory problems and cognitive disorders increases with age. However, many older adults do not experience any significant cognitive decline.

- Neurocognitive disorders caused by neurodegenerative processes include conditions involving dementia (e.g., Alzheimer's disease, vascular cognitive impairment, dementia with Lewy bodies, frontotemporal lobar degeneration) and disorders such as Parkinson's disease and Huntington's disease that have predominant symptoms involving motor dysfunction.

4 What treatments are available for neurocognitive disorders?

- Treatment strategies include physical rehabilitation and cognitive and behavioral therapy. Medications sometimes help control symptoms or slow the progression of some neurocognitive disorders.

5 What do we know about disorders that affect our sleep?

- When excessive sleepiness, ongoing problems initiating or maintaining sleep, or other sleep abnormalities result in daytime distress and impairment, the individual may meet the criteria for one of the sleep disorders.

- Dyssomnias involve difficulties falling asleep or maintaining sleep and excessive daytime sleepiness. They include insomnia disorder, hypersomnolence disorder, narcolepsy, obstructive sleep apnea, and circadian-rhythm sleep–wake disorder.

- Parasomnias involve unusual behaviors or events during sleep or the sleep–wake transition. They include non–rapid eye movement (NREM) sleep arousal disorders, nightmare disorder, and rapid eye movement (REM) sleep behavior disorder.

- Much more is known about the etiology and treatment of the dyssomnias; treatment often focuses on making lifestyle changes, managing stress and worry, and developing a home environment conducive to sleep.

SEXUAL DYSFUNCTIONS, GENDER DYSPHORIA, AND PARAPHILIC DISORDERS

CHRISTINA AND JEREMIAH DECIDED TO SEEK THERAPY after only 8 months of marriage. Both were extremely dissatisfied with their sex life. Jeremiah complained that Christina never initiated sex, found excuses to avoid it, and appeared to fake orgasms during intercourse. Christina complained that Jeremiah's lovemaking was often brief, perfunctory, and without affection. During the therapy sessions, it became clear that Christina had never had a strong interest in sex and seldom became aroused during intercourse. Although Jeremiah had never had difficulty with maintaining an erection, sex with Christina had become progressively worrisome, as he often had difficulty getting hard enough for penetration. Before initiating sex, Jeremiah began to drink heavily to give him "courage" to approach Christina and to alleviate his guilt at "forcing her to have sex." These encounters were often humiliating, as he felt that Christina only agreed to have sex out of pity.

The case of Christina and Jeremiah illustrates the psychological and physiological complexities associated with one of the three groups of disorders discussed in this chapter: *sexual dysfunctions*, which involve problems in the normal sexual response cycle. The two other topics we discuss are *gender dysphoria* (distress resulting from an incongruence between a person's gender identity and assigned gender) and *paraphilic disorders* (problematic sexual urges and fantasies). We begin with a discussion about what constitutes "normal" sexual behavior and conclude the chapter with a discussion of rape, a behavior that has a significant effect on society.

What Is "Normal" Sexual Behavior?

Many people have difficulty dealing with the topic of sexual behavior in an open and direct manner. However, such discussion is important because sex is an integral part of our lives, and because many myths and taboos

1 What are normal sexual behaviors?

2 What do we know about normal sexual responses and sexual dysfunction?

3 What causes gender dysphoria, and how is it treated?

4 What are paraphilic disorders, what causes them, and how are they treated?

5 Is rape an act of sex or aggression?

surround the topic. Much of our understanding of human sexual physiology, practices, and customs comes from the classic studies of researchers such as Alfred Kinsey and his colleagues (A. C. Kinsey, Pomeroy, Martin, & Gebhard, 1953) and William Masters and Virginia Johnson (1966, 1970) who brought the topic of sexuality to the forefront during the 20th century. Further studies such as the *Janus Report on Sexual Behavior* (Janus & Janus, 1993); the National Survey of Sexual Health and Behavior (M. Reese et al., 2010); and the work of contemporary sex researchers have added to our knowledge of sexual functioning.

Despite the quantity of research on the topic, distinguishing between abnormal behavior and harmless variations in sexual preferences is often challenging (McManus, Hargreaves, Rainbow, & Alison, 2013). Definitions of normal sexual behavior vary widely and are influenced by both moral and legal judgments (Potter, 2013). For example, until 2003 some states had laws that defined oral-genital sex as a "perversion" and a "crime against nature," punishable by imprisonment. Today it would make no sense to classify this common sexual practice as abnormal. Sixty-three percent of male respondents ages 20–24 reported engaging in oral sex with female partners and 74 percent of female respondents of the same age reported engaging in oral sex with male partners, according to a comprehensive survey regarding the sexual behavior of U.S. adults (Herbenick et al., 2010). Surveys such as this provide important information about typical sexual practices and have helped clarify what constitutes normal sexual behavior (see Table 14.1).

Understanding what is "normal" is important when classifying or diagnosing sexual problems and behaviors. However, making this differentiation is not an easy task. As you might imagine, it is difficult to define what constitutes "normal" sexual interest, behavior, fantasies, or frequency of sexual activity. To take one example, people report tremendous variation in frequency of sexual outlet or release, according to

Table 14.1 Percentage of Americans Performing Certain Sexual Behaviors in the Past Year (*N* = 5,865)

Sexual Behaviors	Age Groups									
	14–15		16–17		18–19		20–24		25–29	
	Men	Women	Men	Women	Men	Women	Men	Women	Men	Women
Masturbated Alone	62%	40%	75%	45%	81%	60%	83%	64%	84%	72%
Masturbated with Partner	5%	8%	15%	19%	43%	36%	44%	36%	49%	48%
Received Oral from Women	12%	1%	31%	5%	54%	4%	63%	9%	77%	3%
Received Oral from Men	1%	10%	3%	24%	6%	58%	6%	70%	5%	72%
Gave Oral to Women	8%	2%	18%	7%	51%	2%	55%	9%	74%	3%
Gave Oral to Men	1%	12%	2%	22%	4%	59%	7%	74%	5%	76%
Vaginal Intercourse	9%	11%	30%	30%	53%	62%	63%	80%	86%	87%
Received Penis in Anus	1%	4%	1%	5%	4%	18%	5%	23%	4%	21%
Inserted Penis into Anus	3%		6%		6%		11%		27%	

SOURCE: Herbenick et al. (2010).

research by Kinsey and colleagues (1948): One man reported that he had ejaculated only once in 30 years, and another claimed to have averaged 30 orgasms per week for 30 years. Such wide variations make it difficult to determine when to categorize someone as having atypical sexual behavior. Also, using number of orgasms (via intercourse or masturbation) to determine whether sexual behavior is abnormal may introduce gender bias into the definition of "normal" sexual desire since men masturbate and experience more frequent orgasms compared to women (Janus & Janus, 1993). Further, some people may have a high sex drive but not engage in sexual activities, whereas others may have little sexual interest but engage in frequent sexual behaviors for the sake of their partners.

Considering the difficulties in defining "normal," it is not surprising that definitions of sexual disorders are also inexact. In fact, over the past century, psychiatrists in the United States and Europe have pathologized and depathologized a variety of sexual preferences, desires, and behaviors. Revised definitions of what constitutes pathological behaviors or normative sexual practices often occur during the periodic updating of psychiatric classification systems such as the DSM (De Block & Adriaens, 2013).

Cultural norms and values also influence definitions of "normal" sexual behavior. In some cultures or cultural groups, sexual activity is considered appropriate only for procreative purposes (Bhugra, Popelyuk, & McMullen, 2010). Determining normal and abnormal behavior becomes especially difficult when comparing Western and non-Western cultures. Adults in Japan, for example, have 70 percent less sexual intercourse compared to adults in the United States, a pattern also seen in other Asian countries (Durex, 2005). Thus, it is important to take into account cultural variations when considering normative sexual behaviors and constructing definitions of sexual disorders.

	Age Groups								
30–39		40–49		50–59		60–69		70+	
Men	Women	Men	Women	Men	Women	Men	Women	Men	Women
80%	63%	76%	65%	72%	54%	61%	47%	46%	33%
45%	43%	38%	35%	28%	18%	17%	13%	13%	5%
78%	5%	62%	2%	49%	1%	38%	1%	19%	2%
6%	59%	6%	52%	8%	34%	3%	25%	2%	8%
69%	4%	57%	3%	44%	1%	34%	1%	24%	2%
5%	59%	7%	53%	8%	34%	3%	25%	2%	8%
85%	74%	74%	70%	58%	51%	54%	42%	43%	22%
3%	22%	4%	12%	5%	6%	1%	4%	2%	1%
24%		21%		11%		6%		2%	

If legal, moral, and statistical models inadequately differentiate between normal and abnormal sexual behavior, can we simply state that sexual behavior is deviant if it is a threat to society, causes distress to participants, or impairs social or occupational functioning? Using this definition, there would be no objection to defining child sexual abuse, which includes elements of distress and victimization, as deviant behavior. But what about sexual arousal to an inanimate object (fetishism)? This behavior is not a threat to society and frequently does not cause distress to the people involved. Although sexual attraction and fantasies involving nonhuman objects are not the norm, many would argue that there is no need for society or psychiatric classification systems to consider these behaviors as indicative of a mental disorder. There is even greater controversy as to whether gender dysphoria should be considered a psychiatric disorder, especially because much of the suffering associated with this condition stems from discrimination and negative societal reactions. In short, the ambiguities and controversies surrounding all classification systems are particularly relevant with respect to the three groups of sexual disorders discussed in this chapter.

The Sexual Response Cycle

Understanding and treating sexual disorders requires an understanding of the normal sexual response cycle, which traditionally consists of four stages: appetitive (interest and desire), arousal, orgasm, and resolution (Figure 14.1). Empirical findings suggest that it is difficult to distinguish between the desire of the appetitive and arousal stages, because they seem to overlap. Desire and interest, for example, may precede or follow arousal. Although we use a four-stage description, it is best to view the appetitive and arousal stages as intertwined and interactive.

1. The *appetitive phase* is characterized by a person's interest in sexual activity. The person begins to have thoughts or fantasies about sex, feels attracted to another person, or daydreams about sex.
2. The *arousal phase,* which may follow or precede the appetitive phase, involves heightened and intensified arousal resulting from specific and direct sexual stimulation. In a male, blood flow increases in the penis, resulting in an erection. In a female, the breasts swell, nipples become erect, blood engorges the genital region, and the clitoris expands.

Cultural Influences and Sexuality

Sexuality is influenced by how it is viewed in different cultures. Some societies have very rigid social, cultural, and religious taboos associated with exposure of the human body, whereas other societies are more open. Note the dress and behavioral differences between a group of Muslim and U.S.-born American young women shown here.

Amr Abdallah Dalsh/Reuters

Glowimages/Getty Images

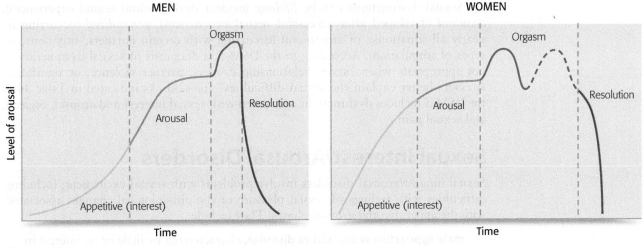

Figure 14.1

Human Sexual Response Cycle

The studies of Masters and Johnson reveal similar normal sexual response cycles for men and women. Note that women may experience more than one orgasm. Sexual disorders may occur at any of the phases, but seldom at the resolution phase.

3. The *orgasm phase* is characterized by involuntary muscular contractions throughout the body and the eventual release of sexual tension. In males, muscles at the base of the penis contract, propelling semen through the penis. In females, the outer third of the vagina contracts rhythmically.

4. The *resolution phase* is characterized by relaxation of the body after orgasm. Males enter a refractory period during which they are unresponsive to sexual stimulation. However, females are capable of multiple orgasms with continued stimulation.

Problems may occur in any of the phases of the sexual response cycle, although they are rare in the resolution phase.

sexual dysfunction a disruption of any part of the normal sexual response cycle that affects sexual desire, arousal, or response

Sexual Dysfunctions

A **sexual dysfunction** is a recurrent and persistent disruption of any part of the normal sexual response cycle involving sexual interest, arousal, or response. The DSM-5 requires that the symptoms associated with a sexual dysfunction be present for at least 6 months and be accompanied by significant distress. People who have no interest in sexual activity or who are unconcerned about an inability to experience an orgasm, for example, would not receive a sexual dysfunction diagnosis. Also, if the sexual problem is mainly due to severe interpersonal relationship problems or another mental condition such as an anxiety disorder, a sexual dysfunction diagnosis would not be made. Epidemiological data suggest that 40–45 percent of adult women and 20–30 percent of adult men have experienced at least one sexual dysfunction (R. W. Lewis et al., 2004). The lifetime prevalence of sexual problems in adults is summarized in Table 14.2.

Table 14.2 Lifetime Prevalence of Sexual Disorders in Men and Women in the 40–80 Age Range for the United States

Condition	Women (%)	Men (%)
Lack of interest in sex	33.2	18.1
Inability to reach orgasm	20.7	12.4
Orgasm reached too quickly	26.2	26.2
Pain during sex	12.7	3.1
Sex not pleasurable	19.7	11.2
Trouble lubricating	21.5	N/A

SOURCE: Laumann, Glasser, Neves, & Moreira (2009).

Sexual dysfunctions can be *lifelong* (evident during initial sexual experiences), *acquired* (developed after successful sexual experiences), *generalized* (occurring in nearly all situations), or *situational* (occurring with certain partners, situations, or types of stimulation). According to the DSM-5, a diagnosis of sexual dysfunction is not appropriate when "severe relationship distress, partner violence, or significant stressors better explain the sexual difficulties" (p. 424). As indicated in Table 14.3, the DSM-5 includes dysfunctions associated with sexual interest and arousal, orgasm, and sexual pain.

Sexual Interest/Arousal Disorders

Sexual interest/arousal disorders involve problems with sexual excitement, including difficulties with feelings of sexual pleasure or the physiological changes associated with the appetitive and arousal phases. They include:

- **male hypoactive sexual desire disorder**, characterized by little or no interest in sexual activities, either actual or fantasized; and

- **female sexual interest/arousal disorder**, characterized by little or no interest in sexual activities, either actual or fantasized, and/or a lack of or diminished arousal to sexual cues during nearly all sexual activities.

Some clinicians estimate that 40–50 percent of all sexual difficulties involve deficits in interest; this is one of the most common complaints of couples seeking sex therapy (Laumann, Glasser, Neves, & Moreira, 2009). Recall that according to the DSM-5, a diagnosis of sexual dysfunction is not appropriate when factors such as severe relationship problems, other mental disorders, or significant stressors play a key role in the sexual difficulties.

male hypoactive sexual desire disorder sexual dysfunction in men that is characterized by a lack of sexual desire

female sexual interest/arousal disorder distressing disinterest in sexual activities or inability to attain or maintain physiological or psychological arousal during sexual activity

Table 14.3 Sexual Dysfunctions

DSM-5 DISORDERS CHART			
Dysfunction[a]	**DSM-5 Definition**	**Prevalence**	**Associated Features**
Male Hypoactive Sexual Desire	Recurrent lack of sexual interest	Up to 15% of men have transient episodes; Less than 2% have chronic symptoms	Increasing prevalence with age
Erectile Dysfunction	Inability to attain or maintain erection sufficient for sexual activity	13%–21% have occasional episodes	Low self-esteem or lack of confidence; fear of failure
Premature Ejaculation	Ejaculation prior to or within 1 minute after vaginal penetration	Up to 30% indicate concern	Fear of not satisfying partner; but only 1%–3% meet the criteria
Delayed Ejaculation	Persistent delay or absence of ejaculation nearly all the time during partnered sex activity	Less than 1% of men	Partner may feel less attractive, feelings of frustration
Female Sexual Interest/ Arousal Disorder	Little or no sexual interest or arousal for sexual activity	30% with symptoms but many do not experience distress	Problems with arousal, pain, orgasm; relationship problem
Female Orgasmic Disorder	Persistent delay or inability to attain an orgasm in nearly all sexual encounters	10%–42% from surveys; nearly 10% never achieve an orgasm in their lifetime	Only mildly related to women's sexual satisfaction
Genito-Pelvic Pain/ Penetration Disorder	Difficulty with vaginal penetration, fear of pain, tightening of pelvic muscles	15%–21% of women report painful intercourse	Fear of penetration, avoidance of sexual activities

[a]All dysfunctions require that the individuals experience "clinically significant distress."
SOURCE: DSM-5; Carvalheira, Træen, & Štulhofer (2014); Pazmany, Bergeron, Van Oudenhove, Verhaeghe, & Enzlin (2013).

This distinction is important because sexual interest or arousal difficulties are often associated with depression or anxiety, relationship issues with the current partner, or current stressful events (Hackett, 2008). It is rare for men to have reduced libido in isolation; it is much more likely to result from a medical condition or other sexual dysfunctions, especially erectile disorder and delayed ejaculation (Corona et al., 2013). In a sample of men between the ages of 18 and 75, a distressing lack of sexual interest was reported by 14.5 percent of the participants, and was most common in men in long-term relationships, who had erectile difficulty, or who did not feel attracted to their partners. Among this group, stress involving work or professional activities was given as a major reason for their lack of interest in sex (Carvalheira, Traeen, & Stulhofer, 2014).

Among a group of women, 31 percent reported experiencing a lack of sexual interest (McCabe & Goldhammer, 2013). For women, difficulties with sexual interest or arousal often result from negative attitudes about sex or early sexual experiences. For example, receiving inaccurate or disturbing sexual information, having been sexually assaulted or molested, or having conflicts with a sexual partner may contribute to limited sexual interest or arousal (Perlman et al., 2007).

Although people with sexual interest/arousal disorders are often capable of experiencing orgasm, they have little interest in, or derive minimal pleasure from, sexual activity. In the following case, relationship problems contributed to the couple's sexual difficulties.

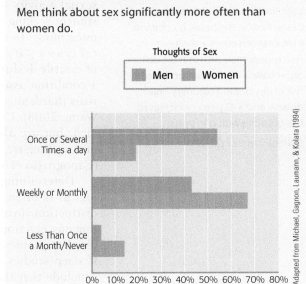

DID YOU KNOW?

Men think about sex significantly more often than women do.

Thoughts of Sex

Men   Women

Once or Several Times a day

Weekly or Monthly

Less Than Once a Month/Never

0% 10% 20% 30% 40% 50% 60% 70% 80%

CASE STUDY   After 5 years of marriage, Rhonda and Michael decided to seek sex therapy because of their unsatisfactory sex life. Although they had enjoyed sex for the first year of their marriage, sexual intercourse had progressively declined: For the past 3 years they have had little or no sexual contact. Rhonda described Michael as "unloving, cold, angry, controlling, and demanding" and explained to the therapist that she does not love or feel sexually interested in Michael. Michael described Rhonda as "punitive, angry, and a vengeful person" and believes she is punishing him for a brief affair he had with a co-worker early in their marriage. Correspondingly, he feels angry, resentful, and cheated of a "normal sex life."

In this case, should Rhonda receive a female sexual interest/arousal disorder diagnosis because of her low sexual desire and limited sexual interest in Michael? Most clinicians would question the legitimacy of such a diagnosis because her lack of desire appears to result from severe relationship difficulties. These interpersonal problems, rather than Rhonda's lack of sexual interest, would be the most appropriate focus of treatment.

Erectile Disorder

CASE STUDY   A 20-year-old college student was experiencing acquired erectile dysfunction. His first episode of erectile difficulty occurred when he attempted sexual intercourse after drinking heavily. Although he knew that his sexual performance was affected by alcohol, he began to have doubts about his sexual ability. During a subsequent sexual encounter, his anxiety and worry increased. When he failed in this next coital encounter, even though he had not been drinking, his anxiety level rose even more. When his erectile difficulties continued, he decided to seek therapy.

In men, inhibited sexual excitement takes the form of an **erectile disorder (ED)**, an inability to attain or maintain an erection sufficient for sexual intercourse or other sexual activity on almost all occasions (Yuan et al., 2014). As was the case of the student seeking therapy, the man may feel fully aroused, yet be unable to engage in intercourse. In the past, people often attributed erectile dysfunction to psychological causes ("It's all in the head"). However, studies indicate that up to 70 percent of erectile dysfunction is due to limited blood flow caused by vascular insufficiency, a condition associated with physiological influences such as diabetes, arteriosclerosis (hardening of the arteries), or traumatic groin injury (R. W. Lewis, Yuan, & Wang, 2008). Complaints regarding erectile dysfunction are common among older men, but are also prevalent in younger individuals. In one study, 26 percent of men seeking treatment for erectile dysfunction were between the ages of 17 and 40 (Capogrosso et al., 2013).

Determining whether erectile dysfunction is primarily biological or psychological is often difficult (Lewis et al., 2008). One procedure used to make this distinction involves recording *nocturnal penile tumescence*—the frequent, spontaneous erections that occur in healthy men during sleep. If a man has a physiological problem, he is unlikely to have these spontaneous erections during sleep. If sleep studies confirm normal erectile activity during sleep, there is reason to conclude that the erectile problems are psychological in nature (Wylie, 2008). In many cases, however, a combination of physical and psychological factors influence erectile difficulties.

Orgasmic Disorders

Orgasmic disorders affect both men and women. Those with this condition experience difficulty or an inability to achieve a satisfactory orgasm after entering the excitement phase and receiving adequate sexual stimulation. Orgasmic difficulties are quite different in men compared to women. In men, the symptoms of orgasmic dysfunction are subsumed under the diagnostic categories of delayed ejaculation and premature ejaculation.

Female Orgasmic Disorder

A woman with **female orgasmic disorder** experiences persistent delay, or inability to achieve an orgasm or a "markedly reduced intensity of orgasmic sensations" (APA, 2013) on nearly all occasions of sexual activity despite receiving "adequate" stimulation. Most women require clitoral stimulation to achieve an orgasm; this may be one of the reasons that only a small percentage of women report consistently experiencing orgasm during sexual intercourse. The diagnosis of female orgasmic disorder is given only if the woman has difficulty achieving an orgasm through clitoral stimulation. Female orgasmic disorder is a frequently reported sexual problem for women (Buster, 2013). In fact, approximately 10 percent of all women have never achieved an orgasm any time during their life (APA, 2013).

Delayed Ejaculation

Delayed ejaculation is the persistent delay or absence of ejaculation after the excitement phase has been reached and sexual activity has been adequate in focus, intensity, and duration. The term is usually restricted to the delay or inability to ejaculate during partnered sexual activity, even with full arousal. For a disorder to be diagnosed, delayed ejaculation must have occurred 75–100 percent of the time for at least 6 months. Due to a lack of consensus in the research, the diagnostic criteria do not address what constitutes a "delay" (APA, 2013). As noted, men who have this dysfunction are usually able to ejaculate when masturbating.

erectile disorder (ED) an inability to attain or maintain an erection sufficient for sexual intercourse

female orgasmic disorder sexual dysfunction involving persistent delay or inability to achieve an orgasm with adequate clitoral stimulation

delayed ejaculation persistent delay or inability to ejaculate within the vagina despite adequate excitement and stimulation

Is Hypersexual Behavior a Sexual Disorder?

Can a person be "oversexed" and have a sexual appetite that requires frequent sex in order to be satisfied? More than 4 percent of people claim to have sex every day; 2 percent of married men and 1 percent of married women report having intercourse more than once a day (Durex, 2001, 2005). Are these people statistically abnormal?

Most sex therapists agree that some individuals seem obsessed with sex, feel compelled to engage in frequent sexual activity, and experience personal distress due to their behavior. In fact, it is estimated that between 3 and 6 percent of U.S. adults exhibit compulsive, impulsive, or addictive sexual behavior (Karila et al., 2013). Terms such as *hypersexuality*, *erotomania*, *nymphomania* (in women), and *satyriasis* (in men) refer to this phenomenon. Golfer Tiger Woods, actors Charlie Sheen and David Duchovny (*The X-Files*, *Californication*), and TV reality star Jesse James (ex-husband of Sandra Bullock) all admitted to "sex addiction" and entered rehabilitation centers for treatment (Thompson, 2014). In these cases, their "compulsions" to have sex with multiple partners resulted in negative personal or professional consequences. Is sexual addiction a real disorder or simply an excuse?

Clinical and research evidence suggests that hypersexuality can result in impairment and distress, so those revising the DSM considered the inclusion of a hypersexual disorder. Although there was a decision not to incorporate this disorder in the DSM-5, most clinicians and researchers agree that some people do have sexual behavior that resembles an addiction. They have recurrent sexual fantasies and urges or they engage in compulsive sexual behavior in response to depression, anxiety, boredom, irritability, or stressful life events. Additionally, they have considerable difficulty reducing or controlling their sexual urges, activities, and fantasies, even when the behaviors cause physical or emotional harm to themselves or others (Weiss, 2012). In addition to personal psychological distress (guilt, shame, anxiety, or depression), the consequences of hypersexual behavior may include relationship problems, divorce or separation, an increased rate of sexually transmitted disease, unintended pregnancies, excessive spending on sexual services, and school or employment dysfunction (Kafka, 2009). Do you know anyone who demonstrates hypersexuality? If so, what do you see as the pros and cons of having their behavioral difficulties recognized as a psychiatric disorder?

Premature (Early) Ejaculation

The inability to satisfy a sexual partner during sexual intercourse is a source of anguish for many men. **Premature (early) ejaculation** involves a distressing and recurrent pattern of having an orgasm with minimal sexual stimulation before, during, or shortly after vaginal penetration; the diagnostic criterion specifies that ejaculation must occur within approximately 1 minute of penetration or attempted penetration (APA, 2013). Premature ejaculation is the most common male sexual dysfunction, affecting approximately 21–33 percent of men (Morales, 2012). However, because DSM-5 added the duration of 1 minute after vaginal penetration to the diagnostic criteria, only 1–3 percent will now meet the criteria for a premature ejaculation diagnosis. Table 14.4 compares responses regarding sexual functioning and satisfaction from men with and without problems with premature ejaculation.

Genito-Pelvic Pain/Penetration Disorder

According to DSM-5, **genito-pelvic pain/penetration disorder** may be diagnosed when a woman experiences distress and difficulty associated with: vaginal penetration during intercourse; pain in the genital or pelvic region during intercourse (**dyspareunia**); fear of pain or vaginal penetration; or tension in the pelvic muscles (APA, 2013). The

premature (early) ejaculation ejaculation with minimal sexual stimulation before, during, or shortly after penetration

genito-pelvic pain/penetration disorder physical pain or discomfort associated with intercourse or penetration; fear, anxiety, and distress are also usually present

dyspareunia recurrent or persistent pain in the genitals before, during, or after sexual intercourse

Sexual Flirtation Common among Teens

Direct expressions of sexual interest are often discouraged in various cultures. Flirting, however, allows for indirect, playful, and romantic sexual overtures toward others. It may occur through verbal communication (tone of voice, pace, and intonation) or body language (eye contact, open stances, hair flicking, or brief touching).

pain and distress associated with genito-pelvic pain/penetration disorder is not caused exclusively by lack of lubrication or by the rare condition, **vaginismus**, which results when involuntary spasms of the outer third of the vaginal wall prevent or interfere with sexual intercourse.

Painful intercourse is relatively common in women under age 40 and is estimated to affect between 15 and 21 percent of women in this age group. As compared to a control group of pain-free women, a sample of women with dyspareunia reported significantly higher levels of distress over body image and their genitals (Pazmany, Bergeron, Van Oudenhove, Verhaeghe, & Enzlin, 2013). As you might expect, many women with genito-pelvic pain/penetration disorder also experience reduced sexual arousal.

Aging and Sexual Dysfunctions

Changes in sexual functioning (decreases in sexual interest, arousal, and activity) are common as we age. It is, therefore, important for clinicians to consider ways in which the aging process affects sexuality. When women reach menopause, estrogen levels drop, and women may experience painful intercourse due to vaginal dryness and thinning of the vaginal wall (Nappi, Kingsberg, Maamari, & Simon, 2013). Older men are at increased risk for prostate problems and cardiovascular difficulties that may increase the risk of erectile disorder (Gooren, 2008). Other illnesses associated with aging such as diabetes, high blood pressure, or heart disease can also affect sexual performance and interest. Hormone replacement therapy, drugs for erectile disorder (Cialis, Levitra, and Viagra), and other medical procedures may help minimize the effects of these organic problems. Additionally, lifestyle modifications such as weight loss, increasing exercise, or decreasing smoking or alcohol consumption can improve sexual functioning in older adults (Glina, Sharlip, & Hellstrom, 2013).

Etiology of Sexual Dysfunctions

Sexual dysfunctions clearly demonstrate the complex interaction of various etiological factors (Bitzer, Giraldi, & Pfaus, 2013). Let's return to the case of Jeremiah and Christina from the chapter opening to illustrate how various etiological factors can contribute to sexual dysfunction. (You may wish to reread the case in order to follow

vaginismus involuntary spasm of the outer third of the vaginal wall that prevents or interferes with sexual intercourse

Table 14.4 Mean Responses of Men with and without Premature Ejaculation

Item	With	Without
1. Over the past month, how was your control over ejaculation during sexual intercourse? (0 = very poor; 4 = good)	0.9	3.0
2. Over the past month, how was your satisfaction with sexual intercourse? (0 = very poor; 4 = very good)	1.9	3.3
3. How distressed are you by how fast you ejaculate during intercourse? (4 = extremely distressed; 0 = not at all)	2.9	0.7
4. To what extent does how fast you ejaculate cause difficulty in your relationship with your partner? (4 = extremely; 0 = not at all)	1.9	0.3

SOURCE: Rowland, Tai, & Brummett (2007).

this multipath analysis.) The following multipath explanation of the couple's sexual difficulties might be operative.

CASE STUDY ANALYSIS Christina and Jerimiah sought sex therapy because Christina did not seem to desire or enjoy sex. Additionally, Jeremiah was experiencing erectile difficulties for the first time in his life. The therapist concluded that these problems were not primarily the result of severe relationship distress. Christina was diagnosed as having a sexual interest/arousal disorder and Jeremiah an erectile disorder. The possibility that Christina could also be experiencing an orgasmic disorder was entertained but eliminated as therapy progressed. It appeared that she was quite capable of being aroused and orgasmic under the right conditions.

Their sexual difficulties involved a variety of interacting factors. Christina's limited interest in sex increasingly strained their sexual relationship and caused Jeremiah to feel anger, guilt, and humiliation and experience difficulty maintaining an erection. After a while, Jerimiah began to drink before initiating sex, which decreased his inhibition and gave him the courage to initiate sex with a reluctant partner; however, alcohol is a central nervous system depressant, a factor that made it more difficult for him to achieve an erection.

When Jeremiah was able to become erect, he quickly entered Christina for fear of losing the erection, and in turn appeared "brief" and "perfunctory" in lovemaking. This caused Christina to feel hurt and rejected. Additionally, the brevity of the sexual encounter did not allow Christina to become sexually aroused; this resulted in insufficient lubrication, painful intercourse, and an inability to achieve an orgasm. Christina then began to fake orgasms in order to please Jeremiah. Jeremiah, however, knew she was faking. He not only blamed himself for the failure but also felt humiliated. As a man, Jeremiah was also affected by cultural scripts—social and cultural beliefs that guide attitudes and behaviors—that associate masculinity with sexual potency. Thus, he began to equate his inability to satisfy Christina with "not being a real man." Given all of these influences, they both found their sexual encounters increasingly unpleasant, a factor that added stress to their relationship and further decreased Christina's interest in sex. The cycle then repeated itself.

As you can see, Jeremiah and Christina's sexual disorders are intertwined and cannot be viewed in isolation. Although the problems began with Christina's low sexual interest, they escalated as Jeremiah began experiencing difficulties achieving and maintaining an erection. Consistent with our case example, research suggests that difficulties with sexual interest, desire, and performance are due to interactions among biological, psychological, social, and sociocultural factors as reflected in our multipath model (Figure 14.2).

Biological Dimension

Environmental and relationship variables influence sexual dysfunction to a greater degree than biological factors (Burri, 2013). However, lower levels of testosterone and higher levels of estrogens such as prolactin have been associated with lower sexual interest in both men and women and with erectile difficulties in men (van Lankveld, 2008). Not surprisingly, drugs that suppress testosterone appear to decrease sexual desire in men (R. W. Lewis et al., 2008). Conversely, the administration of androgens (hormones such as testosterone, which promotes male sexual characteristics) is associated with reports of increased sexual desire in both men and women. The relationship between hormones and sexual behavior, however, is complex and difficult to understand. Many people with reduced sexual desire have normal testosterone levels (Hyde, 2005).

DID YOU KNOW?

In our society, a strong libido is associated with potency, power, attractiveness, sensual pleasure, and health. The search for aphrodisiacs in the form of powdered animal genitals, herbs, secret concoctions, and even drugs such as Viagra is a multibillion-dollar industry.

Figure 14.2

Multipath Model of Sexual Dysfunctions

The dimensions interact with one another and combine in different ways to result in a specific sexual dysfunction.

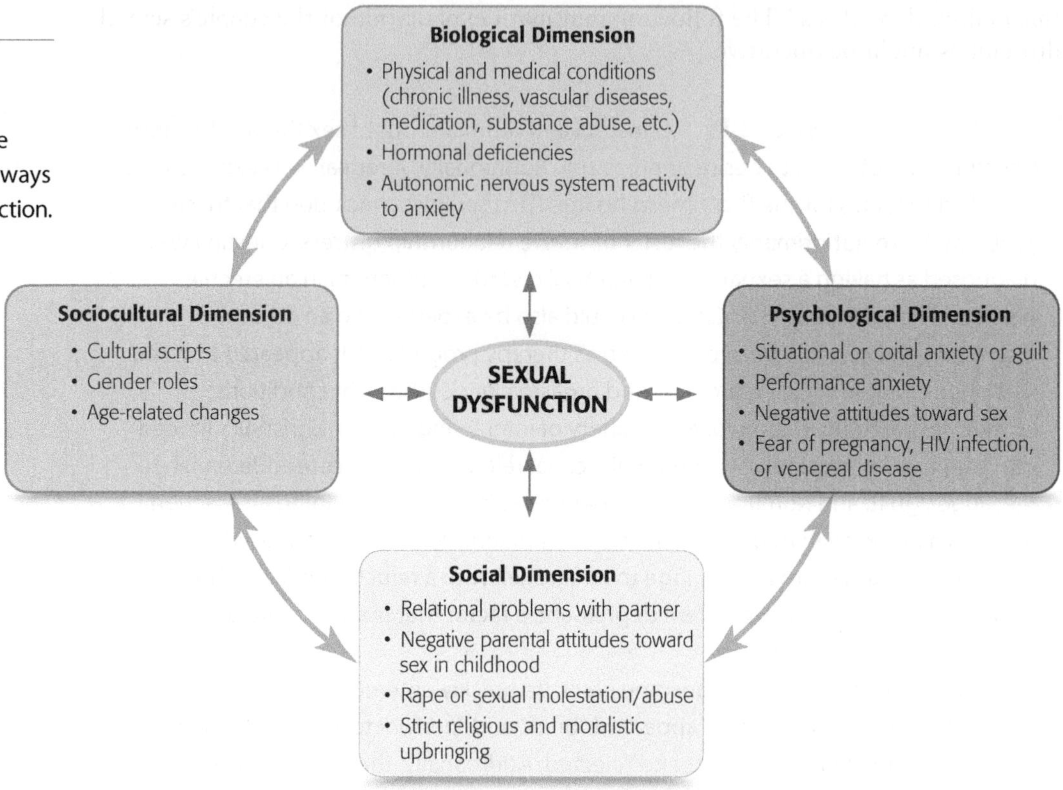

Biological Dimension
- Physical and medical conditions (chronic illness, vascular diseases, medication, substance abuse, etc.)
- Hormonal deficiencies
- Autonomic nervous system reactivity to anxiety

Sociocultural Dimension
- Cultural scripts
- Gender roles
- Age-related changes

SEXUAL DYSFUNCTION

Psychological Dimension
- Situational or coital anxiety or guilt
- Performance anxiety
- Negative attitudes toward sex
- Fear of pregnancy, HIV infection, or venereal disease

Social Dimension
- Relational problems with partner
- Negative parental attitudes toward sex in childhood
- Rape or sexual molestation/abuse
- Strict religious and moralistic upbringing

© Cengage Learning®

Medications that treat medical conditions such as hypertension, ulcers, glaucoma, allergies, and seizures can also affect sex drive. Use of drugs, alcohol use and antidepressant medications are also associated with sexual dysfunctions, as are certain medical conditions (Metzger, Walter, Graf, & Abler, 2013; Ramsey et al., 2013). Indeed, some researchers believe that alcohol abuse is the leading cause of both erectile disorders and premature ejaculation (Arackal & Benegal, 2007). However, not everyone who takes antihypertensive or antidepressant medications, consumes alcohol, or is ill has a sexual dysfunction. In some people these factors may combine with a predisposing personal history or with current stressors to produce problems in sexual function. A complete physical workup—including a medical history, physical exam, and laboratory evaluation—is a necessary first step in assessment. For example, genito-pelvic pain/penetration disorder is often caused by gynecological conditions such as endometriosis (Buster, 2013).

Penile hypersensitivity to physical stimulation may also influence sexual functioning in men. In other words, for some men, premature ejaculation may be physiological (Paik & Laumann, 2006). Men who ejaculate early may be "hardwired" to have a sensitive and more easily triggered sensory and response system (Rowland & McMahon, 2008).

Psychological Dimension

Sexual dysfunctions may result from psychological factors alone or from a combination of psychological and biological factors. Psychological causes for sexual dysfunctions include predisposing or historical factors, as well as more current problems and concerns. Stressful situations and the presence of anxiety disorders tend to inhibit sexual responding and functioning in both women and men (Carvalheira, Traeen, & Stulhofer, 2014; D'ettore, Pucciarelli, & Santarnecchi, 2013). For example, Iraqi and Afghanistan war veterans with PTSD were over 3 times more likely to have a sexual dysfunction compared to veterans without the disorder (Breyer et al., 2014). Guilt, anger, or resentment toward a partner can also interfere with sexual performance (Westheimer & Lopater, 2005). As was the case for Jeremiah and Christina, having a partner with a sexual dysfunction further increases risk of sexual difficulties in the other partner (Jiann, Su, & Tsai, 2013).

Apprehension about sexual functioning plays a key role in erectile disorder, especially for men who report that sex is very important to them or to their partner (Rowland, Lechner, & Burnett, 2012). Men with psychological erectile dysfunction often report anxiety over sexual overtures, including a fear of failing sexually or being seen as sexually inferior, as well as anxiety over the size of their genitals. Performance anxiety and taking on a "spectator role" can exacerbate erectile dysfunction. For example, if a man unexpectedly experiences a problem achieving or maintaining an erection, he may then begin to worry that it will happen again. Instead of enjoying the next sexual encounter and becoming aroused, he monitors or observes his own reactions ("Am I getting an erection?") and becomes a spectator who is anxious and detached from the situation. This can result in sexual failure and increased anxiety during future sexual encounters.

Previous and current sexual experiences may influence a man's sexual expectations and responses in other ways. Men with early ejaculation, for example, report having a lower frequency of sexual intercourse than those without this condition (Rowland & McMahon, 2008). This is significant because even in men without sexual dysfunction, longer intervals between sex results in greater excitement when intercourse occurs. For men with early ejaculation, having fewer sexual experiences may predispose them to greater excitement and arousal. In addition, they may have fewer opportunities to learn how to delay an ejaculatory response. It is important to note that one successful form of sexual therapy for premature ejaculation teaches men to attend more to somatic feedback and to adjust their thoughts and behaviors to delay an impending ejaculation.

Situational anxiety or emotional factors resulting from sexual abuse or other negative childhood sexual experiences often interfere with sexual functioning in women. Other factors associated with sexual dysfunction in women include: having a sexually inexperienced or dysfunctional partner; fear of being an undesirable sexual partner; worry that they will never be able to attain orgasm; concern about pregnancy or sexually transmitted disease; an inability to accept the partner, either emotionally or physically; and misinformation or ignorance about sexuality or sexual techniques (Westheimer & Lopater, 2005).

Negative thoughts ("my partner doesn't really care about me") and dysfunctional beliefs ("sexual desire is sinful") also play a role in female sexual dysfunction. Such thoughts and beliefs are associated with sexual interest/arousal and orgasmic difficulties, as well as painful intercourse (Carvalho, Veríssimo, & Nobre, 2013; Melles et al., 2014). Focusing on one's body can also influence the sexual responsiveness of women. Women who are self-consciousness about their attractiveness or who focus excessively on their bodies experience more difficulty with sexual arousal (Woertman & van den Brink, 2012). Thirty percent of women indicated that a negative body image affected their sex lives and 52 percent reported hiding one or more aspects of their body during sex (Peplau et al., 2008).

Social Dimension

Social upbringing and current relationships both influence sexual functioning. The attitudes parents display toward sex and their expression of affection toward each other can affect their children's attitudes. A strict religious upbringing is associated with sexual dysfunction in both men and women (Carvalho et al., 2013; Masters & Johnson, 1970). Traumatic sexual experiences involving rape or sexual abuse during childhood or adolescence are also factors to consider. Women who have been raped or who were subjected to molestation as children may find it difficult to trust and establish intimacy and exhibit various sexual dysfunctions (Buster, 2013).

Relationship issues are often at the forefront of sexual disorders. Marital satisfaction, for example, is associated with greater levels of sexual arousal and sexual frequency between partners, whereas relationship dissatisfaction can lead to sexual interest and arousal disorders (C. A. Graham et al., 2004). Specifically, sexual satisfaction is

DID YOU KNOW?

In a survey, X-rated film actresses revealed that they were more likely to be bisexual, enjoy sex, have more sexual partners, use more drugs, and have higher self-esteem than a matched sample of women. They were also less likely to have experienced childhood abuse.

SOURCE: Griffith, Mitchell, Hart, Adams, & Gu, 2013

DID YOU KNOW?

Frequency of yearly sex varies among countries, nationalities, and regions:

1. U.S. Americans have the most sex (124 times per year), followed by Greeks (117 times per year), South Africans and Croatians (116 times per year), and New Zealanders (115 times per year).
2. People in Japan (36 times per year), Hong Kong (63 times per year), Taiwan (65 times per year), and China (72 times per year) have the least sex.

SOURCE: Durex, 2001, 2005

increased when relationships are caring, warm, and affectionate and when couples communicate openly about sex and sexual activities (Meston et al., 2008). It is important to note that men and women may define sexual satisfaction differently. For many women, for example, closeness to a partner is more important than the frequency of orgasms or the intensity of sexual arousal.

Sociocultural Dimension

A variety of sociocultural factors can influence sexual attitudes, behavior, and functioning. Although the human sexual response cycle is similar for women and men, gender differences are clearly present: Women have different sexual fantasies than men, are more attuned to relationships in the sexual encounter, and take longer than men to become aroused (Safarinejad, 2006). Likewise, gender differences and biological factors may interact and cause sexual dysfunction. Not surprisingly, women are much more likely to experience sexual interest/arousal difficulties. It is important to note that sex researchers and clinicians who do not take into account these biological differences may unfairly portray women as having a sexual dysfunction.

Cultural scripts about sex result from gender role socialization. It is through this process that we learn social and cultural beliefs and expectations regarding sexual behavior. In U.S. society, men are taught to be sexually assertive whereas women are socialized to avoid initiating sex directly. Cultural scripts for men in the United States may include "sexual potency in men is a sign of masculinity"; "the bigger the sex organ, the better"; and "strong and virile men do not show feelings." For women, scripts include "nice women don't initiate sex"; "women should be restrained and proper in lovemaking"; "men are only after one thing"; and "it is the woman's responsibility to take care of contraception." Because these scripts often guide our sexual attitudes and behaviors, they can exert a major influence on sexual functioning.

Cultural scripts also exist in other nations. For example, people in Asian countries consistently report the lowest frequency of sexual intercourse. Guilt regarding sex may be a contributing factor. In a study of European-Canadian and Chinese-Canadian women, the former group reported less sex guilt and greater sexual desire. Further, Chinese-Canadian women who showed greater acculturation to Western standards reported less guilt and greater sexual desire than their less acculturated counterparts. Cultural differences in sex guilt may be a means by which ethnicity affects reported sexual desire (Woo, Brotto, & Gorzalka, 2012).

Sexual orientation is also a sociocultural influence that may affect sexual responsiveness and sexual dysfunction in gay men and lesbians. Although there are no physiological differences in sexual arousal and response between lesbians and gay men and their heterosexual counterparts, their sexual issues and dysfunctions may differ quite dramatically. For example, problems among heterosexuals most often involve issues with sexual intercourse, whereas sexual concerns among lesbians and gay men may focus on other behaviors (e.g., aversion toward anal eroticism or cunnilingus). Lesbians and gay men must also deal with societal or internalized homophobia, which may inhibit openly expressing affection toward one another (M. S. Schneider, Brown, & Glassgold, 2002). Finally, gay men are forced to deal with the association between sexual activity and HIV infection. These broader contextual issues may create diminished sexual interest or desire, sexual aversion, or negative feelings toward sexual activity (Croteau, Lark, Lidderdale, & Chung, 2005).

Treatment of Sexual Dysfunctions

Many approaches are used to treat sexual dysfunctions, including biological interventions and psychological treatment approaches.

Biological Interventions

Discovering underlying biological issues is an important first step in treating sexual dysfunction (Buster, 2013). Biological interventions may include hormone replacement, special medications, or mechanical means to improve sexual functioning. For example, men with organic erectile dysfunction may be treated with vacuum pumps, suppositories, or penile implants. The penile implant is an inflatable device that, once expanded, produces an erection sufficient for intercourse and ejaculation (see Table 14.5). Approximately 89 percent of men with penile implants and 70 percent of their partners expressed satisfaction with the implants (Center for Male Reproductive Medicine and Microsurgery, 2005), and most said that they would choose the treatment again.

Table 14.5 Treating Erectile Disorders: Medical Interventions

Treatment	Primary Agent	Effects	Drawbacks
Oral medication	Viagra, Levitra, or Cialis	Taken as a pill. Enhances blood flow to the penis and allows many users to achieve normal erections. The drugs are taken before sex, and stimulation is needed for an erection.	Medication side effects including head or stomach pain or nasal congestion.
Surgery	Vascular surgery	Corrects venous leak from a groin injury by repairing arteries to boost blood supply in the penis. Restores the ability to have a normal erection.	Minimal problems when used appropriately with diagnosed condition.
Suppository	Muse (alprotadil)	A tiny pellet is inserted into the penis by means of an applicator 5 to 10 minutes before sex. Erections can last an hour.	Penile aching, minor urethral bleeding or spotting, dizziness, and leg-vein swelling.
Injection therapy	Vasodilating drugs, including Caverject (alprotadil), Edex (alprostadil), and Invicorp (VIP and phentolamine)	Drug is injected directly into the base of the penis 10 minutes to 2 hours before sex, depending on the drug. The drug helps relax smooth-muscle tissues and creates an erection in up to 90% of patients. Erection lasts about an hour.	Pain, bleeding, and scar tissue formation. Erections may not readily subside.
Devices	Vacuum pump	Creates negative air pressure around the penis to induce the flow of blood, which is then trapped by an elastic band encircling the shaft. Pump is used just before sex. Erection lasts until band is removed.	Some difficulty in ejaculation. Penis can become cool and appear constricted in color. Apparatus can be clumsy to use.
	Penile implants	Considered a last resort. A penile prosthesis is implanted in the penis, enabling men to literally "pump themselves up" by pulling blood into it.	Destruction of spongy tissue inside the penis.

Medications are also used to treat erectile disorder. One form of medical treatment for erectile dysfunction involves injecting medication (Alprostadil) into the penis or inserting a suppository with the medication into the opening at the tip of the penis (R. W. Lewis et al., 2008). Within a very short time, blood flow to the area is increased and the man gets a very stiff erection, which may last from 1 to 4 hours. Although men using this method have reported general satisfaction with it, as have their mates, it does have some side effects, including prolonged erections and bruising of the penis.

Oral medications such as Viagra, Levitra, and Cialis are frequently used to treat erectile disorder. In fact, Viagra made headlines in 1998 as a "miracle cure" for men with erectile dysfunction (Read & Mati, 2013). Unlike injectables, Viagra and its competitors do not produce an automatic erection in the absence of sexual stimuli. If a man becomes aroused, the drugs enable the body to follow through the sexual response cycle to completion. The medications do not improve sexual functioning in normally functioning men, nor do they lead to a stiffer erection. However, it is possible that these drugs may act as a placebo in men without erectile dysfunction and thereby improve sexual arousal and performance by stimulating their expectations and fantasies; this psychological boost may then lead to subjective feelings of enhanced pleasure. Viagra has, in fact, been found to increase the level of confidence of men engaging in sexual activity (Seftel et al., 2014).

Although biological treatments are increasingly important in treating sexual dysfunctions, they deemphasize the role of psychological and social factors. Because relationship, sociocultural, and psychological factors are often involved, treatment needs to include more than medications or other biological means to boost sexual interest or desire (Berry, 2013). For example, group therapy plus Viagra is more effective than Viagra alone for treating erectile dysfunction, according to a review by Read and Mati (2013). In fact, group therapy alone produced better results than Viagra alone, which again points out the need for comprehensive treatment.

Psychological Treatment Approaches

Psychological treatment is recommended when relationship or psychological issues, including prior traumatic experiences, play a role in sexual dysfunction. General psychological treatment approaches include the following components (Fruhauf, Gerger, Schmidt, Munder, & Barth, 2013):

Education. The therapist replaces sexual myths and misconceptions with accurate information about sexual anatomy and functioning.

Anxiety reduction. The therapist uses procedures such as desensitization or graded approaches to keep anxiety at a minimum. The therapist explains that constantly observing and evaluating one's performance can interfere with sexual functioning.

Maladaptive thoughts and beliefs. The therapist helps the client identify and change negative thoughts and beliefs that interfere with sexual functioning.

Structured behavioral exercises. The therapist gives a series of graded tasks that gradually increase the amount of sexual interaction between the partners. Each partner takes turns touching and being touched over different parts of the body except for the genital regions. Later the partners fondle the body and genital regions without making demands for sexual arousal or orgasm. Successful sexual intercourse and orgasm are the final stage of the structured exercises.

Communication training. The therapist teaches the partners appropriate ways of communicating their sexual wishes to each other and strategies for effectively resolving relationship conflicts.

In addition to these general psychological treatments, sex therapists can also focus on specific aspects of sexual dysfunction. Some specific nonmedical treatments for other dysfunctions include:

Female orgasmic dysfunction. Both structured behavioral exercises and communication training have been successful in treating sexual arousal disorders in women. Masturbation appears to be the most effective way for women with orgasmic dysfunction to have an orgasm. The procedure involves education about sexual anatomy, visual and tactile self-exploration, use of sexual fantasies and images, and masturbation, both individually and with a partner. High success rates are reported with this procedure, especially for women who have never experienced an orgasm. However, this approach does not necessarily lead to a woman's ability to achieve orgasm during sexual intercourse (Both & Laan, 2009).

Early ejaculation. In one technique, the partner stimulates the penis until the man feels the sensation of impending ejaculation. At this point, the partner momentarily stops the stimulation and then continues it again. This pattern is repeated until the man can tolerate increasingly greater periods of stimulation before ejaculation (Carufel & Trudel, 2006).

Vaginismus. The results of treatment for vaginismus have been uniformly positive. The involuntary spasms or closure of the vaginal muscle can be deconditioned by first training the woman to relax and then inserting successively larger dilators while she is relaxed (Vorvick, 2012).

> **MYTH** Sex is unimportant to older adults. They are averse to being sexually active and are conservative in sexual behavior.
>
> **REALITY** Although sexual activity does decline with age, a major survey of adults ages 57 to 85 found that many older people are sexually active well into their 60s, 70s, and 80s. Fifty-four percent reported having sex at least twice a month, and 23 percent reported having sex at least once weekly. Approximately 50 percent of the respondents younger than age 75 had engaged in oral sex in the previous 2 months (Lindau et al., 2007).

Gender Dysphoria

CASE STUDY Coy Mathis, born a male triplet, has behaved like a girl since she was 18 months old. While her brother Max was consumed with dinosaurs, she was playing with Barbie dolls. By 4, she was telling her mother that something was wrong with her body. Since enrolling in elementary school in Fountain, Colorado, the 6-year-old has presented as female and wears girls' clothing. Her classmates and teachers use female pronouns when referring to her (James, 2013).

Gender dysphoria—previously called *gender identity disorder* or *transsexualism*—is characterized by distress and impairment in functioning that results from a marked incongruence (mismatch) between one's experienced or expressed gender and one's **assigned gender** as a male or female. In other words, individuals who experience gender dysphoria have distress associated with their **transgender identity**—their innate emotional and psychological identity as male or female is opposite from their biological sex. In the case of Coy Mathis, she was born a boy but has identified as a girl since early childhood. It is important to note that gender identity and **sexual orientation** are not the same thing—the sexual orientation of someone with a transgender identity can be heterosexual, gay, lesbian, bisexual, or asexual (Zucker & Cohen-Ketteris, 2008).

Gender dysphoria is diagnosed only when there is significant distress or impairment in functioning resulting from the individual's transgender identity and experiences. Individuals with gender dysphoria may display a strong dislike of their sexual anatomy, a desire for sexual characteristics of their experienced gender, and rejection of objects or activities associated with their assigned gender. In rare cases, the experienced gender may be an alternative gender, distinct from the traditional two genders common across cultures (APA, 2013). Estimates suggest that between 0.25 and 1 percent of the U.S. population have a transgender identity (National Center for Transgender Equality, 2009). However, gender dysphoria is

gender dysphoria   distress and impaired functioning resulting from an incongruence between a person's gender identity and assigned gender

assigned gender   the gender to which a child is socially assigned at birth based on biological sex

transgender identity   a person's innate psychological identification as male or female does not correspond with the person's biological sex

sexual orientation   sexual identity involving the gender to which a person is physically and emotionally attracted

AP Photo/Brennan Linsley

Life as a Transgender Girl

Coy Mathis, left, plays with her sister at their home in Colorado. Biologically, Coy is a boy, but she has self-identified as a girl since early childhood. Her family, friends and classmates all consider her a girl.

relatively rare because many transgender individuals do not experience significant distress or impairment in functioning.

Gender dysphoria is experienced differently at different ages. People with gender dysphoria often begin to report gender-role conflicts early in childhood (Zucker, 2009). A boy may claim that he will grow up to be a woman, demonstrate disgust with his penis, and be interested in toys and activities considered "feminine." He may prefer playing with girls and avoid the aggressive activities commonly enjoyed by boys. Male peers or others frequently label boys with a transgender identity as "sissies." Girls with a transgender identity may insist that they have a penis or will grow one and may exhibit an avid interest in rough-and-tumble play. Nonconformity with stereotypical gender role behavior should not, however, be confused with the pervasive gender incongruence experienced by those with a transgender identity. The strength, pervasiveness, and persistence of gender-incongruent behaviors are a key feature of a transgender identity.

Adults with gender dysphoria often experienced intense feeling of gender incongruence throughout their lives. Because of a lifelong conviction that nature placed them in the wrong body, they are often preoccupied with eliminating their biologically based sexual characteristics and acquiring those of their experienced gender (Lawrence, 2008). As physiological maturation progresses during puberty, dislike for and desire to be rid of their sexual anatomy may strengthen, thus increasing their distress. As puberty sets in, transgender males may begin to shave their legs or bind their genitals, whereas transgender adolescent females may attempt to make their breasts less visible. As their personal identity develops during adolescence, their emotions and reactions may increasingly resemble those of their experienced gender, a factor that further increases gender incongruence. During adolescence and early adulthood, transgender people have an increasing need to be treated and accepted as a member of their experienced gender. It is often under these circumstances that the extent of distress associated with gender incongruence is recognized, treatment is sought, and gender dysphoria is diagnosed.

Etiology of Gender Dysphoria

The etiology of gender dysphoria is unclear. Because it is quite rare, investigators have focused more attention on other disorders. Gender dysphoria appears to be more common in males than in females and occurs in both children and adults (Lawrence, 2008). In all likelihood, a number of variables interact to produce gender dysphoria.

Biological Influences

Biological research suggests that neurohormonal factors and genetics may be involved in the development of a transgender identity (Ghosh & Pataki, 2012). In animal studies, for example, the presence or absence of testosterone early in life appears to influence the organization of brain centers that govern sexual behavior. In human females, early exposure to male hormones has resulted in a more masculine behavior pattern. Thus, it does appear that gender orientation can be influenced by a lack or excess of sex hormones. Interestingly, a study involving physiological indicators of prenatal testosterone exposure found that boys with an early-onset transgender identity appeared to have had less exposure to testosterone compared to matched controls; in fact, their physiological responses were similar to girls in the control group. The transgender girls in the study, however, did not differ significantly from the comparison girls in indicators of prenatal testosterone exposure (Burke, Menks, Cohen-Kettenis, Klink, & Bakker, 2014).

It is important to note, however, that the limited research in this area makes conclusions about hormonal influences very tentative. Some researchers believe that gender identity is malleable. For example, most transgender children have normal hormone levels, raising doubt that biology alone determines masculine and feminine behaviors. Although neurohormonal levels are important, their degree of influence on gender identity in human beings may be minor.

Researchers are also looking into any specific neurological characteristics associated with a transgender identity. Neuroimaging using functional magnetic resonance imaging (fMRI) to compare transgendered individuals who had not yet undergone treatment with matched controls revealed differences in brain connectivity between the groups; however, the neurological differences observed in participants with a transgender identify did not provide insight into etiology. Instead, the findings suggested that transgender individuals may dissociate (detach) bodily emotion from body image, a possible mechanism for coping with their lifelong gender incongruence (Lin et al., 2014). Previous studies have also revealed brain alterations in transgender adults—unique patterns that are associated with psychosocial distress and social exclusion (Ku et al., 2013).

Psychological and Social Influences

Psychological and social explanations for gender dysphoria must also be viewed with caution. Some researchers have hypothesized that childhood experiences influence the development of a transgender identity and gender dysphoria. Factors proposed to contribute to the disorder in boys include parental encouragement of feminine behavior, discouragement of the development of autonomy, excessive attention and overprotection by the mother, the absence of male role models, a relatively powerless or absent father figure, a lack of exposure to male playmates, and encouragement to cross-dress (Zucker & Cohen-Ketteris, 2008). Of course, psychosocial stressors such as stigma, lack of societal acceptance, or difficulty obtaining adequate health care may play a role in the distress and impairment associated with gender dysphoria. In fact, the transgender community has been described as the "most marginalized and underserved population in medicine" (Roberts & Fantz, 2014).

Treatment of Gender Dysphoria

CASE STUDY "I am a woman." This declaration has been frequently voiced by Lana Lawless since her sex reassignment surgery in 2005. Before that date, she had worked for 18 years as a "male" police officer for Rialto, California, in their "gang unit," where Lawless achieved a reputation for being a burly, mean, 245-pound tough cop. "People didn't want to mess with me," she stated. Lawless indicates that beneath her callous exterior, she was always compassionate and sensitive on the inside: "I was always hiding in a straight world. . . . I wanted to be a normal girl." Lawless is notable for another reason as well: She filed and won a lawsuit forcing the Ladies Professional Golf Association (LPGA) to allow her and other transgender persons to compete in their tours (Thomas, 2010).

People with gender dysphoria often decide to pursue gender reassignment therapies, which involve changing their physical characteristics through medical procedures such as hormone treatment or surgery. Hormone therapy (taking hormones associated with the perceived gender) as part of gender reassignment has decreased the distress and psychological reactions associated with gender dysphoria, and has improved the quality of life and sexual functioning in many transgendered individuals (Murad et al., 2010). In addition to hormone therapy, some transgender individuals, such as Lana Lawless, choose to have gender reassignment surgeries that change their existing external genital

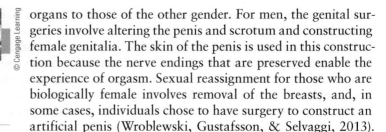

organs to those of the other gender. For men, the genital surgeries involve altering the penis and scrotum and constructing female genitalia. The skin of the penis is used in this construction because the nerve endings that are preserved enable the experience of orgasm. Sexual reassignment for those who are biologically female involves removal of the breasts, and, in some cases, individuals chose to have surgery to construct an artificial penis (Wroblewski, Gustafsson, & Selvaggi, 2013). This procedure is much more complicated and expensive than the male-to-female reassignment. Although just beginning, some health plans now include coverage of hormone therapy or gender-reassignment therapy for transgender individuals (Glicksman, 2013).

Some studies of transgender people indicate positive outcomes for gender reassignment. Many individuals who undergo a female-to-male transition express satisfaction over the outcome of their surgeries, including their sexual functioning (Wierckx et al., 2011). Those who transition to female feel satisfied on an emotional, psychological, and social level but report difficulties with sexual arousal, lubrication, and pain during sex (Weyers et al., 2009). Some research, however, has revealed that transgender individuals who have undergone gender reassignment surgery remain at risk for psychiatric difficulties, including suicidality; these findings suggest that follow-up monitoring of psychological well-being after gender reassignment is important (Dhejne et al., 2011).

Paraphilic Disorders

A **paraphilia** is a condition in which a person's sexual arousal and gratification depends on fantasies or behavior involving socially unacceptable objects, situations, or individuals. According to DSM-5, paraphilias involve sexual interest in non-normative targets or "distorted components of human courtship behavior." The intense and persistent sexual interest associated with a paraphilia can involve unusual erotic behaviors (such as spanking or whipping) or socially unacceptable erotic targets (such as children, animals, or inanimate objects). A **paraphilic disorder** is diagnosed only when the paraphilia harms, or risks harming, others (and is acted on) or causes the individual to experience distress or impairment in social or other areas of functioning. The behaviors associated with paraphilic disorders must have persisted for at least 6 months. Thus, the DSM-5 makes a clear distinction between paraphilias and paraphilic disorders. Such a distinction prevents labeling behavior as pathological just because it is not common behavior. Therefore, a paraphilic disorder is *not* diagnosed if a paraphilia:

1. involves only urges or fantasies, but has not been acted on;
2. has not harmed others or created the potential to harm others;
3. does not impair the person's social, occupational, or other areas of functioning; or
4. does not create anxiety, shame, guilt, loneliness, or sexual frustration or in other ways distress the person.

When the fantasies, urges, or behaviors associated with a paraphilia do not cause personal distress or have the potential to harm to others, a psychiatric diagnosis and intervention is not warranted.

In some cases, diagnosis occurs because the person is severely distressed by or has experienced impairment in social or occupational functioning due to the paraphilia. In other situations, paraphilic disorder is diagnosed when there is evidence or disclosure confirming that the person has acted on paraphilic urges that caused harm, or created risk of harm, to others. This often involves reports from witnesses because many individuals arrested for paraphilic behavior deny engaging in the behavior or otherwise

paraphilia recurring sexual arousal and gratification by means of mental imagery or behavior involving socially unacceptable objects, situations, or individuals

paraphilic disorders sexual disorders in which the person has either acted on or is severely distressed by recurrent urges or fantasies involving nonhuman objects, nonconsenting individuals, or suffering or humiliation

proclaim their innocence. In many cases, paraphilias that harm or interfere with the well-being of others result in arrest and criminal charges.

In all cases, paraphilic disorders are associated with recurrent urges, behaviors, or fantasies involving any of the following three categories (see Table 14.6):

1. nonhuman objects, as in fetishistic and transvestic disorders;

2. nonconsenting others, as in exhibitionistic, voyeuristic, frotteuristic (rubbing against others for sexual arousal), and pedophilic disorders; or

3. real or simulated suffering or humiliation, as in sexual sadism and sexual masochism disorders.

It is not unusual for people to have multiple paraphilias (Langstrom & Zucker, 2005). In one study of sex offenders, almost 50 percent had engaged in a variety of sexually deviant behaviors, averaging between three and four paraphilic disorders and committing more than 500 deviant acts (Rosenfield, 1985). Men who had committed incest, for example, had also molested nonrelatives, exposed themselves, raped adult women, and engaged in voyeurism. In most cultures, paraphilias seem to be much

Table 14.6 Paraphilic Disorders

DSM-5 DISORDERS CHART			
Paraphilia Category	**DSM-5 Definition[a]**	**Prevalence[b]**	**Associated Feature**
Nonhuman objects	**Fetishistic disorder** Sexual attraction and fantasies involving objects or nongenital body parts	Disorder uncommon but fetishistic behavior is not; occurs almost exclusively in males	May rub, smell object and use it in sexual activities Some collect fetish items
	Transvestic disorder Intense sexual arousal from cross-dressing	Fewer than 3% of males report cross-dressing; extremely rare in females	May be aroused by fantasies of being a woman; may masturbate when wearing female clothes
Nonconsenting people	**Exhibitionistic disorder** Urges, acts, or fantasies that involve exposing the genitals to a stranger	Mostly among males; best estimates are 2%–4% of men	May expose to prepubertal children, adults, or both; in general, sexual contact is not sought
	Voyeuristic disorder Urges, acts, or fantasies that involve observing an unsuspecting person disrobing or engaging in sexual activity	Behavior may occur in up to 39% of males From 12% of men and 4% of women may have this disorder	Most common of unlawful sexual behaviors
	Frotteuristic disorder Urges, acts, or fantasies that involve touching or rubbing against a nonconsenting person	Primarily in men; exact figures not available; up to 30% of men may have engaged in frotteuristic acts	Some freely admit behavior but feel no distress or impairment
	Pedophilic disorder Urges, acts, or fantasies that involve sexual contact with a prepubescent child	May occur in up to 3%–5% of males; rare in females	May access child pornography repeatedly; appears to be chronic condition
Pain or humiliation	**Sexual sadism disorder** Sexually arousing urges, fantasies, or acts that involve inflicting physical or psychological suffering	Prevalence estimates of sexual sadism range from 2% to 30%; common in sexually motivated homicides	Extensive use of pornography with themes of pain and suffering; sadism may be a chronic condition
	Sexual masochism disorder Sexual urges, fantasies, or acts that involve being humiliated, bound, or made to suffer	Unknown Up to 18.5% report masochistic fantasies	May extensively use pornography with themes of bondage, being humiliated, or being beaten; may be part of sadomasochistic group

[a]Paraphilias are only diagnosed as a disorder if the urges cause clinically significant distress/ impairment or are acted on with nonconsenting others.
[b]The prevalence of paraphilic disorders is difficult to determine because paraphilic activity is often concealed.
Based on data from Ahlers et al. (2013); APA (2013); Krueger (2010a, 2010b); Långström (2010); Seto (2009).
© Cengage Learning®

more prevalent in males than in females (Gijs, 2008). This finding has led some to speculate that biological factors may account for the unequal distribution.

How common are paraphilias among the general population? In a community sample of German men, 62.4 percent reported at least one paraphilia. The most common were voyeuristic (38.7 percent), fetishistic (35.7 percent), sadistic (24.8 percent), masochistic (18.5 percent), and frotteuristic (15 percent). Less common paraphilias were pedophilic (10.4 percent), transvestic (7.4 percent), and exhibitionistic (4.1 percent). Most of the men who reported paraphilias found them to be intensely sexually arousing. In only 1.7 percent of cases did the respondents report distress over their paraphilias (Ahlers et al., 2011). In addition to the paraphilic disorders we will be discussing, the DSM-5 lists "other specified paraphilic disorders" that include making obscene telephone calls (telephone scatalogia) and sexual urges involving corpses (necrophilia), animals (zoophilia), or feces (coprophilia).

Paraphilic Disorders Involving Nonhuman Objects

Under this category, two forms of paraphilic disorders are evident: fetishistic disorder, which involves attraction or arousal related to a nonliving object (the fetish), and transvestic disorder, which involves cross-dressing for sexual arousal.

Fetishistic Disorder

CASE STUDY   Mr. D. met his wife at a local church and was strongly attracted to her because of her strong religious convictions. When they dated, they occasionally kissed but never had any other sexual contact. Although he loved his wife very much, he was unable to have sexual intercourse with her after their marriage because he could not obtain an erection. However, he had fantasies involving an apron and was able to get an erection and engage in intercourse while wearing an apron. Mrs. D. was upset over this discovery but accepted it because she wanted children. Although using the apron allowed them to consummate their marriage, Mrs. D. was upset about what she considered to be a sexual perversion. Mr. D. also became distressed about his inability to function sexually without the apron.

Fetishistic disorder occurs when there is an extremely strong sexual attraction to or fantasies involving inanimate objects, such as shoes or undergarments, or a specific focus on nongenital body parts such as the feet or toes. As you saw in the case of Mr. D., the fetish is often used as a sexual stimulus during masturbation or sexual intercourse. Many individuals who report having a sexual fetish do not report impairment or distress, and thus do not qualify as having a fetishistic disorder (APA, 2013).

Many heterosexual males find the sight of female undergarments sexually arousing and stimulating; this does not constitute a fetish. An interest in such inanimate objects as panties, stockings, bras, and shoes becomes a sexual fetish when the person is often sexually aroused to the point of erection in the presence of the fetish item, needs the item for sexual arousal during intercourse, chooses sexual partners on the basis of their having the item, or collects the item. To qualify as a fetishistic disorder, the behavior must also cause the individual significant distress or cause harm to others. In many cases the fetish item is enough by itself for complete sexual satisfaction through masturbation, and the person does not seek contact with a partner. Common fetishes include aprons, shoes, undergarments, and leather or latex items. Sexual arousal to fetish items was reported in 35.7 percent of the previously mentioned sample of German men (Ahlers et al., 2011).

fetishistic disorder   sexual attraction and fantasies involving inanimate objects, such as female undergarments

Transvestic Disorder

CASE STUDY   A 26-year-old graduate student referred himself for treatment after he failed an exam in one of his courses. He had been cross-dressing since he was 10 and attributed his exam failure to the excessive amount of time that he spent doing so (four times a week). When he was younger, his cross-dressing had taken the form of masturbating while wearing his mother's high-heeled shoes, but it had gradually expanded to the present stage, in which he dressed completely as a woman, masturbating in front of a mirror. At no time had he experienced a desire to obtain a sex-change operation. He had neither homosexual experiences nor homosexual fantasies. Heterosexual contact had been restricted to heavy petting with occasional girlfriends. (Lambley, 1974, p. 101)

Transvestic disorder occurs when intense sexual arousal is associated with fantasies, urges, or behaviors involving cross-dressing (wearing clothes appropriate to a different gender). This disorder should not be confused with gender dysphoria, in which the individual psychologically identifies with and dresses in accordance with cultural norms for the opposite gender. Although some transgender people and some lesbians and gay men cross-dress, most people who cross-dress are exclusively heterosexual. For a diagnosis of transvestic disorder, the cross-dressing must cause significant distress or impairment in important areas of functioning.

The incidence of transvestic disorder is much higher among men than women (2.8 percent of men and 0.4 percent of women). A higher rate of transvestic behavior (7.4 percent) was reported in the sample of German men (Ahlers et al., 2011). Men who cross-dress often report using pornography, being easily sexually aroused, and engaging in frequent masturbation (Langstrom & Zucker, 2005).

Men with a transvestic paraphilia often wear feminine garments or undergarments during masturbation or sexual intercourse with their partners. Some men with this paraphilia are considered to have *autogynephilia*; that is, they become sexually aroused by thoughts or images of themselves as female. For some individuals, the arousal through cross-dressing may diminish over time and is replaced by feelings of contentment or comfort when cross-dressing (APA, 2013).

©Gertan/Shutterstock.com

Cross-Dressing Behavior or Tranvestic Disorder?

Not all transvestites have a transvestic disorder. Some simply enjoy the activity of cross-dressing and do not experience the intense sexual fantasies, urges, or behaviors associated with tranvestic disorder. Here men are participating in the Hartjesdag (Day of Hearts), an annual cross-dressing carnival in the Netherlands.

Paraphilic Disorders Involving Nonconsenting Persons

This category of disorders involves persistent and powerful sexual fantasies about unsuspecting strangers or acquaintances. The targets are nonconsenting in that they do not choose to be the objects of the attention or sexual behavior.

transvestic disorder   intense sexual arousal obtained through cross-dressing (wearing clothes appropriate to a different gender)

Exhibitionistic Disorder

CASE STUDY   A 19-year-old college student reported that he had daily fantasies of exposing himself and had actually done so on three occasions. The first occurred when he masturbated in front of the window of his dormitory room when women passed by. The other two acts occurred in his car; in each case he asked young women for directions and then exposed his penis and masturbated when they approached. He felt a great deal of anxiety in the presence of women and dated infrequently. (S. C. Hayes, Brownell, & Barlow, 1983)

Exhibitionistic disorder is characterized by urges, acts, or fantasies that involve recurrent episodes of exposing one's genitals to a stranger, often with the intent of shocking the unsuspecting target. In some cases, exhibitionistic disorder is diagnosed when a person acts on exhibitionistic urges, and thereby harms an unconsenting person. In other situations, the person seeks treatment because the behavior is emotionally distressing or results in impairment in important areas of life functioning (APA, 2013). In studies, the prevalence of the disorder ranges from 3.1 percent to 4.1 percent (Ahlers et al., 2011; Långström & Seto, 2006).

Exhibitionistic disorder most commonly occurs in men; their targets are usually adult females. The main goal in exhibitionistic disorder seems to be the sexual arousal that comes from exposing oneself; most individuals with the disorder want no further contact. They may expect to produce surprise, sexual arousal, or disgust in the victim. The act may involve exposing a limp penis or masturbating an erect penis. Most individuals with the disorder are in their 20s—far from being the "dirty old men" of popular myth. Individuals with this paraphilia report lower satisfaction in life, a high level of sexual arousability, and pornography use (Ahlers et al., 2011).

Voyeuristic Disorder

Voyeuristic disorder is characterized by urges, acts, or fantasies that involve observing an unsuspecting person who is naked, disrobing, or engaging in sexual activity. The disorder is diagnosed only in those who are age 18 or older and only when the individual has acted on voyeuristic urges or is distressed by or has experienced impairment in life functioning due to voyeuristic behavior (APA, 2013). "Peeping," as voyeurism is sometimes termed, is considered aberrant when it violates the rights of others, is done in socially unacceptable circumstances, or is preferred to coitus.

Voyeurism is like exhibitionism in that sexual contact is not the goal; viewing an undressed body is the primary motive. Most people who engage in voyeurism are not interested in looking at their spouses or partners; an overwhelming number of voyeuristic acts involve strangers. Observation alone produces sexual arousal and excitement, and the individual often masturbates during this surreptitious activity. Because the act is repetitive and violates the privacy rights of unsuspecting victims, arrest is predictable when a witness or a victim notifies the police. It is estimated that the lifetime prevalence of voyeuristic disorder may be as high as 12 percent in males and 4 percent in females (APA, 2013). Voyeuristic behavior, including adolescent sexual curiosity, is much more common. For example, 38.7 percent of the sample of German men reported engaging in voyeuristic behavior (Ahlers et al., 2011).

Frotteuristic Disorder

CASE STUDY   The 25-year-old man would board trains, stand near unsuspecting women, select one target, and rub his genitals against her body. If no resistance was encountered, he would take this as a positive sign and continue rubbing until orgasm and ejaculation occurred. On weekends, he would begin by watching pornographic movies and then spend the entire day riding trains and engaging in genital rubbing. He was distressed by this behavior but felt unable to control his urges (Kalra, 2013).

exhibitionistic disorder   urges, acts, or fantasies that involve exposing one's genitals to strangers

voyeuristic disorder   urges, acts, or fantasies that involve observing an unsuspecting person disrobing or engaging in sexual activity

Physical contact is the primary motive in **frotteuristic disorder**, which is characterized by recurrent and intense sexual urges, acts, or fantasies that involve touching or rubbing against a nonconsenting person. The inappropriate behaviors of the young man in the case study are consistent with the behaviors exhibited by those with this disorder. The touching, not the coercive nature of the act, is the sexually exciting feature. Similar to other paraphilic disorders, to be diagnosed, the person has acted on or is markedly distressed by the frotteuristic urges. Although up to 30 percent of males in the general population may have engaged in some form of frotteuristic behavior, the prevalence of frotteuristic disorder is difficult to determine (Brannon & Bienenfeld, 2013; Långström, 2010). It may be much more common than thought because the behavior may go unnoticed, be ignored, or be overlooked because it is presumed to be accidental (Patra et al., 2013). In a recent study involving undergraduate students attending an urban university, a high number reported being victims of acts of frotteurism or exhibitionism; these incidents were most frequently associated with using public transportation. The affected students reported feelings of being violated and, in some cases, ongoing psychological distress (Clark, Jeglic, Calkins, & Tatar, 2014).

Pedophilic Disorder

Pedophilic disorder involves an adult obtaining erotic gratification through urges, acts, or fantasies that involve prepubescent or early pubescent children, generally children under age 13. For the diagnosis, the individual must have acted on or be clinically distressed by these urges. In addition, a person must be at least 16 years of age to be diagnosed with this disorder and at least 5 years older than the child (APA, 2013). People with this disorder may victimize children within or outside of their families and may be attracted only to children, or to both children and adults. Additionally, they may be attracted only to males, only to females, or to children of both genders.

Individuals with pedophilia frequently use child pornography for sexual gratification. In fact, some men with pedophilic urges report accessing child pornography but claim they have never attempted to approach a child in a sexual manner (Berlin & Sawyer, 2012). The actual prevalence of pedophilic disorder is not known, but it is estimated that up to 3–5 percent of males may have pedophilic urges; it is rare in women (Brannon & Bienenfeld, 2013; Seto, 2012). Pedophilia is usually considered a lifelong condition, although the intensity of urges may decrease with age (Seto 2009).

Unfortunately, sexual abuse of children is common; it most frequently affects girls, with girls in their early teens having the highest risk of being molested. It is estimated that by age 17, high-impact sexual abuse (genital touching and actual or attempted vaginal or anal penetration) has affected 15 percent of girls and 6 percent of boys. Strikingly, up to 95 percent of child sexual abuse never comes to the attention of authorities (Martin & Silverstone, 2013). Contrary to the popular view of child molesters as strangers, most people who act on pedophilic urges are relatives, friends, or casual acquaintances of their victims (Lussier et al., 2008).

Although many young victims of sexual abuse show no overt symptoms, some do experience physical effects such as poor appetite, headaches, or urinary tract infections; additionally, psychological symptoms including nightmares, difficulty sleeping, decline in school performance, acting-out, or sexually focused behavior may also occur. Some child victims show symptoms of post-traumatic stress disorder. The effects of sexual abuse can be lifelong. One study of women who were survivors of childhood sexual abuse revealed that they often experience a "contaminated identity" characterized by self-loathing, shame, and powerlessness (A. Phillips & Daniluk, 2004).

Pedophilia can also involve **incest**—sexual contact between individuals who are too closely related to marry legally. The cases of incest most frequently reported to law enforcement agencies involve sexual contact between a father and daughter or stepdaughter. Mother–son incest seems to be rare. Although brother–sister incest is more common, most research has focused on father–daughter incest. This type of incestuous relationship generally begins when the daughter is between 6 and 11 years old. Unlike sex between siblings (which may or may not be exploitive), father–daughter incest is

frotteuristic disorder recurrent and intense sexual urges, acts, or fantasies that involve touching or rubbing against a nonconsenting person

pedophilic disorder a disorder in which an adult obtains erotic gratification through urges, acts, or fantasies that involve sexual contact with a prepubescent or early pubescent child

incest sexual relations between people too closely related to marry legally

always exploitive. The girl is especially vulnerable because she depends on her father for emotional support. As a result, victims often feel guilty and powerless.

Psychological symptoms associated with the early eroticization that occurs with father–daughter incest, such as feeling damaged and ashamed, often continue into adulthood and are reflected in high rates of depression and difficulties with adult sexuality and interpersonal relationships (Stroebel et al., 2012). Research comparing survivors of father–daughter and brother–sister incest found that although there were long-term psychosocial effects for both groups, father–daughter incest produced more pervasive damage to self-esteem and psychological functioning (Stroebel et al., 2013a). Similarly, women who experienced sister–sister incest reported ongoing psychological distress and strained family relationships (Stroebel et al., 2013b).

Paraphilic Disorders Involving Pain or Humiliation

CASE STUDY From early adolescence, Peter F., a 41-year-old man, had fantasies of being mistreated, humiliated, and beaten. He recalls becoming sexually excited when envisioning such actions. As he grew older, he experienced difficulty achieving an orgasm unless his sexual partners inflicted pain during sexual activities. He was obsessed with these masochistic sexual acts, which made it difficult for him to concentrate on other matters. He had been married and divorced three times because of his proclivity for demanding that his wives engage in "sex games" that involved having them hurt him. These games involved binding him, spread-eagled on his bed and whipping or biting his upper thighs, sticking pins into his legs, and other forms of torture. During these sessions, he could ejaculate.

Although pain and humiliation are not normally associated with sexual arousal, they play a prominent role in paraphilias involving sadism and masochism. In the case above, Peter had a long-standing paraphilia involving the pain and degradation associated with masochism. **Sexual masochism disorder** is characterized by sexual urges, fantasies, or acts that involve being humiliated, bound, or made to suffer. People who engage in sexual masochism report that they do not seek harm or injury but that they find the sensation of utter helplessness appealing. Because of their passive roles, they are not considered dangerous to others. A sexual masochism disorder diagnosis occurs only if the paraphilia causes distress or impairment in functioning. The prevalence of sexual masochism is unknown (Krueger, 2010a).

Sexual sadism disorder is characterized by sexual arousal associated with urges, fantasies, or acts that involve inflicting physical or psychological suffering on others. Sadistic sexual behavior may include pretend or fantasized infliction of pain; mild to severe cruelty toward partners; or an extremely dangerous, pathological form of sadism that involves mutilation or murder. Estimates regarding the prevalence of sexual sadism range from 2 percent to 30 percent, depending on the definition of sadism employed by the researchers (Krueger, 2010b). As with other paraphilic disorders, the DSM-5 specifies that to receive this diagnosis, a person must have acted on the urges with a nonconsenting person or feel markedly distressed by the behavior.

For some people who participate in sexual sadism or masochism, coitus becomes unnecessary; pain or humiliation alone is sufficient to produce sexual pleasure. Some participants engage in both submissive and dominant roles. Their sexual activities may be carefully scripted and involve mutually agreed upon role-playing (Lussier et al., 2008). In one survey of respondents who participate in sadomasochistic activities involving spanking, whipping, and bondage, only 16 percent were exclusively dominant or submissive. Approximately 40 percent had engaged in behaviors that caused minor pain using ice, hot wax, biting, or face slapping. Fewer than 18 percent had engaged in

sexual masochism disorder sexual urges, fantasies, or acts that involve being humiliated, bound, or made to suffer

sexual sadism disorder sexually arousing urges, fantasies, or acts that involve inflicting physical or psychological suffering on others

more harmful procedures, such as burning or piercing (Brewslow, Evans, & Langley, 1986). Many individuals who practice sadomasochism are aware of the tremendous stigma attached to this practice and are secretive about their sexual behavior. They continue with the practices, however, because they find sadomasochistic sexual activities to be more satisfying than "straight" sex (Stiles & Clark, 2011).

Etiology and Treatment of Paraphilic Disorders

Although it is likely that multiple factors contribute to the development of paraphilic disorders, we still have much to learn about paraphilias. Investigators have attempted to find genetic, neurohormonal, and brain anomalies that might be associated with paraphilic disorders. Some of the research findings conflict with each other; others need replication and confirmation. There is evidence, however, that some men may be biologically predisposed to some paraphilias such as pedophilic disorder (Centre for Addiction and Mental Health, 2007), as pedophiles have been found to have neurological abnormalities, including less white matter. Even if biological factors are found to play a role in the development of paraphilias, psychological factors also contribute in important ways.

Among early attempts to explain paraphilic disorders, psychodynamic theorists proposed that these sexual behaviors represent unconscious conflicts that began in early childhood (Schrut, 2005). Castration anxiety in men, for example, is hypothesized to be an important etiological factor underlying transvestic disorder, fetishistic disorder, exhibitionistic disorder, sexual sadism disorder, and sexual masochism disorder. A man with exhibitionistic disorder, for example, exposes himself to reassure himself that castration has not occurred. The shock that registers on the faces of others assures him that he still has a penis. A man with sexual sadism disorder may protect himself from castration anxiety by inflicting pain. A man with sexual masochism disorder may engage in self-castration through the acceptance of pain, thereby limiting the power of others to castrate him. The psychodynamic treatment of sexual deviations involves helping the client understand the relationship between the sexual behavior and the unconscious conflicts that produce it.

Research looking into the characteristics of sex offenders has provided insight into early psychosocial variables that may influence their behavior. For example, juvenile sex offenders are more likely to have unusual sexual interests, low self-esteem, and anxiety. Additionally, they are more likely to have early exposure to sex, sexual violence, pornography or a history of being sexually victimized (Seto & Lalumière, 2010). In a confidential study involving self-reported pedophiles and users of child pornography who had not yet been detected or arrested for their actions, participants reported long-standing sexual self-regulation difficulties, including high rates of sexual preoccupation and arousal involving a variety of other paraphilias, most commonly voyeurism, sadism, frotteurism, or exhibitionism (Neutze, Grundmann, Scherner, & Beier, 2012).

Learning theorists stress the importance of early conditioning experiences in the etiology of paraphilias (Brannon & Bienenfeld, 2013). In other words, paraphilias may result from accidental associations between sexual arousal and exposure to certain situations, events, acts, or objects. A young boy may develop a fetish for women's panties after he becomes sexually excited watching girls come down a slide with their underpants exposed. He begins to masturbate to fantasies of girls with their panties showing; this behavior could lead to an underwear fetish. Paraphilias often develop during adolescence when sexual interest and arousal are particularly susceptible to conditioning. Additionally, if an adolescent masturbates while engaged in sexually deviant fantasies, the conditioning may hamper the development of normal sexual patterns.

Behavioral approaches to treating sexual deviations have generally involved one or more of the following elements (Kaplan & Krueger, 2012): (a) weakening or eliminating the sexually inappropriate behaviors through processes such as extinction or aversive conditioning; (b) acquiring or strengthening sexually appropriate behaviors; and (c) developing appropriate social skills. The following case study illustrates this approach.

It should be noted that possession of child pornography (the pedophilic stimuli used in this treatment) is considered "legally obscene" and is now against federal law, even for mental health professionals providing treatment to pedophiles.

One of the more unique treatments for exhibitionism involves *aversive behavior rehearsal* (Wickramasekera, 1976), in which shame or humiliation is the aversive stimulus. The technique requires that the person exhibit himself in his usual manner to a preselected audience of women. During the exhibiting act, the person must verbalize a conversation between himself and his penis. He must talk about what he is feeling emotionally and physically and must explain his fantasies regarding what he supposes the female observers are thinking about him. One premise of this technique is that exhibitionism often occurs during a state similar to hypnosis, when the exhibitionist's fantasies are extremely active and his judgment is impaired. This method forces him to experience and examine his actions while being fully aware of what he is doing.

The results of behavioral treatments are generally positive, although the majority of research involves single participants rather than group experimental designs. Additionally, in many studies several different behavioral techniques are incorporated, making it difficult to evaluate specific techniques. In a recent review of research involving treatment for those who sexually abuse children, the results were discouraging—neither psychological nor pharmacological interventions had much effect on reoffending (Långström et al., 2013).

Rape

Rape is a form of sexual aggression that involves *sexual activity* (oral-genital sex, anal intercourse, or vaginal intercourse) performed against a person's will through the use of force, argument, pressure, alcohol or drugs, or authority (McAnulty & Burnette, 2004). Although rape is not a psychological disorder, we believe that the magnitude and seriousness of problems related to rape in U.S. society warrant a discussion of the topic. Rape is an act surrounded by many myths and misconceptions (see Table 14.7).

According to the National Intimate Partner and Sexual Violence survey (Black et al., 2011), the number of rapes in the United States has risen dramatically. An estimated 1.3 million U.S. women and girls are raped each year. It is estimated that 1 in 5 adult women has been raped, with 80 percent experiencing their first rape before age 25 and 12 percent experiencing their first rape at or before age 10. Most women who are raped know their rapist. In fact, 51.1 percent of the woman who were violated in the prior year were raped by an intimate partner and 40.8 percent were raped by an acquaintance. The lifetime prevalence of rape varies by race/ethnicity (African American, 22 percent; European American, 18.8 percent; American Indian/Alaska

rape a form of sexual aggression that involves sexual activity (oral-genital sex, anal intercourse, or vaginal intercourse) performed against a person's will through the use of force, argument, pressure, alcohol or drugs, or authority

Table 14.7 The Facts about Rape

- Anyone can be raped. Rape happens among all age groups, from infants to elderly women; among all economic classes, from rich to poor; among all racial and ethnic groups; and in heterosexual and same-sex relationships.

- Rape happens to both males and females. Statistics show that 1 in 4 girls and 1 in 6 boys are sexually assaulted before they reach the age of 18. About 1 in 6 women and 1 in 11 men are raped after turning 18.

- Rape is an act of violence. Rape is used as a way of dominating, humiliating, and terrifying another person.

- Rape is never the fault of the victim. It has nothing to do with what the victim wore, where the victim went, what the victim did, or whether the victim is "attractive." Only the person committing the assault is to blame. Rape is painful, humiliating, and hurtful. No one ever asks to be raped.

- You are much more likely to be raped by someone you know than by a stranger. Most rapes happen between people of the same race or ethnicity.

- You have the right to say no to sex, even if you have said yes before. You also have the right to stop having sex at any time. You can be raped by someone you have had sex with before, even your spouse or partner.

- Rape is against the law. Not only is rape always wrong, it's also a crime.

SOURCE: Facts and Information (n.d.).

Native, 26.9 percent; multiracial, 33.5 percent). Lesbian and bisexual women report a prevalence of rape equal to or higher than that reported by heterosexual women. Rape statistics are significantly different for men. Approximately 1 in 71 men have experienced rape; more than one fourth of these rapes occurred at or before age 10. Among males who were raped in the prior year, 52.4 percent reported being raped by an acquaintance and 15.1 percent by a stranger.

Men who are sexually aggressive or who try to coerce women into intercourse share certain characteristics (Lussier et al., 2008). They tend to:

1. actively create situations in which sexual encounters may occur;

2. misinterpret women's friendliness as provocation or their protests as insincere;

3. try to manipulate women into sexual encounters by using alcohol (some 70 percent of rapes are associated with alcohol intoxication) or "date rape drugs";

4. attribute failed attempts at sexual encounters to perceived negative features of the woman, thereby protecting their egos;

5. come from environments of parental neglect or physical or sexual abuse;

6. initiate coitus earlier in life than men who are not sexually aggressive; and

7. have more sexual partners than men who are not sexually aggressive.

Sexual aggression by men is quite common; in fact, many men who do not rape also have some of these characteristics. Fifteen percent of one sample of college men reported that they had forced intercourse at least once or twice. In a survey of students enrolled in 32 universities in the United States, more than 50 percent of women reported being the victims of sexual aggression, and 8 percent of men admitted to committing sexual acts that met the legal definition of rape (Hall, 1996; Koss, Gidycz, & Wisniewski, 1987).

Date rape accounts for many of the rapes that involve younger women. For example, between 8 and 25 percent of female college students have reported that they had "unwanted sexual intercourse," and studies have generally found that most college women have experienced some unwanted sexual activity (Abuse, Rape, and Domestic Violence Aid and Resource Collection, 2011). Women seldom report episodes of date rape. Many universities are conducting workshops for students to help them understand that intercourse without consent during a date or other social activity is rape.

DID YOU KNOW?

Some researchers have studied personality patterns associated with committing rape. Rape and sexual coercion are most frequently associated with antisocial and borderline personality disorders.

SOURCE: Schroeder, Iffland, Hill, Berner, & Briken, 2013

Effects of Rape

Rape survivors may experience a cluster of emotional reactions known as the **rape trauma syndrome**; these reactions may include psychological distress, phobic reactions, post-traumatic stress symptoms, or sexual dysfunction (Boyd, 2011). Two phases have been identified in rape trauma syndrome (Koss, 1993):

1. *Acute phase: Disorganization.* During the period immediately following the assault, the rape survivor may have feelings of self-blame, fear, and depression. Survivors may believe they were responsible for the rape (for example, by not locking the door or by being friendly toward the attacker). They may also have a fear that the attacker will return and that they may again be raped or even killed. They may express these emotional reactions and beliefs directly as anger, fear, rage, anxiety, or depression, or conceal them, appearing amazingly calm. Beneath this exterior, however, are signs of tension, including headaches, irritability, restlessness, sleeplessness, and jumpiness.

2. *Long-term phase: Reorganization.* This second phase may last for several years. Survivors begin to deal directly with their feelings and attempt to reorganize their lives. Fears and phobic reactivity may continue in the form of post-traumatic stress disorder, especially in situations with reminders of the traumatic incident. A host of reactions may be present. Many survivors report one or more sexual dysfunctions as the result of the rape; fear of sex and lack of desire or arousal are most common.

Some rape survivors recover quickly, whereas others report problems years after the attack. Feelings of safety and personal vulnerability may be drastically altered following a rape; survivors may feel unsafe in many situations, with these feelings sometimes persisting for decades. It is clear that rape has long-lasting consequences and that family, friends, and acquaintances need to exercise patience and understanding as rape survivors go through the process of healing.

rape trauma syndrome a two-phase syndrome that rape survivors may experience, involving such emotional reactions as psychological distress, phobic reactions, and sexual dysfunction

Etiology of Rape

Various views regarding the motivation for rape have been proposed. Some claim that rape is an act of power and aggression, whereas others contend that sex is the primary motivation for rape. In an influential study of 133 rapists that supported the aggression viewpoint, Groth, Burgess, and Holstrom (1977) distinguished three motivational types:

- The *power rapist*, comprising 55 percent of those studied, is primarily attempting to compensate for feelings of personal or sexual inadequacy by intimidating his target.

- The *anger rapist*, comprising 40 percent of those studied, is angry at women in general; the person is merely a convenient target.

- The *sadistic rapist*, comprising only 5 percent of those studied, derives satisfaction from inflicting pain and may torture or mutilate the victim.

These findings suggest that rape has more to do with power, aggression, and violence than with sex. More recent formulations and findings, however, suggest that rape is also sexually motivated: (a) most rape survivors are in their teens or 20s, an age range associated with sexual attractiveness; (b) most rapists name sexual motivation as the primary reason for their actions; and (c) many rapists have multiple paraphilias (Lussier et al., 2008). Thus, it appears that sexual motivation also plays a role in rapes.

Protesting Rape

The apparent cover-up of an alleged rape involving high school student-athletes in Steubenville, Ohio garnered national attention. Here activists stand in front of the local county courthouse protesting those in the community who supported the male athletes and criticized the rape survivor.

Why Do Men Rape Women?

Two former high school football players were convicted of raping a 16-year-old honor student during several end-of-summer parties in Steubenville, Ohio, in August 2012. The assaults allegedly took place while the girl was severely intoxicated and sometimes unresponsive. The case garnered national attention when it became apparent that teenagers attending the parties sent text messages, made social media posts, and took cell phone pictures and videos of the assaultive behavior, but did not intervene. Further, the local police chief had great difficulty locating witnesses who were willing to come forward and testify. Despite these challenges, the football players were convicted and sentenced to 1 to 2 years in juvenile detention. They are required to register as Level II sex offenders and check in with local law enforcement every 6 months for the next 20 years.

Five adults from the community, including the school district superintendent, also faced a range of charges (obstructing justice, tampering with evidence, lying to authorities, and failing to report suspected child abuse) associated with allegedly covering up the rape in an attempt to protect the football players. Further, some local residents were upset at the girl, charging that she placed herself in a position to be raped and that she had damaged the reputation of the football players and the town's much beloved high school football team. Nationally, there was tremendous support for the girl, including online petitions calling for apologies and an admission by the school superintendent that there was a "rape culture and excessive adulation of male athletes" at Steubenville High (Associated Press, 2014; Macur & Schweber, 2012).

Researchers have proposed a variety of theories regarding the causes of rape. The sociocultural view of rape emphasizes that sexual assault is most likely to occur when there is a "culture" of male dominance and acceptance of rape (McAnulty & Burnette, 2004). This view gained favor with the finding that a significant proportion of men would consider rape if they thought they could get away with it. The bystander and community response to the events in Steubenville appear to be consistent with this perspective.

Sociobiological models, however, posit a very different explanation of rape. Sexual aggression, according to this view, has an evolutionary basis. Sexually aggressive behaviors have evolved as a means of maximizing the reproduction of the human species: Men have a stronger sex drive and have much more to gain in reproductive terms by being able to pass on their genes rapidly to a large number of women, thus increasing their chances of having offspring (L. Ellis, 1991). Ellis (1991) believes that sexual behavior (including the drive to rape) is innate and takes issue with the view that rape is not a sexual crime. He points to the fact that rapists often try to obtain sex by actions such as getting women drunk or falsely pledging love, and argues that many rapists use physical force only after these other tactics fail. He also points out that men are less likely than women to describe rape as motivated by power and anger. Although Ellis believes that the motivation for sexual assault is biological, he acknowledges that the behavior surrounding sexual assault is learned. For example, if sexual aggression is reinforced (or not punished), sexually aggressive behaviors persist.

Sociobiological theories have difficulty explaining differences in the prevalence of rape between societies, changes in rates of rape over time, or the higher rates of rape associated with cultural contexts that support violence. Isolating and testing different propositions concerning the factors that motivate sexual assault have been difficult. Even so, no one—not even those who believe that men have a stronger biological sexual drive—can excuse or condone such behavior. Research suggests that confronting attitudes condoning violence and cultural practices that increase disrespect toward women can reduce the incidence of rape.

For Further Consideration

1. Does the sociobiological perspective seem accurate to you? Can you give examples that support or disprove this perspective?

2. What factors do you think contributed to the Steubenville rape and the bystander and community responses to the rape?

The effect of pornography and media portrayals of violent sex on the prevalence of rape is also of interest to researchers. Exposure to such material may affect sexual attitudes and influence patterns of sexual arousal. These media portrayals may reflect and affect societal values concerning violence and women. A "cultural spillover" theory—namely, that rape tends to be high in cultures or environments that

Resilience in the Aftermath of Rape

In 1989, while jogging through New York's Central Park, Trisha Meili was raped, sodomized, and beaten so savagely that she lost 75 percent of her blood before she was discovered. At the hospital, doctors believed she would not live, but Meili fought valiantly for her life and survived the ordeal. She became known as the "Central Park Jogger," and her case generated a national debate about rape and violence in society. Similar to many women who have experienced a sexual assault, Meili initially found that she had developed the following beliefs in response to her attack: (a) "I have no control over my life," (b) "The world is an unsafe place," (c) "I am unworthy," and (d) "People are not to be trusted" (Mena, 2012). After years of recovery, she finally wrote a book—*I Am the Central Park Jogger: A Story of Hope and Possibility* (Meili, 2003)—which quickly became a best seller. The book is less about rape and assault than about resilience: the hope, healing, and courage of the human spirit.

The story of Trisha Meili exemplifies many of the basic principles that psychologists have discovered about resilience and post-traumatic growth after a rape (J. K. Hill, 2011; Westphal & Bonanno, 2007). Her story is about positive coping; using personal strengths to move forward after the trauma of sexual assault; and the benefits derived from the support of friends, loved ones, communities, and society at large. Resilience research indicates that the ability to overcome adversity, especially in cases of rape, involves intersecting elements that involve: (a) regaining control over the environment and events, (b) having positive social support, (c) moving from defining oneself as a "victim" to a "survivor," and (d) finding a meaningful purpose in life (Hill, 2011). Other suggestions include developing active coping skills (e.g., keeping fit, maintaining a sense of humor) and finding a resilient role model who has recovered from a similar experience (Meichenbaum, 2012).

As Meili describes in her book, supportive social relationships can increase resilience after a sexual assault. Social support from family and friends provides rape survivors with (a) a sense of worth; (b) validation that others love, respect, and value them; and (c) an opportunity to share their thoughts and feelings about the assault in a safe and understanding environment. Unfortunately, rape can alter a person's perception of interpersonal relationships, particularly if the rapist was an acquaintance. This may adversely affect existing social support networks and intimate relationships at a time when the person is most in need. For those who might not have had strong social networks, developing or strengthening supports after a trauma such as rape is imperative.

One of the most potent changes that aided Meili in her healing journey was redefining herself as a survivor rather than a victim. How a woman defines her identity in relationship to a sexual assault is crucial to recovery. Self-identification as a victim implies helplessness, lack of personal control, and a passive rather than an active stance. Being a survivor, however, acknowledges the trauma but also focuses on one's ability to feel in control and overcome adversity. Research suggests that this cognitive shift in self-definition is all-important in the healing journey (Bonanno, 2005).

New York Daily News Archive/Getty Images

Trisha Meili

Finding meaning in life and reestablishing control over one's life can also enhance recovery. Meili, for example, wrote her book to help others overcome a sexual assault. She frequently speaks to groups and organizations about rape recovery and is an active advocate for survivors of rape. These activities have given her meaning in life, hope for the future, and the satisfaction of helping others and having a positive influence on society. For rape survivors, other empowerment activities may include pressing charges and testifying against the offender, taking self-defense classes, becoming an activist, and seeking meaning in the experience. In essence, these actions not only foster a sense of control and purpose in life but also include the larger altruistic goal of creating a safer and more predictable world for others.

encourage violence—has been proposed (L. Baron, Straus, & Jaffee, 1988). Research looking at the relationship between cultural support for violence and rates of rapes in all 50 states found that states with a "culture of violence" had a higher prevalence of rape: When violence is encouraged or condoned, there is a "spillover" effect on rape. Many consider the United States a violent and sexually oriented society; not surprisingly, it has the highest rape rate of countries reporting rape statistics. The incidence of rape in the United States is 4 times higher than in Germany, 13 times higher than in the United Kingdom, and 20 times higher than in Japan (Coalition Educating About Sexual Endangerment, 2011).

Treatment for Rapists

Many people believe that sex offenders are not good candidates for psychiatric treatment or rehabilitation. The most common penalty for rape is imprisonment and, even then, there are high rates of recidivism (repeat offenses) among some sex offenders. Unfortunately, the majority of convicts receive little or no treatment in prison. When intervention occurs, treatment for sexual aggressors (rapists and child abusers) usually incorporates behavioral techniques such as the following (Fedoroff, 2008; Lussier et al., 2008):

1. assessing sexual interests through self-report and measuring erectile responses to different sexual stimuli,
2. reducing deviant interests through aversion therapy (e.g., administering an electric shock when deviant stimuli are presented),
3. reconditioning orgasm or retraining masturbation to increase sexual arousal to appropriate stimuli, and
4. training in social skills to increase interpersonal competence.

Questions remain about the effectiveness of these treatment programs. Although some treatment techniques have shown some success with child molesters and people with exhibitionistic disorder, treatment outcomes have tended to be poor for rapists. Some sex offenders desperately want to end their deviant sexual urges, as can be seen in the following case.

CASE STUDY James Jenkins was in the county jail after having spent seven and one half years in a Virginia prison for molesting three girls. He was waiting in the cell to be transferred to a high-risk sexual offender facility when he asked a guard for a razor so that he could shave for his court appearance. After receiving the razor, he took out the blade, went into the shower, stuffed an apple in his mouth to muffle his screams, castrated himself, and flushed his testicles down the jail toilet. He says he no longer has sexual urges for young girls (Rondeaux, 2006).

This case represents an extreme example. However, surgical castration has been used to treat sexual offenders in many European countries, and results indicate that rates of relapse have been low. Rapists, child molesters, and a sexual murderer who underwent surgical castration all reported a decrease in sexual intercourse, masturbation, and frequency of sexual fantasies. However, some of these men remained sexually active. Chemical castration, which involves the administration of medications that reduce sex drive and sexual activity, is also used with sex offenders. However, these drugs appear to reduce sexual urges much more than actual erectile capability (Fedoroff, 2008).

The Sex Offender Registration and Notification Act (SORNA) requires individuals convicted of sex offenses to register with local authorities and to update their contact information if they move; the period for which registration is required (15 years, 25 years, or life) is determined by the severity of the offense. Additionally, 28 states have "habitual offender" laws that impose a harsher punishment, often a life sentence, on individuals who have received multiple convictions for violent offenses such as rape.

Researchers have attempted to identify risk factors for reoffending among sex offenders and to develop intervention strategies directly associated each risk factor (Ward & Stewart, 2003). These risk factors are:

1. *dispositional*, such as psychopathic or antisocial personality characteristics;
2. *historical*, such as prior history of crime and violence and developmental trauma;
3. *criminogenic*, such as deviant social networks and lack of positive social supports; and
4. *clinical*, such as indicators of substance abuse, psychiatric problems, and poor social functioning.

Treatment then involves using the most empirically sound strategies to alter or minimize the identified risk factors. For example, if a person has a deviant social network, attempts are made to remove the person from such an environment; or, if substance abuse or psychiatric disorders are a concern, treatment is directed toward these conditions. Given the shattered lives associated with sex offenses, controversy is likely to continue regarding the most appropriate treatments and punishments for sex offenders.

Contemporary Trends and Future Directions

As you have seen in this chapter, the DSM-5 has made a clear distinction between paraphilias and paraphilic disorders. This position may change societal views on sexual differences that are not harmful to others. Moving in the same direction, Sweden has removed transvestism, fetishism, and sadomasochism from its official list of mental illnesses. As the head of the National Board of Welfare in Sweden observed, "These diagnoses are rooted in a time when everything other than the heterosexual missionary position were seen as sexual perversions. . . These individuals' sexual preferences have nothing to do with society" (TT/The Local, 2008). However, some forensic professionals express concern that the DSM-5 emphasis on "normal variations" versus paraphilic disorders will have unintended legal ramifications, including the potential for forensic abuse by attorneys and other professionals who defend sex offenders (Wakefield, 2011).

Many support the fact that the DSM-5 now clearly acknowledges that transgender people do not necessarily have a mental disorder. A diagnosis of gender dysphoria is made only when someone with a transgender identity experiences clinically significant distress or impairment. This is clearly a move in the right direction. It is critical that we not pathologize normal biological variations and confuse gender nonconformity with mental illness (Granderson, 2010). Indeed, the need for a diagnostic category of gender dysphoria calls into question our bimodal concepts of gender identity, and highlights the need to address the social stigma experienced by transgender people (Frese & Myrick, 2010). We must also acknowledge that stigma, prejudice, and societal discrimination that affect social relationships, health care, employment, and education may account for much of the distress associated with gender dysphoria. The failure of our society to adequately understand transgender issues not only denies transgender people equal opportunity, but may also be responsible for much of their psychological distress.

There are many indicators that gender dysphoria will eventually be removed as a psychiatric diagnosis. First, there are many parallels between the arguments of advocates and members of the transgender community who oppose the inclusion of gender dysphoria as a mental disorder and those who struggled for years to remove homosexuality as a designated mental disorder (homosexuality was not completely removed from the DSM until 1986). As is true of the gay, lesbian, and bisexual communities, members of the transgender community do not regard their feelings or desires as abnormal (Granderson, 2010). Many hope that future editions of the DSM will go even farther in depathologizing transgender identity and acknowledge that the primary reason for the "clinically significant distress" is negative reactions from society. If there is increased societal openness to transgender people, there may no longer be a need for a diagnostic category of gender dysphoria.

chapter SUMMARY

1 What are normal sexual behaviors?

- There is a wide range of normal sexual behavior; what is considered normal is influenced by moral and legal judgments, as well as cultural norms.

2 What do we know about normal sexual responses and sexual dysfunction?

- The human sexual response cycle has four stages: the appetitive, arousal, orgasm, and resolution phases. Sexual dysfunctions are disruptions of the normal sexual response cycle. They are fairly common in the general population, and treatment is generally successful.

- The multipath model illustrates how biological (hormonal variations and medical conditions), psychological (performance anxieties), social (parental upbringing and attitudes), and sociocultural (cultural scripts) factors contribute to sexual dysfunctions.

3 What causes gender dysphoria, and how is it treated?

- Gender dysphoria involves distress and impairment in functioning that results from a marked mismatch between one's experienced or expressed gender and one's gender assigned at birth.

- Some transgender people take hormones or undergo gender reassignment surgeries to facilitate a transition to their experienced or expressed gender.

4 What are paraphilic disorders, what causes them, and how are they treated?

- Paraphilic disorders occur when a person's sexual arousal and gratification depend on fantasies or behavior involving socially unacceptable objects, situations, or individuals. The diagnosis requires that the individual has acted on these urges with a nonconsenting individual or that the urges produce significant distress. Paraphilias may involve (a) an orientation toward nonhuman objects, (b) repetitive sexual activity with nonconsenting partners, or (c) the association of real or simulated suffering with sexual activity.

- Biological factors such as hormonal or brain abnormalities have been studied as a cause of paraphilic disorders. Psychological factors appear to play a key role in these disorders.

- Treatments are usually behavioral and are aimed at eliminating the disordered sexual behavior while teaching more appropriate behavior.

5 Is rape an act of sex or aggression?

- There appears to be no single motivation for rape; rapists seem to have different motivations and personalities.

- Some researchers feel that sociocultural factors can encourage rape and violence against women.

15

PERSONALITY PSYCHOPATHOLOGY

Chapter Outline

AARON KOPINSKY WAS KNOWN AS A LONER BY HIS CLASSMATES. He seldom participated in social activities, had few friends in his dormitory, and even avoided socializing with his roommate. His favorite pastime seemed to be watching TV programs. Few things seemed to interest Aaron; he did not go to movies and had few hobbies or activities that seemed to give him joy. Yet he did not appear lonely. His college major was forestry, so he frequently went on outings that required long stays in the national forest. While his classmates would huddle around a campfire during the evenings for companionship, Aaron preferred to be by himself.

JENNIFER WANG, A PROJECT MANAGER FOR A SMALL TECHNOLOGY START-UP COMPANY, was described by family, friends, and co-workers as extremely compulsive. At team meetings she was demanding, insistent that things be done correctly in a prescribed manner. She frustrated her colleagues when she posted detailed task lists for each project. Team members were expected to use a red marker to check off each task posted on the bulletin board once the job was completed. They had to do so with a red marker; no other color would do. Jennifer became upset when even the most trivial detail was not completed in accordance with her directions. Everything had to be done flawlessly.

JORDAN MITCHELL WAS "CLUBBING" WITH FRIENDS in San Francisco when he met an attractive prostitute who invited him to a nearby hotel for sex. Despite warnings from his friends to use a condom, he failed to do so. Throughout his life, Jordan was known for being reckless and impulsive. He enjoyed risky and dangerous activities such as racing his car against other willing drivers and discharging his firearm into the sky at night. Jordan bored easily and needed constant excitement. His impulsivity, distractibility, and constant need for change made it difficult for him to hold down a job.

focus
QUESTIONS

1 Can one's personality be pathological?

2 What traits are associated with personality disorders?

3 How does an antisocial personality develop and can it be changed?

4 What problems occur with personality assessment?

5 Are there alternative methods of personality assessment?

Aaron, Jennifer, and Jordan's behaviors, thoughts, and feelings typify how they generally respond to life situations. These behavioral and mental characteristics make each of them unique and thus form the basis of their personalities. In psychology, *personality* means three things. First, it refers to a pattern of recognizable behaviors. Aaron, for example, prefers spending time by himself; he is a loner and avoids almost all social interactions or situations. Jennifer is detail-oriented, perfectionistic, and inflexible. Jordan, in contrast, is impulsive, a thrill seeker and a risk taker. Essentially, all three exhibit a consistency in how they respond to situations. Second, although personality is a psychological characteristic, it is influenced by biological factors (Sterzer, 2010). For example, even at birth, children have differences in **temperament**, including differences in levels of physiological reactivity to outside stimulation (Glenn, Raine, Venables, & Mednick, 2009). This may explain why some people seek or avoid novel situations. Third, we see and respond to the world through the lens of our personality. Aaron, Jennifer, and Jordan behave and respond the way they do because they see the world differently from one another.

Are Aaron, Jennifer, and Jordan's personality patterns considered pathological? That is, can people's characteristic style of responding to situations prove problematic to themselves or others? Certainly, social isolation and friendlessness may be bothersome to most of us, but Aaron does not appear bothered by it. He prefers solitary tasks and situations, and perhaps his major in forestry and desire to become a forest ranger may be the perfect occupational match for him. Jennifer's compulsivity may be irksome to co-workers, but there are advantages to this **trait**. Being orderly and attentive to detail are assets in many situations. However, being governed by rules and habits may decrease her ability to adapt to unexpected problems or situations. On the other hand, Jordan's need for excitement, impulsivity, and risk taking may place both him and others in danger. His personality traits are much more likely to become problematic than are Aaron's or Jennifer's.

Personality Psychopathology

Most of us are fairly consistent and predictable in our outlook on life and in how we approach people and situations. Additionally, most of us we are able to be flexible in how we respond to people and life circumstances. Those of us who are shy, for example, are not necessarily shy in all situations. Individuals with **personality psychopathology**, however, possess rigid patterns of responding that are inflexible, long-standing, and enduring (Abrams & Bromberg, 2007); these dysfunctional personality characteristics are present in nearly all situations.

As we shall see in this chapter, when maladaptive personality characteristics are quite pronounced and the cause of problems for the person or for others, the person may be diagnosed with a personality disorder. Specifically, a diagnosis of a **personality disorder** is characterized by enduring personality patterns (involving behavior, thoughts, emotions, and interpersonal functioning) that are (a) extreme and deviate markedly from cultural expectations, (b) inflexible and pervasive across situations, (c) evident in adolescence or early adulthood and stable over time, and (d) associated with distress and impairment (APA, 2013). Although there are often telltale signs of personality psychopathology in childhood (Sterzer, 2010), clinicians do not usually consider a personality disorder diagnosis until late adolescence or adulthood when personality development is more complete.

People with personality psychopathology often function well enough to get along without aid from others and may not see themselves as having a problem. They often fall under the radar and might be described as odd, peculiar, dramatic, or unusual. For these reasons, many people with personality disorders do not seek help or come to the attention of mental health professionals (Millon, Grossman, Millon, Meagher,

temperament innate mental, physical, and emotional traits

trait a distinguishing quality or characteristic of a person, including a tendency to feel, perceive, behave, or think in a relatively consistent manner

personality psychopathology dysfunctional and maladaptive personality patterns

personality disorder characterized by impairment in self and interpersonal functioning and the presence of pathological personality traits that are relatively inflexible and long-standing

& Ramnath, 2004). As a result, the incidence of personality disorders is difficult to ascertain. The overall lifetime prevalence of personality disorders is estimated to be 9–13 percent, which suggests that these disorders are relatively common in the general population; similarly, personality disorders account for approximately 5–15 percent of those seeking treatment at hospitals and outpatient clinics (Lenzenweger, Lane, Loranger, & Kessler, 2007; Sansone & Sansone, 2011).

DSM-5 delineates two distinct methods of diagnosing and classifying personality psychopathology:

1. a categorical diagnostic model, involving 10 specific personality disorder types, which are each qualitatively distinct clinical syndromes; and

2. an alternative model, including components of both dimensional and categorical assessment.

We will first review the 10 traditional personality disorders and then discuss diagnostic issues associated with personality disorders and the alternative system for personality diagnosis recently included in the DSM-5.

Personality Disorders

The 10 specific personality disorders in the DSM-5 are grouped into three behavior clusters: (1) odd or eccentric behaviors; (2) dramatic, emotional, or erratic behaviors; or (3) anxious or fearful behaviors (see Table 15.1). To diagnose a personality disorder, clinicians use the DSM-5 descriptions of the disorder and determine the degree of match with the individual. We will discuss each of the 10 personality disorders rather briefly. We then provide a multipath analysis of the personality disorder that has the greatest impact on society—antisocial personality disorder.

Cluster A—Disorders Characterized by Odd or Eccentric Behaviors

Three personality disorders are included in Cluster A: *paranoid personality, schizoid personality,* and *schizotypal personality.* These personality disorders share characteristics, including overlapping environmental and genetic risk factors, which are similar to those found in the schizophrenia spectrum disorders (Esterberg, Goulding, & Walker, 2010). There is some evidence that individuals with disorders in this grouping have a greater likelihood of having biological relatives with schizophrenia or other psychotic disorders (APA, 2013).

Paranoid Personality Disorder

CASE STUDY Ralph and Ann married after a brief, intense courtship. The first year of their marriage was relatively happy, although Ralph was very domineering, opinionated, and overprotective. Ann had always known that Ralph was a jealous person who demanded a great deal of attention. She was initially flattered that Ralph would become upset when other men flirted with her because it indicated he cared. It soon became clear, however, that his jealousy was excessive. For example, when Ann came home from shopping later than usual, Ralph would become very hostile and agitated and would demand an accounting of her activities. He often doubted her explanations, and embarrassed Ann by calling her friends or co-workers to confirm her stories.

Table 15.1 Personality Disorders

DISORDERS CHART			
Disorder	**DSM-5 Descriptors**	**Gender Differences**	**Prevalence**
Disorders Characterized by Odd or Eccentric Behaviors			
Paranoid personality disorder[a]	• Pervasive pattern of mistrust and suspiciousness regarding others' motives	Somewhat more common in males	2.3%–4.4%
Schizoid personality disorder[a]	• Socially isolated, emotionally cold, indifferent to others	Somewhat more common in males	3.1%–4.9%
Schizotypal personality disorder	• Peculiar thoughts and behaviors; poor interpersonal relationships	Slightly more common in males	Up to 3.9%
Disorders Characterized by Dramatic, Emotional, or Erratic Behaviors			
Antisocial personality disorder	• Failure to conform to social or legal codes; lack of anxiety and guilt; irresponsible behaviors	Much more common in males	0.6%–4.5%
Borderline personality disorder	• Intense fluctuations in mood, self-image, and interpersonal relationships	Predominantly diagnosed in females	1.6%–5.9%
Histrionic personality disorder[a]	• Self-dramatization, exaggerated emotional expression, and seductive, provocative or attention-seeking behaviors	Mixed findings, but more prevalent in females in clinic settings	0.4%–1.8%
Narcissistic personality disorder	• Exaggerated sense of self-importance; exploitative behavior; lack of empathy	More common in males	0%–6.2%
Disorders Characterized by Anxious or Fearful Behaviors			
Avoidant personality disorder	• Pervasive social inhibition; fear of rejection and humiliation	Equal frequency in men and women	1.4%–5.2%
Dependent personality disorder[a]	• Excessive dependence on others; inability to assume responsibilities; submissive	Unclear, but more frequently diagnosed in women in clinics settings	About 0.5%
Obsessive-compulsive personality disorder	• Perfectionism; controlling interpersonal behavior; devotion to details; rigidity	Twice as common in males	2.1%–7.9%

Note: Symptoms of personality disorders appear early in life. Personality disorders tend to be stable and to endure over time, although symptoms sometimes remit with age. Prevalence figures and gender differences have varied from study to study.

[a]Not included as a diagnostic category in the DSM-5 Alternative Model for Personality Disorders.

SOURCE: Based on APA (2013); Bollini & Walker (2007); J. R. Kuo & Linehan (2009); Sansone & Sansone (2011).

> As the situation progressively worsened, Ralph began to suspect that Ann was having affairs with other men, so he would leave work early to check on Ann. Whenever the phone rang, Ralph insisted on answering it himself. Wrong numbers and male callers took on special significance for him; he felt that they must be trying to contact Ann. Ann found it difficult to discuss her concerns with Ralph. He was always quick to take the offensive, and he expressed very little sympathy or understanding toward her. He thought she and her male friends were playing him for a fool. Thus, Ralph persisted in his pathological jealousy and suspiciousness, even after Ann filed for a divorce.

paranoid personality disorder characterized by distrust and suspiciousness regarding the motives of others

The primary characteristic of **paranoid personality disorder** is a "pervasive distrust and suspiciousness of others such that their motives are interpreted as malevolent"

(APA, 2013, p. 649). People with paranoid personality disorder exhibit unwarranted suspiciousness, hypersensitivity, and reluctance to trust others because they expect to be exploited or mistreated. As was the case with Ralph, they tend to be rigid in their thinking and preoccupied with unfounded beliefs, such as suspicions about the fidelity of their partners. They may seem aloof and lacking in emotion. People with paranoid personality disorder often interpret others' motives negatively, question people's loyalty or trustworthiness, and bear grudges. These beliefs are extremely resistant to change and result in social isolation, difficulties in working with others, and hostility.

The prevalence of paranoid personality disorder ranges from 2.3 to 4.4 percent in U.S. samples (Sansone & Sansone, 2011). As you might expect, many people with this disorder fail to seek treatment because of their suspiciousness and mistrust.

Certain groups, such as refugees and members of minority groups, may display guarded or defensive behaviors not because of a disorder but because of their minority group status, experiences with discrimination, or lack of familiarity with the majority society. To avoid misinterpreting the significance of mistrustful behavior, clinicians assessing members of these groups are careful to clarify the origins of feelings of wariness or suspiciousness.

Causes and Treatment   Paranoid personality traits result from the use of *projection*—a defense mechanism in which unacceptable impulses are denied and attributed to others—according to psychodynamic theorists. In other words, someone with paranoid personality disorder may believe "I am not hostile; they are." From a cognitive-behavioral perspective, individuals with this disorder may filter and interpret the responses of others through an untrusting mental schema such as "Other people have hidden motives," which accounts for their suspiciousness (Bhar, Beck, & Butler, 2012). In terms of treatment, psychotherapy focuses on helping clients reduce their paranoia so they can function better in daily living. However, it may be difficult for therapists to develop rapport due to the client's suspiciousness and difficulty trusting others.

Schizoid Personality Disorder

The most prominent characteristics of **schizoid personality disorder** are "pervasive detachment from social relationships and a restricted range of expression of emotions in interpersonal settings" (APA, 2013, p. 652). People with this disorder have a long history of impairment in social functioning, including social isolation, emotional coldness, and indifference to others. They tend to neither desire nor enjoy close relationships. Many live alone, engage in solitary recreational activities, and are described as withdrawn and reclusive.

Because of a lack of capacity or desire to form social relationships, people with schizoid disorder are perceived by others as peculiar and aloof. They may interact with others in the workplace and similar situations, but their relationships are superficial and frequently awkward. They prefer a hermit-like existence (Esterberg, Goulding, & Walker, 2010). In general, individuals with this disorder prefer social isolation and the single life rather than marriage. When they do marry, their spouses are often unhappy due to their lack of affection and reluctance to participate in family activities. Members of different cultures vary in their social behaviors, and diagnosticians must consider the cultural background of individuals who show schizoid symptoms. The prevalence of this disorder ranges from 3.1 to 4.9 percent in the United States (Sansone & Sansone, 2011).

Causes and Treatment   The relationship between schizoid personality disorder and schizophrenia spectrum disorders (described in Chapter 12) is unclear. One view is that schizoid personality is genetically associated with schizophrenia (APA, 2013). Some studies have shown that schizoid personality disorder is associated with a cold and emotionally impoverished childhood lacking in empathy (Marmar, 1988). Little is known about psychotherapy with individuals with schizoid personality disorder since few seek treatment (Blais, Smallwood, Groves, & Rivas-Vazquez, 2008). They are

schizoid personality disorder   characterized by detachment from social relationships and limited emotional expression

most likely to seek treatment if they are experiencing stress or a crisis, but even then they can be challenging to treat (Thylstrup & Hesse, 2009).

Schizotypal Personality Disorder

CASE STUDY   A 41-year-old man was referred to a community mental health clinic for help in improving his social skills. He had a lifelong pattern of social isolation, had no real friends, and spent long hours worrying that his angry thoughts about his older brother would cause his brother harm. During one interview, he was distant and distrustful. He described in elaborate and often irrelevant detail his rather uneventful and routine daily life. . . . For 2 days he had studied the washing instructions on a new pair of jeans—Did "wash before wearing" mean that the jeans were to be washed before wearing the first time, or did they need, for some reason, to be washed each time before they were worn? . . . He asked the interviewer whether, if he joined the program, he would be required to participate in groups. He said that groups made him very nervous because he felt that if he revealed too much personal information, such as the amount of money that he had in the bank, people would take advantage of him or manipulate him for their own benefit. (Spitzer et al., 1994, pp. 289–290)

People with **schizotypal personality disorder** have odd, eccentric, paranoid, or peculiar thoughts and behaviors and a high degree of discomfort with and reduced capacity for interpersonal relationships (APA, 2013). Many believe they possess magical abilities or special powers (e.g., "I can predict what people will say before they say it"), and some are subject to recurrent illusions (e.g., "I feel that my dead father is watching me"). Speech oddities, such as frequent elaboration, digression, or vagueness in conversation, are often present (Minor & Cohen, 2012). The man in the case study has symptoms that are typical of schizotypal personality disorder: absence of close friends, magical thinking (worrying that his thoughts might harm his brother), conversational oddities, and social anxiety. Up to 3.9 percent of individuals in U.S. community samples have a schizotypal personality disorder (Sansone & Sansone, 2011). Again, the evaluation of individuals must take into account their cultural milieu. For example, superstitious beliefs and hallucinations are common in certain cultures or religions.

Causes and Treatment   Research shows that people with schizotypal personality disorder have abnormalities in cognitive processing that may explain many of their symptoms (Bollini & Walker, 2007). That is, they seem to have problems in thinking and perceiving, which may lead to symptoms of social isolation, hypersensitivity, inappropriate emotional responding, and lack of pleasure from social interactions (Blanchard, Gangestad, Brown, & Horan, 2000). In fact, many characteristics of schizotypal personality disorder resemble those of schizophrenia, although in less serious form. For example, people with schizophrenia exhibit problems in social functioning and information processing—deficits seen in people with schizotypal personality disorder (Goodman, Triebwasser, et al., 2007). Some research has suggested a genetic link between the two disorders (Bollini & Walker, 2007). Additionally, similar temporal lobe abnormalities are seen in those with schizophrenia and people with schizotypal personality disorder, although the latter have larger volume in the prefrontal cortex, which may mitigate (lessen) psychotic symptoms (Hazlett et al., 2014).

Various psychotherapies are used to treat schizotypal personality disorder, such as interpersonal psychotherapy and cognitive-behavioral approaches, as well as group psychotherapy. However, few individuals with schizotypal personality disorder seek therapy.

schizotypal personality disorder   characterized by peculiar thoughts and behaviors and by poor interpersonal relationships

Crime Bosses and Antisocial Personality Disorders

Vito Corleone (played by Marlon Brando) in *The Godfather* and Tony Soprano (played by James Gandolfini) in the TV series *The Sopranos* are both characters who exhibit many of the traits of antisocial personality disorder. Both show a callous disregard for the rights of others and little regret or remorse for cheating, lying, breaking the law, or even killing. However, they also reveal characteristics that are at odds with the diagnosis. Both have deep family relationships, reveal intense loyalty and emotional commitment to their families, and evidence flashes of guilt; Tony Soprano even seeks psychiatric help for his anxiety attacks.

Cluster B—Disorders Characterized by Dramatic, Emotional, or Erratic Behaviors

The group of disorders in Cluster B, characterized by dramatic, emotional, or erratic behaviors, includes four personality disorders: *antisocial, borderline, histrionic,* and *narcissistic*.

Antisocial Personality Disorder

The primary characteristic of **antisocial personality disorder (APD)** is a "pervasive pattern of disregard for and violation of the rights of others" that has occurred since age 15 (APA, 2013). This diagnosis only applies to individuals 18 and older. Chronic antisocial behavioral patterns, such as a failure to conform to social or legal codes, a lack of anxiety and guilt, and irresponsible behaviors, are common with APD. People with this disorder may show little concern about their wrongdoing, which may include lying, using other people, and perpetrating aggressive sexual acts. Relationships with others are superficial and fleeting and involve little loyalty. Those with this disorder seek power over others and often manipulate, deceive, exploit, and con others for their own needs and purposes (Dolan & Fullam, 2010). Clinicians sometimes use the term *psychopath* or *sociopath* to describe individuals with APD, especially those with a pattern of emotional detachment, low levels of anxiety or fear, a bold interpersonal style, and high levels of attention seeking (APA, 2013).

People with APD are prone to engage in unlawful and criminal behavior and have no qualms about violating moral, ethical, or legal codes of conduct (Hare & Neumann, 2009). The following case study of Robert T. exemplifies many of these characteristics.

DID YOU KNOW?

There are differences between those with antisocial personality disorder who are caught breaking the law (criminals) and those who break the law without detection. Those in the latter group have higher cognitive functioning, have greater cardiovascular reactivity to stress, are less likely to come from economically disadvantaged backgrounds, and are more likely to work in white-collar jobs (J. R. Hall & Benning, 2006). These attributes may make them less susceptible to arrest.

antisocial personality disorder (APD) characterized by a failure to conform to social and legal codes, a lack of anxiety and guilt, and irresponsible behaviors

CASE STUDY The epitome of a hard-driven, successful businessman, Robert T. seemed to have it all: enormous financial wealth, an apparently healthy marriage, and, despite his reputation as a ruthless corporate raider, high regard from associates for his business acumen. Then, in less than a year, he lost everything. Stockholders raised questions about nonstandard accounting practices and inappropriate personal use of funds. Robert's financial world collapsed. Lawsuits against him and his company followed, with the trustees finally demanding his resignation. Robert refused to resign and launched a campaign against his own board of directors, accusing them of pursuing a personal vendetta and of conspiring against him. He hired a private detective to dig up dirt on certain trustees and their families, and tried to use that information to intimidate and discredit them. In cases where embarrassing information was lacking, he had no qualms about spreading false rumors. These attempts, however, failed, and Robert was eventually removed from his post. His wife filed for divorce.

It was only after his downfall that the extent of Robert's dishonesty become known. He did not graduate from the Wharton School of Business, as his resume had indicated. He told people that he had been divorced once, but he had been married four times (two of the marriages ended in divorce before age 20); and his fortune did not come from "old money," but from a series of questionable real estate schemes that left investors holding bad debts, which he referred to as "collateral damage." People who knew him in the past often described him as arrogant, deceitful, cunning, and calculating. He showed a disregard for the rights of others, manipulated them, and then discarded them when they served no further use to him. He never expressed regret or remorse for any of his actions.

School records revealed a pattern of juvenile alcohol use, poor grades, frequent lying, and petty theft. At age 14, he was diagnosed with a conduct disorder when school officials became concerned with his fascination for setting fires in the restroom toilets. Nevertheless, the school psychologist described Robert as "very bright, charming, and persuasive."

Robert T. typifies an individual with APD. He exhibits little empathy for others, views them as objects to be manipulated, and has difficulty establishing meaningful and intimate relationships. Robert pushes the boundaries of social convention and often violates moral, legal, and ethical rules for his own personal gain, with little regard for the feelings of others. This characteristic way of handling things is long-standing, and was evident early in life. Similar to others with APD, Robert often blames others, is inflexible in his manner of dealing with life problems, has a callous orientation toward people and appears to feel no remorse about his deceit of others through lying, exaggeration, and manipulation.

In the United States, the prevalence of APD is estimated to be about 0.6–4.5 percent; rates differ by gender, with more men than women diagnosed with the disorder (APA, 2013; Sansone & Sansone, 2011). Estimates of prevalence vary from study to study, however, which may be due to differences in sampling or diagnostic and methodological procedures. People with APD are a difficult population to study because they do not voluntarily seek treatment. Consequently, investigators often locate research participants in prison populations, which presumably contain a relatively large proportion of people with the disorder. APD is much more frequent in urban environments than in rural ones, and among those with lower incomes. Rates of APD appear comparable among European Americans, African Americans, and Latino/Hispanic Americans. Although African Americans have a higher rate of incarceration for crimes, their rates of APD are either equal to or lower than those of other groups (Zukerman, 2003).

The behavior patterns associated with APD are different and distinct from impulse control problems such as pyromania, kleptomania, and intermittent explosive disorder (see Table 15.2) and from behaviors involving social protest or criminal lifestyles. Individuals who violate societal laws or conventions by engaging in civil disobedience are not, as a rule, people with APD because they are usually quite capable of forming meaningful interpersonal relationships and experiencing guilt. They may perceive their violations of rules and norms as acts performed for the greater good. Similarly, engaging in delinquent or adult criminal behavior does not necessarily reflect a personality disorder. Although many convicted criminals do have antisocial characteristics, many others do not. Instead, they may come from a subculture that encourages and reinforces criminal activity; hence, in perpetrating such acts, they are adhering to group norms and codes of conduct.

Borderline Personality Disorder

Individuals with **borderline personality disorder (BPD)** show an enduring pattern of volatile emotional reactions, instability in interpersonal relationships, poor self-image, and impulsive responding (APA, 2013). They lack a strong sense of self-identity and have a fragile self-concept that is easily disrupted by stress. BPD is also characterized by intense fluctuations in mood; hypersensitivity to social threat; and volatile interactions with family, friends, and sometimes even strangers (Herpertz & Bertsch, 2014). People with BPD are impulsive, have chronic feelings of emptiness, and form unstable and intense interpersonal relationships (Goodman, Triebwasser, et al., 2007). They may engage in behaviors with negative consequences such as binge eating, substance abuse, self-injury, verbal aggression, or impulsive shopping (Selby & Joiner, Jr., 2013). They may be quite

Antisocial Personality Disorder in Criminal Populations

Although not all individuals who are incarcerated have an antisocial personality disorder, many people who break the law display many antisocial personality traits. Prisoners who have an antisocial personality disorder have a high risk of re-offending once they are released.

Table 15.2 Impulse Control Disorders

Definitions of some personality disorders include the characteristic of impulsivity. However, there are other mental disorders in which impulse control is a primary characteristic.

1. People with **intermittent explosive disorder**
   - experience recurrent episodes of loss of control over aggressive impulses that result in physical assaults or property damage,
   - display an aggressiveness that is grossly out of proportion to any precipitating stressor or event that may have occurred, and
   - show no signs of general aggressiveness between episodes and may genuinely feel remorse for their actions.

2. People with **kleptomania**
   - chronically fail to resist impulses to steal;
   - do not need the stolen objects for personal use or monetary value, since they usually have enough money to buy the objects and typically discard them, give them away, or surreptitiously return them; and
   - feel irresistible urges and tension before stealing, followed by an intense feeling of relief or gratification after stealing.

3. People with **pyromania**
   - deliberately set fires ;
   - are fascinated by and get intense pleasure or relief from setting the fires, watching things burn, or observing firefighters and their efforts to put out fires; and
   - have fire-setting impulses driven by this fascination rather than by motives involving revenge, sabotage, or financial gains.

© Cengage Learning®

borderline personality disorder (BPD) characterized by intense fluctuations in mood, self-image, and interpersonal relationships

Did Princess Diana Have Borderline Personality Disorder?

Princess Diana, smiling happily in this picture, was known to experience rapid mood swings. Her emotional and behavioral traits, such as impulsiveness, marked fluctuations in mood, chronic feelings of emptiness, and unstable and intense interpersonal relationships, are consistent with a diagnosis of borderline personality disorder. Why do women receive this diagnosis far more frequently than men?

Chris Smith/PhotoEdit

friendly one day and quite hostile the next. Some of the characteristics of BPD can be seen in the following case.

> **CASE STUDY** Dal is an attractive young woman but seems to be unable to maintain a stable sense of self-worth and self-esteem. Her confidence in her ability to "hold on to men" is at a low ebb, having just parted ways with "the love of her life." In the last year alone she confesses to having six "serious relationships". . . "No one f***s with me. I stand my ground, you get my meaning?" She admits that she physically assaulted three of her last six boyfriends, hurled things at them, and, amidst uncontrollable rage attacks and temper tantrums, even threatened to kill them. . . . As she recounts these sad exploits, she alternates between boastful swagger and self-chastising, biting criticism of her own traits and conduct. Her mood swings wildly, in the confines of a single therapy session, between exuberant optimism and unbridled gloom. She sought therapy because she is having intrusive thoughts about killing herself. Her suicidal ideation often manifests in minor acts of self-injury and self-mutilation (Vaknin, 2012).

Individuals with BPD are more likely to show dysfunctional moods, interpersonal problems, poor coping skills, and cognitive distortions than are people without BPD features (J. C. Franklin, Heilbron, Guerry, Bowker, & Blumenthal, 2009). As with Dal, many individuals with BPD exhibit recurrent suicidal behaviors; the number of suicide attempts and completions are higher than average among those who have this disorder (Sherry & Whilde, 2008). Self-destructive behaviors, such as suicide attempts and nonsuicidal self-injury (cutting and self-mutilation), are often triggered by interpersonal conflicts and events (Sansone & Sansone, 2012). Sexual difficulties, such as sexual preoccupation and dissatisfaction, are also common (Zanarini, Parachini, Frankenburg, & Holman, 2003). Because of their behavioral excesses, those with BPD have increased risk of chronic illnesses such as cardiovascular disease, diabetes, and obesity (Iacovino, Powers, & Oltmanns, 2014). People who have BPD sometimes exhibit psychotic symptoms, such as auditory hallucinations (e.g., hearing imaginary voices that tell them to commit suicide), but the symptoms are usually transient (Sieswerda & Arntz, 2007). They are recognized by the individual as unacceptable, alien, and distressing (Oldham, 2006). By contrast, most people with schizophrenia spectrum disorders do not realize that their symptoms are abnormal.

BPD is the most commonly diagnosed personality disorder in both inpatient and outpatient settings (Oldham, 2006). The prevalence of BPD in U.S. community samples ranges from 1.6 to 5.9 percent, and is more common in women (Sansone & Sansone, 2011). Although up to 10 percent of individuals with BPD die by suicide, long-term outcome studies show progressive remission of symptoms over a course of 6 or more years for many individuals with this disorder (Soloff & Chiappetta, 2012). However, remission or recovery is slow and individuals with BPD often have high rates of symptom recurrence (Zanarini, Frankenburg, Reich, & Fitzmaurice, 2012).

Causes and Treatment Difficulty with mood regulation is a central feature of BPD (J. R. Kuo & Linehan, 2009). A biologically based vulnerability to emotional dysregulation may underlie the intense emotional reactivity seen in BPD; in addition, an inability to modulate this hyperreactivity may slow emotional recovery following stressful events (Scott, Levy, & Granger, 2013). In fact, magnetic resonance imaging (MRI) and positron emission tomography (PET) imaging have revealed structural abnormalities in the prefrontal cortex and limbic regions and an atypical pattern of activation in the amygdala among individuals with BPD (Prossin, Love, Koeppe, Zubieta, & Silk, 2010; Richter et al., 2014). These brain regions are associated with mood regulation.

Unstable and intense interpersonal relationships often accompany the difficulties in regulating emotions seen in BPD (J. C. Franklin et al., 2009). According to the cognitive-behavioral perspective, these characteristics are affected by distorted or inaccurate attributions (explanations for others' behaviors or attitudes). Cognitive theorists argue that an individual's basic assumptions about the world play a central role in influencing perceptions, interpretations, and behavioral and emotional responses (Bhar et al., 2012). Individuals with BPD seem to have three basic assumptions: (1) "The world is dangerous," (2) "I am powerless and vulnerable," and (3) "I am inherently unacceptable." Believing in these assumptions, individuals with BPD become fearful, vigilant, guarded, defensive, and reactive.

Similarly, Young, Klosko, and Weishaar (2003) believe that early experiences of neglect or abuse play a role in BPD; unmet childhood needs may result in negative mental frameworks such as concern about being abandoned by loved ones. Viewing relationships through this mental filter leaves the individual hypersensitive and prone to emotional overreactivity in interpersonal situations. There is support for the association between BPD and maladaptive family functioning and childhood trauma such as sexual abuse (Newnham & Janca, 2014; Stepp, Olino, Klein, Seeley, & Lewinsohn, 2013).

Cognitive-behavioral therapy can help individuals with BPD identify negative thoughts and replace them with more adaptive cognitions; this approach has been effective in reducing suicidal acts, dysfunctional beliefs, anxiety, and emotional distress (Davidson, Norrie, & Palmer, 2008). Another form of psychotherapy, schema therapy, combines cognitive-behavioral therapy with psychodynamic techniques; this approach teaches clients to identify and modify maladaptive interpersonal schemas and behaviors. Schema therapy has produced promising results with BPD (Sempértegui, Karreman, Arntz, & Bekker, 2013).

Dialectical behavior therapy (DBT), developed by Linehan (1993) specifically for clients with BPD, was a major breakthrough in the treatment of this challenging disorder. Averting possible suicidal behaviors in clients and strengthening the therapist–client relationship are priorities in DBT. Clients are taught skills that address BPD symptoms, including emotional regulation, distress tolerance, and interpersonal effectiveness (Rizvi, Steffel, & Carson-Wong, 2013). The goals of DBT, in descending order of priority, are to address (1) suicidal behaviors, (2) behaviors that interfere with therapy, (3) behaviors that interfere with quality of life, (4) reactive behaviors, (5) post-traumatic stress behavior, and (6) self-respect behaviors. DBT has proven effective in treating symptoms of DBT, including decreasing suicidal behaviors (Fox, Krawczyk, Staniford, & Dickens, 2014). Because of positive treatment outcomes, DBT is increasingly viewed as the treatment of choice for BPD (Neacsiu, Lungu, Harned, Rizvi, & Linehan, 2014).

CONTINUUM Video Project

Tina: **Borderline Personality Disorder**

"I kinda get high off of making people as uncomfortable as they make me. It's almost my way of really connecting with myself."

Access the Continuum Video Project in MindTap at **www.cengage.com**

© Cengage Learning

Histrionic Personality Disorder

People with **histrionic personality disorder** show a "pervasive pattern of excessive emotionality and attention-seeking" (APA, 2013, p. 667). The term *histrionic* refers to intensely dramatic emotions and behaviors used to draw attention to oneself. Individuals with histrionic personality disorder engage in self-dramatization, exaggerated expression of emotions, and attention-seeking behaviors. The desire for attention may lead to flamboyant acts or flirtatious behaviors (Blais et al., 2008).

Despite superficial warmth and charm, the histrionic person is typically shallow and self-centered. Individuals from different cultures vary in the extent to which they display their emotions, but the histrionic person goes well beyond cultural norms. In the United States, about 0.4 to 1.8 percent of the population may have this disorder (Sansone & Sansone, 2011). Gender differences are not evident, although in clinical settings this disorder is diagnosed more frequently in females (APA, 2013). Histrionic behaviors were apparent in a female client seen by one of the authors, as shown in the following case.

histrionic personality disorder
characterized by extreme emotionality and attention seeking

Dr. Marsha Linehan: Portrait of Resilience

A 17-year-old girl was institutionalized at a psychiatric facility in Connecticut. Doctors considered her among the most seriously disturbed patients they had ever seen (B. Carey, 2011). She habitually cut and burned herself, and would use any sharp object to slash her arms, legs, and midsection. She expressed a desire to die and made attempts at suicide (Grohol, 2011). Because of these constant attempts at self-harm, she was locked in a seclusion room free of any object that she could possibly use to hurt herself. However, this did not prevent her from injuring herself, since she constantly and violently banged her head against the floor or walls.

She was given hours of Freudian analysis, large doses of psychiatric drugs, and, as a last resort, electroconvulsive shock treatments. When discharged 2 years later, doctors gave her little chance of survival.

This is the true story of Dr. Marsha Linehan, a world-renowned psychologist who developed a ground-breaking form of psychotherapy called dialectical behavior therapy (DBT)—a therapeutic approach that successfully treats people with borderline personality disorder and suicidal tendencies. Despite her difficult years and diagnosis of borderline personality disorder, Linehan managed to find the answers to the problems that haunted her and drove her to thoughts of suicide. She went on to receive her PhD in psychology and is now on the faculty at the University of Washington, where the psychological community has embraced her work on DBT, a unique and highly successful therapeutic approach. Her self-healing journey is truly inspirational and speaks to the courage, inner fortitude, and resilience of the human condition. In her own recovery, Linehan has outlined lessons she learned that involve components of a resilient and peaceful life (Emel, 2011):

1. *Real change is possible.* According to conventional wisdom, people with personality disorders have great difficulty changing; some people even say that very little can be done, especially for those with borderline personality disorder. Yet Linehan is a prime example that change is possible, and her DBT incorporates the notion that learning new skills and changing behavior ultimately changes perceptions and emotions.

2. *Accept life as it is, not as it is supposed to be.* Linehan calls this "radical acceptance" and uses her own recovery as an example. The gulf between who she was and what she wanted to be made her hopeless, desperate, and depressed. She despised herself, and her self-harm behaviors symbolized this hatred. Linehan believes that accepting oneself as one truly is represents the first step in combating feelings of self-loathing because it eliminates the discrepancy between an unrealistic ideal and the current state of the person and allows realistic and positive views of the self to develop.

3. *A diagnosis of borderline personality disorder or any disorder is not a life sentence.* According to Linehan, receiving a psychiatric diagnosis often fosters a victim mentality that produces helplessness, dependency, and hopelessness. The person begins to believe that little can be done to overcome the disorder. Linehan teaches her clients to think of themselves as survivors, or people who can control their destiny in life and are capable of overcoming challenges. Such a fundamental change in thinking moves clients from a passive to an active stance.

4. *Find faith and meaning in life.* Linehan's religion and faith in God played an important role in her recovery. Her Catholic faith gave her hope and allowed her to experience an epiphany in 1967 that ultimately led her to develop the core principles of DBT. Since then, Linehan's mission in life has been to help others through the challenges of mental illness.

Dr. Marsha Linehan

Peter Yates/New York Times/Redux

CASE STUDY A 33-year-old real estate agent entered treatment for problems involving severe depression. Her boyfriend had recently told her that she was a self-centered and phony person. He found out that she had been dating other men, despite their understanding that neither would go out with others. Once their relationship ended, her boyfriend refused to communicate with her. The woman then angrily called the boyfriend's employer and told him that unless the boyfriend contacted her, she would commit suicide. He never did call, but instead of attempting suicide, she decided to seek psychotherapy.

The woman dressed in a tight and clinging sweater for her first therapy session. Several times during the session she raised her arms, supposedly to fix her hair, in a very seductive manner. Her conversation was animated and intense. When she was describing the breakup with her boyfriend, she was tearful. Later, she raged over the boyfriend's failure to call her and, at one point, called him a "son of a bitch." Near the end of the session, she seemed upbeat and cheerful, commenting that the best therapy might be for the therapist to arrange a date for her.

None of the behaviors exhibited by this client alone warrants a diagnosis of histrionic personality disorder. In combination, however, her self-dramatization, incessantly drawing attention to herself via seductive behaviors, angry outbursts, manipulative suicidal threats, and lack of genuineness suggest this disorder.

Causes and Treatment Both biological factors, such as autonomic or emotional excitability, and environmental factors, such as parental reinforcement of a child's attention-seeking behaviors or histrionic parental models, may be important influences in the development of histrionic personality disorder (Millon et al., 2004). There is little research on treatment for this disorder (Weston & Riolo, 2007). Psychodynamic therapies focus on establishing a therapeutic alliance with the client and determining why the client craves attention (Horowitz, 2001). Cognitive-behavioral therapy focus on changing irrational cognitions such as: "I should be the center of attention" (Bhar et al., 2012).

Narcissistic Personality Disorder

CASE STUDY Roberto J. was a well-known sociologist at the local community college. He was flamboyant, always seeking attention, and well known for bragging about himself to anyone who would listen. Most people found him superficial and so self-centered that any type of meaningful conversation was nearly impossible. His expertise was in critical race theory, and he had published a few minor articles on topics of racism in professional journals. He saw himself as a great scholar and would often talk about his "accomplishments" to colleagues; Roberto had nominated himself for numerous awards, and asked colleagues to write letters on his behalf. Because his accomplishments were considered mediocre by academic standards, Roberto seldom received any of the awards. Nevertheless, he continued to present himself as a renowned pioneer in the field of race relations.

Roberto came for couples counseling at the request of his wife, who found his self-centered behavior and constant self-orientation alienating. After nearly a year of therapy without significant change in Roberto, his wife filed for divorce.

narcissistic personality disorder
characterized by an exaggerated sense of self-importance, an exploitive attitude, and a lack of empathy

Similar to many people with **narcissistic personality disorder**, Robert has a sense of entitlement, exaggerated self-importance, and superiority. He also seems unconcerned

Narcissistic Behavior

Miranda Priestly (Meryl Streep) in the movie *The Devil Wears Prada* illustrates some of the symptoms of narcissistic personality disorder, including an exaggerated sense of self-importance, an excessive need for admiration, and an inability to accept criticism or rejection. Do you think that narcissistic personality disorder is increasing among young people?

Twentieth Century Fox/Topham/The Image Works

with the feelings of others. The characteristics associated with narcissistic personality disorder include a "pervasive pattern of grandiosity (in fantasy or behavior), need for admiration, and lack of empathy" (APA, 2013, p. 669). People with this disorder require constant attention and admiration, and have difficulty accepting personal criticism. They talk mainly about themselves and show a lack of interest in others. Many fantasize about having power or influence, and they frequently overestimate their talents and importance. For example, they may be impatient or irate if others arrive late for a meeting but may frequently be late themselves and think nothing of it. Although lack of empathy is a primary characteristic of narcissistic personality disorder, the degree of empathic functioning varies among individuals with this disorder (Baskin-Sommers, Krusemark, & Ronningstam, 2014).

Narcissistic traits are common among adolescents and do not necessarily imply that a teenager has a narcissistic personality (APA, 2013). It has been found, however, that people later diagnosed with narcissistic personality disorder were more likely to experience feelings of invulnerability, display risk-taking behavior, and have strong feelings of uniqueness as adolescents (Weston & Riolo, 2007). The prevalence of narcissistic personality disorder varies greatly across studies of U.S. community samples and ranges from 0 to 6.2 percent (Sansone & Sansone, 2011).

Causes and Treatment   Little research exists on the etiology of narcissistic personality disorder. Psychodynamic theorists have hypothesized that the extreme self-focus and lack of empathy shown by individuals with this disorder is due to a lack of parental modeling of empathy during childhood (Kohut, 1977). According to cognitive-behavioral theorists, cognitive schemas such as "Other people should satisfy my needs" are thought to underlie narcissistic characteristics (Bhar et al., 2012).

As with most personality disorders, controlled treatment studies for narcissistic personality disorder are rare; therefore, treatment recommendations are frequently based on clinical experience (Blais et al., 2008). Most individuals with narcissistic personality seek treatment when in a vulnerable state of depression, anxiety, or suicidality (Pincus, Cain, & Wright, 2014). Unfortunately, narcissistic personality disorder is considered very difficult to treat; therapists usually attempt to help clients increase empathy skills, understand the needs of others, and decrease self-involvement (R. L. Leahy, Beck, & Beck, 2005). None of these treatments has met with much success. However, some remission of symptoms does occur. Over a 2-year period, about 53 percent of one sample of individuals with narcissistic personality disorder showed symptom improvement (Vater et al., 2014).

Cluster C—Disorders Characterized by Anxious or Fearful Behaviors

The remaining cluster of personality disorders is characterized by anxious or fearful behaviors. This category includes the *avoidant*, *dependent*, and *obsessive-compulsive* personality disorders.

Avoidant Personality Disorder

> **CASE STUDY** My name is Deb, and I have moderate to severe avoidant personality disorder. . . . I feel like I've had this condition my whole life; there just wasn't a name for it yet. I was considered a very shy, sensitive, overly emotional child. My road to diagnosis began a few years ago when I didn't eat for 4 days because I was afraid someone at the grocery store would talk to me. . . . The fear of being disliked or unwanted is so overwhelming that I'd rather be alone. My daily life involves watching TV or being on the Internet. . . . I hope to be well enough to go watch a parade, see a movie, or attend a carnival and chat with people whom I know (Cooper, 2013).

The essential features of **avoidant personality disorder** are a "pervasive pattern of social inhibition, feelings of inadequacy, and hypersensitivity to negative evaluation" (APA, 2013, p. 672). As in Deb's situation, fear of rejection and humiliation produce a reluctance to enter into social relationships. People with this disorder tend to have a negative sense of self, low self-esteem, and a strong sense of inadequacy. They tend to avoid social situations and relationships and are often socially inept, shy, and withdrawn. They fear humiliation, are overly sensitive to criticism, blame themselves for things that go wrong, and seem to find little pleasure in life.

Unlike some individuals who avoid others because they lack interest, individuals with avoidant personality disorder crave affection and an active social life. They want—but fear—social contact, and this ambivalence is reflected in different ways. For example, many people with this disorder engage in intellectual pursuits or are active in the artistic community. Thus, their need for contact and relationships is woven into their activities. A person with avoidant personality disorder may write poems expressing a need for human intimacy or emphasizing the plight of people who are lonely.

In U.S. community samples, the prevalence of avoidant personality disorder ranges from 1.4 to 5.2 percent (Sansone & Sansone, 2011), and no gender differences are apparent (APA, 2013). People with avoidant personality disorder often have a lifelong pattern of feeling inferior, inadequate, depressed, or anxious (Mahgoub & Hossain, 2007). As with other personality disorders, avoidant personality disorder is considered to be a chronic and enduring condition. However, studies indicate that the symptoms of the disorder change markedly over time and, in cases where symptoms decrease, individuals become more assertive, less submissive, and, more self-assured in social situations (Wright, Pincus, & Lenzenweger, 2013).

Causes and Treatment Some researchers believe that avoidant personality disorder is on a continuum with social anxiety disorder, whereas others see it as a distinct disorder that happens to include the trait of social anxiety. It may be that an avoidant personality results from a complex interaction between early childhood environmental experiences and innate temperament. For example, parental rejection and censure, reinforced by rejecting peers, may lead to the development of mental schema such as "I should avoid unpleasant situations at all costs" (Bhar et al., 2012). Additionally, people with this disorder are caught in a vicious cycle: Because they are preoccupied with rejection, they are constantly alert for signs of negativity or ridicule. This concern leads to many perceived instances of rejection, which cause them to avoid others. Their social skills may then become deficient and invite criticism from others. In other words, their very fear of criticism may lead to criticism.

avoidant personality disorder characterized by a fear of rejection and humiliation and a reluctance to enter into social relationships

Because of the fear of rejection and scrutiny, clients may be reluctant to disclose personal thoughts and feelings during therapy. If the therapist is unable to establish rapport and build a strong therapeutic alliance, the client may discontinue treatment. A number of different therapies, such as cognitive-behavioral, psychodynamic, interpersonal, and pharmacological treatments, are used with avoidant personality disorder. In a preliminary investigation, cognitive-behavioral therapy effectively reduced symptoms and improved the quality of life for clients with this disorder (Rees & Pritchard, 2014).

Dependent Personality Disorder

CASE STUDY Jim was 56, a single man who was living with his 78-year-old widowed mother. When his mother was hospitalized for cancer, Jim decided to see a therapist. He was distraught and depressed over his mother's condition. Jim indicated that he did not know what to do. His mother had always taken care of him, and, in his view, she always knew best. Even when he was young, his mother had "worn the pants" in the family. The only time that he was away from his family was during his 6 years of military service. After he was wounded, he spent several months in a Veterans Administration hospital. He then went to live with his mother. Because of his service-connected injury, Jim was unable to work full time. His mother welcomed him home, and she structured all his activities.

At one point, Jim met and fell in love with a woman, but his mother disapproved of her. During a confrontation between the mother and the woman, each demanded that Jim make a commitment to her. This was quite traumatic for Jim. His mother finally grabbed him and yelled that he must tell the other woman to go. Jim tearfully told the woman that he was sorry, but she must go, and the woman angrily left. While Jim was relating his story, it was clear to the therapist that Jim harbored some anger toward his mother, although he overtly denied any feelings of hostility. His life had always been structured, first by his mother and then by the military. His mother's illness meant that his structured world might crumble.

Dependent personality disorder is a condition in which an individual shows a "pervasive and excessive need to be taken care of that leads to submissive and clinging behavior and fear of separation" (APA, 2013, p. 675). As you saw in Jim's story, his dependency and inability to take responsibility interfered with important life decisions, and resulted in depression, helplessness, and suppressed anger. Individuals with dependent personality disorder lack self-confidence and often subordinate their needs to those of the people on whom they depend. Nevertheless, casual observers may fail to recognize or may misinterpret their dependency and inability to make decisions. Friends may perceive those with dependent personalities as understanding and tolerant, without realizing that they are fearful of doing anything that might disrupt the friendship. Similarly, they may allow their domestic partner to be dominant or abusive for fear that the partner will otherwise leave. Thus, individuals with dependent personality disorder are at high risk of becoming victims of relationship violence (Loas, Cormier, & Perez-Diaz, 2011).

Dependent personality disorder is relatively rare and occurs in about 0.5 percent of the population (Sansone & Sansone, 2011). The prevalence by gender is unclear. In clinical samples, dependent personality disorder is diagnosed more frequently in women. However, other surveys have found similar prevalence rates for men and women (APA, 2013). The individual's environment must be considered before rendering a diagnosis of dependent personality disorder. The socialization process that teaches people to be independent, assertive, and individual rather than group oriented does not occur in all cultures (Sue & Sue, 2013).

dependent personality disorder characterized by submissive, clinging behavior and an excessive need to be taken care of

Causes and Treatment Explanations for dependent personality disorder vary according to theoretical perspective. From the psychodynamic perspective, the disorder is a result of maternal deprivation, which causes fixation at the oral stage of development (Marmar, 1988). Behavioral learning theorists believe that a family or social environment that rewards dependent behaviors and punishes independence may promote dependency. Research findings show that dependency is associated with overprotective, authoritarian parenting (Bornstein, 1997). Presumably, these parenting styles prevent the child from developing a sense of autonomy and self-efficacy.

Cognitive theorists attribute dependent personality disorder to the development of distorted beliefs that discourage independence (Loas et al., 2011). Dependency is not simply a matter of being passive and unassertive. Rather, those with dependent personalities have two deeply ingrained assumptions that affect their thoughts, perceptions, and behaviors. First, they see themselves as inherently inadequate and unable to cope. Second, they conclude that their course of action should be to find someone who can take care of them. Their schema or cognitive framework involves thoughts such as "I need others to help me make decisions or tell me what to do" (Bhar et al., 2012). Different individual and group treatments are used with dependent personality disorder, and, in general, there is more success than with other personality disorders (Perry, 2001).

Obsessive-Compulsive Personality Disorder

CASE STUDY Cecil, a third-year medical student, was referred by his graduate adviser for therapy. The adviser said Cecil was in danger of being expelled from medical school because of his inability to get along with patients and other students. Cecil often berated patients for failing to follow his advice. On one occasion, he told a patient with a lung condition to stop smoking. When the patient indicated he was unable to stop, Cecil angrily told the patient to go for medical treatment elsewhere— that the medical center had no place for a "weak-willed fool." Cecil's relationships with others were similarly strained. He considered many members of the faculty to be "incompetent old deadwood," and he characterized fellow graduate students as "partygoers."

The graduate adviser said that the only reason that Cecil had not been expelled was because several faculty members thought that he was brilliant. Cecil studied and worked 16 hours a day. He was extremely well read and had an extensive knowledge of medical disorders. Although he was always able to provide a careful and detailed analysis of a patient's condition, it took him a great deal of time to do so. His diagnoses tended to cover every disorder that each patient could conceivably have, with a detailed focus on all possible combinations of symptoms.

Obsessive-compulsive personality disorder (OCPD) involves a "pervasive pattern of preoccupation with orderliness, perfectionism, and mental and interpersonal control, at the expense of flexibility, openness, and efficiency" (APA, 2013, p. 676). The person's preoccupation with details and rules leads to an inability to see the big picture. There is a heightened focus on being in control over aspects of one's own life and one's emotions; additionally, there is a strong devotion to minor details and a need to control other people. Individuals with OCPD lack flexibility and their rigid behaviors can significantly impair their occupational and social functioning and affect their quality of life (Pinto, Steinglass, Greene, Weber, & Simpson, 2013). As we saw with Cecil, coworkers may find those with OCPD to be demanding, inflexible, and perfectionistic. In many cases, individuals with OCPD are ineffective on the job, despite devoting long hours to their work.

OCPD is distinct from obsessive-compulsive disorder (OCD), discussed in Chapter 5. The two disorders have similar names, but their clinical manifestations are quite different. Individuals with OCD experience unwanted intrusive thoughts or

obsessive-compulsive personality disorder (OCPD) characterized by perfectionism, a tendency to be interpersonally controlling, devotion to details, and rigidity

Compulsive Behavior

TV detective Adrian Monk, played by Tony Shalhoub in the once popular TV series *Monk*, has some characteristics of obsessive-compulsive personality disorder, including rigidity in thinking and preoccupation with orderliness and cleanliness. However, he also has symptoms of obsessive-compulsive disorder such as fears of contamination and compulsions to perform repetitive behaviors.

Hopper Stone /USA Network /Everett Collection

DID YOU KNOW?

There are both differences and similarities between obsessive-compulsive personality disorder (OCPD) and obsessive-compulsive disorder (OCD):

Characteristics	OCPD	OCD
Rigidity in personality	Yes	Not usual
Preoccupation in thinking	Yes	Yes
Orderliness in general	Yes	Not usual
Need for Control	Yes	Not usual
Perfectionism	Yes	Not usual
Indecisiveness	Yes	Not usual
Intrusive thoughts/behaviors	Not usual	Yes
Need to perform rituals	Not usual	Yes

urges that cause significant distress. On the other hand, OCPD is a pervasive personality and character disturbance. People with OCPD genuinely see their way of functioning as the correct way. They relate to the world though a lens incorporating their own strict standards. In two studies, the prevalence of OCPD ranged from 2.1 to 7.9 percent in U.S. community samples (Sansone & Sansone, 2011). It is diagnosed twice as frequently in males (APA, 2013).

Causes and Treatment   Little research has been done regarding the etiology of OCPD. The disorder appears to occur more frequently among family members, which may be due to genetic or early childhood environmental factors (Blais et al., 2008). Cognitive-behavioral therapy, as well as supportive forms of psychotherapy, has helped some clients (Barber, Morse, Krakauer, Chittams, & Crits-Cristoph, 1997).

The diversity of personality disorders makes it difficult to extensively discuss the etiology and treatment of each. In many cases, we do not have enough knowledge about the disorder to engage in a comprehensive etiological explanation. Yet it is clear that biological, psychological, social, and sociocultural forces influence the development of personality disorders. In the next section, we use our multipath model to discuss one of the better-researched personality disorders: antisocial personality disorder.

Analysis of One Personality Disorder: Antisocial Personality

Although research on most personality disorders has been quite limited, there is more information about antisocial personality disorder (APD) because those with the disorder are often involved with the legal and criminal justice systems. We use our multipath model to explain how the biological, psychological, social, and sociocultural dimensions interact and contribute to the development of APD, as shown in Figure 15.1. In this way, we hope to provide a prototype for understanding the multidimensional development of other personality disorders.

Biological Dimension

The development of APD appears to involve interactions between biological vulnerabilities and environmental adversity (Fairchild, van Goozen, Calder, & Goodyer, 2012). Thus, considerable research has been devoted to trying to uncover the biological basis of APD.

Genetic Influences

It is not uncommon for casual observers to remark that people with antisocial personalities appear to have an inborn tendency toward sensation seeking, impulsivity, aggressiveness, and disregard for others. These speculations are difficult to test, because it is often difficult to distinguish between environmental and hereditary influences on behavior (Sterzer, 2010). Nevertheless, genetic factors are implicated in the development of APD, including the behavioral characteristics observed during childhood and adolescence (Van Hulle et al., 2009).

Support for genetic influences on antisocial behavior comes from research comparing concordance rates for identical or monozygotic twins with those for fraternal or dizygotic twins. Most studies show that monozygotic twins have a higher concordance rate for antisocial tendencies, delinquency, and criminality. Further, some children born to biological parents with antisocial personalities but raised by adoptive parents without such a diagnosis still exhibit higher rates of antisocial characteristics (Eley, Lichtenstein, & Moffitt, 2003).

Although this body of evidence seems to show a strong causal pattern, it must be viewed cautiously for several reasons. First, many of the studies on APD have

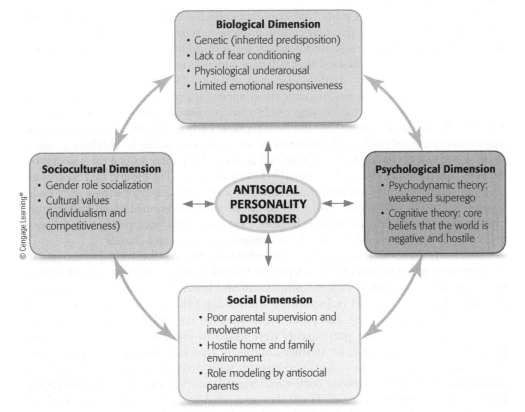

Figure 15.1

Multipath Model of Antisocial Personality Disorder

The dimensions interact with one another and combine in different ways to result in antisocial personality disorder.

drawn research participants from criminal populations; thus, we know less about those with APD in the general population. Second, studies indicating that genetic factors are important do not provide much insight into exactly how hereditary factors influence APD.

Genetic factors do not appear to directly affect antisocial behavior, but may instead influence characteristics, such as risk-taking and impulsivity, that increase the probability that such behavior will occur (Moffitt, 2005). Genetic predisposition also affects people's levels of fearlessness. Antisocial behavior may develop when individuals are fearless or display low levels of anxiety (J. P. Newman, Curtin, et al., 2010). While people who have normal levels of fear avoid risks, stress, and strong stimulation, those with limited fear may seek thrill and adventure. Fearlessness may explain why individuals with APD engage in risky criminal activities or impulsively violate norms and rules (Sterzer, 2010).

Lack of Fear Conditioning and Emotional Responsiveness

One line of research involves the hypothesis that biological abnormalities make people with APD less susceptible to fear and anxiety and therefore less likely to learn from their experiences in situations in which aversive stimuli (or punishment) are involved (Glenn et al., 2009). Because they have less fear about the consequences of their actions, they are less likely to learn to distinguish between appropriate and inappropriate behaviors. A variety of research that points to abnormalities in processing emotions in those with APD supports this position. For example, neuroimaging studies using MRI and PET scans have revealed that individuals with APD have neurological differences in the prefrontal cortex and the limbic amygdala circuitry, regions known to underlie emotional processing (Gao et al., 2010; Schiffer et al., 2014). These differences may help explain why those with APD have difficulty learning from experience and from punishment.

In a major longitudinal study based on data collected some 20 years ago, Gao and colleagues (2010) reasoned that fear conditioning in response to stimuli such as punishment or other negative consequences helps us learn to inhibit antisocial behavior when we are young. They hypothesized that deficient functioning of the amygdala, the part of the brain involved in fear conditioning, may make it difficult for some people to recognize cues that signal threats, making them appear fearless and unconcerned about consequences. Poor fear conditioning would thus predispose individuals to antisocial behavior. Recognizing that this should be detectable early in life, the researchers tested fear conditioning (physiological responses to an unpleasant noise) in children at age 3 using skin conductance measures of fear and arousal. They then probed the association between these findings and adult criminal behavior at age 23. They found that those with criminal records in early adulthood had failed to show fear conditioning in early childhood. It is possible that people with APD do not become conditioned to aversive stimuli; thus, they fail to acquire avoidance behaviors, experience little anticipatory anxiety, and consequently have fewer inhibitions about engaging in antisocial behavior.

Similarly, youth exhibiting antisocial behaviors showed diminished reactivity in the amygdala when shown pictures depicting fearful facial expressions, a finding that may partially explain their lack of compassion and limited emotional responsiveness to others (Brouns et al., 2013). In another study using MRI scans, youth scoring high on psychopathic traits were compared with matched controls in their reactions to photos of painful injuries; participants were asked to imagine that the body in the photograph was theirs and, in another condition, that it belonged to someone else. As compared to the healthy controls, the youth with psychopathic traits showed less activity in the anterior cingulate cortex and amygdala when they were imagining the injury involved another person. Thus, they appeared to demonstrate lower levels of emotional empathy to the plight of others (Marsh et al., 2013).

Arousal and Sensation Seeking

Another line of research proposes that people with APD have lower levels of physiological reactivity and are generally underaroused (Glenn et al., 2009). According to this view, people differ in their sensitivity to arousal—some have high and some have low levels of arousal. Thus, some people may require more stimulation to reach an optimal level of arousal. People with APD may seek excitement and thrills without concern for conventional behavioral standards. Additionally, if those with APD are underaroused, it may take a more intense stimulus to elicit a reaction in them compared to those without this characteristic (J. P. Newman, Curtin, et al., 2010). The lowered levels of reactivity may result in impulsive, stimulus-seeking behaviors in response to boredom.

Psychological Dimension

Psychological explanations of APD fall into three camps: psychodynamic, cognitive, and social learning.

Psychodynamic Perspectives

According to psychodynamic approaches, faulty superego development may cause those with APD to experience little guilt; they are, therefore, more prone to frequent violation of moral and ethical standards. Thus, the personalities of people with APD are dominated by id impulses that operate primarily from the pleasure principle; they impulsively seek immediate gratification and show minimal regard for others (Millon et al., 2004). People exhibiting antisocial behavior patterns presumably did not adequately identify with their parents and thus did not internalize the morals and values of society. Additionally, frustration, rejection, or inconsistent discipline may have resulted in fixation at an early stage of development.

Cognitive Perspectives

Certain core beliefs, and the ways they influence behavior, are emphasized in cognitive explanations of APD (Bhar et al., 2012). These core beliefs operate on an unconscious level, occur automatically, and influence emotions and behaviors. Beck and colleagues

© Greg Epperson/Shutterstock.com

Risk-Taking and Thrill-Seeking Behaviors

People with low anxiety levels are often thrill seekers. The difference between a risk-taking psychopath and an adventurer may largely be a matter of whether the thrill-seeking behaviors are channeled into destructive or constructive acts.

summarized typical cognitions associated with APD (Beck, Freeman, & Associates, 1990, p. 361):

- I have to look out for myself.
- Force or cunning is the best way to get things done.
- Lying and cheating are OK as long as you don't get caught.
- I have been unfairly treated and am entitled to get my fair share by whatever means I can.
- Other people are weak and deserve to be taken.
- I should do whatever I can get away with.
- I can get away with things, so I don't need to worry about bad consequences.

These thoughts arise from what Beck and colleagues refer to as a "predatory strategy." Thus, the worldview of those with APD revolves around a need to perceive themselves as strong and independent so they can survive in a competitive, hostile, and unforgiving world.

Learning Perspectives

Learning theories suggest that people with APD (1) have inherent neurobiological characteristics that impede their learning, and (2) lack positive role models that would help them develop prosocial behaviors. Thus, biology and environmental factors combine in unique ways to influence the development of APD.

As we have seen, some researchers believe that learning deficiencies among individuals with APD are caused by the absence of fear or anxiety and by lowered autonomic reactivity. If so, is it possible to improve their learning by increasing their anxiety or arousal ability? In a now classic study, researchers designed two conditions in which those with APD and control participants performed an avoidance learning task, with electric shock as the unconditioned stimulus (Schachter & Latané, 1964). Under one condition, participants were injected with adrenaline, which presumably increases arousal; under the other, they were injected with a placebo. Those with APD receiving the placebo made more errors in avoiding the shocks than did controls; however, after receiving adrenaline, they tended to perform better than controls. These findings imply that those with APD are more able to learn from negative consequences when their anxiety or arousal is increased.

The *kind* of punishment used in avoidance learning is also an important consideration in evaluating learning deficiencies in those with APD (see Figure 15.2). Whereas those with APD may show learning deficits when faced with physical (electric shock) or social (negative verbal feedback) punishments, they learn as well as controls when the punishment is monetary loss (Schmauk, 1970).

Figure 15.2

Effect of Type of Punishment on Psychopaths and Others

The effects of three different types of punishment on an avoidance learning task are shown for three groups of participants. Although physical or social punishment had little impact on psychopaths' learning, monetary punishment was quite effective.

SOURCE: Schmauk (1970)

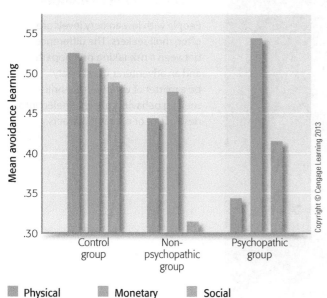

Physical punishment   Monetary punishment   Social punishment

Copyright © Cengage Learning 2013

Social Dimension

Among the many factors that are implicated in ASD, relationships within the family— the primary agent of socialization—are paramount in the development of antisocial patterns. A number of social factors are associated with increased antisocial behavior and limited prosocial behavior among children (J. C. Franklin et al., 2009). First, poor parental supervision and limited parental involvement can increase antisocial behaviors (Loeber, 1990). Additionally, rejection or neglect by one or both parents reduces the opportunity for children to learn socially appropriate behaviors or the value of people as socially reinforcing agents. Both parental separation or absence and inconsistent parenting are associated with APD (K. A. Phillips & Gunderson, 1999). Such situations may lead children to believe that there is little satisfaction in close or meaningful relationships with others and may explain why individuals with APD often misperceive the motives and behaviors of others and have difficulty being empathetic (Benjamin, 1996).

Children's risk of personality dysfunction increases when the adults they live with exhibit antisocial behavior or when they are subjected to neglect, hostility, maltreatment, or abuse (Jaffee, Moffitt, Caspi, & Taylor, 2004). Children from such environments learn that the world is cold, unforgiving, and punitive. Struggle and survival become part of their outlook on life, and they may respond in an aggressive fashion in an effort to control and manipulate the world. Additionally, children living in poverty are twice as likely to develop APD compared to those with a higher socioeconomic status (Lahey, Loeber, et al., 2005).

Sociocultural Dimension

A variety of sociodemographic variables, including social class, race, and gender, are important in both normal and abnormal development (Sue & Sue, 2013). Determining the relative impact of sociocultural factors on APD, however, is complicated.

Gender

Men are more likely to exhibit characteristics of APD compared to women. Thus, there may be different pathways to developing APD that exist along gender lines. For example, women with APD are more likely to report childhood emotional neglect, sexual abuse, and parental use of substances compared to men with APD. Gender also influences the way APD is expressed. Traditional gender-role training by parents may influence antisocial behaviors in children. Traditionally, aggression in males is accepted or even encouraged, whereas aggression in females is discouraged; this may explain why antisocial patterns involving aggression are more prevalent among men than among women (Alegria et al., 2013).

A Successful Psychopath?

Bernard L. Madoff exhibits all the traits of a person with antisocial personality disorder and has often been labeled "a successful psychopath." He lied to family, friends, and investors, manipulated people, experienced feelings of grandiosity, and had a callous disregard for his victims. A seemingly respected power broker on Wall Street, he is reported to have bilked investors out of some $50 billion. He was convicted on 17 felony counts and, on June 29, 2009, sentenced to 150 years in prison.

DON EMMERT/AFP/Getty Images

Whereas men tend to engage in direct acting-out behaviors (e.g., physical aggression), women express themselves in an indirect or passive manner (e.g., spreading rumors or false gossip and rejecting others from their social group), behavior referred to as *relational aggression* (Millon et al., 2004). Other gender differences exist. Men are more likely to exhibit job problems, violence, and traffic offenses, whereas women are more likely to report relationship and occupational problems, engaging in forgery, and harassing or threatening others (Alegria et al., 2013). As gender roles continue to change, one might reasonably expect that antisocial tendencies will increase among females.

Cultural Values

To be born and raised in the United States is to be exposed to the standards, beliefs, and values of U.S. society. One dominant value is that of rugged individualism, which is composed of two assumptions: (a) individualism and independence are viewed as aspects of healthy functioning, and (b) people can and should master and control their own lives (Sue & Sue, 2013). Competition and the ability to effectively manipulate the environment are considered pathways to success; achievement is measured by surpassing the attainment of others. In the extreme, this psychological orientation may fuel the manipulative and aggressive behaviors of people with APD.

Other societies, such as those in some Asian and Latin American countries, possess values and beliefs that are often at odds with individualistic values: Collectivism and interdependence are encouraged, development of the group is valued over the self, and harmony with the universe is preferred over mastery of it. Some have observed that antisocial behavior (e.g., crime and violence) is less likely to occur in Japan and China than in the United States because of these countries' collectivistic orientation, in which harmony and relationships with others are emphasized (Ivey, D'Andrea, Ivey, & Simek-Morgan, 2007). Because traditional Asian values, for example, accentuate harmony, subtlety, and restraint of strong feelings, Asian American clients who seek therapy are less likely than their European American counterparts to engage in behaviors associated with APD such as acting-out (e.g., overt expressions of anger, physical aggression), verbal hostility, substance abuse, and criminal behavior (Sue & Sue, 2013). Thus, it is clear that sociocultural factors may exert a powerful influence on the etiology and manifestation of personality disorders.

Treatment of Antisocial Personality Disorder

APD is not an easy condition to treat. Because people with antisocial traits feel little anxiety, they have little motivation to change their behavior or seek treatment. They are unlikely to see their actions as problematic. If they do seek treatment, they may try to manipulate or con their therapists. Thus, traditional treatment approaches, which require the genuine cooperation of clients, are often ineffective for those with APD. Treatment is most likely to be effective in structured settings in which behavior can be observed and controlled. That is, treatment programs need to provide enough control that those with APD cannot avoid confronting their inability to form close relationships and the effect of their behaviors on others. Such control is sometimes possible when individuals with APD are incarcerated or, for one reason or another, undergo psychiatric hospitalization. In these situations, they may participate in interventions that attempt to change their long-standing patterns of behavior.

Behavior modification programs are sometimes used for those at risk of developing APD, including delinquents with antisocial traits. The most useful treatments focus on decreasing deviant activities, combined with opportunities to learn appropriate behaviors and social skills (Meloy, 2001). Historically, the use of material rewards has been fairly effective in changing antisocial behaviors under controlled conditions (Van Evra, 1983). For example, money or tokens that can be used to purchase items are earned if appropriate behaviors (e.g., punctuality, honesty, discussion of personal problems) are displayed. Once the young people leave the treatment programs, however, they are likely to revert to antisocial activity unless their families and peers help them maintain appropriate behaviors.

Cognitive approaches are also used in treatment. Because individuals with APD are often influenced by dysfunctional beliefs about themselves, the world, and the future, they may have difficulty objectively anticipating possible negative outcomes of their behaviors. Beck, Freeman, and their associates (1990) have advocated that therapists build rapport with clients with APD, attempting to guide clients away from thinking only in terms of self-interest and immediate gratification and toward higher levels of thinking. This might include, for example, recognizing the effects of one's behaviors on others and developing a sense of responsibility. Because cognitive and behavioral approaches assume that antisocial behaviors are learned, treatment programs often target inappropriate behaviors by setting rules and enforcing consequences for rule violations; they teach participants to anticipate consequences of behaviors and practice new ways of interacting with others (Meloy, 2001).

Since longitudinal studies show that the prevalence of APD diminishes with age as individuals become more aware of the social and interpersonal consequences of their behavior, emphasis is placed on intervention with antisocial youth (K. A. Phillips & Gunderson, 1999). Treatment programs often broaden the base of intervention to include not only young clients but also their families and peers. Because people with antisocial traits often seek thrills, they may respond to intervention programs that provide the physical and mental stimulation they need (Farley, 1986).

Current treatment options for people with APD are only minimally effective. Although medication is usually used only when there are comorbid conditions such as depression or substance abuse, a recent study showed promising results with the use of clozapine (an atypical antipsychotic) to reduce impulsive and violent behaviors in a small sample of violent men with APD incarcerated in a high-security hospital setting (Brown et al., 2014).

Mary Kate Denny/PhotoEdit

Treating Antisocial Behaviors

Peers and family are critically important in the treatment of youth with antisocial personality disorder and in maintaining progress made in treatment. Here, a group led by a peer counselor is exploring some of the issues troubling these young people.

CRITICAL THINKING

Sociocultural Considerations in the Assessment of Personality Disorders

In diagnosing a personality disorder, it is important to consider the individual's cultural norms and expectations when considering whether personality traits are maladaptive (APA, 2013). Because culture shapes our habits, customs, values, and personality characteristics, expressions of personality in one culture often differ from those in another culture. Asians in Asia, for example, are more likely to exhibit shyness and *collectivism*, whereas U.S. Americans are more likely to show assertiveness and individualism (Sue & Sue, 2013). Japanese people and individuals from India often display overtly dependent, submissive, and socially conforming behaviors, traits that have negative connotations in U.S. society. Does this mean that the people in Japan and India who conform to these norms have a personality disorder? The behaviors of dependence and submissiveness are influenced by cultural values and norms and, thus, would not reflect personality psychopathology. In fact, in these countries, these traits are considered desirable personality characteristics. As you can see, anyone making judgments about personality functioning and disturbance must consider the individual's cultural, ethnic, and social background (APA, 2013).

Not surprisingly, there are differences in the prevalence and types of personality disorders between countries. For example, although obsessive-compulsive personality disorder is one of the most prevalent personality disorders in the United States and Australia, schizotypal personality disorder is the most common disorder in Iceland and avoidant personality disorder is most prevalent in Norway (Sansone & Sansone, 2011). Additionally, low rates of all personality disorders are found in Asian samples (Ryder, Sun, Dere, & Fung, 2014). What do you think might account for these differences?

Issues with Diagnosing Personality Psychopathology

It has always been challenging to diagnose personality disorders using the current diagnostic system. Diagnosing specific forms of personality disorders has been problematic for several reasons. First, there is poor inter-rater reliability for the personality disorder categories (Pull, 2013). Although diagnosticians generally agree on whether a particular client has a personality disorder, the precise type of personality disorder is where there is less agreement (Reed, 2010). One of the reasons this occurs is because there are overlapping symptoms between the different personality disorders. A person who is diagnosed with paranoid personality disorder, for example, may also have symptoms of and can meet the diagnostic criteria for other personality disorders such as schizotypal, borderline, narcissistic, avoidant, and obsessive-compulsive personality disorders (Zimmerman, Rothschild, & Chelminski, 2005). Thus, for a specific client, one clinician might diagnose a paranoid personality disorder whereas another therapist might consider the same set of behaviors and diagnose a borderline personality. The individual might even receive both diagnoses. As you can see, the reliability of the personality disorder categories is a significant concern.

Second, comorbidity (presence of other disorders) is high with personality disorders, which also reduces diagnostic accuracy. Up to 35 percent of those with PTSD, 47 percent with panic disorder with agoraphobia or generalized anxiety, 48 percent with social phobia, and 52 percent with obsessive-compulsive disorder also have a personality disorder (Latas & Milovanovic, 2014). Additionally, disorders such as depression, bipolar disorder, or substance-use disorders often accompany personality disorders (Lenzenweger, Lane, Loranger, & Kessler, 2007). When personality disorders are comorbid with other disorders, the other disorders are more likely to be diagnosed rather than the personality disorder (Westen et al., 2010).

Third, as we discussed in Chapter 4, an exclusive categorical approach has limitations because categorical diagnoses (1) are based on arbitrary diagnostic thresholds, (2) use an all-or-none method of classification (Reed, 2010), and (3) do not take into account the continuous nature of personality traits (Westen et al., 2010). In reality, people often have personality traits in varying degrees or at various times. Additionally, we all exhibit some of the traits that characterize personality disorders—for example, suspiciousness, dependency, sensitivity to rejection, or compulsiveness—but not to an extreme degree. Alternative methods of determining personality psychopathology have been proposed as a response to these diagnostic issues.

Eluding Capture: Aided by a Personality Disorder?

It took many years for authorities to track down and arrest Ted Kaczynski, the Unabomber, who killed many people over an 18-year period. Formerly a math professor at the University of California, Berkeley, Kaczynski is believed to have had a schizoid personality disorder and to have eluded capture because of his hermit-like existence. He was a loner and did not seem interested in socializing with people. He was finally arrested in his isolated cabin, where he had lived alone for many years.

AP Images/Elaine Thompson

Dimensional Personality Assessment and the DSM-5 Alternative Personality Model

Because of concerns with categorical diagnosis and problems with the reliability and validity of some personality disorder diagnostic categories, members of the DSM-5 Work Group revising the diagnostic criteria for personality disorders proposed discarding the traditional categorical system with the 10 personality disorders we have reviewed in this chapter. They recommended substituting a dimensional model that would involve looking at personality traits on a continuum; a personality disorder diagnosis would occur if a person with maladaptive and pathological personality traits displayed a certain degree of impairment in personality functioning. In other words, the clinician would determine if the person had enough of certain traits to qualify as having a personality disorder. They cited experts in the field of personality who view personality disorders as the extremes of a continuum of normal personality traits (Skodol & Bender, 2009).

Some of these experts argue that considering significant deviations from normal on five key personality dimensions—*extraversion* (sociable), *agreeableness* (good-natured, helpful, and kind), *neuroticism* (emotionally unstable and displaying negative emotionality), *conscientiousness* (thoughtful, organized, and detailed) and *openness to experience* (curiosity, willingness to entertain new ideas and interests)—is the best way to conceptualize personality disorders (Costa & McCrae, 2005; Widiger, 2007). Individuals vary in the extent to which they exhibit any of these factors.

A dimensional approach such as this allows clinicians to consider the degree to which a client possesses specific traits rather than deciding whether or not the client meets the diagnostic criteria for a specific disorder in question (yes or no) as required in a categorical diagnosis (Millon et al., 2004). Using a dimensional approach, clinicians can assess clients on specific traits and then rate the extent to which they possess each trait. For example, rather than deciding if a client meets the diagnostic criteria for a schizoid personality disorder, the clinician could instead describe the client as possessing varying degrees of personality traits such as social withdrawal, social detachment, intimacy avoidance, and so forth.

Although the DSM-5 Personality Work Group favored replacing the categorical system with a dimensional, trait-based model, many clinicians expressed concerns about the complete removal of the traditional diagnostic categories for personality disorders. In particular, clinicians opposed the deletion of certain categories because of their high usage and clinical utility. For example, the following are the percentages of clinicians who use these specific personality categories: borderline (92 percent), antisocial (61 percent), narcissistic (57 percent), and avoidant (51 percent) (Pull, 2013).

In a highly unusual move, the APA Board of Trustees decided to retain the categorical framework of 10 personality disorders in the main text of the DSM-5 and to include an alternative model for personality disorder diagnosis in a separate section of the DSM-5. This alternative model retains some of the categorical diagnoses in a modified form (6 of the 10 traditional personality disorders were retained), but also includes a dimensional classification system based on personality traits. The rationale for including both the traditional and the alternative model of personality disorder diagnosis was to "preserve continuity with current clinical practice, while also introducing a new approach that aims to address numerous shortcomings of the current personality disorders" (APA, 2013, p. 761). Clinicians can choose to use the traditional categorical model or the alternative model when making a personality disorder diagnosis.

The alternative model of personality disorders removed four of the more problematic personality disorders—paranoid, schizoid, histrionic, and dependent. Justification for their removal is based primarily on three lines of evidence:

1. an absence of research on these disorders, making their existence as distinct entities questionable (Skodol & Bender, 2009; Widiger & Trull, 2007);

2. excessive co-occurrence with other personality disorders, making it difficult to differentiate between the different disorders (Zimmerman, Rothschild, & Chelminski, 2005); and

3. the highly questionable reliability and validity of these four categories (Pull, 2013).

Does eliminating certain personality types mean there are no longer paranoid, withdrawn, superficially emotional, or dependent persons who qualify as having a personality disorder? The answer is "no." The new model allows these traits to be considered in a noncategorical fashion. Table 15.3 outlines the four personality disorders

Table 15.3 DSM-5 Personality Disorders and Domain-Trait Descriptions

	DSM-5 Categorical Diagnosis	DSM-5 Alternative Trait Description
Paranoid personality disorder	People with paranoid personality disorder • show unwarranted suspiciousness, hypersensitivity, and reluctance to trust others; and • interpret others' motives as being malevolent, question their loyalty or trustworthiness, persistently bear grudges, or are suspicious of the actions of others.	• The person is described in terms of personality disorder traits such as *suspiciousness, intimacy avoidance, hostility,* and *unusual beliefs.*
Schizoid personality disorder	People with schizoid personality disorder • exhibit social isolation, emotional coldness, and indifference to others; • have a long history of impairment of social functioning; • are reclusive and withdrawn; • do not desire or enjoy close relationships, and have few activities that provide pleasure; and • are perceived as peculiar and aloof and therefore inadequate as dating or marital partners due to lack of capacity or desire to form social relationships.	• The person is described in terms of personality disorder traits such as *social withdrawal, social detachment, intimacy avoidance, restricted affectivity,* and *anhedonia.*
Histrionic personality disorder	People with histrionic personality disorder • engage in self-dramatization, exaggerated expression of emotions, and attention-seeking behaviors; • behave flamboyantly or flirtatiously for attention; • are typically shallow and egocentric, in spite of superficial warmth and charm; and • display emotions well beyond acceptable cultural norms.	• The person is described in terms of personality disorder traits such as *emotional lability* and *histrionism.*
Dependent personality disorder	People with dependent personality disorder • lack self-confidence and subordinate their needs to those of the people on whom they depend; • are fearful of taking the initiative on most matters; • are afraid of disrupting their relationships with others. • see themselves as inherently inadequate and unable to cope; • believe they should find someone who can take care of them; and • often experience feelings of depression, helplessness, and suppressed anger.	• The person is described in terms of personality disorder traits such as *submissiveness, anxiousness,* and *separation insecurity.*

With a DSM-5 categorical diagnosis, the diagnosis is made if the person meets the listed diagnostic criteria. With the alternative trait model, the clinician determines if there is at least moderate impairment in personality functioning in the areas of identity, self-direction, empathy, or intimacy combined with clinical judgment or norm-based assessment that confirms an elevation in pathological personality traits involving 1 of the 5 trait domains or the 25 trait facets.

SOURCE: APA (2013)

that were removed, contrasting the traditional categorical definitions with how they would be described using the alternative approach.

DSM-5 Alternative Personality Model

With the DSM-5 alternative personality model, a diagnosis of personality disorder can be made through two different routes:

1. evidence that the client's pattern of personality traits matches characteristics from one of six specific personality disorder types (antisocial, avoidant, borderline, narcissistic, obsessive-compulsive, or schizotypal); *or*

2. evidence of at least moderate impairment in two key domains of personality functioning (identity, self-direction, empathy, or intimacy) combined with certain specific pathological personality traits.

With both routes, the personality disorder or descriptive personality traits must be pathological and result in at least moderate impairment in personal or interpersonal functioning.

When using the DSM-5 alternative system to diagnose a personality disorder, clinicians first ask the following questions: Does the person have impairment in personality functioning? If so, how severe is the impairment? To answer these questions, the clinician begins by carefully assessing four key areas related to personal and interpersonal personality functioning:

- *Identity*—sense of personal uniqueness, with clear boundaries between oneself and others; capacity to regulate one's emotions; accurate self-appraisal and stable self-esteem

- *Self-direction*—focus on meaningful goals, using self-reflection and positive standards of behavior

- *Empathy*—understanding of and tolerance for others' feelings and perspectives; comprehension of the effects of one's behavior on others

- *Intimacy*—capacity and desire for interpersonal closeness and deep connection with others; respectful interpersonal behavior

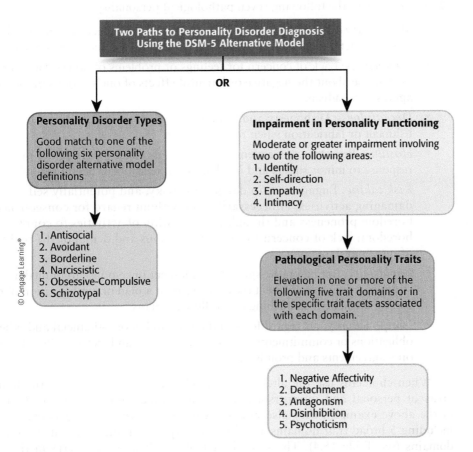

Figure 15.3

Two Paths to Personality Disorder Diagnosis Using the DSM-5 Alternative Model

The clinician measures personality functioning in each of these areas using the DSM-5 five-point Levels of Personality Functioning scale. Using this scale and interviews or other assessment tools, the clinician rates the client on the aforementioned personality characteristics of identity, self-direction, empathy, and intimacy; in each area the rating indicates if there is *no impairment*, or *mild*, *moderate*, *serious*, or *extreme* impairment.

These four key areas of personal and interpersonal personality functioning are addressed when a clinician uses the alternative model to diagnose someone who meets the description of one of the six personality types retained in the alternative model (antisocial, avoidant, borderline, narcissistic, obsessive-compulsive, or schizotypal). Let's take a diagnosis of antisocial personality disorder using the alternative model as an example (APA, 2013, pp. 764–765):

1. Moderate or greater impairment in personality functioning, manifested by characteristic difficulties in two or more of the following four areas:

   - *Identity:* Egocentrism; self-esteem derived from personal gain, power, or pleasure.
   - *Self-direction:* Goal setting based on personal gratification; absence of prosocial internal standards, associated with failure to conform to lawful or culturally normative ethical behavior.
   - *Empathy:* Lack of concern for feelings, needs, or suffering of others; lack of remorse after hurting or mistreating another.
   - *Intimacy:* Incapacity for mutually intimate relationships, as exploitation is a primary means of relating to others, including by deceit and coercion; use of dominance or intimidation to control others.

2. Six or more of the following seven pathological personality traits:

   - *Manipulativeness:* Frequent use of subterfuge to influence or control others; use of seduction, charm, glibness, or ingratiation to achieve one's ends.
   - *Callousness:* Lack of concern for feelings or problems of others; lack of guilt or remorse about the negative or harmful effects of one's actions on others; aggression; sadism.
   - *Deceitfulness:* Dishonesty and fraudulence; misrepresentation of self; embellishment or fabrication when relating events.
   - *Hostility:* Persistent or frequent angry feelings; anger or irritability in response to minor slights and insults; mean, nasty, or vengeful behavior.
   - *Risk taking:* Engagement in dangerous, risky, and potentially self-damaging activities, unnecessarily and without regard for consequences; boredom proneness and thoughtless initiation of activities to counter boredom; lack of concern for one's limitations and denial of the reality of personal danger.
   - *Impulsivity:* Acting on the spur of the moment in response to immediate stimuli; acting on a momentary basis without a plan or consideration of outcomes; difficulty establishing and following plans.
   - *Irresponsibility:* Disregard for—and failure to honor—financial and other obligations or commitments; lack of respect for—and lack of follow-through on—agreements and promises.

When clinicians use the alternative model, they not only address the four key areas of personal and interpersonal personality functioning (shown in Criteria 1 of the above example), they also assess a variety of pathological personality traits, including 5 broad trait domains and 25 facets (specific traits) associated with these domains (see Table 15.4). The second part of the diagnostic criteria in the above example (Criteria 2) focuses on the pathological personality traits associated with antisocial personality disorder. For each of these traits, the clinician uses clinical

Table 15.4 DSM-5 Trait Domains and Related Trait Facets

1. *Negative affectivity* refers to a wide range of negative emotions—such as anxiety, depression, guilt, shame, worry, and so forth—and the behavioral or interpersonal manifestations of those experiences. Emotional stability is the opposite end of this domain. The specific trait facets associated with this domain are
   - emotional lability, anxiousness, separation insecurity, submissiveness, hostility, perseveration, depressivity, suspiciousness, and restricted emotions.

2. *Detachment* involves withdrawal from others, whether the relationships are with intimate acquaintances or strangers. It includes restricted or limited emotional experiences and expressions, especially hedonic capacity (i.e., an inability to experience pleasure or joys in life). Extraversion is the opposite end of this domain. The specific trait facets associated with this domain are
   - withdrawal, avoidance of intimacy, lack of pleasure (anhedonia), depressivity, restricted emotions, and suspiciousness.

3. *Antagonism* refers to negative feelings and behaviors toward others and a corresponding exaggerated sense of self-importance and entitlement. Agreeableness is the opposite end of this domain. The specific trait facets associated with this domain are
   - manipulativeness, deceitfulness, grandiosity, attention seeking, callousness, and hostility.

4. *Disinhibition* involves orientation to the present (including current internal and external stimuli) and seeking immediate gratification. Past learning or future consequences seem minimally important. Conscientiousness is the opposite end of this domain. The specific traits associated with this domain are
   - irresponsibility, impulsivity, distractibility, risk taking, and lack of rigid perfectionism.

5. *Psychoticism* includes behaviors, perceptions, and thoughts or beliefs considered odd, unusual, or bizarre. Lucidity is the opposite end of this domain. The specific traits associated with this domain are
   - unusual beliefs and experiences, eccentricity, and cognitive and perceptual dysregulation.

SOURCE: Based on information from APA (2013).

judgment or norm-based psychological testing to decide if there is a significant elevation or deviation from the norm in these traits.

Clinicians can also assess these same aspects of personal and interpersonal personality functioning and pathological traits when working with clients who have another categorical diagnosis; even if a clinician does not believe a client has a personality disorder, assessment of personality traits can provide important clinical information. For example, evaluation of personality characteristics can provide valuable insight into areas that might interfere with optimal functioning and thus provide guidance for treatment planning.

Contemporary Trends and Future Directions

Personality disorders are considered to be "enduring," "stable," and of "long duration" (APA, 2013). However, recent studies raise questions about these descriptions because research data suggest that personality disorders appear to remit (diminish) more often than previously believed (Gutierrez, 2014). Although many individuals with personality disorders show minimal change or only slow improvement in their maladaptive personality traits, some individuals with personality disorders show rapid symptom remission. Those with the most rapid symptom improvement have fewer comorbid conditions (Hallquist & Lenzenweger, 2013). Researchers are attempting to discover the reason for the different trajectories for personality disorders. In general, this newest research suggests a less pessimistic outlook for individuals with personality psychopathology.

What Personality Traits Best Apply to This Man?

The following case study describes the behavior of a teenager, Roy W. He exhibits some very prominent, maladaptive personality traits. After reading the case, identify Roy's most prominent personality characteristics.

What are Roy's most prominent personality characteristics? If you were making a diagnosis, would a categorical or dimensional perspective be best in attempting to describe and diagnose Roy's condition?

CASE STUDY   Roy W. was an 18-year-old high school senior who was referred by the court for diagnosis and evaluation. He was arrested for stealing a car, something he had done on several other occasions. The court agreed with Roy's mother that he needed evaluation and perhaps psychotherapy. During his interview with the psychologist, Roy was articulate, relaxed, and even witty. He said that stealing was wrong but that he never damaged any of the stolen cars. The last theft occurred because he needed transportation to a beer party (which was located only a mile from his home) and his leg was sore from playing basketball. When the psychologist asked Roy how he got along with young women, he grinned and explained that it is easy to "hustle" them. He then related the following incident:

"About three months ago, I was pulling out of the school parking lot real fast and accidentally sideswiped this other car. The girl who was driving it started to scream at me. God, there was only a small dent on her fender! Anyway, we exchanged names and addresses and I apologized for the accident. When I filled out the accident report later, I said that it was her car that pulled out and hit my car. When she heard about my claim that it was her fault, she had her old man call me. He said that his daughter had witnesses to the accident and that I could be arrested. Bull, he was just trying to bluff me. But I gave him a sob story—about how my parents were ready to get a divorce, how poor we were, and the trouble I would get into if they found out about the accident. I apologized for lying and told him I could fix the dent. Luckily, he never checked with my folks for the real story. Anyway, I went over to look at the girl's car. I really didn't have any idea of how to fix that old heap, so I said I had to wait a couple of weeks to get some tools for the repair job."

"Meanwhile, I started to talk to the girl. Gave her my sob story, told her how nice I thought her folks were. We started to date and I took her out three times. Then one night I laid her. The crummy thing was that she told her folks about it. Can you imagine that? Anyway, her old man called and told me never to get near his precious little thing again. At least I didn't have to fix her old heap. I know I shouldn't lie, but can you blame me? People make such a big thing out of nothing."

As you could see from the description of the DSM-5 alternative model for assessing personality, it is a very complex system. It will be interesting to follow the research arising from this alternative model and to see how frequently clinicians use this alternative diagnostic system. The decision to have two parallel diagnostic systems resulted from the impasse that developed between the DSM-5 Work Group, who advocated for the dimensional classification system, and clinicians, who prefer the traditional categorical system. It is difficult to argue against the Work Group recommendations since research has found that many, if not most, of the traditional personality disorder categories have low reliability and validity. However, since clinicians strongly favored the traditional categorical model and resisted a change to a dimensional system, it remains to be seen if mental health practitioners working outside of research settings will use the alternative methods of diagnosis. Thus, a major question that remains is whether having two systems to diagnose personality disorders will further research into the etiology and treatment of personality disorders or lead to further confusion and more heated debate.

chapter SUMMARY

1 Can one's personality be pathological?

- Personality psychopathology involves inflexible, long-standing personality traits that cause impairment or adaptive failure in the person's everyday life. These traits are usually evident in adolescence and continue into adulthood.

2 What traits are associated with personality disorders?

- DSM-5 lists 10 specific personality disorders; each causes notable impairment in social or occupational functioning or significant distress for the person.

- The three personality disorders considered odd or eccentric include paranoid personality disorder (suspiciousness, hypersensitivity, and mistrust); schizoid personality disorder (social isolation and indifference to others); and schizotypal personality disorder (peculiar thoughts and behaviors).

- The four personality disorders considered dramatic, emotional, or erratic include antisocial personality disorder (failure to conform to social or legal codes of conduct); borderline personality disorder (intense mood and self-image fluctuations); histrionic personality disorder (self-dramatization and attention-seeking behaviors); and narcissistic personality disorder (sense of self-importance and lack of empathy).

- The three personality disorders involving anxiety and fearfulness include avoidant personality disorder (fear of rejection and humiliation); dependent personality disorder (reliance on others and inability to assume responsibility); and obsessive-compulsive personality disorder (perfectionism and interpersonal control).

3 How does an antisocial personality develop and can it be changed?

- Etiological explanations for antisocial personality disorder focus on genetics and neurobiological factors (e.g., lack of fear conditioning and physiological underarousal); psychological factors (beliefs that the world is hostile); social and family environments (antisocial role models); and sociocultural factors (e.g., gender roles and cultural focus on individualism).

- Traditional treatment approaches are not particularly effective with antisocial personality disorder. Treatment is most effective when it occurs in a setting in which behavior can be closely monitored and controlled.

4 What problems occur with personality assessment?

- There is poor inter-rater reliability with the personality disorder categories.

- Diagnosis is complicated by the fact that comorbidity (presence of other disorders) is high with personality disorders.

- Categorical diagnoses are based on arbitrary diagnostic thresholds and do not take into account the continuous nature of personality traits.

5 Are there alternative methods of personality assessment?

- Increasingly, personality disorders are being viewed in a dimensional manner (e.g., as extremes on a continuum of normal personality traits).

- An alternative DSM-5 model for personality disorders focuses on determining if there is evidence of significant impairment in personality functioning in key areas of personality development (identity, self-direction, empathy, or intimacy).

- Clinicians also assess 5 trait domains (negative affectivity, detachment, antagonism, disinhibition, and psychoticism) and 25 associated traits to determine if there is evidence of pathological personality traits.

- The alternative model also includes dimensional definitions for six types of personality disorders: schizotypal, borderline, avoidant, narcissistic, obsessive-compulsive, and antisocial.

16 DISORDERS OF CHILDHOOD AND ADOLESCENCE

Chapter Outline

EIGHT-YEAR-OLD NINA cannot tolerate having her parents out of sight. Upon arriving at school, Nina clings to her mother, refusing to leave the car. Even when her mother walks her to the classroom, Nina cries, screams, and begs her mother not to leave.

    DIAGNOSIS: *separation anxiety disorder*

TEN-YEAR-OLD CASSIE'S PARENTS ARE FRUSTRATED by Cassie's continuing defiance, constant arguments, and vindictiveness. Today Cassie is refusing to come out of her bedroom to greet friends and relatives attending her mother's surprise birthday party. She shouts at her parents, "You can't make me do anything!"

    DIAGNOSIS: *oppositional defiant disorder*

SITTING IN THE PSYCHOLOGIST'S OFFICE, the mother explains that ever since he was in preschool, her son Tyrone, who is now 10, has disrupted classroom instruction. He has difficulty concentrating, is often reprimanded for talking, and is failing most subjects. Throughout the session, Tyrone fidgets in his seat and interrupts his mother.

    DIAGNOSIS: *attention-deficit/hyperactivity disorder*

FIVE-YEAR-OLD AHMED SITS APART FROM THE OTHER CHILDREN, spinning the wheels of a toy truck and humming aloud as if to mimic the sound. Ahmed seems to live in a world of his own, interacting with those around him as if they are inanimate objects.

    DIAGNOSIS: *autism spectrum disorder*

I n this chapter, we discuss psychological disorders occurring in childhood and adolescence. Accurate assessment of mental disorders occurring early in life is not easy; it requires understanding of normal child development and child **temperament**, as well as knowledge about psychiatric disorders. Familiarity with **child psychopathology** (how psychological disorders manifest in children and adolescents) is essential because characteristics that signify mental illness in adults (e.g., difficulty with emotional regulation) often occur in normally developing children. Additionally, symptoms of some disorders are quite different in children compared to adults.

Anxiety about a parent leaving, oppositional behavior, or high levels of activity combined with a short attention span are viewed quite differently depending on the age of the child. We would consider these behaviors typical in a 2- or 3-year-old, but they would be of concern in a 10-year-old. Additionally, children differ in their natural temperament; some children are cautious and slow to warm to new situations, whereas others are energetic, strong willed, and intense in their reactions. Further, child mental health professionals are well aware that the prefrontal cortex, the brain region associated with executive functions such as attention, self-control, and perspective taking, continues developing throughout childhood and adolescence, finally maturing during early adulthood.

To determine if a child has an actual disorder, clinicians consider the child's age and developmental level, as well as environmental factors, asking questions such as these:

- Is the child's behavior significantly different from that of other children of the same age?
- Are the symptoms likely to subside as the child matures?
- Are the behaviors present in most contexts or only in particular settings?
- Are the symptoms occurring because adults are expecting too much or too little of the child?

Clinicians are very cautious when making a diagnosis and weigh the effects of "labeling" on a child's future development against the knowledge that untreated disorders can result in ongoing mental distress.

Childhood disorders are not rare. Face-to-face diagnostic assessment of a representative sample of more than 10,000 U.S. adolescents (ages 13–18) found that almost half had already experienced significant mental health concerns. Nearly one third (31.9 percent) reported symptoms of an anxiety disorder, 19.1 percent demonstrated a behavior disorder, and 14 percent reported symptoms of a depressive or bipolar disorder. Twenty-two percent of the sample reported severe impairment due to their symptoms. Depressive and bipolar disorder symptoms caused the greatest distress. (See Table 16.1 for prevalence, severity, and gender comparisons of specific disorders.) Females reported more depression and post-traumatic stress reactions, whereas males demonstrated more inattention and hyperactivity; more than 40 percent of those surveyed met diagnostic criteria for more than one disorder (Merikangas, He, Burstein, Swanson, et al., 2010). Like adults, children and adolescents often have coexisting disorders (Yoo, Brown, & Luthar, 2009). Unfortunately, in a national sample of 6,483 adolescents (ages 13–18), almost two thirds of those with mental illness received no treatment (Merikangas, He, Burstein, Swendsen, et al., 2011). Of particular concern are the low treatment rates for youth experiencing major depression; this lack of intervention is particularly pronounced for African American, Latino/Hispanic American, and Asian American adolescents (J. R. Cummings & Druss, 2011).

Medication is the most frequent intervention among the children and adolescents who do receive treatment. Recent data from the National Health Interview Survey revealed that an estimated 7.5 percent of youth ages 6–17 years take medication for emotional or behavioral difficulties, including 9.7 percent of boys and 5.2 percent of girls; low-income youth who qualify for subsidized health insurance (Medicaid) are the most likely to take psychotropic medications (Howie, Pastor, & Lukacs, 2014).

temperament innate emotional predisposition or personality traits

child psychopathology the emotional and behavioral manifestation of psychological disorders in children and adolescents

Table 16.1 Lifetime Prevalence of Psychiatric Disorders in Youth Ages 13–18

Disorder	Females (%)	Males (%)	Percentage with Severe Impairment
Generalized anxiety disorder	3.0	1.5	30
Social phobia	11.2	7.0	14
Specific phobia	22.1	15.7	3
Panic disorder	2.6	2.0	9
Post-traumatic stress disorder	8.0	2.3	30
Depression	15.9	7.7	74
Bipolar disorder	3.3	2.6	89
Attention-deficit/hyperactivity disorder	4.2	13.0	48
Oppositional defiant disorder	11.3	13.9	52
Conduct disorder	5.8	7.9	32

SOURCE: Merikangas, He, Burstein, Swanson, et al. (2010).

In fact, critics have expressed outrage over pharmaceutical company practices that encourage doctors to prescribe powerful psychotropic drugs to the newest target group—children and adolescents, particularly groups with state-subsidized insurance such as children in foster care (Osher & Brown, 2014).

Psychiatric disorders are diagnosed only when symptoms cause significant impairment in daily functioning over an extended period. We begin our discussion with internalizing (i.e., emotions directed inward) and externalizing (i.e., disruptive) disorders. We conclude with a look at childhood disorders involving impaired neurological development. The field of child psychopathology is extensive, so we will address many of the disorders only briefly.

Internalizing Disorders among Youth

Disorders involving emotional symptoms that are directed inward are referred to as **internalizing disorders**. As with adults, children and adolescents with internalizing disorders display heightened reactions to trauma, stressors, or negative events, as well as difficulty tolerating distress and regulating their emotions. Anxiety and depressive disorders are the most common internalizing disorders. These disorders are prevalent in early life (see Table 16.1) and are of particular concern because they often lead to substance abuse and suicide (O'Neil, Conner, & Kendall, 2011). Certain behavior patterns among youth with internalizing disorders, such as abrupt changes in behavior or self-destructive or sexualized behavior, can signal the need for assessment to rule out possible sexual abuse (Floyed, Hirsh, Greenbaum, & Simon, 2011).

Anxiety, Trauma, and Stressor-Related Disorders in Early Life

Anxiety, trauma, and stressor-related disorders in childhood or adolescence typically result from a combination of biological predisposition and exposure to environmental

internalizing disorders
conditions involving emotional symptoms directed inward

influences. Anxiety disorders are the most prevalent mental health disorder in childhood and adolescence (Kessler, Petukhova, Sampson, Zaslavsky, & Wittchen, 2012). Among the 32 percent of adolescents who have experienced an anxiety disorder, specific phobias (19 percent) and social phobia (9 percent) are most common (Merikangas, He, Burstein, Swanson, et al., 2010). Specific phobias often begin in early to middle childhood, whereas social phobias typically begin in early to middle adolescence (Rapee, Schniering, & Hudson, 2009).

Youth with anxiety disorders experience extreme feelings of worry, discomfort, or fear when facing unfamiliar or anxiety-provoking situations. Early-onset anxiety can significantly affect academic and social functioning and, if untreated, can lead to adult anxiety disorders (Ginsburg et al., 2014). Children who are inhibited and fearful are at higher risk for anxiety disorders, and overprotective or controlling parenting practices, low parental warmth, or perceived parental rejection can exacerbate the issue (Bayer et al., 2011). Anxiety disorders associated with childhood include:

- **separation anxiety disorder**—severe distress or worry about leaving home, being alone, or being separated from primary caregivers; and

- **selective mutism**—consistent failure to speak in certain social situations.

Children with these disorders display exaggerated autonomic responses and are apprehensive in new situations, preferring to stay at home or in other familiar environments (Kossowsky, Wilhelm, Roth, & Schneider, 2012). Childhood anxiety disorders are most effectively treated with cognitive-behavioral therapy; approximately half of those receiving comprehensive intervention maintain the improvement made during treatment (Compton et al., 2014). Successful treatment for highly anxious children not only reduces the child's anxiety symptoms but also has positive effects on the emotional functioning of parents and has the potential for reducing dysfunctional interactions within the family (Keeton et al., 2013).

Attachment Disorders

Infants and children raised in stressful environments that lack predictable parenting and nurturing sometimes demonstrate significant difficulties with emotional attachments and social relationships (Gleason et al., 2011). Attachment problems can manifest in the inhibited behaviors seen in *reactive attachment disorder* or the excessive attention seeking seen in *disinhibited social engagement disorder*. These childhood stressor and trauma-related disorders are diagnosed only when symptoms are apparent before age 5 and when early circumstances prevent the child from forming stable attachments. Situations that can disrupt attachment include frequent changes in primary caregiver, persistent neglect of physical or psychological safety (including physical abuse), and environments that are devoid of stimulation or affection.

Children with **reactive attachment disorder (RAD)** appear to have little trust that the adults in their lives will attend to their needs; therefore, they do not readily seek or respond to comfort, attention, or nurturing. Children with RAD often behave in a very inhibited or watchful manner, even with family and caregivers. They appear to use avoidance as a psychological defense, and subsequently experience difficulty responding to or initiating social or emotional interactions. Children with RAD rarely show positive emotions and may demonstrate irritability, sadness, or fearfulness when interacting with adults (APA, 2013).

In stark contrast, children with **disinhibited social engagement disorder (DSED)** socialize effortlessly but indiscriminately, and readily become superficially "attached" to strangers or casual acquaintances. They approach and interact with unfamiliar adults in an overly familiar manner (both verbally and physically), while moving away from caregivers. Children with DSED often have a history of harsh punishment or inconsistent parenting in addition to emotional neglect and limited attachment opportunities (APA, 2013).

The course of these disorders depends on the severity of the social deprivation, abuse, neglect, or disruptions in caregiving, as well as subsequent events in the child's

separation anxiety disorder severe distress about leaving home, being alone, or being separated from a parent

selective mutism consistent failure to speak in certain situations

reactive attachment disorder (RAD) a trauma-related disorder characterized by inhibited, avoidant social behaviors and reluctance to seek or respond to attention or nurturing

disinhibited social engagement disorder (DSED) a trauma-related attachment disorder characterized by indiscriminate, superficial attachments and desperation for interpersonal contact

life. Symptoms of RAD often disappear if children begin to receive predictable care-taking and nurturance, whereas symptoms of DSED are more persistent (Zeanah & Gleason, 2010). Issues of mistrust and difficulties with intimate relationships some-times continue into adulthood. Children who are exposed to multiple episodes of mal-treatment are particularly vulnerable to ongoing mental health issues (Kay & Green, 2013). Once RAD or DSED is identified, therapeutic support focuses on building emotional security (Hornor, 2008). Effective intervention includes providing a stable, nurturing environment and opportunities to develop interpersonal trust and social-relational skills. Fortunately, many children raised under difficult circumstances do not show signs of these disorders.

Post-Traumatic Stress Disorder in Early Life

The effects of trauma and resultant post-traumatic stress disorder (PTSD) can be par-ticularly distressing in childhood, as illustrated in the following case study.

> **CASE STUDY** Several months after witnessing her father seriously injure her mother during a domestic dispute, Jenna remained withdrawn; she spoke little and rarely played with her toys. Although a protection order prevented her father from returning home, Jenna became startled whenever she heard the door open and frequently woke up screaming "Stop!" She refused to enter the kitchen, the site of the violent assault.

Youth with PTSD experience recurrent, distressing memories of a shocking expe-rience. As we saw with Jenna, they sometimes desperately want to avoid any cues associated with the event. The trauma that precipitates PTSD can include threats of or direct experience with death, serious injury, or sexual violation. Witnessing or hear-ing about the victimization of others can also result in PTSD, especially when a pri-mary caregiver is involved. Memories of the event may entail (a) distressing dreams; (b) intense physiological or psychological reactions to thoughts or cues associated with the event; (c) episodes of playacting the event (sometimes without apparent dis-tress); or (d) dissociative reactions, in which the child appears to reexperience the trauma or seems unaware of present surroundings. Children who experience trauma may appear socially withdrawn, show few positive emotions, or seem disinterested in activities they previously enjoyed. According to DSM-5, behavioral evidence of PTSD in youth includes angry, aggressive behavior or temper tantrums; difficulty sleeping or concentrating; and exaggerated startle response or vigilance for possible threats (APA, 2013). Lifetime prevalence of PTSD among adolescents is 8 percent for girls and 2.3 percent for boys (Merikangas, He, Burstein, Swanson, et al., 2010). Trauma-focused cognitive-behavioral therapies have proven to be effective in treating child-hood PTSD (Nixon, Sterk, & Pearce, 2012).

Nonsuicidal Self-Injury

> **CASE STUDY** For the past year, Maria has been secretly cutting her forearms and thighs with a razor blade. She has tried to stop; however, when she feels anxious or depressed she thinks of the razor blade and the relief she experiences once she feels the cutting. Maria acknowledges that she has difficulty managing her emotions, particularly when she has conflicts with her parents or her friends. She does not understand why she cuts; she just knows it seems to help her cope when she is feeling upset. The more life hurts, the more she cuts.

Nonsuicidal self-injury (NSSI) is a relatively new phenomenon that involves intention-ally inflicted, superficial wounds. Those who engage in NSSI cut, burn, stab, hit, or

nonsuicidal self-injury (NSSI) intentional, self-inflicted harm intended to provide relief from negative feelings or to induce positive feelings; can also involve a preoccupation with engaging in self-harm

Child Abuse and Neglect

Because the 3-year-old boy had soiled his pants, his mother forced him to sit on the toilet. She told her son that he would not be allowed to get up or eat unless he had a bowel movement. When the son could not comply, the mother pulled him from the toilet seat and lashed his buttocks until they were raw and bleeding.

Child neglect and the physical, emotional, and sexual abuse of children remain a significant national problem (X. Fang, Brown, Florence, & Mercy, 2012). In the United States, 678,810 youth were victims of child neglect or physical or sexual abuse in 2012, including 1,640 who died as a result of their injuries. These distressing statistics are likely an underestimate since many cases of abuse go unreported, particularly cases of child sexual abuse. As seen in Figure 16.1, the majority of deaths from abuse involve children age 3 or younger; in 80 percent of the cases, the perpetrator is one or both parents (U.S. Department of Health and Human Services, 2013).

Why would parents abuse or neglect their own children? We know that multiple factors, including poverty, parental immaturity, and lack of parenting skills, contribute to child maltreatment, and that many adults who abuse were themselves abused as children. Many parents involved in maltreatment are young,

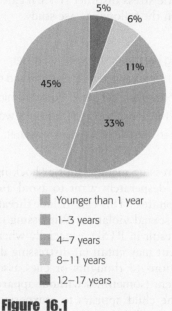

Younger than 1 year
1–3 years
4–7 years
8–11 years
12–17 years

Figure 16.1

Fatalities from Child Abuse or Neglect by Age, 2012

The youngest are the most vulnerable.

SOURCE: U.S. Department of Health and Human Services (2013).

high school dropouts, and under severe stress. Many have personality disorders and low tolerance for frustration, or abuse alcohol and other substances (Leventhal, Martin, & Gaither, 2012). In the case of child sexual abuse, perpetrators are often friends or other family members, and the parent is unaware that the abuse occurred.

Childhood physical or sexual abuse can result in a variety of internalized or externalized symptoms during childhood or adolescence, as well as lifelong physical and psychological consequences such as depression, anxiety, eating disorders, PTSD, and suicidal ideation (Teicher & Samson, 2013). As you might expect, the more maltreatment or trauma a child encounters, the greater the risk of subsequent psychiatric illness (Benjet, Borges, & Medina-Mora, 2010).

Many communities offer parent education and support groups for high-risk families, including families who have come to the attention of child protection agencies. There is a particular need for programs to prevent the maltreatment of infants and young children (Turner, Finkelhor, Ormrod, & Hamby, 2010). What are short-term and long-term consequences of child maltreatment? Why might those who are mistreated as children have an increased risk of becoming abusive themselves?

excessively rub themselves to the point of pain and injury, but without suicidal intent. As we saw with Maria, intense negative thoughts or emotions and a preoccupation with engaging in self-harm (often accompanied by a desire to resist the impulse to self-injure) often precede episodes of self-injury. The DSM-5 has included NSSI as a diagnostic category undergoing further study; for a diagnosis, the individual must display these intentional behaviors at least 5 times over the course of a year. Interpersonal difficulties, negative emotions, or a preoccupation with self-harm often occur just before a self-injury episode. Those who self-injure often expect that it will improve their mood, and many report that the pain produces relief from uncomfortable feelings or a temporary sense of calm and well-being. A secondary motivation for some who practice NSSI is that the self-injurious behavior serves as a form of self-punishment (Darosh & Lloyd-Richardson, 2013). Those who repeatedly self-injure tend to be highly self-critical and have difficulty expressing and regulating their emotions (Klonsky & Glenn, 2011). NSSI is associated with increased risk of substance abuse (Moran et al.

2012) and increased risk of attempted suicide (Kerr, Muehlenkamp, & Turner, 2010). A negative cognitive style and negative self-talk are associated with increased frequency of NSSI and increased likelihood of suicidal behavior (Wolff et al., 2013).

Two thirds of those who engage in NSSI begin the behavior in early adolescence. NSSI occurs with similar frequency in both genders, although males are more likely to hit or burn themselves, whereas females more frequently cut themselves. It is estimated that approximately 14–17 percent of adolescents and young adults have engaged in self-injury at least once; only a minority engage in repeated self-injury. Although adolescent self-harming behavior usually resolves spontaneously, underlying emotional issues such as depression or anxiety often persist (Moran et al., 2012). An effective intervention for adolescents who engage in repeated NSSI is dialectical behavior therapy, which teaches distress tolerance and emotional regulation skills (Shapiro, Heath, & Roberts, 2013).

Mood Disorders in Early Life

Depressive disorders among young people are most prevalent among females and older adolescents (Merikangas, He, Burstein, Swanson, et al., 2010). Environmental factors are a frequent cause of depression in childhood, whereas genetic and other biological factors exert more of an influence during adolescence. Children are especially vulnerable to environmental factors because they lack the maturity and skills to deal with stressors. Conditions such as childhood physical or sexual abuse, parental mental or physical illness, or loss of an attachment figure can increase vulnerability to depression (D. G. Rosenthal, Learned, Liu, & Weitzman, 2012). Like adults, youth with depressive disorders have negative self-concepts and are more likely to engage in self-blame and self-criticism. Adolescents with depression are at high risk of experiencing chronic depressive symptoms, especially if they do not receive treatment (Melvin et al., 2013).

Evidence-based treatment for depression in youth includes individual or group cognitive-behavioral therapy, family-focused therapy, and programs focused on building resilience based on positive psychology principles (Cheung, Kozloff, & Sacks, 2013). Intervention is critical because of the strong association between depressive disorders and adolescent suicidal ideation and suicide attempts (Nock et al., 2013). Using selective serotonin reuptake inhibitors (SSRIs) to treat depressive disorders in youth, however, is an issue because SSRIs may increase suicidality in those younger than age 25. This risk led to U.S. Food and Drug Administration (FDA) warnings regarding the use of these medications for children and adolescents (Hammad, Laughren, & Racoosin, 2006). Subsequent data analysis has indicated that the benefits of using FDA-approved antidepressants may outweigh the risk of increased suicidality, especially among youth who are moderately to severely depressed (Soutullo & Figueroa-Quintana, 2013). Best practices support careful monitoring of suicidality in all children and adolescents who are depressed, with particular attention to those taking antidepressants (Miller, Swanson, Azrael, Pate, & Stürmer, 2014).

Disruptive Mood Dysregulation Disorder

CASE STUDY   As an infant and toddler, Juan was irritable and difficult to please. Temper tantrums, often involving attempts to hit his parents, occurred multiple times daily. Juan's parents had hoped he would outgrow this behavior; but now 8, Juan is still frequently "grumpy" and has continued temper outbursts in many settings.

American Idol 2012/FOX/Getty Images

Demi Lovato

Singer and actress Demi Lovato engaged in disordered eating and nonsuicidal self-injury during early adolescence in an effort to cope with her emotions and in response to bullying from classmates. When receiving treatment for these conditions, it was discovered that her mood swings were also related to undiagnosed bipolar disorder.

DID YOU KNOW?

Adolescents who self-injure often join interactive online groups comprised of other teens who engage in this behavior. Although online communities may help these teens connect with others with similar issues, there is concern that these forums may trigger the urge for self-injury, normalize and reinforce self-injurious behavior, or lead them to believe that stopping the behavior is beyond their control.

SOURCE: Mahdy & Lewis, 2013

Disruptive mood dysregulation disorder?

Many young children have difficulty regulating their emotions and display occasional temper tantrums. However, persistent irritable or angry behavior that continues beyond the preschool years may eventually result in a diagnosis of disruptive mood dysregulation disorder.

disruptive mood dysregulation disorder (DMDD) a childhood disorder involving chronic irritability and significantly exaggerated anger reactions

pediatric bipolar disorder (PBD) a childhood disorder involving depressive and energized episodes similar to the mood swings seen in adult bipolar disorder

Disruptive mood dysregulation disorder (DMDD) is characterized by chronic irritability and severe mood dysregulation, including recurrent episodes of temper triggered by common childhood stressors such as interpersonal conflict or being denied a request. As we saw with Juan, anger reactions are extreme in both intensity and duration, and may involve verbal rage or physical aggression toward people and property. According to DSM-5, DMDD is a depressive disorder; although behavioral symptoms are directed outward, they reflect an irritable, angry, or sad mood state. For a DMDD diagnosis the child's mood between temper episodes must be irritable or angry most of the day, nearly every day. Further, the outbursts are present in at least two settings and occur at least 3 times per week for most months over the course of 1 year. Although the behaviors associated with DMDD often begin in early childhood, this diagnosis is not made until a child is 6 years of age; additionally, the symptoms must be evident before age 10 (APA, 2013). This age requirement ensures that diagnosis is not based on the erratic moods associated with early childhood (e.g., "the terrible 2s") or puberty.

The negative affect associated with DMDD often predicts later depressive and anxiety disorders (Leibenluft, 2011). Clinicians making a diagnosis of DMDD need to rule out pediatric bipolar disorder, due to the overlapping symptoms involving depression and mood changes (see Table 16.2); this differential diagnosis is important because interventions for these two disorders are quite different (Jairam, Prabhuswamy, & Dullur, 2012). Three-month prevalence rates for DMDD have ranged from 0.8 percent to 8.2 percent in community samples. Many children diagnosed with DMDD also have comorbid disorders associated with emotional dysregulation such as depressive disorders or oppositional defiant disorder (Copeland, Angold, Costello, & Egger, 2013; Dougherty et al., 2014).

Pediatric Bipolar Disorder

Pediatric bipolar disorder (PBD) is a serious disorder that parallels the mood variability, depressive episodes, and significant departure from the individual's typical functioning that characterizes adult bipolar disorder (Hauser, Galling, & Correll, 2013). PBD is illustrated in the following case study.

CASE STUDY Anna was a fairly cooperative, engaging child throughout her early years. However, around her 10th birthday, her behavior changed significantly. At times, she experienced periods of extreme moodiness, depression, and high irritability; on other occasions, she displayed boundless energy and talked incessantly, often moving rapidly from one topic to another as she described different ideas and plans. During her energetic periods, she could go for several weeks with minimal sleep.

Youth with PBD display mood changes and distinct periods of elevated energy and activity that may involve diminished need for sleep, distractibility, talkativeness, or inflated self-esteem (see Table 16.2). In addition to experiencing hypomanic/manic episodes, those with PBD may also display recurring depressive episodes or periods of uncharacteristic irritability that alternate with these energized episodes (Hunt et al., 2013). These symptoms can develop gradually or suddenly.

Ace Stock Limited/Alamy

Table 16.2 Disruptive Mood Dysregulation Disorder and Pediatric Bipolar Disorder

DISORDERS CHART				
Disorder	**DSM-5 Criteria**	**Prevalence**	**Age of Onset**	**Course**
Disruptive mood dysregulation disorder (DMDD)	• Recurrent episodes of temper, including verbal rage or physical aggression • Anger response that is exaggerated in intensity and duration • Persistent irritable, angry, or sad mood • Behaviors observed in at least two settings over a 12 month period	2%–5%; more frequently diagnosed in boys	Diagnosis requires onset before age 10 but is often evident in early childhood (diagnosis is not made after age 18)	May improve with maturity; may evolve into a depressive or anxiety disorder; frequently comorbid with ODD
Pediatric bipolar disorder	• Distinct periods of abnormally elevated mood (i.e., manic or hypomanic episodes) • Periodic mood and behavioral changes (e.g., irritability, depression, increased activity, distractibility, or talkativeness; inflated self-esteem) • Bipolar I or bipolar II is diagnosed based on specific symptoms	Less than 1%; affects boys and girls equally	Onset occurs around age 10 through adolescence, about 5 years later than disruptive mood dysregulation disorder	Poor prognosis; often evolves into a chronic psychiatric disorder

SOURCE: APA (2013); Brotman, Schmajuk, et al. (2006); Merikangas, He, Burstein, Swanson, et al. (2010); S. E. Meyer et al. (2009).

As was the case with Anna, the behavior represents a change from the child's normal mood or temperament (APA, 2013). Youth with PBD often demonstrate rapid cycling of moods combined with difficulties in regulating behavior and social-emotional functioning (Olsavsky et al., 2012). Elevated neurological responsiveness to emotional stimuli and various brain abnormalities (A. James et al., 2011; Thomas et al., 2014) have been found in youth with this condition. PBD often occurs in families with a history of the illness and is likely to evolve into adult bipolar disorder or another chronic psychiatric disorder (B. I. Goldstein, 2012). Lifetime prevalence in adolescents is estimated to be 3 percent, with 89 percent of those with PBD reporting severe impairment; there are no significant gender differences in prevalence (Merikangas, He, Burstein, Swanson, et al., 2010). Some experts in the field of PBD believe these prevalence rates are inflated and contend that some clinicians give this diagnosis too liberally, without ensuring that the child or adolescent meets full criteria for hypomania/mania (Weintraub et al., 2014). It is hoped that the new DMDD category will allow for greater diagnostic accuracy.

Medications, therapeutic techniques, and psychosocial intervention for PBD are similar to those used with adult bipolar disorder (Parens & Johnston, 2010). The use of lithium and antipsychotic medications with children, however, concerns some mental health professionals (T. Thomas, Stansifer, & Findling, 2011). Family-focused interventions also help children learn to regulate their mood symptoms (Miklowitz et al., 2013). Unfortunately, emergency room visits and hospitalizations are common for youth with PBD (Berry, Heaton, & Kelton, 2011), as are suicide attempts (Hauser et al., 2013).

DID YOU KNOW?

Bullying can have serious effects on the physical and emotional well-being of children and adolescents. Exposure to bullying during the school years is associated with increased risk of poor health and interpersonal difficulties in adulthood.

SOURCE: Tsitsika et al., 2014

Externalizing Disorders among Youth

Externalizing disorders (sometimes called *disruptive behavior disorders*) include disruptive, impulse control, and conduct disorders—conditions associated with symptoms that are distressing to others. Parenting a child with externalizing behaviors can be challenging

externalizing disorders disruptive behavior disorders associated with symptoms that are socially disturbing and distressing to others.

and can result in negative parent–child interactions, high family stress, and negative feelings about parenting. As you can imagine, these factors can further exacerbate behavioral difficulties. Although early intervention can help interrupt the negative course of these disorders, diagnosing disruptive behaviors is controversial because it is difficult to distinguish externalizing disorders from one another and from the defiance and noncompliance commonly observed in children and adolescents. Diagnosis of a disruptive, impulse control, or conduct disorder requires a persistent pattern of behavior that is (a) atypical for the child's culture, gender, age, and developmental level and (b) severe enough to cause distress to the child or to others or negatively affect social or academic functioning. Disorders in this category include oppositional defiant disorder, intermittent explosive disorder, and conduct disorder.

Oppositional Defiant Disorder

CASE STUDY   Mark's parents and teachers know that when they ask Mark to do something, it is likely that he will argue and refuse to comply. He has been irritable and oppositional since he was a toddler. Mark's parents have given up trying to enlist cooperation; they vacillate between ignoring Mark's hostile, defiant behavior and threatening punishment. However, they are well aware that when Mark is punished, he finds ways to retaliate.

Oppositional defiant disorder (ODD) is characterized by a persistent pattern of angry, argumentative, or vindictive behavior that continues for at least 6 months. These behaviors are directed toward parents, teachers, and others in authority. At least four symptoms involving short-tempered, resentful, blaming, spiteful, or hostile behaviors must be present. Similar to the response of Mark's parents, adults sometimes begin to do whatever they can to avoid conflict, often without success. Although youth with ODD often argue, defy adult requests, and blame others, they do not demonstrate pervasive antisocial behavior or extreme verbal or physical aggression directed toward people, animals, or property (see Table 16.3). ODD is considered mild if symptoms occur only in one setting and severe if the behaviors occur in three or more settings.

Although the symptoms of ODD often resolve, especially with intervention, ODD is associated with interpersonal difficulties in early adulthood (Burke, Rowe, & Boylan, 2014). Additionally, in some cases, youth with ODD begin to demonstrate the more serious rule violations associated with conduct disorder. ODD appears to have two components, one involving negative affect and emotional dysregulation (e.g., angry, irritable mood) and the other involving defiant and oppositional behavior; negative affect predicts future depressive symptoms, whereas oppositional behaviors are more predictive of delinquency and conduct disorder (Cavanagh, Quinn, Duncan, Graham, & Balbuena, 2014). Additionally, approximately half of those with ODD also display inattention and hyperactivity (McBurnett & Pfiffner, 2009).

Intermittent Explosive Disorder

oppositional defiant disorder (ODD) a childhood disorder characterized by negativistic, argumentative, and hostile behavior patterns

intermittent explosive disorder condition involving frequent lower-intensity outbursts or low-frequency, high-intensity outbursts of extreme verbal or physical aggression

Intermittent explosive disorder (IED) is a "prevalent, persistent, and seriously impairing" disorder that is both underdiagnosed and undertreated (McLaughlin et al., 2012). A diagnosis of IED involves (a) recurrent outbursts of extreme verbal or physical aggression that occur approximately twice weekly for at least 3 months (high-frequency/lower-intensity aggressive outbursts) or (b) three outbursts occurring within a 1-year period that involve damage or injury to people, animals, or property (low-frequency/high-intensity outbursts) (Coccaro, Lee, & McCloskey, 2014). The outbursts occur suddenly in response to minor provocation and do not involve premeditation; instead, they are exaggerated angry

Table 16.3 Oppositional Defiant, Intermittent Explosive, and Conduct Disorder

	DISORDERS CHART			
Disorder	**DSM-5 Criteria**	**Prevalence**	**Age of Onset**	**Course**
Oppositional defiant disorder	• Angry, irritable mood • Hostile, defiant, and vindictive behavior • Frequent loss of temper, arguing, and defiance of adult requests • Failure to take responsibility for actions; blaming others • Behaviors continue for at least 6 months	6%–13%; more common in males	Childhood	May resolve, or evolve into a conduct disorder or depressive disorder
Intermittent explosive disorder	• Recurrent outbursts of extreme verbal or physical aggression *or* • 3 outbursts involving physical injury or damage within 1 year • Outbursts are impulsive or anger based and not premeditated • Outbursts cause marked distress or impairment in interpersonal functioning • Behaviors continue for at least 3 months	7.8% in a community sample of adolescents	Age 12 is the average age of onset (must be age 6 for the diagnosis)	May resolve, but anger episodes often continue into adulthood
Conduct disorder	• Aggression or cruelty to people or animals • Fire setting or destruction of property • Theft or deceit (stealing, "conning" others) • Serious rule violations (truancy, running away) • Behaviors continue for at least 12 months	2%–9%; more common in males and in urban settings	Two types: childhood onset and adolescent onset (although onset is rare after age 16)	Prognosis poor with childhood onset; often leads to the criminal behaviors, antisocial acts, and problems in adult adjustment such as antisocial personality disorder

SOURCE: APA (2013); Froehlich, Lanphear, Epstein, et al. (2007); McLaughlin et al. (2012); Merikangas, He, Burstein, Swanson, et al. (2010); Tynan (2008, 2010).

or impulsive reactions that cause distress or impair interpersonal functioning. Unlike the negative mood associated with DMDD, the child's mood is normal between outbursts. A child must be at least 6 years old—an age when children are presumed to have learned to control their aggressive impulses—to receive this diagnosis (APA, 2013).

Not surprisingly, IED is associated with early exposure to familial aggression, violence, and interpersonal trauma (Nickerson, Aderka, Bryant, & Hofmann, 2012). IED may be diagnosed in individuals with attention-deficit/hyperactivity disorder, conduct disorder, or ODD if periodic explosive, aggressive outbursts occur and meet the criteria for IED (Coccaro, 2012). A comprehensive study involving 6,483 adolescents found that 63.3 percent of the adolescents interviewed had experienced anger outbursts in which they destroyed property or threatened violence, or behaved violently. In fact, 7.8 percent of the group had displayed behavior that met the criteria for IED (McLaughlin et al., 2012).

Conduct Disorder

CASE STUDY   Ben, a high school sophomore well known for his ongoing bullying and aggressive behavior, was expelled from school after stabbing another student. Two months later, he was arrested for armed robbery and placed in juvenile detention. Peer relationships at the facility were strained because of Ben's ongoing attempts to intimidate others.

Conduct disorder (CD) is characterized by a persistent pattern of antisocial behavior that reflects dysfunction within the individual (rather than a pattern of behavior accepted within the person's subculture), and includes serious violations of rules and social norms and disregard for the rights of others. Diagnosis of CD requires the presence of at least three different behaviors involving (a) deliberate aggression (bullying, physical fights, use of weapons, cruelty to people or animals, aggressive theft, forced sexual contact); (b) destruction of property, including fire-setting; (c) theft or deceit (stealing, forgery, home or car invasion, "conning others"); or (d) serious violation of rules (staying out at night, truancy, running away). Deliberate rule violations sometimes begin in early childhood and then continue into the school years (Rolon-Arroyo, Arnold, & Harvey, 2014). In many cases, as we saw with Ben, disorderly behavior increases or becomes more serious with age. Boys with CD are often involved in confrontational aggression (e.g., fighting, aggressive theft), whereas girls are more likely to display truancy, substance abuse, or chronic lying. Approximately 2–9 percent of youth meet diagnostic criteria for CD; it is estimated that about half of those with CD also display inattention and hyperactivity (APA, 2013).

According to DSM-5, some youth diagnosed with CD have "limited prosocial emotions"—they display minimal guilt or remorse and are consistently unconcerned about the feelings of others, their own wrongdoing, or poor performance at school or work. They are good at manipulating others and may appear superficially polite and friendly when they have something to gain (APA, 2013). Cruelty, aggression, and a pervasive lack of remorse are common characteristics of this subgroup (R. E. Kahn, Frick, Youngstrom, Findling, & Youngstrom, 2012).

Youth with these callous, unemotional traits are unconcerned about their victims' suffering or about possible punishment for their behavior (Pardini & Byrd, 2012). In fact, they show limited neural responsiveness in brain regions associated with empathy when presented with pictures of other people in pain—a reaction that differs significantly from that displayed by children without antisocial traits (Lockwood et al., 2013). In a study using magnetic resonance imaging (MRI), adolescents with CD and callous traits demonstrated strong pleasure responses to video clips of people experiencing pain and distress (Decety, Michalska, Akitsuki, & Lahey, 2009). Not surprisingly those with these traits are at high risk for continuing criminal behavior (Kahn, Byrd, & Pardini, 2013) and receiving a diagnosis of antisocial personality disorder in adulthood (Lubit, 2012).

The behaviors and criminal acts associated with CD present a significant concern to the public. Some youth advocates endorse widespread screening for CD among young children because early intervention and comprehensive treatment can successfully modify the course of the disorder for some individuals (Hektner, August, Bloomquist, Lee, & Klimes-Dougan, 2014).

Etiology of Externalizing Disorders

Externalizing disorders often begin in early childhood. The etiology of these disorders involves an interaction between biological, psychological, social, and sociocultural factors. Among the externalizing disorders, biological factors appear to exert the greatest influence on the development of CD, the disorder we will focus on in this etiological discussion (Figure 16.2). Antisocial behavior has been linked to brain abnormalities associated with deficits in social information processing, as well as reduced activity in the amygdala in situations associated with fear (Sterzer, 2010); these deficits appear to decrease the ability to learn from rewards and punishments (Byrd, Loeber, & Pardini, 2014). Risk of CD is increased when carriers of the genotype "low-activity MAOA" (an allele associated with fear-regulating circuitry in the amygdala) are subjected to childhood maltreatment (Fergusson, Boden, Horwood, Miller, & Kennedy, 2012). Reduced activity of the autonomic nervous system and an associated increased need for stimulation to achieve optimal arousal is also associated with CD in males; this may account for the risk-taking behaviors associated with the disorder (El-Sheikh, Keiley, & Hinnant, 2009). Elevated stress hormones (cortisol) have been associated with symptoms

conduct disorder (CD) a persistent pattern of behavior that violates the rights of others, including aggression, serious rule violations, and illegal behavior

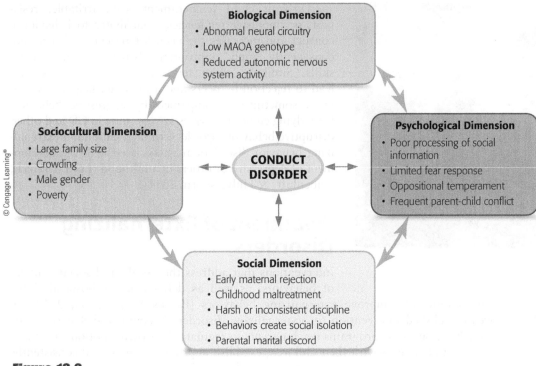

Figure 16.2

Multipath Model of Conduct Disorder

The dimensions interact with one another and combine in different ways to result in a conduct disorder.

of impulsive aggression, whereas low cortisol levels occur in youth with callous and unemotional traits and predatory aggression (Barzman, Patel, Sonnier, & Strawn, 2010).

Both family and social context play a large role in the development of externalizing disorders (Parens & Johnston, 2010). A child's early environment appears to moderate the relationship between individual vulnerability and the age at which antisocial behavior emerges; parents and teachers are able to exert more influence on the behavior of children with antisocial tendencies during childhood compared to adolescence, a period when peer influences predominate (Fairchild, van Goozen, Calder, & Goodyer, 2013).

In some cases, disruptive and aggressive behaviors are associated with harsh or inconsistent discipline (Pederson & Fite, 2014). Disruptive behavior may develop when parents behave in a punitive, inconsistent, or impatient manner in response to typical childhood misbehaviors. Parent–child conflict and power struggles can further intensify inappropriate behaviors. Patterson (1986) formulated a classic psychological-behavioral model of disruptive behavior based on the following pattern of parental reaction to misbehavior:

1. The parent addresses misbehavior or makes an unpopular request.
2. The child responds by arguing or counterattacking.
3. The parent withdraws from the conflict or gives in to the child's demands.

If this pattern develops, the child does not learn to respect rules or authority. An alternate pattern that sometimes occurs involves a vicious cycle of harsh, punitive parental responses to misbehavior, resulting in defiance and disrespect on the part of the child and further coercive parental behaviors (Tynan, 2008). Limited parental supervision, permissive parenting and avoidance of conflict, excessive attention for negative behavior, inconsistent disciplinary practices, and failure to teach prosocial skills or use positive management techniques can further exacerbate disruptive behavior (Bernstein, 2012).

DID YOU KNOW?

Boys are more likely to show direct forms of bullying—intimidating, controlling, or assaulting other children—whereas girls demonstrate more relational aggression, such as using threats of social exclusion.

SOURCE: S. S. Leff & Crick, 2010

Difficult child temperament (e.g., irritable, resistant, or impulsive tendencies) contributes to behavioral conflict and increases the need for parents to learn and consistently apply appropriate behavior management skills. Similarly, these temperamental tendencies can lead to rejection by peers and a blaming, negative worldview, sometimes accompanied by aggressive behavior. Underlying emotional issues are common in CD and other disruptive behavior disorders. In fact, childhood externalizing behavior disorders are associated with the development of depressive disorders in adulthood (Loth, Drabick, Leibenluft, & Hulvershorn, 2014).

Treatment of Externalizing Disorders

Bullying without Remorse

Children and adolescents with conduct disorder frequently engage in aggressive behavior and bully other students. Due to the pervasiveness of bullying behaviors, many schools have implemented curricula aimed at encouraging students to take a stand against bullying.

Interventions that address the family and social context of behaviors, as well as deficits in psychosocial skills, can significantly improve externalizing behaviors (Parens & Johnston, 2010). A well-established intervention for externalizing disorders is cognitive-behavioral parent education; these programs teach parents to regulate their own emotions, increase positive interactions with their children, establish appropriate rules, and consistently implement consequences for inappropriate behavior. Parent-focused interventions can improve both child behavior and parent mental health (Furlong et al., 2013).

CONTROVERSY

Are We Overmedicating Children?

Many medications are prescribed to treat childhood disorders, including antidepressants, tranquilizers, stimulants, and antipsychotics (Jonas, Gu, & Albertorio-Diaz, 2013). Medication use with children and adolescents has increased dramatically in recent years, with many prescriptions written by pediatricians and general practitioners rather than mental health specialists such as child psychiatrists (Olfson, Blanco, Wang, Laje, & Correll, 2014). However, controversy continues regarding overdiagnosis of some childhood disorders, the "quick fix" nature of medication, and the tendency to use medication without first attempting psychotherapy or other interventions (S. M. Berman, Kuczenski, McCracken, & London, 2009). For example, despite strong research supporting psychosocial interventions with ADHD, more than half of all children with ADHD have had no contact with a mental health professional in the previous year (Visser et al., 2014).

Another concern is that many medications prescribed for youth have only been tested on adults; thus, there is insufficient information regarding how these medications might affect the extensive brain development that occurs throughout childhood and adolescence (S. E. Kern, 2009). Many agree that we may not understand all adverse effects of these medications. For example, some antipsychotic medications can triple a child's risk of developing diabetes even in the first year of use (Bobo et al., 2013). Additionally, there is limited evidence supporting the effectiveness of medications for many of the disorders for which they are prescribed (Jacobson, 2014). On the other hand, some contend that medication use with children can ameliorate the symptoms of mental disorders by normalizing brain functioning (Singh & Chang, 2012).

Many believe that medication should be considered only after comprehensive diagnostic evaluation and implementation of alternative interventions. Additionally, medication use is most successful when parents are aware of the specific symptoms being treated, possible side effects, and the prescriber's plan for monitoring progress (American Academy of Child and Adolescent Psychiatry, 2009). How can we determine if medications are prescribed too freely and if their use with children is safe? What can parents do to ensure that adequate assessment and consideration of nonpharmaceutical interventions occur before medication is prescribed?

Psychosocial interventions that focus on teaching youngsters assertiveness and anger management techniques, and building skills in empathy, communication, social relationships, and problem solving, can also produce marked and durable changes in disruptive behaviors (Eyberg et al., 2008). Mobilizing adult mentors who demonstrate empathy, warmth, and acceptance is another effective intervention (Kazdin, Whitley, & Marciano, 2006). Although CD is particularly difficult to treat, success is increased when treatment begins before patterns of antisocial behavior are firmly established (Lubit, 2012). Incarceration within juvenile or adult facilities is the one of the most frequent interventions for youth with CD. Unfortunately, this practice often produces additional behavioral or psychological difficulties rather than rehabilitation, especially when incarceration occurs in adult facilities (Lambie & Randell, 2013).

Elimination Disorders

Although most children handle the developmental milestone of achieving full control over elimination without difficulty, some children experience enuresis or encopresis, which are disorders involving bladder or bowel control. Many children with these elimination disorders experience significant distress and apprehension, sensitivity to real or imagined parental disapproval, and withdrawal from peer relationships. Unsympathetic or impatient responses from caregivers can increase anxiety and distress, further exacerbating the problem (Nevéus, 2011).

Enuresis

Enuresis involves periodic voiding of urine into one's clothes or bed, or onto the floor during the day (urinary incontinence) or night (bedwetting). Enuresis is usually involuntary, although in rare situations it may be intentional (von Gontard, Heron, & Joinson, 2011). Enuresis is most likely to occur during sleep. To be diagnosed with enuresis, the child must be at least 5 years old and must void inappropriately at least twice per week for at least 3 months. Up to 10 percent of 5-year-olds and 5 percent of 10-year-olds experience enuresis; in contrast, only about 1 percent of adolescents and adults exhibit symptoms of enuresis (APA, 2013).

Both psychological and biological factors are associated with enuresis. Psychological stressors (e.g., life situations such as death of a parent or birth of a new sibling), family dysfunction, or the presence of other emotional problems can increase risk (Joinson et al., 2006). Although severe nocturnal enuresis is usually due to hereditary factors, more sporadic bedwetting is associated with social and emotional stressors (von Gontard et al., 2011). Biological influences affected by genetics include delays in physiological maturation and a hypersensitive or small bladder. Providing education and support for the parents and child, setting up reward systems, or using a bedtime urine alarm can all produce successful results (Nevéus, 2011). Medication is sometimes used to prevent bedwetting, often in combination with other techniques such as enuresis alarms (Deshpande, Caldwell, & Sureshkumar, 2012).

Encopresis

Encopresis involves defecating onto one's clothes, the floor, or other inappropriate places. To be diagnosed with encopresis, the child must be at least 4 years old and must have defecated inappropriately at least once a month for at least 3 months. Epidemiological studies report a 0.7 to 4.4 percent prevalence of encopresis in children (Klages et al., 2005; Loening-Baucke, 2007). Intermittent episodes of encopresis can persist for years. The typical pattern for children with encopresis is a history of constipation, resulting in painful defecation and subsequent withholding of bowel movements; this leads to additional constipation, fecal leakage, and involuntary soiling (Dobson & Rogers, 2009). Inattention and hyperactivity are common among children with encopresis (McKeown, Hisle-Gorman, Eide, Gorman, & Nylund, 2013). Intense social problems can arise due to shame, embarrassment, or attempts to conceal the disorder. Ostracism by peers, anger on the part of caregivers, and overall rejection can compound the problem (Dobson & Rogers, 2009). The most common means of treatment includes proper medical evaluation, increasing fluid intake, and parent and child education about toileting regimens (Kuhl et al., 2010).

Neurodevelopmental Disorders

Neurodevelopmental disorders involve impaired development of the brain and central nervous system; symptoms of neurodevelopmental disorders such as difficulties with learning, communication, and behavior become increasingly evident as the child grows and develops. Disorders in this category include tic disorders (such as Tourette's disorder), attention-deficit/hyperactivity disorder, autism spectrum disorders, and intellectual and learning disorders (see Table 16.4).

Tics and Tourette's Disorder

CASE STUDY   James Durbin, a contestant on *American Idol*, had facial and vocal tics as a child and was eventually diagnosed with Tourette's disorder. During his school years he was bullied and teased because of his tics. However, when he would sing, he felt free because his tics completely disappeared (M. Healy, 2011).

Tics are recurrent and sudden, involuntary, nonrhythmic motor movements or vocalizations. **Motor tics** involve various physical behaviors including blinking, grimacing, tapping, jerking the head, flaring the nostrils, and contracting the shoulders. **Vocal tics**

neurodevelopmental disorders conditions involving impaired development of the brain and central nervous system that are evident early in a child's life

tic an involuntary, repetitive movement or vocalization

motor tic a tic involving physical behaviors such as eye blinking, facial grimacing, or head jerking

vocal tic an audible tic such as coughing, grunting, throat clearing, sniffling, or making sudden, vocal outbursts

Table 16.4 Neurodevelopmental Disorders

DISORDERS CHART			
Disorder	**Characteristics**	**Prevalence**	**Course**
Tic disorder	Involuntary, repetitive movements or vocalizations	2%–5%; 4 times as common in males	Sometimes persists into adulthood
Attention-deficit/ hyperactivity disorder	Inattention, hyperactivity, and impulsivity	8%–9%; twice as common in males	Some symptoms may persist into adulthood
Autism spectrum disorder	Qualitative impairment in social communication; restricted, stereotyped interests and activities	0.6%–1%; 4 times as common in males	Course depends on severity, presence of intellectual disability, and intervention
Intellectual disability	Mild, moderate, severe, or profound deficits in intellectual functioning and adaptive behavior	1%–2%; more common in males	Lifelong
Learning disorder	Normal intelligence with significant deficits in basic reading, writing, or math skills	5%; more common in males	May improve with intervention or persist into adulthood

SOURCE: APA (2013); Centers for Disease Control and Prevention (2009b, 2010b); Robertson (2010); U.S. Department of Education, National Center for Education Statistics (2010); Wolanczyk et al. (2008).

include coughing, grunting, throat clearing, sniffling, and sudden, repetitive, and stereotyped outbursts of words. As was the case with James Durbin, tics can be particularly distressing when peers respond with teasing or ridicule. Short-term suppression of a tic is sometimes possible, but often results in subsequent increases in the tic. Many people report feeling tension build before a tic, followed by a sense of relief after the tic occurs. A physician with tics described it this way:

> "This urge comes in the form of a sensation . . . a sensation that is somehow incomplete. To complete and resolve the sensation, the tic must be executed, which provides almost instant relief. . . . The relief is very transient. . . . The sensation comes back again, but often more intensely than before." (Turtle & Robertson, 2008, p. 451)

Tic symptoms often begin in early childhood; however, tics in children are often temporary and disappear without treatment. When a tic has been present for less than a year, a diagnosis of *provisional tic disorder* is given; *chronic motor or vocal tic disorder* refers to tics lasting more than a year (APA, 2013). For those who develop persistent tics, symptoms often peak prior to puberty and decline or disappear during adolescence. Recent neuroimaging studies suggest that this symptom improvement may be due to compensatory, neuroplastic brain reorganization that allows affected teens to suppress and eventually control their tics (Jackson et al, 2013). In some cases, tics continue into adulthood.

Tourette's disorder (TD) is characterized by multiple motor tics (e.g., blinking, grimacing, shrugging, jerking the head or shoulders) and one or more vocal tics (e.g., repetitive throat clearing, sniffing, or grunting) that are present for at least 1 year, although not necessarily concurrently (APA, 2013). Motor movements involving self-harm (e.g., punching oneself) or **coprolalia** (the involuntary uttering of obscenities or inappropriate remarks) occur in about 10 percent of those with TD (Singer, 2005). Comorbid conditions including poor anger control, attention-deficit/hyperactivity disorder, obsessive-compulsive disorder, impulsive behavior, and poor social skills often interfere with quality of life even more than the tics themselves (Cavanna et al., 2013). In a recent meta-analysis, transient tic disorders affected almost 3 percent of youth, whereas only 0.77 percent had Tourette's syndrome; these disorders are much more common in boys (Knight et al., 2012).

Tic disorders are influenced by a variety of etiological factors. Both chronic tic disorder and TD appear to have a genetic basis. Prenatal factors associated with these disorders include maternal alcohol and cannabis use and inadequate maternal weight gain (Mathews et al., 2014). Because TD is highly comorbid with obsessive-compulsive disorder, similar neurochemical abnormalities and brain structures are likely involved (Kurlan, 2013). Stress, negative social interactions, anxiety, excitement, or exhaustion can increase the frequency and intensity of tics (Steinberg, Shmuel-Baruch, Horesh, & Apter, 2013).

Psychotherapy can help with the distress caused by tic symptoms. Additionally, behavioral techniques such as **habit reversal**, which involves teaching a behavior that is incompatible with the tic, is an effective treatment (McGuire et al., 2014). Antipsychotic medications are sometimes used to treat severe tics (Egolf & Coffey, 2014).

Attention-Deficit/Hyperactivity Disorder

CASE STUDY Ron, always on the go as a toddler and preschooler, has had many injuries resulting from his continual climbing and risk taking. In kindergarten, Ron talked incessantly and could not stay seated for group work. In first grade, his distractibility and off-task behavior persisted despite ongoing efforts to help him focus. As part of a comprehensive assessment, his parents took him for a psychological evaluation and a complete physical examination.

Tourette's disorder (TD) a condition characterized by multiple motor tics and one or more vocal tics

coprolalia involuntary utterance of obscenities or inappropriate remarks

habit reversal a therapeutic technique in which a client is taught to substitute new behaviors for habitual behaviors such as a tic

Attention-deficit/hyperactivity disorder (ADHD) is characterized by attentional problems or impulsive, hyperactive behaviors that are atypical for the child's age and developmental level. As was true for Ron, the symptoms often become increasingly apparent once children enter school. According to DSM-5, an ADHD diagnosis requires that symptoms (see Table 16.5) begin before age 12, persist for at least 6 months, and interfere with social or academic functioning. Individuals with ADHD can have problems involving (a) inattention, (b) hyperactivity and impulsivity, or (c) a combination of these characteristics. Symptoms of hyperactivity and impulsivity involve a mixture of excessive movement and a tendency to act without considering the consequences. The distractibility and intense focus on irrelevant environmental stimuli seen in ADHD are due to poor regulation of attentional processes (Contractor, 2012). The easy excitability, impatience, and difficulty with emotional regulation seen in many children with ADHD can significantly impair peer relationships and interfere with optimal academic functioning (Bunford, Evans, & Langberg, 2014).

ADHD can be difficult to diagnose, especially in early childhood, when limited attention, impulsive actions, and high levels of energy are common. Diagnosis relies on observations and input from parents, school personnel, and others knowledgeable about the child's behaviors. To receive a diagnosis of ADHD, a child must display symptoms in at least two settings (APA, 2013). It is necessary to determine if the behaviors are: (a) typical for the child's age, gender, and overall level of development; (b) a normal temperamental variant involving higher than average energy and impulsivity; or (c) an actual disorder involving significantly atypical behaviors that interfere with day-to-day functioning in multiple settings. *Hyperactive* is a confusing term because many people use it to describe all highly energetic children. In fact, family physicians often make ADHD diagnoses and prescribe medication when symptoms of inattention, hyperactivity, and impulsivity are not severe enough to meet DSM diagnostic criteria (Parens & Johnston, 2009).

ADHD is the most frequently diagnosed disorder in preschool and school-age children. One national parent survey revealed that 11 percent of children ages 4 to 17—over 6.4 million children and adolescents—have received an ADHD diagnosis. The number of children diagnosed with ADHD has steadily increased—by approximately 5 percent each year over the last decade. Boys (13.2 percent) are more than twice as likely as girls (5.6 percent) to receive an ADHD diagnosis (Visser et al.,

Table 16.5 Characteristics of Attention-Deficit/Hyperactivity Disorder

Inattention	Hyperactivity and Impulsivity
Poor attention to detail; careless mistakes	Fidgeting
Difficulty sustaining attention	Restlessness
Does not appear to be listening when spoken to	Excessive movement
Poor follow-through with instructions or specific tasks	Excessive loudness
Difficulty organizing tasks	Excessive talking
Avoidance of sustained mental effort	Blurting out answers
Misplacing of important objects	Difficulty waiting for a turn
Distractibility	Interruption of or intrusion on others
Forgetfulness	Impatience

Note: With ADHD, these characteristics occur more frequently than would be expected based on age, gender, and developmental level. A diagnosis of ADHD requires the presence of at least 6 characteristics involving inattention or hyperactivity/impulsivity; the characteristics must be evident before age 12, be present in at least 2 settings, persist for at least 6 months, and interfere with social, academic, or work functioning.
SOURCE: APA (2013).

attention-deficit/hyperactivity disorder (ADHD) childhood-onset disorder characterized by persistent attentional problems and/or impulsive, hyperactive behaviors

2014). Although symptoms of ADHD often improve in late adolescence, follow-up studies suggest that approximately 30 percent of those diagnosed with ADHD experience continued symptoms of inattention, disorganization, or impulsive actions in adulthood (Barbaresi et al., 2013).

ADHD is associated with both behavioral and academic problems (K. Larson et al., 2011). Children with ADHD have the most difficulty in situations that are unstructured or involve insufficient stimulation or tedious activities that require sustained attention (Kooistra, Crawford, Gibbard, Ramage, & Kaplan, 2010). Peer relationships and friendships are also challenging for those with ADHD (Humphreys et al., 2013). Data regarding more than 62,000 U.S. youth (ages 6–17) revealed that two thirds of those with ADHD had other mental health conditions (including CD, ODD, anxiety, or depression) or learning disabilities and other neurodevelopmental disorders; the risk of coexisting conditions is almost 4 times greater among children living in poverty (K. Larson et al., 2011). Youth with ADHD also have a high risk of smoking and use of alcohol and illicit drugs (Gold et al., 2014).

Etiology

Symptoms of ADHD result from multiple etiological factors. ADHD is an early-onset disorder with clear biological as well as psychological, social, and sociocultural etiology.

Biological Dimension   ADHD is a highly heritable disorder, with up to 80 percent of symptoms explainable by genetic factors (Durston, 2010). The exact nature of genetic transmission is unclear because no specific genes strongly link to ADHD symptoms (Faraone & Mick, 2010). It is likely that many of the behaviors associated with ADHD involve multiple genes, each with small effects, and subsequent gene × gene or gene × environment interactions (Ficks & Waldman, 2009). Interestingly, the fact that first-degree relatives of individuals with ADHD have increased risk of both bipolar disorder and schizophrenia suggests that these three disorders have overlapping genetic influences (Larsson et al., 2013).

Different hypotheses regarding neurological mechanisms that produce ADHD symptoms include the following:

- *Functional abnormalities in frontal brain regions associated with executive functions, attention, and inhibition of responses.* Reduced inhibitory mechanisms in the prefrontal cortex can affect impulsivity, organization, and attentional processes (Montauk & Mayhall, 2010). Frontal lobe abnormalities involving networks associated with sustained attention appear to persist into adulthood, even when ADHD symptoms subside (Cubillo, Halari, Smith, Taylor, & Rubia, 2012).

- *Brain structure and circuitry irregularities in regions such as the frontal cortex, cerebellum, and parietal lobes.* Neuroimaging has confirmed these differences, including smaller frontal lobes in children with ADHD, especially those with more severe symptoms (Montauk & Mayhall, 2010). Further, neuroimaging confirms reduced brain connectivity in regions associated with attentional skills and goal-directed actions (Sripada et al., 2014). Additionally, some children with ADHD show slower development of the cerebrum, particularly prefrontal regions associated with attention and motor planning (P. Shaw et al., 2007); this delay (and subsequent catching up) in neurological developmental may explain why many children with ADHD eventually outgrow their disorder.

- *Reductions in neurotransmitters (such as dopamine and GABA) that affect signal flow to and from the frontal lobes.* Reductions in these neurotransmitters are associated with difficulty inhibiting

Interventions for Attention-Deficit/Hyperactivity Disorder

The 6-year-old boy shown here is enrolled in a study called Project Achieve, in which parents and teachers are taught strategies to help minimize problem behaviors. New research shows that providing more structure throughout a child's day can offer a nondrug alternative to help children with attention-deficit/hyperactivity disorder.

George Widman/AP Images

DID YOU KNOW?

Children who come from high-income families have an increased risk of an ADHD diagnosis. What factors might account for this finding?

SOURCE: Getahun et al., 2013

behavioral impulses (Edden, Crocetti, Zhu, Gilbert, & Mostofsky, 2012). Many medications used to treat ADHD target these neurotransmitters (Stergiakouli & Thapar, 2010).

Other biological factors implicated in the development of ADHD include prematurity, perinatal oxygen deprivation, and very low birth weight (D'Onofrio et al., 2013); exposure to lead and PCB (Abelsohn & Sanborn, 2010); viral infections, meningitis, and encephalitis (Millichap, 2008); and maternal smoking or drug or alcohol use during pregnancy (Bandiera et al., 2011). Some researchers believe that certain food additives and unhealthy dietary patterns contribute to hyperactive behaviors (Millichap & Yee, 2012).

Due to ongoing public concerns about a possible relationship between ADHD and synthetic food dyes, the FDA recently held public hearings to answer the question "Are food colors a cause of hyperactivity?" The FDA panel concluded that artificial dyes do not cause ADHD, nor do they represent a significant health problem. However, the FDA did acknowledge that some children appear to have a physiological intolerance for certain synthetic color additives and that these children do demonstrate behavioral changes such as impulsivity and hyperactivity after consuming products with these additives (Weiss, 2012).

Psychological, Social, and Sociocultural Dimensions Many psychological, social, and sociocultural factors are associated with ADHD. Sociocultural and social adversity including family stress, severe marital discord, poverty, family conflicts, maternal psychopathology, paternal criminality, maternal mental disorder, and foster care placement have all been associated with ADHD (G. T. Ray, Croen, & Habel, 2009; T. J. Spencer et al., 2007). Further, children who are inattentive, hyperactive, or impulsive often encounter negative reactions from parents and rejection from peers. This interpersonal conflict may result in psychological reactions (e.g., depression, low self-esteem, rebelliousness) and lack of opportunities to socialize with peers—factors that further exacerbate symptoms (Humphreys et al., 2013). Some argue that differing cultural and regional expectations regarding activity levels, inattentiveness, and academic achievement can explain regional differences in ADHD diagnosis (Figure 16.3). Similarly, parenting practices that encourage exercise and outdoor activity or help prevent children from getting overtired or overaroused are associated with reduced risk of ADHD symptoms (Parens & Johnston, 2009).

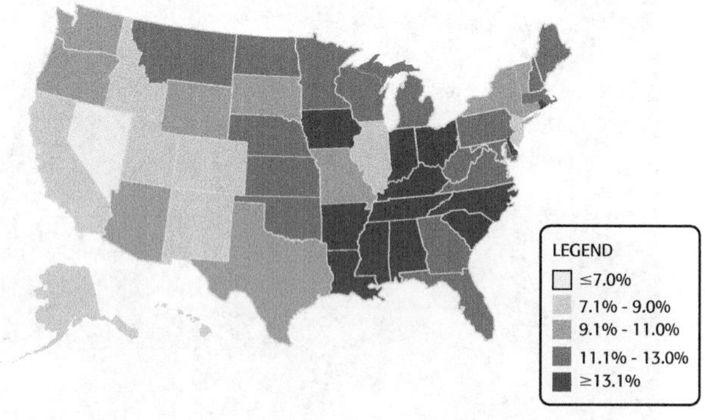
LEGEND
≤7.0%
7.1% - 9.0%
9.1% - 11.0%
11.1% - 13.0%
≥13.1%

Figure 16.3

Percent of Youth (4–17) Ever Diagnosed with Attention-Deficit/Hyperactivity Disorder by State, 2011

The prevalence of parent-reported diagnosis of attention-deficit/hyperactivity disorder (ADHD) varies significantly from state to state, and across geographic regions. The percentage of children diagnosed is highest in southern states (12.6 percent) and lowest in western states (8.1 percent). What might account for the variability in ADHD diagnoses from state to state and region to region?

SOURCE: Centers for Disease Control and Prevention (2014).

Treatment

Stimulant medications such as methylphenidate (Ritalin) have been used to treat ADHD for decades. Although approximately 30 percent of those with ADHD do not improve or experience significant side effects, these medications are considered first-line treatments for ADHD (Gold, Blum, Oscar-Berman, & Braverman, 2014). It is estimated that 69 percent of children diagnosed with ADHD take medication for their symptoms; the likelihood of medication use is greatest (84.4 percent) for those with severe symptoms (Visser at al., 2014). Stimulants work by normalizing neurotransmitter functioning and increasing neurological activation in the frontal cortex, thereby increasing attention and reducing impulsivity. Some treatment trends (e.g., prescribing medications in early childhood, using medication throughout the day rather than just during school hours, and continuing medication use in adulthood) have resulted in increased lifetime medication exposure (Zuvekas & Vitiello, 2012). These trends, combined with increased rates of ADHD diagnoses, likely account for the continued increases in prescription stimulant use in the United States (Figure 16.4). Due

Interventions for Older Youth with Attention-Deficit/Hyperactivity Disorder

Students eat while camping out at the Center for Attention and Related Disorders camp in Connecticut. The 4-week camp matches one instructor with every two campers and provides the structure, discipline, and social order that are helpful for children who have attention-deficit/hyperactivity disorder (ADHD) and similar disorders.

autism spectrum disorder (ASD) a disorder characterized by a continuum of impairment in social communication and restricted, stereotyped interests and activities

to the frequency of misuse and diversion (i.e., giving, selling, or trading) of prescribed short-acting stimulant medications, physicians are educating patients about medication safety and are prescribing medications that are less likely to be abused (Manning, 2013).

There is strong and consistent evidence that behavioral and psychosocial treatments (e.g., parent education, classroom management strategies, behavioral rewards, or self-management training) are highly effective in producing both short-term and long-term reductions in ADHD symptoms (Verma, Balhara, & Mathur, 2011). In fact, some experts argue that parent behavior training (teaching parents to use effective disciplinary practices to deal with the challenging behaviors associated with ADHD) should be used before considering medication, especially with preschool-age children (Charach et al., 2013). Additionally, modifying the environment or social context (e.g., allowing movement or ensuring that schoolwork is sufficiently challenging) can enhance feelings of competence, motivation, and self-efficacy for those with ADHD (Gallichan & Curle, 2008). In fact, simply providing opportunities for moderate exercise can reduce impulsivity and improve academic performance (Pontifex, Saliba, Raine, Picchietti, & Hillman, 2013). Unfortunately, approximately one in five children with ADHD receives no treatment for his or her symptoms (Visser et al., 2014).

Interventions are most successful when services are coordinated and when the child's unique characteristics and social and family circumstances are considered (K. Larson et al., 2011). Some researchers have proposed that symptom severity should guide treatment decisions, with interventions ranging from environmental modifications for mild symptoms to intensive, combined treatment (e.g., behavior management, parenting strategies, and stimulant medication) for severe ADHD symptoms (Pelham & Fabiano, 2008).

Autism Spectrum Disorders

Autism spectrum disorder (ASD) is characterized by significant impairment in social communication skills and by the display of stereotyped interests and behaviors. ASD is designated a spectrum disorder because the symptoms vary significantly—occurring along a continuum from mild to severe and affecting each person in different ways. ASD, estimated to affect approximately 1 out of 68 children in the United States based on precise monitoring of ASD prevalence in 11 selected states, has been increasing at an alarming rate. The estimated prevalence of ASD in the regions monitored increased an astonishing 123 percent between 2002 and 2010. Although the prevalence may be increasing due

Figure 16.4

Medical Consumption of Methylphenidate in the United States and Worldwide, 2003–2009

Methylphenidate is a medication frequently prescribed for attention-deficit/hyperactivity disorder (ADHD). This graph demonstrates that the United States accounts for a large percentage of the use of this medication worldwide, and that from 2003 to 2009 the amount of methylphenidate consumed more than doubled both in the United States and worldwide.

SOURCE: International Narcotics Control Board (2010).

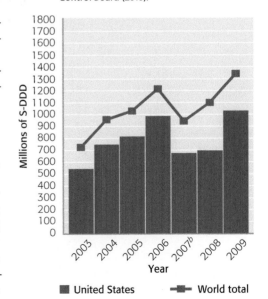

to expanded awareness of the disorder, many experts believe that there are other yet-unknown influences involved. There has been a consistent gender difference in ASD prevalence, with the disorder occurring 5 times more frequently in boys compared to girls (CDC, 2014). As you will see, we still have much to learn about the complex symptoms that affect individuals on the autism spectrum.

Symptoms of Autism Spectrum Disorder

CASE STUDY   Until about 18 months of age, Amy showed normal development—smiling, laughing, babbling, waving to parents, and playing peekaboo. By age 2, she was withdrawn and spoke no words except meaningless phrases from songs. She now spends much of her time rocking back and forth. The only thing that captures her attention is watching animated characters singing and dancing in movies or on television.

CASE STUDY   Danny B. wants chicken and potatoes. He asks for it once, twice . . . ten times. . . . His mother patiently explains that she is fixing spaghetti. "Mom," he asks in a monotone, "why can't we have chicken and potatoes?" If Danny were a toddler, his behavior would be nothing unusual. But Danny is twenty years old. "That's really what life with autism is like," says his mom. "I have to keep laughing. Otherwise, I would cry." (Kantrowitz & Scelfo, 2006, p. 47)

At the beginning of this chapter, we introduced Ahmed, a young child with ASD who spends much of his time humming and spinning the wheels of his toys. The cases of Ahmed, Amy, and Danny give us a glimpse into how ASD presents early in life and in adulthood. In 1943, Leo Kanner, a child psychiatrist, identified a triad of behaviors that have come to define the essential features of ASD: extreme isolation and inability to relate to people, a need for sameness, and significant difficulties with communication. Kanner called the syndrome *infantile autism*, from the Greek *autos* ("self"), to reflect the profound aloneness and detachment of these children. At its core, ASD involves pervasive deficits in social communication (Tanguay, 2011).

ASD is diagnosed when a trained professional documents persistent evidence of the following characteristics (APA, 2013):

1. Deficits in social communication and social interaction.
- *Atypical social-emotional reciprocity.* Interest in social interaction may be limited or totally lacking. For example, there may be no acknowledgement of parents or other family members. Milder symptoms in older children or adults may include one-sided domination of conversation focused on narrow self-interests or failure to understand the back and forth of typical conversations.
- *Atypical nonverbal communication.* There may be little to no eye contact and an absence of meaningful gestures or facial expressions. Milder symptoms may include unusual nonverbal communication (e.g., pushing people aside as if they were objects) or poor social boundaries involving intrusive behaviors or awkward interactions.
- *Difficulties developing and maintaining relationships.* There may be a lack of interest in others or a failure to recognize people's identity or emotions, including treating people as objects or failing to seek physical or emotional contact from caretakers. Those with milder symptoms may have no interest in imaginative play, may be socially inept, or may have difficulty adjusting their behavior to the social context.

2. Repetitive behavior or restricted interests or activities involving at least two of the following:

- *Repetitive speech, movement, or use of objects.* Rhythmic, repetitive, apparently purposeless movements may occur, including banging the head, flapping the arms, rocking the body, spinning objects, whirling in circles, or rhythmically moving fingers. Those with ASD sometimes repetitively stack or spin objects or move them from side to side. There may be repetitive use of language, including **echolalia** (echoing what is heard); incessant repetition of sounds, words, phrases, or nonsensical word combinations; or repetitive, one-sided conversations involving topics of fixated interest.

- *Intense focus on rituals or routines and strong resistance to change.* Common rituals may involve lining up or dropping objects or insistence on the same foods, order of events, or routines. Even small changes in routine can produce agitation and extreme reactions.

- *Intense fixations or restricted interests.* This may involve fascination with certain objects or a repetitive focus on a narrow range of interests.

- *Atypical sensory reactivity.* There may be a lack of reactivity (e.g., apparent indifference to pain, heat, or cold); overreactivity to sensory input (e.g., aversion to touch or certain sounds); or an unusual focus on sensory aspects of objects (e.g., licking or smelling objects or exhibiting an intense interest in moving objects).

The symptoms seen in ASD are not simply developmental delays but represent differences in development that cause impairment in everyday functioning (Lord et al., 2012). ASD symptoms range from mild to severe, and there is wide variation in the characteristics displayed by individuals with ASD. Table 16.6 summarizes the range of symptoms found in ASD.

Although almost half of those with ASD have average or above-average cognitive skills and are considered "high-functioning," approximately one third of those with ASD have significant cognitive impairment (CDC, 2014). Some with low intellectual functioning

Will & Deni McIntyre/Science Source

Identical Twins with Autism Spectrum Disorder

These identical twin boys were both diagnosed with autism spectrum disorder before their second birthday. However, the twins are at opposite ends of the autism spectrum. John, on the left, does not yet speak and engages in many repetitive behaviors such as hand-flapping. In contrast, Sam, on the right, possesses a wealth of information on specific topics such as trains, space, and maps. Sam's greatest struggles involve social interactions, especially with other children.

echolalia repetition of vocalizations made by another person

Table 16.6 Continuum of Symptoms Associated with Autism Spectrum Disorder

Level of Impairment	Social Communication	Restricted Interests and Repetitive Behaviors
Severe (requires very substantial support)	Minimal or absent communication or response to attempts at social interaction	Ongoing repetitive behaviors; intense preoccupation with rituals; extreme distress upon interference with rituals
Moderate (requires substantial support)	Evident difficulties with social communication; noticeably atypical interactions	Fixated interests and frequent repetitive behaviors and rituals that significantly interfere with functioning
Mild[a] (requires support)	Atypical social interactions; difficulty initiating or responding to social communication	Repetitive behaviors and fixated interests that cause some interference with everyday functioning
Not severe enough for ASD diagnosis	Some atypical behaviors and mild deficits in social communication that do not limit or impair everyday functioning	Ritualized behavior, odd mannerisms, or excessive preoccupations that do not interfere with daily functioning
Variation of normal	Social isolation and awkwardness	Odd preoccupations or mannerisms

[a]Those who demonstrate milder symptoms are sometimes referred to as having high-functioning autism or Asperger's syndrome.
SOURCE: Adapted from APA (2013).

Many individuals with autism spectrum disorder have gastro-intestinal symptoms. In many cases, the physiological distress associated with these symptoms may cause maladaptive behaviors. When gastrointestinal symptoms are effectively treated, agitation often decreases.

SOURCE: Chaidez et al., 2013

exhibit *splinter skills*—that is, they do well on isolated tasks such as drawing, puzzle construction, musical ability, or rote memory but perform poorly on tasks requiring language skills and symbolic thinking. These children are referred to as **autistic savants**.

Diagnosis of ASD can be complicated. In fact, although some children diagnosed with ASD show "differences" during infancy, many do not receive an ASD diagnosis until age 4 or later (CDC, 2014). Typical evaluation procedures include autism screening inventories (designed for children 16–30 months of age), clinical observations, parent interviews, developmental histories, communication assessment, and psychological testing. Parent reports and observations are an important part of the diagnostic process. Unfortunately, many of the early indicators of ASD are so subtle (e.g., limited eye gaze) that they are not easily detectible. Recently, however, eye-tracking technology detected steady decreases in eye contact between 2 and 24 months of age among some infants at high risk of ASD. In contrast to the normally developing children who showed progressive increases in eye contact, those who were later diagnosed with ASD showed progressive declines in eye gaze, with the most rapid declines occurring among those who developed the most severe symptoms (Jones & Klin, 2013). The fact that these differences were evident as early as 2 months of age has generated optimism about the possibility of earlier diagnosis. These findings are very significant because eye contact is essential for learning and for normal social development; early diagnosis and intervention might be able to halt or slow down the cascade of events that begins in early life (Daniels, Halladay, Shih, Elder, & Dawson, 2014).

Diagnosis is also delayed because, in some children, there is a period of apparently normal social and intellectual development before ASD symptoms appear, with deterioration of skills beginning around 12 months of age or even later (Ozonoff, Iosif, et al., 2010). Children with this pattern of regression (referred to as *regressive autism*) often develop more severe symptoms compared to autistic children without this pattern (Meilleur & Fombonne, 2009).

Etiology

A great deal of research has focused on the causes of ASD, with the hope of developing early diagnostic procedures and interventions that can prevent, halt, or reverse symptoms. ASD is unique not only because symptoms sometimes appear following a period of relatively normal development, but also because intense, early intervention has reversed progression and even eliminated the disorder in some children. Although psychological effects are important in understanding the course of ASD, biological factors play the most critical role.

Biological Influences on Autism Spectrum Disorder Just as there are a variety of characteristics associated with ASD, it is presumed that multiple factors influence the development of autism spectrum symptoms. Biological researchers are, therefore, approaching the etiology of ASD from a variety of perspectives, including documenting biological processes involved in the development of the disorder, confirming genetic and environmental risk factors, and, most important, elucidating gene × environment interactions (Srivastava & Schwartz, 2014).

Concordance rates for ASD are much higher for monozygotic twins than dizygotic twins, with the heritability of ASD estimated to be around 0.73 percent for males and 0.87 percent for females (Taniai, Nishiyama, Miyachi, Imaeda, & Sumi, 2008). Furthermore, there is a much higher prevalence of ASD (up to 19 percent) among siblings of individuals with ASD compared to the rest of the population (Ozonoff, Young, et al., 2011). Additionally, autistic traits are highly heritable (E. B. Robinson et al., 2011); some siblings who do not develop ASD show atypical social development and communication patterns (Messinger et al., 2013). Taken together, twin and family studies clearly indicate a strong genetic influence on ASD. However, because monozygotic concordance

autistic savant an individual with autism spectrum disorder who performs exceptionally well on certain tasks (e.g., superior rote memory, artistic, or musical skills)

Eliminating the Asperger's Diagnosis: Why the Uproar?

I have aspergers (diagnosed) and my brother has classic autism. I can read and write, I've got a degree, I can dress myself in the morning. My brother however has no communication, bowel problems, he is a man in his 20s who is trapped with the mind of a two year old. He needs help with every aspect of his life. It doesn't do me any good or him any good by you trying to merge what we've got into one condition. (David, 2010)

Prior to DSM-5, **Asperger's syndrome** was the diagnosis given to many individuals on the mild end of the autism spectrum—those with average to above-average cognitive skills, intense focus on narrow interests, and poor social skills involving limited understanding of the rules of social engagement (Ghaziuddin, 2010). The quote above is from a young man on the autism spectrum expressing his opinion about the recent elimination of Asperger's syndrome. Those revising the DSM concluded that the social communication abnormalities, interpersonal relationship difficulties,

desire for sameness, and narrow interests seen in Asperger's syndrome should be incorporated into the autism spectrum disorder (ASD) diagnosis. In other words, the behaviors associated with Asperger's are merely an extension of the autism spectrum, so a separate diagnostic category is redundant (APA, 2013). This decision to eliminate Asperger's syndrome generated strong reactions from individuals with the diagnosis who embrace their uniqueness and who have found social connections within the Asperger's community. They argue that Asperger's is clearly distinct from ASD.

Some experts also supported maintaining the Asperger's category with modifications in diagnostic criteria to include unique features not previously identified, such as socially insensitive communication; verbose, one-sided conversations pertaining to areas of restricted interests; and difficulty with practical use of language (Ghaziuddin, 2010). Do individuals with Asperger's have a point—that they are different from those diagnosed with ASD and that including them on the ASD spectrum will result in increased stigma?

is less than 100 percent and the degree of impairment varies markedly among monozygotic twins pairs with ASD, other factors are etiologically significant as well.

There have been recent unprecedented advances in genome-wide searches for genes and risk alleles associated with ASD, including spontaneous mutations that occur prior to conception or during early prenatal development (Jiang et al., 2013; Willsey et al., 2013). Different genetic factors involving multiple brain regions, including the cerebellum and frontal and temporal lobes, appear to influence different autistic symptoms (Abrahams & Geschwind, 2010). Although the exact mechanisms by which genetic defects translate into impaired brain functioning are not known, research has linked ASD with numerous neurological findings, including:

- unique patterns of metabolic brain activity (Lange et al., 2010);
- reduced gaze toward the eye regions of faces, especially neutral faces, combined with elevated activity in the amygdala in response to human faces (Tottenham et al., 2014);
- abnormally high levels of serotonin, particularly in males with ASD and those who are high-functioning (Brasic, 2010);
- hyperconnectivity throughout the brain (those with the most neural connections experience the most severe social deficits) (Supekar et al., 2013); and
- accelerated growth of the amygdala in early childhood (Nordahl, Scholz, et al., 2012)—accelerated brain growth in boys with regressive autism begins around 4–6 months of age, long before autistic symptoms appear (Nordahl, Lange, et al., 2011).

Accelerated head growth may be an endophenotype (biological marker) for ASD (Constantino et al., 2010). Male infants later diagnosed with ASD exhibited a pattern of rapid head growth 6–9 months after birth (Fukumoto et al., 2010). MRI studies

DID YOU KNOW?

Parents who want to give their offspring a competitive edge sometimes pressure physicians to prescribe medications for the purpose of *neuroenhancement*—using prescription drugs to maximize cognitive or academic functioning. This practice of prescribing drugs for healthy children and adolescents has led some medical organizations to issue ethical position statements strongly discouraging such misuse of medication.

SOURCE: Visser et al., (2014)

of toddlers diagnosed with ASD have confirmed extra growth in multiple regions of the brain (Schumann et al., 2010). The period of accelerated head growth in infancy precedes and overlaps with the onset of autistic symptoms. Conversely, the increasingly severe autistic symptoms displayed by children with ASD in the second year of life correspond with a subsequent period of decelerated growth within the brain (G. Dawson, Munson, et al., 2007). Some boys later diagnosed with ASD showed overall growth acceleration in the first year of life; increased stature was associated with more severe symptoms of ASD and increased likelihood of seizures (Chawarska et al., 2011).

Recent research has focused on the much higher rate of mitochondrial dysfunction found in children with ASD (Giulivi et al., 2010). Mitochondrial dysfunction affects the energy-producing capacity of cells, a process critically important to neural development; some biomarkers of mitochondrial dysfunction correlate with severity of autistic symptoms, especially in children with a history of developmental regression (Rossignol & Frye, 2011). In fact, some children with ASD appear to have genetically based mitochondrial disease (Haas, 2010).

A groundbreaking study involving careful analysis of the postmortem brains of children with ASD (ages 2–15) yielded important insight into the neurological processes underlying autism spectrum symptoms. The researchers found evidence of patchy areas of disrupted neuronal development that occurred during the normal cell-layering process in all six layers of the cortex; these abnormalities were most prevalent in the early-developing layers of the frontal and temporal cortex, areas associated with social-emotional communication skills. These findings suggest that brain abnormalities associated with ASD begin during pregnancy when the brain is forming. The fact that the pathology was in patches may explain why some children can recover from ASD; early intervention may assist the brain to effectively "rewire" and compensate for the early abnormalities (Stoner et al., 2014). Several other groups of researchers have similarly demonstrated that the effects of genetic mutations associated with ASD come into play in specific brain regions during fetal development (between 10 and 24 weeks after conception); these genes influence cell development in brain regions associated with symptoms of ASD (Parikshak et al., 2013; Willsey et al., 2013). Further, comparisons of monozygotic twins with and without ASD have identified the presence of environmentally driven epigenetic alterations in the twin with ASD, changes associated with specific behavioral traits and the expression of genes affecting fetal brain development (Wong et al., 2013). The confluence of these findings—that brain changes associated with ASD occur during fetal development—has generated considerable excitement in the field.

Children who develop ASD appear to have an innate vulnerability that is triggered by environmental factors (Herbert, 2010). Environmental toxins associated with the development of ASD include exposure to air pollutants such as lead, mercury, and other heavy metals (Roberts et al., 2013), certain pesticides (E. M. Roberts et al., 2007), maternal smoking, poor indoor ventilation, and PVC flooring (M. Larsson, Weiss, Janson, Sundell, & Bornehag, 2009). Why might environmental toxins cause ASD in some children and not others? A partial answer to this question may come from research showing that children with ASD and typically-developing children appear to have similar blood levels of both lead (Tian et al., 2011) and mercury (Stamova et al., 2011); however, children with ASD appear to metabolize these toxins differently. It is unclear if toxins or other variables account for the demographic variance in ASD across the United States (Figure 16.5) (Newschaffer et al., 2007).

Searching for Early Indicators of Autism Spectrum Disorder

Researchers are using a variety of technologies to track eye gaze and brain reactions in infants who are at high risk for autism spectrum disorder, especially those who have siblings with the disorder. These technologies are allowing researchers to document differences between children who develop normally and those who begin to display autistic symptoms.

Autism Speaks
Oli Scarff/Getty Images News/Getty Images

Other factors associated with ASD include nutritional deficiencies (Surén et al., 2013), immune system dysregulation (Marques, O'Connor, Roth, Susser, & Bjørke-Monsen, 2013), prematurity (D'Onofrio et al., 2013), and closely spaced pregnancies (Cheslack-Postava, Liu, & Bearman, 2011). Biological mechanisms may also account for the fact that autistic symptoms sometimes improve and then abruptly return when a child with ASD has a fever (L. K. Curran et al., 2007).

Most researchers agree that ASD is a heterogeneous disorder with multiple causes. Fortunately, biological researchers and experts in the field of ASD are working together to search for interventions that produce documentable biological changes; they are encouraged by the neuroplasticity seen in some children who have received intensive, early intervention (Landa, Holman, O'Neill, & Stuart, 2011).

Other Etiological Influences on Autism Spectrum Disorder Early psychological theories pointed to deviant parent–child interactions as the cause of autism. In fact, Kanner (1943), who named the syndrome, originally concluded that cold and unresponsive parenting was responsible for the development of autistic symptoms, describing parents of children with autism as cold, humorless perfectionists. However, Kanner eventually began to recognize that autism is innate. It is now widely agreed that biological factors are the primary cause of ASD.

From a psychological perspective, ASD affects the way a child interacts with the world, which in turn affects how others interact with the child. Many children with ASD seldom make eye contact and seem disinterested in socially connecting with others; instead, they prefer to be alone, do not engage in play, and ignore parental efforts at interaction. As you might imagine, all of these characteristics blunt the development of social skills, further interfering with normal neurological and psychological development. Due to the lack of reciprocal social interaction, family members may eventually make fewer attempts to maintain social connection, further adding to the child's isolation. Additionally, behavioral characteristics associated with ASD often create stress and affect interactions within the family, particularly when parents have limited respite from the day-to-day demands of caretaking (J. L. Taylor & Seltzer, 2010a).

Intervention and Treatment

The prognosis for children with ASD is difficult to predict. Most children diagnosed with ASD retain their diagnosis and require support throughout their lifetime. Some with milder symptoms may be self-sufficient and successfully employed, and function reasonably well in adulthood, although social awkwardness, restrictive interests, or atypical behaviors often persist (C. P. Johnson et al., 2007). In general, those with higher cognitive-adaptive functioning fare better than those who have intellectual disability and severe autistic symptoms.

Some children (including some with severe symptoms) have made a remarkable recovery after receiving early, intense intervention; the most impressive results have occurred among children with higher cognitive and language skills (Mazurek, Kanne, & Miles, 2012). In fact, after intensive intervention, some children no longer meet ASD diagnostic criteria. However, comorbid conditions such as depression, anxiety, inattention, and hyperactivity often remain after ASD symptoms have remitted (Ashburner, Ziviani, & Rodger, 2010). A recent encouraging study involving a sample of children who lost all symptoms of ASD following intensive early intervention found that they are now indistinguishable from their typically developing peers (Fein et al., 2013).

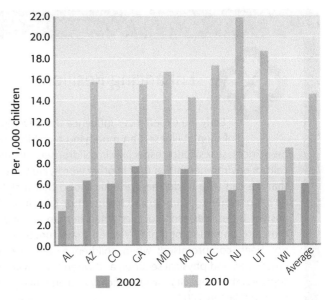

Figure 16.5

Changes in the Prevalence of Autism Spectrum Disorder among 8-Year-Old Children in 10 U.S. States, 2002–2010

The prevalence of autism spectrum disorder among 8-year-old children increased between 2002 and 2010 in all 10 state sites monitored. What might account for these increases and the state-to-state variations in prevalence of the disorder?

SOURCE: Centers for Disease Control and Prevention (2014).

DID YOU KNOW?

In a study involving 600,000 sibling pairs, children born less than 1 year after the birth of a sibling were almost 300 percent more likely to develop ASD compared to children born at least 4 years after a sibling.

SOURCE: Cheslack-Postava et al., 2011

Enhancing Resilience in Youth

Early life experiences influence the development of mental illness. Can modifying a child's environment increase resilience, especially in children who are genetically or environmentally at risk? In other words, are there steps that we can take to decrease the likelihood that a child will develop a mental disorder in childhood or later in life? The answer is yes. Resilience occurs when human adaptive systems are operating optimally—when brain functioning has not been compromised; when children experience social, emotional, and physical security; and when the environment supports their capacity for self-efficacy and effective problem solving (Masten, 2009).

Some interventions increase resilience by reducing potential harm to the developing child. For example, prenatal care and the avoidance of neurotoxins help reduce the risk of conditions that interfere with optimal brain functioning, thus reducing the risk of neurodevelopmental disorders. Other interventions increase resilience by reducing environmental stress—thus providing both biological and psychological benefits to young children (S. E. Taylor, 2010). For example, intervening with parents who are experiencing mental illness or engaging in child maltreatment can

Kevin Peterson/Photodisc/Getty Images

improve behavioral or emotional outcomes in their children (D. G. Rosenthal et al., 2012). Similarly, early intervention when children are experiencing behavioral or emotional difficulties can prevent the downward emotional spiral seen with many disorders (Sapienza & Masten, 2011). With support, children who have been exposed to trauma can experience post-traumatic growth (e.g., increased sense of personal strength or enhanced connection with others) in response to their experiences (Meyerson, Grant, Carter, & Kilmer, 2011). Given the epidemic of mental illness, continued research regarding the best methods for promoting resilience in the face of adversity is a global priority (Masten & Narayan, 2012).

Providing children with experiences that foster competence and healthy development also enhances resilience. Such an approach has the potential to promote positive developmental cascades; that is, increased personal competence not only provides the basis for coping with adversity but also promotes other positive outcomes (Masten, 2011). For example, stimulating home and preschool environments not only enhance cognitive development but also allow children to develop a sense of mastery and optimism. Additionally, positive attachment experiences, quality parenting, and ongoing supportive relationships with positive role models allow children to develop interpersonal trust and coping skills (Masten, 2009). Knowing how to solve problems or regulate emotions allows children to reduce biological reactivity in response to stress or adversity (S. E. Taylor, 2010). Additionally, promotion of a healthy lifestyle (e.g., ensuring adequate sleep, nutrition, and exercise; monitoring television and computer use) can further support physical and psychological resilience (M. E. O'Connell, Boat, & Warner, 2009). One thing is clear—when basic physical, social, and emotional needs are met, youth can develop the strengths that allow them not only to overcome adversity but also to flourish.

Children with ASD are often given multiple medications in an effort to decrease their anxiety, repetitive behaviors, and hyperactivity; however, there is minimal evidence that combining medications is effective (Spencer et al., 2013). Only two medications—the antipsychotics risperidone and aripiprazole—have received FDA approval for the treatment of symptoms of aggression and irritability associated with ASD (Politte, Henry, & McDougle, 2014). Some preliminary randomized controlled studies have found that administration of **oxytocin**, a naturally occurring hormone that affects social bonding, can increase eye gaze and emotional recognition skills in children and adolescents with mild ASD (Andari et al., 2010). Oxytocin increases neural activity in the amygdala and in "social circuits" of the brain, thereby facilitating social attunement (Gordon et al., 2014). Thus far, oxytocin is the only biological

oxytocin a powerful hormone that affects social bonding

intervention to address a core symptom of ASD (social communication) rather than the behavioral challenges associated with the disorder.

ASD causes major disruption in families and unfulfilled lives for many affected children. However, comprehensive treatment programs have enabled many children with ASD to develop some functional skills (Eldevik et al., 2010). Because of the communication and social impairments associated with ASD, skill building in these areas is often a target of intervention. Specialized programs for children with ASD often include:

- a high degree of structure through elements such as predictable routine, visual activity schedules, and clear physical boundaries to minimize distractions;
- intensive, systematically planned, developmentally appropriate educational activities;
- behavior modification procedures to eliminate echolalia and repetitive behaviors and to increase attending behaviors, verbalizations, and social play (Myers et al., 2007);
- parent education regarding behavior management and enhancing communication; and
- opportunities to practice learned skills in new environments, including interactions with typically developing peers.

Interventions that emphasize social communication, reinforcement of appropriate responses to social stimuli, and prevention of repetitive behaviors produce the most significant gains (Helt et al., 2008). Experts in the field believe that it is important for children with ASD to have opportunities for social learning such as interactions with age peers in normal social contexts (Gordon et al., 2014). Training age-level peers in strategies for interacting with children with ASD has also been effective in promoting social interaction (Kasari, Rotheram-Fuller, Locke, & Gulsrud, 2012).

Pivotal response treatment (PRT), a play-based, child-initiated therapeutic approach, focuses on reducing self-stimulating behaviors and developing communication and social skills by targeting "pivotal behaviors" such as motivation, responding to social cues, and initiating social interaction. The PRT approach also uses natural reinforcers—items of interest to the child rather than contrived rewards. PRT, extensively validated for use with young children, is now used as an early intervention with infants at high risk of ASD (Steiner, Gengoux, Klin, & Chawarska, 2013). Given the complexity and high variability of symptoms associated with ASD, treatment approaches are most effective when they are individualized and take into account the individual's skill level, interests, and social-communication strengths.

Intellectual Disability

Intellectual disability (ID), formerly referred to as *mental retardation*, is characterized by significant limitations in intellectual functioning and adaptive behaviors, including:

- significantly below-average general intellectual functioning (ordinarily interpreted as an IQ score of 70 or less on an individually administered IQ test); and
- deficiencies in **adaptive behavior** (e.g., self-care; understanding of health and safety issues; ability to live, work, or plan leisure activities and use community resources; functional use of academic skills) that are greater than would be expected based on age or cultural background.

ID is diagnosed only when low intelligence is accompanied by impaired adaptive functioning. Psychologists have traditionally identified four distinct categories of ID based on IQ score ranges and adaptive behaviors. These categories are (a) *mild* (IQ score 50–55 to 70), (b) *moderate* (IQ score 35–40 to 50–55), (c) *severe* (IQ score 20–25 to 35–40), and (d) *profound* (IQ score below 20–25). Table 16.7 summarizes functional characteristics associated with each of these categories. Social, vocational, and adaptive behaviors can vary significantly not only between categories but also within a given category.

intellectual disability (ID) a disorder characterized by limitations in intellectual functioning and adaptive behaviors

adaptive behavior performance on tasks of daily living, including academic skills, self-care, and the ability to work or live independently

Table 16.7 Adaptive Characteristics Associated with Intellectual Disability

Level	Approximate IQ Range	Characteristics
Mild	50–55 to 70	Daily living and social interaction skills are mildly affected; adaptive difficulties involve conceptual and academic understanding; the individual may need assistance with job skills or independent living; the individual may marry and raise children
Moderate	35–40 to 50–55	The individual may have functional self-care skills and the ability to communicate basic needs; the individual may read a few basic words; lifelong support and supervision are required (e.g., supervised meal preparation, sheltered work)
Severe	20–25 to 35–40	The individual may recognize familiar people; communication skills are limited; lifelong support is required
Profound	Below 20–25	Characteristics are similar to those of severe intellectual disability, with even more extensive care needs

© Cengage Learning®

The American Association on Intellectual and Developmental Disabilities (2012) asserts that, although IQ scores may be used to approximate intellectual functioning for diagnostic purposes, it is much more important to focus on adaptive skills and the nature of psychosocial supports that are needed to maximize functioning. We know that the effects of ID are variable and that individuals with mild or moderate ID often function independently or semi-independently in adulthood. Additionally, with support and intervention, those with more severe ID can make cognitive and social gains and have improved life satisfaction.

Less than 1 percent of students in public schools in the United States are identified as having an ID (U.S. Department of Education, National Center for Education Statistics, 2013). Low- and middle-income countries have double the prevalence of ID compared to higher-income countries (Maulik, Mascarenhas, Mathers, Dua, & Saxena, 2011). Many individuals with ID have coexisting conditions such as ASD (Morin, Cobigo, Rivard, & Lépine, 2010); approximately one fourth have a seizure disorder (World Health Organization, 2011).

Etiology of Intellectual Disability

The etiology of ID differs, to some extent, depending on the level of intellectual impairment. Mild ID is often *idiopathic* (having no known cause), whereas more pronounced ID is often associated with genetic factors, brain abnormalities, or brain injury. Although a variety of biological factors are implicated in ID, psychological, social, and sociocultural factors also play a role in intellectual development and adaptive functioning.

Genetic Factors   In up to 80 percent of cases of ID, the underlying cause is unknown. It is believed that genetic factors that have not yet been identified are responsible for many of these cases; in particular, researchers are working to identify genes that are related to learning and memory. Also, due to the higher prevalence of ID in males, a great deal of research has focused on genes residing on the X chromosome; of the 40 genes that have been identified as contributing to ID, approximately 80 percent are, in fact, on the X chromosome (Kaufman, Ayub, & Vincent, 2010).

Genetic factors that exert an influence on ID include both *genetic variations* and *genetic abnormalities*. ID caused by normal genetic variation reflects the fact that in a normal distribution of any trait (such as intelligence), some individuals fall in the lower range. The normal range of intelligence is considered to lie between the IQ scores of 70 and 130. Some individuals with ID have an IQ that falls at or slightly below the lower end of this normal range (70 or slightly lower) but are otherwise physically and emotionally healthy and have no specific physiological anomalies associated with their cognitive and adaptive difficulties.

The genetic abnormalities associated with ID include chromosomal variations, as well as conditions resulting from inheritance of a single gene. Although genetic abnormalities can result in varying degrees of ID, many individuals with genetically based ID have significant impairment (Raymond et al., 2007). The most common inherited form of ID is **fragile X syndrome**, a condition resulting in limited production of proteins required for brain development. Fragile X syndrome results in mild to severe ID. Females generally have less impairment; males are prone to having communication and social difficulties, including anxious, inattentive, fearful, or aggressive behaviors. Autistic behavior and hyperactivity occur in some individuals with fragile X syndrome (Oliver et al., 2011).

Down syndrome (DS) is the most common and most easily recognized chromosomal disorder resulting in ID (Costa & Scott-McKean, 2013). In the vast majority of cases, an extra copy of chromosome 21 originates during gamete development (involving either the egg or the sperm); this extra chromosome produces the physical and neurological characteristics associated with the condition. DS occurs once in approximately every 691 births. The chance of an egg containing an extra copy of chromosome 21 increases significantly with increasing maternal age. The incidence of DS births to women younger than 30 is less than 1 in 900; the incidence increases to 1 in 400 at age 35, 1 in 70 at age 42, and 1 in 10 at age 49. However, because most pregnancies occur in women younger than age 35, the majority of babies born with DS have young mothers (National Down Syndrome Society, 2014).

Distinctive physical characteristics associated with DS include a single crease across the palm of the hand, slanted eyes, a protruding tongue, and a harsh voice. The majority of individuals with DS have mild to moderate ID; however, minimal intellectual impairment or severe impairment is also possible. With support, many adults with DS have jobs and live semi-independently. Individuals with DS have significantly increased incidence of leukemia and infectious diseases, hearing loss, congenital heart disease, and premature aging. Although medical intervention has improved health outcomes and increased life expectancy, those with DS continue to have a significantly increased risk of early dementia, including early-onset Alzheimer's disease (National Down Syndrome Society, 2014).

Prenatal detection of DS is possible through different techniques, including **amniocentesis**, a screening procedure involving withdrawal of amniotic fluid from the fetal sac. This procedure, performed between the 14th and 18th weeks of pregnancy, involves some risk for both mother and fetus, so it is employed primarily when the chance of finding DS is high (e.g., with women 35 or older). More recently, noninvasive prenatal screening for DS is available early in pregnancy; if the results are positive, confirmatory amniocentesis can be performed (Ohno & Caughey, 2013). There are regional and cultural differences in use of genetic screening and decisions regarding termination of pregnancy; this has produced ethnic/racial differences in DS incidence, with Hispanic mothers being the most likely to give birth to a child with DS (Shin et al., 2009).

Nongenetic Biological Factors ID can result from a variety of environmental influences during the prenatal (from conception to birth), perinatal (just prior to and during the birth process), or postnatal (after birth) period. Many of the circumstances that can cause ID (as well as other neurodevelopmental disorders) are preventable or controllable (Table 16.8). During the prenatal period, the developing fetus is susceptible to viruses and infections (e.g., tuberculosis or German measles), drugs and alcohol, radiation, and poor nutrition. Some risk factors can cause ID both prenatally and after birth. For example, iodine deficiency either during pregnancy or during early infancy can impair intellectual development (World Health Organization, 2011).

Similarly, phenylketonuria (PKU), an inherited condition affecting metabolism, can have prenatal or postnatal effects; if pregnant women with PKU ingest protein or artificial sweeteners, the resultant buildup of a substance called phenylalanine can cause significant intellectual impairment in a developing fetus. This can be prevented if a special diet is followed. Similarly, phenylalanine buildup from undetected and untreated PKU in an infant can cause postnatal brain damage. ID resulting from PKU can be prevented when routine PKU screening is implemented (as is done in the United States, Canada, and many developed countries) and dietary recommendations are followed.

fragile X syndrome an inherited condition involving limited production of proteins required for brain development resulting in mild to severe intellectual disability

Down syndrome (DS) a chromosomal disorder (most frequently involving an extra copy of chromosome 21) that causes physical and neurological abnormalities

amniocentesis a prenatal screening procedure involving withdrawal of amniotic fluid from the fetal sac

Table 16.8 Preventable or Controllable Causes of Neurodevelopmental Disorders

Prenatal (Before Birth)
Severe malnutrition
Alcohol or illicit drugs; prescription medications
Iodine or folic acid deficiency[a]
Maternal infections such as rubella[a] or syphilis
Toxoplasma parasites (from cat feces, undercooked meats, or unwashed produce)
Exposure to radiation
Blood incompatibility (Rh factor)
Maternal chronic disease (heart or kidney disease, diabetes)
Untreated phenylketonuria

Perinatal (Just Before or During Birth)
Severe prematurity[a]
Birth trauma
Asphyxia (lack of oxygen)

Infancy and Childhood
Untreated phenylketonuria
Nutritional deficiencies[a]
Iodine deficiency
Severe lack of stimulation
Chronic lead exposure[a]
Other environmental toxins[a]
Brain infections (e.g., meningitis and encephalitis)
Head injury

[a]These factors have also been implicated in the etiology of autism spectrum disorder.
Adapted from the World Health Organization (2011).

fetal alcohol spectrum effects a continuum of detrimental neurological and behavioral effects resulting from maternal alcohol consumption during pregnancy

fetal alcohol syndrome (FAS) a condition resulting from maternal alcohol consumption during gestation that involves central nervous system dysfunction and altered brain development

Alcohol intake can significantly affect embryonic and fetal development. Although there is a continuum of detrimental neurological and behavioral effects resulting from alcohol consumption during pregnancy (referred to as **fetal alcohol spectrum effects**), the greatest concern is for those children who have **fetal alcohol syndrome (FAS)**. The DSM-5 contains a proposed diagnosis undergoing study (neurobehavioral disorder associated with prenatal alcohol exposure) that encompasses impairment in neurocognitive, behavioral, and adaptive functioning associated with prenatal alcohol exposure; this diagnosis includes children with FAS and those with fetal alcohol spectrum effects (APA, 2013). Although FAS is estimated to occur in less than 1 percent of live births, 2–5 percent of the U.S. population is estimated to have fetal alcohol spectrum effects (P. A. May et al., 2009). Fetal alcohol spectrum effects include reduced cognitive functioning, attentional difficulties, slower information processing, and poor working memory, whereas FAS results in restricted growth, facial abnormalities, and significant dysfunction of the central nervous system and brain (Mattson et al., 2013). Children with fetal alcohol spectrum effects experience difficulty with attention, learning, memory, regulation of emotions, and executive functioning, all of which are associated with the frontal lobe of the brain; markedly delayed development in adaptive behavior, particularly skills of daily living, is also common (Ware et al., 2014).

The most common perinatal birth conditions associated with ID are prematurity and low birth weight. Although most premature infants develop normally, some have neurological problems resulting in learning disorders and ID (Whitaker et al., 2006). During the postnatal period, factors such as head injuries, brain infections, tumors, and prolonged malnutrition can cause brain damage and consequent ID. Exposure to environmental toxins is an increasing concern. Lead, a well-known neurotoxin found in the lead-based paint that was used in many older homes, is associated with both ID and hyperactivity (Abelsohn & Sanborn, 2010).

Psychological, Social, and Sociocultural Dimensions
Psychological, social, and sociocultural factors can affect both intellectual and adaptive functioning. A child's genetic background interacts with environmental factors; children from socioeconomically advantaged homes often experience enriching activities that enhance cognitive development. In contrast, crowded living conditions, lack of adequate health care, poor nutrition, and inadequate educational opportunities place children living in poverty at an intellectual disadvantage and can influence whether they reach their genetic potential (Tucker-Drob, Rhemtulla, Harden, Turkheimer, & Fask, 2011). Similarly, children raised by parents who have mild ID may begin their lives with less intellectual stimulation and learning opportunity, further contributing to a generational pattern of lower intellectual functioning. Additionally, the long-term effects of prematurity appear to be moderated by sociocultural factors such as socioeconomic status and parenting style; supportive parenting or increased socioeconomic resources can enhance ultimate cognitive functioning (D'Onofrio et al., 2013).

An enriching and encouraging home environment, as well as ongoing educational intervention focused on targeted cognitive, academic, self-care, social, and problem-solving skills, can have a strong and positive influence on the development of children with ID (J. D. Thomas et al., 2010). Coping strategies and use of outside resources when raising a child with ID can be highly influenced by sociocultural context. Additionally, religious or cultural beliefs may affect parents' perceptions of their child's condition; for example, some parents may attribute ID to factors such

Risks of Substance Use in Pregnancy

It is common knowledge that alcohol and other drugs can affect a developing fetus. The effects depend on the timing (i.e., the stage of fetal development), as well as the type and amount of substance used. Pregnant women are advised to avoid alcohol throughout pregnancy in order to prevent the physical and cognitive abnormalities associated with fetal alcohol syndrome, the leading cause of preventable intellectual disability (J. D. Thomas, Warren, & Hewitt, 2010). Use of marijuana, cocaine, heroin, or methamphetamine can also lead to neurodevelopmental disorders (Sowell et al., 2010). Of course, in utero substance exposure is often associated with other prenatal and childhood risk

factors, such as poor nutrition, limited prenatal care, a chaotic home environment, and abuse, neglect, or other stressors that can affect brain development (B. M. Lester et al., 2010).

Researchers are attempting to find diagnostic tools to detect drug or alcohol use during pregnancy and to identify newborns affected by maternal substance use; their hope is that early detection will allow for early intervention (Ismail, Buckley, Budacki, Jabbar, & Gallicano, 2010). What are the health, legal, and moral implications of these efforts to detect substance use? Are there other ways to reach out to women who are using substances during pregnancy?

as personal wrongdoing or a curse placed on their family, whereas others believe a child with special needs is a gift from God (Durà-Vilà, Dein, & Hodes, 2010).

Learning Disorders

A **learning disorder (LD)** is diagnosed when someone with at least average intellectual abilities demonstrates development of basic math, reading, or writing skills that is substantially lower than would be expected for the person's chronological age, educational background, and intellectual ability. LD primarily interferes with academic achievement and daily living activities that require reading, writing, or math skills. As with any testing, when an assessment for LD is conducted, care is taken to ensure that testing procedures and test interpretation consider the child's linguistic and cultural background. Specific learning disorders include **dyslexia** (significant difficulties with accuracy or fluency of reading), **dyscalculia** (significant difficulties in understanding quantities, number symbols, or basic arithmetic calculations), and disorders of written expression.

Approximately 5 percent of students in public schools in the United States are diagnosed with LD (U.S. Department of Education, National Center for Education Statistics, 2013). LD occurs twice as frequently in boys. Many children with LD, especially boys, have concurrent disorders such as ADHD (Butterworth & Kovas, 2013). The severity of the disorder varies, and some individuals continue to cope with severe academic deficits in adulthood. Adults with severe LD may experience problems with employment, so it is beneficial if their career choice capitalizes on their abilities and strengths.

Little is currently known about the precise causes of LD. Some children with LD appear to have slower brain maturation and eventually catch up academically. However, others have lifelong differences in neurological processing of information related to basic academic skills. Etiological possibilities for chronic LD include many of the same biological explanations for ID and ADHD (see Table 16.8). Additionally, LD tends to run in families, suggesting a genetic component.

Support for Individuals with Neurodevelopmental Disorders

Many neurodevelopmental disorders produce lifelong disability; therefore, the goal of intervention is to build skills and develop each individual's potential to the fullest extent possible. For those with moderate to severe ID or ASD, such support often

learning disorder (LD) an academic disability characterized by reading, writing, or math skills that are substantially below levels that would be expected based on the person's age, intellectual ability, and educational background

dyslexia a condition involving significant difficulties with reading skills

dyscalculia a condition involving difficulties in understanding mathematical skills or concepts

Work Opportunities for Individuals with Neurodevelopmental Disorders

Many people with Down syndrome and other neurodevelopmental disorders can function well in a supportive work environment. Here a baker's assistant is proudly displaying fresh bread.

begins in infancy and extends across the life span. In the case of ASD, early intervention can result in moderate to significant improvement (G. Dawson, Rogers, et al., 2010). For children with ADHD, LD, mild ID, or mild ASD, support may occur primarily in the school setting. Interventions for LD and mild ID typically involve remedial interventions targeting the area of academic difficulty, whereas supports for ASD and more severe intellectual impairment are generally more comprehensive.

Support in Childhood

When ASD or ID is identified early, children often participate in individualized home-based or school-based programs focused on decreasing inappropriate behaviors and maximizing overall skill development. Parent involvement is an integral part of early intervention programs; parents can help reduce maladaptive behaviors, as well as enhance cognitive, social, and communication development (Scahill et al., 2012). School services are individualized to meet the needs of the child and to maximize learning opportunities, including skills needed for independent or semi-independent living (National Dissemination Center for Children with Disabilities, 2012). Unfortunately, rates of improvement often decrease once school programs are completed; programs terminate following high school graduation, or at age 21 for those with more significant impairment (J. L. Taylor & Seltzer, 2010b).

Support in Adulthood

A number of programs are available for young adults with moderate neurodevelopmental disabilities to learn vocational skills or to participate in work opportunities in a specialized setting. These programs focus on specific job skills, social skills for interacting with co-workers and supervisors, and completing work-related tasks with speed and quality. There is a clear need for more support for those with mild ID or ASD as they make the transition from high school to out-of-school activities, especially for those who are unable to obtain employment without support (J. L. Taylor & Seltzer, 2010a).

Institutionalization of adults with neurodevelopmental disorders is rare. Many adults with special needs live with family members; others live independently or semi-independently within the community. The idea is to provide the least restrictive environment possible—that is, as much independence and personal choice as is safe and practical. Although group arrangements vary considerably from setting to setting, most normalized living arrangements provide opportunities for residents to socialize and to develop independent living skills. Many assisted-living environments promote social interaction with the larger community and continue to support the development of personal competence and independence.

Contemporary Trends and Future Directions

Neglect, maltreatment, inconsistent parenting, bullying, or trauma such as sexual abuse or domestic violence can affect children on multiple levels. Such experiences can exert lifelong influences on biological processes such as the expression of genes or heightened sensitivity of the stress response system. Further, negative early experiences can adversely affect psychological and social functioning. As you have seen throughout this text, many adult mental disorders are rooted in a stressful childhood. Thus, preventing experiences that initiate a negative cascade of events and affect mental health continues to be a high priority. Prevention of environmental exposure to neurotoxins and other factors associated with the development of neurodevelopmental disorders is similarly beneficial.

Developing and implementing evidence-based interventions that promote resilient biological and psychological functioning among children who have experienced maltreatment, trauma, or other factors that may adversely affect their development is also important (Cicchetti, 2013). For example, early intervention when a child displays symptoms such as anxiety, depression, inattention, or antisocial behaviors can help prevent a lifelong pattern of maladaptive symptoms. Such efforts are particularly crucial as adolescents face the physiological, social, and emotional challenges of puberty—a time when the incidence of mental disorders increases significantly, especially among teenage girls (Maughan, Collishaw, & Stringaris, 2013).

Research to address the long-term benefits and risks of pharmacological, social, and psychological interventions remains a high priority (Visser et al., 2014). Parents often play a key role in the intervention process. In many cases, working with a mental health professional can help parents learn strategies to deal with a particularly challenging child or with a child's unique emotional needs. Additionally, individual or group therapy can help children learn to cope with emotions or develop needed social skills. For example, a group-based cognitive-behavioral prevention program showed sustained effects in decreasing the frequency of depressive episodes in adolescents at high risk of depression (Beardslee et al., 2013). Another example is the COPE (Creating Opportunities for Personal Empowerment) Healthy Lifestyles TEEN (Thinking, Emotions, Exercise, Nutrition) program, an easily implemented cognitive-behavioral, skill-building intervention that focuses on a variety of ways in which adolescents can improve their health and overall well-being (Melnyk et al., 2013). There is little doubt that children and adolescents will derive the greatest benefit from preventive efforts and therapies that are empirically based and carefully tailored to the child's or adolescent's gender, developmental level, and specific mental health needs.

chapter SUMMARY

1 What internalizing disorders occur in childhood and adolescence?

- Anxiety disorders are the most common internalizing disorders in youth.
- Trauma- and stressor-related disorders include post-traumatic stress disorder and attachment disorders.
- Nonsuicidal self-injury is most likely to emerge during early adolescence.
- Depressive and bipolar disorders can occur in childhood, but are more prevalent during adolescence.
- Disruptive mood dysregulation disorder involves negative affect and exaggerated responses to anger.

2 What are the characteristics of externalizing disorders?

- Oppositional defiant disorder involves a pattern of hostile, defiant behavior toward authority figures.
- Intermittent explosive disorder involves either high-frequency/low-intensity aggressive outbursts or low-frequency/high-intensity outbursts.
- Conduct disorders involve serious antisocial behaviors and violations of the rights of others.

3 What are elimination disorders?

- Some children experience enuresis or encopresis, which are disorders involving bladder or bowel control.

4 What are neurodevelopmental disorders, and what are their characteristics?

- Motor and vocal tic disorders and Tourette's disorder involve involuntary repetitive movements or vocalizations.
- Attention-deficit/hyperactivity disorder is characterized by inattention, hyperactivity, and impulsivity.
- Autism spectrum disorder involves impairment in social communication and restricted, stereotyped interests and activities.
- Intellectual disability involves limitations in intellectual functioning and adaptive behaviors.
- Learning disorders involve basic reading, writing, or math skills that are substantially below expectations based on age, intelligence, and educational experiences.

17 LAW AND ETHICS IN ABNORMAL PSYCHOLOGY

Chapter Outline

ON JULY 20, 2012, 24-YEAR-OLD JAMES EAGAN HOLMES, described as a shy, intelligent graduate student working toward his doctorate in neuroscience at the University of Colorado, committed a horrendous act. Wearing black tactical clothing with a helmet and a gas mask, Holmes set off tear gas grenades during a screening of the movie *The Dark Knight Rises* in Aurora, Colorado. Then, using a variety of firearms, he killed 12 people and wounded 70 others. He was arrested without resistance outside the theatre. During his first court appearance, his recently dyed, red-orange hair was disheveled and he appeared dazed and unaware of his surroundings. His defense attorney claimed that Holmes committed the massacre during the "throes of a psychotic episode" and that Holmes should be found "not guilty by reason of insanity" (Associated Press, 2012).

The case of James Holmes raises several important issues that will be covered in this chapter. First, what are the components of the insanity defense and do they apply to Holmes? Was he so mentally disturbed that he was unable to tell right from wrong? How did the mental health professionals who evaluated him determine his mental state and what criteria did they use to decide if he was sane or insane at the time of the shooting? Second, prior to withdrawing from his Ph.D. program and prior to the shootings, Holmes met with three mental health professionals at the University of Colorado. Are the conversations he had during these meetings and records from these sessions protected by physician–patient privilege? In other words, is this information admissible as evidence in court proceedings, especially if Holmes does not waive his right to confidentiality? Under what circumstances can privilege and confidentiality be broken? Third, one of those professionals, the psychiatrist, had reportedly been worried about some threatening and homicidal statements made by Holmes during their sessions. Did she have a duty and obligation to warn others about his threats? Dr. Richard Martinez, a forensic psychiatrist and professor at the University of Colorado School of Medicine, stated, "At the moment you determine that there is a credible threat . . . the duty to warn is triggered" (Sallinger, 2012). However, did the duty to warn apply in this situation? Courts, society, and mental health professionals continue to struggle with these complex issues.

1 What are the criteria used to judge insanity, and what is the difference between being insane and being incompetent to stand trial?

2 Under what conditions can a person be involuntarily committed to a mental institution?

3 What rights do mental patients have with respect to treatment and care?

4 Are there situations in which suicide should be an option?

5 What legal and ethical issues guide treatment practices?

RJ Sangosti/Denver Post/Getty Images

Many Unanswered Questions

Colorado theater shooting suspect James Holmes is charged with murdering 12 people and wounding 70 others. He pled "not guilty by reason of insanity." His trial was delayed when prosecutors requested a second evaluation of his sanity. This case also raised questions about the confidentiality of therapist-client communication and the duty to warn the public about a potentially life-threatening situation.

Psychologists and other mental health professionals often participate in the legal system and must deal with the multiple questions posed here. In the past, psychologists primarily evaluated mental competency in criminal cases such as those of James Holmes. Now, determining whether someone is sane or insane is only a small part of the role they play in the judicial system. Psychologists also give expert opinions on child custody, neuropsychological functioning, traumatic injury, and suicide (Table 17.1). The American Psychological Association has even taken on the role of *amicus curiae* (friend of the court), acting in an advisory capacity by filing briefs summarizing social or psychological research that may help inform legal decisions (Clay, 2010). Not only do mental health professionals influence decisions in the legal system, the practice of therapy is also influenced by mental health laws passed at local, state, and federal levels (Pope & Vasquez, 2007).

In this chapter we cover many topics where psychology and the law intersect. We begin by examining some of the issues related to criminal and civil commitment. We then look at patients' rights, including various repercussions of the deinstitutionalization movement and ethical and legal issues associated with suicide. We conclude by examining the legal and ethical parameters of the therapist–client relationship and cultural competence in treatment.

Criminal Commitment

A basic premise of criminal law is that all of us are responsible beings who exercise free will and are capable of choices. If we do something wrong, we are responsible for our actions and should suffer the consequences. **Criminal commitment** is the incarceration of an individual for having committed a crime. Although the field of psychology accepts different perspectives on free will, criminal law does not. Criminal law does recognize, however, that some people lack the ability to assist in their own defense or to discern the ramifications of their actions because they are mentally disturbed. Although they may be technically guilty of a crime, their mental state at the time of the offense might exempt them from legal responsibility. Additionally, they might be mentally incapable of participating in criminal proceedings against them. Let us explore the landmark cases that have influenced how criminal law is applied to individuals who are seriously mentally ill. Standards arising from these cases and some other important guidelines are summarized in Figure 17.1.

Competency to Stand Trial

CASE STUDY On June 5, 2002, Brian David Mitchell kidnapped 14-year-old Elizabeth Smart at knifepoint from her Salt Lake City, Utah, home. The incident set off a massive search effort and evoked intense media coverage. Smart was rescued 9 months later after enduring a horrendous experience that included a forced polygamous "marriage," frequent rapes, and constant threats to her life. Mitchell, a former street preacher, was arrested for the crime, but claimed that God had commanded him to abduct Smart, to enter into a celestial marriage, and to form a religious society of younger females.

Despite his capture and arrest, Mitchell's trial did not begin until November 2010—almost 9 years later. The delays occurred because in three separate court hearings, Mitchell was judged "mentally incapable of assisting in his own defense." In the courtroom he sang hymns and screamed at the judge to "forsake those robes

Table 17.1 The Intersection of Psychology and the Law

The expertise of psychologists is often sought in the legal system. A few of these roles and activities are included here.

Psychological Evaluations in Child Protection Matters	Evaluation for Child Custody in Divorce Proceedings
• Attempt to determine whether abuse or neglect has occurred, whether a child is at risk for harm, and what corrective action, if any, should occur.	• Provide expertise to help courts and social services agencies determine the best interests of the child. • Offer opinions on child well-being, parenting plans, and termination of parental rights in custody cases.

Civil Commitment Determination	Protection of Client Rights
• Become involved in the civil commitment of an individual or the discharge of a person who has been so confined. • Determine whether the person is at risk of harm to the self or others, is too mentally disturbed to practice self-care, or lacks the appropriate resources for care if left alone.	• Become involved in seeing that clients are not grievously wronged by the loss of their civil liberties on the grounds of mental health treatment. • Advise on the right to receive treatment, to refuse treatment, and to live in the least restrictive environment.

Profiling of Criminals	Assessment of Dangerousness
• Work with law enforcement officials in developing profiles of serial killers, mass murderers, or other offenders.	• Assess potential for suicide and homicide, child endangerment, civil commitment, and so on.

Filing of Amicus Briefs	Jury Selection
• Use psychological science to help inform the court as to social science research that is relevant to pending litigation. • Act as a friend of the court by filing amicus briefs (pleadings) that have psychological implications in court cases.	• Aid attorneys in determining whether prospective jurors might favor one side of a case or the other. • Use psychological knowledge in an attempt to screen out individuals who might be biased against clients.

Determination of Sanity or Insanity	Testimony in Malpractice Suits
• At the request of a judge, prosecution, or defense, determine the sanity or insanity of someone accused of a crime. • Present findings via a private hearing to the judge or expert testimony in front of a jury.	• Testify in a civil suit on whether another therapist failed to follow the standards of the profession and is thus guilty of negligence or malpractice. • Determine whether the client bringing the suit incurred psychological harm or damage as a result of the clinician's actions.

Determination of Competency to Stand Trial	Determination of Repressed, Recovered, or False Memories
• Determine whether an individual is mentally competent or sufficiently rational to stand trial and to aid in his or her defense.	• Determine the accuracy and validity of repressed memories—claims by adults that they have recovered memories of childhood abuse.

© Cengage Learning®

and kneel in the dust." His behavior was so bizarre that he was banished from the courtroom several times. As a result, the judge ordered that Mitchell be hospitalized until he was capable of understanding the proceedings. Mitchell refused to participate in psychiatric treatment or to take antipsychotic medication. Finally, following a series of hearings and review of conflicting opinions from various experts who evaluated Mitchell, a federal judge ruled that Mitchell was competent to stand trial. At the trial, the jury rejected his insanity defense and found him guilty. On May 25, 2011, Mitchell was sentenced to life imprisonment without the possibility of parole.

Most court-appointed psychiatrists and psychologists who examined Mitchell declared him not competent to stand trial, although a few believed he was manipulating the system and feigning psychosis. The term **competency to stand trial** refers to a defendant's mental state at the time of psychiatric examination after arrest and

criminal commitment
incarceration of an individual for having committed a crime

competency to stand trial a judgment that a defendant has a factual and rational understanding of the criminal proceedings and can rationally consult with counsel in presenting a defense

**Criminal Commitment and
Mental State of Defendant**

The Insanity Defense

Plea: Innocent by reason of
insanity; refers to mental state at
time of the crime

Competency to Stand Trial

Refers to mental state at time of
psychiatric examination after arrest
and before trial

M'Naghten Rule

Does the person know right from
wrong?

American Law Institute Test

Can the person appreciate the
criminality of the act and conform
his/her behavior to the requirements of the law?

1. Factual understanding of
   proceedings?
2. Rational understanding of
   proceedings?
3. Able to consult with counsel in
   her or his defense?

Irresistible Impulse Test

Did the person lack the willpower
to control his/her actions?

Durham Test

Was the act a product of mental
disease or defect?

© Cengage Learning®

before trial. It has nothing to do with the issue of criminal responsibility, which refers to an individual's mental state or behavior at the time of the offense. Federal law states that an accused person cannot stand trial unless three criteria are satisfied (Fitch, 2007):

- The defendant must have a factual understanding of the proceedings.
- The defendant must have a rational understanding of the proceedings.
- The defendant must be able to rationally consult with counsel in presenting his or her own defense.

These criteria suggest that a defendant who is severely psychotic, for example, could not stand trial because a serious impairment exists. Determination of competency to stand trial is meant to ensure that a person understands the nature of the legal proceedings and is able to help in his or her own defense. The goal is to protect and preserve the civil rights of people who are mentally disturbed. But being judged incompetent to stand trial may have unfair negative consequences as well. A person may be held in custody for an extended period of time, denied the chance to post bail, and isolated from friends and family, all without having been found guilty of a crime.

Such a miscarriage of justice was the focus of a U.S. Supreme Court ruling in the 1972 case of *Jackson v. Indiana.* In that case, a man with mental retardation and brain damage, deaf and unable to speak, was charged with robbery. However, he was found incompetent to stand trial and was incarcerated indefinitely—which in his case probably meant for life, because of the severity and unchanging nature of his disabilities. In other words, it was unlikely that he would ever be judged competent to stand trial on the robbery charges, and thus faced the prospect of being incarcerated for life. His lawyers filed a petition to have him released on the basis of deprivation of **due process**—the legal checks and balances that are guaranteed to everyone, such as the right to receive a fair trial, the right to face one's accusers, the right to present evidence, the right to have counsel, and so on.

The U.S. Supreme Court ruled that a defendant cannot be confined indefinitely solely on the grounds of incompetency. After a reasonable time, a determination must be made as to whether the person is likely or unlikely to regain competency in the foreseeable future. If experts conclude that competency is unlikely, the institution must either release the individual or initiate civil commitment procedures. This is a significant ruling because many more people are committed to prison hospitals because of incompetency determinations than are acquitted on insanity pleas. It is estimated, for example, that approximately 40,000 people in the United States are evaluated each year for competency to stand trial, and as many as 75 percent are determined to be incompetent (Zapf & Roesch, 2006). The *Jackson v. Indiana* decision prompted federal competency hearings in the case of Brian David Mitchell because he could not be held indefinitely without a trial; additionally, prosecutors pushed for another hearing because they did not want the statute of limitations on the charges to expire.

Legal Precedents Regarding the Insanity Defense

The **insanity defense** is a legal argument used by defendants who admit they have committed a crime but plead not guilty because they were mentally disturbed at the time of the crime. The insanity plea recognizes that under specific circumstances, people may not be held accountable for their behavior. As we saw in the case of James Holmes and Brian David Mitchell, defense strategies sometimes involve such a contention—that the defendants are not guilty because they were insane (not of sound mind) at the time of the crime.

In the United States, a number of different standards have been used as legal tests of insanity. One of the earliest is the *M'Naghten* rule. In 1843, Daniel M'Naghten, a mentally disturbed woodcutter from Glasgow, Scotland, claimed that he was commanded by God to kill the English prime minister, Sir Robert Peel. He killed a lesser minister by mistake and was placed on trial, where it became obvious that M'Naghten was quite delusional. Out of this incident emerged the **M'Naghten rule**, popularly known as the "right–wrong" test, which holds that people can be acquitted of a crime if, at the time of the act, they (a) had such defective reasoning that they did not know what they were doing, or (b) were unable to comprehend that the act was wrong. The *M'Naghten* rule has been criticized for being a cognitive test (knowledge of right or wrong) that does not consider motivation or other factors. Further, it is often difficult to evaluate or determine a defendant's awareness or comprehension at the time of the crime.

The second major precedent associated with the insanity defense is the **irresistible impulse test**. In essence, this doctrine says that defendants are not criminally responsible if they lacked the willpower to control their behaviors. Combined with the *M'Naghten* rule, this test broadened the criteria for using the insanity defense. In other words, a not guilty by reason of insanity verdict could be obtained if a jury determined that the defendant did not understand that his or her actions were wrong *or* if the actions resulted from an irresistible impulse to commit the acts (Finnane, 2012). Criticisms of the irresistible impulse defense revolve around what constitutes an irresistible impulse. When, for example, is a person *unable* to exert control (irresistible impulse) rather than *choosing* not to exert control (unresisted impulse)? Is a man who rapes a woman unable to resist his impulses, or is he choosing not to exert control? Neither the mental health profession nor the legal profession has answered this question satisfactorily.

due process constitutional guarantee of fair treatment within the judicial system

insanity defense the legal argument used by defendants who admit that they have committed a crime but plead not guilty because they were mentally disturbed at the time of the offense

M'Naghten rule a cognitive test of legal insanity that inquires whether the accused knew right from wrong when the crime was committed

irresistible impulse test a doctrine that contends that a defendant is not criminally responsible if he or she lacked the willpower to control his or her behavior

Hawaii requires multiple independent evaluations when the insanity defense is employed. In examining 483 evaluating reports on 165 criminal defendants, unanimous agreement regarding insanity was reached in only 55 percent of the cases. Thus, clinicians who evaluated the same defendant for insanity often reached different conclusions. Can a jury trust the conclusions of forensic evaluators regarding insanity?

SOURCE: Gowensmith, Murrie, & Boccaccini, 2013

Legal understandings of the insanity plea were further expanded in the case of *Durham v. United States* (1954), when a U.S. Court of Appeals for the District of Columbia Circuit broadened the *M'Naghten* rule with the so-called "product test," or **Durham standard**. This standard maintains that an accused person should not be considered criminally responsible if his or her unlawful act was the *product* of a mental disease or defect. The intent of the ruling was to (a) give the greatest possible weight to expert evaluation and testimony and (b) allow mental health professionals to define mental illness.

The *Durham* standard also has its drawbacks. The term *product* is vague and difficult to define. Additionally, if the task of defining mental illness is left to mental health professionals, it becomes necessary to consider definitions of mental illness on a case-by-case basis. In many situations, relying on psychiatric testimony serves only to confuse the issues, because both the prosecution and defense bring in psychiatric experts, who often present conflicting opinions (Koocher & Keith-Spiegel, 2008). What we know from cases such as those of James Holmes and Brian David Mitchell is that expert testimony can vary significantly.

In 1962, the *American Law Institute Model Penal Code* provided guidelines to help jurors determine the validity of the insanity defense. The guidelines combine features from the previous standards (Sec. 401, p. 66):

1. A person is not responsible for criminal conduct if at the time of such conduct as a result of mental disease or defect he lacks substantial capacity either to appreciate the criminality of his conduct or to conform his conduct to the requirements of the law.

2. As used in the Article, the terms "mental disease or defect" do not include an abnormality manifested by repeated criminal or otherwise antisocial conduct.

This second point was included to eliminate the insanity defense option for the many criminals diagnosed with an antisocial personality disorder who make a clear decision to violate the law.

In some jurisdictions, the concept of **diminished capacity** has also been incorporated into the American Law Institute standard. *Diminished capacity* is the absence of a *specific intent* to commit the offense as a result of mental impairment. For example, a person under the influence of drugs or alcohol may commit a crime without premeditation or intent; a person who is grieving over the death of a loved one may harm the person responsible for the death. Although diminished capacity is primarily used to guide the sentencing and disposition of defendants, it is sometimes introduced in the trial phase with the hope that the defendant will be convicted of a lesser charge.

Such was the case in the trial of Dan White, a San Francisco supervisor who killed Mayor George Moscone and supervisor Harvey Milk on November 27, 1978. White blamed both individuals for his political demise. During the trial, his attorney used the now-famous "Twinkie defense" (White gorged himself on junk food such as Twinkies, chips, and soda) as a partial explanation for his client's actions. White's attorney attempted to convince the jury that the high sugar content of the junk food affected White's cognitive and emotional state and was partially to blame for his actions. White was convicted only of voluntary manslaughter and was sentenced to less than 8 years in jail. Of course, the citizens of San Francisco were outraged by the verdict and never forgave White. Facing constant public condemnation, he committed suicide after his release.

Insanity Defense Reform

Perhaps no trial has challenged the use of the insanity plea more than the case of John W. Hinckley, Jr., who attempted to assassinate President Ronald Reagan. The jury's verdict that he was not guilty by reason of insanity outraged the public, as well as legal and mental health professionals. Many were concerned that the

Durham standard a test of legal insanity also known as the *product test*—an accused person is not responsible if the unlawful act was the product of a mental disease or defect

diminished capacity law standard allowing defendant to be convicted of a lesser offense due to mental impairment

Public Outrage Over Acquittal Based on Insanity

John Hinckley, Jr. (center), was charged with the attempted murder of President Ronald Reagan. His acquittal by reason of insanity created a furor among the U.S. public over use of the insanity defense. The outrage led Congress to pass the Insanity Defense Reform Act.

criteria for the insanity defense were too broadly interpreted. For quite some time, the Hinckley case aroused such strong emotional reaction that calls for reforms were rampant.

As a result, Congress passed the Insanity Defense Reform Act of 1984, which based the definition of insanity totally on the individual's ability to understand what he or she did. In the wake of the Hinckley verdict, some states adopted alternative pleas, such as "culpable and mentally disabled," "mentally disabled, but neither culpable nor innocent," and "guilty, but mentally ill." These pleas are attempts to separate mental illness from insanity and to hold people responsible for their acts. Such pleas allow jurors to hold defendants responsible for their crimes while also ensuring that they receive treatment for their mental illnesses. Despite attempts at reform, however, states and municipalities continue to use different tests of insanity, with varying outcomes, and the use of the insanity plea remains controversial.

Contemporary Views on the Insanity Defense

The concept of "not guilty by reason of insanity" continues to provoke controversy among legal scholars, mental health practitioners, and the general public. Most defendants who use this defense have a long history of mental illness. James Holmes is an exception to this pattern. Another well-known exception is Andrea Yates, who, on June 30, 2001, waited for her husband to leave for work, filled the bathtub to the very top, and proceeded to drown her five children (ages 7 months to 7 years). After killing her children, she carried them to a bedroom, laid them out next to one another, and covered them with a sheet. She then contacted 911. Afterward, she called her husband and stated, "You need to come home. . . . It's time. I did it." When asked what she meant, Yates responded, "It's the children . . . all of them." When the police arrived, Yates calmly explained how she had killed her five young children.

The case of Andrea Yates shocked the nation. How could a mother possibly commit such an unthinkable act? Her actions were especially heinous because she

DID YOU KNOW?

A frequent misconception shared by both the public and the courts is that having a mental illness makes someone dangerous. Studies have indicated that the vast majority of people with mental disorders are neither violent nor dangerous, including those with psychosis. Risk is increased in those with substance abuse and a history of violence.

SOURCE: Elbogen & Johnson, 2009

murdered her five children in such a methodical manner. During Yates's trial, the prosecution asked for the death penalty, but the defense contended that because she was experiencing severe postpartum depression and postpartum psychosis, she was legally insane and should not be held accountable for her actions. The jury, however, found her guilty. An appeals court subsequently overturned the verdict. During the second trial, another Texas jury found her not guilty by reason of insanity; she has since been confined to a mental hospital. In Yates's case, she had experienced only one previous psychotic breakdown, following the birth of her fourth child.

Determination of guilt when someone who has an ongoing mental illness commits a serious crime can be especially complicated, as you will see in the following case.

CASE STUDY On February 12, 2008, 39-year-old David Tarloff used a meat cleaver to savagely attack and murder Kathryn Faughey, Ph.D., during an attempted robbery. The intended target of the theft was her colleague, Kent Shinbach, M.D., a 70-year-old psychiatrist. Seventeen years earlier, Dr. Shinbach had evaluated and recommended involuntary hospitalization for Tarloff—the first of Tarloff's many hospitalizations. Tarloff had not seen Shinbach for years, but he tracked down his office address after concluding that he "must be rich." Tarloff's plan was to demand $40,000 from Dr. Shinbach so that he could "rescue" his mother from a nursing home and move her to Hawaii where he could take care of her in a villa that he would rent with the stolen money.

When Tarloff finally entered the office suite, he unexpectedly encountered Dr. Faughey and brutally attacked and killed her. When Dr. Shinbach heard Faughey's screams and attempted to come to her aid, he was also viciously assaulted. Ignoring Dr. Shinbach's serious injuries, Tarloff demanded money. Dr. Shinbach testified in court that Tarloff abruptly left when the doctor asked him, "Haven't you done enough harm this evening? Why don't you just leave?" After the attack, Tarloff reportedly threw his bloody clothes away and bought a change of clothing. A few days later, after his arrest, he said he was sorry for killing "that woman" but did not express concern about the serious injuries sustained by Dr. Shinbach; instead, he told detectives that the doctor was "a liar."

During various court appearances, Mr. Tarloff rocked back and forth and appeared to be disoriented. According to his attorneys, Tarloff claimed that he had seen God's eye in tables and floors and that God had approved of his plan to demand money from the psychiatrist. The lawyers explained that Tarloff had been a "normal," well-liked high school student but that he had changed drastically after his first semester of college at Syracuse University. Soon afterward, he was diagnosed with schizophrenia. On numerous occasions over the next 20 years, he was involuntarily hospitalized due to the severity of his mental illness (McKinley, 2014).

Tarloff's attorneys argued that the jury should find him "not guilty by reason of mental disease or defect." His defense attorney called the case "an insane plan by an insane man who was legally insane when it happened." Jury members needed to decide if Tarloff knew right from wrong during his attack. Did his delusions diminish his capacity to understand that his behavior was unlawful?

It took three separate trials before a jury was able to reach a verdict. The first trial, which began in the fall of 2008, was delayed when Tarloff adamantly refused to leave his cell during jury selection. This behavior raised questions about Tarloff's competency to stand trial and led the judge to request that Tarloff receive a mental health evaluation. Based on assessment by two psychiatrists, the judge concluded that Tarloff was not competent to stand trial and ordered him to remain in a secure psychiatric facility until competency was established. Almost 2 years later, it was determined that Tarloff's mental condition had sufficiently stabilized to allow him to understand the proceedings and to assist in his own defense. During the second trial, after 10 days of heated deliberation, the judge conceded that the jury was hopelessly deadlocked; some of the jurors were unable to agree to a guilty verdict, explaining that Tarloff's mental illness clouded his ability to determine right from wrong.

A verdict was finally reached during the third trial. On March 28, 2014, after deliberating for 7 hours, the jurors found Tarloff guilty on all counts, including murder. Some jurors explained that although they recognize that Tarloff has a severe mental illness, they believe that he knew that what he did was wrong. One juror explained: "I believe he's sick to a certain degree but not sick enough to not know right from wrong." Another stated that she had no choice but to find him guilty because of the narrow criteria associated with the insanity defense and voiced her opinion that another choice should have been available to allow him to receive the mental health treatment he needs, "a box for an obviously mentally ill person who knows right from wrong" (McKinley, 2014). The delays in the Tarloff case were due to the severity of his mental illness and the complexities of the case rather than any deliberate attempt to manipulate or exploit the legal system. However, as we saw with the Mitchell case, deliberate delays sometimes occur.

Further, some defendants attempt to feign insanity; fortunately, those who fake are seldom successful. Confessed Hillside Strangler Kenneth Bianchi, for example, attempted to fake mental illness as mitigation for his part in raping, torturing, and murdering a number of girls and young women in the late 1970s. Wanting to use the insanity plea to get a reduced sentence, Bianchi tried to convince psychiatrists that he suffered from dissociative identity disorder. Psychologist and hypnosis expert Dr. Martin Orne exposed his scheme as a fake. The jury concluded that Bianchi was guilty of murder and sentenced him to life in prison without parole.

James Keivom/NY Daily News Archive/Getty Images

Not Guilty by Reason of Mental Disease or Defect?

David Tarloff, who has a longstanding history of schizophrenia, savagely murdered a psychologist and brutally attacked a 70-year-old psychiatrist. Here we see Tarloff soon after his arrest. Although his defense attorney argued that he was insane at the time of the murders, on March 28, 2014, a jury found Tarloff guilty on all charges, including murder.

Popular media has also exploited the fear that a guilty individual might use incompetency to stand trial or an insanity plea to escape criminal responsibility. For example, in the Hollywood film *Primal Fear*, Richard Gere plays a high-powered attorney who is duped into believing that his client has dissociative identity disorder. The client is found not guilty by reason of insanity at the trial, only to have Gere's character discover the ghastly truth: His client convincingly faked his insanity.

In reality, less than 1 percent of defendants use an insanity defense and, even then, in only a small percentage of cases is the defense successful (Kois, Pearson, Chauhan, Goni, & Saraydarian, 2013). Many of the cases discussed in this chapter are the exceptions to the rule; however, they are presented to help illustrate the ways in which psychopathology and the law intersect. These cases

MYTH The insanity defense is often used because defendants who are found not guilty by reason of insanity spend less time in custody (jail, mental health institution, or prison) than those who are convicted.

REALITY As a rule, defendants found not guilty by reason of insanity spend as much if not more time in custody than those who are convicted. They often face a lifetime of judicial oversight even after their release. Further, the plea is infrequently used and seldom successful.

Each state has its own statute that defines civil incompetency or incapacity. Thus, practicing mental health professionals need to be acutely aware of how the states in which they practice define these concepts.

SOURCE: Demakis, 2013

also received significant media attention and helped construct popular opinion about the insanity defense.

In the limited cases where the insanity defense is successfully employed, the defendants usually have past hospitalizations; delusions or paranoia; a previous diagnosis of a serious mental illness such as bipolar disorder or schizophrenia; and few victims were involved. When children or a large number of victims are affected by the crime, the chances for a successful insanity defense diminish dramatically (Conner, 2006). The number of individuals killed and injured by James Holmes in the Aurora shootings may explain why the prosecutors refused to accept a guilty plea in exchange for allowing him to avoid the death penalty (Elliott & Banda, 2013).

Civil Commitment

CASE STUDY She was known only as BL ("Bag Lady") in the area of downtown Oakland, California. By night, she slept on any number of park benches and in storefronts. By day, she could be seen pushing her Safeway shopping cart full of boxes, extra clothing, and garbage, which she collected from numerous trash containers. According to her sister, the woman had lived this way for nearly 10 years, without complaint from local merchants.

Over the previous 6 months, however, BL's behavior had become progressively more intolerable. She had always talked to herself, but recently she had begun shouting and screaming at anyone who approached her. Her use of profanity was graphic, and it was rumored that she urinated in front of local stores. Although she never physically assaulted anyone, her menacing behavior frightened many pedestrians, customers, and shopkeepers. Local law enforcement officials occasionally detained her for short periods, but she always returned to her familiar haunts. Finally, her sister and several merchants requested that the city take action to commit her to a mental institution.

Action is required when people who are severely disturbed behave in a manner that poses a threat to themselves or others. The government has *parens patriae* ("father of the country" or "power of the state") authority, which is the power to commit disturbed individuals for their own best interest. **Civil commitment** is the name of this action; it is the involuntary confinement of individuals judged to be a danger to themselves or others, even though they have not committed a crime. Thus, the commitment of a person in acute distress is purportedly a form of protective confinement and demonstration of concern for the psychological and physical well-being of that person or others. Civil commitment often involves situation such as potential suicide, threatened violence, destruction of property, or a loss of impulse control. Factors relevant to civil commitment are outlined in Figure 17.2.

It is best when civil commitment can be avoided because it has many potentially negative consequences. It may cause major interruption in the person's life, loss of self-esteem, and dependency on others. A possible loss or restriction of civil liberties is another consequence—a point that becomes even more glaring when we consider that the person has actually committed no crime other than making threats, being a nuisance, or assailing people's sensibilities. In the case study, for example, BL had committed no criminal offense, although she had violated many social norms. But at what point do we confine people simply because they display socially inappropriate behavior or fail to conform to our standards of decency?

civil commitment the involuntary confinement of a person judged to be a danger to the self or to others, even though the person has not committed a crime

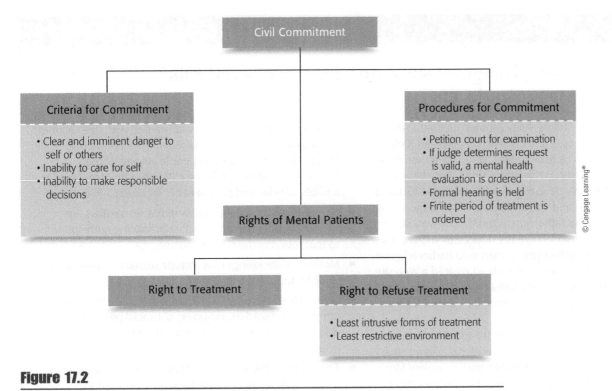

Figure 17.2

Factors in the Civil Commitment of a Nonconsenting Person

Criteria for Commitment

States vary in the criteria used to commit a person, but there are certain general standards. It is not enough that a person is mentally ill; one or more of these additional conditions must exist before involuntary hospitalization is considered (Corey, Callanan, & Corey, 2010).

- *Individuals present a clear and imminent danger to themselves or others.* An example is someone who is displaying suicidal or unsafe behavior (such as walking out on a busy freeway) that places the individual in immediate danger. Threats to harm someone else or behavior viewed as assaultive or destructive are also grounds for commitment.

- *Individuals are unable to care for themselves or do not have the social network to provide for such care.* Most civil commitments are based primarily on this criterion. The details vary, but states generally specify an inability to provide sufficient forms of food (the person is malnourished, food is unavailable, and the person has no feasible plan to obtain it), clothing (attire is not appropriate for the climate, and the person has no plans for obtaining other attire), or shelter (the person has no permanent residence, insufficient protection from climatic conditions, and no logical plans for obtaining adequate housing).

- *Individuals are unable to make responsible decisions about appropriate treatments and hospitalization.* This involves an inability to follow through with needed treatment. As a result, the person's well-being is jeopardized and there is a strong chance of further deterioration in functioning.

- *Individuals are in an unmanageable state of fright or panic.* Such people may behave impulsively or feel that they are on the brink of losing control of their behavior.

DID YOU KNOW?

On April 16, 2007, college student Seung-Hui Cho used two semiautomatic handguns on the Virginia Tech campus to kill 27 students and 5 faculty members before committing suicide with a shot to his head. It was the deadliest mass shooting in modern U.S. history. Although predicting dangerousness is difficult, there was considerable evidence to indicate that Cho was potentially dangerous: (a) He was involved in three stalking incidents on the campus; (b) professors reported that he was menacing and his writings were often intimidating, obscene, and violent; and (c) a mental health professional believed he was a danger to others. Why, then, was Cho not committed—and allowed to purchase firearms? Most likely because a person is innocent until proven guilty and because confinement in the absence of a criminal act violates a person's civil rights.

Predicting Dangerousness and Profiling Serial Killers and Mass Murderers

Seung-Hui Cho (the Virginia Tech shooter), Jeffrey Dahmer (killer of 17 men and boys), and Eric Harris and Dylan Klebold (the Columbine High School killers) were all either serial killers or mass murderers. Were there signs that these individuals were potentially dangerous? Jeffrey Dahmer tortured animals as a small boy and was arrested in 1988 for molesting a child. Even though his father suspected that he was dangerous, Dahmer was released. There is evidence to suggest that Cho was a deeply disturbed young man who harbored great resentment and anger. Harris and Klebold created a Web site that seemed to foretell their proclivity toward violence. In all three situations, potentially dangerous thoughts and behaviors appeared to be ignored.

Lest we be too harsh on psychologists and law enforcement officials, it is important to realize that few serial killers or mass murderers willingly share their deviant sexual or violent fantasies. Furthermore, it is difficult to predict and intervene due to:

1. the lack of one-to-one correspondence between danger signs and possible violence,

2. an increasing awareness that violent behavior often results from many variables, and

3. the recognition that incarceration—both criminal and civil—cannot occur on the basis of potential danger alone.

Nevertheless, tragic experiences with mass murderers and serial killers have led mental health practitioners and law enforcement officials to create profiles to help predict dangerous acts. Let's consider the profile developed to help identify serial killers.

Profile of Serial Killers

Although there is much conjecture in the public regarding serial killers, much of it is inaccurate. The Behavioral Analysis Unit of the FBI published a document about serial killers and shared the following conclusions (FBI, 2008):

■ Most serial killers are not social misfits or noticeably strange. Robert Yates, who killed 17 women in the

Spokane, Washington, area, was married with five children and was a decorated National Guard helicopter pilot. Dennis Rader, who killed 10 people around Wichita, Kansas, was married with two children, a boy scout leader, a public official, and president of his church.

■ Although it is popularly believed that serial killers are primarily white men, their racial distribution corresponds to that found in the U.S. population.

■ Motivation for killings may include sexual fantasies, anger, thrill, financial gain, or attention.

■ Serial killers are rarely insane, although they often have personality disorders, including antisocial personality disorder. Their intelligence ranges from below to above average.

■ There is no single factor that causes someone to become a serial killer; it appears that biological, social, and psychological factors combine in unique ways to produce homicidal behaviors.

■ Neglect and abuse in childhood, substance abuse, eroticizing violence, and personality disorders are common in serial killers.

The American Psychological Association also supports the conclusion that it is difficult to profile serial killers or mass murderers. With respect to perpetrators of mass shootings, it concludes: "In making predictions about the risk for mass shootings, there is no consistent psychological profile or set of warning signs that can be used reliably to identify such individuals in the general population." (Cornell & Guerra, 2013).

For Further Consideration

1. Should we be doing more to develop profiles of mass murderers or serial killers?

2. How can we learn more about these individuals?

3. Is there a risk that inaccurate profiles may harm criminal investigations?

In the past, commitments could be obtained solely on the basis of mental illness and a person's need for treatment, which was often determined arbitrarily. Increasingly, the courts have narrowed the focus of civil commitment procedures and now concentrate primarily on whether people present a danger to themselves or others. How is this potential danger determined? Many people would not consider BL a danger to herself or others. Some, however, might believe that she *could* become assaultive to others or injurious to herself. Are trained mental health professionals able to accurately make such predictions? Let's turn to that question.

Assessing Dangerousness

Mental health professionals have difficulty predicting whether someone, even a person they know well such as a client, will commit dangerous acts. The fact that civil commitments are often based on a determination of **dangerousness**—the person's potential for doing harm to the self or others—makes use of this criterion problematic, particularly when the evaluation is based on a single interview by a mental health professional. The difficulty in predicting potential dangerousness involves four key factors:

1. *The rarer something is, the more difficult it is to predict.* As a group, people with mental illness are not dangerous. Although some evidence suggests that individuals with severe psychotic disorders may have slightly higher rates of violent behavior (Elbogen & Johnson, 2009), the risk is not considered a major concern.

2. *Violence is as much a function of the context in which it occurs as of the person's characteristics.* Although it is theoretically possible for a psychologist to accurately assess an individual's personality, we have little idea about the situations in which people find themselves. A meek and mild person, for example, may display uncontrollable rage when confronted with the tragic death of a loved one.

3. *The best predictor of dangerousness is often past criminal conduct or a history of violence or aggression.* Such a record, however, may be ruled irrelevant or inadmissible by mental health commissions and the courts.

4. *The definition of dangerousness is itself unclear.* Most of us would agree that murder, rape, torture, and physical assaults are dangerous. But are we confining our definition to physical harm only? What about psychological abuse or destruction of property?

When to Intervene?

Aaron Alexis here in a surveillance photo, experienced deteriorating mental health in the months preceding the tragic Navy Yard shootings. On one occasion, he called police to report that three people were following him and talking to him through the walls, ceiling, and floors of his hotel room. However, there was no evidence that he was a danger to himself or others.

Procedures in Civil Commitment

Once someone believes that a person is a threat to himself or herself or to others, civil commitment procedures may be initiated. The rationale for requests for civil commitment is that involuntary confinement will (a) prevent harm to the person or to others, (b) provide appropriate treatment and care, and (c) ensure due process of law (that is, a legal hearing). In many cases, people deemed in need of protective confinement agree to *voluntary commitment* to a period of hospitalization. This process is fairly straightforward, and many believe that it is the preferred avenue for ensuring a positive treatment outcome. *Involuntary commitment* proceedings occur only when the person does not consent to hospitalization.

Involuntary commitment can be a temporary emergency action or may involve a longer period of detention that is determined at a formal hearing. Although states vary in their processes and standards, all recognize that cases arise in which a person is so severely disturbed that immediate detention is required (Demakis, 2013). Thus, states recognize that in-depth hearings take a long time and that delaying commitment might prove adverse to the person or to other individuals.

Formal civil commitment usually follows a similar process, regardless of the state in which it occurs. First, a concerned person, such as a family member, therapist, or family physician, petitions the court for an examination of the person. If the judge believes there is reasonable cause for this action, he or she orders a mental health evaluation. Second, the judge appoints two professionals with no connection to each other to examine the person. In most cases, the examiners are physicians or mental health professionals. Third, a formal hearing is held in which the examiners testify to the person's mental state and any potential dangers. Others, such as family members, friends, or therapists, may also testify. The person is allowed to speak on his or her own behalf and is represented by counsel. Fourth, if it is determined that the person must enter treatment, a finite period may be specified; periods of 6 months to 1 year are common. Some states, however, allow indefinite commitment subject to periodic review and assessment.

dangerousness a person's potential for doing harm to the self or to others

Protection against Involuntary Commitment

Due process procedures are important to ensure that involuntary commitment does not violate a person's civil rights. Some have even argued that criminals are accorded more rights than people who are mentally ill. For example, people accused of a crime are considered innocent until proven guilty in a court of law. Usually, they have the opportunity to post bail and are incarcerated only after a jury trial, and only if a crime has been committed (not if there is only a possibility or even high probability of crime). Yet people who are mentally ill may be confined without a jury trial and without having committed a crime; commitment can occur based on a judgment that they *might* do harm to themselves or others.

In other words, the criminal justice system will not incarcerate people because they *might* harm someone (they must already have done it), but civil commitment is based on possible future harm. It can be argued that in the former case, confinement is punishment, whereas in the latter case it is treatment (for the individual's benefit). Some professionals claim that people who are mentally ill are incapable of determining their own treatment needs, and that, once treated, they will be grateful for the treatment they received. If people resist hospitalization, they are purportedly irrational, which is deemed a symptom of their mental disorder.

Critics do not accept this reasoning. They point out that civil commitment is for the benefit of those initiating commitment procedures (society) and not for the individual. These concerns have prompted and heightened sensitivity toward patient welfare and rights, resulting in a trend toward restricting the powers of the state over the individual.

A Tragic Case of Failure to Predict Dangerousness

Convicted serial killer Jeffrey Dahmer killed at least 17 men and boys over a period of many years. Besides torturing many of his victims, Dahmer admitted to dismembering and devouring their bodies. Although previously convicted of sexual molestation, no one predicted that he was capable of murder. Unsuccessful in his attempt to use the insanity plea, Dahmer was found guilty in 1994 and imprisoned. Another inmate subsequently killed him.

Rights of Mental Patients

Many people in the United States are concerned about the balance of power between the state, our mental institutions, and our citizens. The U.S. Constitution guarantees certain rights such as trial by jury, legal representation, and protection against self-incrimination. The mental health profession has great power, which may be used wittingly or unwittingly to abridge individual freedom. In recent decades, some courts have ruled that commitment for any purpose constitutes a major deprivation of liberty that requires due process protection.

Until 1979, the level of proof required for civil commitments varied from state to state. In a case that set a legal precedent, a Texas man claimed that he was denied due process because the jury that committed him was instructed to use a lower standard than "beyond a reasonable doubt" (a high degree of certainty). The appellate court agreed with the man, but when the case finally reached the Supreme Court in April 1979 (*Addington v. Texas*), the Court ruled that the state must provide only "clear and convincing evidence" (a medium degree of certainty) that a person is mentally ill and potentially dangerous before that person can be committed. Although these standards for confinement are higher than those advocated by most mental health organizations, this ruling represented the first time that the Supreme Court considered any aspect of the civil commitment process.

In 1975 a U.S. district court issued a landmark decision in the case of *Dixon v. Weinberger*. The ruling established the right of individuals to be treated in the **least restrictive environment** possible. This means that people have a right to the least restrictive alternative to freedom that is appropriate to their condition. Only individuals who cannot adequately care for themselves are committed to hospitals. Those who can function acceptably should be given alternative choices, such as halfway houses and other shelters.

Right to Treatment

least restrictive environment the least restrictive alternative to freedom that is appropriate to a person's condition

One of the primary justifications for commitment is that treatment improves a person's mental condition and increases the likelihood that he or she will be able to return

"Doc, I Murdered Someone": Client Disclosures of Violence to Therapists

Basic to a therapeutic relationship is the belief that whatever a client discloses is kept private. However, confidentiality and privilege is not absolute. Most of these exemptions are mandated by law and include abuse or neglect of minors or "vulnerable" adults (Fisher, 2009). The *Tarasoff* ruling also makes it clear that when clients disclose a potential to harm identifiable third parties, therapists have a legal obligation to take actions to ward off the danger. The duty-to-warn principle applies to *future threats of harm*. But what are the legal obligations of therapists who hear from clients that they have committed a *past crime*? What if clients disclose they have assaulted, raped, or even killed someone?

These questions deal with not only legal issues, but moral and ethical ones as well. It may be shocking to many students to know that the law is not clear on this matter. The prevailing consensus is that mental health professionals are not legally required to breach confidentiality when clients inform them that they have committed past crimes (Handelsman et al., 2001).

But how often do therapists hear confessions from their clients about past criminal conduct? The answer is that such confessions do occur. In one survey, many therapists reported occasions when clients mentioned that they had committed violent crimes and were never caught (Walfish,

Barnett, Marlyere, & Zielke, 2010). Out of a sample of 162 doctoral-level psychologists, the percentage of therapists who had heard about various past crimes included the following:

- Confessions of murder: 13 percent
- Sexual assaults/rape: 33 percent
- Physical assaults: 69 percent

In therapy, clients are likely to reveal very intimate secrets about their past feelings, thoughts, and actions. In all likelihood, something shocking, distasteful, or even frightening will be disclosed. Thus, therapists need to be prepared to respond in an appropriate manner, carefully weighing any legal, moral, and therapeutic issues associated with the situation.

For Further Consideration

1. Do you believe that therapists should be required to report a past crime such as murder?

2. Can the *Tarasoff* ruling be interpreted to allow therapists latitude in reporting past crimes? How?

3. If you were the therapist and heard a murder confession, how do you think it would affect you and the therapeutic relationship?

to the community. Is it not deprivation of due process if we confine a person involuntarily and do not provide therapy—the means for release from the institutional setting? Several cases have raised this problem as a constitutional issue. Together, they have determined that mental patients who have been involuntarily committed have a **right to treatment**—a right to receive therapy that would improve their condition.

In 1966, in a lawsuit brought against St. Elizabeth's Hospital in Washington, DC (*Rouse v. Cameron*), the DC Circuit Court held that (a) the right to treatment is a constitutional right, and (b) failure to provide treatment cannot be justified by lack of resources. In the Alabama federal case of *Wyatt v. Stickney* (1972), Judge Frank Johnson specified standards of adequate treatment, such as staff–patient ratios, therapeutic environmental conditions, and professional consensus about appropriate treatment. The court also made it clear that mental patients cannot be forced to work or to engage in work-related activities aimed at maintaining the institution in which they lived. Thus the previously common practice of having patients scrub floors, wash laundry, and cook or serve food was declared unconstitutional. Moreover, patients who volunteer to perform tasks must be paid at least the minimum wage to do them instead of merely receiving token allowances or special privileges. This landmark decision ensured treatment beyond custodial care and protection against neglect and abuse.

Another important case (tried in a U.S. District Court in Florida and affirmed by the U.S. Supreme Court that same year), *O'Connor v. Donaldson* (1975) has also had a major impact on the right to treatment issue. It involved Kenneth Donaldson, who at age 49 was committed for a period of 20 years to the Florida State Hospital

right to treatment the concept that mental patients who have been involuntarily committed have a right to receive therapy for their condition

in Chattahoochee on petition by his father. He was found to be mentally ill, unable to care for himself, easily manipulated, and dangerous. Throughout his confinement, Donaldson petitioned for release, but Dr. O'Connor, the hospital superintendent, determined that Donaldson was "too mentally ill." Finally, Donaldson threatened a lawsuit and was reluctantly discharged by the hospital after 14 years of confinement. He then sued both O'Connor and the hospital, winning an award of $20,000. The monetary award is insignificant compared with the significance of the ruling. Again, the U.S. Supreme Court reaffirmed a patient's right to treatment. It ruled that Donaldson did not receive appropriate treatment and said that the state cannot constitutionally confine nondangerous citizens who are capable of caring for themselves outside of an institution or who have friends or family willing to help them. Further, the court ruled that physicians, as well as institutions, are liable for improper confinements.

One major dilemma in all cases of court-ordered treatment is determining what constitutes treatment. Treatment can range from rest and relaxation to psychosurgery, medication, and aversion therapy. Mental health professionals believe that they are in the best position to make treatment recommendations and evaluate treatment outcome, a position supported by the case of *Youngberg v. Romeo* (1982). The court ruled that Nicholas Romeo, a boy with mental retardation, had a constitutional right to "reasonable care and safety," and it deferred judgment to the mental health professional as to what constitutes appropriate therapy.

Right to Refuse Treatment

The right to refuse treatment is a complicated issue. As you may recall, Brian David Mitchell, the man who kidnapped Elizabeth Smart, was declared mentally incompetent to stand trial, yet for 8 years he steadfastly refused to take antipsychotic medication; this placed him in a position of being indefinitely unable to participate in a trial involving the multiple charges he faced. His attorneys supported his right to refuse treatment and fought government officials on this point. It was only after a federal judge became convinced that Mitchell was manipulating the system that Mitchell was judged competent to stand trial, allowing the trial to proceed. Although it may be easy for us to surmise the reasons that Mitchell's attorneys supported his refusal of treatment, does it make sense for others? Medical patients frequently refuse medical treatment on religious grounds or because the treatment would only prolong a terminal illness. But should mental patients have a right to refuse treatment?

Proponents of the right to refuse treatment argue that many forms of treatment, such as medication or electroconvulsive therapy, may have long-term side effects, as discussed in previous chapters. They also point out that involuntary treatment is generally much less effective than treatment that is accepted voluntarily. People forced into treatment seem to resist it, thereby nullifying the potentially beneficial effects.

The issue of the right to refuse treatment has been addressed by the courts. The case of *Rennie v. Klein* (1978) involved several state hospitals in New Jersey that had a policy of forcibly medicating patients in nonemergency situations. The court ruled that people have a constitutional right to refuse treatment (psychotropic medication) and to have an opportunity for a due process hearing if professionals believe forced treatment is essential to a patient's well-being. In another related case, *Rogers v. Okin* (1979), a Massachusetts court supported these guidelines. Both cases made the point that psychotropic medication was often used to control behavior or as a substitute for treatment. Further, the decisions noted that drugs might actually inhibit recovery.

Courts have usually supported the right to refuse treatment, under certain conditions, and have extended the principle of the least restrictive alternative to include the least intrusive forms of treatment. Generally, psychotherapy is considered less intrusive than somatic or physical therapies (e.g., electroconvulsive therapy and medication). Although this compromise may appear reasonable, other problems present themselves. First, how do we define intrusive treatment? Second, if patients are allowed to refuse certain forms of treatment and if the hospital does not have alternatives for them, can they sue the institution? These questions remain unanswered.

The right to refuse treatment occasionally poses ironies. For example, a U.S. Supreme Court ruling (*Ford v. Wainwright*, 1986) concluded that the government cannot execute someone who is incompetent. Why would someone agree to take medication only to be executed? Some courts have ordered prisoners to take medication based on the assumption that doing so will improve their mental condition. In June 2003, however, the U.S. Supreme Court (*Sell v. United States*) placed strict limits on the ability of the government to forcibly medicate defendants who are mentally ill to make them competent to stand trial. Such actions must, according to the court ruling, be in the "best interest of the defendant."

In restoring competency, alternative reasons for treatment should be considered such as reducing danger to the self or others. If these do not exist the government can seek involuntary treatment only under "limited circumstances." That is, the treatment must be medically appropriate, have no competency-impairing side effects, and be the least intrusive means available. In most cases, defendants who are found incompetent to stand trial appear to willingly accept treatments (Landis, 2012). In one study, over three quarters of those with severe mental illnesses who were found to be incompetent to stand trial were restored to competency after being involuntarily medicated (Herbel & Stelmach, 2007).

Deinstitutionalization

Governmental trends such as the move toward deinstitutionalization can also influence access to treatment, especially for those with severe mental illness. **Deinstitutionalization** is the shifting of responsibility for the care of those who are severely mentally ill from large central institutions to agencies within local communities. When originally formulated in the 1960s and 1970s, the concept excited many mental health professionals. Since its inception, the mental hospital population of patients has dropped 75 percent, the number of state-run mental hospitals has declined dramatically, and there has been a 75 percent decrease in the average daily number of committed patients (J. L. Geller, 2006; Lamb & Weinberger, 2005). The impetus behind deinstitutionalization came from several quarters.

First, there was (and still is) a feeling that large hospitals mainly provide custodial care, that they produce little benefit, and that they may even impede improvement. Court cases discussed earlier (*Wyatt v. Stickney* and *O'Connor v. Donaldson*) exposed the fact that many mental hospitals do little more than warehouse patients. Institutionalization can also foster dependency, promote helplessness, and lower self-sufficiency. The longer people are hospitalized, the more likely they are to remain hospitalized or to be readmitted once released.

Second, beginning in the 1970s, the issue of patient rights began to receive increased attention. Mental health professionals became very concerned about keeping people confined against their will and began to discharge patients soon after their competencies increased. It was believed that **mainstreaming**—integrating people with mental illness back into the community—could be accomplished by providing local outpatient or transition services such as group homes, board-and-care facilities, or halfway houses. In addition, advances in psychopharmacology made it more likely that patients' symptoms would be manageable once they were discharged.

Third, state hospitals were often overcrowded and inadequately staffed due to insufficient funding. Given these overcrowded conditions, mental health administrators viewed the deinstitutionalization movement favorably and supported the rapid release of patients back into communities. State legislative branches encouraged the trend, especially because it reduced the cost of staffing and maintaining large facilities.

What has been the impact of deinstitutionalization on people with mental illness? Critics believe that deinstitutionalization policies have allowed states to relinquish their responsibility to care for people who are unable to care for themselves. There are

deinstitutionalization the shifting of responsibility for the care of mental patients from large central institutions to agencies within local communities

mainstreaming integrating mental patients back into the community

alarming indications that deinstitutionalization has been responsible for placing or "dumping" on the streets many former patients who should have remained institutionalized (Rosenberg & Rosenberg, 2006). Critics believe that people such as the "bag lady" (BL) discussed earlier highlight the human cost and tragedy of deinstitutionalization policies. Many of the mentally ill who live on the streets are severely disabled and have difficulty coping with daily living. Thousands of mentally ill individuals are now homeless, and many of the existing community programs are woefully fragmented and inadequate in delivering needed services. Unfortunately, it is likely that the plight of the severely mentally ill will continue to worsen due to economic pressures facing local governments. For example, between 2009 and 2012, states cut $4.35 billion of public mental health funding from their budgets (Pan, 2013).

The personal toll of inadequate mental health services is immense, as can be seen in the following case.

CASE STUDY   Walter is a 54-year-old DC resident with schizophrenia ... Living on the streets with a mental disorder can often be a hellish experience. Walter describes days filled with long walks and prayer ... "I prayed a lot. I didn't really know what I was going through. I wasn't eating properly. All I know is that prayer kept me going." He usually avoided homeless shelters, apprehensive of the type of people that frequented them. Those fears proved to be sadly justified. Around Walter's 45th birthday, a group of men at a shelter he went to sneaked in alcohol, got drunk, and beat Walter so badly that they broke his jaw (Mukherjee, 2013).

It is becoming apparent that many people with severe mental illness are not receiving treatment. Stories such as Walter's are all too common in communities throughout the United States. Many live on the streets under harsh conditions where they are prone to violent victimization. Others live in nursing homes, board-and-care homes, or group residences. The quality of care in many of these places is marginal, resulting in deterioration in functioning or periodic hospitalization.

Many of the problems that have occurred since the deinstitutionalization movement appear to result from inadequate community resources for meeting the needs of people with chronic mental illness. Many patients released from institutions lacked family or friends who could help them make the transition back into the community; many discharged patients had difficulty finding jobs; many could only find substandard housing; many were inadequately monitored and received no psychiatric treatment; and many become homeless.

It is difficult to estimate how many discharged mental patients joined the ranks of the homeless. We do know that homelessness in the United States, especially in large urban areas, is increasing at an alarming pace. Certainly, it is not difficult to see the number of people who live in transport terminals, parks, flophouses, homeless shelters, cars, and storefronts. It is hard to determine exactly how many of these people are in need of mental health services. However, it is estimated that 30 to 70 percent of the U.S. adults who are homeless have a mental disorder (Hoffman, 2013).

We know that homelessness is associated with poor psychological adjustment and higher arrests and conviction records. The number of individuals who are mentally ill among inmates incarcerated in local, state, and federal prisons more than quadrupled from 1998 to 2006 and has increased operational costs by an additional 50 percent in some county jails. Ironically, spending $2,000 to $3,000 annually to treat individuals who are mentally ill could result in savings of $50,000 for each mentally ill person who is unnecessarily incarcerated (Pan, 2013). The solution, however, is complex, and requires much more than a return to the old institutions of the 1950s. Instead, what we need is easily accessible community-based treatment facilities and outpatient resources geared to meet the comprehensive treatment needs of those with severe mental illness. For patients involved in alternative community programs, the picture is more positive.

The Downside of Deinstitutionalization

Homelessness has become a significant social problem, especially in cities. Many believe that deinstitutionalization contributed to this problem, although it is not clear what proportion of people who are now homeless people previously resided in mental institutions. Unfortunately, scenes such as this one are becoming all too common in large urban areas.

Studies have concluded that programs providing permanent housing, specialized care, and community treatment can reduce homelessness and improve well-being (G. Nelson, Aubry, & Lawrence, 2007).

Moral, Ethical, and Legal Issues Surrounding Suicide

CASE STUDY   In September 2003, after the release of his book *I Ask the Right to Die*, 21-year-old Vincent Humbert's mother administered an overdose of sedatives into his intravenous line, causing his death (C. S. Smith, 2003). Hubert, a French citizen, had serious physical injuries resulting from a traffic accident. He regained consciousness after 9 months in a coma, and was able to hear, think, and reason; however, his only means of communication was with his thumb. With that one thumb, he pointed to letters of the alphabet and wrote a special appeal to French president Jacques Chirac asking for the right to die. His case, and the arrest of his mother for assisting with his death, set off an international debate about the morality and legality of euthanasia.

Ironically, medical science has added fuel to the right-to-die movement. Along with medical technology that extends life comes the reality that we are increasingly lengthening the process of dying. This prolongation has caused many people, especially those who are elderly or terminally ill, to fear being kept alive by artificial means, with no thought to their desires or dignity. Humane and sensitive physicians who believe that the resulting quality of life does not merit heroic measures but whose training impels them to sustain life are caught in the middle of this conflict. In many states, they may face a civil or criminal lawsuit if they agree to allow a patient to die, particularly if the person has no **advance directive** regarding the use of resuscitation or machinery to prolong life.

advance directive   written statement providing guidance for medical and health care decisions in the event the person becomes incapacitated and unable communicate his or her wishes

This brings us to the question: Do people have the right to commit suicide? The act of suicide seems to violate what many of us believe regarding the sanctity of life. Many segments of the population consider suicide immoral. Suicide is both a sin in the canonical law of the Catholic Church and an illegal act according to the secular laws of most countries. Within the United States, many states have laws against suicide. Of course, such laws are difficult to enforce, because the victims are not around to prosecute. Many are beginning to question the legitimacy of such sanctions, however, and are openly advocating a person's right to suicide. In November 1998, Oregon voters passed a physician-assisted suicide act granting physicians the legal right to help end the lives of terminally ill patients. Voters in two other states, Washington and Vermont, have since passed similar legislation. This legislation and related efforts in other states have intensified the debate over whether it is morally, ethically, and legally permissible to allow relatives, friends, or physicians to provide support, means, and actions to carry out a suicide.

Proponents of the right to suicide believe that it can be a rational act and that medical professionals should be allowed to help such patients without fear of legal or professional repercussions. Others argue, however, that suicide is not rational, that many who choose suicide are mentally ill, and that determining "rationality" is fraught with hazards. Some voice the fear that, if suicide is legalized, patients will fall victim to coercion from relatives intent on collecting inheritances or who believe the patient has become a burden. Other critics of assisted suicide fear that in response to medical cost control, medical professionals might encourage people who are terminally ill to choose to die, and that those who are poor and disadvantaged would receive the most encouragement.

Major problems also exist in defining the subjective term *quality of life* as the criterion for deciding between life and death. At what point do we consider quality of life sufficiently poor to justify terminating it? Should society allow people who have been severely injured or disfigured to end their own lives? What about people who are intellectually disabled or seriously mentally ill? Could it be argued that their quality of life is equally poor? Moreover, who decides whether a person is terminally ill? There are recorded cases of "incurable" patients who recovered spontaneously or who responded to newly discovered treatments.

Such questions deal with ethics and human values, and have no easy answers. Yet mental health practitioners cannot avoid these issues. Like their medical counterparts, mental health professionals are trained to intervene to prevent suicide. Strong social, religious, and legal sanctions support this position. Many therapists work with clients who have strong suicidal intent—clients who are not terminally ill but who, for a variety of reasons, view suicide as the answer to their emotional distress. In most situations, their deaths would bring immense pain and suffering to their loved ones. Moreover, as we discussed in Chapter 9, most people who attempt suicide are ambivalent about the act, or find that their suicidal urges pass when their life circumstances improve. Clearly, suicide brings up a number of important social and legal issues and challenges the personal value systems of those considering suicide, their family members, medical and mental health professionals, and those who devise and enforce our laws.

Ethical Guidelines for Mental Health Professionals

Each mental health profession is guided not only by legal rulings, but also by an enforceable code of ethics for its members. For psychologists, the ethical code covers issues such as professional competence, human relations, privacy and confidentiality, advertising, record keeping and fees, required education and training, research, assessment, and therapy. All psychologists are expected to be aware of these guidelines. Being unaware of or misinterpreting these codes is not a defense against a charge of unethical conduct (American Psychological Association, 2010a). We will review sections of the code pertaining to therapist–client relationship issues and cultural competence.

The Therapist–Client Relationship

> **CASE STUDY** A psychiatrist was working with a client named Mary, who had five personalities. He was especially concerned with "Sam," who sometimes demonstrated extreme violence—forcefully throwing chairs and other objects and making threats to injure staff members. Given the potential violence of this aggressive personality, the psychiatrist made certain that restraints were available. During one session, Sam made a threat toward a specific individual—the owner of a grocery store where the client lived. He stated, "I'll kill that guy. You know I will. I've already made a plan and bought a gun. I'm going to shoot him tonight when he gets off work" (Norko, 2008, p. 144). Later, the psychiatric resident sitting in on the case asked the psychiatrist if they should inform the police about Sam's threat. The psychiatrist expressed reluctance, believing such a move would undo the work that they accomplished in therapy. Was the psychiatrist right in his decision? Was he not obligated to protect the possible victim?

The therapist–client relationship involves a number of legal, moral, and ethical issues. We will discuss how they affect cases such as this complex case of dissociative identity disorder. Three primary concerns are issues of confidentiality and privileged communication, the therapist's duty to warn others of a risk posed by a dangerous client, and the therapist's obligation to avoid sexual intimacies with clients.

Confidentiality and Privileged Communication

Basic to the therapist–patient relationship is the premise that therapy involves a deeply personal association in which clients have a right to expect that what they say is kept private. Therapists believe that therapy cannot be effective unless clients trust their therapists and are certain that what they share is confidential. Without this guarantee, clients may not be completely open with their thoughts and may subsequently obtain less benefit from therapy.

Confidentiality is an ethical standard that protects clients from disclosure of information without their consent. Confidentiality, however, is an ethical, not a legal, obligation. **Privileged communication**, a narrower legal concept, protects privacy and prevents the disclosure of confidential communications without a client's permission (Corey, Callanan, et al., 2010). Our society recognizes how important certain confidential relationships are and protects them by law. These relationships are spousal, attorney–client, pastor–congregant, and therapist–client relationships. Psychiatric practices are regulated in all 50 states and the District of Columbia, and most of those jurisdictions have privileged-communication statutes. The Health Information Portability and Accountability Act (HIPAA) further enhanced privacy protections for individuals who seek mental health evaluation or treatment, including protection of therapist records such as notes taken during therapy. An important aspect of the privacy concept is that the holder of the privilege is the client, not the therapist. In other words, if a client waives this privilege, the therapist has no grounds for withholding information.

Exemptions from Privileged Communication   Although states vary considerably, they all recognize certain situations in which communications can be divulged (D. Brown & Srebalus, 2003). Corey and associates (Corey, Callahan, et al., 2010) summarized these conditions:

- In situations that deal with civil or criminal commitment or competency to stand trial, the client has the right to request that privileged information be shared.

confidentiality   an ethical standard that protects clients from disclosure of information without their consent

privileged communication   a therapist's legal obligation to protect a client's privacy and to prevent the disclosure of confidential communications without a client's permission

Figure 17.3

Duty to Warn

Most states have laws that either require or permit mental health professionals to disclose information about clients who may become violent. In some states, the duty to warn about possible danger is mandatory.

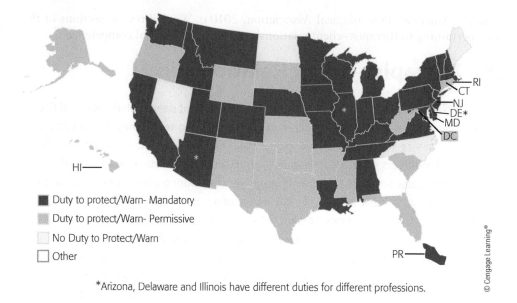

- Duty to protect/Warn- Mandatory
- Duty to protect/Warn- Permissive
- No Duty to Protect/Warn
- Other

© Cengage Learning®

*Arizona, Delaware and Illinois have different duties for different professions.

- Disclosure can also be made when a client who has been in therapy introduces his or her mental condition as a claim or defense in a civil action.

- When the client is younger than 16 or is a dependent elderly person and information leads the therapist to believe that the individual has been a victim of a crime (e.g., incest, rape, or abuse), the therapist must provide such information to the appropriate protective services agency.

- When the therapist has reason to believe that a client presents a danger to himself or herself (such as high risk of suicide) or may potentially harm someone else, the therapist must act to ward off the danger.

As you can see, exemptions from privilege involve a variety of complex situations and decisions. Let's examine one of the important exceptions—the duty to warn.

The Duty to Warn

CASE STUDY In 1968, Prosenjit Poddar—a graduate student from India studying at the University of California, Berkeley—sought therapy from the student health services for depression. Poddar was apparently upset over what he perceived to be a rebuff from another student, Tatiana Tarasoff, whom he claimed to love. During the course of treatment, Poddar informed his therapist that he intended to purchase a gun and kill Tarasoff. Judging Poddar to be dangerous, the psychologist breached the confidentiality of the professional relationship by informing the campus police. The police detained Poddar briefly but freed him because he agreed to stay away from Tarasoff. On October 27, 1969, Poddar went to Tarasoff's home and killed her, first wounding her with a gun and then stabbing her repeatedly with a knife. In the subsequent lawsuit filed by Tarasoff's family, the California Supreme Court made a landmark ruling in 1976 that established what is popularly known as the *duty to warn*—the court ruled that the therapist should have warned not only the police but the intended victim as well.

***Tarasoff* ruling** a California Supreme Court decision that obligates mental health professionals to break confidentiality when their clients pose a clear and imminent danger to another person

The therapist notified his supervisor, the director of the psychiatric clinic, about Poddar's comments because he was extremely concerned that Prosenjit Poddar was dangerous and likely to carry out his threat to harm Tatiana Tarasoff. He also informed the campus police, hoping that they would detain Poddar. Surely the therapist had

A Duty to Warn

Tatiana Tarasoff, a college student, was stabbed to death in 1969 by Prosenjit Poddar, a graduate student at the University of California, Berkeley. Although Poddar's therapist notified the police about threats made by Poddar, the California Supreme Court ruled that the therapist should have also warned Tarasoff.

done all that could be reasonably expected. Not so, ruled the California Supreme Court (*Tarasoff v. the Board of Regents of the University of California*, 1976). In the **Tarasoff ruling**, the court stated that when a therapist determines, according to the standards of the mental health profession, that a client presents a serious danger to another, the therapist is obligated to warn the intended victim. The court went on to say that protective privilege ends where public peril begins. In general, courts have ruled that therapists have a responsibility to protect the public from dangerous acts of violent clients, and have held therapists accountable for (a) failing to predict dangerousness, (b) failing to warn potential victims, (c) failing to initiate commitment proceedings for dangerous individuals, and (d) prematurely discharging dangerous patients from a hospital.

Because of the James Holmes theater shooting in Aurora, Colorado, the governor of Colorado signed House Bill 14-1271 on April 7, 2014, a bill that extends the duty to warn to include not only specifically identified individual targets, but also threats to entities such as buildings or specific locations (parks, etc.) where people might be endangered. Under this law, Colorado mental health professionals must notify the people responsible for the locations or entities, as well as law enforcement, or take other steps such as initiating commitment proceedings. Most but not all states have statues similar to the Tarasoff ruling, but as you can see, state differences do exist (see Figure 17.3).

Criticism of the Duty to Warn   The *Tarasoff* ruling seems to place the therapist in the unenviable role of being a double agent. Therapists have an ethical and legal obligation to their clients, but they also have legal obligations to society. These dual obligations sometimes not only conflict with one another, but they can also be quite ambiguous. Many situations exist in which state courts must rule to clarify the implications and uncertainties of the duty to warn.

When the *Tarasoff* ruling came out, M. Siegel (1979) loudly criticized it, stating that the outcome was a hollow victory for individual parties and was devastating for the mental health professions. He reasoned that if confidentiality had been an absolute policy applied to all situations, then Poddar might have continued his treatment, thus ultimately saving Tarasoff's life. In other words, he wonders if the requirement to notify the authorities led to an escalation of events that resulted in Tatiana Tarasoff's death. Other mental health professionals have echoed this theme in one form or another (Werth et al., 2009). Hostile clients with pent-up feelings and emotions may

DID YOU KNOW?

Prosenjit Poddar served 4 years of a 5-year sentence and was then released on a technicality involving problematic jury instructions regarding diminished capacity. To prevent a retrial, he agreed to leave the United States. He currently lives in India.

SOURCE: Vitelli, 2007

Up to 17 percent of professionals have had some form of sexual contact with their clients. The actual incidence may be much higher, since therapists may be disinclined to admit such behaviors. The majority of the contact involves a male therapist and a female client, but the reverse has also been reported, as have relationships in which the therapist and patient are of the same sex.

SOURCE: National Board for Certification in Occupational Therapy, 2012

be less likely to act out or become violent when allowed to vent their thoughts. The irony, according to critics, is that the duty to warn may actually be counterproductive to its intent to protect potential victims.

The Family Educational Rights and Privacy Act and Confidentiality of College Student Life

CASE STUDY   Elizabeth Shin, a 19-year-old sophomore at the Massachusetts Institute of Technology (MIT), died on April 14, 2000, after she allegedly set herself on fire. Two years after her death, her parents filed a $27 million wrongful death suit against MIT, accusing the university, university psychiatrists, student life staff, and campus police of breach of contract, medical malpractice, and negligence. The Shins contended that MIT staff knew that their daughter had made suicide attempts, cut herself frequently, and was diagnosed with depression, but failed to inform them of her deteriorating mental state. Had they done so, the family asserted, Shin might still be alive today. They further claimed that MIT broke a "business contract" with the family—an agreement they said was implied in Shin's college enrollment at MIT.

Like the *Tarasoff* case, the outcome of the Shins' lawsuit would have had the power to set legal precedent. A ruling could have radically changed the Family Educational Rights and Privacy Act, which prevents colleges and universities from disclosing any personal information about students, even to their parents. Colleges and universities generally assume that students are adults. If they were required to report every concern to parents, students would not have the opportunity to learn to deal with their own problems. Students might also be less inclined to share personal information with school officials if they knew that the information could be reported to their parents.

Yet institutions of higher education are very aware that undergraduate students seem to have more mental health needs than ever before. One national study of counseling center client problems over 13 years revealed that students are entering college with more severe problems than in the past (Benton, Robertson, Tseng, Newton, & Benton, 2003). The Shin's lawsuit never tested the issue of student confidentiality and privacy, however, because the case was settled out of court in 2005 for an undisclosed sum and with an agreement between MIT and the family that Shin died by accident rather than suicide.

Sexual Relationships with Clients

According to the ethical code for psychologists, sexual intimacies are prohibited with current clients, the relatives or partners of current clients, or former clients for a minimum of 2 years after termination of therapy. Even after 2 years, sexual intimacy with a former client would not be acceptable "except in the most unusual circumstances" (American Psychological Association, 2010a). Unfortunately, such contact does occur—the most common civil complaint related to psychotherapy involves sexual intimacies between a therapist and a current or former client (Corey et al., 2010).

Traditionally, mental health practitioners have emphasized the importance of separating and creating boundaries between their personal and professional lives. This separation is emphasized because therapists need to be objective and because becoming emotionally involved with a client may interfere with therapy. A therapist who is personally involved with a client may be less confrontational, may fulfill his or her own needs at the expense of the client's, and may unintentionally exploit the client because of his or her position (Corey & Corey, 2010). Although some people question the premise that a social or personal relationship interferes with therapy, professional codes make it clear that personal relations, especially sexual intimacy, are inappropriate. Fortunately, the vast majority of psychologists behave in a professional manner.

Cultural Competence and the Mental Health Profession

The American Psychological Association (2010a) emphasizes the importance of therapists possessing competence in understanding the effects of diversity issues involving age, gender, race, ethnicity, culture, national origin, religion, sexual orientation, gender identity, disability, language, or socioeconomic status. Most mental health professionals agree that psychological theories, our understandings of mental disorders, and contemporary approaches to therapy are culture bound; that is, they are based on the highly individualistic values of middle- to upper-class European Americans (Sue & Sue, 2013). Unfortunately, services offered to clients from diverse backgrounds often fail to consider the clients' life experiences. Further, inadequate cultural competence not only results in poor sensitivity and understanding of client needs, but may also be oppressive and discriminatory toward minority populations. These concerns apply not only to ethnic minorities but also to other marginalized groups such as women, gay men and lesbians, people with disabilities, and so forth.

In a historic move, the American Psychological Association adopted guidelines on multicultural education, training, research, practice, and organizational change for psychologists (2003). These comprehensive guidelines emphasize the importance of culturally sensitive work with racial and ethnic minorities and make it clear that service providers need to become aware of how their own culture, life experiences, attitudes, values, and biases have influenced them. The guidelines also emphasize the importance of cultural and environmental factors in diagnosis and treatment, and the importance of respecting and incorporating traditional healing approaches that are intrinsic to a client's culture. Finally, therapists are encouraged to learn more about cultural issues and seek consultation when confronted with culture-specific problems. The American Psychological Association (2010a), in its most recent *Ethical Principles of Psychologists and Code of Conduct*, has made it clear that working with clients from different cultures is unethical unless the mental health professional has adequate training and expertise in multicultural psychology.

Inherent in all of these documents is a call for cultural competence—if therapists ignore the racial and cultural backgrounds of their clients or have inadequate training in working with a culturally diverse population, the result may be biased, discriminatory, and unethical treatment. From this perspective, mental health professionals have a moral and professional responsibility to become culturally competent if they work with people who differ from them in terms of race, culture, ethnicity, gender, sexual orientation, and so forth.

Mental health professionals who provide culturally appropriate treatment strive toward attaining three goals (Sue & Sue, 2013):

1. becoming aware of and dealing with the biases, stereotypes, and assumptions that affect their practice;

2. becoming aware of the values and worldviews of clients from different cultures; and

3. developing appropriate intervention strategies that take into account the social, cultural, historical, and environmental factors that influence clients from diverse cultures.

Fortunately, a focus on how multicultural factors can influence the development of mental disorders is evident throughout the DSM-5 (APA, 2013).

Changing Demographics and Therapy

Therapists often participate in multicultural training in preparation for work with clients from a variety of cultural backgrounds. Here therapists discuss their personal experiences during a diversity training activity.

JLP/Jose L. Pelaez/Corbis

Using Positive Psychology to Build Soldier Resilience: An Ethical Dilemma?

Throughout this text, we have extolled the virtues of positive psychology and a strength-based approach to viewing the human condition. Positive psychology has made many contributions to our understanding of resilience and the protective factors that may help safeguard against mental disorders. Positive psychology prompts us to focus on factors that enhance mental health; to value prevention and resilience; and to embrace assets and strengths. But can the basic tenets and principles of positive psychology be misused and misapplied? If so, would that not raise moral and ethical questions?

Such is the case with an intervention that created a major controversy within the psychological community—the Comprehensive Soldier Fitness (CSF) program being implemented by the U.S. Army (G. W. Casey, 2011; Cornum, Matthews, & Seligman, 2011). Using research findings and principles derived from positive psychology, the U.S. Army embarked on an effort to increase the psychological strength and positive performance of soldiers and to reduce any maladaptive responses to military trauma and demands. The goal is to increase soldiers' resilience as they face threat of injury or death, sleep deprivation, separation from family and friends, extreme climates, and the trauma of taking the life of enemy combatants. Such an undertaking is especially important during times of war. For example, during the wars in Iraq and Afghanistan, approximately 70 percent of soldiers were exposed to traumatic events. This exposure resulted in high rates of post-traumatic stress disorder, alcohol abuse, suicide, and depression (Cornum et al., 2011).

The CSF training develops psychological resilience in soldiers using an evidence-based approach that strengthens emotional, social, family, and spiritual fitness to ward off the stresses of military life and combat. Just as physical training focuses on physical preparedness for military combat, CSF increases the mental fitness of soldiers by strengthening their psychological assets and preparing them to participate in high-risk actions such as going on patrols, killing or injuring their enemies, and interrogating captives (Cornum et al., 2011). Preliminary evidence suggests that the CSF program is effective (Algoe & Fredrickson, 2011; Cacioppo, Reis, & Zautra, 2011; Tedeschi & McNally, 2011), although questions have been raised regarding the adequacy of the research design in these studies (Eidelson & Soldz, 2012; Sagalyn, 2012)

On the surface, the CSF program appears to have very worthy goals—providing the best care possible for those who serve in the military. Yet a number of psychologists have raised serious moral and ethical objections to the use of positive psychology in the CSF program. They assert that the basic premise of the program is flawed and misguided (Eidelson, Pilisuk, & Soldz, 2011; J. Krueger, 2011; Phipps, 2011). Among their objections are the following:

- The use of positive psychology in the military operates under the assumption that war is unavoidable and that, as a result, it is the patriotic duty of psychologists to help the military make our men and women more resilient in combat. Critics vehemently question this assumption, and instead advocate the use of positive psychology principles to reduce conflict between nations, to prevent war, and to promote peace.

- War is horrific and exposes combatants to gruesome sights and situations. Reactions of distress or repugnance are natural, healthy, and humane responses. To train soldiers to experience less distress when encountering or perpetuating death, destruction, and inhumane acts is a frightening prospect. To teach soldiers, for example, to feel better about killing is morally and ethically questionable.

- Psychologists who use positive psychology to help the military are deceiving themselves. The CSF client is the Army and not the individual soldier. The Army demands discipline, efficiency, and obedience, and attempts to standardize behavior. It is naive to think that the CSF program would put soldiers' psychological needs ahead of the goals of the Army.

R. D. Laing, an existential psychiatrist, once asked the question, "Is schizophrenia a 'sick' response in a 'healthy' society, or is it a 'healthy' response to a 'sick' one?" Psychologists

©S. F/Shutterstock/Shutterstock.com

Using Positive Psychology to Build Soldier Resilience: An Ethical Dilemma?—cont'd

who object to using psychological principles to aid the military seem to be asking a similar question about war and military objectives. If war is unnatural, unhealthy, and pathological, are we using positive psychology to help soldiers adjust to a "sick" situation? Is it appropriate for psychologists to lend their considerable expertise in human behavior for military purposes if the outcome involves objectionable goals? We must remember that psychological science can be used for any number of purposes, both good and bad.

chapter SUMMARY

1 What are the criteria used to judge insanity, and what is the difference between being insane and being incompetent to stand trial?

- People can be acquitted of a crime using an insanity defense if they (a) did not know right from wrong (*M'Naghten* rule), (b) were unable to control their behavior (irresistible impulse), or (c) acted out of a mental disease or defect (*Durham* decision). The American Law Institute guidelines attempt to define insanity by combining aspects of these three standards.

- Competency to stand trial refers to defendants' mental state (whether they can rationally aid attorneys in their own defense) at the time they are evaluated, not at the time of the offense.

2 Under what conditions can a person be involuntarily committed to a mental institution?

- People who have committed no crime can be confined against their will if it can be shown that they (a) present a clear and imminent danger to themselves or others, (b) are unable to care for themselves, (c) are unable to make responsible decisions about appropriate treatment and hospitalization, or (d) are in an unmanageable mental state.

- It is very difficult to predict dangerousness, because such acts often depend on many external situations and not solely on personal attributes.

3 What rights do mental patients have with respect to treatment and care?

- Court rulings have established that mental patients have the right to receive treatment and the right to refuse treatment.

- Deinstitutionalization, the shifting of responsibility for the care of mental patients from large central institutions to agencies within the local community, has left many individuals with severe mental illness fewer opportunities for adequate services. Some view this as a violation of patient rights.

4 Are there situations in which suicide should be an option?

- This question is difficult to answer, particularly when a person is terminally ill and wishes to end his or her suffering. A few states allow physician-assisted suicide under these circumstances.

5 What legal and ethical issues guide treatment practices?

- Confidentiality and privileged communication are crucial to the therapist–client relationship. Exceptions involve (a) civil or criminal commitment and determinations of competency to stand trial, (b) a client's involvement in court actions in which the client's mental condition is introduced, (c) concern that child abuse or elder abuse has occurred, or (d) a client poses a danger to himself or herself or to others.

- The *Tarasoff* decision makes therapists responsible for warning a potential victim in order to avoid liability.

- Sexual misconduct by therapists is considered to be one of the most serious of all ethical violations.

- It is important to consider diversity involving factors such as culture, ethnicity, and gender in therapy. Adequate training and expertise in multicultural psychology is important for therapists treating members of marginalized groups.

GLOSSARY

abnormal psychology the scientific study whose objectives are to describe, explain, predict, and modify behaviors associated with mental disorders

abstinence refraining from use of alcohol, drugs, or other addictive substances

acculturative stress the psychological, physical, and social pressures experienced by individuals who are adapting to a new culture

acute stress disorder disorder characterized by flashbacks, hypervigilance, and avoidance symptoms that last up to 1 month after exposure to a traumatic stressor

adaptive behavior performance on tasks of daily living, including academic skills, self-care, and the ability to work or live independently

addiction compulsive drug-seeking behavior and a loss of control over drug use

adjustment disorder condition involving reactions to life stressors that are disproportionate to the severity or intensity of the event or situation

adrenal gland releases sex hormones and other hormones, such as cortisol, in response to stress

advance directive written statement providing guidance for medical and health care decisions in the event the person becomes incapacitated and unable communicate his or her wishes

agoraphobia an intense fear of being in public places where escape or help may not be readily available

alcohol poisoning toxic effects resulting from rapidly consuming alcohol or ingesting a large quantity of alcohol; can result in impaired breathing, coma, and death

alcoholic person who has become dependent on alcohol and who exhibits characteristics of an alcohol-use disorder

alcoholism broad term referring to a condition in which the individual is dependent on alcohol and has difficulty controlling drinking

alleles the gene pair responsible for a specific trait

alogia lack of meaningful speech

Alzheimer's disease dementia involving memory loss and other declines in cognitive and adaptive functioning

amniocentesis a prenatal screening procedure involving withdrawal of amniotic fluid from the fetal sac

amygdala brain structure associated with the processing, expression, and memory of emotions, especially anger and fear

analogue study an investigation that attempts to replicate or simulate, under controlled conditions, a situation that occurs in real life

anhedonia inability to experience pleasure from previously enjoyed activities

anorexia nervosa an eating disorder characterized by low body weight, an intense fear of becoming obese, and body image distortion

antipsychotic medication medicine developed to counteract symptoms of psychosis

antisocial personality disorder (APD) characterized by a failure to conform to social and legal codes, a lack of anxiety and guilt, and irresponsible behaviors

anxiety an anticipatory emotion that produces bodily reactions that prepare us for "fight or flight"

anxiety disorder fear or anxiety symptoms that interfere with an individual's day-to-day functioning

anxiety sensitivity trait involving fear of physiological changes within the body

anxiolytics a class of medications that reduce anxiety

anxious distress symptoms of motor tension, difficulty relaxing, pervasive worries, or feelings that something catastrophic will occur

asociality minimal interest in social relationships

assigned gender the gender to which a child is socially assigned at birth based on biological sex

asthma a chronic inflammatory disease of the airways in the lungs

asymptomatic without symptoms

atherosclerosis condition involving the progressive thickening and hardening of the walls of arteries due to an accumulation of fats and cholesterol along their inner linings

attention-deficit/hyperactivity disorder (ADHD) childhood-onset disorder characterized by persistent attentional problems and/or impulsive, hyperactive behaviors

attenuated psychosis syndrome condition being researched that involves distressing or disabling early signs of delusions, hallucinations, or disorganized speech that emerged or became progressively worse over the previous year; reality testing remains relatively intact

attributional style characteristic way of explaining why a positive or negative event occurred

atypical antipsychotics newer antipsychotic medications that are chemically different and less likely to produce the side effects associated with first-generation antipsychotics

aura a visual or physical sensation (e.g., tingling of an extremity or flashes of light) that precedes a headache

autism spectrum disorder a disorder characterized by a continuum of impairment in social communication and restricted, stereotyped interests and activities

autistic savant an individual with autism spectrum disorder who performs exceptionally well on certain tasks

autonomic nervous system coordinates basic physiological functions and regulates physical responses associated with emotional reactions

avoidant personality disorder characterized by a fear of rejection and humiliation and a reluctance to enter into social relationships

avolition lack of motivation; an inability to take action or become goal oriented

axon extension on the neuron cell body that sends signals to other neurons, muscles, and glands

base rate the rate of natural occurrence of a phenomenon in the population studied

behavioral inhibition shyness

behavioral models models of psychopathology concerned with the role of learning in abnormal behavior

behavioral undercontrol personality trait associated with rebelliousness, novelty seeking, risk taking, and impulsivity

beta-amyloid plaques clumps of beta-amyloid proteins found in the spaces between neurons

binge drinking episodic intake of five or more alcoholic beverages for men or four or more drinks for women

binge eating rapid consumption of large quantities of food

binge-eating disorder an eating disorder that involves the consumption of large amounts of food over a short period of time with accompanying feelings of loss of control and distress over the excess eating

biofeedback training a physiological and behavioral approach in which an individual receives information regarding particular autonomic functions and is rewarded for influencing those functions in a desired direction

biological viewpoint the belief that mental disorders have a physical or physiological basis

biological vulnerability genetic or physiological susceptibility

biopsychosocial model perspective suggesting that interactions between biological, psychological, and social factors cause mental disorders

bipolar I disorder diagnosis involves at least one manic episode that has impaired social or occupational functioning; the person may or may not experience depression or psychotic symptoms

bipolar II disorder diagnosis involves at least one major depressive episode and at least one hypomanic episode

blood pressure the measurement of the force of blood against the walls of the arteries and veins

body dysmorphic disorder condition involving a preoccupation with a perceived physical defect or excessive concern over a slight physical defect

body mass index (BMI) an estimate of body fat calculated on the basis of a person's height and weight

borderline personality disorder characterized by intense fluctuations in mood, self-image, and interpersonal relationships

brain pathology a dysfunction or disease of the brain

brief psychotic disorder psychotic episodes with a duration of at least 1 day but less than 1 month

bulimia nervosa an eating disorder in which episodes involving rapid consumption of large quantities of food and a loss of control over eating are followed by purging, excessive exercise, or fasting in an attempt to compensate for binges

cardiovascular pertaining to the heart and blood vessels

case study an intensive study of one individual that relies on clinical data, such as observations, psychological tests, and historical and biographical information

catatonia a condition characterized by marked disturbance in motor activity—either extreme excitement or motoric immobility

cathartic method a therapeutic use of verbal expression to release pent-up emotional conflicts

caudate nuclei brain region that regulates transmission of impulses warning that something is amiss

cerebral contusion bruising of the brain, often resulting from a blow that causes the brain to forcefully strike the skull

cerebral cortex the outermost layers of brain tissue; covers the cerebrum

cerebral laceration open head injury in which brain tissue is torn, pierced, or ruptured

cerebrum the largest part of the brain, consisting of the right and left hemisphere

child psychopathology the emotional and behavioral manifestation of psychological disorders in children and adolescents

chronic traumatic encephalopathy a progressive, degenerative condition involving brain damage resulting from multiple episodes of head trauma

circadian rhythm an internal clock or daily cycle of internal biological rhythms that influence various bodily processes such as body temperature and sleep–wake cycles

circadian rhythm sleep disorder sleep disturbance due to a disrupted sleep–wake cycle

civil commitment the involuntary confinement of a person judged to be a danger to the self or to others, even though the person has not committed a crime

classical conditioning a process in which responses to new stimuli are learned through association

cluster headache excruciating stabbing or burning sensations located in the eye or cheek

cognitive models explanations based on the assumption that conscious thought mediates an individual's emotional state or behavior in response to a stimulus

cognitive restructuring cognitive strategy that attempts to alter unrealistic thoughts associated with conditions such as phobias

cognitive symptoms symptoms of schizophrenia involving problems with attention, memory and developing a plan of action

comorbid the presence of two or more disorders in the same person

comorbidity co-occurrence of different disorders

competency to stand trial a judgment that a defendant has a factual and rational understanding of the criminal proceedings and can rationally consult with counsel in presenting a defense

compulsion the need to perform acts or mental tasks to reduce anxiety

concordance rate degree of similarity between twins with respect to a trait or disorder

concussion trauma-induced changes in brain functioning, typically caused by a blow to the head

conditioned response in classical conditioning, a learned response to a previously neutral stimulus that has acquired some of the properties of the unconditioned stimulus with which it has been paired

conditioned stimulus in classical conditioning, a previously neutral stimulus that has acquired some of the properties of the unconditioned stimulus with which it has been paired

conduct disorder a persistent pattern of behavior that violates the rights of others, including aggression, serious rule violations, and illegal behavior

confidentiality an ethical standard that protects clients from disclosure of information without their consent

controlled drinking consuming no more than a predetermined amount of alcohol

conversion disorder (functional neurological symptom disorder) condition involving sensory or motor impairment suggestive of a neurological disorder but with no underlying medical cause

coprolalia involuntary utterance of obscenities or inappropriate remarks

coronary heart disease disease process involving the narrowing of cardiac arteries, resulting in the restriction or partial blockage of the flow of blood and oxygen to the heart

correlation the extent to which variations in one variable are accompanied by increases or decreases in a second variable

cortisol hormone released by the adrenal gland in response to stress

co-rumination extensively discussing negative feelings or events with peers or others

couples therapy a treatment aimed at helping couples understand and clarify their communications, role relationships, unfulfilled needs, and unrealistic or unmet expectations

course usual pattern that a disorder follows

criminal commitment incarceration of an individual for having committed a crime

critical periods a specific time in early development during which there is heightened sensitivity to environmental influences or experiences

cross-cutting measure assesses common symptoms that are not specific to one disorder

cultural relativism the belief that lifestyles, cultural values, and worldviews affect the expression and definition of mental disorders

cultural universality the assumption that a fixed set of mental disorders exists whose manifestations and symptoms are similar across cultures

culture the configuration of shared values, beliefs, attitudes, and behaviors that is transmitted from one generation to another by members of a particular group and symbolized by artifacts, roles, expectations, and institutions

cyclothymic disorder condition involving milder hypomanic symptoms that are consistently interspersed with milder depressed moods for at least 2 years

dangerousness a person's potential for doing harm to the self or to others

defense mechanism in psychoanalytic theory, an ego-protection strategy that shelters the individual from anxiety, operates unconsciously, and distorts reality

deficit model early attempt to explain differences in minority groups that contended that differences are the result of "cultural deprivation"

deinstitutionalization the shifting of responsibility for the care of mental patients from large central institutions to agencies within local communities

delayed ejaculation persistent delay or inability to ejaculate within the vagina despite adequate excitement and stimulation

delirium an acute state of confusion involving diminished awareness, disorientation, and impaired attentional skills

delirium tremens life-threatening withdrawal symptoms that can result from chronic alcohol use

delusion a false belief that is firmly and consistently held

delusional disorder persistent delusions without other unusual or odd behaviors; tactile and olfactory hallucinations related to the delusional theme may be present

dementia condition with symptoms involving deterioration in cognition and independent functioning

Dementia with Lewy bodies (DLB) dementia involving visual hallucinations, cognitive fluctuations, and atypical movements

dendrite short, rootlike structure on the neuron cell body that receives signals from other neurons

dependent personality disorder characterized by submissive, clinging behavior and an excessive need to be taken care of

dependent variable a variable that is expected to change when an independent variable is manipulated in a psychological experiment

depersonalization/derealization disorder dissociative condition characterized by feelings of unreality concerning the self and the environment

depressant a substance that causes a slowing of responses and generalized depression of the central nervous system

depression a mood state characterized by sadness or despair, feelings of worthlessness, and withdrawal from others

detoxification phase of alcohol or drug treatment during which the body is purged of intoxicating substances

diastolic pressure arterial force exerted when the heart is relaxed and the ventricles of the heart are filling with blood

diathesis-stress theory view that people inherit a predisposition to develop illness (diathesis) and that certain environmental forces (stressors) may activate the predisposition, resulting in a disorder

diminished capacity law standard allowing defendant to be convicted of a lesser offense due to mental impairment

diminished emotional expression reduced display of observable verbal and nonverbal behaviors that communicate internal emotions

disconfirmatory evidence information that contradicts a delusional belief

discrimination unjust or prejudicial treatment toward a person based on the person's actual or perceived membership in a certain group

disinhibited social engagement disorder a trauma-related attachment disorder characterized by indiscriminate, superficial attachments and desperation for interpersonal contact

disordered eating physically or psychologically unhealthy eating behavior such as chronic overeating or dieting with the goal of losing or controlling weight or managing emotions

disruptive mood dysregulation disorder a childhood disorder involving chronic irritability and significantly exaggerated anger reactions

dissociative amnesia sudden partial or total loss of important personal information or recall of events due to psychological factors

dissociative anesthetic a substance that produces a dreamlike detachment

dissociative disorders a group of disorders, including dissociative amnesia, dissociative identity disorder, and depersonalization/derealization disorder, all of which involve some sort of dissociation, or separation, of a part of the person's consciousness, memory, or identity

dissociative fugue episode involving complete loss of memory of one's life and identity, unexpected travel to a new location, or assumption of a new identity

dissociative identity disorder a condition in which two or more distinct personality states appear to exist in one person, including experiences of possession; also known as *multiple-personality disorder*

dopamine hypothesis the suggestion that schizophrenia may result from excess dopamine activity at certain synaptic sites

double-blind design experimental design in which neither those helping with the experiment nor the participants are aware of experimental conditions

Down syndrome a chromosomal disorder (most frequently involving an extra copy of chromosome 21) that causes physical and neurological abnormalities

dream analysis psychoanalytic technique focused on interpreting the hidden meanings of dreams

drug-drug interactions when the effect of a medication is changed, enhanced, or diminished when taken with another drug, including herbal substances

due process constitutional guarantee of fair treatment within the judicial system

Durham standard a test of legal insanity also known as the *product test*—an accused person is not responsible if the unlawful act was the product of a mental disease or defect

dyscalculia a condition involving difficulties in understanding mathematical skills or concepts

dyslexia a condition involving significant difficulties with reading skills

dyspareunia recurrent or persistent pain in the genitals before, during, or after sexual intercourse

dyssomnias disorders involving abnormalities in the quality, amount, or timing of sleep

echolalia repetition of vocalizations made by another person

elevated mood a mood state involving extreme confidence and exaggerated feelings of energy and well-being

emotional lability unstable and rapidly changing emotions and mood

empowerment increasing one's sense of personal strength and self-worth

endophenotype measurable characteristics (neurochemical, endocrinological, neuroanatomical, cognitive, or neuropsychological) that can give clues regarding the specific genes involved in a disorder

enteric nervous system (ENS) an independent neural system involved with digestion; capable of signaling the brain regarding stress and other emotions

epidemiological research the study of the prevalence and distribution of mental disorders in a population

epigenetics field of biological research focused on understanding how environmental factors influence gene expression

epigenome chemical compounds found outside of the genome that modify gene expression; although the epigenome does not change DNA within the genome, epigenetic changes can be passed on to new cells during cell division and can be inherited

epinephrine hormone released by the adrenal gland in response to physical or mental stress; also known as *adrenaline*

erectile disorder (ED) an inability to attain or maintain an erection sufficient for sexual intercourse

etiological model model developed to explain the cause of a disorder

etiology cause or origin of a disorder

euphoria exceptionally elevated mood; exaggerated feeling of well-being

evidence-based practice treatment decisions based on best current research combined with clinician judgment and client needs

evidence-based therapies treatment techniques that have strong research support

excoriation (skin-picking) disorder distressing and recurrent compulsive picking of the skin resulting in skin lesions

executive functioning mental processes that involve the planning, organizing, and attention required to meet short-term and long-term goals

exhibitionistic disorder urges, acts, or fantasies that involve exposing one's genitals to strangers

existential approach a set of philosophical attitudes that focus on human alienation, the individual in the context of the human condition, and personal responsibility to others as well as to oneself

exorcism treatment method in which prayers, noises, emetics, flogging, and starvation were used to cast evil spirits out of an afflicted person's body

expansive mood person may feel extremely confident or self-important and behave impulsively

experiment a technique of scientific inquiry in which a prediction is made about two variables; the independent variable is then manipulated in a controlled situation, and changes in the dependent variable are measured

experimental hypothesis a prediction concerning how an independent variable will affect a dependent variable in an experiment

exposure therapy a treatment approach based on extinction principles that involves gradual or rapid exposure to feared objects or situations

expressed emotion (EE) a negative communication pattern found among some relatives of individuals with schizophrenia

external validity the degree to which findings of a particular study can be generalized to other groups or conditions

externalizing disorders disruptive behavior disorders associated with symptoms that are socially disturbing and distressing to others.

extinction decrease or cessation of a behavior due to the gradual weakening of a classically or operantly conditioned response

extrapyramidal symptoms side effects of antipsychotic medications that affect a person's gait, movement, or posture

factitious disorder condition in which a person deliberately induces or simulates symptoms of physical or mental illness with no apparent incentive other than attention from medical personnel or others

factitious disorder imposed on another a pattern of falsification or production of physical or psychological symptoms in another individual

factitious disorder imposed on self symptoms of illness are deliberately induced, simulated, or exaggerated, with no apparent external incentive

family systems model explanation that assumes that the behavior of one family member directly affects the entire family system

fear an intense emotion experienced in response to a threatening situation

fear extinction elimination of conditioned fear responses associated with a fear-arousing stimulus

female orgasmic disorder sexual dysfunction involving persistent delay or inability to achieve an orgasm with adequate clitoral stimulation

female sexual interest/arousal disorder distressing disinterest in sexual activities or inability to attain or maintain

physiological or psychological arousal during sexual activity

fetal alcohol spectrum effects a continuum of detrimental neurological and behavioral effects resulting from maternal alcohol consumption during pregnancy

fetal alcohol syndrome (FAS) a condition resulting from maternal alcohol consumption during gestation that involves central nervous system dysfunction and altered brain development

fetishistic disorder sexual attraction and fantasies involving inanimate objects, such as female undergarments

field study an investigative technique in which behaviors and events are observed and recorded in their natural environment

first-generation antipsychotics a group of medications originally developed to combat psychotic symptoms by reducing dopamine levels in the brain; also called *conventional* or *typical antipsychotics*

flight of ideas rapidly changing or disjointed thoughts

flooding a technique that involves inducing a high anxiety level through continued actual or imagined exposure to a fear-arousing situation

fragile X syndrome an inherited condition involving limited production of proteins required for brain development resulting in mild to severe intellectual disability

free association psychoanalytic therapeutic technique in which clients are asked to say whatever comes to mind for the purpose of revealing their unconscious thoughts

frontotemporal lobar degeneration dementia involving degeneration in the frontal and temporal lobes of the brain causing declines in language and behavior

frotteuristic disorder recurrent and intense sexual urges, acts, or fantasies that involve touching or rubbing against a nonconsenting person

functional imaging procedures that provide data regarding physiological and biochemical processes occurring within the brain

GABA gamma-aminobutyric acid, an inhibitory neurotransmitter involved in inducing sleep and relaxation

gateway drug a substance that leads to use of additional substances that are even more lethal

gender dysphoria distress and impaired functioning resulting from an incongruence between a person's gender identity and assigned gender

gene expression the process by which information encoded in a gene is translated into a specialized function or phenotype

generalized anxiety disorder condition characterized by persistent, high levels of anxiety and excessive worry over many life circumstances

genes segments of DNA coded with information needed for the biological inheritance of various traits

genetic linkage studies studies that attempt to determine whether a disorder follows a genetic pattern

genetic mutations an alteration in a gene that changes the instructions within the gene

genito-pelvic pain/penetration disorder physical pain or discomfort associated with intercourse or penetration

genome the complete set of DNA in a cell; the human genome consists of approximately 21,000 genes located in the nucleus of every cell

genotype a person's genetic makeup

glia cells that support and protect neurons

grandiosity an overvaluation of one's significance or importance

gray matter brain tissue comprised of the cell bodies of neurons and glia

group therapy a form of therapy that involves the simultaneous treatment of two or more clients and may involve more than one therapist

habit reversal a therapeutic technique in which a client is taught to substitute new behaviors for habitual behaviors such as a tic

hallucination a sensory experience (such as an image, sound, smell, or taste) that seems real but that does not exist outside of the mind

hallucinogen a substance that induces perceptual distortions and heightens sensory awareness

heavy drinking chronic alcohol intake of more than two drinks per day for men and more than one drink per day for women

hemorrhagic stroke a stroke involving leakage of blood into the brain

heredity the genetic transmission of personal characteristics

heterogeneous different or diverse

hippocampus structure involved with the formation, organization, and storing of emotionally relevant memories

histrionic personality disorder characterized by extreme emotionality and attention seeking

hoarding disorder condition involving congested living conditions due to accumulation of items and distress over the thought of discarding them

homeostasis ability to maintain internal equilibrium by adjusting physiological processes

hormones regulatory chemicals that influence various physiological activities, such as metabolism, digestion, growth, and mood

humanism a philosophical movement that emphasizes human welfare and the worth and uniqueness of the individual

humanistic perspective the optimistic viewpoint that people are born with the ability to fulfill their potential and that abnormal behavior results from disharmony between a person's potential and self-concept

Huntington's disease (HD) a genetic disease characterized by involuntary twitching movements and eventual dementia

hypersomnolence (excessive sleepiness) disorder condition involving difficulty waking up after sleeping and excessive daytime sleepiness or prolonged unrefreshing sleep

hypertension a chronic condition, which increases risk of stroke and heart disease, characterized by a systolic blood pressure of 140 or higher or a diastolic pressure of 90 or higher

hyperthermia significantly elevated body temperature

hypervigilance state of ongoing anxiety in which the person is constantly tense and alert for threats

hypnotics a class of medications that induce sleep

hypomania a milder form of mania involving increased levels of activity and goal-directed behaviors combined with an elevated, expansive, or irritable mood

hypothalamic-pituitary-adrenal (HPA) axis the system involved in stress and trauma reactions and regulation of body processes such as "fight or flight" responses

hypothalamus brain structure that regulates bodily drives, such as hunger, thirst, and sexual response, and body conditions, such as body temperature and circadian rhythms

hypothesis a tentative explanation for certain facts or observations

hysteria an outdated term referring to excessive or uncontrollable emotion, sometimes resulting in somatic symptoms (such as blindness or paralysis) that have no apparent physical cause

iatrogenic disorder a condition unintentionally produced by a therapist's actions and treatment strategies

iatrogenic effects unintended effects of an intervention—such as an unintended change in behavior resulting from a medication or a psychological technique used in treatment

illness anxiety disorder persistent health anxiety and/or concern that one has an undetected physical illness

impulsivity tendency to act quickly without careful thought

incest sexual relations between people too closely related to marry legally

incidence number of new cases of a disorder that appear in an identified population within a specified time period

independent variable a variable or condition that an experimenter manipulates to determine its effect on a dependent variable

inferiority model early attempt to explain differences in minority groups that contended that racial and ethnic minorities are somehow inferior to the majority population

insanity defense the legal argument used by defendants who admit that they have committed a crime but plead not guilty because they were mentally disturbed at the time of the offense

insomnia disorder chronic difficulty falling asleep or remaining asleep

intellectual disability a disorder characterized by limitations in intellectual functioning and adaptive behaviors

intermittent explosive disorder condition involving frequent lower-intensity outbursts or low-frequency, high-intensity outbursts of extreme verbal or physical aggression

internal validity the degree to which changes in the dependent variable are due solely to the effect of changes in the independent variable

internalizing disorders conditions involving emotional symptoms directed inward

interoceptive conditioning when internal bodily sensations of fear and anxiety that have preceded panic attacks serve as signals for new panic attacks

intoxication pattern of problem behaviors or psychological changes associated with use or abuse of a substance

intrapsychic psychological processes occurring within the mind

irresistible impulse test a doctrine that contends that a defendant is not criminally responsible if he or she lacked the willpower to control his or her behavior

ischemic stroke a stroke due to reduced blood supply caused by a clot or severe narrowing of the arteries supplying blood to the brain

learned helplessness a learned belief that one is helpless and unable to affect outcomes

learning disorder (LD) an academic disability characterized by reading, writing, or math skills that are substantially below levels that would be expected based on the person's age, intellectual ability, and educational background

least restrictive environment the least restrictive alternative to freedom that is appropriate to a person's condition

lethality capability of causing death

lifetime prevalence the percentage of people in the population who have had a disorder at some point in their lives

limbic system group of deep brain structures associated with emotions, decision making, and memory formation

localized amnesia lack of memory for a specific event or events

longitudinal research method that involves observing, assessing, or evaluating a group of people over a long period of time

loosening of associations continual shifting from topic to topic without any apparent logical or meaningful connection between thoughts

M'Naghten rule a cognitive test of legal insanity that inquires whether the accused knew right from wrong when the crime was committed

mainstreaming integrating mental patients back into the community

major depressive disorder (MDD) condition diagnosed if someone (without a history of hypomania/mania) experiences a depressive episode involving severe depressive symptoms that have negatively affected functioning most of the day, nearly every day, for at least 2 full weeks

major depressive episode a period involving severe depressive symptoms that have impaired functioning for at least 2 full weeks

major neurocognitive disorder condition involving significant decline in independent living skills and one or more areas of cognitive functioning

male hypoactive sexual desire disorder sexual dysfunction in men that is characterized by a lack of sexual desire

malingering feigning illness for an external purpose

managed health care the industrialization of health care, whereby large organizations in the private sector control the delivery of services

mania mental state characterized by very exaggerated activity and emotions including euphoria, excessive excitement, or irritability that result in impairment in social or occupational functioning

MDD with a seasonal pattern major depressive episodes occur seasonally more than nonseasonally; at least two seasonal episodes of severe depression have occurred ending at a predictable time of year

medically induced coma a deliberately induced state of deep sedation that allows the brain to rest and heal

mental disorder psychological symptoms or behavioral patterns that reflect an underlying psychobiological dysfunction, are associated with distress or disability, and are not merely an expectable response to common stressors or losses

mental health professional health care practitioners (such as psychologists, psychiatrists, psychiatric nurses, social workers, or mental health counselors) whose services focus on improving mental health or treating mental illness

mental illness a mental health condition that negatively affects a person's emotions, thinking, behavior, relationships with others, or overall functioning

meta-analysis statistical method in which researchers combine and analyze the results from numerous studies focused on the same or similar phenomena

metabolic syndrome a medical condition associated with obesity, diabetes, high cholesterol, and hypertension

migraine headache moderate to severe head pain resulting from abnormal brain activity affecting the cranial blood vessels and nerves

mild neurocognitive disorder condition involving a modest decline in at least one major cognitive area

mindfulness nonjudgmental awareness of thoughts, feelings, physical sensations, and the environment

mixed features concurrent hypomanic/manic and depressive symptoms

model an analogy used by scientists, usually to describe or explain a phenomenon or process they cannot directly observe

modeling process of learning by observing models (and later imitating them)

modeling therapy procedure involving observation of a nonphobic individual

successfully coping with a feared phobic object or situation

moderate drinking a lower-risk pattern of alcohol intake (no more than one or two drinks per day)

mood emotional state or prevailing frame of mind

moral treatment movement crusade to institute more humane treatment of people with mental illness

motivational enhancement therapy a therapeutic approach that addresses ambivalence and helps clients consider the advantages and disadvantages of changing their behavior

motor tic a tic involving physical behaviors such as eye blinking, facial grimacing, or head jerking

multicultural model contemporary view that emphasizes the importance of considering a person's cultural background and related experiences when determining normality and abnormality

multicultural psychology a branch of psychology that focuses on culture, race, ethnicity, gender, age, socioeconomic class, and other similar factors in its effort to understand behavior

multipath model a model that provides an organizational framework for understanding the numerous influences on the development of mental disorders, the complexity of their interacting components, and the need to view disorders from a holistic framework

multiple-baseline study a single-participant experimental design in which baselines on two or more behaviors or the same behavior in two or more settings are obtained prior to intervention

muscle dysmorphia extreme dissatisfaction with one's muscularity

myelin white, fatty material that surrounds and insulates axons

myelination process by which myelin sheaths increase the efficiency of signal transmission between nerve cells

narcissistic personality disorder characterized by an exaggerated sense of self-importance, an exploitive attitude, and a lack of empathy

negative appraisal interpreting events as threatening

negative reinforcement increasing the frequency or magnitude of a behavior by removing something aversive

negative symptoms symptoms of schizophrenia associated with an inability or decreased ability to initiate actions or speech, express emotions, or feel pleasure

neural circuits signal-relaying network of interconnected neurons

neural stem cells uncommitted cells that can be stimulated to form new neurons and glia

neurocognitive disorder a disorder that occurs when brain dysfunction affects thinking processes, memory, consciousness, or perception

neurodegeneration declining brain functioning due to progressive loss of brain structure, neurochemical abnormalities, or the death of neurons

neurodevelopmental disorders conditions involving impaired development of the brain and central nervous system that are evident early in a child's life

neurofibrillary tangles twisted fibers of tau protein found inside nerve cells

neurogenesis birth and growth of new neurons

neuron nerve cell that transmits messages throughout the body

neuropeptides small molecules that can directly and indirectly influence a variety of hormones and neurotransmitters

neuroplasticity the process by which the brain changes to adapt to environmental changes or to compensate for injury

neurotransmitter any of a group of chemicals that help transmit messages between neurons

nightmare disorder condition involving frightening dreams that produce awakening

nonsuicidal self-injury self-harm intended to provide relief from negative feelings or to induce a positive mood state

normal blood pressure the normal amount of force exerted by blood against the artery walls; systolic pressure is less than 120 and diastolic pressure is less than 80

obesity a condition involving a body mass index (BMI) greater than 30

observational learning theory theory that suggests that an individual can acquire new behaviors by watching other people perform them

obsession intrusive, repetitive thought or image that produces anxiety

obsessive-compulsive disorder condition characterized by intrusive, repetitive anxiety-producing thoughts or a strong need to perform acts to reduce anxiety

obsessive-compulsive personality disorder (OCPD) characterized by perfectionism, a tendency to be interpersonally controlling, devotion to details, and rigidity

obstructive sleep apnea a breathing-related sleep disorder involving partial or complete upper-airway obstruction

operant behavior voluntary and controllable behavior, such as walking or thinking, that "operates" on an individual's environment

operant conditioning theory of learning that holds that behaviors are controlled by the consequences that follow them

operational definition concrete description of the variables that are being studied

opioid a painkilling agent that depresses the central nervous system, such as heroin and prescription pain relievers

oppositional defiant disorder (ODD) a childhood disorder characterized by negativistic, argumentative, and hostile behavior patterns

optimal human functioning qualities such as subjective well-being, optimism, resilience, hope, courage, ability to cope with stress, self-actualization, and self-determinism

orbitofrontal cortex brain region associated with planning and decision making

other specified feeding or eating disorder a seriously disturbed eating pattern that does not fully meet criteria for another eating disorder diagnosis

oxytocin a powerful hormone that affects social bonding

panic attack episode of intense fear accompanied by symptoms such as a pounding heart, trembling, shortness of breath, and fear of losing control or dying

panic disorder condition involving recurrent, unexpected panic attacks with apprehension over future attacks or behavioral changes to avoid attacks

paranoid ideation suspiciousness about the actions or motives of others

paranoid personality disorder characterized by distrust and suspiciousness regarding the motives of others

paraphilia recurring sexual arousal and gratification by means of mental imagery or behavior involving socially unacceptable objects, situations, or individuals

paraphilic disorders sexual disorders in which the person has either acted on or is severely distressed by recurrent urges or fantasies involving nonhuman objects, nonconsenting individuals, or suffering or humiliation

parasomnias sleep abnormalities occurring during sleep or in the sleep–wake transition

Parkinson's disease a progressive disorder characterized by poorly controlled motor movements sometimes followed by cognitive decline

pediatric bipolar disorder a childhood disorder involving depressive and energized episodes similar to the mood swings seen in adult bipolar disorder

pedophilic disorder a disorder in which an adult obtains erotic gratification through urges, acts, or fantasies that involve sexual contact with a prepubescent or early pubescent child

penetrance the proportion of individuals carrying a specific variant of a gene (allele or genotype) who also express the associated trait (phenotype)

persecutory delusions beliefs of being targeted by others

persistent complex bereavement disorder proposed disorder that involves persistent sorrow or preoccupation continuing a year after the death of a loved one

persistent depressive disorder (dysthymia) condition involving chronic depressive symptoms that are present most of the day for more days than not during a 2-year period with no more than 2 months symptom-free

personality disorder characterized by impairment in self and interpersonal functioning and the presence of pathological personality traits that are relatively inflexible and long-standing

personality psychopathology dysfunctional and maladaptive personality patterns

personalized medicine use of a person's genetic profile to guide decisions about prevention and treatment of disease and mental disorders

phenotype observable physical and behavioral characteristics resulting from the interaction between the genotype and the environment

phobia a strong, persistent, and unwarranted fear of a specific object or situation

physiological dependence state of adaptation that occurs after chronic exposure to a substance; can result in craving and withdrawal symptoms

pituitary gland stimulates hormones associated with growth, sexual and reproductive development, metabolism, and stress responses

placebo an ineffectual or sham treatment, such as an inactive substance, used as a control in an experimental study

placebo effect improvement produced by expectations of a positive treatment outcome

plaque sticky material (composed of fat, cholesterol, and other substances) that builds up on the walls of veins or arteries

pleasure principle the impulsive, pleasure-seeking aspect of our being, from which the id operates

polymorphic variation a common mutation of a gene

polymorphisms a common DNA mutation or variation of a gene

positive psychology the philosophical and scientific study of positive human functioning and the strengths and assets of individuals, families, and communities

positive reinforcement desirable actions or rewards that increase the likelihood that a particular behavior will occur

positive symptoms symptoms of schizophrenia that involve unusual thoughts or perceptions, such as delusions, hallucinations, disordered thinking, or bizarre behavior

possession the replacement of a person's sense of personal identity with a supernatural spirit or power

post-traumatic stress disorder (PTSD) disorder characterized by flashbacks, hypervigilance, avoidance, and other symptoms that last for more than 1 month and that occur as a result of exposure to extreme trauma

predisposition a susceptibility to certain symptoms or disorders

prefrontal cortex the outer layer of the prefrontal lobe responsible for inhibiting instinctive responses and performing complex cognitive behavior such as managing attention, behavior, and emotions

prefrontal lobotomy a surgical procedure in which the frontal lobes are disconnected from the remainder of the brain

prehypertension a condition believed to be a precursor to hypertension, stroke, and heart disease, characterized by systolic blood pressure of 120 to 139 and diastolic pressure from 80 to 89

prejudice an unfair, preconceived judgment about a person or group based on their supposed characteristics

premature (early) ejaculation ejaculation with minimal sexual stimulation before, during, or shortly after penetration

premenstrual dysphoric disorder condition involving distressing and disruptive symptoms of depression, irritability, and tension that occur the week before menstruation

premorbid before the onset of major symptoms

pressured speech rapid, frenzied, or loud, disjointed communication

prevalence the percentage of individuals in a targeted population who have a particular disorder during a specific period of time

privileged communication a therapist's legal obligation to protect a client's privacy and to prevent the disclosure of confidential communications without a client's permission

prognosis prediction of the probable outcome of a disorder, including the chances of full recovery

projective personality test testing involving responses to ambiguous stimuli, such as inkblots, pictures, or incomplete sentences

protective factors conditions or attributes that lessen or eliminate the risk of a negative psychological or social outcome

provisional diagnosis an initial diagnosis based on currently available information

psychache a term created to describe the unbearable psychological hurt, pain, and anguish associated with suicide

psychiatric epidemiology the study of the prevalence of mental illness in a society

psychoactive substance a substance that alters mood, thought processes, or other psychological states

psychoanalysis therapy to uncover repressed material, to help clients achieve insight into inner motivations and desires, and to resolve childhood conflicts that affect current relationships

psychodiagnosis assessment and description of an individual's psychological symptoms, including inferences about what might be causing the psychological distress

psychodynamic model model that views disorders as the result of childhood trauma or anxieties and that holds that many of these childhood-based anxieties operate unconsciously

psychogenic originating from psychological causes

psychological assessment the process of gathering information and drawing conclusions about the traits, skills, abilities, emotional functioning, and psychological problems of an individual

psychological autopsy the systematic examination of existing information after a person's death for the purpose

of understanding and explaining the person's behavior

psychological flexibility the ability to mentally and emotionally adapt to situational demands

psychological resilience the capacity to effectively adapt to and bounce back from stress, trauma, and other adversity

psychological viewpoint the belief that mental disorders are caused by psychological and emotional factors rather than biological influences

psychopathology the study of the symptoms, causes, and treatments of mental disorders

psychopharmacology study of the effects of medications on thoughts, emotions, and behaviors

psychophysiological disorder any physical disorder that has a strong psychological basis or component

psychosexual stages in psychodynamic theory, the sequence of stages—oral, anal, phallic, latency, and genital—through which human personality develops

psychosis condition involving loss of contact with or distorted view of reality, including disorganized thinking, false beliefs, or seeing or hearing things that are not there

psychotherapy a program of systematic intervention with the purpose of improving a client's behavioral, emotional, or cognitive symptoms

psychotic symptoms loss of contact with reality that may involve disorganized thinking, false beliefs, or seeing or hearing things that are not there

psychotropic medications drugs that treat or manage psychiatric symptoms by influencing brain activity associated with emotions and behavior

pure dysthymic syndrome the individual meets the criteria for persistent depressive disorder (dysthymia) and has not had a major depressive episode in the previous 2 years

purge to rid the body of unwanted calories by means such as self-induced vomiting or misuse of laxatives, diuretics, or other medications

rape a form of sexual aggression that involves sexual activity (oral-genital sex, anal intercourse, or vaginal intercourse) performed against a person's will through the use of force, argument, pressure, alcohol or drugs, or authority

rape trauma syndrome a two-phase syndrome that rape survivors may experience, involving such emotional reactions as psychological distress, phobic reactions, and sexual dysfunction

rapid cycling the occurrence of four or more mood episodes per year in someone with bipolar disorder

reactive attachment disorder a trauma-related disorder characterized by inhibited, avoidant social behaviors and reluctance to seek or respond to attention or nurturing

reality principle an awareness of the demands of the environment and of the need to adjust behavior to meet these demands, from which the ego operates

reappraisal minimizing negative responses by looking at a situation from various perspectives

recovery movement philosophy that with appropriate treatment and support those with mental illness can improve and live satisfying lives even with any limitations caused by their illness

reinforcer anything that influences the frequency or magnitude of a behavior

relapse a return to drug or alcohol use after a period of abstention

relaxation training a therapeutic technique in which a person acquires the ability to relax the muscles of the body in almost any circumstance

reliability degree to which a measure or procedure yields the same results repeatedly

REM sleep behavior disorder condition involving dream-related vocalizations and motor behaviors that occur during REM sleep

remission a diminution in the seriousness of an illness

remit diminish or disappear

repressed memory memory of a traumatic event has been repressed and is, therefore, unavailable for recall

resilience the ability to recover quickly from stress or adversity

resistance during psychoanalysis, a process in which the client unconsciously attempts to impede the analysis by preventing the exposure of repressed material

response prevention technique in which an individual is prevented from performing a compulsive behavior

restricted affect severely diminished or limited emotional responsiveness

reuptake the reabsorption of a neurotransmitter after an impulse has been transmitted across the synapse

right to treatment the concept that mental patients who have been involuntarily committed have a right to receive therapy for their condition

rumination repeatedly thinking about concerns or details of past events

schema mental framework for organizing and interpreting information

schizoaffective disorder a condition involving the existence of both symptoms of schizophrenia and major depressive or manic symptoms

schizoid personality disorder characterized by detachment from social relationships and limited emotional expression

schizophrenia disorder characterized by severely impaired cognitive processes, personality disintegration, mood disturbance, and social withdrawal

schizophrenia spectrum group of disorders that range in severity and that have similar clinical features, including some degree of reality distortion

schizophreniform disorder psychotic episodes with a duration of at least 1 month but less than 6 months

schizotypal personality disorder characterized by peculiar thoughts and behaviors and by poor interpersonal relationships

scientific method a method of inquiry that provides for the systematic collection of data, controlled observation, and the testing of hypotheses

sedatives a class of drugs that have a calming or sedating effect

selective amnesia an inability to remember certain details of an event

selective mutism consistent failure to speak in certain situations

self-actualization an inherent tendency to strive toward the realization of one's full potential

self-efficacy belief in one's ability to succeed in a specific situation

self-schema stable set of beliefs and assumptions about the self that are based on the person's experiences, values, and perceived capabilities

self-stigma acceptance of prejudice and discrimination based on internalized negative societal beliefs or stereotypes

separation anxiety disorder severe distress about leaving home, being alone, or being separated from a parent

serotonin a neurotransmitter associated with mood, sleep, appetite, and impulsive behavior

sexual dysfunction a disruption of any part of the normal sexual response cycle that affects sexual desire, arousal, or response

sexual masochism disorder sexual urges, fantasies, or acts that involve being humiliated, bound, or made to suffer

sexual orientation sexual identity involving the gender to which a person is physically and emotionally attracted

sexual sadism disorder sexually arousing urges, fantasies, or acts that involve inflicting physical or psychological suffering on others

single-blind design experimental design in which only the participants are unaware of the purpose of the research

single-participant experiment an experiment performed on a single individual in which some aspect of the person's behavior is used as a control or baseline for comparison with future behaviors

sleep inertia significant grogginess and impaired alertness after sleeping or napping

sleep terrors episodes of intense fear that occur during deep sleep

social anxiety disorder an intense fear of being scrutinized in social or performance situations

social stigma negative societal beliefs about a group, including the view that the group is somehow different from other members of society

sociocultural factors such as gender, sexual orientation, spirituality, religion, socioeconomic status, race/ethnicity or culture that can exert an effect on mental health

somatic symptom and related disorders broad grouping of psychological disorders that involve physical symptoms or anxiety over illness, including somatic symptom disorder, illness anxiety disorder, conversion disorder (functional neurological symptom disorder), and factitious disorder

somatic symptom disorder condition involving a pattern of reporting distressing physical symptoms combined with extreme concern about health or fears of having an undiagnosed medical condition

somatic symptom disorder with predominant pain distressing and disruptive somatic symptoms involving severe or lingering pain

somatic symptoms physical or bodily symptoms

specific phobia an extreme fear of a specific object (such as snakes) or situation (such as being in an enclosed place)

specifier specific features associated with a diagnostic category

spirituality belief in an animating life force or energy beyond what we can perceive with our senses

standardization the use of identical procedures in the administration of tests

standardization sample the comparison group on which test norms are based

statistical significance the likelihood that a research finding is not due to chance alone

stereotype an oversimplified, often inaccurate, image or idea about a group of people

stimulant a substance that energizes the central nervous system

stress the internal psychological or physiological response to a stressor

stressor an external event or situation that places a physical or psychological demand on a person

stroke a sudden halting of blood flow to a portion of the brain, leading to brain damage

structural imaging procedures that allow for visualization of brain anatomy

substance abuse pattern of excessive or harmful use of any substance for mood-altering purposes

substance-use disorder condition in which cognitive, behavioral, and physiological symptoms contribute to the continued use of alcohol or drugs despite significant substance-related problems

subtype mutually exclusive subgrouping within a diagnosis

suicidal ideation thoughts about suicide

suicide the intentional, direct, and conscious taking of one's own life

suicidologist a professional who studies the manifestation, dynamics, and prevention of suicides

sympathetic nervous system part of the nervous system that automatically performs functions such as increasing heart rate, constricting blood vessels, and raising blood pressure

synapse tiny gap that exists between the axon of the sending neuron and the dendrites of the receiving neuron

syndrome certain symptoms that tend to occur regularly in clusters

synergistic effect the result of chemicals (or substances) interacting to multiply one another's effects

systematic desensitization treatment technique involving repeated exposure to a feared stimulus while a client is in a competing emotional or physiological state such as relaxation

systematized amnesia loss of memory for certain categories of information

systolic pressure force on blood vessels when the heart contracts

tarantism a form of mass hysteria prevalent during the Middle Ages, characterized by wild raving, jumping, dancing, and convulsing

***Tarasoff* ruling** a California Supreme Court decision that obligates mental health professionals to break confidentiality when their clients pose a clear and imminent danger to another person

temperament innate mental, physical, and emotional traits

tension headache head pain produced by prolonged contraction of the scalp and neck muscles, resulting in constriction of the blood vessels and steady pain

theory a group of principles and hypotheses that together explain some aspect of a particular area of inquiry

theory of mind the ability to recognize that others have emotions, beliefs, and desires that may be different from one's own

tic an involuntary, repetitive movement or vocalization

tolerance decreases in the effects of a substance that occur after chronic use

Tourette's disorder a condition characterized by multiple motor tics and one or more vocal tics

trait a distinguishing quality or characteristic of a person, including a tendency to feel, perceive, behave, or think in a relatively consistent manner

transference process by which a client undergoing psychoanalysis reenacts early conflicts by applying to the analyst feelings and attitudes that the person has toward significant others

transgender identity a person's innate psychological identification as male or female does not correspond with the person's biological sex

transient ischemic attack (TIA) a "mini-stroke" resulting from temporary blockage of arteries

transvestic disorder intense sexual arousal obtained through cross-dressing (wearing clothes appropriate to a different gender)

traumatic brain injury (TBI) a physical wound or internal injury to the brain

treatment plan a proposed course of therapy, developed collaboratively by a therapist and client, that addresses the client's most distressing mental health symptoms

treatment-resistant depression depressive episode that has not improved despite an adequate trial of antidepressant medication or other traditional forms of treatment

trephining a surgical method from the Stone Age in which part of the skull was chipped away to provide an opening through which an evil spirit could escape

trichotillomania recurrent and compulsive hair pulling that results in hair loss and causes significant distress

unconditioned response in classical conditioning, the unlearned response made to an unconditioned stimulus

unconditioned stimulus in classical conditioning, the stimulus that elicits an unconditioned response

universal shamanic tradition set of beliefs and practices from non-Western indigenous traditions that assume that special healers are blessed with powers to act as intermediaries or messengers between the human and spirit worlds

vaginismus involuntary spasm of the outer third of the vaginal wall that prevents or interferes with sexual intercourse

validity degree to which an instrument measures what it was developed to measure

vascular neurocognitive disorder condition involving decline in cognitive skills due to reduced blood flow to the brain

vocal tic an audible tic such as coughing, grunting, throat clearing, sniffling, or making sudden, vocal outbursts

voyeuristic disorder urges, acts, or fantasies that involve observing an unsuspecting person disrobing or engaging in sexual activity

white matter brain tissue comprised of myelinated nerve pathways

withdrawal adverse physical and psychological symptoms that occur after reducing or ceasing intake of a substance

REFERENCES

AAPA (Asian American Psychological Association). (2012). Suicide among Asian Americans. Retrieved from http://www.apa.org/pi/oema/resources/ethnicity-health/asian-american/suicide-fact-sheet.pdf

Aas, M., Djurovic, S., Athanasiu, L., Steen, N. E., Agartz, I., Lorentzen, S., . . . Melle, I. (2012). Serotonin transporter gene polymorphism, childhood trauma, and cognition in patients with psychotic disorders. *Schizophrenia Bulletin, 38,* 15–22.

Abbate-Daga, G., Amianto, F., Delsedime, N., De-Bacco, C., & Fassino, S. (2013). Resistance to treatment in eating disorders: A critical challenge. *BMC Psychiatry, 13,* 294. doi:10.1186/1471-244X-13-294

Abdulhamid, I., & Pataki, C. (2011). Pediatric Munchausen syndrome by proxy. Retrieved from http://emedicine.medscape.com/article/917525-overview#aw2aab6b7

Abelsohn, A. R., & Sanborn, M. (2010). Lead and children: Clinical management for family physicians. *Canadian Family Physician, 56,* 531–535.

Aboraya, A., Chumber, P., & Altaha, B. (2009). The treatment-resistant catatonia patient. *Current Psychiatry, 8,* 66–69.

Aboud, F., & Miller, L. (2007). Promoting peer intervention in name-calling. *South African Journal of Psychology, 37,* 803–819.

Abouzaid, S., Tian, H., Zhou, H., Kahler, K. H., Harris, M., & Kim, E. (2014). Economic burden associated with extrapyramidal symptoms in a medicaid population with schizophrenia. *Community Mental Health Journal, 50,* 51–58.

Abrahams, B. S., & Geschwind, D. H. (2010). Connecting genes to brain in the autism spectrum disorders. *Archives of Neurology, 67,* 395–399.

Abramowitz, J. S., Metzer-Brody, S., Leserman, J., Killenberg, S., Rinaldi, K., Mahaffey, B. L., . . . Pedersen, C. (2010). Obsessional thoughts and compulsive behaviors in a sample of women with postpartum mood symptoms. *Archives of Women's Mental Health, 13,* 523–530.

Abramowitz, J. S., Taylor, S., & McKay, D. (2010). Hypochondriasis and severe health anxiety. In D. McKay, J. S. Abramowitz, & S. Taylor (Eds.), *Cognitive-behavioral therapy for refractory cases: Turning failure into success* (pp. 327–346). Washington, DC: American Psychological Association Press.

Abrams, R. C., & Bromberg, C. E. (2007). Personality disorders in the elderly. *Psychiatric Annals, 37,* 123–127.

Abuse, Rape, and Domestic Violence Aid and Resource Collection, An. (2011). Rape and sexual assault statistics. Retrieved from http://www.aardvarc.org/rape/about/statistics.shtml

Addington v. Texas, 99 S. Ct. 1804 (1979).

Addington, J., & Addington, D. (2009). Three-year outcome of treatment in an early psychosis program. *Canadian Journal of Psychiatry, 54,* 626–630.

Adler, A. (1929/1964). *Social interest: A challenge to mankind.* New York, NY: Capricorn Books.

Adler, J., & Rogers, A. (1999, January 11). The new war against migraines. *Newsweek, 133,* 46–52.

Agras, W. S., Crow, S. J., Halmi, K. A., Mitchell, J. E., Wilson, G. T., & Kraemer, H. C. (2000). Outcome predictors for the cognitive behavior treatment of bulimia nervosa: Data from a multisite study. *American Journal of Psychiatry, 157,* 1302–1308.

Agrawal, A., Verweij, K. J., Gillespie, N. A., Heath, A. C., Lessov-Schlaggar, C. N., Martin, N. G., . . . Lynskey, M. T. (2012). The genetics of addiction—A translational perspective. *Translational Psychiatry, 2,* e140. doi:10.1038/tp.2012.54

Ahlers, C. J., Schaefer, G. A., Mundt, I. A., Roll, S., Englert, H., Willich, S. N., & Beier, K. M. (2011). How unusual are the contents of paraphilias? Paraphilia-associated sexual arousal patterns in a community-based sample of men. *Journal of Sexual Medicine, 8,* 1362–1370.

Ahmed, I., Cook, T., Genen, L., & Schwartz, R. A. (2014). Body dysmorphic disorder. Retrieved from http://emedicine.medscape.com/article/291182-overview#aw2aab6b2b3

Akbarian, S., & Halene, T. (2013). Neuroepigenetics of suicide. *American Journal of Psychiatry, 170,* 462–465.

Akinaga, M. (2013). Japanese Actroid robots—Latest human robots. Retrieved October 12, 2013, from http://wordsinjapanese.com/japanese-actroid-robot-latest-human-robots.php

Akinbami, L. J., Moorman, J. E., & Liu, X. (2011). Asthma prevalence, health care use, and mortality: United States, 2005–2009. *National Health Statistics Report, 12*(32), 1–14.

Albert, M. A., Glynn, R. G., & Buring, J. (2010, November). Women with high job strain have 40 percent increased risk of heart disease. Presented at the Annual Meetings of the American Heart Association, Chicago, IL.

Alcantara, C., Casement, M. D., & Lewis-Fernandez, R. (2013). Conditional risk for PTSD among Latinos: A systematic review of racial/ethnic differences and sociocultural explanations. *Clinical Psychology Review, 33,* 107–119.

Alcantara, C., & Gone, J. P. (2008). Suicide in Native American communities. In F. Leong & M. M. Leach (Eds.), *Ethnic suicides* (pp. 173–199). New York, NY: Routledge.

Alcantara, C., & Gone, J. P. (2014). Multicultural issues in the clinical interview and diagnostic process. In F. T. L. Leong, L. Comas-Diaz, G. C. Nagayama Hall, V. C. McLoyd, & J. E. Trimble (Eds.), *APA handbook of multicultural psychology. Vol. 2: Applications and training* (pp. 153–163). Washington, DC: APA.

Alegria, A. A., Blanco, C., Petry, N. M., Skodol, A. E., Liu, S. M., Grant, B., & Hasin, D. (2013). Sex differences in antisocial personality disorder: Results from the National Epidemiological Survey on Alcohol and Related Conditions. *Personality Disorders, 4,* 214–222.

Alexander, F. G., & Selesnick, S. T. (1966). *The history of psychiatry.* New York, NY: Harper & Row.

Alexander, G. C., Gallagher, S. A., Mascola, A., Moloney, R. M., & Stafford, R. S. (2011). Increasing off-label use of antipsychotic medications in the United States, 1995–2008. *Pharmacoepidemiology and Drug Safety, 20*(2), 177–184. doi:10.1002/pds.2082

Alford, G. S., Morin, C., Atkins, M., & Schuen, L. (1987). Masturbatory extinction of deviant sexual arousal: A case study. *Behavior Therapy, 18,* 265–271.

Algoe, S. B., & Fredrickson, B. L. (2011). Emotional fitness and the movement of affective science from lab to field. *American Psychologist, 66,* 35–42.

Ali, S., Nathani, M., Jabeen, S., Yazdani, I., Mouton, C. D., Bailey, R. K., . . . Riley, W. J. (2013). Alcohol: The lubricant to suicidality. *Innovations in Clinical Neuroscience, 10,* 20–29.

Alladi, S., Bak, T. H., Duggirala, V., Surampudi, B., Shailaja, M., Shukla, A. K., . . . Kaul, S. (2013). Bilingualism delays age at onset of dementia, independent of education and immigration status. *Neurology, 81,* 1938–1944.

Allanson, J., Bass, C., & Wade, D. T. (2002). Characteristics of patients with persistent severe disability and medically unexplained neurological symptoms: A pilot study. *Journal of Neurology, Neurosurgery and Psychiatry, 73,* 307–309.

Allen, J. P., Chango, J., Szwedo, D., Schad, M., & Marston, E. (2012). Predictors of susceptibility to peer influence regarding substance use in adolescence. *Child Development, 83,* 337–350.

Allen, K. L., Byrne, S. M., Oddy, W. H., & Crosby, R. D. (2013). Early onset binge eating and purging eating disorders: Course and outcome in a population-based study of adolescents. *Journal of Abnormal Child Psychology, 41,* 1083–1096.

Allen, S. S., Allen, A. M., & Pomerleau, C. S. (2009). Influence of phase-related variability in premenstrual symptomatology, mood, smoking withdrawal, and smoking behavior during ad libitum smoking, on smoking cessation outcome. *Addictive Behavior, 34,* 107–111.

Alloy, L. B., & Abramson, L. Y. (2010). The role of the behavioral approach system (BAS) in bipolar spectrum disorders. *Current Directions in Psychological Science, 19,* 189–194.

Alloy, L. B., Abramson, L. Y., Walshaw, P. D., Gerstein, R. K., Keyser, J. D., Whitehouse, W. G., . . . Harmon-Jones, E. J. (2009). Behavioral approach system (BAS)–relevant cognitive styles and bipolar spectrum disorders: Concurrent and prospective associations. *Journal of Abnormal Psychology, 118,* 459–471.

Alstadhaug, K. B., Hernandez, A., Naess, H., & Stovner, L. J. (2012). Migraine among Norwegian neurologists. *Headache, 52,* 1369–1376.

Althouse, B. M., Allem, J.-P., Childers, M. A., Dredze, M., & Ayers, J. W. (2014). Population health concerns during the United States' Great Recession. *American Journal of Preventive Medicine, 46,* 166–170.

Alvy, L. M. (2013). Do lesbian women have a better body image? Comparisons with heterosexual women and model of lesbian-specific factors. *Body Image, 11,* 524–534.

Amador, X. (2003). Poor insight in schizophrenia: Overview and impact on medication compliance. Retrieved from http://www.xavieramador.com/files/cns-special-report-on-insight.pdf

American Academy of Child and Adolescent Psychiatry. (2009). Practice parameter on the use of psychotropic medication in children and adolescents. *Journal of the American Academy of Child & Adolescent Psychiatry, 48,* 961–973.

American Academy of Neurology. (2013). AAN issues updated sports concussion guideline: Athletes with suspected concussion should be removed from play. Retrieved from https://www.aan.com/PressRoom/Home/PressRelease/1164

American Association of University Women. (2011). Crossing the line: Sexual harassment at school. Retrieved from http://www.aauw.org/learn/research/crossingtheline.cfm

American Association of University Women. (2013). The simple truth about the gender pay gap. Retrieved from http://www.aauw.org/research/the-simple-truth-about-the-gender-pay-gap

American Association on Intellectual and Developmental Disabilities. (2012). FAQ on intellectual disability. Retrieved from http://www.aaidd.org/content_104.cfm

American College Health Association. (2012). *National College health assessment. Reference Group Data Report, Spring 2012.* Hanover, MD: American College Health Association.

American Heart Association. (2010). *Heart disease and stroke statistics: 2010 update.* Dallas, TX: American Heart Association.

American Heart Association. (2013). Is broken heart syndrome real? Retrieved from http://www.heart.org/HEARTORG/Conditions/More/Cardiomyopathy/Is-Broken-Heart-Syndrome-Real_UCM_448547_Article.jsp

American Law Institute. (1962). *Model penal code: Proposed official draft.* Philadelphia, PA: Author.

American Medical Association. (2011, June 21). AMA adopts new policies at annual meeting. Retrieved from http://www.ama-assn.org/ama/pub/news/news/a11-new-policies.page

American Psychiatric Association. (2000). *Diagnostic and statistical manual of mental disorders* (4th ed., text rev.). Washington, DC: American Psychiatric Publishing.

American Psychiatric Association. (2006). Treatment recommendations for patients with eating disorders. *American Journal of Psychiatry, 163,* 5–54.

American Psychiatric Association (APA). (2013). *Diagnostic and statistical manual of mental disorders* (5th ed.). Arlington, VA: American Psychiatric Publishing.

American Psychological Association. (2003). Guidelines on multicultural education, training, research, practice, and organizational change for psychologists. *American Psychologist, 58,* 377–402.

American Psychological Association. (2010a). *Ethical principles of psychologists and code of conduct.* Washington, DC: Author.

American Psychological Association. (2010b). *Stress in America.* Washington, DC: Author.

American Psychological Association (2013). APA report on gun violence identifies precursors and promising solutions. Retrieved from http://www.apa.org/news/press/releases/2013/12/gun-violence.aspx

American Psychological Association. (2014). *Stress in America: Are teens adopting adults' stress habits?* Washington, DC: Author.

American Psychological Association, Task Force on the Sexualization of Girls. (2007). Report of the task force on the sexualization of girls. Retrieved from http://www.apa.org/pi/women/programs/girls/report.aspx

American Society of Addiction Medicine. (2012). White paper on state-level proposals to legalize marijuana. Retrieved from http://www.asam.org

Amir, L., Voracek, M., Yousef, S., Galadari, A., Yammahi, S., Sadeghi, M.-R., . . . Dervic, K. (2013). Suicidal behavior and attitudes among medical students in the United Arab Emirates. *Crisis, 34,* 116–123.

Amir, N., & Taylor, C. T. (2012). Combining computerized home-based treatments for generalized anxiety disorder: An attention modification program and cognitive behavioral therapy. *Behavior Therapy, 43,* 546–559.

Amminger, G. P., Schafer, M. R., Papageorgiou, K., Klier, C. M.,

Cotton, S. M., Harrigan, S. M., . . . Berger, G. E. (2010). Long-chain omega-3 fatty acids for indicated prevention of psychotic disorders: A randomized, placebo-controlled trial. *Archives of General Psychiatry, 67,* 146–154.

Andari, E., Duhamel, J. R., Zalla, T., Herbrecht, E., Leboyer, M., & Sirigu, A. (2010). Promoting social behavior with oxytocin in high-functioning autism spectrum disorders. *Proceedings of the National Academy of Sciences, 107,* 4389–4394.

Anderson, J. A., Mizgalewicz, A., & Illes, J. (2013). Triangulating perspectives on functional neuroimaging for disorders of mental health. *BMC Psychiatry, 13,* 208.

Anderson, K. N., & Bradley, A. J. (2013). Sleep disturbance in mental health problems and neurodegenerative disease. *Nature and Science of Sleep, 5,* 61–75.

Anderson, K. W., Taylor, S., & McLean, P. H. (1996). Panic disorder associated with blood-injury reactivity: The necessity of establishing functional relationships among maladaptive behaviors. *Behavior Therapy, 27,* 463–472.

Anderson, S. E., Gooze, R. A., Lemeshow, S., & Whitaker, R. C. (2012). Quality of early maternal-child relationship and risk of adolescent obesity. *Pediatrics, 129,* 132–140.

Andrade, C. (2013). Augmenting selective serotonin reuptake inhibitors with clomipramine in obsessive-compulsive disorder: Benefits and risks. *Journal of Clinical Psychiatry, 74,* 1128–1133.

Andrade, P., Noblesse, L. H., Temel, Y., Ackermans, L., Lim, L. W., Steinbusch, H. W., & Visser-Vandewalle, V. (2010). Neurostimulatory and ablative treatment options in major depressive disorder: A systematic review. *Acta Neurochirugia, 152,* 565–577.

Andresen, R., Oades, L., & Caputi, P. (2003). The experience of recovery from schizophrenia: Towards an empirically validated stage model. *Australian and New Zealand Journal of Psychiatry, 37,* 586–594.

Andrews, G., Cuijpers, P., Craske, M. G., McEvoy, P., & Titov, N. (2010). Computer therapy for the anxiety and depressive disorders is effective, acceptable and practical health care: A meta-analysis. *PLOS One, 5,* e13196.

Andrews, G., Hobbs, J. J., Borkovec, T. D., Beesdo, K., Craske, M. G., Heimberg, R. G., . . . Stanley, M. A. (2010). Generalized worry disorder: A review of DSM-IV generalized anxiety disorder and options for DSM-V. *Depression and Anxiety, 27,* 137–147.

Angrisani, L., Cutolo, P. P., Formisano, G., Nosso, G., & Vitolo, G. (2013). Laparoscopic adjustable gastric banding versus Roux-en-Y gastric bypass: 10-year results of a prospective, randomized trial. *Surgery for Obesity and Related Diseases, 9,* 405–413.

Ani, C., Reading, R., Lynn, R., Forlee, S., & Garralda, E. (2013). Incidence and 12-month outcome of non-transient childhood conversion disorder in the U.K. and Ireland. *British Journal of Psychiatry, 202,* 413–418.

Anorexia Nervosa and Associated Disorders. (2014). Eating disorder statistics. Retrieved from http://www.anad.org/get-information/about-eating-disorders/eating-disorders-statistics

Anthenelli, R. M. (2010). Focus on: Comorbid mental health disorders. Retrieved from http://pubs.niaaa.nih.gov/publications/arh40/109-117.htm

Anthony, W. A. (1993). Recovery from mental illness: The guiding vision of the mental health service system in the 1990s. *Psychosocial Rehabilitation Journal, 16,* 11–23.

Antypa, N., Serretti, A., & Rujescu, D. (2013). Serotonergic genes and suicide: A systematic review. *European Neuropsychopharmacology, 23,* 1125–1142.

Aoki, H., Kato, R., Hirano, K., Suzuki, T., Kato, K., & Inuma, M. (2003). A case of sudden unexplained nocturnal death from overlooked Brugada syndrome at a pre-employment check-up. *Journal of Occupational Health, 45,* 70–73.

APA Presidential Task Force on Evidence-Based Practice. (2006). Evidence-based practice in psychology. *American Psychologist, 61,* 271–285.

Arackal, B. S., & Benegal, V. (2007). Prevalence of sexual dysfunction in male subjects with alcohol dependence. *Indian Journal of Psychiatry, 49,* 109–120.

Arboleda-Fiórez, J., & Stuart, H. (2012). From sin to science: Fighting the stigmatization of mental illnesses. *Canadian Journal of Psychiatry, 57,* 457–463.

Arcelus, J., Haslam, M., Farrow, C., & Meyer, C. (2013). The role of interpersonal functioning in the maintenance of eating psychopathology: A systematic review and testable model. *Clinical Psychology Review, 33,* 156–167.

Arnsberg, F. K., Johannesson, K. B., & Michel, P.-O. (2013). Prevalence and duration of PTSD in survivors 6 years after a natural disaster. *Journal of Anxiety Disorders, 27,* 347–352.

Arria, A. M., Caldeira, K. M., O'Grady, K. E., Vincent, K. B., Johnson, E. P., & Wish, E. D. (2008). Nonmedical use of prescription stimulants among college students: Associations with attention-deficit–hyperactivity disorder and polydrug use. *Pharmacotherapy, 28,* 156–169.

Arseneault, L., Cannon, M., Fisher, H. L., Polanczyk, G., Moffitt, T. E., & Caspi, A. (2011). Childhood trauma and children's emerging psychotic symptoms: A genetically sensitive longitudinal cohort study. *American Journal of Psychiatry, 168,* 65–72.

Arzy, S., Collette, S., Wissmeyer, M., Lazeyras, F., Kaplan, P. W., & Blanke, O. (2011). Psychogenic amnesia and self-identity: A multimodal functional investigation. *European Journal of Neurology, 18,* 1422–1425.

Ashburner, J., Ziviani, J., & Rodger, S. (2010). Surviving in the mainstream: Capacity of children with autism spectrum disorders to perform academically and regulate their emotions and behavior at school. *Research in Autism Spectrum Disorders, 4,* 18–27.

Ashley, W. (2014). The angry black woman: The impact of pejorative stereotypes on psychotherapy with black women. *Social Work and Public Health, 29,* 27–34.

Associated Press. (1998, August 14). Psychiatrist is sued over multiple bad personalities. *Seattle Post Intelligencer,* p. A12.

Associated Press. (2001, April 22). Two therapists found guilty in rebirthing therapy death. *Bellingham Herald,* p. A3.

Associated Press. (2007a, January 26). Man loses memory, wanders for 25 days. Retrieved from www.msnbc.msn.com/id/16829260/print/1/displaymode/1098

Associated Press. (2007b, August 10). *Too many studies use college students as guinea pigs.* Retrieved from www.printthis.clickability.com/pt/cpt?action5cpt&title5Psych

Associated Press. (2012, July 20). Who is James Egan Holmes? Retrieved from http://www.toledoblade.com/Nation/2012/07/20/Suspect-described-2.html

Associated Press. (2014). Steubenville football coach pleads no contest. Retrieved from http://www.huffingtonpost.com/2014/04/22/matt-belardine-no-contest_n_5193024.html

Association for Frontotemporal Degeneration. (2014). Diagnosis. Retrieved from http://www.theaftd.org/frontotemporal-degeneration/diagnosis

Association for Psychological Science. (2007, March 2). Genes and stressed-out parents lead to shy kids. *Science Daily.* Retrieved from http://www.sciencedaily.com/releases/2007/03/070302111100.htm

Asthma and Allergy Foundation of America. (2007). Asthma facts and figures. Retrieved from http://www.aafa.org/display.cfm?id58&sub542

Auerbach, R. P., Ho, M. H., & Kim, J. C. (2014). Identifying cognitive and interpersonal predictors of adolescent depression. *Journal of Abnormal Child Psychology. 42,* 913–924

Ayllon, T., Haughton, E., & Hughes, H. B. (1965). Interpretation of symptoms: Fact or fiction. *Behaviour Research and Therapy, 3,* 1–7.

Babusa, B., & Túry, F. (2011). Nosological classification and assessment of muscle dysmorphia. *Psychiatria Hungarica, 26,* 158–166.

Badgaiyan, R. D. (2011). Neurotransmitter imaging: Basic concepts and future perspectives. *Current Medical Imaging Reviews, 7,* 98–103.

Bagalman, E., & Napili, A. (2013). *Prevalence of mental illness in the United States: Data sources and estimates.* Congressional Record Service. Washington, DC: U.S. Government Printing Office.

Bagge, C. L., Glenn, C. R., & Lee, H.-J. (2013). Quantifying the impact of recent negative life events on suicide attempts. *Journal of Abnormal Psychology, 122,* 359–368.

Baglioni, C., Battagliese, G., Feige, B., Spiegelhalder, K., Nissen, C., Voderholzer, U., . . . Riemann, D. (2011). Insomnia as a predictor of depression: A meta-analytic evaluation of longitudinal epidemiological studies. *Journal of Affective Disorders, 135,* 10–19.

Bahrampour, T. (2013, June 3). Baby boomers are killing themselves at an alarming rate, raising question: Why? Retrieved from http://www.washingtonpost.com/local/baby-boomers-are-killing-themselves-at-an-alarming-rate-begging-question-why/2013/06/03/d98acc7a-c41f-11e2-8c3b-0b5e9247e-8ca_print.html

Bailey, P. E., & Henry, J. D. (2010). Separating component processes of theory of mind in schizophrenia. *British Journal of Clinical Psychology, 49,* 43–52.

Baillie, L. E., Gabriele, J. M., & Penzien, D. B. (2014). A systematic review of behavioral headache interventions with an aerobic exercise component. *Headache, 54,* 40–53.

Bakbak, B., Gedik, S., Koktekir, B. E., & Okka, M. (2012). Cluster headache with ptosis responsive to intranasal lidocaine application: A case report. *Journal of Medical Case Reports, 15;6:64.*

Baker, J. H., Mitchell, K. S., Neale, M. C., & Kendler, K. S. (2010). Eating disorder symptomatology and substance use disorders: Prevalence and shared risk in a population based twin sample. *International Journal of Eating Disorders, 43,* 648–658.

Baker, J. L., Olsen, L. W., & Sorensen, T. I. A. (2007). Childhood body-mass index and the risk of coronary heart disease in adulthood. *New England Journal of Medicine, 357,* 2329–2337.

Baker, K. (2010). "It's not me" to "it was me, after all." *Psychoanalytic Social Work, 17,* 79–98.

Baker, L. D., Frank, K., Foster-Schubert, K., Green, P. S., Wilkinson, C. W., McTiernan, A., . . . Craft, S. (2010). Effects of aerobic exercise on mild cognitive impairment: A controlled trial. *Archives of Neurology, 67,* 71–79.

Baker, S. P., Hu, G., Wilcox, H. C., & Baker, T. D. (2013). Increase in suicide by hanging/suffocation in the U.S., 2000–2010. *American Journal of Preventive Medicine, 44,* 146–149.

Baker, T. B., McFall, R. M., & Shoham, V. (2008). Current status and future prospects of clinical psychology: Toward a scientifically principled approach to mental and behavioral health care. *Psychological Science in the Public Interest, 9,* 67–103.

Bakker, A., Spinhoven, P., Van Balkom, A. J. L. M., & Van Dyck, R. (2002). Relevance of assessment of cognitions during panic attacks in the treatment of panic disorder. *Psychotherapy and Psychosomatics, 71,* 158–162.

Balami, J. S., Chen, R., & Grunwald, I. Q. (2011). Neurological complications of acute ischaemic stroke. *The Lancet Neurology, 10*(4), 357–371.

Balazs, J., Miklosi, M., Kereszteny, A., Hoven, C. W., Carli, V., Wasserman, C., . . . Wasserman, D. (2013). Adolescent subthreshold-depression and anxiety: Psychopathology, functional impairment and increased suicide risk.

Journal of Child Psychology and Psychiatry, 54, 670–677.

Balci, K., Utku, U., Asil, T., & Celik, Y. (2011). Ischemic stroke in young adults: Risk factors, subtypes, and prognosis. *Neurologist, 17,* 16–20.

Baldassano, C. F. (2006). Illness course, comorbidity, gender, and suicidality in patients with bipolar disorder. *Journal of Clinical Psychiatry, 67*(Suppl 11), 8–11.

Bale, T. L., Baram, T. Z., Brown, A. S., Goldstein, J. M., Insel, T. R., McCarthy, M. M., . . . Nestler, E. J. (2010). Early life programming and neurodevelopmental disorders. *Biological Psychiatry, 68,* 314–319.

Baliki, M. N., Petre, B., Torbey, S., Herrmann, K. M., Huang, L., Schnitzer, T. J., . . . Apkarian, A. V. (2012). Corticostriatal functional connectivity predicts transition to chronic back pain. *Nature Neuroscience, 15,* 1117–1119.

Ballard, C., Corbett, A., & Jones, E. L. (2011). Dementia: Challenges and promising developments. *The Lancet Neurology, 10,* 7–9.

Ballenger, J. C., Davidson, J. R. T., Lecrubier, Y., Nutt, D. J., Borkovec, T. D., Rickels, K., . . . Wittchen, H. U. (2000). Consensus statement on generalized anxiety disorder from the International Consensus Group on depression and anxiety. *Journal of Clinical Psychiatry, 62,* 53–58.

Ballew, L., Morgan, Y., & Lippmann, S. (2003). Intravenous diazepam for dissociative disorder: Memory lost and found. *Psychosomatics, 44,* 346–349.

Ban, T. A. (2007). Fifty years chlorpromazine: A historical perspective. *Neuropsychiatric Disease and Treatment, 3,* 495–500.

Bande, C. S., & Garcia-Alba, C. (2008). Munchausen syndrome by proxy: A dilemma for diagnosis. *Roschachiana, 29,* 183–200.

Bandiera, F. C., Richardson, A. K., Lee, D. J., He, J. P., & Merikangas, K. R. (2011). Secondhand smoke exposure and mental health among children and adolescents. *Archives of Pediatrics & Adolescent Medicine, 165,* 332–338.

Banducci, A. N., Hoffman, E. M., Lejuez, C. W., & Koenen, K. C. (2014). The impact of childhood abuse on inpatient substance users: Specific links with risky sex, aggression, and emotion dysregulation. *Child Abuse and Neglect, 38,* 928–938.

Bandura, A. (1982). Self-efficacy mechanism in human agency. *American Psychologist, 37,* 122–147.

Bandura, A. (1997). *Self-efficacy: The exercise of self-control.* New York, NY: Freeman.

Bandura, A., & Rosenthal, T. L. (1966). Vicarious classical conditioning as a function of arousal level. *Journal of Personality and Social Psychology, 13,* 173–199.

Banerjee, G., & Roy, S. (1998). Determinants of help-seeking behaviour of families of schizophrenic patients attending a teaching hospital in India: An indigenous explanatory model. *International Journal of Social Psychiatry, 44,* 199–214.

Bang, J., Price, D., Prentice, G., & Campbell, J. (2009). ECT treatment for two cases of dementia-related pathological yelling. *Journal of Neuropsychiatry and Clinical Neuroscience, 20,* 379–380.

Baratta, M. V., Rozeske, R. R., & Maier, S. F. (2013). Understanding stress resilience. *Frontiers in Behavioral Neuroscience, 7,* 1–2.

Barbaresi, W. J., Colligan, R. C., Weaver, A. L., Voigt, R. G., Killian, J. M., & Katusic, S. K. (2013). Mortality, ADHD, and psychosocial adversity in adults with childhood ADHD: A prospective study. *Pediatrics, 131,* 637–644.

Barber, J. P., Morse, J. Q., Krakauer, I. D., Chittams, J., & Crits-Cristoph, K. (1997). Change in obsessive-compulsive and avoidant personality disorders following time-limited supportive-expressive therapy. *Journal of Psychotherapy, 34,* 133–143.

Barbui, C., Cipriani, A., Patel, V., Ayuso-Mateos, J. L., & van Ommeren, M. (2011). Efficacy of anti-depressants and benzodiazepines in minor depression: Systematic review and meta-analysis. *British Journal of Psychiatry, 198,* 11–16.

Barch, D. (2013). The CAINS: Theoretical and practical advances in the assessment of negative symptoms in schizophrenia. *American Journal of Psychiatry, 170,* 133–135.

Bardone-Cone, A. M., & Cass, K. M. (2007). What does viewing a pro-anorexia website do? An experimental examination of website exposure and moderating effects. *International Journal of Eating Disorders, 40,* 537–548.

Bargenquast, R., & Schweitzer, R. D. (2013). Enhancing sense of recovery and self-reflectivity in people with schizophrenia: A pilot study of Metacognitive Narrative Psychotherapy. *Psychology and Psychotherapy: Theory, Research and Practice.* doi:10.1111/papt.12019

Barlow, M. R. (2011). Memory for complex emotional material in dissociative identity disorder. *Journal of Trauma and Dissociation, 12,* 53–66.

Barnett, E., Moyers, T. B., Sussman, S., Smith, C., Rohrbach, L. A., Sun, .P, & Spruijt-Metz, D. (2014). From counselor skill to decreased marijuana use: Does change talk matter? *Journal of Substance Abuse Treatment, 46,* 498–505.

Barnett, J. H., McDougall, F., Xu, M. K., Croudace, T. J., Richards, M., & Jones, P. B. (2012). Childhood cognitive function and adult psychopathology: Associations with psychotic and non-psychotic symptoms in the general population. *British Journal of Psychiatry, 201,* 124–130.

Baron, L., Straus, M. A., & Jaffee, D. (1988). Legitimate violence, violent attitudes, and rape: A test of the cultural spillover theory. *Annals of the New York Academy of Sciences, 528,* 79–110.

Barrera, T. L., & Norton, P. J. (2010). Quality of life impairment in generalized anxiety disorder, social phobia, and panic disorder. *Journal of Anxiety Disorders, 23,* 1086–1090.

Bart, G. (2012). Maintenance medication for opiate addiction: The foundation of recovery. *Addictive Diseases, 31,* 207–225.

Bartik, W., Maple, M., Edwards, H., & Kiernan, M. (2013). Adolescent survivors after suicide: Australian young people's bereavement narratives. *Crisis, 34,* 211–217.

Barton, J. (2004, September 29). Mental health centers feel storm surge: Calls for help climb after hurricanes. *Columbian* (Vancouver, WA), p. A3.

Barzman, D. H., Patel, A., Sonnier, L., & Strawn, J. R. (2010). Neuroendocrine aspects of pediatric aggression: Can hormone measures be clinically useful? *Journal of Neuropsychiatric Disease and Treatment, 6,* 691–697.

Bashir, A., Lipton, R. B., Ashina, S., & Ashina, M. (2013). Migraine and structural changes in the brain: A systematic review and meta-analysis. *Neurology, 81,* 1260–1268.

Baskin-Sommers, A., Krusemark, E., & Ronningstam, E. (2014, February 10). Empathy in narcissistic personality disorder: From clinical and empirical perspectives. *Personality Disorders: Theory, Research, and Treatment.*

Baslet, G., & Hill, J. (2011). Case report: Brief mindfulness-based psychotherapeutic intervention during inpatient hospitalization in a patient with conversion and dissociation. *Clinical Case Studies, 10,* 95–109.

Bassett, E. & Moore, S. (2013). Gender differences in the social pathways linking neighborhood disadvantage to depressive symptoms in adults. PLoS One, 17;8(10):e76554. doi: 10.1371/journal.pone.0076554. eCollection 2013.

Bassetti, C., & Aldrich, M. S. (1997). Idiopathic hypersomnia: A series of 42 patients. *Brain, 120,* 1423–1435.

Bateman, R. J., Aisen, P. S., De Strooper, B., Fox, N. C., Lemere, C. A., Ringman, J. M., . . . Xiong, C. (2011). Autosomal-dominant Alzheimer's disease: A review and proposal for the prevention of Alzheimer's disease. *Alzheimer's Research & Therapy, 3,* 1–13.

Bates, M. J., & Bowles, S. V. (2012). Review of well-being in the context of suicide prevention and resilience. Retrieved from http://ftp.rta.nato.int/public//PubFullText/RTO/MP%5CRTO-MP-HFM-205///MP-HFM-205-29.doc

Battiste, N., & Effron, L. (2012). EDNOS: Deadliest eating disorder is quietly the most common. Retrieved from http://news.yahoo.com/ednos-deadliest-eating-disorder-quietly-most-common-204016641—abc-news-health.html

Baugh, C. M., Stamm, J. M., Riley, D. O., Gavett, B. E., Shenton, M. E., Lin, A., . . . Stern, R. A. (2012). Chronic traumatic encephalopathy: Neurodegeneration following repetitive concussive and subconcussive brain trauma. *Brain Imaging and Behavior, 6,* 244–254.

Bava, S., Jacobus, J., Thayer, R. E., & Tapert, S. F. (2013). Longitudinal changes in white matter integrity among adolescent substance users. *Alcoholism, Clinical and Experimental Research, Supplement 1,* E181–E189.

Bayer, J. K., Rapee, R. M., Hiscock, H., Ukoumunne, O. C., Mihalopoulos, C., & Wake, M. (2011). Translational research to prevent internalizing problems early in childhood. *Depression and Anxiety, 28,* 50–57.

Beard, C., Moitra, E., Weisberg, R. B., & Keller, M. B. (2010). Characteristics and predictors of social phobia course in a longitudinal study of primary-care patients. *Depression and Anxiety, 27,* 839–845.

Bearden, C. E., Woogen, M., & Glahn, D. C. (2010). Neurocognitive and neuroimaging predictors of clinical outcome in bipolar disorder. *Current Psychiatry Reports, 12,* 499–504.

Beardslee, W. R., Brent, D. A., Weersing, V. R., Clarke, G. N., Porta, G., Hollon, S. D., . . . Garber, J. (2013). Prevention of depression in at-risk adolescents: Longer-term effects. *JAMA Psychiatry, 70*(11), 1161–1170. doi:10.1001/jamapsychiatry.2013.295

Beauchamp, G. A., Ho, M. L., & Yin, S. (2014). Variation in suicide occurrence by day and during major American holidays. *Journal of Emergency Medicine.* doi:10.1016/j.jemermed.2013.09.023 [Epub ahead of print]

Beck, A. T. (1976). *Cognitive therapy and emotional disorders.* New York, NY: International Universities Press.

Beck, A. T. (1985). Cognitive therapy, behavior therapy, psychoanalysis, and pharmacotherapy: A cognitive continuum. In M. Mahoney & A. Freeman (Eds.), *Cognition and psychotherapy* (pp. 197–220). New York, NY: Plenum Press.

Beck, A. T., Freeman, A. F., & Associates. (1990). *Cognitive therapy of personality disorders.* New York, NY: Guilford Press.

Beck, A. T., Grant, P. M., Huh, G. A., Perivoliotis, D., & Chang, N. A. (2013). Dysfunctional attitudes and expectancies in deficit syndrome schizophrenia. *Schizophrenia Bulletin, 39,* 43–51.

Beck, A. T., Ward, C. H., Mendelson, M., Mock, J. E., & Erbaugh, J. (1961). An inventory for measuring depression. *Archives of General Psychiatry, 4,* 561–571.

Beck, A. T., & Weishaar, M. E. (2010). Cognitive therapy. In R. J. Corsini & D. Wedding (Eds.), *Current psychotherapies* (9th ed., pp. 301–322). Belmont, CA: Brooks/Cole.

Becker, A. E. (2004). Television, disordered eating, and young women in Fiji: Negotiating body image and identity during rapid social change. *Cultural Medical Psychiatry, 28,* 533–559.

Becker, A. E., Burwell, R. A., Herzog, D. B., Hamburg, P., & Gilman, S. E. (2002). Eating behaviours and attitudes following prolonged exposure to television among ethnic Fijian adolescent girls. *British Journal of Psychiatry, 180,* 509–514.

Becker, A. E., & Kleiman, A. (2013). Mental health and the global agenda. *New England Journal of Medicine, 369,* 66–73.

Becker, B., Scheele, D., Moessner, R., Maier, W., & Hurlemann, R. (2013). Deciphering the neural signature of conversion blindness. *American Journal of Psychiatry, 170,* 121.

Beghi, M., & Rosenbaum, J. F. (2010). Risk factors for fatal and nonfatal repetition of suicide attempt: A critical appraisal. *Current Opinions in Psychiatry, 23,* 349–355.

Begum, M., & McKenna, P. J. (2011). Olfactory reference syndrome: A systematic review of the world literature. *Psychological Medicine, 41,* 453–461.

Bellack, A. S. (2006). Scientific and consumer models of recovery in schizophrenia: Concordance, contrasts, and implications. *Schizophrenia Bulletin, 32,* 432–442.

Bello, N. T., & Hajnal, A. (2010). Dopamine and binge eating behaviors. *Pharmacology, Biochemistry and Behavior, 97,* 25–33.

Belluck, P. (2010, June 20). Hallucinations in hospital pose risk to elderly. *New York Times.* Retrieved from http://www.nytimes.com

Belsky, D. W., Moffitt, T. E., Baker, T. B., Biddle, A. K., Evans, J. P., Harrington, H., . . . Caspi, A. (2013). Polygenic risk and the developmental progression to heavy, persistent smoking and nicotine dependence: Evidence from a 4-decade longitudinal study. *JAMA Psychiatry, 70,* 534–542.

Benazzi, F. (2007). Bipolar II disorder: Epidemiology, diagnosis and management. *CNS Drugs, 21,* 727–740.

Bender, E. (2013, April 2). AACAP helps psychiatrists address patients' cultural factors. *Psychiatric News, 48,* 1–3.

Bender, L. (1938). A visual motor gestalt test and its clinical use. *Research Monographs of the American Orthopsychiatric Association, 3*(11), 176.

Bender, R. E., & Alloy, L. B. (2011). Life stress and kindling in bipolar disorder: Review of the evidence and integration with emerging biopsychosocial theories. *Clinical Psychology Review, 31,* 383–398.

Benedict, J. G., & Donaldson, D. W. (1996). Recovered memories threaten all. *Professional Psychology: Research and Practice, 27,* 427–428.

Bener, A., Al-Hamaq, A. O., & Dafeeah, E. E. (2014). A two fold risk of metabolic syndrome in a sample of patients with schizophrenia: Do consanguinity and family history increase risk? *Diabetes & Metabolic Syndrome, 8,* 24–29.

Benes, F. M. (2009). Neural circuitry models of schizophrenia: Is it dopamine, GABA, glutamate, or something else? *Biological Psychiatry, 65,* 1003–1005.

Benjet, C., Borges, G., & Medina-Mora, M. E. (2010). Chronic childhood adversity and onset of psychopathology during three life stages: Childhood, adolescence and adulthood. *Journal of Psychiatric Research, 44,* 732–740.

Bennett, M. P., & Lengacher, C. A. (2006). Humor and laughter may influence health. *Evidence Based Complementary Alternative Medicine, 3,* 61–63.

Bennett, M. P., Zeller, J. M., Rosenberg, L., & McCann, J. (2003). The effect of mirthful laughter on stress and natural killer cell activity. *Alternative Therapies in Health and Medicine, 9,* 38–45.

Bennett, S. A., Beck, J. G., & Clapp, J. D. (2009). Understanding the relationship between posttraumatic stress disorder and trauma cognitions: The impact of thought control strategies. *Behaviour Research and Therapy, 47,* 1018–1023.

Benowitz, N. L. (2010). Nicotine addiction. *New England Journal of Medicine, 362,* 2295–2303.

Benton, S. A., Robertson, J. M., Tseng, W.-C., Newton, F. B., & Benton, S. L. (2003). Changes in counseling center client problems across 13 years. *Professional Psychology: Research and Practice, 34,* 66–72.

Benton, T. D., Ifeagwu, J. A., Aronson, S. C., & Talavera, F. (2012). Acute stress disorder. Retrieved from http://emedicine.medscape.com/article/292759-overview#aw2aab6b6

Benyamina, A., Lecacheux, M., Blecha, L., Reynaud, M., & Lukasiewcz, M. (2008). Pharmacotherapy and psychotherapy in cannabis withdrawal and dependence. *Expert Reviews in Neurotherapy, 8,* 479–491.

Ben-Zeev, D., Kaiser, S. M., Brenner, C. J., Begale, M., Duffecy, J., & Mohr, D. C. (2013). Development and usability testing of FOCUS: A smartphone system for self-management of schizophrenia. *Psychiatric Rehabilitation Journal.* Advance online publication. doi:10.1037/prj0000019

Berenbaum, H. (2013). Classification and psychopathology research. *Journal of Abnormal Psychology, 122,* 894–901.

Berg, K. C., Crosby, R. D., Cao, L., Peterson, C. B., Engel, S. G., Mitchell, J. E., & Wonderlich, S. A. (2013). Facets of negative affect prior to and following binge-only, purge-only, and binge/purge events in women with bulimia nervosa. *Journal of Abnormal Psychology, 122,* 111–118.

Bergemann, N., Parzer, P., Jaggy, S., Auler, B., Mundt, C., & Maier-Braunleder, S. (2008). Estrogen and comprehension of metaphoric speech in women suffering from schizophrenia: Results of a double-blind, placebo-controlled trial. *Schizophrenia Bulletin, 34,* 1172–1181.

Berger, W., Mendlowicz, M. V., Marques-Portella, C., Kinrys, G., Fontenelle, L. F., Marmar, C. R., Figueira, I. (2009). Pharmacologic alternatives to antidepressants in posttraumatic stress disorder: A systematic review. *Progress in Neuropsychopharmacology and Biological Psychiatry, 33,* 169–180.

Bergstrom, R. L., & Neighbors, C. (2006). Body image disturbance and the social norms approach: An integrative review of the literature. *Journal of Social and Clinical Psychology, 25,* 975–1000.

Berk, L., Hallam, K. T., Colom, F., Vieta, E., Hasty, M., Macneil, C., & Berk, M. (2010). Enhancing medication adherence in patients with bipolar disorder. *Human Psychopharmacology, 25,* 1–16.

Berlim, M. T., & Turecki, G. (2007). Definition, assessment, and staging of treatment-resistant refractory major depression: A review of current concepts and methods. *Canadian Journal of Psychiatry, 52,* 46–54.

Berlin, F. S., & Sawyer, D. (2012). Potential consequences of accessing child pornography over the Internet and who is accessing it. *Sexual Addiction & Compulsivity, 19,* 30–40.

Berman, A. L. (2006). Risk management with suicidal patients. *Journal of Clinical Psychology: In Session, 62,* 171–184.

Berman, J. (2010, February 23). The media's contribution to eating disorders [Web log post]. Retrieved from http://doctorjenn.com/wordpress/2010/02/the-media%E2%80%99s- contribution-to-eating-disorders

Berman, S. M., Kuczenski, R., McCracken, J. T., & London, E. D. (2009). Potential adverse effects of amphetamine treatment on brain and behavior: A review. *Molecular Psychiatry, 14,* 123–142.

Bernal, G., & Saez-Santiago, E. (2006). Culturally centered psychosocial interventions. *Journal of Community Psychology, 34,* 121–132.

Bernard, C., Helmer, C., Dilharreguy, B., Amieva, H., Auriacombe, S., Dartigues, J. F., . . . Catheline, G. (2014). Time course of brain volume changes in the preclinical phase of Alzheimer's disease. *Alzheimer's & Dementia. 10,* 143–151.

Bernstein, E. B. (2012). Conduct disorder. Retrieved from http://emedicine.medscape.com/article/918213-overview

Berry, E. A., Heaton, P. T., & Kelton, C. M. (2011). National estimates of the inpatient burden of pediatric bipolar disorder in the United States. *Journal of Mental Health Policy and Economics, 14,* 115–123.

Berry, M. D. (2013). Historical revolutions in sex therapy: A critical examination of men's sexual dysfunctions and their treatment. *Journal of Sex and Marital Therapy, 39,* 21–39.

Bersamin, M. M., Zamboanga, B. L., Schwartz, S. J., Donnellan, M. B., Hudson, M., Weisskirch, R. S., . . . Caraway, S. J. (2014). Risky business: Is there an association between casual sex and mental health among emerging adults? *Journal of Sex Research, 51,* 43–51.

Bertholet, N., Faouzi, M., Studer, J., Daeppen, J. B., & Gmel, G. (2013). Perception of tobacco, cannabis, and alcohol use of others is associated with one's own use. *Addiction Science & Clinical Practice, 8,* 15. doi:10.1186/1940-0640-8-15

Beseler, C. L., Taylor, L. A., Kraemer, D. T., & Leeman, R. F. (2012). A latent class analysis of DSM-IV alcohol use disorder criteria and binge drinking in undergraduates. *Alcoholism: Clinical and Experimental Research, 36,* 153–161.

Beucke, J. C., Sepulcre, J., Talukdar, T., Linnman, C., Zschenderlein, K., Endrass, T., . . . Kathmann, N. (2013). Abnormally high degree connectivity of the orbitofrontal cortex in obsessive-compulsive disorder. *American Journal of Psychiatry, 70,* 619–629.

Bhalla, R. N. (2013). Schizophreniform disorder. Retrieved from http://emedicine.medscape.com/article/2008351-overview

Bhalla, R. N., & Ahmed, I. (2011). Schizophreniform disorder. Retrieved from http://emedicine.medscape.com/article/2008351-overview

Bhar, S. S., Beck, A. T., & Butler, A. C. (2012). Beliefs and personality disorders: An overview of the Personality Beliefs Questionnaire. *Journal of Clinical Psychology, 68,* 88–100.

Bhugra, D., Popelyuk, D., & McMullen, I. (2010). Paraphilias across cultures: Contexts and controversies. *Journal of Sex Research, 47,* 242–256.

Bianchi, K. N., & Carter, M. M. (2012). An experimental analysis of disgust sensitivity and fear of contagion in spider and blood injection injury phobia. *Journal of Anxiety Disorders, 26,* 753–761.

Bienvenu, O. J., Davydow, D. S., & Kendler, K. S. (2011). Psychiatric "diseases" vs. behavioral disorders and degree of genetic influence. *Psychological Medicine, 41,* 33–40.

Bigard, A. (2010). Risks of energy drinks in youth. *Archives of Pediatrics, 17,* 1625–1631.

Billioti de Gage, S., Bégaud, B., Bazin, F., Verdoux, H., Dartigues, J. F., Pérès K., . . . Pariente, A. (2012). Benzodiazepine use and risk of dementia: Prospective population based study. *British Medical Journal, 345,* e6231. doi:10.1136/bmj.e6231

Biondi, M., & Picardi, A. (2003). Attribution of improvement to medication and increased risk of relapse of panic disorder with agoraphobia: Reply. *Psychotherapy and Psychosomatics, 72,* 110–111.

Bisson, J. I., Roberts, N. P., Andrew, M., Cooper, R., & Lewis, C. (2013). Psychological therapies for chronic post-traumatic stress disorder (PTSD) in adults. *Cochrane Database of Systematic Reviews,* Issue 12. Art. no.: CD003388. doi:10.1002/14651858.CD003388.pub4

Bitzer, J., Giraldi, A., & Pfaus, J. (2013). Sexual desire and hypoactive sexual desire disorder in women. Introduction and overview. Standard operating procedure. *Journal of Sexual Medicine, 10,* 36–49.

Bjornsson, A. S., Didie, E. R., & Phillips, K. A. (2010). Body dysmorphic disorder. *Dialogues in Clinical Neuroscience, 12,* 221–232.

Bjornsson, A. S., Dyck, I., Moitra, E., Stout, R. L., Weisberg, R., Keller, M. B., Phillips, K. A. (2011). The clinical course of body dysmorphic disorder in the Harvard/Brown Anxiety Research Project (HARP). *Journal of Nervous and Mental Disease, 199,* 55–57.

Bjornsson, A. S., Sibrava, N. J., Beard, C., Moitra, E., Weisberg, R. B., Benítez, C., & Keller, M. B. (2014). Two-year course of generalized anxiety disorder, social anxiety disorder, and panic disorder with agoraphobia in a sample of Latino adults. *Journal of Consulting and Clinical Psychology.* doi: 10.1037/a0036565

Black, D. L., Cawthon, B., Robert, T., Moser, F., Caplan, Y. H., & Cone, E. J. (2009). Multiple drug ingestion by ecstasy abusers in the United States. *Journal of Analytical Toxicology, 33,* 143–147.

Black, M. C. (2011). Intimate partner violence and adverse health consequences. *American Journal of Lifestyle Medicine, 5,* 428–439.

Black, M. C., Basile, K. C., Breiding, M. J., Smith, S. G., Walters, M. L., Merrick, M. T., . . . Stevens, M. R. (2011). *The National Intimate Partner and Sexual Violence Survey (NISVS): 2010 summary report.* Atlanta, GA: National Center for Injury Prevention and Control, Centers for Disease Control and Prevention.

Blacker, K. J., Herbert, J. D., Forman, E. M., & Kounios, J. (2012). Acceptance-versus change-based pain management: The role of psychological acceptance. *Behavior Modification, 36,* 37–48.

Blais, M. A., Smallwood, P., Groves, J. E., & Rivas-Vazquez, R. A. (2008). Personality and personality disorders. In T. A. Stern, J. F. Rosenbaum, M. Fava, J. Biederman, & S. L. Rauch (Eds.), *Massachusetts General Hospital comprehensive clinical psychiatry.* Philadelphia, PA: Elsevier Mosby.

Blanchard, J. J., Gangestad, S. W., Brown, S. A., & Horan, W. P. (2000). Hedonic capacity and schizotypy revisited: A taxometric analysis of social anhedonia. *Journal of Abnormal Psychology, 109,* 87–95.

Blashill, A. J., & Safren, S. A. (2014). Sexual orientation and anabolic-androgenic steroids in US adolescent boys. *Pediatrics. 133,* 469–475.

Blashill, A. J., & Vander Wal, J. S. (2009). Mediation of gender role conflict and eating pathology in gay men. *Psychology of Men and Masculinity, 10,* 204–217.

Blaze, D. (2013). Neurocognitive disorders in DSM-5. *American Journal of Psychiatry, 170,* 585–587.

Bloch, M. H., & Pittenger, C. (2010). The genetics of obsessive-compulsive disorder. *Current Psychiatry Reviews, 6,* 91–103.

Bloomberg, D. (2000, January/February). Bennett Braun case settled: Two-year loss of license, five years probation. *Skeptical Inquirer, 7–8.*

Blum, S., Luchsinger, J. A., Manly, J. J., Schupf, N., Stern, Y., Brown, T. R., . . . Brickman, A. M. (2012). Memory after silent stroke: Hippocampus and infarcts both matter. *Neurology, 78,* 38–46.

Blume, H. K., Brockman, L. N., & Breuner, C. C. (2012). Biofeedback therapy for pediatric headache: Factors associated with response. *Headache, 52,* 1377–1386.

Boardman, J. D., Blalock, C. L., Pampel, F. C., Hatemi, P. K., Heath, A. C., & Eaves, L. J. (2011). Population composition, public policy, and the genetics of smoking. *Demography, 48,* 1517–1533.

Bobo, W. V. (2013). Asenapine, iloperidone and lurasidone: Critical appraisal of the most recently approved pharmacotherapies for schizophrenia in adults. *Expert Review in Clinical Pharmacology, 6,* 61–91.

Bobzean, S. A., Denobrega, A. K., & Perrotti, L. I. (2014). Sex differences in the neurobiology of drug addiction. *Experimental Neurology.* doi:10.1016/j.expneurol.2014.01.022 [Epub ahead of print]

Bochukova, E. G., Huang, N., Keogh, J., Henning, E., Purmann, C., Blaszczyk, K., . . . Farooqui, I. S. (2010). Large, rare chromosomal deletions associated with severe early-onset obesity. *Nature, 463,* 666–669.

Bock, M. A. (2007). The impact of social-behavioral learning strategy training on the social interaction skills of four students with Asperger syndrome. *Focus on Autism and Other Developmental Disabilities, 22,* 88–95.

Bodell, L. P., Joiner, T. E., & Keel, P. K. (2013). Comorbidity-independent risk for suicidality increases with bulimia nervosa but not with anorexia nervosa. *Journal of Psychiatric Research, 47,* 617–621.

Bodell, L. P., Smith, A. R., Gordon, K. T., Holm-Denoma, J. M., & Joiner, T. E. (2011). Low social support and negative life events predict later bulimic symptoms. *Eating Behaviors, 12,* 44–48.

Boeding, S. E., Paprocki, C. M., Baucom, J. S., Abramowitz, M. C., Wheaton, M. L. E., & Fischer, M. S. (2013). Let me check that for you: Symptom accommodation in romantic partners of adults with obsessive compulsive disorder. *Behaviour Research and Therapy, 51,* 316–322.

Boehm, J. K., Peterson, C., Kivimaki, M., & Kubzansky, L. D. (2011). Heart health when life is satisfying: Evidence from the Whitehall II cohort study. *European Heart Journal, 32,* 2672–2677.

Boehmer, U., Bowen, D. J., & Bauer, G. R. (2007). Overweight and obesity in sexual-minority women: Evidence from population-based data. *American Journal of Public Health, 29,* 1134–1140.

Boettcher, J., Åström, V., Påhlsson, D., Schenstrom, O., Andersson, G., & Carlbring, P. (2014). Internet-based mindfulness treatment for anxiety disorders: A randomized controlled trial. *Behavior Therapy, 45,* 241–253.

Bohman, H., Jonsson, U., Päären, A., von Knorring, L., Olsson, G., & von Knorring, A. L. (2012). Prognostic significance of functional somatic symptoms in adolescence: A 15-year community-based follow-up study of adolescents with depression compared with healthy peers. *BMC Psychiatry, 12,* 90. doi:10.1186/1471-244X-12-90

Bohne, A., Keuthen, N. J., Wilhelm, S., Deckersbach, T., & Jenike, M. A. (2002). Prevalence of symptoms of body dysmorphic disorder and its correlates: A cross-cultural comparison. *Psychosomatics, 43,* 486–490.

Bokszczanin, A. (2008). Parental support, family conflict, and overprotectiveness: Predicting PTSD symptom levels of adolescents 28 months after a natural disaster. *Anxiety, Stress, & Coping, 21,* 325–335.

Bola, J. R., Kao, D. T., & Soydan, H. (2012). Antipsychotic medication for early-episode schizophrenia. *Schizophrenia Bulletin, 38,* 23–25.

Bolier, L., Haverman, M., Westerhof, G. J., Riper, H., Smit, F., & Bohlmeijer, E. (2013). Positive psychology interventions: A meta-analysis of randomized controlled studies. *BMC Public Health, 13,* 119.

Bollini, A. M., & Walker, E. F. (2007). Schizotypal personality disorder. In W. O. Donohus, K. A. Fowler, & S. O. Lilienfeld (Eds.), *Personality disorders: Toward the DSM-V* (pp. 32–40). Los Angeles, CA: Sage.

Bolton, J. M., Au, W., Leslie, W. D., Martens, P. J., Enns, M. W., Roos, L. L., . . . Sareen, J. (2013). Parents bereaved by offspring suicide: A population-based longitudinal case-control study. *JAMA Psychiatry, 70,* 158–167.

Bonanno, G. A. (2005). Resilience in the face of potential trauma. *Current Directions in Psychological Science, 14,* 135–138.

Bond, E. (2012). Virtually anorexic—Where's the harm? A research study on the risks of pro-anorexia websites. Retrieved from http://www.ucs.ac.uk/SchoolsAndNetwork/UCSSchools/SchoolofAppliedSocialSciences/Virtually%20Anorexic.pdf

Boone, L., Soenens, B., Braet, C., & Goossens, L. (2010). An empirical typology of perfectionism in early-to-mid adolescents and its relation with eating disorder symptoms. *Behaviour Research and Therapy, 48,* 686–691.

Boothroyd, L. G., Tovée, M. J., & Pollet, T. V. (2012). Visual diet versus associative learning as mechanisms of change in body size preferences. *PLOS One,* 7(11), e48691. doi:10.1371/journal.pone.0048691

Bootzin, R. R., & Bailey, E. T. (2005). Understanding placebo, nocebo, and iatrogenic treatment effects. *Journal of Clinical Psychology, 61,* 87.

Borch-Jacobsen, M. (1997). Sybil—The making of a disease: An interview with Dr. Herbert Spiegel. *New York Review of Books, 44,* 60–64.

Bornstein, R. F. (1997). Dependent personality disorder in the DSM-IV and beyond. *Clinical Psychology, 4,* 175–187.

Borzekowski, D. L. G., Schenk, S., Wilson, J. L., & Peebles, R. (2010). E-ana and e-mia: A content analysis of pro–eating disorder Web sites. *American Journal of Public Health, 100,* 1526–1534.

Both, S., & Laan, E. (2009). Directed masturbation: A treatment for female orgasmic dysfunction. In W. T. O'Donohue & J. E. Fisher (Eds.), *General principles and empirically supported techniques of cognitive behavior therapy* (pp. 256–264). Hoboken, NJ: John Wiley.

Boudreault, S. (2011). Top six Charlie Sheen rantings, with analysis [Web log post]. Retrieved from http://celebs.gather.com/viewArticle.action?articleId5281474979115776

Bourget, D., & Whitehurst, L. (2007). Amnesia and crime. *Journal of the American Academy of Psychiatry and the Law, 35,* 469–480.

Bouquegneau, A., Dubois, B. E., Krzesinski, J. M., & Delanaye, P. (2012). Anorexia nervosa and the kidney. *American Journal of Kidney Disease, 60,* 299–307.

Bowden, C. L. (2010). Diagnosis, treatment, and recovery maintenance in bipolar depression. *Journal of Clinical Psychiatry, 71,* e01.

Bowlby, J. (1969). *Attachment.* New York, NY: Basic Books.

Boyd, C. (2011, April). *The impacts of sexual assault on women.* Australian Institute of Family Studies: Melbourne, Australia.

Boyington, J. E. A., Carter-Edwards, L., Piehl, M., Hutson, J., Langdon, D., & McManus, S. (2008). Cultural attitudes toward weight, diet, and physical activity among overweight African American girls. *Preventing Chronic Disease, 5,* 1–9.

Bradley, B., Davis, T. A., Wingo, A. P., Mercer, K. B., & Ressler, K. J. (2013). Family environment and adult resilience: Contributions of positive parenting and the oxytocin receptor gene. *European Journal of Psychotraumatology.* eCollection 2013. doi:10.3402/ejpt.v4i0.21659

Brady, J. E., & Li, G. (2014). Trends in alcohol and other drugs detected in fatally injured drivers in the United States, 1999–2010. *American Journal of Epidemiology. 179,* 692–699.

Braff, D. L., Freedman, R., Schork, N. J., & Gottesman, I. I. (2007). Deconstructing schizophrenia: An overview of the use of endophenotypes in order to understand a complex disorder. *Schizophrenia Bulletin, 33,* 21–25.

Brand, B., & Loewenstein, R. J. (2010, October). Dissociative disorders: An overview of assessment, phenomenology, and treatment. *Psychiatric Times,* 62–69. Retrieved from https://www.cmellc.com/landing/pdf/A10001101.pdf

Brand, B. L., Classen, C. C., McNary, S. W., & Zaveri, P. (2009). A review of dissociative disorders treatment studies. *Journal of Nervous and Mental Disease, 197,* 646–654.

Brand, B. L., McNary, S. W., Myrick, A. C., Classen, C. C., Lanius, R., Loewenstein, R. J., . . . Putnam, F. W. (2013). A longitudinal naturalistic study of patients with dissociative disorders treated by community clinicians. *Psychological Trauma: Theory, Research, Practice and Policy, 5,* 301–308.

Brand, B. L., Myrick, A. C., Loewenstein, R. J., Classen, C. C., Lanius, R., McNary, S. W. . . . Putnam, F. W. (2012). A survey of practices and recommended treatment interventions among expert therapists treating patients with dissociative identity disorder and dissociative disorder not otherwise specified. *Psychological Trauma: Theory, Research, Practice, and Policy,* 4, 490-500.

Brand, M., Eggers, C., Reinhold, N., Fujiwara, E., Kessler, J., Heiss, W-D., Markowitsch, H. J. (2009). Functional brain imaging in 14 patients with dissociative amnesia reveals right inferolateral prefrontal hypometabolism. *Psychiatry Research: Neuroimaging, 174,* 32–39.

Brand, S., & Kirov, R. (2011). Sleep and its importance in adolescence and in common adolescent somatic and psychiatric conditions. *International Journal of General Medicine, 4,* 25–42.

Brandl, E. J., Muller, D. J., & Richter, M. A. (2012). Pharmacogenetics of obsessive-compulsive disorders. *Pharmacogenomics, 13,* 71–81.

Brannigan, G. G., Decker, S. L., & Madsen, D. H. (2004). *Innovative features of the Bender-Gestalt II and expanded guidelines for the use of the Global Scoring System* (Bender Visual-Motor Gestalt Test, 2nd ed., Assessment Service Bulletin No. 1). Itasca, IL: Riverside.

Brannon, G. E. (2013). Schizoaffective disorder. Retrieved from http://emedicine.medscape.com/article/294763-overview

Brannon, G. E., & Bienefeld, D. (2012). Schizoaffective disorder. Retrieved from http://emedicine.medscape.com/article/294763-overview

Brannon, G. E., & Bienenfeld, D. (2013). History and mental status examination. Retrieved from http://emedicine.medscape.com/article/293402-overview

Brannon, G. E., & Dunayevich, E. (2011). Munchausen syndrome by proxy. Retrieved from http://emedicine.medscape.com/article/295258-overview#showall

Brasic, J. R. (2010). PET scanning in autism spectrum disorders. Retrieved from http://emedicine.medscape.com/article/1155568-overview

Brauser, D. (2013). Mixed reaction to FDA approval of ADHD brain-wave test. Retrieved from http://www.medscape.com/viewarticle/809079

Breese-McCoy, S. J. (2011). Postpartum depression: An essential overview for the practitioner. *Southern Medical Journal, 104,* 128–132.

Breier, A. (2011). Anxiety disorders and antipsychotic drugs: A pressing need for more research. *American Journal of Psychiatry, 168,* 1012–1014.

Breitborde, N. J. K., Lopez, S. R., & Nuechterlein, K. H. (2009). Expressed emotion, human agency, and schizophrenia: Toward a new model for the EE-relapse association. *Cultural and Medical Psychiatry, 33,* 41–60.

Brent, D. A. (2009). Youth depression and suicide: Selective serotonin reuptake inhibitors treat the former and prevent the latter. *Canadian Journal of Psychiatry, 54,* 76–77.

Brent, D. A., & Melhem, N. (2008). Familial transmission of suicidal behavior. *Psychiatric Clinics of North America, 31,* 157–177.

Breslau, J., Borges, G., Tancredi, D., Saito, N., Kravitz, R., Hinton, L., . . . Aguilar-Gaxiola, S. (2011). Migration from Mexico to the United States and subsequent risk for depressive and anxiety disorders: A cross-national study. *Archives of General Psychiatry, 68,* 428–433.

Bresnahan, M., Begg, M. D., Brown, A., Schaefer, C., Sohler, N., Insel B., . . . Susser, E. (2007). Race and risk of schizophrenia in a US birth cohort: Another example of health disparity? *International Journal of Epidemiology, 36,* 751–758.

Breuer, J., & Freud, S. (1957). *Studies in hysteria.* New York, NY: Basic Books. (Original work published 1895)

Brewerton, T. D., & Costin, C. (2011). Treatment results of anorexia nervosa and bulimia nervosa in a residential treatment program. *Eating Disorders, 19,* 117–131.

Brewslow, N., Evans, L., & Langley, J. (1986). Comparisons among heterosexual, bisexual, and homosexual male sadomasochists. *Journal of Homosexuality, 13,* 83–107.

Breyer, B. N., Cohen, B. E., Bertenthal, D., Rosen, R. C., Neylan, T. C., & Seal, K. H. (2014). Sexual dysfunction in male Iraq and Afghanistan war veterans: Association with posttraumatic stress disorder and other combat-related mental health disorders: A population-based cohort study. *Journal of Sexual Medicine, 11,* 75–83.

Brière, F. N., Rohde, P., Shaw, H., & Stice, E. (2014). Moderators of two indicated cognitive-behavioral depression prevention approaches for adolescents in a school-based effectiveness trial. *Behavior Research & Therapy, 53,* 55–62.

Briggs, E. S., & Price, I. R. (2009). The relationship between adverse childhood experience and obsessive-compulsive symptoms and beliefs: The role of anxiety, depression, and experiential avoidance. *Journal of Anxiety Disorders, 23,* 1037–1046.

Brim, S. N., Rudd, R. A., Funk, R. H., & Callahan, D. B. (2008). Asthma prevalence among US children in underrepresented minority populations: American Indian/Alaska Native, Chinese, Filipino, and Asian Indian. *Pediatrics, 122,* 217–222.

Britton, J. C., Lissek, S., Grillon, C., Norcross, M. A., & Pine, D. S. (2011). Development of anxiety: The role of threat appraisal and fear learning. *Depression and Anxiety, 28,* 5–17.

Broeren, S., Lester, K. J., Muris, P., & Field, A. P. (2011). They are afraid of the animal, so therefore I am too: Influence of peer modeling on fear beliefs and approach–avoidance behaviors towards animals in typically developing children. *Behaviour Research and Therapy, 49,* 50–57.

Brooks, J. O., Goldberg, J. F., Ketter, T. A., Miklowitz, D. J., Calabrese, J. R., Bowden, C. L., & Thase, M. E. (2011). Safety and tolerability associated with second-generation antipsychotic polytherapy in bipolar disorder: Findings from the Systematic Treatment Enhancement Program for Bipolar Disorder. *Journal of Clinical Psychiatry, 72,* 240–247.

Brooks, S., Prince, A., Stahl, D., Campbell, I. C., & Treasure, J. (2011). A systematic review and meta-analysis of cognitive bias to food stimuli in people with disordered eating behavior. *Clinical Psychology Review, 31,* 37–51.

Brooks-Harris, J. E. (2008). *Integrative multitheoretical psychotherapy.* Boston, MA: Lahaska Press.

Brotman, M. A., Schmajuk, M., Rich, B. A., Dickstein, D. P., Guyer, A. E., Costello, E. J., . . . Leibenluft, E. (2006). Prevalence, clinical correlates, and longitudinal course of severe mood dysregulation in children. *Biological Psychiatry, 60,* 991–997.

Brouns, B. H., de Wied, M. A., Keijsers, L., Branje, S., van Goozen, S. H., & Meeus, W. H. (2013). Concurrent and prospective effects of psychopathic traits on affective and cognitive empathy in a community sample of late adolescents. *Journal of Child Psychology and Psychiatry, 54,* 969–976.

Brown, D., Larkin, F., Sengupta, S., Romero-Ureclay, J. L., Ross, C. C., Gupta, N., . . . Das, M. (2014). Clozapine: An effective treatment for seriously violent and psychopathic men with antisocial personality disorder in a UK high-security hospital. *CNS Spectrums, 3,* 1–12.

Brown, D., & Srebalus, D. J. (2003). *Introduction to the counseling profession.* Boston, MA: Allyn & Bacon.

Brown, G. K., Ten Have, T., Henriques, G. R., Xie, S. X., Hollander, J. E., & Beck, A. T. (2005). Cognitive therapy for the prevention of suicide attempts: A randomized controlled trial. *Journal of the American Medical Association, 294,* 563–570.

Brown, G. W., Ban, M., Craig, T. K., Harris, T. O., Herbert, J., & Uher, R. (2013). Serotonin transporter length polymorphism, childhood maltreatment, and chronic depression: A specific gene–environment interaction. *Depression and Anxiety, 30,* 5–13.

Brown, J., McKone, E., & Ward, J. (2010). Deficits of long-term memory in Ecstasy users are related to cognitive complexity of the task. *Psychopharmacology, 209,* 51–67.

Brown, R. J. (2004). Psychological mechanisms of medically unexplained symptoms: An integrative conceptual model. *Psychological Bulletin, 130,* 793–812.

Brown, R. J., & Lewis-Fernández, R. (2011). Culture and conversion disorder: Implications for DSM-5. *Psychiatry: Interpersonal and Biological Processes, 74,* 187–206.

Brown, T. A., & Keel, P. K. (2012). Current and emerging directions in the treatment of eating disorders. *Substance Abuse, 6,* 33–61.

Brown, W. A. (2012). *The placebo effect in clinical practice.* New York, NY: Oxford University Press.

Browne, B. (2011). Sinister secrets in the sky. Retrieved from http://coto2.word press.com/2011/02/05/sinister-secrets-in-the-ky-and-morgellons-disease

Bruch, H. (1978). Obesity and anorexia nervosa. *Psychosomatics, 19,* 208–221.

Bruch, M. A., & Heimberg, R. G. (1994). Differences in perceptions of parental and personal characteristics between generalized and nongeneralized social phobics. *Journal of Anxiety Disorders, 8,* 155–168.

Bruchmüller, K., Margraf, J., & Schneider, S. (2012). Is ADHD diagnosed in accord with diagnostic criteria? Overdiagnosis and influence of client gender on diagnosis. *Journal of Consulting and Clinical Psychology, 80,* 128–138.

Brunner, E. J., Shipley, M. J., Britton, A. R., Stansfeld, S. A., Heuschmann, P. U., Rudd, A. G., . . . Kivimaki, M. (2014). Depressive disorder, coronary heart disease, and stroke: Dose-response and reverse causation effects in the Whitehall II cohort study. *European Journal of Preventive Cardiology, 21,* 340–346.

Bruno, R., Matthews, A. J., Topp, L., Degenhardt, L., Gomez, R., & Dunn, M. (2009). Can the severity of dependence scale be usefully applied to "Ecstasy"? *Neuropsychobiology, 60,* 137–147.

Brunoni, A. R., Fraguas, R., & Fregni, F. (2009). Pharmacological and combined interventions for the acute depressive episode: Focus on efficacy and tolerability. *Journal of Therapeutics and Clinical Risk Management, 5,* 897–910.

Bruss, M. B., Morris, J., & Dannison, L. (2003). Prevention of childhood obesity: Sociocultural and familial factors. *Journal of the American Dietetic Association, 103,* 1042–1045.

Bryan, C. J. (2013). Repetitive traumatic brain injury (or concussion) increases severity of sleep disturbance among deployed military personnel. *Sleep, 36,* 941–946.

Bryan, C. J., & Clemans, T. A. (2013). Repetitive traumatic brain injury, psychological symptoms, and suicide risk. *JAMA Psychiatry, 15,* 1–6.

Bryant, K. (2001, February 20). Eating disorders: In their own words. *Atlanta Journal-Constitution,* p. B4.

Bryant, R. A. (2013). An update of acute stress disorder. *PTSD Research Quarterly, 24,* 1–7.

Bryant, R. A., & Das, P. (2012). The neural circuitry of conversion disorder and its recovery. *Journal of Abnormal Psychology, 121,* 289–296.

Bucchianeri, M. M., Serrano, J. L., Pastula, A., & Corning, A. F. (2014). Drive for muscularity is heightened in body-dissatisfied men who socially compare. *Eating Disorders, 22,* 221–232.

Buchanan, A., Binder, R., Norko, M., & Swartz, M. (2012). Psychiatric violence risk assessment. *American Journal of Psychiatry, 169,* 340.

Buchanan, B. G., Rossell, S. L., Maller, J. J., Toh, W. L., Brennan, S., & Castle, B. J. (2013). Brain connectivity in body dysmorphic disorder compared with controls: A diffusion tensor imaging study. *Psychological Medicine, 43,* 2513–2521.

Buckels, E. E., Trapnell, P. D., & Paulhus, D. L. (2014). Trolls just want to have fun. Personality and individual differences. Retrieved from http://dx.doi.org/10.1016/j.paid.2014.01.016

Bulik, C. M., & Kendler, K. S. (2000). "I am what I (don't) eat": Establishing an identity independent of an eating disorder. *American Journal of Psychiatry, 157,* 1755–1760.

Bulik, C. M., Thornton, L. M., Root, T. L., Pisetsky, E. M., Lichtenstein, P., & Pedersen, N. L. (2010). Understanding the relation between anorexia nervosa and bulimia nervosa in a Swedish national twin sample. *Biological Psychiatry, 67,* 71–77.

Bull, C. B. (2004). Binge eating disorder. *Current Opinion in Psychiatry, 17,* 43–48.

Bullen, C., Howe, C., Laugesen, M., McRobbie, H., Parag, V., Williman, J., & Walker, N. (2013). Electronic cigarettes for smoking cessation: A randomised controlled trial. *Lancet, 382,* 1629–1637.

Bullying statistics 2009. (2009). Retrieved from http://www.bullyingstatistics.org/content/bullying-statistics-2009.html

Bunford, N., Evans, S. W., & Langberg, J. M. (2014). Emotion dysregulation is associated with social impairment among young adolescents with ADHD. *Journal of Attention Disorders.* doi: 10.1177/1087054714527793

Buodo, G., Ghisi, M., Novara, C., Scozzari, S., Di Natale, A., & Sanavio, E. (2011). Assessment of cognitive functions in individuals with post-traumatic symptoms after work-related accidents. *Journal of Anxiety Disorders, 25,* 64–70.

Burbach, J. P. (2011). What are neuropeptides? *Methods in Molecular Biology, 789,* 1–36.

Bureau of Labor Statistics. (2013). American time use survey—2012 results. Retrieved from http://www.bls.gov/tus

Burgess, K., Rubin, K. H., Cheah, C., & Nelson, L. (2001). Socially withdrawn children: Parenting and parent-child relationships. In R. Crozier & L. E. Alden (Eds.), *The self, shyness and social anxiety: A handbook of concepts, research, and interventions* (pp. 137–158). New York, NY: Wiley.

Burke, J. D., Rowe. R., & Boylan, K. (2014). Functional outcomes of child and adolescent oppositional defiant disorder symptoms in young adult men. *Journal of Child Psychology & Psychiatry, 55,* 264–272.

Burke, S. M., Menks, W. M., Cohen-Kettenis, P. T., Klink, D. T., & Bakker, J. (2014). Click-evoked otoacoustic emissions in children and adolescents with gender identity disorder. *Archives of Sexual Behavior.* retrieved from http://dare.ubvu.vu.nl/bitstream/handle/1871/51287/chapter_2.pdf?sequence56

Burnham, J. J. (2009). Contemporary fears of children and adolescents: Coping and resiliency in the 21st century. *Journal of Counseling and Development, 87,* 28–33.

Burri, A. (2013). Bringing sex research into the 21st century: Genetic and epigenetic approaches on female sexual function. *Journal of Sex Research, 50,* 318–328.

Burrows, R. D., Slavec, J. J., Nangle, D. W., & O'Grady, A. C. (2013). ERP, medication, and brief hospitalization in the treatment of an adolescent with severe BDD. *Clinical Case Studies, 12,* 3-21.

Burstein, M., & Ginsburg, G. S. (2010). The effect of parental modeling of anxious behaviors and cognitions in school-aged children: An experimental pilot study. *Behaviour Research and Therapy, 48,* 506–515.

Burton, C., McGorm, K., Weller, D., & Sharpe, M. (2010). Depression and anxiety in patients repeatedly referred to secondary care with medically unexplained symptoms: A case-control study. *Psychological Medicine, 41*(3), 555–563.

Buster, J. E. (2013). Managing female sexual dysfunction. *Fertility and Sterility, 100,* 905–915.

Butcher, J. N. (1990). *The MMPI-2 in psychological treatment.* New York, NY: Oxford University Press.

Butcher, J. N. (2010). Personality assessment from the nineteenth to the early twenty-first century: Past achievements and contemporary challenges. *Annual Review of Clinical Psychology, 6,* 1–20.

Butler, L. D., Duran, R. E. F., Jasiukaitis, P., Koopman, C., & Spiegel, D. (1996). Hypnotizability and traumatic experience. *American Journal of Psychiatry, 153,* 42–59.

Butler, S. F., Black, R., Serrano, J., Wood, M., & Budman, S. (2010). Characteristics of prescription opioid abusers in treatment: Prescription opioid use history, age, use patterns, and functional severity. *Journal of Opioid Management, 6,* 239–241, 246–252.

Butterworth, B., & Kovas, Y. (2013). Understanding neurocognitive developmental disorders can improve education for all. *Science, 340*(6130), 300. doi:10.1126/science.1231022

Butz, M. R., Evans, F. B., & Webber-Dereszynski, R. L. (2009). A practitioner's complaint and proposed direction: Munchausen syndrome by proxy, factitious disorder by proxy, and fabricated and/or induced illness in children. *Professional Psychology: Research and Practice, 40,* 31–38.

Byrd, A. L., Loeber, R., & Pardini, D. A. (2014). Antisocial behavior, psychopathic features and abnormalities in reward and punishment processing in youth. *Clinical Child & Family Psychology Review, 17*, 125–156.

Byrne, R. E., & Morrison, A. P. (2013, August 24). Young people at risk of psychosis: Their subjective experiences of monitoring and cognitive behaviour therapy in the early detection and intervention evaluation 2 trial. *Psychology and Psychotherapy: Theory, Research and Practice.* doi:10.1111/papt.12013 [Epub ahead of print]

Bystritsky, A., Kerwin, L., Noosha, N., Natoli, J. L., Abrahami, N., Klap, R., . . . Young, A. S. (2010). Clinical and subthreshold panic disorder. *Depression and Anxiety, 27*, 381–389.

Cacioppo, J. T., Reis, H. T., & Zautra, A. J. (2011). The value of social fitness with an application to the military. *American Psychologist, 66*, 43–51.

Calhoun, S. L., Fernandez-Mendoza, J., Vgontzas, A. N., Liao, D., & Bixler, E. O. (2014). Prevalence of insomnia symptoms in a general population sample of young children and preadolescents: Gender effects. *Sleep Medicine, 15*, 91–95.

Callaghan, R. C., Cunningham, J. K., Allebeck, P., Arenovich, T., Sajeev, G., Remington, G., . . . Kish, S. J. (2012). Methamphetamine use and schizophrenia: A population-based cohort study in California. *American Journal of Psychiatry, 169*, 389–396.

Calzo, J. P., Corliss, H. L., Blood, E. A., Field, A. E., & Austin, S. B. (2013). Development of muscularity and weight concerns in heterosexual and sexual minority males. *Health Psychology, 32*, 42–51.

Cameron, A., Palm, K., & Follette, V. (2010). Reaction to stressful life events: What predicts symptom severity? *Journal of Anxiety Disorders, 24*, 645–649.

Campos, M. S., Garcia-Jalon, E., Gilleen, J. K., David, A. S., Peralta, V., & Cuesta, M. J. (2011). Premorbid personality and insight in first-episode psychosis. *Schizophrenia Bulletin, 37*, 52–60.

Canas, F. (2005). Mechanisms of action of atypical antipsychotics. *CNS Spectrums, 8*, 5–11.

Canavera, K. E., Ollendick, T. H., May, J. T. E., & Pincus, D. B. (2010). Clinical correlates of comorbid obsessive-compulsive disorder and depression in youth. *Child Psychiatry and Human Development, 41*, 583–594.

Canfield, M., Keller, C., Frydrych, L., Ashrafiuon, L., Purdy, C. H., & Blondell, R. (2010). Prescription opioid use among patients seeking treatment for opioid dependence. *Journal of Addiction Medicine, 4*, 108–113.

Cannon, T. D., Cadenhead, K., Cornblatt, B., Woods, S. W., Addington, J., Walker, E., . . . Heinssen, R. (2008). Prediction of psychosis in youth at high clinical risk: A multisite longitudinal study in North America. *Archives of General Psychiatry, 65*, 28–32.

Cantor, D. W., & Fuentes, M. A. (2008). Psychology's response to managed care. *Professional Psychology: Research and Practice, 39*, 638–645.

Caplan, P. J. (1995). *They say you're crazy.* Reading, MA: Addison-Wesley.

Capogrosso, P., Colicchia, M., Ventimiglia, E., Castagna, G., Clementi, M. C., Suardi, N., . . . Salonia, A. (2013). One patient out of four with newly diagnosed erectile dysfunction is a young man—Worrisome picture from the everyday clinical practice. *Journal of Sexual Medicine, 10*, 1833–1841.

Cardno, A. G., & Owen, M. J. (2014, February 24). Genetic relationships between schizophrenia, bipolar disorder, and schizoaffective disorder. *Schizophrenia Bulletin, 40*, 504–515.

Carels, R. A., Cacciapaglia, H., Perez-Benitez, C. I., Douglass, O., Christie, S., & O'Brien, W. H. (2003). The association between emotional upset and cardiac arrhythmias during daily life. *Journal of Consulting and Clinical Psychology, 71*, 613–618.

Carey, B. (2011, June 23). Expert on mental illness reveals her own fight. *New York Times.* Retrieved from http://www.nytimes.com

Carey, K. B., Scott-Sheldon, L., Carey, M. P., & DeMartini, K. S. (2007). Individual-level interventions to reduce college student drinking: A meta-analytic review. *Addictive Behaviors, 32*, 2469–2494.

Carlson, E. B., Dalenberg, C., & McDade-Montez, E. (2012). Dissociation in posttraumatic stress disorder part I: Definitions and review of research. *Psychological Trauma: Theory, Research, Practice, and Policy, 4*, 479–489.

Carlson, L. E., Speca, M., Faris, P., & Patel, K. D. (2007). One year pre-post intervention follow-up of psychological, immune, endocrine and blood pressure outcomes of mindfulness-based stress reduction (MBSR) in breast and prostate cancer outpatients. *Brain and Behavioral Immunology, 21*, 1038–1049.

Carmichael, S. (2010, June 17). Debenhams reveals tricks of the trade and axes digitally enhanced models. *London Evening Standard.* Retrieved from http://www.standard.co.uk

Carper, T. L, Negy, C., & Tantleff-Dunn, S. (2010). Relations among media influence, body image, eating concerns, and sexual orientation in men: A preliminary investigation. *Body Image, 7*, 301–309.

Carrasco, M., Volkmar, F. R., & Bloch, M. H. (2012). Pharmacologic treatment of repetitive behaviors in autism spectrum disorders: Evidence of publication bias. *Pediatrics, 129*, e1301–e1310.

Carroll, K. M., & Onken, L. S. (2005). Behavioral therapies for drug abuse. *American Journal of Psychiatry, 162*, 1452–1460.

Carroll, L. (2011, July 6). Eating disorders stalk women into adulthood. Retrieved from http://today.msnbc.msn.com

Carta, M. G., Balestrieri, M., Murru, A., & Hardoy, M. C. (2009). Adjustment disorder: Epidemiology, diagnosis and treatment. *Clinical Practice and Epidemiology in Mental Health, 26*(5), 15. doi:10.1186/1745-0179-5-15

Carter, J. S., & Garber, J. (2011). Predictors of the first onset of a major depressive episode and changes in depressive symptoms across adolescence: Stress and negative cognitions. *Journal of Abnormal Psychology, 120*, 779–796.

Carter, R. T., Mazzula, S., Victoria, R., Vazquez, R., Hall, S., Smith, S.,, . . . Williams, B. (2013). Initial development of the race-based Traumatic Stress Symptom Scale: Assessing the emotional impact of racism. *Psychological Trauma: Theory, Research, Practice, and Policy, 5*, 1–9.

Cartwright, S. (1851, May). Report on the diseases and physical peculiarities of the Negro race. *DeBow's Review, XI*, 64–69.

Carufel, F., & Trudel, G. (2006). Effects of a new functional-sexological treatment for premature ejaculation. *Journal of Sex & Marital Therapy, 32*, 97–114.

Carvalheira, A., Træen, B., & Štulhofer, A. (2014). Correlates of men's sexual interest: A cross-cultural study. *Journal of Sexual Medicine, 11*, 154–164.

Carvalho, J., Veríssimo, A., & Nobre, P. J. (2013). Cognitive and emotional determinants characterizing women with persistent genital arousal disorder. *Journal of Sexual Medicine, 10,* 1549–1558.

Casey, B. J., Ruberry, E. J., Libby, V., Glatt, C. E., Hare, T., Soliman, F., . . . Tottenham, N. (2011). Transitional and translational studies of risk for anxiety. *Depression and Anxiety, 28,* 18–28.

Casey, D. E. (2006). Implications of the CATIE trial on treatment: Extrapyramidal symptoms. *CNS Spectrums, 11,* 25–31.

Casey, G. W. (2011). Comprehensive Soldier Fitness: A vision for psychological resilience in the U.S. Army. *American Psychologist, 66,* 1–3.

Casey, P. (2009). Adjustment disorder: Epidemiology, diagnosis and treatment. *CNS Drugs, 23,* 927–938.

Casey, P., & Doherty, A. (2013). Adjustment disorders: Diagnostic and treatment issues. *Psychiatric Times.* Retrieved from http://www.psychiatric-times.com/adjustment-disorders-diagnostic-and-treatment-issues

Caspi, A., Sugden, K., Moffitt, T. E., Taylor, A., Craig, I. W., Harrington, H., . . . Poulton, R. (2003). Influence of life stress on depression: Moderation by a polymorphism in the 5-HTT gene. *Science, 301,* 386–389.

Cassidy, F. (2010). Insight in bipolar disorder: Relationship to episode subtypes and symptom dimensions. *Journal of Neuropsychiatric Disease and Treatment, 6,* 627–631.

Castelnuovo, G. (2010, July 2). Empirically supported treatments in psychotherapy: Towards an evidence-based or evidence-biased psychology in clinical settings? *Frontiers in Psychology.* Published online. doi:10.3389/fpsyg.2010.00027

Catalina, M. L., Gomez, M. V., & de Cos, A. (2008). Prevalence of factitious disorder with psychological symptoms in hospitalized patients. *Actas Espanolas de Psiquiatria, 36,* 345–349.

Cather, C. (2005). Functional cognitive-behavioural therapy: A brief, individual treatment for functional impairments resulting from psychotic symptoms in schizophrenia. *Canadian Journal of Psychiatry, 50,* 258–263.

Cavanagh, K., Strauss, C., Cicconi, F., Griffiths, N., Wyper, A., & Jones, F. (2013). A randomised controlled trial of a brief online mindfulness-based intervention. *Behaviour Research and Therapy, 51,* 573–578.

Cavanagh, M., Quinn, D., Duncan, D., Graham, T., & Balbuena, L.

(2014). Oppositional defiant disorder is better conceptualized as a disorder of emotional regulation. *Journal of Attention Disorders.* doi: 10.1177/1087054713520221[Epub ahead of print]

Cavanna, A. E., Luoni, C., Selvini, C., Blangiardo, R., Eddy, C. M., Silvestri, P. R., . . . Termine, C. (2013). Disease-specific quality of life in young patients with Tourette syndrome. *Pediatric Neurology, 48,* 111–114.

Cavedini, P., Zorzi, C., Piccinni, M., Cavallini, M. C., & Bellodi, L. (2010). Executive dysfunctions in obsessive-compulsive patients and unaffected relatives: Searching for a new intermediate phenotype. *Biological Psychiatry, 67,* 1178–1184.

Center for Male Reproductive Medicine and Microsurgery. (2005). Penile implants (prosthesis) surgery. Retrieved from http://www.maleinfertility.org/penileimplants.html

Centers for Disease Control and Prevention. (2009). Prevalence of autism spectrum disorders—Autism and Developmental Disabilities Monitoring Network, United States, 2006. Retrieved from http://www.cdc.gov/mmwr/preview/mmwrhtml/ss5810a1.htm

Centers for Disease Control and Prevention. (2010a). Increasing prevalence of parent-reported attention-deficit/hyperactivity disorder among children—United States, 2003 and 2007. *Morbidity and Mortality Weekly Report, 59,* 1439–1443.

Centers for Disease Control and Prevention. (2010b). Vital signs: State-specific obesity prevalence among adults—United States, 2009. *Morbidity and Mortality Weekly Report, 59,* 1–5.

Centers for Disease Control and Prevention. (2010c). Youth risk behavior surveillance—United States, 2009. *Morbidity and Mortality Weekly Report Surveillance Summary, 59*(SS-5), 1–142.

Centers for Disease Control and Prevention. (2011). CDC investigation of unexplained dermopathy. Retrieved from http://www.cdc.gov/unexplained-dermopathy

Centers for Disease Control and Prevention. (2012a). Epilepsy. Retrieved from http://www.cdc.gov/epilepsy/basics/faqs.htm

Centers for Disease Control and Prevention. (2012b). Vital signs: Binge drinking prevalence, frequency, and

intensity among adults—United States, 2010. *Morbidity and Mortality Weekly Report, 61,* 14–19.

Centers for Disease Control and Prevention. (2013). FastStats: Asthma. Retrieved from http://www.cdc.gov/nchs/fastats/asthma.htm

Centers for Disease Control and Prevention. (2014). Childhood obesity facts. Retrieved from http://www.cdc.gov/obesity/data/childhood.html

Centers for Disease Control and Prevention Web-based Injury Statistics Query and Reporting System. (2013). Leading causes of death reports. Retrieved from www.cdc.gov/injury/wisqars/fatal_injury_reports.html

Centre for Addiction and Mental Health. (2007, October 23). Are some men predisposed to pedophilia? *Science Daily.* Retrieved from www.sciencedaily.com/releases/2007/10/071022120203.htm

Cerasa, A., Quattrone, A., Piras, F., Mangone, G., Magariello, A., Fagioli, S., . . . Spalletta, G. (2013). 5-HTTLPR, anxiety and gender interaction moderates right amygdala volume in healthy subjects. *Social Cognitive and Affective Neuroscience.* doi:10.1093/scan/nst144

Cha, C. B., Najmi, S., Park, J. M., Finn, C. T., & Nock, M. K. (2010). Attentional bias toward suicide-related stimuli predicts suicidal behavior. *Journal of Abnormal Psychology, 119,* 616–622.

Chadwick, P., Kaur, H., Swelam, M., Ross,. S., & Ellett, L. (2011). Experience of mindfulness in people with bipolar disorder: A qualitative study. *Psychotherapy Research, 21,* 277–285.

Chaidez, V., Hansen, R. L., & Hertz-Picciotto, I. (2014). Gastrointestinal problems in children with autism, developmental delays or typical development. *Journal of Autism & Developmental Disorders, 44,* 1117–1127.

Chalder, M., Elgar, F. J., & Bennett, P. (2006). Drinking and motivations to drink among adolescent children of parents with alcohol problems. *Alcohol and Alcoholism, 41,* 107–113.

Challacombe, F., & Salkovskis, P. (2009). A preliminary investigation of the impact of maternal obsessive-compulsive disorder and panic disorder on parenting and children. *Journal of Anxiety Disorders, 23,* 848–847.

Champion, H. R., Holcomb, J. B., & Young, L. A. (2009). Injuries from explosions. *Journal of Trauma, 66,* 1468–1476.

Chan, J. S. Y., Yan, J. H., & Payne, V. G. (2013). The impact of obesity and exercise on cognitive aging. *Frontiers in Aging Neuroscience, 5,* 97. doi:10.3389/fnagi.2013.00097

Chan, R. C. K., Di, X., McAlonan, G. M., & Gong, Q.-Y. (2011). Brain anatomical abnormalities in high-risk individuals, first-episode, and chronic schizophrenia: An activation likelihood estimation meta-analysis of illness progression. *Schizophrenia Bulletin, 37,* 177–188.

Chambliss, C. H. (2000). *Psychotherapy and managed care: Reconciling research and reality.* Boston, MA: Allyn & Bacon.

Chandler-Laney, P. C., Hunter, G. R., Ard, J. D., Roy, J. L., Brock, D. W., & Gower, B. A. (2009). Perception of others' body size influences weight loss and regain for European American but not African American women. *Health Psychology, 28,* 414–418.

Chaney, M. P., Filmore, J. M., & Goodrich, K. M. (2011). No more sitting on the sidelines: Practical strategies for working with LGBT clients on issues of heterosexism and transphobia, coming out and bullying. *Counseling Today, 53,* 34–37.

Chapman, C., Gilger, K., & Chestnutt, A. (2010). The challenge of eating disorders on a college campus. *Counseling Today, 53,* 44–45.

Chappell, P. (2013, January 14). U.S. military's suicide rate surpassed combat deaths in 2012. Retrieved from http://www.npr.org/blogs/thetwo-way/2013/01/14/169364733/u-s-militarys-suicide-rate-surpassed-combat-deaths-in-2012

Charach, A., Carson, P., Fox, S., Ali, M. U., Beckett, J., & Lim, C. G. (2013). Interventions for preschool children at high risk for ADHD: A comparative effectiveness review. *Pediatrics, 131,* e1584–e1604.

Charland, L. C. (2007). Benevolent theory: Moral treatment at the York Retreat. *History of Psychiatry, 18,* 61–80.

Chartier, K., & Caetano, R. (2010). Ethnicity and health disparities in alcohol research. *Alcohol Research & Health, 33*(1/2), 152–160. Retrieved from http://pubs.niaaa.nih.gov/publications/arh40/152-160.pdf

Chatburn, A., Coussens, S., & Kohler, M. J. (2013). Resiliency as a mediator of the impact of sleep on child and adolescent behavior. *Nature and Science of Sleep, 6,* 1–9.

Chawarska, K., Campbell, D., Chen, L., Shic, F., Klin, A., & Chang, J. (2011).

Early generalized overgrowth in boys with autism. *Archives of General Psychiatry, 68,* 1021–1031.

Chekoudjian, C. B. (2009). The subjective experience of PMS: A sociological analysis of women's narratives. (Unpublished master's thesis.) University of South Florida, Tampa, FL. Retrieved from http://scholarcommons.usf.edu/etd/1895

Cheng, M. (2013). Belgium considering new euthanasia law for kids. Retrieved from http://www.nbcnews.com/health/belgium-considering-new-euthanasia-law-kids-8C11512194

Cheng, Y., Xu, J., Nie, B., Luo, C., Yang, T., Li, H., . . . Xu, X. (2013). Abnormal resting-state activities and functional connectivities of the anterior and the posterior cortexes in medication-naïve patients with obsessive-compulsive disorder. *PLOS One, 8,* e67478.

Chentsova-Dutton, Y. E., Tsai, J. L., & Gotlib, I. H. (2010). Further evidence for the cultural norm hypothesis: Positive emotion in depressed and control European American and Asian American women. *Cultural Diversity and Ethnic Minority Psychology, 16,* 284–295.

Cherian, A. V., Math, S. B., Kandavel, T., & Reddy, Y. C. (2014). A 5-year prospective follow-up study of patients with obsessive-compulsive disorder treated with serotonin reuptake inhibitors. *Journal of Affective Disorders, 154,* 387–394.

Cheslack-Postava, K., Liu, K., & Bearman, P. S. (2011). Closely spaced pregnancies are associated with increased odds of autism in California sibling births. *Pediatrics, 127,* 246–253.

Cheung, A. H., Kozloff, N., & Sacks, D. (2013). Pediatric depression: An evidence-based update on treatment interventions. *Current Psychiatry Reports, 5,* 381. doi:10.1007/s11920-013-0381-4

Chiao, J. Y., Cheon, B. K., Pornpattananangkul, N., Mrazek, A. J., & Blizinsky, K. D. (2013). Cultural neuroscience: Progress and promise. *Psychological Inquiry, 24,* 1–19.

Chin, J. T., Hayward, M., & Drinnan, A. (2009). "Relating" to voices: Exploring the relevance of this concept to people who hear voices. *Psychology and Psychotherapy: Theory, Research and Practice, 81,* 1–17.

Choi, S. H., Lee, H., Chung, T. S., Park, K. M., Jung, Y. C., Kim, S. I., & Kim, J. J. (2012). Neural network functional

connectivity during and after an episode of delirium. *American Journal of Psychiatry, 169,* 498–507.

Chollet, F., Tardy, J., Albucher, J., Thalamas, C., Berard, E., Lamy, C., . . . Loubinoux, I. (2011). Fluoxetine for motor recovery after acute ischaemic stroke (FLAME): A randomised placebo-controlled trial. *The Lancet Neurology, 10*(2), 123–130. doi:10.1016/S1474-4422(10)70314-8

Chopra, S., & Bienenfeld, D. (2011). Delusional disorder. Retrieved from http://emedicine.medscape.com/article/292991-overview

Chopra, S., & Khan, R. A. (2009). Delusional disorder. Retrieved from http://emedicine.medscape.com/article/292991

Christakis, N. A., & Fowler, J. H. (2007). The spread of obesity in a large social network over 32 years. *New England Journal of Medicine, 357,* 370–379.

Christensen, H., Griffiths, K. M., & Farrer, L. (2009). Adherence in Internet interventions for anxiety and depression. *Journal of Medical Internet Research, 11,* e13.

Christensen, R. C. (2012). The development of posttraumatic stress disorder following an unusual life event: A case report. *Innovations in Clinical Neuroscience, 9,* 26–28.

Christie, A. M., & Barling, J. (2009). Disentangling the indirect links between socioeconomic status and health: The dynamic roles of work stressors and personal control. *Journal of Applied Psychology, 94,* 1466–1478.

Chuang, L. C., Kao, C. F., Shih, W. L., & Kuo, P. H. (2013). Pathway analysis using information from allele-specific gene methylation in genome-wide association studies for bipolar disorder. *PLOS One, 8,* e53092. doi:10.1371/journal.pone.0053092

Chung, W. S., Clarke, L. E., Wang, G. X., Stafford, B. K., Sher, A., Chakraborty, C., . . . Barres, B. A. (2013). Astrocytes mediate synapse elimination through MEGF10 and MERTK pathways. *Nature, 504,* 394–400.

Churchill, R., Moore, T. H. M., Furukawa, T. A., Caldwell, D. M., Davies, P., Jones, H., . . . Hunot, V. (2013). "Third wave" cognitive and behavioural therapies versus treatment as usual for depression. *Cochrane Database of Systematic Reviews,* Issue 10. Art. no.: CD008705. doi:10.1002/14651858.CD008705.pub2

Cicchetti, D. (2013). Annual research review: Resilient functioning in maltreated children—past, present, and future perspectives. *Journal of Child Psychology & Psychiatry, 54,* 402–422.

Cicero, D. C., Kerns, J. G., & McCarthy, D. M. (2010). The Aberrant Salience Inventory: A new measure of psychosis proneness. *Psychological Assessment, 22,* 688–701.

Cipriani, A., Hawton, K., Stockton, S., & Geddes, J. R. (2013). Lithium in the prevention of suicide in mood disorders: Updated systematic review and meta-analysis. *British Medical Journal, 346,* f3646. doi:10.1136/bmj.f3646

Cisler, J. M., Adams, T. G., Brady, R. E., Bridges, A. J., Lohr, J. M., & Olatunji, B. O. (2011). Unique affective and cognitive processes in contamination appraisals: Implications for contamination fear. *Journal of Anxiety Disorders, 25,* 28–35.

Clabough, E. B. (2013) Huntington's disease: The past, present, and future search for disease modifiers. *Yale Journal of Biological Medicine, 86,* 217–233.

Clark, M., Gosnell, M., Witherspoon, J., Huck, J., Hager, M., Junkin, D., . . . Robinson, T. L. (1984, December 3). A slow death of the mind. *Newsweek, 104*(22), 56–62.

Clark, R. (2006). Perceived racism and vascular reactivity in black college women: Moderating effects of seeking social support. *Health Psychology, 25,* 20–25.

Clark, S. K., Jeglic, E. L., Calkins, C., & Tatar, J. R. (2014). More than a nuisance: The prevalence and consequences of frotteurism and exhibitionism. *Sexual Abuse: A Journal of Research and Treatment.* doi: 10.1177/1079063214525643

Clay, R. A. (2010). Psychology's voice is heard. *APA Monitor, 41,* 22.

Clay, R. A. (2012, January). Yes, recovery is possible. *Monitor on Psychology,* 53–55.

Cloitre, M., Stovall-McClough, K. C., Nooner, K., Zorbas, P., Cherry, S., Jackson, C. L., . . . Petkova, E. (2010). Treatment for PTSD related to childhood abuse: A randomized control trial. *American Journal of Psychiatry, 167,* 915–924.

Cloninger, C. R., & Dokucu, M. (2008). Somatoform and dissociative disorders. In S. H. Fatemi & P. J. Clayton (Eds.), *The medical basis of psychiatry* (pp. 181–194). Totawa, NJ: Humana Press.

Cloud, J. (2011, January 15). The troubled life of Jared Loughner. *Time.* Retrieved from http://www.time.com

Coalition Educating About Sexual Endangerment. (2011). Rape statistics. Retrieved from http://oak.cats.ohiou.edu/,ad361896/anne/cease/number spage.html

Coccaro, E. F. (2012). Intermittent explosive disorder as a disorder of impulsive aggression for DSM-5. *American Journal of Psychiatry, 169,* 577–588.

Coccaro, E. F., Lee, R., & McCloskey, M. S. (2014). Validity of the new A1 and A2 criteria for DSM-5 intermittent explosive disorder. *Comprehensive Psychiatry, 55,* 260–267.

Cody, M. G., & Teachman, M. W. (2011). Global and local evaluations of public speaking performance in social anxiety. *Behavior Therapy, 42,* 601–611.

Coelho, C. M., & Purkis, H. (2009). The origins of specific phobias: Influential theories and current perspectives. *Review of General Psychology, 13,* 335–348.

Cohen, N. (2009, July 28). A Rorschach cheat sheet on Wikipedia? *New York Times.* Retrieved from http://www.nytimes.com

Cohen, S., Frank, E., Doyle, W. J., Skoner, D. P., Rabin, B. S., & Gwaltney, J. M. (1998). Types of stressors that increase susceptibility in the common cold in healthy adults. *Health Psychology, 17,* 214–223.

Coleman, D., Kaplan, M. S., & Casey, J. T. (2011). The social nature of male suicide: A new analytical model. *International Journal of Men's Health, 10,* 240–252.

Collins, J. (2013, April 26). SC woman pleads guilty, mentally ill in 4 slayings. Retrieved from http://news.yahoo.com/sc-woman-pleads-guilty-mentally-ill-4-slayings-191300209.html

Collip, D., Wigman, J. T. W., Lin, A., Nelson, B., Oorschot, M., Vollebergh, W. A. M., . . . Yung, A. R. (2013). Dynamic association between interpersonal functioning and positive symptom dimensions of psychosis over time: A longitudinal study of healthy adolescents. *Schizophrenia Bulletin, 39,* 179–185.

Coltheart, M., Langdon, R., & McKay, R. (2007). Schizophrenia and monothematic delusions. *Schizophrenia Bulletin, 33,* 642–647.

Combs, D. R., Adams, S. D., Penn, D. L., Roberts, D., Thiegreen, J., & Stem, P. (2007). Social cognition and interaction training (SCIT) for inpatients with schizophrenia spectrum disorders: Preliminary findings. *Schizophrenia Research, 91,* 112–116.

Compas, B. E., Forehand, R., Thigpen, J. C., Keller, G., Hardcastle, E. J., Cole, D., . . . Roberts, L. (2011). Family group cognitive-behavioral preventive intervention for families of depressed parents: 18- and 24-month outcomes. *Journal of Consulting and Clinical Psychology, 79,* 488–499.

Compton, S. N., Peris, T. S., Almirall, D., Birmaher, B., Sherrill, J., Kendall, P. C., . . . Albano, A. M. (2014). Predictors and moderators of treatment response in childhood anxiety disorders: Results from the CAMS trial. *Journal of Consulting and Clinical Psychology, 82,* 212–224.

Comtois, K. A., & Linehan, M. M. (2006). Psychosocial treatments of suicidal behaviors: A practice-friendly review. *Journal of Clinical Psychology: In Session, 62,* 161–170.

Conner, K. (2006). Factors in a successful use of the insanity defense. Is there more to insanity than a state of mind? *Internet Journal of Criminology.* Retrieved from http://loh.loswego.k12.or.us/noblem/docs/psy2_Insanity_Defense_Study.pdf

Connolly, K. R., Helmer, A., Cristancho, M. A., Cristancho, P., & O'Reardon, J. P. (2012). Effectiveness of transcranial magnetic stimulation in clinical practice post-FDA approval in the United States: Results observed with the first 100 consecutive cases of depression at an academic medical center. *Journal of Clinical Psychiatry, 73,* e567–e573. doi:10.4088/JCP.11m07413

Conradi, H. J., Ormel, J., & de Jonge, P. (2010). Presence of individual (residual) symptoms during depressive episodes and periods of remission: A 3-year prospective study. *Psychological Medicine, 8,* 1–10.

Constantino, J. N., Majmudar, P., Bottini, A., Arvin, M., Virkud, Y., Simons, P., & Spitznagel, E. J. (2010). Infant head growth in male siblings of children with and without autism spectrum disorders. *Neurodevelopmental Disorders, 2,* 39–46.

Contractor, Z. (2012). Attention deficit hyperactivity disorder. Retrieved from http://emedicine.medscape.com/article/912633-overview

Conway, C. R., Chibnall, J. T., Gebara, M. A., Price, J. L., Snyder, A. Z.,

Mintun, M. A., . . . Sheline, Y. I. (2013). Association of cerebral metabolic activity changes with vagus nerve stimulation antidepressant response in treatment-resistant depression. *Brain Stimulation, 6,* 788–797.

Conwell, Y., Van Orden, K., & Caine, E. D. (2011). Suicide in older adults. *Psychiatric Clinics of North America, 34,* 451–468.

Cooper, D. (2013). First person: Avoidant personality disorder often means hiding from the world. Retrieved from news. yahoo.com/first-person-avoidant-personality-disorder-often-means-hiding-152700170.html

Copeland, W. E., Angold, A., Costello, E. J., & Egger, H. (2013). Prevalence, comorbidity, and correlates of DSM-5 proposed disruptive mood dysregulation disorder. *American Journal of Psychiatry, 170,* 173–179.

Copeland, W. E., Wolke, D., Angold, A., & Costello, E. J. (2013). Adult psychiatric outcomes of bullying and being bullied by peers in childhood and adolescence. *JAMA Psychiatry, 70,* 419–426.

Coppola, M., & Mondola, R. (2012). 3,4-Methylenedioxypyrovalerone (MDPV): Chemistry, pharmacology and toxicology of a new designer drug of abuse marketed online. *Toxicology Letters, 208,* 12–15.

Corcoran, J., & Walsh, J. (2010). *Clinical assessment and diagnosis in clinical social work practice.* New York, NY: Oxford University Press.

Cordova, M. J., Cunningham, L. L. C., Carlson, C. R., & Andrykowski, M. A. (2001). Social constraints, cognitive processing, and adjustment to breast cancer. *Journal of Consulting and Clinical Psychology, 69,* 706–711.

Corey, G. (2013). *Theory and practice of counseling and psychotherapy.* Belmont, CA: Brooks/Cole.

Corey, G., Callanan, P., & Corey, M. S. (2010). *Issues and ethics in the helping professions.* Belmont, CA: Brooks/Cole.

Corey, G., & Corey, M. S. (2010). *Codes of ethics for the helping professions.* Belmont, CA: Brooks/Cole.

Cornell, D., & Guerra, N. G. (2013). Gun violence: Prediction, prevention, and policy. Retrieved from http://www.apa .org/pubs/info/reports/gun-violence-prevention.aspx?item52

Cornic, F., Consoli, A., & Cohen, D. (2007). Catatonia in children and adolescents. *Psychiatric Annals, 37,* 19–26.

Cornish, M. A., & Wade, N. G. (2010). Spirituality and religion in group counseling: A literature review with practice guidelines. *Professional Psychology: Research and Practice, 41,* 398–404.

Cornum, R., Matthews, M. D., & Seligman, M. E. P. (2011). Comprehensive Soldier Fitness: Building resilience in a challenging institutional context. *American Psychologist, 66,* 4–9.

Corona, G., Rastrelli, G., Ricca, V., Jannini, E. A., Vignozzi, L., Monami, M., . . . Maggi, M. (2013). Risk factors associated with primary and secondary reduced libido in male patients with sexual dysfunction. *Journal of Sexual Medicine, 10,* 1074–1089.

Correll, C. U., Manu, P., Olshanskiv, V., Napolitano, B., Kane, J. M., & Malhotra, A. K. (2010). Cardiometabolic risk of second-generation antipsychotic medications during first-time use in children and adolescents. *Journal of the American Medical Association, 302,* 1765–1773.

Corrigan, P. W., & Rao, D. (2012). On the self-stigma of mental illness: Stages, disclosure, and strategies for change. *Canadian Journal of Psychiatry, 57,* 464–469.

Corrigan, P. W., Sokol, K. A., & Rusch, N. (2013). The impact of self-stigma and mutual help programs on the quality of life of people with serious mental illnesses. *Community Mental Health Journal, 49,* 1–6.

Cortina, L. M., & Kubiak, S. P. (2006). Gender and posttraumatic stress: Sexual violence as an explanation for women's increased risk. *Journal of Abnormal Psychology, 115,* 753–759.

Coryell, W., Fiedorowicz, J. G., Solomon, D., Leon, A. C., Rice, J. P., & Keller, M. B. (2012). Effects of anxiety on the long-term course of depressive disorders. *British Journal of Psychiatry, 200,* 210–215.

Cosci, F. (2012). The psychological development of panic disorder: Implications for neurobiology and treatment. *Revista Brasileira de Psiquiatria, 34,* 9–19.

Cosgrove, L., & Krimsky, S. (2012). A comparison of DSM-IV and DSM-5 panel members' financial associations with industry: A pernicious problem persists. *PLOS Medicine, 9*(3), e1001190. doi:10.1371/journal. pmed.1001190

Costa, A. C., & Scott-McKean, J. J. (2013). Prospects for improving brain function in individuals with Down syndrome. *CNS Drugs, 27,* 679–702.

Costa, P. T., Jr., & McCrae, R. R. (2005). A five-factor model perspective on personality disorders. In S. Strack (Ed.), *Handbook of personality and psychopathology* (pp. 442–461). Hoboken, NJ: Wiley.

Costafreda, S. G., Fu, C. H., Picchioni, M., Toulopoulou, T., McDonald, C., Walshe, M., . . . McGuire, P. K. (2011). Pattern of neural responses to verbal fluency shows diagnostic specificity for schizophrenia and bipolar disorder. *BioMed Central Psychiatry, 11,* 18. doi:10.1186/1471-244X-11-18

Cottler, L. B., Leung, K. S., & Abdallah, A. B. (2009). Test–re-test reliability of DSM-IV adopted criteria for 3,4-methylenedioxymethamphetamine (MDMA) abuse and dependence: A cross-national study. *Addiction, 104,* 1679–1690.

Cottrell, D., & Boston, P. (2002). Practitioner review: The effectiveness of systemic family therapy for children and adolescents. *Journal of Child Psychology and Psychiatry, 43,* 573–586.

Cougnard, A., Marcelis, M., Myin-Germeys, I., De Graaf, F., Vollebergh, W., Krabbendam, L., . . . Van Os, J. (2007). Does normal developmental expression of psychosis combine with environmental risk to cause persistence of psychosis? A psychosis proneness-persistence model. *Psychological Medicine, 37,* 513–527.

Courtet, P., Gottesman, I. I., Jollant, F., & Gould, T. D. (2011) The neuroscience of suicidal behaviors: What can we expect from endophenotype strategies? *Translational Psychiatry, 1,* pii: e7.

Courtney, K. E., & Polich, J. (2009). Binge drinking in young adults: Data, definitions, and determinants. *Psychological Bulletin, 135,* 142–156.

Cousins, N. (1979). *Anatomy of an illness.* New York, NY: Norton.

Cowley, G., & Underwood, A. (1997, May 26). Why Ebonie can't breathe. *Newsweek,* 58–63.

Craddock, N., & Sklar, P. (2013). Genetics of bipolar disorder. *Lancet, 381,* 1654–1662.

Craigmyle, N. A. (2013). The beneficial effects of meditation: Contribution of the anterior cingulate and locus coeruleus. *Frontiers in Psychology, 4,* 731. doi:10.3389/fpsyg.2013.00731

Crepeau-Hobson, M. F., & Leech, N. L. (2013). The impact of exposure to peer suicidal self-directed violence on youth suicidal behavior: A critical review of the literature. *Suicide and Life-Threatening Behavior, 44,* 58–77.

Crews, F., & Boettiger, C. A. (2009). Impulsivity, frontal lobes and risk for addiction. *Pharmacology Biochemistry and Behavior, 88,* 237–247.

Crosby, R. D., Wonderlich, S. A., Engel, S. G., Simonich, H., Smyth, J., & Mitchell, J. E. (2009). Daily mood patterns and bulimic behaviors in the natural environment. *Behaviour Research and Therapy, 47,* 181–188.

Croteau, J. M., Lark, J. S., Lidderdale, M. A., & Chung, Y. B. (2005). *Deconstructing heterosexism in the counseling professions.* Thousand Oaks, CA: Sage.

Crow, S. J., Peterson, C. B., Swanson, S. A., Raymond, N. C., Specker, S., Eckert, E. D., & Mitchell, J. E. (2009). Increased mortality in bulimia nervosa and other eating disorders. *American Journal of Psychiatry, 166,* 1342–1346.

Crum, R. M., Mojtabai, R., Lazareck, S., Bolton, J. M., Robinson, J., Sareen, J., . . . Storr, C. L. (2013). A prospective assessment of reports of drinking to self-medicate mood symptoms with the incidence and persistence of alcohol dependence. *JAMA Psychiatry, 70,* 718–726.

Cryan, J. F., & Dinan, T. G. (2012). Mind-altering microorganisms: The impact of the gut microbiota on brain and behaviour. *Nature Reviews: Neuroscience, 13,* 701–712.

Csipke, E., & Horne, O. (2007). Pro-eating disorder websites: Users' opinions. *European Eating Disorders Review, 15,* 196–206.

Cubillo, A., Halari, R., Smith, A., Taylor, E., & Rubia, K. (2012). A review of fronto-striatal and fronto-cortical brain abnormalities in children and adults with attention deficit hyperactivity disorder (ADHD) and new evidence for dysfunction in adults with ADHD during motivation and attention. *Cortex, 48,* 194–215.

Cuijpers, P., Sijbrandij, M., Koole, S., Huibers, M., Berking, M., & Andersson, G. (2014). Psychological treatment of generalized anxiety disorder: A meta-analysis. *Clinical Psychology Review, 34,* 130–140.

Culbert, K. M., Burt, S. A., McGue, M., Iacono, W. G., & Klump, K. L. (2009). Puberty and the genetic diathesis of disordered eating attitudes and behaviors. *Journal of Abnormal Psychology, 118,* 788–796.

Culbertson, C. S., Bramen, J., Cohen, M. S., London, E. D., Olmstead, R. E., Gan, J.J., . . . Brody, A. L. (2011). Effect of bupropion treatment on brain activation induced by cigarette-related cues in smokers. *Archives of General Psychiatry, 68*(5), 505–515. doi:10.1001/archgenpsychiatry.2010.193

Cummings, J. R., & Druss, B. G. (2011). Racial/ethnic differences in mental health service use among adolescents with major depression. *Journal of the American Academy of Child & Adolescent Psychiatry, 50,* 106–107.

Curran, L. K., Newschaffer, C. J., Lee, L. C., Crawford, S. O., Johnston, M. V., & Zimmerman, A. W. (2007). Behaviors associated with fever in children with autism spectrum disorders. *Pediatrics, 120,* 1386–1392.

Cutting, L. P., & Docherty, N. M. (2000). Schizophrenia outpatients' perceptions of their parents: Is expressed emotion a factor? *Journal of Abnormal Psychology, 109,* 266–272.

Dahlstrom, W. G., & Welsh, G. S. (1965). *An MMPI handbook.* Minneapolis, MN: University of Minnesota Press.

Dalenberg, C. J., Brand, B. L., Gleaves, D. H., Dorahy, M. J., Loewenstein, R. J., Cardeña, E., . . . Spiegel, D. (2012). Evaluation of the evidence for the trauma and fantasy models of dissociation. *Psychological Bulletin, 138*(3), 550–588. doi:10.1037/a0027447

Dalrymple, K. L., & Zimmerman, M. (2011). Age of onset of social anxiety disorders in depressed outpatients. *Journal of Anxiety Disorders, 25,* 131–137.

Daly, M. C., Oswald, A. J., Wilson, D., & Wu, S. (2011). Dark contrasts: The paradox of high rates of suicide in happy places. *Journal of Economic Behavior & Organization, 80,* 435–442.

Dammeyer, M. D., Nightingale, N. N., & McCoy, M. L. (1997). Repressed memory and other controversial origins of sexual abuse allegations: Beliefs among psychologists and clinical social workers. *Child Maltreatment, 2,* 252–263.

Dams-O'Conner, K., Martens, M. P., & Anderson, D. A. (2006). Alcohol-related consequences among women who want to lose weight. *Eating Behaviors, 7,* 188–195.

Damsa, C., Ruether, K. A., Moussaly, K., Adam, E., Vaney, C., & Berclaz, O. (2009). Greater evidence of dissociative symptoms noted in general practitioners attending an educational session on dissociation. *American Journal of Psychiatry, 166,* 1190–1191.

Daniels, A. M., Halladay, A. K., Shih, A., Elder, L. M., & Dawson, G. (2014). Approaches to enhancing the early detection of autism spectrum disorders: A systematic review of the literature. *Journal of the American Academy of Child & Adolescent Psychiatry, 53,* 141–152.

Daniulaityte, R., Falck, R., & Carlson, R. G. (2012). "I'm not afraid of those ones just 'cause they've been prescribed": Perceptions of risk among illicit users of pharmaceutical opioids. *International Journal of Drug Policy, 122,* 201–207.

Dannahy, L., Hayward, M., Strauss, C., Turton, W., Harding, E., & Chadwick, P. (2011). Group person-based cognitive therapy for distressing voices: Pilot data from nine groups. *Journal of Behavior Therapy and Experimental Psychiatry, 42,* 111–116.

Dao, J. (2011, December 1). After duty, dogs suffer like soldiers. *New York Times.* Retrieved from http://www.nytimes.com

Dardick, H. (2004, February 13). Psychiatric patient tells of ordeal in treatment. *Chicago Tribune,* p. 1.

Darosh, A. G., & Lloyd-Richardson, E. E. (2013). Exploring why students self-injure: The functions of nonsuicidal self-injury. *School Psychology Forum, 7,* 111–120.

Darwish, M., Kirby, M., D'Andrea, D. M., Yang, R., Hellriegel, E. T., & Robertson, P., Jr. (2010). Pharmacokinetics of armodafinil and modafinil after single and multiple doses in patients with excessive sleepiness associated with treated obstructive sleep apnea: A randomized, open-label, crossover study. *Clinical Therapeutics, 32,* 2074–2087.

Das-Munshi, J., Bécares, L., Boydell, J. E., Dewey, M. E., Morgan, C., Stansfeld, S. A., & Prince, M. J. (2012). Ethnic density as a buffer for psychotic experiences: Findings from a national survey (EMPIRIC). *British Journal of Psychiatry, 201,* 282–290.

Davidson, K., Norrie, J., & Palmer, S. (2008). The effectiveness of cognitive behavior therapy for borderline personality disorder: Results from the borderline personality disorder study of cognitive therapy (BOSCOT) trial. *Journal of Personality Disorders, 20,* 450–465.

Davies, P. G., Spencer, S. J., & Steele, C. M. (2005). Clearing the air: Identity safety moderates the effects of stereotype threat on women's leadership aspirations. *Journal of Personality and Social Psychology, 88,* 276–287.

Davis, G. P., Compton, M. T., Wang, S., Levin, F. R., & Blanco, C. (2013). Association between cannabis use, psychosis, and schizotypal personality disorder: Findings from the National Epidemiologic Survey on Alcohol and Related Conditions. *Schizophrenia Research, 151,* 197–202.

Davis, L., Uezato, A., Newell, J. M., & Frazier, E. (2008). Major depression and comorbid substance use disorders. *Current Opinion in Psychiatry, 21,* 14–18.

Dawson, D. A., Goldstein, R. B., & Grant, B. F. (2007). Rates and correlates of relapse among individuals in remission from DSM-IV alcohol dependence: A 3-year follow-up. *Alcoholism: Clinical and Experimental Research, 31,* 2036–2045.

Dawson, G., Munson, J., Webb, S. J., Nalty, T., Abbott, R., & Toth, K. (2007). Rate of head growth decelerates and symptoms worsen in the second year of life in autism. *Biological Psychiatry, 61,* 458–464.

Dawson, G., Rogers, S., Munson, J., Smith, M., Winter, J., Greenson, J., . . . Varley, J. (2010). Randomized, controlled trial of an intervention for toddlers with autism: The Early Start Denver model. *Pediatrics, 125,* 17–23.

Deacon, B. J. (2013). The biomedical model of mental disorder: A critical analysis of its validity, utility, and effects on psychotherapy research. *Clinical Psychology Review, 33,* 846–851.

DeAngelis, T. (2009, April). Fostering lives worth living. *Monitor on Psychology, 40,* 56.

De Leo, D., Milner, A., Fleischmann, A., Bertolote, J., Collings, S., Amadeo, S., . . . Wang, X. (2013). Suicidal behaviors across different areas of the world. *Crisis, 34,* 156–163.

De Backer, W. (2013). Obstructive sleep apnea/hypopnea syndrome. *Panminerva Medica, 55,* 191–195.

De Berardis, D., Marini, S., Fornaro, M., Srinivasan, V., Iasevoli, F., Tomasetti, C., . . . di Giannantonio, M. (2013). The melatonergic system in mood and anxiety disorders and the role of agomelatine: Implications for clinical practice. *International Journal of Molecular Science, 14,* 12458–12483.

De Block, A., & Adriaens, P. R. (2013). Pathologizing sexual deviance: A history. *Journal of Sex Research, 50,* 276–298.

Decety, J., Michalska, K. J., Akitsuki, Y., & Lahey, B. B. (2009). Atypical empathic responses in adolescents with aggressive conduct disorder: A functional MRI investigation. *Biological Psychology, 80,* 203–211.

Declercq, T., Petrovic, M., Azermai, M., Vander Stichele, R., De Sutter, A. I., van Driel, M. L., & Christiaens, T. (2013). Withdrawal versus continuation of chronic antipsychotic drugs for behavioural and psychological symptoms in older people with dementia. *Cochrane Database of Systematic Reviews.* doi:10.1002/14651858.CD007726.pub2

De Coteau, T., Anderson, J., & Hope, D. (2006). Adapting manualized treatments: Treating anxiety disorders among Native Americans. *Cognitive and Behavioral Practice, 13,* 304–309.

Dedovic, K., Wadiwalla, M., Engert, V., & Pruessner, J. C. (2009). The role of sex and gender socialization in stress reactivity. *Developmental Psychology, 4,* 45–55.

De Geus, E. J. C., Kupper, N., Boomsma, D. I., & Snieder, H. (2007). Bivariate genetic modeling of cardiovascular stress reactivity: Does stress uncover genetic variance? *Psychosomatic Medicine, 69,* 356–364.

Degnan, K. A., & Fox, N. A. (2007). Behavioral inhibition and anxiety disorders: Multiple levels of a resilience process. *Development and Psychopathology, 19,* 729–746.

de Kleine, R. A., Hendriks, G.-J., Smits, J. A., Broekman, T. G., & van Minnen, A. (2014). Prescriptive variables for D-cycloserine augmentation of exposure therapy for posttraumatic stress disorder. *Journal of Psychiatric Research, 48,* 40–46.

de la Fuente-Sandoval, C., León-Ortiz, P., Azcárraga, M., Stephano, S., Favila, R., Díaz-Galvis, L., . . . Graff-Guerrero, A. (2013). Glutamate levels in the associative striatum before and after 4 weeks of antipsychotic treatment in first-episode psychosis: A longitudinal proton magnetic resonance spectroscopy study. *JAMA Psychiatry, 70,* 1057–1066.

DeLany, J. P., Jakicic, J. M., Lowery, J. B., Hames, K. C., Kelley, D. E., & Goodpaster, B. H. (2013, December 19). African American women exhibit similar adherence to intervention but lose less weight due to lower energy requirements. *International Journal of Obesity.* doi:10.1038/ijo.2013.240

De Leo, D. (2009). Cross-cultural research widens suicide prevention horizons. *Crisis, 30,* 59–62.

Dell, P. F. (2013). Three dimensions of dissociative amnesia. *Journal of Trauma & Dissociation, 14,* 25–39.

Dell, P. F., & Eisenhower, J. W. (1990). Adolescent multiple personality disorder: A preliminary study of eleven cases. *Journal of the American Academy of Child & Adolescent Psychiatry, 29,* 359–366.

Del Re, A. C., Flückiger, C., Horvath, A. O., Symonds, D., & Wampold, B. E. (2012). Therapist effects in the therapeutic alliance-outcome relationship: A restricted-maximum likelihood meta-analysis. *Clinical Psychology Review, 32,* 642–649.

Demakis, D. J. (2013). State statutory definitions of civil incompetency/incapacity: Issues for psychologists. *Psychology, Public Policy, and Law, 19,* 331–342.

De Martino, E. (2005). *The land of remorse: A study of southern Italian tarantism* (translated by D. L. Zinn with an introduction by V. Crapanzano). London, UK: Free Association Books.

Denis, C., Lavie, E., Fatséas, M., & Auriacombe, M. (2006). Psychotherapeutic interventions for cannabis abuse and/or dependence in outpatient settings. *Cochrane Database of Systematic Reviews, 19,* CD005336. doi:10.1002/14651858.CD005336.pub2

Denney, J. T. (2010). Family and household formations and suicide in the United States. *Journal of Marriage and Family, 72,* 202–213.

Denney, J. T., Rogers, R. G., Krueger, P. M., & Wadsworth, T. (2009). Adult suicide mortality in the United States: Marital status, family size, socioeconomic status, and differences by sex. *Social Science Quarterly, 90,* 1167–1185.

de Rossi, P. (2010). *Unbearable lightness: A story of loss and gain.* Chicago, IL: Atria.

DeRubeis, R. J., Siegle, G. J., & Hollon, S. D. (2008). Cognitive therapy vs. medications for depression: Treatment outcomes and neural mechanisms. *National Review of Neuroscience, 9,* 788–796.

Desbonnet, L., O'Tuathaigh, C. M. P., & Waddington, J. L. (2012). Modeling schizophrenia. *Expert Review in Clinical Pharmacology, 5,* 667–676.

Deshmukh, A. (2012, November). Women more likely than men to develop "broken heart syndrome." Presented at the Meetings of the American Heart Association, Gainesville, FL.

Deshpande, A. V., Caldwell, P. H., & Sureshkumar, P. (2012). Drugs for nocturnal enuresis in children (other than desmopressin and tricyclics). *Cochrane Database of Systematic Reviews, 12*, CD002238. doi:10.1002/14651858.CD002238.pub2

de Simone, V., Kaplan, L., Patronas, N., Wassermann, E. M., & Grafman, J. (2006). Driving abilities in frontotemporal dementia patients. *Dementia and Geriatric Cognitive Disorders, 23*, 1–7.

Desmond, S., Price, J., Hallinan, C., & Smith, D. (1989). Black and white adolescents' perceptions of their weight. *Journal of School Health, 59*, 353–358.

DeStefano, F., Price, C. S., & Weintrau, E. S. (2013). Increasing exposure to antibody- stimulating proteins and polysaccharides in vaccines is not associated with risk of autism. *Journal of Pediatrics, 163*, 561–567.

Detka, J., Kurek, A., Basta-Kaim, A., Kubera, M., Lason, W., & Budziszewska, B. (2013). Neuroendocrine link between stress, depression and diabetes. *Pharmacological Reports, 65*, 1591–1600.

D'ettore, D., Pucciarelli, M., & Santarnecchi, E. (2013). Anxiety and female sexual functioning: An empirical study. *Journal of Sex & Marital Therapy, 39*, 216–240.

Devita-Raeburn, E. (2007). The Morgellons mystery. *Psychology Today*. Retrieved from http://www.psychology-today.com

De Young, K. P., Zander, M., & Anderson, D. A. (2014). Beliefs about the emotional consequences of eating and binge eating frequency. *Eating Behaviors, 15*, 31–36.

Dhabhar, F. S. (2013). Psychological stress and immunoprotection versus immunopathology in the skin. *Clinical Dermatology, 31*, 18–30.

Dhejne, C., Lichtenstein, P., Boman, M., Johansson, A. L., Långström, N., & Landén, M. (2011). Long-term follow-up of transsexual persons undergoing sex reassignment surgery: Cohort study in Sweden. *PLOS One, 6*, e16885. doi:10.1371/journal.pone.0016885

Diamond, A. (2009). The interplay of biology and the environment broadly defined. *Developmental Psychology, 45*, 1–8.

Dickerson, S. S., & Kemeny, M. E. (2004). Acute stressors and cortisol responses: A theoretical integration and synthesis of laboratory research. *Psychological Bulletin, 130*, 355–391.

Diflorio, A., & Jones, I. (2010). Is sex important? Gender differences in bipolar disorder. *International Review of Psychiatry, 22*, 437–452.

DiFranza, J. R., Savageau, J. A., Fletcher, K., Pbert, L., O'Loughlin, J., McNeill, A. D., . . . Wellman, R. J. (2007). Susceptibility to nicotine dependence: The Development and Assessment of Nicotine Dependence in Youth 2 study. *Pediatrics, 120*, 974–983.

DiGangi, J. A., Gomez, D., Mendoza, L., Jason, L. A., Keys, C. B., & Koenen, K. C. (2013). Pretrauma risk factors for posttraumatic stress disorder: A systematic review of the literature. *Clinical Psychology Review, 33*, 728–744.

DiGrande, L., Neria, Y., Brackbill, M., Pulliam, P., & Galea, S. (2011). Longterm posttraumatic stress symptoms among 3,271 civilian survivors of the September 11, 2001, terrorist attacks on the World Trade Center. *American Journal of Epidemiology, 173*, 271–281.

Diles, K. (2013). My story. Retrieved from https://www.save.org/index.cfm?fuseaction5home.viewPage&page_id584B187C2-D156-503D-6B56FA19D6126E5B&previewMode5true&r51

Dilks, S., Tasker, F., & Wren, B. (2010). Managing the impact of psychosis: A grounded theory exploration of recovery processes in psychosis. *British Journal of Clinical Psychology, 49*, 87–107.

Dimsdale, J. E. (2011). Medically unexplained symptoms: A treacherous foundation for somatoform disorders? *Psychiatric Clinics of North America, 34*, 511–513.

Dimsdale, J. E., & Levenson, J. (2013). What's next for somatic symptom disorder? *American Journal of Psychiatry, 170*, 1393–1395.

Ding, K., Chang, G. A., & Southerland, R. (2009). Age of inhalant first time use and its association to the use of other drugs. *Journal of Drug Education, 39*, 261–272.

Di Paola, F., Faravelli, C., & Ricca, V. (2010). Perceived expressed emotion in anorexia nervosa, bulimia nervosa, and binge-eating disorder. *Comprehensive Psychiatry, 51*, 401–405.

Dirmann, T. (2003, September 8). Ex-Spice Girl Geri Halliwell: How I beat my eating disorder. *US Weekly*, 60.

Dixon v. Weinberger, 498 F. 2d 202 (1975).

Doane, L. D., & Zeiders, K. H. (2013). Contextual moderators of momentary cortisol and negative affect in adolescents' daily lives. *Journal of Adolescent Health, 54*, 536–542.

Dobbs, D. (2009). The post-traumatic stress trap. *Scientific American, 300*(4), 64–69.

Dobkin, R. D., Allen, L. A., & Menza, M. (2006). A cognitive-behavioral treatment package for depression in Parkinson's disease. *Psychosomatics, 47*, 259–263.

Dobson, K. S., Hollon, S. D., Dimidjian, S., Schmaling, K. B., Kohlenberg, R. J., Gallop, R. J., . . . Jacobson, N. S. (2008). Randomized trial of behavioral activation, cognitive therapy, and antidepressant medication in the prevention of relapse and recurrence in major depression. *Journal of Consulting and Clinical Psychology, 76*, 468–477.

Dobson, P., & Rogers, J. (2009). Assessing and treating faecal incontinence in children. *Nursing Standards, 24*, 49–56.

Dodick, D. W., & Gargus, J. J. (2008). Why migraines strike. *Scientific American, 299*(2), 56–63.

Doka, K. J. (2013). Grief and the DSM: A brief Q&A. Retrieved from http://www.huffingtonpost.com/kenneth-j-doka/grief-and-the-dsm_b_3340216.html

Dolan, M. C., & Fullam, R. (2010). Emotional memory and psychopathic traits in conduct disordered adolescents. *Personality and Individual Differences, 48*, 327–331.

Dolezsar, C. M., McGrath, J. J., Herzig, A. J., & Miller, S. B. (2014). Perceived racial discrimination and hypertension: A comprehensive systematic review. *Health Psychology, 33*, 20–34.

Dollinger, S. J. (1983). A case of dissociative neurosis (depersonalization disorder) in an adolescent treated with family therapy and behavior modification. *Journal of Consulting and Clinical Psychology, 15*, 479–484.

Dominguez, M. D. G., Saka, M. C., Lieb, R., Wittchan, H.-U., & Van Os, J. (2010). Early expression of negative/disorganized symptoms predicting psychotic experiences and subsequent clinical psychosis: A 10-year study. *Am J Psychiatry, 167*, 1075–1082.

Dominguez, M. D. G., Wichers, M., Lieb, R., Wittchen, H.-U., & Van Os, J. (2011). Evidence that onset of clinical psychosis is an outcome of progressively more persistent subclinical psychotic experiences: An 8-year cohort study. *Schizophrenia Bulletin, 37*, 84–93.

Domschke, K., Stevens, S., Pfleiderer, B., & Gerlach, A. L. (2010). Interoceptive sensitivity in anxiety and anxiety disorders: An overview and integration of neurobiological findings. *Clinical Psychology Review, 30,* 1–11.

Donegan, E., & Dugas, M. J. (2012). Generalized anxiety disorder: A comparison of symptom change in adults receiving cognitive-behavioral therapy or applied relaxation. *Journal of Consulting and Clinical Psychology, 80,* 490–496.

Dong, Q., Yang, B., & Ollendick, T. H. (1994). Fears in Chinese children and adolescents and their relations to anxiety and depression. *Journal of Child Psychology and Psychiatry, 35,* 351–363.

D'Onofrio, B. M., Class, Q. A., Rickert, M. E., Larsson, H., Långström, N., & Lichtenstein, P. (2013). Preterm birth and mortality and morbidity: A population-based quasi-experimental study. *JAMA Psychiatry, 70,* 1231–1240.

Donoghue, K., Doody, G. A., Murray, R. M., Jones, P. B., Morgan, C., Dazzan, P., . . . Maccabe J. H. (2014). Cannabis use, gender and age of onset of schizophrenia: Data from the ÆSOP study. *Psychiatry Research, 215,* 528–532.

Dorahy, M. J., Shannon, C., Seagar, L., Corr, M., Stewart, K., Hanna, D., . . . Middleton, W. (2009). Auditory hallucinations in dissociative identity disorder and schizophrenia with and without a childhood trauma history: Similarities and differences. *Journal of Nervous and Mental Disease, 197,* 892–898.

Dougan, B. K., Horswill, M. S., & Geffen, G. M. (2014). Do injury characteristics predict the severity of acute neuropsychological deficits following sports-related concussion? A meta-analysis. *Journal of the International Neuropsychological Society, 20,* 81–87.

Dougherty, L. R., Smith, V. C., Bufferd, S. J., Carlson, G. A., Stringaris, A., Leibenluft, E., & Klein, D. N. (2014). DSM-5 disruptive mood dysregulation disorder: Correlates and predictors in young children. *Psychological Medicine, 21,* 1–12.

Doughty, O. J., Lawrence, V. A., Al-Mousawi, A., Ashaye, K., & Done, D. J. (2009). Overinclusive thought and loosening of associations are not unique to schizophrenia and are produced in Alzheimer's dementia. *Cognitive Neuropsychiatry, 14,* 149–164.

Dovidio, J. F., Kawakami, K., Smoak, N., & Gaertner, S. L. (2009). Implicit measures of attitudes. In R. Petty, R. Faxio, & P. Brinol (Eds.), *Implicit measures*

(pp. 165–192). New York, NY: Psychology Press.

Doward, J. (2013). Psychiatrists under fire in mental health battle. Retrieved from http://www.theguardian.com/society/2013/may/12/psychiatrists-under-fire-mental-health

Downey, R., III, Gold, P. M., Rowley, J. A., Wickramasinghe, H., Sharma, S., Talavera, F., . . . Mosenifar, Z. (2013). Obstructive sleep apnea. Retrieved from http://emedicine.medscape.com/article/295807-overview#a0156

Dragt, S., Nieman, D. H., Becker, H. E., van de Fliert, R., Dingemans, P. M., de Hann, L., . . . Linszen, D. H. (2010). Age of onset of cannabis use is associated with age of onset of high-risk symptoms for psychosis. *Canadian Journal of Psychiatry, 55,* 165–171.

Draxler, H., & Hiltunen, A. J. (2012). A modification of enhanced cognitive behavioral therapy for anorexia nervosa: A case study. *Clinical Case Studies, 11,* 201–217.

Dreher, D. E. (2013). Abnormal psychology in the Renaissance. In T. G. Plante (Ed.), *Abnormal psychology across the ages.* Vol. I: *History and conceptualizations* (pp. 33–50). Santa Barbara, CA: Praeger/ABC-CLIO.

Drum, D. J., Brownson, C., Denmark, A. B., & Smith, S. E. (2009). New data on the nature of suicidal crisis in college students: Shifting the paradigm. *Professional Psychology: Research and Practice, 40,* 213–222.

Dudley, R., Siitarinen, J., James, I., & Dodson, G. (2009). What do people with psychosis think caused their psychosis? A Q methodology study. *Behavioural and Cognitive Psychotherapy, 37,* 11–24.

Dulai, R., & Kelly, S. L. (2009). A case of the body snatchers. *Current Psychiatry, 8,* 56–65.

Dunham, D. (2012). "Skinny doesn't sell" so disturbing trend has models airbrushed to look fatter. Retrieved from http://www.blisstree.com/2012/08/23/beauty-shopping/skinny-doesnt-sell-so-disturbing-trend-has-models-airbrushed-to-look-fatter-592/#ixzz2rzQZwz2E

Dunkley, D. M., Masheb, R. M., & Grilo, C. M. (2010). Child maltreatment, depressive symptoms, and body dissatisfaction in patients with binge eating disorder: The mediating role of self-criticism. *International Journal of Eating Disorders, 43,* 274–281.

Durà-Vilà, G., Dein, S., & Hodes, M. (2010). Children with intellectual disability: A gain not a loss: Parental beliefs and family life. *Clinical Child Psychology and Psychiatry, 5,* 171–184.

Durex. (2001). Global sex survey. Retrieved from http://www.durex.com/uk/globalsexsurvey/2005results.asp

Durex. (2005). Global sex survey 2005 results. Retrieved from www.durex.com/uk/globalsexsurvey/2005results.asp

Durham v. United States, 214 F. 2d 862, 874–875 (D.C. Cir. 1954).

Durkheim, É. (1951). *Suicide.* New York, NY: Free Press. (Original work published 1897)

Durso, L. E., Latner, J. D., White, M. A., Masheb, R. M., Blomquist, K. K., Morgan, P. T., & Grilo, C. M. (2012). Internalized weight bias in obese patients with binge eating disorder: Associations with eating disturbances and psychological functioning. *International Journal of Eating Disorders, 45,* 423–427.

Durston, S. (2010). Imaging genetics in ADHD. *Neuroimage, 53,* 832–838.

Dworkin, A. (2009, November 11). After stroke, Portland woman's brain on the rebound [Web log post]. Retrieved from http://www.oregonlive.com/health/index.ssf/2009/11/after_stroke_portland_womans_b.html

Dzokoto, A. A., & Adams, G. (2005). Understanding genital-shrinking epidemics in West Africa: Koro, juju, or mass psychogenic illness? *Culture, Medicine and Psychiatry, 29,* 53–78.

Eack, S. M., Bahorik, A. L., Newhill, C. E., Neighbors, H. W., & Davis, L. E. (2012). Interviewer-perceived honesty as a mediator of racial disparities in the diagnosis of schizophrenia. *Psychiatric Services, 63,* 875–880.

Ebdlahad, S., Nofzinger, E. A., James, J. A., Buysse, D. J., Price, J. C., & Germain, A. (2013). Comparing neural correlates of REM sleep in posttraumatic stress disorder and depression: A neuroimaging study. *Psychiatry Research, 214,* 422–428.

Eberhart, N. K. (2011). Maladaptive schemas and depression: Tests of stress generation and diathesis-stress models. *Journal of Social and Clinical Psychology, 30,* 75–104.

Edden, R. A., Crocetti, D., Zhu, H., Gilbert, D. L., & Mostofsky, S. H. (2012). Reduced GABA concentration in attention-deficit/hyperactivity disorder. *Archives of General Psychiatry, 69,* 750–753.

Eddy, K. T., Tanofsky-Kraff, M., Thompson-Brenner, H., Hertzog, D. B., Brown, T. A., & Ludwig, D. S. (2007). Eating disorder pathology among overweight treatment-seeking youth: Clinical correlates and cross-sectional risk modeling. *Behaviour Research and Therapy, 45,* 2360–2367.

Edenberg, H. J. (2012). Genes contributing to the development of alcoholism: An overview. *Alcohol Research, 34,* 336–338.

Edens, J. F., Davis, K. M., Fernandez Smith, K., & Guy, L. S. (2013). No sympathy for the devil: Attributing psychopathic traits to capital murderers also predicts support for executing them. *Personality Disorders, 4,* 175–181.

Edmondson, D., Richardson, S., Fausett, J. K., Falzon, L., Howard, V. J., & Kronish, I. M. (2013). Prevalence of PTSD in survivors of stroke and transient ischemic attack: A meta-analytic review. *PLOS One, 8*(6), e66435. doi:10.1371/journal.pone.0066435

Edvardsen, J., Torgersen, S., Røysamb, E., Lygren, S., Skre, I., Onstad, S., & Oien, P. A. (2008). Heritability of bipolar spectrum disorders: Unity or heterogeneity? *Journal of Affective Disorders, 106,* 229–240.

Eftekhari, A., Ruzek, J. I., Crowley, J. J., Rosen, C. S., Greenbaum, M. A., & Karlin, B. E. (2013). Effectiveness of national implementation of prolonged exposure therapy in Veterans Affairs care. *JAMA Psychiatry, 70,* 949–955.

Egido, J. A., Castillo, O., Roig, B., Sanz, I., Herrero, M. R., Garay, M. T., . . . Fernandez, C. (2012). Is psycho-physical stress a risk factor for stroke? A case-control study. *Journal of Neurology, Neurosurgery, and Psychiatry, 83,* 1104–1110.

Egolf, A., & Coffey, B. J. (2014). Current pharmacotherapeutic approaches for the treatment of Tourette syndrome. *Drugs Today, 50,* 159–179.

Ehrlich, S., Pfeiffer, E., Salbach, H., Lenz, K., & Lehmkuhl, U. (2008). Factitious disorder in children and adolescents: A retrospective study. *Psychosomatics, 49,* 392–398.

Eidelman, P., Gershon, A., Kaplan, K., McGlinchey, E., & Harvey, A. G. (2012). Social support and social strain in inter-episode bipolar disorder. *Bipolar Disorders, 14,* 628–640.

Eidelman, P., Talbot, L. S., Gruber, J., & Harvey, A. G. (2010). Sleep, illness course, and concurrent symptoms in inter-episode bipolar disorder. *Journal of Behavior Therapy and Experimental Psychiatry, 41,* 145–149.

Eidelson, R., Pilisuk, M., & Soldz, S. (2011). The dark side of Comprehensive Soldier Fitness. *American Psychologist, 66,* 643–644.

Eidelson, R., & Soldz, S. (2012). Does Comprehensive Soldier Fitness work? CSF research fails the test. Retrieved from http://www.ethicalpsychology.org/Eidelson-&-Soldz-CSF_Research_Fails_the_Test.pdf

Eisenberg, M. A., Andrea, J., Meehan, W., & Mannix, R. (2013). Time interval between concussions and symptom duration. *Pediatrics, 132,* 8–17.

Eisenberg, M. E., & Neumark-Sztainer, D. (2010). Friends' dieting and disordered eating behaviors among adolescents five years later: Findings from Project EAT. *Journal of Adolescent Health, 47,* 67–73.

Elbogen, E. B., & Johnson, S. C. (2009). The intricate link between violence and mental disorder. *Archives of General Psychiatry, 66,* 152–161.

Elder, T. (2010). The importance of relative standards in ADHD diagnosis: Evidence based on exact birth dates. *Journal of Health Economics, 29,* 641–656.

Eldevik, S., Hastings, R. P., Hughes, J. C., Jahr, E., Eikeseth, S., & Cross, S. (2010). Using participant data to extend the evidence base for intensive behavioral intervention for children with autism. *American Journal of Intellectual and Developmental Disabilities, 115,* 381–405.

Eley, T. C., Lichtenstein, P., & Moffitt, T. E. (2003). A longitudinal behavioral genetic analysis of the etiology of aggressive and nonaggressive antisocial behavior. *Development and Psychopathology, 15,* 383–402.

El-Gabalawy, R., Cox, B., Clara, I., & Mackenzie, C. (2010). Assessing the validity of social anxiety disorder subtypes using a nationally representative sample. *Journal of Anxiety Disorders, 24,* 244–249.

Elkashef, A., Vocci, F., Huestis, M., Haney, M., Budney, A., Gruber, A., & el-Guebaly, N. (2008). Marijuana neurobiology and treatment. *Substance Abuse, 29,* 17–29.

Elklit, A., & Christiansen, D. M. (2010). ASD and PTSD in rape victims. *Journal of Interpersonal Violence, 25,* 1470–1488.

Elliott, D., & Banda, P. S. (2013). Prosecutors not ready to agree to Holmes plea. Retrieved from http://bigstory.ap.org/article/prosecutors-not-ready-agree-holmes-plea

Elliott, R. (2002). The effectiveness of humanistic therapies. In D. J. Cain & J. Seeman (Eds.), *Humanistic psychotherapies: Handbook of research and practice* (pp. 57–81). Washington, DC: American Psychological Association.

Elliot, R.-L., Campbell, L., Hunter, M., Cooper, G., Melville, J., McCabe, K., . . . Loughland, C. (2014). When I look into my baby's eyes . . . Infant emotion recognition by mothers with borderline personality disorder. *Infant Mental Health Journal, 35,* 21–32.

Ellis, A. (1989). Rational-emotive therapy. In R. J. Corsini & D. Wedding (Eds.), *Current psychotherapies* (pp. 197–238). Itasca, IL: Peacock.

Ellis, A. (1997). The evolution of Albert Ellis and rational emotive behavior therapy. In J. K. Zeig (Ed.), *The evolution of psychotherapy: The third conference.* New York, NY: Brunner/Mazel.

Ellis, A. (2008). Rational emotive behavior therapy. In R. J. Corsini & D. Wedding (Eds.), *Current psychotherapies* (8th ed., pp. 187–222). Belmont, CA: Brooks/Cole.

Ellis, D. M., & Hudson, J. L. (2010). The metacognitive model of generalized anxiety disorder in children and adolescents. *Clinical Child and Family Psychology Review, 13,* 151–163.

Ellis, L. (1991). A synthesized (biosocial) theory of rape. *Journal of Consulting and Clinical Psychology, 59,* 631–642.

Ellison-Wright, I., & Bullmore, E. (2010). Anatomy of bipolar disorder and schizophrenia: A meta-analysis. *Schizophrenia Research, 117,* 1–12.

El-Sheikh, M., Keiley, M., & Hinnant, J. B. (2009). Developmental trajectories of skin conductance level in middle childhood: Sex, race, and externalizing behavior problems as predictors of growth. *Biological Psychology, 83,* 116–124.

Elwyn, T. S., Ahmed, I., & Dunayevich, E. (2014). Factitious disorder imposed on self. Retrieved from http://emedicine.medscape.com/article/291304-overview

Emel, B. (2011, July 1). 2 Key components to a resilient and peaceful life [Web log post]. Retrieved from http://www.thebounceblog.com/2011/07/01/2-key-components-to-a-resilient-and-peaceful-life

Engelhard, I. M., de Jong, P. J., van den Hout, M. A., & van Overveld, M.

(2009). Expectancy bias and the persistence of posttraumatic stress. *Behaviour Research and Therapy, 47,* 887–892.

Enoch, M. A. (2012). The influence of gene-environment interactions on the development of alcoholism and drug dependence. *Current Psychiatry Reports, 14,* 150–158.

Enterman, J. H., & van Dijk, D. (2011). The curious case of a catatonic patient. *Schizophrenia Bulletin, 37,* 235–237.

Epperson, C. N., Steiner, M., Hartlage, S. A., Eriksson, E., Schmidt, P. J., Jones, I., & Yonkers, K. A. (2012). Premenstrual dysphoric disorder: Evidence for a new category for DSM-5. *Am J Psychiatry, 169,* 465–475.

Epstein, J. A., Banga, H., & Botvina, G. J. (2007). Which psychosocial factors moderate or directly affect substance use among inner-city adolescents? *Addictive Behaviors, 32,* 700–713.

Epstein, L. H., Leddy, J. J., Temple, J. L., & Faith, M. S. (2007). Food reinforcement and eating: A multilevel analysis. *Psychological Bulletin, 133,* 884–906.

Erdely, S. R. (2004, March). What women sacrifice to be thin. *Redbook, 202*(3), 114–120.

Erickson, E. H. (1968). *Identity: Youth and crisis.* New York, NY: Norton.

Ersche, K. D., Turton, A. J., Pradhan, S., Bullmore, E. T., & Robbins, T. W. (2010). Drug addiction endophenotypes: Impulsive versus sensation-seeking personality traits. *Biological Psychiatry, 68,* 770–773.

Eshun, S., & Gurung, R. A. R. (Eds.). (2009). *Introduction to culture and psychopathology, in culture and mental health: Sociocultural influences, theory, and practice.* Oxford, UK: Wiley-Blackwell.

Ester. (2013). Ester's story. Retrieved from https://www.save.org/ester

Esterberg, M. L., Goulding, S. M., & Walker, E. L. (2010). A personality disorders: schizotypal, schizoid and paranoid personality disorders in childhood and adolescence. *Journal of Psychopathology and Behavioral Assessment, 32,* 515–528.

Etter, J. F., & Bullen, C. (2014). A longitudinal study of electronic cigarette users. *Addictive Behavior, 39,* 491–494.

Ettinger, U., Schmechtig, A., Toulopoulou, T., Borg, C., Orrells, C., Owens, S., . . . Picchioni, M. (2012). Prefrontal and striatal volumes in monozygotic twins concordant and disconcordant for schizophrenia. *Schizophrenia Bulletin, 38,* 192–203.

Evans-Lacko, S., Brohan, E., Mojtabai, R., & Thornicroft, G. (2012). Association between public views of mental illness and self-stigma among individuals with mental illness in 14 European countries. *Psychological Medicine, 42,* 1441–1452.

Ewing, C. P. (1998, February). Indictment fuels repressed-memory debate. *APA Monitor,* p. 52.

Eyberg, S. M., Nelson, M. M., & Boggs, S. R. (2008). Evidence-based psychosocial treatments for children and adolescents with disruptive behavior. *Journal of Clinical Child and Adolescent Psychology, 37,* 215–237.

Ezra, Y., Gotkine, M., Goldman, S., Adahan, H. M., & Ben-Hur, T. (2012). Hypnotic relaxation vs amitriptyline for tension-type headache: Let the patient choose. *Headache, 52,* 785–791.

Faces and Voices of Recovery. (2014). How many people in the U.S are in recovery? Retrieved from http://www.facesandvoicesofrecovery.org/about/faq2.php

Facts and Information. (n.d.). Retrieved from http://www.sfwar.org/facts.html

Fagiolini, A. (2008). Medical monitoring in patients with bipolar disorder: A review of data. *Journal of Clinical Psychiatry, 69,* e16.

Fairburn, C. G., Cooper, Z., Doll, H. A., Norman, P., & O'Connor, M. (2000). The natural course of bulimia nervosa and binge eating disorder in young women. *Archives of General Psychiatry, 57,* 659–665.

Fairchild, G., van Goozen, S. H., Calder, A. J., & Goodyer, I. M. (2013). Research review: Evaluating and reformulating the developmental taxonomic theory of antisocial behaviour. *Journal of Child Psychology and Psychiatry, 54,* 924–940.

Fallon, E. A., Harris, B. S., & Johnson, P. (2014). Prevalence of body dissatisfaction among a United States adult sample. *Eating Behaviors, 15,* 151–158.

Fals-Stewart, W., & O'Farrell, T. J. (2003). Behavioral family counseling and naltrexone for male opioid-dependent patients. *Journal of Consulting and Clinical Psychology, 71,* 432–442.

Fang, F. C., Steen, R. G., & Casadevall, A. (2012). Misconduct accounts for the majority of retracted scientific publications. *Proceedings of the National Academy of Sciences of the United States of America, 109,* 17028–17033.

Fang, X., Brown, D. S., Florence, C. S., & Mercy, J. A. (2012). The economic burden of child maltreatment in the United States and implications for prevention. *Child Abuse and Neglect, 36,* 156–165.

Faraone, S. V., & Mick, E. (2010). Molecular genetics of attention deficit hyperactivity disorder. *Psychiatric Clinics of North America, 33,* 159–180.

Farchione, T. J., Fairholme, C. P., Ellard, K. K., Boisseau, C. L., Thompson-Hollands, J., Carl, J. R., . . . Barlow, D. H. (2012). Unified protocol for transdiagnostic treatment of emotional disorders: A randomized controlled trial. *Behavior Therapy, 43,* 666–678.

Farley, F. (1986). World of the type T personality. *Psychology Today, 20,* 45–52.

Farquhar, J. C., & Wasylkiw, L. (2007). Media images of men: Trends and consequences of body conceptualization. *Psychology of Men and Masculinity, 8,* 145–160.

Fattore, L., & Fratta, W. (2010). How important are sex differences in cannabinoid action? *British Journal of Pharmacology, 160,* 544–548.

Faul, M., Xu, L., Wald, M. M., & Coronado, V. G. (2010). Traumatic brain injury in the United States: Emergency department visits, hospitalizations, and deaths 2002–2006. Atlanta, GA: Centers for Disease Control and Prevention, National Center for Injury. Retrieved from http://www.cdc.gov/traumaticbraininjury/tbi_ed.html

Faulk, C., & Dolinoy, D. C. (2011). Timing is everything: The when and how of environmentally induced changes in the epigenome of animals. *Epigenetics, 6,* 791–797.

FBI. (2008). Serial murder: Multi-disciplinary perspectives for investigators. Retrieved from http://www.fbi.gov/stats-services/publications/serial-murder/serial-murder-july-2008-pdf

Fedoroff, J. P. (2008). Treatment of paraphilic sexual disorders. In D. Rowland & L. Incrocci (Eds.), *Handbook of sexual and gender identity disorders* (pp. 563–586). Hoboken, NJ: Wiley.

Fein, D., Barton, M., Eigsti, I. M., Kelley, E., Naigles, L., Schultz, R. T., . . . Tyson, K. (2013). Optimal outcome in individuals with a history of autism. *Journal of Child Psychology & Psychiatry, 54,* 195–205.

Feinstein, J. S., Adolphs, R., Damasio, A., & Tranel, D. (2011). The human amygdala and the induction and experience of fear. *Current Biology, 21,* 1–5.

Feinstein, J. S., Duff, M. C., & Tranela, D. (2010). Sustained experience of emotion after loss of memory in patients with amnesia. *Proceedings of the National Academy of Sciences, 107,* 7674–7679.

Fenton, M. C., Keyes, K. M., Martins, S. S., & Hasin, D. S. (2010). The role of a prescription in anxiety medication use, abuse, and dependence. *American Journal of Psychiatry, 167,* 1247–1253.

Fergusson, D. M., Boden, J. M., Horwood, L. J., Miller, A., & Kennedy, M. A. (2012). Moderating role of the MAOA genotype in antisocial behaviour. *British Journal of Psychiatry, 200,* 116–123.

Fernández, A., Mendive, J. M., Salvador-Carulla, L., Rubio-Valera, M., Luciano, J. V., Pinto-Meza, A., . . . Serrano-Blanco, A. (2012). Adjustment disorders in primary care: Prevalence, recognition and use of services. *British Journal of Psychiatry, 201,* 137–142.

Fernández-Cabana, M., García-Caballero, A., Alves-Pérez, M. T., García-García, M. J., & Mateos, R. (2013). Suicidal traits in Marilyn Monroe's Fragments. *Crisis, 34,* 124–130.

Ferner, R. E., & Aronson, J. K. (2013). Laughter and MIRTH (Methodical Investigation of Risibility, Therapeutic and Harmful): Narrative synthesis. *British Medical Journal, 347,* f7274.

Ferrari, A. J., Charlson, F. J., Norman, R. E., Flaxman, A. D., Patten, S. B., Vos, T., & Whiteford, H. A. (2013). The epidemiological modelling of major depressive disorder: Application for the Global Burden of Disease Study 2010. *PLOS One, 8,* e69637. doi:10.1371/journal.pone.0069637

Ferrier-Auerbach, A. G., & Martens, M. P. (2009). Perceived incompetence moderates the relationship between maladaptive perfectionism and disordered eating. *Eating Disorders, 17,* 333–344.

Ficks, C. A., & Waldman, I. D. (2009). Gene-environment interactions in attention-deficit/hyperactivity disorder. *Current Psychiatry Reports, 11,* 387–392.

Field, A. E., Sonneville, K. R., Crosby, R. D., Swanson, S. A., Eddy, K. T., Camargo, C. A., Jr., . . . Micali, N. (2014). Prospective associations of concerns about physique and the development of obesity, binge drinking, and drug use among adolescent boys and young adult men. *JAMA Pediatrics, 168,* 34–39.

Field, A. P., Ball, J. E., Kawycz, N. J., & Moore, H. (2007). Parent-child relationships and verbal information pathway to fear in children: Two preliminary experiments. *Behavioural and Cognitive Psychotherapy, 35,* 473–486.

Finkelhor, D., Ormrod, R., Turner, H., & Hamby, S. L. (2005). The victimization of children and youth: A comprehensive national survey. *Child Maltreatment, 10,* 5–25.

Finnane, M. (2012). "Irresistible impulse": Historicizing a judicial innovation in Australian insanity jurisprudence. *History of Psychiatry, 23,* 454–468.

Fischer, S., Stojek, M., & Hartzell, E. (2010). Effects of multiple forms of childhood abuse and adult sexual assault on current eating disorder symptoms. *Eating Behaviors, 11,* 190–192.

Fisher, H. L., Jones, P. B., Fearon, P., Craig, T. K., Dazzan, P., Morgan, K., . . . Morgan, C. (2010). The varying impact of type, timing and frequency of exposure to childhood adversity on its association with adult psychotic disorder. *Psychological Medicine, 40,* 1967–1978.

Fisher, M. A. (2009). Replacing "who is the client?" with a different ethical question. *Professional Psychology: Research and Practice, 40,* 1–7.

Fitch, W. L. (2007). AAPL practice guidelines for the forensic psychiatric evaluation of competence to stand trial: An American legal perspective. *Journal of American Psychiatric Law, 35,* 509–513.

Flegal, K. M., Carroll, M. D., Kit, B. K., & Ogden, C. L. (2012). Prevalence of obesity and trends in the distribution of body mass index among US adults, 1999–2010. *Journal of the American Medical Association, 307,* 491–497.

Flegal, K. M., Kit, B. K., Orpana, H., & Graubard, B. I. (2013). Association of all-cause mortality with overweight and obesity using standard body mass index categories: A systematic review and meta-analysis. *Journal of the American Medical Association, 309,* 71–82.

Flink, I. K., Nicholas, M. K., Boersma, K., & Linton, S. J. (2009). Reducing the threat value of chronic pain: A preliminary replicated single-case study of interoceptive exposure versus distraction in six individuals with chronic back pain. *Behaviour Research and Therapy, 47,* 721–728.

Flint, A. J., Gearhardt, A. N., Corbin, W. R., Brownell, K. D., Field, A. E., & Rimm, E. B. (2014, January 22). Food addiction scale measurement in 2 cohorts of middle-aged and older women. *American Journal of Clinical Nutrition, 99,* 578–586.

Flores, E., Tschann, J. M., Dimas, J. M., Pasch, L. A., & de Groat, C. L. (2010). Perceived racial/ethnic discrimination, posttraumatic stress symptoms, and health risk behaviors among Mexican American adolescents. *Journal of Counseling Psychology, 57,* 264–273.

Floyed, R. L., Hirsh, D. A., Greenbaum, V. J., & Simon, H. K. (2011). Development of a screening tool for pediatric sexual assault may reduce emergency-department visits. *Pediatrics, 128,* 221–226.

Foa, E., Gillihan, S., & Bryant, R. (2013). Challenges and successes in dissemination of evidence-based treatments for posttraumatic stress: Lessons learned from prolonged exposure therapy for PTSD. *Psychological Science in the Public Interest, 14,* 65–111.

Foa, E. B., & Kozak, M. J. (1995). DSM-IV field trial: Obsessive-compulsive disorder. *American Journal of Psychiatry, 152,* 90–96.

Foley, D. L., & Morley, K. I. (2011). Systematic review of early cardiometabolic outcomes of the first treated episode of psychosis. *Archives of General Psychiatry, 68,* 609–616. doi:10.1001/archgenpsychiatry.2011.2

Foote, B., Smolin, Y., Kaplan, M., Legatt, M. E., & Lipschitz, D. (2006). Prevalence of dissociative disorders in psychiatric outpatients. *American Journal of Psychiatry, 163,* 623–629.

Ford v. Wainwright, 477 U.S. 399 (1986).

Fornaro, M., & Giosue, P. (2010). Current nosology of treatment resistant depression: A controversy resistant to revision. *Clinical Practice and Epidemiology in Mental Health, 6,* 20–24.

Forno, E., & Celedón, J. C. (2009). Asthma and minorities: Socioeconomic status and beyond. *Current Opinion in Allergy and Clinical Immunology, 9,* 154–160.

Foroud, T., Edenberg, H. J., & Crabbe, J. C. (2010). Genetic research: Who is at risk for alcoholism? Retrieved from http://pubs.niaaa.nih.gov/publications/arh40/64-75.htm

Forsyth, J. K., Ellman, L. M., Tanskanen, A., Mustonen, U., Huttunen, M. O., Suvisaari, J., & Cannon, T. D. (2013). Genetic risk for schizophrenia, obstetric complications, and adolescent school outcome: Evidence for gene-environment interaction. *Schizophrenia Bulletin, 39,* 1067–1076.

Fortier, C. B., Leritz, E. C., Salat, D. H., Venne, J. R., Maksimovskiy, A. L., Williams, V., . . . McGlinchey, R. E. (2011). Reduced cortical thickness in abstinent alcoholics and association with alcoholic behavior alcoholism. *Clinical and Experimental Research, 35*, 2193–2201.

Foster, J. A., & MacQueen, G. (2008). Neurobiological factors linking personality traits and major depression. *La Revue Canadienne de Psychiatrie, 53*, 6–13.

Foti, D. J., Kotov, R., Guey, L. T., & Bromet, E. J. (2010). Cannabis use and the course of schizophrenia: 10 year follow-up after first hospitalization. *American Journal of Psychiatry, 167*, 987–993.

Fottrell, E., Tollman, S., Byass, P., Golooba-Mutebi, F., & Kahn, K. (2012). The epidemiology of "bewitchment" as a lay-reported cause of death in rural South Africa. *Journal of Epidemiology and Community Health, 66*, 704–709.

Fountoulakis, K. N., Kontis, D., Gonda, X., & Yatham, L. N. (2013). A systematic review of the evidence on the treatment of rapid cycling bipolar disorder. *Bipolar Disorder, 15*, 115–137.

Fournier, J. C., DeRubeis, R. J., Hollon, S. D., Dimidjian, S., Amsterdam, J. D., & Fawcett, J. (2010). Antidepressant drug effects and depression severity: A patient-level meta-analysis. *Journal of the American Medical Association, 303*, 47–53.

Fournier, A. K., Hall, E., Ricke, P., & Storey, B. (2013). Alcohol and the social network: The effect of online social networking sites on perceived college drinking norms. *Psychology of Popular Media Culture, 2*(2), 86–95.

Fox, C. L., Towe, S. L., Stephens, R. S., Walker, D. D., & Roffman, R. A. (2011). Motives for cannabis use in high-risk adolescent users. *Psychology of Addictive Behaviors, 25*, 492–500.

Fox, E., Krawczyk, K., Staniford, J., & Dickens, G. L. (2014, February). A service evaluation of a 1-year dialectical behaviour therapy programme for women with borderline personality disorder in a low secure unit. *Behavioural and Cognitive Psychotherapy, 13*, 1–16. [Epub ahead of print]

Fox, N. A., Henderson, H. A., Marshall, P. J., Nichols, K. E., & Ghera, M. M. (2005). Behavioral inhibition: Linking biology and behavior within a developmental framework. *Annual Review of Psychology, 56*, 235–262.

Frances, A. (2009). A warning sign to the road to DSM-V: Beware of its unintended consequences. *Psychiatric Times, 26*, 1–4.

Frances, A. (2013). The new crisis in confidence in psychiatric diagnosis. *Annals of Internal Medicine, 159*, 221–222.

Francis, A. (2014). Teen trying experimental treatment for narcolepsy. Retrieved from http://news.ninemsn.com.au/world/2014/01/07/14/17/teen-trying-experimental-treatment-for-narcolepsy

Franko, D. L., Keshaviah, A., Eddy, K. T., Krishna, M., Davis, M. C., Keel, P. K., & Herzog, D. B. (2013). A longitudinal investigation of mortality in anorexia nervosa and bulimia nervosa. American Journal of Psychiatry, 170, 917–925.

Frank, D. L., Khorshid, L., Kiffer, J. F., Moravec, C. S., & McKee, M. G. (2010). Biofeedback in medicine: Who, when, why and how? *Mental Health in Family Medicine, 7*, 85–91.

Frankenburg, F. R. (2010). Schizophrenia. Retrieved from http://emedicine.medscape.com/article/288259-overview

Franklin, J. C., Heilbron, N., Guerry, J. D., Bowker, K. B., & Blumenthal, T. D. (2009). Antisocial and borderline personality disorder symptomalogies are associated with decreased prepulse inhibition: The importance of optimal experimental parameters. *Personality and Individual Differences, 47*, 439–443.

Franklin, T., Wang, Z., Suh, J. J., Hazan, R., Cruz, J., Li, Y., . . . Childress, A. R. (2011). Effects of varenicline on smoking cue–triggered neural and craving responses. *Archives of General Psychiatry, 68*(5), 516–526. doi:10.1001/archgenpsychiatry.2010.190

Franklin, T. B., Russig, H., Weiss, I. C., Graff, J., Linder, N., Michalon, A., . . . Mansuy, I. M. (2010). Epigenetic transmission of the impact of early stress across generations. *Biological Psychiatry, 68*, 408–415.

Franko, D. L., Keshaviah, A., Eddy, K. T., Krishna, M., Davis, M. C., Keel, P. K., & Herzog, D. B. (2013). A longitudinal investigation of mortality in anorexia nervosa and bulimia nervosa. *American Journal of Psychiatry, 170*, 917–925.

Franko, D. L., Thompson-Brenner, H., Thompson, D. R., Boisseau, C. L., Davis, A., Forbush, K. T., . . . Wilson, G. T. (2012). Racial/ethnic differences in adults in randomized clinical trials of binge eating disorder. *Journal of Consulting and Clinical Psychology, 80*, 186–195.

Frazel, S., & Grann, M. (2006). The population impact of severe mental illness on violent crime. *American Journal of Psychiatry, 163*, 1397–1403.

Frazier, P., Anders, S., Perera, S., Tomich, P., Tennen, H., Park, C., & Tashiro, T. (2009). Traumatic events among undergraduate students: Prevalence and associated symptoms. *Journal of Counseling Psychology, 56*, 450–460.

Frederick, C. B., Snellman, K., & Putnam, R. D. (2014). Increasing socioeconomic disparities in adolescent obesity. *Proceedings of the National Academy of Sciences, 111*, 1338–1342.

Fredrickson, B. L. (2013). Learning to self-generate positive emotions. In D. Hermans, B. Rimé, & B. Mesquita (Eds.), *Changing emotions*. London, UK: Psychology Press.

Freed, G. L., Clark, S. J., Butchart, A. T., Singer, D. C., & Davis, M. M. (2010). Parental vaccine safety concerns in 2009. *Pediatrics, 125*, 654–659.

Freedman, R., Lewis, D. A., Michels, R., Pine, D. S., Schultz, S. K., Tamminga, C. A., . . . Yager, J. (2013). The initial field trials of DSM-5: New blooms and old thorns. *American Journal of Psychiatry, 170*, 1–5.

Freeman, D., McManus, S., Brugha, T., Meltzer, H., Jenkins, R., & Bebbington, P. (2010). Concomitants of paranoia in the general population. *Psychological Medicine, 41*(5), 923–936.

Freis, S. D., & Gurung, R. A. R. (2013). A Facebook analysis of helping behavior in online bullying. *Psychology of Popular Media Culture, 2*, 11–19.

Frese, F. J., III, Knight, E. L., & Saks, E. (2009). Recovery from schizophrenia: With views of psychiatrists, psychologists, and others diagnosed with this disorder. *Schizophrenia Bulletin, 35*, 370–380.

Frese, F. J., III, & Myrick, K. J. (2010). On consumer advocacy and the diagnosis of mental disorders. *Professional Psychology: Research and Practice, 41*, 495–501.

Freud, S. (1938). The psychopathology of everyday life. In A. B. Brill (Ed.), *The basic writings of Sigmund Freud*. New York, NY: Modern Library.

Freud, S. (1949). *An outline of psychoanalysis*. New York, NY: Norton.

Freudenmann, R. W., & Lepping, P. (2009). Delusional infestation. *Clinical Microbiology Reviews, 22*, 690–732.

Freudenreich, O., Kontos, N., Tranulis, C., & Cather, C. (2010). Morgellons disease, or antipsychotic-responsive delusional parasitosis, in an HIV patient: Beliefs in the age of the Internet. *Psychosomatics, 51*, 453–459.

Frewen, P. A., Evans, E. M., Maraj, N., Dozois, D. J. A., & Partridge, K. (2008). Letting go: Mindfulness and negative automatic thinking. *Cognitive Therapy Research, 32,* 758–774.

Freyer, T., Kloppel, S., Tuscher, O., Kordon, A., Zurowski, B., Kuelz, A. K., . . . Voderholzer, U. (2011). Frontostriatal activation in patients with obsessive-compulsive disorder before and after cognitive behavior therapy. *Psychological Medicine, 41,* 211–216.

Friedman, J. H., & LaFrance, W. C., Jr. (2010). Psychogenic disorders: The need to speak plainly. *Archives of Neurology, 67,* 753–755.

Friedman, M. J. (2013). Toward rational pharmacotherapy for posttraumatic stress disorder: Reprise. *American Journal of Psychiatry, 170,* 944–946.

Friedman, R. A. (2004, October 18). A patient's suicide, a psychiatrist's pain. *New York Times,* p. F6.

Friedman, R. A. (2012, September 25). A call for caution on antipsychotic drugs. *New York Times.* Retrieved from http://www.nytimes.com/2012/09/25/health/a-call-for-caution-in-the-use-of-antipsychotic-drugs.html?_r50

Friedman, R. A., & Michels, R. (2013). How should the psychiatric profession respond to the recent mass killings? *American Journal of Psychiatry, 170,* 455–458.

Friedman, S. (2007). *Just for boys.* Vancouver, BC: Salah Books.

Friedrich, W. N., Fisher, J., Broughton, D., Houston, M., & Shafran, C. (1998). Normative sexual behavior in children: A contemporary sample. *Pediatrics, 101,* 1–8.

Frodl, T., Reinhold, E., Koutsouleris, N., Donohoe, G., Bondy, B., Reiser, M., . . . Meisenzahl, E. M. (2010). Childhood stress, serotonin transporter gene and brain structures in major depression. *Neuropsychopharmacology, 35,* 1383–1390.

Froehlich, T. E., Lanphear, B. P., Epstein, J. N., Barbaresi, W. J., Katusic, S. K., & Kahn, R. S. (2007). Prevalence and treatment of ADHD in a national sample of U.S. children. *Archives of Pediatrics & Adolescent Medicine, 161,* 857–864.

Frohm, K. D., & Beehler, G. P. (2010). Psychologists as change agents in chronic pain management practice: Cultural competence in the health care system. *Psychological Services, 7,* 115–125.

Frojd, S., Ranta, K., Kaltiala-Heino, R., & Marttunen, M. (2011). Associations of social phobia and general anxiety with alcohol and drug use in a community sample of adolescents. *Alcohol and Alcoholism, 46*(2), 192–199. doi:10.1093/alcalc/agq096

Frühauf, S., Gerger, H., Schmidt, H. M., Munder, T., & Barth, J. (2013). Efficacy of psychological interventions for sexual dysfunction: A systematic review and meta-analysis. *Archives of Sexual Behavior, 42,* 915–933.

Fry, J. P., & Neff, R. A. (2010). Periodic prompts and reminders in health promotion and health behavior interventions: Systematic review. *Journal of Medical Internet Research, 11,* e16.

Fryar, C. D., Gu, Q., & Ogden, C. L. (2012). Anthropometric reference data for children and adults: United States, 2007–2010. National Center for Health Statistics. *Vital Health Statistics, 11*(252).

Frye, L. A., & Spates, C. R. (2012). Prolonged exposure, mindfulness, and emotion regulation for the treatment of PTSD. *Clinical Case Studies, 11,* 184–200.

Fukumoto, A., Hashimoto, T., Mori, K., Tsuda, Y., Arisawa, K., & Kagami, S. (2010). Head circumference and body growth in autism spectrum disorders. *Brain Development.* Retrieved from http://www.ncbi.nlm.nih.gov/pubmed/20934821

Fullana, M. A., Mataix-Cols, D., Caspi, A., Harrington, H., Grisham, J. R., Moffitt, T. E., Poulton, R. (2009). Obsessions and compulsions in the community: Prevalence, interference, help-seeking, developmental stability, and co-occurring psychiatric conditions. *American Journal of Psychiatry, 166,* 329–336.

Fuller-Thompson, E. (2012). Evidence supporting an independent association between childhood physical abuse and lifetime suicidal ideation. *Suicide and Life-Threatening Behavior,* 279–291.

Fulton, J. J., Marcus, D. K., & Merkey, T. (2011). Irrational health beliefs and health anxiety. *Journal of Clinical Psychology, 67,* 527–538.

Furer, P., & Walker, J. R. (2005). Treatment of hypochondriasis with exposure. *Journal of Contemporary Psychotherapy, 35,* 251–267.

Furlong, M., McGilloway, S., Bywater, T., Hutchings, J., Smith, S. M., & Donnelly, M. (2013). Cochrane review: Behavioural and cognitive-behavioural group-based parenting programmes for early-onset conduct problems in children aged 3 to 12 years. *Evidence-Based Child Health, 8,* 318–692.

Furness, P., Glazebrook, C., Tay, J., Abbas, K., & Slaveska-Hollis, K. (2009). Medically unexplained physical symptoms in children: Exploring hospital staff perceptions. *Child Clinical Psychology and Psychiatry, 14,* 575–587.

Gage, F. H., & Temple, S. (2013). Neural stem cells: Generating and regenerating the brain. *Neuron, 80,* 588–601.

Gagne, D. A., Von Holle, A., Brownley, K. A., Runfola, C. D., Hofmeier, S., Branch, K. E., & Bulik, C. M. (2012). Eating disorder symptoms and weight and shape concerns in a large web-based convenience sample of women ages 50 and above: results of the Gender and Body Image (GABI) study. *International Journal of Eating Disorders, 45,* 832–844.

Galea, S., Ahern, J., Resnick, H., Kilpatrick, D., Bucuvalas, M., Gold, J., & Vlahov, D. (2002). Psychological sequelae of the September 11 terrorist attacks in New York City. *New England Journal of Medicine, 346,* 982–987.

Galimberti, D., & Scarpini, E. (2012). Progress in Alzheimer's disease. *Journal of Neurology, 259,* 201–211.

Gallagher, M. G., Naragon-Gainey, K., & Brown, T. A. (2014). Perceived control is a transdiagnostic predictor of cognitive-behavior therapy outcome for anxiety disorders. *Cognitive Therapy and Research, 38,* 10–22.

Gallagher, M. W., Payne, L. A., White, K. S., Shear, K. M., Woods, S. W., Gorman, J. M., & Barlow, D. H. (2013). Mechanisms of change in cognitive behavioral therapy for panic disorder: The unique effects of self-efficacy and anxiety sensitivity. *Behaviour Research and Therapy, 51,* 767–777.

Gallichan, D. J., & Curle, C. (2008). Fitting square pegs into round holes: The challenge of coping with attention-deficit hyperactivity disorder. *Clinical Child Psychology and Psychiatry, 13,* 343–363.

Gallup. (2013). Religion. Retrieved from http://www.gallup.com/poll/159785/rise-religious-nones-slows-2012.aspx

Galvez, J. F., Thommi, S., & Ghaemi, S. (2011). Positive aspects of mental illness: A review in bipolar disorder. *Journal of Affective Disorders, 128,* 185–190.

Gao, Y., Raine, A., Venables, P. H., Dawson, M. E., & Mednick, S. A.

(2010). Association of poor childhood fear conditioning and adult crime. *American Journal of Psychiatry, 167,* 56–60.

Gara, M. A., Vega, W. A., Arndt, S., Escamilla, M., Fleck, D. E., Lawson, W. B., . . . Strakowski, S. M. (2012). Influence of patient race and ethnicity on clinical assessment in patients with affective disorders. *Archives of General Psychiatry, 69,* 593–600.

Garber, J., & Cole, D. A. (2010). Intergenerational transmission of depression: A launch and grow model of change across adolescence. *Developmental Psychopathology, 22,* 819–830.

Garcia-Toro, M., Rubio, J. M., Gili, M., Roca, M., Jin, C. J., Liu, S. M., . . . Blanco, C. (2013). Persistence of chronic major depression: A national prospective study. *Journal of Affective Disorders, 151,* 306–312.

Gardner, A. (2011, March 1). Is Charlie Sheen bipolar? *Health.* Retrieved from http://www.health.com

Garety, P. A., Bebbington, P., Fowler, D., Freeman, D., & Kuipers, E. (2007). Implications for neurobiological research of cognitive models of psychosis: A theoretical paper. *Psychological Medicine, 37,* 1377–1391.

Garrett, M., & Silva, R. (2003). Auditory hallucinations, source monitoring, and the belief that "voices" are real. *Schizophrenia Bulletin, 29,* 445–451.

Gasecki, D., Kwarciany, M., Nyka, W., & Narkiewicz, K. (2013). Hypertension, brain damage and cognitive decline. *Current Hypertension Reports, 15,* 547–558.

Gates, G. J. (2011). How many people are lesbian, gay, bisexual, and transgender? Retrieved from http://williamsinstitute. law.ucla.edu/wp-content/uploads/ Gates-How-Many-People-LGBT-Apr-2011.pdf

Gawrysiak, M., Nicholas, C., & Hopko, D. R. (2009). Behavioral activation for moderately depressed university students: Randomized controlled trial. *Journal of Counseling Psychology, 56,* 468–475.

Gayle, D. (2013). Transsexual, 44, elects to die by euthanasia after botched sex-change operation turned him into a "monster." Retrieved from http:// www.dailymail.co.uk/news/article-2440086/Belgian-transsexual-Nathan-Verhelst-44-elects-die-eutha nasia-botched-sex-change-operation. html#ixzz2jVDTgguM

Gaynor, K., Ward, T., Garety, P., & Peters, E. (2013). The role of safety-seeking behaviours in maintaining threat appraisals in psychosis. *Behaviour Research & Therapy, 51,* 75–81.

Geddes, J. R., & Miklowitz, D. J. (2013). Treatment of bipolar disorder. *Lancet, 381,* 1672–1682.

Gelauff, J., Stone, J., Edwards, M., & Carson, A. (2014). The prognosis of functional (psychogenic) motor symptoms: A systematic review. *Journal of Neurology, Neurosurgery, and Psychiatry, 85,* 220-226

Geller, J. L. (2006). A history of private psychiatric hospitals in the USA: From start to finish. *Psychiatric Quarterly, 77,* 1–41.

Gentile, J. P., Dillon, K. S., & Gillig, P. M. (2013). Psychotherapy and pharmacotherapy for patients with dissociative identity disorder. *Innovations in Clinical Neuroscience, 10,* 22–29.

George, M. S., Taylor, J. J., & Short, B. (2013). Treating the depressions with superficial brain stimulation methods. *Handbook of Clinical Neurology, 116,* 399–413.

Gerrard, M., Stock, M. L., Roberts, M. E., Gibbons, F. X., O'Hara, R. E., Weng, C. Y., & Wills, T. A. (2012). Coping with racial discrimination: The role of substance use. *Psychology of Addictive Behavior, 26,* 550–560.

Gerson, R., & Rappaport, N. (2013). Traumatic stress and posttraumatic stress disorder in youth: Recent research findings on clinical impact, assessment, and treatment. *Journal of Adolescent Health, 52,* 137–143.

Geschwind, N., Peeters, F., Van Os, J., Drukker, M., & Wichers, M. (2011). Mindfulness training increases momentary positive emotions and reward experience in adults vulnerable to depression. A randomized controlled trial. *Journal of Consulting and Clinical Practice, 79,* 618–628.

Getahun, D., Jacobsen, S. J., Fassett, M. J., Chen, W., Demissie, K., & Rhoads, G. G. (2013). Recent trends in childhood attention-deficit/hyperactivity disorder. *JAMA Pediatrics, 167,* 282–288.

Ghaemi, S. N. (2010a). Levels of evidence. *Psychiatric Times, 27,* 1–4.

Ghaemi, S. N. (2010b). *The rise and fall of the biopsychosocial model: Reconciling art and science in psychiatry.* Baltimore, MD: Johns Hopkins University Press.

Gharaibeh, N. (2009). Dissociative identity disorder: Time to remove it from DSM-V? *Current Psychiatry, 8,* 30–37.

Ghaziuddin, M. (2010). Should the DSM-V drop Asperger syndrome? *Journal of Autism and Developmental Disorders, 40,* 1146–1148.

Ghaznavi, S., & Deckersbach, T. (2012). Rumination in bipolar disorder: Evidence for an unquiet mind. *Biology of Mood & Anxiety Disorders, 2,* 2.

Ghezzi, L., Scarpini, E., & Galimberti, D. (2013). Disease-modifying drugs in Alzheimer's disease. *Drug Design, Development and Therapy, 7,* 1471–1478.

Ghisi, M., Chiri, L. R., Marchetti, I., Sanavio, E., & Sica, C. (2010). In search of specificity: "Not just right experiences" and obsessive-compulsive symptoms in non-clinical and clinical Italian individuals. *Journal of Anxiety Disorders, 24,* 879–886.

Ghosh, S., & Pataki, C. (2012). Gender identity. Retrieved from http://emedi cine.medscape.com/article/917990-overview#aw2aab6b3

Gibbons, R. D., Brown, C. H., Hur, K., Davis, J., & Mann, J. J. (2012). Suicidal thoughts and behavior with antidepressant treatment: Reanalysis of the randomized placebo-controlled studies of fluoxetine and venlafaxine. *Archives of General Psychiatry, 69,* 580–587.

Giesbrecht, T., Lynn, S. J., Lilienfeld, S. O., & Merckelbach, H. (2008). Cognitive processes in dissociation: An analysis of core theoretical assumptions. *Psychological Bulletin, 134,* 617–647.

Gigante, A.D., Bond, D.J., Lafer, B., Lam, R.W., Young, L.T., Yatham, L.N., (2012). Brain glutamate levels measured by magnetic resonance spectroscopy in patients with bipolar disorder: a meta-analysis. Bipolar Disorder, 14, 478–487.

Gijs, L. (2008). Paraphilia and paraphilia-related disorders: An introduction. In D. Rowland & L. Incrocci (Eds.), *Handbook of sexual and gender identity disorders* (pp. 491–528). Hoboken, NJ: Wiley.

Gilbert, B. D., & Christopher, M. S. (2010). Mindfulness-based attention as a moderator of the relationship between depressive affect and negative cognitions. *Cognitive Therapy and Research, 34,* 514–521.

Gilbert, S. C. (2003). Eating disorders in women of color. *Clinical Psychology: Science and Practice, 10,* 1–16.

Gillham, J. E., Chaplin, T. M., Reivich, K. J., & Hamilton, J. (2008). Preventing depression in early adolescent girls: The Penn Resiliency and Girls in Transition Programs. In C. LeCroy & J. Mann

(Eds.), *Handbook of prevention and intervention programs for adolescent girls* (pp. 123–161). Hoboken, NJ: Wiley.

Gillig, P. M. (2013). Psychogenic nonepileptic seizures. *Innovations in Clinical Neuroscience, 10*, 15–18.

Ginsburg, G. S., Becker, E. M., Keeton, C. P., Sakolsky, D., Piacentini, J., Albano, A. M., . . . Kendall, P. C. (2014). Naturalistic follow-up of youths treated for pediatric anxiety disorders. *JAMA Psychiatry, 71*, 310–318.

Ginzburg, K., & Solomon, Z. (2010). Trajectories of stress reactions and somatization symptoms among war veterans: A 20-year longitudinal study. *Psychological Medicine, 41*, 353–362.

Giulivi, C., Zhang, Y., Omanska-Klusek, A., Ross-Inta, C., Wong, S., Hertz-Picciotto, I., . . . Pessah, I. N. (2010). Mitochondrial dysfunction in autism. *Journal of the American Medical Association, 304*, 2389–2396.

Glantz, S. A., Iaccopucci, A., Titus, K., & Polansky, J. R. (2012). Smoking in top-grossing US movies. *Prevention of Chronic Diseases, 9*, 120170. doi: http://dx.doi.org/10.5888/pcd9.120170

Glasner-Edwards, S., Mooney, L. J., Marinelli-Casey, P., Hillhouse, M., Ang, A., & Rawson, R. A. (2010). Psychopathology in methamphetamine-dependent adults 3 years after treatment. *Drug and Alcohol Review, 29*, 12–20.

Gleason, M. M., Fox, N. A., Drury, S., Smyke, A., Egger, H. L., Nelson, C. A., . . . Zeanah, C. H. (2011). Validity of evidence-derived criteria for reactive attachment disorder: Indiscriminately social/disinhibited and emotionally withdrawn/inhibited types. *Journal of the American Academy of Child & Adolescent Psychiatry, 50*, 216–231.

Glenn, A. L., Raine, A., Venables, P. H., & Mednick, S. A. (2009). Early temperamental and psychophysiological precursors of adult psychopathic personality. *Personality Disorders: Theory, Research, and Treatment, S*, 46–60.

Glicksman, E. (2013). Transgender today. *APA Monitor, 44*, 36–39.

Glina, S., Sharlip, I. D., & Hellstrom, W. J. (2013). Modifying risk factors to prevent and treat erectile dysfunction. *Journal of Sexual Medicine, 10*, 115–119.

Global Initiative for Asthma. (2010). Global strategy for asthma management and prevention. Retrieved from http://www.ginasthma.org

Glozier, N., Martiniuk, A., Patton, G., Ivers, R., Li, Q., Hickie, I., . . . Stevenson, M. (2010). Short sleep duration in prevalent and persistent psychological distress in young adults: The DRIVE study. *Sleep, 33*, 1139–1145.

Glynn, S. M., Cohen, A. N., Dixon, L. B., & Niv, N. (2006). The potential impact of the recovery movement on family interventions for schizophrenia: Opportunities and obstacles. *Schizophrenia Bulletin, 32*, 451–463.

Go, A. S., Mozaffarian, D., Roger, V. L., Benjamin, E. J., Berry, J. D., Borden, W. B., . . . Turner, M. B. (2013). Heart disease and stroke statistics—2013 update: A report from the American Heart Association. *Circulation, 127*, 143–152.

Go, A. S., Mozaffarian, D., Roger, V. L., Benjamin, E. J., Berry, J. D., Blaha, M. J., . . ., American Heart Association Statistics Committee and Stroke Statistics Subcommittee. (2014). Heart disease and stroke statistics—2014 update: A report from the American Heart Association. *Circulation, 129*, e28–e292.

Godfrin, K. A., & van Heeringen, C. (2010). The effects of mindfulness-based cognitive therapy on recurrence of depressive episodes, mental health and quality of life: A randomized controlled study. *Behaviour Research and Therapy, 48*, 738–746.

Godlee, F., Smith, J., & Marcovitch, H. (2011). Wakefield's article linking MMR vaccine and autism was fraudulent. *British Medical Journal, 342*, c7452. doi:10.1136/bmj.c7452

Godoy, A., & Haynes, S. N. (2011). Clinical case formulation. *European Journal of Psychological Assessment, 27*, 1–3.

Goff, D. C. (1993). Reply to Dr. Armstrong. *Journal of Nervous and Mental Disease, 181*, 604–605.

Goff, D. C., & Simms, C. A. (1993). Has multiple personality disorder remained consistent over time? *Journal of Nervous and Mental Disease, 181*, 595–600.

Gogtag, N. (2008). Cortical brain development in schizophrenia: Insights from neuroimaging studies in childhood-onset schizophrenia. *Schizophrenia Bulletin, 34*, 30–36.

Gold, M. S., Blum, K., Oscar-Berman, M., & Braverman, E. R. (2014). Low dopamine function in attention deficit/hyperactivity disorder: Should genotyping signify early diagnosis in children? *Postgraduate Medicine, 126*, 153–177.

Goldapple, K., Segal, Z., Garson, C., Lau, M., Bieling, P., Kennedy, S., & Mayberg, H. (2004). Modulation of cortical-limbic pathways in major depression: Treatment-specific effects of cognitive behavior therapy. *Archives of General Psychiatry, 61*, 34–41.

Goldberg, C. (2009). The mental status exam (MSE). Retrieved from http://meded.ucsd.edu/clinicalmed/mental.htm

Goldberg, D. (2006). The aetiology of depression. *Psychological Medicine, 36*, 1341–1347.

Goldberg, D. P., Krueger, R. F., Andrews, G., & Hobbs, M. J. (2009). Emotional disorders: Cluster 4 of the proposed meta-structure for DSM-V and ICD-11. *Psychological Medicine, 39*, 2043–2059.

Golden, R. N., Gaynes, B. N., Ekstrom, R. D., Hamer, R. M., Jacobsen, F. M., Suppes, T., . . . Nemeroff, C. B. (2005). The efficacy of light therapy in the treatment of mood disorders: A review and meta-analysis of the evidence. *American Journal of Psychiatry, 162*, 656–662.

Goldfein, J. A., Devlin, M. J., & Spitzer, R. L. (2000). Cognitive behavioral therapy for the treatment of binge eating disorder: What constitutes success? *American Journal of Psychiatry, 157*, 1051–1056.

Goldin, P. R., Ziv, M., Jazaieri, H., Werner, K., Kraemer, H., Heimberg, R. G., & Gross, J. J. (2012). Cognitive reappraisal self-efficacy mediates the effects of individual cognitive-behavioral therapy for social anxiety disorder. *Journal of Consulting and Clinical Psychology, 80*, 1034–1040.

Goldman, S. M., Quinlan, P. J., Ross, G. W., Marras, C., Meng, C., Bhudhikanok, G. S., . . . Tanner, C. M. (2012). Solvent exposures and Parkinson disease risk in twins. *Annals of Neurology, 71*, 776–784.

Goldstein, B. I. (2012). Recent progress in understanding pediatric bipolar disorder. *Archives of Pediatrics & Adolescent Medicine, 166*, 362–371.

Goldstein, G., & Beers, S. (2004). *Comprehensive handbook of psychological assessment, intellectual and neuropsychological assessment* (Vol. 1). New York, NY: John Wiley.

Goldston, D. B., Molock, S. D., Whitbeck, L. B., Murakami, J. L., Zayas, L. H., & Hall, G. C. N. (2008). Cultural considerations in adolescent suicide prevention and psychosocial treatment. *American Psychologist, 63*, 14–31.

Gonsiorek, J. C., Richards, P. S., Pargament, K. I., & McMinn, M. R. (2009). Ethical challenges and opportunities at the edge: Incorporating spirituality and religion into psychotherapy. *Professional Psychology: Research and Practice, 40,* 385–395.

Goodman, M., Triebwasser, J., Shah, S., & New, A. S. (2007). Neuroimaging in personality disorders: Current concepts, findings, and implications. *Psychiatric Annals, 37,* 100–104, 107–108.

Goodwin, B. E., Sellbom, M., & Arbisi, P. A. (2013). Posttraumatic stress disorder in veterans: The utility of the MMPI–2–RF validity scales in detecting overreported symptoms. *Personality Assessment, 25,* 671–678.

Goodwin, R. D., Bandiera, F. C., Steinberg, D., Ortega, A. N., & Feldman, J. M. (2012). Asthma and mental health among youth: Etiology, current knowledge, and future directions. *Expert Review of Respiratory Medicine, 6,* 1–10.

Gooley, J. J., Rajaratnam, S. M., Brainard, G. C., Kronauer, R. E., Czeisler, C. A., & Lockley, S. W. (2010). Spectral responses of the human circadian system depend on the irradiance and duration of exposure to light. *Science Translational Medicine, 2,* 31–33.

Gooren, L. (2008). Androgens and endocrine function in aging men: Effects on sexual and general health. In D. Rowland & L. Incrocci (Eds.), *Handbook of sexual and gender identity disorders* (pp. 122–153). Hoboken, NJ: Wiley.

Gordon, I., Vander Wyk, B. C., Bennett, R. H., Cordeaux, C., Lucas, M. V., Eilbott, J. A., . . . Pelphrey, K. A. (2014). Oxytocin enhances brain function in children with autism. *Proceedings of the National Academy of Sciences U S A, 110,* 20953–20958.

Gotlib, I. H., & Joormann, J. (2010). Cognition and depression: Current status and future directions. *Annual Review of Clinical Psychology, 6,* 285–312.

Gottesman, I. I. (1978). Schizophrenia and genetics: Where are we? Are you sure? In L. C. Wynne, R. L. Cromwell, & S. Matthysse (Eds.), *The nature of schizophrenia: New approaches to research and treatment* (pp. 59–69). New York, NY: Wiley.

Gottesman, I. I. (1991). *Schizophrenia genesis.* New York, NY: Freeman.

Gottesman, I. I., & Gould, T. D. (2003). The endophenotype concept in psychiatry: Etymology and strategic intentions. *American Journal of Psychiatry, 160,* 636–645.

Gould, M. S. (2007). Suicide contagion (clusters). Retrieved from http://suicide-andmentalhealthassociationinternational.org/suiconclus.html

Gould, M. S., Kalafat, J., Harrismunfakh, J. L., & Kleinman, M. (2007). An evaluation of crisis hotline outcomes. Part 2: Suicidal callers. *Suicide and Life-Threatening Behavior, 37,* 338–352.

Gowensmith, W. N., Murrie, D. C., & Boccaccini, M. T. (2013). How reliable are forensic evaluations of legal sanity? *Law and Human Behavior, 37,* 98–106.

Goyal, D., Gay, C., & Lee, K. (2009). Fragmented maternal sleep is more strongly correlated with depressive symptoms than infant temperament at three months postpartum. *Archives of Women's Mental Health, 12,* 229–237.

Goyette, B. (2012) Foxconn workers talked out of suicide protest at factory in China. Retrieved from: http://www.nydailynews.com/news/world/mayor-talks-foxconn-electronics-workers-suicide-protest-factory-china-article-1.1004584

Grabe, H. J., Schwahn, C., Appel, K., Mahler, J., Schulz, A., Spitzer, C., . . . Volzke, H. (2010). Childhood maltreatment, the corticotropin-releasing hormone receptor gene and adult depression in the general population. *American Journal of Medical Genetics Part B: Neuropsychiatric Genetics, 153B,* 1483–1493.

Grabe, S., & Hyde, J. S. (2006). Ethnicity and body dissatisfaction among women in the United States: A meta-analysis. *Psychological Bulletin, 132,* 622–640.

Grabe, S., Ward, L. M., & Hyde, J. S. (2008). The role of the media in body image concerns among women: A meta-analysis of experimental and correlational studies. *Psychological Bulletin, 134,* 460–476.

Grados, M. A., Specht, M. W., Sung, H. M., & Fortune, D. (2013). Glutamate drugs and pharmacogenetics of OCD: A pathway-based exploratory approach. *Expert Opinion on Drug Discovery, 8,* 1515–1527.

Graf, W. D., Nagel, S. K., Epstein, L. G., Miller, G., Nass, R., & Larriviere, D. (2013). Pediatric neuroenhancement: Ethical, legal, social, and neurodevelopmental implications. *Neurology, 80,* 1251–1260.

Graham, C. A., Sanders, S. A., Milhausen, R. R., & McBride, K. R. (2004). Turning on and turning off: A focus group study of the factors that affect women's sexual arousal. *Archives of Sexual Behavior, 33,* 527–538.

Graham, J. R. (2005). *MMPI-2: Assessing personality and psychopathology* (4th ed.). New York, NY: Oxford University Press.

Graham, R. (2012). Mass hysteria in upstate New York. Retrieved from http://www.slate.com/articles/double_x/doublex/2012/01/mass_hysteria_in_up state_new_york_why_lori_brownell_and_13_other_teenage_girls_are_show ing_tourette_s_like_sy mptoms_.html

Granderson, L. Z. (2010, December 3). Sports, gender, questions and hate. Retrieved from http://sports.espn .go.com/espn/commentary/news/story?id55879536

Granello, D. H. (2010). The process of suicide risk assessment: Twelve core principles. *Journal of Counseling and Development, 88,* 363–370.

Granello, D. H., & Granello, P. F. (2007). *Suicide: An essential guide for helping professionals and educators.* Boston, MA: Allyn & Bacon.

Grann, M., & Langstrom, N. (2007). Actuarial risk assessment: To weigh or not to weigh? *Criminal Justice and Behavior, 34,* 22–36.

Grant, I., & Adams, K. M. (2009). *Neuropsychological assessment of neuropsychiatric and neuromedical disorders* (3rd ed.). New York, NY: Oxford University Press.

Grant, V. V., Stewart, S. H., O'Connor, R. M., Blackwell, E., & Conrod, P. J. (2007). Psychometric evaluation of the five-factor modified drinking motives questionnaire—revised in undergraduates. *Addictive Behaviors, 32*(11), 2611–2632.

Gray, B. (2008). Hidden demons: A personal account of hearing voices and the alternative of the hearing voices movement. *Schizophrenia Bulletin, 34,* 1006–1007.

Graziottin, A., & Serafini, A. (2009). Depression and the menopause: Why antidepressants are not enough? *Menopause International, 15,* 76–81.

Green, M. F. (2007). Cognition, drug treatment, and functional outcome in schizophrenia: A tale of two transitions. *American Journal of Psychiatry, 164,* 992–994.

Green, S., Lambon Ralph, M. A., Moll, J., Deakin, J. F., & Zahn, R. (2012). Guilt-selective functional disconnection of anterior temporal and subgenual cortices in major depressive disorder. *Archives of General Psychiatry, 69,* 1014–1021.

Green, S., Moll, J., Deakin, J. F., Hulleman, J., & Zahn, R. (2013). Proneness to decreased negative emotions in major depressive disorder when blaming others rather than oneself. *Psychopathology, 46,* 34–44.

Greenberg, W. M. (2010). Obsessive-compulsive disorder. Retrieved from http://emedicine.medscape.com/article/287681-print

Greenberger, E., Chen, C., Tally, S. R., & Dong, Q. (2000). Family, peer, and individual correlates of depressive symptomatology among U.S. and Chinese adolescents. *Journal of Consulting and Clinical Psychology, 68,* 209–219.

Greenfield, B. (2013). Too-skinny model ban takes effect in Israel. Retrieved from http://shine.yahoo.com/fashion/too-skinny-model-ban-takes-effect-israel-213500942.html

Greer, T. L., & Trivedi, M. H. (2009). Exercise in the treatment of depression. *Current Psychiatry Reports, 11,* 466–472.

Gregory, R. J., & Jindal, S. (2006). Factitious disorder on an inpatient psychiatry ward. *American Journal of Orthopsychiatry, 76,* 31–36.

Grekin, E. R., & Sher, K. J. (2006). Alcohol dependence symptoms among college freshmen: Prevalence, stability and person-environment interactions. *Experimental and Clinical Psychopharmacology, 14,* 329–338.

Gressier, F., Calati, R., Balestri, M., Marsano, A., Alberti, S., Antypa, N., & Serretti, A. (2013). The 5-HTTLPR polymorphism and posttraumatic stress disorder: A meta-analysis. *Journal of Traumatic Stress, 26,* 645–653.

Griffith, J. D., Mitchell, S., Hart, C. L., Adams, L. T., & Gu, L. L. (2013). Pornography actresses: An assessment of the damaged goods hypothesis. *Journal of Sex Research, 50,* 621–632.

Grilo, C. M., White, M. A., & Masheb, R. M. (2012). Significance of overvaluation of shape and weight in an ethnically diverse sample of obese patients with binge-eating disorder in primary care settings. *Behavior Research and Therapy, 50,* 298–303.

Groenewold, N. A., Opmeer, E. M., de Jonge, P., Aleman, A., & Costafreda, S. G. (2013). Emotional valence modulates brain functional abnormalities in depression: Evidence from a meta-analysis of fMRI studies. *Neuroscience & Biobehavioral Reviews, 37,* 152–163.

Grohol, J. (2011, June 27). Marsha Linehan acknowledges her own struggle with bornderline personality disorder [Web log post]. Retrieved from http://psychcentral.com/blog/archives/2011/06/27/marsha-linehan-acknowledges-her-own-struggle-with-borderline-personality-disorder

Groth, A. N., Burgess, A. W., & Holstrom, L. (1977). Rape: Power, anger, and sexuality. *American Journal of Psychiatry, 134,* 1239–1243.

Groth-Marnat, G. (2009). *Handbook of psychological assessment* (5th ed.). New York, NY: John Wiley.

Gruber, S. A., Sagar, K. A., Dahlgren, M. K., Racine, M., & Lukas, S. E. (2012). Age of onset of marijuana use and executive function. *Psychology of Addictive Behaviors, 26,* 496–506.

Grund, J. P., Latypov, A., & Harris, M. (2013). Breaking worse: The emergence of krokodil and excessive injuries among people who inject drugs in Eurasia. *International Journal of Drug Policy, 24,* 265–274.

Guerreiro, R., Wojtas, A., Bras, J., Carrasquillo, M., Rogaeva, E., Majounie, E., . . . Hardy, J. (2013). TREM2 variants in Alzheimer's disease. *New England Journal of Medicine, 368,* 117–127.

Guerry, J. D., & Hastings, P. D. (2011). In search of HPA axis dysregulation in child and adolescent depression. *Clinical Child and Family Psychology Review, 14,* 135–160.

Gujar, N., Yoo, S. S., Hu, P., & Walker, M. P. (2011). Sleep deprivation amplifies reactivity of brain reward networks, biasing the appraisal of positive emotional experiences. *Journal of Neuroscience, 31,* 4466–4474.

Gupta, H. V., Farrell, A. M., & Mittal, M. K. (2014). Transient ischemic attacks: Predictability of future ischemic stroke or transient ischemic attack events. *Therapeutics and Clinical Risk Management, 10,* 27–35.

Gupta, S., & Bonanno, G. A. (2010). Trait self-enhancement as a buffer against potentially traumatic events: A prospective study. *Psychological Trauma: Theory, Research, Practice, and Policy, 2,* 83–92.

Gur, R. E., Calkins, M. E., Gur, R. C., Horan, W. P., Nuechterlein, K. H., Seidman, L. J., & Stone, W. S. (2007). The Consortium on the Genetics of Schizophrenia: Neurocognitive endophenotypes. *Schizophrenia Bulletin, 33,* 49–55.

Gutiérrez, F. (2014). The course of personality pathology. *Current Opinion in Psychiatry, 27,* 78–83.

Guyll, M., Cutrona, C., Burzette, R., & Russell, D. (2010). Hostility, relationship quality, and health among African American couples. *Journal of Consulting and Clinical Psychology, 78,* 646–654.

Haagsma, J. A., Ringburg, A. N., van Lieshout, E. M., van Beeck, E. F., Patka, P., Schipper, I. B., & Polinder, S. (2012). Prevalence rate, predictors and long-term course of probable posttraumatic stress disorder after major trauma: A prospective cohort study. *BMC Psychiatry, 12,* 236. doi:10.1186/1471-244X-12-236

Haas, A., Eliason, M., Mays, V., Mathy, R., Cochran, S., D'Angelli, A., & Clayton, P. (2011). Suicide and suicide risk in lesbian, gay, bisexual, and transgender populations: Review and recommendations. *Journal of Homosexuality, 58,* 10–51.

Haas, R. H. (2010). Autism and mitochondrial disease. *Developmental Disabilities Research Review, 16,* 144–153.

Hackett, G. I. (2008). Disorders of male sexual desire. In D. Rowland & L. Incrocci (Eds.), *Handbook of sexual and gender identity disorders* (pp. 5–31). Hoboken, NJ: Wiley.

Haeffel, G. J. (2010). When self-help is no help: Traditional cognitive skills training does not prevent depressive symptoms in people who ruminate. *Behavior Research and Therapy, 48,* 152–157.

Hagermoser Sanetti, L. M., & Kratochwill, T. R. (Eds.). (2014). *Treatment integrity: A foundation for evidence-based practice in applied psychology.* Washington, DC: American Psychological Association.

Haijma, S. V., Van Haren, N., Cahn, W., Koolschijn, P. C., Hulshoff Pol, H. E., & Kahn, R. S. (2013). Brain volumes in schizophrenia: A meta-analysis in over 18,000 subjects. *Schizophrenia Bulletin, 39,* 1129–1138.

Hajek, T., Kopecek, M., Höschl, C., & Alda, M. (2012). Smaller hippocampal volumes in patients with bipolar disorder are masked by exposure to lithium: A meta-analysis. *Journal of Psychiatry & Neuroscience, 37,* 333–343.

Haley, J. (1963). *Strategies of psychotherapy.* New York, NY: Grune & Stratton.

Haley, J. (1987). *Problem-solving therapy* (2nd ed.). New York, NY: Jossey-Bass.

Haley, J. (2003, October 31). Defendant's wife testifies about his multiple personas. *Bellingham Herald*, p. B4.

Hall, G. C. (1996). *Theory-based assessment, treatment, and prevention of sexual aggression*. New York, NY: Oxford University Press.

Hall, G. C. N., & Yee, A. (2014). Evidence-based practice. In F. T. L. Leong, L. Comas-Diaz, G. C. N. Hall, V. McLoyd, & J. Trimble (Eds.), *APA handbook of multicultural psychology*. Vol. 2: *Applications and training* (pp. 59–79). Washington, DC: APA.

Hall, J. R., & Benning, S. D. (2006). The "successful psychopath": Adaptive and subclinical manifestations of psychopathy in the general population. In C. J. Patrick (Ed.), *Handbook of psychopathy* (pp. 456–478). New York, NY: Guilford Press.

Hall, M. J., Levant, S., & DeFrances, C. J. (2012) Hospitalization for stroke in U.S. hospitals, 1989–2009. *NCHS Data Brief, 95*, 1–8.

Hallak, J. E. C., Crippa, J. A. S., & Zuardi, A. W. (2000). Treatment of koro with citalopram. *Journal of Clinical Psychology, 61*, 951–952.

Hallquist, M. N., & Lenzenweger, M. F. (2013). Identifying latent trajectories of personality disorder symptom change: Growth mixture modeling in the longitudinal study of personality disorders. *Journal of Abnormal Psychology, 122*, 138–155.

Halmi, K. A., Bellace, D., Berthod, S., Ghosh, S., Berrettini, W., Brandt, H. A., . . . Strober, M. (2012). An examination of early childhood perfectionism across anorexia nervosa subtypes. *International Journal of Eating Disorders, 45*, 800–807.

Halmi, K. A., Sunday, S. R., Strober, M., Kaplan, A., Woodside, D. B., Fichter M., . . . Kaye, W. H. (2000). Perfectionism in anorexia nervosa: Variation by clinical subtype, obsessionality, and pathological eating disorder. *American Journal of Psychiatry, 157*, 1799–1805.

Hamer, M., Kivimaki, M., Stamatakis, E., & Batty, G. D. (2012). Psychological distress as a risk factor for death from cerebrovascular disease. *Canadian Medical Association Journal,184*, 1461–1466.

Hamer, M., O'Donnell, K., Lahiri, A., & Steptoe, A. (2010). Salivary cortisol responses to mental stress are associated with coronary artery calcification in healthy men and women. *European Heart Journal, 31*, 424–429.

Hamilton, B. E., Miniño, A. M., Martin, J. A., Kochanek, K. D., Strobino, D. M., & Guyer, B. (2007). Annual summary of vital statistics: 2005. *Pediatrics, 119*, 345–360.

Hammad, T. A., Laughren, T., & Racoosin, J. (2006). Suicidality in pediatric patients treated with antidepressant drugs. *Archives of General Psychiatry, 63*, 332–339.

Hammen, C. (2006). Stress generation in depression: Reflections on origins, research, and future directions. *Journal of Clinical Psychology, 62*, 1065–1082.

Handelsman, M., Walfish, S., & Hess, A. K. (Eds.). (2001). *Learning to become ethical: Succeeding in graduate school: The career guide for psychology students*. Mahwah, NJ: Erlbaum.

Hanewinkel, R., Isensee, B., Sargent, J. D., & Morgenstern, M. (2011). Cigarette advertising and teen smoking initiation. *Pediatrics, 127*(2), e271–e278. doi:10.1542/peds.2010-2934

Hanford, N., & Figueiro, M. (2013). Light therapy and Alzheimer's disease and related dementia: Past, present, and future. *Journal of Alzheimer's Disease, 33*, 913–922.

Hankey, G. J. (2011). Stroke: Fresh insights into causes, prevention, and treatment. *The Lancet Neurology, 10*, 2–3.

Hankin, B. L. (2008). Rumination and depression in adolescence: Investigating symptom specificity in a multiwave prospective study. *Journal of Clinical Child and Adolescent Psychology, 37*, 701–713.

Hankin, B. L. (2009). Development of sex differences in depressive and co-occurring anxious symptoms during adolescence: Descriptive trajectories and potential explanations in a multiwave prospective study. *Journal of Clinical Child and Adolescent Psychology, 38*, 460–472.

Hanrahan, F., Field, A. P., Jones, F. W., & Davey, G. C. (2013). A meta-analysis of cognitive therapy for worry in generalized anxiety disorder. *Clinical Psychology Review, 33*, 120–132.

Hanson, A. J., Bayer-Carter, J. L., Green, P. S., Montine, T. J., Wilkinson, C. W., Baker, L. D., . . . Craft, S. (2013). Effect of apolipoprotein E genotype and diet on apolipoprotein E lipidation and amyloid peptides: Randomized clinical trial. *JAMA Neurology, 70*, 972–980.

Hansen, L., Kingdon, D., & Turkington, D. (2006). The ABCs of cognitive-behavioral therapy for schizophrenia. *Psychiatric Times, 23*, 49–53.

Harbin, J. M., Gelso, C. J., & Rojas, A. E. P. (2013). Therapist work with client strengths: Development and validation of a measure. *The Counseling Psychologist*. Published online before print, February 5, 2013. doi: 10.1177/0011000012470570

Hare, R. D., & Neumann, C. S. (2009). Psychopathy: Assessment and forensic implications. *Canadian Journal of Psychiatry, 54*, 791–802.

Hargreaves, D. A., & Tiggemann, M. (2009). Muscular ideal media images and men's body image: Social comparison processing and individual vulnerability. *Psychology of Men and Masculinity, 10*, 109–119.

Harmon, K. G., Drezner, J. A., Gammons, M., Guskiewicz, K. M., Halstead, M., Herring, S. A., . . . Roberts, W. O. (2013). American Medical Society for Sports Medicine position statement: Concussion in sport. *British Journal of Sports Medicine, 47*, 15–26.

Harris, J. C. (2010). Asylum at Saint-Rémy. *Archives of General Psychiatry, 67*, 666.

Harrow, M., Grossman, L. S., Jobe, T. H., & Herbener, E. S. (2005). Do patients with schizophrenia ever show periods of recovery? A 15-year multi-follow-up study. *Schizophrenia Bulletin, 31*, 723–734.

Harrow, M., & Jobe, T. H. (2013). Does long-term treatment of schizophrenia with antipsychotic medications facilitate recovery? *Schizophrenia Bulletin, 39*, 962–965.

Hartling, L., Abou-Setta, A. M., Dursun, S., Mousavi, S. S., Pasichnyk, D., & Newton, A. S. (2012). Antipsychotics in adults with schizophrenia: Comparative effectiveness of first-generation versus second-generation medications: A systematic review and meta-analysis. *Annals of Internal Medicine, 157*, 498–511.

Hartmann, A., Zeeck, A., & Barrett, M. S. (2010). Interpersonal problems in eating disorders. *International Journal of Eating Disorders, 43*, 619–627.

Harvey, C. J., Gehrman, P., & Espie, C. A. (2014). Who is predisposed to insomnia: A review of familial aggregation, stress-reactivity, personality and coping style. *Sleep Medicine Reviews, 18*, 237–247.

Harvey, P. O., Zaki, J., Lee, J., Ochsner, K., & Green, M. F. (2013). Neural substrates of empathic accuracy in people with schizophrenia. *Schizophrenia Bulletin, 39*, 617–628.

Harvey, W. T., Bransfield, R. C., Mercer, D. E., Wright, A. J., Ricchi, R. M., & Leitao, M. M. (2009). Morgellons disease, illuminating an undefined illness: A case series. *Journal of Medical Case Reports, 3,* 8243.

Hashimoto, M. (2014, February 6). No time for Ethan Couch, no justice for his many victims. Retrieved from http://dallasmorningviewsblog.dallasnews.com/2014/02/no-time-for-ethan-couch-no-justice-for-his-many-victims.html

Hasin, D. S., Goodwin, R. D., Stinson, F. S., & Grant, B. F. (2005). Epidemiology of major depressive disorder: Results from the National Epidemiologic Survey on Alcoholism and Related Conditions. *Archives of General Psychiatry, 62,* 1097–1106.

Hasin, D. S., Stinson, F. S., Ogburn, E., & Grant, B. F. (2007). Prevalence, correlates, disability, and comorbidity of DSM-IV alcohol abuse and dependence in the United States: Results from the National Epidemiologic Survey on Alcohol and Related Conditions. *Archives of General Psychiatry, 64,* 830–842.

Hathaway, S. R., & McKinley, J. C. (1943). *Manual for the Minnesota Multiphasic Personality Inventory.* New York, NY: Psychological Corporation.

Hatsukami, D. K., Stead, L. F., & Gupta, P. C. (2008). Tobacco addiction. *Lancet, 371,* 2027–2038.

Hattingh, C. J., Ipser, J., Tromp, S. A., Syal, S., Lochner, C., Brooks, S. J., & Stein, D. J. (2013). Functional magnetic resonance imaging during emotion recognition in social anxiety disorder: An activation likelihood meta-analysis. *Frontiers in Human Neuroscience, 6,* 347. doi:10.3389/fnhum.2012.00347

Hatzenbuehler, M. L. (2011). The social environment and suicide attempts in lesbian, gay, and bisexual youth. *Pediatrics, 127,* 896–903.

Hauer, P. (2010). Systemic affects of methamphetamine use. *South Dakota Medicine: Journal of the South Dakota State Medical Association, 63*(8), 285–287.

Haugaard, J. J. (2000). The challenge of defining child sexual abuse. *American Psychologist, 55,* 1036–1039.

Haupt, M., Sheldon, S. H., & Loghmanee, D. (2013) Just a scary dream? A brief review of sleep terrors, nightmares, and rapid eye movement sleep behavior disorder. *Pediatric Annals, 42,* 211–216.

Hausenblas, H. A., Campbell, A., Menzel, J. E., Doughty, J., Levine, M., & Thompson, J. K. (2013). Media effects of experimental presentation of the ideal physique on eating disorder symptoms: A meta-analysis of laboratory studies. *Clinical Psychology Review, 33,* 168–181.

Hauser, M., Galling, B., & Correll, C. U. (2013). Suicidal ideation and suicide attempts in children and adolescents with bipolar disorder: A systematic review of prevalence and incidence rates, correlates, and targeted interventions. *Bipolar Disorders, 15,* 507–523.

Häuser, W., & Wolfe, F. (2013). The somatic symptom disorder in DSM 5 risks mislabeling people with major medical diseases as mentally ill. *Journal of Psychosomatic Research, 75,* 586–587.

Hawkins, J. D., Oesterle, S., Brown, E. C., Monahan, K. C., Abbott, R. D., Arthur, M. W., & Catalano, R. F. (2012). Sustained decreases in risk exposure and youth problem behaviors after installation of the Communities That Care prevention system in a randomized trial. *Archives of Pediatrics & Adolescent Medicine, 166,* 141–148.

Hayes, E., Gavrilidis, E., & Kulkarni, J. (2012). The role of oestrogen and other hormones in the pathophysiology and treatment of schizophrenia. *Schizophrenia Research and Treatment.* Retrieved from http://www.hindawi.com/journals/sprt/2012/540273/ref

Hayes, S. C., Brownell, K. D., & Barlow, D. H. (1983). Heterosocial skills training and covert sensitization: Effects on social skills and sexual arousal in sexual deviants. *Behaviour Research and Therapy, 21,* 383–392.

Hayley, S., & Litteljohn, D. (2013). Neuroplasticity and the next wave of antidepressant strategies. *Frontiers in Cellular Neuroscience, 7,* 218. doi:10.3389/fncel.2013

Hayward, M., Berry, K., & Ashton, A. (2011). Applying interpersonal theories to the understanding of and therapy for auditory hallucinations: A review of the literature and directions for further research. *Clinical Psychology Review, 31,* 1313–1323.

Hazlett, E. A., Lamade, R.V., Graff, F. S., McClure, M. M., Kolaitis, J. C., Goldstein, K. E., . . . Moshier, E. (2014). Visual-spatial working memory performance and temporal gray matter volume predict schizotypal personality disorder group membership. *Schizophrenia Research, 152,* 350–357.

Headaches. (2006). *Journal of the American Medical Association, 295,* 2320–2322.

Healy, M. (2011). "Idol" finalist Durbin is singing through Tourette's. *USA Today.* Retrieved from http://www.usatoday.com

Heaton, R. K., Clifford, D. B., Franklin, D. R., Jr., Woods, S. P., Ake, C., Vaida, F., . . . Grant, I. (2010). HIV-associated neurocognitive disorders persist in the era of potent antiretroviral therapy: CHARTER study. *Neurology, 75,* 2087–2096.

Hebert, K. K., Cummins, S. E., Hernández, S., Tedeschi, G. J., & Zhu, S. (2011). Current major depression among smokers using a state quitline. *American Journal of Preventive Medicine, 40,* 47–53.

Hebert, L. E., Weuve, J., Scherr, P. A., & Evans, D. A. (2013). Alzheimer disease in the United States (2010–2050) estimated using the 2010 census. *Neurology, 80,* 1778–1783.

Heinssen, R. K., & Cuthbert, B. N. (2001). Barrier to relationship formation in schizophrenia: Implications for treatment, social recovery, and translational research. *Psychiatry, 64,* 126–132.

Heinz, A. J., Wu, J., Witkiewitz, K., Epstein, D. H., & Preston, K. L. (2009). Marriage and relationship closeness as predictors of cocaine and heroin use. *Addictive Behavior, 34,* 258–263.

Hektner, J. M., August, G. J., Bloomquist, M. L., Lee, S., & Klimes-Dougan, B. (2014). A 10-year randomized controlled trial of the Early Risers conduct problems preventive intervention: Effects on externalizing and internalizing in late high school. *Journal of Consulting & Clinical Psychology, 82,* 355–360.

Hellstrom, K., Fellenius, J., & Öst, L.-G. (1996). One versus five sessions of applied tension in the treatment of blood phobia. *Behaviour Research and Therapy, 34,* 101–112.

Helt, M., Kelley, E., Kinsbourne, M., Pandey, J., Boorstein, H., Herbert, M., & Fein, D. (2008). Can children with autism recover? If so, how? *Neuropsychological Review, 18,* 339–366.

Hepp, U., Stulz, N., Unger-Köppel, J., & Ajdacic-Gross, V. (2012). Methods of suicide used by children and adolescents. *European Child and Adolescent Psychiatry, 21,* 67–73.

Herbel, B. L., & Stelmach, H. (2007). Involuntary medication treatment for competency restoration of 22 defendants with delusional disorder. *Journal of the American Academy of Psychiatry and Law, 35,* 47–59.

Herbenick, D., Reece, M., Schick, V., Sanders, S. A., Dodge, B., & Fortenberry, J. D. (2010). Sexual behavior in the United States from a national probability sample of men and women ages 14–94. *Journal of Sexual Medicine, 7,* 255–265.

Herbert, M. R. (2010). Contributions of the environment and environmentally vulnerable physiology to autism spectrum disorders. *Current Opinions in Neurology, 23,* 103–110.

Hernandez, A., & Sachs-Ericsson, N. (2006). Ethnic differences in pain reports and the moderating role of depression in a community sample of Hispanic and Caucasian participants with serious health problems. *Psychosomatic Medicine, 68,* 121–127.

Herpertz, S. C., & Bertsch, K. (2014). The social-cognitive basis of personality disorders. *Current Opinion in Psychiatry, 27,* 73–77.

Herringa, R. J., Birn, R. M., Ruttle, P. L., Burghy, C. A., Stodola, D. E., Davidson, R. J., & Essex, M. J. (2013). Childhood maltreatment is associated with altered fear circuitry and increased internalizing symptoms by late adolescence. *Proceedings of the National Academy of Science U S A, 110,* 19119–19124.

Herrnstein, R. J., & Murray, C. (1994). *The bell curve: Intelligence and class structure in American life.* New York, NY: Free Press.

Hettema, J. M. (2010). Genetics of depression. *Focus, 8,* 316–322.

Hicks, T. V., Leitenberg, H., Barlow, D. H., & Gorman, K. M. (2005). Physical, mental, and social catastrophic cognitions as prognostic factors in cognitive-behavioral and pharmacological treatments for panic disorder. *Journal of Consulting and Clinical Psychology, 73,* 506–514.

Hilbert, A., Bishop, M. E., Stein, R. I., Tanofsky-Kraff, M., Swenson, A. K., Welch, R. R., & Wilfley, D. E. (2012). Long-term efficacy of psychological treatments for binge eating disorder. *British Journal of Psychiatry, 200,* 232–237.

Hilbert, A., & Tuschen-Caffier, B. (2007). Maintenance of binge eating through negative mood: A naturalistic comparison of binge eating disorder and bulimia nervosa. *International Journal of Eating Disorders, 40,* 521–527.

Hill, S. K., Reilly, J. L., Keefe, R. S., Gold, J. M., Bishop, J. R., Gershon, E. S., . . . Sweeney, J. A. (2013). Neuropsychological impairments in schizophrenia and psychotic bipolar disorder: Findings from the Bipolar-Schizophrenia Network on Intermediate Phenotypes (B-SNIP) study. *American Journal of Psychiatry, 170,* 1275–1284.

Hill, A. L., Rand, D. G., Nowak, M. A., & Christakis, N. A. (2010). Infectious disease modeling of social contagion in networks. *PLOS Computational Biology, 6* (11), e1000968. doi:10.1371/journal.pcbi.1000968

Hill, J. K. (2011). *Victims of Crime Research Digest, issue no. 2.* Retrieved from http://www.justice.gc.ca/eng/pi/rs/rep-rap/rd-rr/rd09_2-rr09_2/p1.html

Hiller, R. M., Lovato, N., Gradisar, M., Oliver, M., & Slater, A. (2014). Trying to fall asleep while catastrophising: What sleep-disordered adolescents think and feel. *Sleep Medicine, 15,* 96–103.

Hiller, W., Leibbrand, R., Rief, W., & Fichter, M. M. (2002). Predictors of course and outcome in hypochondriasis after cognitive-behavioral treatment. *Psychotherapy and Psychosomatics, 71,* 318–327.

Hines, M. (2011). Gender development and the human brain. *Annual Review of Neuroscience, 34,* 69–88.

Hinton, D. E., & Lewis-Fernández, R. (2011). The cross-cultural validity of posttraumatic stress disorder: Implications for DSM-5. *Depression and Anxiety, 28,* 783–801.

Hinton, D. E, Nickerson, A., & Bryant, R. A. (2011). Worry, worry attacks, and PTSD among Cambodian refugees: A path analysis investigation. *Social Science & Medicine, 72,* 1817–1825.

Hirshfeld-Becker, D. R., Biederman, J., Henin, A., Faraone, S. V., Davis, S., Harrington, K., . . . Jerrold, F. (2007). Behavioral inhibition in preschool children at risk is a specific predictor of middle childhood social anxiety: A five-year follow-up. *Journal of Developmental and Behavioral Pediatrics, 28,* 225–233.

Ho, B.-C., Andreasen, N. C., Ziebell, S., Pierson, R., & Magnotta, V. (2011). Long-term antipsychotic treatment and brain volumes. *Archives of General Psychiatry, 68,* 128–137.

Ho, M., Garnett, S. P., Baur, L., Burrows, T., Stewart, L., Neve, M., & Collins, C. (2012). Effectiveness of lifestyle interventions in child obesity: Systematic review with meta-analysis. *Pediatrics, 130,* 1647–1671.

Hobza, C. L., & Rochlen, A. B. (2009). Gender role conflict, drive for muscularity, and the impact of ideal media portrayals on men. *Psychology of Men & Masculinity, 10,* 120–130.

Hoehn-Saric, R., McLeod, D. R., Funderburk, F., & Kowalski, P. (2004). Somatic symptoms and physiologic responses in generalized anxiety disorder and panic disorder: An ambulatory monitor study. *Archives of General Psychiatry, 61,* 913–921.

Hoffman, P. (2013, May 6). More mentally ill becoming homeless because states won't help. Retrieved from http://truth-out.org/opinion/item/16193-more-mentally-ill-becoming-homeless-because-states-wont-help

Hofmann, S. F., Asnaani, A., & Hinton, D. E. (2010). Cultural aspects in social anxiety and social anxiety disorder. *Depression and Anxiety, 27,* 1117–1127.

Hofmann, S. G. (2014). D-cycloserine for treating anxiety disorders: Making good exposures better and bad exposures worse. *Depression and Anxiety, 31,* 175–177.

Hofmann, S. G., Meuret, A. E., Rosenfield, D., Suvak, M. K., Barlow, D. H., Gorman, J., Woods, S. W. (2007). Preliminary evidence for cognitive mediation during cognitive-behavioral therapy of panic disorder. *Journal of Consulting and Clinical Psychology, 75,* 374–379.

Hofmann, S. G., Smits, J. A., Rosenfield, D., Simon, N., Otto, M. W., Meuret, A. E., . . . Pollack, M. H. (2013). D-cycloserine as an augmentation strategy with cognitive-behavioral therapy for social anxiety disorder. *American Journal of Psychiatry, 170,* 751–758.

Hofmann, S. G., Wu, J. Q., & Boettcher, H. (2013). D-cycloserine as an augmentation strategy for cognitive behavioral therapy of anxiety disorders. *Biology of Mood & Anxiety Disorders, 3,* 11. doi:10.1186/2045-5380-3-11

Hoge, E. A., Worthington, J. J., Nagurney, J. T., Chang, Y., Kay, E. B., Feterowski, C. M., . . . Pitman, R. K. (2012). Effect of acute posttrauma propranolol on PTSD outcome and physiological responses during script-driven imagery. *CNS Neuroscience & Therapeutics, 18,* 21–27.

Hollender, M. H. (1980). The case of Anna O.: A reformulation. *American Journal of Psychiatry, 137,* 797–800.

Hollon, S. D., Stewart, M. O., & Strunk, D. (2006). Enduring effects for cognitive behavior therapy in the treatment of depression and anxiety. *Annual Review of Psychology, 57,* 285–315.

Holmqvist, V. N., & Walsh, K. (2014). Web- vs telehealth-based delivery of cognitive behavioral therapy for insomnia: A randomized controlled trial. *Sleep Medicine, 15,* 187–195.

Holt-Lunstad, J., Smith, T. B., & Layton, B. (2010). Social relationships and mortality risk: A meta-analytic review. *PLOS Medicine, 7*(7), e1000316. doi:10.1371/journal.pmed.1000316

Hölzel, B. K., Hoge, E. A., Greve, D. N., Gard, T., Creswell, J. D., Brown, K. W., . . . Lazar, S. W. (2013). Neural mechanisms of symptom improvements in generalized anxiety disorder following mindfulness training. *NeuroImage Clinical, 2,* 448–458.

Honda, K., & Goodwin, R. D. (2004). Cancer and mental disorders in a national community sample. *Psychotherapy and Psychosomatics, 73,* 235–242.

Honea, R. A., Thomas, G. P., Harsha, A., Anderson, H. S., Donnelly, J. E., Brooks, W. M., & Burns, J. M. (2009). Cardiorespiratory fitness and preserved medial temporal lobe volume in Alzheimer disease. *Alzheimer Disease and Associated Disorders, 23,* 188–197.

Hornor, G. (2008). Reactive attachment disorder. *Journal of Pediatric Health Care, 22,* 234–239.

Hornor, G. (2013). Posttraumatic stress disorder. *Journal of Pediatric Health Care, 27,* 29–38.

Hornung, O. P., & Heim, C. M. (2014). Gene-environment interactions and intermediate phenotypes: Early trauma and depression. *Frontiers in Endocrinology, 5,* 14. eCollection 2014.

Horowitz, M. J. (2001). Histrionic personality disorder. In G. O. Gabbard (Ed.), *Treatment of psychiatric disorders* (pp. 2293–2307). Washington, DC: American Psychiatric Press.

Houenou, J., Frommberger, J., Carde, S., Glasbrenner, M., Diener, C., Leboyer, M., & Wessa, M. (2011). Neuroimaging-based markers of bipolar disorder: Evidence from two meta-analyses. *Journal of Affective Disorders, 132,* 344–355.

Howard, M. O., Perron, B. E., Sacco, P., Ilgen, M., Vaughn, M. G., Garland, E., & Freedentahl, S. (2010). Suicide ideation and attempts among inhalant users: Results from the National Epidemiologic Survey on Alcohol and Related Conditions. *Suicide and Life-Threatening Behavior, 40,* 276–286.

Howard, M. O., Perron, B. E., Vaughn, M. G., Bender, K. A., & Garland, E. (2010). Inhalant use, inhalant-use disorders, and antisocial behavior: Findings from the National Epidemiologic Survey on Alcohol and Related Conditions (NESARC). *Journal of Studies on Alcohol and Drugs, 71,* 201–209.

Howe, E. (2010). What psychiatrists should know about genes and Alzheimer's disease. *Psychiatry, 7,* 45–51.

Howe, E. (2011). Nonmedical treatment of patients with dementia. *Innovation in Clinical Neuroscience, 8,* 18–25.

Howe, E. (2013). Clinical implications of the new diagnostic guidelines for dementia. *Innovations in Clinical Neuroscience, 10,* 32–38.

Howes, O. D., Kambeitz, J., Kim, E., Stahl, D., Slifstein, M., Abi-Dargham, A., & Kapur, S. (2012). The nature of dopamine dysfunction in schizophrenia and what this means for treatment. *Archives of General Psychiatry, 69,* 776–786. doi:10.1001/archgenpsychiatry.2012.169

Howie, L. D., Pastor, P. N., & Lukacs, S. L. (2014). Use of medication prescribed for emotional or behavioral difficulties among children aged 6–17 years in the United States, 2011–2012. NCHS data brief, no 148. Hyattsville, MD: National Center for Health Statistics.

Howland, R. H. (2011). Sleep interventions for the treatment of depression. *Journal of Psychosocial Nursing and Mental Health Services, 49,* 17–20.

Howlett, S., & Reuber, M. (2009). An augmented model of brief psychodynamic interpersonal therapy for patients with nonepileptic seizures. *Psychotherapy: Research, Practice, Training, 46,* 125–138.

Howley, J., & Ross, C. A. (2003). The structure of dissociative fugue: A case report. *Journal of Trauma & Dissociation, 4,* 109–124.

Hoyer, J., Burmann, I., Kieseler, M. L., Vollrath, F., Hellrung, L., Arelin, K., . . . Sacher, J. (2013). Menstrual cycle phase modulates emotional conflict processing in women with and without premenstrual syndrome (PMS)—A pilot study. *PLOS One, 8,* e59780. doi:10.1371/journal.pone.0059780

Hsu, L., Woody, S. R., Lee, H. J., Peng, Y., Zhou, X., & Ryder, A. G. (2012). Social anxiety among East Asians in North America: East Asian socialization or the challenge of acculturation? *Cultural Diversity and Ethnic Minority Diversity, 18,* 181–191.

Hudson, J. I., Hiripi, E., Pope, H. G., & Kessler, R. C. (2007). The prevalence and correlates of eating disorders in the National Comorbidity Survey Replication. *Biological Psychiatry, 61,* 348–358.

Huffman, J. C., DuBois, C. M., Healy, B. C., Boehm, J. K., Kashdan, T. B., Celano, C. M., . . . Lyubomirsky, S. (2014). Feasibility and utility of positive psychology exercises for suicidal inpatients. *General Hospital Psychiatry, 36,* 88–94.

Hughes, V. (2012). Roots of post-trauma resilience sought in genetics and brain changes. Retrieved from http://www.scientificamerican.com/article.cfm?id5roots-post-trauma-resilience-sought-genetics-brain-changes

Huijbregts, K. M., van der Feltz-Cornelis, C. M., van Marwijk, H. W., de Jonge, F. J., van der Windt, D. A., & Beekman, A. T. (2010). Negative association of concomitant physical symptoms with the course of major depressive disorder: A systematic review. *Journal of Psychosomic Research, 68,* 511–519.

Humphreys, C. L., Rubin, J. S., Knudson, R. M., & Stiles, W. B. (2005). The assimilation of anger in a case of dissociative identity disorder. *Counselling Psychology Quarterly, 18,* 121–132.

Humphreys, K. L., Katz, S. J., Lee, S. S., Hammen, C., Brennan, P. A., & Najman, J. M. (2013). The association of ADHD and depression: Mediation by peer problems and parent-child difficulties in two complementary samples. *Journal of Abnormal Psychology, 122,* 854–867.

Hunsley, J. (2007). Addressing key challenges in evidence-based practice in psychology. *Professional Psychology: Research and Practice, 38,* 113–121.

Hunt, J., Case, B. G., Birmaher, B., Stout, R. L., Dickstein, D. P., Yen, S., . . . Keller, M. B. (2013). Irritability and elation in a large bipolar youth sample: Relative symptom severity and clinical outcomes over 4 years. *Journal of Clinical Psychiatry, 74,* e110–e117. doi:10.4088/JCP.12m07874

Hunter, E. C. M., Salkovskis, P. M., & David, A. S. (2014). Attributions, appraisals and attention for symptoms in depersonalisation disorder. *Behaviour Research and Therapy, 53,* 20–29.

Huntjens, R. J. C., Verschuere, B., & McNally, R. J. (2012). Inter-identity autobiographical amnesia in patients with dissociative identity disorder. *PLOS One, 7*(7), e40580. doi:10.1371/journal.pone.0040580

Hurd, M. D., Martorell, P., Delavande, A., Mullen, K. J., & Langa, K. M. (2013). Monetary costs of dementia in the United States. *New England Journal of Medicine, 368,* 1326–1334.

Hussong, A. M., Jones, D. J., Stein, G. L., Baucom, D. H., & Boeding, S. (2011). An internalizing pathway to alcohol use and disorder. *Psychology of Addictive Behaviors, 25,* 390–404.

Hyde, J. S. (2005). *Biological substrates of human sexuality.* Washington, DC: American Psychological Association.

Iacovino, J. M., Gredysa, D. M., Altman, M., & Wilfley, D. E. (2012). Psychological treatments for binge eating disorder. *Current Psychiatry Report, 14,* 432–446.

Iacovino, J. M., Powers, A. D., & Oltmanns, T. F. (2014). Impulsivity mediates the association between borderline personality pathology and body mass index. *Personality and Individual Differences, 56,* 100–104.

Iancu, I., Sarel, A., Avital, A., Abdo, B., Joubran, S., & Ram, E. (2011). Shyness and social phobia in Israeli Jewish vs Arab students. *Comprehensive Psychiatry, 52,* 708–714.

Imuta, K., Scarf, D., Pharo, H., & Hayne, H. (2013). Drawing a close to the use of human figure drawings as a projective measure of intelligence. *PLOS One, 8*(3), e58991. doi:10.1371/journal.pone.0058991

Insel, T., Cuthbert, B., Garvey, M., Heinssen, R., Pine, D. S., Quinn, K., . . . Wang, P. (2010). Research domain criteria (RDoC): Toward a new classification framework for research on mental disorders. *American Journal of Psychiatry, 167,* 748–751.

International Narcotics Control Board. (2010). Psychotropic substances: Statistics for 2009. Retrieved from http://www.incb.org/pdf/technical-reports/psychotropics/2010/Psychotropic_Substances_Publication_2010.pdf

International Society for the Study of Trauma and Dissociation. (2011). Guidelines for treating dissociative identity disorder in adults, third revision: Summary version. *Journal of Trauma & Dissociation, 12,* 188–212.

IsHak, W. W., Rasyidi, E., Saah, T., Vasa, M., Ettekal, A., & Fan, A. (2010). Factitious disorder case series with variations of psychological and physical symptoms. *Primary Psychiatry, 17,* 40–43.

Ishak, W. W., Ugochukwu, C., Bagot, K., Khalili, D., & Zaky, C. (2012). Energy drinks: Psychological effects and impact on well-being and quality of life—A literature review. *Innovations in Clinical Neuroscience, 9,* 25–34.

Irani, F., & Siegel, S. J. (2006). Predicting outcome in schizophrenia. *Psychiatric Times, 23,* 69–71.

Irizarry, L. (2004, August 8). Widespread starvation: A proliferation of Web sites are promoting anorexia, which shows that sometimes, there is no safety in numbers. *New Orleans Times-Picayune,* p. 1.

Irwin, H. J. (1998). Attitudinal predictors of dissociation: Hostility and powerlessness. *Journal of Psychology, 132,* 389–404.

Isaac, M., Elias, B., Katz, L. Y., Belik, S. L., Deane, F. P., Enns, M. W., . . . Swampy Cree Suicide Prevention Team (12 members). (2009). Gatekeeper training as a preventative intervention for suicide: A systematic review. *La Revue Canadienne de Psychiatrie, 54,* 260–268.

Isenberg-Grzeda, E., Kutner, H. E., & Nicolson, S. E. (2012). Wernicke-Korsakoff-syndrome: Under-recognized and under-treated. *Psychosomatics, 53,* 507–516.

Islam, L., Scarone, S., & Gambini, O. (2011). First- and third-person perspectives in psychotic disorder and mood disorders with psychotic features. *Schizophrenia Research and Treatment.* Retrieved from http://www.hindawi.com/journals/sprt/2011/769136

Ismail, S., Buckley, S., Budacki, R., Jabbar, A., & Gallicano, I. (2010). Screening, diagnosing and prevention of fetal alcohol syndrome: Is this syndrome treatable? *Developmental Neuroscience, 32,* 91–100.

Ivey, A. E., D'Andrea, M., Ivey, M. B., & Simek-Morgan, L. (2007). *Theories of counseling and psychotherapy: A multicultural perspective* (2nd ed.). Boston, MA: Allyn & Bacon.

Jack, C. R., & Holtzman, D. M. (2013). Biomarker modeling of Alzheimer's disease. *Neuron, 80,* 1347–1358.

Jacka, F. N., Kremer, P. J., Beark, M., de Silva-Sanigorski, A. M, Moodie, M., Leslie, E. R., . . . Swinburn, B. A. (2011). A prospective study of diet quality and mental health in adolescents. *PLOS One, 6*(9), e24805. doi:10.1371/journal.pone.0024805

Jacka, F. N., Pasco, J. A., Mykletun, A., Williams, L. J., Hodge, A. M., O'Reilly, S. L., . . . Berk, M. (2010). Association between Western and traditional diets and depression and anxiety in women. *American Journal of Psychiatry, 167,* 305–311.

Jackson, C., Geddes, R., Haw, S., & Frank, J. (2012). Interventions to prevent substance use and risky sexual behaviour in young people: A systematic review. *Addiction, 107,* 733–747.

Jackson, C. A., & Mishra, G. D. (2013). Depression and risk of stroke in midaged women: A prospective longitudinal study. *Stroke, 44,* 1555–1560.

Jackson, S. R., Parkinson, A., Manfredi, V., Millon, G., Hollis, C., & Jackson, G. M. (2013). Motor excitability is reduced prior to voluntary movements in children and adolescents with Tourette syndrome. *Journal of Neuropsychology, 7,* 29–44.

Jackson, T., & Chen, H. (2010). Sociocultural experiences of bulimic and non-bulimic adolescents in a school-based Chinese sample. *Journal of Abnormal Child Psychology, 38,* 69–76.

Jacobs, E., & D'Esposito, M. (2011). Estrogen shapes dopamine-dependent cognitive processes: Implications for women's health. *Journal of Neuroscience, 31,* 5286–5293.

Jacobsen, P. B., Bovbjerg, D. H., Schwartz, M. D., Hudis, C. A., Gilewski, T. A., & Norton, L. (1995). Conditioned emotional distress in women receiving chemotherapy for breast cancer. *Journal of Consulting and Clinical Psychology, 63,* 108–114.

Jacobson, R. (2014). Should children take antipsychotic drugs? Retrieved from http://www.scientificamerican.com/article/should-children-take-antipsychotic-drugs

Jaffe, J., Robinson, L., & Segal, J. (2013). Coping with suicidal thoughts: The first steps. Retrieved from http://beta.helpguide.org/mental/suicide_help.htm

Jaffee, S. R., Moffitt, T. E., Caspi, A., Taylor, A., & Arsenault, L. (2002). Influence of adult domestic violence on children's externalizing and internalizing problems: An environmentally informative twin study. *Journal of the American Academy of Child & Adolescent Psychiatry, 41,* 1095–1103.

Jagdeo, A., Cox, B. J., Stein, M. B., & Sareen, J. (2009). Negative attitudes toward help seeking for mental illness in 2 population-based surveys from the

United States and Canada. *Canadian Journal of Psychiatry, 54,* 757–766.

Jairam, R., Prabhuswamy, M., & Dullur, P. (2012). Do we really know how to treat a child with bipolar disorder or one with severe mood dysregulation? Is there a magic bullet? *Depression Research and Treatment.* Retrieved from http://www.hindawi.com/journals/drt/2012/967302/967302

Jakubowski, P., & Lange, A. J. (1978). *The assertive option: Your rights and responsibilities.* Champaign, IL: Research Press.

James, A., Hough, M., James, S., Burge, L., Winmill, L., Nijhawan, S., . . . Zarei, M. (2011). Structural brain and neuropsychometric changes associated with pediatric bipolar disorder with psychosis. *Bipolar Disorders, 13,* 16–27.

James, D. C. (2013). Weight loss strategies used by African American women: Possible implications for tailored messages. *Journal of Human Nutrition and Dietetics, 26,* 71–77.

Janjua, A., Rapport, D., & Ferrara, G. (2010). The woman who wasn't there. *Current Psychiatry, 9,* 62–72.

Janssen, K. (1983). Treatment of sinus tachycardia with heart-rate feedback. *Psychiatry and Human Development, 17,* 166–176.

Janus, S. S., & Janus, C. L. (1993). *The Janus report on sexual behavior.* New York, NY: Wiley.

Jaremka, L. M., Fagundes, C. P., Peng, J., Bennett, J. M., Glaser, R., Malarkey, W. B., & Kiecolt-Glaser, J. K. (2013). Loneliness promotes inflammation during acute stress. *Psychological Science, 24,* 1089–1097.

Jauch-Chara, K., & Oltmanns, K. M. (2014, January 3). Obesity—A neuropsychological disease? Systematic review and neuropsychological model. Progress in Neurobiology. pii: S0301-0082(13)00141-X. doi:10.1016/j.pneurobio.2013.12.001 [Epub ahead of print]

Jeffries, F. W., & Davis, P. (2013). What is the role of eye movements in eye movement desensitization and reprocessing (EMDR) for post-traumatic stress disorder (PTSD)? A review. *Behavioral and Cognitive Psychotherapy, 41,* 290–300.

Jellinger, K. A. (2008). Morphologic diagnosis of "vascular dementia"—A critical update. *Journal of Neurological Science, 270,* 1–12.

Jenike, M. A. (2001). A forty-five-year-old woman with obsessive-compulsive disorder. *Journal of the American Medical Association, 285,* 2121–2128.

Jenkins, J. H., Strauss, M. E., Carpenter, E. A., Miller, D., Floersch, J., & Sajatovic, M. (2005). Subjective experience of recovery from schizophrenia-related disorders and atypical antipsychotics. *International Journal of Social Psychiatry, 51,* 211–227.

Jepsen, E. K. K., Langeland, W., Sexton, H., & Heir, T. (2014). Inpatient treatment for early sexually abused adults: A naturalistic 12-month follow-up study. *Psychological Trauma: Theory, Research, Practice, and Policy, 6,* 142-151.

Jepson, J. A. (2013). Teach them to be self-aware. *Schizophrenia Bulletin, 39,* 483–484.

Jiang, Y. H., Yuen, R. K., Jin, X., Wang, M., Chen, N., Wu, X., . . . Scherer, S. W. (2013). Detection of clinically relevant genetic variants in autism spectrum disorder by whole-genome sequencing. *American Journal of Human Genetics, 93,* 249–263.

Jiann, B.-P., Su, C.-C., & Tsai, J.-Y. (2013). Is female sexual function related to the male partners' erectile function? *Journal of Sexual Medicine, 10,* 420–429.

Joelving, F. (2011). One in 16 U.S. surgeons consider suicide: Survey. *Archives of Surgery, 146(1),* 54–62.

Johns, L. C., Cannon, M., Singleton, N., Murray, R. M., Farrell, M., Brugha, T., . . . Metzer, H. (2004). Prevalence and correlates of self-reported psychotic symptoms in the British population. *British Journal of Psychiatry, 185,* 298–305.

Johnson, C. P., Myers, S. M., & Council on Children with Disabilities. (2007). Identification and evaluation of children with autism spectrum disorders. *Pediatrics, 120,* 1183–1215.

Johnson, D. P., Penn, D. L., Fredrickson, B. L., Meyer, P. S., Kring, A. M., & Brantley, M. (2009). Loving-kindness meditation to enhance recovery from negative symptoms of schizophrenia. *Journal of Clinical Psychology: In Session, 65,* 499–509.

Johnson, D. W., & Johnson, F. P. (2003). *Joining together.* Boston, MA: Allyn & Bacon.

Johnson, J. G., Cohen, P., Kasen, S., & Brook, J. S. (2006). Dissociative disorders among adults in the community, impaired functioning, and axis I and II comorbidity. *Journal of Psychiatric Research, 40,* 131–140, 2006.

Johnson, J. G., Cohen, P., Smailes, E. M., Kasen, S., & Brook, J. S. (2002). Television viewing and aggressive behavior during adolescence and adulthood. *Science, 295,* 2468–2471.

Johnson, K. A., Farris, S. G., Schmidt, N. B., Smits, J. A., & Zvolensky, M. J. (2013). Panic attack history and anxiety sensitivity in relation to cognitive-based smoking processes among treatment-seeking daily smokers. *Nicotine and Tobacco Research, 15,* 1–10.

Johnson, S. L., Edge, M. D., Holmes, M. K., & Carver, C. S. (2012). The behavioral activation system and mania. *Annual Review of Clinical Psychology, 8,* 243–267.

Johnston, L. D., O'Malley, P. M., Miech, R. A., Bachman, J. G., & Schulenberg, J. E. (2014). *Monitoring the Future national results on drug use: 1975–2013: Overview, key findings on adolescent drug use.* Ann Arbor, MI: Institute for Social Research, University of Michigan.

Joiner, T. E. (2005). *Why people die by suicide.* Cambridge, MA: Harvard University Press.

Joiner, T. E., Van Orden, K. A., Witte, T. K., Selby, E. A., Ribeiro, J. D., Lewis, R., & Rudd, M. D. (2009). Main predictions of the interpersonal-psychology theory of suicidal behavior: Empirical tests in two samples of young adults. *Journal of Abnormal Psychology, 118,* 634–646.

Joinson, C., Heron, J., Butler, U., & von Gontard, A. (2006). Psychological differences between children with and without soiling problems. *Pediatrics, 117,* 1575–1584.

Joinson, C., Heron, J., Lewis, G., Croudace, T., & Araya, R. (2011). Timing of menarche and depressive symptoms in adolescent girls from a UK cohort. *British Journal of Psychiatry, 198,* 17–23.

Jonas, B. S., Gu, Q., & Albertorio-Diaz, J. R. (2013). Psychotropic medication use among adolescents: United States, 2005–2010. *NCHS Data Brief, 135,* 1–8.

Jonas, D. E., Cusack, K., Forneris Wilkins, T. M., Sonis, J., Middleton, J. C., Feltner, C., . . . Gaynes, B. N. (2013). *Psychological and pharmacological treatments for adults with posttraumatic stress disorder.* Rockville, MD: Agency for Healthcare Research and Quality. Retrieved from http://www.ncbi.nlm.nih.gov/books/NBK137702

Jones, A. W., Holmgren, A., & Ahlner, J. (2013). Toxicology findings in suicides: Concentrations of ethanol and other drugs in femoral blood in victims of hanging and poisoning in relation to age and gender of the deceased. *Journal of Forensic and Legal Medicine, 20,* 842–847.

Jones, C., Leung, N., & Harris, G. (2007). Dysfunctional core beliefs in eating disorders: A review. *Journal of Cognitive Psychotherapy: An International Quarterly, 21,* 156–171.

Jones, W., & Klin, A. (2013). Attention to eyes is present but in decline in 2–6-month-old infants later diagnosed with autism. *Nature, 504,* 427–431.

Josselson, R., & Matilla, H. (2012). The humanity of the psychotic patient and the human approach by the therapist: A relational and intersubjective meeting. *Pragmatic Case Studies in Psychotherapy, 8,* 36–48.

Jovanovic, T., Sakoman, A. J., Kozarić-Kovačić, D., Meštrović, A. H., Duncan, E. J., Davis, M., & Norrholm, S. D. (2013). Acute stress disorder versus chronic posttraumatic stress disorder: Inhibition of fear as a function of time since trauma. *Depression and Anxiety, 30,* 217–224.

Ju, Y. E., McLeland, J. S., Toedebusch, C. D., Xiong, C., Fagan, A. M., Duntley, S. P., . . . Holtzman, D. M. (2013). Sleep quality and preclinical Alzheimer disease. *JAMA Neurology, 70,* 587–593.

Juang, L. P., & Cookston, J. T. (2009). Acculturation, discrimination, and depressive symptoms among Chinese American adolescents: A longitudinal study. *Journal of Primary Prevention, 30,* 475–496.

Judd, L. L., Schettler, P. J., Akiskal, H., Coryell, W., Fawcett, J., Fiedorowicz, J. G., . . . Keller, M. B. (2012). Prevalence and clinical significance of subsyndromal manic symptoms, including irritability and psychomotor agitation, during bipolar major depressive episodes. *Journal of Affective Disorders, 138,* 440–448.

Jupp, B., & Lawrence, A. J. (2010). New horizons for therapeutics in drug and alcohol abuse. *Pharmacological Therapy, 125,* 138–168.

Kaddena, R. M., Litt, M. D., Kabela-Cormiera, E., & Petrya, N. M. (2007). Abstinence rates following behavioral treatments for marijuana dependence. *Addictive Behaviors, 32,* 1220–1236.

Kafka, M. P. (2009). Hypersexual disorder: A proposed diagnosis for DSM-V. *Archives of Sexual Behavior, 39*(2), 377–400. doi:10.1007/s10508-009-9574-7

Kahn, R. E., Byrd, A. L., & Pardini, D. A. (2013). Callous–unemotional traits robustly predict future criminal offending in young men. *Law & Human Behavior, 37,* 87–97.

Kahn, R. E., Frick, P. J., Youngstrom, E., Findling, R. L., & Youngstrom, J. K. (2012). The effects of including a callous–unemotional specifier for the diagnosis of conduct disorder. *Journal of Child Psychology and Psychiatry, 53,* 271–282.

Kalra, G. (2013). The depressive façade in a case of compulsive sex behavior with frottage. *Indian Journal of Psychiatry, 55,* 183–186.

Kaltenthaler, E., Parry, G., Beverley, C., & Ferriter, M. (2008). Computerised cognitive-behavioural therapy for depression: Systematic review. *British Journal of Psychiatry, 193,* 181–184.

Kamarck, T. W., Muldoon, M. F., Shiffman, S. S., & Sutton-Tyrrell, K. (2007). Experiences of demand and control during daily life are predictors of carotid progression among healthy men. *Health Psychology, 26,* 324–332.

Kamat, S. A., Rajagopalan, K., Pethick, N., Willey, V., Bullano, M., & Hassan, M. J. (2008). Prevalence and humanistic impact of potential misdiagnosis of bipolar disorder among patients with major depressive disorder in a commercially insured population. *Academy of Managed Care Pharmacy, 14,* 631–642.

Kanaan, R., Armstrong, D., & Wessely, S. (2009). Limits to truth-telling: Neurologists' communication in conversion disorder. *Parent Education and Counseling, 77,* 296–301.

Kanfer, J., Busch, A., & Rusch, L. (2009). *Behavioral activation: Distinctive features.* New York, NY: Routledge.

Kangas, M. (2013). DSM-5 trauma and stress-related disorders: Implications for screening for cancer-related stress. *Frontiers in Psychiatry, 4,* 122. doi:10.3389/fpsyt.2013.00122

Kannai, R. (2009). Munchausen by mommy. *Families, Systems, & Health, 27,* 105–112.

Kanner, L. (1943). Autistic disturbances of affective content. *Nervous Child, 2,* 217–240.

Kanter, J. W., Puspitasari, A. J., Santos, M. M., & Nagy, G. A. (2012). Behavioural activation: History, evidence and promise. *British Journal of Psychiatry, 200,* 361–363.

Kantrowitz, B., & Scelfo, J. (2006, November 27). What happens when they grow up? *Newsweek,* pp. 47–53.

Kapalko, J. (2010, June 18). Pro-ana websites abound. *Salon.* Retrieved from http://www.salon.com

Kaplan, M. S., & Krueger, R. B. (2012). Cognitive-behavioral treatment of the paraphilias. *Israel Journal of Psychiatry & Related Sciences, 49,* 291–296.

Kaplan, M. S., McFarland, B. H., Huguet, N., Conner, K., Caetano, R., Giesbrecht, N., & Nolte, K. B. (2012). Acute alcohol intoxication and suicide: A gender-stratified analysis of the National Violent Death Reporting System. *Injury Prevention, 19,* 38–43.

Karatsoreos, I. N., & McEwen, B. S. (2013). Annual research review: The neurobiology and physiology of resilience and adaptation across the life course. *Journal of Child Psychology and Psychiatry, 54,* 337–347.

Karceski, S. (2013). Alzheimer disease: Which test is best? *Neurology, 81,* e32.

Karg, K., Burmeister, M., Shedden, K., & Sen, S. (2011). The serotonin transporter promoter variant (5–HTTLPR), stress, and depression meta-analysis revisited: Evidence of genetic moderation. *Archives of General Psychiatry, 68*(5), 444–454. doi:10.1001/archgenpsychiatry.2010.189

Karila, L., Wéry, A., Weinstein, A., Cottencin, O., Reynaud, M., & Billieux, J. (2013). Sexual addiction or hypersexual disorder: Different terms for the same problem? A review of the literature. *Current Pharmaceutical Design, 20,* 4012–4020.

Kariuki-Nyuthe, C., Gomez-Mancilla, B., & Stein, D. J. (2014). Obsessive compulsive disorder and the glutamatergic system. *Current Opinion in Psychiatry, 27,* 32–37.

Karno, M., & Golding, J. M. (1991). Obsessive-compulsive disorder. In L. N. Robins & D. A. Regier (Eds.), *Psychiatric disorders in America: The Epidemiologic Catchment Area study* (pp. 204–219). New York, NY: Free Press.

Karra, E., O'Daly, O. G., Choudhury, A. I., Yousseif, A., Millership, S., & Neary, M. T., . . . Batterham, R. L. (2013). A link between FTO, ghrelin, and impaired brain food-cue responsivity. *Journal of Clinical Investigation, 123,* 3539-3551.

Kasari, C., Rotheram-Fuller, E., Locke, J., & Gulsrud., A. (2012). Making the connection: Randomized controlled trial of social skills at school for children with autism spectrum disorders. *Journal of Child Psychology and Psychiatry, 53,* 431–439.

Kasen S., Wickramaratne, P., & Gameroff, M. J. (2013, May 29). Religiosity and longitudinal change in psychosocial functioning in adult offspring of depressed parents at high risk for major depression. *Depression and Anxiety.* doi:10.1002/da.22131

Kasen, S., Wickramaratne, P., Gameroff, M. J., & Weissman, M. M. (2012). Religiosity and resilience in persons at high risk for major depression. *Psychological Medicine, 42,* 509–519.

Kashdan, T. B., Ferssizidis, P., Farmer, A. S., Adams, L. M., & McKnight, P. E. (2013). Failure to capitalize on sharing good news with romantic partners: Exploring positivity deficits of socially anxious people with self-reports, partner-reports, and behavioral observations. *Behaviour Research and Therapy, 51,* 656–668.

Kashdan, T. B., & Rottenberg, J. (2010). Psychological flexibility as a fundamental aspect of health. *Clinical Psychology Review, 30,* 865–878.

Kastelan, A., Franciskovic, T., Moro, L., Roncevic-Grzeta, I., Grkovic, J., Jurcan, V., . . . Girotto, I. (2007). Psychotic symptoms in combat-related posttraumatic stress disorder. *Military Medicine, 172,* 273–277.

Kato, K., Sullivan, P. F., Evengard, B., & Pedersen, N. L. (2009). A population-based twin study of functional somatic syndromes. *Psychological Medicine, 39,* 497–505.

Katon, W. J. (2010). Asthma, suicide risk, and psychiatric comorbidity. *American Journal of Psychiatry, 167,* 1020–1022.

Katzer, A., Oberfeld, D., Hiller, W., Gerlach, A. L., & Witthoft, M. (2012). Tactile perceptual processes and their relationship to somatoform disorders. *Journal of Abnormal Psychology, 121,* 530–543.

Kaufman, L., Ayub, M., & Vincent, J. B. (2010). The genetic basis of non-syndromic intellectual disability: A review. *Journal of Neurodevelopmental Disorders, 2,* 182–209.

Kay, C., & Green, J. (2013). Reactive attachment disorder following early maltreatment: Systematic evidence beyond the institution. *Journal of Abnormal Child Psychology, 41,* 571–581.

Kaye, S., Darke, S., & Duflou, J. (2009). Methylenedioxy-methamphetamine (MDMA)–related fatalities in Australia: Demographics, circumstances, toxicology and major organ pathology. *Drug and Alcohol Dependence, 104,* 254–261.

Kaye, W. H., Wierenga, C. E., Bailer, U. F., Simmons, A. N., Wagner, A., & Bischoff-Grethe, A. (2013). Does a shared neurobiology for foods and drugs of abuse contribute to extremes of food ingestion in anorexia and bulimia nervosa? *Biological Psychiatry, 73,* 836–842.

Kaynak, O., Meyers, K., Caldeira, K. M., Vincent, K. B., Winters, K. C., & Arria, A. M. (2013). Relationships among parental monitoring and sensation seeking on the development of substance use disorder among college students. *Addictive Behavior, 38,* 1457–1463.

Kazdin, A. E., Whitley, M., & Marciano, P. L. (2006). Child-therapist and parent-therapist alliance and therapeutic change in the treatment of children referred for oppositional, aggressive, and antisocial behavior. *Journal of Child Psychology and Psychiatry, 47,* 436–445.

Kean, C. (2011). Battling with the life instinct: The paradox of the self and suicidal behavior in psychosis. *Schizophrenia Bulletin, 37,* 4–7.

Kearney, D. J., McDermott, K., Malte, C., Martinez, M., & Simpson, T. L. (2012). Association of participation in a mindfulness program with measures of PTSD, depression and quality of life in a veteran sample. *Journal of Clinical Psychology, 68,* 101–116.

Keating, G. M., & Lyseng-Williamson, K. A. (2010). Varenicline: A pharmacoeconomic review of its use as an aid to smoking cessation. *Pharmacoeconomics, 28,* 231–254.

Keel, P. K., Forney, K. J., Brown, T. A., & Heatherton, T. F. (2013). Influence of college peers on disordered eating in women and men at 10-year follow-up. *Journal of Abnormal Psychology, 122,* 105–110.

Keeton, C. P., Ginsburg, G. S., Drake, K. L., Sakolsky, D., Kendall, P. C., Birmaher, B., . . . Walkup, J. T. (2013). Benefits of child-focused anxiety treatments for parents and family functioning. *Depression & Anxiety, 30,* 865–872.

Keita, G. P. (2012, March). Psychology's role in the recovery movement. *Monitor on Psychology, 43.*

Kelleher, I., & Cannon, M. (2010). Psychotic-like experiences in the general population: Characterizing a high-risk group for psychosis. *Psychological Medicine, 41*(1), 1–6. doi:10.1017/S0033291710001005

Kelleher, I., Keeley, H., Corcoran, P., Lynch, F., Fitzpatrick, C., Devlin, N., . . . Cannon, M. (2012). Clinicopathological significance of psychotic experiences in non-psychotic young people: Evidence from four population-based studies. *British Journal of Psychiatry, 201,* 26–32.

Kelleher, I., Keeley, H., Corcoran, P., Ramsay, H., Wasserman, C., Carli, V., . . . Cannon, M. (2013). Childhood trauma and psychosis in a prospective cohort study: Cause, effect, and directionality. *American Journal of Psychiatry, 170,* 734–741.

Keller, R. M., & Calgay, C. E. (2010). Microaggressive experiences of people with disabilities. In D. W. Sue (Ed.), *Microaggressions and marginality: Manifestation, dynamics and impact* (pp. 241–267). Hoboken, NJ: Wiley.

Kellogg, N. D. (2009). Clinical report—The evaluation of sexual behaviors in children. *Pediatrics, 124,* 992–998.

Kelly, J. F., Stout, R. L., Magill, M., Tonigan, J. S., Pagano, M. E. (2011). Spirituality in recovery: A lagged mediational analysis of Alcoholics Anonymous' principal theoretical mechanism of behavior change. *Alcoholism: Clinical & Experimental Research, 35,* 454–463.

Kelly, V. L., Barker, H., Field, A. P., Wilson, C., & Reynolds, S. (2010). Can Rachman's indirect pathways be used to un-learn fear? A prospective paradigm to test whether children's fears can be reduced using positive information and modeling a non-anxious response. *Behaviour Research and Therapy, 48,* 164–170.

Keltner, N. G., & Dowben, J. S. (2007). Psychobiological substrates of posttraumatic stress disorder: Part 1. *Perspectives in Psychiatric Care, 43,* 97–101.

Kendall, P. C., Khanna, M. S., Edson, A., Cummings, C., & Harris, M. S. (2011). Computers and psychosocial treatment for child anxiety: Recent advances and ongoing efforts. *Depression and Anxiety, 28,* 58–66.

Kendall-Tackett, K. (2009). Psychological trauma and physical health: A psychoneuroimmunology approach to etiology of negative health effects and possible interventions. *Psychological Trauma: Theory, Research, Practice, and Policy, 1,* 35–48.

Kendler, K. S., & Prescott, C. A. (2006). *Genes, environment, and psychopathology: Understanding the causes of psychiatric and substance use disorders.* New York, NY: Guilford Press.

Kendzor, D. E., Businelle, M. S., Reitzel, L. R., Castro, Y., Vidrine, J. I., Mazas, C. A., . . . Wetter, D.W. (2014). The influence of discrimination on smoking cessation among Latinos. *Drug and Alcohol Dependence, 136,* 143–148.

Kern, S. E. (2009). Challenges in conducting clinical trials in children: Approaches for improving performance. *Expert Review of Clinical Pharmacology, 2*(6), 609–617.

Kerr, P. L., Muehlenkamp, J. J., & Turner, J. M. (2010). Nonsuicidal self-injury: A review of current research for family medicine and primary care physicians. *Journal of the American Board of Family Medicine, 23,* 240–259.

Kersting, A., Brähler, E., Glaesmer, H., & Wagner, B. (2011). Prevalence of complicated grief in a representative population-based sample. *Journal of Affective Disorders, 131,* 339–343.

Kessing, L. V., Hellmund, G., Geddes, J. R., Goodwin, G. M., & Andersen, P. K. (2011). Valproate v. lithium in the treatment of bipolar disorder in clinical practice: Observational nationwide register-based cohort study. *British Journal of Psychiatry, 199,* 57–63.

Kessler, D., Lewis, G., Kaur, S., Wiles, N., King, M., Weich, S., . . . Peters, T. J. (2009). Therapist-delivered Internet psychotherapy for depression in primary care: A randomized controlled trial. *Lancet, 374,* 628–634.

Kessler, R. C. (2003). Epidemiology of women and depression. *Journal of Affective Disorders, 74,* 5–13.

Kessler, R. C., Akiskal, H. S., Ames, M., Birnbaum, H., Greenberg, P., Hirschfeld, R. M.,. . . Wang, P. S. (2006). Prevalence and effects of mood disorders on work performance in a nationally representative sample of U.S. workers. *American Journal of Psychiatry, 163,* 1561–1568.

Kessler, R. C., Berglund, P., Demler, O., Jin, R., Merikangas, K. R., & Walters, E. E. (2005). Lifetime prevalence and age-of-onset distribution of DSM-IV disorders in the National Comorbidity Survey Replication. *Archives of General Psychiatry, 62,* 593–602.

Kessler, R. C., Chiu, W. T., Demler, O., & Walters, E. E. (2005). Prevalence, severity, and comorbidity of 12-month DSM-IV disorders in the National Comorbidity Survey Replication. *Archives of General Psychiatry, 62,* 617–627.

Kessler, R. C., Petukhova, M., Sampson, N. A., Zaslavsky, A. M., & Wittchen, H.-U. (2012). Twelve-month and lifetime prevalence and lifetime morbid risk of anxiety and mood disorders in the United States. *International Journal of Methods in Psychiatric Research, 21,* 169–184.

Ketter, T. A. (2010). Diagnostic features, prevalence, and impact of bipolar disorder. *Journal of Clinical Psychiatry, 71,* e14.

Keyes, K. M., Hatzenbuehler, M. L., Grant, B. F., & Hasin, D. S. (2012). Stress and alcohol: Epidemiologic evidence. *Alcohol Research, 34,* 391–400.

Khadka, S., Meda, S. A., Stevens, M. C., Glahn, D. C., Calhoun, V. D., Sweeney, J. A., . . . Pearlson, G. D. (2013). Is aberrant functional connectivity a psychosis endophenotype? A resting state functional magnetic resonance imaging study. *Biological Psychiatry, 74,* 458–466.

Kidd, T., Hamer, M., & Steptoe, A. (2011). Examining the association between adult attachment style and cortisol responses to acute stress. *Psychoneuroendocrinology, 36,* 771–779.

Kidger, J. (2011). The association between bankruptcy and hospital-presenting attempted suicide: A record linkage study. *Suicide and Life-Threatening Behavior, 41,* 676–684.

Kiecolt-Glaser, J. (2009). Is stress a risk factor for cancer? *U.S. News and World Report.* Retrieved from http://health .usnews.com/health-news/blogs/health-advice/2009/02/19/is-stress-a-risk-factor-for-cancer.html

Kikuchi, H., Fujii, T., Abe, N., Suzuki, M., Takagi, M., Mugikura, S., . . . Mori, E. (2010). Memory repression: Brain mechanism underlying dissociative amnesia. *Journal of Cognitive Neuroscience, 22,* 602–613.

Kilpatrick, D. G., Amstadter, A. B., Resnick, H. S., & Ruggiero, K. J. (2007). Rape-related PTSD: Issues and interventions. *Psychiatric Times, 24,* 1–3.

Kilpatrick, D. G., Koenen, K. C., Ruggiero, K. J., Acierno, R., Galea, S., Resnick, H. S., . . . Gelernter, J. (2008). The serotonin transporter genotype and social support and moderation of post-traumatic stress disorder and depression in hurricane-exposed adults. *American Journal of Psychiatry, 164,* 1693–1699.

Kilpeläinen, T. O., Qi, L., Brage, S., Sharp, S. J., Sonestedt, E., Demerath, E., . . . Loos, R. J. F. (2011). Physical activity attenuates the influence of *FTO* variants on obesity risk: A meta-analysis of 218,166 adults and 19,268 children. *PLOS Medicine, 8*(11), e1001116. doi:10.1371/journal.pmed.1001116

Kim, S. H., Schneider, S. M., Bevans, M., Kravitz, L., Mermier, C., Qualls, C., & Burge, M. R. (2013). PTSD symptom reduction with mindfulness-based stretching and deep breathing exercise: Randomized controlled clinical trial of efficacy. *Journal of Clinical Endocrinology and Metabolism, 98,* 2984–2992.

Kim, S. Y., Chen, Q., Li, J., Huang, X., & Moon, U. J. (2009). Parent-child acculturation, parenting, and adolescent depressive symptoms in Chinese immigrant families. *Journal of Family Psychology, 23,* 426–437.

Kim, Y., & Berrios, G. E. (2001). Impact of the term schizophrenia on the culture of ideograph: The Japanese experience. *Schizophrenia Bulletin, 27,* 181–185.

King, C. A., & Merchant, C. R. (2008). Social and interpersonal factors relating to adolescent suicidality: A review of the literature. *Archives of Suicide Research, 12,* 181–196.

King, N. J., Eleonora, G., & Ollendick, T. H. (1998). Etiology of childhood phobias: Current status of Rachman's three pathways theory. *Behavior Research and Therapy, 36,* 297–309.

Kinsey, A. C., Pomeroy, W. B., & Martin, C. E. (1948). *Sexual behavior in the human male.* Philadelphia, PA: Saunders.

Kinsey, A. C., Pomeroy, W. B., Martin, C. E., & Gebhard, P. H. (1953). *Sexual behavior in the human female.* Philadelphia, PA: Saunders.

Kirk-Sanchez, N. J., & McGough, E. L. (2014). Physical exercise and cognitive performance in the elderly: Current perspectives. *Clinical Interventions in Aging, 9,* 51–62.

Kisch, J., Leino, E. V., & Silverman, M. M. (2005). Aspects of suicidal behavior, depression and treatment in college students: Results from the spring 2000 National College Health Assessment Survey. *Suicide and Life-Threatening Behavior, 35,* 3–13.

Kissin, I. (2013). Long-term opioid treatment of chronic nonmalignant pain: Unproven efficacy and neglected safety? *Journal of Pain Research, 6,* 513–529.

Klages, T., Geller, B., Tillman, R., Bolhofner, K., & Zimerman, B. (2005). Controlled study of encopresis and enuresis in children with a prepubertal and early adolescent bipolar I disorder phenotype. *Journal of the American Academy of Child & Adolescent Psychiatry, 44,* 1050–1057.

Klauke, B., Deckert, J., Reif, A., Pauli, P., & Domschke, K. (2010). Life events in panic disorder—An update on "candidate stressors." *Depression and Anxiety, 27,* 716–730.

Kleeman, J. (2011, February 25). Sick note: Faking illness online. *Guardian.* Retrieved from http://www.guardian-news.com

Kleim, B., Grey, N., Wild, J., Nussbeck, F. W., Stott, R., Hackmann, A., . . . Ehlers, A. (2013). Cognitive change predicts symptom reduction with cognitive therapy for posttraumatic stress disorder. *Journal of Consulting and Clinical Psychology, 81,* 383–393.

Kleinhaus, K., Harlap, S., Perrin, M. C., Manor, O., Weiser, M., Harkavy-Friedman, J. M., . . . Malaspina, D. (2012). Catatonic schizophrenia: A cohort prospective study. *Schizophrenia Bulletin, 38,* 331–337.

Kleinman, A. (2004). Culture and depression. *New England Journal of Medicine, 351,* 951–953.

Klemm, W. (2010). Traumatic memories, part II. Post-traumatic stress treatment. Retrieved from http://www.psychology-today.com/blog/memory-medic/201009/traumatic-memories-part-ii-post-traumatic-stress-treatment

Klimes-Dougan, B., Klingbeil, D. A., & Meller, S. J. (2013). Suicide-prevention programs on the help-seeking attitudes and behaviors of youths. *Crisis, 34,* 82–97.

Kline, T. J. (2005). *Psychological testing: A practical approach to design and evaluation.* Thousand Oaks, CA: Sage.

Klonsky, E. D., & Glenn, C. R. (2011). Non-suicidal self-injury: What independent practitioners should know. Retrieved from http://www.42online.org/node/163

Klopfer, B., & Davidson, H. (1962). *The Rorschach technique.* New York, NY: Harcourt, Brace & World.

Kluft, R. P. (1987). Dr. Kluft replies. *American Journal of Psychiatry, 144,* 125.

Knabb, J. J., Vogt, R. G., & Newgren, K. P. (2011). MMPI-2 characteristics of the old order Amish: A comparison of clinical, nonclinical and United States normative samples. *Psychological Assessment, 23,* 865–875.

Knapik, G. P., Martsolf, D. S., Draucker, C. B., & Strickland, K. D. (2010).

Attributes of spirituality described by survivors of sexual violence. *Qualitative Report, 15,* 644–657.

Knight, T., Steeves, T., Day, L., Lowerison, M., Jette., N, & Pringsheim, T. (2012). Prevalence of tic disorders: A systematic review and meta-analysis. *Pediatric Neurology, 47,* 77–90.

Kobayashi, I., Cowdin, N., & Mellman, T. A. (2012). One's sex, sleep, and post-traumatic stress disorder. *Biology of Sex Differences, 3,* 29.

Koerner, K. & Linehan, M. M. (2011). *Doing dialectical behavior therapy: A practical guide.* New York, NY: Guilford Press.

Kohler, J. (2001, March 30). Therapists on trial in death of girl, 10. *Washington Post,* p. A19.

Kohut, H. (1977). *The restoration of the self.* Chicago, IL: University of Chicago Press.

Kois, L., Pearson, J., Chauhan, P., Goni, M., & Saraydarian, L. (2013). Competency to stand trial among female inpatients. *Law and Human Behavior, 37,* 231–240.

Kollannoor-Samuel, G., Wagner, J., Damio, G., Segura-Pérez, S., Chhabra, J., Vega-López, S., & Pérez-Escamilla, R. (2011). Social support modifies the association between household food insecurity and depression among Latinos with uncontrolled type 2 diabetes. *Journal of Immigrant and Minority Health, 13,* 982–989.

Kolli, V., Sharma, A., Amani, M., Bestha, D., & Chaturvedi, R. (2013). Letter to the editor—"Meow meow" (mephedrone) and catatonia. *Innovations in Clinical Neuroscience, 10,* 10–16.

Kong, L. C., Tap, J., Aron-Wisnewsky, J., Pelloux, V., Basdevant, A., Bouillot, J. L., . . . Clément, K. (2013). *American Journal of Clinical Nutrition, 98,* 16–24.

Koob, G. F. (2013). Addiction is a reward deficit and stress surfeit disorder. *Frontiers* in Psychiatry, 4, doi: 10.3389/fpsyt.2013.00072. eCollection

Koob, G. F., Buck, C. L., Cohen, A., Edwards, S., Park, P. E., Schlosburg, J. E., . . . George, O. (2014). Addiction as a stress surfeit disorder. *Neuropharmacology, 76*(pt B), 370–382. doi:10.1016/j.neuropharm.2013.05.024

Koocher, G. P., & Keith-Spiegel, P. (2008). *Ethics in psychology and the mental health profession: Standards and cases* (3rd ed.). Oxford, UK: Oxford University Press.

Kooistra, L., Crawford, S., Gibbard, B., Ramage, B., & Kaplan, B. J. (2010). Differentiating attention deficits in children with fetal alcohol spectrum disorder or attention-deficit-hyperactivity disorder. *Developmental Medicine & Child Neurology, 52,* 205–211.

Kopelman, M. D. (2002). Disorders of memory. *Brain, 125,* 2152–2190.

Koss, M. P., Gidycz, C. A., & Wisniewski, N. (1987). The scope of rape: Incidence and prevalence of sexual aggression and victimization in a national sample of higher education students. *Journal of Consulting and Clinical Psychology, 55,* 162–170.

Kossowsky, J., Wilhelm, F. H., Roth, W. T., & Schneider, S. (2012). Separation anxiety disorder in children: Disorder-specific responses to experimental separation from the mother. *Journal of Child Psychology and Psychiatry, 53,* 178–187.

Kosten, T., Domingo, C., Orson, F., & Kinsey, B. (2014). Vaccines against stimulants: Cocaine and MA. *British Journal of Clinical Pharmacology, 77,* 368–374.

Koszewska, I., & Rybakowski, J. K. (2009). Antidepressant-induced mood conversions in bipolar disorder: A retrospective study of tricyclic versus non-tricyclic antidepressant drugs. *Neuropsychobiology, 59,* 12–16.

Koszycki, D., Taljaard, M., Segal, Z., & Bradwejn, J. (2011). A randomized trial of sertraline, self-administered cognitive behavior therapy, and their combination for panic disorder. *Psychological Medicine, 41,* 371–381.

Kotwicki, R., & Harvey, P. D. (2013). Systematic study of structured diagnostic procedures in outpatient psychiatric rehabilitation: A three-year, three-cohort study of the stability of psychiatric diagnoses. *Innovations of Clinical Neuroscience, 10,* 14–19.

Kowal, S. L., Dall, T. M., Chakrabarti, R., Storm, M. V., & Jain, A. (2013). The current and projected economic burden of Parkinson's disease in the United States. *Movement Disorders, 28,* 311–318.

Kponee, K. Z., Siegel, M., & Jernigan, D. H. (2014). The use of caffeinated alcoholic beverages among underage drinkers: Results of a national survey. *Addictive Behavior, 39,* 253–258.

Kraepelin, E. (1923). *Textbook of psychiatry* (8th ed.). New York, NY: Macmillan. (Original work published 1883)

Kraus, R. P., & Nicholson, I. R. (1996). AIDS-related obsessive compulsive disorder: Deconditioning based in fluoxetine-induced inhibition of anxiety. *Journal of Behavior Therapy and Experimental Psychiatry, 27*, 51–56.

Kroll, J. (2007, July 1). No-suicide contracts as a suicide prevention strategy. *Psychiatric Times, 24*, 2.

Kroon, J. S., Wohlfarth, T. D., Dieleman, J., Sutterland, A. L., Storosum, J. G., Denys, D., . . . Sturkenboom, M. C. (2013). Incidence rates and risk factors of bipolar disorder in the general population: A population-based cohort study. *Bipolar Disorders, 15*, 306–313.

Krueger, J. (2011). Shock without awe. *American Psychologist, 66*, 642–643.

Krueger, R. B. (2010a). The DSM diagnostic criteria for sexual masochism. *Archives of Sexual Behavior, 39*, 346–356.

Krueger, R. B. (2010b). The DSM diagnostic criteria for sexual sadism. *Archives of Sexual Behavior, 39*, 325–345.

Krystal, A. D. (2012). Psychiatric disorders and sleep. *Neurologic Clinics, 30*, 1389–1413.

Ku, H. L., Lin, C. S., Chao, H. T., Tu, P. C., Li, C. T., Cheng, C. M., . . . Hsieh, J. C. (2013). Brain signature characterizing the body-brain-mind axis of transsexuals. *PLOS One, 8*, e70808. doi:10.1371/journal.pone.0070808

Kubany, E. S., Hill, E. E., Owens, J. A., Iannce-Spencer, C., McCaig, M. A., Tremayne, K. J., & William, P. L. (2004). Cognitive trauma therapy for battered women with PTSD (CTT-BW). *Journal of Consulting and Clinical Psychology, 72*, 3–18.

Kuehn, B. M. (2010). Integrated care key for patients with both addiction and mental illness. *Journal of the American Medical Association, 303*, 1905–1907.

Kuehnle, K., & Connell, M. (2009). *The evaluation of child sexual abuse allegations: A comprehensive guide to assessment and testimony.* Hoboken, NJ: John Wiley.

Kuhl, E. S., Hoodin, F., Rice, J., Felt, B. T., Rausch, J. R., & Patton, S. R. (2010). Increasing daily water intake and fluid adherence in children receiving treatment for retentive encopresis. *Journal of Pediatric Psychology, 35*, 1144–1151.

Kung, S., Espinel, Z., & Lapid, M. I. (2012). Treatment of nightmares with prazosin: A systematic review. *Mayo Clinic Proceedings, 87*, 890–900.

Kung, W. W., & Lu, P. C. (2008). How symptom manifestations affect help seeking for mental health problems among Chinese Americans. *Journal of Nervous and Mental Disease, 196*, 46–54.

Kuo, C.-J., Chen, V. C.-H., Lee, W.-C., Chen, W. J., Ferri, C. P., Stewart, R., . . . Ko, Y.-C. (2010). Asthma and suicide mortality in young people: A 12-year follow-up study. *American Journal of Psychiatry, 167*, 1092–1099.

Kuo, J. R., & Linehan, M. M. (2009). Disentangling emotion processes in borderline personality disorder: Physiological and self-reported assessment of biological vulnerability, baseline intensity, and reactivity to emotionally evocative stimuli. *Journal of Abnormal Psychology, 118*, 531–544.

Kupfer, D. (2013). *Chair of DSM-5 task force discusses future of mental health research.* Arlington, VA: American Psychiatric Association.

Kuramoto, S. J., Runeson, B., Stuart, E. A., Lichtenstein, P., & Wilcox, H. C. (2013). Time to hospitalization for suicide attempt by the timing of parental suicide during offspring early development. *JAMA Psychiatry, 70*, 149–157.

Kuramoto, S., Stuart, E. A., Runeson, B., Lichtenstein, P., Långström, N., & Wilcox, H. C. (2010). Maternal or paternal suicide and offspring's psychiatric and suicide-attempt hospitalization risk. *Pediatrics, 126*, 1026–1032.

Kurlan, R. M. (2013). Treatment of Tourette syndrome. *Neurotherapeutics, 11*, 161–165.

Kusek, K. (2001, May). Could a fear wreak havoc on your life? *Cosmopolitan, 230*(5), 182–184.

Kuss, D. J. (2013). Internet gaming addiction: Current perspectives. *Psychological Research and Behavior Management, 6*, 125–137.

Kvaale, E. P., Gottdiener, W. H., & Haslam, N. (2013). Biogenic explanations and stigma: A meta-analytic review of associations among lay people. *Social Science & Medicine, 96*, 95–103.

Kvaale, E. P., Haslam, N., & Gottdiener, W. H. (2013). The "side effects" of medicalization: A meta-analytic review of how biogenetic explanations affect stigma. *Clinical Psychology Review, 33*, 782–794.

Lab, D. D., & Moore, E. (2005). Prevalence and denial of sexual abuse in a male psychiatric inpatient population. *Journal of Traumatic Stress, 18*, 323–330.

Labonté, B., Suderman, M., Maussion, G., Lopez, J. P., Navarro-Sánchez, L., Yerko, V., . . . Turecki, G. (2013) Genome-wide methylation changes in the brains of suicide completers. *American Journal of Psychiatry, 170*, 511–520.

Labonté, B., Suderman, M., Maussion, G., Navaro, L., Yerko, V., Mahar, I., . . . Gustavo, T. (2012). Genome-wide epigenetic regulation by early-life trauma. *Archives of General Psychiatry, 69*, 722–731.

Labonté, B., & Turecki, G. (2010). The epigenetics of suicide: Explaining the biological effects of early life environmental adversity. *Archives of Suicide Research, 14*, 291–310.

Labrie, J. W., Napper, L. E., & Hummer, J. F. (2014). Normative feedback for parents of college students: Piloting a parent based intervention to correct misperceptions of students' alcohol use and other parents' approval of drinking. *Addictive Behaviors, 39*, 107–113.

Ladouceur, R., Freeston, M. H., Rheaume, J., Dugas, M. J., Gagnon, F., Thibodeau, N., Fournier, S. (2000). Strategies used with intrusive thoughts: A comparison of OCD patients with anxious and community controls. *Journal of Abnormal Psychology, 109*, 179–187.

Lahey, B. B., Loeber, R., Burke, J. D., & Applegate, B. (2005). Predicting future antisocial personality disorder in males from a clinical assessment in childhood. *Journal of Consulting and Clinical Psychology, 73*, 389–399.

Lam, D. (2009). Can the behavioral approach system (BAS) dysregulation theory help us to understand psychosocial interventions in bipolar disorders? *Clinical Psychology: Science and Practice, 16*, 476–477.

Lam, R. W., Levitt, A. J., Levitan, R. D., Enns, M. W., Morehouse, R., Michalak, E. E., & Tam, E. M. (2006). The Can-SAD study: A randomized controlled trial of the effectiveness of light therapy and fluoxetine in patients with winter seasonal affective disorder. *American Journal of Psychiatry, 163*, 805–812.

Lamb, H. R., & Weinberger, I. E. (2005). One year follow up of persons discharged from a locked intermediate care facility. *Psychiatric Services, 56*, 198–201.

Lambiase, M. J., Kubzansky, L. D., & Thurston, R. C. (2014). Prospective study of anxiety and incident stroke. *Stroke, 45*, 438–443.

Lambie, I., & Randell, I. (2013). The impact of incarceration on juvenile offenders. *Clinical Psychology Review, 33*, 448–459.

Lambley, P. (1974). Treatment of transvestism and subsequent coital problems. *Journal of Behavior Therapy and Experimental Psychiatry, 5*, 101–102.

Lampert, E. J., Roy Choudhury, K. R., Hostage, C. A., Petrella, J. R., & Doraiswamy, P. M. (2013). Prevalence of Alzheimer's pathologic endophenotypes in asymptomatic and mildly impaired first-degree relatives. *PLOS One, 8*, e60747.

The Lancet Neurology. (2010). Dispelling the stigma of Huntington's disease. *The Lancet Neurology, 9*, 751. doi:10.1016/S1474-4422(10)70170-8

Landa, R. J., Holman, K. C., O'Neill, A. H., & Stuart, E. A. (2011). Intervention targeting development of socially synchronous engagement in toddlers with autism spectrum disorder: A randomized controlled trial. *Journal of Child Psychology and Psychiatry, 52*, 22–23.

Landau, S. M., Marks, S. M., Mormino, E. C., Rabinovici, G. D., Oh, H., O'Neil, J. P., . . . Jagust, W. J. (2012). Association of lifetime cognitive engagement and low b-amyloid deposition. *Archives of Neurology, 69*, 623–629. doi:10.1001/archneurol.2011.2748

Landis, E. E. (2012). Restoration of competency. Retrieved from http://lawandjusticegov.org/psychology-and-law/criminal-competencies/98-restoration-of-competency.html

Landrigan, P. J. (2010). What causes autism? Exploring the environmental contribution. *Current Opinions in Pediatrics, 22*, 219–225.

Laney, C., & Loftus, E. F. (2005). Traumatic memories are not necessarily accurate memories. *Canadian Journal of Psychiatry, 50*, 823–828.

Lange, N., Dubray, M. B., Lee, J. E., Froimowitz, M. P., Froehlich, A., Adluru, N., . . . Lainhart, J. E. (2010). Atypical diffusion tensor hemispheric asymmetry in autism. *Autism Research, 3*(6), 350–358. doi:10.1002/aur.162

Långström, N. (2010). The DSM diagnostic criteria for exhibitionism, voyeurism, and frotteurism. *Archives of Sexual Behavior, 39*, 317–324.

Långström, N., Enebrink, P., Laurén, E. M., Lindblom, J., Werkö, S., & Hanson, R. K. (2013). Preventing sexual abusers of children from reoffending: Systematic review of medical and psychological interventions. *British Medical Journal, 9*, 347:f4630. doi:10.1136/bmj.f4630

Långström, N., & Seto, M. C. (2006). Exhibitionistic and voyeuristic behavior in a Swedish National Population Survey. *Archives of Sexual Behavior, 35*, 427–435.

Langstrom, N., & Zucker, K. J. (2005). Transvestic fetishism in the general population: Prevalence and correlates. *Journal of Sex and Marital Therapy, 31*, 87–95.

Large, M., Sharma, S., Compton, M. T., Slade, T., & Nielssen, O. (2011). Cannabis use and earlier onset of psychosis: A systematic meta-analysis. *Archives of General Psychiatry, 68*, 555–561. doi:10.1001/archgenpsychiatry.2011.5

Larkin, K. T., & Zayfert, C. (1996). Anger management training with mild essential hypertensive patients. *Journal of Behavioral Medicine, 19*, 415–433.

Larsen, S. E., & Fitzgerald, L. F. (2011). PTSD symptoms and sexual harassment: The role of attributions and perceived control. *Journal of Interpersonal Violence, 26*, 2555–2567.

Larson, K., Russ, S. A., Kahn, R. S., & Halfon, N. (2011). Patterns of comorbidity, functioning, and service use for US children with ADHD, 2007. *Pediatrics, 127*(3), 462–470. doi:10.1542/peds.2010-0165

Larsson, B., & Fischtel, Å. (2012). Headache prevalence and characteristics among school children as assessed by prospective paper diary recordings. *Journal of Headache and Pain, 13*, 129–136. doi:10.1007/s10194-011-0410-9

Larsson, H., Rydén, E., Boman, M., Långström, N., Lichtenstein, P., & Landén, M. (2013). Risk of bipolar disorder and schizophrenia in relatives of people with attention-deficit hyperactivity disorder. *British Journal of Psychiatry, 203*, 103–106.

Larsson, M., Weiss, B., Janson, S., Sundell, J., & Bornehag, C. G. (2009). Associations between indoor environmental factors and parental-reported autistic spectrum disorders in children 6–8 years of age. *Neurotoxicology, 30*, 822–831.

Latas, M., & Milovanovic, S. (2014). Personality disorders and anxiety disorders: What is the relationship? *Current Opinion in Psychiatry, 27*, 57–61.

Latimer, W., & Zur, J. (2010). Epidemiologic trends of adolescent use of alcohol, tobacco, and other drugs. *Child and Adolescent Psychiatric Clinics of North America, 19*, 451–464.

Laumann, E. O., Glasser, D. B., Neves, R. C. S., & Moreira, E. D. (2009). A population-based survey of sexual activity, sexual problems and associated help-seeking behavior patterns in mature adults in the United States of America. *International Journal of Impotence Research, 21*, 171–178.

Lavakumar, M., Garlow, S. J., & Schwartz, A. C. (2011). A case of returning psychosis. *Current Psychiatry, 10*, 51–57.

Lavelle, M., Healey, P. G., & McCabe, R. (2013). Is nonverbal communication disrupted in interactions involving patients with schizophrenia? *Schizophrenia Bulletin, 39*, 1150–1158.

Lawrence, A. A. (2008). Gender identity disorders in adults: Diagnosis and treatment. In D. Rowland & L. Incrocci (Eds.), *Handbook of sexual and gender identity disorders* (pp. 423–456). Hoboken, NJ: Wiley.

Lazarov, O., Mattson, M. P., Peterson, D. A., Pimplika, S. W., & van Praag, H. (2010). When neurogenesis encounters aging and disease. *Trends in Neuroscience, 33*, 569–579.

lcouvrely Binging & purging: Bulimia [online forum comment]. Retrieved from http://www.caloriesperhour.com/forums/forum25/656.html

Leahey, T. M., Crowther, J. H., & Ciesla, J. A. (2011). An ecological momentary assessment of the effects of weight and shape social comparisons on women with eating pathology, high body dissatisfaction, and low body dissatisfaction. *Behavior Therapy, 42*, 197–210.

Leahy, R. L., Beck, J., & Beck, A. T. (2005). Cognitive therapy for the personality disorders. In S. Strack (Ed.), *Handbook of personality and psychopathology* (pp. 442–461). Hoboken, NJ: Wiley.

Leary, P. M. (2003). Conversion disorder in childhood: Diagnosed too late, investigated too much? *Journal of the Royal Society of Medicine, 96*, 436–444.

LeBel, E. P., & Peters, K. R. (2011). Fearing the future of empirical psychology: Bem's (2011) evidence of Psi as a case study of deficiencies in modal research practice. *Review of General Psychology, 15*, 371–379.

Leckman, J. F., Denys, D., Simpson, H. B., Mataix-Cols, D., Hollander, E., Saxena, S., . . . Stein, D. J. (2010). Obsessive-compulsive disorder: A review of the diagnostic criteria and possible subtypes and dimensional specifiers for DSM-V. *Depression and Anxiety, 27,* 507–527.

Lecomte, T., Mueser, K. T., MacEwan, W., Thornton, A. E., Buchanan, T., Bouchard, V., . . . Honer, W. G. (2013). Predictors of persistent psychotic symptoms in persons with methamphetamine abuse receiving psychiatric treatment. *Journal of Nervous and Mental Disease, 201,* 1085–1089.

LeCrone, H. (2007). BED sometimes thought of as overeating takes over one's life. Retrieved from http://proquest.umi.com.ezproxy.library.wwu.edu/pqdweb?index52

Lee, C. M., Geisner, I. M., Patrick, M. E., & Neighbors, C. (2010). The social norms of alcohol-related negative consequences. *Psychology of Addictive Behaviors, 24*(2), 342–348.

Lee, C. W., & Cuijpers, P. (2013). A meta-analysis of the contribution of eye movements in processing emotional memories. *Journal of Behavior Therapy & Experimental Psychiatry, 44,* 231–239.

Lee, S., Lam, K., Kwok, K., & Fung, C. (2010). The changing profile of eating disorders at a tertiary psychiatric clinic in Hong Kong (1987–2007). *International Journal of Eating Disorders, 43,* 307–314.

Lee, Y., & Lin, P.-Y. (2010). Association between serotonin transporter gene polymorphism and eating disorders: A meta-analytic study. *International Journal of Eating Disorders, 43,* 498–504.

Lee, Y. J., & Jeong, D. U. (2014, January 16). Obstructive sleep apnea syndrome is associated with higher diastolic blood pressure in men but not in women. *American Journal of Hypertension, 27,* 325–330.

Leeies, T. M., Pagura, J., Sareen, J., & Bolton, J. M. (2010). The use of alcohol and drugs to self-medicate symptoms of posttraumatic stress disorder. *Depression and Anxiety, 27*(8), 731–736.

Leer, A., Engelhard, I. M., Altink, A., & van den Hout, M. A. (2013). Eye movements during recall of aversive memory decreases conditioned fear. *Behaviour Research & Therapy, 51,* 633–640.

Leff, J. (1994). Working with the families of schizophrenic patients. *British Journal of Psychiatry, 164,* 71–76.

Leff, S. S., & Crick, N. R. (2010). Interventions for relational aggression: Innovative programming and next steps in research and practice. *School Psychology Review, 39,* 504–507.

Le Grange, D., Lock, J., Loeb, K., & Nicholls, D. (2010). Academy for eating disorders position paper: The role of the family in eating disorders. *International Journal of Eating Disorders, 43,* 1–5.

Lehman, A. F., & Steinwachs, D. M. (1998). At issue: Translating research into practice: The schizophrenia patient outcome research team (PORT) treatment recommendations. *Schizophrenia Bulletin, 24,* 1–10.

Lehman, E. J., Hein, M. J., Baron, S. L., & Gersic, C. M. (2012). Neurodegenerative causes of death among retired National Football League players. *Neurology, 79,* 1970–1974.

Lehrer, P. M., Vaschillo, E., Vaschillo, B., Lu, S.-E., Scardella, A., Siddique, M., & Habib, R. H. (2004). Biofeedback treatment for asthma. *Chest, 126,* 352–361.

Leibenluft, E. (2011). Severe mood dysregulation, irritability, and the diagnostic boundaries of bipolar disorder in youths. *American Journal of Psychiatry, 168,* 129–142.

Leiknes, K. A., Finset, A., Moum, T., & Sandanger, I. (2008). Overlap, comorbidity, and stability of somatoform disorders and the use of current versus lifetime criteria. *Psychosomatics, 49,* 152–162.

Leisure, C. (2013). Living with OCD: We are unique, not abnormal. Retrieved from http://news.yahoo.com/living-ocd-unique-not-abnormal-175100233.html

Lejuez, C. W., Hopko, D. R., Acierno, R., Daughters, S. B., & Pagoto, S. L. (2011). Ten year revision of the brief behavioral activation treatment for depression: Revised treatment manual. *Behavior Modification, 35,* 111–161.

Lomonick, M. D. (2004). In search of Sleep. *Time, 164,* pg. 100

Lenzenweger, M. F., Lane, M. C., Loranger, A. W., & Kessler, R. C. (2007). Personality disorders in the National Comorbidity Survey Replication. *Biological Psychiatry, 62,* 553–564.

Leonard, B. E. (2010). The concept of depression as a dysfunction of the immune system. *Current Opinion in Immunology, 6,* 205–212.

Leonardo, E. D., & Hen, R. (2006). Genetics of affective and anxiety disorders. *Annual Review of Psychology, 57,* 117–137.

Leong, F. T., & Leach, M. M. (2008). *Ethnic suicides.* New York, NY: Routledge.

Lerman, C., & Audrain-McGovern, J. (2010). Reinforcing effects of smoking: More than feeling. *Biological Psychiatry, 67,* 699–701.

Lervolino, A. C., Perroud, N., Fullana, M. A., Guipponi, M., Cherkas, L., Collier, D. A., & Mataix-Cols, D. (2009). Prevalence and heritability of compulsive hoarding: A twin study. *American Journal of Psychiatry, 166,* 1156–1161.

Lespérance, F., Frasure-Smith, N., St-André, E., Turecki, G., Lespérance, P., & Wisniewski, S. R. (2011). The efficacy of omega-3 supplementation for major depression: A randomized controlled trial. *Journal of Clinical Psychiatry, 72,* 1054–1062.

Lester, B. M., Lagasse, L. L., Shankaran, S., Bada, H. S., Bauer, C. R., & Lin, R. (2010). Prenatal cocaine exposure related to cortisol stress reactivity in 11-year-old children. *Journal of Pediatrics, 157,* 288–295.

Lester, D. (2008). Theories of suicide. In F. Leong & M. M. Leach (Eds.), *Ethnic suicides* (pp. 39–53). New York, NY: Routledge.

Levenson, J. C., Frank, E., Cheng, Y., Rucci, P., Janney, C. A., Houck, P., . . . Fagiolini, A. (2010). Comparative outcomes among the problem areas of interpersonal psychotherapy. *Depression and Anxiety, 27,* 434–440.

Leventhal, J. M., Martin, K. D., & Gaither, J. R. (2012). Using US data to estimate the incidence of serious physical abuse in children. *Pediatrics, 129,* 458–464.

Levi, J., Vinter, S., St. Laurent, R., & Segal, R. M. (2010). *F as in fat: How obesity threatens America's future.* Washington, DC: Trust for America's Health. Retrieved from http://healthy-americans.org/report/88

Levine, M. D., Perkins, K. A., Kalarchian, M. K., Cheng, Y., Houck, P. R., Slane, J. D., & Marcus, M. D. (2010). Bupropion and cognitive behavioral therapy for weight-concerned women smokers. *Archives of Internal Medicine, 170,* 543–550.

Levinson, D. F. (2006). The genetics of depression: A review. *Biological Psychiatry, 60,* 84–92.

Levkovitz, Y., Harel, E. V., Roth, Y., Braw, Y., Most, D., & Zangen, A. (2009). Deep transcranial magnetic stimulation over the prefrontal cortex: Evaluation of antidepressant and cognitive effects in depressive patients. *Brain Stimulation, 2,* 188–200.

Levy, L. B., & O'Hara, M. W. (2010). Psychtherapeutic interventions for depressed, low-income women: A review of the literature. *Clinical Psychology Review, 30,* 934–950.

Lew-Starowicz, M. (2012). Shared psychotic disorder with sexual delusions. *Archives of Sexual Behavior, 41,* 1515–1520.

Lewinsohn, P. M., Hoberman, H. M., Teri, L., & Hautzinger, M. (1985). An integrative theory of depression. In S. Reiss & R. R. Bootzin (Eds.), *Theoretical issues in behavioral therapy* (pp. 331–359). Orlando, FL: Academic Press.

Lewinsohn, P. M., Muñoz, R. F., Youngren, M. A., & Zeiss, A. M. (1994). *Control your depression* (rev. ed.). New York, NY: Fireside.

Lewis, G., Rice, F., Harold, G.T., Collishaw, S., & Thapar, A. (2011). Investigating environmental links between parent depression and child depressive/anxiety symptoms using an assisted conception design. *Journal of the American Academy of Child & Adolescent Psychiatry, 50,* 451-459.

Lewis, R. W., Fugl-Meyer, K. S., Bosch, R., Fugl-Meyer, A. R., Laumann, E. O., Lizza, E., & Martin-Morales, A. (2004). Epidemiology/risk factors of sexual dysfunction. *Journal of Sexual Medicine, 1,* 35–39.

Lewis, R. W., Yuan, J., & Wang, R. (2008). Male sexual arousal disorder. In D. L. Rowland & L. Incrocci (Eds.), *Handbook of sexual and gender identity disorders* (pp. 32–63). Hoboken, NJ: Wiley.

Lewis-Fernández, R., Hinton, D. E., Laria, A. J., Patterson, E. H., Hofmann, S. G., Craske, M. G., . . . Liao, B. (2010). Culture and the anxiety disorders: Recommendations for DSM-V. *Depression and Anxiety, 27,* 212–229.

Lewy Body Dementia Association. (2014). Lewy body dementia symptoms and diagnostic criteria. Retrieved from http://www.lbda.org/content/symptoms

Li, C. T., Bai, Y. M., Huang, Y. L., Chen, Y. S., Chen, T. J., Cheng, J. Y., & Su, T. P. (2012). Association between antidepressant resistance in unipolar depression and subsequent bipolar disorder: Cohort study. *British Journal of Psychiatry, 200,* 45–51.

Li, G., Wang, L. Y., Shofer, J. B., Thompson, M. L., Peskind, E. R., McCormick, W., . . . Larson, E. B. (2011). Temporal relationship between depression and dementia: Findings from a large community-based 15-year follow-up study. *Archives of General Psychiatry, 68,* 970–977.

Liao, Y., Knoesen, N. P., Castle, D. J., Tang, J., Deng, Y., Bookun, R., . . . Liu, T. (2010). Symptoms of disordered eating, body shape, and mood concerns in the male and female Chinese medical students. *Comprehensive Psychiatry, 51,* 516–523.

Liberman, R. P., Kopelowicz, A., & Young, A. S. (1994). Biobehavioral treatment and rehabilitation of schizophrenia. *Behavior Therapy, 25,* 89–107.

Lichtenstein, E., Zhu, S., & Tedeschi, G. J. (2010). Smoking cessation quitlines: An underrecognized intervention success story. *American Psychologist, 65,* 252–261.

Lie, D. A. (2012). The many faces of depression. Retrieved from http://www.medscape.com/viewarticle/768764

Lieberman, J. A., Stroup, T. S., McEvoy, J. P., Swartz, M. S., Rosenheck, R. A., Perkins, D. O., . . . Clinical Antipsychotic Trials of Intervention Effectiveness (CATIE) Investigators. (2005). Effectiveness of antipsychotic drugs in patients with chronic schizophrenia. *New England Journal of Medicine, 353,* 1209–1223.

Lilienfeld, S. O., Lynn, S. J., Kirsch, I., Chaves, J. F., Sarbin, T. R., Ganaway, G. K., & Powell, R. A. (1999). Dissociative identity disorder and the sociocognitive model: Recalling the lessons of the past. *Psychological Bulletin, 125,* 507–523.

Lilienfeld, S. O., Lynn, S. J., & Lohr, J. M. (2004). *Science and pseudoscience in clinical psychology.* New York, NY: Guilford Press.

Lilly, M. M., Pole, N., Best, S. R., Metzler, T., & Marmar, C. R. (2009). Gender and PTSD: What can we learn from female police officers. *Journal of Anxiety Disorders, 23,* 767–774.

Lin, C. S., Ku, H. L., Chao, H. T., Tu, P. C., Li, C. T., Cheng, C. M., . . . Hsieh, J. C. (2014). Neural network of body representation differs between transsexuals and cissexuals. *PLOS One, 9,* e85914. doi:10.1371/journal.pone.0085914

Lin, K. C., Chung, H. Y., Wu, C. Y., Liu, H. L., Hsieh, Y. W., Chen, I-H., . . . Wai, Y. Y. (2010). Constraint-induced therapy versus control intervention in patients with stroke: A functional magnetic resonance imaging study. *American Journal of Physical and Medical Rehabilitation, 89,* 177–185.

Lindau, S. T., Schumm, L. P., Laumann, E. O., Levinson, W., O'Muircheartaigh, C. A., & Waite, L. J. (2007). A study of sexuality and health among older adults in the United States. *New England Journal of Medicine, 357,* 762–774.

Lindfors, O., Knekt, P., Virtala, E., & Laaksonen, M. A. (2012). The effectiveness of solution-focused therapy and short- and long-term psychodynamic psychotherapy on self-concept during a 3-year follow-up. *Journal of Nervous and Mental Disease, 200,* 946–953.

Lindner, K., Lacefield, K., Dunn, S. T., & Dunn, M. E. (2014). The use of videoconference in the treatment of panic disorder with agoraphobia in a housebound woman: A case study. *Clinical Case Studies, 13,* 146–166.

Lindstrom, C. M., Cann, A., Calhoun, L. G., & Tedeschi, R. G. (2013). The relationship of core belief challenge, rumination, disclosure, and sociocultural elements to posttraumatic growth. *Psychological Trauma: Theory, Research, Practice, and Policy, 5,* 50–55.

Linehan, M. M. (1993). *Cognitive-behavioral treatment of borderline personality disorder.* New York, NY: Guilford Press.

Linehan, M. M., Comtois, K. A., Murray, A. M., Brown, M. Z., Gallop, R. J., Heard, H. L., . . . Lindenboim, M. (2006). Two-year randomized controlled trial and follow-up of dialectical behavior therapy vs therapy by experts for suicidal behaviors and borderline personality disorder. *Archives of General Psychiatry, 63,* 757–766.

Linn, V. (2004, June 26). Headache "beast" holds tight grip on sufferers. *Seattle Post-Intelligencer,* p. A1.

Lipsitz, J. D., & Markowitz, J. C. (2013). Mechanisms of change in interpersonal therapy (IPT). *Clinical Psychology Review, 33,* 1134–1147.

Liptak, A. (2010, May 17). Extended civil commitment of sex offenders is upheld. *New York Times,* p. A3.

Lipton, R. B., Bigal, M. E., Diamond, M., Freitag, F., Reed, M. L., & Stewart, W. F. (2007). Migraine prevalence, disease burden, and the need for preventive therapy. *Neurology, 68,* 343–349.

Lis, J. (2011, May 17). Ban on stick-thin models passes Knesset hurdle. *Haaretz.* Retrieved from http://www.haaretz.com

Litvan, I., Goldman, J. G., Tröster, A. I., Schmand, B. A., Weintraub, D., Petersen, R. C., . . . Emre, M. (2012). Diagnostic criteria for mild cognitive impairment in Parkinson's disease: Movement Disorder Society Task Force guidelines. *Movement Disorders, 27,* 349–356.

Liu, B., Lavebratt, C., Nordqvist, T., Fandiño-Losada, A., Theorell, T., Forsell, Y., & Lundberg, I. (2013).

Working conditions, serotonin transporter gene polymorphism (5-HTTLPR) and anxiety disorders: A prospective cohort study. *Journal of Affective Disorders, 151,* 652–659.

Liu, R. T., & Alloy, L. B. (2010). Stress generation in depression: A systematic review of the empirical literature and recommendations for future study. *Clinical Psychology Review, 30,* 582–593.

Lo, C. C., & Cheng, T. C. (2012) Discrimination's role in minority groups' rates of substance-use disorder. *American Journal of Addiction, 21,* 150–156.

Loas, G., Cormier, J., & Perez-Diaz, F. (2011). Dependent personality disorder and physical abuse. *Psychiatry Research, 185,* 167–170.

Lockwood, P. L., Sebastian, C. L., McCrory, E. J., Hyde, Z. H., Gu, X., De Brito, S. A., & Viding, E. (2013). Association of callous traits with reduced neural response to others' pain in children with conduct problems. *Current Biology, 23,* 901–905.

Loeber, R. (1990). Development and risk factors of juvenile antisocial behavior and delinquency. *Clinical Psychology Review, 10,* 1–42.

Loening-Baucke, V. (2007). Prevalence rates for constipation and faecal and urinary incontinence. *Archives of Disease in Childhood, 92,* 486–489.

Loewenstein, R. J. (1994). Diagnosis, epidemiology, clinical course, treatment, and cost effectiveness of treatment for dissociative disorders and MPD: Report submitted to the Clinton Administration Task Force on Health Care Reform. *Dissociation, 7,* 3–11.

Loftus, E. (2003). Memory in Canadian courts of law. *Canadian Psychology, 44,* 207–212.

Loftus, E. F., Garry, M., & Hayne, H. (2008). Repressed and recovered memory. In E. Borgida & S. T. Fiske (Eds.), *Beyond common sense: Psychological science in the courtroom* (pp. 177–194). Malden, MA: Blackwell Publishing.

Lohoff, F. W. (2010). Overview of the genetics of major depressive disorder. *Current Psychiatry Reports, 12,* 539–546.

Lommen, M. J. J., Engelhard, I. M., Sijbrandij, M., van den Hout, M. A., & Hermans, D. (2013). Pre-trauma individual differences in extinction learning predict posttraumatic stress. *Behaviour Research and Therapy, 51,* 63–67.

Lomonick, M. D. (2004). In search of sleep. *Time, 164,* 100.

Loo, C., Katalinic, N., Mitchell, P. B., & Greenberg, B. (2011). Physical treatments for bipolar disorder: A review of electroconvulsive therapy, stereotactic surgery and other brain stimulation techniques. *Journal of Affective Disorders, 132,* 1–13.

Lopez, S. R., Hipke, K. N., Polo, A. J., Jenkins, J. H., Karno, M., Vaughn, C., & Snyder, K. S. (2004). Ethnicity, expressed emotion, attributions, and course of schizophrenia: Family warmth matters. *Journal of Abnormal Psychology, 113,* 428–439.

Lopez-Duran, N. (2010, March 19). Re: Autism and Asperger's in the DSM-V: Thoughts on clinical utility [Web log comment]. Retrieved from http://www.child-psych.org/2010/02/autism-and-aspergers-in-the-dsm-v-going-beyond-the-politics.html

Lorains, F. K., Stout, J. C., Bradshaw, J. L., Dowling, N. A., & Enticott, P. G. (2014). Self-reported impulsivity and inhibitory control in problem gamblers. *Journal of Clinical and Experimental Neuropsychology, 36,* 144–157.

Lord, C., Petkova, E., Hus, V., Gan, W., Lu, F., Martin, D. M., . . . Risi, S. (2012). A multisite study of the clinical diagnosis of different autism spectrum disorders. *Archives of General Psychiatry, 69,* 306–313.

Loth, A. K., Drabick, D. A., Leibenluft, E., & Hulvershorn, L. A. (2014). Do childhood externalizing disorders predict adult depression? A meta-Analysis. *Journal of Abnormal Child Psychology.* DOI 10.1007/s10802-014-9867-8 [Lövdén, M., Xu, W., & Wangy, H.-X. (2013). Lifestyle change and the prevention of cognitive decline and dementia: What is the evidence? *Current Opinion in Psychiatry, 26,* 239–243.

Lovejoy, M. (2001). Disturbances in the social body: Differences in body image and eating problems among African American and white women. *Gender and Society, 15,* 239–261.

Lubit, R. H. (2012). Oppositional defiant disorder. Retrieved from http://emedicine.medscape.com/article/918095-overview

Lubit, R. H., Bonds, C. L., II, & Lucia, M. A. (2013). Sleep disorders. Retrieved from http://emedicine.medscape.com/article/287104-overview

Luca, M., Vecchio, C., Luca, A., & Calandra, C. (2012). Haloperidol augmentation of fluvoxamine in skin picking disorder: A case report. *Journal of Medical Case Reports, 6,* 219–233.

Lucas, M., Mekary, R., Pan, A., Mirzaei, F., O'Reilly, E. J., Willett, W. C., . . . Ascherio, A. (2011). Relation between clinical depression risk and physical activity and time spent watching television in older women: A 10-year prospective follow-up study. *American Journal of Epidemiology, 174,* 1017–1027.

Lucas, M., O'Reilly, E. J., Pan, A., Mirzaei, F., Willett, W. C., Okereke, O. I., & Ascherio, A. (2013, July 2). Coffee, caffeine, and risk of completed suicide: Results from three prospective cohorts of American adults. *World Journal of Biological Psychiatry,* pp. 1–10.

Ludwig, J., Marcotte, D. E., & Norberg, K. (2009). Anti-depressants and suicide. *Journal of Health Economics, 28,* 659–676.

Lundh, A., Sismondo, S., Lexchin, J., Busuioc, O. A., & Bero, L. (2012). Industry sponsorship and research outcome. *Cochrane Database of Systematic Reviews, 12.* doi:10.1002/14651858.MR000033.pub2

Luoma, J. B., Hayes, S. C., & Walser, R. D. (2007). *Learning ACT: An acceptance and commitment therapy skills-training manual for therapists.* Oakland, CA: New Harbinger & Reno, NV: Context Press.

Lurie, A. (2011). Obstructive sleep apnea in adults: Epidemiology, clinical presentation, and treatment options. *Advances in Cardiology, 46,* 1–42.

Lussier, P., McCann, K., & Beauregard, E. (2008). The etiology of sexual deviance. In D. Rowland & L. Incrocci (Eds.), *Handbook of sexual and gender identity disorders* (pp. 529–562). Hoboken, NJ: Wiley.

Luxton, D. D., Osenbach, J. E., Reger, M. A., Smolenski, D. J., Skopp, N. A., Bush, N. E., & Gahm, G. A. (2012). *Department of Defense suicide events report, 2011.* Washington, DC: Department of Defense.

Lyke, M. L. (2004, August 27). Once a "people person," vet couldn't leave home. *Seattle Post-Intelligencer,* p. A8.

Lyketsos, C. G., Targum, S. D., Pendergrass, J. C., & Lozano, A. M. (2012). Deep brain stimulation: A novel strategy for treating Alzheimer's disease. *Innovations in Clinical Neuroscience, 9,* 10–17.

Lykken, D. T. (1982). Fearlessness: Its carefree charm and deadly risks. *Psychology Today, 16,* 20–28.

Lyon, G. J., Abi-Dargham, A., Moore, H., Lieberman, J. A., Javitch, J. A., &

Sulzer, D. (2011). Presynaptic regulation of dopamine transmission in schizophrenia. *Schizophrenia Bulletin, 37,* 108–117.

Lysaker, P. H., & Roe, D. (2012). The processes of recovery from schizophrenia: The emergent role of integrative psychotherapy. *Journal of Psychotherapy Integration, 22,* 287–297.

Machover, K. (1949). *Personality projection in the drawing of the human figure: A method of personality investigation.* Springfield, IL: Thomas.

Mackenzie, S., Wiegel, J. R., Mundt, M., Brown, D., Saewyc, E., Heiligenstein, E., . . . Fleming, M. (2011). Depression and suicide ideation among students accessing campus health care. *American Journal of Orthopsychiatry, 81,* 101–107.

Macur, J., & Schweber, N. (2012). Rape case unfolds on Web and splits city. Retrieved from http://www.nytimes.com/2012/12/17/sports/high-school-football-rape-case-unfolds-online-and-divides-steubenville-ohio.html?pagewanted5all

Maddi, S. R. (2002). The story of hardiness: Twenty years of theorizing, research and practice. *Consulting Psychology Journal, 54,* 173–185.

Madsen, K. A., Weedn, A. E., & Crawford, P. B. (2010). Disparities in the peaks, plateaus, and declines in prevalence of high BMI among adolescents. *Pediatrics, 126,* 434–442.

Maguen, S., Luxton, D. D., Skopp, N. A., & Madden, E. (2012). Gender differences in traumatic experiences and mental health in active duty soldiers redeployed from Iraq and Afghanistan. *Journal of Psychiatric Research, 46,* 311–316.

Mahdy, J. C., & Lewis, S. P. (2013). Nonsuicidal self-injury on the Internet: An overview and guide for school mental health professionals. *School Psychology Forum,* 148–160.

Mahgoub, N., & Hossain, A. (2006). A 28-yearold woman and her 58-year-old mother with a shared psychotic disorder. *Psychiatric Annals, 36,* 306–309.

Mahgoub, N., & Hossain, A. (2007). A 60-year-old woman with avoidant personality disorder. *Psychiatric Annals, 37,* 10–12.

Mahler, M. (1968). *On human symbiosis and the vicissitudes of individuation.* New York, NY: International University Press.

Maier, S. F., & Watkins, L. R. (2010). Role of the medial prefrontal cortex in coping and resilience. *Brain Research, 1355,* 52–60.

Maines, R. P. (1999). *The technology of orgasm: "Hysteria," the vibrator, and women's sexual satisfaction.* Baltimore, MD: Johns Hopkins University Press.

Maisel, N. C., Blodgett, J. C., Wilbourne, P. L., Humphreys, K., & Finney, J. W. (2013). Meta-analysis of naltrexone and acamprosate for treating alcohol use disorders: When are these medications most helpful? *Addiction, 108,* 275–293.

Malik, A. B. (2013). Neuropsychological evaluation. Retrieved from http://emedicine.medscape.com/article/317596-overview#a30

Mallett, K. A., Varvil-Weld, L., Borsari, B., Read, J. P., Neighbors, C., & White, H. R. (2013). An update of research examining college student alcohol-related consequences: New perspectives and implications for interventions. *Alcoholism: Clinical & Experimental Research, 37,* 709–716.

Mancebo, M. C., Eisen, J. L., Sibrava, N. J., Dyck, I. R., & Rasmussen, S. A. (2011). Patient utilization of cognitive-behavior therapy for OCD. *Behavior Therapy, 42,* 399–412.

Manchikanti, L., Fellows, B., Ailinani, H., & Pampati, V. (2010). Therapeutic use, abuse, and nonmedical use of opioids: A ten-year perspective. *Pain Physician, 13,* 401–435.

Mancuso, C. E., Tanzi, M. G., & Gabay, M. (2004). Paradoxical reactions to benzodiazepines: Literature review and treatment options. *Pharmacotherapy, 24,* 1177–1185.

Mann, J. J., Arango, V. A., Avenevoli, S., Brent, D. A., Champagne, F. A., Clayton, P., . . . Wenzel, A. (2009). Candidate endophenotypes for genetic studies of suicidal behavior. *Biological Psychiatry, 65,* 556–563.

Mann, J. J., & Haghighi, F. (2010). Genes and environment: Multiple pathways to psychopathology. *Biological Psychiatry, 68,* 403–404.

Mann, K., & Hermann, D. (2010). Individualized treatment in alcohol-dependent patients. *European Archives of Psychiatry and Clinical Neuroscience, 2,* S116–S120.

Mann, T., Tomiyama, A. J., Westling, E., Lew, A.-M., Samuels, B., & Chatman, J. (2007). Medicare's search for effective obesity treatments: Diets are not the answer. *American Psychologist, 62,* 220–233.

Manning, J. S. (2013). Strategies for managing the risks associated with ADHD medications. *Journal of Clinical Psychiatry, 74,* e19. doi:10.4088/JCP.12077tx2c

Manuel, A., & Wade, T. D. (2013). Emotion regulation in broadly defined anorexia nervosa: Association with negative affective memory bias. *Behaviour Research and Therapy, 51,* 417–424.

Marangell, L. B., Dennehy, E. B., Miyahara, S., Wisniewski, S. R., Bauer, M. S., Rapaport, M. H., & Allen, M. H. (2009). The functional impact of subsyndromal depressive symptoms in bipolar disorder: Data from STEP-BD. *Journal of Affective Disorders, 114,* 58–67.

Marar, M., McIlvain, N. M., Fields, S. K., & Comstock, R. D. (2012). Epidemiology of concussions among United States high school athletes in 20 sports. *American Journal of Sports Medicine, 40,* 747–755.

Marceaux, J. C., & Melville, C. L. (2011). Twelve-step facilitated versus mapping-enhanced cognitive-behavioral therapy for pathological gambling: A controlled study. *Journal of Gambling Studies, 27,* 171–190.

Marchand, E., Ng, J., Rohde, P., & Stice, E. (2010). Effects of an indicated cognitive-behavioral depression prevention program are similar for Asian American, Latino, and European American adolescents. *Behavior Research and Therapy, 48,* 821–825.

Marjoribanks, J., Brown, J., O'Brien, P. M., & Wyatt, K. (2013). Selective serotonin reuptake inhibitors for premenstrual syndrome. *Cochrane Database of Systematic Reviews, 6,* CD001396. doi:10.1002/14651858.CD001396.pub3

Mark, T. L., Levit, K. R., Vandivort-Warren, R., Buck, J. A., & Coffey, R. M. (2011). Changes in US spending on mental health and substance abuse treatment, 1986–2005, and implications for policy. *Health Affairs, 30,* 284–292.

Markarian, Y., Larson, M. J., Aldea, M. A., Baldwin, S. A., Good, D., Berkeljon, A., . . . McKay, D. (2010). Multiple pathways to functional impairment in obsessive-compulsive disorder. *Clinical Psychology Review, 30,* 78–88.

Markus, C. R., & De Raedt, R. (2011). Differential effects of 5-HTTLPR genotypes on inhibition of negative emotional information following acute stress exposure and tryptophan challenge. *Neuropsychopharmacology, 36,* 819–826.

Marmar, C. R. (1988). Personality disorders. In H. H. Goldman (Ed.), *Review of general psychiatry* (pp. 401–424). Norwalk, CT: Appleton & Lange.

Marques, A. H., O'Connor, T. G., Roth, C., Susser, E., & Bjørke-Monsen, A. L. (2013). The influence of maternal prenatal and early childhood nutrition and maternal prenatal stress on offspring immune system development and neurodevelopmental disorders. *Frontiers in Neuroscience, 7*, 120. doi:10.3389/fnins.2013.00120

Marras, C., Armstrong, M. J., Meaney, C. A., Fox, S., Rothberg, B., Reginold, W., . . . Duff-Canning, S. (2013). Measuring mild cognitive impairment in patients with Parkinson's disease. *Movement Disorders, 28*, 626–633.

Marris, E. (2006). Mysterious "Morgellons disease" prompts U.S. investigation. *Nature, 12*, 982.

Marsh, A. A., Finger, E. C., Fowler, K. A., Adalio, C. J., Jurkowitz, I. T., Schechter, J. C., . . . Blair, R. J. (2013). Empathic responsiveness in amygdala and anterior cingulate cortex in youths with psychopathic traits. *Journal of Child Psychology and Psychiatry, 8*, 900–910.

Marsh, W. K., Ketter, T. A., & Rasgon, N. L. (2009). Increased depressive symptoms in menopausal age women with bipolar disorder: Age and gender comparison. *Journal of Psychiatric Research, 43*, 798–802.

Marshall, R. D., Bryant, R. A., Amsel, L., Suh, E. J., Cook, J. M., & Neria, Y. (2007). The psychology of ongoing threat: Relative risk appraisal, the September 11 attacks, and terrorism-related fears. *American Psychologist, 62*, 304–316.

Marshall, S. A., Landau, M. E., Carroll, C. G., Schwieters, B., Llewellyn, A., Liskow, B. I., . . . Bienenfeld, D. (2013). Conversion disorders. Retrieved from http://emedicine.medscape.com/article/287464-overview

Marsolek, M. R., White, N. C., & Litovitz, T. L. (2010). Inhalant abuse: Monitoring trends by using poison control data, 1993–2008. *Pediatrics, 125*, 906–913.

Martin, C. G., Cromer, L. D., Deprince, A. P., & Freyd, J. J. (2013). The role of cumulative trauma, betrayal, and appraisals in understanding trauma symptomatology. *Psychological Trauma, 52*, 110–118.

Martin, E. K., & Silverstone, P. H. (2013). How much child sexual abuse is "below the surface," and can we help adults

identify it early? *Frontiers in Psychiatry, 4*, 58. doi:10.3389/fpsyt.2013.00058

Martin, P. R., & MacLeod, C. (2009). Behavioral management of headache triggers: Avoidance of triggers is an inadequate strategy. *Clinical Psychology Review, 29*, 483–495.

Martin, L. A., Neighbors, H. W., & Griffith, D. M. (2013). The experience of symptoms of depression in men vs women: Analysis of the National Comorbidity Survey Replication. *JAMA Psychiatry, 70*, 1100–1106.

Martinez-Taboas, A. (2005). Psychogenic seizures in an espiritismo context: The role of culturally sensitive psychotherapy. *Psychotherapy: Theory, Research, Practice, Training, 42*, 6–13.

Martins, S. S., & Alexandre, P. K. (2009). The association of Ecstasy use and academic achievement among adolescents in two US national surveys. *Addictive Behaviors, 34*, 9–16.

Masataka, N., & Shibasaki, M. (2012). Premenstrual enhancement of snake detection in visual search in healthy women. *Scientific Reports.* Retrieved from http://www.nature.com/srep/2012/120308/srep00307/full/srep00307.html. doi:10.1038/srep00307

Mason, M. (2006, October 24). Is it disease or delusion? U.S. takes on a dilemma. *New York Times.* Retrieved from http://www.nytimes.com

Mason, S. M., Flint, A. J., Field, A. E., Austin, S. B., & Rich-Edwards, J. W. (2013). Abuse victimization in childhood or adolescence and risk of food addiction in adult women. *Obesity, 21*, 775–781.

Masten, A. S. (2009). Ordinary magic: Lessons from research on resilience in human development. *Education Canada, 49*, 28–32. Retrieved from http://www.cea-ace.ca/education-canada/article/ordinary-magic-lessons-research-or-resilience-human-development

Masten, A. S. (2011). Resilience in children threatened by extreme adversity: Frameworks for research, practice, and translational synergy. *Development and Psychopathology, 23*, 493–506.

Masten, A. S., Faden, V. B., Zucker, R. A., & Spear, L. P. (2008). Underage drinking: A developmental framework. *Pediatrics, 121*(Suppl 4), S235–S251.

Masten, A. S., & Narayan, A. J. (2012). Child development in the context of disaster, war, and terrorism: Pathways of risk and resilience. *Annual Review of Psychology, 63*, 227–257.

Masters, K. S., & Hooker, S. A. (2013). Religiousness/spirituality, cardiovascular disease, and cancer: Cultural integration for health research and intervention. *Journal of Consulting and Clinical Psychology, 81*, 206–216.

Masters, W. H., & Johnson, V. E. (1966). *Human sexual response.* Boston, MA: Little, Brown.

Masters, W. H., & Johnson, V. E. (1970). *Human sexual inadequacy.* London, UK: Churchill.

Mataix-Cols, D., Boman, M., Monzani, B., Rück, C., Serlachius, E., Långström, N., & Lichtenstein, P. (2013). Population-based, multigenerational family clustering study of obsessive-compulsive disorder. *JAMA Psychiatry, 70*, 709–717.

Mathews, C. A., & Grados, M. A. (2011). Familiality of Tourette syndrome, obsessive-compulsive disorder and attention-deficit/hyperactivity disorder: Heritability analysis in a large sib-pair sample. *Journal of the American Academy of Child & Adolescent Psychiatry, 50*, 46–54.

Mathis, C. A., & Klunk, W. E. (2013). Imaging tau deposits in vivo: Progress in viewing more of the proteopathy picture. *Neuron, 79*, 1035–1037.

Mathews, C. A., Scharf, J. M., Miller, L. L., Macdonald-Wallis, C., Lawlor, D. A., & Ben-Shlomo, Y. (2014). Association between pre- and perinatal exposures and Tourette syndrome or chronic tic disorder in the ALSPAC cohort. *British Journal of Psychiatry, 204*, 40–45.

Mattson, S. N., Roesch, S. C., Glass, L., Deweese, B. N., Coles, C. D., Kable, J. A., . . . Riley, E. P. (2013). Further development of a neurobehavioral profile of fetal alcohol spectrum disorders. *Alcohol: Clinical & Experimental Research, 37*, 517–528.

Matwiyoff, G., & Lee-Chiong, T. (2010). Parasomnias: An overview. *Indian Journal of Medical Research, 131*, 333–337.

Maughan, B. (2013). Editorial: "Better by design"—Why randomized controlled trials are the building blocks of evidence-based practice. *Journal of Child Psychology and Psychiatry, 54*, 225–226.

Maughan, B., Collishaw, S., & Stringaris, A. (2013). Depression in childhood and adolescence. *Journal of the Canadian Academy of Child & Adolescent Psychiatry, 22*, 35–40.

Maulik, P. K., Mascarenhas, M. N., Mathers, C. D., Dua, T., & Saxena, S. (2011). Prevalence of intellectual disability: A meta-analysis of population-based studies. *Research on Developmental Disabilities, 32,* 419–436.

May, P. A., Gossage, J. P., Kalberg, W. O, Robinson, L. K., Buckley, D., Manning, M., & Hoyme, H. E. (2009). Prevalence and epidemiologic characteristics of FASD from various research methods with an emphasis on recent in-school studies. *Developmental Disabilities Research Reviews, 15,* 176–192.

Mayhew, S. L., & Gilbert, P. (2008). Compassionate mind training with people who hear malevolent voices: A case series report. *Clinical Psychology and Psychotherapy, 15,* 113–138.

Mayo, C., Kaye, A. D., Conrad, E., Baluch, A., & Frost, E. (2010). Update on anesthesia considerations for electroconvulsive therapy. *Middle Eastern Journal of Anesthesiology, 20,* 493–498.

Mazurek, M. O., Kanne, S. M., & Miles, J. H. (2012). Predicting improvement in social-communication symptoms of autism spectrum disorders using retrospective treatment data. *Research in Autism Spectrum Disorders, 6,* 535–545.

McAllister, T. W., Flashman, L. A., Maerlender, A., Greenwald, R. M., Beckwith, J. G., Tosteson, T. D., . . . Turco, J. H. (2012). Cognitive effects of one season of head impacts in a cohort of collegiate contact sport athletes. *Neurology, 78*(22), 1777–1784.

McAnulty, R. D., & Burnette, M. M. (2004). *Fundamentals of exploring human sexuality: Making healthy decisions.* New York, NY: Allyn & Bacon.

McBurnett, K., & Pfiffner, L. J. (2009). Treatment of aggressive ADHD in children and adolescents: Conceptualization and treatment of comorbid behavior disorders. *Postgraduate Medicine, 121,* 158–165.

McCabe, H. T., Wilsnack, S. E., West, B. T., & Boyd, C. J. (2010). Victimization and substance use disorders in a national sample of heterosexual and sexual minority women and men. *Addiction, 105*(12), 2130–2140. doi:10.1111/j.1360-0443. 2010.03088.x

McCabe, M. P., & Goldhammer, D. L. (2013). Prevalence of women's sexual desire problems: What criteria do we use? *Archives of Sexual Behavior, 42,* 1073–1078.

McCabe, R., & Priebe, S. (2004). Explanatory models of illness in schizophrenia: Comparison of four ethnic groups. *British Journal of Psychiatry, 185,* 25–30.

McCabe, R. E., Miller, J. L., Laugesen, N., Antony, M. M., & Young, L. (2010). The relationship between anxiety disorders in adults and recalled childhood teasing. *Journal of Anxiety Disorders, 24,* 238–243.

McCarron, R. M. (2006). Somatization in the primary care setting. *Psychiatric Times, 23,* 32–36.

McCarter, S. J., Boswell, C. L., St Louis, E. K., Dueffert, L. G., Slocumb, N., Boeve, B. F., . . . Tippmann-Peikert, M. (2013). Treatment outcomes in REM sleep behavior disorder. *Sleep Medicine, 14,* 237–242.

McClung, C. A. (2007). Circadian genes, rhythms and the biology of mood disorders. *Pharmacology and Therapeutics, 114,* 222–232.

McCracken, L. M., & Larkin, K. T. (1991). Treatment of paruresis with in vivo desensitization: A case report. *Journal of Behavior Therapy and Experimental Psychiatry, 22,* 57–62.

McDaniel, S. H., & Speice, J. (2001). What family psychology has to offer women's health: The examples of conversion, somatization, infertility treatment, and genetic testing. *Professional Psychology: Research and Practice, 32,* 44–51.

McDermott, P. A., Watkins, M. W., & Rhoad, A. M. (2013). Whose IQ is it? Assessor bias variance in high-stakes psychological assessment. *Psychological Assessment, 26,* 207–214.

McElroy, S. L., Frye, M. A., Hellemann, G., Altshuler, L., Leverich, G. S., Suppes, T., . . . Post, R. M. (2011). Prevalence and correlates of eating disorders in 875 patients with bipolar disorder. *Journal of Affective Disorders, 128,* 191–198.

McGlashan, T. H., & Woods, S. (2011). Early antecedents and detection of schizophrenia. *Psychiatric Times, 28,* 1–6.

McGorm, K., Burton, C., Weller, D., Murray, G., and Sharpe, M. (2010). Patients repeatedly referred to secondary care with symptoms unexplained by organic disease: Prevalence, characteristics, and referral pattern. *Family Practice, 27,* 479–486.

McGowan, P. O. (2013, September 26). Epigenomic mechanisms of early adversity and HPA dysfunction: Considerations for PTSD research. *Frontiers in Psychiatry, 4,* 110.

McGrath, C. L., Kelley, M. D., Holzheimer, P. E., III, Dunlop, B. W., Craighead, W. E., Franco, R., . . . Mayberg, H. S. (2013). Toward a neuroimaging treatment selection biomarker for major depressive disorder. *JAMA Psychiatry, 70,* 821–829.

McGrath, J., Welham, J., Scott, J., Varghese, D., Degenhardt, L., Hayatbakhsh, M. R., . . . Najman, J. M. (2010). Association between cannabis use and psychosis-related outcomes using sibling pair analysis in a cohort of young adults. *Archives of General Psychiatry, 67,* 440–447.

McGuire, J. F., Piacentini, J., Brennan, E. A., Lewin, A. B., Murphy, T. K., Small, B. J., & Storch, E. A. (2014). A meta-analysis of behavior therapy for Tourette syndrome. *Journal of Psychiatric Research, 50,* 106–112.

McHugh, P. R. (2009). Multiple personality disorder (dissociative identity disorder). Retrieved from http://www.psycom.net/mchugh.html

McKinley, J. C., Jr. (2014). Life sentence is imposed in '08 killing of therapist. Retrieved from http://www.nytimes.com/2014/05/03/nyregion/david-tarloff-is-given-life-sentence-for-08-killing-of-psychologist.html?_r50

McKnight, R. F., Adida, M., Budge, K., Stockton, S., Goodwin, G. M., & Geddes, J. R. (2012). Lithium toxicity profile: A systematic review and meta-analysis. *Lancet, 379,* 721–728.

Miklowitz, D. J., Price, J., Holmes, E. A., Rendell, J., Bell, S., Budge, K., . . . Geddes, J. R. (2012). Facilitated Integrated Mood Management for adults with bipolar disorder. *Bipolar Disorders, 14,* 185–197.

Miklowitz, D. J., Schneck, C. D., Singh, M. K., Taylor, D. O., George, E. L., Cosgrove, V. E., . . . Chang, K. D. (2013). Early intervention for symptomatic youth at risk for bipolar disorder: A randomized trial of family-focused therapy. *Journal of American Academy of Child & Adolescent Psychiatry, 52,* 121–131.

McIntosh, V. V. W., Carter, F. A., Bulik, C. M., Frampton, C. M. A., & Joyce, P. R. (2010). Five-year outcome of cognitive behavioral therapy and exposure with response: Prevention for bulimia nervosa. *Psychological Medicine, 41*(5), 1061–1071. doi:10.1017/S0033291710001583

McKay, D., & Storch, E. A. (2014). Treatment of childhood obsessive-compulsive disorder. *Clinical Case Studies, 13,* 3–8.

McKee, A. C., Stern, R. A., Nowinski, C. J., Stein, T. D., Alvarez, V. E., Daneshvar, D. H., . . . Cantu, R. C. (2013). The spectrum of disease in chronic traumatic encephalopathy. *Brain, 136,* 43–64.

McKetin, R., Lubman, D., Baker, A. L., Dawe, S., & Ali, R. L. (2013). Dose-related psychotic symptoms in chronic methamphetamine users: Evidence from a prospective longitudinal study. *JAMA Psychiatry, 70,* 319–324.

McKibben, J. B., Bresnick, M. G., Wiechman Askay, S. A., & Fauerbach, J. A. (2008). Acute stress disorder and posttraumatic stress disorder: A prospective study of prevalence, course, and predictors in a sample with major burn injuries. *Journal of Burn Care and Research, 29,* 22–35.

McLaughlin, K. A., Green, J. G., Hwang, I., Sampson, N. A., Zaslavsky, A. M., & Kessler, R. C. (2012). Intermittent explosive disorder in the National Comorbidity Survey Replication Adolescent Supplement. *Archives of General Psychiatry, 69,* 1131–1139.

McLaughlin, K. A., Hatzenbuehler, M. L., & Keyes, K. M. (2010). Responses to discrimination and psychiatric disorders among black, Hispanic, female, and lesbian, gay, and bisexual individuals. *American Journal of Public Health, 100,* 1477–1484.

McLay, R. N., Graap, K., Spira, J., Perlman, K., Johnston, S., Rothbaum, B. O., ... Rizzo, A. (2012). Development and testing of virtual reality exposure therapy for post-traumatic stress disorder in active duty service members who served in Iraq and Afghanistan. *Military Medicine, 177,* 635–642.

McLean, C. P., & Anderson, E. R. (2009). Brave men and timid women? A review of gender differences in fear and anxiety. *Clinical Psychology Review, 29,* 496–505.

McLean, S. A., Paxton, S. J., & Wertheim, E. H. (2010). Factors associated with body dissatisfaction and disordered eating in women in midlife. *International Journal of Eating Disorders, 43,* 527–536.

McManus, F., Surawy, C., Muse, K., Vazquez-Montes, M., & Williams, J. M. G. (2012). A randomized clinical trial of mindfulness-based cognitive therapy versus unrestricted services for health anxiety (hypochondriasis). *Journal of Consulting and Clinical Psychology, 80,* 817–828.

McManus, M. A., Hargreaves, P., Rainbow, L., & Alison, L. J. (2013). Paraphilias: Definition, diagnosis and treatment. Retrieved from http://www.ncbi.nlm.nih.gov/pmc/articles/PMC3769077

McNally, R. J. (2007). Dispelling confusion about traumatic dissociative amnesia. *Mayo Clinic Proceedings, 82,* 1083–1087.

Mealer, M., Jones, J., Newman, J., McFann, K. K., Rothbaum, B., & Moss, M. (2013). The presence of resilience is associated with a healthier psychological profile in intensive care unit (ICU) nurses: Results of a national survey. *International Journal of Nursing Studies, 49,* 292–299.

Medina, J. J. (2008). Neurobiology of PTSD: Part 1. *Psychiatric Times, 25*(1), 29–33.

Mednick, L. M., & Claar, R. L. (2012). Treatment of severe blood-injection-injury phobia with the applied-tension method: Two adolescent case examples. *Clinical Case Studies, 11,* 24–34.

Medway, C., & Morgan, K. (2014). Review: The genetics of Alzheimer's disease; putting flesh on the bones. *Neuropathology and Applied Neurobiology, 40,* 97–105.

Meehl, P. E. (1962). Schizotaxia, schizotypia, schizophrenia. *American Psychologist, 17,* 827–838.

Meeks, J. (2004). *AFPPA 2003: Headache management—Evaluation and treatment.* Retrieved from www.medscape.com/viewarticle/467744

Meichenbaum, D. (2007). Stress inoculation training: A preventative and treatment approach. In P. M. Lehrer et al. (Eds.), *Principles and practice of stress management* (pp. 497–518). New York, NY: Guilford Press.

Meichenbaum, D. (2012). *Important facts about resilience: A consideration of research findings about resilience and implications for assessment and treatment.* Retrieved from http://www.melissainstitute.org/documents/facts_resilience.pdf

Meier, M. H., Caspi, A., Ambler, A., Harrington, H., Houts, R., Keefe, R. S., . . . Ward, A. (2012). Persistent cannabis users show neuropsychological decline from childhood to midlife. *Proceedings of the National Academy of Science, 109,* E2657–E2664.

Meili, T. (2003). *I am the Central Park Jogger: A story of hope and possibility.* New York, NY: Scribner.

Meilleur, A. A., & Fombonne, E. J. (2009). Regression of language and non-language skills in pervasive developmental disorders. *Intellectual Disabilities Research, 53,* 115–124.

Meiser-Stedman, R., Dalgleish, T., Gluckman, E., Yule, W., & Smith, P. (2009). Maladaptive cognitive appraisals mediate the evolution of post-traumatic stress reactions: A 6-month follow-up of child and adolescent assault and motor vehicle accident survivors. *Journal of Abnormal Psychology, 118,* 778–787.

Melago, C. (2009, October 15). Ralph Lauren firing of "too fat" size 4 Filippa Hamilton raises ire of women, body-image experts. *New York Daily News.* Retrieved from http://www.nydailynews.com

Melka, S. E., Lancaster, S. L., Adams, L. J., Howarth, E. A., & Rodriguez, B. F. (2010). Social anxiety across ethnicity: A confirmatory factor analysis of the FNE and SAD. *Journal of Anxiety Disorders, 24,* 680–685.

Melles, R. J., ter Kuile, M. M., Dewitte, M., van Lankveld, J. J.D.M., Brauer, M., & Lyons, M. J. (2014). Erectile dysfunction, vascular risk, and cognitive performance in late middle age. *Psychology of Aging, 29,* 163–172.

Melnyk, B. M., Jacobson, D., Kelly, S., Belyea, M., Shaibi, G., Small, L., . . . Marsiglia, F. F. (2013). Promoting healthy lifestyles in high school adolescents: A randomized controlled trial. *American Journal of Preventive Medicine, 45,* 407–415.

Meloy, J. R. (2001). Antisocial personality disorder. In G. O. Gabbard (Ed.), *Treatment of psychiatric disorders* (pp. 2251–2271). Washington, DC: American Psychiatric Publishing.

Melvin, G. A., Dudley, A. L., Gordon, M. S., Ford, S., Taffe, J., & Tonge, B. J. (2013). What happens to depressed adolescents? A follow-up study into early adulthood. *Journal of Affective Disorders, 151,* 298–305.

Memon, M. A. (2013). Brief psychotic disorder. Retrieved from http://emedicine.medscape.com/article/294416-overview

Mena, A. (2012). Rape trauma syndrome: The journey to healing belongs to everyone. Retrieved from http://www.adkanenough.com/rape-trauma-syndrome.html

Menge, H., Schimmelmann, B. G., Koch, E., Bailey, B., Parzer, P., Günter, M., . . . Resch, F. (2009). Basic symptoms in the general population and in psychotic and non-psychotic psychiatric adolescents. *Schizophrenia Research, 111,* 32–38.

Mercan, S., Altunay, I. K., Taskintuna, N., Ogutcen, O., & Kayaoglu, S. (2007). Atypical antipsychotic drugs in the treatment of delusional parasitosis. *International Journal of Psychiatry in Medicine, 37,* 29–37.

Mercer, J. (2013). Deliverance, demonic possession, and mental illness: Some considerations for mental health professionals. *Mental Health, Religion & Culture, 16,* 595–611.

Merikangas, K. R. (2013). Contributions of epidemiology to our understanding of migraine. *Headache, 53,* 230–246.

Merikangas, K. R., Akiskal, H. S., Angst, J., Greenberg, P. E., Hirschfeld, R. M., Petukhova, M., & Kessler, R. C. (2007). Lifetime and 12-month prevalence of bipolar spectrum disorder in the National Comorbidity Survey Replication. *Archives of General Psychiatry, 64,* 543–552.

Merikangas, K. R., He, J.-P., Burstein, M., Swanson, S. A., Avenevoli, S., Cui, L., . . . Swendsen, J. (2010). Lifetime prevalence of mental disorders in U.S. adolescents: Results from the National Comorbidity Survey Replication–Adolescent Supplement (NCS-A). *Journal of the Academy of Child & Adolescent Psychiatry, 49,* 980–989.

Merikangas, K. R., He, J.-P., Burstein, M., Swendsen, J., Avenevoli, S., Case, B., . . . Olfson, M. (2011). Service utilization for lifetime mental disorders in U.S. adolescents: Results of the National Comorbidity Survey–Adolescent Supplement (NCS-A). *Journal of the American Academy of Child & Adolescent Psychiatry, 50,* 32–45.

Merikangas, K. R., Jin, R., He, J.-P., Kessler, R. C., Lee, S., Sampson, N. A., . . . Zarkov, Z. (2011). Prevalence and correlates of bipolar spectrum disorder in the world mental health survey initiative. *Archives of General Psychiatry, 68,* 241–251.

Merrill, J. E., Read, J. P., & Barnett, N. P. (2013). The way one thinks affects the way one drinks: Subjective evaluations of alcohol consequences predict subsequent change in drinking behavior. *Psychology of Addictive Behavior, 27,* 42–51.

Merritt, M. M., Bennett, G. G., Jr., Williams, R. B., Edwards, C. L., & Sollers, J. J., III. (2006). Perceived racism and cardiovascular reactivity and recovery to personally relevant stress. *Health Psychology, 25,* 364–369.

Merry, S. N., Stasiak, K., Shepherd, M., Frampton, C., Fleming, T. & Lucassen, M. F. G. (2012). The effectiveness of SPARX, a computerized self help intervention for adolescents seeking help for depression: Randomized controlled non-inferiority trial. *British Medical Journal, 344,* e2598. doi: 10.1136/bmj.e2598

Merryman, K. (1997, July 17). Medical experts say Roberts may well have amnesia: Parts of her life match profile of person who might lose memory. *Tacoma News Tribune,* pp. A8–A9.

Messinger, D., Young, G.S., Ozonoff, S., Dobkins, K., Carter, A., Zwaigenbaum, L., . . . Sigman, M. (2013). Beyond autism: A baby siblings research consortium study of high-risk children at three years of age. *Journal of the American Academy of Child & Adolescent Psychiatry, 52,* 300–308.

Meston, C. M., Seal, B. N., & Hamilton, L. D. (2008). Problems with arousal and orgasm in women. In D. Rowland & L. Incrocci (Eds.), *Handbook of sexual and gender identity disorders* (pp. 188–219). Hoboken, NJ: Wiley.

Metzger, C. D., Walter, M., Graf, H., & Abler, B. (2013). SSRI-related modulation of sexual functioning is predicted by pre-treatment resting state functional connectivity in healthy men. *Archives of Sexual Behavior, 42,* 935–947.

Metzger, N. (2013). Battling demons with medical authority: Werewolves, physicians and rationalization. *History of Psychiatry, 24,* 341–355.

Mewton, L., Slade, T., McBride, O., Grove, R., & Teesson, M. (2011). An evaluation of the proposed DSM-5 alcohol use disorder criteria using Australian national data. *Addiction, 106*(5), 941–950. doi:10.1111/j.1360-0443.2010.03340.x

Meyer, G. J., Finn, S. E., Eyde, L. D., Kay, G. G., Moreland, K. L., Dies, R. R., . . . Reed, G. M. (2001). Psychological testing and psychological assessment: A review of evidence and issues. *American Psychologist, 56,* 128–165.

Meyer, G. J., Finn, S. E., Eyde, L. D., Kay, G. G., Moreland, K. L., Dies, R. R., (2003). Psychological testing and psychological assessment: A review of the evidence and issues. In A. E. Kazdin (Ed.), *Methodological issues and strategies in clinical research* (pp. 265–345). Washington, DC: American Psychological Association.

Meyer, S. E., Carlson, G. A., Youngstrom, E., Ronsaville, D. S., Martinez, P. E., Gold, P. W., . . . Radke-Yarrow, M. (2009). Long-term outcomes of youth who manifested the CBCL-pediatric bipolar disorder phenotype during childhood and/or adolescence. *Journal of Affective Disorders, 113,* 227–235.

Meyera, P. S., Johnson, D. P., Parks, A., Iwanskia, C., & Penn, D. L. (2012). Positive living: A pilot study of group positive psychotherapy for people with schizophrenia. *Journal of Positive Psychology, 7,* 239–248.

Meyerson, D. A., Grant, K. E., Carter, J. S., & Kilmer, R. P. (2011). Posttraumatic growth among children and adolescents: A systematic review. *Clinical Psychology Review, 31,* 949–964.

Mezulis, A. H., Priess, H. A., & Hyde, J. S. (2011). Rumination mediates the relationship between infant temperament and adolescent depressive symptoms. *Depression Research and Treatment, 487873.*

Michael, R. T., Gagnon, J. H., Laumann, E. O., & Kolata, G. (1994). *Sex in America: A definitive survey.* New York, NY: Little, Brown.

Michal, M., Koechel, A., Canterino, M., Adler, J., Reiner, I., Vossel, G., . . . Gamer, M. (2013). Depersonalization disorder: Disconnection of cognitive evaluation from autonomic responses to emotional stimuli. *PLOS One, 8*(9), e74331. doi:10.1371/journal.pone.0074331

Michalak, E. E., Torres, I. J., Bond, D. J., Lam, R. W., & Yatham, L. N. (2013). The relationship between clinical outcomes and quality of life in first-episode mania: A longitudinal analysis. *Bipolar Disorders, 15,* 188–198.

Michl, L. C., McLaughlin, K. A., Shepherd, K., & Nolen-Hoeksema, S. (2013). Rumination as a mechanism linking stressful life events to symptoms of depression and anxiety: Longitudinal evidence in early adolescents and adults. *Journal of Abnormal Psychology, 122,* 339–352.

Midei, A. J., & Matthews, K. A. (2009). Social relationships and negative emotional traits are associated with central adiposity and arterial stiffness in health adolescents. *Health Psychology, 28,* 347–353.

Midei, A. J., Matthews, K. A., Chang, Y. F., & Bromberger, J. T. (2013). Childhood physical abuse is associated with incident metabolic syndrome in mid-life women. *Health Psychology, 32,* 121–127.

Mielke, M. M., Vemuri, P., & Rocca, W. A. (2014). Clinical epidemiology of Alzheimer's disease: Assessing sex and gender differences. *Clinical Epidemiology, 6,* 37–48.

Miettunen, J., Tormanen, S., Murray, G. K., Jones, P. B., Maki, P., Ebeling,

H., . . . Veijola, J. (2008). Association of cannabis use with prodromal symptoms of psychosis in adolescence. *British Journal of Psychiatry, 192,* 470–471.

Mihalopoulos, C., Harris, M., Henry, L., Harrigan, S., & McGorry, P. (2009). Is early intervention in psychosis cost-effective over the long term? *Schizophrenia Bulletin, 35,* 909–918.

Milillo, D. (2008). Sexuality sells: A content analysis of lesbian and heterosexual women's bodies in magazine advertisements. *Journal of Lesbian Studies, 12,* 381–386.

Miller, A. B., Esposito-Smythers, C., Weismoore, J. T., & Renshaw, K. D. (2013). The relation between child maltreatment and adolescent suicidal behavior: A systematic review and critical examination of the literature. *Clinical Child and Family Psychology Review, 16,* 146–172.

Miller, D. B., & O'Callaghan, J. P. (2013). Personalized medicine in major depressive disorder—Opportunities and pitfalls. *Metabolism, 62,* S34–S39. doi:10.1016/j.metabol.2012.08.021

Miller, E. S., Chu, C., Gollan, J., & Gossett, D. R. (2013). Obsessive-compulsive symptoms during the postpartum period. A prospective cohort. *Journal of Reproductive Medicine, 58,* 115–122.

Miller, G. E., Lachman, M. E., Chen, E., Gruenewald, T. L., Karlamangla, A. S., & Seeman, T. E. (2011). Pathways to resilience: Maternal nurturance as a buffer against the effects of childhood poverty on metabolic syndrome at midlife. *Psychological Science, 22,* 1591–1599.

Miller, J. M., Brennan, K. G., Ogden, T. R., Oquendo, M. A., Sullivan, G. M., Mann, J. J., & Parsey, R. V. (2009). Elevated serotonin 1A binding in remitted major depressive disorder: Evidence for a trait biological abnormality. *Neuropsychopharmacology, 34,* 2275–2284.

Miller, M., & Kantrowitz, B. (1999, January 25). Unmasking Sybil. *Newsweek,* pp. 66–68.

Miller, M., Swanson, S. A., Azrael, D., Pate, V., & Stürmer, T. (2014). Antidepressant dose, age, and the risk of deliberate self-harm. *JAMA Internal Medicine, 174,* 899–909.

Miller, M. N., & Pumariega, A. J. (2001). Culture and eating disorders: A historical and cross-cultural review. *Psychiatry, 64,* 93–110.

Miller, R., & Prosek, E. A. (2013). Proposed changes to the DSM-5 for vulnerable

populations. *Journal of Counseling & Development, 91,* 359–366.

Miller, T. C., & Zwerdling, D. (2010, June 9). With traumatic brain injuries, soldiers face battle for care. Retrieved from http://www.npr.org/templates/story/story.php?storyId5127542820

Millichap, J. G. (2008). Etiologic classification of attention-deficit/hyperactivity disorder. *Pediatrics, 121,* e358–e365.

Millichap, J. G., & Yee, M. M. (2012). The diet factor in attention-deficit/hyperactivity disorder. *Pediatrics, 129,* 330–337.

Millon, T., Grossman, S., Millon, C., Meagher, S., & Ramnath, R. (2004). *Personality disorders in modern life.* Hoboken, NJ: Wiley.

Mineka, S., & Zinbarg, R. (2006). A contemporary learning theory perspective on the etiology of anxiety disorders. *American Psychologist, 61,* 10–26.

Minich, D. M., & Bland, J. S. (2013). Personalized lifestyle medicine: Relevance for nutrition and lifestyle recommendations. *The Scientific World Journal.* Retrieved from http://www.hindawi.com/journals/tswj/2013/129841

Minor, K. S., & Cohen, A. S. (2012). The role of atypical semantic activation and stress in odd speech: Implications for individuals with psychometrically defined schizotypy. *Journal of Psychiatric Research, 46,* 1231–1236.

Minuchin, S. (1974). *Families and family therapy.* Cambridge, MA: Harvard University Press.

Mischoulon, D., Eddy, K. T., Keshaviah, A., Dinescu, D., Ross, S. L., Kass, A. E., . . . Herzog, D. B. (2011). Depression and eating disorders: Treatment and course. *Journal of Affective Disorders, 130,* 470–477.

Misselhorn, C., Pompe, U., & Stapleton, M. (2013). Ethical considerations regarding the use of social robots in the fourth age. *GeroPsychology, 26,* 121–133.

Mitchell, A. J., Chan, M., Bhatti, H., Halton, M., Grassi, L., Johansen, C., & Meader, N. (2011). Prevalence of depression, anxiety, and adjustment disorder in oncological, haematological, and palliative-care settings: A meta-analysis of 94 interview-based studies. *Lancet Oncology, 12,* 160–174.

Mitrouska, I., Bouloukaki, I., & Siafakas, N. M. (2007). Pharmacological approaches to smoking cessation. *Pulmonary Pharmacological Therapy, 20,* 220–32.

Mittal, V. A., Ellman, L. M., & Cannon, T. D. (2008). Gene-environment interaction and covariation in schizophrenia: The role of obstetric complications. *Schizophrenia Bulletin, 34,* 1083–1094.

Miu, A. C., Vulturar, R., Chiş, A., Ungureanu, L., & Gross, J. J. (2013). Reappraisal as a mediator in the link between 5-HTTLPR and social anxiety symptoms. *Emotion, 13,* 1012–1022.

Mizrahi, R. (2010). Advances in PET analyses of stress and dopamine. *Neuropsychopharmacology, 35,* 348–349.

Moens, E., Braet, C., & Van Winckel, M. (2010). An 8 year follow-up of treated obese children: Children's process and parental predictors of successful treatment. *Behaviour Research and Therapy, 48,* 626–633.

Moezzi, 2014 Depressionn and Bipolar Support Alliance: Life Unlimited Stories. Retrieved from http://www.dbsalliance.org/site/PageServer?pagename5peer_life_unlimited

Moffitt, T. E. (2005). The new look of behavioral genetics in developmental psychopathology: Gene-environment interplay in antisocial behaviors. *Psychological Bulletin, 131,* 533–554.

Mohr, D. C., Cox, D., & Merluzzi, N. (2005). Self-injection anxiety training: Successful treatment for patients unable to self-inject injectable medication. *Multiple Sclerosis, 11,* 182–185.

Mohr, J. J., Weiner, J. L., Chopp, R. M., & Wong, S. J. (2009). Effects of client bisexuality on clinical judgment: When is bias most likely to occur? *Journal of Counseling Psychology, 56,* 164–175.

Moisse, K., & Davis, L. (2012, January 27). Erin Brockovich launches investigation into tic illness affecting N.Y. teenagers. Retrieved from http://abcnews.go.com/Health/Wellness/erin-brockovich-launches-investigation-tic-illness-affecting-ny/story?id515456672

Mojtabai, R., & Olfson, M. (2010). National trends in psychotropic medication polypharmacy in office-based psychiatry. *Archives of General Psychiatry, 67,* 26–36.

Molz-Adams, A., Shapero, B. G., Pendergast, L. H., Alloy, L. B., & Abramson, L. Y. (2014). Self-referent information processing in individuals with bipolar spectrum disorders. *Journal of Affective Disorders, 152,* 483–490.

Moncrieff, J. (2012). Questioning the "neuroprotective" hypothesis: Does drug treatment prevent brain damage in early psychosis or schizophrenia? *British Journal of Psychiatry, 198,* 85–87.

Monk, C. S., Nelson, E. E., McClure, E. B., Mogg, K., Bradley, B. P., Leibenluft, E., . . . Pine, D. S. (2006). Ventrolateral prefrontal cortex activation and attentional bias in response to angry faces in adolescents with generalized anxiety disorder. *American Journal of Psychiatry, 163,* 1091–1097.

Montauk, S. L., & Mayhall, C. A. (2010). Attention deficit hyperactivity disorder. Retrieved from http://emedicine. medscape.com/article/912633-print

Monteith, T., & Sprenger, T. (2010). Tension type headache in adolescence and childhood: Where are we now? *Current Pain and Headache Reports, 14,* 424–430.

Montoya, I. D., & Vocci, F. (2008). Novel medications to treat addictive disorders. *Current Psychiatry Reports, 10,* 392–398.

Monzani, B., Rijsdijk, F., Cherkas, L., Harris, J., Keuthen, N., & Mataix-Cols, D. (2012b). Prevalence and heritability of skin picking in an adult community sample: A twin study. *American Journal of Medical Genetics, 159,* 605–610.

Moodley, R. (2005). Shamanic performances: Healing through magic and the supernatureal. In R. Moodley & W. West (Eds.), *Integrating traditional healing practices into counseling and psychotherapy* (pp. 2–14). Thousand Oaks, CA: Sage.

Moore, B. A., & Budney, J. (2003). Relapse in outpatient treatment for marijuana dependence. *Journal of Substance Abuse Treatment, 25,* 85–89.

Moore, C. S., Grant, M. D., Zink, T. A., Panizzon, M. S., Franz, C. E., Logue, M. W., . . . Lyons, M. J. (2014). Erectile dysfunction, vascular risk, and cognitive performance in late middle age. *Psychology of Aging, 29,* 163–172.

Moore, T. H. M., Zammit, S., Lingford-Hughes, A., Barnes, T. R. E., Jones, P. B., Burke, M., & Lewis, G. (2007). Cannabis use and risk of psychotic or affective mental health outcomes: A systematic review. *Lancet, 370,* 319–328.

Moos, R. H. (2005). Iatrogenic effects of psychosocial interventions for substance use disorders: Prevalence, predictors, prevention. *Addiction, 100,* 595–604.

Moos, R. H., & Moos, B. S. (2006). Participation in treatment and Alcoholics Anonymous: A 16-year follow-up of initially untreated individuals. *Journal of Clinical Psychology, 62,* 735–750.

Morales, A. (2012). Evolving therapeutic strategies for premature ejaculation: The search for on-demand treatment—Topical versus systemic. *Canadian Urological Association Journal, 6,* 380–385.

Morales, E., & Norcross, J. C. (2010). Evidence-based practices with ethnic minorities: Strange bedfellows no more. *Journal of Clinical Psychology: In Session, 66,* 821–829.

Moran, P., Coffey, C., Romaniuk, H., Olsson, C., Borschmann, R., Carlin, J. B., & Patton, G. C. (2012). The natural history of self-harm from adolescence to young adulthood: A population-based cohort study. *Lancet, 379,* 236–243.

Moran, R. J., Symmonds, M., Dolan, R. J., & Friston, K. J. (2014). The brain ages optimally to model its environment: Evidence from sensory learning over the adult lifespan. *PLOS Computational Biology, 10,* e1003422.

Morbidity and Mortality Weekly Report (MMWR). (2013). Suicide among adults aged 35–64 years—United States, 1999–2010. *MMWR, 62,* 321–325.

Moreno, M. A., Christakis, D. A., Egan, K. G., Brockman, L. N., & Becker, T. (2012). Associations between displayed alcohol references on Facebook and problem drinking among college students. *Archives of Pediatrics & Adolescent Medicine, 166,* 57–163.

Morgan, C. J., Muetzelfeldt, L., & Curran, H. V. (2010). Consequences of chronic ketamine self-administration upon neurocognitive function and psychological wellbeing: A 1-year longitudinal study. *Addiction, 105,* 121–133.

Morgan Consoli, M. L., & Llamas, J. D. (2013). The relationship between Mexican American cultural values and resilience among Mexican American college students: A mixed methods study. *Journal of Counseling Psychology, 60,* 617–624.

Morillo, C., Belloch, A., & Garcia-Soriano, G. (2007). Clinical obsessions in obsessive-compulsive patients and obsession-relevant intrusive thoughts in non-clinical, depressed and anxious subjects: Where are the differences? *Behaviour Research and Therapy, 45,* 1319–1333.

Morin, D., Cobigo, V., Rivard, M., & Lépine, M. (2010). Intellectual disabilities and depression: How to adapt psychological assessment and intervention. *Canadian Psychology, 51,* 185–193.

Moritz, S., Favrod, J., Andreou, C., Morrison, A. P., Bohn, F., Veckenstedt, R., . . . Karow, A. (2013). Beyond the usual suspects: Positive attitudes towards positive symptoms is associated with medication noncompliance in psychosis. *Schizophrenia Bulletin, 39,* 917–922.

Morley, T. E., & Moran, G. (2011). The origins of cognitive vulnerability in early childhood: Mechanisms linking early attachment to later depression. *Clinical Psychology Review, 31,* 1071–1082.

Morris, C. D., Miklowitz, D., & Waxmonsky, J. A. (2007). Family-focused treatment for bipolar disorder in adults and youth. *Journal of Clinical Psychology: In Session, 63,* 433–445.

Morris, J. C. (2012). Revised criteria for mild cognitive impairment may compromise the diagnosis of Alzheimer disease dementia. *Archives of Neurology, 69,* 700–708.

Morris, M. C., Ciesla, J. A., & Garber, J. (2008). A prospective study of the cognitive-stress model of depressive symptoms in adolescents. *Journal of Abnormal Psychology, 117,* 719–734.

Morris, M. C., Ciesla, J. A., & Garber, J. (2010). A prospective study of stress autonomy versus stress sensitization in adolescents at varied risk for depression. *Journal of Abnormal Psychology, 119,* 341–354.

Morris, R., Griffiths, O., Le Pelley, M. E., & Weickert, T. W. (2013). Attention to irrelevant cues is related to positive symptoms in schizophrenia. *Schizophrenia Bulletin, 39,* 575–582.

Morrison, A. P., French, P., Stewart, S. L. K., Birchwood, M., Fowler, D., Gumley, A. I., . . . Dunn, G. (2012). Early detection and intervention evaluation for people at risk of psychosis: Multisite randomised controlled trial. *British Medical Journal, 344,* e2233. doi:10.1136/bmj.e2233

Morriss, R. (2012). Role of mental health professionals in the management of functional somatic symptoms in primary care. *British Journal of Psychiatry, 200,* 444–445.

Morrow, R. L., Garland, E. J., Wright, J. M., Maclure, M., Taylor, S., & Dormuth, C. R. (2012). Influence of relative age on diagnosis and treatment of attention-deficit/hyperactivity disorder in children. *Canadian Medical Association Journal, 184,* 755–762.

Mostofsky, E., Maclure, M., Sherwood, J. B., Tofler, G. H., Muller, J. E., & Mittleman, M. A. (2012). Risk of acute myocardial infarction after the death of a significant person in one's life: The determinants of myocardial infarction onset study. *Circulation, 125,* 491–496.

Mott, J. M., Sutherland, R. J., Williams, W., Lanier, S. H., Ready, D. J., & Teng, E. J. (2012). Patient perspectives on the effectiveness and tolerability of group-based exposure therapy for posttraumatic stress disorder: Preliminary self-report findings from 20 veterans. *Psychological Trauma: Theory, Research, Practice, and Policy, 5,* 453–461.

Moukheiber, A., Rautureau, G., Perez-Diaz, F., Soussignan, R., Dubal, S., Jouvent, R., Pelissolo, A. (2010). Gaze avoidance in social phobia: Objective measure and correlates. *Behaviour Research and Therapy, 48,* 147–151.

Mueller, A., Mitchell, J. E., Crosby, R. D., Glaesmer, H., & de Zwaan, M. (2009). The prevalence of compulsive hoarding and its association with compulsive buying in a German population-based sample. *Behaviour Research and Therapy, 47,* 705–709.

Mueser, K. T., Sengupta, A., Schooler, N. R., Bellack, A. S., Xie, H., Glick, I. D., & Keith, S. J. (2001). Family treatment and medication dosage reduction in schizophrenia: Effects on patient social functioning, family attitudes, and burden. *Journal of Consulting and Clinical Psychology, 69,* 3–12.

Mufaddel, A., Osman, O. T., Almugaddam, F., & Jafferany, M. (2013). A review of body dysmorphic disorder and its presentation in different clinical settings. *Primary Care Companion to CNS Disorders, 15*(4). pii:PCC.12r01464

Muhlberger, A., Wiedemann, G., Herrmann, M. J., & Pauli, P. (2006). Phylo- and ontogenetic fears and expectations of danger: Differences between spider- and flight-phobic subjects in cognitive and physiological responses to disorder-specific stimuli. *Journal of Abnormal Psychology, 115,* 580–589.

Mujoomdar, M., Cimon, K., & Nkansah, E. (2010). Dialectical behaviour therapy in adolescents for suicide prevention: Systematic review of clinical-effectiveness. *CADTH Technological Review, 1*(1), e0104.

Mukherjee, S. (2013). This town: What it's like being homeless with a mental illness in Washington DC. Retrieved from http://thinkprogress.org/health/2013/08/28/2310961/mentally-homeless-district

Mulkens, S. A. N., de Jong, P. J., & Merckelbach, H. (1996). Disgust and spider phobia. *Journal of Abnormal Psychology, 105,* 464–468.

Müller, C. A., Geisel, O., Banas, R., & Heinz, A. (2014). Current pharmacological treatment approaches for alcohol dependence. *Expert Opinion in Pharmacotherapy, 15,* 471–481.

Muller, R. J. (2006). A woman who refused treatment for a paranoid psychosis. *Psychiatric Times, 23,* 422–424.

Müller, T. D., & Tschöp, M. H. (2013). Ghrelin—A key pleiotropic hormone-regulating systemic energy metabolism. *Endocrine Development, 25,* 91–100.

Munder, T., Brütsch, O., Leonhart, R., Gerger, H., & Barth, J. (2013). Researcher allegiance in psychotherapy outcome research: An overview of reviews. *Clinical Psychology Review, 33,* 501–511.

Munsey, C. (2010). Medicine or menace? Psychologists' research can inform the growing debate over legalizing marijuana. *APA Monitor, 41*(6), 50.

Murad, M. H., Elamin, M. B., Garcia, M. Z., Mullan, R. J., Murad, A., Erwin, P. J., & Montori, V. M. (2010). Hormonal therapy and sex reassignment: A systematic review and meta-analysis of quality of life and psychosocial outcomes. *Clinical Endocrinology, 72,* 214–231.

Muris, P., & Dietvorst, R. (2006). Underlying personality characteristics of behavioral inhibition in children. *Child Psychiatry and Development, 36,* 437–445.

Muris, P., Merckelbach, H., & Clavan, M. (1997). Abnormal and normal compulsions. *Behaviour Research and Therapy, 35,* 249–252.

Muris, P., Merckelbach, H., & Collaris, R. (1997). Common childhood fears and their origins. *Behaviour Research and Therapy, 35,* 929–936.

Muris, P., van Zwol, L., Huijding, J., & Mayer, B. (2010). Mom told me scary things about this animal: Parents installing fear beliefs in their children via the verbal information pathway. *Behaviour Research and Therapy, 48,* 341–346.

Murphy, H., & Perera-Delcourt, R. (2014). "Learning to live with OCD is a little mantra I often repeat": Understanding the lived experience of obsessive-compulsive disorder (OCD) in the contemporary therapeutic context. *Psychology and Psychotherapy, 87,* 111–125.

Murphy, S. L., Xu, J., & Kochanek, K. D. (2013). Deaths: Final data for 2010. *National Vital Statistics Reports, 61,* 1–118.

Murray, C. K., Reynolds, J. C., Schroeder, J. M., Harrison, M. B., Evans, O. M., & Hospenthal, D. R. (2005). Spectrum of care provided at an Echelon II medical unit during Operation Iraqi Freedom. *Military Medicine, 170,* 516–520.

Murray, H. A., & Morgan, H. (1938). *Explorations in personality.* New York, NY: Oxford University Press.

Murray, S. B., Rieger, E., Touyz, S. W., & De la Garza Garcia, Y. (2010). Muscle dysmorphia and the DSM-V conundrum: Where does it belong? A review paper. *International Journal of Eating Disorders, 43,* 483–491.

Muscatell, K. A., Slavich, G. M., Monroe, S. M., & Gotlib, I. H. (2009). Stressful life events, chronic difficulties, and the symptoms of clinical depression. *Journal of Nervous and Mental Diseases, 197,* 154–c160.

Muse, K., McManus, F., Hackmann, A., Williams, M., & Williams, M. (2010). Intrusive imagery in severe health anxiety: Prevalence, nature and links with memory and maintenance cycles. *Behaviour Research and Therapy, 48,* 792–798.

Mustafa, B., Evrim, O., & Sari, A. (2005). Secondary mania following traumatic brain injury. *Journal of Neuropsychiatry and Clinical Neuroscience, 17,* 122–124.

Mustanski, B., & Liu, R. T. (2013). A longitudinal study of predictors of suicide attempts among lesbian, gay, bisexual, and transgender youth. *Archives of Sexual Behavior, 42,* 437–448.

Myers, S. G., & Wells, A. (2013). An experimental manipulation of metacognition: A test of the metacognitive model of obsessive-compulsive symptoms. *Behaviour Research & Therapy, 51,* 177–184.

Myers, S. M., Johnson, C. P., & Council on Children with Disabilities. (2007). Management of children with autism spectrum disorders. *Pediatrics, 120,* 1162–1182.

Myers, T. A., & Crowther, J. H. (2009). Social comparison as a predictor of body satisfaction. *Journal of Abnormal Psychology, 118,* 683–698.

Nademanee, K., Veerakul, G., Nimmannit, S., Chaowakul, V., Bhuripanyo, K., Likittanasombat, K., . . . Tatsanavivat, P. (1997). Arrhythmogenic marker for sudden unexplained death syndrome in Thai men. *Circulation, 96,* 2595–2600.

Naeem, F., Waheed, W., Gobbi, M., Ayub, M., & Kingdon, D. (2011). Preliminary evaluation of culturally sensitive CBT for depression in Pakistan: Findings from Developing Culturally Sensitive CBT Project (DCCP). *Behavioral and Cognitive Psychotherapy, 39,* 165–173.

Nagano, J., Kakuta, C., Motomura, C., Odajima, H., Sudo, N., Nishima, S., & Kubo, C. (2010). The parenting attitudes and the stress of mothers predict the asthmatic severity of their children: A prospective study. *BioPsychoSocial Medicine, 4,* 12. doi:10.1186/1751-0759-4-12

Naggiar, S. (2012). "Broken heart" syndrome can be triggered by stress, grief. Retrieved from: http://vitals.nbcnews.com/_news/2012/09/24/14072649-broken-heart-syndrome-can-be-triggered-by-stress-grief?lite

Namiki, C., Yamada, M., Yoshida, H., Hanakawa, T., Fukuyama, H., & Murai, T. (2008). Small orbitofrontal traumatic lesions detected by high resolution MRI in a patient with major behavioral changes. *Neurocase, 14,* 474–479.

Nappi, R. E., Kingsberg, S., Maamari, R., & Simon, J. (2013). The CLOSER (CLarifying Vaginal Atrophy's Impact On SEx and Relationships) survey: Implications of vaginal discomfort in postmenopausal women and in male partners. *Journal of Sexual Medicine, 10,* 2232–2241.

Nardi, A. E., Freire, R. C., Mochcovitch, M. D., Amrein, R., Levitan, M. N., King, A. L., . . . Versiani, M. (2012). A randomized, naturalistic, parallel-group study for the long-term treatment of panic disorder. *Journal of Clinical Psychopharmacology, 32,* 120–126.

Nashoni, E., Yaroslavsky, A., Varticovschi, P., Weizman, A., & Stein, D. (2010). Alterations in QT dispersion in the surface electrocardiogram of female adolescent inpatients diagnosed with bulimia nervosa. *Comprehensive Psychiatry, 51,* 406–411.

Nasrallah, H. A. (2009). Diagnosis 2.0. Are mental illnesses diseases, disorders, or syndromes? *Current Psychiatry, 8,* 14–16.

National Board for Certification in Occupational Therapy. (2012). Sexual misconduct by professionals. Retrieved from http://www.nbcot.org/index.php?option5com_content&view5article&id5128%3Asexual-misconduct-by-professionals&catid52&Itemid5119

National Cancer Institute. (2012). Psychological stress and cancer. Retrieved from http://www.cancer.gov/cancertopics/factsheet/Risk/stress

National Center for Health Statistics. (2012). *Health, United States, 2011: With special feature on socioeconomic status and health.* Hyattsville, MD: Library of Congress.

National Center for Trangender Equality. (2009). Understanding transgender. Retrieved from http://transequality.org/Resources/NCTE_UnderstandingTrans.pdf

National Dissemination Center for Children with Disabilities. (2012). Intellectual disability. Retrieved from http://nichcy.org/disability/specific/intellectual

National Down Syndrome Society. (2014). What is Down syndrome? Retrieved from https://www.ndss.org/Down-Syndrome/What-Is-Down-Syndrome/

National Institute of Child Health and Human Development. (2011a). Down syndrome. Retrieved from http://www.nichd.nih.gov/health/topics/down_syndrome.cfm

National Institute of Child Health and Human Development. (2011b). Fragile X syndrome. Retrieved from http://www.nichd.nih.gov/health/topics/fragile_x_syndrome.cfm

National Institute of Mental Health. (2009). Anxiety disorders. Retrieved from http://www.nimh.nih.gov/health/publications/anxiety-disorders/nimhanxiety.pdf

National Institute of Mental Health. (2010). *Social phobia (social anxiety disorder).* NIMH publication no. TR 10-4678, revised 2010. U.S. Department of Health and Human Services, National Institutes of Health.

National Institute of Mental Health. (2011a). Depression. Retrieved from http://www.nimh.nih.gov/health/publications/depression/depression-booklet.pdf

National Institute of Mental Health. (2011b). Eating disorders. Retrieved from http://www.nimh.nih.gov/health/publications/eating-disorders/index.shtml

National Institute of Mental Health. (2013a). *Generalized anxiety disorder.* NIH Publication No. TR 10-4677. U.S. Department of Health and Human Services, National Institutes of Health.

National Institute of Mental Health. (2013b). *Obsessive-compulsive disorder.* NIH Publication No. TR 10-4676. U.S. Department of Health and Human Services, National Institutes of Health.

National Institute of Mental Health. (2013c). *Panic disorder.* NIH Publication No. TR 10-4679. U.S. Department of Health and Human Services, National Institutes of Health.

National Institute of Mental Health. (2014). Eating disorders. Retrieved from http://www.nimh.nih.gov/health/publications/eating-disorders/index.shtml#pub1

National Institute of Neurological Disorders and Stroke. (2012). Headache: Hope through research. Retrieved from http://www.ninds.nih.gov/disorders/headache/detail_headache.htm

National Institute of Neurological Disorders and Stroke. (2014). NINDS Parkinson's disease information page. Retrieved from http://www.ninds.nih.gov/disorders/parkinsons_disease/parkinsons_disease.htm

National Institutes of Health. (2013). Suicide and suicidal behavior. Retrieved from http://www.nlm.nih.gov/medlineplus/ency/article/001554.htm

National Sleep Foundation. (2014). How sleep works. Retrieved from http://www.sleepfoundation.org/primary-links/how-sleep-works

National Stroke Association. (2014). Unique symptoms in women. Retrieved from http://www.stroke.org/site/PageServer?pagename5WOMSYMP

Naumann, E., Tuschen-Caffier, B., Voderholzer, U., & Svaldi, J. (2014). On the role of sadness in the psychopathology of anorexia nervosa. *Psychiatry Research, 215,* 711–717.

Navaneelan, T. (2013). Suicide rates: An overview. Retrieved from http://www.statcan.gc.ca/pub/82-624-x/2012001/article/11696-eng.htm

Neacsiu, A. D., Lungu, A., Harned, M. S., Rizvi, S. L., & Linehan, M. M. (2014). Impact of dialectical behavior therapy versus community treatment by experts on emotional experience, expression, and acceptance in borderline personality disorder. *Behaviour Research and Therapy, 53,* 47–54.

Neal-Barnett, A., Flessner, C., Franklin, M. E., Woods, D. W., Keuthen, N. J., & Stein, D. W. (2010). Ethnic differences in trichotillomania: Phenomenology, interference, impairment, and treatment efficacy. *Journal of Anxiety Disorders, 24,* 553–558.

Neerakal, I., & Srinivasan, K. (2003). A study of the phenomenology of panic attacks in patients from India. *Psychopathology, 36,* 92–97.

Negreponti, A. (2012). Surviving anorexia. Retrieved from http://www.huffingtonpost.com/amalia-negreponti/anorexia_b_1364462.html

Neighbors, L., & Sobal, J. (2007). Prevalence and magnitude of body weight and shape dissatisfaction among university students. *Eating Behaviors, 9,* 429–439.

Nelson, B., & Yung, A. R. (2011). Should a risk syndrome for first episode psychosis be included in the DSM-5? *Current Opinion in Psychiatry, 24,* 128–133.

Nelson, G., Aubry, T., & Lawrence, A. (2007). A review of the literature on the effectiveness of housing and support, assertive community treatment, and intensive case management interventions for persons with mental illness who have been homeless. *American Journal of Orthopsychiatry, 77,* 350–361.

Neng, J. M., & Weck, F. (2014). Attribution of somatic symptoms in hypochondriasis. *Clinical Psychology and Psychotherapy.* doi: 10.1002/cpp.1871.

Nervi, A., Reitz, C., Tang, M. X., Santana, V., Piriz, A., Reyes, D., . . . Mayeux, R. (2011). Familial aggregation of dementia with Lewy bodies. *British Archives of Neurology, 68,* 90–93.

Nestler, E. J., & Malenka, R. C. (2004). The addicted brain. *Scientific American, 290,* 50–57.

Neugebauer, R. (1979). Medieval and early modern theories of mental illness. *Archives of General Psychiatry, 36,* 477–483.

Neumark-Sztainer, D., Hannan, P. J., & Stat, M. (2000). Weight-related behaviors among adolescent girls and boys. *Archives of Pediatrics & Adolescent Medicine, 154,* 569–577.

Neumark-Sztainer, D., Wall, M., Story, M., & Fulkerson, J. A. (2004). Are family meal patterns associated with disordered eating behaviors among adolescents? *Journal of Adolescent Health, 35,* 350–359.

Neutze, J., Grundmann, D., Scherner, G., & Beier, K. M. (2012). Undetected and detected child sexual abuse and child pornography offenders. *International Journal of Law and Psychiatry, 35,* 168–175.

Nevéus, T. (2011). Nocturnal enuresis—Theoretic background and practical guidelines. *Pediatric Nephrology, 26,* 1207–*1214.*

Newman, C. F. (2010). The case of Gabriel: Treatment with Beckian cognitive therapy. *Journal of Constructivist Psychology, 23,* 25–41.

Newman, J. P., Curtin, J. J., Bertsch, J. D., & Baskin-Sommers, A. R. (2010). Attention moderates the fearlessness of psychopathic offenders. *Biological Psychiatry, 67,* 66–70.

Newnham, E. A., & Janca, A. (2014). Childhood adversity and borderline personality disorder: A focus on adolescence. *Current Opinion in Psychiatry, 27,* 68–72.

Newschaffer, C. J., Croen, L. A., Daniels, J., Giarelli, E., Grether, J. K., Levy, S. E., . . . Windham, G. C. (2007). The epidemiology of autism spectrum disorders. *Annual Review of Public Health, 28,* 235–258.

Nichols, M. P., & Schwartz, R. C. (2005). *The essentials of family therapy.* New York, NY: Allyn & Bacon.

Nickerson, A., Aderka, I. M., Bryant, R. A., & Hofmann, S. G. (2012). The relationship between childhood exposure to trauma and intermittent explosive disorder. *Psychiatry Research, 197,* 128–134.

Niederkrotenthaler, T., Fu, K.-W., Yip, P. S. F., Fong, D. Y. T., Stack, S., Cheng, Q., & Pirkis, J. (2012). Changes in suicide rates following media reports on celebrity suicide: A meta-analysis. *Journal of Epidemiology and Community Health, 66,* 1037–1042.

Nielsen, S., Hillhouse, M., Thomas, C., Hasson, A., & Ling, W. (2013). A comparison of buprenorphine taper outcomes between prescription opioid and heroin users. *Journal of Addictive Medicine, 7,* 33–38.

Nierenberg, A. A., Akiskal, H. S., Angst, J., Hirschfeld, R. M., Merikangas, K. R., Petukhova, M., & Kessler, R. C. (2010). Bipolar disorder with frequent mood episodes in the National Comorbidity Survey Replication (NCS-R). *Molecular Psychiatry, 15,* 1075–1087.

Nillni, Y. I., Rohan, K. J., Bernstein, A., & Zvolensky, M. J. (2010). Premenstrual distress predicts panic-relevant responding to a CO2 challenge among young adult females. *Journal of Anxiety Disorder, 24,* 416–422.

Nisbett, R. E. (2005). Heredity, environment, and race differences in IQ: A commentary on Rushton and Jensen (2005). *Psychology, Public Policy, and Law, 11,* 302–310.

Nixon, R., Sterk, J., & Pearce, A. (2012). A randomized trial of cognitive behaviour therapy and cognitive therapy for children with posttraumatic stress disorder following single-incident trauma. *Journal of Abnormal Child Psychology, 40,* 327–337.

Nobel, L., Mayo, N. E., Hanley, J., Nadeau, L., & Daskalopoulou, S. S. (2014). MyRisk_Stroke Calculator: A personalized stroke risk assessment tool for the general population. *Journal of Clinical Neurology, 10,* 1–9.

Nock, M. K., Green, J. G., Hwang, I., McLaughlin, K. A., Sampson, N. A., Zaslavsky, A. M., & Kessler, R. C. (2013). Prevalence, correlates, and treatment of lifetime suicidal behavior among adolescents: Results from the National Comorbidity Survey Replication Adolescent Supplement. *JAMA Psychiatry, 70,* 300–310.

Nock, M. K., Stein, M. B., Heeringa, S. G., Ursano, R. J., Colpe, L. J., Fullerton, C. S., . . . Kessler, R. C. (2014). Prevalence and correlates of suicidal behavior among soldiers. *JAMA Psychiatry, 71,* 514–522.

Nolen-Hoeksema, S. (2004). Gender differences in depression. In T. F. Oltmanns & R. E. Emery (Eds.), *Current directions in abnormal psychology* (pp. 49–55). Upper Saddle River, NJ: Prentice Hall.

Nolen-Hoeksema, S. (2012). Emotion regulation and psychopathology: The role of gender. *Annual Review of Clinical Psychology, 8,* 161–187.

Nolen-Hoeksema, S., Girgus, J. S., & Seligman, M. E. (1992). Predictors and consequences of childhood depressive symptoms: A 5-year longitudinal study. *Journal of Abnormal Psychology, 101,* 405–422.

Noll, J. G., Shenk, C. E., & Putnam, K. T. (2009). Childhood sexual abuse and adolescent pregnancy: A meta-analytic update. *Journal of Pediatric Psychology, 34,* 366–378.

Norcross, J. C. (2004). Empirically supported treatments (ESTs): Context, consensus, and controversy. *Register Report, 30,* 12–14.

Nordahl, C. W., Lange, N., Li, D. D., Barnett, L. A., Lee, A., Buonocore, M. H., . . . Amaral, D. G. (2011). Brain enlargement is associated with regression in preschool-age boys with autism spectrum disorders. *Proceedings of the National Academy of Sciences U S A, 108,* 20195–20200.

Nordahl, C. W., Scholz, R., Yang, X., Buonocore, M. H., Simon, T., Rogers, S., & Amaral, D. G. (2012). Increased rate of amygdala growth in children aged 2 to 4 years with autism spectrum disorders: A longitudinal study. *Archives of General Psychiatry, 69,* 53–61.

Nordentoft, M., & Hjorthoj, C. (2007). Cannabis use and risk of psychosis in later life. *Lancet, 370,* 293–294.

Nordstrom, B. R., & Levin, F. R. (2007). Treatment of cannabis use disorders: A review of the literature. *American Journal of Addiction, 16,* 331–342.

Norfleet, M. A. (2002). Responding to society's needs: Prescription privileges for psychologists. *Journal of Clinical Psychology, 58,* 599–610.

Norko, M. A. (2008). Duty to warn and dissociative identity disorder. *American Medical Association Journal of Ethics, 10,* 144–149.

Norton, P. J., & Barrera, T. L. (2012). Transdiagnostic versus diagnosis-specific CBT for anxiety disorders: A preliminary randomized controlled noninferiority trial. *Depression and Anxiety, 29,* 874–882.

Noveck, J., & Tompson, T. (2007). Poll: Family, friends make youths happy. Retrieved from http://www.usatoday.com/news/topstories/2007-08-19-1958101914_x.htm

Noyes, R., Jr., Stuart, S., Watson, D. B., & Langbehn, D. R. (2006). Distinguishing between hypochondriasis and somatization disorder: A review of the existing literature. *Psychotherapy and Psychosomatics, 75,* 270–281.

Nuevo, R., Chatterji, S., Verdes, E., Naidoo, N., Arango, C., & Ayuso-Mateos, J. L. (2012). The continuum of psychotic symptoms in the general population: A cross-national study. *Schizophrenia Bulletin, 38,* 475–485.

Nutt, D. J., King, L. A., & Phillip, L. D. (2010). Drug harms in the UK: A multicriteria decision analysis. *Lancet, 376*(9752), 1558–1565.

Oberndorfer, T. A., Frank, G. K., Simmons, A. N., Wagner, A., McCurdy, D., Fudge, J. L., . . . Kaye, W. H. (2013). Altered insula response to sweet taste processing after recovery from anorexia and bulimia nervosa. *American Journal of Psychiatry, 170,* 1143–1151.

O'Brien, M. P., Gordon, J. L., Bearden, C. E., Lopez, S. R., Kopelowicz, A., & Cannon, T. D. (2006). Positive family environment predicts improvement in symptoms and social functioning among adolescents at imminent risk for onset of psychosis. *Schizophrenia Research, 81,* 269–275.

O'Brien, W. H., & Carhart, V. (2011). Functional analysis in behavioral medicine. *European Journal of Psychological Assessment, 27,* 4–16.

O'Connell, K. A., Hosein, V. L., Schwartz, J. E., & Leibowitz, R. Q. (2007). How does coping help people resist lapses during smoking cessation? *Health Psychology, 26,* 77–84.

O'Connell, M. E., Boat, T., & Warner, K. E. (2009). *Preventing mental, emotional, and behavioral disorders among young people: Progress and possibilities.* Washington, DC: National Academies Press. Retrieved from http://www.nap.edu/catalog.php?record_id512480

O'Connor v. Donaldson, 95 S. Ct. 2486 (1975).

Odlaug, B. L., Kim, S. W., & Grant, J. E. (2010). Quality of life and clinical severity in pathological skin picking and trichotillomania. *Journal of Anxiety Disorders, 24,* 823–829.

O'Donnell, M. J., Xavier, D., Liu, L., Zhang, H., Chin, S. L., Rao-Melacini, P., . . . Yusuf, S. (2010). Risk factors for ischaemic and intracerebral haemorrhagic stroke in 22 countries (the INTERSTROKE study): A case-control study. *Lancet, 376,* 112–123.

Ogden, C. L., Fryar, C. D., Carroll, M. D., & Flegal, K. M. (2004). *Mean body weight, height, and body mass index, United States 1960–2002: Advance data from vital and health statistics (no. 347).* Hyattsville, MD: National Center for Health Statistics.

Ohayon, M. M. (2012). Determining the level of sleepiness in the American population and its correlates. *Journal of Psychiatric Research, 46,* 422–427.

Ohayon, M. M., Dauvilliers, Y., & Reynolds, C. F. (2012). Operational definitions and algorithms for excessive sleepiness in the general population: Implications for DSM-5 nosology. *Archives of General Psychiatry, 69,* 71–79.

Ohayon, M. M., Mahowald, M. W., Dauvilliers, Y., Krystal, A. D., & Léger, D. (2012). Prevalence and comorbidity of nocturnal wandering in the U.S. adult general population. *Neurology, 78,* 1583–1589.

Ohno, M., & Caughey, A. (2013). The role of noninvasive prenatal testing as a diagnostic versus a screening tool—A cost-effectiveness analysis. *Prenatal Diagnostics, 33,* 630–635.

Okazaki, S., Liu, J. F., Longworth, S. L., & Minn, J. Y. (2002). Asian American–white American differences in expressions of social anxiety: A replication and extension. *Cultural Diversity and Ethnic Minority Psychology, 8,* 234–247.

Okereke, O. I., Prescott, J., Wong , J.-Y. Y., Han, J., Rexrode, K. M., & De Vivo, I. (2012). High phobic anxiety is related to lower leukocyte telomere length in women. *PLOS One, 7*(7), e40516. doi:10.1371/journal.pone.0040516

Olatunji, B. O., Etzel, E. N., Tomarken, A. J., Ciesielski, B. G., & Deacon, B. (2011). The effects of safety behaviors on health anxiety: An experimental investigation. *Behaviour Research and Therapy, 49,* 719–728.

Olatunji, B. O., Rosenfield, D., Tart, C. D., Cottraux, J., Powers, M. B., & Smits, J. A. (2013). Behavioral versus cognitive treatment of obsessive-compulsive disorder: An examination of outcome and mediators of change. *Journal of Consulting and Clinical Psychology, 81,* 415–428.

Oldham, J. M. (2006). Integrated treatment for borderline personality disorder. *Psychiatric Annals, 36,* 361–362, 364–369.

Olfson, M., Blanco, C., Wang, S., Laje, G., & Correll, C. U. (2014). National trends in the mental health care of children, adolescents, and adults by office-based physicians. *JAMA Psychiatry, 71,* 81–90.

Olfson, M., & Marcus, S. C. (2008). A case-control study of antidepressants and attempted suicide during early phase treatment of major depressive episodes. *Journal of Clinical Psychiatry, 69,* 425–432.

Oliver, C., Berg, K., Moss, J., Arron, K., & Burbidge, C. (2011). Delineation of behavioral phenotypes in genetic syndromes: Characteristics of autism spectrum disorder, affect and hyperactivity. *Journal of Autism and Developmental Disorders, 41,* 1019–1032. doi:10.1007/s10803-010-1125-5

Olmos, J. M., Valero, C., Gomez del Barrio, A., Amando, J. A., Hernandez, J. L., Menendez-Arango, J., & Gonzalez-Macia, J. (2010). Time course of bone loss in patients with anorexia nervosa. *International Journal of Eating Disorders, 43,* 537–542.

Olsavsky, A. K., Brotman, M. A., Rutenberg, J. G., Muhrer, E. J., Deveney, C. M., Fromm, S. J., . . . Leibenluft, E. (2012). Amygdala hyperactivation during face emotion processing in unaffected youth at risk for bipolar disorder. *Journal of the American Academy of Child & Adolescent Psychiatry, 51,* 294–303.

Olshansky, S. J. (2011). Aging of US presidents. *Journal of the American Medical Association, 306,* 2328–2329.

Olsson, A., Nearing, K. I., & Phelps, E. A. (2007). Learning fears by observing others: The neural systems of social fear transmission. *Scan, 2,* 3–11.

O'Neil, K. A., Conner, B. T., & Kendall, P. C. (2011). Internalizing disorders and substance use disorders in youth: Comorbidity, risk, temporal order, and implications for intervention. *Clinical Psychology Review, 31,* 104–112.

Ooteman, W., Naassila, M., Koeter, M. W., Verheul, R., Schippers, G. M., Houchi, H., . . . van den Brink, W. (2009). Predicting the effect of naltrexone and acamprosate in alcohol-dependent patients using genetic indicators. *Addictive Biology, 14,* 328–337.

Oquendo, M. A., Baca-García, E., Mann, J. J., & Giner, J. (2008). Issues for DSM-V: suicidal behavior as a separate diagnosis on a separate axis. *American Journal of Psychiatry, 165,* 1383–1384.

Oquendo, M. A., Currier, D., Liu, S. M., Hasin, D. S., Grant, B. F., & Blanco, C. (2010). Increased risk for suicidal behavior in comorbid bipolar disorder and alcohol use disorders: Results from the National Epidemiologic Survey on Alcohol and Related Conditions (NESARC). *Journal of Clinical Psychiatry, 71,* 902–909.

Oregon Public Health Division. (2013). Oregon's Death with Dignity Act—2012. Retrieved from http://public.health.oregon.gov/ProviderPartnerResources/EvaluationResearch/DeathwithDignityAct/Documents/year15.pdf

Ortiz, R. M. (2011, October). Physiology of cardiovascular disease: Gender disparities. Presented at the meeting of the American Physiological Society, Jackson, MS.

Osbourne, L. (2001, May 6). Regional disturbances. *New York Times Magazine.* Retrieved from http://www.nytimes.com/2001/05/06/magazine/06LATAH.html?pagewanted5all

Osher, C. N., & Brown, J. (2014). Drug firms have used dangerous tactics to drive sales to treat kids. Retrieved from http://www.denverpost.com/investigations/ci_25561024/drug-firms-have-used-dangerous-tactics-drive-sales

Öst, L.-G. (1987). Age of onset in different phobias. *Journal of Abnormal Psychology, 96,* 223–229.

Öst, L.-G. (1992). Blood and injection phobia: Background and cognitive, physiological, and behavioral variables. *Journal of Abnormal Psychology, 101,* 68–74.

Ostchega, Y., Yoon, S. S., Hughes, J., & Louis, T. (2008). Hypertension awareness, treatment, and control—Continued disparities in adults: United States, 2005–2006. *National Center for Health Statistics, 3,* 1–8.

Oster, T. J., Anderson, C. A., Filley, C. M., Wortzel, H. S., & Arciniegas, D. B. (2007). Quetiapine for mania due to traumatic brain injury. *CNS Spectrums, 12,* 764–769.

Otiniano-Verissimo, A. D., Gee, G. C., Ford, C. L., & Iguchi, M. Y. (2014). Racial discrimination, gender discrimination, and substance abuse among Latina/os nationwide. *Cultural Diversity and Ethnic Minority Psychology, 20,* 43–51.

Otto, M. W., McHugh, R. K., Simon, N. M., Farach, F. J., Worthington, J. J., & Pollack, M. H. (2010). Efficacy of CBT for benzodiazepine discontinuation in patients with panic disorder: Further evaluation. *Behaviour Research and Therapy, 48,* 720–727.

Owen, P. R. (2012). Portrayals of schizophrenia by entertainment media: A content analysis of contemporary movies. *Psychiatric Services, 63,* 655–659.

Ozomaro, U., Wahlestedt, C., & Nemeroff, C.B. (2013). Personalized medicine in psychiatry: Problems and promises. *BMC Medicine, 11,* 132. doi:10.1186/1741-7015-11-132

Ozonoff, S., Iosif, A. M., Baguio, F., Cook, I. C., Hill, M. M., . . . Sigman, M. (2010). A prospective study of the emergence of early behavioral signs of autism. *Journal of the American Academy of Child & Adolescent Psychiatry, 49,* 256–266.

Ozonoff, S., Young, G. S., Carter, A., Messinger, D., Yirmiya, N., Zwaigenbaum, L., . . . Stone, W. L. (2011). Recurrence risk for autism spectrum disorders: A baby siblings research consortium study. *Pediatrics, 128,* e488–495. [Epub 2011 Aug 15]

Paik, A., & Laumann, E. O. (2006). Prevalence of women's sexual problems in the USA. In I. Goldstein, C. M. Meston, S. R. Davis, & A. M. Traish (Eds.), *Women's sexual function and dysfunction* (pp. 23–33). London, UK: Taylor & Francis.

Pail, G., Huf, W., Pjrek, E., Winkler, D., Willeit, M., Praschak-Rieder, N., & Kasper, S. (2011). Bright-light therapy in the treatment of mood disorders. *Neuropsychobiology, 64,* 152–162.

Palavras, M. A., Kaio, G. H., Mari, J., & Claudino, A. M. (2011). A review of the state of the art of the scientific literature on binge eating disorder in Latin America. *Revista Brasileria Psiquiatrica, 33*(Suppl 1), S81–S108.

Palazzolo, D. L. (2013). Electronic cigarettes and vaping: A new challenge in clinical medicine and public health. A literature review. *Frontiers in Public Health, 1,* 56. eCollection.

Palfi, S., Gurruchaga, J. M., Ralph, G. S., Lepetit, H., Lavisse, S., Buttery, P. C., . . . Mitrophanous, K. A. (2014). Long-term safety and tolerability of ProSavin, a lentiviral vector-based gene therapy for Parkinson's disease: A dose escalation, open-label, phase 1/2 trial. *Lancet, 383,* 1138–1146.

Pan, A., Sun, Q., Okereke, O. I., Rexrode, K. M., & Hu, F. B. (2011). Depression and risk of stroke morbidity and mortality: A meta-analysis and systematic review. *Journal of the American Medical Association, 306,* 1241–1249.

Pan, D. (2013). Map: Which states have cut treatment for the mentally ill the most? Retrieved from http://www.motherjones.com/mojo/2013/04/map-states-cut-treatment-for-mentally-ill

Pandey, G. N. (2013). Biological basis of suicide and suicidal behavior. *Bipolar Disorders, 15,* 524–541.

Papadopoulous, F. C., Ekbom, A., Brandt, L., & Ekselius, L. (2009). Excess mortality, causes of death and prognostic factors in anorexia nervosa. *British Journal of Psychiatry, 194,* 10–17.

Papousek, I., Reiser, E. M., Schulter, G., Fink, A., Holmes, E. A., Niederstätter, H., . . . Weiss, E. M. (2013). Serotonin transporter genotype (5-HTTLPR) and electrocortical responses indicating the sensitivity to negative emotional cues. *Emotion, 13,* 1173–1181.

Paquette, M. (2007). Morgellons: Disease or delusions? *Perspectives in Psychiatric Care, 43,* 67–68.

Paras, M. L., Murad, M. H., Chen, L. P., Goranson, E. N., Sattler, A. L., Colbenson, K. M., . . . Zirkzadeh, A. (2009). Sexual abuse and lifetime diagnosis of somatic disorders: A systematic review and meta-analysis. *Journal of the American Medical Association, 302,* 550–561.

Pardini, D. A., & Byrd, A. L. (2012). Perceptions of aggressive conflicts and others' distress in children with callous-unemotional traits: "I'll show you who's boss, even if you suffer and I get in trouble." *Journal of Child Psychology and Psychiatry, 53,* 283–291.

Parens, E., & Johnston, J. (2009). Facts, values, and attention-deficit hyperactivity disorder (ADHD): An update on the controversies. *Child and Adolescent Psychiatry and Mental Health, 3,* 1–17.

Parens, E., & Johnston, J. (2010). Controversies concerning the diagnosis and treatment of bipolar disorder in children. *Childhood and Adolescent Psychiatry and Mental Health, 10,* 4–9.

Parikshak, N. N., Luo, R., Zhang, A., Won, H., Lowe, J. K., Chandran, V., . . . Geschwind, D. H. (2013). Integrative functional genomic analyses implicate specific molecular pathways and circuits in autism. *Cell, 155,* 1008–1021.

Parish, B. S., & Yutzy, S. H. (2011). Somatoform disorders. In R. E. Hales, S. C. Yudofsky, & G. O. Babbard (Eds.), *Essentials of psychiatry* (3rd ed., pp. 229–254). Arlington, VA: American Psychiatric Publishing.

Parker, S., Nichter, M., Vuckovic, N., Sims, C., & Ritenbaugh, C. (1995). Body image and weight concerns among African-American and white adolescent females: Differences that make a difference. *Human Organization, 54,* 103–114.

Parsons, J. T., Grov, C., & Kelly, B. C. (2009). Club drug use and dependence among young adults recruited through time-space sampling. *Public Health Reports, 124*(2), 246–254.

Partnership for a Drug-Free America & MetLife Foundation. (2010). 2009 parents and teens attitude tracking study. Retrieved from http://drugfreetexas.org/wp-content/files_mf/1267570941PATS_Full_Report_2009_PDF.pdf

Pascoe, E. A., & Richman, L. S. (2009). Perceived discrimination and health: A meta-analytic review. *Psychological Bulletin, 135,* 531–554.

Patel, S. B., Poston, J. T., Pohlman, A., Hall, J. B., & Kress, J. P. (2014). Rapidly reversible, sedation-related delirium versus persistent delirium in the ICU. *American Journal of Respiratory Critical Care Medicine, 189,* 658–665.

Patihis, L., Ho, L.Y., Tingen, I.W., Lilienfeld, S. O., & Loftus, E. F. (2014). Are the "memory wars" over? A scientist-practitioner gap in beliefs about repressed memory. *Psychological Science, 25,* 519–530.

Patra, A. P., Bharadwaj, B., Shaha, K. K., Das, S., Rayamane, A. P., & Tripathi, C. S. (2013). Impulsive frotteurism: A case report. *Medicine, Science, and the Law, 53,* 235–238.

Patterson, G. R. (1986). Performance models for antisocial boys. *American Psychologist, 41,* 432–444.

Patton, G. C., Tollit, M. M., Romaniuk, H., Spence, S. H., Sheffield, J., & Sawyer, M. G. (2011). A prospective study of the effects of optimism on adolescent health risks. *Pediatrics, 127,* 306–316.

Paulozzi, L., Baldwin, G., Franklin, G., Kerlikowske, R. G., Jones, C. M., Ghiya, N., & Popovic, T. (2012). CDC grand rounds: Prescription drug overdoses, a U.S. epidemic. *Morbidity & Mortality Weekly Report, 61,* 10–13.

Pazmany, E., Bergeron, S., Van Oudenhove, L., Verhaeghe, J., & Enzlin, P. (2013). Body image and genital self-image in pre-menopausal women with dyspareunia. *Archives of Sexual Behavior, 42,* 999–1010.

Pearce, L. R., Atanassova, N., Banton, M. C., Bottomley, B., van der Klaauw, A. A., Revelli, J. P., . . . Farooqi, I. S. (2013). KSR2 mutations are associated with obesity, insulin resistance, and impaired cellular fuel oxidation. *Cell, 155,* 765–777.

Pearce, M. S., Salotti, J. A., Little, M. P., McHugh, K., Lee, C., Kim, K. P., . . . de Gonzalez, A. (2012). Radiation exposure from CT scans in childhood and subsequent risk of leukaemia and brain tumours: A retrospective cohort study. *Lancet, 380,* 499–505.

Pearson, M. L., Selby, J. V., Katz, K. A., Cantrell, V., Braden, C. R., Parise, M. E., . . . Eberhard, M. L. (2012). Clinical, epidemiologic, histopathologic and molecular features of an unexplained dermopathy. *PLOS One, 7,* 1–23.

Pearson, M. R., D'Lima, G. M., & Kelley, M. (2011). Self-regulation as a buffer of the relationship between parental alcohol misuse and alcohol-related outcomes in first-year college students. *Addictive Behaviors, 36,* 1309–1312.

Pederson, C. A., & Fite, P. J. (2014). The impact of parenting on the associations between child aggression subtypes and oppositional defiant disorder symptoms. *Child Psychiatry & Human Development.* DOI: 10.1007/s10578-014-0441-y

Peira, N., Fredrikson, M., & Pourtois, G. (2014). Controlling the emotional heart: Heart rate biofeedback improves cardiac control during emotional reactions. *International Journal of Psychophysiology, 91,* 225-231.

Pelham, W. E., & Fabiano, G. A. (2008). Evidence-based psychosocial treatment for ADHD: An update. *Journal of Clinical Child and Adolescent Psychology, 37,* 184–214.

Pelkonen, M., Marttunen, M., Henriksson, M., & Lönnqvist, J. (2007). Adolescent adjustment disorder: Precipitant stressors and distress symptoms of 89 outpatients. *European Psychiatry, 22,* 288–295.

Pelletier, L. G., & Dion, S. C. (2007). An examination of general and specific motivational mechanisms for the relations between body dissatisfaction and eating behaviors. *Journal of Social and Clinical Psychology, 26,* 303–333.

Pemberton, C. K., Neiderhiser, J. M., Leve, L. D., Natsuaki, M. N., Shaw, D. S., Reiss, D., & Ge, X. (2010). Influence of parental depressive symptoms on adopted toddler behaviors: An emerging developmental cascade of genetic and environmental effects. *Developmental Psychopathology, 22,* 803–818.

Pendlebury, S. T. (2012). Review: Depression is associated with an increased risk of developing stroke. *Evidence-Based Mental Health, 15*(1), 6.

Penn, D. L., Mueser, K. T., Tarrier, N., Gloege, A., Cather, C., Serrano, D., & Otto, M. W. (2004). Supportive therapy for schizophrenia: Possible mechanisms and implications for adjunctive psychosocial treatments. *Schizophrenia Bulletin, 30,* 101–112.

Peplau, L. A., Frederick, D. A., Yee, C., Maisel, N., Level, J., & Ghavami, N. (2008). Body image satisfaction in heterosexual, gay, and lesbian adults. *Archives of Sexual Behavior, 38,* 713–725.

Perkins, H. W., Linkenbach, J. W., Lewis, M. A., & Neighbors, C. (2010). Effectiveness of social norms media marketing in reducing drinking and driving: A statewide campaign. *Addictive Behaviors, 35,* 866–874.

Perkins, K. A. (2009). Sex differences in nicotine reinforcement and reward: Influences on the persistence of tobacco smoking. *The Motivational Impact of Nicotine and its Role in Tobacco Use: Nebraska Symposium on Motivation, 55,* 1–27.

Perlis, R. H., Ostacher, M., Fava, M., Nierenberg, A. A., Sachs, G. S., & Rosenbaum, J. F. (2010). Assuring that double-blind is blind. *American Journal of Psychiatry, 167,* 250–252.

Perlis, R. H., Smoller, J. W., Mysore, J., Sun, M., Gillis, T., Purcell, S., . . . Gusella, J. (2010). Prevalence of incompletely penetrant Huntington's disease alleles among individuals with major depressive disorder. *American Journal of Psychiatry,167*, 574–579.

Perlman, C. M., Martin, L., Hirdes, J. P., & Curtin-Telegdi, N. (2007). Prevalence and predictors of sexual dysfunction in psychiatric inpatients. *Psychosomatics, 48*, 309–318.

Perrone, M. (2013). Female libido drug remains in limbo. Retrieved from http://news.msn.com/science-technology/female-libido-drug-remains-in-limbo

Perry, J. C. (2001). Dependent personality disorder. In G. O. Gabbard (Ed.), *Treatment of psychiatric disorders* (pp. 2353–2368). Washington, DC: American Psychiatric Press.

Pescosolido, B. A., Martin, J. K., Long, S., Medina, T. R., Phelan, J. C., & Link, B. G. (2010). "A disease like any other"? A decade of change in public reactions to schizophrenia, depression, and alcohol dependence. *American Journal of Psychiatry, 167*, 1321–1330.

Peters, S. A., Huxley, R. R., & Woodward, M. (2013). Smoking as a risk factor for stroke in women compared with men: A systematic review and meta-analysis of 81 cohorts, including 3,980,359 individuals and 42,401 strokes. *Stroke, 44*, 2821–2828.

Petersen, L., Sørensen, T. I. A., Andersen, P. K., Mortensen, P. B., & Hawton, K. (2013). Genetic and familial environmental effects on suicide—An adoption study of siblings. *PLOS One, 8*(10), e77973. doi:10.1371/journal.pone.0077973

Petersen, R. C. (2011). Mild cognitive impairment. *New England Journal of Medicine, 364*, 2227–2234.

Peterson, A. L., Luethcke, C. A., Borah, E. V., Borah, A. M., & Young-McCaughan, S. (2011). Assessment and treatment of combat-related PTSD in returning war veterans. *Journal of Clinical Psychology in Medical Settings, 18*, 164–175.

Peterson, C., & Seligman, M. (2005). *Character strengths and virtue: A handbook and classification.* New York, NY: Oxford University Press.

Peterson, C. B., Thuras, P., Ackard, D. M., Mitchell, J. E., Berg, K., Sandager, N., . . . Crow, S. J. (2010). Personality dimensions in bulimia nervosa, binge eating disorder, and obesity. *Comprehensive Psychiatry, 51*, 31–36.

Peterson, R. A. (2001). On the use of college students in social science research: Insights from a second-order meta-analysis.

Journal of Consumer Research, 28, 450–461.

Peterson, R. E., Latendresse, S. J., Bartholome, L. T., Warren, C. S., & Raymond, N. C. (2012). Binge eating disorder mediates links between symptoms of depression, anxiety, and caloric intake in overweight and obese women. *Journal of Obesity, 2012*, 407103.

Petry, N. M., Alessi, S. M., Carroll, K. M., Hanson, T., MacKinnon, S., Rounsaville, B., & Sierra, S. (2006). Contingency management treatments: Reinforcing abstinence versus adherence with goal-related activities. *Journal of Consulting and Clinical Psychology, 74*, 592–601.

Pezawas, L., Meyer-Lindenberg, A., Drabant, E. M., Verchinski, B. A., Munoz, K. E., Kolachana, B. S., . . . Weinberger, D. R. (2005). 5-HTTLPR polymorphism impacts human cingulated amygdala interactions: A genetic susceptibility mechanism for depression. *Nature Neuroscience, 8*, 828–834.

Pezdek, K., Blandon-Gitlin, I., & Gabbay, P. (2006). Imagination and memory: Does imagining implausible events lead to false autobiographical memories? *Psychonomic Bulletin and Review, 13*, 764–769.

Phillips, A., & Daniluk, J. C. (2004). Beyond "survivor": How childhood sexual abuse informs the identity of adult women at the end of the therapeutic process. *Journal of Counseling and Development, 82*, 177–184.

Phillips, K. A. (2005). *The broken mirror: Understanding and treating body dysmorphic disorder* (2nd ed., revised). New York, NY: Oxford University Press.

Phillips, K. A., & Gunderson, J. G. (1999). Personality disorders. In R. E. Hales, S. C. Yudofsky, & J. A. Talbott (Eds.), *Textbook of psychiatry* (pp. 795–823). Washington, DC: American Psychiatric Publishing.

Phillips, K. A., Pagano, M. E., Menard, W., & Stout, R. L. (2006). A 12-month follow-up study of the course of body dysmorphic disorder. *American Journal of Psychiatry, 163*, 907–912.

Phillips, K. A., Stein, D. J., Rauch, S. L., Hollander, E., Fallon, B. A., Barsky, A., . . . Leckman, J. (2010). Should an obsessive-compulsive spectrum grouping of disorders be included in DSM-V? *Depression and Anxiety, 27*, 528–555.

Phillips, K. A., Wilhelm, S., Koran, L. M., Didie, E. R., Fallon, B. A., Feusner, J.,

Stein, D. J. (2010). Body dysmorphic disorder: Some key issues for DSM-V. *Depression and Anxiety, 27*, 573–591.

Phillips, M. L., & Kupfer, D. J. (2013). Bipolar disorder diagnosis: Challenges and future directions. *Lancet, 38*, 1663–1671.

Phipps, S. (2011). Positive psychology and war: An oxymoron. *American Psychologist, 66*, 641–642.

Piazza-Gardner, A. K., & Barry, A. E. (2013). Appropriate terminology for the alcohol, eating, and physical activity relationship. *Journal of American College Health, 61*, 311–313.

Picardi, A. (2009). Rating scales in bipolar disorder. *Current Opinion in Psychiatry, 22*, 42–49.

Pies, R. (2012). Are antidepressants effective in the acute and long-term treatment of depression? *Innovations in Clinical Neuroscience, 9*, 31–40.

Pigeon, W. R., Pinquart, M., & Conner, K. (2012). Meta-analysis of sleep disturbance and suicidal thoughts and behaviors. *Journal of Clinical Psychiatry, 73*, e1160–e1167.

Pilotto, A., Padovani, A., & Borroni, B. (2013). Clinical, biological, and imaging features of monogenic Alzheimer's disease. *Biomedical Research International.* Retrieved from http://dx.doi.org/10.1155/2013/689591

Pincus, A. L. (2011). Some comments on nosology, diagnostic process, and narcissistic personality disorder in DSM-5: Proposal for personality and personality disorders. *Personality Disorders: Theory, Research, and Treatment, 2*, 41–53.

Pincus, A. L., Cain, N. M., & Wright, A. G. (2014). Narcissistic grandiosity and narcissistic vulnerability in psychotherapy. *Personality Disorders.* ,DOI: 10.1037/per0000031

Pincus, D. B., May, J. E., Whitton, S. W., Mattis, S. G., & Barlow, D. H. (2010). Cognitive-behavioral treatment of panic disorder in adolescence. *Journal of Clinical Child and Adolescent Psychology, 39*, 638–649.

Pinheiro, A. P., Raney, T. J., Thornton, L. M., Fichter, M. M., Berrentini, W. H., Goldman, D., . . . Bulik, C. M. (2010). Sexual functioning in women with eating disorders. *International Journal of Eating Disorder, 43*, 123–129.

Pinto, A., Steinglass, J. E., Greene, A. L., Weber, E. U., & Simpson, H. B. (2013, November 4). Capacity to delay reward differentiates obsessive-compulsive disorder and obsessive compulsive personality disorder. *Biological Psychiatry, 75*, 653–659.

Piper, A., & Merskey, H. (2004). The persistence of folly: A critical examination of dissociative identity disorder. Part 1: The excesses of an improbable concept. *Canadian Journal of Psychiatry, 49*, 592–600.

Piper, M. E., Cook, J. W., Schlam, T. R., Jorenby, D. E., & Baker, T. B. (2010). Anxiety diagnoses in smokers seeking cessation treatment: Relations with tobacco dependence, withdrawal, outcome and response to treatment. *Addiction, 106*, 418–427. doi:10.1111/j.1360-0443.2010.03173.x

Pizarro, J., Silver, R. C., & Prause, J. (2006). Physical and mental health costs of traumatic war experiences among Civil War veterans. *Archives of General Psychiatry, 63*, 193–200.

Plante, T. G. (2013). *Abnormal psychology across the ages*. Santa Barbara, CA: Praeger.

Poels, M. M., Ikram, M. A., van der Lugt, A., Hofman, A., Niessen, W. J., Krestin, G. P., . . . Vernooij, M. W. (2012). Cerebral microbleeds are associated with worse cognitive function. *Neurology, 78*, 326–333.

Polanczyk, G., Moffitt, T. E., Arseneault, L., Cannon, M., Ambler, A., Keefe, R. S. E., . . . Caspi, A. (2010). Etiological and clinical features of childhood psychotic symptoms: Results from a birth cohort. *Archives of General Psychiatry, 67*, 328–338.

Poletti, M., & Bonuccelli, U. (2013). Acute and chronic cognitive effects of levodopa and dopamine agonists on patients with Parkinson's disease: A review. *Therapeutic Advances in Psychopharmacology, 3*, 101–113.

Politte, L. C., Henry, C. A., & McDougle, C. J. (2014). Psychopharmacological interventions in autism spectrum disorder. *Harvard Review of Psychiatry, 22*, 76–92.

Polosa, R., Rodu, B., Caponnetto, P., Maglia, M., & Raciti, C. (2013). A fresh look at tobacco harm reduction: The case for the electronic cigarette. *Harm Reduction Journal, 10*, 19. doi:10.1186/1477-7517-10-19

Pompili, M., Gonda, X., Serafini, G., Innamorati, M., Sher, L., Amore, M., . . . Girardi, P. (2013). Epidemiology of suicide in bipolar disorders: A systematic review of the literature. *Bipolar Disorders, 15*, 457–490.

Pontifex, M. B., Saliba, B. J., Raine, L. B., Picchietti, D. L., & Hillman, C. H. (2013). Exercise improves behavioral, neurocognitive, and scholastic performance in children with attention-deficit/hyperactivity disorder. *Journal of Pediatrics, 162*, 543–551.

Pope, H. G., Jr., Barry, S., Bodkin, A., & Hudson, J. I. (2006). Tracking scientific interest in the dissociative disorders: A study of scientific publication output, 1984–2003. *Psychotherapy and Psychosomatics, 75*, 19–24.

Pope, H. G., Jr., Gruber, A. J., Mangweth, B., Bureau, B., deCol, C., Jouvent, R., & Hudson, J. I. (2000). Body image perception among men in three countries. *American Journal of Psychiatry, 157*, 1297–1301.

Pope, H. G., Jr., & Hudson, J. I. (2007). *"Repressed memory" challenge*. Retrieved from www.butterfliesandwheels.com/printer_friendly.php?num5177

Pope, H. G., Jr., Poliakoff, M. B., Parker, M. P., Boynes, M., & Hudson, J. I. (2009). Response to R. E. Goldsmith, R. E. Cheit, & M. E. Wood, "Evidence of dissociative amnesia in science and literature: Culture-bound approaches to trauma." *Journal of Trauma & Dissociation, 10*, 254–257.

Pope, K. S., & Vasquez, M. J. T. (2007). *Ethics in psychotherapy and counseling*. Hoboken, NJ: Wiley.

Porter, J. (2012). Stress, high school, tics and secondary stress response. Retrieved from http://www.stressstop.com/blog/read-entry.php?eid542

Posner, J., Hellerstein, D. J., Gat, I., Mechling, A., Klahr, K., Wang, Z., . . . Peterson, B. S. (2013). Antidepressants normalize the default mode network in patients with dysthymia. *JAMA Psychiatry, 70*, 373–382.

Potenza, M. N., Balodis, I. M., Franco, C. A., Bullock, S., Xu, J., Chung, T., & Grant, J. E. (2013). Neurobiological considerations in understanding behavioral treatments for pathological gambling. *Psychology of Addictive Behaviors, 27*, 380–392.

Potter, R., Patterson, B. W., Elbert, D. L., Ovod, V., Kasten, T., Sigurdson, W., . . . Bateman, R. J. (2013). Increased in vivo amyloid-b42 production, exchange, and loss in presenilin mutation carriers. *Science Translational Medicine, 5*, 189ra77.

Poulsen, S., Lunn, S., Daniel, S. I., Folke, S., Mathiesen, B. B., Katznelson, H., & Fairburn, C. G. (2013). A randomized controlled trial of psychoanalytic psychotherapy or cognitive-behavioral therapy for bulimia nervosa. *American Journal of Psychiatry, 171*, 109–116.

Powell, L. H., Calvin, J. E., III, & Calvin, J. E., Jr. (2007). Effective obesity treatments. *American Psychologist, 62*, 234–246.

Powell, N. D., Tarr, A. J., & Sheridan, J. F. (2013). Psychosocial stress and inflammation in cancer. *Brain, Behavior, and Immunity, 30*, 41–47.

Powers, M. B., Halpern, J. M., Ferenschak, M. P., Gillihan, S. J., & Foa, E. B. (2010). A meta-analytic review of prolonged exposure for posttraumatic stress disorder. *Clinical Psychology Review, 30*, 635–641.

Powsner, S. (2013). Conversion disorder in emergency medicine. Retrieved from http://emedicine.medscape.com/article/805361-overview

Prati, G., & Pietrantoni, L. (2009). Optimism, social support, and coping strategies as factors contributing to posttraumatic growth: A meta-analysis. *Journal of Loss and Trauma, 14*, 364–388.

Pratt, L. A., Brody, D. J., & Gu, Q. (2011). *Antidepressant use in persons aged 12 and over: United States, 2005–2008* (NCHS Data Brief No. 76). Hyattsville, MD: National Center for Health Statistics.

Preda, A. (2012). Primary hypersomnia. Retrieved from http://emedicine.medscape.com/article/291699-overview#aw2aab6b2b2aa

Preece, M. H., Horswill, M. S., & Geffen, G. M. (2010). Driving after concussion: The acute effect of mild traumatic brain injury on drivers' hazard perception. *Neuropsychology, 24*, 493–503.

Price, C. S., Thompson, W. W., Goodson, B., Weintraub, E. S., Croen, L. A., Hinrichsen, V. L., . . . DeStafano, F. (2010). Prenatal and infant exposure to thimerosal from vaccines and immunoglobulins and risk of autism. *Pediatrics, 126*, 656–664.

Price, J., Cole, V., & Goodwin, G. M. (2009). Emotional side effects of selective serotonin reuptake inhibitors: Qualitative study. *British Journal of Psychiatry, 195*, 211–217.

Prince, M., Bryce, R., & Ferri, C. (2011). *World Alzheimer report 2011: The benefits of early diagnosis and intervention*. London, UK: Alzheimer's Disease International. Retrieved from http://www.alz.co.uk/research/WorldAlzheimerReport2011.pdf

Prossin, A. R., Love, T. M., Koeppe, R. A., Zubieta, J. K., & Silk, K. R. (2010). Dysregulation of regional endogenous opioid function in borderline personality disorder. *American Journal of Psychiatry, 167,* 925–933.

Proudfoot, J., Doran, J., Manicavasagar, V., & Parker, G. (2010). The precipitants of manic/hypomanic episodes in the context of bipolar disorder: A review. *Journal of Affective Disorders, 133,* 381–387.

Proudfoot, J. G. (2004). Computer-based treatment for anxiety and depression: Is it feasible? Is it effective? *Neuroscience and Biobehavioral Reviews, 28,* 353–363.

PubMed. (2010). Narcissistic personality disorder. Retrieved from http://www.ncbi.nlm.nih.gov/pubmedhealth/PMH0001930

Puhl, R. M., & Heuer, C. A. (2009). The stigma of obesity: A review and update. *Obesity, 17,* 941–964.

Puhl, R. M., Peterson, J. L., & Luedicke, J. (2013). Weight-based victimization: Bullying experiences of weight loss treatment-seeking youth. *Pediatrics, 131,* e1–e9.

Pulcu, E., Lythe, K., Elliott, R., Green, S., Moll, J., Deakin, J. F., & Zahn, R. (2014). Increased amygdala response to shame in remitted major depressive disorder. *PLOS One, 9,* e86900. doi:10.1371/journal.pone.0086900

Pull, C. B. (2013). Too few or too many? Reactions to removing versus retaining specific personality disorders in DSM-5. *Current Opinion in Psychiatry, 26,* 73–78.

Pumariega A. J., Rothe, E., Mian, A., Carlisle, L., Toppelberg, C. , Harris, T., . . . Smith, J. (2013). Practice parameter for cultural competence in child and adolescent psychiatric practice. *Journal of the American Academy of Child & Adolescent Psychiatry, 52,* 1101–1115.

Purdon, C., & Clark, D. A. (2005). *Overcoming obsessional thoughts.* Oakland, CA: New Harbinger.

Purse, M. (2013). Brief reactive psychosis—An inside story. Retrieved from http://bipolar.about.com/od/interviews/a/brief-reactive-psychosis-experience.htm

Quinn, S. O. (2012). Credibility, respectability, suggestibility, and spirit travel: Lurena Brackett and animal magnetism. *History of Psychology, 15,* 273–282.

Qureshi, I. A., & Mehler, M. F. (2014). Epigenetics of sleep and chronobiology.

Current Neurology and Neuroscience Reports, 14, 432.

Qureshi, S. U., Kimbrell, T., Pyne, J. M., Magruder, K. M., Hudson, T. J., Petersen, N. J., . . . Kunik, M. E. (2010). Greater prevalence and incidence of dementia in older veterans with post-traumatic stress disorder. *Journal of the American Geriatrics Society, 58,* 1627–1633. doi:10.1111/j.1532-5415.2010.02977.x

Rabinowitz, J., Levine, S. Z., Haim, R., & Hafner, H. (2007). The course of schizophrenia: Progressive deterioration, amelioration or both? *Schizophrenia Research, 91,* 254–258.

Rachman, S. (2012). Health anxiety disorders: A cognitive construal. *Behaviour Research and Therapy, 50,* 502–512.

Rachman, S., Elliott, C. M., Shafran, R., & Radomsky, A. S. (2009). Separating hoarding from OCD. *Behaviour Research and Therapy, 47,* 520–522.

Rachman, S., Marks, I. M., & Hodgson, R. (1973). The treatment of obsessive compulsive neurotics by modeling and flooding in vivo. *Behaviour Research and Therapy, 11,* 463–471.

Radonic, E., Rados, M., Kalember, P., Bajs-Janovic, M., Folnegovic-Smalc, V., & Henigsberg, N. (2011). Comparison of hippocampal volumes in schizophrenia, schizoaffective and bipolar disorder. *Collegium Antropologicum, 35,* 249–252.

Ramachandraih, C. T., Subramanyam, N., Bar, K. J., Baker, G., & Yeragani, V. K. (2011). Antidepressants: From MAOIs to SSRIs and more. *Indian Journal of Psychiatry, 53,* 180–182.

Ramachandran, V. (2013). Social media project monitors keywords to prevent suicide. Retrieved from http://mashable.com/2013/08/20/durkheim-project-social-media-suicide

Ramsey, S. D., Zeliadt, S. B., Blough, D. K., Moinpour, C. M., Hall, I. J., Smith, J. L., . . . Penson, D. F. (2013). Impact of prostate cancer on sexual relationships: A longitudinal perspective on intimate partners' experiences. *Journal of Sexual Medicine, 10,* 3135–3143.

Ramos, R. (1998). *An ethnographic study of Mexican American inhalant abusers in San Antonio.* Austin, TX: Texas Commission on Alcohol and Drug Abuse. Retrieved from http://www.dshs.state.tx.us/sa/research/populations/Inhale98S.pdf

Rand Corporation. (2010). Invisible wounds: Mental health and cognitive care needs

of America's returning veterans. Retrieved from http://www.rand.org/pubs/research_briefs/RB9336/index1.html

Rao, V., Handel, S., Vaishnavi, S., Keach, S., Robbins, B., Spiro, J., . . . Berlin, F. (2007). Psychiatric sequelae of traumatic brain injury: A case report. *American Journal of Psychiatry, 164,* 728–735.

Rapee, R. M., Schniering, C. A., & Hudson, J. L. (2009). Anxiety disorders during childhood and adolescence: Origins and treatment. *Annual Review of Clinical Psychology, 5,* 311–341.

Rashid, T., & Ostermann, R. F. (2009). Strength-based assessment in clinical practice. *Journal of Clinical Psychology, 65,* 488–498.

Rathbone, C. J., Moulin, C. J., & Conway, M. A. (2009). Autobiographical memory and amnesia: Using conceptual knowledge to ground the self. *Neurocase: The Neural Basis of Cognition, 15,* 405–418.

Raval, A. P., Borges-Garcia, R., Diaz, F., Sick, T. J., & Bramlett, H. (2013). Oral contraceptives and nicotine synergistically exacerbate cerebral ischemic injury in the female brain. *Translational Stroke Research, 4,* 402–412.

Ravindran, A. V., Smith, A., Cameron, C., Bhatla, R., Cameron, I., Georgescu, T. M., & Hogan, M. J. (2009). Toward a functional neuroanatomy of dysthymia: A functional magnetic resonance imaging study. *Journal of Affective Disorders, 119,* 9–15.

Ray, G. T., Croen, L. A., & Habel, L. A. (2009). Mothers of children diagnosed with attention-deficit/hyperactivity disorder: Health conditions and medical care utilization in periods before and after birth of the child. *Medical Care, 47,* 105–114.

Raymond, F. L., Tarpey, P. S., Edkins, S., Tofts, C., O'Meara, S., Teague, J., . . . Futreal, P. A. (2007). Mutations in ZDHHC9, which encodes a palmitoyl-transferase of NRAS and HRAS, cause X-linked mental retardation associated with a marfanoid habitus. *American Journal of Human Genetics, 80,* 982–987.

Razani, J., Nordin, S., Chan, A., & Murphy, C. (2010). Semantic networks for odors and colors in Alzheimer's disease. *Neuropsychology, 24,* 291–299.

Read, J., & Mati, E. (2013). Erectile dysfunction and the Internet: Drug company manipulation of public and professional opinion. *Journal of Sex and Marital Therapy, 39,* 541–559.

Reas, D. L., & Grilo, C. M. (2014, January 25). Current and emerging drug treatments for binge eating disorder. *Expert Opinion on Emerging Drugs, 19,* 99-142.

Rector, N. A., Beck, A. T., & Stolar, N. (2005). The negative symptoms of schizophrenia: A cognitive perspective. *Canadian Journal of Psychiatry, 50,* 247-257.

Redolfi, S., Arnulf, I., Pottier, M., Lajou, J., Koskas, I., Bradley, T. D., & Similowski, T. (2011). Attenuation of obstructive sleep apnea by compression stockings in subjects with venous insufficiency. *American Journal of Respiratory and Critical Care Medicine, 183,* A6161.

Reed, B., Villeneuve, S., Mack, W., Decarli, C., Chui, H. C., & Jagust, W. (2013). Associations between serum cholesterol levels and cerebral amyloidosis. *JAMA Neurology, 71,* 195-200.

Reed, G. M. (2010). Toward ICD-11: Improving the clinical utility of WHO's International Classification of Mental Disorders. *Professional Psychology: Research and Practice, 41,* 457-464.

Reed, I. (2007). Why Salem made sense: Culture, gender, and the Puritan persecution of Witchcraft, *Cultural Sociology, 1,* 209-234.

Rees, C. S., & Pritchard, R. (2014). Brief cognitive therapy for avoidant personality disorder. *Psychotherapy.* doi: 10.1037/a0035158

Reese, H. E., McNally, R. J., & Wilhelm, S. (2011). Reality monitoring in patients with body dysmorphic disorder. *Behavior Therapy, 42,* 387-398.

Reese, M., Herbenick, D., Schick, V., Sanders, S. A., Dodge, B., & Fortenberry, J. D. (2010). Background and considerations on the National Survey of Sexual Health and Behavior (NSSHB) from the investigators. *Journal of Sexual Medicine, 7,* 243-245.

Reeves, A., Stuckler, D., McKee, M., Gunnell, D., Chang, S. S., & Basu, S. (2012). Increase in state suicide rates in the USA during economic recession. *Lancet, 380,* 1813-1814.

Reger, G. M., Durham, T. L., Tarantino, K. A., Luxton, D. D., Holloway, K. M., & Lee, J. A. (2013). Deployed soldiers' reactions to exposure and medication treatments for PTSD. *Psychological Trauma: Theory, Research, Practice, and Policy, 5,* 309-316.

Reichenberg, A., & Harvey, P. D. (2007). Neuropsychological impairments in schizophrenia: Integration of performance-based and brain imaging findings. *Psychological Bulletin, 133,* 833-858.

Reiman, E. M., Quiroz, Y. T., Fleisher, A. S., Chen, K., Velez-Pardo, C., Jimenez-Del-Rio, M., . . . Lopera, F. (2012). Brain imaging and fluid biomarker analysis in young adults at genetic risk for autosomal dominant Alzheimer's disease in the presenilin 1 E280A kindred: A case-control study. *Lancet Neurology, 11,* 1048-1056.

Reinelt, E., Aldinger, M., Stopsack, M., Schwahn, C., John, U., Baumeister, S. E., . . . Barnow, S. (2014, January 10). High social support buffers the effects of 5-HTTLPR genotypes within social anxiety disorder. *European Archives of Psychiatry and Clinical Neuroscience.* [Epub ahead of print]

Reinhold, N., & Markowitsch, H. J. (2009). Retrograde episodic memory and emotion: A perspective from patients with dissociative amnesia. *Neuropsychologia, 47,* 2197-2206.

Relton, C. L., & Davey Smith, G. (2012). Two-step epigenetic mendelian randomization: A strategy for establishing the causal role of epigenetic processes in pathways to disease. *International Journal of Epidemiology, 41,* 161-176.

Rennie v. Klein, 462 F. Supp. 1131 (D.N.J. 1978).

Ressler, K. J., & Rothbaum, B. O. (2012). Augmenting obsessive-compulsive disorder treatment: From brain to mind. *JAMA Psychiatry, 70,* 1129-1131.

Reynolds, R. M. (2013). Glucocorticoid excess and the developmental origins of disease: Two decades of testing the hypothesis—2012 Curt Richter Award Winner. *Psychoneuroendocrinology, 38,* 1-11.

Rhea, D. J., & Thatcher, W. G. (2013). Ethnicity, ethnic identity, self-esteem, and at-risk eating disordered behavior differences of urban adolescent females. *Eating Disorders, 21,* 223-237.

Richards, E. P. (2010). Phenotype v. genotype: Why identical twins have different fingerprints. Retrieved from http// www.forensic-evidence.com/site/ID/ ID_Twins.html

Richards, J. C., Alvarenga, M., & Hof, A. (2000). Serum lipids and their relationships with hostility and angry affect and behaviors in men. *Health Psychology, 19,* 393-398.

Richardson, L. F. (1998). Psychogenic dissociation in childhood: The role of the counseling psychologist. *Counseling Psychologist, 26,* 69-100.

Richardson, S. M., & Paxton, S. J. (2010). An evaluation of a body image intervention based on risk factors for body dissatisfaction: A controlled study with adolescent girls. *International Journal of Eating Disorders, 43,* 112-122.

Richardson, T., Stallard, P., & Velleman, S. (2010). Computerised cognitive behavioural therapy for the prevention and treatment of depression and anxiety in children and adolescents: A systematic review. *Clinical Child and Family Psychology Review, 13,* 275-290.

Richardson, J. R., Roy, A., Shalat, S. L., von Stein, R. T., Hossain, M. M., Buckley, B., . . . German, D. C. (2014). Elevated serum pesticide levels and risk for Alzheimer disease. *JAMA Neurology, 71,* 284-290.

Richwine, J. (2009). IQ and immigration policy. Retrieved from ProQuest Dissertations and Theses.

Richey, S. M., & Krystal, A. D. (2011). Pharmacological advances in the treatment of insomnia. *Current Pharmaceutical Design, 17,* 1471-1475.

Ridaura, V. K., Faith, J. J., Rey, F. E., Cheng, J., Duncan, A. E., Kau, A. L., . . . Gordon, J. I. (2013). Gut microbiota from twins discordant for obesity modulate metabolism in mice. *Science, 341,* 1241214.

Ridley, C. R. (2005). *Overcoming unintentional racism in counseling and therapy* (2nd ed.). Thousand Oaks, CA: Sage.

Ridley, C. R., Mollen, D., & Kelly, S. M. (2011). Beyond microskills: Toward a model of counseling competence. *The Counseling Psychologist, 39,* 825-864.

Rieber, R. W. (2006). *The bifurcation of the self: The history and theory of dissociation and its disorders.* New York, NY: Springer.

Rieker, P. P., & Bird, C. E. (2005). Rethinking gender differences in health: Why we need to integrate social and biological perspectives. *Journal of Gerontology, 60,* S40-S47.

Rihmer, Z., & Gonda, X. (2011). Antidepressant-resistant depression and antidepressant-associated suicidal behaviour: The role of underlying bipolarity. *Depression Research and Treatment, 2011,* 906462. doi:10.1155/2011/906462

Rinck, M., & Becker, E. S. (2006). Spider fearful individuals attend to threat, then quickly avoid it: Evidence from eye movements. *Journal of Abnormal Psychology, 115,* 231-238.

Ritchie, K., Norton, J., Mann, A., Carrière, I., & Ancelin, M. L. (2013). Late-onset agoraphobia: General population incidence and evidence for a clinical subtype. *American Journal of Psychiatry, 170,* 790–798.

Ritz, T., Meuret, A. E., & Simon, E. (2013). Cardiovascular activity in blood-injection-injury phobia during exposure: Evidence for diphasic response patterns? *Behaviour Research and Therapy, 51,* 460–468.

Ritz, T., Meuret, A. E., Trueba, A. F., Fritzsche, A., & von Leupoldt, A. (2013). Psychosocial factors and behavioral medicine interventions in asthma. *Journal of Consulting and Clinical Psychology, 81,* 231–250.

Rivara, F. P., Koepsell, T. D., Wang, J., Temkin, N., Dorsch, A., Vavilala, M. S., . . . Jaffe, K. M. (2011). Disability 3, 12, and 24 months after traumatic brain injury among children and adolescents. *Pediatrics, 128,* e1129-e1138.

Rizvi, S. L., Steffel, L. M., & Carson-Wong, A. (2013). An overview of dialectical behavior therapy for professional psychologists. *Professional Psychology: Research and Practice, 44,* 73–80.

Roberts, A., & Smith, M. (2014). Horrific taboo: Female circumcision on the rise in U.S. Retrieved from http://www.nbc news.com/news/world/horrific-taboo-female-circumcision-rise-u-s-n66226

Roberts, A. L., Gilman, S. E., Breslau, J., Breslau, N., & Koenen, K. C. (2010). Race/ethnic differences in exposure to traumatic events, development of post-traumatic stress disorder, and treatment-seeking for post-traumatic stress disorder in the United States. *Psychological Medicine, 41*(1), 71–83. doi:10.1017/S0033291710000401

Roberts, A. L., Lyall, K., Hart, J. E., Laden, F., Just, A. C., Bobb, J. F., . . . Weisskopf, M. G. (2013). Perinatal air pollutant exposures and autism spectrum disorder in the children of Nurses' Health Study II participants. *Environmental Health Perspectives, 121,* 978–984.

Roberts, E. M., English, P. B., Grether, J. K., Windham, G. C., Somberg, L., & Wolff, C. (2007). Maternal residence near agricultural pesticide applications and autism spectrum disorders among children in the California Central Valley. *Environmental Health Perspectives, 115,* 1482–1489.

Roberts, R., Wells, G. A., Stewart, A. F., Dandona, S., & Chen, L. (2010). The genome-wide association study—A new era for common polygenic disorders. *Journal of Translational Cardiovascular Research, 3,* 173–182.

Roberts, T. K., & Fantz, C. (2014). Barriers to quality health care for the transgender population. *Clinical Biochemistry, 47,* 983–987.

Robertson, W. C., Jr. (2010). Tourette syndrome and other tic disorders. Retrieved from http://emedicine.medscape.com/article/1182258-overview

Robinson, E. B., Koenen, K. C., McCormick, M. C., Munir, K., Hallett, V., Happé, F., . . . Ronald, A. (2011). Evidence that autistic traits show the same etiology in the general population and at the quantitative extremes (5%, 2.5%, and 1%). *Archives of General Psychiatry, 68,* 1113–1121.

Robinson, J., Cox, G., Malone, A., Williamson, M., Baldwin, G., Fletcher, K., & O'Brien, M. (2013). A systematic review of school-based interventions aimed at preventing, treating, and responding to suicide-related behavior in young people. *Crisis, 34,* 164–182.

Robinson, T. E., Yager, L. M., Cogan, E. S., & Saunders, B. T. (2014). On the motivational properties of reward cues: Individual differences. *Neuropharmacology, 76 Pt B,* 450–459. doi:10.1016/j.neuropharm.2013.05.040

Robison, E. J., Shankman, S. A., & McFarland, B. R. (2009). Independent associations between personality traits and clinical characteristics of depression. *Journal of Nervous and Mental Disease, 197,* 476–483.

Rodebaugh, T. L. (2009). Social phobia and perceived friendship quality. *Journal of Anxiety Disorders, 23,* 872–878.

Roder, V., Mueller, D. R., Mueser, K. T., & Brenner, H. D. (2006). Integrated psychological therapy (IPT) for schizophrenia: Is it effective? *Schizophrenia Bulletin, 32,* 81–93.

Rodewald, F., Wilhelm-Gobling, C., Emrich, H. M., Reddemann, L., & Gast, U. (2011). Axis-I comorbidity in female patients with dissociative identity disorder and dissociative disorder not otherwise specified. *Journal of Nervous and Mental Disease, 199,* 122–131.

Rodriguez, C. I., Kegeles, L. S., Levinson, A., Feng, T., Marcus, S. M., Vermes, D., . . . Simpson, H. B. (2013). Randomized controlled crossover trial of ketamine in obsessive-compulsive disorder: Proof-of-concept. *Neuropsychopharmacology, 38,* 2475–2483.

Roecklein, K. A., Schumacher, J. A., Miller, M. A., & Ernecoff, N. C. (2012). Cognitive and behavioral predictors of light therapy use. *PLOS One, 7,* e39275. doi:10.1371/journal.pone.0039275

Rogers v. Okin (1979). 478 F. Supp. 1342 (D. Mass.1979), 634 F.2d 650 (1st Cir. 1980).

Rogers, C. H., Floyd, F. J., Seltzer, M. M., Greenberg, J., & Hong, J. (2008). Long-term effects of the death of a child on parents' adjustment in midlife. *Journal of Family Psychology, 22,* 203–211.

Rogers, C. R. (1959). A theory of therapy, personality, and interpersonal relationships, as developed in client-centered framework. In S. Koch (Ed.), *Psychology: A study of science* (Vol. 3, pp. 123–148). New York, NY: McGraw-Hill.

Rogers, C. R. (1961). *On becoming a person.* Boston, MA: Houghton Mifflin.

Rogers, J. R. (1992). Suicide and alcohol: Conceptualizing the relationship from a cognitive-social paradigm. *Journal of Counseling and Development, 70,* 540–543.

Rogers-Wood, N. A., & Petrie, T. A. (2010). Body dissatisfaction, ethnic identity, and disordered eating among African American women. *Journal of Counseling Psychology, 57,* 141–153.

Rohrmann, S., Hopp, H., & Quirin, M. (2008). Gender differences in psychophysiological responses to disgust. *Journal of Psychophysiology, 22,* 65–75.

Rohsenow, D. J., Monti, P. M., Martin, R. A., Michalec, E., & Abrams, D. B. (2000). Brief coping skills treatment for cocaine abuse: 12-month substance use outcomes. *Journal of Consulting and Clinical Psychology, 68,* 515–520.

Rolfe, A., & Burton, C. (2013). Reassurance after diagnostic testing with a low pretest probability of serious disease: Systematic review and meta-analysis. *JAMA Internal Medicine, 173,* 407–416.

Rolland, Y., van Kan, G. A., & Vellas, B. (2010). Healthy brain aging: Role of exercise and physical activity. *Clinics in Geriatric Medicine, 26,* 75–87.

Rollnick, S., Miller, W. R., & Butler, C. C. (2008). *Motivational interviewing in health care: Helping patients change behavior.* New York, NY: Guilford Press.

Rolon-Arroyo, B., Arnold, D. H., & Harvey, E. A. (2014). The predictive utility of conduct disorder symptoms in preschool children: A 3-year follow-up study. *Child Psychiatry and Human Development, 45,* 329–337.

Romero, N., Sanchez, A., & Vazquez, C. (2014). Memory biases in remitted depression: The role of negative cognitions at explicit and automatic processing levels. *Journal of Behavior Therapy and Experimental Psychiatry, 45,* 128–135.

Rondeaux, C. (2006). Can castration be a solution for sex offenders? Retrieved from http://www.washingtonpost.com/wp-yn/content/article/2006/07/04/AR2006070400960_pf.html

Rose, S. C., Bisson, J., Churchill, R., & Wessely, S. (2009). Psychological debriefing for preventing post traumatic stress disorder (PTSD). Retrieved from http://www.thecochranelibrary.com/SpringboardWebApp/userfiles/ccoch/file/PTSD/CD000560.pdf

Rosen, H. J., & Levenson, R. W. (2009). The emotional brain: Combining insights from patients and basic science. *Neurocase, 15,* 173–181.

Rosenberg, J., & Rosenberg, S. (2006). *Community mental health: Challenges for the 21st century.* New York, NY: Routledge.

Rosenfarb, I. S., Bellack, A. S., & Aziz, N. (2006). Family interactions and the course of schizophrenia in African American and white patients. *Journal of Abnormal Psychology, 115,* 112–120.

Rosenfarb, I. S., Goldstein, M. J., Mintz, J., & Nuechterlein, K. H. (1995). Expressed emotion and subclinical psychopathology observable within the transactions between schizophrenic patients and their family members. *Journal of Abnormal Psychology, 104,* 259–267.

Rosenfeld, B. (2004). *Assisted suicide and the right to die.* New York, NY: Guilford Press.

Rosenfeld, J. V., McFarlane, A. C., Bragge, P., Armonda, R. A., Grimes, J. B., & Ling, G. S. (2013). Blast-related traumatic brain injury. *Lancet Neurology, 12,* 882–893.

Rosenfield, A. H. (1985). Discovering and dealing with deviant sex. *Psychology Today, 19,* 8–10.

Rosenhan, D. L. (1973). On being sane in insane places. *Science, 179,* 250–258.

Rosenkranz, M. A., Davidson, R. J., Maccoon, D. G., Sheridan, J. F., Kalin, N. H., & Lutz, A. (2013). A comparison of mindfulness-based stress reduction and an active control in modulation of neurogenic inflammation. *Brain, Behavior and Immunity, 27,* 174–184.

Rosenthal, D. (1970). *Genetic theory and abnormal behavior.* New York, NY: McGraw-Hill.

Rosenthal, D. G., Learned, N., Liu, Y., & Weitzman, M. (2013). Characteristics of fathers with depressive symptoms. *Maternal and Child Health Journal, 17,* 119–128.

Rosner, R. I. (2012). Aaron T. Beck's drawings and the psychoanalytic origin story of cognitive therapy. *History of Psychology, 15,* 1–18.

Ross, C. A. (2011). Possession experiences in dissociative identity disorder: A preliminary study. *Journal of Trauma and Dissociation, 12,* 393–400.

Ross, C. A., Anderson, G., Fleisher, W. P., & Norton, G. R. (1991). The frequency of multiple personality disorder among psychiatric inpatients. *American Journal of Psychiatry, 148,* 1717–1720.

Ross, K., Freeman, D., Dunn, G., & Garety, P. (2011). Can jumping to conclusion be reduced in people with delusions? An experimental investigation of a brief reasoning training module. *Schizophrenia Bulletin, 37,* 324–333.

Rossignol, D. A., & Frye, R. E. (2012). Mitochondrial dysfunction in autism spectrum disorders: A systematic review and meta-analysis. *Molecular Psychiatry, 17,* 290–314.

Rossler, W., Riecher-Rossler, A. R., Angst, J., Murray, R., Gamma, A., Eich, D., . . . Gross, V. A. (2007). Psychotic experiences in the general population: A twenty-year prospective study. *Schizophrenia Research, 92,* 1–14.

Rothe, M., & Blaut, M. (2013). Evolution of the gut microbiota and the influence of diet. *Beneficial Microbes, 4,* 31–37.

Rouleau, C. R., & von Ranson, K. M. (2011). Potential risks of pro-eating disorder websites. *Clinical Psychology Review, 31,* 525–531.

Rouse v. Cameron, 373 F. 2d 451 (D.C. Cir. 1966).

Rowland, D. L., Lechner, K. H., & Burnett, A. L. (2012). Factors contributing to psychoaffective differences among men with sexual dysfunction in response to a partnered sexual experience. *Journal of Sex and Marital Therapy, 38,* 115–127.

Rowland, D. L., & McMahon, C. G. (2008). Premature ejaculation. In D. L. Rowland & L. Incrocci (Eds.), *Handbook of sexual and gender identity disorders* (pp. 68–95). Hoboken, NJ: Wiley.

Rowland, D. L., Tai, W., & Brummett, K. (2007). Interactive processes in ejaculatory disorders: Psychophysiological considerations. In E. Janssen (Ed.), *The psychophysiology of sex* (pp. 227–243).

Bloomington, IN: Indiana University Press.

Roy, A., Carli, V., & Sarchiapone, M. (2011). Resilience mitigates the suicide risk associated with childhood trauma. *Journal of Affective Disorders, 133,* 591–594.

Roy-Byrne, P. P., Craske, M. G., & Stein, M. B. (2006). Panic disorder. *Lancet, 368,* 1023–1032.

Rozen, T. D. (2010). Cluster headache with aura. *Current Pain and Headache Reports, 15,* 98–100. doi:10.1007/s11916-010-0168-9

Rozen, T. D., & Fishman, R. S. (2012). Cluster headache in the United States of America: Demographics, clinical characteristics, triggers, suicidality, and personal burden. *Headache, 52,* 99–113. doi:10.1111/j.1526-4610.2011.02028.x

Rucker, J. H., & McGuffin, P. (2010). Polygenic heterogeneity: A complex model of genetic inheritance in psychiatric disorders. *Biological Psychiatry, 68,* 312–313.

Rudaz, M., Craske, M. G., Becker, E. S., Ledermann, T., & Margraf, J. (2010). Health anxiety and fear of fear in panic disorder and agoraphobia vs. social phobia: A prospective longitudinal study. *Depression and Anxiety, 27,* 404–411.

Rudd, M. D., Goulding, J., & Bryan, C. (2011, May). Student veterans: A National survey exploring psychological symptoms and suicide risk. Presentation at the Meetings of the American Psychological Association, Washington, DC.

Rudd, M. D., Joiner, T., & Rajab, M. H. (2004). *Treating suicidal behavior.* New York, NY: Guilford Press.

Rudigera, J. A., & Winstead, B. A. (2013). Body talk and body-related co-rumination: Associations with body image, eating attitudes, and psychological adjustment. *Body Image, 11,* 462–471.

Rudolph, K. D., Flynn, M., Abaied, J. L., Groot, A., & Thompson, R. (2009). Why is past depression the best predictor of future depression? Stress generation as a mechanism of depression continuity in girls. *Journal of Clinical Child and Adolescent Psychology, 38,* 473–485.

Rumpel, J. A., Ahmedani, B. K., Peterson, E. L., Wells, K. E, Yang, M., Levin, A. M., . . . Williams, L. K. (2012). Genetic ancestry and its association with asthma exacerbations among African American subjects with asthma. *Journal of Allergy and Clinical Immunology, 130,* 1302–1306.

Rusch, N., Corrigan, R. N., Todd, A. R., & Bodenhausen, G. V. (2010). Implicit self-stigma in people with mental illness. *Journal of Nervous Mental Disease, 198*, 150–153.

Russell, J. J., Moskowitz, D. S., Zuroff, D. C., Bleau, Z. P., & Young, S. N. (2010). Anxiety, emotional security and the interpersonal behavior of individuals with social anxiety disorder. *Psychological Medicine, 41*, 545–554. doi:10.1017/S0033291710000863

Rusyniak, D. E. (2011). Neurologic manifestations of chronic methamphetamine abuse. *Neurologic Clinics, 29*, 641–655.

Rutter, M. (2006). Implications of resilience concepts for scientific understanding. *Annals of the New York Academy of Sciences, 1094*, 1–12.

Ryder, A. G., Sun, J., Dere, J., & Fung, K. (2014). Personality disorders in Asians: Summary, and a call for cultural research. *Asian Journal of Psychiatry, 7*, 86–88.

Rynn, M., Puliafico, A., Heleniak, C., Rikhi, P., Ghalib, K., & Vidair, H. (2011). Advances in psychopharmacology for pediatric anxiety disorders. *Depression and Anxiety, 28*, 76–87.

Rytwinski, N. K., Scur, M. D., Feeny, N. C., & Youngstrom, E. A. (2013). The co-occurrence of major depressive disorder among individuals with posttraumatic stress disorder: A meta-analysis. *Journal of Traumatic Stress, 26*, 299–309.

Sack, R. L., Auckley, D., Auger, R. R., Carskadon, M. A., Wright, K. P., Jr., & Vitiello, M. V. (2007). Circadian rhythm sleep disorders: Part I, basic principles, shift work and jet lag. *Sleep, 30*, 1460–1483.

Sadeh, N., & McNiel, D. E. (2013). Facets of anger, childhood sexual victimization, and gender as predictors of suicide attempts by psychiatric patients after hospital discharge. *Journal of Abnormal Psychology, 122*, 879–890.

Safarinejad, M. R. (2006). Female sexual dysfunction in a population-based study in Iran: Prevalence and associated risk factors. *International Journal of Impotence Research, 18*, 382–395.

Sagalyn, D. (2012). Health experts question army report on psychological training. Retrieved from http://www.pbs.org/newshour/updates/military-jan-june12-csf_training_01-02

Sajatovic, M., Ignacio, R. V., West, J. A., Cassidy, K. A., Safavi, R., Kilbourne, A. M., & Blow, F. C. (2009). Predictors of nonadherence among individuals with bipolar disorder receiving treatment in a community mental health clinic. *Comprehensive Psychiatry, 50*, 100–107.

Saklofske, D. H., Hildebrand, D. K., & Gorsuch, R. L. (2000). Replication of the factor structure of the Wechsler Adult Intelligence Scale—Third Edition with a Canadian sample. *Psychological Assessment, 12*, 436–439.

Saks, E. R. (2007). *The center cannot hold: My journey through madness.* New York, NY: Hyperion.

Saks, E. R. (2013). Successful and schizophrenic. Retrieved from http://www.nytimes.com/2013/01/27/opinion/sunday/schizophrenic-not-stupid.html?_r50

Sakuma-Sasai, T., & Inoue, Y. (2013). Rapid eye movement (REM) sleep behavior disorder in older adults. *Nihon Rinsho, 71*, 1853–1857.

Sakuragi, S., Sugiyama, Y., & Takeuchi, K. (2002). Effect of laughing and weeping on mood and heart rate variability. *Journal of Physiological Anthropology and Applied Human Science, 21*, 159–165.

Salgado-Pineda, P., Caclin, A., Baeza, I., Junque, C., Bernardo, M., Blin, O., & Funlupt, P. (2007). Schizophrenia and the frontal cortex: Where does it fail? *Schizophrenia Research, 91*, 73–81.

Sallinger, R. (2012). James Holmes saw three mental health professionals before shooting. Retrieved from http://www.alipac.us/f19/james-holmes-saw-three-mental-health-professionals-before-shooting-262890

Salvatore, G., Russo, B., Russo, M., Popolo, R., & Dimaggio, G. (2012). Metacognition-oriented therapy for psychosis: The case of a woman with delusional disorder and paranoid personality disorder. *Journal of Psychotherapy Integration, 22*, 314–329.

Salvatore, P., Bhuvaneswar, C., Tohen, M., Khalsa, H. M., Maggini, C., & Baldessarini, R. J. (2014, February 7). Capgras' syndrome in first-episode psychotic disorders. *Psychopathology, 47*, 261–269.

Samarrai, F. (2013). New Center for Open Science designed to increase research transparency, provide free technologies for scientists. Retrieved from https://news.virginia.edu/content/new-center-open-science-designed-increase-research-transparency-provide-free-technologies

SAMHSA. (2009). Suicide assessment five-step evaluation and triage. Retrieved from http://store.samhsa.gov/shin/content//SMA09-4432/SMA09-4432.pdf

SAMHSA. (2012a). *National strategy for suicide prevention 2012: How you can play a role in preventing suicide.* Washington, DC: SAMHSA.

SAMHSA. (2012b). *Results from the 2010 National Survey on Drug Use and Health: Mental health findings.* Rockville, MD: SAMHSA.

SAMHSA. (2012c). Treatment Episode Data Set (TEDS): 2000–2010. National Admissions to Substance Abuse Treatment Services. DASIS Series S-61, HHS Publication No. (SMA) 12-4701. Rockville, MD: Substance Abuse and Mental Health Services Administration.

Sánchez-Ortuño, M. M., & Edinger, J. D. (2012). Cognitive-behavioral therapy for the management of insomnia comorbid with mental disorders. *Current Psychiatry Reports, 14*, 519–528.

Sánchez-Villegas, A., & Martínez-González, M. A. (2013). Diet, a new target to prevent depression? *BMC Medicine, 11*, 3. doi:10.1186/1741-7015-11-3

Sand, E., Gordon, K. H., & Bresin, K. (2013). The impact of specifying suicide as the cause of death in an obituary. *Crisis, 34*, 63–66.

Sansone, R. A., & Sansone, L. A. (2011). Personality pathology and its influence on eating disorders. *Innovations in Clinical Neuroscience, 8*, 14–18.

Sansone, R. A., & Sansone, L. A. (2012). Medically self-sabotaging behavior and its relationship with borderline personality. *Primary Care Reports, 18*, 37–47.

Santiago, P. N., Ursano, R. J., Gray, C. L., Pynoos, R. S., Spiegel, D., Lewis-Fernandez, R., . . . Fullerton, C. S. (2013). A systematic review of PTSD prevalence and trajectories in DSM-5 defined trauma exposed populations: Intentional and non-intentional traumatic events. *PLOS One, 8*(4), e59236. doi:10.1371/journal.pone.0059236

Sapienza, J. K., & Masten, A. S. (2011). Understanding and promoting resilience in children and youth. *Current Opinion in Psychiatry, 24*, 267–273.

Sar, V. (2011). Epidemiology of dissociative disorders: An overview. *Epidemiology Research International.* 404538. Retrieved from http://dx.doi.org/10.1155/2011/404538

Sasaki, A., de Vega, W. C., & McGowan, P. O. (2013). Biological embedding in mental health: An epigenomic perspective. *Biochemistry and Cellular Biology, 91,* 14–21.

Satir, V. (1967). A family of angels. In J. Haley & L. Hoffman (Eds.), *Techniques of family therapy* (pp. 99–113). New York, NY: Basic Books.

Satow, R. (1979). Where has all the hysteria gone? *Psychoanalytic Review, 66,* 463–477.

Sattler, S., Sauer, C., Mehlkop, G., & Graeff, P. (2013). The rationale for consuming cognitive enhancement drugs in university students and teachers. *PLOS One, 8,* e68821. doi:10.1371/journal.pone.0068821

Sauer, S. E., Burris, J. L., & Carlson, C. R. (2010). New directions in the management of chronic pain: Self-regulation theory as a model for integrative clinical psychology practice. *Clinical Psychology Review, 30,* 805–814.

Saunders, S. M., Miller, M., & Bright, M. M. (2010). Spiritually conscious psychological care. *Professional Psychology: Research and Practice, 41,* 355–362.

Savely, V. R., Leitao, M. M., & Stricker, R. B. (2006). The mystery of Morgellons disease: Infection or delusion? *American Journal of Clinical Dermatology, 7,* 1–5.

Saver, J. L., Fonarow, G. C., Smith, E. E., Reeves, M. J., Grau-Sepulveda, M. V., Pan, W., . . . Schwamm, L. H. (2013). Time to treatment with intravenous tissue plasminogen activator and outcome from acute ischemic stroke. *Journal of the American Medical Association, 309,* 2480–2488.

Savica, R., Grossardt, B. R., Bower, J. H., Boeve, B. F., Ahlskog, J. E., & Rocca, W. A. (2013). Incidence of dementia with Lewy bodies and Parkinson disease dementia. *JAMA Neurology, 70,* 1396–1402.

Savitz, J. B., Rauch, S. L., & Drevets, W. C. (2013). Clinical application of brain imaging for the diagnosis of mood disorders: The current state of play. *Molecular Psychiatry, 18,* 528–539.

Savolainen, K., Eriksson, J. G., Kajantie, E., Lahti, M., & Räikkönen, K. (2014). The history of sleep apnea is associated with shorter leukocyte telomere length: The Helsinki Birth Cohort Study. *Sleep Medicine, 15,* 209–212.

Saxena, S. (2011). Psychotherapy of compulsive hoarding. *Journal of Clinical Psychology: In Session, 67,* 477–484.

Scahill, L., McDougle, C. J., Aman, M. G., Johnson, C., Handen, B., Bearss, K., . . . Vitiello, B. (2012). Effects of risperidone and parent training on adaptive functioning in children with pervasive developmental disorders and serious behavioral problems. *Journal of the American Academy of Child & Adolescent Psychiatry, 51,* 36–46.

Schachter, S., & Latané, B. (1964). Crime, cognition, and the autonomic nervous system. *Nebraska Symposium on Motivation, 12,* 221–274.

Schaefer, H. H. (1970). Self-injurious behavior: Shaping "head banging" in monkeys. *Journal of Applied Behavior Analysis, 3,* 111–116.

Schaefer, S. M., Morozink, B. J., van Reekum, C. M., Lapate, R. C., Norris, C. J., Ryff, C. D., & Davidson, R. J. (2013). Purpose in life predicts better emotional recovery from negative stimuli. *PLOS One, 8*(11), e80329. doi:10.1371/journal.pone.0080329

Schauer, M., & Elbert, T. (2010). Dissociation following traumatic stress: Etiology and treatment. *Journal of Psychology, 218,* 109–127.

Scheel, M. J., Davis, C. K., & Henderson, J. D. (2013). Therapist use of client strengths: A qualitative study of positive processes. *The Counseling Psychologist, 41,* 392–427.

Schiffer, B., Pawliczek, C., Müller, B., Forsting, M., Gizewski, E., Leygraf, N., & Hodgins, S. (2014, January 28). Neural mechanisms underlying cognitive control of men with lifelong antisocial behavior. *Psychiatry Research: Neuroimaging, 222,* 43–51.

Schmauk, F. J. (1970). Punishment, arousal, andavoidance learning. *Journal of Abnormal Psychology, 76,* 325–335.

Schmetze, A. D., & McGrath, R. (2014). Phencyclidine (PCP)-related psychiatric disorders. Retrieved from http://emedicine.medscape.com/article/290476-overview

Schmidt, N. B. (2012). Innovations in the treatment of anxiety psychopathology: Introduction. *Behavior Therapy, 43,* 465–467.

Schmidt, N. B., Buckner, J. D., Pusser, A., Woolaway-Bickel, K., Preston, J. L., & Norr, A. (2012). Randomized controlled trial of False Safety Behavior Elimination Therapy: A unified cognitive behavioral treatment for anxiety psychopathology. *Behavior Therapy, 43,* 518–532.

Schmidt, N. B., Keough, M. E., Mitchell, M. A., Reynolds, E. K., MacPherson, L., Zvolensky, M. J., . . . Lejuez, C. W. (2010). Anxiety sensitivity: Prospective prediction of anxiety among early adolescents. *Journal of Anxiety Disorders, 24,* 503–508.

Schmidt, N. B., Richey, J., Buckner, J. D., & Timpano, K. R. (2009). Attention training for generalized social anxiety disorder. *Journal of Abnormal Psychology, 118,* 5–14.

Schmidt, U., Kaltwasser, S. F., & Wotjak, C. T. (2013). Biomarkers in posttraumatic stress disorder: Overview and implications for future research. *Disease Markers, 35,* 43–54.

Schmitt, A., Malchow, B., Hasan, A., & Falkai, P. (2014). The impact of environmental factors in severe psychiatric disorders. *Frontiers in Neuroscience, 8,* 19. eCollection 2014.

Schneider, M. S., Brown, L. S., & Glassgold, J. M. (2002). Implementing the resolution on appropriate therapeutic responses to sexual orientation: A guide for the perplexed. *Professional Psychology: Research and Practice, 33,* 265–276.

Schneider, S., Peters, J., Bromberg, U., Brassen, S., Miedl, S. F., Banaschewski, T., . . . Büchel, C. (2012). Risk taking and the adolescent reward system: A potential common link to substance abuse. *American Journal of Psychiatry, 169,* 39–46.

Schneier, F. R., Neria, Y., Pavlicova, M., Hembree, E., Suh, E. J., Amsel, L., & Marshall, R. D. (2012). Combined prolonged exposure therapy and paraxetine for PTSD related to the World Trade Center attack: A randomized controlled trial. *American Journal of Psychiatry, 169,* 80–88.

Schnittker, J. (2010). Gene-environment correlations in the stress-depression relationship. *Journal of Health and Social Behavior, 51,* 229–243.

Schofield, P., Ashworth, M., & Jones, R. (2011). Ethnic isolation and psychosis: Re-examining the ethnic density effect. *Psychological Medicine, 41,* 1263–1269.

Schonfeldt-Lecuona, C., Connemann, B. J., Spitzer, M., & Herwig, U. (2003). Transcranial magnetic stimulation in the reversal of motor conversion disorder. *Psychotherapy and Psychosomatics, 72,* 286–290.

Schooler, D., & Daniels, E. A. (2014). "I am not a skinny toothpick and proud of it": Latina adolescents' ethnic identity and responses to mainstream media images. *Body Image, 11,* 11–18.

Schosser, A., Butler, A. W., Ising, M., Perroud, N., Uher, R., Ng, M. Y., . . . Lewis, C. M. (2011). Genomewide association scan of suicidal thoughts and behaviour in major depression. *PLOS One, 6*(7), e20690. doi:10.1371/journal.pone.0020690

Schreiber, F. R. (1973). *Sybil.* Chicago, IL: Regnery.

Schreier, A., Wolke, D., Thomas, K., Horwood, J., Hollis, C., Gunnell, D., . . . Harrison, G. (2009). Prospective study of peer victimization in childhood and psychotic symptoms in a nonclinical population at age 12 years. *Archives of General Psychiatry, 66,* 527–536.

Schröder, A., Rehfeld, E., Ornbøl, E., Sharpe, M., Licht, R. W., & Fink, P. (2012). Cognitive-behavioural group treatment for a range of functional somatic syndromes: Randomised trial. *British Journal of Psychiatry, 200,* 499–507.

Schroeder, M., Iffland, J. S., Hill, A., Berner, W., & Briken, P. (2013). Personality disorders in men with sexual and violent criminal offense histories. *Journal of Personality Disorders, 27,* 519–530.

Schrut, A. (2005). A psychodynamic (non-Oedipal) and brain function hypothesis regarding a type of male sexual masochism. *Journal of the American Academy of Psychoanalysis and Dynamic Psychiatry, 33,* 333–349.

Schulte, I. E., & Petermann, F. (2011). Familial risk factors for the development of somatoform symptoms and disorders in children and adolescents: A systematic review. *Child Psychiatry and Human Development, 42,* 569–583.

Schulte, I. E., Petermann, F., & Noeker, M. (2010). Functional abdominal pain in childhood: From etiology to maladaptation. *Psychotherapy and Psychosomatics, 79,* 73–86.

Schultz, E. S., Gruzieva, O., Bellander, T., Bottai, M., Hallberg, J., Kull, I., . . . Pershagen, G. (2012). Traffic-related air pollution and lung function in children at 8 years of age: A birth cohort study. *American Journal of Respiratory and Critical Care Medicine,186,* 1286–1291.

Schulz, A. J., Gravlee, C. C., Williams, D. R., Israel, B. A., Mentz, G., & Rowe, Z. (2006). Discrimination, symptoms of depression, and self-rated health among African American women in Detroit: Results from a longitudinal analysis. *American Journal of Public Health, 96,* 1265–1270.

Schumann, C. M., Bloss, C. S., Barnes, C. C., Wideman, G. M., Carper, R. A., . . . Courchesne, E. (2010). Longitudinal magnetic resonance imaging study of cortical development through early childhood in autism. *Journal of Neuroscience, 30,* 4419–4427.

Schuster, R., Bornovalova, M., & Hunt, E. (2012). The influence of depression on the progression of HIV: Direct and indirect effects. *Behavior Modification, 36,* 87–119.

Schutz, E., Sailer, U., Al Nima, A., Rosenberg, P., Arnten, A.-C., Archer, T., & Garcia, D. (2013). The affective profile in the USA: Happiness, depression, life satisfaction, and happiness-increasing strategies. PeerJ1:e156. doi:107717/peerj.156.

Schweckendiek, J., Klucken, T., Merz, C. J., Tabbert, K., Walter, B., Ambach, W., . . . Stark, R. (2011). Weaving the (neuronal) web: Fear learning in spider phobia. *NeuroImage, 54,* 681–688.

Schweitzer, P. J., Zafar, U., Pavlicova, M., & Fallon, B. A. (2011). Long-term follow-up of hypochondriasis after selective serotonin reuptake inhibitor treatment. *Journal of Clinical Psychopharmacology, 31,* 365–368.

Schwerdtfeger, A. (2011). Battling the stigma of mental illness. Retrieved October 8, 2013, from http://voices.yahoo.com/battling-stigma-mental-illness-9114619.html?cat572&override_id5131114%3Fcat%3D5

Scott, C., & Resnick, P. J. (2009). Assessing potential for harm: Would your patient injure himself or others? *Current Psychiatry, 24,* 26–33.

Scott, L. N., Levy, K. N., & Granger, D. A. (2013). Biobehavioral reactivity to social evaluative stress in women with borderline personality disorder. *Personality Disorders, 4,* 91–100.

Scudellari, M. (2013, July 1). Worried sick. Retrieved from http://www.the-scientist.com/?articles.view/articleNo/36126/title/Worried-Sick

Seery, M. D. (2011). Resilience: A silver lining to experiencing adverse life events? *Current Directions in Psychological Science, 20,* 390–394.

Seery, M. D., Holman, E. A., & Silver, R. C. (2010). Whatever does not kill us: Cumulative lifetime adversity, vulnerability, and resilience. *Journal of Personality and Social Psychology, 99,* 1025–1041.

Seftel, A. D., Rosen, R. C., Hayes, R. P., Althof, S., Goldfisher, E., Shen, W., &

Sontag, A. (2014). Effect of once-daily tadalafil on confidence and perceived difficulty in performing sexual intercourse in men who were incomplete responders to as-needed PDE5 inhibitor treatment. *International Journal of Clinical Practice, 68,* 841–849.

Segarra, R., Ojeda, N., Zabala, A., García, J., Catalán, A., Eguíluz, J., & Gutiérrez, M. (2012). Similarities in early course among men and women with a first episode of schizophrenia and schizophreniform disorder. *European Archives of Psychiatry and Clinical Neuroscience, 262,* 95–105.

Segerstrom, S. C., & Sephton, S. E. (2010). Optimistic expectancies and cell-mediated immunity: The role of positive affect. *Psychological Science, 21,* 448–455.

Sehlmeyer, C., Dannlowski, U., Schoning, S., Kugel, H., Pyka, M., Pfleiderer, B., . . . Konrad, C. (2011). Neural correlates of trait anxiety in fear extinction. *Psychological Medicine, 41,* 789–798. doi:10.1017/S0033291710001248

Seife, C. (2012). Is drug research trustworthy? The pharmaceutical industry funnels money to prominent scientists who are doing research that affects its products—and nobody can stop it. *Scientific American, 307,* 56–63.

Seitz, V. (2007). The impact of media spokeswomen on teen girls' body image: An empirical assessment. *Business Review, 7,* 228–236.

Selby, E. A., & Joiner, T. E., Jr. (2013). Emotional cascades as prospective predictors of dysregulated behaviors in borderline personality disorder. *Personality Disorders, 4,* 168–174.

Seligman, M. E., Ernst, R. M., Gillham, J., Reivich, K., & Linkins, M. (2009). Positive education: Positive psychology and classroom interventions. *Oxford Review of Education, 35,* 293–311.

Seligman, M. E. P. (1975). *Helplessness.* San Francisco, CA: Freeman.

Seligman, M. E. P. (2007). Coaching and positive psychology. *Australian Psychologist, 42,* 266–287.

Seligman, M. E. P., & Csikszentmihalyi, M. (2000). Positive psychology: An introduction. *American Psychologist, 55,* 5–14.

Sell v. United States, 539 U.S. 166. (2003).

Seltman, R. E., & Matthews, B. R. (2012). Frontotemporal lobar degeneration: Epidemiology, pathology, diagnosis and management. *CNS Drugs, 26,* 841–870.

Seminowicz, D. A., Shpaner, M., Keaser, M. L., Krauthamer, G. M., Mantegna, J., Dumas, J. A., . . . Naylor, M. R. (2013). Cognitive-behavioral therapy increases prefrontal cortex gray matter in patients with chronic pain. *Journal of Pain, 14,* 1573–1584.

Sempértegui, G. A., Karreman, A., Arntz, A., & Bekker, M. H. (2013). Schema therapy for borderline personality disorder: A comprehensive review of its empirical foundations, effectiveness and implementation possibilities. *Clinical Psychology Review, 33,* 426–447.

Serafini, G., Pompili, M., Lindqvist, D., Dwivedi, Y., & Girardi, P. (2013). The role of neuropeptides in suicidal behavior: A systematic review. *Biomed Research International,* 687575.

Serpe, G. (2009). Tyra's alleged stalker goes on trial. Retrieved from http://www.eonline.com/news/119280/tyras-alleged-stalker-goes-on-trial

Seto, M. C. (2009). Pedophilia. *Annual Review of Clinical Psychology, 5,* 391–407.

Seto, M. C. (2012). Is pedophilia a sexual orientation? *Archives of Sexual Behavior, 41,* 231–236.

Seto, M. C., & Lalumière, M. L. (2010). What is so special about male adolescent sexual offending? A review and test of explanations through meta-analysis. *Psychological Bulletin, 136,* 526–575.

Setodji, C. M., Martino, S. C., Scharf, D. M., & Shadel, W. G. (2013). Friends moderate the effects of pro-smoking media on college students' intentions to smoke. *Psychology of Addictive Behavior, 27,* 256–261.

Sgobba, C. (2011). Frown towns. *Men's Health.* Retrieved from http://www.menshealth.com

Shah, M., Adams-Huet, B., Rao, S., Snell, P., Quittner, C., & Garg, A. (2013). The effect of dietary counseling on nutrient intakes in gastric banding surgery patients. *Journal of Investigative Medicine, 61,* 1165–1172.

Shalev, I., Entringer, S., Wadhwa, P. D., Wolkowitz, O. M., Puterman, E., Lin, J., & Epel, E. S. (2013). Stress and telomere biology: A lifespan perspective. *Psychoneuroendocrinology, 38,* 1835–1842.

Shapiro, A., Heath, N., & Roberts, E. (2013). Treatment of nonsuicidal self-injury: Critical review and implications for school applications. *School Psychology Forum,* 121–135.

Sharma, S., Moon, C. S., Khogali, A., Haidous, A., Chabenne, A., Ojo, C., . . . Ebadi, M. (2013). Biomarkers in Parkinson's disease (recent update). *Neurochemistry International, 63,* 201–229.

Shaw, P., Eckstrand, K., Sharp, W., Blumenthal, J., Lerch, J. P., Greenstein, D., . . . Rapoport, J. L. (2007). Attention-deficit/hyperactivity disorder is characterized by a delay in cortical maturation. *Proceedings of the National Academy of Sciences, 104,* 19649–19654.

Shawyer, F., Farhall, J., Mackinnon, A., Trauer, T., Sims, E., Ratcliff, K., . . . Copolov, D. (2012). A randomised controlled trial of acceptance-based cognitive behavioural therapy for command hallucinations in psychotic disorders. *Behaviour Research and Therapy, 50,* 110–121.

Sheehan, W., Sewall, B., & Thurber, S. (2005). Dissociative identity disorder and temporal lobe involvement: Replication and a cautionary note. *Psychiatry On-Line.* Retrieved from www.priory.com/psych.htm

Shelby, G. D., Shirkey, K. C., Sherman, A. L., Beck, J. E., Haman, K., Shears, A. R., . . . Walker, L. S. (2013). Functional abdominal pain in childhood and long-term vulnerability to anxiety disorders. *Pediatrics, 132,* 475–482.

Shelley-Ummenhofer, J., & MacMillan, P. D. (2007). Cognitive-behavioural treatment for women who binge eat. *Canadian Journal of Dietetic Practice and Research, 68,* 139–142.

Shelton, R. C., Osuntokun, O., Heinloth, A. N., & Corya, S. A. (2010). Therapeutic options for treatment-resistant depression. *CNS Drugs, 24,* 131–161.

Sher, K. J., Dick, D. M., Crabbe, J. C., Hutchison, K. E., O'Malley, S. S., & Heath, A. C. (2010). Consilient research approaches in studying gene 3 environment interactions in alcohol research. *Addiction Biology, 15,* 200–216.

Sherin, J. E., & Nemeroff, C. B. (2011). Post-traumatic stress disorder: The neurobiological impact of psychological trauma. *Dialogues in Clinical Neuroscience, 13,* 263–278.

Sherry, A., & Whilde, M. R. (2008). Borderline personality disorder. In M. Hersen & J. Rosqvist (Eds.), *Handbook of psychological assessment, case conceptualization, and treatment: Vol. 1. Adults* (pp. 403–437). Hoboken, NJ: Wiley.

Shiban, Y., Pauli, P., & Mühlberger, A. (2013). Effect of multiple context exposure on renewal in spider phobia. *Behaviour Research and Therapy, 51,* 68–74.

Shih, R. A., Miles, J., Tucker, J. S., Zhou, A. J., & D'Amico, E. J. (2010). Racial/ethnic differences in adolescent substance use: Mediation by individual, family, and school factors. *Journal of the Study of Alcohol and Other Drugs, 71,* 640–651.

Shin, H., Kim, M. H., Lee, S. J., Lee, K. H., Kim, M. J., Kim, J. S., & Cho, J. W. (2013). Decreased metabolism in the cerebral cortex in early-stage Huntington's disease: A possible biomarker of disease progression? *Journal of Clinical Neurology, 9,* 21–25.

Shin, M., Besser, L. M., Kucik, J. E., Lu, C., Siffel, C., Correa, A., & CSABA. (2009). Prevalence of Down syndrome among children and adolescents in 10 regions of the United States. *Pediatrics, 124,* 1565–1571.

Shmueli-Blumberg, D., Hu, L., Allen, C., Frasketi, M., Wu, L. T., & Vanveldhuisen, P. (2013). The National Drug Abuse Treatment Clinical Trials Network Data Share project: Website design, usage, challenges, and future directions. *Clinical Trials, 10,* 977–986.

Shneidman, E. S. (1998). *The suicidal mind.* New York: Oxford University Press.

Shorey, R. C., & Stuart, G. L. (2012). Manualized cognitive-behavioral treatment of social anxiety disorder: A case study. *Clinical Case Studies, 11,* 35–47.

Shorter, E. (2010). Disease versus dimension in diagnosis: Response to Dr. van Praag. *Canadian Journal of Psychiatry, 55,* 63.

Shrivastava, A., Shah, N., Johnston, M., Stitt, L., & Thakar, M. (2010). Predictors of long-term outcome of first-episode schizophrenia: A ten-year follow-up study. *Indian Journal of Psychiatry, 52,* 320–326.

Sibitz, I., Unger, A., Woppmann, A., Zidek, T., & Amering, M. (2011). Stigma resistance in patients with schizophrenia. *Schizophrenia Bulletin, 37,* 316–323.

Sibolt, G., Curtze, S., Melkas, S., Pohjasvaara, T., Kaste, M., Karhunen, P. J., . . . Erkinjuntti, T. (2013). Post-stroke depression and depression-executive dysfunction syndrome are associated with recurrence of ischemic stroke. *Cerebrovascular Diseases, 36,* 336–343.

Sibrava, N. J., Beard, C., Bjornsson, A. S., Moitra, E., Weisberg, R. B., & Keller,

M. B. (2013). Two-year course of generalized anxiety disorder, social anxiety disorder, and panic disorder in a longitudinal sample of African American adults. *Journal of Consulting and Clinical Psychology, 81,* 1052–1062.

Siebert, D. C., & Wilke, D. J. (2007). High-risk drinking among young adults: The influence of race and college enrollment. *American Journal of Drug & Alcohol Abuse, 33,* 843–850.

Siegel, M. (1979). Privacy, ethics, and confidentiality. *Professional Psychology, 10,* 249–258.

Sierra, M. (2012). *Depersonalization: A new look at a neglected syndrome.* New York, NY: Cambridge University Press.

Sieswerda, S., & Arntz, A. (2007). Successful psychotherapy reduces hypervigilance in borderline personality disorder. *Behavioral and Cognitive Psychotherapy, 35,* 387–402.

Silberg, J. L., Maes, H., & Eaves, L. J. (2010). Genetic and environmental influences on the transmission of parental depression to children's depression and conduct disturbance: An extended children of twins study. *Journal of Child Psychology and Psychiatry, 51,* 734–744.

Silberstein, S. D. (1998). *Migraine and other headaches: A patient's guide to treatment.* Chicago, IL: American Medical Association.

Silveri, M. M. (2012). Adolescent brain development and underage drinking in the United States: Identifying risks of alcohol use in college populations. *Harvard Review of Psychiatry, 20,* 189–200.

Sim, L. A., Lebow, J., & Billings, M. (2013). Eating disorders in adolescents with a history of obesity. *Pediatrics, 132,* e1026–e1030.

Sim, L. A., Sadowski, C. M., Whiteside, S. P., & Wells, L. A. (2004). Family-based therapy for adolescents with anorexia nervosa. *Mayo Clinic Proceedings, 79,* 1305–1308.

Simeon, D., Gross, S., Guralnik, O., Stein, D. J., Schmeidler, J., & Hollander, E. (1997). Feeling unreal: Thirty cases of DSM-III-R depersonalization disorder. *American Journal of Psychiatry, 154,* 1107–1113.

Simmons, A. M. (2002, January 13). Eating disorders on rise for South African blacks. *Los Angeles Times,* p. A3.

Simon, G. E., & VonKorff, M. (1991). Somatization and psychiatric disorder in the NIMH Epidemiologic Catchment Area study. *American Journal of Psychiatry, 148,* 1494–1500.

Simon, H., & Zieve, D. (2012). Narcolepsy. Retrieved from http://umm.edu/health/medical/reports/articles/narcolepsy

Simons, T. (2014). Local bowler finds renewed energy with silver cross sleep apnea treatment. Retrieved from http://joliet.patch.com/groups/silver-cross-health/p/local-bowler-finds-renewed-energy-with-silver-cross-sleep-apnea-treatment

Simpson, H. B., Foa, E. B., Liebowitz, M. R., Huppert, J. D., Cahill, S., Maher, M. J., . . . Campeas, R. (2013). Cognitive-behavioral therapy vs risperidone for augmenting serotonin reuptake inhibitors in obsessive-compulsive disorder: A randomized clinical trial. *American Journal of Psychiatry, 70,* 1190–1199.

Sin, N. L., & Lyubomirsky, S. (2009). Enhancing well-being and alleviating depressive symptoms with positive psychology interventions: A practice friendly meta-analysis. *Journal of Clinical Psychology, 65,* 467–487.

Singer, H. S. (2005). Tourette's syndrome: From behaviour to biology. *Lancet Neurology, 4*(3), 149–159.

Singh, A. A., Hays, D. G., & Watson, L. S. (2011). Strength in the face of adversity: Resilience strategies of transgender individuals. *Journal of Counseling and Development, 89,* 20–27.

Singh, B. S. (2007). *Managing somatoform disorders.* Retrieved from www.mja.com.au/public/mentalhealth/articles/singh/singh.html

Singh, M. K., & Chang, K. D. (2012). The neural effects of psychotropic medications in children and adolescents. *Child & Adolescent Psychiatry Clinics of North America, 21,* 753–771.

Singh, M. K., & Crystal, H. A. (2013). Muscle contraction tension headache. Retrieved from http://emedicine.medscape.com/article/1142908-overview

Sinha-Deb, K., Sarkar, S., Sood, M., & Khandelwall, S. K. (2013). Wires in the body: A case of factitious disorder. *Indian Journal of Psychological Medicine, 35,* 209–221.

Sivec, H. J., & Montesano, V. L. (2013). Clinical process examples of cognitive behavioral therapy for psychosis. *Psychotherapy, 50,* 458–463.

Skinner, B. F. (1990). Can psychology be a science of mind? *American Psychologist, 45,* 1206–1210.

Skinner, M. D., Lahmek, P., Pham, H., & Aubin, H. J. (2014). Disulfiram efficacy in the treatment of alcohol dependence: A meta-analysis. *PLOS One, 9,* e87366. doi:10.1371/journal.pone.0087366

Skodol, A. E., & Bender, D. S. (2009). The future of personality disorders in DSM-V? *American Journal of Psychiatry, 166,* 388–390.

Slavich, G. M., O'Donovan, A., Epel, E. S., & Kemeny, M. E. (2010). Black sheep get the blues: A psychobiological model of social rejection and depression. *Neuroscience and Biobehavioral Reviews, 35,* 39–45.

Slavich, G. M., Way, B. M., Eisenberger, N. I., & Taylor, S. E. (2010). Neural sensitivity to social rejection is associated with inflammatory responses to social stress. *Proceedings of the National Academy of Sciences of the USA, 107,* 14817–14822.

Sleegers, K., Lambert, J. C., Bertram, L., Cruts, M., Amouyel, P., & Van Broeckhoven, C. (2010). The pursuit of susceptibility genes for Alzheimer's disease: Progress and prospects. *Trends in Genetics, 26,* 84–93.

Sloane, C., Burke, S. C., Cremeens, J., Vail-Smith, K., & Woolsey, C. (2010). Drunkorexia: Calorie restriction prior to alcohol consumption among college freshman. *Journal of Alcohol & Drug Education, 54*(2), 17–34.

Slotema, C. W., Blom, J. D., Hoek, H. W., & Sommer, I. E. (2010). Should we expand the toolbox of psychiatric treatment methods to include repetitive transcranial magnetic stimulation (rTMS)? A meta-analysis of the efficacy of rTMS in psychiatric disorders. *Journal of Clinical Psychiatry, 71,* 873–884.

Smith, A. D., Smith, S. M., de Jager, C. A., Whitbread, P., Johnston, C., Agacinski, G., . . . Refsum, H. (2010). Homocysteine-lowering by B vitamins slows the rate of accelerated brain atrophy in mild cognitive impairment: A randomized controlled trial. *PLOS One, 5*(9), e12244. doi:10.1371/journal.pone.0012244

Smith, A. R., Fink, E. L., Anestis, M. D., Ribeiro, J. D., Gordon, K. H., Davis, H., . . . Joiner, T. E., Jr. (2012). Exercise caution: Over-exercise is associated with suicidality among individuals with disordered eating. *Psychiatry Research, 206,* 246–255.

Smith, A. R., Hawkeswood, S. E., Bodell, L. P., & Joiner, T. E. (2011). Muscularity versus leanness: An examination of body ideals and predictors of disordered eating in heterosexual and gay college students. *Body Image, 8,* 232–236.

Smith, B. L. (2012). Inappropriate prescribing. *Monitor on Psychology, 43,* 36.

Smith, C. (2002, August 7). Persecuted parents or protected children? *Seattle Post Intelligencer,* pp. A1, A10.

Smith, C. S. (2003, September 27). Son's wish to die, and mother's help, stir French debate. *New York Times,* pp. A1, A4.

Smith, G. C., Clarke, D. M., Handrinos, D., Dunsis, A., & McKenzie, D. P. (2000). Consultation-liaison psychiatrists' management of somatoform disorders. *Psychosomatics, 41,* 481–489.

Smith, L. (2010). *Psychology, poverty, and the end of social exclusion.* New York, NY: Teachers College Press.

Smith, L., & Reddington, R. M. (2010). Class dismissed: Making the case for the study of classist microaggressions. In D. W. Sue (Ed.), *Microaggressions and marginality: Manifestation, dynamics and impact* (pp. 269–285). Hoboken, NJ: Wiley.

Smith, M., Segal, J., & Robinson, L. (2013). Suicide prevention. Retrieved from http://www.helpguide.org/mental/suicide_prevention.htm

Smith, P. N., Cukrowicz, K. C., Poindexter, E. K., Hobson, V., & Cohen, L. M. (2010). The acquired capability for suicide: A comparison of suicide attempters, suicide ideators, and non-suicidal controls. *Depression and Anxiety, 27,* 871–877.

Smith, S. L., & Choueiti, M. (2010). Gender disparity on screen and behind the camera in family films. Retrieved from http://www.theeenadavisinstitute.org/downloads/FullStudy_GenderDisparityFamilyFilms.pdf

Smoller, J., Shiedly, B., & Tsuang, M. T. (Eds.). (2008). *Psychiatric genetics: Applications in clinical practice.* Washington, DC: American Psychiatric Publishing.

Snorrason, I., Smari, J., & Olafsson, R. P. (2011). Motor inhibition, reflection impulsivity, and trait impulsivity in pathological skin picking. *Behavior Therapy, 42,* 521–532.

Snyder, J. S., Soumier, A., Brewer, M., Pickel, J., & Cameron, H. A. (2011). Adult hippocampal neurogenesis buffers stress responses and depressive behaviour. *Nature, 476,* 458–461.

So, J. K. (2008). Somatization as a cultural idiom of distress: Rethinking mind and body in a multicultural society. *Counselling Psychology Quarterly, 21,* 167–174.

Soehle, M., Kayser, S., Ellerkmann, R. K., & Schlaepfer, T. E. (2014). Bilateral bispectral index monitoring during and after electroconvulsive therapy compared with magnetic seizure therapy for treatment-resistant depression. *British Journal of Anaesthesia, 112,* 695–702.

Sola, C. L., Chopra, A., & Rastogi, A. (2010). Sedative, hypnotic, anxiolytic use disorders. Retrieved from http://emedicine.medscape.com/article/290585-overview

Sollman, M. J., Ranseen, J. D., & Berry, D. T. R. (2010). Detection of feigned ADHD in college students. *Psychological Assessment, 22,* 325–335.

Soloff, P. H., & Chiappetta, L. (2012). Subtyping borderline personality disorder by suicidal behavior. *Journal of Personality Disorders, 26,* 468–480.

Solovitch, S. (2014). Conspiracy of silence. When the psychiatrist has bp. Retrieved from http://www.bphope.com/Item.aspx/102/conspiracy-of-silence-when-the-psychiatrist-has-bp

Soreff, S. (2013). Suicide. Retrieved from http://emedicine.medscape.com/article/2013085-overview#aw2aab6b2

Soreff, S., & McInnes, L. A. (2014). Bipolar affective disorder. Retrieved from http://emedicine.medscape.com/article/286342-overview

Sørensen, H. J., Mortensen, E. L., Schiffman, J., Reinisch, J. M., Maeda, J., & Mednick, S. A. (2010). Early developmental milestones and risk of schizophrenia: A 45-year follow-up of the Copenhagen Perinatal Cohort. *Schizophrenia Research, 118,* 41–47.

Sorensen, P., Birket-Smith, M., Wattar, U., Buemann, I., & Salkovskis, P. (2011). A randomized clinical trial of cognitive behavioural therapy versus no intervention for patients with hypochondriasis. *Psychological Medicine, 41,* 431–441.

Soria, V., Martínez-Amorós, E., Escaramís, G., Valero, J., Pérez–Egea, R., Garcia, C., . . . Urretavizcaya, M. (2010). Differential association of circadian genes with mood disorders: CRY1 and NPAS2 are associated with unipolar major depression and CLOCK and VIP with bipolar disorder. *Neuropsychopharmacology, 35,* 1279–1289.

Sorkin, A., Weinshall, D., & Peled, A. (2008). The distortion of reality perception in schizophrenia patients, as measured in virtual reality. *Studies in Health Technology and Informatics, 132,* 475–480.

Soutullo, C., & Figueroa-Quintana, A. (2013). When do you prescribe antidepressants to depressed children? *Current Psychiatry Reports, 15,* 366. doi:10.1007/s11920-013-0366-3

Sowell, E. S., Leow, A. D., Bookheimer, S. Y., Smith, L. M., O'Connor, M. J., Kan, E., . . . Thompson, P. M. (2010). Differentiating prenatal exposure to methamphetamine and alcohol versus alcohol and not methamphetamine using tensor-based brain morphometry and discriminant analysis. *Journal of Neuroscience, 30,* 3876–3885.

Spanos, N. P. (1978). Witchcraft in histories of psychiatry: A critical analysis and an alternative conceptualization. *Psychological Bulletin, 85,* 417–439.

Spanos, N. P. (1994). Multiple identity enactments and multiple personality disorder: A sociocognitive perspective. *Psychological Bulletin, 116,* 143–165.

Spence, S. H., Donovan, C. L., March, S., Gamble, A., Anderson, R., Prosser, S., . . . Kenardy, J. (2008). Online CBT in the treatment of child and adolescent anxiety disorders: Issues in the development of BRAVE–ONLINE and two case illustrations. *Behavioural and Cognitive Psychotherapy, 36,* 411–430.

Spencer, D., Marshall, J., Post, B., Kulakodlu, M., Newschaffer, C., Dennen, T., . . . Jain, A. (2013). Psychotropic medication use and polypharmacy in children with autism spectrum disorders. *Pediatrics, 132,* 833–840.

Spencer, T. J., Biederman, J., & Mick, E. (2007). Attention-deficit/hyperactivity disorder: Diagnosis, lifespan, comorbidities, and neurobiology. *Journal of Pediatric Psychology, 32,* 631–642.

Spencer-Thomas, S., Hindman, J., & Conrad, J. (2012) Man therapy: An innovative approach to suicide prevention for working aged men. Retrieved from http://carsonjspencer.org/programs/man-therapy

Spiegel, D. (2006). Recognizing traumatic dissociation. *American Journal of Psychiatry, 163,* 566–568.

Spiegel, D., Loewenstein, R. J., Lewis-Fernández, R., Sar, V., Simeon, D., Vermetten, E., . . . Dell, P. F. (2011). Dissociative disorders in DSM-5. *Depression and Anxiety, 28,* 824–852.

Spiegelhalder, K., Regen, W., Nanovska, S., Baglioni, C., & Riemann, D. (2013). Comorbid sleep disorders in neuropsychiatric disorders across the life cycle. *Current Psychiatry Reports, 5,* 364.

Spielmans, G. I., Jureidini, J., Healy, D., & Purssey, R.(2013). Inappropriate data and measures lead to questionable conclusions. *JAMA Psychiatry, 70,* 121–123.

Spira, A. P., Gamaldo, A. A., An, Y., Wu, M. N., Simonsick, E. M., Bilgel, M., . . . Resnick, S. M. (2013). Self-reported sleep and b-amyloid deposition in community-dwelling older adults. *JAMA Neurology, 70,* 1537–1543.

Spira, A. P., Rebok, G. W., Stone, K. L., Kramer, J. H., & Yaffe, K. (2012). Depressive symptoms in oldest-old women: Risk of mild cognitive impairment and dementia. *American Journal of Geriatric Psychiatry, 20,* 1006–1015.

Spitzer, R. L., Gibbon, M., Skodol, A. E., Williams, J. B., & First, M. B. (Eds.). (1994). *DSM-IV: Casebook* (pp. 121–122). Washington, DC: American Psychiatric Publishing.

Springen, K. (2006, December 7). Study looks at pro-anorexia web sites. Retrieved from www.msnbc.msn.com/id/16098915/site/newsweek/print

Sripada, C., Kessler, D., Fang, Y., Welsh, R. C., Prem Kumar, K., & Angstadt, M. (2014). Disrupted network architecture of the resting brain in attention-deficit/hyperactivity disorder. *Human Brain Mapping.* doi:10.1002/hbm.22504

Srivastava, A. K., & Schwartz, C. E. (2014). Intellectual disability and autism spectrum disorders: Causal genes and molecular mechanisms. *Neuroscience & Biobehavioral Reviews.* doi:10.1016/j.neubiorev.2014.02.015 [Staal, W. G., Pol, H. E. H., Schnack, H. G., van Haren, N. E. M., Seifert, M., & Kahn, R. S. (2001). Structural abnormalities in chronic schizophrenia at the extremes of the outcome spectrum. *American Journal of Psychiatry, 158,* 1140–1142.

Stahl, S. M. (2007). The genetics of schizophrenia converge upon the NMDA glutamate receptor. *CNS Spectrums, 12,* 583–588.

Stahl, S. M., & Wise, D. D. (2008). The potential role of a corticotrophin-releasing factor receptor–1 antagonist in psychiatric disorders. *CNS Spectrums, 13,* 467–478.

Stalberg, G., Ekerwald, H., & Hultman, C. M. (2004). At issue: Siblings of patients with schizophrenia: Sibling bond, coping patterns, and fear of possible schizophrenia heredity. *Schizophrenia Bulletin, 30,* 445–451.

Stambor, Z. (2006). Stressed out nation. *Monitor on Psychology, 37,* 28–29.

Stamova, B., Green, P. G., Tian, Y., Hertz-Picciotto, I., Pessah, I. N., Hansen, R., . . . Sharp, F. R. (2011). Correlations between gene expression and mercury levels in blood of boys with and without autism. *Neurotoxicity Research, 19,* 31–48.

Staniloiu, A., & Markowitsch, H. J. (2010). Searching for the anatomy of dissociative amnesia. *Journal of Psychology, 218,* 96–108.

Stanley, B., Brown, G., Brent, D. A., Wells, K., Poling, K., Curry, J., . . . Hughes, J. (2009). Cognitive-behavioral therapy for suicide prevention (CBT-SP): Treatment model, feasibility, and acceptability. *Journal of the American Academy of Child & Adolescent Psychiatry, 48,* 1005–1013.

Stanley, M. A., Beck, J. G., Novy, D. M., Averill, P. M., Swann, A. C., Diefenbach, G. J., & Hopko, D. R. (2003). Cognitive-behavioral treatment of late-life generalized anxiety disorder. *Journal of Consulting and Clinical Psychology, 71,* 309–319.

Stark, J. (2004, July 25). Twin sisters, a singular affliction. *Bellingham Herald,* p. A1.

Startup, H., Freeman, D., & Garety, P. A. (2006). Persecutory delusions and catastrophic worry in psychosis: Developing the understanding of delusion distress and persistence. *Behaviour Research and Therapy, 45,* 523–537.

Stavro, K., Pelletier, J., & Potvin, S. (2013). Widespread and sustained cognitive deficits in alcoholism: A meta-analysis. *Addiction Biology, 18,* 203–213.

Steck, E. L., Abrams, L. M., & Phelps, L. (2004). Positive psychology in the prevention of eating disorders. *Psychology in the Schools, 41,* 111–117.

Stefanidis, E. (2006). Being rational. *Schizophrenia Bulletin, 32,* 422–423.

Steiger, A. E., Allemand, M., Robins, R. W., & Fend, H. A. (2014). Low and decreasing self-esteem during adolescence predict adult depression two decades later. *Journal of Personality and Social Psychology, 106,* 325–338.

Steiger, H., & Bruce, K. R. (2007). Phenotypes, endophenotypes, and genotypes in bulimia spectrum eating disorders. *Canadian Journal of Psychiatry, 52,* 220–227.

Stein, A., Craske, M. G., Lehtonen, A., Harvey, A., Savage-McGlynn, E., Davies, B., . . . Counsell, N. (2012). Maternal cognitions and mother–infant interaction in postnatal depression and generalized anxiety disorder. *Journal of Abnormal Psychology, 121,* 795–809.

Stein, D. J., Scott, K., Haro Abad, J. M., Aguilar-Gaxiola S., Alonso, J., Angermeyer, M., . . . Von Korff, M. (2010). Early childhood adversity and later hypertension: Data from the World Mental Health Survey. *Annals of Clinical Psychiatry, 22*(1), 19–28.

Steinberg, J. S., Arshad, A., Kowalski, M., Kukar, A., Suma, V., Vloka, M., . . . Rozanski, A. (2004). Increased incidence of life-threatening ventricular arrhythmias in implantable defibrillator patients after the World Trade Center attack. *Journal of the American College of Cardiology, 44,* 1261–1264.

Steinberg, T., Shmuel-Baruch, S., Horesh, N., & Apter, A. (2013). Life events and Tourette syndrome. *Comprehensive Psychiatry, 54,* 467–473.

Steinbrecher, N., & Hiller, W. (2011). Course and prediction of somatoform disorder and medically unexplained symptoms in primary care. *General Hospital Psychiatry, 33,* 318–326.

Steiner, A. M., Gengoux, G. W., Klin, A., & Chawarska, K. (2013). Pivotal response treatment for infants at-risk for autism spectrum disorders: A pilot study. *Journal of Autism & Developmental Disorders, 43,* 91–102.

Steiner, T. J., MacGregor, E. A., & Davies, P. T. G. (2007). *Guidelines for all healthcare professionals in the diagnosis and management of migraine, tension-type, cluster and medication-overuse headache* (3rd ed.). Hull, UK: British Association for the Study of Headache.

Steiner, A. P. & Redish, A. D. (2014). Behavioral and neurophysiological correlates of regret in rat decision-making on a neuroeconomic task. *Nature Neuroscience, 17,* 995–1002.

Steinhausen, H. C. (2009). Outcome of eating disorders. *Child and Adolescent Psychiatric Clinics of North America, 18,* 225–242.

Steinhausen, H. C., & Weber, S. (2009). The outcome of bulimia nervosa: Findings from one-quarter century of research. *American Journal of Psychiatry, 166,* 1331–1341.

Steketee, G., Frost, R. O., Tolin, D. F., Rasmussen, J., & Brown, T. A. (2010). Waitlist-controlled trial of cognitive behavior therapy for hoarding disorder. *Depression and Anxiety, 27,* 476–484.

Stepp, S. D., Olino, T. M., Klein, D. N., Seeley, J. R., & Lewinsohn, P. M. (2013). Unique influences of adolescent antecedents on adult borderline personality disorder features. *Personality Disorders, 4,* 223–229.

Stergiakouli, E., & Thapar, A. (2010). Fitting the pieces together: Current research on the genetic basis of attention-deficit/hyperactivity disorder (ADHD). *Journal of Neuropsychiatric Disease and Treatment, 6,* 551–560.

Sternberg, R. J. (2004). Culture and intelligence. *American Psychologist, 59,* 325–338.

Sterzer, P. (2010). Born to be criminal? What to make of early biological risk factors for criminal behavior. *American Journal of Psychiatry, 167,* 1–3.

Stetka, B. S., Christoph, U., & Correll, M. D. (2013, May 21). A guide to DSM-5. *Medscape.* Retrieved from http://www.medscape.com/viewarticle/803884_1

Stevenson, T., Thalman, L., Christie, H., & Poluha, W. (2012). Constraint-induced movement therapy compared to dose-matched interventions for upper-limb dysfunction in adult survivors of stroke: A systematic review with meta-analysis. *Physiotherapy Canada, 64,* 397–413.

Stice, E. (2001). A prospective test of the dual-pathway model of bulimic pathology: Mediating effects of dieting and negative affect. *Journal of Abnormal Psychology, 110,* 124–135.

Stice, E., Marti, C. N., & Rohde, P. (2013). Prevalence, incidence, impairment, and course of the proposed DSM-5 eating disorder diagnoses in an 8-year prospective community study of young women. *Journal of Abnormal Psychology, 122,* 445–457.

Stice, E., Marti, C. N., Shaw, H., & Jaconis, M. (2009). An 8-year longitudinal study of the natural history of threshold, subthreshold, and partial eating disorders from a community sample of adolescents. *Journal of Abnormal Psychology, 118,* 587–597.

Stice, E., & Shaw, H. (2004). Eating disorder prevention programs: A meta-analytic review. *Psychological Bulletin, 130,* 206–227.

Stice, E., Shaw, H., Bohon, C., Marti, C. N., & Rohde, P. (2009). A meta-analytic review of depression prevention programs for children and adolescents: Factors that predict magnitude of intervention effects. *Journal of Consulting and Clinical Psychology, 77,* 486–503.

Stiles, B. L., & Clark, R. E. (2011). BDSM: A subcultural analysis of sacrifices and delights. *Deviant Behavior, 32,* 158–189.

Stitzer, M., Petry, N., & Peirce, J. (2010). Motivational incentives research in the National Drug Abuse Treatment Clinical Trials Network. *Journal of Substance Abuse Treatment, 38*(Suppl 1), S61–S69.

Stober, G. (2006). Genetic correlates of the nosology of catatonia. *Psychiatric Annals, 37,* 37–44.

Stone, L. B., Hankin, B. L., Gibb, B. E., & Abela, J. R. (2011). Co-rumination predicts the onset of depressive disorders during adolescence. *Journal of Abnormal Psychology, 120,* 752–757.

Stoner, R., Chow, M. L., Boyle, M. P., Sunkin, S. M., Mouton, P. R., Roy, S., . . . Courchesne, E. (2014). Patches of disorganization in the neocortex of children with autism. *New England Journal of Medicine, 370,* 1209–1219.

Stoolmiller, M., Wills, T. A., McClure, A. C., Tanski, S. E., Worth, K. A., Gerrard, M., & Sargen, J. D. (2012). Comparing media and family predictors of alcohol use: A cohort study of US adolescents. *British Medical Journal Open, 2,* e000543.

Story, M., Neumark-Sztainer, D., Sherwood, N., Stang, J., & Murray, D. (1998). Dieting status and its relationship to eating and physical activity behaviors in a representative sample of U.S. adolescents. *Journal of the American Dietetic Association, 98,* 1127–1135.

Stossel, S. (2014). Surviving anxiety. Retrieved from www.theatlantic.com/magazine/archive/2014/01/surviving_anxiety/355741

St-Pierre-Delorme, M.-E., Lalonda, M. P., Perreault, V., Koszegi, N., & O'Connor, K. (2011). Inference-based therapy for compulsive hoarding: A clinical case study. *Clinical Case Studies, 10,* 291–303.

Strakowski, S. M., Fleck, D. E, DelBello, M. P., Adler, C. M., Shear, P. K., Kotwal, R., & Arndt, S. (2010). Impulsivity across the course of bipolar disorder. *Bipolar Disorder, 12,* 285–297.

Strakowski, S. M., Adler, C. M., Almeida, J., Altshuler, L. L., Blumberg, H. P., Chang, K. D., . . . Townsend, J. D. (2012). The functional neuroanatomy of bipolar disorder: A consensus model. *Bipolar Disorders, 14,* 313–325.

Strand, S. L. (2013). Post-concussive syndrome in a female basketball player: A case study. *Open Access Journal of Sports Medicine, 4,* 23–25.

Strenziok, M., Krueger, F., Despande, G., Lenrook, R. K., van der Meer, E., & Grafman, J. (2010). Frontal-parietal regulation of media violence exposure in adolescents: A multi-method study. *Social Cognitive and Affective Neuroscience, 6,* 537–547. doi:10.1093/scan/nsq079

Striegel-Moore, R. H., & Bulik, C. M. (2007). Risk factors in eating disorders. *American Psychologist, 62,* 181–198.

Strober, M., Freeman, R., Diamond, C. L. J., & Kaye, W. (2000). Controlled family study of anorexia nervosa and bulimia nervosa: Evidence of shared liability and transmission of partial syndromes. *American Journal of Psychiatry, 157,* 393–401.

Stroebel, S. S., O'Keefe, S. L., Beard, K. W., Kuo, S. Y., Swindell, S., & Stroupe, W. (2013a). Brother-sister incest: Data from anonymous computer-assisted self interviews. *Journal of Child Sexual Abuse, 22,* 255–276.

Stroebel, S. S., O'Keefe, S. L., Griffee, K., Kuo, S. Y., Beard, K. W., & Kommor, M. J. (2013b). Sister-sister incest: Data from an anonymous computerized survey. *Journal of Child Sexual Abuse, 22,* 695–719.

Stroud, C. B., Davila, J., Hammen, C., and Vrshek-Schallhorn, S. (2011). Severe and nonsevere events in first onsets versus recurrences of depression: Evidence for stress sensitization. *Journal of Abnormal Psychology, 120,* 142–154.

Stuart, H. (2012). The stigmatization of mental illnesses. *Canadian Journal of Psychiatry, 57,* 455–456.

Stuart, S., & Noyes, R., Jr. (2005). Treating hypochondriasis with interpersonal psychotherapy. *Journal of Contemporary Psychotherapy, 35,* 269–283.

Substance Abuse and Mental Health Services Administration. (2010a, June 18). Trends in emergency department visits involving nonmedical use of narcotic pain relievers. *The DAWN Report.* Retrieved from http://www.oas.samhsa.gov/2k10/dawn016/opioided.htm

Substance Abuse and Mental Health Services Administration. (2010b). *Results from the 2009 National Survey on Drug Use and Health: Mental health findings* (Office of Applied Studies, NSDUH Series H–39, HHS Publication No. SMA 10–4609). Rockville, MD.

Substance Abuse and Mental Health Services Administration. (2012). *Results from the 2010 National Survey on Drug Use and Health: Mental health* findings (NSDUH Series H-42, HHS Publication No. SMA 11-4667). Rockville, MD.

Substance Abuse and Mental Health Services Administration . (2013a). *Results from the 2012 National Survey on Drug Use and Health: Summary of national findings.* (NSDUH Series H-46, HHS Publication No. SMA 13-4795.) Rockville, MD: Substance Abuse and Mental Health Services Administration.

Substance Abuse and Mental Health Services Administration. (2013b). Update on emergency department visits involving energy drinks: A continuing public health concern. Retrieved from http://www.samhsa.gov/data/2k13/DAWN126/sr126-energy-drinks-use.htm

Sue, D. W. (2010). *Microaggressions in everyday life: Race, gender and sexual orientation.* Hoboken, NJ: Wiley.

Sue, D. W., & Sue, D. (2013). *Counseling the culturally diverse: Theory and practice* (6th ed.). Hoboken, NJ: Wiley.

Sugawara, J., Tarumi, T., & Tanaka, H. (2010). Effect of mirthful laughter on vascular function. *American Journal of Cardiology, 15,* 856–859.

Suglia, S. F., Solnick, S., & Hemenway, D. (2013). Soft drinks consumption is associated with behavior problems in 5-year-olds. *Journal of Pediatrics, 163,* 1323-1328.

Sui, X., LaMonte, M. J., Laditka, J. N., Hardin, J. W., Chase, N., Hooker, S. P., & Blair, S. N. (2007). Cardiorespiratory fitness and adiposity as mortality predictors in older adults. *Journal of the American Medical Association, 298,* 2507–2516.

Suicide Prevention Resource Center. (2013). *Suicide attempts among racial/ethnic populations In the United States.* Newton, MA: Education Development Center, Inc.

Sullivan, E. V., Harris, R. A., & Pfefferbaum, A. (2010). Alcohol's effects on brain and behavior. Retrieved from http://pubs.niaaa.nih.gov/publications/arh40/127-143.htm

Sundel, M., & Sundel, S. S. (1998). Psychopharmacoslogical treatment of panic disorder. *Research of Social Work Practice, 8,* 426–451.

Sundstrom, E. (2004). First person account: The clogs. *Schizophrenia Bulletin, 30,* 191–192.

Sung, J., Woo, J. M., Kim, W., Lim, S. K., & Chung, E. J. (2012). The effect of cognitive behavior therapy–based

"forest therapy" program on blood pressure, salivary cortisol level, and quality of life in elderly hypertensive patients. *Clinical and Experimental Hypertension, 34,* 1–7.

Suominen, K., Mantere, O., Valtonen, H., Arvilommi, P., Leppämäki, S., & Isometsä, E. (2009). Gender differences in bipolar disorder type I and II. *Acta Psychiatrica Scandanavica, 120,* 464–473.

Supekar, K., Uddin, L. Q., Khouzam, A., Phillips, J., Gaillard, W. D., Kenworthy, L. E., . . . Menon, V. (2013). Brain hyperconnectivity in children with autism and its links to social deficits. *Cell Reports, 5,* 738–747.

Supic, G., Jagodic, M., & Magic, Z. (2013). Epigenetics: A new link between nutrition and cancer. *Nutrition and Cancer, 65,* 781–792.

Surén, P., Roth, C., Bresnahan, M., Haugen, M., Hornig, M., Hirtz, D., . . . Stoltenberg, C. (2013). Association between maternal use of folic acid supplements and risk of autism spectrum disorders in children. *Journal of the American Medical Association, 309,* 570–577.

Surtees, P. B., Wainwright, N. W. J., Luben, R., Wareham, N. J., Bingham, S. A., & Khaw, K.-T. (2010). Mastery is associated with cardiovascular disease mortality in men and women at apparently low risk. *Health Psychology, 29,* 412–420.

Sutin, A. R., & Terracciano, A. (2013). Perceived weight discrimination and obesity. *PLOS One, 8*(7), e70048. doi:10.1371/journal.pone.0070048

Suzuki, K., Takei, N., Kawai, M., Minabe, Y., & Mori, N. (2003). Is *taijin kyofusho* a culture-bound syndrome? *American Journal of Psychiatry, 160,* 1358.

Suzuki, L., & Aronson, J. (2005). The cultural malleability of intelligence and its impact on the racial/ethnic hierarchy. *Psychology, Public Policy, and Law, 11,* 320–327.

Svaldi, J., Caffier, D., Blechert, J., & Tuschen-Caffier, B. (2009). Body-related film clip triggers desire to binge in women with binge eating disorder. *Behaviour Research and Therapy, 47,* 790–795.

Svoboda, E. (2006, December 5). All the signs of pregnancy except one: A baby. *New York Times.* Retrieved from http://www.nytimes.com

Swami, V., & Voracek, M. (2013). Associations among men's sexist attitudes,

objectification of women, and their own drive for muscularity. *Psychology of Men & Masculinity, 14,* 168–174.

Swann, A. C., Steinberg, J. L., Lijffijt, M., Moeller, G. F. (2009). Continuum of depressive and manic mixed states in patients with bipolar disorder: Quantitative measurement and clinical features. *World Psychiatry, 8,* 166–172.

Swanson, S. A., & Colman, I. (2013). Association between exposure to suicide and suicidality outcomes in youth. *Canadian Medical Association Journal, 185,* 870–877.

Swanson, S. A., Crow, S. J., LeGrange, D., Swendsen, J., & Merikangas, K. R. (2011). Prevalence and correlates of eating disorders in adolescents: Results from the National Comorbidity Survey Replication–Adolescent Supplement. *Archives of General Psychiatry, 68,* 714–723.

Swart, M. L., van Schagen, A. M., Lancee, J., & van den Bout, J. (2013). Prevalence of nightmare disorder in psychiatric outpatients. *Psychotherapy and Psychosomatics, 82,* 267–268.

Sweeney, C. T., Sembower, M. A., Ertischek, M. D., Shiffman, S., & Schnoll, S. H. (2013). Nonmedical use of prescription ADHD stimulants and preexisting patterns of drug abuse. *Journal of Addictive Diseases, 32,* 1–10.

Swendsen, J., Burstein, M., Case, B., Conway, K. P., Dierker, L., He, J., & Merikangas, K. R. (2012). Use and abuse of alcohol and illicit drugs in US adolescents: Results of the National Comorbidity Survey–Adolescent Supplement. *Archives of General Psychiatry, 69,* 390–398.

Szasz, T. S. (1987). Justifying coercion through theology and therapy. In J. K. Zeig (Ed.), *The evolution of psychotherapy* (pp. 158–174). New York, NY: Brunner/Mazel.

Szyf, M., & Bick, J. (2013). DNA methylation: A mechanism for embedding early life experiences in the genome. *Child Development, 84,* 9–57.

Szymkowicz, S. M., Finnegan, N., & Dale, R. M. (2013). A 12-month naturalistic observation of three patients receiving repeat intravenous ketamine infusions for their treatment-resistant depression. *Journal of Affective Disorders, 147,* 416–420.

Takahashi, T., Tsunoda, M., Miyashita, M., Ogihara, T., Okada, Y., Hagiwara, T., . . . Amano, N. (2011). Comparison of diagnostic names of mental illnesses in medical documents before and after the adoption of a new Japanese translation of "schizophrenia." *Psychiatry and Clinical Neurosciences, 65,* 89–94.

Takeuchi, H., Suzuki, T., Remington, G., Bies, R. R., Abe, T., Graff-Guerrero, A., . . . Uchida, H. (2012). Effects of risperidone and olanzapine dose reduction on cognitive function in stable patients with schizophrenia: An open-label, randomized, controlled, pilot study. *Schizophrenia Bulletin, 39,* 993–998.

Takeuchi, J. (2000). Treatment of a biracial child with schizophreniform disorder: Cultural formulation. *Cultural Diversity and Ethnic Minority Psychology, 6,* 93–101.

Talavage, T. M., Nauman, E. A., Breedlove, E. L., Yoruk, U., Dye, A. E., Morigaki, K., . . . Leverenz, L. J. (2010). Functionally-detected cognitive impairment in high school football players without clinically-diagnosed concussion. *Journal of Neurotrauma.* Advance online publication. doi:10.1089/neu.2010.1512

Talleyrand, R. M. (2010). Eating disorders in African American girls: Implications for counselors. *Journal of Counseling and Development, 88,* 319–325.

Tan, R., Gould, R. V., Combes, H., & Lehmann, S. (2014). Distress, trauma, and recovery: Adjustment to first episode psychosis. *Psychology and Psychotherapy: Theory, Research and Practice, 87,* 80–95.

Tanguay, P. E. (2011). Autism in DSM-5. *American Journal of Psychiatry, 168,* 1142–1144.

Taniai, H., Nishiyama, T., Miyachi, T., Imaeda, M., & Sumi, S. (2008). Genetic influences on the broad spectrum of autism: Study of proband-ascertained twins. *American Journal of Medical Genetics. Part B, Neuropsychiatric Genetics, 147B,* 844–849.

Tarasoff v. the Board of Regents of the University of California, 17 Cal. 3d 435, 551 P.2d 334, 131 Cal. Rptr. 14, 83 Ad. L. 3d 1166 (1976).

Taylor, J. L., & Seltzer, M. M. (2010a). Changes in the autism behavioral phenotype during the transition to adulthood. *Journal of Autism and Developmental Disorders, 40,* 431–446.

Taylor, J. L., & Seltzer, M. M. (2010b). Employment and post-secondary educational activities for young adults with autism spectrum disorders during the transition to adulthood. *Journal of Autism and Developmental Disorders,*

41, 566–574. doi:10.1007/s10803-010-1070-3

Taylor, K. N., Harper, S., & Chadwick, P. (2009). Impact of mindfulness on cognition and affect in voice hearing: Evidence from two case studies. *Behavioural and Cognitive Psychotherapy, 37,* 397–402.

Taylor, S., Asmundson, G. J. G., & Coons, M. J. (2005). Current directions in the treatment of hypochondriasis. *Journal of Cognitive Psychotherapy: An International Quarterly, 19,* 285–304.

Taylor, S., Jang, K. L., Stein, M. B., & Asmundson, G. J. G. (2008). A behavioral-genetic analysis of cognitive-behavioral model of hypochondriasis. *Journal of Cognitive Psychotherapy: An International Quarterly, 22,* 143–154.

Taylor, S. E. (2010). How psychosocial resources enhance health and wellbeing. In S. Donaldson, M. Csikszentmihalyi, & J. Nakamura (Eds.), *Applied positive psychology.* New York, NY: Routledge.

Teachman, B. A., Marker, C. D., & Clerkin, E. M. (2010). Catastrophic misinterpretations as a predictor of symptom change during treatment for panic disorder. *Journal of Consulting and Clinical Psychology, 24,* 300–308.

Tedeschi, R. G., & McNally, R. J. (2011). Can we facilitate posttraumatic growth in combat veterans? *American Psychologist, 66,* 19–24.

Teicher, M. H., Andersen, S. L., Polcari, A., Anderson, C. M., & Navalta, C. P. (2002). Developmental neurobiology of childhood stress and trauma. *Psychiatric Clinics of North America, 25,* 397–426.

Teicher, M. H., & Samson, J. A. (2013). Childhood maltreatment and psychopathology: A case for ecophenotypic variants as clinically and neurobiologically distinct subtypes. *American Journal of Psychiatry, 170,* 1114–1133.

Tejada-Vera, B. (2013). Mortality from Alzheimer's disease in the United States: Data for 2000 and 2010. *NCHS Data Brief, 116,* 1–8.

Terman, L. M., & Merrill, M. A. (1960). *Stanford-Binet intelligence scale.* Boston, MA: Houghton Mifflin.

Terry-McElrath, Y. M., O☒Malley, P. M., & Johnston, L. D. (2014). Energy drinks, soft drinks, and substance use among United States secondary school students. *Journal of Addiction Medicine, 8,* 6–13.

Thakker-Varia, S., & Alder, J. (2009). Neuropeptides in depression: Role of

VGF. *Behavioral Brain Research, 197,* 262–278.

Thanos, P. K., Michaelides, M., Piyis, Y. K., Wang, G. J., & Volkow, N. D. (2008). Food restriction markedly increases dopamine D2 receptor (D2R) in a rat model of obesity as assessed with in-vivo muPET imaging ([(11)C] raclopride) and in-vitro ([(3)H] spiperone) autoradiography. *Synapse, 62,* 50–61.

Thom, A., Sartory, G., & Johren, P. (2000). Comparison between one-session psychological treatment and benzodiazepine in dental phobia. *Journal of Consulting and Clinical Psychology, 68,* 378–387.

Thomas, J. D., Warren, K. R., & Hewitt, B. G. (2010). Fetal alcohol spectrum disorders: From research to policy. *Alcohol Research & Health, 33,* 118–126.

Thomas, J. J., Vartanian, L. R., & Brownell, K. D. (2009). The relationship between eating disorder not otherwise specified (EDNOS) and officially recognized eating disorders: Meta-analysis and implications for DSM. *Psychological Bulletin, 135,* 407–433.

Thomas, K. (2010, October 12). Transgender woman sues L.P.G.A. over policy. *New York Times,* p. B13.

Thomas, K. (2013, March 18). U.S. drug costs dropped in 2012, but rises loom. *New York Times,* p. A1.

Thomas, P. (1995). Thought disorder or communication disorder: Linguistic science provides a new approach. *British Journal of Psychiatry, 166,* 287–290.

Thomas, T., Stansifer, L., & Findling, R. L. (2011). Psychopharmacology of pediatric bipolar disorders in children and adolescents. *Pediatric Clinics of North America, 58,* 173–187.

Thompson, D., Jr. (2014). When sex is a problem for the rich and famous. Retrieved from http://www.everyday health.com/sexual-health-pictures/ celebs-sex-addiction.aspx#/slide-1

Thompson, J. K., & Stice, E. (2004). Thin-ideal internalization: Mounting evidence for a new risk factor for body-image disturbance and eating pathology. In T. F. Oltmanns & R. E. Emery (Eds.), *Current directions in abnormal psychology* (pp. 97–101). Upper Saddle River, NJ: Prentice Hall.

Thompson, M., & Gibbs, N. (2012, July 23). Why can't the army win the war on suicide? *Time,* pp. 23–31.

Thompson, P. M., Vidal, C., Giedd, J. N., Gochman, P., Blumenthal, J., Nicolson, R., . . . Rapoport, J. L. (2001). Mapping adolescent brain change reveals dynamic wave of accelerated gray matter loss in very early-onset schizophrenia. *Proceedings of the National Academy of Sciences, 98,* 11650–11655.

Thorndike, R. L., Hagen, E. P., & Sattler, J. M. (1986). *The Stanford-Binet intelligence scale: Guide for administration and scoring* (3rd ed.). Chicago, IL: Riverside.

Thorpe, S. J., Barnett, J., Friend, K., & Nottingham, K. (2011). The mediating roles of disgust sensitivity and danger expectancy in relation to hand washing behaviour. *Behavioural and Cognitive Psychotherapy, 39,* 175–190.

Thorup, A., Waltoft, B. L., Pedersen, C. B., Mortensen, P. B., & Nordentoft, M. (2007). Young males have a higher risk of developing schizophrenia: A Danish register study. *Psychological Medicine, 37,* 479–484.

Thun, M. J., Carter, B. D., Feskanich, D., Freedman, N. D., Prentice, R., Lopez, A. D., . . . Gapstur, S. M. (2013). 50-year trends in smoking-related mortality in the United States. *New England Journal of Medicine, 368,* 351–364.

Thurston, R. C., & Kubzansky, L. D. (2009). Women, loneliness, and incident coronary heart disease. *Psychosomatic Medicine, 71,* 836–842.

Thylstrup, B., & Hesse, M. (2009). "I am not complaining"—Ambivalence construct in schizoid personality disorder. *American Journal of Psychotherapy, 63,* 147–167.

Tian, Y., Green, P. G., Stamova, B., Hertz-Picciotto, I., Pessah, I. N., Hansen, R., . . . Sharp, F. R. (2011). Correlations of gene expression with blood lead levels in children with autism compared to typically developing controls. *Neurotoxicity Research, 19,* 1–13.

Tierney, J. (1988, July 3). Research finds lower-level workers bear brunt of workplace stress. *Seattle Post Intelligencer,* pp. K1–K3.

Tietjen, G. E., Khubchandani, J., Herial, N. A., & Shah, K. (2012). Adverse childhood experiences are associated with migraine and vascular biomarkers. *Headache, 52,* 920–929.

Timberlake, D. S., Hopfer, C. J., Rhee, S. H., Friedman, N. P., Haberstick, B. C., Lessem, J. M., & Hewitt, J. K. (2007). College attendance and its effect on drinking behaviors in a longitudinal study of adolescents. *Alcoholism: Clinical and Experimental Research, 31,* 1020–1030.

Tindle, H. A., Chang, Y.-F., Kuller, L. H., Manson, J. E., Robinson, J. G., Rosal, M. C., . . . Matthews, K. A. (2009). Optimism, cynical hostility, and incident coronary heart disease and mortality in the Women's Health Initiative. *Circulation, 120,* 656–662.

Ting, L., & Panchanadeswaran, S. (2009). Barriers to help-seeking among immigrant African American women survivors of partner abuse: Listening to women's own voices. *Journal of Aggression, Maltreatment & Trauma, 18,* 817–838.

Tobin, J. J., & Friedman, J. (1983). Spirits, shamans, and nightmare death: Survivor stress in a Hmong refugee. *American Journal of Orthopsychiatry, 53,* 439–448.

Tolin, D. F., Meunier, S. A., Frost, R. O., & Steketee, G. (2011). Hoarding among patients seeking treatment for anxiety disorders. *Journal of Anxiety Disorders, 25,* 43–48.

Tolin, D. F., Steenkamp, M. M., Marx, B. P., & Litz, B. T. (2010). Detecting symptom exaggeration in combat veterans using the MMPI-2 symptom validity scales: A mixed group validation. *Psychological Assessment, 22,* 729–736.

Torpey, D. C., & Klein, D. N. (2008). Chronic depression: Update on classification and treatment. *Current Psychiatry Reports, 10,* 458–464.

Tottenham, N., Hertzig, M. E., Gillespie-Lynch, K., Gilhooly, T., Millner, A. J., & Casey, B. J. (2014). Elevated amygdala response to faces and gaze aversion in autism spectrum disorder. *Social & Cognitive Affective Neuroscience, 9,* 106–117.

Touyz, S., Le Grange, D., Lacey, H., Hay, P., Smith, R., Maguire, S., . . . Crosby, R. D. (2013). Treating severe and enduring anorexia nervosa: A randomized controlled trial. *Psychological Medicine, 43,* 2501–2511.

Trampe, D., Stapel, D. A., & Siero, F. W. (2010). On models and vases: Body dissatisfaction and proneness to social comparison effects. *Journal of Personality and Social Psychology, 92,* 106–118.

Trautmann, E., & Kroner-Herwig, B. (2010). A randomized controlled trial of Internet-based self-help training for recurrent headache in children and adolescents. *Behaviour Research and Therapy, 48,* 28–37.

Treichel, J. (2011). Ignoring cultural factors can compromise therapy. Retrieved from: http://psychnews. psychiatryonline.org/newsarticle. aspx?articleid5115860

Trichotillomania. (2010). Retrieved from http://www.ncbi.nlm.nih.gov/pubmed health/PMH0002485

Triffleman, E. G., & Pole, N. (2010). Future directions in studies of trauma among ethnoracial and sexual minority samples. *Journal of Consulting and Clinical Psychology, 78,* 490–497.

Trinh, J., & Farrer, M. (2013). Advances in the genetics of Parkinson disease. *Nature Reviews Neurology, 9,* 445–454.

Trivedi, M. H., Greer, T. L., Church, T. S., Carmody, T. J., Grannemann, B. D., . . . Blair, S. N. (2011). Exercise as an augmentation treatment for nonremitted major depressive disorder: A randomized, parallel dose comparison. *Journal of Clinical Psychiatry, 72,* 677–684.

Troister, T., & Holden, R. R. (2010). Comparing psychache, depression, and hopelessness in their associations with suicidality: A test of Shneidman's theory of suicide. *Personality and Individual Differences, 49,* 689–693.

Trudel-Fitzgerald, C., Boehm, J. K., Kivimaki, M., & Kubzansky, L. D. (2014). Taking the tension out of hypertension: A prospective study of psychological well being and hypertension. *Journal of Hypertension, 32,* 1222–1228.

Trust for America's Health. (2013). F as in fat: How obesity threatens America's future 2013. Retrieved from http:// healthyamericans.org/report/108

Tsai, G. E., Condie, D., Wu, M.-T., & Chang, I.-W. (1999). Functional magnetic resonance imaging of personality switches in a woman with dissociative identity disorder. *Harvard Review of Psychiatry, 7,* 119–122.

Tsang, H. W., Leung, A. Y., Chung, R. C., Bell, M., & Cheung W. M. (2010). Review on vocational predictors: A systematic review of predictors of vocational outcomes among individuals with schizophrenia: An update since 1998. *Australia and New Zealand Journal of Psychiatry, 44,* 495–504.

Tsitsika, A. K., Barlou, E., Andrie, E., Dimitropoulou, C., Tzavela, E. C., Janikian, M., & Tsolia, M. (2014). Bullying behaviors in children and adolescents: "An ongoing story." *Frontiers in Public Health, 2,* 7. eCollection 2014.

TT/The Local. (2008, November 17). Transvestism "no longer a disease" in Sweden. Retrieved from http://www .thelocal.se/20081117/15728

Tucker, B. T. P., Woods, D. W., Flessner, C. A., Franklin, S. A., & Franklin, M. E. (2011). The skin picking impact project: Phenomenology, interference, and treatment utilization of pathological skin picking in a population-based sample. *Journal of Anxiety Disorders, 25,* 88–95.

Tucker, C. (2012). New research aimed at mental health: U.S. veterans struggle with pain, stigma of post-traumatic stress. *Nations Health, 42,* 1–12.

Tucker-Drob, E. M., Rhemtulla, M., Harden, K. P., Turkheimer, E., & Fask, D. (2011). Emergence of a gene 3 socioeconomic status interaction on infant mental ability between 10 months and 2 years. *Psychological Science, 22,* 125–133.

Tully, E. C., Iacono, W. G., & McGue, M. (2010). Changes in genetic and environmental influences on the development of nicotine dependence and major depressive disorder from middle adolescence to early adulthood. *Developmental Psychopathology, 22,* 831–848.

Tunks, E. R., Weir, R., & Crook, J. (2008). Epidemiologic perspective on chronicpain treatment. *Canadian Journal of Psychiatry, 53,* 235–242.

Turetsky, B. I., Calkins, M. E., Light, G. A., Olincy, A., Radant, A. D., & Swerdlow, N. R. (2007). Neurophysiological endophenotypes of schizophrenia: The viability of selected candidate measures. *Schizophrenia Bulletin, 33,* 69–78.

Turk, D. C., Swanson, K. S., & Tunks, E. R. (2008). Psychological approaches in the treatment of chronic pain patients—When pills, scalpels, and needles are not enough. *Canadian Journal of Psychiatry, 53,* 213–223.

Turner, E. H., Knoepflmacher, D., & Shapley, L. (2012). Publication bias in antipsychotic trials: An analysis of efficacy comparing the published literature to the U.S. Food and Drug Administration database. *PLOS Medicine, 9*(3), e1001189. doi:10.1371/journal.pmed.1001189

Turner, E. H., Matthews, A. M., Linardatos, E., Tell, R. A., & Rosenthal, R. (2008). Selective publication of antidepressant trials and its influence on apparent efficacy. *New England Journal of Medicine, 358,* 252–257.

Turner, H. A., Finkelhor, D., Ormrod, R., & Hamby, S. L. (2010). Infant victimization in a nationally representative sample. *Pediatrics, 126,* 44–52.

Turtle, L., & Robertson, M. M. (2008). Tics, twitches, tales: The experiences of Gilles de la Tourette's syndrome. *American Journal of Orthopsychiatry, 78,* 449–455.

Tuttle, J. P., Scheurich, N. E., & Ranseen, J. (2010). Prevalence of ADHD diagnosis and nonmedical prescription stimulant use in medical students. *Academic Psychiatry, 34,* 220–223.

Tynan, W. D. (2008). Oppositional defiant disorder. Retrieved from http://emedicine.medscape.com/article/918095-print

Tynan, W. D. (2010). Conduct disorder. Retrieved from http://emedicine.medscape.com/article/918213-print

Ucok, A. (2007). Other people stigmatize . . . But, what about us? Attitudes of mental health professionals towards patients with schizophrenia. *Archives of Neuropsychiatry, 44,* 108–116.

Ungar, M., & Liebenberg, L. (2013). Ethnocultural factors, resilience, and school engagement. *School Psychology International, 34,* 514–526.

United Nations. (2013). The Millennium Development Goals report. Retrieved from http://www.un.org/millennium goals/reports.shtml

United Nations Office on Drugs and Crime. (2013). *World drug report.* New York, NY: United Nations.

University of Michigan. (2010, October 28). Friends with cognitive benefits: Mental function improves after certain kinds of socializing. *Science Daily.* Retrieved from http://www.sciencedaily.com/releases/2010/10/101028113817.htm

Ursache, A., Blair, C., Stifter, C., & Voegtline, K. (2013). Emotional reactivity and regulation in infancy interact to predict executive functioning in early childhood. *Developmental Psychology, 49,* 127–137.

U.S. Census Bureau. (2012). Most children younger than age 1 are minorities, Census Bureau Reports. Retrieved from http://www.census.gov/newsroom/releases/archives/population/cb12-90.html

U.S. Department of Commerce. (2011). *Women in America.* Washington, DC: U.S. Government Printing Office.

U.S. Department of Education, National Center for Education Statistics. (2010). Digest of education statistics, 2009 (NCES 2010-013). Retrieved from http://nces.ed.gov/pubs2010/2010013_0.pdf

U.S. Department of Education, National Center for Education Statistics. (2013). Digest of education statistics, 2012 (NCES 2014-015). Retrieved from https://nces.ed.gov/fastfacts/display.asp?id564

U.S. Department of Health and Human Services. (2013). Child maltreatment 2012. Retrieved from http://www.acf.hhs.gov/programs/cb/resource/child-maltreatment-2012

U.S. Food and Drug Administration. (2007). Anti-depressant use in children, adolescents, and adults. Retrieved from http://www.fda.gov/NewsEvents/Newsroom/PressAnnouncements/2007/ucm108905.htm

U.S. Food and Drug Administration. (2011). FDA drug safety communication: Antipsychotic drug labels updated on use during pregnancy and risk of abnormal muscle movements and withdrawal symptoms in newborns. Retrieved from http://www.fda.gov/Drugs/DrugSafety/ucm243903.htm

United States v. Comstock. 560 U.S. (2010).

Vahid, B., & Marik, P. E. (2007, September suppl). Severe emphysema associated with cocaine smoking: A case study. *Journal of Respiratory Diseases,* pp. 12–20.

Vaknin, S. (2012). The borderline patient—A case study. Retrieved from http://www.healthyplace.com/personality-disorders/malignant-self-love/borderline-patient-a-case-study

Valentí, M., Pacchiarotti, I., Rosa, A. R., Bonnín, C. M., Popovic, D., Nivoli, A. M., . . . Vieta, E. (2011). Bipolar mixed episodes and antidepressants: A cohort study of bipolar I disorder patients. *Bipolar Disorders, 13,* 145–154.

Valor, L. M., & Guiretti, D. (2013). What's wrong with epigenetics in Huntington's disease? *Neuropharmacology 80,* 103–114.

van Almen, K. L. M., & van Gerwen, L. J. (2013). Prevalence and behavioral styles of fear of flying. *Aviation Psychology and Applied Human Factors, 3,* 39–43.

Van Ameringen, M., Simpson, W., Patterson, B., Dell'Osso, B., Fineberg, N., Hollander, E., . . . Zohar, J. (2014). Pharmacological treatment strategies in obsessive compulsive disorder: A cross-sectional view in nine international OCD centers. *Journal of Psychopharmacology, 28,* 596–602.

van den Hout, M. A., & Engelhard, I. M. (2012). How does EMDR work? *Journal of Experimental Psychopathology, 3,* 724–738.

van der Gaag, M., Nieman, D. H., Rietdijk, J., Dragt, S., Ising, H. K., Klaassen, R. M., . . . Linszen, D. H. (2012). Cognitive behavioral therapy for subjects at ultrahigh risk for developing psychosis: A randomized controlled clinical trial. *Schizophrenia Bulletin, 38,* 1180–1188.

van der Gaag, M., Stant, A. D., Wolters, K. J. K., Burkens, E., & Wiersma, D. (2011). Cognitive behavioral therapy for persistent and recurrent psychosis in people with schizophrenia-spectrum disorder: Cost-effectiveness analysis. *British Journal of Psychiatry, 198,* 59–65.

Vander Wal, J. S. (2012). Night eating syndrome: A critical review of the literature. *Clinical Psychology Review, 32,* 49–59.

van der Werf, M., Thewissen, V., Dominguez, M. D., Lieb, R., Wittchen, H., & Van Os, J. (2011). Adolescent development of psychosis as an outcome of hearing impairment: A 10–year longitudinal study. *Psychological Medicine, 41,* 477–485.

van der Werff, S. J., van den Berg, S. M., Pannekoek, J. N., Elzinga, B. M., & van der Wee, N. J. (2013). Neuroimaging resilience to stress: A review. *Frontier of Behavioral Neuroscience, 7,* 39. doi:10.3389/fnbeh.2013.00039

Vandrey, R., & Haney, M. (2009). Pharmacotherapy for cannabis dependence: How close are we? *CNS Drugs, 23,* 543–553.

Van Evra, J. P. (1983). *Psychological disorders of children and adolescents.* Boston, MA: Little, Brown.

Van Gundy, K., Cesar, J., & Rebellon, C. (2010). A life-course perspective on the "gateway hypothesis." *Journal of Health and Social Behavior, 51,* 244–259.

van Hartevelt, T. J., Cabral, J., Deco, G., Møller, A., Green, A. L., Aziz, T. Z., & Kringelbach, M. L. (2014). Neural plasticity in human brain connectivity: The effects of long term deep brain stimulation of the subthalamic nucleus in Parkinson's disease. *PLOS One, 9,* e86496.

Van Heeringen, C., & Marusic, A. (2003). Understanding the suicidal brain. *British Journal of Psychiatry, 183,* 282–284.

Van Hulle, C. A., Waldman, I. D., D'Onofrio, B. M., Rodgers, J. L., Rathouz, P. J., & Lahey, B. B. (2009). Developmental structure of genetic influences on antisocial behavior across

childhood and adolescence. *Journal of Abnormal Psychology, 118,* 711–721.

van Lankveld, J. (2008). Problems with sexual interest and desire in women. In D. Rowland & L. Incrocci (Eds.), *Handbook of sexual and gender identity disorders* (pp. 154–187). Hoboken, NJ: Wiley.

Van Noppen, B., & Steketee, G. (2009). Testing a conceptual model of patient and family predictors of obsessive compulsive disorder (OCD) symptoms. *Behaviour Research and Therapy, 47,* 18–25.

van Strien, T., Snoek, H. M., van der Zwaluw, C. S., & Engels, R. C. (2010). Parental control and the dopamine D2 receptor gene (DRD2) interaction on emotional eating in adolescence. *Appetite, 54,* 255–261.

Varga, M., Dukay-Szabó, S., Túry, F., & van Furth, E. F. (2013). Evidence and gaps in the literature on orthorexia nervosa. *Eating and Weight Disorders, 18,* 103–111.

Värnik, P. (2012). Suicide in the world. *International Journal of Environmental Research and Public Health, 9,* 760–771.

Vasey, M. W., Vilensky, M. R., Heath, J. H., Harbaugh, C. N., Buffington, A. G., & Fazio, R. H. (2012). It was as big as my head, I swear! Biased spider estimation in spider phobia. *Journal of Anxiety Disorders, 26,* 20–24.

Vassallo, M., Durant, J., Biscay, V., Lebrun-Frenay, C., Dunais, B., Laffon, M., . . . Dellamonica, P. (2014). Can high central nervous system penetrating antiretroviral regimens protect against the onset of HIV-associated neurocognitive disorders? *AIDS, 28,* 493–501.

Vassilopoulos, S. P., Banerjee, R., & Prantzalou, C. (2009). Experimental modification of interpretation bias in socially anxious children: Changes in interpretation, anticipated interpersonal anxiety, and social anxiety symptoms. *Behaviour Research and Therapy, 47,* 1085–1089.

Vasterling, J. J., Brailey, K., Proctor, S. P., Kane, R., Heeren, T., & Franz, M. (2012). Neuropsychological outcomes of mild traumatic brain injury, post-traumatic stress disorder and depression in Iraq-deployed US Army soldiers. *British Journal of Psychiatry, 201,* 186–192.

Vater, A., Ritter, K., Strunz, S., Ronningstam, E. F., Renneberg, B., & Roepke, S. (2014, February 10). Stability of

narcissistic personality disorder: Tracking categorical and dimensional rating systems over a two-year period. *Personal Disord.* [Epub ahead of print]

Vedantam, S. (2005). Racial disparities found in pinpointing mental illness. Retrieved from http://www.washingtonpost.com/wp-dyn/content/article/2005/06/27/AR2005062701496.html

Veling, W., Selten, J.-P., Mackenbach, J. P., & Hoek, H. W. (2007). Symptoms at first contact for psychotic disorder: Comparison between native Dutch and ethnic minorities. *Schizophrenia Research, 95,* 30–38.

Velligan, D. I., Weiden, P. J., Sajatovic, M., Scott, J., Carpenter, D., Ross, R., & Docherty, J. P. (2009). The expert consensus guideline series: Adherence problems in patients with serious and persistent mental illness. *Journal of Clinical Psychiatry, 70*(Suppl 4), 1–46.

Ventura, M. I., Baynes, K., Sigvardt, K. A., Unruh, A. M., Acklin, S. S., Kirsch, H. E., & Disbrow, E. A. (2012). Hemispheric asymmetries and prosodic emotion recognition deficits in Parkinson's disease. *Neuropsychologia, 50,* 1936–1945.

Verboom, C. E., Sentse, M., Sijtsema, J. J., Nolen, W. A., Ormel, J., & Penninx, B. W. (2011). Explaining heterogeneity in disability with major depressive disorder: Effects of personal and environmental characteristics. *Journal of Affective Disorders, 132,* 71–81.

Verdon, B. (2011). The case of thematic tests adapted to older adults. *Rorschachiana, 32,* 46–71.

Verma, R., Balhara, Y. P., & Mathur, S. (2011). Management of attention-deficit hyperactivity disorder. *Journal of Pediatric Neuroscience, 6,* 13–18.

Viding, E., & Blakemore, S. (2007). Endophenotype approach to developmental psychopathology: Implications for autism research. *Behavior Genetics, 37,* 51–60.

Vigod, S. N., & Stewart, D. (2009). Emergent research in the cause of mental illness in women across the lifespan. *Current Opinion in Psychiatry, 22,* 396–400.

Vilhauer, J. S., Young, S., Kealoha, C., Borrmann, J., Ishak, W. W., Rapaport, M.H.,. . . Mirocha, J. (2011). Treating major depression by creating positive expectations for the future: A pilot study for the effectiveness of future-directed therapy (FDT) on symptom severity and quality of life. *CNS Neuroscience and Therapeutics, 18,* 102–109. doi:10.1111/j.1755-5949.2011.00235.x

Villagonzalo, K. A., Dodd, S., Ng, F., Mihaly, S., Langbein, A., & Berk, M. (2011). The relationship between substance use and posttraumatic stress disorder in a methadone maintenance treatment program. *Comprehensive Psychiatry, 52,* 562–566. doi:10.1016/j.comppsych.2010.10.001

Vincent, M. A., & McCabe, M. P. (2000). Gender differences among adolescents in family, and peer influences on body dissatisfaction, weight loss, and binge eating disorders. *Journal of Youth and Adolescence, 29,* 205–221.

Visser, S., Danielson, M., Bitsko, R., Holbrook, J. R., Kogan, M. D., Ghandour, R. M., . . . Blumberg, S. J. (2014). Trends in the parent-report of health care provider-diagnosis and medication treatment for ADHD disorder: United States, 2003–2011. *Journal of the American Academy of Child & Adolescent Psychiatry, 53,* 34–46.

Vitelli, R. (2007). The Tarasoff decision. Retrieved from http://ezinearticles.com/?The-Tarasoff-Decision&id5827885

Vogel, D. L., Bitman, R. L., Hammer, J. H., & Wade, N. G. (2013). Is stigma internalized? The longitudinal impact of public stigma on self-stigma. *Journal of Counseling Psychology, 60,* 311–316.

Vogt, D., Vaughn, R., Glickman, M. E., Schultz, M., Drainoni, M.-L., Elwy, R., . . . Eisen, S. (2011). Gender differences in combat-related stressors and their association with post-deployment mental health in a nationally representative sample of U.S. OEF/OIF veterans. *Journal of Abnormal Psychology, 120,* 797–806.

Vöhringer, P. A., Barroilhet, S. A., Amerio, A., Reale, M. L., Alvear, K., Vergne, D., & Ghaemi, S. N. (2013). Cognitive impairment in bipolar disorder and schizophrenia: A systematic review. *Frontiers in Psychiatry, 4,* 87. doi:10.3389/fpsyt.2013.00087

Volbrecht, M. M., & Goldsmith, H. H. (2010). Early temperamental and family predictors of shyness and anxiety. *Developmental Psychology, 46,* 1192–1205.

Volkow, N. D., Wang, G. J., Tomasi, D., & Baler, R. D. (2013). Obesity and addiction: Neurobiological overlaps. *Obesity Reviews, 14,* 2–18.

von Gontard, A., Heron, J., & Joinson, C. (2011). Family history of nocturnal enuresis and urinary incontinence: Results from a large epidemiological study. *Journal of Urology, 185,* 2303–2306.

von Lojewski, A., & Abraham, S. (2014). Personality factors and eating disorders: Self-uncertainty. *Eating Behaviors, 15,* 106–109.

Voon, V., Gallea, C., Nattori, N., Bruno, M., Ekanayake, V., & Hallett, M. (2010). The involuntary nature of conversion disorder. *Neurology, 74,* 223–228.

Vorvick, L. J. (2012). Vaginismus. Retrieved from http://www.ncbi.nlm.nih.gov/pubmedhealth/PMH0002457

Wade, T., George, W. M., & Atkinson, M. (2009). A randomized controlled trial of brief interventions of body dissatisfaction. *Journal of Consulting and Clinical Psychology, 77,* 845–854.

Wagner, J., & Abbott, G. (2007). Depression and depression care in diabetes: Relationship to perceived discrimination in African Americans. *Diabetes Care, 30,* 364–366.

Wagner, K. D., Ritt-Olson, A., Chou, C. P., Pokhrel, P., Duan, L., Baezconde-Garbanati, L., . . . Unger, J. B. (2010). Associations between parental family structure, family functioning, and substance use among Hispanic/Latino adolescents. *Psychology of Addictive Behaviors, 24,* 98–108.

Wainwright, L. D., Glentworth, D., Haddock, G., Bentley, R., & Lobban, F. (2014). What do relatives experience when supporting someone in early psychosis? *Psychology and Psychotherapy: Theory, Research, and Practice.* doi:10.1111/papt.12024

Wakefield, H., & Underwager, R. (1993). Misuse of psychological tests in forensic settings: Some horrible examples. *American Journal of Forensic Psychology, 11,* 55–57.

Wakefield, J. C. (2011). DSM-5 proposed diagnostic criteria for sexual paraphilias: Tensions between diagnostic validity and forensic utility. *International Journal of Law & Psychiatry, 34,* 195–209.

Wakefield, J. C. (2013). The DSM-5 debate over the bereavement exclusion: Psychiatric diagnosis and the future of empirically supported treatment. *Clinical Psychology Review, 33,* 825–845.

Walfish, S., Barnett, J. E., Marlyere, K., & Zielke, R. (2010). "Doc, there's something I have to tell you": Patient disclosure to their psychotherapist of unprosecuted murder and other violence. *Ethics and Behavior, 20,* 311–323.

Walker, E., & Tessner, K. (2008). Schizophrenia. *Perspectives on Psychological Science, 3,* 30–37.

Walker, J. R., & Furer, P. (2008). Interoceptive exposure in the treatment of health anxiety and hypochondriasis. *Journal of Cognitive Psychotherapy, 22,* 367–380.

Walkup, J. (1995). A clinically based rule of thumb for classifying delusions. *Schizophrenia Bulletin, 21,* 323–331.

Wallace, E. R., & Gach, J. (2008). *History of psychiatry and medical psychology with an epilogue on psychiatry and the mind-body relation.* New York, NY: Springer.

Walsh, J. L., Senn, T. E., & Carey, M. P. (2013). Longitudinal associations between health behaviors and mental health in low-income adults. *Translational Behavioral Medicine, 3,* 104–113.

Walsh, K., Danielson, C. K., McCauley, J. L., Saunders, B. E., Kilpatrick, D. G., & Resnick, H. S. (2012). National prevalence of posttraumatic stress disorder among sexually revictimized adolescent, college, and adult household-residing women. *Archives of General Psychiatry, 69,* 935–942.

Walsh, R., & Shapiro, S. L. (2006). The meeting of meditative disciplines and Western psychologies. *American Psychologist, 61,* 227–239.

Walter, H. J. (2001). Substance abuse and substance use disorders. In G. O. Gabbard (Ed.), *Treatment of psychiatric disorders* (pp. 325–338). Washington, DC: American Psychiatric Publishing.

Wang, G. J., Volkow, N. D., Logan, J., Pappas, N. R., Wong, C. T., Zhu, W., . . . Fowler, J. S. (2001). Brain dopamine and obesity. *Lancet, 357,* 354–357.

Wang, K. T., Wong, Y. J., & Fu, C.-C. (2013). Moderation effects of perfectionism and discrimination on interpersonal factors and suicide ideation. *Journal of Counseling Psychology, 60,* 367–378.

Wang, X. P., & Ding, H. L. (2008). Alzheimer's disease: Epidemiology, genetics, and beyond. *Neuroscience Bulletin, 24,* 105–109.

Wang, Y., Yi, J., He, J., Chen, G., Li, L., Yang, Y., & Zhu, X. (2013). Cognitive emotion regulation strategies as predictors of depressive symptoms in women newly diagnosed with breast cancer. *Psycho-oncology, 23,* 93–99.

Wang, Y. P., & Andrade, L. H. (2013). Epidemiology of alcohol and drug use in the elderly. *Current Opinions of Psychiatry, 26*, 343–348.

Ward, M. P., & Irazoqui, P. P. (2010). Evolving refractory major depressive disorder diagnostic and treatment paradigms: Toward closed-loop therapeutics. *Frontiers in Neuroengineering, 3*, 7.

Ward, T., & Stewart, C. A. (2003). The treatment of sex offenders: Risk management and good lives. *Professional Psychology: Research and Practice, 34*, 353–360.

Ware, A. L., Glass, L., Crocker, N., Deweese, B. N., Coles, C. D., Kable, J. A., . . . Mattson, S. N. (2014). Effects of prenatal alcohol exposure and attention-deficit/hyperactivity disorder on adaptive functioning. *Alcohol: Clinical & Experimental Research, 38*, 1439–1447.

Warner, R. (2009). Recovery from schizophrenia and the recovery model. *Current Opinion in Psychiatry, 22*, 374–380.

Warner, R. (2010). Does the scientific evidence support the recovery model? *The Psychiatrist, 34*, 3–5.

Warren, Z. E., Sanders, K. B., & Veenstra-VanderWeele, J. (2010). Identity crisis involving body image in a young man with autism. *American Journal of Psychiatry, 167*, 1299–1303.

Wartik, N. (1994, February). Fatal attention. *Redbook*, 62–69.

Washington Post. (2012). *Washington Post*–Kaiser Family Foundation poll of black women in America. Retrieved from http://www.washingtonpost.com/wp-srv/special/nation/black-women-in-america

Watkins, E. R., Taylor, R. S., Byng, R., Baeyens, C., Read, R.,Pearson, K., & Watson, L. (2012). Guided self-help concreteness training as an intervention for major depression in primary care: A Phase II randomized controlled trial. *Psychological Medicine, 42*, 1359–1371. doi:10.1017/S0033291711002480

Watson, J. B., & Rayner, R. (1920). Conditioned emotional reactions. *Journal of Experimental Psychology, 3*, 1–14.

Watson, N. F., Harden, K. P., Buchwald, D., Vitiello, M. V., Pack, A. I., Strachan, E., & Goldberg, J. (2014). Sleep duration and depressive symptoms: A gene-environment interaction. *Sleep, 37*, 351–358.

Watt, M. C., O'Connor, R. M., Stewart, S. H., Moon, E. C., & Terry, L. (2008). Specificity of childhood learning experiences in relation to anxiety sensitivity and illness/injury sensitivity: Implications for health anxiety and pain. *Journal of Cognitive Psychotherapy: An International Quarterly, 22*, 128–143.

Webb, T. L., Joseph, J., Yardley, L., & Michie, S. J. (2010). Using the Internet to promote health behavior change: A systematic review and meta-analysis of the impact of theoretical basis, use of behavior change techniques, and mode of delivery on efficacy. *Journal of Medical Internet Research, 12*, e4.

Wechsler, D. (1981). *Wechsler adult intelligence scale.* New York, NY: Harcourt, Brace, Jovanovich.

Weems, C. F., Hayward, C., Killen, J., & Taylor, C. B. (2002). A longitudinal investigation of anxiety sensitivity in adolescence. *Journal of Abnormal Psychology, 111*, 471–477.

Weems, C. F., Pina, A. A., Costa, N. M., Watts, S. E., Taylor, L. K., & Cannon, M. F. (2007). Predisaster trait anxiety and negative affect predict posttraumatic stress in youth after Hurricane Katrina. *Journal of Counseling and Clinical Psychology, 75*, 154–159.

Wehmeier, P. M., Barth, N., & Remschmidt, H. (2003). Induced delusional disorder. *Psychopathology, 36*, 37–45.

Wei, Y., Szumilas, M., & Kutcher, M. (2010). Effectiveness on mental health of psychological debriefing for crisis intervention in schools. *Educational Psychology Review, 22*, 339–347.

Weiner, I. B., & Greene, R. L. (2008). *Handbook of personality assessment.* Hoboken, NJ: John Wiley & Sons.

Weinhold, B. (2006). Epigenetics: The science of change. *Environmental Health Perspective, 114*, 160–167.

Weintraub, M., Youngstrom, E. A., Marvin, S. E., Podell, J. L., Walshaw, P. D., Kim, E. Y., . . . Miklowitz, D. J. (2014). Diagnostic profiles and clinical characteristics of youth referred to a pediatric mood disorders clinic. *Journal of Psychiatric Practice, 20*, 154–162.

Weiss, N. H., Tull, M. T., Lavender, J., & Gratz, K. L. (2013). Role of emotion dysregulation in the relationship between childhood abuse and probable PTSD in a sample of substance abusers. *Child Abuse and Neglect, 37*, 944–954.

Weiss, R. (2012). Hypersexuality: Symptoms of sexual addiction. Retrieved from http://psychcentral.com/lib/hypersexuality-symptoms-of-sexual-addiction/00011488

Weisz, J. R., Weiss, B., Suwanlert, S., & Chaiyasit, W. (2006). Culture and youth psychopathology: Testing the syndromal sensitivity model in Thai and American adolescents. *Journal of Consulting and Clinical Psychology, 74*, 1098–1107.

Welham, J., Isohanni, M., Jones, P., & McGrath, J.(2009). The antecedents of schizophrenia: A review of birth cohort studies. *Schizophrenia Bulletin, 35*, 603–623.

Wells, A. (2005). The metacognitive model of GAD: Assessment of meta-worry and relationship with DSM-IV generalized anxiety disorder. *Cognitive Therapy and Research, 29*, 107–121.

Wells, A. (2009). *Metacognitive therapy for anxiety and depression.* New York, NY: Guilford Press.

Wells, R. E., Yeh, G. Y., Kerr, C. E., Wolkin, J., Davis, R. B., Tan, Y., . . . Kong, J. (2013). Meditation's impact on default mode network and hippocampus in mild cognitive impairment: A pilot study. *Neuroscience Letters, 556*, 15–19.

Wells, T. T., & Beevers, C. G. (2010). Biased attention and dysphoria: Manipulating selective attention reduces subsequent depressive symptoms. *Cognition and Emotion, 24*, 719–728.

Werner, S., Malaspina, D., & Rabinowitz, J. (2007). Socioeconomic status at birth is associated with risk of schizophrenia: Population-based multilevel study. *Schizophrenia Bulletin, 33*, 1373–1378.

Werth, J. L., Weifel, R., & Benjamin, G. A. H. (2009). *The duty to protect: Ethical, legal, and professional considerations for mental health professionals.* Washington, DC: American Psychological Association.

Westberg, J. (2010, July 30). Abilify commercials: There's something missing—and it might make you even more depressed. Retrieved from http://www.examiner.com/article/abilify-commercials-there-s-something-missing-and-it-might-make-you-even-more-depressed

Westen, D., Defife, J. A., Bradley, B., & Hilsenroth, M. J. (2010). Prototype personality diagnosis in clinical practice: A viable alternative to DSM-5 and ICD-11. *Professional Psychology: Research and Practice, 41*, 482–487.

Westheimer, R. K., & Lopater, S. (2005). *Human sexuality: A psychosocial perspective.* Baltimore, MD: Lippincott Williams & Wilkins.

Weston, C. G., & Riolo, S. A. (2007). Childhood and adolescent precursors to adult personality disorders. *Psychiatric Annals, 37,* 114–120.

Westphal, M., & Bonanno, G. A. (2007). Posttraumatic growth and resilience to trauma: Different sides of the same coin or different coins? *Applied Psychology: An International Review, 56,* 417–427.

Weyers, S., Elaut, E., De Sutter, P., Gerris, J., T'Sjoen, G., Heylens, G., . . . Verstraelen, H. (2009). Long-term assessment of the physical, mental, and sexual health among transsexual women. *Journal of Sexual Medicine, 6,* 752–760.

Whealin, J. M., Stotzer, R., Nelson, D., Li, F., Liu-Tom, H. T., & Pietrzak, R. H. (2013). Evaluating PTSD prevalence and resilience factors in a predominantly Asian American and Pacific Islander sample of Iraq and Afghanistan Veterans. *Journal of Affective* Disorders, 150, 1062–1068.

Whitaker, A. H., Feldman, J. F., Lorenz, J. M., Shen, S.,McNicholas, F., Nieto, M., . . . Paneth, N. (2006). Motor and cognitive outcomes in nondisabled low-birth-weight adolescents: Early determinants. *Archives of Pediatrics & Adolescent Medicine, 160,* 1040–1046.

White, E. K., & Warren, C. S. (2013). Body checking and avoidance in ethnically diverse female college students. *Body Image, 11,* 583–590.

White, K. S., Craft, J. M., & Gervino, E. V. (2010). Anxiety and hypervigilance to cardiopulmonary sensations in non-cardiac chest pain patients with and without psychiatric disorders. *Behaviour Research and Therapy, 48,* 394–401.

White, L., McDermott, J., Degnan, K., Henderson, H., & Fox, N. (2011). Behavioral inhibition and anxiety: The moderating roles of inhibitory control and attention shifting. *Journal of Abnormal Child Psychology, 39,* 735–747.

The White House, Office of the Press Secretary. (2011). Statement by the President on change of condolence letter policy . Retrieved from http://www.whitehouse.gov/thepress-office/2011/07/06/statement-president-change-condolence-letter-policy

Whitmer, D. A., & Woods, D. L. (2013). Analysis of the cost effectiveness of a suicide barrier on the Golden Gate Bridge. *Crisis, 34,* 98–106.

Wickramasekera, I. (1976). Aversive behavior rehearsal for sexual exhibitionism. *Behavioral Therapy, 1,* 167–176.

Wicks, S., Hjern, A., & Dalman, C. (2010). Social risk or genetic liability for psychosis? A study of children born in Sweden and reared by adoptive parents. *American Journal of Psychiatry, 167,* 1240–1246.

Wicks, S., Hjern, A., Gunnell, D., Lewis, G., & Dalman, C. (2005). Social adversity in childhood and the risk of developing psychosis: A national cohort study. *American Journal of Psychiatry, 162,* 1652–1657.

Widiger, T. A. (2007). Current controversies in nosology and diagnosis of personality disorders. *Psychiatric Annals, 37,* 93–99.

Widiger, T. A., & Trull, T. J. (2007). Plate tectonics in the classification of personality disorder: Shifting to a dimensional model. *American Psychologist, 62,* 71–83.

Wierckx, K., Van Caenegem, E., Elaut, E., Dedecker, D., Van de Peer, F., Toye, K., . . . T'Sjoen, G. (2011). Quality of life and sexual health after sex reassignment surgery in transsexual men. *Journal of Sexual Medicine, 8,* 3379–3388.

Wiersma, D., Nienhuis, F. J., Sloof, C. J., & Giel, R. (1998). Natural course of schizophrenic disorders: A fifteen-year follow-up of a Dutch incidence cohort. *Schizophrenia Bulletin, 24,* 75–85.

Wilfley, D. E., Pike, K. M., Dohm, F.-A., Striegel-Moore, R. H., & Fairburn, C. G. (2001). Bias in binge eating disorder: How representative are recruited clinic samples? *Journal of Consulting and Clinical Psychology, 69,* 383–388.

Wilhelm, S., Phillips, K. A., Didie, E., Buhlmann, U., Greenberg, J. L., Fama, J. M., . . . Steketee, G. (2014). Modular cognitive-behavioral therapy for body dysmorphic disorder: A randomized controlled trial. *Behavior Therapy, 45,* 314–327.

Wilhelm, S., Phillips, K. A., Fama, J. M., Greenberg, J. L., & Steketee, G. (2011). Modular cognitive-behavioral therapy for body dysmorphic disorder. *Behavior Therapy, 42,* 624–633.

Willenbring, M. L. (2010). The past and future of research on treatment of alcohol dependence. Retrieved from http://pubs.niaaa.nih.gov/publications/arh40/55-63.htm

Williams, D. R., González, H. M., Neighbors, H., Nesse, R., Abelson, J. M., Sweetman, J., & Jackson, J. S. (2007). Prevalence and distribution of major depressive disorder in African Americans, Caribbean blacks, and non-Hispanic whites: Results from the National Survey of American Life.

Archives of General Psychiatry, 64, 305–315.

Williams, M. T., Abramowitz, J. S., & Olatunji, B. O. (2012). The relationship between contamination cognitions, anxiety, and disgust in two ethnic groups. *Journal of Behavior Therapy and Experimental Psychiatry, 43,* 632–637.

Williams, P. G., Smith, T. W., & Jordan, K. D. (2010). Health anxiety and hypochondriasis: Interpersonal extensions of the cognitive behavioral perspective. In G. Beck (Ed.), *Interpersonal processes in the anxiety disorders: Implications for understanding psychopathology and treatment* (pp. 261–284). New York, NY: American Psychological Association.

Williamson, D., Robinson, M. E., & Melamed, B. (1997). Patient behavior, spouse responsiveness, and marital satisfaction in patients with rheumatoid arthritis. *Behavior Modification, 21,* 97–106.

Williamson, S. (2009). The relationship between severity of childhood sexual abuse and adult perceptions of intimacy with internalized shame as a mediator. (Unpublished master's thesis.) Provo, UT: Brigham Young University.

Willis, A. W., Bradley, A., Evanoff, M. L., Criswell, S. R., & Racette, B. A. (2010). Geographic and ethnic variation in Parkinson disease: A population-based study of US Medicare beneficiaries. *Neuroepidemiology, 34,* 143–151.

Willsey, A. J., Sanders, S. J., Li, M., Dong, S., Tebbenkamp, A. T., Muhle, R. A., . . . State, M. W. (2013). Coexpression networks implicate human midfetal deep cortical projection neurons in the pathogenesis of autism. *Cell, 155,* 997–1007.

Wilson, D., Frontera, A., Thomas, G., & Duncan, E. (2014). Screening for atrial fibrillation in patients with obstructive sleep apnea to reduce ischemic strokes. *International Journal of Cardiology, 172,* 297–298.

Wilson, G. T. (2011). Treatment of binge eating disorder. *Psychiatric Clinics of North America, 34,* 773–783.

Wilson, R. S., Scherr, P. A., Schneider, J. A., Tang, Y., & Bennett, D. A. (2007). Relation of cognitive activity to risk of developing Alzheimer disease. *Neurology, 69,* 1911–1920.

Winkler, A., Dörsing, B., Rief, W., Shen, Y., & Glombiewski, J. A. (2013). Treatment of Internet addiction: A meta-analysis.

Clinical Psychology Review, 33, 317–329.

Winter, J. (2013). Police warned Navy about gunman's mental instability 6 weeks ago, report says. Retrieved from http://www.foxnews.com/us/2013/09/18/navy-yard-shooter-heard-voices-through-walls-thought-people-sending-vibrations/#ixzz2fFS8OFbo

Wise, R. A., & Koob, G. F. (2014). The development and maintenance of drug addiction. *Neuropsychopharmacology, 39*, 254–262.

Witek-Janusek, L., Albuquerque, K., Chroniak, K. R., Croniak, C., Durazo-Arvizu, R., & Mathews, H. L. (2008). Effect of mindfulness based stress reduction on immune function, quality of life and coping in women newly diagnosed with early stage breast cancer. *Brain and Behavioral Immunology, 22*, 969–981.

Wittchen, H.-U., Gloster, A. T., Beesdo-Baum, K., Fava, G. A., & Craske, M. G. (2010). Agoraphobia: A review of the diagnostic classificatory position and criteria. *Depression and Anxiety, 27*, 113–133.

Wittchen, H.-U., & Hoyer, J. (2001). Generalized anxiety disorder: Nature and course. *Journal of Clinical Psychiatry, 62*, 15–21.

Wittstein, I. S., Thiemann, D. R., Lima, J. A. C., Baughman, K. L., Schulman, S. P., Gerstenblith, G., . . . Champion, H. C. (2005). Neurohumoral features of myocardial stunning due to sudden emotional stress. *New England Journal of Medicine, 352*, 539–548.

Woertman, L., & van den Brink, F. (2012). Body image and female sexual functioning and behavior: A review. *Journal of Sex Research, 49*, 184–211.

Wolanczyk, S. R., Wolanczyk, T., Gawrys, A., Swirszcz, K., Stefanoff, E., Kaminska, A., . . . Brynska, A. (2008). Prevalence of tic disorder among school children in Warsaw, Poland. *European Child and Adolescent Psychiatry, 17*, 171–178.

Woliver, R. (2000, March 26). 44 personalities, but artist shines. *New York Times*, pp. 6–9.

Wollschlaeger, B. (2007). The science of addiction: From neurobiology to treatment. *Journal of the American Medical Association, 298*, 809–810.

Wolff, J., Frazier, E. A., Esposito-Smythers, C., Burke, T., Sloan, E., & Spirito, A. (2013). Cognitive and social factors associated with NSSI and suicide attempts in psychiatrically hospitalized adolescents. *Journal of Abnormal Child Psychology, 41*, 1005–1013.

Wolpe, J. (1958). *Psychotherapy by reciprocal inhibition*. Stanford, CA: Stanford University Press.

Wolpe, J. (1973). *The practice of behavior therapy*. New York, NY: Pergamon.

Won, C., Mahmoudi, M., Qin, L., Purvis, T., Mathur, A., & Mohsenin, V. (2014). The impact of gender on timeliness of narcolepsy diagnosis. *Journal of Clinical Sleep Medicine, 15*, 89–95.

Wong, J. M., Na, B., Regan, M. C., & Whooley, M. A. (2013, September 30). Hostility, health behaviors, and risk of recurrent events in patients with stable coronary heart disease: Findings from the Heart and Soul Study. *Journal of the American Heart Association, 2*, e000052. doi:10.1161/JAHA.113.000052

Wong, M. M., & Brower, K. J. (2012). The prospective relationship between sleep problems and suicidal behavior in the National Longitudinal Study of Adolescent Health. *Journal of Psychiatric Research, 46*, 953–959.

Wong, S. S., Zhou, B., Goebert, D., & Hishinuma, E. S. (2013). The risk of adolescent suicide across patterns of drug use: A nationally representative study of high school students in the United States from 1999 to 2009. *Social Psychiatry and Psychiatric Epidemiology, 48*, 1611–1620.

Woo, J. S., Brotto, L. A., & Gorzalka, B. B. (2012). The relationship between sex guilt and sexual desire in a community sample of Chinese and Euro-Canadian women. *Journal of Sex Research, 49*, 290–298.

Wood, M. D., Capone, C., Laforge, R., Erickson, D. J.,& Brand, N. H. (2007). Brief motivational intervention and alcohol expectancy challenge with heavy drinking college students: A randomized factorial study. *Addictive Behaviors, 32*, 2509–2528.

Wood, J. M., Lilienfeld, S. O., Nezworski, M. T., Garb, H. N., Allen, K. H., & Wildermuth, J. L. (2010). Validity of Rorschach inkblot scores for discriminating psychopaths from nonpsychopaths in forensic populations: A meta-analysis. *Psychological Assessment, 22*, 336–349.

Woods, J. M., & Nashat, M. (2012). Psychoanalysis and the Rorschach. *Rorschachiana, 33*, 95–99.

Woods, B., Aguirre, E., Spector, A. E., & Orrell, M. (2012, February 15). Cognitive stimulation to improve cognitive functioning in people with dementia. *Cochrane Database of Systematic Reviews, 2*, CD005562.

Woods, N. F., Mitchell, E. S., Percival, D. B., & Smith-DiJulio, K. (2009). Is the menopausal transition stressful? Observations of perceived stress from the Seattle Midlife Women's Health Study. *Menopause, 16*, 90–97.

World Health Organization. (2011). Mental retardation: From knowledge to action. Retrieved from http://www.searo.who.int/en/Section1174/Section1199/Section1567/Section1825_8090.htm

World Health Organization. (2013). Obesity and overweight. Retrieved from http://www.who.int/mediacentre/factsheets/fs311/en

World Health Organization. (2014) Why tobacco is a public health priority. Retrieved from http://www.who.int/tobacco/health_priority/en/

Worley, C. B., Feldman, M. D., & Hamilton, J. C. (2009). The case of factitious disorder versus malingering. *Psychiatric Times, 26*, 1–4.

Wright, A. G., Pincus, A. L., & Lenzenweger, M. F. (2013). A parallel process growth model of avoidant personality disorder symptoms and personality traits. *Personality Disorders, 4*, 230–238.

Wroblewski, P., Gustafsson, J., & Selvaggi, G. (2013). Sex reassignment surgery for transsexuals. *Current Opinion in Endocrinology, Diabetes, and Obesity, 20*, 570–574.

Wrosch, C., Schulz, R., Miller, G. E., Lupien, S., & Dunne, E. (2007). Physical health problems, depressive mood, and cortisol secretions in old age: Buffer effects of health engagement control strategies. *Health Psychology, 26*, 341–349.

Wu, E. Q., Birnbaum, H. G., Shi, L., Ball, D. E., Kessler, R. C., Moulism, M., & Aggarwal, J. (2005). The economic burden of schizophrenia in the United States in 2002. *Journal of Clinical Psychology, 66*, 1122–1129.

Wu, L., Ringwalt, C., Weiss, R. D., & Blazer, D. G. (2009). Hallucinogen-related disorders in a national sample of adolescents: The influence of Ecstasy/MDMA use. *Drug and Alcohol Dependence, 104*, 156–166.

Wunderink, L., Nieboer, R. M., Wiersma, D., Sytema, S., & Nienhuis, F. J. (2013). Recovery in remitted first-episode psychosis at 7 years of follow-up of an early dose reduction/discontinuation or maintenance treatment strategy: Long-term follow-up of a 2-year randomized clinical trial. *JAMA Psychiatry, 70,* 913–920.

Wyatt v. Stickney, 344 F. Supp. 373 (Ala. 1972).

Wyatt, S. (2006, May). Positive influence of religion and spirituality on blood pressure in the Jackson Heart Study. Paper presented at the annual Scientific Meeting of American Society of Hypertension, New York, NY.

Wylie, K. (2008) Erectile dysfunction. *Advance in Psychosomatic Medicine, 29,* 33–49.

Xia, J., Merinder, L. B., & Belgamwar, M.R. (2011). Psychoeducation for schizophrenia. *Cochrane Database of Systemic Reviews.* doi:10.1002/14651858.CD002831.pub2

Xu, Y., Schneider, F., Heimberg, R. G., Princisvalle, K., Liebowitz, M. R., Wang, S., & Blanco, C. (2012). Gender differences in social anxiety disorder: Results from the National Epidemiologic Sample on Alcohol and Related Conditions. *Journal of Anxiety Disorders, 26,* 12–19.

Yadin, E., & Foa, E. B. (2009). How to reduce distress and repetitive behaviors in patients with OCD. *Current Psychiatry, 8,* 19–23.

Yalom, I. D. (2005). *The theory and practice of group psychotherapy.* New York, NY: Basic Books.

Yanek, L. R., Kral, B. G., Moy, T. F., Vaidya, D., Lazo, M., Becker, L. C., & Becker, D. M. (2013, June 28). Effect of positive well-being on incidence of symptomatic coronary artery disease. *American Journal of Cardiology, 112,* 1120–1125.

Yang, L. H., & WonPat-Borja, A. J. (2007). Psychopathology among Asian Americans. In F. T. L. Leong, A. Ebreo, L. Kinoshita, A. G. Inman, M. Fu, & L. H. Yang (Eds.), *Handbook of Asian American psychology* (pp. 379–405). Thousand Oaks, CA: Sage.

Yates, W. R. (2013). Somatoform disorders. Retrieved from http://emedicine.medscape.com/article/294908-overview

Yates, W. R. (2014). Anxiety disorders. Retrieved from http://emedicine.medscape.com/article/286227-clinical

Yeager, D., Walton, G., & Cohen, G. L. (2013). Addressing achievement gaps with psychological interventions. *Phi Delta Kappan, 94,* 62–65.

Yeater, E. A., Treat, T. A., Viken, R. J., & McFall, R. M. (2010). Cognitive processes underlying women's risk judgments: Associations with sexual victimization history and rape myth acceptance. *Journal of Counseling and Clinical Psychology, 78,* 375–386.

Yeh, P. H., Gazdzinski, S., Durazzo, T. C., Sjöstrand, K., & Meyerhoff, D. J. (2007). Hierarchical linear modeling (HLM) of longitudinal brain structural and cognitive changes in alcohol-dependent individuals during sobriety. *Drug and Alcohol Dependence, 91,* 195–204.

Yehuda, R., Cai, G., Golier, J. A., Sarapas, C., Galea, S., Ising, M., . . . Buxbaum, J. D. (2009). Gene expression patterns associated with posttraumatic stress disorder follow exposure to the World Trade Center attacks. *Biological Psychiatry, 66,* 708–711.

Yeung, A., & Deguang, H. (2002). Somatoform disorders. *Western Journal of Medicine, 176,* 253–256.

Yong, E. (2013). Psychologists strike a blow for reproducibility. Retrieved from: http://www.nature.com/news/psychologists-strike-a-blow-for-reproducibility-1.14232

Yoo, J. P., Brown, P. J., & Luthar, S. S. (2009). Children with co-occurring anxiety and externalizing disorders: Family risks and implications for competence. *American Journal of Orthopsychiatry, 79,* 532–540.

Young, J. A., & Tolentino, M. (2011). Neuroplasticity and its applications for rehabilitation. *American Journal of Therapeutics, 18,* 70–80.

Young, J. E., Klosko, J. S., & Weishaar, M. E. (2003). *Schema therapy: A practitioner's guide.* New York, NY: Guilford Press.

Youngberg v. Romeo, 457 U. S. 307 (1982).

Yuan, Y., Zhang, Z., Gao, B., Peng, J., Cui, W., Song, W., . . . Guo, Y. (2014). The Self-estimation Index of Erectile Function–No Sexual Intercourse (SIEF-NS): A multidimensional scale to assess erectile dysfunction in the absence of sexual intercourse. *Journal of Sexual Medicine, 11,* 1201–1207.

Zaidi, Z. F. (2012). Gender differences in human brain: A review. *The Open Anatomy Journal, 2,* 37–55.

Zammit, S., Kounali, D., Cannon, M., David, A. S., Gunnell, D., Heron, J., . . . Lewis, G. (2013). Psychotic experiences and psychotic disorders at age 18 in relation to psychotic experiences at age 12 in a longitudinal population-based cohort study. *American Journal of Psychiatry, 170,* 742–750.

Zammit, S., Owen, M. J., Evans, J., Heron, J., & Lewis, G. (2011). Cannabis, *COMT* and psychotic experiences. *British Journal of Psychiatry, 199,* 380–385.

Zanarini, M. C., Frankenburg, F. R., Reich, D. B., & Fitzmaurice, G. (2012). Attainment and stability of sustained symptomatic remission and recovery among patients with borderline personality disorder and axis II comparison subjects: A 16-year prospective follow-up study. *American Journal of Psychiatry, 169,* 476–483.

Zanarini, M. C., Parachini, E. A., Frankenburg, F. R., & Holman, J. B. (2003). Sexual relationship difficulties among borderline patients and Axis II comparison subjects. *Journal of Nervous and Mental Disease, 191,* 479–482.

Zapf, P. A., & Roesch, R. (2006). Competency to stand trial: A guide for evaluators. In A. K. Hess & J. B. Weiner (Eds.), *Handbook of forensic psychology* (pp. 305–331). Hoboken, NJ: Wiley.

Zaroff, C. M., Davis, J. M., Chio, P. H., & Madhavan, D. (2012). Somatic presentations of distress in China. *Australian and New Zealand Journal of Psychiatry, 46,* 1053–1057.

Zeanah, C. H., Egger, H. L., Smyke, A. T., Nelson, C. A., Fox, N. A., Marshall, P. J., & Guthrie, D. (2009). Institutional rearing and psychiatric disorders in Romanian preschool children. *American Journal of Psychiatry, 166,* 777–785.

Zeanah, C. H., & Gleason, M. M. (2010). Reactive attachment disorder: A review for DSM-V. Retrieved from http://www.dsm5.org/Proposed%20Revision%20Attachments/APA%20DSM-5%20Reactive%20Attachment%20Disorder%20Review.pdf

Zeeck, A., Weber, S., Sandholz, A., Joos, A., & Hartmann, A. (2011). Stability of long-term outcome in bulimia nervosa: A 3-year follow-up. *Journal of Clinical Psychology, 67,* 318–327.

Zeiders, K. H., Umaña-Taylor, A. J., & Derlan, C. L. (2013). Trajectories of depressive symptoms and self-esteem in Latino youths: Examining the role of gender and perceived discrimination. *Developmental Psychology, 49,* 951–963.

Zerdzinski, M. (2008). Olfactory obsessions—Individual cases or one of the symptoms of obsessive-compulsive disorder? An analysis of 2 clinical cases. *Archives of Psychiatry and Psychotherapy, 3,* 23–27.

Zhang, A. Y., & Snowden, L. R. (1999). Ethnic characteristics of mental disorders in five U.S. communities. *Cultural Diversity and Ethnic Minority Psychology, 5,* 134–146.

Zhang, T.-Y., & Meaney, M. J. (2010). Epigenetics and the environmental regulation of the genome and its function. *Annual Review of Psychology, 61,* 439–466.

Zhang, W., & Li, N. (2011). Prevalence, risk factors, and management of prehypertension. *International Journal of Hypertension, 2011.* 605359. doi:10.4061/2011/605359

Zimmerman, M., Martinez, J. A., Attiullah, N., Friedman, M., Toba, C., Boerescu, D. A., & Rahgeb, M. (2012). Why do some depressed outpatients who are in remission according to the Hamilton Depression Rating Scale not consider themselves to be in remission? *Journal of Clinical Psychiatry, 73,* 790–795.

Zimmerman, M., Rothschild, L., & Chelminski, I. (2005). The prevalence of DSM-IV personality disorders in psychiatric outpatients. *American Journal of Psychiatry, 162,* 1911–1918.

Zito, J. M., Burcu, M., Ibe, A., Safer, D. J., & Magder, L. S. (2013). Antipsychotic use by Medicaid-insured youths: Impact of eligibility and psychiatric diagnosis across a decade. *Psychiatric Services, 64,* 223–229.

Zohar, J., Hollander, E., Stein, D. J., Westenberg, H. G. M., & Cape Town Consensus Group. (2007). Consensus statement. *CNS Spectrums, 12,* 59–63.

Zondervan, R. L., Hahn, P. F., Sadow, C. A., Liu, B., & Lee, S. I. (2013). Body CT scanning in young adults: Examination indications, patient outcomes, and risk of radiation-induced cancer. *Radiology, 267,* 460–469.

Zucker, K. J. (2009). The DSM diagnostic criteria for gender identity disorder in children. *Archives of Sexual Behavior, 39,* 477–498. doi:10.1007/s10508-009-9540-4

Zucker, K. J., & Cohen-Ketteris, P. T. (2008). Gender identity disorder in children and adolescents. In D. Rowland & L. Incrocci (Eds.), *Handbook of sexual and gender identity disorders* (pp. 376–422). Hoboken, NJ: Wiley.

Zukerman, M. (2003). Are there racial and ethnic differences in psychopathic personality? A critique of Lynn's (2002) racial and ethnic differences in psychopathic personality. *Personality and Individual Differences, 35,* 1463–1469.

Zuvekas, S. H., & Vitiello, B. (2012). Stimulant medication use in children: A 12-year perspective. *American Journal of Psychiatry, 169,* 160–166.

NAME INDEX

Davila, J., 245
Davis, C. K., 79
Davis, G. P., 378
Davis, J., 105, 275
Davis, J. M., 23
Davis, K. M., 492
Davis, L., 106, 236
Davis, L. E., 384
Davis, M. M., 105
Davis, P., 178
Davis, T. A., 38
Dawe, S., 378
Dawson, D. A., 353
Dawson, G., 526, 528, 536
Dawson, M. E., 514
De-Bacco, C., 316
De Backer, W., 427
De Berardis, D., 241
De Block, A., 435
de Cos, A., 203
De Coteau, T., 133
De Geus, E. J. C., 189
de Groat, C. L., 175
de Jong, P. J., 139, 140, 173
de Jonge, P., 238, 240
de Kleine, R. A., 141
de la Fuente-Sandoval, C., 378
De la Garza Garcia, Y., 298
De Leo, D., 286
De Martino, E., 17
De Raedt, R., 244
de Rossi, P., 300
de Simone, V., 405
de Vega, W. C., 47
De Young, K. P., 304, 307
de Zwaan, M., 159
Deacon, B., 202
Deacon, B. J., 21
Deakin, J. F., 29
DeAngelis, T., 291
Decety, J., 514
Decker, S. L., 86
Deckersbach, T., 156, 261
Deckert, J., 131
Declercq, T., 423
Dedovic, K., 249
DeFrances, C. J., 412
DeGeneres, P., 299, 300
Degnan, K., 132
Degnan, K. A., 132
Deguang, H., 210
Dein, S., 535
Del Re, A. C., 62
Delanaye, P., 300
DeLany, J. P., 320
Delayande, A., 404
Dell, P. F., 212, 219
Demakis, D. J., 550, 553
DeMartini, K. S., 354
Demler, O., 128, 133, 235, 256
Denis, C., 356
Denmark, A. B., 269
Dennehy, E. B., 262
Denney, J. T., 284

Denobrega, A. K., 351
Depp, J., 136
Dere, J., 493
Derlan, C. L., 247
DeRubeis, R. J., 254
Desbonnet, L., 378
Deshmukh, A., 180
Deshpande, A. V., 517
Desmond, S., 311
D'Esposito, M., 379
DeStefano, F., 105
Detka, J., 240
D'ettore, D., 144
Devita-Raeburn, E., 394
Devlin, M. J., 303, 318
Dhabhar, F. S., 187
Dhejne, C., 452
Di, X., 377
Di Paola, F., 307
Diamond, A., 71
Diamond, C. L. J., 313
Diana, Princess of Wales, 478
Diaz, F., 412
Dick, D. M., 346
Dickens, G. L., 479
Dickerson, S. S., 191
Didie, E. R., 154
Dietvorst, R., 140
Diflorio, A., 259
DiFranza, J. R., 339
DiGangi, J. A., 173
DiGrande, L., 169
Diles, K., 273
Dilks, S., 26
Dillon, K. S., 217
Dimaggio, G., 392
Dimas, J. M., 175
Dimsdale, J. E., 199, 201
Dinan, T. G., 49
Ding, K., 342
Dion, S. C., 308
Dirmann, T., 302
Dix, D., 19, 20
Dixon, L. B., 27, 366
D'Lima, G. M., 350
Doane, L. D., 38
Dobbs, D., 174
Dobkin, R. D., 423
Dobson, K. S., 254
Dobson, P., 518
Docherty, N. M., 383
Dodick, D. W., 183
Dodson, G., 383
Doherty, A., 167
Dohm, F.-A., 303
Doka, K. J., 166
Dokucu, M., 197
Dolan, M. C., 475
Dolan, R. J., 416
Dolezsar, C. M., 192
Dolinoy, D. C., 47
Doll, H. A., 305
Dollinger, S. J., 223
Domingo, C., 355

Dominguez, M. D. G., 374
Domschke, K., 131, 146
Donaldson, D. W., 222
Donaldson, K., 555–556
Done, D. J., 370
Donegan, E., 149
Dong, Q., 140, 247
D'Onofrio, B. M., 522, 529, 534
Donoghue, K., 340
Donovan, C. L., 143
Dorahy, M. J., 221
Doraiswamy, P. M., 418
Doran, J., 260
Dörsing, B., 358
Dougan, B. K., 411
Dougherty, L. R., 510
Doughty, O. J., 370
Dovidio, J. F., 68
Doward, J., 99
Dowling, N. A., 357
Downey, R., III, 427
Dozois, D. J. A., 254
Drabick, D. A., 516
Dragt, S., 378
Draucker, C. B., 108
Draxler, H., 301
Dredze, M., 182
Dreher, D. E., 18
Drevets, W. C., 264
Dreyfus, R., 14
Drinnan, A., 369–370
Drukker, M., 246
Drum, D. J., 269, 276
Druss, B. G., 504
Dua, T., 532
Dubois, B. E., 300
Duchovny, D., 441
Dudley, R., 383
Duff, M. C., 416
Duflou, J., 343
Dugas, M. J., 149
Dulai, R., 368
Dullur, P., 510
Dunayevich, E., 205
Duncan, D., 512
Duncan, E., 427
Dunkley, D. M., 307
Dunn, G., 369
Dunn, M. E., 146
Dunn, S. T., 146
Dunne, E., 191
Dunsis, A., 208
Durà-Vilà, G., 535
Duran, R. E. F., 221
Durazzo, T. C., 414
Durkheim, É., 284
Durso, L. E., 306
Durston, S., 521
Dwivedi, Y., 280
Dworkin, A., 419
Dyck, I., 155
Dyck, I. R., 160
Dzokoto, A. A., 209

Eack, S. M., 384
Eaves, L. J., 245
Ebdlahad, S., 241
Eberhart, N. K., 244
Edden, R. A ., 522
Eddy, K. T., 321
Edenberg, H. J., 349, 350
Edens, J. F., 492
Edge, M. D., 260
Edinger, J. D., 429
Edmondson, D., 171
Edson, A., 143
Edvardsen, J., 260
Edwards, C. L., 192
Edwards, H., 270
Edwards, M., 203
Effron, L., 301, 305, 306, 316
Eftekhari, A., 178
Egan, K. G., 347
Egger, H., 510
Egolf, A., 519
Ehrlich, S., 205
Eidelman, P., 261, 264
Eidelson, R., 566
Eisen, J. L., 160
Eisenberg, M. A., 411
Eisenberg, M. E., 308, 310
Eisenberger, N. I., 245
Eisenhower, J. W., 219
Ekbom, A., 300
Ekerwald, H., 391
Ekselius, L., 300
El-Gabalawy, R., 135
El-Sheikh, M., 514
Elbert, T., 212
Elbogen, E. B., 395, 553
Elder, L. M., 526
Elder, T., 520
Eldevik, S., 531
Eleonora, G., 139
Eley, T. C., 488
Elgar, F. J., 346
Elkashef, A., 355
Elklit, A., 171
Ellerkmann, R. K., 49
Ellett, L., 264
Elliot, R.-L., 478
Elliott, C. M., 154
Elliott, D., 550
Elliott, R., 62
Ellis, A., 243
Ellis, D. M., 150
Ellison-Wright, I., 261
Ellman, L., 380
Elwyn, T. S., 205
Emrich, H. M., 217
Engelhard, I. M., 173, 178
Engels, R. C., 313
Engert, V., 249
Enoch, M. A., 351
Enterman, J. H., 371
Enticott, P. G., 357
Enzlin, P., 438, 442
Epel, E. S., 245

Hossain, A., 368, 483
Hostage, C. A., 418
Houenou, J., 261
Houston, M., 109
Howard, M. O., 342
Howarth, E. A., 85
Howe, E., 415, 423, 424
Howes, O. D., 378
Howie, L. D., 504
Howland, R. H., 241, 252
Howlett, S., 202
Howley, J., 215
Hoyer, J., 150, 248
Hsu, L., 140
Hu, F. B., 412
Hu, G., 270
Hu, P., 233, 264
Huang, X., 247
Hudson, J. I., 110, 219
Hudson, J. L., 150, 299, 302, 303, 506
Huffman, J. C., 272
Hughes, H. B., 55
Hughes, J., 182
Hughes, V., 174
Huh, G. A., 381
Huijbregts, K. M., 232
Huijding, J., 140
Hulleman, J., 29
Hultman, C. M., 391
Hulvershorn, L. A., 516
Hummer, J. F., 358
Humphreys, C. L., 217
Humphreys, K., 353
Humphreys, K. L., 521, 522
Hunsley, J., 106
Hunt, J., 510
Hunter, E. C. M., 223
Huntjens, R. J. C., 218
Hur, K., 105, 275
Hurd, M. D., 404
Hurlemann, R., 203, 206
Hussong, A. M., 345
Huxley, R. R., 412, 424
Hyde, J. S., 243, 310, 311, 314, 443

Iaccopucci, A., 348
Iacono, W. G., 239, 313
Iacovino, J. M., 324, 478
Iancu, I., 141
Ibe, A., 388
Ifeagwu, J. A., 171
Iffland, J. S., 462
Iguchi, M. Y., 348
Illes, J., 99
Imaeda, M., 526
Imuta, K., 82
Ingram, J., 215
Innocent VIII, Pope, 17
Inoue, Y., 428
Insel, T., 99
Irani, F., 374
Irazoqui, P. P., 251

Irizarry, L., 301
Irwin, H. J., 220
Isaac, M., 287
Isenberg-Grzeda, E., 423
Isensee, B., 348
IsHak, W. W., 204, 205, 336, 425
Islam, L., 365, 368, 381
Ismail, S., 535
Isohanni, M., 381
Ivey, A. E., 66, 492
Ivey, M. B., 66, 492
Iwanskia, C., 366

Jabbar, A., 535
Jack, C. R., 417, 430
Jacka, F. N., 246
Jackson, C., 350
Jackson, J., 14
Jackson, M., 270, 333, 334
Jackson, P., 270
Jackson, S. R., 519
Jackson, T., 308
Jacobs, E., 379
Jacobsen, P. B., 139
Jacobson, R., 516
Jacobus, J., 341
Jaconis, M., 305
Jaffe, J., 278
Jaffee, D., 465
Jaffee, S. R., 491
Jafferany, M., 155
Jagdeo, A., 13
Jagodic, M., 47
Jain, A., 420
Jairam, R., 510
Jakubowski, P., 57
James, A., 511
James, D. C., 321, 322, 449
James, I., 383
James, J., 441
James, W., 20
Janca, A., 479
Jang, K. L., 206
Janjua, A., 216, 219, 223
Janson, S., 528
Janssen, K., 193
Janus, C. L., 434, 435
Janus, S. S., 434, 435
Jaremka, L. M., 190
Jasiukaitis, P., 221
Jauch-Chara, K., 320, 324
Jeffries, F. W., 178
Jeglic, E. L., 457
Jellinger, K. A., 414
Jenike, M. A., 153, 156
Jenkins, J. H., 387
Jeong, D. U., 427
Jepsen, E. K. K., 225
Jepson, J. A., 369
Jernigan, D. H., 344
Jiang, Y. H., 527
Jiann, B.-P., 445
Jimenez, T., 283

Jin, R., 133, 235, 238, 255, 256, 258, 259
Jindal, S., 211
Jobe, T. H., 373, 388
Joelving, F., 270
Johannesson, K. B., 170
Johns, L. C., 109
Johnson, C., 267–268
Johnson, C. P., 529
Johnson, D. P., 366, 372
Johnson, D. W., 63
Johnson, E. P., 63
Johnson, J., 529
Johnson, J. G., 114, 212, 213, 216, 217
Johnson, K. A., 417, 430
Johnson, P., 298
Johnson, S. C., 395, 553
Johnson, S. L., 260
Johnson, V. E., 434, 437, 438, 445
Johnston, L. D., 336, 338, 340, 341, 342, 343, 346, 347, 348
Johnston, M., 374
Johren, P., 111
Joiner, T., 284
Joiner, T. E., 272, 284, 303, 310
Joiner, T. E., Jr., 477
Joinson, C., 248, 517
Jollant, F., 280
Jonas, B. S., 177, 505, 516
Jones, A. W., 283
Jones, C., 306
Jones, D. J., 345
Jones, E. L., 415
Jones, F. W., 150
Jones, I., 259
Jones, P., 381
Jones, R., 384
Jones, W., 526
Joos, A., 303
Jordan, K. D., 208
Jorenby, D. E., 346
Joseph, J., 251
Josselson, R., 117
Jovanovic, T., 173
Joyce, P. R., 316
Ju, Y. E., 418
Juang, L. P., 247
Judd, L. L., 258
Jupp, B., 352
Jureidini, J., 105, 250, 276

Kabela-Cormiera, E., 355
Kaczynski, T., 494
Kaddena, R. M., 355
Kafka, M. P., 441
Kahn, K., 18
Kahn, R. E., 514
Kahn, R. S., 514
Kaio, G. H., 312
Kajantie, E., 427
Kalafat, J., 290
Kalra, G., 456
Kaltenthaler, E., 251

Kaltiala-Heino, R., 149
Kaltwasser, S. F., 171
Kamarck, T. W., 190
Kamat, S. A., 238
Kambeitz, J., 378
Kanaan, R., 209
Kandavel, T., 160
Kanfer, J., 253
Kangas, M., 166
Kannai, R., 205
Kanne, S. M., 529
Kanner, L., 524, 529
Kanter, J. W., 253
Kantrowitz, B., 224, 524
Kao, C. F., 260
Kao, D. T., 374
Kapalko, J., 297
Kaplan, B. J., 521
Kaplan, J., 406
Kaplan, K., 261
Kaplan, L., 405
Kaplan, M., 219
Kaplan, M. S., 286, 459
Karatsoreos, I. N., 38
Karceski, S., 402, 423
Karg, K., 239, 240
Karila, L., 441
Kariuki-Nyuthe, C., 158
Karno, M., 159
Karra, E., 320
Karreman, A., 479
Kasari, C., 531
Kasen, S., 19, 114, 212, 213, 246
Kashdan, T. B., 135, 243
Kastelan, A., 373, 395
Katalinic, N., 263
Kato, K., 206
Katon, W. J., 186
Katzer, A., 206
Kaufman, L., 532
Kaur, H., 264
Kawai, M., 141
Kawakami, K., 68
Kawycz, N. J., 140
Kay, C., 507
Kaye, A. D., 252
Kaye, S., 343
Kaye, W., 313
Kaye, W. H., 313
Kaynak, O., 346
Kayser, S., 49
Kazdin, A. E., 517
Kearney, D. J., 178
Keating, G. M., 356
Keel, P. K., 303, 308, 316
Keeton, C. P., 506
Keiley, M., 514
Keisha, 302
Keita, G. P., 27
Keith-Spiegel, P., 546
Kelleher, I., 374, 382, 398
Keller, M. B., 135
Keller, R. M., 65
Kelley, M., 350

Mick, E., 521
Midei, A. J., 189, 191
Miettunen, J., 378
Mihalopoulos, C., 374
Miklowitz, D. J., 262, 263, 264
Miles, J., 348
Miles, J. H., 529
Milillo, D., 310
Miller, A., 509
Miller, A. B., 282
Miller, D. B., 264
Miller, E. S., 159
Miller, G. E., 132, 191
Miller, J. L., 140
Miller, J. M., 240
Miller, L., 275
Miller, M., 19, 224, 250, 509
Miller, M. A., 252
Miller, M. N., 312
Miller, R., 96
Miller, T. C., 408
Miller, W. R., 352
Millichap, J. G., 522
Millon, C., 470, 471
Millon, T., 470, 471, 481, 487, 489, 492, 495
Milovanovic, S., 494
Minabe, Y., 141
Mineka, S., 129
Minich, D. M., 38
Minor, K. S., 474
Minuchin, S., 64
Mischoulon, D., 307
Misselhorn, C., 30
Mitchell, A. J., 167
Mitchell, B. D., 542–543, 545, 556
Mitchell, D., 546
Mitchell, E. S., 248
Mitchell, J. E., 159
Mitchell, K. S., 346
Mitchell, P. B., 263
Mitrouska, I., 356
Mittal, M. K., 412
Mittal, V. A., 380
Miu, A. C., 133
Miyachi, T., 526
Mizgalewicz, A., 99
M'Naghten, D., 545
Mock, J. E., 83
Moens, E., 322
Moessner, R., 203, 206
Moezzi, M., 257, 357
Moffitt, T. E., 488, 491
Mohr, D. C., 138
Mohr, J. J., 83
Moisse, K., 106
Moitra, E., 135
Mojtabai, R., 14, 388
Moll, J., 29
Mollen, D., 99
Moloney, R. M., 388
Molz-Adams, A., 261
Moncrieff, J., 374
Mondola, R., 342

Monroe, M., 268, 287
Monroe, S. M., 245
Montauk, S. L., 521
Monteith, T., 184
Montesano, V. L., 390
Monti, P. M., 355
Montoya, I. D., 355
Monzani, B., 156
Moodley, R., 67
Moon, E. C., 208
Moon, U. J., 247
Moore, B. A., 352, 355
Moore, C. S., 440
Moore, E., 108, 281
Moore, H., 140
Moore, S., 246
Moore, T. H. M., 376
Moorman, J. E., 184
Moos, B. S., 353
Moos, R. H., 122, 353
Morales, A., 441
Morales, E., 22, 123
Moran, P., 509
Moran, R. J., 416
Moravec, C. S., 193
Moreira, E. D., 438, 439
Moreno, M. A., 347
Morgan, C. J., 338
Morgan, H., 81
Morgan, K., 418
Morgan, Y., 215
Morgan Consoli, M. L., 38
Morgenstern, M., 348
Mori, N., 141
Morillo, C., 153
Morin, C., 460
Morin, D., 532
Moritz, S., 369, 387
Morley, K. I., 387, 388
Morris, J., 312
Morrison, A. P., 398
Morse, J. Q., 486
Mortensen, P. B., 280, 379
Moscone, G., 546
Moskowitz, D. S., 135
Mostofsky, S. H., 522
Mott, J. M., 177
Moukheiber, A., 135
Moulin, C. J., 408
Moum, T., 207
Mrazek, A. J., 24
Muehlenkamp, J. J., 509
Mueller, A., 159
Mueser, K. T., 391
Muetzelfeldt, L., 338
Mufaddel, A., 155
Muguen, S., 175
Muhlberger, A., 138
Mühlberger, A., 142
Mujoomdar, M., 291
Mukherjee, S., 558
Muldoon, M. F., 190
Mulkens, S. A. N., 139, 140
Mullen, K. J., 404

Müller, C. A., 353
Muller, D. J., 159
Muller, R. J., 393
Müller, T. D., 315
Munder, T., 107, 448
Muñoz, R. F., 241
Munsey, C., 341, 355
Munson, J., 528
Murad, M. H., 451
Muris, P., 136, 140, 153
Murphy, C., 416
Murphy, H., 160
Murphy, S. L., 268, 285, 286
Murray, C., 85
Murray, C. K., 408
Murray, D., 311
Murray, G., 201
Murray, H. A., 81
Murray, S. B., 298
Murrie, D. C., 546
Murru, A., 176
Muscatell, K. A., 245
Muse, K., 208, 212
Mustafa, B., 261
Mustanski, B., 285
Myers, S. G., 158
Myers, S. M., 531
Myers, T. A., 305, 309
Myrick, K. J., 466

Na, B., 191
Nadeau, L., 414
Nademanee, K., 181
Naeem, F., 254
Naess, H., 183
Nagano, J., 63
Naggiar, S., 179
Nagy, G. A., 253
Najmi, S., 283
Namiki, C., 408
Nangle, D. W., 154
Nanovska, S., 430
Napili, A., 12
Napper, L. E., 358
Nappi, R. E., 442
Naragon-Gainey, K., 419
Narayan, A. J., 530
Nardi, A. E., 147
Narkiewicz, K., 415
Nashat, M., 81
Nashoni, E., 302
Naumann, E., 301
Navaneelan, T., 284
Neacsiu, A. D., 479
Neal-Barnett, A., 156
Neale, M. C., 346
Nearing, K. I., 139
Neerakal, I., 147
Neff, R. A., 251
Negreponti, A., 297
Ncgy, C., 310
Neighbors, C., 307, 334, 347
Neighbors, H. W., 384

Neighbors, L., 307
Nelson, B., 374
Nelson, G., 559
Nelson, L., 140
Nemeroff, C. B., 173, 264
Neng, J. M., 208
Neria, Y., 169
Nervi, A., 419
Nestler, E. J., 349, 353
Neugebauer, R., 15
Neumann, C. S., 475
Neumark-Sztainer, D., 298, 308, 310, 311, 321
Neutze, J., 459
Neves, R. C. S., 438, 439
Névéus, T., 517
Newell, J. M., 236
Newgren, K. P., 85
Newhill, C. E., 384
Newman, C. F., 247
Newman, J. P., 488, 489
Newnham, E. A., 479
Newschaffer, C. J., 528
Newton, F. B., 564
Newton, I., 15
Ng, J., 254
Nicholas, C., 241
Nicholas, M. K., 211
Nicholls, D., 308
Nichols, M. P., 64, 131
Nicholson, I. R., 153
Nichter, M., 311
Nickerson, A., 171, 513
Nicolson, S. E., 423
Nieboer, R. M., 388
Nielsen, S., 355
Nielssen, O., 379
Nienhuis, F. J., 373, 388
Nierenberg, A. A., 258
Nightingale, N. N., 110
Nillni, Y. I., 147
Nisbett, R. E., 86
Nishiyama, T., 526
Niv, N., 27, 366
Nixon, R., 507
Nkansah, E., 291
Nobel, L., 414
Nobre, P. J., 445
Nock, M. K., 268, 283, 509
Noeker, M., 208
Nolen-Hoeksema, S., 133, 149, 243, 264
Noll, J. G., 109
Norberg, K., 275
Norcross, J. C., 22, 29, 123
Norcross, M. A., 131
Nordahl, C. W., 527
Nordentoft, M., 376, 379
Nordin, S., 416
Nordstrom, B. R., 355
Norfleet, M. A., 27
Norko, M., 6
Norko, M. A., 561

Polansky, J. R., 348
Pole, N., 175, 176
Poletti, M., 423
Poliakoff, M. B., 110
Polich, J., 332
Politte, L. C., 530
Pollack, M. H., 177
Pollet, T. V., 323
Polosa, R., 339
Poluha, W., 422
Pomerleau, C. S., 356
Pomeroy, W. B., 434
Pompe, U., 30
Pompili, M., 259, 280
Pontifex, M. B., 523
Pope, H. G., 302, 303
Pope, H. G., Jr., 110, 219, 298
Pope, K. S., 542
Popelyuk, D., 435
Popolo, R., 392
Pornpattananangkul, N., 24
Porter, J., 106
Posner, J., 240
Poston, J. T., 406
Potenza, M. N., 358, 359
Potter, R., 89, 417, 434
Potvin, S., 414
Poulsen, S., 316
Pourtois, G., 193
Powell, L. H., 322
Powell, N. D., 187
Powers, A. D., 478
Powers, M. B., 177
Prabhuswamy, M., 510
Pradhan, S., 346
Prantzalou, C., 140
Prati, G., 174
Pratt, L. A., 249
Prause, J., 170
Preda, A., 426
Preece, M. H., 410
Prentice, G., 403
Prescott, C. A., 120, 137, 145, 149, 349
Preston, K. L., 355
Pretlow, R., 323
Price, C. S., 105
Price, D., 403
Price, I. R., 159
Price, J., 252, 311
Priebe, S., 385
Priess, H. A., 243
Prince, A., 313
Prince, M., 403, 405
Pritchard, R., 484
Prosek, E. A., 96
Prosser, S., 143
Prossin, A. R., 478
Proudfoot, J., 260
Proudfoot, J. G., 251
Pruessner, J. C., 249
Pucciarelli, M., 144
Puhl, R. M., 321
Pulcu, E., 245

Pull, C. B., 494, 495
Pulliam, P., 169
Pumariega, A. J., 99, 312
Purdon, C., 152
Purkis, H., 138
Purse, M., 395
Purssey, R., 105, 250, 276
Puspitasari, A. J., 253
Putnam, K. T., 109
Putnam, R. D., 322

Quinn, D., 512
Quinn, S. O., 21
Quirin, M., 140
Qureshi, I. A., 429
Qureshi, S. U., 404

Rabinowitz, J., 373, 384
Rachman, S., 153, 154, 207
Racine, M., 341
Raciti, C., 339
Racoosin, J., 509
Radcliffe, D., 136
Radomsky, A. S., 154
Radonic, E., 397
Räikkönen, K., 427
Rainbow, L., 434
Raine, A., 470, 514
Raine, L. B., 523
Rajab, M. H., 284
Ramachandraih, C. T., 239
Ramachandran, V., 295
Ramage, B., 521
Ramnath, R., 470, 471
Ramos, R., 341
Ramsey, S. D., 444
Rand, D. G., 321
Randell, I., 517
Ranseen, J., 337
Ranseen, J. D., 83
Ranta, K., 149
Rao, D., 13, 15, 98
Rao, V., 401
Rapee, R. M., 506
Rappaport, N., 173
Rapport, D., 216
Rasgon, N. L., 259
Rashid, T., 77
Rasmussen, J., 160
Rasmussen, S. A., 160
Rastogi, A., 335
Rathbone, C. J., 408
Rauch, S. L., 264
Raval, A. P., 412
Ravindran, A. V., 240
Ray, G. T., 522
Raymond, F. L., 533
Raymond, N. C., 319
Rayner, R., 138
Razani, J., 416
Read, J., 448
Read, J. P., 346
Reading, R., 198, 202, 203
Reagan, R., 416, 546

Reas, D. L., 317
Rebellon, C., 341
Rebok, G. W., 418
Rector, N. A., 372, 381
Reddemann, L., 217
Reddington, R. M., 66
Reddy, Y. C., 160
Redolfi, S., 110
Reed, G. M., 494
Reed, I., 18
Rees, C. S., 484
Reese, H. E., 154
Reese, M., 434
Reeves, A., 286
Reeves, K., 137
Regan, M. C., 191
Regen, W., 430
Reger, G. M., 177
Reich, D. B., 478
Reichenberg, A., 371, 377
Reif, A., 131
Reiman, E. M., 417
Reinelt, E., 133
Reinhold, N., 212
Reis, H. T., 566
Reivich, K. J., 246
Relton, C. L., 47
Remschmidt, H., 393
Renshaw, K. D., 282
Resnick, H. S., 171
Resnick, P. J., 10
Ressler, K. J., 38, 157
Reuber, M., 202
Rexrode, K. M., 412
Reynaud, M., 335
Reynolds, C. F., 426, 428
Reynolds, R. M., 264
Reynolds, S., 144
Rhea, D. J., 311
Rhemtulla, M., 534
Rhoad, A. M., 83
Ricca, V., 307
Rice, F., 245
Rich-Edwards, J. W., 321
Richards, E. P., 120
Richards, J. C., 191
Richards, P. S., 19
Richardson, J. R., 403
Richardson, L. F., 219
Richardson, N., 409
Richardson, S. M., 323
Richardson, T., 251
Richey, J., 140
Richey, S. M., 429
Richman, L. S., 192
Richter, M. A., 159
Richwine, J., 85
Ricke, P., 347
Ridaura, V. K., 320
Ridley, C. R., 66, 99
Rieber, R. W., 222
Rief, W., 211, 358
Rieger, E., 298
Rieker, P. P., 248

Riemann, D., 430
Rihmer, Z., 259
Rinck, M., 140
Ringwalt, C., 338
Riolo, S. A., 481, 482
Ritchie, K., 137
Ritenbaugh, C., 311
Ritz, T., 136, 142, 186, 191
Rivara, F. P., 415
Rivard, M., 532
Rivas-Vazquez, R. A., 473
Rizvi, S. L., 479
Robbins, T. W., 346
Roberts, A., 435
Roberts, A. L., 171, 175
Roberts, E., 509
Roberts, E. M., 528
Roberts, N. P., 377
Roberts, T. K., 451
Robertson, J. M., 564
Robertson, M. M., 519
Robertson, W. C., Jr., 518
Robins, R. W., 242
Robinson, E. B., 287, 526
Robinson, L., 278, 287, 289
Robinson, M. E., 207
Robinson, T. E., 353
Robison, E. J., 241
Rochlen, A. B., 298
Roder, V., 391
Rodewald, F., 217
Rodger, S., 529
Rodriguez, B. F., 85
Rodriguez, C. I., 158
Rodu, B., 339
Roe, D., 386
Roecklein, K. A., 252
Roesch, R., 545
Roffman, R. A., 345
Rogers, A., 183
Rogers, C. H., 273
Rogers, J., 518
Rogers, J. R., 283
Rogers, R. G., 284
Rogers, S., 536
Rogers-Wood, N. A., 311
Rohan, K. J., 147
Rohde, P., 254, 299
Rohrmann, S., 140
Rohsenow, D. J., 355
Rojas, A. E. P., 77
Rolfe, A., 190
Rolland, Y., 424
Rollnick, S., 352
Rolon-Arroyo, B., 514
Romeo, N., 556
Romero, N., 243
Rondeaux, C., 465
Ronningstam, E., 482
Rorschach, H., 81
Rose, S. C., 177
Rosen, H. J., 407
Rosenbaum, J. F., 288
Rosenberg, J., 558

Shapiro, A., 509
Shapiro, S. L., 67
Shapley, L., 123
Sharlip, I. D., 442
Sharma, A., 378, 379
Sharma, S., 420, 430
Sharpe, M., 201
Shaw, H., 305
Shaw, P., 521
Shawyer, F., 390, 398
Shedden, K., 239
Sheehan, W., 219
Sheen, C., 97, 441
Shelby, G. D., 506
Sheldon, S. H., 427
Shelley-Ummenhofer, J., 317
Shelton, R. C., 249
Shen, Y., 358
Shenk, C. E., 109
Shepherd, K., 243, 264
Sher, K. J., 346
Sheridan, J. F., 187
Sherin, J. E., 173
Sherry, A., 478
Sherwood, N., 311
Shiban, Y., 142
Shibasaki, M., 137
Shiedly, B., 120
Shields, B., 14
Shiffman, S. S., 190, 388
Shih, A., 526
Shih, R. A., 348
Shih, W. L., 260
Shin, E., 564
Shin, H., 420
Shin, M., 533
Shinbach, K., 548
Shmuel-Baruch, S., 519
Shmueli-Blumberg, D., 359
Shneidman, E. S., 269, 282
Shoham, V., 107
Shorey, R. C., 135
Short, B., 50, 252
Shorter, E., 90
Shrivastava, A., 374
Sibitz, I., 374
Sibolt, G., 423
Sibrava, N. J., 135, 150, 160
Sica, C., 158
Sick, T. J., 412
Siebert, D. C., 346, 347
Siegel, M., 344, 563
Siegel, S. J., 374
Siero, F. W., 306
Sierra, M., 216
Sieswerda, S., 478
Siitarinen, J., 383
Sijbrandij, M., 173
Silberg, J. L., 245
Silberstein, S. D., 184
Silk, K. R., 478
Silva, R., 370
Silver, R. C., 170
Silveri, M. M., 349

Silverman, M. M., 277
Silverstone, P. H., 457
Sim, L. A., 316, 318
Simek-Morgan, L., 66, 492
Simeon, D., 216
Simmons, A. N., 313
Simms, C. A., 219, 221
Simon, G. E., 207
Simon, H., 429
Simon, H. K., 505
Simon, J., 442
Simon, N., 177
Simons, T., 426
Simpson, H. B., 160, 485
Simpson, T. L., 178
Sims, C., 311
Sin, N. L., 246
Singer, D. C., 105
Singer, H. S., 519
Singh, A. A., 24
Singh, B. S., 202
Singh, M. K., 184, 516
Sinha-Deb, K., 205
Sismondo, S., 108
Sivec, H. J., 390
Sizemore, C., 222, 224
Sjöstrand, K., 414
Skinner, M. D., 353
Sklar, P., 260, 261
Skodol, A. E., 405, 495
Skopp, N. A., 175
Slade, T., 96, 379
Slater, A., 428
Slavec, J. J., 154
Slaveska-Hollis, K., 200
Slavich, G. M., 245
Sleegers, K., 421
Sloane, C., 346, 351
Sloof, C. J., 373
Slotema, C. W., 253
Smailes, E. M., 114
Smallwood, P., 473
Smari, J., 156
Smart, E., 542
Smith, A., 521
Smith, A. D., 423
Smith, A. R., 303, 310
Smith, B., 81
Smith, B. L., 50
Smith, C., 50
Smith, C. S., 559
Smith, D., 311
Smith, G. C., 208
Smith, J., 526
Smith, L., 65, 66, 192
Smith, M., 287, 289, 435
Smith, P., 174
Smith, P. N., 271, 284
Smith, S. E., 269
Smith, S. L., 309
Smith, T. W., 208
Smith-DiJulio, K., 248
Smits, J. A., 141, 417, 430
Smoak, N., 68

Smolin, Y., 219
Smoller, J., 120
Smoller, J. W., 420
Snellman, K., 322
Snieder, H., 189
Snoek, H. M., 313
Snorrason, I., 156
Snowden, L. R., 153, 159
Snyder, J. S., 240
Sobal, J., 307
Soehle, M., 49
Soenens, B., 306
Sokol, K. A., 14
Sola, C. L., 335
Soldz, S., 566
Sollers, J. J., III, 192
Sollman, M. J., 83
Solnick, S., 113
Soloff, P. H., 478
Solomon, Z., 206
Solovitch, S., 396
Sommer, I. E., 253
Sonnier, L., 515
Sood, M., 205
Soreff, S., 260, 268, 270, 282, 283
Sørensen, H. J., 381
Sorensen, P., 201
Sorensen, T. I. A., 280, 318
Sorkin, A., 370
Soumier, A., 240
Southerland, R., 342
Soutullo, C., 250, 509
Sowell, E. S., 535
Soydan, H., 374
Spanos, N. P., 15, 221
Spates, C. R., 169, 174
Spear, L. P., 350
Speca, M., 194
Specht, M. W., 160
Spector, A. E., 424
Speice, J., 199
Spence, S. H., 143
Spencer, D., 530
Spencer, S. J., 98
Spencer, T. J., 522
Spencer-Thomas, S., 286
Spiegel, D., 212, 213, 214, 217, 219
Spiegel, H., 222
Spiegelhalder, K., 430
Spielman, G. I., 105, 250, 252, 276
Spinhoven, P., 148
Spira, A. P., 418
Spitzer, M., 203
Spitzer, R. L., 303, 318, 405
Sprenger, T., 184
Springen, K., 301
Srebalus, D. J., 561
Srinivasan, K., 147
Sripada, C., 521
Srivastava, A. K., 526
St. Laurent, R., 321

St-Pierre-Delorme, M.-E., 153, 159, 160
Stafford, R. S., 388
Stahl, D., 313
Stahl, S. M., 173, 239, 240, 380
Stalberg, G., 391
Stallard, P., 251
Stamatakis, E., 191
Stambor, Z., 192
Stamova, B., 528
Stang, J., 311
Staniford, J., 479
Staniloiu, A., 219
Stanley, B., 291
Stanley, M. A., 150
Stansifer, L., 511
Stant, A. D., 389
Stapel, D. A., 306
Stapleton, M., 30
Stark, J., 368
Startup, H., 367
Stat, M., 298
Stavro, K., 414
Stead, L. F., 356
Steck, E. L., 323
Steele, C. M., 98
Steen, R. G., 123
Steenkamp, M. M., 154
Stefanidis, E., 365
Steffel, L. M., 479
Steiger, A. E., 242
Steiger, H., 312, 313
Stein, A., 150
Stein, D., 302
Stein, D. J., 151, 156, 157
Stein, G. L., 345
Stein, M. B., 13, 130, 146, 206
Steinberg, D., 191
Steinberg, J. L., 259
Steinberg, T., 519
Steinbrecher, N., 200
Steiner, A. M., 531
Steiner, T. J., 183
Steinglass, J. E., 485
Steinhausen, H. C., 301, 303
Steinwachs, D. M., 382
Steketee, G., 83, 159, 160
Stelmach, H., 557
Stephens, R. S., 345
Stepp, S. D., 479
Steptoe, A., 174, 189
Stergiakouli, E., 522
Sterk, J., 507
Sternberg, R. J., 85, 86
Sterzer, P., 470, 487, 488, 514
Stetka, B. S., 91, 96
Stevens, S., 146
Stevenson, T., 422
Stewart, C. A., 466
Stewart, D., 248
Stewart, M. O., 253, 259
Stewart, S. H., 208, 346
Stice, E., 254, 299, 302, 305, 309
Stifter, C., 132

Stiles, B. L., 459
Stiles, W. B., 217
Stiller, B., 262
Stinson, F. S., 333
Stitt, L., 374
Stitzer, M., 352, 355
Stober, G., 371
Stockton, S., 262
Stojek, M., 109
Stolar, N., 372, 381
Stone, E., 14
Stone, J., 203
Stone, K. L., 418
Stone, L. B., 243
Stone, S., 394
Stoner, R., 528
Stoolmiller, M., 348
Storey, B., 347
Storm, M. V., 420
Storrch, E. A., 160
Story, M., 311, 321
Stossel, S., 161
Stout, J. C., 357
Stout, R. L., 155
Stovner, L. J., 183
Strakowski, S. M., 233, 261
Strand, S. L., 410
Straus, M. A., 465
Strawn, J. R., 515
Strenziok, M., 58
Stricker, R. B., 394
Strickland, K. D., 108
Striegel-Moore, R. H., 303, 313
Stringaris, A., 537
Strober, M., 313
Stroebel, S. S., 458
Stroud, C. B., 245
Strunk, D., 253, 259
Stuart, E. A., 273, 529
Stuart, G. L., 135
Stuart, H., 13, 26
Stuart, S., 200, 208, 210
Studer, J., 347
Štulhofer, A., 438, 439, 444
Stulz, U., 270
Stürmer, T., 250, 509
Subramanyam, N., 239
Sue, D., 10, 11, 19, 22, 23, 24, 35, 64, 65, 66, 67, 99, 182, 285, 484, 491, 492, 493, 565
Sue, D. W., 10, 11, 19, 22, 23, 24, 35, 64, 65, 66, 67, 99, 182, 285, 484, 491, 492, 493, 565
Sugawara, J., 188
Sugden, K., 239, 245
Sugiyama, Y., 188
Suglia, S. F., 113
Sui, X., 319
Sullivan, E. V., 333
Sullivan, P. F., 206
Sumi, S., 526
Sun, J., 493
Sun, Q., 412
Sundel, M., 141

Sundel, S. S., 141
Sundell, J., 528
Sung, H. M., 160
Sung, J., 193
Suominen, K., 259
Supekar, K., 527
Supic, G., 47
Surawy, C., 212
Surén, P., 529
Sureshkumar, P., 517
Surtees, P. B., 190
Susser, E., 529
Sutin, A. R., 321
Sutton-Tyrrell, K., 190
Suwanlert, S., 507
Suzuki, K., 141
Suzuki, L., 86
Svaldi, J., 301, 304
Svoboda, E., 211
Swami, V., 306
Swann, A. C., 259
Swanson, K. S., 200, 207
Swanson, S. A., 128, 250, 275, 305, 504, 505, 506, 507, 509, 511, 513
Swart, M. L., 428
Swartz, M., 6
Sweeney, C. T., 336, 388
Swelam, M., 264
Swendsen, J., 305, 347, 504
Symmonds, M., 416
Symonds, D., 62
Sytema, S., 388
Szasz, T. S., 11
Szumilas, M., 177
Szwedo, D., 347
Szyf, M., 47
Szymkowicz, S. M., 78

Tai, W., 442
Takahashi, T., 384
Takei, N., 141
Takeuchi, H., 388
Takeuchi, J., 385
Takeuchi, K., 188
Talavage, T. M., 410
Talavera, F., 171
Talbot, L. S., 264
Taljaard, M., 141
Talleyrand, R. M., 311
Tally, S. R., 247
Tan, R., 364
Tanaka, H., 188
Tang, Y., 416
Tanguay, P. E., 524
Taniai, H., 526
Tanofsky-Kraff, M., 321
Tantleff-Dunn, S., 310
Tanzi, M. G., 141
Tapert, S. F., 341
Tarasoff, T., 562, 563
Targum, S. D., 423
Tarloff, D., 548–549
Tarr, A. J., 187

Tarumi, T., 188
Tasker, F., 26
Tatar, J. R., 457
Tay, J., 200
Taylor, A., 491
Taylor, C. B., 147
Taylor, C. T., 162
Taylor, E., 529
Taylor, J. J., 50, 252
Taylor, J. L., 529, 534
Taylor, K. N., 391
Taylor, L. A., 334
Taylor, R. S., 255
Taylor, S., 206, 208, 210
Taylor, S. E., 142, 190, 245, 530
Teachman, B. A., 146
Teachman, M. W., 135
Tedeschi, G. J., 345, 356
Tedeschi, R. G., 171, 566
Teesson, M., 96
Teicher, M. H., 219, 508
Tejada-Vera, B., 414
Tell, R. A., 108, 251
Temple, J. L., 313–315
Temple, S., 45
Teri, L., 242
Terman, L. M., 85
Terracciano, A., 321
Terry, L., 208
Terry-McElrath, Y. M., 336
Tessner, K., 382
Thakar, M., 374
Thakker-Varia, S., 45
Thalman, L., 422
Thanos, P. K., 320
Thapar, A., 245, 522
Thatcher, W. G., 311
Thayer, R. E., 341
Thom, A., 111
Thomas, C., 355
Thomas, G., 427
Thomas, J. D., 534, 535
Thomas, J. J., 305
Thomas, K., 335
Thomas, O., 410
Thomas, P., 370
Thomas, T., 511
Thommi, S., 261
Thompson, D., Jr., 441
Thompson, J. K., 309
Thompson, M., 275
Thompson, P. M., 377
Thompson, R., 249
Thompson, W., 321
Thorndike, R. L., 85
Thornicroft, G., 14
Thornton, B. B., 136
Thornton, L. M., 313
Thorpe, S. J., 156
Thorup, A., 379
Thun, M. J., 356
Thurber, S., 219
Thurman, U., 136
Thurston, R. C., 191, 192

Thylstrup, B., 474
Tian, Y., 528
Tierney, J., 181
Tietjen, G. E., 190
Tiggemann, M., 306
Timberlake, D. S., 334
Timberlake, J., 137
Timpano, K. R., 140
Tindle, H. A., 191
Ting, L., 66
Tingen, I. W., 215
Titov, N., 251, 254
Titus, K., 348
Tobin, J. J., 182
Todd, A. R., 13
Tolentino, M., 412, 422
Tolin, D. F., 83, 154, 160
Tollman, S., 18
Tomarken, A. J., 202
Tomasi, D., 358
Tompson, T., 243
Torpey, D. C., 236
Torres, I. J., 256
Touyz, S. W., 298, 316
Tovée, M. J., 323
Towe, S. L., 345
Træen, B., 438, 439, 444
Trampe, D., 306
Tranel, D., 130
Tranela, D., 416
Tranulis, C., 394
Trapnell, P. D., 477
Trautmann, E., 193
Treasure, J., 313
Treat, T. A., 65
Treichel, J., 95
Triffleman, E. G., 175
Trinh, J., 420, 430
Trivedi, M. H., 246, 252
Troister, T., 282
Trudel, G., 449
Trudel-Fitzgerald, C., 190
Trull, T. J., 495
Trueba, A. F., 136, 186
Tsai, G. E., 219
Tsai, J. L., 231
Tsang, H. W., 374
Tschann, J. M., 175
Tschöp, M. H., 315
Tseng, W.-C., 564
Tsitsika, A. K., 511
Tsuang, M. T., 120
Tsunoda, M., 384
Tucker, B. T. P., 151, 156
Tucker, C., 165
Tucker, J. S., 348
Tucker-Drob, E. M., 534
Tuke, W., 18
Tull, M. T., 346
Tully, E. C., 239
Tunks, E. R., 200, 207, 208
Turecki, G., 281
Turetsky, B. I., 377
Turk, D. C., 200, 207

Turkaly, F., 277
Turkheimer, E., 534
Turkington, D., 389
Turner, E. H., 108, 123, 251
Turner, H., 109
Turner, H. A., 508
Turner, J. M., 509
Turtle, L., 519
Turton, A. J., 346
Túry, F., 155
Tuschen-Caffier, B., 301, 304
Tuttle, J. P., 337
Tynan, W. D., 513, 515

Ucok, A., 384
Uezato, A., 236
Ugochukwu, C., 336
Umaña-Taylor, A. J., 247
Underwager, R., 82
Underwood, A., 186
Ungar, M., 38
Unger, A., 374
Unger-Köppel, J., 270
Ungureanu, L., 133
Ursache, A., 132
Utku, U., 412

Vahid, B., 337
Valentí, M., 258
Valor, L. M., 430
van Almen, K. L. M., 129
Van Balkom, A. J. L. M., 148
van den Bout, J., 428
van den Brink, F., 445
van den Hout, M. A., 173, 178
van der Gaag, M., 389, 398
van der Werf, M., 395
van der Zwaluw, C. S., 313
van Dijk, D., 371
Van Dyck, R., 148
Van Evra, J. P., 492
van Gerwen, L. J., 129
Van Gogh, V., 19
van Goozen, S. H., 487, 515
Van Gundy, K., 341
van Hartevelt, T. J., 423
Van Heeringen, C., 269
van Heeringen, C., 254
Van Hulle, C. A., 487
van Kan, G. A., 424
van Lankveld, J., 443
van Minnen, A., 141
Van Noppen, B., 159
van Ommeren, M., 251
Van Orden, K., 277, 279, 284
Van Os, J., 246, 374, 376
Van Oudenhove, L., 438, 442
van Overveld, M., 173
van Praag, H., 415, 417
van Schagen, A. M., 428
van Strien, T., 313
van Winckel, M., 322
van Zwol, L., 136, 153
Vander Wal, J. S., 310, 319

Vandivort-Warren, R., 12
Vandrey, R., 355
Vang Xiong, 182
Värnik, P., 293
Vartanian, L. R., 305
Varticovschi, P., 302
Vasey, M. W., 140
Vasquez, M. J. T., 542
Vassallo, M., 421
Vassilopoulos, S. P., 140
Vasterling, J. J., 408
Vater, A., 482
Vazquez, C., 243
Vazquez-Montes, M., 212
Vecchio, C., 156
Vedantam, S., 95
Veenstra-VanderWeele, J., 118
Veling, W., 384
Vellas, B., 424
Velleman, S., 251
Velligan, D. I., 263
Venables, P. H., 470, 514
Ventura, M. I., 420
Verboom, C. E., 65, 245
Verdon, B., 81
Verhaeghe, J., 438, 442
Verhelst, N., 293
Verissimo, A., 445
Verma, R., 523
Verschuere, B., 218
Vgontzas, A. N., 425
Viding, E., 119
Vigod, S. N., 248
Viken, R. J., 65
Vilhauer, J. S., 254
Villagonzalo, K. A., 345
Vincent, J. B., 532
Vincent, M. A., 308
Vinter, S., 321
Virtala, E., 53
Visser, S., 516, 520, 522, 523, 527, 537
Vitiello, B., 522
Vitolo, G., 322
Vocci, F., 355
Voderholzer, U., 301
Voegtline, K., 132
Vogel, D. L., 98
Vogt, D., 175
Vogt, R. G., 85
Vöhringer, P. A., 262
Volkmar, F. R., 123
Volkow, N. D., 320, 358
von Gontard, A., 517
von Leupoldt, A., 136, 186
von Lojewski, A., 307
von Ranson, K. M., 301
von Sacher-Masoch, L., 458
Voon, V., 203
Voracek, M., 306
Vorvick, L. J., 449
Vrshek-Schallhorn, S., 245
Vuckovic, N., 311
Vulturar, R., 133

Waddington, J. L., 378
Wade, D. T., 207
Wade, N. G., 19, 98
Wade, T., 306, 323
Wade, T. D., 301
Wadiwalla, M., 249
Wadsworth, T., 284
Wagner, A., 313
Wagner, B., 237
Wagner, J., 247
Wagner, K. D., 347
Waheed, W., 254
Wahlestedt, C., 264
Wainwright, L. D., 364, 382
Wakefield, H., 82
Wakefield, J. C., 96
Wald, M. M., 409
Waldman, I. D., 521
Walfish, S., 555
Walker, D. D., 345
Walker, E., 382
Walker, E. F., 472, 474
Walker, E. L., 471, 473
Walker, H., 217
Walker, J. R., 200, 201, 208
Walker, M. P., 233, 264
Walkup, J., 369
Wall, M., 321
Wallace, E. R., 15
Walser, R. D., 60
Walsh, J., 77
Walsh, J. L., 345
Walsh, K., 170, 429
Walsh, R., 67
Walshaw, P. D., 261
Walter, M., 18
Walters, E. E., 128, 133, 235, 256
Walters, H. J., 344
Waltoft, B. L., 379
Walton, G., 38
Wampold, B. E., 62
Wang, G. J., 320, 358
Wang, K. T., 285
Wang, S., 378, 516
Wang, Y., 194
Wang, Y. P., 327
Wangy, H.-X., 415, 424
Ward, C. H., 83
Ward, J., 343
Ward, L. M., 314
Ward, M. P., 251
Ward, T., 368, 466
Ware, A. L., 534
Warner, K. E., 530
Warner, R., 26, 366, 374, 391
Warren, C. S., 306, 319
Warren, K. R., 535
Warren, Z. E., 118
Wartik, N., 205
Wassermann, E. M., 405
Wasylkiw, L., 310
Watkins, E. R., 255
Watkins, L. R., 132
Watkins, M. W., 83

Watson, D. B., 200
Watson, J. B., 138
Watson, L. S., 24
Watson, N. F., 241
Watt, M. C., 208
Wattar, U., 201
Way, B. M., 245
Webb, T. L., 251
Webber-Dereszynski, R. L., 205
Weber, E. U., 485
Weber, S., 303
Wechsler, D., 85
Weck, F., 208
Weedn, A. E., 312
Weems, C. F., 133, 147, 173
Wehmeier, P. M., 393
Wei, Y., 177
Weinberger, I. E., 557
Weiner, I. B., 76
Weiner, J. L., 83
Weinhold, B., 121
Weinshall, D., 370
Weintrau, E. S., 105
Weintraub, M., 511
Weir, R., 208
Weisberg, R. B., 135
Weishaar, M. E., 58, 479
Weismoore, J. T., 282
Weiss, B., 507, 528
Weiss, N. H., 346
Weiss, R., 441, 522
Weiss, R. D., 338
Weissman, M. M., 246
Weisz, J. R., 507
Weitzman, M., 509
Weizman, A., 302
Welham, J., 381
Weller, D., 201
Wells, A., 150, 158
Wells, L. A., 316
Wells, R. E., 424
Wells, T. T., 254
Welsh, G. S., 84
Werner, S., 384
Werth, J. L., 563
Wessely, S., 177, 209
West, B. T., 346
Westberg, J., 388
Westen, D., 494
Westenberg, H. G. M., 157
Westheimer, R. K., 444, 445
Weston, C. G., 481, 482
Westphal, M., 464
Weyer, J., 18
Weyers, S., 452
Whealin, J. M., 175
Whilde, M. R., 478
Whitaker, A. H., 534
Whitaker, R. C., 321
White, D., 546
White, E. K., 306
White, K. S., 201, 208
White, L., 132
White, M. A., 304

SUBJECT INDEX

sociocultural dimension, 245–249
symptoms, 230
treatment of, 249–255
Derealization, 170, 215–216
Designer drugs, 342, 343
Deterministic genes, 421
Detoxification, 352
Developmental factors, 94
Deviance, 8, 9
Devil Wears Prada, The, 482
Dexedrine, 336
Dextromethorphan (DXM), 330t, 338
Dhat syndrome, 209
Diagnosis, 89–98
Diagnostic and Statistical Manual of Disorders (DSM), 90–92. *See also Diagnostic and Statistical Manual of Disorders (DSM)*
dimensional perspective, 93–95
personality psychopathy, and, 494–495
Diagnostic and Statistical Manual of Disorders (DSM), 20
contemporary diagnostic trends/future directions, 98–99
dimensional model of mental disorders, 93–95
DSM-5 classification system, evolution of, 96–98
DSM-5 disorders, 91
interrater reliability, 90–92
objections to classification/labeling, 98
Diagnostic and Statistical Manual of Disorders 5 (DSM-5), 8
Dialectical behavior therapy (DBT), 479
borderline personality disorder (BPD), 479
overview, 60
suicide, 291
Diastolic pressure, 181
Diathesis-stress theory, 71
Diazepam, 141
DID. *See* Dissociative identity disorder (DID)
Dietary counseling, 322
Dieting, 306, 322
Diffusion tensor imaging (DTI), 88t, 89
Dimensional model of mental disorders, 93
Diminished capacity, 546
Diminished emotional expression, 372
Disconfirmatory bias, 158

Disconfirmatory evidence, 368
Discrimination, 13
Discrimination based, 247
"Diseases and Peculiarities of the Negro Race" (Cartwright), 24
Disgust, 139
Disinhibited social engagement disorder (DSED), 506
Displacement, 52t
Disruptive behavior disorders. *See* Externalizing disorders among youth
Disruptive mood dysregulation disorder (DMDD), 509–510
Dissociative amnesia, 212–215
Dissociative anesthetic, 338
Dissociative disorders, 91t, 213t
biological dimension, 220–221
contemporary trends/future directions, 225–226
defined, 212
depersonalization/derealization disorder, 215–216
dissociative amnesia, 212
dissociative fugue, 215
dissociative identity disorder (DID), 216–219
etiology of, 218–223
hypnosis, as therapy, 214
localized amnesia, 212–215
multipath model of, 220f
psychological dimension, 222–223
treatment of, 223–225
Dissociative fugue, 215
Dissociative identity disorder (DID), 216–219
Dissociative trance states, 219
Distress, 8–9
Distress tolerance, in dialectical behavior therapy, 60
Disulfiram, 353
Dixon v. Weinberger, 554
Dizygotic (DZ) twins, 120
DLB. *See* Dementia with Lewy bodies (DLB)
DMDD. *See* Disruptive mood dysregulation disorder (DMDD)
Dopamine, 44t
Dopamine hypothesis, 378
Double-blind design, 112–113
Down syndrome (DS), 533
Draw-a-person tests, 82
Dream analysis, 52
Drug-drug interactions, 50
Drug revolution in psychiatry, 27–28
Drug use. *See* Substance-related and other addictive disorders

DS. *See* Down syndrome (DS)
DSED. *See* Disinhibited social engagement disorder (DSED)
DSM. *See Diagnostic and Statistical Manual of Disorders (DSM)*
DTI. *See* Diffusion tensor imaging (DTI)
Due process, 545
Durham standard, 546
Durham v. United States, 546
Durkheim Project, 294
Duty to warn, 562–564
DXM. *See* Dextromethorphan (DXM)
Dyscalculia, 535
Dyslexia, 535
Dyspareunia, 441
Dysregulation model of bipolar disorder, 260
Dyssomnias
circadian rhythm sleep disorder, 427
defined, 425
hypersomnolence disorder, 426
insomnia disorder, 425
narcolepsy, 426
obstructive sleep apnea, 426–427
Dysthymia, 236
Dystonia, 387
DZ twins. *See* Dizygotic (DZ) twins

E-cigarettes, 339
Early ejaculation, 438t, 441
Eating conditions not elsewhere classified, 305
Eating disorders, 91t, 299t
anorexia nervosa, 299–302. *See also* Anorexia nervosa
binge-eating disorder, 303–305
biological dimension, 313–315
bulimia nervosa, 302–303
contemporary trends/future directions, 322–323
defined, 297–298
eating conditions not elsewhere classified, 305
etiology of, 305–315
multipath model of, 306f
obesity, 318–322. *See also* Obesity
prevention programs, 317
psychological dimension, 305–307
social dimension, 307–308
sociocultural dimension, 308–313
treatment of, 315–318

Echolalia, 525
Ecstasy (MDMA), 330t, 338, 342–343, 344
ECT. *See* Electroconvulsive therapy (ECT)
ED. *See* Erectile disorder (ED)
Edex, 447t
EEG. *See* Electroencephalography (EEG)
Elderly, and suicide, 277–279
Electroconvulsive therapy (ECT), 49, 252
Electroencephalography (EEG), 80, 87–88, 402
Electronic cigarettes, 339
Elevated mood, 232
Elimination disorders, 517–518
Ellis's A-B-C theory of personality, 58, 59, 59f
EMDR. *See* Eye movement desensitization and reprocessing (EMDR)
Emotional lability, 233
Emotional regulation
in dialectical behavior therapy, 60
psychophysiological disorders, 194
Emotional responses, 41–42
Emotional symptoms
depression, 231
hypomania/mania, 232–233
Empowerment, 15
Encopresis, 517–518
Endophenotypes
defined, 119, 156
schizophrenia, 377
suicide, and, 281
ENS. *See* Enteric nervous system (ENS)
Enteric nervous system (ENS), 43
Enuresis, 517
Environmental factors, 94, 189
Environmental support, 424
Epidemiological research, 122
Epigenetic research, 121, 281
Epigenetics, 47
Epigenome, 46
Epinephrine, 43, 44t, 173
Erectile disorder (ED), 438t, 440, 447, 447t, 448
Erotomania, 393, 441
Espiritismo, 103
Estrogen, 379
Eszopiclone, 429
Ethical issues
client disclosures of violence to therapists, 555
Comprehensive Soldier Fitness (CSF) program, 566–567
confidentiality, 561
cultural competence of therapists, 565

Breathing-Related Sleep Disorders

Obstructive Sleep Apnea Hypopnea/
Central Sleep Apnea/Sleep-Related
Hypoventilation/Circadian Rhythm
Sleep-Wake Disorders

Parasomnias

Non-Rapid Eye Movement Sleep Arousal
Disorders/Nightmare Disorder/Rapid
Eye Movement Sleep Behavior Disorder/
Restless Legs Syndrome/Substance/
Medication-Induced Sleep Disorder/
Other Specified Insomnia Disorder/
Unspecified Insomnia Disorder/Other
Specified Hypersomnolence Disorder/
Unspecified Hypersomnolence Disorder/
Other Specified Sleep-Wake Disorder/
Unspecified Sleep-Wake Disorder

Sexual Dysfunctions

Delayed Ejaculation/Erectile Disorder/
Female Orgasmic Disorder/Female
Sexual Interest/Arousal Disorder/
Genito-Pelvic Pain/Penetration
Disorder/Male Hypoactive Sexual Desire
Disorder/Premature (Early) Ejaculation/
Substance/Medication-Induced Sexual
Dysfunction/Other Specified Sexual
Dysfunction/Unspecified Sexual
Dysfunction

Gender Dysphoria

Gender Dysphoria/Other Specified
Gender Dysphoria/Unspecified
Gender Dysphoria

Disruptive, Impulse-Control, and Conduct Disorders

Oppositional Defiant Disorder/Intermittent
Explosive Disorder/Conduct Disorder/
Antisocial Personality Disorder/
Pyromania/Kleptomania/Other
Specified Disruptive, Impulse-Control,
and Conduct Disorder/Unspecified
Disruptive, Impulse-Control, and
Conduct Disorder

Substance-Related and Addictive Disorders

Substance-Related Disorders

Alcohol-Related Disorders: Alcohol Use
Disorder/Alcohol Intoxication/Alcohol
Withdrawal/Other Alcohol-Induced
Disorders/Unspecified Alcohol-Related
Disorder

Caffeine-Related Disorders: Caffeine
Intoxication/Caffeine Withdrawal/Other
Caffeine-Induced Disorders/Unspecified
Caffeine-Related Disorder

Cannabis-Related Disorders: Cannabis
Use Disorder/Cannabis Intoxication/
Cannabis Withdrawal/Other Cannabis-
Induced Disorders/Unspecified
Cannabis-Related Disorder

Hallucinogen-Related Disorders:
Phencyclidine Use Disorders/
Other Hallucinogen Use Disorder/
Phencyclidine Intoxication/Other
Hallucinogen Intoxication/Hallucinogen
Persisting Perception Disorder/Other
Phencyclidine-Induced Disorders/
Other Hallucinogen-Induced Disorders/
Unspecified Phencyclidine-Related
Disorders/Unspecified Hallucinogen-
Related Disorders

Inhalant-Related Disorders: Inhalant Use
Disorder/Inhalant Intoxication/Other
Inhalant-Induced Disorders/Unspecified
Inhalant-Related Disorders

Opioid-Related Disorders: Opioid Use
Disorder/Opioid Intoxication/Opioid
Withdrawal/Other Opioid-Induced
Disorders/Unspecified Opioid-Related
Disorder

Sedative-, Hypnotic-, or Anxiolytic-
Related Disorders: Sedative, Hypnotic,
or Anxiolytic Use Disorder/Sedative,
Hypnotic, or Anxiolytic Intoxication/
Sedative, Hypnotic, or Anxiolytic
Withdrawal/Other Sedative-, Hypnotic-,
or Anxiolytic-Induced Disorders/
Unspecified Sedative-, Hypnotic-,
or Anxiolytic-Related Disorder

Stimulant-Related Disorders: Stimulant
Use Disorder/Stimulant Intoxication/
Stimulant Withdrawal/Other Stimulant-
Induced Disorders/Unspecified
Stimulant-Related Disorder

Tobacco-Related Disorders: Tobacco Use
Disorder/Tobacco Withdrawal/Other
Tobacco-Induced Disorders/Unspecified
Tobacco-Related Disorder

Other (or Unknown) Substance-Related
Disorders: Other (or Unknown)
Substance Use Disorder/Other (or
Unknown) Substance Intoxication/Other
(or Unknown) Substance Withdrawal/
Other (or Unknown) Substance-Induced
Disorders/Unspecified Other (or
Unknown) Substance-Related Disorder

Non-Substance-Related Disorders

Gambling Disorder

Neurocognitive Disorders

Delirium

Major and Mild Neurocognitive Disorders

Major or Mild Neurocognitive Disorder
Due to Alzheimer's Disease

Major or Mild Frontotemporal
Neurocognitive Disorder

Major or Mild Neurocognitive Disorder
with Lewy Bodies

Major or Mild Vascular Neurocognitive
Disorder

Major or Mild Neurocognitive Disorder
Due to Traumatic Brain Injury

Substance/Medication-Induced Major or
Mild Neurocognitive Disorder

Major or Mild Neurocognitive Disorder
Due to HIV Infection

Major or Mild Neurocognitive Disorder
Due to Prion Disease

Major or Mild Neurocognitive Disorder
Due to Parkinson's Disease

Major or Mild Neurocognitive Disorder
Due to Huntington's Disease

Major or Mild Neurocognitive Disorder
Due to Another Medical Condition

Major and Mild Neurocognitive Disorders
Due to Multiple Etiologies

Unspecified Neurocognitive Disorder

Personality Disorders

Cluster A Personality Disorders

Paranoid Personality Disorder/Schizoid
Personality Disorder/Schizotypal
Personality Disorder

Cluster B Personality Disorders

Antisocial Personality Disorder/Borderline
Personality Disorder/Histrionic
Personality Disorder/Narcissistic
Personality Disorder

Cluster C Personality Disorders

Avoidant Personality Disorder/Dependent
Personality Disorder/Obsessive-
Compulsive Personality Disorder

Other Personality Disorders

Personality Change Due to Another
Medical Condition/Other Specified
Personality Disorder/Unspecified
Personality Disorder

DSM-5 CLASSIFICATIONS

Neurodevelopmental Disorders

Intellectual Disabilities

Intellectual Disability (Intellectual Developmental Disorder)/Global Developmental Delay/Unspecified Intellectual Disability (Intellectual Developmental Disorder)

Communication Disorders

Language Disorder/Speech Sound Disorder/Childhood-Onset Fluency Disorder (Stuttering)/Social (Pragmatic) Communication Disorder/Unspecified Communication Disorder

Autism Spectrum Disorder

Autism Spectrum Disorder

Attention-Deficit/Hyperactivity Disorder

Attention-Deficit/Hyperactivity Disorder/Other Specified Attention-Deficit/Hyperactivity Disorder/Unspecified Attention-Deficit/Hyperactivity Disorder

Specific Learning Disorder

Motor Disorders

Developmental Coordination Disorder/Stereotypic Movement Disorder

Tic Disorders

Tourette's Disorder/Persistent (Chronic) Motor or Vocal Tic Disorder/Provisional Tic Disorder/Other Specified Tic Disorder/Unspecific Tic Disorder

Other Neurodevelopmental Disorders

Other Specified Neurodevelopmental Disorder/Unspecified Neurodevelopmental Disorder

Schizophrenia Spectrum and other Psychotic Disorders

Schizotypal (Personality) Disorder
Delusional Disorder
Brief Psychotic Disorder
Schizophreniform Disorder
Schizophrenia
Schizoaffective Disorder
Substance/Medication-Induced Psychotic Disorder
Psychotic Disorder Due to Another Medical Condition
Catatonia Associated with Another Mental Disorder
Catatonic Disorder due to Another Medical Condition

Unspecified Catatonia
Other Specified Schizophrenia Spectrum and Other Psychotic Disorder
Unspecified Schizophrenia Spectrum and Other Psychotic Disorder

Bipolar and Related Disorders

Bipolar I Disorder/Bipolar II Disorder/Cyclothymic Disorder/Substance/Medication-Induced Bipolar and Related Disorder/Bipolar and Related Disorder Due to Another Medical Condition/Other Specified Bipolar and Related Disorder/Unspecified Bipolar and Related Disorder

Depressive Disorders

Disruptive Mood Dysregulation Disorder/Major Depressive Disorder/Persistent Depressive Disorder (Dysthymia)/Premenstrual Dysphoric Disorder/Substance/Medication-Induced Depressive Disorder/Depressive Disorder Due to Another Medical Condition/Other Specified Depressive Disorder/Unspecified Depressive Disorder

Anxiety Disorders

Separation Anxiety Disorder/Selective Mutism/Specific Phobia/Social Anxiety Disorder (Social Phobia)/Panic Disorder/Panic Attack Specifier/Agoraphobia/Generalized Anxiety Disorder/Substance/Medication-Induced Anxiety Disorder/Anxiety Disorder Due to Another Medical Condition/Other Specified Anxiety Disorder/Unspecified Anxiety Disorder

Obsessive-Compulsive and Related Disorders

Obsessive-Compulsive Disorder/Body Dysmorphic Disorder/Hoarding Disorder/Trichotillomania (Hair-Pulling Disorder)/Excoriation (Skin-Picking) Disorder/Substance/Medication-Induced Obsessive-Compulsive and Related Disorder/Obsessive-Compulsive and Related Disorder Due to Another Medical Condition/Other Specified Obsessive-Compulsive and Related Disorder/Unspecified Obsessive-Compulsive and Related Disorder

Trauma- and Stressor-Related Disorders

Reactive Attachment Disorder/Disinhibited Social Engagement Disorder/Post-traumatic Stress Disorder (includes Posttraumatic Stress Disorder for Children 6 Years and Younger)/Acute Stress Disorder/Adjustment Disorders/Other Specified Trauma- and Stressor-Related Disorder/Unspecified Trauma- and Stressor-Related Disorder

Dissociative Disorders

Dissociative Identity Disorder/Dissociative Amnesia/Depersonalization/Derealization Disorder/Other Specified Dissociative Disorder/Unspecified Dissociative Disorder

Somatic Symptom and Related Disorders

Somatic Symptom Disorder/Illness Anxiety Disorder/Conversion Disorder (Functional Neurological Symptom Disorder)/Psychological Factors Affecting Other Medical Conditions/Factitious Disorder (includes Factitious Disorder Imposed on Self, Factitious Disorder Imposed on Another)/Other Specified Somatic Symptom and Related Disorder/Unspecified Somatic Symptoms and Related Disorder

Feeding and Eating Disorders

Pica/Rumination Disorder/Avoidant/Restrictive Food Intake Disorder/Anorexia Nervosa (Restricting type, Binge-eating/Purging type)/Bulimia Nervosa/Binge-Eating Disorder/Other Specified Feeding or Eating Disorder/Unspecified Feeding or Eating Disorder

Elimination Disorders

Enuresis/Encopresis/Other Specified Elimination Disorder/Unspecified Elimination Disorder

Sleep-Wake Disorders

Insomnia Disorder/Hypersomnolence Disorder/Narcolepsy

Paraphilic Disorders

Voyeuristic Disorder/Exhibitionist Disorder/Frotteuristic Disorder/Sexual Masochism Disorder/Sexual Sadism Disorder/Pedophilic Disorder/Fetishistic Disorder/Transvestic Disorder/ Other Specified Paraphilic Disorder/ Unspecified Paraphilic Disorder

Other Mental Disorders

Other Specified Mental Disorder Due to Another Medical Condition/Unspecified Mental Disorder Due to Another Medical Condition/Other Specified Mental Disorder/Unspecified Mental Disorder

Medication-Induced Movement Disorders and Other Adverse Effects of Medication

Neuroleptic-Induced Parkinsonism/Other Medication-Induced Parkinsonism/ Neuroleptic Malignant Syndrome/ Medication-Induced Acute Dystonia/ Medication-Induced Acute Akathisia/ Tardive Dyskinesia/Tardive Dystonia/ Tardive Akathisia/Medication-Induced Postural Tremor/Other Medication-Induced Movement Disorder/ Antidepressant Discontinuation Syndrome/Other Adverse Effect of Medication

Other Conditions That May Be a Focus of Clinical Attention

Relational Problems
Problems Related to Family Upbringing
Other Problems Related to Primary Support Group

Abuse and Neglect
Child Maltreatment and Neglect Problems
Adult Maltreatment and Neglect Problems

Educational and Occupational Problems
Educational Problems
Occupational Problems

Housing and Economic Problems
Housing Problems
Economic Problems

Other Problems Related to the Social Environment

Problems Related to Crime or Interaction with the Legal System

Other Health Service Encounters for Counseling and Medical Advice

Problems Related to Other Psychosocial, Personal, and Environment Circumstances

Other Circumstances of Personal History
Problems Related to Access to Medical and Other Health Care
Nonadherence to Medical Treatment

DSM-5 DISORDERS FOR FURTHER STUDY

The *DSM-5* Task Force judged that these disorders do not currently have sufficient supporting data for inclusion in *DSM-5* and therefore require further study. In fact, only a few of these proposed disorders will ultimately meet criteria, and others will be excluded from further consideration. Many of the more interesting disorders are discussed in one or more appropriate chapters.

Attenuated Psychosis Syndrome
Key features include delusions, hallucinations, or disorganized speech that distresses and disables the individual; the symptoms are like psychosis but not extreme enough to be considered a full psychotic disorder.

Depressive Episodes with Short-Duration Hypomania
Key features of this disorder are depressive episodes and episodes resembling hypomanic episodes but having a shorter duration (at least 2 days but below the 4-day minimum for hypomanic episodes).

Persistent Complex Bereavement Disorder
Key feature is intense grief for a year or more after the death of someone close to the bereaved individual.

Caffeine Use Disorder
Key features of this disorder are excessive caffeine use and an inability to control use.

Internet Gaming Disorder
Key features of this disorder are the fixation on Internet games and continually playing them, at the expense of school, work, and/or social interactions.

Neurobehavioral Disorder Associated with Prenatal Alcohol Exposure
The key feature is diminished behavioral, cognitive, or adaptive functioning due to prenatal alcohol exposure.

Suicidal Behavior Disorder
Key feature is a suicide attempt within the past 2 years that is not related to confusion or delirium.

Nonsuicidal Self-Injury
Key feature is repeated, yet nonserious, self-inflicted bodily damage. The individual engages in these acts due to interpersonal problems, negative feelings, or uncontrollable and/or intense thoughts about the act of injuring themselves.

Source: American Psychiatric Association. (2013). *Diagnostic and statistical manual of mental disorders* (5th ed.). Arlington, VA: American Psychiatric Association.

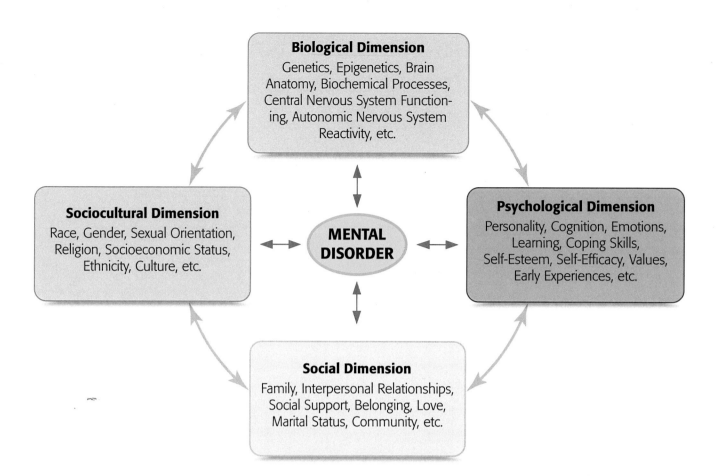

Multipath Model of Mental Disorders

The multipath model operates under several assumptions:

- No one theoretical perspective is adequate to explain the complexity of the human condition and the development of mental disorders.

- There are multiple pathways to and influences on the development of any single disorder. Explanations of abnormal behavior must consider biological, psychological, social, and sociocultural elements.

- Not all dimensions contribute equally to a disorder. In the case of some disorders, current research suggests that certain etiological forces have the strongest influence on the development of the specific disorder. Additionally, our understanding of mental disorders often evolves as further investigation provides new insight into contributing factors.

- The multipath model is integrative and interactive. It acknowledges that factors may combine in complex and reciprocal ways so that people exposed to the same influences may not develop the same disorder and that different individuals exposed to different factors may develop similar mental disorders.

- The biological and psychological strengths and assets of a person and positive aspects of the person's social and sociocultural environment can help protect against psychopathology, minimize symptoms, or facilitate recovery from mental illness.